The Computer Desktop Encyclopedia

2nd Edition

ALAN FREEDMAN

The Computer Desktop Encyclopedia

Second Edition

AMACOM

American Management Association

New York • Atlanta • Boston • Chicago • Kansas City • San Francisco • Washington, D.C.
Brussels • Toronto • Mexico City

This publication is designed to provide accurate and authoritative
information in regard to the subject matter covered. It is sold with the
understanding that the publisher is not engaged in rendering legal,
accounting, or other professional service. If legal advice or other
expert assistance is required, the services of a competent professional
person should be sought.

Library of Congress Cataloging-in-Publication Data

Freedman, Alan
    Computer desktop encyclopedia / Alan Freedman. -- 2nd ed.
        p.   cm.
    ISBN 0-8144-7985-5
    1. Computers--Dictionaries.   I. Title.
QA76.15.F732   1999
004'.03--dc21   98-32408
                                                        CIP

Printing number

10   9   8   7   6   5   4   3   2   1

*To my mother,
who had the vision to send me
to "automation school" in 1960*

ILLUSTRATIONS: Peter Felperin, Alan Freedman, Irma Lee Morrison,
Eric Jon Nones, Joseph D. Russo
EDITORIAL/PRODUCTION: Irma Lee Morrison
COPY EDITING: Mary McCann
BOOK DESIGN & TYPOGRAPHY: Cedar Waxwing Design, Rosemont, NJ
PUBLISHING SOFTWARE: PageMaker 6.5
FONTS: Garamond, Arial and Courier

A Note from the Author

The purpose of *Computer Desktop Encyclopedia* is to provide a meaningful definition of every important computer concept, term and buzzword used in the world of computers from micro to mainframe. Major hardware and software products are included as well as backgrounders on the companies that make them. Many historical photos of the first computers and electronic devices are in this book to remind us of the extraordinary acceleration of the technology of our era. All of this has come about in little over a hundred years, since the harnessing of electricity. It is a good idea to stop and smell the roses as we race towards the newest and the fastest.

It is also the purpose of this book to make sense out of this industry in general. As impossible a task as that may be, I have been trying for the past 20 years. What started out as a 300-term compendium for my computer seminars has now become my life's work. And, for that, I am very grateful, because I am interested in all the facets of this industry. I am lucky to have had a wide variety of experience in this field, and I am very lucky to have expert professionals who have been willing to help.

The degree of technical explanation chosen for each term is based on the term. Fundamental terms are explained for the lay person. More technical terms are explained with other technical terms, because, at some point, we have to assume a base knowledge without starting from scratch. However, all the terms used in this book are defined in the book.

I hope you find this book helpful and enjoyable. If there are concepts or products you feel should be included in the next edition, please let me know. Chances are they may have already been added to our floppy and CD-ROM versions, which are updated more frequently; however, I would love to hear from you and review your suggestions. Please write, fax, e-mail or call. Thank you very much for purchasing *Computer Desktop Encyclopedia*.

Alan Freedman

The Computer Language Company Inc.
5521 State Park Road
Point Pleasant, PA 18950
215 297-8082 fax 8424
E-mail: freedman@computerlanguage.com

Table of Contents

Acknowledgments

It woud be impossible to put a book like this together without the help of hundreds of technical engineers and public relations people who work for the hardware and software companies that make up this industry. In addition, many readers of my of current and previous editions of *The Computer Glossary* have contributed terms, suggestions and comments. For all of you that have willingly helped me, I thank you very much for your assistance. For those of you who made the experience akin to pulling teeth, well, thank you too. I appreciate your help.

I'd like to give a special acknowledgement to the following professionals who have continued to help me year after year. Thanks again to:

> *David Chappell*, Chappell Associates
> *Thom Drewke*, Technical Directions
> *James J. Farrell, III*, Motorola, Inc.
> *Max B. Fetzer*, Envirotronics
> *Lynn F. Thompson*, Cadmus Communications
> *Peter Hermsen*, MRC Computing
> *Clive "Max" Maxfield*, Intergraph Computer Systems
> *Terry O'Donnel*, Adobe Systems
> *Jim Stroh*, LXD Inc.
> *Paul and Jan Witte*, Originetics

I would like to thank the staff at AMACOM who have worked on this project for more than a decade, including *Hank Kennedy, Weldon Rackley, Ray O'Connell, Steve Arkin* and *Lydia Lewis*. Thanks for believing in me and for your continued support.

Most of all, an extra special thank you to *Irma Lee Morrison*, my wife and partner. Your contribution has always been the most significant, because you are truly my inspiration. I love you dearly Irmalee.

Basic Concepts and Vocabulary

The entries in the following list are the fundamental terms for the topics indicated. Review them and use them as a springboard to other concepts and terms.

Fundamentals
analog
digital
binary
hardware
software
bit
byte
data
computer
computer system
operating system
application software
system software
chip
PC
bus

Graphics & Multimedia
graphics
paint program
drawing program
CAD
MPC
CD
CD-ROM
CD-R
virtual reality

Communications
communications
modem
LAN
client
server
client/server
client/server development system
enterprise networking
peer-to-peer communications
gateway
router
hub
Ethernet
Token Ring
OSI
NetWare
TCP/IP
Internet
World Wide Web
Web browser
HTTP
HTML

Application Development
information system
field
record
file
database
DBMS
data dictionary
functional specification
systems analysis & design
system development cycle
prototyping
DSS
OLAP database
Systemantics

Programming
programming language
source language
machine language
assembly language
high-level language
object-oriented programming

Advanced Concepts
multitasking
multiprocessing
SMP
MPP
virtual memory
virtual machine
RISC
computer architecture
pipeline processing
memory protection
address modes
relocatable code
standards & compatibility

Interesting Stuff
RTFM
flame
salary survey
hot topics and trends
space/time
object technology
software vendors
hardware vendors
emoticons
Easter Egg
Year 2000 problem
how to spoof your technical friend
holographic storage

Look Up the Acronym!

DOS PMOS APA OCR RARP DME CPE HSB SIMM APC HGC TOF
CAP ALU SSD TPS VHS UDP VBR DDC CISC AIX TSR TTL ZAK
CSMA/CD VM VESA MPP PMMU SDRAM PVC ROM OTPROM FEC
T3 EDFA HMOS ACK FPU SAS TCP/IP CGA EOT RISC MMI VLAN
DASD VAD ECL CGM AFP PGP SOHO CRT WFW JPEG ONC XBM
DDP EPP GAS PRML CMOS PR/SM GDM SSE EPROM BIOS YUV
SMD VSAM EOF VBE FRAM TXD GIF DHCP RCS FEP ZIF TDMA
SOCKS WFM ADPCM RAS PIF FPGA PRAM DAC CHRP OSR2
FQDN REXX EMS CORBA GSOS SOJ APPN GUI SVC TDM HPIB
ICMP SIDF HTML FDX GPC VAR SQL ECC CSU/DSU DIN RAM
TSOP QUAM TXD ORB DFSMS JAD UART SGRAM TFT ICSA VLIW
SNA PROM RBOC PRN CDMA FDDI ARP DRAM ESD HLS RAD
CNE DCE A/UX GARP EIGRP ONA IOW GDI IPX EDA FED SOM
IBIS PDN HSRP SPICE BPR XML UPC RDBMS DVD HDTV TIFF
DLS IMTC GNU MPEG CAV DNA UNC ICCP HSM BMP UCR FSN
MPC VSAT RCDD IRC SPID DES OLE FUD IHV TCO EMM SVR5
GSMP ICS PCL HDA FOIRL ADRS SPX VBE DDCMP IP RTUA RPQ
EBCDIC MIC LSI SIPP FDMA JEIDA IDAPI COM GXC EOL XDR
LEO DMA SCO JNI DAT IAP EIA UUCP HPR JCL GBPS HPFS
ASCII MIB ICR DIB LSAPI TIF HMOS XIP RFS IPS CGA DAO
EEPROM ISO EAM MIME PDQ HDL NIST PCMCIA DPMI KHZ
LMDS BCD VDT VBE LDAP JMAPI MIPS TLA HTTP JAR FCB
ICAP MHZ JBOD GPSS LQ INT JES RMI IMS MAN KBPS JTAG
DEN MGA MHS SLC ROM EIDE GAL NCGA MTF NLSP DEC ITSP
NTFS HiPPI ECMA WAN GSM MS PCI OODBMS DHTML KB MOPS
CR/LF NCOS MSN SMA MIDI ST POP LCD OCX LATA IGES NIC
GIGO IANA HLLAPI IPDS QNX JTC1 MIMD PSW OEM OORDBMS
ACAP LPT1 TA NMI JDK PNNI NCSC HFS SVN RFC UDF IOS
DCOM NCB HP-MFM NURB UX JAM MEO RMA LUNI PnP PVN
MDF MICR SDLC KB PFB IDE NT VADSL IMAP JTAG PCM OCE
NAT PPS QAM RIP SAP MSMQ ESA HDLC SCSI MCA NDIS DIMM
GEO ODBC FEP RF JFIF MCSE LANE TTY XCMD NUMA FAT NASI
GQL LAN NGM MRP OODB TIA PQFP FPU DDS MMX SONET OSF
RLE BRI SGML MCB TQFP SDF QIC UMA QBE LED MCM HST
NAK SIR PUMA RSVP LBA PU MVS POS ITAA SMP PMMU MOV
LU SOIC MSO Z-CAV PFM ABI TSO CCW EMI ISA PCB SCO ODMA
RACF GVPN VAP NLQ BTLZ CAM DDBMS FSK SDH DFP CCITT
HIPO SPL INIT LIFO SHTML UAE TLD MLPPP NTAS

Most entries in this book are by acronym only.

A

A:

The designation for the first floppy disk drive in a PC. In PCs that have two floppy drives, the 3.5" drive is typically A:, and the 5.25" drive is B:.

A+ certification

See *CompTIA*.

AA

(Auto Answer) See *modem*.

AAUI

(Apple AUI) Apple's version of the Ethernet AUI connector. See *AUI* and *10Base5*.

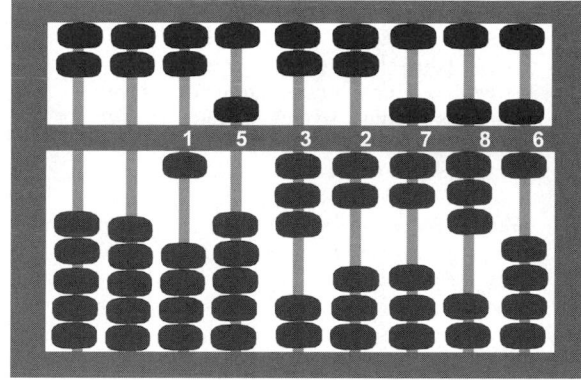
An Abacus

abacus

One of the earliest counting instruments. Similar devices predate the Greek and Roman days. It uses sliding beads in columns that are divided in two by a center bar. The top is "heaven," where each of two beads is worth 5 when moved to the center bar. The bottom is "earth," where each of five beads is worth 1 when moved toward the center. See *biquinary code*.

ABAP/4

The Development Workbench part of SAP's R/3 software suite. See *R/3*.

A/B box

A manual switch box with two inputs (A and B) or two outputs, depending on usage. It typically connects two peripherals to one computer or one peripheral to two computers. See *data switch*.

ABC

(Atanasoff-Berry Computer) The first electronic digital computer. Completed in 1942 by Iowa State Professor John Atanasoff and graduate student Clifford Berry, it employed many of the principles of all future computers. For example, although physically in the form of rotating drums, its memory used capacitors that were constantly being recharged like today's dynamic RAM.

It used a standard IBM card reader for input and an odometer-like device for output. For interim storage, Atanasoff devised a base-2 punch and reader that could very quickly store 1,500 bits on paper sheets by electrostatically burning holes in them. The ABC could solve 29 linear equations with 29 unknowns in one 24-hour day, a marvel for its time.

John Mauchly, cobuilder of the ENIAC, began corresponding with Atanasoff in 1940 and visited him in 1941. Although Eckert and Mauchly's machine gained international attention,

ABC Computer
(Photo courtesy of Charles Babbage Institute, University of Minnesota.)

the ABC was recognized years later. A 1973 court overturned an ENIAC patent, stating that the basic ideas of the modern computer came from Atanasoff. In 1990, 87-year-old Atanasoff was awarded the National Medal of Technology, and, in 1997, a team from Iowa State University completed a replica of the machine, which took three years to build. It worked exactly as it was supposed to.

abend

(ABnormal END) Also called a *crash* or *bomb*, it occurs when the computer is presented with instructions or data it cannot recognize or the program is reaching beyond its protective boundary. It is the result of erroneous software logic or hardware failure.

When the abend occurs, if the program is running in a personal computer under a single-task (one program at a time) operating system, such as DOS, the computer locks up and has to be rebooted. Multitasking operating systems with memory protection halt the offending program allowing remaining programs to continue.

If you consider what goes on inside a computer, you might wonder why it doesn't crash more often. A large mainframe's memory can easily contain several billion storage cells (bits). Within every second, millions of these cells change their state from uncharged to charged to uncharged. If only one cell fails, the computer can abend.

ABI

(Application Binary Interface) A specification for a particular hardware platform and operating system. It is one step beyond the application program interface (API), which defines the calls from the application to the operating system. The ABI defines the API plus the machine language for a particular CPU family. An API does not ensure runtime compatibility, but an ABI does, because it defines the machine language, or runtime, format. See illustration on next page.

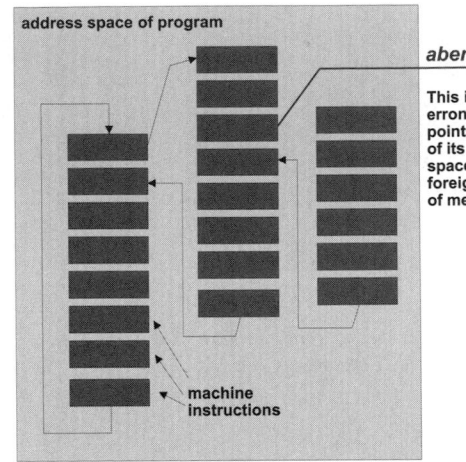

address space of program

abend

This instruction erroneously points outside of its address space into a foreign region of memory.

machine instructions

Abending

Abending, or crashing, often occurs when the program points outside of its address space. This diagram depicts the anatomy of a program. "The Data" refers to constants used within the program and the input/output areas that hold the data while it is being processed. "The Processing" refers to the program's logic embodied in the flow chart and physically implemented as thousands of machine instructions (the columns).

Abilene

A high-speed backbone network for Internet2 and other research projects developed by the University Corporation for Advanced Internet Development (UCAID) and named after a pioneering railroad outpost in the American West. Announced in April 1998, it is expected to provide an alternate to the vBNS backbone for Internet2 and initially operate at 2.4 Gbps (OC-48). Companies such as 3Com, MCI, Nortel, Cisco and Qwest have donated equipment worth more than $500 million. See *Internet2*.

ablative WORM

An optical disk technology in which the creation of the bit permanently alters the recording material, and the data cannot be changed.

abort

(1) To exit a function or application without saving any data that has been changed.

(2) To stop a transmission.

ABR

(1) (AutoBaud Rate detect) The analysis of the first characters of a message to determine its transmission speed and number of start and stop bits.

(2) (Available Bit Rate) An asynchronous transfer mode (ATM) level of service that adjusts bandwidth according to the congestion levels in the network.

absolute

In programming, a mathematical function that always returns a positive number. For example, ABS(25-100) yields 75, not -75.

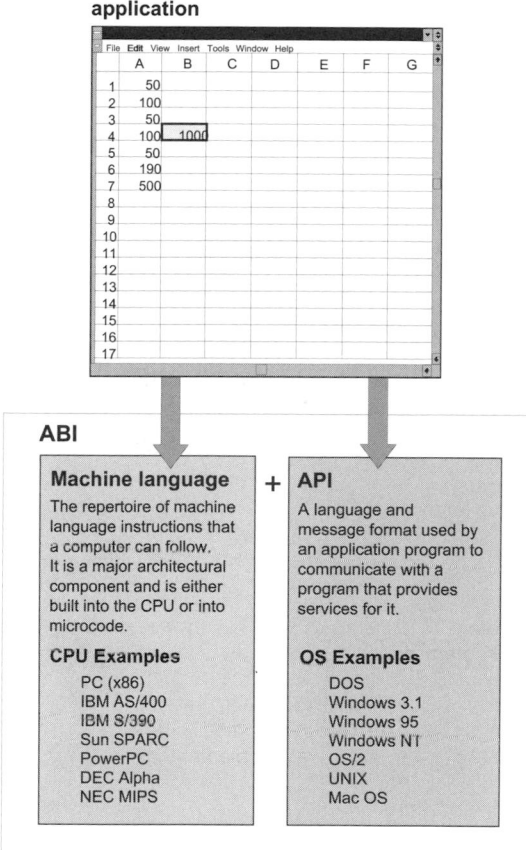

application

ABI

Machine language + **API**

The repertoire of machine language instructions that a computer can follow. It is a major architectural component and is either built into the CPU or into microcode.

A language and message format used by an application program to communicate with a program that provides services for it.

CPU Examples

PC (x86)
IBM AS/400
IBM S/390
Sun SPARC
PowerPC
DEC Alpha
NEC MIPS

OS Examples

DOS
Windows 3.1
Windows 95
Windows NT
OS/2
UNIX
Mac OS

ABI and API Relationship

absolute address

An explicit identification of a memory location, peripheral device, or location within a device. For example, memory byte 107,443, disk drive 2 and sector 238 are absolute addresses. The computer uses absolute addresses to reference memory and peripherals. See *base address* and *relative address*.

absolute path

Same as *full path*.

absolute URL

A URL that specifies the full path to the document page, which includes the domain name. Contrast with *relative URL*.

absolute vector

In computer graphics, a vector with end points designated in absolute coordinates. Contrast with *relative vector*.

absolute zero

The theoretical temperature at which molecular activity ceases. It is -273.15 degrees Celsius and -459.67 degrees Farhrenheit.

abstract class

Also called an *abstract superclass*, in object technology, it is a class created as a master structure. No objects of an abstract class are created, rather subclasses of the abstract class are defined with their own variations, and the subclasses are used to create the actual objects.

abstract data type

A unique data type that is defined by the programmer. It may refer to an object class in object-oriented programming or to a special data type created in traditional, non-OOP languages. See *abstraction, object-oriented programming* and *data type*.

abstraction

In object technology, determining the essential characteristics of an object. Abstraction is one of the basic principles of object-oriented design, which allows for creating user-defined data types, known as objects. See *object technology* and *encapsulation*.

abstract superclass

See *abstract class* and *superclass*.

AC

(Alternating Current) The common form of electricity from power plant to home/office. Its direction is reversed 60 times per second in the U.S.; 50 times in Europe. Contrast with *DC*.

AC-3

A Dolby Digital audio recording technology with surround sound. Used on DVD movie discs, it provides six channels, known as 5.1: front left, right and center and rear left and right plus subwoofer.

ACAP

(Application Configuration Access Protocol) A protocol for storing configuration information in a central server. It is designed to enhance e-mail functions for remote users by providing a central location for personal address books and client application preferences.

ACATS

(**A**dvisory **C**ommittee on **A**dvanced **T**elevision **S**ervice) The FCC committee that recommended the new Digital TV standard for the U.S. See *DTV*.

Accelerated Graphics Port

See *AGP*.

accelerator

A key combination used to activate a task. See *accelerator board* and *graphics accelerator*.

accelerator board

An add-in board that replaces the existing CPU with a higher performance CPU. See *graphics accelerator*.

ACCELL/SQL

A fourth-generation language from Unify Corporation, Sacramento, CA, that runs on UNIX platforms and supports Oracle, Ingres, Informix, Sybase and Unify databases. Introduced in 1985 as the Interactive Development System, it was the first database-independent 4GL for UNIX.

acceptable use policy

The conduct expected from a person using a computer or service. ISPs, online services and BBSs provide their customers with an acceptable use policy (AUP), which may prohibit spamming or commercial usage. Schools and universities provide AUPs for students using the computer lab, which defines unacceptable behavior.

acceptance test

A test performed by the end user to determine if the system is working according to the specifications in the contract.

access

To store data on and retrieve data from a disk or other peripheral device. See *access arm, access method* and *Microsoft Access*.

access arm

The mechanical arm that moves the read/write head across the surface of a disk similar to a tone arm on a phonograph. The access arm is directed by instructions in the operating system to move the read/write head to a specific track on the disk. The rotation of the disk positions the read/write head over the required sector.

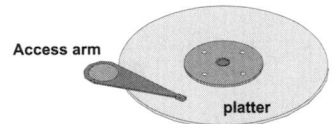

access charge

The charge imposed by a communications service or telephone company for the use of its network.

access code

(1) An identification number and/or password used to gain access into a computer system.

(2) The number used as a prefix to a calling number in order to gain access to a particular telephone service.

access concentrator

See *remote access concentrator*.

access control

The management of permissions for logging onto a computer or network. See *access control list* and *security*.

access control list

A set of data associated with a file, directory or other resource that defines the permissions that users and/or groups have for accessing it.

access control protocol

The technology used to authenticate a user logging onto a computer or network.

access denied

The system is unable to retrieve the file you are requesting. This often means that the file you want to open is already open in another application. It may also mean that the file has been purposefully made unavailable. See *hidden file*.

access line

The line from a customer site to a telephone company's central office.

access method

A software routine that is part of the operating system or network control program which performs the storing/retrieving or transmitting/receiving of data. It is also responsible for detecting a bad transfer of data caused by hardware or network malfunction and correcting it if possible.

Tape Access Methods

With tapes, the *sequential access method* is always used for storing data, which places the next block of data after the previous one.

Disk Access Methods

For disks, indexed access methods are widely used to keep track of records and files. The index is a table of contents for each file or each record within the file. The sequential method is also used when retrieval of individual records is not required. For example, the *indexed sequential access method* (ISAM) combines both methods by providing an index that is kept in sequential order. For fastest retrieval, the *direct access method* uses a formula to convert the record's identifying field, such as account number, into a physical storage address.

Communications Access Methods

Communications access methods, such as IBM's TCAM and VTAM, transfer data between a host computer and remote terminals. These routines prepare the data for transmission by placing the data into frames with appropriate control codes. These methods reference layers 3, 4 and 5 of the OSI model.

LAN access methods, such as CSMA/CD (Ethernet) and token passing (Token Ring), transfer data to and from connected computers on the network. These methods reference layers 1 and 2 of the OSI model.

accessory card

Same as *expansion board*.

access provider

See *ISP* and *online services*.

access rights

The privileges that are granted to a user, or perhaps to a program, to read, write and erase files in the computer system. Access rights can be tied to a particular server, to directories within that server or to specific programs and data files.

access router

See remote access router.

access server

See *remote access server* and *communications server*.

access time

(1) Memory access time is how long it takes for a character in memory to be transferred to or from the CPU. In a personal computer, fast RAM chips have an access time of 70 nanoseconds or less. SDRAM chips have a burst mode that obtains the second and subsequent characters in 10 ns or less.

(2) Disk access time is an average of the time between initiating a request and obtaining the first data character. In includes command processing, seek time and latency. Fast hard disks have access times of 10 milliseconds (ms) or less. This is a common speed measurement, but disk performance is influenced by channel speed (transfer rate), interleaving and caching. See *cache, seek time* and *latency*.

access token

In Windows NT, an internal security card that is generated when users log on. It contains the security IDs (SIDs) for the user and all the groups the user belongs to. A copy of the access token is assigned to every process launched by the user.

account

See *user account, guest account* and *account number.*

accounting machine

An early office machine used to compute and prepare invoices and payroll, etc., using magnetic stripe ledger cards or punched cards.

account number

The number assigned to an employee, customer, vendor or product for identification. Although it may contain only numeric digits, it is often stored as a character field, so that parts of the account number can be searched independently. For example, the number could contain a territory code, and records could be selected by state or region.

Accounting Machine System
The IBM accounting machine (left), keypunch and sorter (right) were the main ingredients of a punched-card data processing system up until the late 1960s. After keypunching, the cards were sorted into account number sequence, and the accounting machine printed the details and accumulated the totals. *(Photo courtesy of IBM Corporation.)*

accounts payable software

Financial software that deals with money owed by the organization to vendors. It summarizes the amounts owed, handles partial payments and vendor credits and also manages vendor terms, sales taxes payable and 1099s.

accounts receivable software

Financial software that deals with money owed to the organization. It provides reports on aging (amounts uncollected over time) and collection reports as well as credit memos and payment history.

accumulator

A hardware register used to hold the results or partial results of arithmetic and logical operations.

accuracy

How correct an answer is. The accuracy obtained from calculations depends on using bug-free computer chips as well as the quality of the input. Contrast with *precision*, which refers to the number of digits, or exactness, in an answer.

ACD

(Automatic Call Distributor) A computerized phone system that routes incoming telephone calls to the next available operator or agent. ACDs are the electronic heart of call centers, which are widely used in telephone sales and service departments of all organizations. The ACD responds to the caller with a voice menu and connects the call to an appropriate individual.

ACE

(Advanced Computing Environment) An open standard based on UNIX and Windows NT introduced in 1991 by MIPS Computer Systems and others. Although later disbanded, its purpose was to provide users a migration path from x86 PCs to MIPS RISC machines.

ACF

(Advanced Communications Function) An official product line name for IBM SNA programs, such as VTAM (ACF/VTAM), NCP (ACF/NCP), etc.

ACGNJ

(**A**mateur **C**omputer **G**roup of **N**ew **J**ersey) See *user group* and *Trenton Computer Festival*.

ACH

(**A**utomated **C**learing **H**ouse) A system of the U.S. Federal Reserve Bank that provides electronic funds transfer (EFT) between banks. It is used for all kinds of fund transfer transactions, including direct deposit of paychecks and monthly debits for routine payments to vendors. The ACH is separate and distinct from the various bank card networks that process credit card transactions.

ACIS

(**A**lan **C**harles **I**an **S**patial) A 3-D modeling engine from Spatial Technology Inc., Boulder, CO. ACIS is the 3-D kernel used in a wide variety of 3-D CAD programs including MicroStation Modeler, CorelCAD and, as of release 13, the venerable AutoCAD.

ACK

(**ACK**nowledgment code) The communications code sent from a receiving station to a transmitting station to indicate that it is ready to accept data. It is also used to acknowlege the error-free receipt of transmitted data. Contrast with *NAK*.

acknowledgment code

See *ACK*.

ACM

(**A**ssociation for **C**omputing **M**achinery, New York, www.acm.org) A membership organization founded in 1947 dedicated to advancing the arts and sciences of information processing. In addition to awards and publications, ACM also maintains special interest groups (SIGs) in the computer field.

Acoustic Coupler

acoustic coupler

A device that connects a terminal or computer to the handset of a telephone. It contains a shaped foam bed that the handset is placed in, and it may also contain the modem.

ACP

(**A**ssociate **C**omputer **P**rofessional) The award for successful completion of an examination in computers offered by the ICCP.

ACPI

(**A**dvanced **C**onfiguration and **P**ower **I**nterface) A power management specification developed by Intel, Toshiba and Microsoft that makes hardware status information available to the operating system. ACPI enables a PC to turn its peripherals on and off for improved power management especially in portables. It also allows the PC to be turned on and off by external devices, so that the touch of a mouse or the press of a key will "wake up" the machine. ACPI support is expected in Windows 98. See *OnNow*.

Acrobat

Document exchange software from Adobe that allows documents created on one platform to be displayed and printed exactly the same on another. An Acrobat driver works with most applications to convert DOS, Windows, UNIX and Mac documents into the Portable Document Format (PDF), which is displayed on the target machine with a free Acrobat reader. Fonts are either embedded within the PDF document, or to save space, the Acrobat reader (Acroread) can simulate the page layout with only two fonts. The style will differ, but the sizes and weights of the characters will reproduce correctly to maintain the same positioning of the text on the page.

Acrobat Exchange lets you view, print, annotate and collate electronic documents. It includes the PDF Writer driver for creating PDF files from most applications and also lets users add bookmarks and hypertext links to their documents. Acrobat Distiller is used to convert PostScript files into the PDF Format and allows for the creation of thumbnails. See *Acroread*.

Acroread

(**ACRO**bat **READ**er) The reader for Adobe Acrobat documents. Acroread is available free from the Adobe Web site (www.adobe.com). See *Acrobat*.

ACS

(Asynchronous Communications Server) See *remote access server*.

ACT!

A popular contact manager from Symantec that runs under DOS, Windows, Mac, Lotus Notes and various PDAs, including the Newton, HP and Psion palmtops. Originally a DOS-only program for contact names, ACT! has evolved into a comprehensive application for the sales professional and includes a full-featured word processor, activity scheduler and report generator. It also provides connectivity to fax and e-mail.

active addressing

A variety of techniques that are used to improve the quality of passive matrix LCD screens. See *LCD*.

Active Channel

An information delivery system from Microsoft that provides a platform for "pushing" information to users from Internet content providers as well as from internal intranets. Active Channels, which are supported in Internet Explorer Version 4.0 and Windows 98, are based on Microsoft's Channel Definition Format (CDF). Windows 98 provides a Channel Bar that can be viewed on the desktop. See *Active Desktop*.

active component

A device that adds intelligence in some manner to the signal or data that passes through it. For example, in networking, an active hub regenerates fading input pulses into new, strong output pulses. In contrast, a passive hub is just a junction box that does not affect the passing data.

Active Desktop

Enhanced functionality on the desktop that is part of Internet Explorer 4.0 and Windows 98. It enables Web pages to be turned into Desktop Items that reside on the desktop and be updated automatically. A Web page can also be turned into wallpaper, allowing a workgroup home page to be readily visible on each user's computer with links to related information on the intranet. Active Desktop supports Active Channels, which are subscriber-based content delivery systems from Internet Web sites or company intranet sites. See *Active Channel*.

Active Directory

An advanced, hierarchical directory service that comes with Windows NT 5.0. It is LDAP compliant and built on the Internet's Domain Naming System (DNS). Workgroups are given domain names, just like Web sites, and any LDAP-compliant client (Windows, Mac, UNIX, etc.) can gain access to it. Active Directory can function in a heterogeneous, enterprise network and encompass other directories including NDS and NIS+. Cisco is supporting it in its IOS router operating system. See *directory service*.

active hub

The central connecting device in a network that regenerates signals. Contrast with *passive hub* and *intelligent hub*. See *hub*.

The Channel Bar
This is the default Active Channel Bar on the first Windows 98 desktops. Clicking any item launches the browser so that you can subscribe. The Channel Guide lets you browse through the thousands of offerings from third parties that are made available via Microsoft's Web site.

active matrix

An LCD technology used in flat panel computer displays. It produces a brighter and sharper display with a broader viewing angle than passive matrix screens. Active matrix technology uses a thin film transistor at each pixel and is often designated as a "TFT screen." See *passive matrix* and *LCD*.

ActiveMovie

A video programming interface (API) from Microsoft for Windows 95/98 and NT that provides playback of MPEG, AVI and QuickTime video as well as WAV audio. It can decode MPEG movies in software and display them full screen at 24 fps on a 90MHz Pentium.

Active Server Page

A Web page that contains programming code written in VB Script or Jscript. It was developed by Microsoft starting with Version 3.0 of its Internet Information Server (IIS). When the IIS server encounters an Active Server page that is requested by the browser, it executes the embedded program. Active Server Pages are Microsoft's alternative to CGI scripts, which allow Web pages to interact with databases and other programs. Active Server Pages use an .ASP extension.

active star

See *active hub*.

Active Streaming Format

See *ASF*.

ActiveX

A brand name from Microsoft for various technologies based on its Component Object Model (COM), many of which are targeted for the Internet. See *COM, ActiveX control, ActiveX Server Component, OLE* and *COM automation*.

ActiveX automation

See *COM automation*.

ActiveX component

A software module based on Microsoft's Component Object Model (COM) architecture. Increasingly, Microsoft is using the term ActiveX to refer to a variety of its COM-based technologies. See *ActiveX control, ActiveX Documents, ActiveX Server Component* and *COM*.

ActiveX control

A software module based on Microsoft's Component Object Model (COM) architecture. It enables a program to add

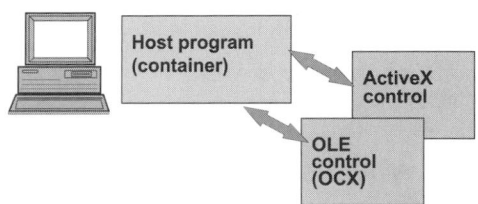

STAND-ALONE MACHINE (CLIENT or SERVER)

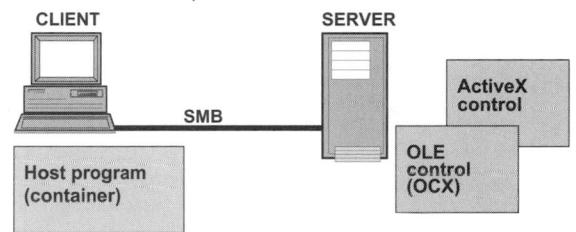

STORED ON A LAN, RUN LOCALLY

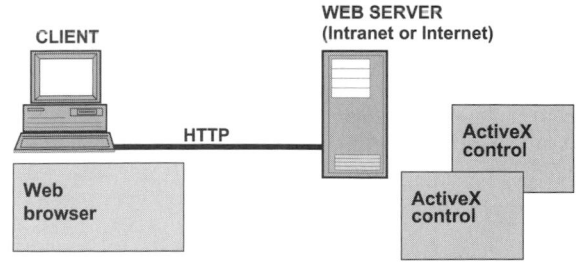

STORED ON A WEB SITE, RUN LOCALLY

ActiveX Controls

ActiveX controls can be stored locally or remotely, but they are run locally.

functionality by calling ready-made components that blend in and appear as normal parts of the program. They are typically used to add user interface functions, such as 3-D toolbars, a notepad, calculator or even a spreadsheet.

On the Internet or on an intranet, ActiveX controls can be linked to a Web page and downloaded by an ActiveX-compliant Web browser. ActiveX controls turn Web pages into software pages that can perform just like any program that is launched from a server.

ActiveX controls were originally called *OLE controls* or *OCXs*, which were Microsoft's second generation component architecture (VBXs were the first). OLE controls were renamed ActiveX and their interface requirements were reduced to speed up downloading from slow-speed Internet connections. See *COM, OLE, COM automation, OCX* and *VBX.*

ActiveX Documents

Extensions to Microsoft's OLE compound document architecture that allow a container application to use the full capabilities of server applications. For example, starting with Version 3.0, Internet Explorer (IE) is an ActiveX Documents container. Microsoft Office applications and the HTML viewer used in IE are ActiveX Document servers. Thus, IE can view a Web page, an Excel spreadsheet or a Word document by launching the appropriate server application.

Microsoft's Binder, which is an ActiveX Documents container, can print Excel spreadsheets and Word documents with the full printing and formatting capabilities of Excel and Word.

Formerly Document Objects, or DocObjects, the documents associated with ActiveX Documents are now called ActiveX Documents objects.

ActiveX-enabled browser

A Web browser that supports Microsoft's ActiveX component technology. It is built into Microsoft's Internet Explorer and is available as a plug-in for Netscape Navigator. See *ActiveX control* and *ScriptActive.*

ActiveX Server Component

A server-side software module constructed as an ActiveX component that is stored on a Windows client/server system or a Windows Web site. On a Web site, ActiveX Server Components can be called from Active Server Pages.

ACTOR

An earlier Windows object-oriented programming language for PCs developed by The Whitewater Group Inc., Evanston, IL.

ACTS

(Automated Computer Time Service) An NIST service that provides an ultra-accurate time based on several atomic clocks. ACTS lets computers using NIST software dial up the service and obtain the current time.

actuator

A mechanism that causes a device to be turned on or off, adjusted or moved. The component that moves the head assembly on a disk drive or an arm of a robot is called an actuator.

Ada

A high-level programming language developed by the U.S. Department of Defense along with the European Economic Community and many other organizations. It was designed for embedded applications and process control but is also used for logistics applications. Ada is a Pascal-based language that is very comprehensive.

Ada was named after Augusta Ada Byron (1815-1852), Countess of Lovelace and daughter of Lord Byron. She was a mathematician and colleague of Charles Babbage, who was developing his Analytical Engine. Some of her programming notes for the machine have survived, giving her the distinction of being the first documented programmer in the world.

The following Ada program converts Fahrenheit to Celsius:

```
with Text_IO;
procedure Convert is
package Int_IO is new Text_IO.Integer_IO(Integer);
Fahrenheit : Integer;
begin
  Text_IO.Put_Line("Enter Fahrenheit");
  Int_IO.Get(Fahrenheit);
  Text_IO.Put("Celsius is ");
  Int_IO.Put((Fahrenheit-32) * 5 / 9);
  Text_IO.New_Line;
end Convert;
```

ADABAS

A database management systems (DBMS) from Software AG, Reston, VA, (www.sagus.com), for IBM mainframes, VAXes, UNIX and Windows. It is an inverted list DBMS with relational capabilities. A 4GL called NATURAL, text retrieval, GIS processing, SQL and distributed database functions are also available. Introduced in 1969, it was one of the first DBMS's.

ADAPSO

See *ITAA*.

adapter

A device that allows one system to connect to and work with another. An adapter is often a simple circuit that converts one set of signals to another; however, the term often refers to devices which are more accurately called controllers. For example, display adapters (video cards), network adapters (NICs) and SCSI host adapters perform extensive processing, but they are still called adapters. See *host adapter* and *expansion bus*.

adapter card

See *adapter* and *expansion board*.

adaptive bridge

A network bridge that remembers destination addresses in order to route subsequent packets more quickly. Most bridges are this type.

adaptive compression

A data compression technique that dynamically adjusts the algorithm used based on the content of the data being compressed.

adaptive equalization

A transmission technique that dynamically adjusts its modulation method based on the quality of the line.

adaptive routing

The ability to select a new communications path to get around heavy traffic or a node or circuit failure.

adaptor

An alternate spelling of adapter.

ad banner

See *banner ad*.

ADC

(1) See *A/D converter*.
(2) (Advanced Data Connector) See *RDS*.

analog in   **digital out**
0 1 1 0 0 0 1 0 1 1 0

A/D Converter

ADCCP

(Advanced Data Communications Control Procedure) An ANSI communications protocol that is similar to the SDLC and HDLC protocols.

A/D converter

(Analog/Digital converter) A device that converts continuously varying analog signals from instruments that monitor such conditions as movement, temperature, sound, etc., into binary code for the computer. It may be contained on a single chip or can be one circuit within a chip. See *modem* and *codec*. Contrast with *D/A converter*.

AD/Cycle

(Application Development/Cycle) SAA-compliant software from IBM that provides a system for managing systems development. It provides a structure for storing information about all phases of an information system including systems analysis and design, database design and programming.

add-drop multiplexor

A device that multiplexes lower-speed electrical and optical channels into a high-speed optical channel. It is used to connect individual lines into backbone trunks. For example, an ADM might connect to a SONET ring on its high-speed side and to several T1s on its low-speed side. See DWDM.

adder

An elementary electronic circuit that adds the bits of two numbers together.

add-in, add-on

Refers to hardware modules, such as printed circuit boards, that are designed to be plugged into a socket within the computer.

address

(1) The number of a particular memory or peripheral storage location. Like post office boxes, each byte of memory and each disk sector has its own unique address. Programs are compiled into machine language, which references actual addresses in the computer.

(2) As a verb, to manage or work with. For example, "the computer can address 16MB of memory."

addressable cursor

A screen cursor that can be programmed to move to any row or column on the screen.

address bus

An internal channel from the CPU to memory across which the addresses of data (not the data) are transmitted. The number of lines (wires) in the address bus determines the amount of memory that can be directly addressed as each line carries one bit of the address. For example, the 8088 CPU has 20 address lines and can address 1,048,576 bytes. The 68020 has 32 address lines and can address four gigabytes.

Various swapping and switching techniques can be added to the hardware that allow a computer to use more memory than is directly addressable by its address bus. See *EMS*.

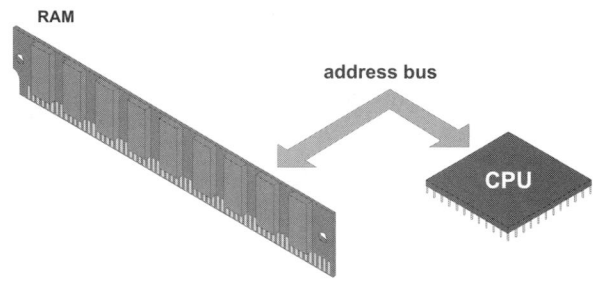

RAM

address bus

CPU

address mode

The method by which an instruction references memory. In *indexed addressing*, an instruction address is modified by the contents of an index register before execution. In *indirect addressing*, the instruction points to another address. Ultimately, in order to do any actual processing, the instruction must derive an *absolute address*, which is the real, physical address where the required data is located.

address register

A high-speed circuit that holds the addresses of data to be processed or of the next instruction to be executed.

address resolution

Obtaining a physical address that is ultimately needed to perform an operation. All instructions executing at the machine level require a physical memory, storage or network node address when referencing the actual hardware. Machine addresses are derived using table lookups and/or algorithms.

In a network, a "where is?" request is broadcast onto the network, and the logical address (name) is turned into a physical address (machine number), either by the recipient node or by a router that maintains a list of address translations.

address space

A computer's address space is the total amount of memory that can be addressed by the computer. For example, the Pentium can address 4GB of physical memory and 64TB of virtual memory.

A program's address space is the actual memory used by the program when running. It may refer to physical memory (RAM chips) or to virtual memory (disk) or to a combination of both.

Computer Desktop Encyclopedia

address translation

Transforming one address into another. For example, assemblers and compilers translate symbolic addresses into machine addresses. Virtual memory systems translate a virtual address into a real address. See also *address resolution*.

adds, moves and changes

See *moves-adds-changes*.

ADE

(Application Development Environment) An IBM approach for developing applications that will run in all SAA environments. The development software is client/server based, and the main functions reside in the host.

ADF

(Application Development Facility) An IBM programmer-oriented mainframe application generator that runs under IMS.

ad hoc query

A non-standardized inquiry. An ad hoc query is composed to answer a question when the need arises.

Ad Lib

An earlier sound card from Ad Lib, Inc., Quebec City, that, for a while, was the de facto standard for synthesized background music for computer games. It was a precursor to the MIDI standard.

admin

See *network administrator* and *system administrator*.

administrator

See *data administrator, database administrator, network administrator* and *system administrator*.

ADO

(Active Data Objects) A programming interface from Microsoft that is designed as "the" Microsoft standard for data access. First used with Internet Information Server, it is expected to become available for all Microsoft programming languages and applications. ADO is a COM object. See *RDO, DAO, OLE DB* and *ODBC*.

Adobe

(Adobe Systems, Inc., Mountain View, CA, www.adobe.com) The leading graphics and desktop publishing software company. Founded in 1982 by Dr. John Warnock, Adobe helped pioneer desktop publishing with its fonts and applications. Initially developed for the Macintosh, Adobe's PostScript fonts have become the standard among graphics and printing service bureaus. Adobe PhotoShop and Adobe Type Manager are examples of world-class software that spearheaded the industry. With Adobe's 1995 acquisitions of PageMaker and FrameMaker, Adobe has become the preeminent graphics design and desktop publishing software company.

Adobe fonts

See *PostScript*.

Adobe Illustrator

A full-featured drawing program for Windows and Macintosh from Adobe. It provides sophisticated tracing and text manipulation capabilities as well as color separations. Included is Adobe Type Manager and a selection of Type 1 fonts. Illustrator was originally developed for the Mac in 1987 and, up until Version 7.0, which was introduced in 1997, the Mac version included more features. The Macintosh version is the most widely-used drawing and composition program for the Mac platform.

Adobe Type Align

Software from Adobe that is used to align text to different shapes; for example, wrapping text around a circle or along the borders of an irregular or multi-sided object.

Adobe Type Manager

A PostScript font utility for the Macintosh and Windows from Adobe. It scales Type 1 fonts into screen fonts and prints them on non-PostScript dot matrix and HP laser printers. For printing fonts, current versions of ATM download font bitmaps to the printer. Earlier versions sent a bitmap of the entire page of text to the printer.

ATM technology is built into OS/2 and NeXTstep, and was originally developed to provide WYSIWYG screen fonts for the Mac. Since Windows does not render PostScript fonts on screen, ATM is widely used to do so. Both work together. Under Windows, ATM scales Type 1 fonts, while Windows 3.1 scales TrueType fonts. See *ATM.INI* and *PostScript*.

ADP

(1) (Automatic Data Processing) Synonymous with data processing (DP), electronic data processing (EDP) and information processing.

(2) (Automatic Data Processing, Inc., Roseland, NJ, www.adp.com) A nationwide computer services organization that specializes in payroll processing.

ADPCM

(Adaptive Differential PCM) An advanced PCM technique that converts analog sound into digital data and vice versa. Instead of coding an absolute measurement at each sample point, it codes the difference between samples and can dynamically switch the coding scale to compensate for variations in amplitude and frequency.

ADPCM Levels A and B sample at 37.8KHz creating 8-bit and 4-bit resolution (size of sample) respectively. Level C is 18.9KHz, 4-bit. See *PCM* and *sampling rate*.

ADP system

(Automatic Data Processing system) Same as *computer system*.

ADRS

(A Departmental Reporting System) An IBM mainframe report writer.

ADS

(AutoCAD Development System) A facility that allows C routines to be run from within AutoCAD.

ADSL

See *DSL*.

ADSM

(ADSTAR Distributed Storage Manager) A comprehensive software system for backup, HSM and disaster recovery from IBM. It can back up data from more than 25 client and server platforms to an ADSM server running on any IBM platform, HP-UX, Solaris or Windows NT. It extracts data from popular databases including DB2, Oracle, Sybase and Lotus Notes. ADSM uses its own RDBMS to keep track of all storage management functions. As of Version 3.0, it supports adminstration via a Web-based interface.

ADT

(Asynchronous Data Transfer) A transmission technique used in ISDN PBXs that dynamically allocates bandwidth. See also *abstract data type* and *tool* (as in application development tool).

Advanced Data Connector

See *RDS*.

Advanced Revelation

A DOS application development system from Revelation Technologies, Inc., Cambridge, MA, (www.revelation.com). It includes the R/BASIC programming language and supports SQL, DB2, Oracle and other databases. The Windows counterpart is OpenInsight for Workgroups and uses the BASIC+ language.

AdvanceNet

HP's early network strategy that included OSI, SNA and various networking standards along with its proprietary networking. In the mid 1980s, HP moved from proprietary networking to open standards.

ADW

See *Key:Enterprise.*

AES

(Advanced Encryption Standard) A state-of-the-art encryption standard that is being developed by the NIST. It is expected to replace DES. See *NIST* and *DES.*

(2) (Audio Engineering Society, Inc., New York, www.aes.org) A membership association devoted to audio technology research and development, marketing and education. Founded in 1948, technical standards have been continually developed under the its auspices. AES is dedicated to ensuring that audio quality is maintained in the digital world.

(3) (Automated Export System) A U.S. Customs Service application that tracks goods exported to foreign countries.

AFC

(Application Foundation Classes) A class library from Microsoft that provides an application framework and graphics, graphical user interface (GUI) and multimedia routines for Java programmers. AFC Enterprise Libraries include support for data access, directory services, transactions and distributed objects. AFC is compatible with AWT and runs in Windows and other JVM environments. See *JFC, AWT* and *IFC.*

AFE

(Apple File Exchange) A Macintosh utility that converts data files between Mac and PC formats. It also includes a file translator between IBM's DCA format and MacWrite; however, MacLink Plus Translators can be used for additional capability.

AFIPS

(American Federation of Information Processing Societies Inc.) An organization founded in 1961 dedicated to advancing information processing in the U.S. It was the U.S. representative of IFIP and umbrella for 11 membership societies. In 1990, it was dissolved and superseded by FOCUS.

AFM file

(Adobe Font Metrics file) A file that contains font metric information for a Type 1 PostScript font. See *PFA file, PFB file* and *PostScript.*

AFP

(Advanced Function Presentation) A page description language from IBM introduced in 1984 initially as Advanced Function Printing. It was first developed for mainframes and then brought down to minis and workstations. AFP is implemented on the various platforms by Print Services Facility (PSF) software, which generates the native IBM printer language, IPDS, and depending on the version, PostScript and LaserJet PCL as well. IBM calls AFP a "printer architecture" rather than a page description language.

AFP printer

A printer that natively accepts the AFP page description language. IBM makes desktop AFP printers and third parties make network printers that support AFP.

AFS

A distributed file system for large, widely-dispersed UNIX networks from Transarc Corporation, Pittsburgh, PA. It is noted for its ease of administration and expandability and stems from Carnegie-Mellon's Andrew File System.

AFSMI

(Association For Service Management International, Fort Myers, FL, www.asfmi.org) A membership organization dedicated to the advancement of executives and managers in the high-tech services and support industry. Founded in 1976, benefits include industry studies and publications, education, career placement and an annual conference and exhibition.

After Dark

A popular screen saver program for Macs and PCs from Berkeley Systems, Inc., that allows the user to develop custom animations. After Dark popularized the "flying toaster" display in 1989.

agent

A software routine that waits in the background and performs an action when a specified event occurs. For example, agents could transmit a summary file on the first day of the month or monitor incoming data and alert the user when a certain transaction has arrived. Agents are also called *intelligent agents*. When used with PDAs, they are often called *personal agents*. See *workflow*.

aggregate

To gather, collect or assemble. For example, "to aggregate data" means to gather separate sets of data. As a noun, "aggregate data" is data that has been collected from two or more sources.

AGP

(Accelerated Graphics Port) A high-speed graphics port from Intel that provides a direct connection between the display adapter and memory at 66MHz, twice the speed of the 33MHz PCI bus. A clock doubling technique boosts speed to 133MHz. AGP-equipped motherboards have only one AGP slot, which requires an AGP-compliant display adapter.

The PCI slot that would normally host the display adapter can be used for another device. The AGP slot is brown and slightly shorter than the white PCI slot. It is also located about an inch farther back. AGP is expected to give a large boost to 3-D graphics performance.

AGPset

A chipset that supports the Accelerated Graphics Port. See *Intel chipsets*.

AI

(Artificial Intelligence) Devices and applications that exhibit human intelligence and behavior including robots, expert systems, voice recognition, natural and foreign language processing. It also implies the ability to learn or adapt through experience.

In the future, everything we now know and think about a computer will change. By the turn of the century, you should be able to converse with the average computer. Future systems will ask you what help you need and automatically call in the appropriate applications to aid you in solving your problem.

In the 1990s, the AI buzzword will be abused to the hilt as it will refer to any and all advancements. However, the acid test of AI was defined in the 1940s by the English scientist, Alan Turing, who said, "A machine has artificial intelligence when there is no discernible difference between the conversation generated by the machine and that of an intelligent person."

Note: The term intelligence refers to processing capability; therefore, every computer is intelligent. But, artificial intelligence implies human-like intelligence. An ironic twist in terminology.

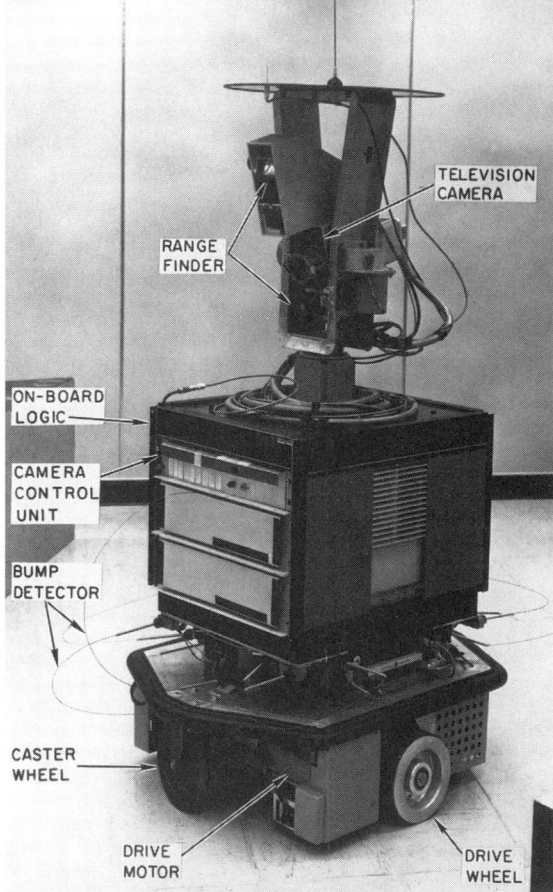

Shakey the Robot
Developed in 1969 by the Stanford Research Institute, Shakey was the first fully-mobile robot with artificial intelligence. Shakey is seven feet tall and was named after its rather unstable movements. *(Photo courtesy of The Computer Museum, Boston.)*

AIFC, AIFF file
(Audio Interchange File Format) A digital audio file format from Apple that is used on the Macintosh. It uses the .AIF extension and breaks apart the file into chunks. The Common chunk holds file parameters such as sampling rate, and the Sound Data chunk contains the digital sound. AIFC and AIFF-C are compressed versions of the format.

AI file
(Adobe Illustrator file) A vector graphics file created in Adobe Illustrator.

AIIM
(Association for Information and Image Management International, Silver Spring, MD, www.aiim.org) A membership organization founded in 1943 devoted to creating industry standards and disseminating information about the document management industry. Its Document Management Alliance (DMA) task group has developed a common programming interface for document management systems (see *DMA*).

AIM
(Apple/IBM/Motorola) The alliance of Apple, IBM and Motorola, which developed the PowerPC chip, Taligent, Kaleida, etc. See *Apple*.

AIS
(Adobe IntelliSelect) Software from Adobe that enables a printer to automatically detect the printer language being used (PostScript, PCL, HPGL) and to switch to that mode of operation.

AIT
(Advanced Intelligent Tape) A magnetic tape techology from Sony that uses 8mm cassette-style cartridges that hold 25GB. It uses advanced metal evaporated (AME) media and includes a built-in head cleaner and an EEPROM chip that stores tape status and indexing information. The Memory in Cassette (MIC) feature enables fast forwarding to a selected partition. The cartridges are very similar in appearance to Exabyte 8mm tapes, but are not the same. AIT drive numbers have an SDX prefix. For a summary of all storage technologies, see *storage*.

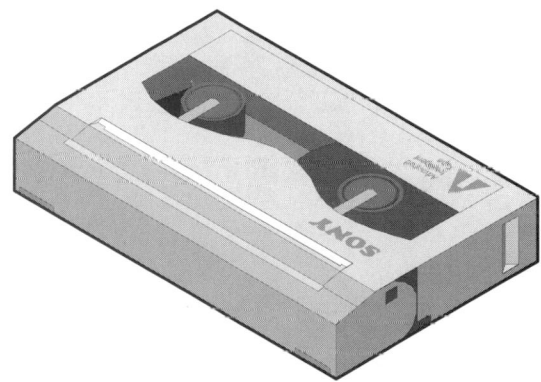

AIT Cartridge
Sony's AIT cartridges contain a memory chip that stores tape status and user information that enables fast forwarding to a selected partition.

AITP
(Association of Information Technology Professionals, Park Ridge, IL, www.aitp.org) Formerly the Data Processing Management Association (DPMA), it is a membership organization founded in 1951 devoted to providing professional development to individuals in the information systems field. It originated the CDP examinations which were later administrated by the ICCP. It was renamed AITP in 1996.

AIX
(Advanced Interactive eXecutive) IBM's version of UNIX, which runs on 386 and higher PCs, RS/6000 workstations and 390 mainframes. It is based on AT&T's UNIX System V with Berkeley extensions.

alarm filtering
In network management, the ability to pinpoint the device that has failed. If one device in a network fails, others may fail as a result and cause alarms. Without alarm filtering, the management console reports all deteriorating devices with equal attention.

A-Law
An ITU standard for converting analog data into digital form using pulse code modulation (PCM). Europe uses A-Law, while North America and Japan use mu-Law (u-Law). See *PCM* and *mu-Law*.

ALC

(Assembly Language Coding) A generic term for IBM mainframe assembly languages.

Aldus

The software company that pioneered desktop publishing with its PageMaker program for the Macintosh. Aldus was acquired by Adobe.

Aldus FreeHand

See *Macromedia Freehand*.

Aldus Persuasion

A desktop presentation program for the Mac from Adobe. It is used to create output for overheads, handouts, speaker notes and film recorders and provides sophisticated transition features (fades, gravel, swipes, etc.).

algebraic expression

One or more characters or symbols associated with algebra; for example, A+B=C or A/B.

ALGOL

(ALGOrithmic Language) A high-level compiler language that was developed as an international language for the expression of algorithms between people and between people and machines. ALGOL-60 (1960) was simple and widely used in Europe. ALGOL-68 (1968) was more complicated and scarcely used, but was the inspiration for Pascal.

The following example changes Fahrenheit to Celsius:

```
fahrenheit
begin
  real fahr;
  print ("Enter Fahrenheit ");
  read (fahr);
  print ("Celsius is ", (fahr-32.0) * 5.0/9.0);
end
finish
```

algorithm

A set of ordered steps for solving a problem, such as a mathematical formula or the instructions in a program. The terms algorithm and logic are synonymous. Both refer to a sequence of steps to solve a problem. However, an algorithm implies an expression that solves a complex problem rather than the overall input-process-output logic of typical business programs.

alias

(1) An alternate name used for identification, such as for naming a field or a file.

(2) A phony signal created under certain conditions when digitizing voice.

aliasing

In computer graphics, the stair-stepped appearance of diagonal lines. See *anti-aliasing*.

allClear

A flowcharting program for Windows from Clear Software, Inc., Newton, MA. It originally used a scripting language for chart creation; however, as of allClear III, it also provides visual chart building, allowing the user to easily switch between graphical and language modes.

ALL-IN-1

Office systems software from Digital for the VAX series. It provides a menu to all of Digital's office systems programs, including word processing, appointment calendars and e-mail systems.

allocate

To reserve a resource such as memory or disk. See *memory allocation*.

allocation unit

Same as *cluster*.

alloy

A mixture of two or more metals or a mixture of metal and some other substance in order to alter the end product to fit a particular requirement. For example, solder is an alloy of tin and lead.

all points addressable

See *APA*.

ALOHA

A type of TDMA transmission system developed by the University of Hawaii used for satellite and terrestrial radio links. In the traditional ALOHA system, packets are transmitted as required, and, like Ethernet's CSMA/CD method, collisions can occur. A "Slotted ALOHA" system triggers transmission starts by a clock and reduces the number of collisions.

Alpha

A family of RISC-based, 64-bit CPUs and computer systems from Digital. The first model introduced in early 1992 was the 150MHz 21064-AA, considered equivalent to a Cray-1 on a single chip. Subsequent Alpha models have continued to blaze the trails for high-speed microprocessors with clock rates up to 600MHz. Digital's Alpha-based servers and workstations run under Digital Unix, OpenVMS and Windows NT.

alpha channel

Eight bits in a 32-bit graphics pixel that is used as a separate layer for representing levels of transparency in an object.

Alpha Four, Five

A database program from SoftQuad International, Inc., Toronto, that is noted for its ease of use. Alpha programs read and write dBASE files directly. Alpha Four for DOS provides scripts for customizing applications. Alpha Five for Windows includes Xbasic, a BASIC-like programming language that incorporates database commands. These products were developed by Alpha Software, Burlington, MA, which was maintained as SoftQuad's U.S. headquarters.

alphageometric, alphamosaic

A very-low-resolution display technique that uses elementary graphics symbols in its character set.

alphanumeric

The use of alphabetic letters mixed with numbers and special characters as in name, address, city and state. The text you're reading is alphanumeric.

alpha test

The first test of newly developed hardware or software in a laboratory setting. The next step is a *beta test* with actual users.

Altair 8800

A microcomputer kit introduced in late 1974 from Micro Instrumentation and Telemetry Systems (MITS). It sold for $400 and used an 8080 microprocessor. In 1975, it was packaged with the Microsoft MBASIC interpreter written by Paul Allen and Bill Gates. Although computer kits were advertised earlier by others, an estimated 10,000 Altairs were sold, making it the first commercially successful microcomputer.

Altair 8800 Computer
The first successful microcomputer and the first commercial computer that came with a Microsoft product. *(Photo courtesy of The Computer Museum, Boston.)*

AltaVista

(www.altavista.digital.com) A search site on the Web that searches other search sites. Developed by Digital, the AltaVista software is also available in a variety of versions for searching inhouse intranets and databases. AltaVista's LiveTopics feature classifies search results further by organizing them by categories. See *Web search sites.*

alternate routing

The ability to use another transmission line if the regular line is busy.

alt key

A keyboard key that is pressed with a letter or digit key to command the computer. For example, in Windows, holding down the alt key and pressing F displays the File menu. Pressing Alt-Tab toggles between applications.

Alto

The personal computer from Xerox that pioneered the mouse/icon/desktop environment. Developed at PARC, it was the progenitor of Xerox's Star and Apple's Lisa and Mac. Designed in 1973 with 128K RAM, 608x808 screen, 2.5MB removable hard disk and built-in Ethernet. About 1,000 Altos were in use by 1979.

ALU

(Arithmetic Logic Unit) The high-speed CPU circuit that does calculating and comparing. Numbers are transferred from memory into the ALU for calculation, and the results are sent back into memory. Alphanumeric data is sent from memory into the ALU for comparing. The results are tested by GOTOs; for example, IF ITEMA EQUALS ITEMB GOTO UPDATE ROUTINE.

Some chips have multiple ALUs that allow for simultaneous calculations. For example, Chromatic Research's Mpact media processor chip has 450 of them. It allows audio, video and other multimedia processes to be performed simultaneously.

AM

(Amplitude Modulation) A transmission technique that blends the data signal into a carrier by varying (modulating) the amplitude of the carrier. See *modulate.*

Am386, Am486, Am586

Designations for AMD's 386-, 486- and low-end Pentium-compatible CPU chips.

Amazon.com

The largest bookstore on the World Wide Web. In March 1997, it announced that it had more than 2.5 million titles available for sale online, including one million out-of-print books that are still popular. Obviously, its name is its URL (www.amazon.com).

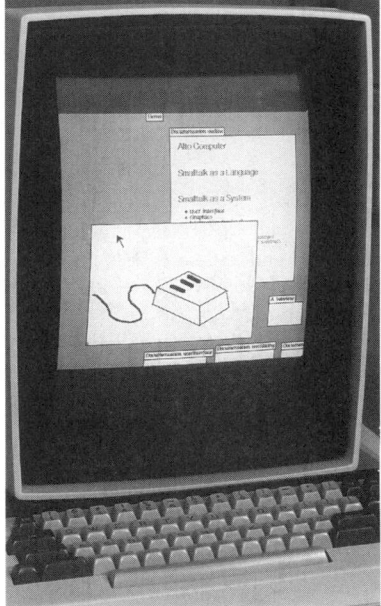

Alto Computer
The first graphical user interface created for business purposes was working more than 10 years before the Macintosh was introduced. *(Photo courtesy of Xerox Corporation.)*

An ALU in the Early Days
This was an arithmetic logic unit you could admire. The equivalent electronics of the ALU in Honeywell's Datamatic 1000 could fit on the head of a pin today. *(Photo courtesy of Honeywell, Inc.)*

ambient

Surrounding. For example, ambient temperature and humidity are atmospheric conditions that exist at the moment.

AMD

(Advanced Micro Devices, Inc., Sunnyvale, CA, www.amd.com) A manufacturer of flash memories, programmable logic devices, embedded processors and x86-compatible CPUs. Founded in 1969 by W. J. (Jerry) Sanders III and seven others, AMD has become a competitor to Intel, and its chips are used by many PC makers, including Compaq. Am486, K5 and K6 are AMD brand names.

Amdahl

(Amdahl Corporation, Sunnyvale, CA, www.amdahl.com) A computer manufacturer founded in 1970 by Dr. Gene Amdahl, chief architect of the IBM System/360. In 1975, Amdahl installed its first IBM-compatible mainframe, the 470/V6. Although not the first to make IBM-compatible mainframes, it succeeded where others failed. Today, Amdahl still offers a line of IBM-compatible mainframes along with UNIX based SPARC servers from Sun. However, more of the company's revenues are derived from software and consulting services.

In 1979, Amdahl left the company he founded to form Trilogy, which tried without success to make the world's largest chip based on wafer scale integration. See *Trilogy* and *CDS*.

Amdahl's First Computer
In 1975, Dr. Amdahl stands beside the Wisconsin Integrally Synchronized Computer (WISC), which he designed in 1950. It was built in 1952. *(Photo courtesy of Dr. Gene M. Amdahl.)*

Amdahl's law

"Overall system speed is governed by the slowest component." By Gene Amdahl, chief architect of IBM's first mainframe series and founder of Amdahl Corporation and other companies. Amdahl's law applied to networking. The slowest device in the network will determine the maximum speed of the network. See *laws*.

AMI BIOS

A PC BIOS from American Megatrends, Inc., Norcross, GA, (www.megatrends.com). AMI BIOSs have been widely used in PCs.

Amiga

A personal computer series from Amiga International, Inc., (www.amiga.de), subsidiary of Gateway 2000. The Amigas were originally introduced by Commodore in 1985. The first model was the A1000 with 256KB of RAM and powered by a 7MHz 68000 CPU. Amigas gained a reputation early on as advanced graphics and multimedia machines and NewTek's Video Toaster application brought it to the forefront of economical, high-end video editing.

Subsequent machines include the A500 and A600 home computers and A2000, A1200, A3000 and A4000 models. Commodore went into bankruptcy in 1994, and the technology was purchased by Escom AG, a German PC maker, who created the Amiga Technologies subsidiary. In 1997, Amiga Technologies was purchased by Gateway 2000 and renamed Amiga International. See *Commodore*.

AMLCD

(Active Matrix LCD) See *active matrix*.

amorphous

Unorganized or vague. A lack of structure. For example, the amorphous state of a spot on a rewritable optical disk means that the laser beam will not be reflected from it, which is in contrast to a crystalline state which will reflect light. See *crystalline*.

amp

(AMPere) A unit of electrical current in a circuit. *Volts* measure the force or pressure behind the current. *Watts* are a total measurement of power derived from multiplying amps times volts. See *volt* and *watt*.

ampere

See *amp*.

amplitude

The strength or volume of a signal, usually measured in decibels.

AMPS

(Advanced Mobile Phone Service) The analog cellular mobile phone system in North and South America and more than 35 other countries. It uses the FDMA transmission technology. AMPS is the cellular equivalent of POTS. See *D-AMPS* and *N-AMPS*.

analog

A representation of an object that resembles the original. Analog devices monitor conditions, such as movement, temperature and sound, and convert them into analogous electronic or mechanical patterns. For example, an analog watch represents the planet's rotation with the rotating hands on the watch face. Telephones turn voice vibrations into electrical vibrations of the same shape. Analog implies continuous operation in contrast with digital, which is broken up into numbers.

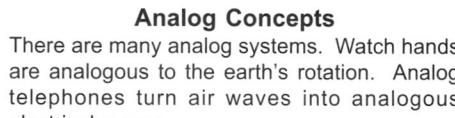

Analog Concepts
There are many analog systems. Watch hands are analogous to the earth's rotation. Analog telephones turn air waves into analogous electrical waves.

Advantages and Disadvantages Of Analog Techniques

Traditionally, audio and video recording has been analog. Sound, which is continuously varying air vibrations, is converted into analogous electrical vibrations. Video cameras scan their viewing area a line at a time and convert the infinitely varying intensities of light into analogous electrical signals.

The ability to capture the subtle nature of the real world is the single advantage of analog techniques. However, once captured, modern electronic equipment, no matter how advanced, cannot copy analog signals perfectly. Third and fourth generations of audio and video recordings show marked deterioration.

By converting analog signals into digital, the original audio or video data can be preserved indefinitely and copied over and over without deterioration. Once continuously varying analog signals are measured and converted into digital form, they can be stored and transmitted without loss of integrity due to the accuracy of digital methods.

The key to conversion is the amount of digital data that is created from the analog signal. The shorter the time interval between samples and the more data recorded from that sample, the more the digital encoding reflects the original signal.

analog camera

The traditional video camera. It records images as rows of continuous waves of red, green and blue intensities on videotape. Contrast with *digital camera*. See *analog, analog video* and *raster*.

analog channel

In communications, a channel that carries voice or video in analog form as a varying range of electrical frequencies. Contrast with *digital channel*.

analog computer

A device that processes infinitely varying signals, such as voltage or frequencies. A thermometer is a simple analog computer. As the temperature varies, the mercury moves correspondingly. Although special-purpose, complex analog computers are built, almost all computers are digital. Digital methods provide programming flexibility.

analog copy machine

The traditional copy machine that duplicates the image to be copied with the use of light and lenses. Contrast with *digital copy machine*.

analog monitor

A video monitor that accepts analog signals from the computer (digital to analog conversion is performed in the display adapter). It may accept only a narrow range of display resolutions; for example, only VGA or VGA and Super VGA, or it may accept a wide range of signals including TV. See *multiscan monitor* and *RGB monitor*. Contrast with *digital monitor*.

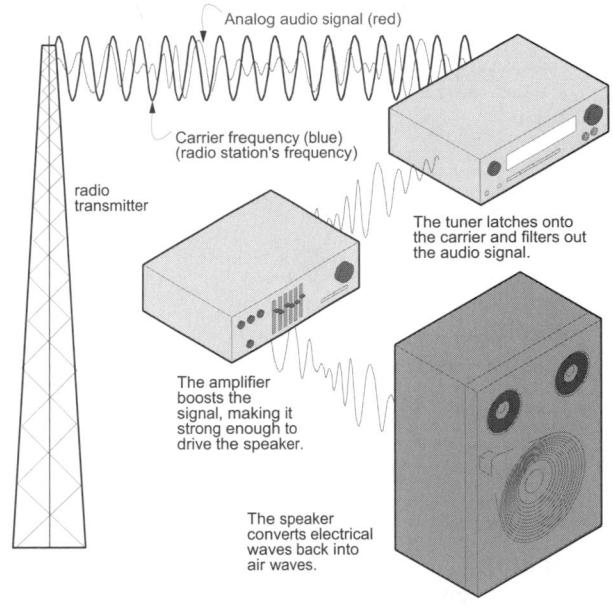

Analog Radio

Radio broadcasting uses analog transmission. The sound waves are wrapped in a carrier frequency unique to each station in the area. The sound is maintained in analog form throughout the entire chain from recording microphone to the listener's speaker.

analog phone

The original telephone technology, which converts air vibrations into an analogous electrical frequency. Unless a key telephone system or digital PBX is used, most homes and small offices still use analog phones, and the local loop is mostly analog. See *local loop*.

analog-to-digital converter

See *A/D converter*.

analog video

The original video recording method which stores continuous waves of red, green and blue intensities. In analog video, the number of rows are fixed, but the number of columns are infinite, because the signals are uninterrupted across each row. Contrast with *digital video*. See *analog camera* and *raster*.

analysis

See *systems analysis & design*.

analyst

See *systems analyst, business analyst* and *industry analyst*.

analytical database engine

Software that provides multiple views into a database of numerical information. The data is maintained in a non-redundant database, and the views are displayed in a traditional spreadsheet interface. See *spreadsheet* and *TM1*. See also *OLAP*.

Analytical Engine

A programmable calculator designed by British scientist Charles Babbage in the mid 1830s. Although it was never completed due to a lack of funds and constant redesign, it was a major advance because it contained the principles of the stored program computer.

Babbage's colleague and close friend, Augusta Ada Byron, the Countess of Lovelace and daughter of the poet Lord Byron, explained the machine's concepts to the public. Her programming notes have survived making her the first official computing machine programmer in the world. The Ada programming language was named after her. See *Difference Engine*.

anchor

In desktop publishing, a format code that keeps a graphic near or next to a text paragraph. If text is added, causing the paragraph to move to a subsequent page, the graphic image is moved along with it. See also *hypertext anchor*.

ANDF

(Architecture Neutral Distributed Format) Developed by The Open Group (formerly OSF), ANDF provides a method for developing shrink-wrapped UNIX software. ANDF is a pseudo, or intermediate, language that developers would generate their programs in. Each target machine would have an ANDF compiler that creates the machine language for that environment. ANDF never made it.

Analytical Engine
Programming the Analytical Engine might have been a bit more tedious than programming one of today's computers. *(Photo courtesy of Charles Babbage Institute, University of Minnesota.)*

AND-OR-NOT

The fundamental operations of Boolean logic. AND is true if both inputs are true, OR is true if any input is true, and NOT is an inverter; the output is always the opposite. For more details, see *Boolean logic*.

angstrom

A unit of measurement equal to .1 nanometer, which is approximately 1/250 millionth of an inch. Ten angstroms equal one nanometer. Angstroms are used to measure the wavelengths of light and the elements in a chip. The size of an atom is from three to 10 angstroms.

ANI

(Automatic Number Identification) A telephone service that provides the telephone number of the incoming call. ISDN supports ANI by carrying the calling telephone number in the D channel.

animated graphics

See *animation*.

animation

Moving diagrams or cartoons that are made up of a sequence of images displayed one after the other. Animation files take up much less disk space than a true video sequence.

Computer Desktop Encyclopedia

anisotropic

Refers to properties, such as transmission speed, that vary depending on the direction of measurement. Contrast with *isotropic*.

anode

In electronics, a positively charged receiver of electrons that flow from the negatively charged *cathode*.

anomaly

Abnormality or deviation. It is a favorite word among computer people when complex systems produce output that is inexplicable.

anonymous FTP

An FTP site on the Internet that contains files that can be downloaded by anyone. The anonymous FTP directory is isolated from the rest of the system and will generally not accept uploads from users.

ANS

(ANS Communications, Inc, Purchase, NY, www.ans.net) An ISP, Internet backbone and provider of private data network services, founded in 1990 as Advanced Network & Services, Inc., by IBM, MCI and Merit (consortium of Michigan universities). The original ANS was formed as a non-profit network services provider for NFSnet, but later added commercial customers through its for-profit ANS CO+RE (COmmercial REsearch) subsidiary.

In 1995, ANS CO+RE was acquired by AOL and changed its name to ANS Communications. The non-profit arm of Advanced Network & Services, (www.advanced.org), moved into Internet-based education. In 1997, WorldCom acquired ANS from AOL.

ANSI

(American National Standards Institute, New York, www.ansi.org) A membership organization founded in 1918 that coordinates the development of U.S. voluntary national standards in both the private and public sectors. It is the U.S. member body to ISO and IEC. Information technology standards pertain to programming languages, EDI, telecommunications and physical properties of diskettes, cartridges and magnetic tapes.

ANSI character set

The ANSI-standard character set that defines 256 characters. The first 128 are ASCII, and the second 128 contain math and foreign language symbols, which are different than those on the PC. See *extended ASCII*.

ANSI.SYS

A DOS driver used for screen control (cursor movement, clearing the screen, etc.) and as a keyboard macro processor to assign commands to a function key or reassign awkwardly placed keys. A few early applications required ANSI.SYS.

ANSI terminal

A display terminal that follows commands in the ANSI standard terminal language. Uses escape sequences to control the cursor, clear the screen and set colors, for example. Communications programs support the ANSI terminal mode and often default to this terminal emulation for dial-up connections to online services and BBSs.

answer only modem

A modem capable of answering a call, but not initiating one.

ant

See *crawler*.

anti-aliasing

Smoothing the jagged appearance of diagonal lines in a bitmapped image. The pixels that surround the edges of the line are changed to varying shades of gray or color in order to blend the sharp edge into the background. This technique is also called *dithering*, but when it is applied to diagonal and curved lines, it is called anti-aliasing. See ilustrations on next page.

Antifuse

A PLD technology from Actel Corporation, Sunnyvale, CA, (www.actel.com), that works the opposite of typical programmable chip methods. Instead of creating open circuits (blowing the fuse), connections are made between elements.

antivirus

A program that detects and removes a virus.

ANVIL

A family of CADD/CAM software packages from Manufacturing and Consulting Services Inc., Scottsdale, AZ. ANVIL products include 2 1/2-D and 3-D mechanical engineering systems for PCs, workstations, minis and mainframes.

AOCE

(Apple Open Collaboration Environment) Extensions to the Macintosh System 7 operating system from Apple that provide a technology framework for sharing services across a multiplatform enterprise. PowerTalk and PowerShare are the first AOCE products.

AO/DI

(Always On/Dynamic ISDN) A connection between an ISDN customer and an information service provider using the X.25-based D channel, which is a signalling channel that is always active. AO/DI uses 9.6 Kbps of the 16 Kbps D channel and switches to a circuit-switched B channel when more bandwidth is required. It enables low-bandwidth traffic, such as e-mail, newsfeeds, automatic data collection and credit card verifications, to be handled quickly and cost effectively. See *ISDN*.

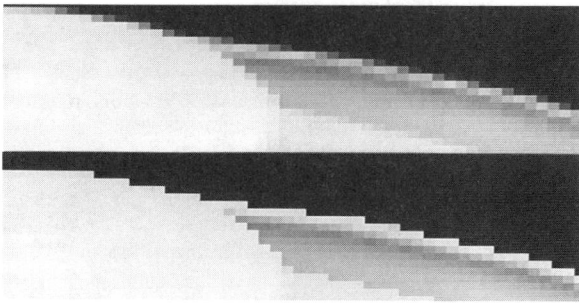

Anti-aliasing
This teapot, a famous first example of anti-aliasing, was programmed at the University of Utah. *(Photos courtesy of Computer Sciences Department, University of Utah.)*

AOL

(America Online, Inc., Dulles, VA, www.aol.com) The world's largest online information service with access to the Internet, e-mail, chat rooms and a variety of databases and services. In November 1997, it reached 10 million customers. AOL's Windows and Macintosh software displays all major functions on one screen, which has been appealing to the newcomer to the online experience.

In 1995, AOL acquired ANS CO+RE, a network services provider, which two years later, it sold to WorldCom in exchange for CompuServe's customer base, which WorldCom acquired at the same time. WorldCom continues to provide AOL's network services.

AOL's marketing campaign to freely distribute its trial software in unprecedented numbers has worked well, as new members have signed on in record numbers. AOL diskettes have even wound up in dry-ice-frozen packages of filet mignons.

When sending e-mail to an AOL customer via the Internet, the **aol.com** is the last part of the address; for example: **jjones@aol.com**. See *ANS* and *online services*.

APA

(All Points Addressable) Refers to an array (bitmapped screen, matrix, etc.) in which all bits or cells can be individually manipulated.

Apache

(1) (A "patchy" server) A widely-used public domain, UNIX-based Web server from the Apache Group (www.apache.org). It is based on, and is a plug-in replacement for, NCSA's HTTPd server Version 1.3. The name came from a body of existing code and many "patch files."

(2) A PowerPC CPU from IBM optimized for commercial processing.

APC

(1) (American Power Conversion Corporation, West Kingston, RI, www.apcc.com) The leading manufacturer of UPS systems and surge suppressors, founded in 1981 by Rodger Dowdell, Neil Rasmussen and Emanual Landsman, three electronic power engineers who had worked at MIT. Although created to develop solar electricity, the company introduced its first UPS system three years later as government funding for solar energy dissipated.

(2) (Application Performance Characterization) A graphics benchmark that tests actual application performance. See *GPC*.

APCUG

(Association of Personal Computer User Groups, Washington, DC, www.apcug.org) A non-profit organization dedicated to fostering communication among and between user groups and between user groups and vendors.

aperture card

A punched card that holds a frame of microfilm.

aperture grille

The technology used for illuminating phosphors in Sony's Trinitron monitors. See *slot mask*.

API

(Application Program Interface) A language and message format used by an application program to communicate with the operating system or other system program such as a database management system (DBMS). APIs are implemented by writing function calls in the program, which provide the linkage to a specific subroutine for execution. Thus, an API implies that some program module or routine is either already in place or that must be linked in to perform the tasks requested by the function call. See *ABI* and *interface*.

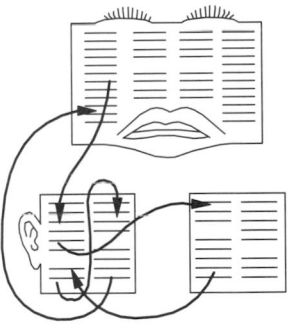

PROGRAMS TALK TO EACH OTHER!

APIC

(Advanced Programmable Interrupt Controller) An Intel chip that provides symmetric multiprocessing (SMP) for its Pentium systems. It can support up to 60 processors. See *OpenPIC*.

APL

(A Programming Language) A high-level mathematical programming language noted for its brevity and matrix generation capabilities. Developed by Kenneth Iverson in the mid 1960s, it runs on micros to mainframes and is often used to develop mathematical models. It is primarily an interpreted language, but compilers are available.

APL uses unique character symbols and, before today's graphical interfaces, required special software or ROM chips to enable the computer to display and print them. APL is popular in Europe.

APM

(Advanced Power Management) An API from Intel and Microsoft for battery-powered computers that lets programs communicate power requirements to slow down and speed up components.

app

See *application*.

APPC

(Advanced Program-to-Program Communications) A high-level communications protocol from IBM that allows one program to interact with another program across the network. It supports client/server and distributed computing by providing a common programming interface across all IBM platforms. It provides commands for managing a session, sending and receiving data and transaction security and integrity (two-phase commit).

APPC software is either part of, or optionally available, on all IBM and many non-IBM operating systems. Since APPC has only supported SNA, which utilizes the LU 6.2 protocol for session establishment, APPC and LU 6.2 have been considered synonymous.

In the past, APPC commands have differed across platforms. However, the CPI-C interface defines a standard set of APPC verbs.

app code

(APPlication code) Instructions in a program that actually process data.

append

To add to the end of an existing structure.

Apple

(Apple Computer, Inc., Cupertino, CA, www.apple.com) A manufacturer of personal computers and the industry's most fabled story. Founded in a garage by Steve Wozniak and Steve Jobs and guided by Mike Markkula, Apple blazed the trails for the personal computer industry.

Apple was formed on April Fool's Day in 1976. After introducing the Apple I at the Palo Alto Homebrew Computer Club, 10 retail stores were selling them by the end of the year.

In 1977, it introduced the Apple II, a fully-assembled computer with 4K RAM for $1,298. Its open architecture encouraged third-party vendors to build plug-in hardware enhancements. This, plus sound and color graphics, caused Apple IIs to become the most widely used computer in the home and classroom. They were also used in business primarily for the innovative VisiCalc software that was launched on it.

In 1983, Apple introduced the Lisa, the forerunner of the Macintosh. Lisa was aimed at the corporate market, but was soon dropped in favor of the Mac. As a graphics-based machine, the Mac was successful as a low-cost desktop publishing system. Although praised for its ease of use, its slow speed, small monochrome screen and closed architecture didn't excite corporate buyers.

In 1987, the Mac II offered higher speed, larger screens in color and traditional cabinetry that allowed third-party cards to be plugged in more easily. Numerous models were added and widely accepted. In

The Two Steve's
Wozniak and Jobs (left to right) pioneered the microcomputer revolution. Wozniak's engineering and Job's charisma truly built a legend. Here they hold the motherboard from the Apple I, Apple's first computer. *(Photo courtesy of Apple Computer, Inc.)*

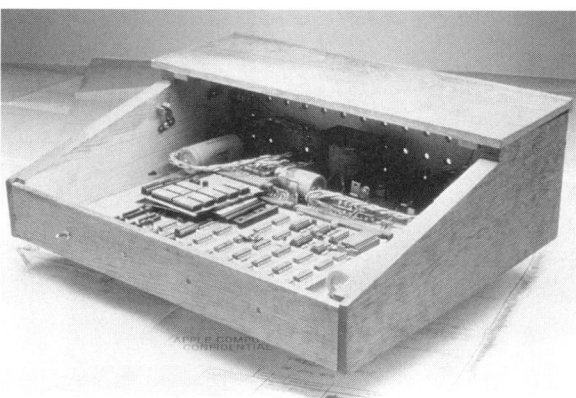

The Apple I
Rather humble beginnings, yet the Apple I led to the very successful Apple II series, which thrived for many years. *(Photo courtesy of Apple Computer, Inc.)*

1991, Apple surprised the industry by announcing an alliance with IBM to form several companies to develop hardware and software together. All the new efforts were eventually folded back into Apple and IBM, but the major product of this alliance for Apple was the PowerPC chip. In 1994, Apple introduced its first PowerMacs, and all subsequent Macintoshes eventually moved from the Motorola 680x0 architecture to the PowerPC.

Apple has stood alone in a sea of IBM and IBM-compatible PCs for more than a decade and a half. It has watched its graphical interface copied more with each incarnation of Windows and watched its market share drop simultaneously. Macintosh sales are estimated to be about 4% of the personal computer market. In late 1994, Apple began to license its OS to system vendors with the hopes of creating a Macintosh clone industry, which pundits felt should have been done years ago. Three years later, it pulled the plug on the clones, baffling almost every analyst that follows the company.

In late 1996, Apple announced its acquisition of NeXT Computer, which brought Steve Jobs back to the company he founded. It also gave Apple NeXT's OpenStep environment to be turned into Apple's next-generation operating system known as Rhapsody.

In 1998, Apple announced that Rhapsody was out and that only parts of OpenStep would be used in the next Mac operating system called Mac OS X (the X is Roman numeral X). Also in that year, Apple introduced the iMac, a low-priced Internet-ready Mac with a new look and the first personal computer with only a CD-ROM drive and no floppy disk.

Will Jobs inspire the company to greatness once again? Can Apple find ways to capture market share? Two things are a certainty. Mac users are extremely loyal, and surprises are always in store in the computer industry. Stay tuned!

Apple Desktop Bus

The Macintosh communications port for keyboards, mice, trackballs, graphics tablets and other input devices.

Apple II

The personal computer family from Apple that pioneered the microcomputer revolution. It was widely used in schools and home and actually still made until 1994. It used the 8-bit 6502 microprocessor running at 1MHz, an 8-bit bus and the Apple DOS or ProDOS operating systems. AppleSoft BASIC was built into ROM. With a Z80 microprocessor board plugged in, Apple IIs could run CP/M programs, which were the predominant desktop business software of the time.

Apple key

The original name of the Command key.

Apple menu

The menu at the top left side of a Macintosh screen that is always available to provide access to desk accessories.

AppleScript

A comprehensive command language used for automating tasks that is part of the System 7 operating system from Apple, starting with System 7 Pro. AppleScript provides a command line interface to the Macintosh similar to the way DOS commands are used in a PC.

AppleShare

Software from Apple that turns a

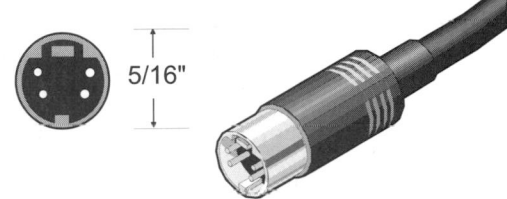

5/16"

Apple Desktop Bus Connector
ADB plugs and sockets look a lot like PS/2 connectors, but use a different pin configuration.

The Original Apple II
This was the very first Apple II in 1978. A TV set was often used as a monitor in the beginning. *(Photo courtesy of Apple Computer, Inc.)*

Macintosh into a file server. It works in conjunction with the Mac operating system and can coexist with other Macintosh applications in a non-dedicated mode.

AppleShare PC

Software for PCs from Apple that allows a PC to connect to an AppleTalk network. It requires a LocalTalk PC Card from Apple for ISA PCs, or a LocalTalk Card from DayStar Communications for Micro Channel PCs.

AppleSoft BASIC

Apple's version of BASIC that comes with Apple II models. It is installed in firmware and is always available.

applet

A small application, such as a utility program or limited-function spreadsheet or word processor. Java programs are usually called Java applets, because they are relatively small in size. See *crapplet*.

AppleTalk

Apple's local area network architecture introduced in 1985. It supports Apple's proprietary LocalTalk access method as well as Ethernet and Token Ring. The AppleTalk network manager and the LocalTalk access method are built into all Macintoshes and LaserWriters.

With other products from Apple and third parties, AppleTalk can run in PCs, VAXs and UNIX workstations. Since AppleTalk is patterned after the OSI model, it is a routable protocol that contains a network layer (OSI layer 3).

AppleTalk Filing Protocol

A client/server protocol used in AppleTalk communications networks. In order for non-Apple networks to access data in an AppleShare server, their protocols must translate into the AFP language.

AppleWorks

An integrated software package for the Mac and Windows from Apple. Originally ClarisWorks, it includes a word processor, spreadsheet, database and drawing program. It provides compound document creation that lets you, for example, insert a spreadsheet into your text document.

AppleWorks was originally the name for Apple's integrated package for the Apple II, which was introduced in 1983.

application

(1) A specific use of the computer, such as for payroll, inventory and billing. For a list of major application software categories, see *application software*.

(2) Same as *application program* and *software package*.

application centric

Focusing on the application as the foundation or starting point. In an application-centric system, the program is loaded first, which in turn is used to create or edit a particular type of data structure (text, spreadsheet, image, etc.). Contrast with *document centric*. See *component software*.

application developer

An individual that develops a business application and usually performs the duties of a systems analyst and application programmer.

application development environment

The combination of hardware and software used to develop an application. See *application development system* and *ADE*.

application development language

Same as *programming language*.

application development system

A programming language and associated utility programs that allow for the creation, development and running of application programs. Many database management systems (DBMSs) include a complete application development system along with a query language, report writer and the capability to interactively create and manage database files.

An application development system may also provide a full-scale application generator or various degrees of automatic application generation. An application development system that does not include its own database provides links to other databases via SQL, ODBC and other interfaces.

A client/server application development system is one in which the end product runs on a local area network. A two-tiered system splits the software between client and server. A three-tiered system splits the software between client, application server and database server. The application server provides the business logic in this case. See *client/server development system* and *application generator*.

Application Error

The error that occurs when a Windows program generates a GPF (General Protection Fault). The GPF usually causes the program to terminate, or "crash."

application framework

(1) The building blocks of an application.

(2) A class library that provides the foundation for programming an object-oriented application.

application gateway

See *proxy server*.

application generator

Software that generates application programs from descriptions of the problem rather than by traditional programming. It is at a higher level and easier to use than a high-level programming language. One statement or descriptive line may generate a huge routine or an entire program. However, application generators always have limits as to what they can be used for. Generators used for complex program development allow if-then-else programming to be expressed along with the simpler descriptive entries.

The goal with application generators and computer-aided software engineering (CASE) has always been to create a program by describing it, not programming it. The problem with such high-level systems is that either the resulting code is too slow or certain functions simply cannot be performed at all. As a result, commercial programs are rarely written in these languages; they are used for business information systems and often only for creating prototypes that are later reprogrammed in COBOL or C.

As computers run faster, they are capable of absorbing the excess code generated by higher-level products. In time, it is expected that the machine efficiency demanded of today's hardware may not be as critical and higher-level development tools may become the norm, relegating lower-level languages to a handful of highly-skilled and very highly-paid individuals. See *application development system*.

application layer

The software in the OSI protocol stack (layer 7 of 7) that provides the starting point of the communications session. See *OSI* and *TCP/IP abc's*.

application level gateway

See *proxy server*.

application notes

Instructions and recommendations from the vendor provided in addition to the normal reference manuals.

application package

A software package that is created for a specific purpose or industry.

application partitioning

Separating an application into components that run on clients and multiple servers in a client/server environment. Programming languages and development systems that support this architecture, known as *three-tier client/server*, may allow the program to be developed as a whole and then separated into pieces later. Development systems are differentiated by their ability to perform partitioning as a mainstream function in a high-level language or with visual programming (drag & drop) versus having to write chunks of code in C.

Application partitioning is an important capability for migrating legacy systems onto client/server environments. In many business applications, there is a lot of processing that should be done centrally in a server and not in each client machine. Such programs are either too demanding and process intensive for the client or they represent proprietary business logic that should not be replicated all over the enterprise. The centralized mainframe has always made a lot of sense for many applications. Partitioning the logic onto multiple servers emulates this approach in a client/server environment.

Who's Doing It?

Application partitioning can always be accomplished by writing 3GL code. However, with today's push for rapid application development (RAD), writing in a traditional programming language takes time. Newer client/server development systems such as Forte and DYNASTY provide application partitioning at the 4GL level, and it is being included in upgrades to existing development systems.

The OSF's Distributed Computing Environment (DCE) standard is also used for three-tier client/server, because it provides a standard for accessing programs and databases no matter where they are located.

application processor

A computer that processes data in contrast with one that performs control functions, such as a front end processor or database machine.

application program

Any data entry, update, query or report program that processes data for the user. It includes the generic productivity software (spreadsheets, word processors, database programs, etc.) as well as custom and packaged programs for payroll, billing, inventory and other accounting purposes. For a list of major application software categories, see *application software*. See also *program*. Contrast with *system program*.

application program interface

See *API*.

application program library

Application programs used by an organization.

application programmability

The customizability of an off-the-shelf application with the use of a macro or scripting language. For example, VBA (Visual Basic for Applications) is widely used to customize Windows applications. See *VBA*.

application programmer

An individual who writes application programs in a user organization. Most programmers are application programmers. Contrast with *systems programmer*.

application proxy

See *proxy server*.

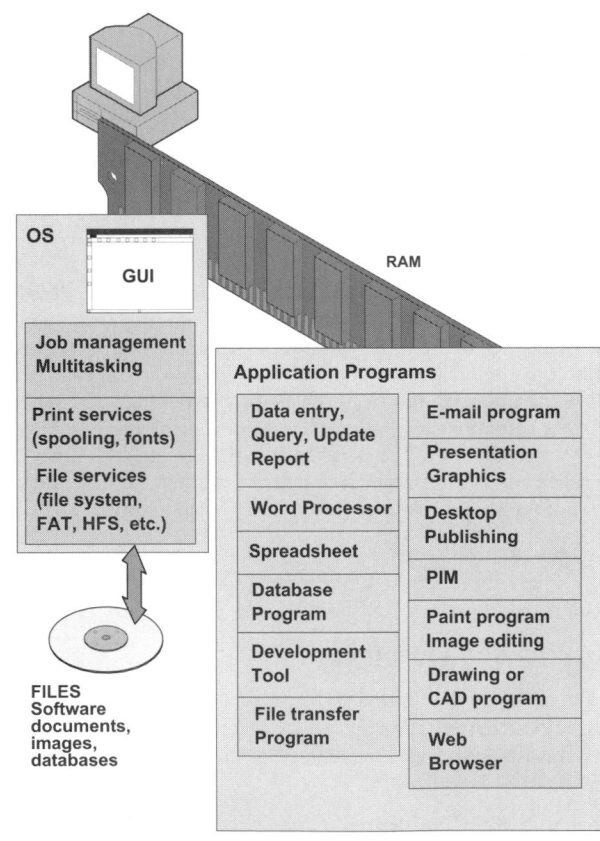

Application Programs

This diagram shows the typical application programs that run in a desktop computer. It also shows the major components of the operating

application server

(1) A computer in a LAN that performs data processing. In a two-tier client/server environment, the application server does the database processing (DBMS), and the client machine performs the business logic. In a three-tier client/server environment, an independent application server performs the business logic.

The operating system used to run the application server determines the server's effectiveness to process data for multiple users simultaneously. The quality of the algorithms used to manage time slices and to share resources are the most critical.

(2) A server in a LAN that contains applications shared by network clients. In this case, it functions as a remote disk drive for storing applications and is more accurately called a *file server*.

application sharing

A data conferencing capability that lets two or more users interactively work on the same application at the same time. The application is loaded and running in only one machine; however, keystrokes are transmitted from and screen changes are transmitted to the other participants. Application sharing provides the same capability as remote control software. See *application viewing* and *T.120*.

application software

Following are the major categories of application programs (software packages). See *application program*.

application suite

A set of applications designed to work together. It typically includes word processing, spreadsheet, presentation graphics and database programs. Some of the programs may be available separately, while others come only in the bundle. Microsoft Office, Corel Wordperfect Suite and Lotus SmartSuite are the major business application suites for Windows.

Although Windows provides integration features such as cut and paste and compound document creation, the suites provide additional tools to move data from one application more easily into another. In addition, common functions such as spell checking can be installed once and shared among all programs.

While no single application suite has the best program in each category, they have become popular because they come on one CD-ROM, are upgradable as a single unit and training is available for the whole package. Microsoft Office is the leading product.

application viewing

A data conferencing capability that lets two or more users view the same application at the same time. All users may be able to highlight different parts of the document, spreadsheet or database, but only the user at the machine where the application is loaded can actually edit it. See *application sharing* and *T.120*.

APPLICATION SOFTWARE

DATABASEPROGRAMS (Data Management)
Create and edit master and transaction records. Interactive editing of data. Ask questions, summarize, sort, print reports.

WORD PROCESSING
Create and edit text files. Replaces all typewriter functions. Some programs provide rudimentary desktop publishing.

SPREADSHEET
Create and edit rows and columns of numbers for budgets and financials and "what if " analysis. Multidimensional spreadsheets provide different slices, or views, of data quickly. Advanced financial planning systems provide goal seeking as well as statistical calculations.

PRESENTATION GRAPHICS
Create slide shows, do freehand drawing and turn numbers into 2-D and 3-D business graphics.

COMMUNICATIONS AND ELECTRONIC MAIL
Send/receive data and mail via modem and the network.

Integrated Package or Suite

DESKTOP PUBLISHING
Merge text and graphics and provide complete control over page layout for printing. More precise than word processing programs.

PIM (Personal Information Manager)
Organize random information for fast retrieval. Includes such features as a telephone list with automatic dialing, calendar, scheduler and tickler.

PROJECT MANAGEMENT
Keep track of a project and determine the impact of changes. The "critical path" is computed, which monitors all tasks that will slow down the entire project if delayed.

CAD (Vector graphics)
Create drawings for illustration and industrial design.

IMAGING (Raster graphics)
Scan documents and paint pictures into TV-like images.

DIAGRAMMING PROGRAM
Create drawings of interconnected symbols, such as network diagrams and organization charts. When symbols are moved, the lines stay connected.

CONTACT MANAGER
Keep track of prospects, names, addresses, appointments. Similar to a PIM, but specialized for sales activities.

MATHEMATICAL
Create, run and print complex mathematical equations.

SCIENTIFIC
Analyze real-world events by simulating them on high-speed computers or supercomputers.

MULTIMEDIA (Games and Education)
Multimedia adds graphics, sound and video for interactive games, encyclopedias and other references and educational courseware of all kinds.

VERTICAL MARKETS
Data entry, query, update and report programs customized for an industry such as banking and insurance. Either off-the-shelf or custom programmed, vertical market software is the most specialized type of information system available.

WEB BROWSER
"Surf the Web." Access the largest body of information in the world, shop online and be entertained.

APPN

(Advanced Peer-to-Peer Networking) Extensions to IBM's SNA communications that provide the necessary flexibility to enable direct communication between users anywhere on the network. Features includes improved administration, intermediate node routing and dynamic network services. APPN makes use of LU 6.2 protocols and is implemented in an SNA Node Type 2.1.

Approach

A relational database from Lotus that is also part of Lotus' SmartSuite set. It provides the ability to graphically create Windows applications using industry standard database formats, such as dBASE and Paradox. It includes macros and the ability to attach programming statements to data, providing a way to automate many kinds of applications.

APT

(Automatic Programmed Tools) A high-level programming language used to generate instructions for numerical control machines.

aptitude tests

The following organizations provide aptitude and proficiency tests in programming and computer topics.

Berger Series

A set of proficiency and aptitude tests from Psychometrics, Inc., Sherman Oaks, CA, (www.psy-test.com). Tests are available for many programming languages, including Ada, C, C++, CICS, COBOL, IBM 360/370 Assembler, Xbase and Visual Basic. Tests for MVS and UNIX are also available. Aptitude tests include B-APT for people with no programming experience, B-APT AF for the experienced and B-SYS for systems programming. All tests are paper and pencil, multiple-choice, administered by the recruiting or hiring firm. Psychometrics provides results by phone and by mail.

Prove It!

A set of software-based proficiency tests developed by Know It All, Inc., Philadelphia, PA, (www.knowitallinc.com). The tests, available on disks, cover a wide range of technical and clerical skills. The company also makes Prove It.Com, a subscription-based, Internet version of 65 tests for assessing various computer programming and related technical skills. Tests are available for one-time or continued use.

TekCheck

A series of more than 90 online tests developed by Bookman Consulting, Inc., New York, (www.tekchek.com), to measure programmer proficiency. Companies and employment/recruiting firms administer tests from their locations, send the results to Bookman and receive assessments within a couple of days. The series includes tests for C, C++, COBOL, CICS, DB2, Lotus Notes, Oracle, PowerBuilder, RPG and Visual Basic.

Wolfe-Spence Programming Aptitude Tests

A set of tests for programming, systems programming and systems analysis offered by Walden Personnel Testing & Training, Inc., Montreal, Canada, (www.waldentesting.com). Completed test booklets are faxed to U.S scoring centers in New Jersey. Walden faxes back detailed evaluation report on each candidate.

NOCTI

Technical Skills Tests Developed by the National Occupational Competency Testing Institute, available through Wonderlic Personnel Tests, Inc., Libertyville, IL. Wonderlic offers job-specific tests that assess the candidate's knowledge of a trade or profession. Tests are available for computer programming, computer technology, CAD/CAM and graphics/imaging. The company also offers Hay Aptitude tests to identify candidates who can work quickly and accurately with alphanumeric data.

arbitration

A set of rules for allocating machine resources, such as memory or peripheral devices, to more than one user or program.

Computer Desktop Encyclopedia

ARC, ARC+Plus

(1) PC compression programs from System Enhancement Associates, Inc., Clifton, NJ. ARC was one of the first compression utilities to become popular in the early 1980s. ARC+Plus provides enhanced features and speed.

(2) The ARC extension was previously used by PKWARE Inc. in its PKARC program.

(3) (Advanced RISC Computing) An open system specification based on the MIPS R3000 and R4000 CPUs. It includes EISA and TURBOchannel buses.

Archie

(ARCHIvE) An Internet utility used to search for file names. There are approximately 30 computer systems throughout the Internet, called "Archie servers," that maintain catalogs of files available for downloading from various FTP sites. Periodically, Archie servers search FTP sites throughout the Internet and record information about the files they find. If you do not have Archie, some Internet hosts let you log on via Telnet as user "archie." See *FTP*.

architecture

See *computer architecture, network architecture* and *software architecture*.

architecture neutral

Refers to software that is designed without regard to the target platform. Software is often written to maximize the performance of a specific hardware platform, but such software must be modified to make it run on other hardware. It is always a tradeoff. The more specialized the software, the faster the performance of the hardware, but the more difficult to make the software work on other platforms. See *intermediate language*.

archive

(1) To copy data onto a different disk or tape for backup or data retention purposes. Archived files are normally compressed to maximize storage media, and such compression programs may be called archiver or archiving programs.

(2) To save data onto the disk.

archive attribute

A file classification that indicates whether the file has been updated since the last backup.

archive formats

Following are popular data compression and archiving formats.

.ARC Compressed archive. Requires ARC from SEAware, PKARC, or Vernon Buerg's tiny, free ARCE or ARC-E programs to extract. Macintosh program ArcMac and UNIX program arc5521 will also work.

.ARJ A compressed archive requiring the ARJ program to uncompress. Requires UNARJ. No Macintosh equivalent is available.

.BTOA Binary to ASCII. A binary file in text format that must be converted back to binary with the UNIX program BTOA or the Windows/DOS program ATOB. (No Mac equivalent.) The file extension .atob is, of course, ASCII to Binary.

.CP or .CPIO Archives created by UNIX CPIO (copy-in/copy-out) tape archiving program. An early competitor to TAR. UNIX users may use the PAX (Portable Archive Exchange) program to deal with such files or with .TAR files. For DOS/Windows users, the program to get is PAX2EXE. (No Mac equivalent.)

.CPT A Macintosh file created by Compactor. (No DOS/Windows equivalent.)

.EXE Compression programs such as PKZIP and LHA have the ability to create "self-extracting" archive files. These are executable files because they have the decompression program built into them, and that's what you run. When you key in the name or double click the filename, the archive contents are extracted automatically.

.gz A compressed archive requiring a UNIX interpretation of PKZIP, specifically the GZIP (GNU Zip) program from the GNU Project. Get GZIP or GUNZIP for DOS/Windows machines. (No Mac equivalent.)

.Hqx or **.hqx** A Macintosh compression format. Requires the Mac program BinHex, the DOS/Windows program XBIN or the UNIX program MCVERT to convert.

.LHA or **.LZH** A DOS compressed archive requiring the use of the public domain program LHA, which can handle archives created by its predecessor if you specify the /O (for "old version") switch. LHA or WinZip are good choices for DOS/Windows users. Mac users should get MacLHarc.

.PAK A DOS compressed archive created by the PAK program. Rarely seen these days. (No Mac equivalent.)

.PIT A file created by the Macintosh program PackIt. DOS/Windows users can use UNPACKIT.

.SEA A Macintosh self-extracting archive. (No DOS/Windows equivalent.)

.shar, **.sh**, or **.Shar** A "shell archive" created by the UNIX SHAR program. Use UNSHAR to uncompress. There are versions for both Wintel machines and the Macintosh.

.SIT A compressed archive created with the Macintosh Stuffit or Stuffit Deluxe program from Aladdin Systems, Inc. DOS/Windows users should use UNSTUFF or UNSIT.

.taz or **.tgz** Short for ".tar.z". Use the GZIP program first on such files, and then TAR. No Mac equivalent for GZIP, but there is one for TAR.

.tar or **-tar** "Tape ARchive" files are packed into a single file by the UNIX TAR program. Use TAR to unpack. Macintosh users should look for UNTAR.

.UU or **.UUE** A binary file in ASCII format requiring the UUDECODE program or a clone to convert back into binary form. DOS/Window users should use UUDECODE by Richard Marks since it is the best version. Macintosh users should look for UUTOOL.

.Z Upper case "Z." A compressed file requiring the UNIX UNCOMPRESS program or a clone, such as the DOS program U16 or the Mac program MacCompress.

.z Lower case "z." Usually indicates an archive requiring the free GZIP program from GNU Project. To reduce confusion, newer versions of the GZIP program create files ending in .gz instead.

.ZIP Compressed archive created by PKZIP, WinZip, or a similar program. Mac owners may use ZipIt, UnZip or Stuffit Expander.

.ZOO Compressed archive created by the ZOO program, which is required to uncompress it. DOS/Windows users use ZOO. Macintosh users use MaxBooz.

ARCNET

(**A**ttached **R**esource **C**omputer **NET**work) The first local area network (LAN) introduced in 1968 by Datapoint Corporation. It connects up to 255 nodes in a star topology at 2.5 Mbits/sec over twisted pair or coax. A 20 Mbits/sec version was introduced in 1989. Although not as popular as Ethernet and Token Ring, many ARCNET networks were sold due to their lower-cost adapters. Gateways can connect ARCNET to mini and mainframe networks.

ARCNET is a data link protocol and functions at the data link and physical levels of the OSI model (1 and 2). It uses the token passing access method. See *data link protocol* and *OSI*.

ARDIS

(The ARDIS Company, Lincolnshire, IL, www.ardis.com) A joint venture of IBM and Motorola that provides wireless data transmission in the 800MHz FM band. It covers more than 400 metropolitan areas in the U.S., Puerto Rico and the Virgin Islands. ARDIS, which originally stood for Advanced National Radio Data Service, was the first wireless data network in the U.S.

areal density
The number of bits per square inch of storage surface. It typically refers to disk drives, where the number of bits per inch times the number of tracks per inch yields the areal density. The areal density of disk storage devices has increased dramatically since IBM introduced the RAMAC, the first hard disk computer in 1956.

The RAMAC had an areal density of 2000 bits per square inch. Current-day disk drives have areal densities of several hundred million bits per square inch. In 1996, IBM introduced its 2.5" Travelstar magnetic disks with capacities exceeding two gigabytes and an areal density of 1.3 billion bits per square inch. In its labs, IBM has demonstrated optical disks with 2.5 billion bits per square inch.

It is expected that by the year 2000, areal densities of disk drives will range from 10 to 30 billion bits per square inch. See *holographic storage* and *atomic force microscope*.

arg
See *argument*.

argument
In programming, a value that is passed between programs, subroutines or functions. Arguments are independent items, or variables, that contain data or codes. When an argument is used to customize a program for a user, it is typically called a *parameter*.

ARIN
(American Registry for Internet Numbers, Herndon, VA, www.arin.net) An organization founded in 1997 to dispense IP addresses in North and South America, the Caribbean and sub-Saharan Africa. This was previous handled by the InterNIC, which manages domain names. The European and Asian counterparts of ARIN are Researux IP Europeens (RIPE) and Asia Pacific Network Information Center (APNIC). See *IP address* and *InterNIC*.

arithmetic coding
A statistical data compression method that converts strings of data into single floating point numbers between 0 and 1.

arithmetic expression
(1) In mathematics, one or more characters or symbols associated with arithmetic, such as **1+2=3** or **8*6**.

(2) In programming, a non-text expression.

arithmetic operators
Symbols for arithmetic functions: + add, - subtract, * multiply, / divide. See *precedence*.

arithmetic overflow
The result from an arithmetic calculation that exceeds the space designated to hold it.

arithmetic underflow
The result from an arithmetic calculation that is too small to be expressed properly. For example, in floating point, a negative exponent can be generated that is too large (too small a number) to be stored in its allotted space.

ARJ
A compression program for backup archiving from ARJ Software, Inc., Norwood, MA, (www.arjsoftware.com). Introduced in the early 1990s and created by Robert Jung (the RJ in ARJ), ARJ never achieved the popularity of PKZIP, although it is considered a worthy competitor. See *JAR*.

ARM chips
A family of RISC-based microprocessors and microcontrollers from Advanced RISC Machines, Los Gatos, CA, (www.arm.com). ARM chips are high-speed CPUs that are known for their small die size and low power requirements. They are widely used in PDAs and other hand-held devices, including games and phones, as well as a large variety of consumer products. The StrongARM chip is a high-speed version jointly developed with Digital.

ARM was formed in 1990 by Acorn Computers, Apple and VLSI Technology. Its designs are licensed to various semiconductor manufacturers. See *StrongARM* and *Thumb*.

aromaware

Vaporware that is programmed in Java. See *vaporware*.

ARP

(Address Resolution Protocol) A TCP/IP protocol used to obtain a node's physical address. A client station broadcasts an ARP request onto the network with the IP address of the target node it wishes to communicate with, and the node with that address responds by sending back its physical address so that packets can be transmitted. ARP returns the layer 2 address for a layer 3 address.

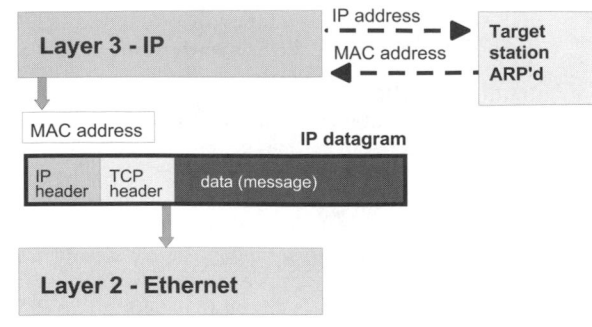

ARP'ing

The IP protocol broadcasts the IP address of the destination station onto the network, and the node with that address responds.

Since an ARP gets the message to the target machine, one might wonder why bother with IP addresses in the first place. The reason is that ARP requests are broadcast onto the network, requiring every station in the subnet to process the request. See *RARP*.

ARPAnet

(Advanced Research Projects Agency NETwork) The research network funded by the U.S. Advanced Research Projects Agency (ARPA). The software was developed by Bolt, Beranek and Newman (BBN), and Honeywell 516 minicomputers were the first hardware used as packet switches. ARPAnet was launched in 1969 at four sites including two University of California campuses, the Stanford Research Institute and the University of Utah.

In late 1972, the ARPAnet was demonstrated at the International Conference on Computers in Washington, DC. This was the first public demonstration of packet switching. Over the next decade, ARPAnet spawned other networks, and in 1983 with more than 300 computers connected, its protocols were changed to TCP/IP. In that same year, the unclassified military Milnet network was split off from ARPAnet.

As TCP/IP and gateway technologies matured, more disparate networks were connected, and the ARPAnet became known as "the Internet" and "the Net." Starting in 1987, the National Science Foundation began developing a high-speed backbone between its supercomputer centers. Intermediate networks of regional ARPAnet sites were formed to hook into the backbone, and commercial as well as non-profit network service providers were formed to handle the operations.

Over time, backbones by other federal agencies and organizations were formed and interlinked. In 1995, commercial Internet service providers took control of the major backbones, and the Internet continues to grow every day.

ARQ

(Automatic Repeat reQuest) A method of handling communications errors in which the receiving station requests retransmission if an error occurs.

array

An ordered arrangement of data elements. A vector is a one dimensional array, a matrix is a two-dimensional array. Most programming languages have the ability to store and manipulate arrays in one or more dimensions. Multi-dimensional arrays are used extensively in scientific simulation and mathematical processing; however, an array can be as simple as a pricing table held in memory for instant access by an order entry program. See *subscript*.

array element

One item in an array.

Price list in one-dimensional array						
Item	Amount	Item	Amount	Item	Amount	etc.
0001	016.43	0002	005.44	0003	110.00	0004

Sales figures in two-dimensional array					
	Jan	Feb	Mar	Apr	etc.
Product A	24484	09880	45884	83304	
Product B	67300	12372	37461		
Product C	20011	10029			
etc.					

array processor

A computer, or extension to its arithmetic unit, that is capable of performing simultaneous computations on elements of an array of data in some number of dimensions. Common uses include analysis of fluid dynamics and rotation of 3-D objects, as well as data retrieval, in which elements in a database are scanned simultaneously. See *vector processor* and *math coprocessor*.

artifact

Some distortion of an image or sound caused by a limitation or malfunction in the graphics and sound hardware or software.

artificial intelligence

See *AI*.

artificial language

A language that has been predefined before it is ever used. Contrast with *natural language*.

artificial life

An evolving computer science that models the behavior of biological systems. The models are used to study evolution as well as to apply the algorithms to a variety of problems in such fields as engineering, robotics and drug research.

AS

(1) (Application System) An IBM mainframe 4GL that runs under MVS. It was originally designed for non-computer people and includes commands for planning, budgeting and graphics. However, a programmer can also produce complex applications. It also provides computer conferencing.

(2) See *autonomous system*.

AS/400

(Application System/400) An IBM minicomputer series introduced in 1988 that runs under the OS/400 operating system. It is IBM's midrange series of computer systems used primarily for business applications, most of which are written in RPG III and COBOL.

The AS/400 was designed to supersede the System/36 and System/38, IBM's prior midrange computers. The AS/400 is an enhanced version of the System/38, which includes an integrated relational database management system. Since System/38 programs can be run without change in the AS/400, System/38s were readily exchanged for AS/400s. However, in order to run System/36 applications, the programs have to be recompiled.

In 1994, IBM introduced the AS/400 Advanced System/36, a PowerPC-based version of the AS/400 that natively runs the System/36 SSP operating system and its applications.

The AS/400 serves in a variety of networking configurations: as a host or intermediate node to other AS/400s and System/3x machines, as a remote system to mainframe-controlled networks and as a network server to PCs.

AS/400

The AS/400 is IBM's primary minicomputer line for small to medium-sized businesses. It has been an outstanding success. This is a low-end model of the second generation of AS/400s, which are housed in black cabinets. *(Photo courtesy of IBM Corporation.)*

AS/400 Integrated PC Server

Formerly the File Server I/O Processor (FSIOP) and now the IPCS, it is a CPU add-on to the AS/400 from IBM. It turns the AS/400 into a file server for PC networks, supporting network operating systems such as Windows NT, NetWare and OS/2. Initially powered by a 486, it migrated to the Pentium Pro.

ascender

The part of lowercase b, d, f, h, k, l, and t, that extends above the body of the letters.

ASCII

(American Standard Code for Information Interchange) Pronounced "ask-ee." A binary code for text as well as communications and printer control. It is used for most communications and is the built-in character code in most minicomputers and all personal computers.

ASCII is a 7-bit code providing 128 character combinations, the first 32 of which are control characters. Since the common storage unit is an 8-bit byte (256 combinations) and ASCII uses only 7 bits, the extra bit is used differently depending on the computer.

For example, the PC uses the additional values for foreign language and graphics symbols (see ASCII chart below). In the Macintosh, the additional values can be user-defined. See *hex chart* and *Unicode*.

ASCII art

Pictures created with normal text characters. This is done by hand or with programs that convert scanned images into ASCII characters. The following image was created by ASCII artist Joan Stark of Westlake, Ohio. ASCII art is very imaginative. For a wide variety of Joan's work as well as that of other artists, visit her gallery on the Web at www.geocities.com/SoHo/7373. See *GIFSCII*.

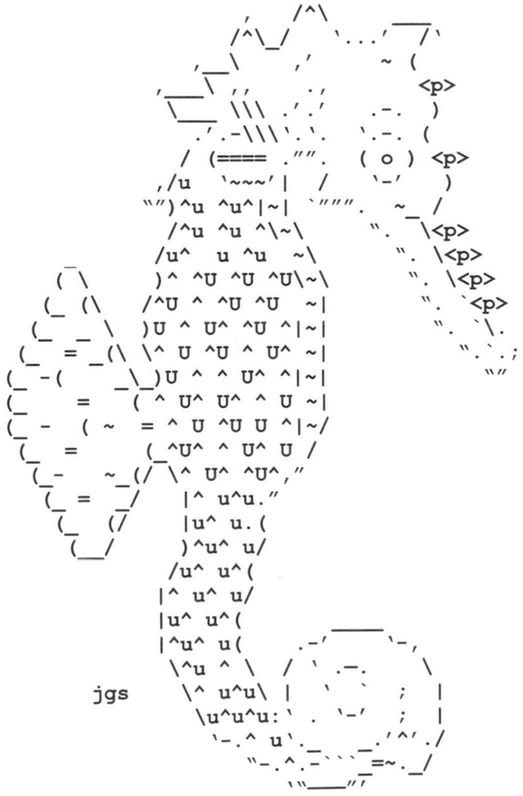

```
                          ,   /^\
                        /^\_/   `...,' /¯`
                 ,__\       ,'         ~  (
             ,__\  , ,       .,             <p>
             \___  \\\ .'.'       .-.       )
           .'`.-\\\`.`.     `.-. (
           / (==== ."".     ( o )  <p>
          ,/u `~~~'|  /      `-'    )
         `"")^u ^u^|~|  `""".    ~ _/
          /^u ^u ^\~\         ".  `\<p>
          /u^  u ^u  ~\         ".  \<p>
   _      )^ ^U ^U ^U\~\         ".  \<p>
  ( \    /^U ^ ^U ^U  ~|          ". `<p>
  (_ (\   )U ^ U^ ^U ^|~|           ". `\.
 (_  _ \ \^ U ^U ^ U^ ~|            ".`.`.;
 (_  = _(\ \^ U ^U ^ U^ ~|              ".`.`.;
 (_ -(   _\_)U ^ ^ U^ ^|~|               \"/
 (_   =  ( ^ U^ U^ ^ U ~|
 (_  - ( ~  = ^ U ^U U ^|~/
  (_  =     (_^U^ ^ U^ U /
   (_-  ~_(/ \^ U^ ^U^,"
    (_  =  _/   |^ u^u."
     (_  (/     |u^ u.(
      (__/      )^u^ u/
               /u^ u^(
               |^ u^ u/
               |u^ u^(
               |^u^ u(        _____
                \^u ^ \  / `-.-.  `-,
   jgs           \^ u^u\ |  `  `   ;  \
                  \u^u^u:`.  `-'   ;  |
                   `-.^ u`._     ,'^'./
                    "-.^.-``‾`=~._/
                       \"\___"7
```

ASCII chart

```
┌─────────────────────────────────────────┬───────────────────────┐
│          Standard ASCII                  │    Extended ASCII     │
│   The first 32 characters are            │        (DOS)          │
│          control codes.                  │                       │
├─────────────────────────────────────────┼───────────────────────┤
```

0	Null	33	!	81	Q	128	Ç	174	«	220	▄
1	Start of heading	34	"	82	R	129	ü	175	»	221	▌
2	Start of text	35	#	83	S	130	é	176	░	222	▐
3	End of text	36	$	84	T	131	â	177	▒	223	▀
4	End of transmit	37	%	85	U	132	ä	178	▓	224	α
5	Enquiry	38	&	86	V	133	à	179	│	225	β
6	Acknowledge	39	'	87	W	134	å	180	┤	226	Γ
7	Audible bell	40	(	88	X	135	ç	181	╡	227	π
8	Backspace	41	)	89	Y	136	ê	182	╢	228	Σ
9	Horizontal tab	42	*	90	Z	137	ë	183	╖	229	σ
10	Line feed	43	+	91	[	138	è	184	╕	230	µ
11	Vertical tab	44	,	92	\	139	ï	185	╣	231	τ
12	Form feed	45	-	93	]	140	î	186	║	232	Φ
13	Carriage return	46	.	94	^	141	ì	187	╗	233	Θ
14	Shift out	47	/	95	_	142	Ä	188	╝	234	Ω
15	Shift in	48	0	96	`	143	Å	189	╜	235	δ
16	Data link escape	49	1	97	a	144	É	190	╛	236	∞
17	Device control 1	50	2	98	b	145	æ	191	┐	237	ø
18	Device control 2	51	3	99	c	146	Æ	192	└	238	∈
19	Device control 3	52	4	100	d	147	ô	193	┴	239	∩
20	Device control 4	53	5	101	e	148	ö	194	┬	240	≡
21	Neg. acknowledge	54	6	102	f	149	ò	195	├	241	±
22	Synchronous idle	55	7	103	g	150	û	196	─	242	≥
23	End trans. block	56	8	104	h	151	ù	197	┼	243	≤
24	Cancel	57	9	105	i	152	ÿ	198	╞	244	⌠
25	End of medium	58	:	106	j	153	Ö	199	╟	245	⌡
26	Substitution	59	;	107	k	154	Ü	200	╚	246	÷
27	Escape	60	<	108	l	155	¢	201	╔	247	≈
28	File separator	61	=	109	m	156	£	202	╩	248	°
29	Group separator	62	>	110	n	157	¥	203	╦	249	·
30	Record separator	63	?	111	o	158	₧	204	╠	250	·
31	Unit separator	64	@	112	p	159	ƒ	205	═	251	√
32	Blank space	65	A	113	q	160	á	206	╬	252	ⁿ
		66	B	114	r	161	í	207	╧	253	²
		67	C	115	s	162	ó	208	╨	254	■
		68	D	116	t	163	ú	209	╤	255	
		69	E	117	u	164	ñ	210	╥		
		70	F	118	v	165	Ñ	211	╙		
		71	G	119	w	166	ª	212	╘		
		72	H	120	x	167	º	213	╒		
		73	I	121	y	168	¿	214	╓		
		74	J	122	z	169	⌐	215	╫		
		75	K	123	{	170	¬	216	╪		
		76	L	124	¦	171	½	217	┘		
		77	M	125	}	172	¼	218	┌		
		78	N	126	~	173	¡	219	█		
		79	O	127	⌂						
		80	P								

ASCII Characters (Decimal)

These are the standard ASCII characters (0-127), plus the extended ASCII characters as implemented in the DOS PC. This chart shows the values in decimal (0-255).

ASCII file

A file that contains data made up of ASCII characters. It is essentially raw text just like the words you're reading now. Each byte in the file contains one character that conforms to the standard ASCII code. Program source code, batch files, macros and scripts are straight text and stored as ASCII files. Text editors (Notepad, DOS Editor, Brief, etc.) and a few word processors, such as XyWrite, create ASCII files as their native file format.

ASCII text files become a common denominator between applications that do not import each other's formats. If both applications can import and export ASCII files, you can transfer your files between them. Almost all word processors import and export ASCII files, as well as many database and spreadsheet programs, although the latter may handle only a variation of this format known as comma delimited.

In non-ASCII, proprietary file formats, the actual text (name, address, etc.) is still ASCII, but there are codes in a header at the beginning of the file and codes are often embedded throughout the file. If you were to open a spreadsheet, database or graphics file with a text editor, it will generally display what appears like garble on screen.

Users familiar with DOS have often experienced this when using the Type command to display the contents of a file that was not just plain text. For example, if you were to "Type" one of the WMF picture files in this Encyclopedia, such as:

```
C:\CDE\PICTURES>type x86.wmf
```

you would get an erratic display and lots of beeps, because many of the codes in the file coincidentally contain the same binary patterns as line feeds, returns and the bell character, which are all ASCII control characters. The terms ASCII file, ASCII text file, text file and TXT file are synonymous. Contrast with *binary file*.

ASCII sort

The sequential order of ASCII data. In ASCII code, lower case characters follow upper case. True ASCII order would put the words DATA, data and SYSTEM into the following sequence:

```
DATA    SYSTEM    data
```

ASCII terminal

A simple input/output device that transmits and receives ASCII data. See *dumb terminal*.

ASCII text

Alphanumeric characters that are not in any proprietary file format. See *ASCII file*.

ASCII value

The numerical value, or order, of an ASCII character. There are 128 standard ASCII characters, numbered from 0 to 127. Extended ASCII adds another 128 values and goes to 255. The numbers are typically represented in decimal or in hexadecimal.

ASF

(Active Streaming Format) Microsoft's streaming media format. It is used in NetShow and is expected to become the standard format for RealAudio and RealVideo. See *NetShow*.

Ashton-Tate

A software company founded in 1980 by Hal Lashlee and George Tate to market dBASE II, which was created by Wayne Ratliff. The company developed and acquired other products, including Framework, MultiMate and dBASE Mac. In the mid 1980s, Ashton-Tate was one of the hottest software companies in the personal computer business. In 1991, it was acquired by Borland, which dispensed with all products except dBASE.

ASIC

(Application Specific Integrated Circuit) Pronounced "A-sick." A chip that is custom designed for a specific application rather than a general-purpose chip such as a microprocessor. There are many varieties of ASIC manufacturing, including custom built circuits from scratch, which is the most time consuming and complicated, to using gate arrays, standard cells and programmable logic devices. See *gate array, standard cell, PLD, CSIC* and *ASSP*.

askSam

A text management system for PCs from askSam Systems, Perry FL, (www.asksam.com). It holds unstructured text as well as standard data fields. The product is noted for its flexible text retrieval and hypertext capabilities.

ASM

(1) (Association for Systems Management) An international membership organization based in Cleveland, Ohio. Founded in 1947 and disbanded in 1996, it sponsored conferences in all phases of administrative systems and management.

(2) The file extension for assembly language source programs.

ASMO

(Advanced Storage Magneto-Optic) An enhanced magneto-optic, rewritable disk that holds 6GB. Using 120 mm (CD size) disks, ASMO evolved from a 7GB MO specification.

ASMP

(ASymmetric MultiProcessing) A multiprocessing design in which each CPU is assigned a particular program or part of a program that it executes for the duration of the session. Contrast with *SMP*, in which all the CPUs function as a resource pool taking whatever tasks need to be processed next. See *MPP*.

ASN

(1) (Autonomous System Number) A unique identifier of an autonomous system on the Internet. More than 7,000 ASNs have been assigned to ISPs and NSPs. ISPs usually have only one ASN, but NSPs may have more than one. ASNs are maintained in the Routing Arbiter Database (RADB). See *autonomous system, ISP* and *NSP*.

(2) (Advance Ship Notice) A notice sent by the vendor to the customer indicating what merchandise has been shipped. It enables the receiver to identify a package's contents electronically without having to open it.

ASN.1

(Abstract Syntax Notation.1) The rules for defining data structures transmitted over an OSI network.

ASP

(1) (Association of Shareware Professionals, Muskegon, MI, www.asp-shareware.org) A trade organization for shareware founded in 1987. Author members submit products to ASP, which are approved, virus checked and distributed monthly via CD to member vendors. CDs are periodically made available to the public.

(2) (Active Server Page) See *Active Server Page*.

aspect ratio

The ratio of width to height of an object. The aspect ratio of the screen of a standard computer monitor and TV set is 4:3. The high-definition TV (HDTV) format is 16:9.

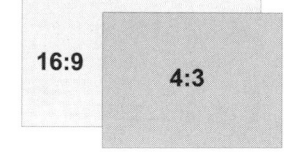

ASPI

(Advanced SCSI Programming Interface) An interface specification developed by Adaptec, Inc., Milpitas, CA, that provides a common language between drivers and SCSI host adapters. Drivers written to the ASPI interface can access peripherals that reside on different versions of SCSI host adapter hardware.

The ASPI Manager is the software that supports the ASPI interface. ASPI drivers call ASPI functions to access SCSI peripherals. The ASPI Manager for the SCSI host adapter processes these function calls and generates the appropriate SCSI commands to the SCSI peripherals. In DOS, the driver and ASPI Manager are combined in one module.

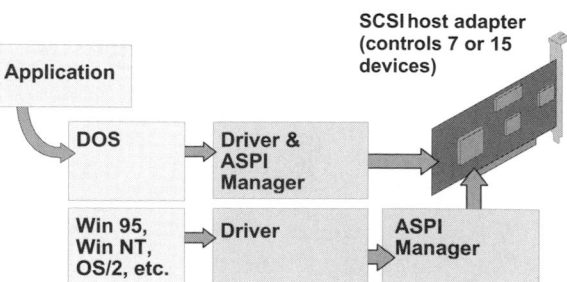

assembler

Software that translates assembly language into machine language. Contrast with *compiler*, which is used to translate a high-level language, such as COBOL or C, into assembly language first and then into machine language.

assembly language

A programming language that is one step away from machine language. Each assembly language statement is translated into one machine instruction by the assembler. Programmers must be well versed in the computer's architecture, and, undocumented assembly language programs are difficult to maintain. It is hardware dependent; there is a different assembly language for each CPU series.

In the past, control programs (operating systems, database managers, etc.) were written in assembly language to maximize the machine's performance. Today, C is often used instead. Like assembly language, C can manipulate the bits at the machine level, but it is also portable to different computer platforms. There are C compilers for most computers.

Although often used synonomously, assembly language and machine language are not the same. Assembly language is turned into machine language. For example, the assembly instruction COMPARE A,B is translated into COMPARE contents of memory bytes 2340-2350 with 4567-4577 (where A and B happen to be located). The physical binary format of the machine instruction is specific to the computer it's running in.

Assembly languages are quite different between computers as is evident in the example below, which takes 16 lines of code for the mini and 82 lines for the micro. The example changes Fahrenheit to Celsius.

```
         PC (Intel x86)                                HP 3000

cseg    segment para public 'CODE'      begin
        assume  cs:cseg,ds:cseg          intrinsic  read,print,binary,ascii;
start:                                   array buffer(0:17);
        jmp     start1                   array string(0:3);
msgstr  db      'Enter Fahrenheit '      byte array b'string(*) = string;
crlf    db      13,10,'$'                integer ftemp, ctemp, len;
nine    db      9                          move buffer:= "Enter Fahrenheit ";
five    db      5                          print (buffer,-30,%320);
outstr  db      'Centrigrade is $'        len:=read (string,-4);
start1: push    ds                         ftemp:= binary(b'string,len);
        push    cs                         ctemp:= (ftemp-32) * 5 / 9;
        pop     ds                         len:= ascii(ctemp,1-,b'string);
        mov     dx,offset cseg:msgstr      move buffer:= "Celsius is ";
        mov     ah,9                       move buffer(14) := string, (-len);
        int     21h                        print (buffer,-32,%0);
sloop:                                   end
cent:   call    getnumb
        test    ax,ax
        je      exit
        push    ax
        mov     dx,offset cseg:outstr
        mov     ah,9
        int     21h
        pop     ax
        sub     ax,32
        jns     c1
        push    ax
        mov     dl,'-'
        mov     ah,6
        int     21h
        pop     ax
        neg     ax
c1:     mul     five
        div     nine
        call    putval
        mov     dx,offset cseg:crlf
        mov     ah,9
```

Computer Desktop Encyclopedia

```
        PC (Intel x86)
        continued...

        int     21h              llr:    mov     dx,offset cseg:crlf
        jmp     sloop                    mov     ah,9
exit:   pop     ds                       int     21h
        mov     ah,4ch                   mov     ax,bx
        int     21h                      ret
getnumb:                         putval: xor     bx,bx
        xor     bx,bx                    push    bx
llp:    mov     dl,0ffh                  mov     bx,10
        mov     ah,1             llg:    xor     dx,dx
        int     21h                      div     bx
        cmp     al,0dh                   add     dx,'0'
        je      llr                      push    dx
        sub     al,'0'                   test    ax,ax
        jb      llr                      jne     llg
        cmp     al,'9'           bloop:  pop     dx
        ja      llr                      test    dx,dx
        xor     ah,ah                    je      endx
        shl     bx,1                     mov     ah,6
        add     ax,bx                    int     21h
        shl     bx,1                     jmp     bloop
        shl     bx,1             endx:   ret
        add     bx,ax            cseg    ends
        jmp     llp                      end     start
```

assignment statement

In programming, a compiler directive that places a value into a variable. For example, **counter=0** creates a variable named counter and fills it with zeros. The VARIABLE=VALUE syntax is common among programming languages.

associating files

See *file association*.

associative storage

Storage that is accessed by comparing the content of the data stored in it rather than by addressing predetermined locations.

ASSP

(Application Specific Standard Part) Another term for an ASIC chip. See also *CSIC*.

AST

(AST Computer, Irvine, CA, www.ast.com) A PC manufacturer founded in 1980 by Albert Wong, Safi Qureshey and Tom Yuen (A, S and T). It offers a complete line of PCs and sells through its dealer channel. AST was initially known for its line of add-in memory boards for the PC, including the Rampage and SixPak Plus boards. In 1993, AST acquired Tandy Corporation's PC manufacturing facilities.

asymmetric compression

A data compression technique that typically takes more time to compress than it does to decompress. Some asymmetric compression methods take longer to decompress, which would be suited for backup files that are constantly being compressed and rarely decompressed. Contrast with *symmetric compression*.

asymmetric encryption

Same as *public key cryptography*.

asymmetric modem

A full-duplex modem that transmits data in one direction at one speed and simultaneously in the other direction at another speed. Contrast with *ping pong*. See *V.90*.

asymmetric system

(1) A system in which major components or properties are different.

(2) In video compression, a system that requires more equipment to compress the data than to decompress it.

asynchronous

Refers to events that are not synchronized, or coordinated, in time. The following are considered asynchronous operations. The interval between transmitting A and B is not the same as between B and C. The ability to initiate a transmission at either end. The ability to store and forward messages. Starting the next operation before the current one is completed. Contrast with *synchronous*.

asynchronous communications server

See *ACS*.

asynchronous I/O

Overlapping input and output with processing. Both the hardware and the software must be designed for this capability. The peripherals must be able to run independent of the CPU, and the software must be designed to manage it.

asynchronous protocol

A communications protocol that controls an asynchronous transmission, for example, ASCII, TTY, Kermit and Xmodem. Contrast with *synchronous protocol*.

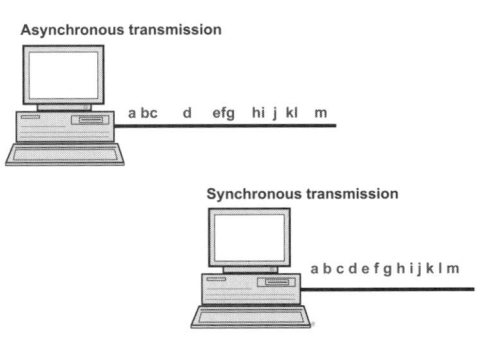

asynchronous transmission

The transmission of data in which each character is a self-contained unit with its own start and stop bits. Intervals between characters may be uneven. It is the common method of transmission between a computer and a modem, although the modem may switch to synchronous transmission to communicate with the other modem. Also called *start/stop transmission*. Contrast with *synchronous transmission*.

AT

(Advanced Technology) IBM's first 286-based PC, introduced in 1984. It was the most advanced machine in the PC line and featured a new keyboard, 1.2MB floppy and 16-bit data bus. AT-class machines run considerably faster than XTs (8088-based PCs). See *PC*.

AT&T

(American Telephone & Telegraph Company, New York, www.att.com) The largest long distance carrier in the U.S. It was founded in 1885 and was once the largest corporation in America. On January 1, 1984, it was relieved of its operating telephone companies by Federal court order. AT&T has gone through a major change from the world's largest monopoly to a competitive enterprise. Its early ventures into the PC market were modest, but in 1991, AT&T acquired NCR, a seasoned computer company, which it later renamed AT&T GIS.

In 1995, AT&T announced its intentional breakup into three

IBM AT
The fastest PC in 1984. Users were amazed at the extraordinary speed of the 286 with its huge 20MB hard disk. *(Photo courtesy of IBM Corporation.)*

independent companies: AT&T for telecommunications, Lucent Technologies for manufacturing of telecom equipment and AT&T GIS for computers, renamed NCR once again.

AT&T GIS

(AT&T Global Information Solutions) The new name of the NCR Corporation when it was acquired by AT&T in 1991. In 1996, AT&T spun off AT&T GIS as an independent company and restored its original name. See *NCR*.

AT&T WorldNet

One of the world's largest Internet service providers, providing dial-up access to the Net in more than 700 cities and 150 countries. To get started with the service, customers must download an application from the company's Web site at www.att.com/worldnet.

ATA, ATA-2, ATA-3, ATA-4

(AT Attachment) The specifications for IDE drives. See *IDE*.

ATAPI

(AT Attachment Packet Interface) The specification for IDE tape drives and CD-ROMs. See *IDE*.

Atari

(Atari Computer, Sunnyvale, CA) A video game manufacturer founded in 1972 by Nolan Bushnell, who named the company after a word used in the Japanese game of Go. Atari became famous for "Pong," a video game that simulated Ping-Pong on a TV set. In 1976, Atari was sold to Warner Communications which came out with a game computer dubbed the Atari Video Computer System. In 1978, the Atari 400 and 800 home computers were introduced, which were very successful. It later introduced the 600XL and 1200XL models.

In 1984, Atari was sold to Jack Tramiel and investors, which introduced the ST personal computer line in 1985 to compete with the Macintosh. The STs were advanced machines that were available up into the 1990s, but although popular, they received limited application support. Atari made attempts at offering IBM-compatible PCs, but was not successful in that arena. In late 1992, it introduced the Falcon multimedia computer, but soon shut down its R&D. At the end of 1993, it introduced its Jaguar video game, but sales were not sufficient to grow the company. In 1996, Atari merged with JTS Corporation. A large amount of inventory still existed at the time, but was not made available to the general public.

Atari 400

Sporting a whopping 16K of RAM and 8K of ROM, the Atari 400 was used mostly for games, which were contained in ROM cartridges that plugged into the unit. Atari computers helped spearhead the personal computer revolution in the early 1980s. *(Image courtesy of Kevan Heydon, Kevan's Computer Bits.)*

AT Attachment

See *ATA*.

AT bus

Refers to the 16-bit bus introduced with the IBM AT. It was an early term for the ISA bus.

AT class

Refers to second-generation PCs that use the 286 CPU and the 16-bit AT (ISA) bus. In the mid 1980s, AT class machines were the high-speed PCs of the day.

AT command set

A series of machine instructions used to activate features on an intelligent modem. Developed by

Hayes Microcomputer Products, Inc., and formally called the Hayes Standard AT Command Set, it is used entirely or partially by most every modem manufacturer. AT is a mnemonic code for ATtention, which is the prefix that initiates each command to the modem. See *Hayes Smartmodem*.

ATE

(Automatic Test Equipment) Machines that test electronic systems, primarily chips. See *EDA* and *DTA*.

AT interface

See *AT bus*. See also *ATA*.

AT keyboard

An 84-key keyboard provided with the PC AT. It corrected the non-standard placement of the PC's return and left shift keys. See *PC keyboard* and *Enhanced keyboard*.

ATM

(1) See also *ATM machine* and *Adobe Type Manager*.

(2) (**A**synchronous **T**ransfer **M**ode) A network technology for both LANs and WANs that supports realtime voice and video as well as data. The topology uses switches that establish a logical circuit from end to end, which guarantees a quality of service (QoS) for that transmission. However, unlike telephone switches that dedicate circuits end to end, unused bandwidth in ATM's logical circuits can be appropriated whenever available. For example, idle bandwidth in a videoconference circuit can be used to transfer data.

ATM is also highly scalable and supports transmission speeds of 1.5, 25, 100, 155, 622 and 2488 Mbps. ATM is also running as slow as 9.6 Kbps between ships at sea. An ATM switch can be added into the middle of a switch fabric to enhance total capacity, and the new switch is automatically updated using ATM's PNNI routing protocol.

Cell Switching

ATM works by transmitting all traffic as fixed-length, 53-byte cells. This fixed unit allows very fast switches to be built, because the processing associated with variable-length packets is eliminated (finding the end of the frame). The small ATM packet also ensures that voice and video can be inserted into the stream often enough for realtime transmission.

Quality of Service (Qos)

The ability to speficy a quality of service is one of ATM's most important features, allowing voice and video to be transmitted smoothly. Constant Bit Rate (CBR) guarantees bandwidth for realtime voice and video. Available Bit Rate (ABR) adjusts bandwidth according to congestion levels for LAN traffic. Unspecified Bit Rate (UBR) provides a best effort for remote users. Realtime variable Bit Rate (rt-VBR) supports interactive multimedia that requires minimal delays, and non-realtime variable bit rate (nrt-VBR) is used for bursty transaction traffic.

Integration with Legacy LANs

Network applications use protocols, such as TCP/IP, IPX, AppleTalk and DECnet, and there are tens of millions of Ethernet and Token Ring clients in existence. ATM has to coexist with these legacy protocols and networks. MPOA is an ATM standard that routes legacy protocols while preserving ATM quality of service.

LANE (LAN Emulation) interconnects legacy LANs by encapsulating Ethernet and Token Ring frames into LANE packets and then converting them into ATM cells. It supports existing protocols without changes to Ethernet and Token Ring clients, but uses MPOA route servers or traditional routers for internetworking between LAN segments.

ATM - Dead and Growing

When ATM came on the scene in the early 1990s, it was thought to be the beginning of a new era in networking, because it was both a LAN and WAN technology that could start at the desktop and go straight through to the remote office. In addition, ATM's ability to provide quality of service from end to end was highly praised as many envisioned a future world of realtime videoconferencing from desktop to desktop. However, the scenario did not evolve as quickly as expected, because huge numbers of Ethernets and Token Rings were in place, and faster versions of Ethernet along with Ethernet switches provided a simpler way to solve bandwidth congestion.

ATM equipment was expensive by comparison; the standards were confusing, and they took longer to be finalized. Very few ATM adapters wound up in desktop machines, except for demanding applications, and although ATM was widely implemented as a backbone technology, after Gigabit Ethernet was announced, "ATM is dead" was acclaimed throughout the networking community.

But a funny thing happened on the way to the graveyard. By the late 1990s, the ghosts were still breathing, and ATM equipment revenues began to increase. Over the years, ATM has been deployed as a backbone technology by major enterprises and all the major ISPs. The bugs have slowly been worked out, and the interfaces between Ethernet networks, which initially seemed complicated, are working solid and enjoying outstanding throughput over the ATM backbone.

ATM continues to be installed for mission critical network backbones. For example, Level 3 Communications, a multi-billion dollar startup, which is building a full service fiber network based on IP, is using ATM switches at its core. While router vendors claim they can deliver quality of service over IP-routed networks without ATM, today, ATM is the only game in town that guarantees it.

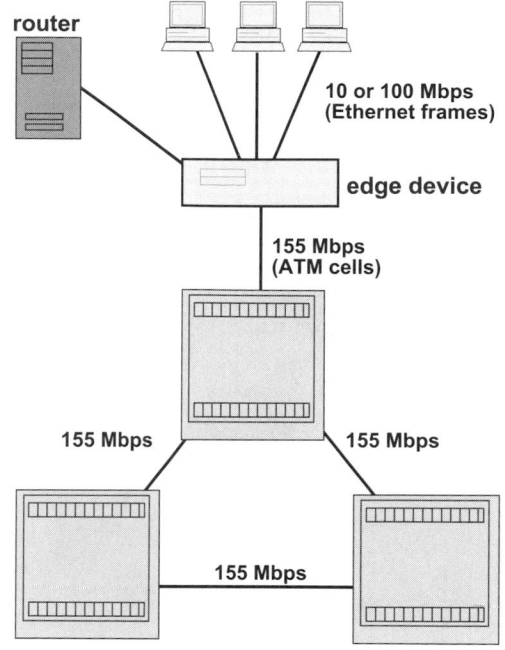

ATM Topology
This diagram shows ATM switches used as a network backbone, or "switch fabric." The edge device is an Ethernet switch with a high-speed ATM link. It converts LAN packets, such as Ethernet and Token Ring, into ATM cells and vice versa.

ATM25, ATM155
Refers to 25 and 155 Mbps ATM operations or equipment. See *ATM*.

ATM Forum
A membership organization founded in 1991 to promote ATM networking technology. It works with ANSI and the ITU to set standards. Its first specification in 1992 defined the User-Network Interface (UNI). Technical committees work on various projects in order to accelerate standards.

ATM.INI
A Windows configuration file that contains the locations of installed Type 1 fonts. It contains the path to both the PFB and PFM files.

ATM machine
(Automatic Teller Machine) A banking terminal that accepts deposits and dispenses cash. Stand alone or online to a central computer, ATMs are activated by inserting a cash or credit card that contains the user's account number on a magnetic str

ATM NIC
A network interface card (NIC) that transmits and receives Asynchronous Transfer Mode traffic. It is plugged into the bus of a client station or server.

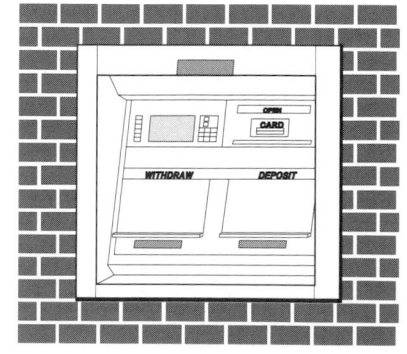

ATM Machine
What would life be without them?

AT motherboard

A motherboard that uses the same form factor as the original IBM AT, typically 12x13.5". It was superseded by the 9x10" Baby AT motherboard. See *ATX motherboard*.

atom

In list processing languages, a single element in a list.

atomic

Indivisible. An atomic operation, or atomicity, implies an operation that must be performed entirely or not at all. For example, if machine failure prevents a transaction to be processed to completion, the system will be rolled back to the start of the transaction. See *two-phase commit*.

atomic force microscope

A device used to detect atoms in a molecule. In 1992, IBM demonstrated a prototype atomic force microscope for recording data. Its pyramid-shaped tip was heated by a laser and pressed against the surface of a disk to form an indentation (a bit). Such a device might be capable of storing 30 billion bits per square inch in the future.

attach a file

To link a file to an e-mail message so that they travel to their destination together. Any type of file can be attached; for example, a database, spreadsheet, graphics or program file. Even a text file that might elaborate more on the message being sent can be attached. See *how to transfer a file over the Internet*.

attached processor

An additional CPU connected to the primary CPU in a multiprocessing environment. It operates as an extension of the primary CPU and shares the system software and peripheral devices.

attaching a file

See *how to transfer a file over the Internet*.

attenuation

Loss of signal power in a transmission.

atto

Quintillionth (10 to the -18th power). See *space/time*.

attribute

(1) In relational database management, a field within a record.

(2) For printers and display screens, a characteristic that changes a font, for example, from normal to boldface or underlined, or from normal to reverse video.

(3) See *file attribute*.

ATX motherboard

A motherboard that superseded the widely-used Baby AT design. ATX rotates the CPU and memory 90 degrees, allowing full-length boards in all sockets.

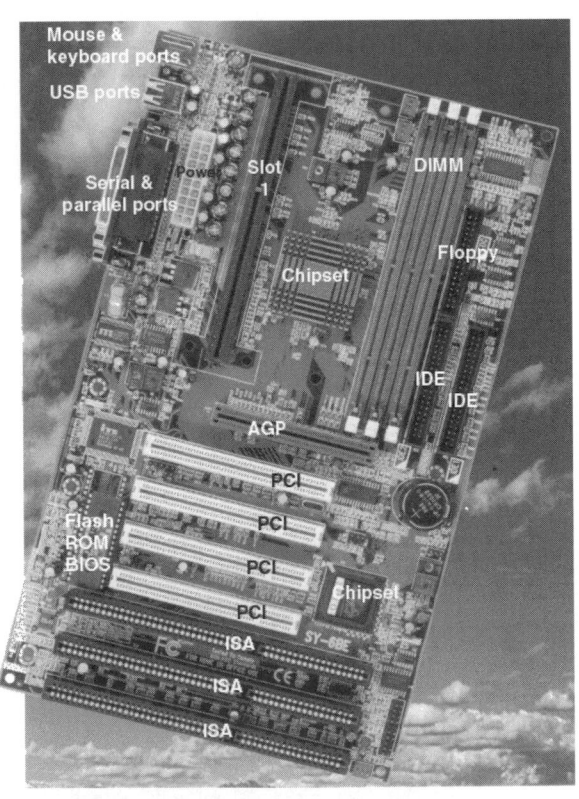

The ATX Motherboard

The motherboard glues all the components together via its various slots. Slot 1 is for the CPU. DIMM slots hold memory modules, and the AGP, PCI and ISA slots hold the various adapter cards. Control for the IDE and floppy disk drives as well as the USB, mouse, keyboard and serial and parallel ports are built in. *(Photo courtesy of Soyotek, Inc.)*

The power supply blows air over the CPU rather than pulling air through the chassis. The Micro ATX is a smaller version of the ATX with fewer slots. See *Baby AT motherboard*.

audio

The range of frequencies within human hearing (approx. 20Hz at the low to a high of 20,000Hz).

Traditional audio devices are analog, because they handle sound waves in an analogous form. Radios maintain the audio signal as rippling waves from antenna to speaker. Sound waves are "carved" into plastic phonograph records, and audio tape records sound as magnetic waves.

Audio is processed in a computer by converting the analog signal into a digital code using various techniques, such as PCM. See *RealAudio*.

audio adapter, audio board, audio card

Same as *sound card*.

audio cassette

The common 1/8" inch tape module used in portable music players, home stereos and car radio/tape systems. Sound is recorded in analog format on audio cassettes. See *cassette*.

audio CD

The music compact disc (CD) format that has replaced the phonograph record. Starting in the early 1990s, certain stereo amplifiers and receivers have come on the market without a phono input, making the definitive statement that analog phonograph records are history! See *CD* and *Red Book*.

audio codec

A hardware circuit that converts sound into digital code and vice versa using one of several analog to digital conversion methods such as PCM or ADPCM. If the codec is specialized for human voice, it is known as a speech codec, voice codec or vocoder.

Although the term generally refers to a chip, it may also refer to just the audio compression method, which can be performed in software. See *speech codec*.

audio compression

Encoding digital audio to take up less storage space and transmission bandwidth. The PCM and ADPCM methods are commonly used for audio compression. See *audio codec* and *data compression*.

audioconferencing

An audio communications session among three or more people that are geographically dispersed. It is provided by a conference function in a PBX or multiline telephone or by the telephone companies. See *videoconferencing* and *data conferencing*.

audiographics

Realtime data conferencing combined with audio capability. See *data conferencing* and *T.120*.

audio on demand

The ability to start delivering an audio program to an individual Web browser whenever the user requests it. See *streaming audio*.

audio response

See *voice response*.

audio server

A computer that delivers streaming audio for audio on demand applications. Audio servers may be computers that are specialized for this purpose. The term may just refer to the software that performs this service. See *streaming audio*.

audiotex, audiotext

A voice response application that allows users to enter and retrieve information over the telephone. See *IVR*.

audiovisual

Audio and/or video capability.

audit

An examination of systems, programming and datacenter procedures in order to determine the efficiency of computer operations.

audit software

Specialized programs that perform a variety of audit functions, such as sampling databases and generating confirmation letters to customers. It can highlight exceptions to categories of data and alert the examiner to possible error. Audit software often includes a non-procedural language that lets the auditor describe the computer and data environment without detailed programming.

audit trail

A record of transactions in an information system that provides verification of the activity of the system. The simplest audit trail is the transaction itself. If a person's salary is increased, the change transaction includes the date, amount of raise and name of authorizing manager.

A more elaborate audit trail can be created when the system is being verified for accuracy; for example, samples of processing results can be recorded at various stages. Item counts and hash totals are used to verify that all input has been processed through the system.

AU file

(AUdio file) A digital audio file format from Sun that is used on the Internet and can be played by a Java program. It provides toll-quality sound and uses the .AU extension. It generally uses the u-Law (mu-Law) encoding method, and raw u-Law files and AU files are the same except for the file header.

AUI

(Attachment Unit Interface) The network interface used with standard Ethernet. On the adapter card, it is a 15-pin socket. A transceiver, which taps into the Ethernet cable, plugs into the socket. See *10Base5*.

AUP

See *acceptable use policy*.

authentication

Verifying the identity of a user that is logging onto a computer system or verifying the integrity of a transmitted message. See *password, digital signature, IP spoofing* and *biometrics*.

authentication token

A security device given to authorized users who keep them in their possession. To log onto the network, the card may be read directly like a credit card, or it may display a changing number that is typed in as a password. See *SecurID card*.

authoring program

Software that allows for the creation of tutorials, CBT courseware, Web sites, CD-ROMs and other interactive programs. Authoring packages generally provide high-level visual tools that enable a complete system to be designed without writing any programming code. See *Web authoring software* and *HTML editor*.

authorization code

An identification number or password that is used to gain access to a local or remote computer system.

Authorware

A popular multimedia authoring program from Macromedia that is widely used for creating interactive learning programs on Windows and Macintosh.

auto

(AUTOmatic) Refers to a wide variety of devices that perform unattended operation.

auto answer

A modem feature that accepts a telephone call and establishes the connection. See *auto dial*.

auto attendant

A voice store and forward system that replaces the human operator and directs callers to the appropriate extensions or voice mailboxes.

auto baud detect

A modem feature that detects the highest speed of the called modem and switches to it.

autobaud rate

See *ABR*.

auto bypass

The ability to bypass a terminal or other device in a network if it fails, allowing the remaining devices to continue functioning.

AutoCAD

A full-featured CAD program from Autodesk Inc., Sausalito, CA, (www.autodesk.com), that runs on PCs, VAXs, Macs and UNIX workstations. Originally developed for CP/M machines, it was one of the first major CAD programs for personal computers and became an industry standard. There are countless third-party add-on packages that are available for AutoCAD, and many graphics applications import and export AutoCAD's DXF file format.

autochanger

A mechanism that moves disks or tapes from a storage bin to a drive for reading (playing) and writing. See *tape library, CD-ROM changer* and *CD-ROM server*.

autocoder

An IBM assembly language for 1960s-vintage 1400 and 7000 series computers.

auto dial

A modem feature that opens the line and dials the telephone number of another computer to establish connection. See *auto answer*.

AUTODIN

(**AUTO**matic **DI**gital **N**etwork) The worldwide communications network of the U.S. Defense Communications System.

AUTOEXEC.BAT

(**AUTO**matic **EXEC**ute **BAT**ch) A DOS batch file that is executed when the computer is started. It is stored in the root directory. DOS install programs may edit your AUTOEXEC.BAT and CONFIG.SYS files during installation. For example, they may want to add the new directory to the path or to set an environment variable. They made also need to add a new driver. You are generally informed that this is being done and often shown the changes as they are made. The original files are usually renamed with a different extension and left on the disk.

autoflow

Wrapping text around a graphic image or from one page to the next.

auto line feed

A feature that moves the cursor or print head to the next line when a CR (carriage return) is sensed. PCs put a LF (line feed) after the CR and do not use this feature. The Mac uses only a CR for end of line and requires it.

autoloader

(1) A mechanism that inserts disk or tape into a drive sequentially. For example, a diskette duplicator autoloader holds a stack of floppies that are fed to the drive one after the other.

(2) Same as *autochanger*.

auto logon

Performing the complete log-on sequence necessary to gain entry into a computer system without user intervention.

automata theory

An open-ended computer science discipline that concerns an abstract device called an "automaton," which performs a specific computational or recognition function. Networks of automata are designed to mimic human behavior.

automate

To turn a set of manual steps into an operation that goes by itself.

automatic data processing

Same as *data processing*.

automatic design optimization

Using the computer to achieve the most efficient design of a product. Finite element analysis (FEA) and other methods are used. In the past, design engineers have performed a combination of manual and automated methods to accomplish design optimization. They have applied FEA to parts of a CAD drawing, determined what components needed work and then redrew the object manually. Increasingly, software that is tightly integrated with the CAD program can perform the analysis and automatically redraw the object.

automatic feature negotiation

The ability of a modem to adjust to the speed, error control and data compression method of the modem at the other end of the line.

A Vision of Automation
Artist Unknown, Circa 1895
A hundred years ago, the concept of the future lacked one major ingredient... the computer! *(Photo courtesy of Rosemont Engineering.)*

automation

The replacement of manual operations by computerized methods. Office automation refers to integrating clerical tasks such as typing, filing and appointment scheduling. Factory automation refers to computer-driven assembly lines. See also *COM automation* and *tape library*.

automation client, controller, server

See *COM automation*.

automation product

See *tape library*.

automounting

Making remote files available to a client at the time the file is accessed. Remote directories are associated with a local directory on the client ahead of time, and the mounting takes places the first time a remote file is opened by the client.

autonegotiate

To automatically determine the correct settings. The term is often used with communications and networking. For example, Ethernet 10/100 cards, hubs and switches can determine the highest speed of the node they are connected to and adjust their transmission rate accordingly.

autonomous system

A network that is administered by a single set of management rules that are controlled by one person, group or organization. Autonomous systems often use only one routing protocol, although multiple protocols can be used. The core of the Internet is made up many autonomous systems. See *ASN, routing protocol* and *path vector protocol*.

auto redial

A modem, fax or telephone feature that redials a busy number a fixed number of times.

auto reliable

A modem feature that enables it to send to a modem with or without built-in error detection and compression.

auto resume

A feature that lets you stop working on the computer and take up where you left off later without having to reload applications. Memory contents are stored on disk or kept active by battery or AC power.

autorun

A feature that automatically launches a program without manual intervention. In Windows 95/98 and NT, CD-ROMs and floppies can automatically launch an introductory menu right after the disk is inserted into the drive.

autosave

Saving data to the disk at periodic intervals without user intervention.

auto scroll

To scroll by dragging the mouse pointer beyond the edge of the current window or screen. It is used to move around a virtual screen as well as to highlight text blocks and images that are larger than the current window.

autosizing

The ability of a monitor to maintain the same rectangular image size when changing from one resolution to another.

autostart routine

Instructions built into the computer and activated when it is turned on. The routine performs diagnostic tests, such as checking the computer's memory, and then loads the operating system and passes control to it.

autotrace

A routine that converts a bitmap into a vector graphics image. It scans the bitmap and turns the dark areas into vectors (lines). Once a bitmap has been turned into vectors, individual components of the drawing can be scaled independently.

This process usually creates many more vectors than if the picture were drawn in a drawing program in the first place. In order to faithfully reproduce the original, the conversion routine will generate a vector for the slightest deviation in a line. However, extraneous vectors can be deleted afterwards.

A/UX

Apple's version of UNIX for the Macintosh, which is based on AT&T's UNIX System V with Berkeley extensions. A/UX is no longer supported.

auxiliary memory

A high-speed memory bank used in mainframes and supercomputers. It is not directly addressable by the CPU, rather it functions like a disk. Data is transferred from auxiliary memory to main memory over a high-bandwidth channel. See *auxiliary storage*.

auxiliary storage

External storage devices, such as disk and tape.

A/V

(Audio/Visual, Audio/Video) Refers to equipment used in audio and video applications, such as microphones, videotape machines (VCRs) and sound systems.

availability

The measurement of a system's uptime. See *uptime* and *high availability*.

avatar

An image you select or create to represent yourself in a 3-D chat site on the Web. In order to interact with these sites, you need a VRML plug-in. Avatar is a Sanskrit word that means the incarnation of a god on earth. See *VRML*.

AV drive

(Audio Visual drive) A hard disk drive that is optimized for audio and video applications. Transferring analog high-fidelity audio and video signals onto a digital disk and playing them back at high performance levels requires a drive that can sustain continuous reads and writes without interruption. AV drives are designed to postpone thermal recalibration when reading and writing so that long data transfers will not be interrupted, and frames will not be lost.

AVI

(Audio Video Interleaved) A Windows multimedia video format from Microsoft. It interleaves standard waveform audio and digital video frames (bitmaps) to provide reduced animation at 15 fps at 160x120x8 resolution. Audio is 11,025Hz, 8-bit samples.

avionics

The electronic instrumentation and control equipment used in airplanes and space vehicles.

Award BIOS

A PC BIOS from Award Software, Inc., Los Gatos, CA, (www.award.com). Award BIOS chips have been installed in more than 50 million computers.

AWC

(Association for Women in Computing, San Francisco, CA, www.awc-hq.org) A membership organization, founded in 1978, dedicated to the advancement of women in computing. It publishes newsletters, hosts seminars and annual conferences and recognizes distinguished women in the field with its Augusta Ada Lovelace award.

awk

(Aho Weinberger Kernighan) A UNIX programming utility developed in 1977 by Aho, Weinberger and Kernighan. Due to its unique pattern-matching syntax, it is often used in data retrieval and data transformation. DOS versions are also available.

AWT

(Abstract Windowing Toolkit) A class library from Sun that provides an application framework and graphical user interface (GUI) routines for Java programmers. AWT is included in the Java Foundation Classes (JFC). See *JFC, AFC* and *IFC*.

Axiant

An application development system from Cognos for client/server environments. Built on Cognos' PowerHouse 4GL, it supports Windows and Macintosh clients and a variety of databases and UNIX servers. Cognos' Impromptu query language and PowerPlay EIS/DSS system are components. Also included is the WATCOM/SQL database.

AXP

A family of computer systems from Digital that use the Alpha CPU chip. This series is expected to take Digital throughout the 1990s and beyond.

AYT

Digispeak for "are you there?"

azimuth

The trajectory of an angle measured in degrees going clockwise from a base point. A disk azimuth alignment test checks for the correct positioning of the read/write head to the track.

B:

The designation for the second floppy disk drive in a PC. In PCs that have two floppy drives, the 3.5" drive is typically A:, and the 5.25" drive is B:. Since the 5.25" floppy is obsolete, the B: is rarely seen anymore.

B1

The computer system security level required by the Department of Defence (DOD). See *NCSC*.

BAAN IV

An integrated family of client/server applications from Baan Company, Menlo Park, CA, (www.baan.com). It includes manufacturing, distribution, finance, transportation, service, project and features enterprise modeling via its Orgware modules. Earlier versions of the software were named TRITON.

Baby AT motherboard

A smaller motherboard (9x10") that superseded the one used in the original IBM AT (12x13.5"). The Baby AT motherboard has been widely used in 386, 486 and Pentium PCs. It was superseded by the ATX motherboard. See *ATX motherboard*.

Bachman tools

A variety of systems design, database administration and system performance measurement products from Bachman Information Systems, Inc., Burlington, MA.

backbone

In communications, the part of a network that handles the major traffic. It employs the highest-speed transmission paths in the network and may also run the longest distance. Smaller networks are attached to the backbone.

A backbone can span a large geographic area or be as small as a backplane in a single cabinet. See *collapsed backbone*.

backdoor

See *trapdoor*.

back end

The support components of a computer system. It typically refers to the database management system (DBMS), which is the storehouse for the data.

Baby AT Motherboard

This is the model SY-5EH motherboard from Soyotek, which is a later version of the original Baby AT. It includes support for DIMM memory, AGP adapters and USB, which came on the scene in the late 1990s. Socket 7 is used for Intel chips and x86 clones from companies such as AMD and Cyrix. *(Photo courtesy of Soyotek, Inc.)*

back-end CASE

CASE tools that generate program code. Contrast with *front-end CASE*.

back end processor

Same as *database machine*.

backfile conversion

Scanning older documents that reside in a file cabinet. Service bureaus specialize in this conversion process.

background

(1) The non-interactive processing in the computer. See *foreground/background*.

(2) The base, or backdrop color. In order to distinguish any image on screen, whether text or graphics, there must be a contrasting background color.

background ink
A highly reflective OCR ink used to print the parts of the form not recognized by a scanner.

background noise
An extraneous signal that has crept into a line, channel or circuit.

background processing
Processing in which the program is not visibly interacting with the user. Most personal computers use operating systems that run background tasks only when foreground tasks are idle, such as between keystrokes. Advanced multitasking operating systems let background programs be given any priority from low to high.

backing storage
Same as *auxiliary storage*.

backlit
An LCD screen that has its own light source from the back of the screen, making the background brighter and characters appear sharper.

BackOffice
A suite of network server software products from Microsoft that includes Windows NT Server, SQL Server, Systems Management Server (SMS), SNA Server and Mail Server.

backplane
An interconnecting device that may or may not have intelligence, but typically has sockets that cards (boards) plug into. Although resistors may be used, a passive backplane adds no processing in the circuit. An intelligent backplane, or active backplane, may have microprocessor or controller-driven circuitry that adds a little or a lot of processing. See *bus*.

backside cache
A memory cache that has a dedicated channel to the CPU, enabling it run at the full speed of the CPU. See *inline cache* and *lookaside cache*.

backslash
The backslash symbol (\) is used as a separator between folder and file names in DOS, Windows and OS/2 when the full path to a file is written out. For example, the path **c:\cde\cde.exe** points to the CDE.EXE file in the CDE folder on the C: drive.

When the universal naming convention (UNC) is used, double backslash (\\) characters serve as a prefix to the server name (see *UNC*).

Just the Worst!
The backslash character was the worst symbol that could ever have been chosen for this purpose. Not only is the backslash key not located in a standard place on the keyboard, but Internet addresses use forward slashes since they come from UNIX. The irony is that the DOS path syntax was copied from UNIX, but somebody must have felt compelled to show originality of authorship and thus reversed the separator symbols. Now both methods are in our faces day after day. See *path*.

backsolver
See *solver*.

backspace
(1) To move the screen cursor one column to the left, deleting the character that was in that position. A backspace to the printer moves the print head one column to the left.

(2) To move to the previous block on a magnetic tape.

back up
To make a copy of important data onto a different storage medium for safety.

backup

Additional resources or duplicate copies of data on different storage media for emergency purposes. See *backup types*.

backup & recovery

The combination of manual and machine procedures that can restore lost data in the event of hardware or software failure. Routine backup of databases and logs of computer activity are part of a backup & recovery program. See *checkpoint/restart*.

backup copy

A disk, tape or other machine readable copy of a data or program file. Making backup copies is a discipline most computer users learn the hard way— after a week's work is lost.

backup disk

A disk used to hold duplicate copies of important files. Floppy disks and disks cartridges are used for backup disks.

backup power

An additional power source that can be used in the event of power failure. See *UPS*.

backup tape

See *tape backup*.

backup types

The selection of files for backup purposes.

Full Backup
Backs up all selected files.

Differential Backup
Backs up selected files that have been changed. Used when only the latest version of a file is required.

Incremental Backup
Backs up selected files that have been changed, but if a file has been changed for the second or subsequent time since the last full backup, the file doesn't replace the already-backed-up file, rather it is appended to the backup medium. This is used when each revision of a file must be maintained.

Delta Backup
Similar to an incremental backup, but backs up only the actual data in the selected files that has changed, not the files themselves.

Backus-Naur form

Also known as Backus normal form, it was the first metalanguage to define programming languages. Introduced by John Backus in 1959 to describe the ALGOL 58 language, it was enhanced by Peter Naur and used to define ALGOL 60.

backward chaining

In AI, a form of reasoning that starts with the conclusion and works backward. The goal is broken into many subgoals or sub-subgoals which can be solved more easily. Known as top-down approach. Contrast with *forward chaining*.

backward compatible

Same as *downward compatible*.

BackWeb

An Internet delivery system from BackWeb Technologies, Inc., San Jose, CA, (www.backweb.com) that provides a platform for "pushing" information from content providers to users. The information can be anything from news, stock quotes and multimedia presentations to virus and software upgrades. The BackWeb server, which can also be used on intranets, can host multiple channels of information. The BackWeb client software is free and available from their Web site.

Bad command or file name
A DOS error message that means DOS does not understand the command you entered, or it cannot find the program you asked it to run.

bad font
A scalable font that is poorly programmed. If a font programmer does not follow the rules when coding a Type 1 or TrueType font, problems can occur when the rasterizer (RIP) tries to convert it into bitmaps for display or printing.

bad sector
A segment of disk storage that cannot be read or written due to a physical problem in the disk. Bad sectors on hard disks are marked by the operating system and bypassed. If data is recorded in a sector that becomes bad, file recovery software, and sometimes special hardware, must be used to restore it.

BAK file
(BAcKup file) A DOS and OS/2 file extension for backup files.

BAL
(1) (Basic Assembly Language) The assembly language for the IBM 370/3000/4000 mainframe series.

(2) (Branch And Link) An instruction used to transfer control to another part of the program.

ballistic gain
A trackball or mouse feature that changes cursor travel relative to hand speed. The faster the ball is moved, the farther the cursor is moved.

baloon help
On-screen help displayed in a cartoon-style dialogue box that appears when the pointer (cursor) is placed over the object in question.

balun
(BALanced UNbalanced) A device that connects a balanced line to an unbalanced line; for example, a twisted pair to a coaxial cable. A balanced line is one in which both wires are electrically equal. In an unbalanced line, such as a coax, one line has different properties than the other.

Balun
The BNC connector on the left connects to coaxial cable. The screw connectors on the right connect to telephone style twisted wire pairs. *(Photo courtesy of Black Box Corporation.)*

band
(1) The range of frequencies used for transmitting a signal. A band is identified by its lower and upper limits; for example, a 10MHz band in the 100 to 110MHz range.

(2) A contiguous group of tracks that are treated as a unit.

(3) A rectangular section of a page that is created and sent to the printer. See *band printing*.

(4) The printing element in a band printer.

band pass filter
An electronic device that prohibits all but a specific range of frequencies to pass through it.

band printer
A line printer that uses a metal band, or loop, of type characters as its printing mechanism. The band contains a fixed set of embossed characters that can only be changed by replacing the band. The band spins horizontally around a set of hammers, one for each print column. When the required character in the band has revolved to the selected print column, the hammer pushes the paper into the ribbon and against the embossed image of the letter, digit or symbol.

Band printers can print up to approximately 2,000 lpm and can exist in very harsh industrial environments, although they are mostly used in datacenters. Band printers and line matrix printers are the two surviving line printer technologies.

Band printer is not to be confused with "band printing," which is a method for sending output to the printer. See *band printing* and *printer*.

band printing

Printing a page by creating the output in several rectangular sections, or bands, rather than the entire page. It enables a printer with limited memory to print a full page of text and graphics. Most dot matrix printers and some laser printers benefit from this approach. This is not to be confused with *band printer*, which is hardware.

bandwidth

The transmission capacity of an electronic line such as a communications network, computer bus or computer channel. It is expressed in bits per second, bytes per second or in Hertz (cycles per second). When expressed in Hertz, the frequency may be a greater number than the actual bits per second, because the bandwidth is the difference between the lowest and highest frequencies transmitted. See *video bandwidth*. See illustration on next page.

bang path

An address for sending e-mail via UUCP that specifies the entire route to the destination computer. It separates each host name with an exclamation point, which is known as a bang. For example, the bang path **midearth!shire!bilbo!jsmith** would go to the JSMITH user account on the BILBO host, which is reached by first going to MIDEARTH and then SHIRE. See *UUCP*.

bank

An arrangement of identical hardware components.

bank switching

Engaging and disengaging electronic circuits. Bank switching is used when the design of a system prohibits all circuits from being addressed or activated at the same time, requiring that one unit be turned on while the others are turned off.

banner ad

A graphic image used on Web sites to advertise a product. Banner ads are typically rectangles about 460 pixels wide by 60 pixels deep. See *interstitial ad*.

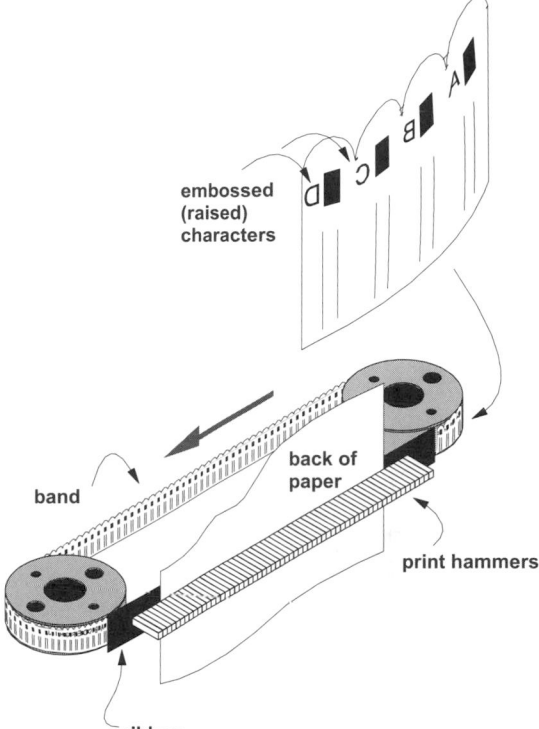

embossed (raised) characters

band

back of paper

print hammers

ribbon

Band Printer Mechanism
When the required character in the band has revolved to the selected print column, the hammer pushes the paper into the ribbon and against the embossed image of the letter or digit.

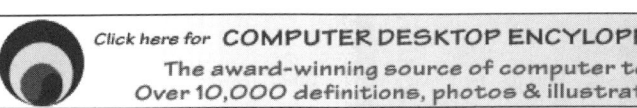

BAPC

(Bandwidth Allocation Control Protocol) An IETF standard for adding and dropping the second B channel during an ISDN session. Working in conjunction with Multilink PPP, it enables sending and receiving devices to negotiate the required bandwidth.

BAPCo

(Business Applications Performance Corporation, Santa Clara, CA, www.bapco.com) A nonprofit organization founded in 1991 that provides a series of SYSmark brand benchmarks for testing software in the PC client/server and laptop environment. It also has a benchmark for battery life. See *benchmark*.

BAPI

(**Business API**) An interface to one of SAP's R/3 applications. It enables third-party developers to write enhancements that interact with the R/3 modules. See *R/3*.

bar chart

A graphical representation of information in the form of bars. See *business graphics*.

bar code

The printed code used for recognition by a bar code reader (scanner). Traditional one-dimensional bar codes use the bar's width as the code, but encode just an ID or account number. Two-dimensional bar codes, such as PDF417 from Symbol Technology, are read horizontally and vertically. PDF417 holds 1,800 characters in an area the size of a postage stamp. See *UPC* and *point of sale*.

bar code reader

A scanning device specialized for reading bar codes and converting them into either the ASCII or EBCDIC digital character code. See *bar code* and *point of sale*.

barrel distortion

A screen distortion in which the sides bow out. Contrast with *pincushioning*.

barrel printer

Same as *drum printer*.

base

(1) A starting or reference point.

(2) In a bipolar transistor, the line that activates the switch. Same as *gate* in a CMOS transistor.

(3) A multiplier in a numbering system. In a decimal system, each digit position is worth 10x the position to its right. In binary, each digit position is worth 2x the position to its right.

base64

An encoding method that converts binary data into ASCII text and vice versa and is one of the methods used by MIME. Base64 divides each three bytes of the original data into four 6-bit units, which it represents as four 7-bit ASCII characters. This typically increases the original file by about a third.

base address

The starting address (beginning point) of a program or table. See *base/displacement* and *relative address*.

0 ‖25700‖‖00220‖

One-Dimensional Bar Code

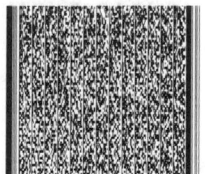

Two-Dimensional Bar Code

This PDF417 bar code image developed by Symbol Technology contains the entire Gettysburg address. *(Photo courtesy of Symbol Technology, Inc.)*

LAN Technologies	Bandwidth
Ethernet	10 Mbps (shared)
Switched Ethernet	10 Mbps (node to node)
Fast Ethernet	100 Mbps
Gigabit Ethernet	1000 Mbps
Token Ring	4, 16 Mbps
Fast Token Ring	100, 128 Mbps
FDDI/CDDI	100 Mbps
ATM	25, 45, 155, 622. 2488 Mbps +

To compute actual network throughput, divide bps (bits per sec) by 10 for bytes per second. Then halve the amount to account for overhead. Thus, in a 10 Mbps Ethernet network, there is only 500 thousand bytes per second of usable bandwidth. That means a 10 meg file will take 20 seconds to send. The 10 million bits per second doesn't sound so fast anymore, does it?

WAN Technologies	Bandwidth
UNSWITCHED PRIVATE LINES (point to point)	
T1	24 x 64 Kbps = 1.5 Mbps
T3	672 x 64 Kbps = 44.7 Mbps
Fractional T1	N x 64 Kbps
SWITCHED SERVICES	
Dial-up via modem	9.6, 14.4, 28.8, 33.6, 56 Kbps
ISDN	BRI 64-128 Kbps PRI 1.544 Mbps
Switched 56/64	56 Kbps, 64 Kbps
Packet switched (X.25)	56 Kbps
Frame relay	56 Kbps to 45 Mbps
SMDS	45, 155 Mbps
ATM	25, 45, 155, 622, 2488 Mbps +

Computer Desktop Encyclopedia

base alignment

The alignment of a variety of font sizes on a baseline.

baseband

A communications technique in which digital signals are placed onto the transmission line without change in modulation. It is usually limited to a few miles and does not require the complex modems used in broadband transmission. Common baseband LAN techniques are token passing ring (Token Ring) and CSMA/CD (Ethernet).

In baseband, the full bandwidth of the channel is used, and simultaneous transmission of multiple sets of data is accomplished by interleaving pulses using TDM (time division multiplexing). Contrast with *broadband* transmission, which transmits data, voice and video simultaneously by modulating each signal onto a different frequency, using FDM (frequency division multiplexing).

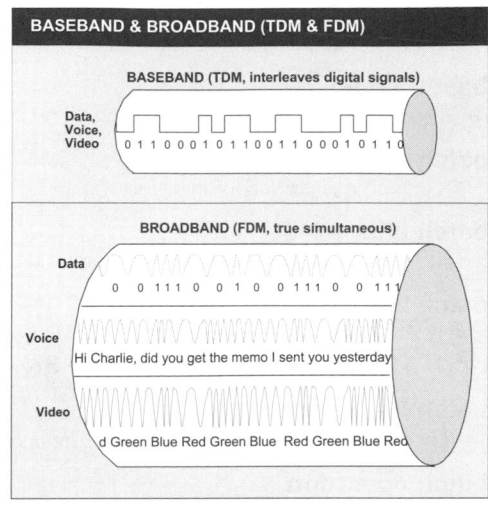

base/displacement

A machine architecture that runs programs no matter where they reside in memory. Addresses in a machine language program are displacement addresses, which are relative to the beginning of the program. At runtime, the hardware adds the address of the current first byte of the program (base address) to each displacement address and derives an absolute address for execution.

All modern computers use some form of base/displacement or offset mechanism in order to to run multiple programs in memory at the same time.

base font

The default font used for printing if none other is specified.

baseline

The horizontal line to which the bottoms of lowercase characters (without descenders) are aligned. See *typeface*.

baselining tool

A network monitor that analyzes communications usage in order to establish routine traffic patterns.

base station

An earth-based transmitting and receiving station for cellular phones, paging services and other wireless transmission systems. See *earth station*.

BASIC

(Beginners All purpose Symbolic Instruction Code) A programming language developed by John Kemeny and Thomas Kurtz in the mid 1960s at Dartmouth College. Originally developed as an interactive, mainframe timesharing language, it has become widely used on small computers.

BASIC is available in both compiler and interpreter form. As an interpreter, the language is conversational and can be debugged a line at a time. BASIC is also used as a quick calculator.

BASIC is considered one of the easiest programming languages to learn. Simple programs can be quickly written on the fly. However, BASIC is not a structured language, such as Pascal, dBASE or C, and it's easy to write spaghetti code that's difficult to decipher later.

The following BASIC example converts Fahrenheit to Celsius:

```
10 INPUT "Enter Fahrenheit "; FAHR
20 PRINT "Celsius is ", (FAHR-32) * 5 / 9
```

basic cell

The group of transistors and resistors replicated many times on a gate array chip. See *gate array*.

BASIC in ROM

A BASIC interpreter stored in a read only memory chip that is available to the user at all times.

bastion host

A computer system in a network that is fortified against illegal entry and attack. See *firewall*.

batch

A group, or collection, of items.

batch data entry

Entering a group of source documents into the computer.

batch file

(1) A file containing data that is processed or transmitted from beginning to end.

(2) A file containing instructions that are executed one after the other. See *BAT file* and *shell script*.

batch file transfer

The consecutive transmission of two or more files.

batch operation

Some action performed on a group of items at one time.

batch processing

Processing a group of transactions at one time. Transactions are collected and processed against the master files (master files updated) at the end of the day or some other time period. Contrast with *transaction processing*. See *transaction processing* for illustration.

Batch and Transaction Processing

Information systems typically use both batch and transaction processing methods. For example, in an order processing system, transaction processing is the continuous updating of the customer and inventory files as orders are entered.

At the end of the day, batch processing programs generate picking lists for the warehouse. At the end of some period, batch programs print invoices and management reports.

batch program (batch job)

A non-interactive (non-conversational) program such as a report listing or sort.

batch session

Transmitting or updating an entire file. Implies a non-interactive or non-interruptible operation from beginning to end. Contrast with *interactive session*.

batch stream

A collection of batch processing programs that are scheduled to run in the computer.

batch terminal

A terminal that is designed for transmitting or receiving blocks of data, such as a card reader or printer.

batch total

The sum of a particular field in a collection of items used as a control total to ensure that all data has been entered into the computer. For example, using account number as a batch total, all account numbers would be summed manually before entry into the computer. After entry, the total is checked with the computer's sum of the numbers. If it does not match, source documents are manually checked against the computer's listing.

batch window

The time available for an intensive batch processing operation such as a disk backup.

BAT file

(BATch file) A file of DOS or OS/2 commands, which are executed one after the other. It has a .BAT extension and is created with a text editor. See *DOS batch file*.

batteries

See *lead acid, lithium ion, lithium polymer, nickel cadmium, nickel hydride* and *zinc air*.

BatteryMark

A Ziff-Davis benchmark that tests battery life on notebook computers running Windows 95/98. It requires a special hardware device to perform the test. See *ZDBOp*.

baud

The signalling rate of a line, which is the number of transitions (voltage or frequency changes) that are made per second. The term has often been erroneously used to specify bits per second. However, only at very low speeds is baud equal to bps; for example, 300 baud is the same as 300 bps. Beyond that, one baud can be made to represent more than one bit. For example, a V.22bis modem generates 1200 bps at 600 baud.

baudot code

Pronounced "baw-doh." One of the first standards for international telegraphy developed in the late 19th century by Emile Baudot. It uses five bits per character.

baud rate

A redundant reference to baud. Baud is a rate.

Bay Networks

(Bay Networks, Inc., Santa Clara, CA, www.baynetworks.com) A communications products company that was formed in 1994 as a merger of SynOptics Communications, Santa Clara, CA and Wellfleet Communications, Billerica, MA. The name was derived from their locations: the California Bay and the Bay State. At the time of the merger, SynOptics was number #1 in hubs, and Wellfleet was number #2 in routers.

bayonet connector

A plug and socket that uses a connecting mechanism to lock them together. One part is pushed into the other and turned. BNC and ST connectors are examples of bayonet connectors.

BBN

(Bolt, Beranek and Newman) A consulting firm that participated in the development of some of the most extensive networks in the world, including ARPANET, which evolved into the Internet. It was founded in 1948 as a consulting service in acoustics by Dr. Richard Bolt and Dr. Leo Beranek. Two years later, Robert Newman became a partner.

In 1997, BBN was acquired by GTE and was merged into its network services organization, which was renamed GTE Internetworking (www.bbn.com).

BBNS

(BroadBand Networking Services) A Broadband ISDN-compliant networking architecture from IBM. It includes a number of enhancements such as guaranteed quality of service, traffic rerouting upon failure and rerouting of higher-priority connections.

BBS

(1) (Bulletin Board System) A computer system used as an information source and forum for a particular interest group. They were widely used in the U.S. to distribute shareware and drivers and had their heyday before the World Wide Web took off. A BBS functions somewhat like a stand-alone Web site, but without graphics. However, unlike Web sites, each BBS has its own telephone number to dial into.

Today, BBSs are still used throughout the world where there is much less direct Internet access, and many serve as e-mail gateways to the Internet. Some BBSs are still in use in the U.S. and software companies may continue to maintain them as alternatives to their Web sites for downloading drivers.

A general-purpose communications program such as Crosstalk or Qmodem Pro is used to access a BBS. The address list in a communications program stores telephone numbers just like an e-mail program's address list holds e-mail addresses.

(2) (BIOS Boot Specification) A Plug and Play BIOS format that enables the user to determine the boot sequence. See *OPROM*.

bcc:

(**B**lind **C**arbon **C**opy) The field in an e-mail header that names additional recipients for the message. It is similar to carbon copy (cc:), but the names do not appear in the recipient's message. Not all e-mail systems support bcc:, in which case the "hidden" names will appear.

BCD

(**B**inary **C**oded **D**ecimal) The storage of numbers in which each decimal digit is converted into binary and is stored in a single character or byte. For example, a 12-digit number would take 12 bytes. See *numbers*.

BCS

(1) (The **B**oston **C**omputer **S**ociety) A personal computer users group founded in 1977 by Jonathan Rotenberg and disbanded in 1996. The BCS was one of the first sources for education and technical information about personal computers. At its height in the late 1980s, it had more than 30,000 members, although more than 100,000 were involved at one time or another. The Computer Museum maintains a Web site for some groups that have continued on their own (www.bcs.org).

(2) (The **B**ritish **C**omputer **S**ociety, Swindon, Wiltshire, England, www.bcs.org.uk) The chartered body for information technology professionals, founded in 1957. It sets standards, conducts exams, advises Parliament and disseminates awards for excellence in computing. The BCS was a founding member of the Council for European Professional Informatics Societies (CEPIS).

(3) (**B**inary **C**ompatibility **S**tandard) See *ABI*.

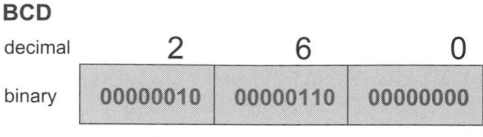

BCD

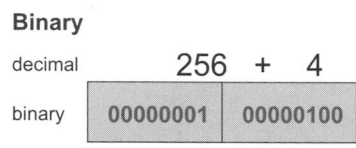

Binary

BCD and Binary

The BCD method codes each decimal digit in binary and stores it in its own byte. The binary method converts the entire decimal number into a binary number. In the binary example above, the 1 in the left byte is the ninth bit starting from the rightmost bit in the right byte (256-128-64-32-16-8-4-2-1-0).

BDC

(**B**ackup **D**omain **C**ontroller) In a Windows NT server, a copy of the Primary Domain Controller (PDC). The BDC is periodically synchronized with the PDC. See *PDC*.

BDOS error

See *read error* and *write error*.

BDPA

(**B**lack **D**ata **P**rocessing **A**ssociates, Washington, DC, www.bdpa.org) A membership organization founded in 1975 by Earl A. Pace Jr. and David Wimberly. It is the largest national professional organization representing minorities in the information industry. BDPA provides a forum for exchanging ideas through its monthly meetings, seminars, workshops and annual conferences. Membership is open to members of all races.

Be

(**Be**, Inc., Menlo Park, CA, www.be.com) A computer company founded in 1990 by Jean Louise Gassee, former head of R&D at Apple. It developed the PowerPC-based BeBox computer, which runs under the BeOS operating system. The BeBox and BeOS are designed for digital audio, video and 3-D graphics applications. There are versions of BeOS for the BeBox, PowerPC-based Macintoshes and Pentiums.

beaconing

A continuous signalling of error conditions on a LAN.

bead

(1) A small programming subroutine. A sequence of beads that are strung together is called a *thread*.

(2) The insulator surrounding the inner wire of a coaxial cable.

BEA TUXEDO

A TP monitor from BEA Systems, Inc., Sunnyvale, CA, (www.beasys.com), that runs on a variety of UNIX-based computers. Originally developed by AT&T and sold as source code, Novell acquired it, enhanced it and offered it as shrink-wrapped software for various UNIX servers. It was later sold to BEA. BEA TUXEDO and Transarc's Encina are the major TP monitors in the UNIX client/server environment.

BeBox

See *Be*.

BEDO RAM

See *EDO RAM*.

behavior

In object technology, the processing that an object can perform.

bell character

The control code used to sound an audible bell or tone in order to alert the user (ASCII 7, EBCDIC 2F).

Bell compatible

A modem that is compatible with modems originally introduced by the Bell Telephone System.

Bellcore

(Bell Communications Research, Piscataway, NJ, www.bellcore.com) The research and development organization created at Divestiture and jointly owned by the regional Bell telephone companies (RBOCs). It is also involved in communications issues of the U.S. government regarding national security and emergency preparedness.

Bell Labs

The research and development center of Lucent Technologies, formerly AT&T. Bell Labs is one of the most renowned scientific laboratories in the world.

bells and whistles

Refers to all the advanced functions that are known to be available in an application or system. Contrast with *plain vanilla*.

Bell System

AT&T and the Bell Telephone Companies before Divestiture. See *Divestiture* and *RBOC*.

benchmark

A performance test of hardware and/or software. There are various programs that very accurately test the raw power of a single machine, the interaction in a single client/server system (one server/multiple clients) and the transactions per second in a transaction processing system. However, it is next to impossible to benchmark the performance of an entire enterprise network with a great degree of accuracy. See *ZDBOp*, *BAPCo*, *Linpack*, *Dhrystones*, *Whetstones*, *Khornerstones*, *SPEC* and *GPC*.

The Real Bell
Alexander Graham Bell was born in Scotland in 1847 and died in 1922. His famous sentence "Mr. Watson, come here, I want to see you," were the first words to travel over a wire, ringing in the birth of electronic communications. *(Photo courtesy of AT&T.)*

benign virus

A prank virus that does not cause damage. It does such things as randomly displaying a message on screen declaring "Peace on Earth" or causing the computer to make a clicking sound every time a key is pressed on some famous person's birthday. Fortunately, most viruses are benign.

Bento

A data structure used to store embedded documents in an OpenDoc compound document. Bento, which stands for lunch box in Japanese, provides a "container" to hold the data and a format for defining its contents.

BeOS

See *Be*.

BER

(1) (Basic Encoding Rules) One method for encoding information in the OSI environment. For example, it defines how Boolean data is coded.

(2) (Bit Error Rate) The average number of bits transmitted in error.

Berger Series

See *aptitude tests*.

Berkeley extensions

See *BSD UNIX*.

Bernoulli Box

An early removable disk drive from Iomega. Introduced in 1983 with a SCSI interface and 8" 10MB cartridges, it provided an extremely-reliable, transportable storage medium for personal computers at near hard disk speeds. In 1987, 5.25" 20MB disks were introduced and later 44 and 90MB. The MultiDisk 150 drive accepts 35, 65, 90, 105 and 150MB cartridges. In 1994, the 230MB disk was introduced with backward compatibility to the 44MB disks.

Bernoulli Cartridge
This is an example of a third-generation Bernoulli cartridge. The Bernoulli was the first removable storage for personal computers, which proved very reliable.

Unlike a hard disk in which the read/write head flies over a rigid disk, the Bernoulli floppy is spun at high speed and bends up close to the head. Upon power failure, a hard disk must retract the head to prevent a crash, whereas the Bernoulli disk naturally bends down. See *Bernoulli principle*. For a summary of all storage technologies, see *storage*.

Bernoulli principle

The Swiss scientist, Daniel Bernoulli (1700-1782), demonstrated that, in most cases, the pressure in a fluid (air, water, gas, etc.) decreases as the fluid moves faster. This explains in part why a wing lifts an airplane and why a baseball curves.

best-effort service

A communications service that makes no guarantees regarding the speed with which data will be transmitted to the recipient or that the data will even be delivered entirely.

best-of-class

A product considered to be superior within a certain category of hardware or software. It does not mean absolute best overall; for example, the best-of-class in a low-priced category may be seriously inferior to the best product on the market, which could sell for ten times as much.

Beta

The first home VCR format, known as Betamax. Developed by Sony, it used 1/2" tape cassettes. Beta Hi-fi added CD-quality audio, and SuperBeta improved the image. The Beta format succumbed to VHS, which is the standard 1/2" VCR format today. See *Betamaxed*.

Betamaxed

A superior technology that is overtaken by a lesser one. It comes from Sony's Betamax 1/2" magnetic tape format that was always considered superior to VHS, but did not survive.

beta test
A test of hardware or software that is performed by users under normal operating conditions. See *alpha test*.

betaware
Software in beta test that has been provided to a large number of users in advance of the formal release.

BeyondMail
A Windows-based mail program from Banyan Systems Inc., Westboro, MA, (www.banyan.com) that works with Banyan's own Intelligent Messaging and Novell's MHS messaging systems. It includes a variety of pre-formatted message forms that can be programmed to access ODBC-compliant databases directly. It provides message distribution into selected folders, automatic filtering and forwarding and a tickler. An optional calendaring module is available.

Bezier
In computer graphics, a curve that is generated using a mathematical formula which assures continuity with other Bezier curves. It is mathematically simpler, but more difficult to blend than a b-spline curve. Within CAD and drawing programs, Bezier curves are typically reshaped by moving the handles that appear off of the curve.

BFR
(Big Fast Router) A routing switch (or switch router). See *layer 3 switch*.

BFT
(Binary File Transfer) An extension to the fax protocol that allows transmission of raw data. A page of text is transmitted faster than a bitmap of the page and is displayed at normal printer resolution at the receiving side.

BGA
(Ball Grid Array) A surface mount chip package that uses a grid of solder balls as its connectors. It is noted for its compact size, high lead count and low inductance, which allows lower voltages to be used. BGAs come in plastic and ceramic varieties. See *chip package*.

BGP
A routing protocol that is used to span autonomous systems on the Internet. It is a robust, sophisticated and scalable protocol that was developed by the Internet Engineering Task Force (IETF). BGP4 supports the CIDR addressing scheme, which has increased the number of available IP addresses on the Internet. BGP was designed to supersede EGP, the orginal exterior gateway protocol. It is also known as a path vector protocol. See *CIDR* and *routing protocol*.

bias
The voltage used to control or stabilize an electronic circuit.

BiCMOS
(BIpolarCMOS) A type of integrated circuit that uses both bipolar and CMOS technologies. The logic gate is primarily made of CMOS, but its output stage uses bipolar transistors, which can handle higher current.

BICSI
(Building Industry Consulting Services International) A membership organization devoted to advancing its members in the field of distributing low-level electronics within a building. It publishes the Telecommunications Distribution Methods Manual and coordinates the testing for the RCDD (Registered Communications Distribution Designer), which is a certificate for excellence in telecommunications distribution design in commercial, campus and multi-family buildings.

bidirectional
The ability to move, transfer or transmit in both directions.

bidirectional printer
A printer that prints alternate lines from right to left.

bi-endian
The ability to switch between big endian and little endian ordering. For example, the PowerPC is a bi-endian CPU.

BIFF
(Binary Interchange File Format) A spreadsheet file format that holds data and charts, introduced with Excel Version 2.2.

bifurcate
To divide into two.

Big Blue
A nickname for IBM coined from the blue covers on most of its earlier mainframes.

big endian
The order of bytes in a word in which the most significant byte or digits are placed leftmost in the structure. This is the way humans deal with normal arithmetic. However, some CPUs are built using the little endian method, which is just the opposite and places the least significant digits on the left. Since numbers are calculated by the CPU starting with the least significant digits, little endian numbers are already set up for the required processing order.

A bi-endian machine, such as the PowerPC, is built to handle both types of byte ordering.

In the following example, the decimal number 23,041 (equivalent to 5A01 in hex) is shown in the big endian byte order and little endian byte order.

```
Big endian          Little endian
(Motorola 680x0)    (Intel x86)
5A01                015A
```

Bigfoot
See *Web white pages*.

big iron
Refers to mainframes.

bilinear filtering, bilinear interpolation

bilinear texture mapping
A texture mapping technique that produces a reasonably realistic image. An algorithm is used to map a screen pixel location to a corresponding point on the texture map. A weighted average of the attributes (color, alpha, etc.) of the four surrounding texels is computed and applied to the screen pixel. This process is repeated for each pixel forming the object being textured.

The term bilinear refers to the performing of interpolations in two dimensions (horizontal and vertical). The top and bottom pairs of each texel quadrant are averaged (horizontal) and then their results are averaged (vertical). This method is often used in conjunction with MIP mapping. See *texture map, MIP mapping, point sampling* and *trilinear interpolation*.

billion
One thousand times one million (10^9). See *space/time*.

bill of materials
The list of components that make up a system. For example, a bill of materials for a house would include the cement block, lumber, shingles, doors, windows, plumbing, electric, heating and so on. Each subassembly also contains a bill of materials; the heating system is made up of the furnace, ducts, etc. A bill of materials "implosion" links component pieces to a major assembly, while a bill of materials "explosion" breaks apart each assembly or subassembly into its component parts.

The first hierarchical databases were developed for automating bills of materials for manufacturing organizations in the early 1960s.

bin
(BINary) A popular directory name for storing executable programs, device drivers, etc. (binary files).

Computer Desktop Encyclopedia

binaries

Executable programs in machine language.

binary

Meaning two. The principle behind digital computers. All input to the computer is converted into binary numbers made up of the two digits 0 and 1 (bits). For example, when you press the "A" key on your personal computer, the keyboard generates and transmits the number 01000001 to the computer's memory as a series of pulses. The 1 bits are transmitted as high voltage; the 0 bits are transmitted as low. The bits are stored as charged and uncharged memory cells in the computer or as microscopic magnets on disk and tape. Display screens and printers convert the binary numbers into visual characters.

The electronic circuits that process these binary numbers are also binary in concept. They are made up of on/off switches (transistors) that are electrically opened and closed. The current flowing through one switch turns on (or off) another switch, and so on. These switches open and close in nanoseconds and picoseconds (billionths and trillionths of a second).

A computer's capability to do work is based on its storage capacity (memory and disk) and internal transmission speed. Greater storage capacities are achieved by making the memory cell or magnetic spot smaller. Faster transmission rates are achieved by shortening the time it takes to open and close the switch. In order to increase computer performance, we keep improving binary devices.

How Binary Numbers Work

Binary numbers are actually simpler than decimal numbers as they use only the digits 0 and 1 instead of 0 through 9.

In decimal, when you add 9 and 1, you get 10. But, if you break down the steps you find that by adding 9 and 1, what you get first is a result of 0 and a carry of 1. The carry of 1 is added to the digits in the next position on the left. In the following example, the carry becomes part of the answer since there are no other digits in that position.

```
carry-- 1
         9
       + 1
        10
```

The following example adds 1 ten times in succession. Note that the binary method has more carries than the decimal method. In binary, 1 and 1 are 0 with a carry of 1.

Binary	Decimal		Binary	Decimal
0	0			
+ 1	+ 1		+ 1	+ 1
1	1		110	6
+ 1	+ 1		+ 1	+ 1
10	2		111	7
+ 1	+ 1		+ 1	+ 1
11	3		1000	8
+ 1	+ 1		+ 1	+ 1
100	4		1001	9
+ 1	+ 1		+ 1	+ 1
101	5		1010	10

binary code

A coding system made up of binary digits. See *BCD, data code* and *numbers*.

binary coded decimal

See *BCD*.

binary compatible

Refers to any data, hardware or software structure (data file, machine code, instruction set, etc.) in binary form that is 100% identical to another. It most often refers to executable programs.

binary field

A field that contains binary numbers. It may refer to the storage of binary numbers for calculation purposes, or to a field that is capable of holding any information, including data, text, graphics images, voice and video. See *LOB*.

binary file

A file that uses all eight bits of the byte. Machine language programs (executable programs), graphics files, databases, spreadsheets and most word processing files fall into this category. Almost all files except for simple ASCII text files are binary files.

The distinction is meaningful when transmitting mail over the Internet. SMTP (Simple Mail Transfer Protocol) supports ASCII characters, which use only seven bits. When binary files are attached to e-mail messages, they must be converted into a 7-bit temporary text format, such as MIME, UUcoding or BinHex, and restored to their original 8-bit format at the receiving end. Full-blown e-mail programs (not light versions) support the popular encoding methods.

binary file transfer

Sending a file from one location to another in which all eight bits of the byte are transmitted either intact or via some encoding scheme. See *binary file*. See also *BFT*.

binary format

(1) Numbers stored in pure binary form in contrast with *BCD* form. See *binary numbers*.

(2) Information stored in a binary coded form, such as data, text, images, voice and video. See *binary file, binary field* and *LOB*.

(3) A file transfer mode that transmits any type of file without loss of data.

binary notation

The use of binary numbers to represent values.

binary numbers

Numbers stored in pure binary form. Within one byte (8 bits), the values 0 to 255 can be held. Two contiguous bytes (16 bits) can hold values from 0 to 65,535. See *numbers* and *BCD*.

binary search

A technique for quickly locating an item in a sequential list. The desired key is compared to the data in the middle of the list. The half that contains the data is then compared in the middle, and so on, either until the key is located or a small enough group is isolated to be sequentially searched.

binary standard

A standard that has been specified at a working level. Standards organizations often provide specifications that can be interpreted in different ways by vendors. A binary standard implies that there is no possible interpretation, because all the details (fields, variables, messages, etc.) have been defined at the bits and bytes level.

binary synchronous

See *bisync*.

binary tree

A data structure in which each node contains one parent and no more than two children.

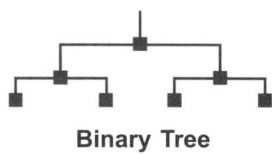

Binary Tree

binary values

The following table shows the maximum number of numeric combinations in a binary structure with all bits set to zero equivalent to one combination. For example, in one bit, which can be 0 or 1, there are two possible values.

Just as 99 is the largest decimal number in two decimal digits, 11 is the largest binary number in two binary digits. The decimal equivalent of the largest binary number in a group of bits is one less than the

Computer Desktop Encyclopedia

total number of values. For example, in four bits, which provides 16 values, the largest binary number is 1111 or 15 in decimal.

The decimal equivalent of the largest binary numbers as well as the binary numbers themselves are displayed below for up to 16 bits.

Bits		Total Values	Largest binary number Decimal equiv.	Binary
1		2	1	1
2		4	3	11
3		8	7	111
4		16	15	1111
5		32	31	1 1111
6		64	63	11 1111
7		128	127	111 1111
8		256	255	1111 1111
9		512	511	1 1111 1111
10	1K	1,024	1,023	11 1111 1111
11	2K	2,048	2,047	111 1111 1111
12	4K	4,096	4,095	1111 1111 1111
13	8K	8,192	8,191	1 1111 1111 1111
14	16K	16,384	16,383	11 1111 1111 1111
15	32K	32,768	32,767	111 1111 1111 1111
16	64K	65,536	65,535	1111 1111 1111 1111
17	128K	131,072		
18	256K	262,144		
19	512K	524,288		
20	1M	1,048,576		
21	2M	2,097,152		
22	4M	4,194,304		
23	8M	8,388,608		
24	16M	16,777,216		
25	32M	33,554,432		
26	64M	67,108,864		
27	128M	134,217,728		
28	256M	268,435,456		
29	512M	536,870,912		
30	1G	1,073,741,824		
31	2G	2,147,483,648		
32	4G	4,294,967,296		
33	8G	8,589,934,592		
34	16G	17,179,869,184		
35	32G	34,359,738,368		
36	64G	68,719,476,736		
37	128G	137,438,953,472		
38	256G	274,877,906,944		
39	512G	549,755,813,888		
40	1T	1,099,511,627,776		

bind

(1) In programming, to link or assign one routine or address to another. The operation is accomplished by setting pointers or indexes to the appropriate locations in memory or disk or by copying codes from one variable into another. See *binding time* and *linkage editor*.

(2) In a communications network, to establish a software connection between one protocol and another. Data flows from the application to the transport protocol to the network protocol to the data link protocol and then onto the network. Binding the protocols creates the internal pathway.

(3) (BIND) (Berkeley Internet Name Domain) A public domain DNS server that is available for most versions of UNIX.

Binder

A Microsoft Office workbook file that lets users combine related documents from different Office applications. The documents can be viewed, saved, opened, e-mailed and printed as a group. The Binder is an ActiveX Documents container, and Office applications, such as Excel and Word, are ActiveX Documents servers. The documents are known as ActiveX Documents objects, which were formerly known as DocObjects. See *ActiveX Documents*.

bindery

A NetWare file used for security and accounting in NetWare 2.x and 3.x. A bindery pertains only to the server it resides in and contains the names and passwords of users and groups of users authorized to log in to that server. It also holds information about other services provided by the server to the client (print, modem, gateway, etc.).

NDS (NetWare Directory Service) is the bindery counterpart in NetWare 4.x, but NDS is global oriented, manages multiple servers and provides a naming service, which the bindery does not. Bindery emulation software enables NetWare 2.x and 3.x clients to access services on NetWare 4.x servers. See *NDS*.

bindings

A set of linkages or assignments. See *bind*.

binding time

(1) In program compilation, the point in time when symbolic references to data are converted into physical machine addresses.

(2) In programming languages, when a variable is assigned its type (integer, string, etc.). Traditional compilers and assemblers provide early binding and assign types at compilation. Object-oriented languages provide late binding and assign types at runtime when the variable receives a value from the keyboard or other source.

BinHex

A utility and encoding format that originated on the Macintosh which is used to convert binary files into 7-bit ASCII for communications over Internet e-mail. Files formatted in BinHex use the .HQX extension. See *MIME, UUcoding* and *Wincode*.

biochip

See *gene chip*.

biomechanics

The study of the anatomical principles of movement. Biomechanical applications on the computer employ stick modeling to analyze the movement of athletes as well as racing horses.

biometrics

Means biological measurements and refers to eyes, voice, hand and fingerprints, which are used for authentication. See *authentication*.

bionic

A machine that is patterned after principles found in humans or nature; for example, robots. It also refers to artificial devices implanted into humans replacing or extending normal human functions.

BIOS

(Basic Input Output System) Although BIOSs were created more than 40 years ago as routines for handling input and output, the term generally refers to the PC's system BIOS, which is stored on a chip and provides an interface between the operating system and the peripheral hardware. The BIOS supports all peripheral technologies and internal services such as the realtime clock (time and date).

On startup, the BIOS tests the system and prepares the computer for operation by querying the

CMOS configuration settings and searching for other BIOSs on the plug-in boards and setting up pointers (interrupt vectors) in memory to access those routines. It then loads the operating system and passes control to it. The BIOS accepts requests from the drivers as well as the application programs.

BIOSs must periodically be updated to keep pace with new peripheral technologies. If the BIOS is stored on a ROM chip (ROM BIOS), it must be replaced. Newer BIOSs are stored on a flash memory chip that can be upgraded via software. See *CMOS setup*.

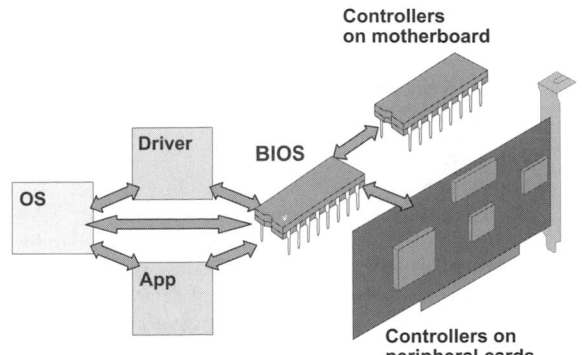

BIOS Interaction

On startup, the BIOS searches all peripheral controllers in the system to obtain the current configuration, which it makes available to the software.

biosensor

A device that detects and analyzes body movement, temperature or fluids and turns it into an electronic signal. It may be worn (headgear, bracelet, etc.) or used in a handheld or stationary unit. See *data glove*.

BIOS setup

Same as *CMOS setup*.

bipolar

A category of high-speed microelectronic circuit design, which was used to create the first transistor and the first integrated circuit. The most common variety of bipolar chip is TTL (transistor transistor logic). Emitter coupled logic (ECL) and integrated injection logic (I2L) are also part of the bipolar family.

Today, bipolar and CMOS are the two major transistor technologies. Most all personal computers use CMOS, and even large mainframes that have traditionally used bipolar have given way to CMOS designs. CMOS uses far less energy than bipolar.

However, bipolar transistors are still widely used for high radio frequency (RF) applications that reach into the gigahertz range, which CMOS technology cannot handle.

The bipolar transistor works by pulsing a line called the *base*, which allows current to flow from the *emitter* to the *collector*, or vice versa depending on the design.

bipolar transmission

A digital transmission technique that alternates between positive and negative signals. The 1s and 0s are determined by varying amplitudes at both polarities while non-data is zero amplitude.

BIPS

(Billion Instructions Per Second) See *MIPS*.

biquinary code

Meaning two-five code. A system for storing decimal digits in a four-bit binary number. The biquinary code was used in the abacus. See *abacus*.

birefringence

Using a crystal to split light into two frequencies that travel at different speeds and at right angles to each other. It's used to filter out a color in an LCD display.

bis

Second version. It means twice in Old Latin, or encore in French. Ter means three. For example, V.27bis and V.27ter are the second and third versions of the V.27 standard.

BISDN

(Broadband **ISDN**) A second-generation ISDN standard that uses fiber optic cables for speeds of 155 Mbps and higher. BISDN's bottom three layers of implementation comprise ATM (asynchronous transfer mode), which by itself is gaining ground as a networking technology for LANs and WANs.

bison

The Free Software Foundation's version of yacc.

bistable circuit

Same as *flip-flop*.

bisync

(**BI**nary **SYNC**hronous) A major category of synchronous communications protocols used in mainframe networks. Bisync communications require that both sending and receiving devices are synchronized before transmission of data is started. Contrast with *asynchronous* transmission.

bisynchronous

See *bisync*.

bit

(**BI**nary digi**T**) The smallest element of computer storage. It is a single digit in a binary number (0 or 1). The bit is physically a transistor or capacitor in a memory cell, a magnetic domain on disk or tape, a reflective spot on optical media or a high or low voltage pulsing through a circuit.

Groups of bits make up storage units in the computer, called characters, bytes, or words, which are manipulated as a group. The most common is the byte, made up of eight bits and equivalent to one alphanumeric character.

Bits are widely used as a measurement for transmission. Ten megabits per second means that ten

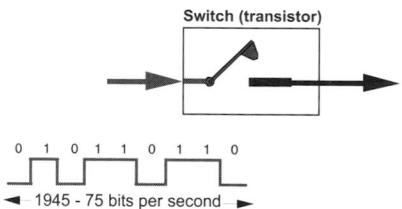

Transmission - Making it Faster

The bit is transmitted as a pulse of high or low voltage. Speed is increased by making the transistors open and close faster, which is a combination of making the microscopic elements within the transistor smaller and more durable.

Transmitting pulses internally in the computer is much simpler than out over a network, where they are influenced by long distances and interference. The telephone companies have been the pioneers in installing high-speed optical trunks throughout the country.

The Bit

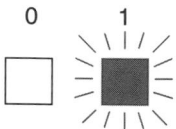

The bit is the smallest element of computer storage. It is a positive or negative magnetic spot on disk and tape and charged cells in memory.

Bits on magnetic disk

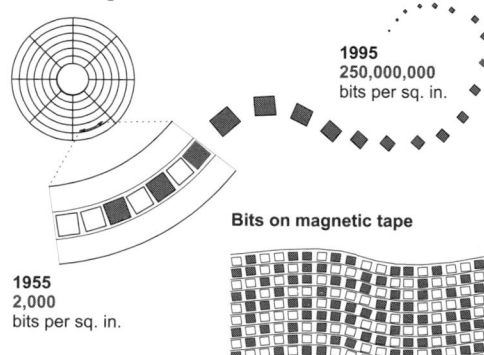

1995
250,000,000
bits per sq. in.

1955
2,000
bits per sq. in.

Bits on magnetic tape

The Byte

A byte is 8 binary digits, or cells.

Bytes in memory
In a 16 megabyte memory, there are 16 million of these 8-bit structures.

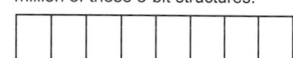

Storage - Making it Smaller

Making the spot or cell smaller increases the storage capacity. Our disks hold staggering amounts of data compared to 10 years ago, yet we still want more. Look up *holographic storage* for a look into a fascinating future storage technology.

million pulses are transmitted per second. A 16-bit bus means that there are 16 wires transmitting the bit at the same time.

Measurements for storage devices, such as disks, files and databases, are given in bytes rather than bits. See *space/time*.

bitblt

(**BIT BL**ock Transfer) In computer graphics, a hardware feature that moves a rectangular block of bits from main memory into display memory. It speeds the display of moving objects (animation, scrolling) on screen.

A hardware bitblt provides fastest speed, but bitblts are also implemented in software even in non-graphics systems. For example, text scrolls faster when it is copied as a contiguous block (bitblt) to the next part of the window rather than processing every character on every line. See *stretch blt*.

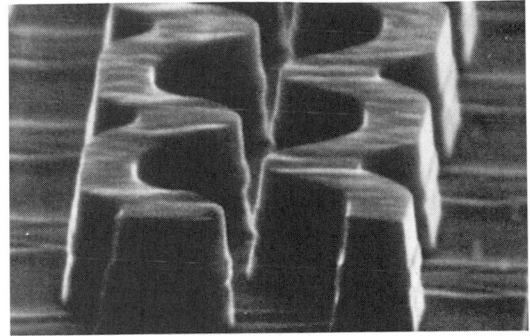

A Memory Bit

This is one storage cell in a 16-megabit dynamic RAM memory chip. There are 16,777,216 of these in the chip, which is about a quarter of an inch square. *(Photo courtesy of IBM Corporation.)*

bit bucket

An imaginary trash can. The phrase "it went into the bit bucket" means the data was lost.

bit cell

A boundary in which a single bit is recorded on a tape or disk.

bit density

The number of bits that can be stored within a given physical area.

bit depth

(1) The number of bits used to hold a pixel. Also called *color depth* and *pixel depth*, the bit depth determines the number of colors that can be displayed at one time. Digital video requires at least 15 bits, while 24 bits produces photorealistic colors.

```
Color depth    Number of colors
 4-bits        16
 8-bits        256
15-bits        32,768
16-bits        65,536
24-bits        16,777,216
32-bits        16,777,216 + alpha channel
```

(2) Bit depth can refer to any coding system that uses numeric values to represent something. The depth, or number of bits, determines how many discrete items can be represented.

bite

See *byte*.

bit error rate

See *BER*.

bit flipping

Same as *bit manipulation*.

bit level device

A device, such as a disk drive, that inputs and outputs data bits. Contrast with *pulse level device*.

bit manipulation

Processing individual bits within a byte. Bit-level manipulation is very low-level programming, often done in graphics and systems programming.

bitmap

A binary representation in which a bit or set of bits corresponds to some part of an object such as an image or font. For example, in monochrome systems, one bit represents one pixel on screen. For gray scale or color, several bits in the bitmap represent one pixel or group of pixels. The term may also refer to the memory area that holds the bitmap.

A bitmap is usually associated with graphics object in which the bits are a direct representation of the pict image. However, bitmaps can be used to represent and keep track of anything, where each bit location is assigned a different value or condition.

bitmapped font

A set of dot patterns for each letter and digit in a particular typeface (Times Roman, Helvetica, etc.) for a specified type size (10 points, 12 points, etc.). Bitmapped typefaces are either purchased in groups of pre-generated point sizes, or, for a wide supply of fonts, font generators allow the user to create a variety of point sizes. Bitmapped fonts take up disk space for each point size. Contrast with *scalable font*. See *font* and *font generator*.

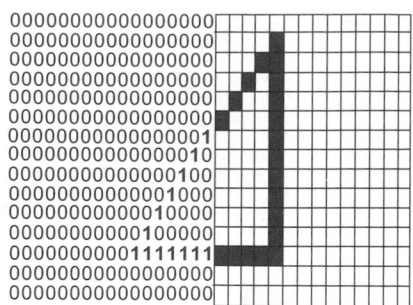

A Monochrome Bitmap
The left half of this diagram shows the bits in the bitmap, and the right half depicts what would show on screen. In monochrome systems, one bit is used to represent one pixel. Images that are scanned into the computer are turned into bitmaps, and bitmaps can be created in a paint program.

bitmapped graphics

In computer graphics, a technique for representing a picture image as a matrix of dots. Also known as "raster graphics," it is the digital counterpart of analog TV. However, unlike TV, which uses one standard format in the U.S. known as NTSC, there are dozens of bitmapped graphics formats, including GIF, TIF, BMP, JPG and PCX (see *graphics formats*). See *graphics*. Contrast with *vector graphics*.

BITNET

A worldwide communications network founded in 1981 that served higher education and research. Well known for its LISTSERV software for managing electronic mailing lists, for years, BITNET was the world's largest computer-based, higher-education network. It was gradually supplanted by the Internet.

bit-oriented protocol

A communications protocol that uses individual bits within the byte as control codes, such as IBM's SDLC. Contrast with *byte-oriented protocol*.

bit parallel

The transmission of several bits at the same time, each bit travelling over a different wire in the cable.

bit pattern

A specific layout of binary digits.

bit plane

A segment of memory used to control an object, such as a color, cursor or sprite. Bit planes may be reserved parts of a common memory or independent memory banks each designed for one purpose.

bit rate

The transmission speed of binary coded data. Same as *data rate*.

bit serial

The transmission of one bit after the other on a single line or wire.

bit slice processor

A logic chip that is used as an elementary building block for the computer designer. Bit slice processors usually come in 4-bit increments and are strung together to make larger processors (8 bit, 12 bit, etc.).

Computer Desktop Encyclopedia

bit specifications

Everything in the digital world is measured in bits and bytes. Bits are a measurement of different components and functions depending on what is being referenced. Following are the most common. See also *binary values*.

(1) The size of the computer's internal word, or registers, which is the amount of data the CPU can compute at the same time. If the clock rates are the same (50MHz, 100MHz, etc.) and the basic architectures are equal, a 32-bit computer works twice as fast internally as a 16-bit computer.

(2) The size of the computer's data bus, which is the pathway over which data is transferred between memory and the CPU and between memory and the peripheral devices. If the bus clock rates are equal, a 16-bit bus transfers data twice as fast as an 8-bit bus.

(3) The size of the address bus, which determines how much memory the CPU can address directly. Each bit doubles the number, for example, 20-bits addresses 1,048,576 bytes; 24-bits addresses 16,772,216 bytes. See *binary values*.

(4) The number of colors that can be displayed at one time. This is called *bit depth, color depth* and *pixel depth*. Unless some of the memory is used for cursor or sprite movement, an 8-bit display adapter generates 256 colors; 16-bit, 64K colors; 24-bit, 16.8 million colors. See *alpha channel* and *bit depth*.

Bit specifications, such as 64-bit and 128-bit, refer to the display adapter's architecture, which affects speed, not the number of colors. See *64-bit graphics accelerator* and *128-bit graphics accelerator*.

(5) The quality of sound based on the number of bits in the samples taken. A 16-bit sample yields a number with 65,536 increments compared to 256 in an 8-bit sample. See *8-bit sample* and *16-bit sample*.

bit stream

The transmission of binary signals.

bit stuffing

Adding bits to a transmitted message in order to round out a fixed frame or to break up a pattern of data bits that could be misconstrued for control codes.

bit twiddler

Same as *hacker*.

bit wise

See *bitwise* and *bit manipulation*.

bitwise

Dealing with bits rather than larger structures such as a byte. Bitwise operators are programming commands or statements that work with individual bits. See *bit manipulation*.

BIX

(Byte Information Exchange, Cambridge, MA, www.bix.com) An online database of computer knowledge from BYTE magazine, designed to help users fix problems and obtain info on hardware and software products. See *online services*.

black box

A custom-made electronic device, such as a protocol converter or encryption system. Yesterday's black boxes often become today's off-the-shelf products.

Black Box Corporation

(Black Box Corporation, Pittsburgh, PA, www.blackbox.com) An organization that specializes in selling communications and LAN products. It offers expert services, custom solutions and hard-to-find products. It also provides free, 24-hour tech support.

The Black Box
A black box doesn't have to look like a box. It can be any contraption that is custom made for an application.

The company's original name was Expandor, Inc., which offered manual printer switches known as "black boxes." Its catalog was eventually named the Black Box catalog, and later the company changed its name.

Black Screen of Death

A Windows 95 error that causes the computer to lock up, and the screen turns black. The solution is to reboot. See *Blue Screen of Death*.

blank character

A space character that takes up one byte in the computer just like a letter or digit. When you press the space bar on a personal computer keyboard, the ASCII character with a numeric value of 32 is created.

blank squash

The removal of blanks between items of data. For example, the Trim function in dBASE removes trailing blanks. The expression **trim(city) + ", " + state** concatenates city and state with a blank squash resulting in DALLAS, TX rather than DALLAS   TX.

bleed

Printing at the very edge of the paper. Many laser printers, including all LaserJets up to the 11x17" 4V, cannot print to the very edge, leaving a border of approximately 1/4". In commercial printing, bleeding is generally more expensive, because wider paper is often used, which is later cut to size.

Blenheim shows

(The Blenheim Group, Fort Lee, NJ) A major producer of trade shows that organized more than 40 IT expositions around the world, PC EXPO being the largest and most notable. Blenheim was acquired by Miller Freeman in late 1996. See *Miller Freeman*.

blip

A mark, line or spot on a medium, such as microfilm, that is optically sensed and used for timing or counting purposes.

blitting

Using a bitblt to transfer data.

bloatware

Software that is so overloaded with functionality that its performance suffers. At the very least, it takes a long time to load the program. Software vendors seem to have the perception that more is always better.

BLOB

(Binary Large OBject) Borland's term for a LOB. See *LOB*.

block

(1) A group of disk or tape records that is stored and transferred as a single unit.

(2) A group of bits or characters that is transmitted as a unit.

(3) A group of text characters that has been marked for moving, copying, saving or other operation.

block device

A peripheral device that transfers a group of bytes (block, sector, etc.) of data at a time such as a disk. Contrast with *character device*.

block diagram

A chart that contains squares and rectangles connected with arrows to depict hardware and software interconnections. For program flow charts, information system flow charts, circuit diagrams and communications networks, more elaborate graphical representations are usually used.

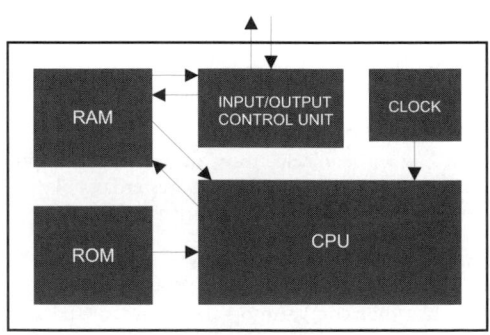

Block Diagram of a Computer

blocking factor

The number of records in a block.

blocking software

See *Web filtering* and *parental control software*.

block move
The ability to mark a contiguous segment of text or data and move it.

block multiplexor channel
A high-speed mode of operation within IBM's parallel channel. See *parallel channel*.

blow
To write code or data into a PROM chip by blowing the fuses of the 0 bits. The 1 bits are left alone.

blow up
Same as *crash*, *bomb* or *abend*.

blue laser
A type of laser capable of writing bits with up to five times greater density than the infrared lasers commonly used. In 1993, IBM demonstrated a recording density of 2.5 billion bits per square inch on a magneto-optic disk. It is expected that blue lasers will be commercially used in a few years.

blue screen
See *color key*.

Blue Screen of Death
A Windows NT error that causes the computer to lock up, and the screen turns blue. The solution is to reboot. See *Black Screen of Death*.

BMP file
(Bit MaP file) Also known as a "bump" file, it is a Windows and OS/2 bitmapped graphics file format. It is the Windows native bitmap format, and every Windows application has access to the BMP software routines in Windows that support it. BMP files provide formats for 2, 16, 256 or 16 million colors (1-bit, 4-bit, 8-bit and 24-bit color). BMP files use the .BMP or .DIB extensions (DIB stands for Device-Independent Bitmap).

BNC connector
(British Naval Connector) A commonly used plug and socket for audio, video and networking applications. BNCs connect two-wire coaxial cable (signal and ground) using a bayonet mount. After the plug is inserted, the bayonette mechanism causes the pins to be pinched into the locking groove when the plug is turned. See *RCA connector* for illustration.

BNF
See *Backus-Naur form*.

board
See *card*, *printed circuit board* and *BBS*.

board level
Electronic components that are mounted on a printed circuit board instead of in a cabinet or finished housing.

boardware
Same as *board level*.

BOC
(Bell Operating Company) One of 22 telephone companies that was formerly part of AT&T and now part of one of the seven regional Bell telephone companies.

body text
The base font used for text in a paragraph. In many desktop publishing programs, any paragraph that is not tagged separately is assigned the body text style.

body type
The typeface and size commonly used for text in paragraph copy. Typically 10 points.

BOF

(Beginning Of File) The status of a file when it is first opened or when an instruction or command has reset the file pointer.

boilerplate

A common phrase or expression used over and over. Boilerplate is stored on disk and copied into the document as needed. See *stationery*.

boldface

Characters that are heavier and darker on printed output and brighter than normal on a display screen.

boldface attribute

A code that turns normal characters into boldface characters on a printer or display screen.

boldface font

A set of type characters that are darker and heavier than normal type. In a boldface font, all characters have been designed as bold characters.

bomb

Same as *abend* and *crash*.

BOMP

(Bill Of Materials Processor) One of the first DBMSs used for bill of materials explosion in the early 1960s from IBM. A subsequent version, DBOMP, was used in manufacturing during the 1970s.

bonded modem

See *channel bonding*.

bonding

Tying two or more devices together to function as one. See *channel bonding* and *ISDN*.

Bongo

A visual interface builder for Java from Marimba that includes a variety of ready-to-use controls, known as "interface widgets." Bongo output can be directly published as Castanet channels. See *Castanet*.

Booch

An object-oriented analysis and design method developed by Grady Booch, chief scientist of Rational Software. See *object references* and *Rational Rose*.

bookmark

A stored location for quick retrieval at a later date. Web browsers provide bookmarks that contain the addresses (URLs) of favorite sites. Most electronic references, large text databases and help systems provide bookmarks that mark a location users want to revisit in the future.

Some of the First Boilerplate
Throughout the 1940s and up until the mid 1970s, Auto-typist machines from the American Automatic Typewriter Company provided reliable document processing. *(Photos courtesy of TMC/Compco, Inc.)*

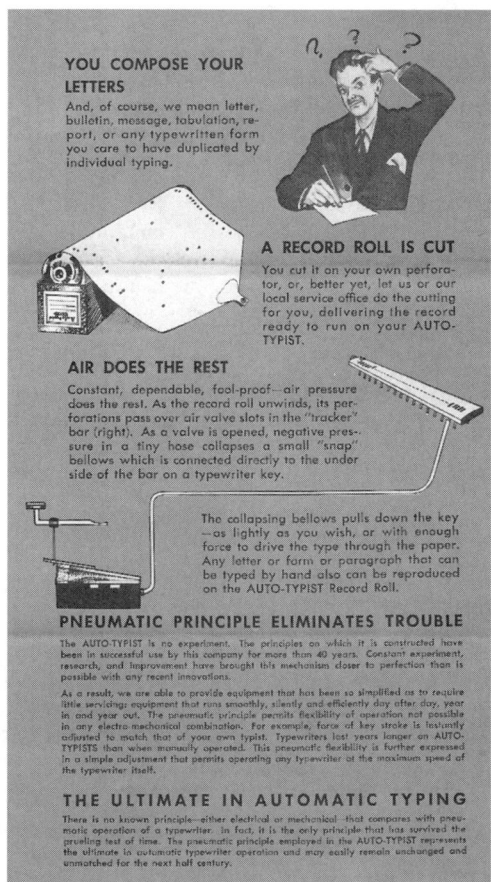

Computer Desktop Encyclopedia

Boolean data

Yes/no or true/false data.

Boolean expression

A statement using Boolean operators that expresses a condition which is either true or false.

Boolean logic

The "mathematics of logic," developed by English mathematician George Boole in the mid 19th century. Its rules govern logical functions (true/false). As add, subtract, multiply and divide are primary operations of arithmetic, AND, OR and NOT are the primary operations of Boolean logic. Boolean logic is turned in logic gates on circuit boards, and various permutations are used, including NAND, NOR, XOR and XNOR. The rules, or truth tables, for Boolean AND, OR and NOT are shown on the right. See *logic gate*.

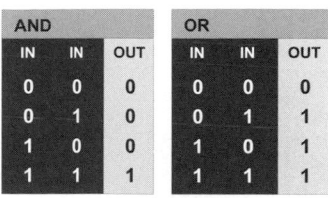

AND			OR		
IN	IN	OUT	IN	IN	OUT
0	0	0	0	0	0
0	1	0	0	1	1
1	0	0	1	0	1
1	1	1	1	1	1

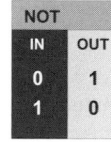

NOT	
IN	OUT
0	1
1	0

Curious About the Chip?

Wired in patterns of Boolean logic and in less space than a postage stamp, transistors inside one of today's high-speed chips collectively open and close trillions of times every second. If you're curious about how it really works down deep in the layers of the silicon, read the rest of "Boolean logic," then "chip" and, finally, "transistor." It's a fascinating venture into a microscopic world.

The logic of AND, OR and NOT is implemented as transistors, which are electronic switches that are opened and closed by being pulsed. If you don't understand every last detail below, keep on going. It will come together at the end. You can always review.

AND

AND requires both inputs to be present in order to provide output. Because the AND gate is wired in series, both inputs must pulse both switches closed, and current flows from the source to the output.

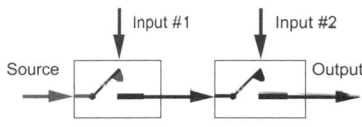

OR

OR requires one input to be present in order to provide output. Because the OR gate is wired in parallel, either one or both inputs will generate output.

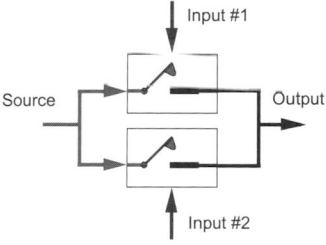

NOT

NOT reverses the input. If there is no pulse on the input line, the source goes directly to output, as in the diagram above. If there is a pulse on the input line, switch #1 is closed. The switch #1 current goes to switch #2 and pulses it open (it's a reverse switch), and the source current is impeded.

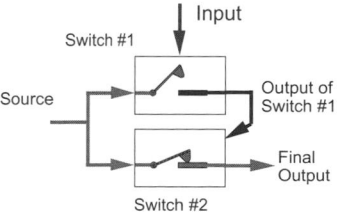

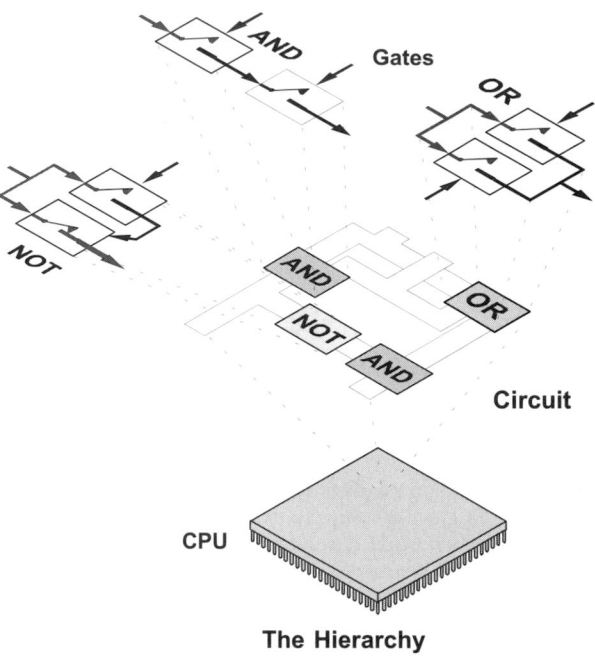

Gates

Circuit

CPU

The Hierarchy

The gates make up circuits, and circuits make a logical devices, such as a CPU. We're going to look at a circuit that is present in every computer. It adds one bit to another.

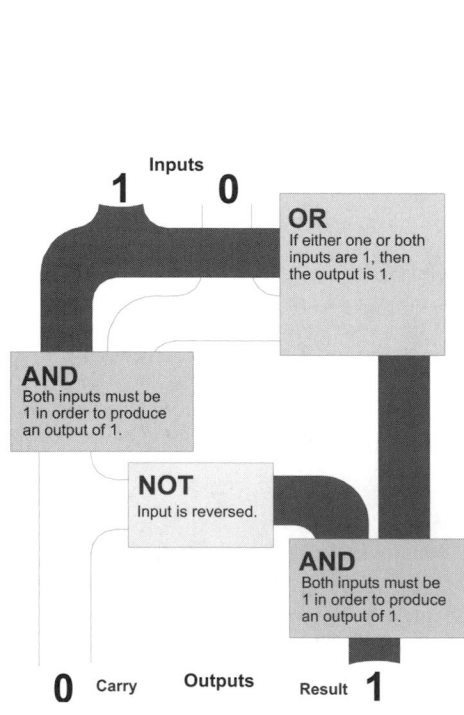

Inputs

1 **0**

OR
If either one or both inputs are 1, then the output is 1.

AND
Both inputs must be 1 in order to produce an output of 1.

NOT
Input is reversed.

AND
Both inputs must be 1 in order to produce an output of 1.

0 Carry   **Outputs**   Result **1**

The Half-Adder Circuit

Trace the current through the example above. See how AND, OR and NOT react to their inputs. The 1 is represented by the red line (flow of current), and the 0 by no line. If it makes sense to you, try it yourself below.

```
    0    0    0    1    1  ◄── Carry bit
    0    0    1    1
  + 0  + 1  + 0  + 1
Result bit ►  0    1    1    0
```

Adding Two Bits Together

The half-adder circuit adds one bit to another and yields a one-bit result with one carry bit. This circuit in combination with a shift register, which moves over to the next bit, is how a string of binary numbers are added. This diagram shows the four possible binary additions for two bits.

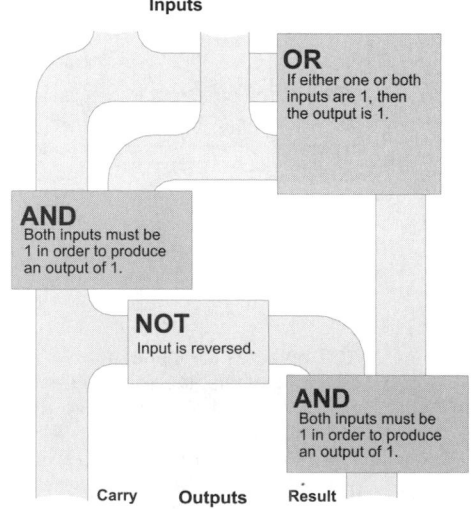

Inputs

OR
If either one or both inputs are 1, then the output is 1.

AND
Both inputs must be 1 in order to produce an output of 1.

NOT
Input is reversed.

AND
Both inputs must be 1 in order to produce an output of 1.

Carry   **Outputs**   Result

Try It

Try your Boolean skill. Pick any combination of 0 and 1 and see if you can get the right answer. Review the combinations above.

Ready For More?
If you get the sense of how a circuit works inside the chip, it's time to see how the chip itself is built. Look up *chip* in this Encyclopedia. Also, if you are seriously interested in digital electronics, "Bebop to the Boolean Boogie" by Clive "Max" Maxfield, is must reading. It is informative, understandable and downright enjoyable. (HighText Publishing, 1995, ISBN 1-878707-22-1)

Boolean operator
One of the Boolean logic operators such as AND, OR and NOT.

Boolean search
A search for specific data. It implies that any condition can be searched for using the Boolean operators AND, OR and NOT. For example, the English language request: "Search for all Spanish and French speaking employees who have MBAs, but don't work in Sales." is expressed in the following dBASE command:

```
list for degree = "MBA" .and. (language = "Spanish" .or. language = "French")
    .and. .not. department = "Sales"
```

boot
Causing the computer to start executing instructions. Personal computers contain built-in instructions in a ROM chip that are automatically executed on startup. These instructions search for the operating system, load it and pass control to it. Starting up a large computer may require more button pushing and keyboard input.

The term comes from "bootstrap," since bootstraps help you get your boots on, booting the computer helps it get its first instructions. The term is often used erroneously for application software. You might hear for example, "let's boot WordPerfect," whereas the correct usage is "load WordPerfect." See *cold boot, warm boot* and *clean boot*.

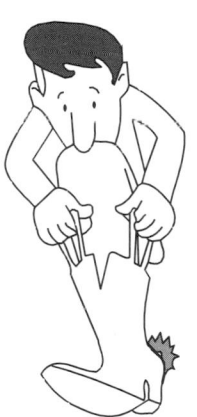

bootable CD-ROM
A CD-ROM that can boot its own operating system. It is used to install the operating system on a brand new machine. See *bootable disk*.

bootable disk
A disk that contains the operating system in a form ready to load into the computer. It usually refers to a floppy disk that contains the operating system in its boot sectors; however, increasingly, CD-ROMs are being made bootable. Desktop computers are usually configured to look for a bootable floppy in the primary floppy drive at startup (A: in a PC). If it is not found, it boots from the hard disk.

It's a good idea to make a bootable disk for your personal computer in case the hard disk doesn't boot some day. That way, you'll be able to start the computer and access important data. In Windows 95/98, select Startup Disk from the ADD/REMOVE PROGRAMS control panel.

bootable floppy
See *bootable disk*.

boot drive
A disk drive that contains the operating system.

boot failure
The inability to locate and/or read the operating system from the designated disk.

BOOTP

(**BOOT**strap Protocol) A TCP/IP protocol used by a diskless workstation or network computer (NC) to obtain its IP address and other network information such as server address and default gateway. Upon startup, the client station sends out a BOOTP request in a UDP packet to the BOOTP server, which returns the required information. Unlike RARP, which uses only the layer 2 (Ethernet) frame for transport, the BOOTP request and response use an IP broadcast function that can send messages before a specific IP address is known. See *RARP*.

boot record

See *boot sector*.

boot ROM

A memory chip that allows a workstation to be booted from the server or other remote station. See *remote boot*.

boot sector

Reserved sectors on disk that are used to load the operating system. On startup, the computer looks for the master book record (MBR) or something similarly named, which is typically the first sector in the first partition of the disk. The MBR contains pointers to the first sector of the partition that contains the operating system, and that sector contains the instructions that cause the computer to boot the operating system.

bootstrap

See *boot*.

boot virus

A virus written into the boot sectors of a floppy disk. If the floppy is booted, it infects the system. For example, the Michelangelo virus, which destroys data on March 6th, Michelangelo's birthday, infects a computer if the virus diskette is left in the drive and booted inadvertently when the computer is turned back on.

Borland

The original name of INPRISE Corporation. See *INPRISE*.

Borland C++

An ANSI C and C++ compiler from INPRISE for DOS and Windows applications. It is Turbo C-compatible and its debugger supports Windows programs written in Microsoft C. It includes application frameworks for Windows (ObjectWindows) and DOS (Turbo Vision). Borland C++ for OS/2 is also available.

Borland Database Engine

Software from INPRISE that runs on a Windows client and unifies database access across multiple platforms. Using INPRISE's own IDAPI interface, it provides a middleware layer between the client and numerous databases, including dBASE, Paradox, Oracle, SQL Server, DB2, Informix, Interbase and ODBC-compliant databases. It used to be available separately, but has since been built into all of INPRISE's language products.

boss screen

A fake business-like screen that can be quickly popped up over a game when the boss walks in.

bot

(1) (ro**BOT**) A program used on the Internet that performs a repetitive function such as posting a message to multiple newsgroups or searching for information. Bots are also used to keep a channel open on the Internet Relay Chat (IRC). Increasingly, the term is used for all variety of macros and intelligent agents that are Internet or Web related.

(2) (BOT) Beginning of tape. Similar to BOF.

Boundary Routing

3Com's trade name for remote office routing, which it pioneered. See *remote-office router*.

Computer Desktop Encyclopedia

boundary scan

See *scan technology*.

Bourne shell

The original command line processor for UNIX. See *C Shell, Korn Shell* and *UNIX*.

box

Slang for hardware. A box can be a PC or server or any device, although it is typically one that processes information. For example, a "UNIX box" is just another way of saying "UNIX computer."

Boyer-Moore algorithm

A formula that speeds up searching for text. Instead of comparing each character in the target area, the pointer is moved ahead by several bytes based on the last non-matching characters.

bozo filter

A feature of certain e-mail programs that allows you to delete unread, unwanted mail based on words in the message header.

bpi

(Bits Per Inch) The measurement of the number of bits stored in a linear inch of a track on a recording surface, such as on a disk or tape.

bpp

(Bits Per Pixel) See *bit depth*.

BPR

(Business Process Reengineering) See *reengineering*.

B protocol

A file transfer protocol from CompuServe. Quick B is a faster version only for downloading. Later versions of B will automatically select Quick B.

bps

(Bits Per Second) The measurement of the speed of data transfer in a communications system.

bracket

In programming, brackets (the [and] characters) are used to enclose numbers and subscripts. For example, in the C statement **int menustart** [4] = {2,9,15,22}; the [4] indicates the number of elements in the array, and the contents are enclosed in brackets. In the C expression, **if (ABCbuff [501] == '\x1')**, the [501] indicates the 501st byte of the ABC buffer (starting with 0).

brains

A computer's "brains" are its central processing unit. See *CPU*.

branch

(1) A machine instruction that switches the CPU to another location in the program (in memory). In assembly languages, branch and jump instructions provide the branch. In high-level languages, the goto statement provides the branch. For example, "IF A EQUALS B GOTO MATCH_ROUTINE." See *branch prediction*.

(2) A connection between two blocks in a flowchart or two nodes in a network.

branch prediction

In CPU instruction execution, predicting the outcome of a branch so that those instructions may be executed in parallel with the current instructions. If the CPU guesses the wrong branch, it will take extra machine cycles to go back and execute the correct one; however, on average, if the prediction algorithms are good, overall performance is increased. See *predication* and *branch*.

braze

To solder using metals with a very high melting point, such as with an alloy of zinc and copper.

BRB

Digispeak for "be right back."

breadboard

A thin plastic board full of holes used to hold components (transistors, chips, etc.) that are wired together. It is used to develop electronic prototypes or one-of-a-kind systems.

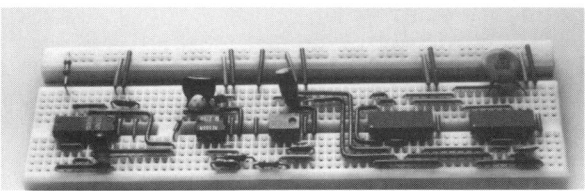

Breadboard
(Photo courtesy of 3M Company.)

break

To temporarily or permanently stop executing, printing or transmitting.

break key

A keyboard key that is pressed to stop the execution of the current program or transmission.

breakout box

A device inserted into a multiple-line cable for testing purposes that provides an external connecting point to each wire. A small LED may be attached to each line, which glows when a signal is present.

breakpoint

The location in a program used to temporarily halt the program for testing and debugging. Lines of code in a source program are marked for break points. When those instructions are about to be executed, the program stops, allowing the programmer to examine the status of the program (registers, variables, etc.). After inspection, the programmer can step through the program one line at a time or cause the program to continue running either to the end or to the next break point, whichever comes first.

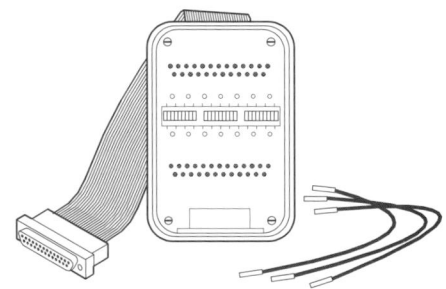

Breakout Box

bridge

(1) To cross from one circuit, channel or element over to another.

(2) A device that connects two LAN segments together, which may be of similar or dissimilar types, such as Ethernet and Token Ring. Bridges are inserted into a network to improve performance by keeping traffic contained within smaller segments.

Bridges maintain address tables of the nodes on the network through experience. They learn which addresses were successfully received through which output ports by monitoring which station acknowledged receipt of the address.

Bridges work at the data link layer (OSI layer 2), whereas routers work at the network layer (layer 3). Bridges are protocol independent; routers are protocol dependent. Bridges are faster than routers because they do not have to read the protocol to glean routing information.

Bridges with more than two ports (multiport bridges) perform a switching function. Today's LAN switches are really multiport bridges that can switch at full wire speed. See *transparent bridge, repeater, router, gateway* and *hub*. See *LAN* for illustration.

bridge router

A communications device that provides the functions of a bridge and router. See *bridge* and *router*.

bridgeware

Hardware or software that converts data or translates programs from one format into another.

Brief

An early text editor for DOS programming from Borland. It provided automatic indentation and the ability to edit different parts of a source program at the same time.

Computer Desktop Encyclopedia

Briefcase

In Windows 95/98, a system folder used for synchronizing files between two computers, typically a desktop and laptop computer. Files to be worked on are placed into a Briefcase, which is then transferred to the second machine via floppy, cable or network. The Briefcase is then brought back to the original machine after its contents have been edited on the second machine, and a special update function replaces the original files with the new ones.

brightness

The light level on a display screen. Contrast with *contrast*.

British Telecom

The telephone and communications carrier that provides services in Great Britain and Northern Ireland. It used to be a division of the British Post Office, but was privatized in 1984 under Margaret Thatcher's regime.

broadband

(1) High-speed transmission. The term is commonly used to refer to communications lines or services at T1 rates (1.544 Mbps) and above.

(2) A technique for transmitting data, voice and video using the same frequency division multiplexing (FDM) technique as cable TV. Modems are required for this method, because the digital data has to be modulated onto the line. Contrast with *baseband*.

broadcast

To transmit data to everybody on the network or network segment. Contrast with *narrowcast*. See *multicast*.

broadcast fax

The ability to send a fax to multiple recipients, which is very worthwhile when you need to disseminate faxes to several colleagues at once. Not so worthwhile however is receiving unsolicited faxes about something that you have no interest in. See *junk faxes*.

broadcast storm

Excessive transmission of broadcast traffic in a network. Broadcast storms can be lessened by properly designing and balancing the number of nodes on each network segment.

broadcast traffic

In a network, message traffic that is sent out to everybody on a network segment. Broadcasts are issued for address resolution when the location of a user or server is not known. They may occur when clients and servers come online and identify themselves. Sometimes, network devices continually announce their presence. In all cases, the broadcast has to reach all possible networks and stations that might potentially respond. Contrast with *multicast*.

brochureware

A Web site that advertises a product but contains only the equivalent of a paper brochure with no interactivity. The Web is not encumbered by the size of paper and offers the ability to show endless views and details of a product, make recommendations based on user input, download demos (of software), compute order totals, even remember what you asked the last time you visited. All this is missing in brochureware.

Brook's law

"Adding manpower to a late software project makes it later." By Fred Brooks, author of "The Mythical Man-Month." The extra human communications required to add another member to a programming team is considerably more than anyone ever expects. It of course depends on the experience and sophistication of the programmers involved and the quality of the documentation, which is often sparse. See *laws*.

brouter

(Bridging ROUTER) See *bridge router*.

browse

(1) To view the contents of a file or a group of files. Browser programs generally let you view data by scrolling through the documents or databases. In a database program, the browse mode often lets you edit the data. See *Web browser*.

(2) To view and edit a flow chart of a system created in a program specialized for visual system design or to view and edit a class hierarchy of objects in an object-oriented programming language.

(3) In Windows, the Browse button lets you view the file names in your disk directories. Clicking on the names of the drives and directories switches you to those locations.

browser

A program that lets you look through a set of data. See *Web browser* and *browse*.

browser box

See *Internet appliance*.

browser cache

Pronounced "browser cash." A temporary storage area in memory or on disk that holds the most recently-downloaded Web pages. As you link from page to page on the Web, caching those pages in memory lets you quickly go back to a page without having to download it from the Web again. When you quit the browser session, those pages are stored on disk. The Web browser lets you set the amount of space to use and the length of time to hold them.

BrowserComp

A benchmark from Ziff-Davis that tests a Web browser, including its ability to handle pages with JavaScript, VBScript, audio, video and style sheets. See *ZDBOp*.

BSC

(Binary Synchronous Communications) See *bisync*.

BSDL

(Boundary Scan Description Language) A IEEE language used to describe structures for boundary scan testing. See *scan technology*.

BSD socket

A communications interface in UNIX first introduced in BSD UNIX. See *UNIX socket*.

BSD UNIX

(Berkeley Software Distribution UNIX) A version of UNIX developed by the Computer Systems Research Group of the University of California at Berkeley from 1979 to 1993. BSD enhancements, known as the "Berkeley Extensions," include networking, virtual memory, task switching and large file names (up to 255 chars.). BSD's UNIX was distributed free, with a charge only for the media. USL code is contained in most BSD versions, and users require a valid USL license in such cases.

Bill Joy ran the group until 1982 when he co-founded Sun Microsystems, bringing 4.2BSD with him as the foundation of SunOS. The last BSD version released by BSD was 4.4BSD.

Berkeley Software Design, Inc., Colorado Springs, CO (www.bsdi.com), a private company founded in 1991, continues to develop BSD code.

b-spline

In computer graphics, a curve that is generated using a mathematical formula which assures continuity with other b-splines. See *spline* and *NURB*.

BT

See *British Telecom*.

BTA

(Business Technology Association, Kansas City, MO, www.btanet.org) A membership association of office equipment dealers founded in 1994. It is a merger of NOMDA (National Office Machine Dealers Association), founded in 1926, with LANDA and AIMED (LAN Dealers Association and Affiliated Independent Mailing Equipment Dealers). Publications, training seminars and conferences are provided for members.

BTAM

(Basic Telecommunications Access Method) IBM communications software used in bisynch, non-SNA mainframe networks. Application programs must interface directly with the BTAM access method.

BT font

(BitsTream font) Refers to fonts from Bitstream Inc., Cambridge, MA. See *FaceLift* and *FontWare*.

BTLZ

(British Telecom Lempel Ziv) A data compression algorithm based on the Lempel-Ziv method that can achieve up to 4x the throughput of 2400 and 9600 bps modems.

B-tree

(Balanced-tree) A technique for organizing indexes. In order to keep access time to a minimum, it stores the data keys in a balanced hierarchy that continually realigns itself as items are inserted and deleted. Thus, all nodes always have a similar number of keys.

B+tree is a version of B-tree that maintains a hierarchy of indexes while also linking the data sequentially, providing fast direct access and fast sequential access. IBM's VSAM uses this.

Btrieve

A database manager for NetWare, Windows 95/98 and Windows NT from Btrieve Technologies, Inc., Austin, TX. It allows for the creation of indexed files, using the b-tree organization method. Btrieve functions can be called from within many common programming languages. Btrieve was originally developed by Novell for NetWare. In 1994, it was sold to Btrieve Technologies, which was founded by former Novell employees. See *Xtrieve*.

BTW

Digispeak for "by the way."

bubble

A bit in bubble memory or a symbol in a bubble chart.

bubble chart

A chart that uses bubble-like symbols often used to depict data flow diagrams.

Bubble Jet

Canon's trade name for its thermal drop on demand ink jet printer technology. The ink is heated, which produces a bubble that expands and ejects the ink out of the nozzle. As the bubble cools, the vacuum created draws fresh ink back into the nozzle.

bubble memory

A solid state semiconductor and magnetic storage device suited for rugged applications. It is about as fast as a slow hard disk and holds its content without power.

It is conceptually a stationary disk with spinning bits. The unit, only a couple of square inches in size, contains a thin film magnetic recording layer. Globular-shaped bubbles (bits) are electromagnetically generated in circular strings inside this layer. In order to read or write the bubbles, they are rotated past the equivalent of a read/write head.

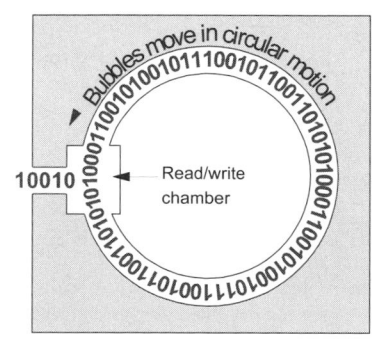

Bubble Memory
This is a conceptual drawing of how a bubble memory circuit works.

bubble sort

A multiple-pass sorting technique that starts by sequencing the first two items, then the second with the third, then the third with the fourth and so on until the end of the set has been reached. The process is repeated until all items are in the correct sequence.

bucket

Another term for a variable. It's just a place to store something.

buckyballs

A form of carbon expected to have use in a wide variety of applications including computer chips. They are also known as "buckminsterfullerenes," because the 60 atoms that make up their spherical molecule resemble Buckminster Fuller's geodesic domes. Buckyballs were identified in 1985 by three scientists who later received a Nobel prize for the discovery. Buckyballs are used as a building block for many experimental materials. See *buckytubes*.

buckytubes

Also called *nanotubes*, they are a form of carbon that resembles a cylinder or tube. Accidentally discovered by a Japanese researcher in 1990 while making buckyballs, they have potential for use in a variety of applications including electronic instruments and circuitry. With a tensile strength 100 times greater than steel at about one quarter the weight, buckytubes are considered the strongest material for their weight known to mankind. See *buckyballs*.

BUF

(BUFfer gate) A logic gate that generates the same output as the input. It is used as a relay to increase power, to add some delay in the circuit and to isolate signals. See *logic gate*.

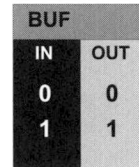

BUF	
IN	OUT
0	0
1	1

buffer

A reserved segment of memory used to hold data while it is being processed. In a program, buffers are created to hold some amount of data from each of the files that will be read or written. A buffer may also be a small hardware memory bank used for special purposes.

buffer flush

The transfer of data from memory to disk. Whenever you command your application to save the document you're working on, the program is actually flushing its buffer (writing the contents of one or more reserved areas of memory to the hard disk).

Go Flush Your Cold Buffer!

Try this one out on your colleagues. A cold buffer is a reserved area of memory that contains data, which hasn't been updated for a while. Cold buffers are flushed at periodic intervals. More importantly, this phrase sounds as strange as they get. Better yet, try "go flush your cold buffer into your SCSI DASD" (pronounced scuzzy dazdy). Be sure to say this without cracking a smile, and expect quite a grin from a systems professional. If your friend doesn't understand this phrase, be sure to recommend a good computer dictionary!

buffer pool

An area of memory reserved for buffers.

buffer underrun

See *underrun*.

bug

A persistent error in software or hardware. If the bug is in software, it can be corrected by changing the program. If the bug is in hardware, new circuits have to be designed.

Although the derivation of bug is generally attributed to the moth that was found squashed between the points of an electromechanical relay in a computer in the 1940s, the term was already in use in the late 1800s. See *bug fix* and *software bug*. Contrast with *glitch*.

A Note from the Author

On October 19, 1992, I found my first "real bug." When I fired up my laser printer, it printed blotchy pages. Upon inspection, I found a bug lying belly up in the trough below the corona wire. The printer worked fine after removing it!

bug compatible

A hardware device that contains the same design flaws as the original.

bug fix

A revised program file or patch that corrects a software bug. See *bug, patch* and *hot fix*.

bug inheritance
Software bugs that are brought down from a higher-level class in an object-oriented system.

build
(1) A version of a program, typically one still in testing. Although a version number is usually given to a released product, sometimes, a build number is used instead. See *gold code*.

(2) To program (write lines of code).

bulk storage
Storage that is not used for high-speed execution. May refer to auxiliary memory, tape or disk.

Bull
(Bull North America, Billerica, MA, www.bull.com) The U.S. branch of Compagnie des Machines Bull. Bull is a worldwide computer and information services company with offices in more than 85 countries. It was founded in France in 1933 by Norwegian engineer Fredrik Rosing Bull, who created a revolutionary adding-sorting machine in 1921.

In the 1960s, Bull partnered with GE in computer development in France. When Honeywell took over GE's computer business in 1970, its French division became Honeywell Bull. In 1987, Honeywell turned all its computer business over to Bull. For a while, both Honeywell and NEC had ownership in the company, which was named Bull HN. Today, all operations are under the Bull name. See *Honeywell*.

bulletin board
See *BBS*.

bump file
(BuMP file) See *BMP file*.

bump mapping
In computer graphics, a technique for simulating rough textures by creating irregularities in shading.

BUNCH
(Burroughs, Univac, NCR, Control Data and Honeywell) IBM's competitors after RCA and GE got out of the computer business.

bundle
To sell hardware and software as a single product or to combine several software packages for sale as a single unit. Contrast with *unbundle*.

bunny suit
The protective clothing worn by an individual in a clean room that keeps human bacteria from infecting the chip-making process. The outfit makes people look like oversized rabbits.

burn
To write a write-once optical medium such as a CD-R disc.

burn in
To test a new electronic system by running it for some length of time. Weak components often fail within the first few hours of use.

Burroughs
See *Unisys*.

Burst EDO
See *EDO RAM*.

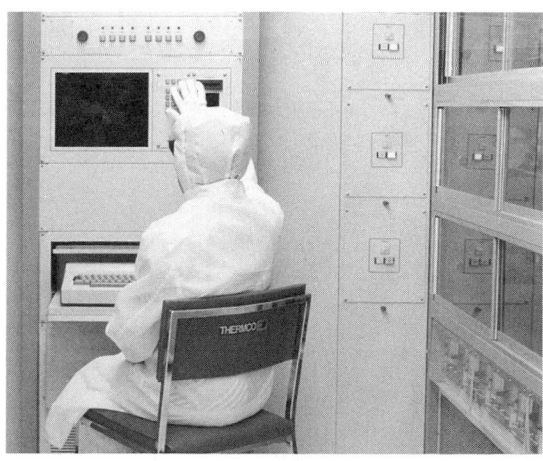

Bunny Suit
Getting into a bunny suit is an elaborate procedure with as many as 100 steps. All workers in a clean room must wear them. *(Photo courtesy of VLSI Technology, Inc.)*

burster

A mechanical device that separates continuous paper forms into cut sheets. A burster can be attached to the end of a collator, which separates multipart forms into single parts.

burst mode

A high-speed transmission mode in a communications or computer channel. Under certain conditions, the system sends a burst of data at higher speed for a limited amount of time. For example, a multiplexor channel may suspend transmitting several streams of data and send one high-speed transmission using the entire bandwidth.

bursty

Refers to data that is transferred or transmitted in short, uneven spurts. LAN traffic is typically bursty. Contrast with *streaming data*.

bus

A common pathway, or channel, between multiple devices. The computer's internal bus is known as the local bus, or processor bus. It provides a parallel data transfer path between the CPU and main memory and to the peripheral buses. A 16-bit bus transfers two bytes at a time over 16 wires; a 32-bit bus uses 32 wires, etc. The bus is comprised of two parts: the address bus and the data bus. Addresses are sent over the address bus to signal a memory location, and the data is transferred over the data bus to that location.

Various buses have been used in the PC, including the ISA, EISA, Micro Channel, VL-bus and PCI bus. Examples of other peripheral buses are NuBus, TURBOchannel, VMEbus, MULTIBUS and STD bus.

Another type of bus is a network bus. For example, some Ethernets use a serial bus, which is a common cable connecting all stations. A data packet, which contains the address of the destination station, is broadcast to all nodes at the same time, and the recipient computer responds by accepting it. Data is transmitted serially (one bit after the other) over the cable. See *local bus* and *software bus*.

Why Is It Called a Bus?

The term was coined after a real bus, the concept being that a bus stops at all the bus stops en route. In an electronic bus, the signals go to all stations connected to it. A weak analog perhaps, but the term will live forever.

bus and tag channel

A common name for the parallel channel between IBM mainframes and peripherals. One set of cables carries the data (the bus), and another set is for control information (the tag). IBM's OEM Information publication (OEMI) is another term for this. See *parallel channel* and *ESCON*.

bus attached

Connected directly to the computer's peripheral bus using a hardware interface such as SCSI, IDE, SSA or ESCON.

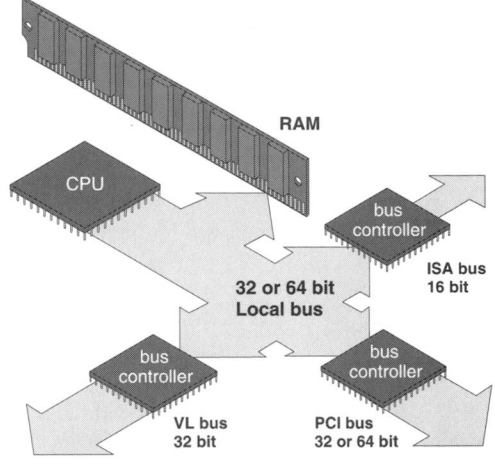

Local and Peripheral Buses
Expansion boards (cards, adapters, etc.) plug into the computer's bus and signals and data pass between the peripheral device and memory.

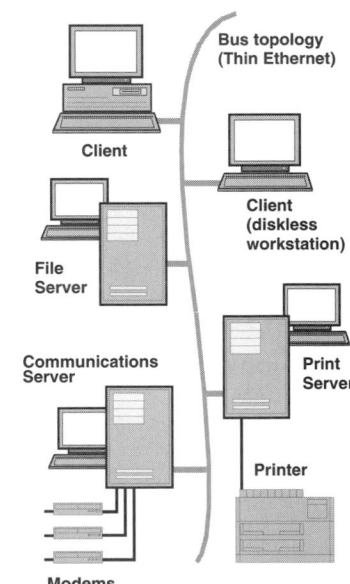

LAN Bus
10Base5 "Thick" Ethernet and 10Base2 "Thin" Ethernet use a bus topology, which is a common cable between all stations. All packets are broadcast onto the cable and each station "listens" for its address.

bus bridge

A device that connects two similar or dissimilar busses together, such as two VMEbuses or a VMEbus and a Futurebus. This is not the same as a communications bridge, which connects network segments together. See *bridge*.

bus card

An expansion board (card) that plugs into the computer's expansion bus.

bus extender

(1) A board that pushes a printed circuit board out of the way of surrounding boards for testing purposes. It plugs into an expansion slot, and the expansion board plugs into the bus extender.

(2) A device that extends the physical distance of a bus. See *repeater*.

(3) A device that increases the number of expansion slots. It is either an expansion board containing multiple expansion slots, or an expansion board that cables to a separate housing that contains the slots and its own power supply.

business analyst

An individual who analyzes the operations of a department or functional unit with the purpose of developing a general systems solution to the problem that may or may not require automation. The business analyst, who is often part of a user department, can provide insights into its operation for the systems analyst that reports to the information systems department.

Business Basic

A version of the BASIC programming language derived from the original Dartmouth BASIC created by Kemeny and Kurtz. It was first developed by MAI Systems Corporation with later versions known as Thoroughbred Basic from Thoroughbred Software International, Inc., Somerset, NJ, and BBxPROGRESSION/4 from Basis International, Ltd, Irvine, CA.

business graphics

Numeric data represented in graphic form. While line graphs, bar charts and pie charts are the common forms of business graphics, there are dozens of others types. The ability to generate business graphics is often included in spreadsheet and presentation graphics programs.

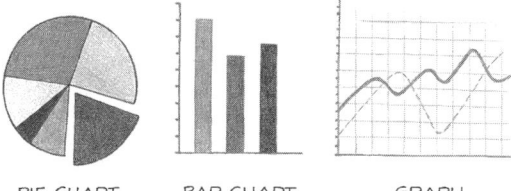

PIE CHART   BAR CHART   GRAPH

Common Graphics Types

business logic

The part of an application program that performs the required data processing of the business. It refers to the routines that perform the data entry, update, query and report processing, and more specifically to the processing that takes place behind the scenes. A client application is made up of a user interface and the business logic. A server application may be mostly business logic.

Both client and server applications also require communications links, but the network infrastructure, like the user interface, is not part of the business logic.

business machine

Any office machine, such as a typewriter or calculator, that is used in clerical and accounting functions. The term has traditionally excluded computers and terminals.

BusinessMiner

A data mining tool from Business Objects that runs under all versions of Windows. It can extract data from dBASE, Excel, SPSS and ASCII files and other relational databases that have been brought into BusinessObjects. BusinessMiner identifies trends and influential factors automatically, which saves users from manually slicing and dicing the data to come up with the same results. See *BusinessObjects* and see *data mining* for illustration.

Business Objects

(1) (Business Objects, San Jose, CA, www.businessobjects.com) The leading software company specializing in decision support tools for the business market. Founded in France in 1990 by Bernard Liautaud and Denis Payre, Business Objects was the first to integrate query, reporting and OLAP into one product, using a patented semantic layer that shields end users from the complexities of making a query. Products include its flagship BusinessObjects software, BusinessQuery for Excel and BusinessMiner data mining program.

The use of the word "objects" refers to "items," not object technology, as the company was founded and its products were created before object-oriented programming became popular. See *BusinessObjects*.

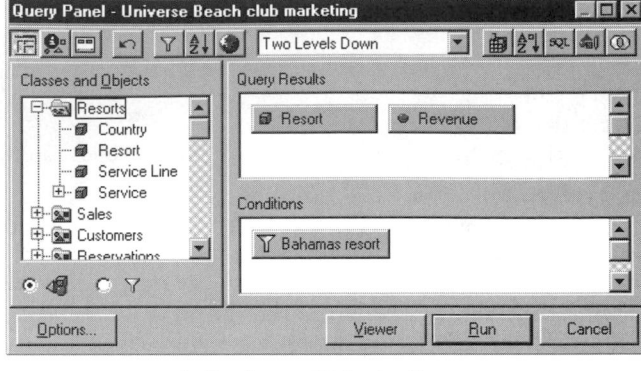

A BusinessObjects Query

Once the business objects have been defined, users simply drag and drop the icons from the window on the left into the windows on the right. *(Screen shot courtesy of Business Objects.)*

(2) (business objects) A broad category of business processes that are modeled as objects. A business object can be as large as an entire order processing system or a small process within an information system. See *object technology* and *object-oriented programming*.

BusinessObjects

A query, reporting and analysis tool from Business Objects that runs under all versions of Windows and various UNIX clients. It is the leading decision support tool in the business market, providing access to a wide variety of databases, including Oracle, INFORMIX and DB2. As data is extracted from the database, it is stored as multidimensional OLAP cubes that can be easily sliced and diced into different views.

BusinessObjects uses a patented semantic layer that shields users from the complexities of table names and relationships. Once the semantic layer has been defined, users work with familiar "business objects" such as product, customer and revenue.

The use of the word "objects" refers to "items," not object technology, as the company and products were created before object-oriented programming became popular.

business process reengineering

See reengineering.

bus mastering

A bus design that allows the peripheral controllers (plug-in boards) to access the computer's memory independently of the CPU. It allows data transfers to take place between the peripheral device and memory while the CPU is performing other tasks.

bus mouse

A mouse that plugs into an expansion board instead of the serial port. This type of mouse was somewhat popular in the 1980s. Its connector looks like a PS/2 connector, but the pin configurations are different and not compatible.

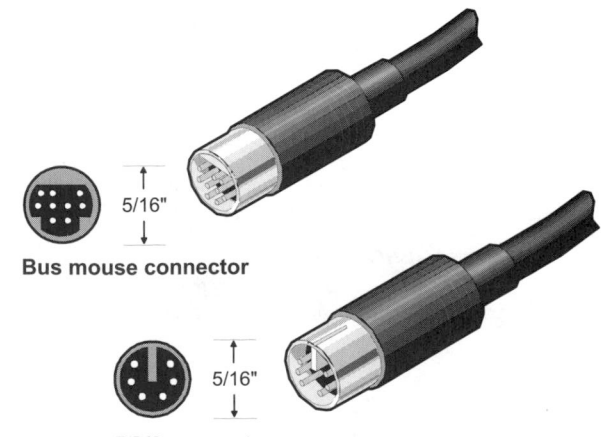

Bus mouse connector

5/16"

PS/2 connector

5/16"

Bus Mouse and PS/2 Connectors Look Alike

The plug on a bus mouse looks similar to the common PS/2 connector, but it has a different pin structure.

Butterfly Switch

A parallel processing topology from BBN Advanced Computers Inc., Cambridge, MA, that mimics a crossbar and provides high-speed switching of data between nodes. It can also be used to create a hypercube topology.

button

(1) A knob, such as on a printer or a mouse, which is pushed with the finger to activate a function.

(2) A simulated button on screen that is "pushed" by clicking it with the mouse.

buzzwords

A term used to refer to what is current or "in" in the field. Buzzwords are hot for a while and then either become mainstream or fade away.

BX chipset

See *Intel chipsets*.

bypass

In communications, to avoid the local telephone company by using satellites and microwave systems.

byte

(BinarY TablE) The common unit of computer storage from micro to mainframe. It is made up of eight binary digits (bits). A ninth bit may be used in the memory circuits as a parity bit for error checking.

On-screen Button
The button on the left is in its normal state. The one on the right has been depressed. When a button is clicked, it simulates the physical depression of a real button by offsetting the icon a few pixels and switching the shadow lines from the right and bottom to the top and left edges.

A byte holds the equivalent of a single character, such as the letter A, a dollar sign or decimal point. For numbers, a byte can hold a single decimal digit (0 to 9), two numeric digits (packed decimal) or a number from 0 to 255 (binary numbers).

Byte Specifications

The primary specifications of hardware are rated in bytes; for example, a 40-megabyte (40M or 40MB) disk holds 40 million characters of instructions and data. A one-megabyte (1M or 1MB) memory allows one million characters of instructions and data to be stored internally for processing.

With database files and word processing documents, the file size is slightly larger than the number of data characters stored in it. Word processing files contain embedded codes for layout settings (margins, tabs, boldface); therefore, a 100,000-byte document implies slightly less than 100,000 characters of text (approx. 30 pages). Database files contain codes that describe the structure of the records, thus, a 100,000-byte database file holds somewhat less than 100,000 characters of data.

Unlike data and text, a 100,000-byte graphics file is not indicative of the size of the image contained in it. There are many graphics standards, and the higher the image quality, the more bytes are needed to represent it. A low-resolution graphics file can take as little as 8,000 bytes, while high-resolution files can take 100,000 or more bytes per picture. See *bit* for illustration.

byte addressable

A computer that can address each byte of memory independently of the others. In today's computers, all of memory is usually byte addressable, which is why memory is used for processing. Units (fields) of data can be worked on independently. Contrast with *word addressable*.

byte code

An intermediate language that is executed by a runtime interpreter. Visual Basic and Java source programs are compiled into byte code, which are then executed by their respective interpreters.

byte ordering

See *big endian*.

byte-oriented protocol

A communications protocol that uses control codes made up of full bytes. The bisynchronous protocols used by IBM and other vendors are examples. Contrast with *bit-oriented protocol*.

Updated quarterly on CD-ROM

The book is available on CD-ROM for Windows PCs.
*More than **12,000 entries!***
*More than **1,200 illustrations, diagrams** and **photos!***

Call (888) 815-3772

C

C

A high-level programming language developed at Bell Labs that is able to manipulate the computer at a low level like assembly language. During the last half of the 1980s, C became the language of choice for developing commercial software.

C can be compiled into machine languages for almost all computers. For example, UNIX is written in C and runs in a wide variety of micros, minis and mainframes.

C is written as a series of functions that call each other for processing. Even the body of the program is a function named "main." Functions are very flexible, allowing programmers to choose from the standard library that comes with the compiler, to use third party functions from other C suppliers, or to develop their own.

Compared to other high-level programming languages, C appears complicated. Its intricate appearance is due to its extreme flexibility. C was standardized by ANSI (X3J11 committee) and ISO in 1989. See *Turbo C, Borland C++, Microsoft C* and *Visual C++*.

The following C example converts fahrenheit to centigrade:

```
main()    {
float fahr;
printf("Enter Fahrenheit ");
scanf("%f", &fahr);
printf("Celsius is %f\n", (fahr-32)*5/9);
        }
```

The Origin of C

C was developed to allow UNIX to run on a variety of computers. After Bell Labs' Ken Thompson and Dennis Ritchie created UNIX and got it running on several PDP computers, they wanted a way to easily port it to other machines without having to rewrite it from scratch. Thompson created a language called B, a simpler version of a language called BCPL, itself a version of CPL. Later, in order to improve B, Thompson and Ritchie created C.

C:

The designation for the primary hard disk in a PC.

C++

An object-oriented version of C created by Bjarne Stroustrup. C++ has become popular because it combines traditional C programming with OOP capability. Smalltalk and other original OOP languages did not provide the familiar structures of conventional languages such as C and Pascal. Microsoft's Visual C++ is the most widely-used C++ compiler. See *Visual C++* and *Borland C++*.

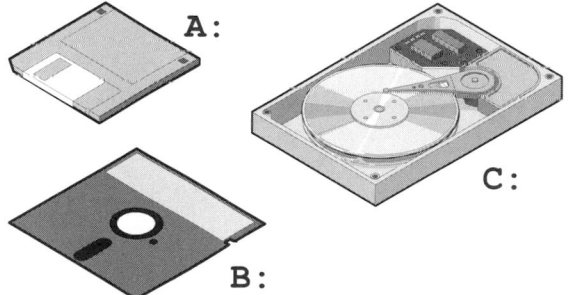

C2

The minimum security level defined by the National Computer Security Center. See *NCSC*.

C6

See *WinChip*.

C8x

A family of RISC-based digital signal processing (DSP) chips from TI designed for multimedia applications such as videoconferencing. The chips are designed with a master processor, floating point unit, video controller and multiple parallel DSP processors with a crossbar switch that lets them access 50KB of built-in static RAM. The C80 (TMS320C80) contains four and the C82 (TMS320C82) chip contains two DSP processors.

CA

(1) (Computer Associates International, Inc., Islandia, NY, www.cai.com) The world's largest diversified software vendor offering more than 500 applications from micro to mainframe. Founded in 1976 by Charles Wang and three associates, its first product was CA-SORT, a very successful IBM mainframe utility. Its first personal computer software was SuperCalc, one of the first spreadsheets. CA has grown via numerous acquisitions over the years, and in 1989, was the first independent software company to reach $1 billion dollars in sales. Its fiscal 1996 revenues are more than $3.5 billion. CA product names all contain the CA prefix.

(2) (Certificate Authority) An organization that issues digital certificates (digital IDs) and makes its public key widely available to its intended audience. See *digital certificate*.

CAB file

(**CAB**inet file) A file format from Microsoft used to hold compressed files on its distribution disks. The Windows 95/98 Extract program is run at the DOS command line to decompress the files. For example, to view the content of the WIN95_02.CAB file in the \WIN95 directory on the E: drive, you would use the **/d** (display) switch as follows:

Charles Wang
Wang developed the world's largest software company that covers all segments of the industry from micro to mainframe. *(Photo courtesy of Computer Associates International, Inc.)*

```
C:\>extract e:\win95\win95_02.cab  /d
```

To copy and decompress EDIT.COM from that same CAB file into the current directory, you would type:

```
C:\ANYWHERE>extract e:\win95\win95_02.cab edit.com
```

cable

A flexible metal or glass wire or group of wires. All cables used in electronics are insulated with a material such as plastic or rubber.

cable categories

The following categories are based on their transmission capacity. The majority of new wiring installations use Category 5 UTP wire in order to be able to run or upgrade to the faster network technologies that will require it. Categories 1 through 5 are based on the EIA/TIA-568 standard.

Category	Cable type	Application
1	UTP	Analog voice
2	UTP	Digital voice
		1 Mbps data
3	UTP, STP	16 Mbps data
4	UTP, STP	20 Mbps data
5	UTP, STP	100 Mbps data
6	Coax	100 Mbps+ data
7	Fiber optic	100 Mbps+ data

cable Internet

Internet access via cable TV. There are two kinds of service. One uses a cable modem to connect to a computer, and the other uses an enhanced cable box that provides Internet access directly at the TV. Both of these differ from WebTV, which requires a phone line. See *cable modem, WorldGate* and *WebTV*.

cable matcher

Same as *gender changer*.

cable modem

A modem used to connect a computer to a cable TV service that provides Internet access. Cable modems can dramatically increase the bandwidth between the user's computer and the Internet service provider. Most cable modems link to an Ethernet adapter in the PC making the service online all the time; however, the bandwidth will vary depending on how many customers are using the Web at the same time. See *cable Internet, Internet appliance* and *WebTV*.

cable telephony

Telephone service provided by a cable TV company.

cabletext

A videotex service that uses coaxial cable. See *videotex*.

Cabletron

(Cabletron Systems, Rochester, NH, www.cabletron.com) A communications products company that was founded in 1983 by S. Robert Levine and Craig Benson. What began as a part-time venture in a garage evolved into a billion dollar company by 1996. Cabletron is known for its modular hubs and switches that support Ethernet, Token Ring, FDDI, SNA and ATM. Cabletron introduced the first intelligent hub and continues to have the largest installed base. The company is also known for providing a complete networking strategy, which includes comprehensive technical support as well as the advanced SPECTRUM network management software.

cable TV

The transmission of TV programs into the home and office via coaxial cable. Cable TV organizations have tremendous potential for new services since they are already wired into so many homes. See *cable Internet, data broadcast* and *CATV*.

cache

Pronounced "cash." A temporary storage area for instructions and data that is closer to the CPU's speed. The larger the cache, the faster the performance, since there is a greater chance that the instruction or data required next is already in the cache. The chief measurement of a cache is its hit rate, which is the percentage of all accesses that are satisfied by the data in the cache.

Cache used to refer to only memory and disk caches (explained below) that function as temporary "look-ahead" storage. With the advent of the Web, the term is used to refer to more permanent storage. When Web pages are "cached" on a server, they can be stored for

Cable Modem

A cable modem provides high-speed access to a desktop computer.

Cable Internet

Cable Internet delivers Internet service to the TV via an enhanced set-top cable box.

WebTV

WebTV delivers Internet access to the TV using an analog modem over a telephone line.

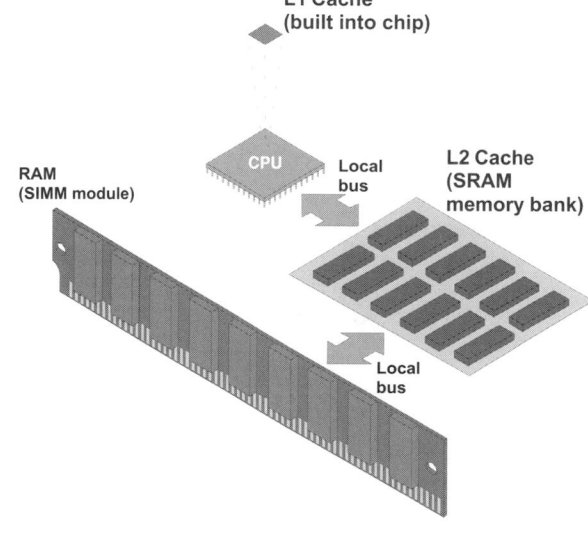

L1 Cache (built into chip)
RAM (SIMM module) CPU Local bus L2 Cache (SRAM memory bank) Local bus

long periods of time; thus, the term is also used to mean "stored for future use," not just within the current session. See *browser cache*.

Memory Caches

A memory cache, or CPU cache, is a memory bank that bridges main memory and the CPU. It is faster than main memory and allows instructions to be executed and data to be read at higher speed. Instructions and data are transferred to the cache in blocks, using some kind of look-ahead algorithm. The more sequential the instructions in the routine being accessed, and the more sequential the order of the data being read, the more chance the next desired item will still be in the cache, and the greater improvement in performance.

A level 1 (L1) cache is a memory bank built into or packaged within the chip. A level 2 cache (L2) is a group of memory chips on the motherboard. Increasing a Level 2 cache may speed up some applications and amount to nothing on others. Both types are used together. In PCs, the cache is made up of static RAM (SRAM) chips, while dynamic RAM (DRAM) chips are used for main memory.

Disk Caches

A disk cache is a section of main memory or memory on the controller board that bridges the disk and the CPU. When the disk is read, a larger block of data is copied into the cache. If subsequent requests for data can be satisfied in the cache, a much slower disk access is not required.

If the cache is used for writing, data is queued up at high speed and then written to disk during idle machine cycles by the caching program. If the cache is built into the hardware, the disk controller figures out when to do it.

DOS and Windows 3.x use the SmartDrive caching program. Windows 95/98 uses Vcache. See *write back cache, write through cache, pipeline burst cache, lookaside cache, inline cache* and *backside cache*.

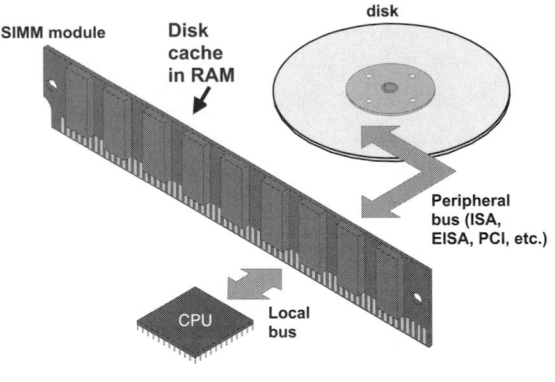

cache coherency

Managing a cache so that data is not lost or overwritten. For example, when data is updated in a cache, but not yet transferred to its target memory or disk, the chance of corruption is greater. Cache coherency is obtained by well-designed algorithms that keep track of the cache. It is even more critical in symmetric multiprocessing (SMP) where memory is shared by multiple processors.

cache server

A dedicated network server or a service within a server that caches Web pages in order to speed up access to information that has already been retrieved by a previous user. See *ICP* and *CARP*.

caching controller

A disk controller with a built-in cache. See *cache*.

CA-Clipper

An application development system from Computer Associates. Originally a dBASE compiler, it evolved into a programming language with many unique features that supports dBASE and non-dBASE databases. Clipper generates DOS programs, but third-party products enable it to create Windows applications. Clipper was originally developed by Nantucket Corporation.

CAD

(Computer-Aided Design) Using computers to design products. CAD systems are high-speed workstations or desktop computers using CAD software and input devices such as graphic tablets and scanners. CAD output is a printed design or electronic input to CAM systems (see *CAD/CAM*).

CAD software is available for generic design or specialized uses, such as architectural, electrical and mechanical design. CAD software may also be highly specialized for creating products such as printed circuits and integrated circuits.

The most elaborate and complex form of CAD is solid modeling, which allows objects to be created with real-world characteristics. For example, objects can be sectioned (sliced down the middle) to reveal their internal structure. See *wireframe modeling, surface modeling, solid modeling, graphics* and *CAE.*

CADAM

A full-featured IBM mainframe CAD application, which includes 3-D capability, solid modeling and numerical control. Originally developed by Lockheed for internal use, it was distributed by IBM starting in the late 1970s. In 1989, IBM purchased the Lockheed subsidiary, CADAM, Inc.

CA-DATACOM/DB

A relational database management system (DBMS) from Computer Associates that runs on PCs, IBM minis and mainframes. There are many options and add-ons that support the product all under the CA-DATACOM umbrella, such as CA-DATACOM/CICS Services and CA-DATACOM/SQL Option.

CA-dBFast

A dBASE-compatible application development system from Computer Associates. It provides over 200 language extensions to dBASE allowing dBASE or xBASE programs to be converted to Windows applications.

CAD/CAM

(Computer-Aided Design/Computer-Aided Manufacturing) The integration of CAD and CAM. Products designed by CAD are direct input into the CAM system. For example, a device is designed and its electronic image is translated into a numerical control programming language, which generates the instructions for the machine that makes it.

CADD

(Computer-Aided Design and Drafting) CAD systems with additional features for drafting, such as dimensioning and text entry.

CADDS 5

A 3-D solid modeling CAD program that runs on Windows NT and UNIX from Computervision, Bedford, MA, (www.computervision.com). It is very popular software that provides a huge variety of packaging options based on application requirements.

caddy

A plastic container that holds a CD or DVD disc for added protection. The bare disc is placed in the caddy, and the caddy is inserted into the drive. A caddy is not a jewel case. A jewel case protects the disc for transportation. A caddy protects the disc while reading and writing.

caddyless

A tray load drive that does not use a caddy for added protection. See *caddy.*

CADKEY

An integrated 2-D drafting and 3-D design system for Windows from Baystate Technologies, Marlborough, MA, (www.cadkey.com). It offers a total design solution with solids creation and built-in DXF and IGES translators. Over 200 manufacturing systems link to CADKEY through its CADL programming language.

CADS

(Computer-Aided Dispatch System) An intelligent vehicle dispatch system that uses mobile data terminals and a GIS.

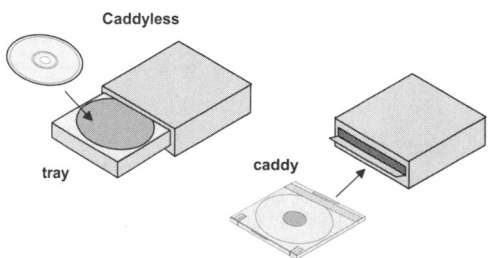

Tray Load versus Caddy Load
Earlier drives always used a caddy. Today, some drives still require one for added protection.

CAE

(1) (Computer-Aided Engineering) Software that analyzes designs which have been created in the computer or that have been created elsewhere and entered into the computer. Different kinds of engineering analyses can be performed, such as structural analysis and electronic circuit analysis.

(2) (Common Application Environment) Software development platform that is specified by X/Open.

CA-Easytrieve

An application development system for IBM mainframes, DOS and OS/2 from Computer Associates. It includes 4GL query and reporting capabilities and can access many IBM mainframe and PC database formats. UNIX and Windows versions forthcoming. Easytrieve was originally developed by Pansophic Systems.

Cafe

A Java development package for Windows and the Macintosh from Symantec. It was Symantec's first development environment for Java, which was superseded by Visual Cafe. See *Visual Cafe*.

caffeine based

Any program written in Java. See *Java*.

CaffeineMark

A Java benchmark from Pendragon Software Corporation, Buffalo Grove, IL, (www.webfayre.com). It is used to measure the speed of a Java Virtual Machine (Java interpreter) running on a particular hardware platform. See *Java*.

CAI

(1) (Computer-Assisted Instruction) Same as *CBT*.

(2) See *CA*.

CA-IDMS

A relational DBMS from Computer Associates that runs on minis and mainframes. IDMS (Integrated Data Management System) was developed at GE in the 1960s and marketed by Cullinane, later renamed Cullinet and then acquired by CA in 1989. There are a variety of CA-IDMS products, such as CA-IDMS/R for the relational DBMS, CA-IDMS/DDS for its distributed version and so on.

CA-Ingres

The original version of CA-OpenIngres from Computer Associates. See *CA-OpenIngres*.

CAL

(1) (Computer-Assisted Learning) Same as *CBT*.

(2) (Conversational Algebraic Language) A timesharing language from the University of California.

calculated field

A numeric or date field that derives its data from the calculation of other fields. Data is not entered into a calculated field by the user.

calculator

A machine that provides arithmetic capabilities. It accepts keypad input and displays results on a readout and/or paper tape. Unlike a computer, it cannot handle alphabetic data.

Caldera

(Caldera, Inc., Orem, UT, www.caldera.com)

A software company that specializes in operating systems, founded in 1994 by Bryan Sparks and Ray Noorda, the patriarch of Novell. Caldera's primary products are OpenLinux and DR-DOS. OpenLinux is a UNIX-like Linux operating system combined with a complete suite of related tools, and DR-DOS is a

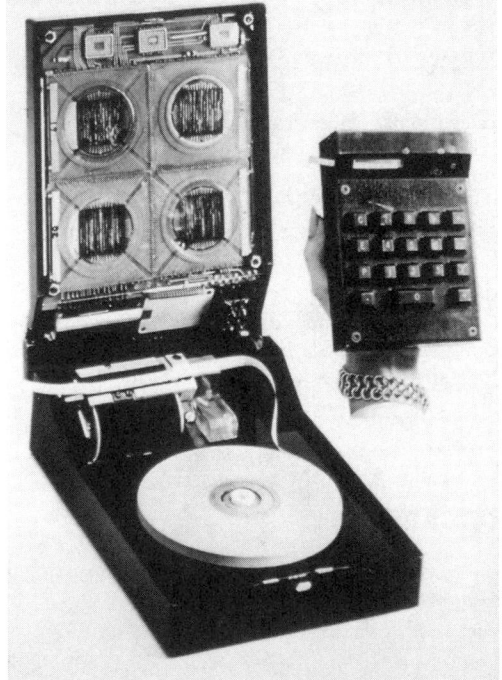

The First Hand-held Calculator
In 1967, Texas Instruments introduced the first hand-held calculator. The opened unit in the picture shows the paper tape used as output. *(Photo courtesy of Texas Instruments, Inc.)*

DOS-compatible operating system, which it acquired from Novell in 1996.

As the current owner of DR-DOS, which was originally developed by Digital Research, Caldera owns the history of the product, which was nearly driven out of the market in the early 1990s by Microsoft. As a result, Caldera is the first company to bring a private antitrust lawsuit against Microsoft, which will be brought to court in the summer of 1999. Caldera intends to prove that Microsoft used its monopoly status to prevent it from continuing to offer DR-DOS. These claims are outlined on Caldera's Web site.

calendaring

Using an electronic calendar to keep track of events. Calendars can be set up to alert you at a certain time or at recurring times. Group calendaring can alert an entire team as well as let users view each other's calendars. It often includes group scheduling, which allows a user to set up a meeting with project members. Team members are automatically e-mailed, and the program waits for the collective reponses.

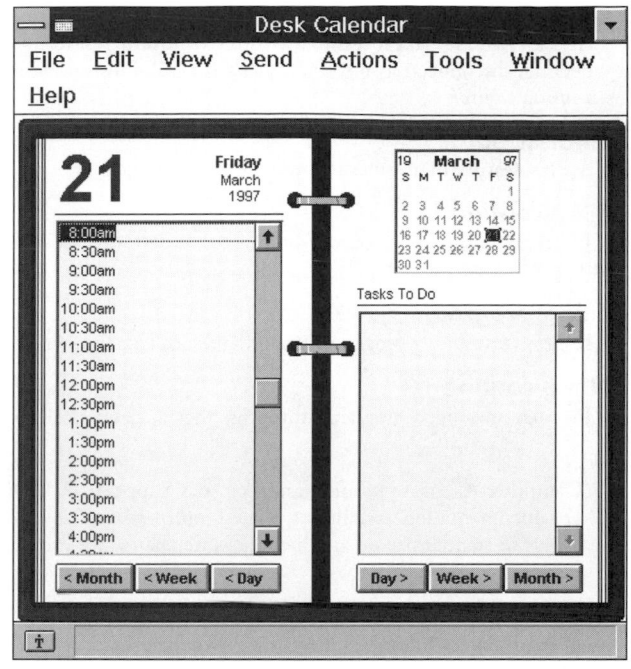

GroupWise Calendars
Electronic calendars generally provide multiple views including day, week and month. Fourteen calendar views are available in Novell's GroupWise collaboration system. This is an example from Version 4.1.

CA-Librarian

A version control system for IBM mainframes from Computer Associates. Librarian's master files can be simultaneously accessed on shared disks by different operating systems. Librarian was originally developed by ADR, Inc.

call

(1) In programming, a statement that requests services from another subroutine or program. The call is physically made to the subroutine by a branch instruction or some other linking method which is created by the assembler, compiler or interpreter. The routine that is called is responsible for returning control to the calling program after it has finished processing.

(2) In communications, the action taken by the transmitting station to establish a connection with the receiving station in a dial-up network.

call by reference

In programming, a call to a subroutine that passes addresses of the parameters used in the subroutine.

call by value

In programming, a call to a subroutine that passes the actual data of the parameters used in the subroutine.

call center

A company department that handles telephone sales and/or service. Call centers use automatic call distributors (ACDs) to route calls to the appropriate agent or operator. See *ACD* and *Web-enabled call center*.

call control

Also known as "call processing," it is the controlling of telephone and PBX functions. It includes connecting, disconnecting and transferring the call, but it does not affect the content of the call. Contrast with *media control*.

call distributor

A PBX feature that routes incoming calls to the next available agent or operator.

called routine

In programming, a program subroutine that performs a task and is accessed by a call or branch instruction in the program.

calling program

In programming, a program that initiates a call to another program.

calling routine

In programming, a program subroutine that initiates a call to another program routine.

CALS

(Computer-Aided Acquisition and Logistics Support) A DOD initiative for electronically capturing military documentation and linking related information. The CALS bitmap format was developed in the mid 1980s to standardize on graphics data interchange for electronic publishing for the federal government.

CAM

(1) (Computer-Aided Manufacturing) The automation of manufacturing systems and techniques, including numerical control, process control, robotics and materials requirements planning (MRP). See *CAD/CAM*.

(2) (Common Access Method) An ANSI standard interface that provides a common language between drivers and SCSI host adapters. It is primarily supported by Future Domain and NCR. See *SCSI*.

(3) (Content Addressable Memory) Same as *associative storage*.

CA-ManMan/X

A comprehensive manufacturing application from Computer Associates that runs under UNIX on VAX and HP platforms. It covers all aspects of manufacturing management including planning, tracking and shop floor control. CA-ManMan/X was originally ManMan (Manufacturing Management), developed by Ask Computer Systems, Inc.

camera ready

Printed material that serves as original artwork for commercial printing. Camera-ready material is photographed, and the films are made into plates for the printing presses. Camera ready implies high-resolution text and graphics. See *resolution* and *high-resolution*.

campus

Two or more buildings located in close proximity. For example, a campus backbone implies a high-speed transmission system, such as FDDI or ATM, running between several buildings all within a geographic area that may be only a couple of hundred feet or as much as several hundred yards long.

candela

A unit of measurement of the intensity of light. An ordinary wax candle generates one candela. See *lumen*.

Candle

(Candle Corporation, Santa Monica, CA, www.candle.com) A leading software company specializing in performance monitoring and systems availability tools for the mainframe environment. It was founded in 1976 by Aubrey Chernick, who developed OMEGAMON, the first realtime performance monitor for MVS. Candle provides a wide variety of products for managing systems and applications, and in 1996, expanded into middleware.

canned program

A software package that provides a fixed solution to a problem. Canned business applications should be analyzed carefully as they usually cannot be changed much, if at all.

canned routine

A program subroutine that performs a specific processing task.

canonical synthesis

The process of designing a model of a database without redundant data items. A canonical model, or schema, is independent of the hardware and software that will process the data.

Canvas

A drawing, image editing and page layout program for Windows 95/98 and NT and the Mac from Deneba Software, Miami, FL, (www.deneba.com). While most other programs specialize in either drawing or image editing, Canvas combines numerous illustration (vector graphics) and image editing tools (bitmapped graphics) in one application. It also includes presentation graphics capabilities for producing on-screen slide shows.

CA-OpenIngres

A relational database management system (DBMS) from Computer Associates that runs on Windows NT, OS/2, VAXs and most UNIX platforms. CA-OpenIngres is an enhanced version of Ingres, one of the first heavyweight DBMSs and noted for its advanced features. For example, Ingres was the first major DBMS to include triggers and stored procedures.

Ingres was originally developed by Relational Technology, founded in 1980 to market a commercial version of "INteractive Graphics and REtrieval System," which was developed at the University of California at Berkeley in the early 1970s. The company was renamed Ingres Corporation, then later acquired by the Ask Group and eventually Computer Associates.

CA-OpenRoad

A client/server development system from Computer Associates that runs on Windows, X terminal and OS/2 clients. It supports the major SQL databases including CA-OpenIngres. CA-OpenRoad was originally Windows 4GL from Ingres, but supported only the Ingres database.

CAP

(1) (Competitive Access Provider) An organization that competes with the established telecommunications provider in an area.

(2) (Carrierless Amplitude Phase) A type of ADSL service. See *DSL*.

Capability Maturity Model

See *SEI*.

capacitor

An electronic component that holds a charge. It comes in varying sizes for use in power supplies. It is also constructed as microscopic cells in dynamic RAM chips.

CA-Panvalet

A version control system for IBM mainframes from Computer Associates that keeps track of source code, JCL and object modules. Panvalet was originally developed by Pansophic Systems. CA-PAN/LCM is a similar product for PCs, which also provides interfaces to mainframe systems, such as CA-Panvalet and CA-Librarian.

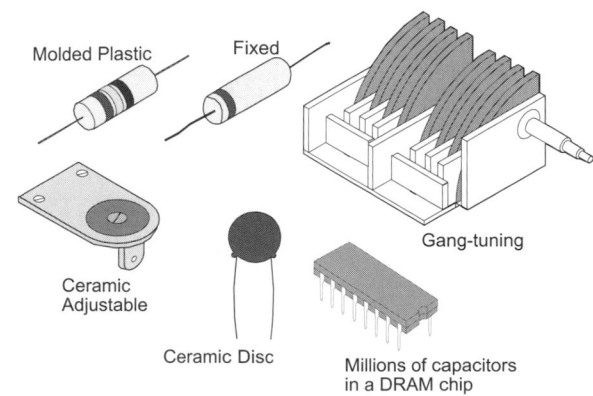

Molded Plastic   Fixed

Gang-tuning

Ceramic Adjustable

Ceramic Disc

Millions of capacitors in a DRAM chip

Capacitors

capstan

On magnetic tape drives, a motorized cylinder that traps the tape against a free-wheeling roller and moves it at a regulated speed.

capture buffer

A reserved memory area for holding an incoming transmission.

CAR

(Computer-Assisted Retrieval) Systems that use the computer to keep track of text documents or records stored on paper or on microform. The computer is used to derive the location of a requested item, which must be manually retrieved from a shelf, bin, or microform.

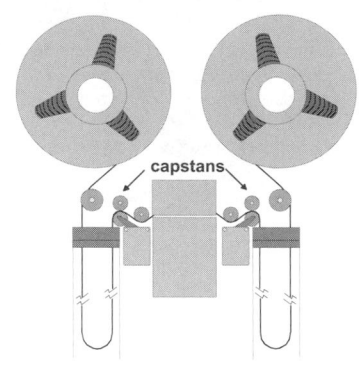

capstans

CA-RAMIS

A fourth-generation retrieval language for IBM mainframes and PCs from Computer Associates. Originally developed by Mathematica, RAMIS was later acquired by Martin Marietta Data Systems, On-Line Software, then CA in 1991. The earliest version of RAMIS was one of the first database packages with a non-procedural language for IBM mainframes.

Carbon Copy

Remote control software for DOS and Windows from Microcom, Inc., Norwood, MA, (www.microcom.com). Carbon Copy integrates well with Microcom's modem and remote access hardware.

card

See *expansion board, printed circuit board, magnetic stripe, punched card* and *HyperCard*.

CardBus

The 32-bit version of the PC Card. See *PC Card*.

card cage

A cabinet or metal frame that holds printed circuit cards.

card column

A vertical column that is used to represent a single character of data by its pattern of punched holes. The common IBM card contains 80 card columns.

card image

The representation of punched cards in which each hole in the card is represented by a bit on tape or disk.

**Card
Board
Adapter
Controller**

Called by different names, this printed circuit board expands the computer's ability to work with a peripheral device, whose controlling electronics are not built into the motherboard.

In a PC, it plugs into a slot in the ISA, EISA or PCI bus.

cardinality

A quantity relationship between elements. For example, one-to-one, one-to-many and many-to-one express cardinality. See *cardinal number*.

cardinal number

The number that states how much or how many. In "record 43 has 7 fields," the 7 is cardinal. See *cardinality*. Contrast with *ordinal number*.

card punch

(1) An early peripheral device that punches holes into cards at 100 to 300 cards per minute.

(2) Same as *keypunch machine*.

card reader

(1) A peripheral device that reads magnetic stripes on the back of a credit card.

(2) An early peripheral device that reads punched cards at 500 to 2,000 cards/minute. The code is detected by light patterns created by the holes in the card.

card services

Software that manages PC Cards. See *PC Card*.

CA-Realizer

An application development system for Windows and OS/2 from Computer Associates. It is based on a superset of BASIC and includes visual tools and the ability to incorporate routines written in C, Pascal and other languages. Realizer was originally developed by Within Technologies.

caret

The small up-arrow on the "6" key (shift-6) on a typewriter keyboard. It is sometimes used as a symbol for the control key; for example, ^Y means Ctrl-Y.

CARP

(Cache Array Routing Protocol) A protocol from Microsoft that is used by one proxy server to query another for a cached Web page without having to go to the Internet to retrieve it. CARP allows arrays of cache servers to be used and managed as a single entity, which avoids redundancy and supports failover and load balancing. See *ICP* and *proxy server*.

carpal tunnel syndrome

The compression of the main nerve to the hand due to scarring or swelling of the surrounding soft tissue in the wrist (area formed by carpal bones on top and muscle tendons below). Caused by trauma, arthritis and improper positioning of the wrist, it can result in severe damage to the hands. See *RSI*.

carriage

A printer or typewriter mechanism that holds the platen and controls paper feeding and movement.

carriage return

See *return key*.

carrier

An alternating current that vibrates at a fixed frequency, used to establish a boundary, or envelope, in which a signal is transmitted. Carriers are commonly used in radio transmission (AM, FM, TV, microwave, satellite, etc.) in order to differentiate transmitting stations. For example, an FM station's channel number is actually its carrier frequency. The FM station merges (modulates) its audio broadcast (data signal) onto its carrier and transmits the combined signal over the airwaves. At the receiving end, the FM tuner latches onto the carrier frequency, filters out the audio signal, amplifies it and sends it to the speaker.

Carriers can be used to transmit several signals simultaneously. For example, multiple voice, data and/or video signals can travel over the same line with each residing in its own carrier vibrating at a different frequency. See *analog* for illustration.

carrier based

A transmission system that generates a fixed frequency (carrier) to contain the data being transmitted.

carrier detect

A signal that indicates a connection has been made by sensing a carrier frequency on the line. See *RS-232* and *modem*.

carrier frequency

A unique frequency used to "carry" data within its boundaries. It is measured in cycles per second, or Hertz. See *carrier* and *FDM*.

Carterfone decision

The FCC decree in 1968 that permitted users to connect their own telephone equipment to the public telephone system.

cartridge

A removable storage module that contains magnetic or optical disks, magnetic tape or memory chips. Cartridges are inserted into slots in the drive, printer or computer. See *font cartridge* and *cassette*. For a complete summary of removable tape, disk and optical cartridges, see *storage*.

CAS

(1) (Communications Application Specification) A programming interface from Intel and DCA for activating functions in fax/modems. Introduced in 1988, Intel provides both the boards and the chips. CAS has not been widely used.

(2) (Column Address Strobe) A clock signal in a memory chip used to pinpoint the column of a particular bit in a row-column matrix. See *RAS*.

cascade

A connected series of devices or images. It often implies that the second and subsequent device takes over after the previous one is used up. For example, cascading tapes in a dual-tape backup system means the second tape is written after the first one is full. In a PC (286 and up), a second IRQ chip is cascaded to the first, doubling the number of interrupts.

Cascading Style Sheets

See *CSS*.

CASE

(Computer-Aided Software Engineering or Computer-Aided Systems Engineering) Software that is used in any and all phases of developing an information system, including analysis, design and programming. For example, data dictionaries and diagramming tools aid in the analysis and design phases, while application generators speed up the programming phase.

CASE tools provide automated methods for designing and documenting traditional structured programming techniques. The ultimate goal of CASE is to provide a language for describing the overall system that is sufficient to generate all the necessary programs. See also *case statement*.

case-based reasoning

An AI problem solving technique that catalogs experience into "cases" and matches the current problem to the experience. Such systems are easier to maintain than rule-based expert systems, because changes require adding new cases without the complexity of adding new rules. It is used in many areas including pattern recognition, diagnosis, troubleshooting and planning.

case cracker

A tool used to "crack" open the cases of various laptop computers. The early Macintosh cases and many laptop cases are designed to snap together. The spatula-like ends of the case cracker make it easier to pry open the case without damaging it.

case sensitive

Distinguishing lower case from upper case. In a case sensitive language, "abc" is considered different data than "ABC."

case statement

In programming, a variation of the if-then-else statement that is used when several ifs are required in a row. The following C example tests the variable KEY1 and performs functions based on the results.

```
switch (key1)   {
   case '+':  add();  break;
   case '-':  subtract();  break;
   case '*':  multiply();  break;
   case '/':  divide();  break;
            }
```

Computer Desktop Encyclopedia

cassette

A removable magnetic tape storage module that contains supply and takeup reels (hubs) like an audio or videotape. DAT, 8mm and Magstar MP tapes use the cassette-style cartridge.

Castanet

Java-based delivery software for the Internet and intranets from Marimba. Castanet automatically pushes application updates and other published content into client machines. Castanet Transmitter is a server program that manages "Castanet channels," which are content streams. Castanet Tuner is client software that looks for selected channels. Castanet Tuner is built into Netscape Netcaster. See *Bongo*.

casting

In programming, the conversion of one data type into another. See also *Webcast, narrowcast, multicast* and *broadcast*.

cat

(conCATenate) A UNIX command that displays the contents of a file.

catalog

A directory of disk files or files used in an application. Also any map, list or directory of storage space used by the computer.

Category 3, 5, etc.

See *cable categories*.

CA-Telon

An application generator from Computer Associates that generates COBOL and PL/I code for IBM mainframes and COBOL code for AS/400s. Development can be performed on mainframes or PCs. Telon was originally developed by Pansophic Systems.

cathode

In electronics, a device that emits electrons, which flow from the negatively charged cathode to the positively charged anode. Cathodes are used in CRTs and diodes.

CATIA

A family of 2-D and 3-D CAD programs from IBM. CATIA was one of the first CAD programs to provide 3-D solid modelling. The program was developed by Dassault Aviation, a French aerospace company. CATIA runs on IBM mainframes, RS/6000 and HP 9000 workstations with other platforms expected in the future.

CATV

(Community Antenna TV) The original name for cable TV, which used a single antenna at the highest location in the community.

CAU

(Controlled Access Unit) An intelligent hub from IBM for Token Ring networks. Failed nodes are identified by the hub and reported via IBM's LAN Network Manager software.

CA-Unicenter

Systems management software from Computer Associates that supports a variety of servers, including Sun, HP, Digital, IBM and NetWare. Unicenter TNG (The Next Generation) manages the global enterprise, including networks, systems, applications and databases regardless of location.

CAV

(Constant Angular Velocity) Rotating a disk at a constant speed. Since the length of the inner tracks are smaller than the outer tracks, the same clock frequency for recording causes the innermost track to be the most dense and the outermost track to be the least dense. In order to utilize the space more efficiently, zoned CAV (Z-CAV) breaks the disk into multiple zones and uses a different clock frequency for each zone. The innermost track of each zone is the most dense for that zone.

Partial CAV (P-CAV), also known as CAV/CLV, breaks the disk into only two zones. It varies the disk rotation (CLV) for the inner zone and then switches to constant speed (CAV) for the outer one. Contrast with *CLV*.

CAVE

(Computer Automatic Virtual Environment) A virtual reality system that uses projectors to display images on three or four walls and the floor. Special glasses make everything appear as 3-D images and also track the path of the user's vision. CAVE was the first virtual reality system to let multiple users participate in the experience simultaneously. It was developed by the Electronic Visualization Laboratory at the University of Illinois in the early 1990s. Contrast with *HMD*.

CA-Visual Objects

An object-oriented client/server development system from Computer Associates that is used to develop Windows applications. It provides visual programming tools and a programming language that evolved from Clipper. CA-Visual Objects supports ODBC and SQL databases and includes a compiler for generating Windows EXEs and DLLs.

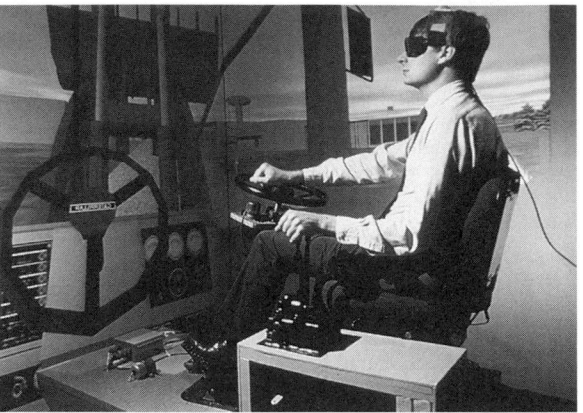

A CAVE System
Pyramid Systems' CAVE products, which license technology from the University of Illinois, can be used to simulate training environments as in this heavy machinery example. The steering wheel on the left of this simulated Caterpillar bulldozer meets the real steering wheel in virtual space, and it appears to the man as the wheel he is turning. *(Photo courtesy of Pyramid Systems, Inc.)*

CB

(Citizen's Band) The frequency band for public radio transmission in the 27 MHz range.

CBD

(Component Based Development) Building applications with components (objects). See *component software*.

CBEMA

See *ITI*.

CBR

(1) (Computer-Based Reference) Reference materials accessible by computer in order to help people do their jobs quicker. For example, this database on disk!

(2) (Constant Bit Rate) A uniform transmission rate. For example, realtime voice and video traffic requires a CBR. In ATM, CBR guarantees bandwidth for the peak cell rate of the application.

(3) See *case-based reasoning*.

CB simulator

See *computer conferencing*.

CBT

(Computer-Based Training) Using the computer for training and instruction. CBT programs are called *courseware* and provide interactive training sessions for all disciplines. It uses graphics extensively, as well as CD-ROM and LaserDisc.

CBT courseware is developed with authoring languages, such as Adroit, PILOT and Demo II, which allow for the creation of interactive sessions.

CBX

(Computerized Branch eXchange) Same as *PBX*.

cc:

(Carbon Copy) The field in an e-mail header that names additional recipients for the message. See *bcc:*.

CCA

(1) (Common Cryptographic Architecture) Cryptography software from IBM for MVS and DOS applications.

(2) (Compatible Communications Architecture) A Network Equipment Technology protocol for transmitting asynchronous data over X.25 networks.

(3) (Communications Control Architecture) The U.S. Navy network that includes an ISDN backbone called BITS (Base Information Transfer System).

CCC/Harvest

A software configuration management (SCM) system for client/server environments from Platinum Technology, Oakbrook Terrace, IL, (www.platinum.com). On the server, it runs on all major UNIX platforms and Windows NT. Windows, OS/2 and UNIX are supported on the client. Other related products include CCC/Manager for VAXes and CCC/LCM for mainframes.

CCD

(1) (Charge Coupled Device) An electronic memory that can be charged by light. CCDs can hold a variable charge, which is why they are used in cameras and scanners to record variable shades of light. CCDs are analog, not digital, and are made of a special type of MOS transistor. Analog to digital (ADC) converters quantify the variable charge into a discrete number of colors. See *digital camera* for illustration.

(2) (Consumer Computing Device) A low-cost consumer-oriented product that contains a computer, such as a PDA, Internet appliance or specialized mobile device.

CCFL, CCFT

(Cold Cathode Fluorescent Lamp, Tube) A type of light source for a backlit screen. It weighs more and uses more power than other backlights.

CCIA

(Computer and Communications Industry Association, Washington, DC, www.ccianet.org) A membership organization composed of computer and communications firms. It represents their interests in domestic and foreign trade, and, working with the NIST, keeps members advised of regulatory policy.

CCIE

(Cisco Certified Internetwork Expert) A certification for competency in internetworking devices and concepts and Cisco routers specifically. It is administered by Cisco Systems, San Jose, CA, as well as Drake testing centers throughout the U.S. and Canada.

CCIR 601

An international standard for digital video designed to encompass both NTSC and PAL analog signals. It requires 27MB per second and uses three signals: one 13.5MB/sec luminance (gray scale) and two 6.75MB/sec chrominance (color). It provides an NTSC-equivalent resolution of 720x486 pixels at 30 fps.

CCIR 601 was established in 1987 by CCIR (Consultative Commitee for International Radio), SMPTE and the European Broadcasting Union.

CCIS

(Common Channel Interoffice Signaling) A telephone communications technique that transmits voice and control signals over separate channels. Control signals are transmitted over a packet-switched digital network, providing faster connects and disconnects and allowing data, such as calling number, to be included. See *CCS*.

CCITT

See *ITU*.

cc:Mail

A widely-used messaging system from Lotus that runs on PC LANs. Originally developed by cc:Mail, Inc., Mountain View, CA, Lotus acquired the company in 1991. Mail-enabled applications that are written to the VIM programming interface can use the cc:Mail system.

CCP

(Certified Computer Professional) The award for successful completion of a comprehensive examination on computers offered by the ICCP. See *ICCP*.

CCS

(1) (Common Communications Support) SAA specifications for communications, which includes data streams (DCA, 3270), application services (DIA, DDM), session services (LU 6.2) and data links (X.25, Token Ring).

(2) (Common Channel Signaling) An integral part of ISDN known as "Signaling System 7," which advances the CCIS method for transmitting control signals. It allows call forwarding, call waiting, etc., to be provided anywhere in the network.

(3) (Common Command Set) The de facto instruction set between a SCSI-1 adapter and a hard disk.

(4) (Continuous Composite Servo) A technique for aligning the read/write head over a track in an optical disk by sensing special tracking grooves in the disk.

(5) (100 Call Seconds) A unit of measurement equal to 100 seconds of conversation. One hour = 36 CCS.

CCW

(Continuous Composite Write) A magneto-optic disk technology that emulates a WORM (Write Once Read Many) disk. It uses firmware in the drive to ensure that data cannot be erased and rewritten.

CD

(Compact Disc) A digital audio disc that contains up to 74 minutes of hi-fi stereo sound. Introduced in 1982, the disc is a plastic platter 120mm (4.75") in diameter, recorded on one side, with individual selections playable in any sequence.

Sound is converted into digital code by sampling the sound waves 44,056 times per second and converting each sample into a 16-bit number. It requires approximately 1.5 million bits of storage for each second of stereo hi-fi sound.

Other forms of CDs, such as CD-ROM, CD-I and Video CD, all stem from the audio CD, which is also known as Compact Disc-Digital Audio (CD-DA). See also *carrier detect*.

The Books

Documentation for various CD formats are found in books commonly known by the color of their covers.

```
Red Book     - Audio CDs (CD-DA)
Yellow Book - CD-ROM
Orange Book - Write-once (Photo CD, CD-R)
Green Book   - CD-I
White Book   - Video CD
Blue Book    - CD Plus
```

What Happened to the Phonograph?

The audio CD was introduced in the U.S. in 1983. Three years later, sales of CDs and CD players exceeded sales of LPs and turntables.

Unlike phonograph records, in which the platter contains "carved sound waves," CDs are recorded in digital form as microscopic pits (binary code) covered by a clear, protective plastic layer. Instead of a needle vibrating in the groove, a laser shines onto the pits and the reflections are decoded. Audio CDs, as well as CD-ROMs, use a spiral recording track just like the phonograph record.

Digital sound is so clear because the numbers are turned into sound electronically. There's no needle pops and clicks as there are with phonograph records (there's also no tape hiss if the original recording was digital). In addition, the CD can handle a wider range of volume (dynamic range), providing more realism. A soft whisper can be interrupted by a loud cannon blast. If a phonograph record were recorded with that much dynamic range, the needle would literally jump out of the groove.

CD+G

(CD+Graphics) An audio CD format that allows images to be stored in subcode channels. It has primarily been used to store lyrics in Karaoke (sing along) discs.

CD32

A specialized Amiga computer from Commodore that was introduced in 1993. It played audio CDs, CD-ROMs and the Karaoke CD+G format.

CDA

(Compound Document Architecture) A compound document format from Digital that creates hot links between documents. See *compound document*.

CD audio

Same as *CD* and *DAD*.

CD burner

A CD-R machine. See *CD-R*.

CDC

See *Control Data* and *century date change*.

CD-DA

(Compact Disc-Digital Audio) The formal designation for the original compact disc format, which was designed for audio only. Since "CD" is used loosely for all compact disc formats, CD-DA differentiates a music disc or player from its data counterparts, such as CD-ROM, CD-R and CD-RW. See *CD*.

CDDA

(Compact Disc Digital Audio) See *CD*.

CDDI

(Copper Distributed Data Interface) A version of FDDI that uses UTP (unshielded twisted pair) wires rather than optical fiber. The term is a trademark of Crescendo Communications, Sunnyvale, CA. ANSI's standard for FDDI over UTP is officially TP-PMD (Twisted Pair-Physical Media Dependent).

CD-E

(Compact Disc-Erasable) The original name for rewritable CDs (CD-RWs). See *CD-RW*.

CDE

(1) (Common Desktop Environment) A graphical user interface standard for open systems from The Open Group. It is based on Motif with elements from HP, IBM and others and was originally managed by COSE. All the major UNIX vendors support CDE.

CDE also provides remote program launching and the ability to suspend and resume applications in their own workspace. CDE branding is governed by X/Open (The Open Group). See also *CD-E*.

(2) (Cooperative Development Environment) A client/server application development system from Oracle Corporation that evolved into Develper/2000 and Designer/2000.

(3) (Computer Desktop Encyclopedia) What you are reading at this very moment.

cdev

(Control Panel DEVice) Customizable settings in the Macintosh Control Panel that pertain to a particular program or device. Cdevs for the mouse, keyboard and startup disk, among others, come with the Mac. Others are provided with software packages and utilities.

CD Extra

See *CD Plus*.

CDF

(1) (Central Distribution Frame) A connecting unit (typically a hub) that acts a central distribution point to all the nodes in a zone or domain. See *MDF*.

(2) (Channel Definition Format) The file format used in Microsoft's Active Channel push technology. See *Active Channel*.

CDFS

(CD-ROM File System) The file system that handles CD-ROMs in Windows 95/98. It is the 32-bit version of the 16-bit MSCDEX.EXE used in DOS/Windows 3.1.

CD-I

(Compact Disc-Interactive) A compact disc format developed by Philips and Sony that holds data, audio, still video and animated graphics. It provides up to 144 minutes of CD-quality stereo, 9.5 hours of AM-radio-quality stereo or 19 hours of monophonic audio.

CD-I includes an operating system standard as well as proprietary hardware methods for compressing the data further in order to display video images. CD-I discs require a CD-I player and will not play in a CD-ROM player. The standard specification for the CD-I format is contained in a document entitled the Green Book. See *CD, CD-ROM* and *DVD*.

CDIA

See *CompTIA*.

CDIF

(CASE Data Interchange Format) An EIA standard for exchanging data between CASE tools.

CDIP

(CERamic Dual In-line Package) A DIP chip made of ceramic materials. It uses gold-plated leads attached to two sides by brazing and a metal lid bonded to the chip with a metal seal. See *DIP, CERDIP, CERQUAD* and *chip package*.

CD jukebox

A jukebox for audio CDs. CD-ROM jukeboxes are also called CD jukeboxes. See *CD-ROM server*.

CDMA

(Code Division Multiple Access) A digital cellular phone technology from Qualcomm, Inc., San Diego, CA, (www.qualcomm.com), that operates in the 800MHz and 1.9GHz (PCS) bands. CDMA phones are noted for their excellent call quality and long battery life, and some phones can switch between both bands.

CDMA uses a spread spectrum technique that codes each digital packet and allows multiple calls to be placed on one channel, boosting caller capacity 20 to 35 times that of the analog network. See *FDMA, TDMA, CDPD* and *spread spectrum*.

CDP

(Certificate in Data Processing) An earlier award for the successful completion of an examination in hardware, software, systems analysis, programming, management and accounting, offered by the ICCP. See *ICCP*.

CDPD

(Cellular Digital Packet Data) A digital wireless transmission system that uses the cellular network. Based on IBM's CelluPlan II, it moves data at 19.2Kbps over ever-changing unused intervals in the voice channels. It has been implemented by IBM, AT&T and most major telephone companies. See *FDMA, TDMA* and *CDMA*.

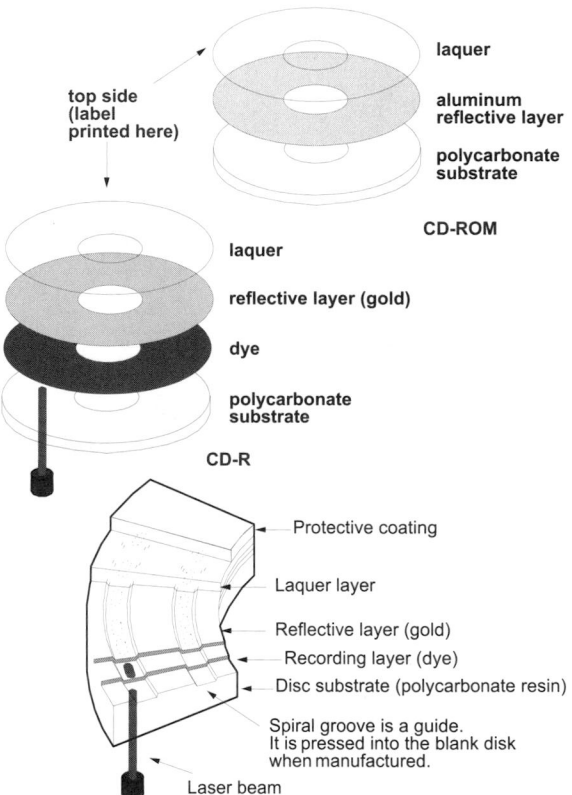

CD-R and CD-ROM Layers

Both gold and silver are used for the reflective layer on a CD-R disc. Fresh out of the box, a CD-R disc is entirely reflective lands, because the dye layer is transparent. In order to create the equivalent of a pit, the laser deforms the dye, making it darker and less reflective. On CD-ROMs, the lands and pits are molded into the plastic which is covered by an aluminum reflective coating. To see how a laser reads a CD-ROM, see *CD-ROM*.

CD Plus

Also called *CD Extra, Enhanced CD* and *Enhanced CD-ROM*, it is a compact disc format that contains both audio and data. It uses the multisession capability to store up to 98 audio tracks in the first session and one CD-ROM XA data track in the second session. Audio CD players will play the first session and ignore the second. A multisession CD-ROM drive (all new drives are today) will read the last session first, and the software in the data session can cause the audio session to be played. See *Mixed Mode CD*.

CD-R

(CD-Recordable) A recordable CD-ROM technology using a disc that can be written only once. The drive that writes the CD-R disc is often called a one-off machine and can also be used as a regular CD-ROM reader. CD-Rs create the equivalent of pits in the disc by altering the reflectivity of a dye layer. Different dyes can be used, including cyanine (green), pthalo-cyanine (yellow-gold) and metal-azo (blue).

CD-R discs are used for beta versions and original masters of CD-ROM material as well as a means to distribute large amounts of data to a small number of recipients. CD-Rs are also used for archiving data. A major advantage over other media is that they can be read in any CD-ROM reader.

To record a full 650MB disc takes from 20 minutes to an hour depending on the speed of the drive. While this may be suitable for archiving or small distributions, large numbers of CD-ROMs are duplicated on a pressing machine from a master plate derived from the original CD-R recording. See *CD UDF*. For a summary of all storage technologies, see *storage*. See illustration on opposite page.

CDRAM

(Cached **DRAM**) A high-speed DRAM memory chip developed by Mitsubishi that includes a small SRAM cache.

CD recorder

See *CD-R*.

CD-ROM

(Compact Disc Read Only Memory) A compact disc format used to hold text, graphics and hi-fi stereo sound. It's like an audio CD, but uses a different track format for data. The audio CD player cannot play CD-ROMs, but CD-ROM players can play audio discs.

CD-ROMs hold 650MB of data, which is equivalent to about 250,000 pages of text or 20,000 medium-resolution images. Sometimes 680MB is used as the capacity, depending on whether the total number of bytes (681,984,000) is divided by 1,000,000 or 1,048,576 (see *binary values*).

A CD-ROM drive (player, reader) connects to a controller card, which is plugged into one of the computer's expansion slots. Earlier drives used a proprietary interface and came with their own card, requiring a free expansion slot in the computer. Today, CD-ROMs use SCSI or EIDE and can be installed without taking up an extra slot.

The first CD-ROM drives transferred data at 150KB per second. Speeds doubled to 300KB and continued upward to as much as 32 times the original. Access times range from 80 to 120ms. See *CD-R, CD-RW* and *DVD*. For a summary of optical and all other storage technologies, see *storage*.

CD-ROM audio cable

A cable used to send audio CD sound into the computer's sound system. When playing audio CDs, CD-ROM drives output analog sound to both a headphones jack and external connector, just like a CD player. Unlike the digital sound on a CD-ROM disk, which is passed via the computer's bus to the sound card, the CD-ROM audio cable passes analog sound to the sound card.

MPC Level 2 defines a standard four-pin cable; however, earlier cards and drives have used connectors with from three to six pins. Finding the right cable has been a problem. Earlier drives have no connector. One advantage of a multimedia upgrade kit is that it includes the card, drive and the right cable.

In lieu of this connection, a stereo cable from the headphones jack of the drive to the AUDIO IN of the sound card can always be used.

CD-ROM changer

A CD-ROM drive that holds a small number of CD-ROMs for individual use on a desktop computer. Although it can swap discs, it typically contains only one drive and can only read one at a time. See *CD-ROM server*.

CD-ROM Extensions

The software required to use a CD-ROM drive on a PC running DOS. It allows CD-ROM drives to be addressed like a hard disk and take the next available drive letter; for example, drive D: in a system with one hard disk. Microsoft's CD-ROM Extensions are in the file MSCDEX.EXE. The installation program for a CD-ROM drive installs the CD-ROM driver and MSCDEX.EXE.

Windows 95/98 includes the CD-ROM File System (CDFS), which is a 32-bit version of MSCDEX.EXE. If MSCDEX.EXE is found when installing, it is replaced with CDFS.

CD-ROM jukebox, CD-ROM server, CD-ROM tower

A CD-ROM reader designed for network use. It can be configured as a tower or jukebox. Towers contain several drives, and each drive holds one CD-ROM. Jukeboxes hold from a couple dozen to hundreds of discs, but have only a small number of drives. A robotic mechanism moves the discs to the drives as required. See *CD-ROM changer*.

CD-ROM XA

(CD-ROM eXtended Architecture) A CD-ROM enhancement introduced in 1988 by Philips, Sony and Microsoft that lets text and pictures be narrated by allowing concurrent audio and video. It provides up to 9.5 hours of AM-quality stereo or 19 hours of monophonic audio. CD-ROM XA drives are required for Kodak's Photo CD discs.

CD-ROM XA functions as a bridge between CD-ROM and CD-I, since CD-ROM XA discs will play on a CD-I player. CD-ROM XA uses a standard CD-ROM player, but requires a CD-ROM XA controller card in the computer. See *CD-I*.

CDRS

(Conceptual Design and Rendering System) Software from Parametric Technology Corporation, Waltham, MA, (www.ptc.com), that is used to test OpenGL performance. See *CDRS-03* and *OPC*.

CDRS-03

A modeling and rendering viewset of the Viewperf benchmark, which is used to test OpenGL performance. See *OPC* and *CDRS*.

CD-RW

(CD-ReWritable) A rewritable CD-ROM technology. CD-RW drives can also be used to write CD-R discs, and they can read CD-ROMs. But, CD-RW disks have a lower reflectivity than CD-ROMs and CD-Rs, and newer MultiRead CD-ROM drives are required to read them. Initially known as CD-E (for CD-Erasable), a CD-RW disk can be rewritten a thousand times.

CD-RW disks can be used to master CD-ROMs, and the same software used for CD-R creation supports this application. However, unlike CD-Rs, in which the entire disc or an entire track is recorded at once, CD-RWs support UDF (Universal Disk Format), which is similar to the file system on a hard

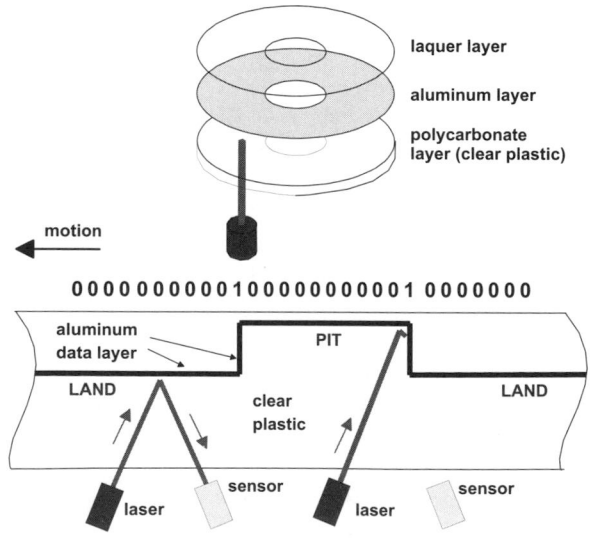

Reading a CD-ROM

Digital data is carved into the CD-ROM as pits (low spots) and lands (high spots). As the laser shines into the moving pits and lands, a sensor detects a change in reflection when it encounters a transition from pit to land or land to pit. Each transition is a 1. The lack of transitions are 0s. There is only one laser in a drive. Two are used here to illustrate the difference in reflection.

disk. Using variable packet writing, small numbers of files can be appended, and using fixed packet writing, files can be added and deleted. The fixed packet approach requires preformatting like a floppy disk, but takes considerably longer.

CD-RWs use phase change technology to alter the reflectivity of the disk's surface. This is similar to Panasonic's PD (phase change dual) drive, which reads and writes rewritable phase change disks and also reads CD-ROMs. However, the Panasonic phase change disks are only usable in the PD drive. See *phase change* and *DVD*. For a summary of all storage technologies, see *storage*.

CDS

(Commercial Data Servers, Inc., Sunnyvale, CA, www.cdatas.com) A manufacturer of entry-level, IBM-compatible mainframes, designed to replace surviving 43xx and 9370 machines. Founded in 1994 by Gene Amdahl, Bill O'Connell and Ray Williams, CDS is expected to produce a high-end mainframe using cryogenic techniques in the 1998 timeframe. See *Trilogy* and *Amdahl*.

CDSL

See *DSL*.

CD tower

See *CD-ROM server*.

CDTV

(Commodore Dynamic Total Vision) A multimedia and video game technology from Commodore that has been superseded by the CD32 system. It also plays audio CDs.

CD UDF

(CD Universal Data Format) A CD-R and CD-RW format introduced in 1996 that allows data to be recorded in packets rather than in a continuous stream. This format is similar to a hard disk and enables small numbers of files to be added. It also eliminates underruns where the computer cannot keep up with the recording process. See *CD-RW*.

How a CD-ROM Is Made

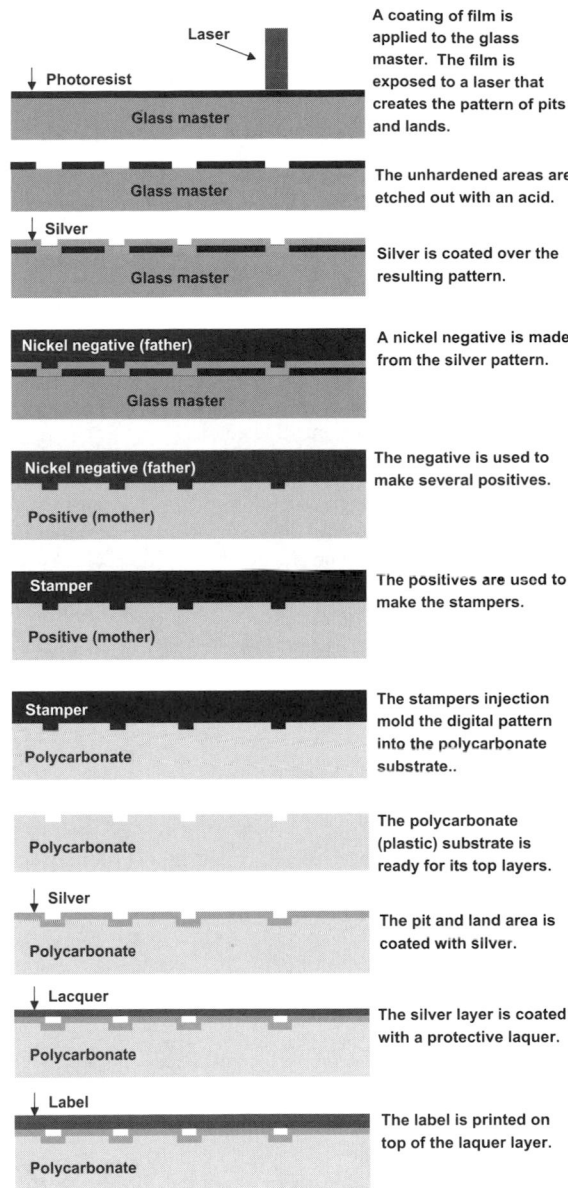

A coating of film is applied to the glass master. The film is exposed to a laser that creates the pattern of pits and lands.

The unhardened areas are etched out with an acid.

Silver is coated over the resulting pattern.

A nickel negative is made from the silver pattern.

The negative is used to make several positives.

The positives are used to make the stampers.

The stampers injection mold the digital pattern into the polycarbonate substrate..

The polycarbonate (plastic) substrate is ready for its top layers.

The pit and land area is coated with silver.

The silver layer is coated with a protective laquer.

The label is printed on top of the laquer layer.

CDV

(1) (Compressed Digital Video) The compression of full-motion video for high-speed, economical transmission.

(2) (CD Video) A small videodisc (5" diameter) that provides five minutes of video with digital sound plus an additional 20 minutes of audio. Most LaserDisc players can also play CDVs.

CE

See *Windows CE, customer engineer* and *consumer electronics*.

CeBIT

(www.cebit.de) The world's largest information technology show hosted in Hannover, Germany. In 1996, 6500 exhibitors from around the world drew more than 600,000 attendees. The show is held in March.

CEbus

(**C**onsumer **E**lectronics **bus**) An EIA standard for a control network.

CE device

A hand-held computer or other device that is managed by the Windows CE operating system. See *Windows CE*.

Ceefax

A teletext service of the British Broadcasting Corporation.

CEG

(**C**ontinous **E**dge **G**raphics) A VGA RAMDAC chip from Edsun Labs that adds anti-aliasing on the fly. It can also calculate intermediate shades, thus providing thousands of colors on an 8-bit board that normally generates only 256 colors.

Celeron

A family of low-cost Pentium II chips from Intel that was introduced in the summer of 1998. The first model (266MHz) does not include an external L2 cache and runs slower than counterpart chips with the cache. Subsequent models have 128KB of L2 cache. Celeron chips are designed for consumer PCs. See *Pentium II*.

cell

(1) An elementary unit of storage for data (bit) or power (battery).

(2) In a spreadsheet, the intersection of a row and column.

Cello

One of the first Web browsers, introduced by Cornell University in 1993.

cell relay

A transmission technology that uses small fixed-length packets (cells) that can be switched at high speed. It is easier to build a switch that switches fixed-length packets than variable ones. ATM uses a type of cell relay technology.

cell switch

A network device that switches fixed packets, such as an ATM switch. Contrast with *frame switch*.

cell switching

Using cell switches to forward fixed-length packets in a network. Contrast with *frame switching*. See *ATM*.

CELP

(**C**ode **E**xcited **L**inear **P**redictive) A speech compression method that achieves high compression ratios along with toll quality audio. LD-CELP (Low-Delay CELP) provides near toll quality audio by using a smaller sample size that is processed faster, resulting in lower delays. LD-CELP was developed by Dr. Raymond Chen when he was at AT&T. Chen was also involved with CELP.

CELP socket

(**C**ard **E**dge **L**ow **P**rofile socket) A socket from Intel used for plugging in SIMM modules containing cache memory, known as "cache on a stick," or COAST. It replaced the tedious job of adding and removing individual DIP memory chips.

Centaur

(Centaur Technology, Inc., Austin, TX, www.winchip.com, subsidiary of Integrated Devices Technology, IDT) An x86-compatible CPU manufacturer founded in 1995 by Glenn Henry. In 1997, it introduced its first Pentium MMX-class chips. See *WinChip*.

centering cone

A short plastic or metal cone used to align a 5.25" floppy disk to the drive spindle. It is inserted into the diskette's center hole when the drive door is closed.

centimeter

A unit of measurement that is 1/100th of a meter or approximately 4/10ths of an inch (0.39 inch).

centralized processing

Processing performed in one or more computers in a single location. All terminals in the organization are connected to the central computers. Contrast with *distributed computing* and *decentralized processing*.

Are We Doing a 180?

The Windows terminal and network computer (NC) are a move towards centralized computing, or thin client computing, once again. This trend towards centralization stems from the high cost of overloaded PCs, which have caused network administration headaches in large organizations.

The Windows terminal works similarly to a mainframe or minicomputer terminal in that all the application processing is done in a central computer (Windows NT server). The NC differs in that it does the processing in the client machine, but keeps nothing locally. All the software is retrieved from the central server. See *Windows terminal, network computer* and *thin client*.

central office

A local telephone company switching facility that covers a geographic area such as a small town or a part of a city. It is where subscribers' telephone lines in the local loop are connected to intracity and intercity trunks. There are more than 25,000 central offices in the U.S.

central processing unit, central processor

See *CPU*.

CENTREX

PBX services provided by a local telephone company. Switching is done in the telephone company's central office. Some services do the switching at the customer's site, but control it in the central office.

Centronics

A standard 36-pin parallel interface for connecting printers and other devices to a computer. It defines the plug, socket and signals used and transfers data asynchronously up to 200 Kbytes/sec. The plug has 18 contacts each on the top and bottom. The socket contains one opening with matching contacts.

This de facto standard was developed by Centronics Corporation, maker of the first successful dot matrix printers. The printer was introduced in 1970, and the company was bought by Genicom Corporation in 1987. See *printer cable*.

locking handles

Centronics Connectors

Centronics connectors are used on most printers. A larger 50-pin variation is used on SCSI-1 devices.

Centura

A high-level development system for 32-bit Windows applications from Centura Software Corporation (formerly Gupta Software), Menlo Park, CA, (www.centurasoft.com). It includes a 4GL, a replication facility for OLE clients, web publishing and three-tier client/server support. Centura is the 32-bit counterpart of the widely-used 16-bit SQLWindows. Code developed with SQLWindows migrates easily to Centura.

century date change

The change from 1999 to 2000. See *Year 2000 problem*.

CEO

(Comprehensive Electronic Office) Office software from Data General introduced in 1981. It includes word processing, e-mail, spreadsheets, business graphics and desktop accessories.

CERDIP

(**CER**amic **D**ual **I**n-line **P**ackage) A type of ceramic DIP chip. It uses a ceramic lid that is bonded to the chip with a glass seal. See *DIP, CDIP, CERQUAD* and *chip package.*

CERN

(Conseil Europeen pour la Recherche Nucleaire, Geneva, Switzerland, www.cern.ch) CERN is the European Laboratory for Nuclear Research where the World Wide Web was developed to enhance collaboration on research documents pertaining to particle physics. A complete Web server software package is available at no charge from CERN.

CERQUAD

(**CER**amic **QUAD**pack) A square, ceramic, surface mount chip package. It uses a ceramic lid that is bonded to the chip with a glass seal. It has pins on all four sides that wrap under like those of a PLCC package. See *CERDIP, CDIP* and *PLCC.*

certificate authority

See *CA.*

Certificate in Computer Programming

See *CCP.*

certification

See *CCIE, CCP, CompTIA, Microsoft Certified Professional, NetWare certification, Xplor* and *aptitude tests.*

CFG file

(**C**on**Fi****G**uration file) A file that contains startup information required to launch a program or operating system. Same as *INI file.*

CGA

(**C**olor/**G**raphics **A**dapter) An IBM video display standard that provided low-resolution text and graphics. It was the first graphics standard for the IBM PC and has been superseded by EGA and VGA. CGA requires a digital RGB Color Display monitor. See *PC display modes.*

CGI

(1) (**C**omputer **G**raphics **I**nterface) A device independent graphics language for display and printing that stemmed from GKS.

(2) (**C**omputer-**G**enerated **I**mage) A picture created in the computer. See *computer animation.*

(3) See *CGI script.*

cgi-bin

The directory on a Web server in which CGI scripts are typically stored. CGI scripts are text files, not binary files, but the "bin" designation has traditionally been used for any directory that holds programs. See *CGI script.*

CGI script

(**C**ommon **G**ateway **I**nterface script) A small program written in a script language such as Perl that functions as the glue between HTML pages and other programs on the Web server. For example, a CGI script would allow search data entered on a Web page to be sent to the DBMS (database management system). It would also format the results of that search onto an HTML page, which is sent back to the user.

CGI scripts have been the initial mechanism used to make Web sites interact with databases and other programs. Java and JavaScript programs and ActiveX components are expected to perform much of this processing in the future. See *cgi-bin.*

CGM

(**C**omputer **G**raphics **M**etafile) A standard format for interchanging graphics images. CGM stores images primarily in vector graphics, but also provides a raster format. Earlier GDM and VDM formats have been merged into CGM. There are many non-standard varieties of CGM in use.

Computer Desktop Encyclopedia

chad

A piece of paper that is punched out on a punched card, paper tape or on the borders of continuous forms. A chadded form is when the holes are cut completely through. A chadless form is when the chads are still attached to one edge of the hole.

chained list

A group of items in which each item contains the location of the next item in sequence.

chaining

Linking items or records to form a chain. Each link in the chain points to the next item.

chain printer

An early line printer that used type slugs linked together in a chain as its printing mechanism. The chain spins horizontally around a set of hammers. When the desired character is in front of the selected print column, the corresponding hammer hits the paper into the ribbon and onto the character in the chain. Chain and train printers gave way to band printers in the early 1980s.

challenge/response

An authentication method used to verify the legitimacy of users logging onto the network. When a user logs on, the server uses account information to send a "challenge" number back to the user. The user enters the number into a credit-card sized token card that generates a response which is sent to the server.

change control

See *version control*.

change file

A transaction file used to update a master file.

change management

See *version control* and *configuration management*.

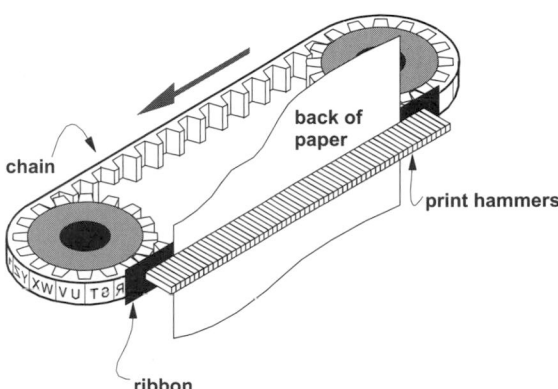

Chain Printer Mechanism

When the required character in the chain has revolved to the selected print column, the hammer pushes the paper into the ribbon and against the type slug of the letter or digit.

channel

(1) A high-speed metal or optical fiber pathway between the computer and the control units of the peripheral devices. Channels are used in mainframes and high-end machines. Each channel is an independent unit that can transfer data concurrently with other channels as well as the CPU. For example, in a 10-channel computer, 10 streams of data are being transmitted to and from the CPU at the same time. In contrast, the bus in a personal computer serves as a common, shared channel between all devices. Each device must wait for its turn on the bus.

(2) In communications, any pathway between two computers or terminals. It may refer to the physical medium, such as coaxial cable, or to a specific carrier frequency (subchannel) within a larger channel or wireless medium.

(3) Information on a particular subject that is transmitted into the user's computer from a Webcast site via the user's browser or push client. It is the Internet's counterpart of the TV or radio channel. See *Webcast, push client* and *push technology*.

(4) The distributor/dealer sales channel. Vendors that sell in the channel rely on the sales ability of their dealers and the customer relationships they have built up over the years. Such vendors may or may not compete with the channel by selling direct to customers via mail order.

channel bank

A multiplexor that merges several low-speed voice or data lines into one high-speed (typically T1) line and vice versa. Channel banks use TDM (time division multiplexing) to combine the different signals into one. See *TDM*.

channel bonding

Doubling transmission speed by spreading the data over two lines. ISDN modems use channel bonding to split the data stream into two 64 Kbps channels, which use both lines in an ISDN BRI service. Bonded analog modems use channel bonding to split the data into two 56 Kbps or two 33.6 Kbps channels, which require two analog telephone lines.

The MPPP (MultiLink PPP) protocol is typically required to support dual channels to an Internet service provider (ISP), and bonded analog modems may require same-brand devices at both ends. See *MPPP, V.34* and *V.90*.

channel program

Instructions executed by a peripheral channel. The channel executes the channel program independently of the CPU, allowing concurrent operations to take place in the computer.

chaos

The science that deals with the underlying order of the seemingly random nature of the universe. See *fractals*.

CHAP

(Challenge Handshake Authentication Protocol) An access control protocol that dynamically encrypts the user's ID and password. The logon procedure in the user's machine obtains a key from the CHAP server, which it uses to encrypt the username and password before transmitting it. See *PAP*.

character

(1) A single alphabetic letter, numeric digit, or special symbol such as a decimal point or comma. A character is equivalent to a byte; for example, 50,000 characters take up 50,000 bytes.

(2) The term character is also used to describe command-driven systems. For example, in the phrase "it supports Mac, Windows and character interfaces," character refers to the line-at-a-time text entry used with dumb terminals.

character based

Same as *text based*.

character cell

A matrix of dots used to form a single character on a display screen or printer. For example, an 8x16 cell is made up of 16 rows each containing eight dots. Character cells are displayed and printed contiguously; therefore the design of each letter, digit or symbol within the cell must include surrounding blank space.

character code

A digital coding system for alphanumeric characters. See *ASCII* and *EBCDIC*.

character data

Alphanumeric data or text. Contrast with *numeric data*.

character device

A peripheral device that transfers data one byte at a time at a time, such as a parallel or serial port. Contrast with *block device*.

character field

A data field that holds alphanumeric characters. Contrast with *numeric field*.

character generator

(1) Circuitry that converts data characters into dot patterns for a display screen.

(2) A device that creates tex t characters that are superimposed onto video frames.

Computer Desktop Encyclopedia

character graphics

A set of special symbols strung together like letters of the alphabet to create elementary graphics and forms, as in the following example:

characteristic

In logarithms and floating point, the number that indicates where the decimal point is placed.

Character Map

A Windows utility that displays all the characters in a particular font. See *Win 9x Typing special characters*.

character mode

Same as *text mode*.

character-oriented protocol

See *byte-oriented protocol*.

character pitch

The measurement of the number of characters per inch. See *cpi*.

character printer

A printer that prints one character at a time. The typical character printer is the dot matrix printer. See *printer*.

character recognition

The ability of a machine to recognize printed text. See *OCR* and *MICR*.

character set

A group of unique symbols used for display and printing. Character sets for alphabet-based languages, such as English and Spanish, generally contain 256 symbols, which is the number of combinations one byte can hold. Except for special fonts, such as Dingbats, Wingdings and the Greek Symbol font, the symbols are the same for the first 128 characters. The letters may have different styling due to their typeface, but an M still looks like an M with each character set, for example.

The second 128 characters differ depending on the font/character set chosen. See *ASCII chart* for the actual characters in the PC-8 character set, which was defined for the original IBM PC. See *extended ASCII*.

character string

A group of alphanumeric characters. Contrast with *numeric data*.

Character Studio

A plug-in for 3D Studio that enables two-footed characters (people, cartoons, robots, etc.) to be animated automatically. A generic skeleton is used to define the path of movement, and the user's own character design is overlaid onto it. See *3D Studio*.

character tag

In desktop publishing, a code embedded in the text that defines a style for the word or phrase that follows it. It defines typeface, size, leading, letter spacing and other settings. See *paragraph tag*.

character terminal

A display screen without graphics capability.

CHARGECARD

An earlier hardware memory manager for 286s from ALL Computers Inc., Toronto, that turned

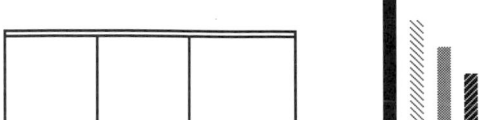

The DOS OEM Font
The characters at the upper end (extended ASCII) of the character set in the original DOS font allowed elementary forms and bar charts to be printed as in this example.

The Character Printer
The desktop dot matrix printer is the typical character printer. It is also called a *serial dot matrix printer* or *serial matrix printer*.

extended memory into EMS and used high memory (640-1024K) for drivers and TSRs. The 286 chip was removed and plugged into the CHARGECARD, which was plugged back into the socket.

charge coupled device
See *CCD*.

Charisma
An earlier presentation graphics program for Windows from Micrografx that included a comprehensive media manager for managing large libraries of image, sound and video clips.

charting program
Software used to create business graphics, charts and diagrams. See *business graphics* and *diagramming program*.

chassis
Pronounced "chah-see," it is a physical structure that holds everything or that everything is attached to. A computer's cabinet is often called the chassis.

chat
A realtime conferencing capability between two or more users on a LAN, BBS or the Internet. The chat is accomplished by typing on the keyboard, not speaking. Each keystroke is transmitted as it is pressed. See *Internet Relay Chat*.

chat mode
An option in a communications program that turns on the chat function.

chat room
An interactive discussion (by keyboard) about a specific topic that is hosted on a BBS, online service or the Internet. See *3-D chat* and *Internet Relay Chat*.

chat window
A text window used for conferencing between two or more users. See *chat room*.

Cheapernet
See *Ethernet*.

check bits
A calculated number used for error checking. The number is derived by some formula from the binary value of one or more bytes of data. See *parity checking, checksum* and *CRC*.

check box
A small box on screen that simulates the equivalent symbol on a paper form. When the box is clicked, the box displays an X or a checkmark to indicate that option has been selected.

check digit
A numeric digit used to ensure that account numbers are correctly entered into the computer. Using a formula, a check digit is calculated for each new account number, which then becomes part of the number, often the last digit.

When an account number is entered, the data entry program recalculates the check digit and compares it to the check digit entered. If the digits are not equal, the account number is considered invalid.

checkpoint/restart
A method of recovering from a system failure. A checkpoint is a copy of the computer's memory that is periodically saved on disk along with the current register settings (last instruction executed, etc.). In the event of any failure, the last checkpoint serves as a recovery point.

When the problem has been fixed, the restart program copies the last checkpoint into memory, resets all the hardware registers and starts the computer from that point. Any transactions in memory after the last checkpoint was taken until the failure occurred will be lost.

checksum
A value used to ensure data is transmitted without error. It is created by adding the binary value of each alphanumeric character in a block of data and sending it with the data. At the receiving end, a new

checksum is computed and matched against the transmitted checksum. A non-match indicates an error.

Just as a check digit tests the accuracy of a single number, a checksum tests a block of data. Checksums detect single bit errors and some multiple bit errors, but are not as effective as the CRC method.

chiclet keyboard

A keyboard with flat, squared-off keys that resemble chiclets (gum). Used on low-cost devices, it is unsuitable for continuous typing.

chief technical officer

See *CTO*.

child

(1) In database management, the data that is dependent on its parent. See *parent-child*.

(2) A component that is subordinate to a higher-level component. See *child menu, child program* and *child window*.

child menu

A secondary or submenu that is displayed on screen when a certain option in the "parent" menu is selected.

child program

A secondary or subprogram called for and loaded into memory by the main program. See *parent program*.

child window

A secondary window on screen that is displayed within the main overall window of the application.

chip

A set of microminiaturized, electronic circuits that are designed for use as processors and memory in computers and countless consumer and industrial products. Chips are the driving force in this industry. Small chips can hold from a handful to tens of thousands of transistors. They look like tiny chips of aluminum, no more than 1/16" square by 1/30" thick, which is where the term "chip" came from. Large chips, which can be more than a half inch square, hold millions of transistors. It is actually only the top one thousandth of an inch of a chip's surface that holds the circuits. The rest of it is just a base. The terms *chip*, *integrated circuit* and *microchip* are synonymous.

An entire computer on a single chip.

Types of Chips by Function

Logic Chip

A single chip can perform some or all of the functions of a processor. A microprocessor is an entire processor on a single chip. Desktop and portable computers use one microprocessor for their CPU while larger computers may employ several types of microprocessors as well as hundreds or thousands of specialized logic chips.

Memory Chip

Random access memory (RAM) chips contain from a couple of hundred thousand to several million storage cells (bits). They are the computer's working storage and require constant power to keep their bits charged. Firmware chips, such as ROMs, PROMs, EPROMs, and EEPROMs are permanent memory chips that hold their content without power.

Computer on a Chip

Also called a *microcontroller*, or MCU, it is a single chip that contains the processor, RAM, ROM, I/O control unit, and a timing clock. It is used in myriads of consumer and industrial products by the hundreds of millions each year.

Analog/Digital and DSP

A single chip can perform the conversion between analog and digital signals. A programmable CPU called a *DSP* (digital signal processor) is also used in many analog/digital conversions. It contains fast instructions sequences commonly used in such applications.

Special Purpose Chip

Chips used in low-cost consumer items (watches, calculators, etc.) as well as higher-cost products (video games, automobile control, etc.) may be designed from scratch to obtain economical and effective performance. Today's ASIC chips can be quickly created for any special purpose.

Logic Array and Gate Array

These chips contain logic gates which have not been tied together. A final set of steps applies the top metal layer onto the chip stringing the logic gates together into the pattern required by the customer. This method eliminates much of the design and fabrication time for producing a chip.

Bit Slice Processor

Bit slice chips contain elementary electronic circuits that serve as building blocks for the computer architect. They are used to custom-build a processor for specialized purposes.

How the Chip Came About

Revolution

In 1947, the semiconductor industry was born at AT&T's Bell Labs with the invention of the *transistor* by John Bardeen, Walter Brattain and William Shockley. The transistor, fabricated from solid materials that could change their electrical conductivity, would eventually replace all the bulky, hot, glass vacuum tubes used as electronic amplifiers in radio and TV and as on/off switches in computers. By the late 1950s, the giant first-generation computers were giving way to smaller, faster and more reliable transistorized machines.

Evolution

The original transistors were discrete components; each one was soldered onto a circuit board to connect to other individual transistors, resistors and diodes. Since hundreds of transistors were made on one round silicon wafer and cut apart only to be reconnected again, the idea of building them in the required pattern to begin with was obvious. In the late 1950s, Jack Kilby of TI and Robert Noyce of Fairchild Semiconductor created the *integrated circuit*, a set of interconnected transistors and resistors on a single chip.

Since then, the number of transistors that have been put onto a single chip has increased exponentially, from a handful in the early 1960s to millions by the late 1980s. Today, a million transistors take up no more space than the first transistor.

A byproduct of miniaturization is speed. The shorter the distance a pulse travels, the faster it gets there. The

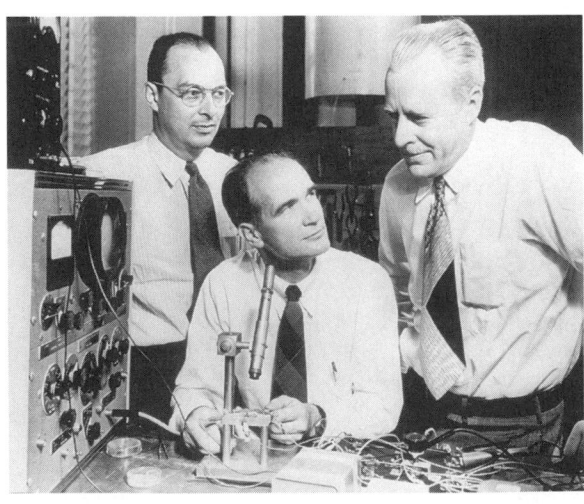

Drs. Bardeen, Shockley and Brattain (1947)
(Photo courtesy of AT&T.)

Computer Desktop Encyclopedia

smaller the elements in the transistor, the faster it switches. Speed is measured in billionths and trillionths of a second.

Logic and Memory
In first- and second-generation computers, internal main memory was made of such materials as tubes filled with liquid mercury, magnetic drums and magnetic cores. As integrated circuits began to flourish in the 1960s, design breakthroughs allowed memories to also be made of semiconductor materials. Thus, logic circuits, the "brains" of the computer, and memory circuits, its internal workspace, were moving along the same miniaturization path.

By the end of the 1970s, it was possible to put a processor, working memory (RAM), permanent memory (ROM), a control unit for handling input and output and a timing clock on the same chip.

Within 25 years, the transistor on a chip grew into the computer on a chip. When the awesome UNIVAC I was introduced in 1951, you could literally open the door and walk inside. Who would have believed the equivalent electronics would some day be built into your watch.

The Making of a Chip

Computer circuits carry electrical pulses from one point to another. The pulses flow through transistors (on/off switches) that open or close when electrically activated. The current flowing through one switch effects the opening or closing of another and so on. Transistors are wired together in patterns of Boolean logic. Logic gates make up circuits. Circuits make up CPUs and other electronic systems.

From Logic to Plumbing
All circuits were originally designed in some manner by humans. Today, many logic functions reside in libraries, and designers pick and choose modules from a menu. There is always a little bit of "glue logic" necessary to interconnect them however, and this still must be done logic gate by logic gate. If a required function is not predesigned, that part will have to be created gate by gate. In addition, if the purpose of the final chip is to be the "fastest" and "greatest" of all chips of its kind, most likely all the logic will be designed from scratch.

Computers make computers. The computer converts the logical circuit design into transistors, diodes and resistors. From there the whole thing is turned into a plumber's nightmare that connects millions of components together. After inspection by technicians, the electronic images are transferred to machinery that creates glass, lithographic plates, called *photomasks*.

The photomask is the actual size of the chip, replicated many times to fit on a round silicon wafer, which is generally 6 to 12" in diameter. Transistors are built

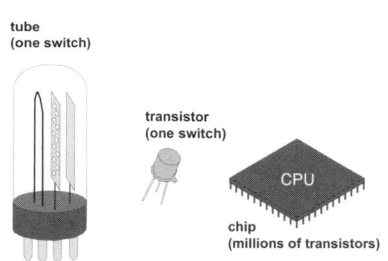

Tube to Transistor to Chip

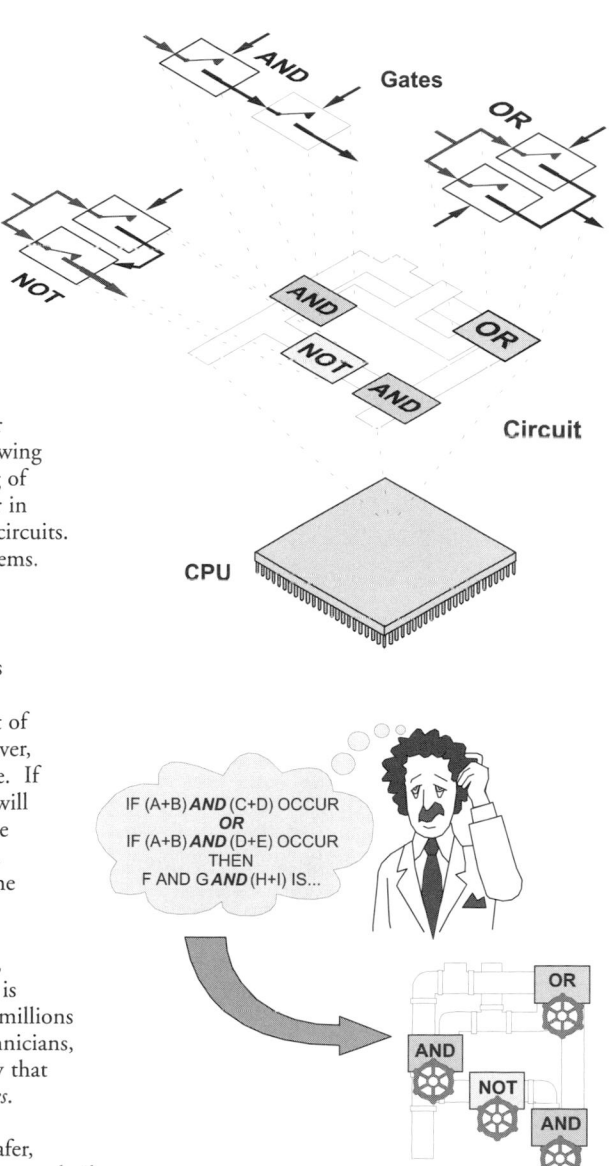

Gates

Circuit

CPU

IF (A+B) **AND** (C+D) OCCUR
OR
IF (A+B) **AND** (D+E) OCCUR
THEN
F AND G **AND** (H+I) IS...

OR

AND

NOT

AND

by creating subterranean layers in the silicon, and a different photomask is created for each layer.

Chips Are Just Rocks

The base material of a chip is usually silicon, although materials such as sapphire and gallium arsenide are also used. Silicon is found in quartz rocks and is purified in a molten state. It is then chemically combined (doped) with other materials to alter its electrical properties. The result is a silicon crystal ingot up to eight inches in diameter that is either positively (p-type) or negatively charged (n-type). *Wafers*, about 1/30th of an inch thick, are cut from this "crystal salami."

Inspecting the Plumbing
(Photo courtesy of Elxsi Corporation.)

silicon ingot

wafer

1/30"

Drawing the Ingot
The silicon ingot is being drawn from a scalding furnace containing molten silicon. High-speed saws will slice it into wafers about as thick as a dime, which will then be ground thinner and polished like a mirror. *(Photo courtesy of Texas Instruments, Inc.)*

Building the Layers

Circuit building starts out by adhering a layer of silicon dioxide insulation on the wafer's surface. The insulation is coated with film and exposed to light through the first photomask, hardening the film and insulation below it. The unhardened areas are etched away exposing the silicon base below. By shooting a gas under heat and pressure into the exposed silicon (diffusion), a sublayer with different electrical properties is created beneath the surface.

Through multiple stages of masking, etching, and diffusion, the sublayers on the chip are created. The final stage lays the top metal layer (usually aluminum), which interconnects the transistors to each other and to the outside world.

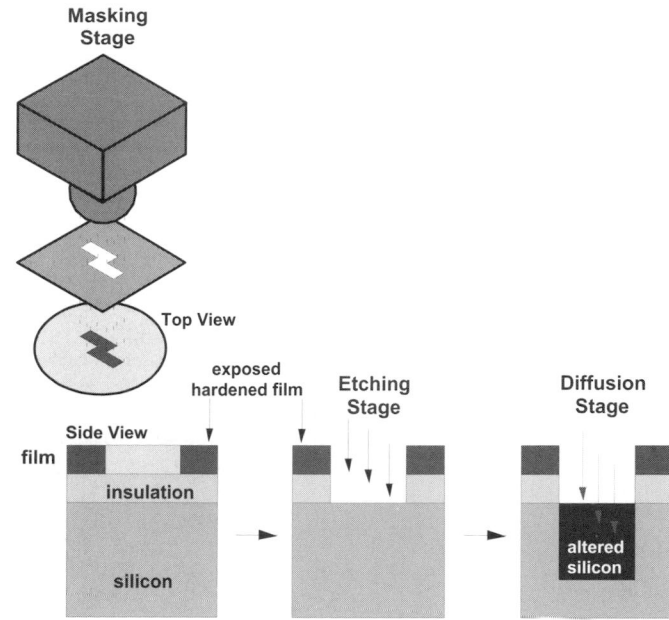

Each chip is tested on the wafer, and bad chips are marked for elimination. The chips are sliced out of the wafer, and the good ones are placed into packages (DIPs, PQFPs, etc.). The chip is connected to the package with tiny wires, then sealed and tested as a complete unit.

Chip making is extremely precise. Operations are performed in a "clean room," since air particles can mix with the microscopic mixtures and easily render a chip worthless. Depending on the design complexity, more chips can fail than succeed.

Inspecting Wafers

The lady is wearing a "bunny suit," but is not wearing a mask, because the wafers have already been manufactured. *(Photo courtesy of Hewlett-Packard Company.)*

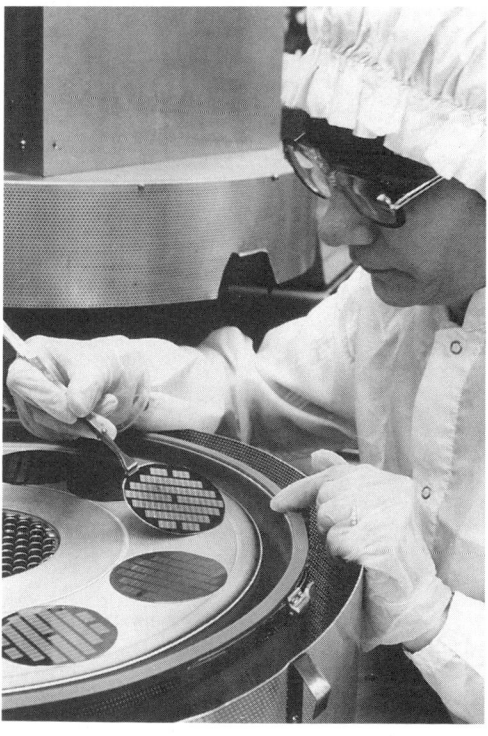

The Future

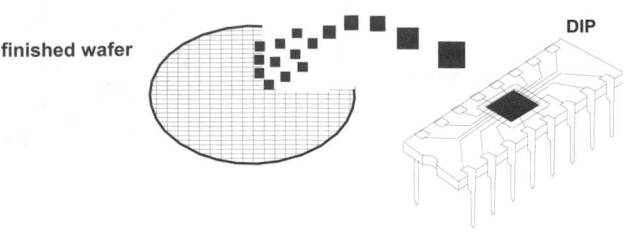

finished wafer   DIP

There is a never-ending thirst for putting more circuits onto a chip. In order to miniaturize elements of a transistor even more, electron beam lithography will be used to expose the mask patterns directly onto the wafer, eliminating the photomask process entirely.

Just as integrated circuits eliminated cutting apart the transistors only to be reconnected again, eventually *wafer scale integration* will eliminate cutting apart the chips only to be tied together with other chips. All the computer circuitry will be built on one chip.

As we're trying to make the chip wider, we're also trying to make it deeper. Instead of adding more circuits across the surface, we are experimenting with building overlapping layers. Within the next 10 years, today's supercomputer will fit within a cubic inch.

For a detailed look into the making of a transistor, see *transistor*.

chip card

See *smart card* and *memory card*.

chip carrier

(1) The package that a chip is mounted in. See *chip package*.

(2) A chip package with connectors on all sides. See *leaded chip carrier* and *leadless chip carrier*.

chip container

See *chip package*.

chip cooler

See *CPU cooler*.

chip housing

See *chip package*.

chip jewelry

High-tech jewelry and accessories, such as tie clips, money clips, pins and earrings, made from outdated electronic components.

Packaging the Chip
This machine bonds the chips to the metal structure that will be connected to the pins of the chip housing and carry the signals to and from the circuit board. *(Photo courtesy of Texas Instruments, Inc.)*

chip on board

A bare chip that is mounted directly on the printed circuit board. After the wires are attached, a "blob" of epoxy or plastic is used to cover the chip and its connections.

chip on chip

A 3-D cube of chips, using bare chips mounted one over the other with spacers in between. As this technology matures, it is expected that up to 100 chips can be used in one cube.

chip package

The housing that chips come in for plugging into (socket mount) or soldering onto (surface mount) the printed circuit board. See *CDIP, CERDIP, CERQUAD, CLCC, DIP, flatpack, PLCC, QFP, MCM, SOP, SOIC, SOJ, TSOP* and *ZIP*.

chipset

A group of chips designed to work as a unit to perform a function. For example, a modem chipset contains all the primary circuits for transmitting and receiving. A PC chipset provides the electronic interfaces between all subsystems. See *PC chipset*.

Chkdsk

A DOS utility program that looks for lost clusters on the hard disk. It also reports the current amount of free memory and disk space. Although still on the Windows 95/98 distribution disk, it has been replaced by ScanDisk. See *lost cluster*.

CHK file

(CHecKdisk file) The file extension applied to unlinked files by the DOS ScanDisk utility and Chkdsk command. See *ScanDisk*.

CHMOS

(High-density **CMOS**) A chip with a high density of CMOS transistors.

Chooser

A Macintosh desk accessory that allows the user to select a printer, file server or network device, such as a network modem.

chroma key

Chroma means color. See *color key*.

chromatic dispersion

The spreading of light rays within an optical fiber, which causes decreased bandwidth.

chrominance

The color information in a video signal. See *luminance, saturation* and *hue*.

CHRP

(Common Hardware Reference Platform) A specification intended to make the PowerPC a standard platform. Also known as the PowerPC Reference Platform (PPCP), it defines minimum hardware requirements such as ports, sockets, bootstrap ROM and cache. Introduced in 1995, the first CHRP systems became available from Motorola in 1997. Since OS/2, NT, Solaris and NetWare support for the PowerPC has been halted, CHRP serves as a standard for Macintosh clones.

CICS

(Customer Information Control System) A TP monitor from IBM that was originally developed to provide transaction processing for IBM mainframes. It controls the interaction between applications and users and lets programmers develop screen displays without detailed knowledge of the terminals used. It provides terminal routing, password security, transaction logging for error recovery and activity journals for performance analysis.

CICS has also been made available on non-mainframe platforms including the RS/6000, AS/400 and OS/2-based PCs.

CICS commands are written along with and into the source code of the applications, typically COBOL, although assembly language, PL/I and RPG are also used. CICS implements SNA layers 4, 5 and 6.

CICS programmer

A programmer versed in CICS commands as well as in the programming language used to develop the application.

CID

(Configuration, Installation and Distribution) IBM software for controlling software distribution throughout a network from a central source.

CIDR

(Classless Inter-Domain Routing) A method for creating additional addresses on the Internet, which are given to Internet service providers (ISPs) that in turn delegate them to their customers. CIDR reduces the burden on Internet routers by aggregating routes so that one IP address represents thousands of addresses that are serviced by a major backbone provider. All packets sent to any of those addresses are sent to the ISP such as MCI or Sprint. In 1990, there were about 2,000 routes on the Internet. Five years later, there were more than 30,000. Without CIDR, the routers would not have been able to support the increasing number of Internet sites.

Instead of the fixed 7, 14 and 21 bits used in the Class A-B-C network IDs, CIDR uses a variable network ID from 13 to 27 bits. For example, the CIDR address 204.12.01.42/24 indicates that the first 24 bits are used for network ID. See *IP address*.

CIE

(Commission Internationale de l'Eclairage) A color model defined in 1931 that represents all possible colors in a three-dimensional color space. All of the variants of CIE (CIELAB, CIELUV, CIEXYZ, etc.) use values of lightness, red-green and yellow-blue to represent a color. The CIE Chromaticity Diagram is a two-dimensional drawing of this model.

CIF

(1) (Common Intermediate Format) A standard video format used in videoconferencing. CIF formats are defined by their resolution, and standards both above and below the original resolution have been established. The original CIF is also known as Full CIF (FCIF). The bit rates in the chart below are for uncompressed color frames.

CIF Format		Resolution	Bit Rate at 30 fps (Mbps)
SQCIF	(Sub Quarter CIF)	128 x 96	4.4
QCIF	(Quarter CIF)	176 x 144	9.1
CIF	(Full CIF, FCIF)	352 x 288	36.5
4CIF	(4 x CIF)	704 x 576	146.0
16CIF	(16 x CIF)	1408 x 1152	583.9

(2) (Cells In Frames) A networking technology developed by Cornell University that allows ATM backbones to be used with Ethernet LANs. CIF utilizes the inherent quality of service in ATM, which allows for realtime voice and video, all the way to the Ethernet end station by placing the ATM cell within the Ethernet frame. It differs from LAN Emulation, in which Ethernet packets are encapsulated into LAN Emulation packets and then converted into ATM cells.

CIF is implemented by replacing the Ethernet hub with a switch or multiplexor known as a CIF Attachment Device (CIF-AD). CIF drivers are used in the client stations.

CIFS

(Common Internet File System) An enhanced version of the SMB file sharing protocol for the Internet. It allows Web applications to share data over the Internet and intranets and is Microsoft's counterpart to Sun's WebNFS. CIFS supports file access only and not printer sharing. See *SMB, WebNFS* and *DFS*.

CI Labs

(Component Integration Labs, Sunnyvale, CA, www.cilabs.com) The vendor consortium that managed OpenDoc. It dissolved in June of 1997.

CIM

(1) (Computer-Integrated Manufacturing) Integrating office/accounting functions with automated factory systems. Point of sale, billing, machine tool scheduling and supply ordering are part of CIM.

(2) (CompuServe Information Manager) The software provided by CompuServe for installation in a subscriber's computer to access available services.

(3) (Common Information Model) A model for describing management information from the DMTF. CIM is implementation independent, allowing different management applications to collect the required data from a variety of sources. CIM includes schemas for systems, networks, applications and devices, and new schemas will be added. It also provides mapping techniques for interchange of CIM data with MIB data from SNMP agents and MIF data from DMI-compliant systems. See *JMAPI* and *WBEM*.

cine-oriented

A film-image orientation like that of movie film, in which the tops of the frames run perpendicular to the outer edge of the medium. See *comic-strip oriented* for illustration.

Computer Desktop Encyclopedia

Cinepak

A video compression/decompression algorithm from SuperMac Technologies, Sunnyvale, CA, that is used to compress movie files. It is widely used on the Macintosh and is included in Windows 95/98.

CIO

(Chief Information Officer) The executive officer in charge of all information processing in an organization. The CIO's job is demanding and one that may not receive the same praise and rewards as other executives. Information systems in an organization is often taken for granted until something breaks down, which is when the CIO catches hell.

The CIO is responsible for explaining to executive managment the complex nightmare this industry has gotten itself into over the past 30 years and why equipment must be constantly retrofitted or replaced. Justifying new expenditures can be the most difficult part of the job. See *salary survey*.

cipher

An encoded character. See *ciphertext* and *cryptography*.

ciphertext

Data that has been coded (enciphered, encrypted, encoded) for security purposes. See *cryptography*.

CIR

(Committed Information Rate) In a frame relay system, a method for sharing a virtual circuit by assigning an appropriate bandwidth to a node. Frame relay carriers define and package CIRs differently; however, the CIR is generally an average, not a fixed transfer rate. For example, if a terminal is assigned a 16Kbps CIR, it could transmit 64Kbps for a quarter of a second and still be within the limits.

circuit

(1) A set of electronic components that perform a particular function in an electronic system.

(2) Same as *communications channel*.

circuit analyzer

(1) A device that tests the validity of an electronic circuit.

(2) In communications, same as *data line monitor*.

circuit board

Same as *printed circuit board*.

circuit breaker

A protective device that opens a circuit upon sensing a current overload. Unlike a fuse, it can be reset.

circuit card

Same as *printed circuit board*.

circuit cellular

The transmission of data over the cellular network using a voice channel and modem similar to using land-based modems. Contrast with *packet cellular*. See *wireless*.

circuit switching

The temporary connection of two or more communications channels. Users have full use of the circuit until the connection is terminated. Circuit switching is used by the telephone company for its voice networks in order to guarantee steady, consistent service for two people engaged in a telephone conversation. See *connection oriented*. Contrast with *packet switching* and *message switch*.

CIS

(1) (CompuServe Information Service) See *CompuServe*.

(2) (Card Information Structure) A data structure on a PC Card that contains information about the card's contents. It allows the card to describe its configuration requirements to its host computer.

CIS B

(CompuServe Information Service B) A proprietary communications protocol from CompuServe that is used for transferring files. See *B protocol*.

CISC

(Complex Instruction Set Computer) Pronounced "sisk." The traditional architecture of a computer which uses microcode to execute very comprehensive instructions. Instructions may be variable in length and use all addressing modes, requiring complex circuitry to decode them. Contrast with *RISC*.

Cisco

(Cisco Systems, Inc., San Jose, CA, www.cisco.com) A leading manufacturer of networking equipment, including routers, bridges, frame switches and ATM switches, dial-up access servers and network management software. Cisco was founded in 1984 by Leonard Bosack and Sandra Lerner, a married couple both employed by Stanford University. Initially targeting universities, it sold its first router in 1986. Starting in the early 1990s, Cisco has made numerous acquisitions, including Crescendo Communications (CDDI), Newport Systems Solutions (software-based routers), Kalpana and Catalyst (frame switches) and LightStream and StrataCom (ATM switches).

Citrix

(Citrix Systems, Inc., Ft. Lauderdale, FL, www.citrix.com) Founded in 1989, it is a company that specializes in multiuser server software. Its Windows NT-based WinFrame server uses Citrix's Intelligent Console Architecture (ICA) to send only screen changes to the client machines. Citrix technology is expected to be built into future versions of Windows NT by Citrix and Microsoft. See *WinFrame*. See also *Cyrix*.

CIX

(Commercial Internet eXchange Association, Herndon, VA, www.cix.org) Pronounced "kicks," it is a membership organization that promotes the development of a level playing field for ISPs. Founded in 1991 by Rick Adams, Marty Schofstall and Susan Estrada, it created the first public, commercial interconnect point on the Internet, originally in Santa Clara, California, and later in Palo Alto. Instead of bilateral peering agreements between two parties as is common on other NAPs, CIX is multilateral, whereby all members must exchange traffic with each other. See *NAP* and *peering*.

CKO

(Chief Knowledge Officer) The executive officer responsible for exchanging knowledge within an organization. CKOs determine how research storehouses and all other expertise throughout the enterprise can be shared by all departments. They work closely with the CIO to provide the necessary information retrieval systems.

The large U.S. accounting firms were the first to develop this position in the mid 1990s. Although more extensive, the CKO's focus is somewhat like that of the data administrator, a popular position in the 1970s and 1980s, whose responsibility it was to model data for the entire enterprise, crossing all departmental lines.

CL/1

(Connectivity Language/1) A database language from Apple that lets a Macintosh access an SQL-based database in another computer. CL/1 applications communicate with the CL/1 client program in the Mac, and the client program communicates with the CL/1 server program in the host computer.

cladding

The plastic or glass sheath that is fused to and surrounds the core of an optical fiber. The cladding's mirror-like coating keeps the light waves reflected inside the core. The cladding is covered with a protective outer jacket.

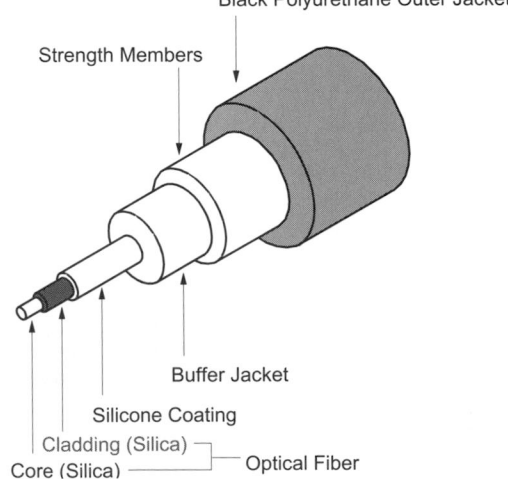

Black Polyurethane Outer Jacket

Strength Members

Buffer Jacket

Silicone Coating

Cladding (Silica) ⌐
Core (Silica) ──────── └── Optical Fiber

Cladding

The cladding covers the inner core of the fiber which is the actual pathway that the light travels through.

clamping ring

The part of a 5.25" floppy disk drive that presses the disk onto the spindle. It is usually part of the centering cone.

Clarion

A family of application development systems for DOS and Windows from TopSpeed Corporation, Pompano Beach, FL, (www.topspeed.com). It provides a comprehensive set of tools for development, including a screen builder, 4GL and application generator. It includes a compiler that is known for generating fast executables. It also includes a data dictionary and drivers for popular databases. TopSpeed Corporation was formerly Clarion Software Corporation.

Claris

(Claris Corporation, Santa Clara, CA) A software subsidiary of Apple that was separated from the corporation (although mostly owned by it) in 1988 and then bought back in 1990. In 1998, Apple turned Claris Corporation into FileMaker, Inc., to focus on database and Web software. FileMaker Pro and Claris Home Page were the products retained by FileMaker.

Claris CAD

A full-featured 2-D CAD program for the Macintosh from Claris that is noted for its ease of use. It provides an easy-to-learn path into CAD, while offering most features found in CAD programs.

ClarisWorks

See *AppleWorks*.

Clarke belt

The geosynchronous (also geostationary) orbit that satellites are placed into. It was named after Arthur C. Clarke who proposed the concept in 1945. See *GEO*.

class

In object technology, a user-defined data type that defines a collection of objects that share the same characteristics. An object, or class member, is one instance of the class. Concrete classes are designed to be instantiated. Abstract classes are designed to pass on characteristics through inheritance. See *instantiate*.

Class 1 fax, Class 2 fax

See *fax/modem*.

Class A, B

See *FCC Class*.

Classical IP

An IETF standard for transmitting IP traffic in an ATM network. IP protocols contain IP addresses that have to be converted into ATM addresses, and Classical IP performs this conversion, as long as the destination is within the same subnet. Classical IP does not support routing between networks. The Classical IP-enabled driver in the end station sends out an ARP request to a Classical IP-enabled ARP server, which returns the ATM address.

class library

A set of ready-made software routines (class definitions) that programmers use for writing object-oriented programs. For example, a class library is commonly available to provide graphical user interface (GUI) functions such as windowing routines, buttons, scroll bars and other elements. These class definitions also include their inheritance characteristics, if applicable.

class variable

In object-oriented programming, a variable used by the class definition. Contrast with *instance variable*. See *class*.

claymation

A form of stop-motion animation that uses actual clay figures which are molded into different positions for each frame. See *stop-motion animation*.

CLCC

(Ceramic Leadless Chip Carrier) A square, ceramic chip package that uses metal pads for contact and comes in both socket mount and surface mount varieties. See *chip package*.

clean boot

Booting the computer without loading anything but the main part of the operating system.

clean room

A room in which the air is highly filtered in order to keep out impurities. Chip fabrication plants use clean rooms where the air is completely exchanged as much as seven times per minute. Workers go through an elaborate procedure to gown themselves in the "bunny suits" which are required to keep them from contaminating the atmostphere.

ClearCase

A software configuration management (SCM) system for client/server environments from Pure Atria, Sunnyvale, CA, (www.pureatria.com). It supports all the major UNIX platforms as well as Windows NT.

clear memory

To reset all RAM and hardware registers to a zero or blank condition. Rebooting the computer may or may not clear memory, but turning the computer off and on again guarantees that memory is cleared.

clear to send

See *CTS*.

Taking an Air Shower
After gowning, this man is taking an "air" shower to purify the outside of his suit before entering the clean room. *(Photo courtesy of Intel Corporation.)*

CLEC

(Competitive Local Exchange Carrier) An organization offering local telephone services. Although most CLECs are established as a telecommunications service organization, any large company, university or city government has the option of becoming a CLEC and supplying its own staff with dial tone at reduced cost. It must have a telephone switch, satisfy state regulations, pay significant filing fees and also make its services available to outside customers. This was all sanctioned by the Telecommunications Act of 1996. Contrast with *ILEC*. See *ELEC* and *TELRIC*.

CLI

(Call Level Interface) A database programming interface from the SQL Access Group, an SQL membership organization. SAG's CLI is an attempt to standardize the SQL language for database access. Microsoft's ODBC conforms to the CLI, but adds its own extensions. Under CLI, SQL statements are passed directly to the server without being recompiled.

click

To select an object by pressing the mouse button when the cursor is pointing to the required menu option, icon or hypertext link.

Click! disk

A low-cost, portable disk drive technology from Iomega that is expected in 1998. It uses 40MB removable cartridges that are half the size of a credit card and expected to sell for $10. External drives are designed for notebooks, digital cameras, PDAs and other hand-held devices. An internal model is expected for OEM use. See *latest disk drives*. For a summary of all storage technologies, see *storage*.

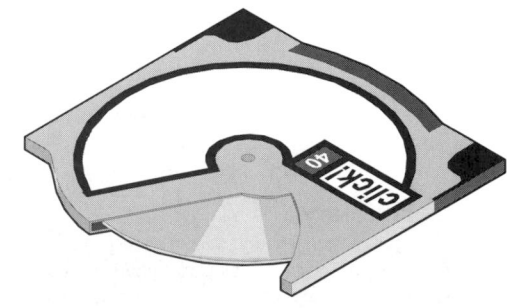

Click! Cartridge
Click! drives are aimed at handheld devices that require removable storage, such as PDAs and digital cameras.

clickable map
Same as *image map*.

click and drag
Using a pointing device, such as a mouse, to latch onto an icon on screen and move it to some other location. When the screen pointer is over the icon of the object, the mouse button is clicked to grab it. The button is held down while the object is moved ("dragged") to its destination. Then the mouse button is released.

click disk
See *click! disk*.

ClickNet
A network diagramming program for Windows from PinPoint Software Corporation, San Jose, CA, (www.pinpt.com). It keeps the lines connected to the objects when they are moved and also allows a database to be linked to diagram objects for equipment and network documentation. More than 2,300 predefined images and 80 management reports are included.

click potato
The cyberspace version of the couch potato.

clickstream
The trail of mouse clicks made by a user performing a particular operation on the computer. It often refers to linking from one page to another on the World Wide Web.

click through
On the Web, the act of linking to a third party. Click-through rates are used to measure the effectiveness of one site persuading a user to go to another site. On "click-through advertising," royalties may be paid on this number.

clicktract
See *clickwrap*.

clickwrap
The equivalent of shrinkwrap on the Internet. A clickwrap contract, or clicktract, is a notice that requires a user to agree to certain conditions before proceeding to the next page.

client
(1) A workstation or personal computer in a client/server environment. See *client/server* and *fat client*.

(2) One end of the spectrum in a request/supply relationship between programs. See *X Window* and *OLE*.

client application
An application running in a workstation or personal computer on a network. See also *OLE*.

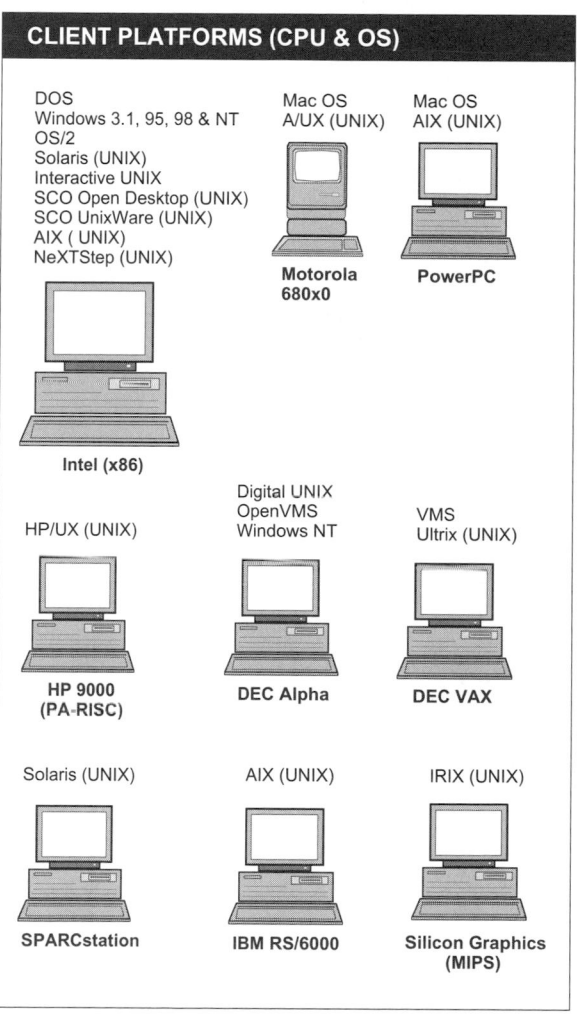

CLIENT PLATFORMS (CPU & OS)

Clients
These are the major hardware platforms used in local and enterprise-wide networks today along with the operating systems that run on them.

client-client-server

An Apple architecture that allows users with remote devices, such as laptops and PDAs, to have easy access to their desktop machines (clients) as well as to the servers.

client machine

A user's workstation that is attached to a network. The term can also refer to a portable computer that is plugged into the network. See *client* and *client/server*.

client program

Software that runs in the user's PC or workstation. Contrast with *server program*, which resides in a server in the network.

client/server

An architecture in which the client (personal computer or workstation) is the requesting machine and the server is the supplying machine, both of which are connected via a local area network (LAN) or wide area network (WAN). Since the early 1990s, client/server has been the buzzword for building applications on LANs in contrast to centralized minis and mainframes with dedicated terminals.

The client contains the user interface and may perform some or all of the application processing.

Servers can be high-speed microcomputers, minicomputers or even mainframes. A database server maintains the databases and processes requests from the client to extract data from or update the database. An application server provides additional business processing for the clients.

The term client/server is sometimes used to contrast a peer-to-peer network, in which any client can also act as a server. In that case, client/server means nothing more than having a dedicated server.

However, client/server architecture means more than dedicated servers. Simply downloading files from or sharing programs and databases on a server is not true client/server either. True client/server implies that the application was originally designed to run on a network and that the network infrastructure provides the same quality of service as traditional mini and mainframe information systems.

The network operating system (NOS) together with the database management system (DBMS) and transaction monitor (TP monitor) are responsible for integrity and security. Some of these products have gone through many client/server versions by now and have finally reached industrial strength.

Non-Client/Server

In non-client/server architecture, the server is nothing more than a remote disk drive. The user's machine does all the processing. If many users routinely perform lengthy searches, this can bog down the network, because each client has to pass the entire database over the net. At 1,000 bytes per record, a 10,000 record database requires 10MB of data be transmitted.

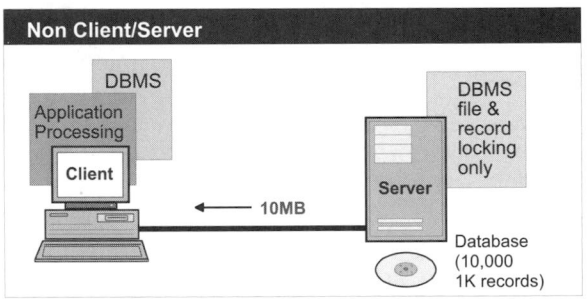

Two-Tier Client/Server

Two-tier client/server is really the foundation of client/server. The database processing is done in the server. An SQL request is generated in the client and transmitted to the server. The DBMS searches locally and returns only matching records. If 50 records met the criteria, only 50K would be transmitted. This reduces traffic in the LAN.

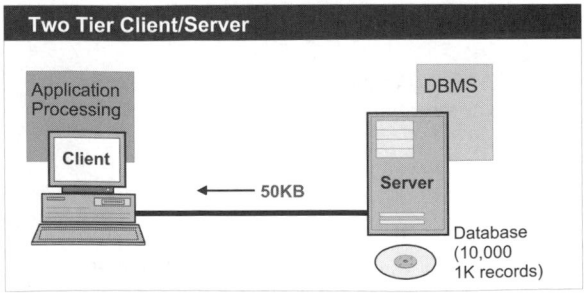

Computer Desktop Encyclopedia

Three-Tier Client/Server

Many applications lend themselves to centralized processing. If they contain proprietary algorithms, security is improved. Upgrading is also simpler. Sometimes, programs are just too demanding to be placed into every client PC. In three-tier client/server, application processing is performed in one or more servers.

Three Tier Client/Server

client/server architecture

An environment in which the application processing is divided between client workstations and servers. It implies the use of desktop computers interacting with servers in a network in contrast to processing everything in a large centralized mainframe. See *client/server*.

client/server development system

An application development system used to create applications for a client/server environment. A comprehensive system generally includes a GUI builder for creating one or all of the major GUIs: Windows, Mac and Motif, a fourth-generation language for creating the business logic, an interpreter and/or compiler and debugging tools. It provides support for many of the major database management systems (Oracle, Sybase, Informix, etc.), and it may include its own DBMS.

For enterprise-wide client/server development, a system may allow for application partitioning, which separates parts of the application onto different machines. Such systems support the major server environments (UNIX, NetWare, NT, etc.) in order to accommodate the dispersion of business logic onto multiple computers. It may also include software configuration management capabilities that provide version control and bug tracking.

Almost any language can be used to develop the client front ends in a client/server application. For example, Visual Basic is very popular for such purposes. However, a client/server system implies that client-to-server connections and application partitioning are written at a higher level than a 3GL programming language. It implies that there is little or no "tweaking" to make things happen. See *client/server* and *application partitioning*. Following is a list of client/server development tools in alphabetical order.

Axiant	JAM
CA-OpenRoad	Key:Enterprise
CA-Visual Objects	ObjectPro
Centura	ObjectView
COOL:Gen	OMNIS
Corel Paradox	Passport IntRprise
C/S ELEMENTS	PowerBuilder
Delphi Client/Server	Progress
Developer/2000	SQLWindows
DYNASTY	Superbase
Enfin/Object Studio	Team Enterprise Developer
ESL	UNIFACE
Forte	Unify VISION
GEMBASE	Visual Basic
INFORMIX-New Era	Visual dBASE

client/server environment

A networking environment that is made up of clients and servers running applications designed for client/server architecture. See *client/server*.

client/server network

(1) A communications network that uses dedicated servers. In this context, the term is used to contrast it with a *peer-to-peer network*, which allows any client to also be a server.

(2) A network that is processing applications designed for client/server architecture. See *client/server*.

client/server protocol

A communications protocol that provides a structure for requests between client and server in a network. It refers to OSI layer 7.

client-side

Refers to any operation that is performed at the client workstation. Contrast with *server-side*.

CLINKS

(Connectors are the weakest **LINKS**) The first devices to be checked when the network fails are the plugs and sockets. All networks should be constructed with CLINKS as the golden rule. Coined by American Business Telephones, Inc.

clip art

A set of canned images used to illustrate word processing and desktop publishing documents.

clipboard

A reserved section of memory that is used as a temporary holding area when you copy and paste or cut and paste from one application to another. After you copy or cut data from your application, it is viewable in the clipboard. If you cut data from an application and do not paste it into another, and you do not save the clipboard's contents as a file, then the data is gone.

Clipper

(1) See *CA-Clipper*.

(2) A family of 32-bit RISC microprocessors from Intergraph that were used in earlier graphics workstations.

(3) A cryptography chip endorsed by the U.S. government for general use that would let authorities unscramble the data if needed.

clipping

Cutting off the outer edges or boundaries of a word, signal or image. In rendering an image, clipping removes any objects or portions thereof that are not visible on screen. See *scissoring*.

clipping level

A disk's ability to maintain its magnetic properties and hold its content. A high-quality level range is 65-70%; low quality is below 55%.

clobbering memory

Erroneously writing into an area of memory that contains instructions and data that are still being worked on. See *memory* and *memory allocation*.

clock

An internal timing device. Using a quartz crystal, the CPU clock breathes life into the CPU by feeding it a constant flow of pulses. For example, a 200MHz CPU receives 200 million pulses per second. Similarly, in a communications device, the clock synchronizes the data pulses between sender and receiver.

A realtime clock keeps track of the time of day and makes this data available to the software. A timesharing clock interrupts the CPU at regular intervals and allows the operating system to divide its time between active users and/or applications. See *per clock*.

clock battery

See *CMOS battery*.

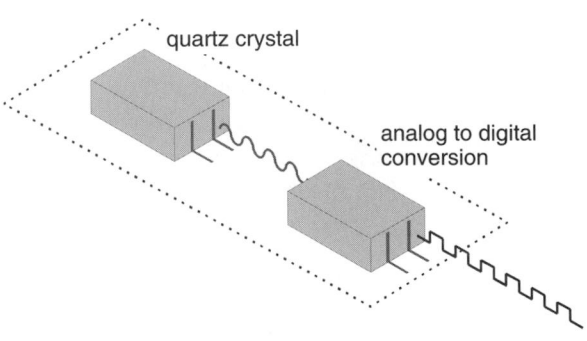

quartz crystal

analog to digital conversion

The CPU Clock
The quartz crystal generates continuous waves, which are converted into digital pulses.

clock/calendar

An internal time clock and month/year calendar that is kept active with a battery. Its output allows software to remind users of appointments, to determine the age of a transaction and to activate tasks at specified times.

clock doubling

Doubling the internal processing speed of a CPU while maintaining the original clock speed for I/O (transfers in/out of the chip). Intel popularized the technique with its Speed Doubler chips. See *486* and *clock tripling*.

clock pulse

A signal used to synchronize the operations of an electronic system. Clock pulses are continuous, precisely spaced changes in voltage. See *clock speed*.

clock speed

The internal heartbeat of a computer. The clock circuit uses fixed vibrations generated from a quartz crystal to deliver a steady stream of pulses to the CPU. See *Mhz*.

clock tick

One increment, or pulse, of the CPU clock. See *clock speed*.

clock tripling

Tripling the internal processing speed of a CPU while maintaining the original clock speed for I/O (transfers in/out of the chip). See *DX4*.

clone

A device that works like the original, but does not necessarily look like it. It implies 100% functional compatibility. See *cloning software*.

cloning software

Software that copies the full image of a hard disk to another machine via direct cable or the network. Cloning saves time setting up new machines by eliminating the installation of the operating system and each individual application.

close

To disengage a disk or tape file that has been opened for reading and writing. The close procedure generally prompts the user to save any changes made to the disk before it releases the file. Contrast with *open*.

closed

With regard to a switch, closed is "on." Open is "off."

closed architecture

A system whose technical specifications are not made public. Contrast with *open architecture*.

closed shop

An environment in which only data processing staff is allowed access to the computer. Contrast with *open shop*.

closed system

A system in which specficiations are kept proprietary to prevent third-party hardware or software from being used. Contrast with *open system*.

cloud

See *network cloud*.

CLSID

(CLasS ID) The identification of a COM object. Applications that support Microsoft's COM architecture register their objects as class IDs (CLSIDs). See *COM*.

cluster

(1) Also called an *allocation unit*, it is some number of disk sectors that are treated as a unit. This is the smallest unit of storage the operating system can manage. For example, on a PC with a 200MB hard disk, the smallest cluster is eight sectors (8 x 512 bytes) or 4K. On a 2GB disk, the cluster is 32K. That means a 1K file takes up 32K on the disk, wasting an inordinate amount of space. In mid 1996, Windows 95 installed on new PCs introduced a 32-bit file allocation table (FAT32), which decreased the cluster size to 4K. See *FAT32, OSR2* and *lost cluster*.

Following are the cluster sizes that DOS/Windows uses starting with DOS 4.0. The disk size is the partition size. One physical hard disk may have multiple partitions; for example, C: and D: could be on the same hard disk.

```
FAT16
Disk Size              Cluster Size
   0 -   127MB            2K
 128 -   255MB            4K
 256 -   511MB            8K
 512 - 1023MB            16K
1024 - 2047MB            32K


FAT32
   0 - 8181MB             4K
```

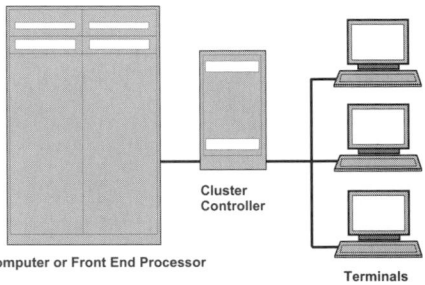

Cluster
Controller

Computer or Front End Processor

Terminals

(2) Two or more systems working together. See *clustering*.

cluster controller

A control unit that manages several peripheral devices, such as terminals or disk drives.

clustering

Using two or more systems that work together. It generally refers to multiple computer systems that are linked together in order to handle variable workloads or to provide continued operation in the event one fails. Each computer may be a multiprocessor system itself. For example, a cluster of four computers, each with four CPUs, would provide a total of 16 CPUs processing simultaneously.

Cluster Server

See *Microsoft Cluster Server*.

CLUT

(Color Look Up Table) See *color palette*.

CLV

(Constant Linear Velocity) Rotating a disk at varying speeds. By changing speed depending on which track is being accessed, the density of bits in each track can be made uniform. This allows the outer tracks to hold more data than the inner tracks and fully utilizes the disk space. CLV is used on optical media such as CDs and DVDs. In practice, the rotation does not change precisely from every track to the next. A data buffer provides some flexibility for changing speed across some number of tracks.

Zoned CLV (Z-CLV) breaks the disk into several zones (typically 24 on a DVD-RAM disk) and changes the speed within each zone rather than uniformly across the entire platter. Contrast with *CAV*.

CM

See *configuration management*.

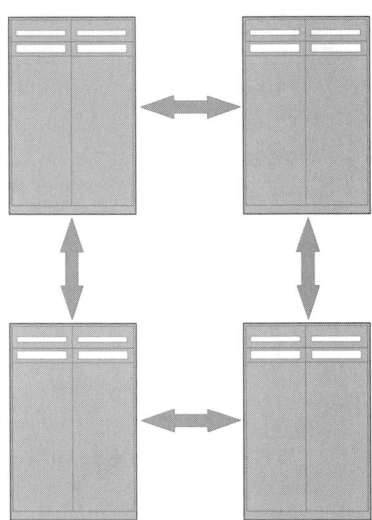

Clustering

A cluster of computer systems provides fault tolerance and load balancing. If one system fails, one or more additional systems are still available. Load balancing distributes the workload over multiple systems.

Computer Desktop Encyclopedia

CM/2

(Communications Manager/2) A communications program for OS/2 from IBM that provides terminal emulation to IBM mainframes, AS/400s and VAXes and supports APPN and APPC protocols.

CMC

(Common Messaging Calls) A programming interface specified by the XAPIA as the standard messaging API for X.400 and other messaging systems. CMC is intended to provide a common API for applications that want to become mail enabled.

CMI

(Computer-Managed Instruction) Using computers to organize and manage an instructional program for students. It helps create test materials, tracks the results and monitors student progress.

CMIP

(Common Management Information Protocol) Pronounced "C-mip." A network monitoring and control standard from ISO. CMOT (CMIP over TCP) is a version that runs on TCP/IP networks, and CMOL (CMIP over LLC) runs on IEEE 802 LANs (Ethernet, Token Ring, etc.).

CMIS

(Common Management Information Services) Pronounced "C-miss." An OSI standard that defines the functions for network monitoring and control.

CMM

(Capability Maturity Model) See *SEI*.

CMOL

See *CMIP*.

CMOS

(1) (Complementary MOS) Pronounced "C moss." The most widely-used type of integrated circuit for digital processors and memories. Virtually everything is CMOS today. Even mainframe CPUs are CMOS based. CMOS uses PMOS and NMOS transistors wired together in a certain manner that causes less power to be used than PMOS-only or NMOS-only circuits. See *PMOS* and *NMOS*.

(2) See *CMOS memory*.

CMOS based

An integrated circuit fabricated using CMOS technology. Most logic chips and CPU chips have been CMOS based for some time. Even mainframes, which have used ultra-fast bipolar chip technology in the past, are giving way to CMOS-based models. See *Parallel Enterprise Server*.

CMOS battery

A battery that maintains the time, date, hard disk and other configuration settings in the CMOS memory. See *CMOS setup*.

CMOS machine

See *Parallel Enterprise Server* and *Multiprise*.

CMOS mainframes

See *Parallel Enterprise Server* and *Multiprise*.

CMOS memory

(1) A small, battery-backed memory bank in a personal computer that holds configuration settings. See *CMOS setup*.

(2) Memory made of CMOS. See *CMOS*.

CMOS RAM

See *CMOS memory*.

CMOS setup

A small, battery-backed memory bank in a personal computer that holds configuration settings such as drive types, port speeds and modes, time, date and other system information. In a PC, if disk drives are added, removed or changed, the parameters in the CMOS memory must be updated in order for the operating system to recognize the new devices. Although newer PCs can detect new drives and update their CMOS memory automatically, older ones require manual editing.

The BIOS allows editing of the CMOS settings at startup. Immediately after turning the machine on, a message is displayed such as "Press Del for Setup," which informs you which key to press to enter the CMOS setup area. If there is no message on screen, refer to your system manual (RTFM!). Some of the CMOS settings are quite arcane and only changed by experienced technicians. See *hard disk configuration*.

CMOT

See *CMIP*.

CMS

(1) (Conversational Monitor System) Software that provides interactive communications for IBM's VM operating system. It allows a user or programmer to launch an application from a terminal and interactively work with it. The CMS counterpart in MVS is called TSO. Contrast with *RSCS*, which provides batch communications for VM.

(2) (Call Management System) An AT&T call accounting package for its PBXs.

(3) See *color management system*.

CMYK

(Cyan Magenta Yellow blacK) The color model used for printing. In theory, cyan, magenta and yellow (CMY) can print all colors, but inks are not pure and black comes out muddy. Black ink is required for quality printing. See *colors* and *RGB*.

CNA

(Certified NetWare Administrator) See *NetWare certification*.

CNC

(Computerized Numerical Control) See *numerical control*.

CNE

(Certified NetWare Engineer) See *NetWare certification*.

CNI

(1) (Certified NetWare Instructor) See *NetWare certification*.

(2) (Coalition for Networked Information, Washington, DC, www.cni.org) A partnership of the Association of Research Libraries, CAUSE and EDUCOM, founded in 1990. Its mission is to advance education and intellectual productivity by the use of high-performance networks and computers.

CO

See *central office*.

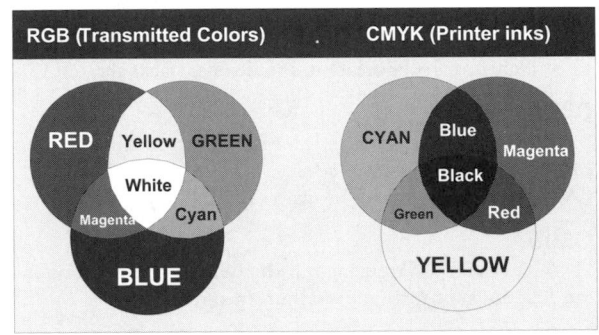

Color Mixing Methods

The two major methods for creating colors are RGB and CMY. RGB uses red, green and blue to create transmitted colors. CMY uses cyan, magenta and yellow to create printed colors. In theory, equal parts of cyan, magenta and yellow ink make black, but the blacks tend to be muddy. Thus, a pure black fourth ink is always used. This is the four color process, called CMYK (K for blacK).

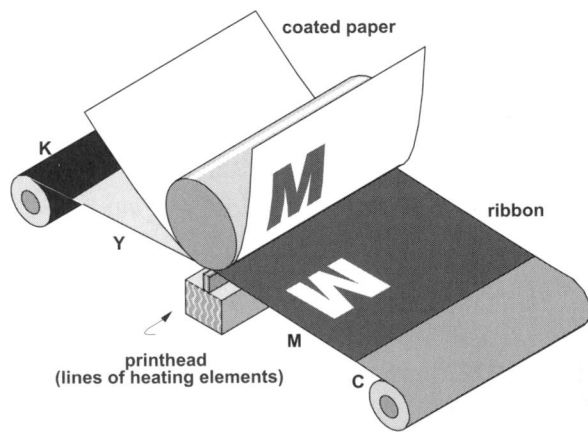

CMYK Ribbon

This diagram shows a four-color dye sublimation or thermal wax transfer ribbon. There is a panel of dye or wax-based ink for each of the CMYK colors. In these printing technologies, the ribbon panels are as large as the page that is printed.

coax adapter

Same as *3270 emulator*. The board is sometimes called a coax adapter because of its coaxial cable connection to the IBM cluster controller.

coaxial cable (coax)

A high-capacity cable used in communications and video, commonly called co-ax. It contains an insulated solid or stranded wire surrounded by a solid or braided metallic shield, wrapped in a plastic cover. Fire-safe teflon coating is optional.

Although similar in appearance, there are several types of coaxial cable, each designed with a different width and impedance for a particular purpose (TV, baseband, broadband). Coax provides a higher bandwidth than twisted wire pair. See *cable categories*.

main wire

insulation

ground

insulation

Coaxial Cable
Coax is a two-wire cable. The inner wire is the primary conductor, and the metal sheath is used for ground.

COB

See *chip on board*.

COBOL

(COmmon Business Oriented Language) A high-level programming language that has been the primary business application language on mainframes and minis. It is a compiled language and was one of the first high-level languages developed. Formally adopted in 1960, it stemmed from a language called Flowmatic in the mid 1950s.

COBOL is a very wordy language. Although mathematical expressions can also be written like other programming languages (see example below), its verbose mode is very readable for a novice. For example, **multiply hourly-rate by hours-worked giving gross-pay** is self-explanatory. COBOL is structured into the following divisions:

```
Division name     Contains
IDENTIFICATION    Program identification.
ENVIRONMENT       Types of computers used.
DATA              Buffers, constants, work areas.
PROCEDURE         The processing (program logic).
```

The following COBOL example converts a Fahrenheit number to Celsius. To keep the example simple, it performs the operation on the operator's terminal rather than a user terminal.

```
IDENTIFICATION DIVISION.
PROGRAM-ID.   EXAMPLE.

ENVIRONMENT DIVISION.
CONFIGURATION SECTION.
SOURCE-COMPUTER.   IBM-370.
OBJECT-COMPUTER.   IBM-370.

DATA DIVISION.
WORKING-STORAGE SECTION.
77 FAHR   PICTURE 999.
77 CENT   PICTURE 999.

PROCEDURE DIVISION.
DISPLAY 'Enter Fahrenheit ' UPON CONSOLE.
ACCEPT FAHR FROM CONSOLE.
COMPUTE CENT = (FAHR- 32) * 5 / 9.
DISPLAY 'Celsius is ' CENT UPON CONSOLE.
GOBACK.
```

IBM COBOLs

In 1994, IBM dropped support of OS/VS COBOL, which conforms to ANSI 68 and ANSI 74 standards and limits a program's address space to 16 bits. IBM's VS COBOL II (1984) and COBOL/370 (1991) conform to ANSI 85 standards and provide 31-bit addressing, which allows programs to run "above the line."

COBOL/370 is more compliant with AD/Cycle, has more string, math and date functions, including four-digit years, allows development through a PC window and provides enhanced runtime facilities.

COBOL Workbench

See *Micro Focus*.

CobWeb

(1) A Web page that has not been updated in a long time.

(2) A Web page that is rarely downloaded because the references to it are obscure or the subject is simply uninteresting.

Coda

(1) Web authoring software from RandomNoise, Inc., San Francisco, CA, (www.randomnoise.com). It is used to generate very sophisticated Web sites that are built in Java rather than HTML codes. The client plug-in is expected to be included with the major browsers. Coda itself is written in Java.

(2) A software company based in the U.K. that produces accounting software for mainframes, VAX and client/server environments. The parent company is the Coda Group, Plc. with U.S. offices in Manchester, NH.

CODASYL

(COnference on DAta SYstems Languages) An organization founded in 1959 by the U.S. Department of Defense. It evolved into a variety of volunteer committees and ultimately disbanded by the mid 1990s. CODASYL was widely known for its definition of COBOL, but it was also involved with the network database model and the data description language (DDL) for defining database schemas.

code

(1) A set of machine symbols that represents data or instructions. See *data code* and *machine language*.

(2) Any representation of one set of data for another. For example, a parts code is an abbreviated name of a product, product type or category. A discount code is a percentage.

(3) To write a program. See *source code* and *lines of code*.

(4) To encode for security purposes. See *cryptography*.

codec

(COder-DECoder or COmpressor/DECompressor) A hardware circuit that converts analog sound, speech or video to digital code. It typically includes both analog to digital and digital to analog conversion (coder/decoder) as well as compression and decompression (compressor/decompressor).

A codec may provide only the A/D and D/A conversion (coder/decoder) or just the compression and decompression (compressor/decompressor). However, if the codec is used for general-purpose data compression such as for text and graphics files, it typically refers to software rather than a chip. See *audio codec, speech codec, video codec* and *data compression*.

code density

The amount of space that an executable program takes up in memory. Code density is important in PDAs and hand-held devices that contain a limited amount of memory. See *Thumb*.

code generator

See *application generator* and *macro recorder*.

code name

An internal name given to a product under development. For example, Chicago was the code name for Windows 95.

code page

In DOS 3.3 and higher, a table that sets up the keyboard and display characters for various foreign languages.

coder

(1) A junior, or trainee, programmer who writes simple programs or writes the code for a larger program that has been designed by someone else.

(2) Person who assigns special codes to data.

Computer Desktop Encyclopedia

CodeView

A Microsoft debugger for programs written with Microsoft C and CodeView-compatible compilers. Like other modern debuggers, it links source and object program letting the programmer step through the source code as the program is executed.

coercivity

On magnetic media, the amount of electrical energy required to change the polarization of a bit. The coercivity of hard disks ranges from 500 to 2000 Oersted. On magneto-optic media, it takes between 5000 to 10,000 Oersted. See *Oersted*.

COFF

(Common Object File Format) A UNIX System V machine language format.

Cognos

(Cognos Inc., Ottawa, Canada, www.cognos.com) A software company that specializes in application development and 4GL tools. Founded in 1969 as a consulting firm, its PowerHouse 4GL was introduced in the late 1970s for midrange systems. Products include the PowerPlay EIS/DSS system, Impromptu report and query language and Axiant client/server development system.

COGO

(COordinate GeOmetry) A programming language used for solving civil engineering problems.

COLD

(Computer Output to LaserDisc) Archiving large volumes of transactions on optical media. Instead of printing large paper reports or producing microfilm or microfiche, data is stored on optical disks. The advantage of COLD over COM (Computer Output Microfilm) for high-volume, archival storage is that optical disks can be directly accessed just like a hard disk.

cold boot

Starting the computer by turning power on. Turning power off and then back on again clears memory and many internal settings. Some program failures will lock up the computer and require a cold boot to use the computer again. In other cases, only a warm boot is required. See *boot, warm boot* and *clean boot*.

ColdFire

A 680x0 CPU architecture from Motorola that has been specialized for embedded systems. It is faster and smaller than previous 680x0 chips and also contains fewer instructions. ColdFire is targeted for use in consumer electronics devices.

cold fusing

See *fusing*.

Cold Fusion

An application development tool from Allaire Corporation, Cambridge, MA, (www.allaire.com), for writing Web pages that interact with databases. Instead of writing tedious CGI and Perl scripts, operations are coded in the Cold Fusion Markup Language as tags embedded in the Web pages. The Cold Fusion engine, which interfaces with a Windows-based Web server, interprets the codes, accesses the database and delivers the results as HTML pages for the Web browser.

cold start

Same as *cold boot*.

collaboration products

See *e-mail, groupware, data conferencing* and *videoconferencing*.

collaborative browsing

Synchronizing browser access to the same sites. As one user browses the Web, the other users trail along automatically and link to and view the same pages from their browsers.

collapsed backbone

A network configuration that provides a backbone in a centralized location, to which all subnetworks are attached. A collapsed backbone is implemented in a router or switch that uses a high-speed backplane that can handle the simultaneous traffic of all or most all of its ports at full wire speed. See *router* for illustration.

collating sequence
The sequence, or order, of the character set built into a computer. See *ASCII*.

collator
(1) A punched card machine that merges two decks of cards into one or more stacks.

(2) A utility program that merges records from two or more files into one file.

collector
One side of a bipolar transistor. When the base is pulsed, current flows from the emitter to the collector, or vice versa depending on the design. See *drain*.

collision detection
See *CSMA/CD*.

co-location
Placing equipment owned by a customer or competitor in an organization's own facility. Telephone companies often allow co-location in order to provide the best interconnection between devices.

color bits
The number of bits associated with each pixel that represent its color. See *bit depth*.

color calibration
The matching of colors to a base color, such as a Pantone color, or from one device to another; for example, screen and printer output.

color cycling
In computer graphics, a technique that simulates animation by continuously changing colors rather than moving the objects. Also called *color lookup table animation*.

color depth
Same as *bit depth*.

color gamut
The entire range of colors available on a particular device such as a monitor or printer. A monitor, which displays RGB signals, has a much greater color gamut than a printer, which uses CMYK inks. See *color management system*.

color graphics
The ability to display graphic images in colors.

color key
(1) A technique for superimposing a video image onto another. For example, to float a car on the ocean, the car image is placed onto a blue background. The car and ocean images are scanned together. The ocean is made to appear in the resulting image wherever background (blue) exists in the car image. The ocean is cancelled wherever the car appears (no background).

(2) In prepress, a high-quality sample of printed output that is used as a comp for the customer and a guide for the printer. It is made by exposing the CMYK negatives onto four acetate films which are developed. When overlaid on top of each other, they simulate the printed results. See *match print*.

color lookup table
See *color palette*.

color management system
Software that translates the colors of an original image into the truest representation obtainable on the output device. Color management works from a profile of the output device, typically a digital printer or offset press, and works backward to the source of the material such as a scanner.

Starting from the colors in real life, the color gamut decreases as it moves to analog film to a digital scanner to a printer. A monitor is also capable of displaying a greater range of colors than the printing process. Color management takes all of these factors into consideration.

color map
See *color palette*.

color mode
See *bit depth* and *color model*.

color model
A system used to represent color for display and printing. See *RGB, CIE, CMYK, HSV, HLS* and *YIQ*.

color palette
Also called a *color lookup table, lookup table, index map, color table* or *color map*, it is a commonly-used method for saving file space when creating 8-bit color images. Instead of each pixel containing its own red, green and blue values, which would require 24 bits, each pixel holds an 8-bit value, which is an index number into the color palette. The color palette contains 256 predefined RGB values from 0 to 255.

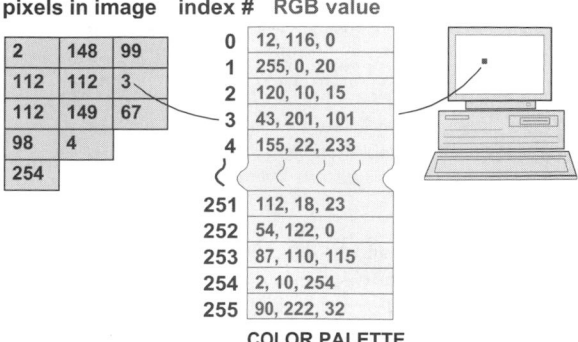

pixels in image   index #   RGB value

index #	RGB value
0	12, 116, 0
1	255, 0, 20
2	120, 10, 15
3	43, 201, 101
4	155, 22, 233
251	112, 18, 23
252	54, 122, 0
253	87, 110, 115
254	2, 10, 254
255	90, 222, 32

COLOR PALETTE

Color Palette Index
The pixels in the image contain an index number, which points to the RGB value in the color palette. The RGB values are the ones use by the display system.

Two or more 256-color (8 bit) images generally cannot display correctly side by side on a 256-color display, because there are too many colors for the system to handle. If the images have very similar colors, there may be little discrepancy, but if they are different, one or more images will suffer. The remedy is to average the palettes in an image editor or to reduce the number of colors to 128 for each (7 bit) image. See *bit depth*.

color plasma
See *plasma display*.

color printer
A printer that prints in color using three (CMY) or four (CMYK) colors of ink, toner or dye. Four color ribbons have been used in dot matrix printers, but these are rare today. See *printer*.

colors
The perception of the different wavelengths of light. It is possible to create almost all visible colors using two systems of primary colors. Transmitted colors use red, green and blue (RGB), and reflected colors use cyan (light blue), magenta (purplish-red), yellow and black (CMYK). Color displays use RGB (colors are added to create white) and color printing uses CMYK (colors are subtracted to create white).

color separation
Separating a picture by colors in order to make negatives and plates for color printing. The four-color process requires four separations: cyan, magenta, yellow and black (CMYK). See *OPI* and *DCS*.

color space
A 3-D model of the three attributes of a color, which are hue, value and saturation (chroma).

color space conversion
Changing one color signal into another. It typically refers to converting YUV analog video into digital RGB video. See *YUV*.

ColorSpan
(ColorSpan Corporation, Eden Prarie, MN, www.colorspan.com) A manufacturer of wide-format color printers. Founded in 1985 as LaserMaster Corporation, it was originally involved in high-resolution upgrades for LaserJet printers, followed by a line of laser printers and plain paper imagesetters. In 1997, it changed its name to focus on its line of wide-format ink jet printers that it introduced in 1993.

color table
See *color palette*.

column

A vertical set of data or components. Contrast with *row*.

column move

Relocating a rectangular block of characters within a text document or a column in a spreadsheet.

COM

(1) (Component Object Model) A component software architecture from Microsoft, which defines a structure for building program routines (objects) that can be called up and executed in a Windows environment. This capability is built into Windows 95/98 and Windows NT 4.0. Parts of Windows itself and Microsoft's own applications are also built as COM objects. COM provides the interfaces between objects, and Distributed COM (DCOM) allows them to run remotely. COM is used in the following ways.

COM Objects

COM objects can be small or large. They can be written in several programming languages, and they can perform any kind of processing. A program can call the object whenever it needs its services. Objects can be run remotely (DCOM) over the network in a distributed objects environment. Depending on their usage, COM objects are also called *ActiveX components* as Microsoft increasingly uses the term ActiveX for its component architecture.

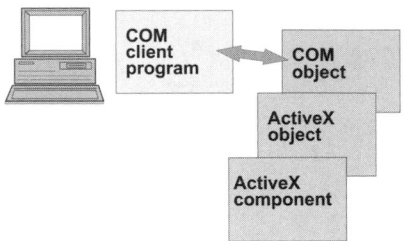

STAND-ALONE MACHINE (CLIENT or SERVER)

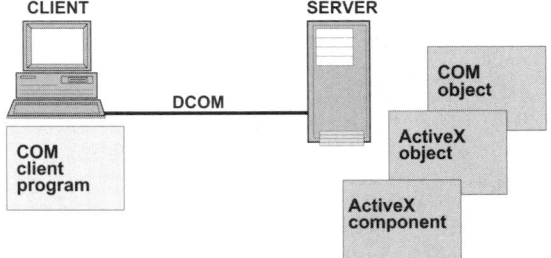

DISTRIBUTED OBJECTS (RUN OVER THE NETWORK)

COM Objects

Any kind of program, small or large, can be written as a COM object. It can be run locally or remotely via DCOM. The terms COM object, ActiveX object and ActiveX component are synonymous.

Automation (OLE automation, ActiveX automation)

Standard applications, such as word processors and spreadsheets, can be written to expose their internal functions as COM objects, allowing them to be "automated" instead of manually selected from a menu. For example, a script could be written to extract data from a database, summarize and chart it in a spreadsheet and place the results into a text document. See *COM automation*.

Controls (OLE controls, ActiveX controls)

Applications can invoke COM objects, called *controls*, that blend in and become just another part of the program. An industry of third-party, ready-made controls for the Windows programmer has been created. ActiveX controls can also be downloaded from the Internet to make a Web page perform any kind of processing. See *ActiveX control*.

Compound Documents and ActiveX Documents

Microsoft's OLE compound documents are based on COM, which lets one document be embedded within or linked to another (see *OLE*). ActiveX Documents are extensions to OLE that allow a Web browser, for example, to view not only Web pages, but any kind of document (see *ActiveX Documents*).

Programming Interfaces

Increasingly, Microsoft is making its standard programming interfaces conform to the COM object model so that there is continuity between all interfaces. See *DAO, ADO* and *OLE DB*.

It's Confusing

Microsoft first used the term OLE to refer to its COM-based architecture, then later dropped that designation in favor of ActiveX. Since both OLE and ActiveX are based on COM, the term COM is also used. As a result, any combination of the words COM, OLE and ActiveX followed by the words control, object and component may mean the same thing, or they may not, depending on context.

(2) (Computer Output Microfilm) Creating microfilm or microfiche from the computer. A COM machine receives print-image output from the computer either online or via tape or disk and creates a film image of each page.

COM+

Enhancements to the Microsoft Component Object Model (COM) that enable programmers to develop COM objects more easily. For example, COM+ allows native C++ calls to be translated into the correct COM call. In addition, instead of defining COM interfaces in the traditional IDL language, they can be defined by more familiar programming syntax.

COM1

In a PC, the logical name assigned to the first serial port. Two serial ports, or COM ports, are provided on a PC to connect a mouse and modem. Typically the mouse is on COM1, and the modem on COM2, but this is not mandatory. Any serial device can be connected to either serial port.

The COM1 and COM2 names are used to inform the operating system of the physical connections that have been made. The term originated before the days of the mouse, when the serial port was primarily used for modem COMmunications.

DOS versions up to 3.2 support COM1 and COM2. Starting with Version 3.3, DOS supports up to COM4, and Windows 95/98 supports COM5 and higher. Contrast with *LPT1*.

COM/ActiveX

Refers to Microsoft's component software, which is based on COM objects. ActiveX technologies are based on COM; however, ActiveX is also used as an umbrella term for COM objects.

COM automation

A particular usage of Microsoft's COM-based component software architecture that lets applications expose their internal functions as COM objects. Called *automation, OLE automation* or *ActiveX automation*, it enables tasks that are normally selected from menus to be "automated." For example, a small script could be written to extract data from a database, put it into a spreadsheet, summarize and chart it, all without manual intervention.

Virtually any internal routine can be written as a COM object and its interfaces exposed to other programs. Microsoft applications such as Word and Excel are written as COM objects, and not only do they allow their functions to be automated, but they offer programmers a toolbox of functions that can save them the time and effort of writing similar routines themselves.

combo box

A combination text box and list box. It normally displays as a single line item, but can be opened into a list by clicking its arrow.

COMDEX

(SOFTBANK COMDEX, Needham, MA, www.comdex.com) A trade show originally created for computer dealers and distributors.

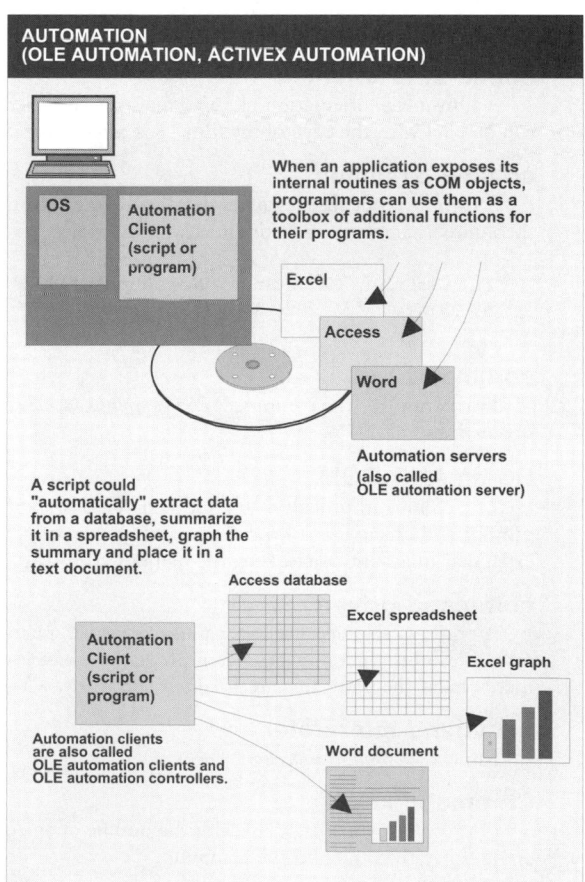

**AUTOMATION
(OLE AUTOMATION, ACTIVEX AUTOMATION)**

OS
Automation Client (script or program)

When an application exposes its internal routines as COM objects, programmers can use them as a toolbox of additional functions for their programs.

Excel
Access
Word

Automation servers (also called OLE automation server)

A script could "automatically" extract data from a database, summarize it in a spreadsheet, graph the summary and place it in a text document.

Access database

Excel spreadsheet

Excel graph

Automation Client (script or program)

Automation clients are also called OLE automation clients and OLE automation controllers.

Word document

COMDEX stands for Computer Dealers Exposition; however, large numbers of end users attend. COMDEX was originally developed by The Interface Group, which was acquired by the Japanese SOFTBANK Corporation in 1995. The first COMDEX/Fall in 1979 had 157 exhibitors and 4,000 attendees. Now, more than 2,000 exhibitors and 200,000 people attend each year.

COMDEX/Spring, which began in 1981 with 237 exhibitors and 11,000 attendees, is about half the size of COMDEX/Fall.

COMDEX/Fall in Las Vegas takes over the entire city and is the largest computer show in the U.S. Housed in both major convention centers and several hotels, shuttle buses escort attendees between sites. Waiting in a long line for a bus can become a welcome relief after walking the massive corridors of COMDEX. COMDEX Las Vegas is exhausting, and fascinating.

Comdisco

(Comdisco, Inc., Rosemont, IL, www.comdisco.com) A technology services company, originally founded as Computer Discount Company in 1969 by Ken Pontikes. It is the largest independent computer and network equipment leasing company and a leader in network services, asset management and business continuity services. By 1997, Comdisco provided help for more than 250 disaster recovery incidents.

Comensa

A datacenter control system from MAXM Systems Corporation, McLean, VA, (www.maxm.com), that is used to monitor a variety of minicomputers and mainframes. It can set off audio alarms if problems occur.

COM file

(1) (COMmand file) An executable DOS or OS/2 program that takes up less than 64K and fits within one segment. It is an exact replica of how it looks in memory. See *EXE file*.

(2) A VMS file containing commands to be executed.

comic-strip oriented

A film-image orientation like a comic strip, in which the tops of the frames run parallel with the edge of the film. See *cine-oriented* for illustration.

comma delimited

A record layout that separates data fields with a comma and usually surrounds character data with quotes, for example:

```
"Pat Smith","Main St.","New Hope","PA","18950"
"K. Jones","34 8th Ave.","Syosset","NY","11724"
```

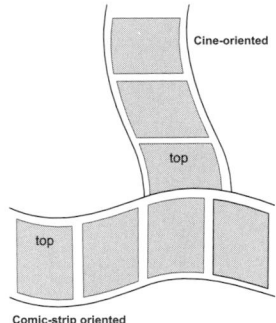

Comic-strip oriented

command

Instruction for the computer. See *command-driven, menu-driven* and *function*.

COMMAND.COM

The command processor in DOS and Windows 95/98. COMMAND.COM displays the DOS prompt and executes the DOS commands you type in. The COMMAND.COM in Windows has been expanded to accommodate long file names.

command-driven

A program that accepts commands as typed-in phrases. It is usually harder to learn, but may offer more flexibility than a menu-driven program. Once learned, command-driven programs may be faster to use, because the user can state a request succinctly. Contrast with *menu-driven*.

command interpreter

Same as *command processor*.

Command key

On Apple keyboards, a key with the outline of an Apple, a propeller, or both. It is pressed along with another key to command the computer.

command language

A special-purpose language that accepts a limited number of commands, such as a query language, job control language (JCL) or command processor. Contrast with *programming language*, which is a general purpose language.

command line

In a command-driven system, the area on screen that accepts typed-in commands.

command mode

An operating mode that causes the computer or modem to accept commands for execution.

command processor

A system program that accepts a limited number of user commands and converts them into the machine commands required by the operating system or some other control program or application. COMMAND.COM is the command processor that accompanies DOS. See *4DOS*.

command prompt

The symbol displayed in a command-driven system that indicates it is ready for user input. For example, in DOS, **C:\BUDGET>** would be the command prompt when the working drive is C: and the working directory is BUDGET.

command queuing

The ability to store multiple commands and execute them one at a time.

command set

Same as *instruction set*.

command shell

Same as *command processor*.

comment

A descriptive statement in a source language program that is used for documentation.

comment out

To disable lines of code in a program by surrounding them with comment-start and comment-stop characters.

commerce server

See *merchant server*.

commercial software

Software that is designed and developed for sale to the general public. See *software package*.

Commodore

One of the first personal computer companies. In 1977, Commodore Business Machines, West Chester, PA, introduced the PET computer and launched the personal computer industry along with Apple and Radio Shack. In 1982, it introduced the Commodore 64 (64K RAM) and later the Commodore 128. These were popular home computers, and over 10 million were sold.

In 1985, the Amiga series was introduced, which continued to offer advanced imaging and video capabilities at affordable prices. A line of IBM-compatible PCs were also introduced, but the Amiga series was Commodore's mainstay until May 1994, when it went into bankruptcy. See *Amiga*.

The Commodore PET
In 1977, the Commodore PET, Apple II and TRS-80 launched the personal computer industry. The $595 PET, which stood for Personal Electronic Transactor, contained its own tape cassette (on the left) and a whopping 12K of memory. *(Photo courtesy of Commodore Business Machines, Inc.)*

common carrier

A government-regulated organization that provides telecommunications services for public use, such as AT&T, the telephone companies, ITT, MCI and Western Union.

Common Gateway Interface

See *CGI script*.

Common Ground

Document exchange software from Hummingbird Communications, North York, Ontario, (www.hummingbird.com), that converts a Windows or Macintosh document into a proprietary file format for viewing on other machines. The viewer allows multiple documents to be displayed at the same time. The Common Ground file format is called DigitalPaper.

Common OS API

A specification for a standard UNIX programming interface endorsed in 1993 by major UNIX vendors. It led to Spec 1170, which led to the Single UNIX Specification.

comm port

May refer to any serial communications port or specifically to the serial ports on a PC. See *COM1*.

comm program

See *communications program*.

communications

The electronic transfer of information from one location to another. *Data communications* refers to digital transmission, and *telecommunications* refers to analog and digital transmission, including voice and video.

The Protocol

The way communications systems "talk to" each other is defined in a set of standards called *protocols*. Protocols work in a hierarchy starting at the top with the user's program and ending at the bottom with the plugs, sockets and electrical signals. See *communications protocol* and *OSI*.

Personal Computer Communications

Personal computer communications takes several forms.

Via Modem

Data can be transferred between two distant personal computers by using modems, a telephone line and a communications program in each computer.

Between Two Computers

Data can be transferred between two local computers by cabling them together with a null modem cable and a file transfer program in each computer.

As a Remote Terminal

Personal computers can act like a remote terminal to a mini or mainframe. For example, a 3270 emulation board, such as Attachmate's Irma board, plugs into a personal computer and turns it into an IBM mainframe terminal.

On a Network

Personal computers can be part of a local area network (LAN), in which databases and printers are shared among users. If the LAN interconnects with mini and mainframe networks, then personal computers can communicate with larger computers.

Increasingly, LANs of personal computers are running applications previously delegated to minis and mainframes. These applications are designed as "client/server" applications, which duplicate the integrity, security and transaction processing requirements of the larger computers.

Minicomputer Communications

Minicomputer communications systems control as many as several hundred terminals connected to a single computer system. They support a variety of low-speed dial-up terminals and higher-speed local terminals. With larger minicomputers, the communications processing is handled in separate machines, called *communications controllers*.

Minicomputers are designed with communications in mind. The communications programs and operating systems are often integrated and provide simpler operation than mainframes.

Minicomputers can connect to a mainframe by emulating a mainframe terminal, in which case, the mainframe thinks it's talking to another user terminal. Minicomputers can connect directly to some LANs, or to all LANs via a gateway, which converts the protocols.

Mainframe Communications

Mainframe systems can control several thousand remote terminals. They support a variety of low-speed dial-up terminals and high-speed local terminals.

Large mainframes use separate machines, called *communications controllers* or *front end processors*, to handle the communications processing. These machines take the data from the mainframes and package it for transmission over the network. They also strip the communications codes from the incoming messages and send pure data to the mainframes for processing.

Mainframes set the standards for communications. It's usually up to the mini and micro vendors to provide compatibility with the mainframe systems.

Analog vs Digital Communications

The most common form of long-distance communications has been the telephone system, which, up until a few years ago, transmitted only voice frequencies. This technique, known as *analog* communications, has been error prone, because the electronic frequencies get mixed together with unwanted signals (noise) that are nearby.

In analog telephone networks, amplifiers are placed in the line every few miles to boost the signal, but they cannot distinguish between signal and noise. Thus, the noise is amplified along with the signal. By the time the receiving person or machine gets the signal, it may be impossible to decipher it.

In a *digital* network, only two (binary) distinct frequencies or voltages are transmitted. Instead of amplifiers, repeaters are used, which analyze the incoming signal and regenerate a new outgoing signal. Any noise on the line is filtered out at the next repeater. When data is made up of only two signals (0 and 1), it can be more easily distinguished from the garble. Digital is simple!

Communications Act

The establishment of the Federal Communications Commission (FCC) in 1934, the regulatory body for interstate and foreign telecommunications. Its mission is to provide high-quality services at reasonable cost to everyone in the U.S. on a nondiscriminatory basis.

communications channel

Also called a *circuit* or *line*, it is a pathway over which data is transferred between remote devices. It may refer to the entire physical medium, such as a telephone line, optical fiber, coaxial cable or twisted wire pair, or, it may refer to one of several carrier frequencies transmitted simultaneously within the line.

communications controller

A peripheral control unit that connects several communications lines to a computer and performs the actual transmitting and receiving as well as various message coding and decoding activities.

Communications controllers are typically nonprogrammable units designed for specific protocols and communications tasks. Contrast with *front end processor*, which can be programmed for a variety of protocols and network conditions.

communications network

The transmission channels interconnecting all client and server stations as well as all supporting hardware and software.

The First Analog Communications
In 1876, Alexander Graham Bell sent the first electronic communications over a wire when he said, "Mr. Watson, come here, I want to see you." *(Photo courtesy of AT&T.)*

communications parameters

The basic settings for modem transmission, which include bit rate (14400 bps, 28800 bps, etc.), parity (none, even, odd), number of data bits (7 or 8) and number of stop bits (typically 1). The latter three are often expressed together; for example, N-8-1, which means No parity, 8 data bits and 1 stop bit.

communications program

Software that manages the transmission of data between computers, typically via modem and the serial port. Such programs were very popular for connecting to BBSs before the Internet took off. Comm programs include several file transfer protocols and can also emulate dumb terminals for dialing into minis and mainframes. See *communications protocol*.

communications protocol

Hardware and software standards that govern transmission between two stations. On personal computers, communications programs offer a variety of protocols (Zmodem, Ymodem, Kermit, etc.) to transfer files via modem. Internet connections typically use a combination of PPP and TCP/IP.

On LANs, data link protocols such as Ethernet, Token Ring and FDDI provide the access method (OSI layers 1 and 2) that moves packets from station to station, and higher level protocols, such as TCP/IP, SPX/IPX and NetBIOS/NetBEUI (OSI layers 3, 4 and 5), to control and route the transmission.

The following is a conceptual exchange that would be managed by a communications protocol.

Are you there? **Yes, I am.** Are you ready to receive? **Yes, I am.** Here comes the message—bla, bla, bla— did you get it? **Yes, I did.** Here comes the next part— bla, bla, bla— did you get it? **No, I didn't.** Here it comes again— bla, bla, bla— did you get it? **Yes, I did.** There is no more. Goodbye. **Goodbye.**

communications satellite

A radio relay station in orbit above the earth that receives, amplifies and redirects analog and digital signals contained within a carrier frequency. There are three kinds. Geostationary (GEO) satellites are in ordbit 22,282 miles above the earth and rotate with the earth, thus appearing stationary. The downlink from GEOs back to earth can be localized into small areas or cover as much as a third of the earth's surface.

Low-earth orbit (LEO) satellites

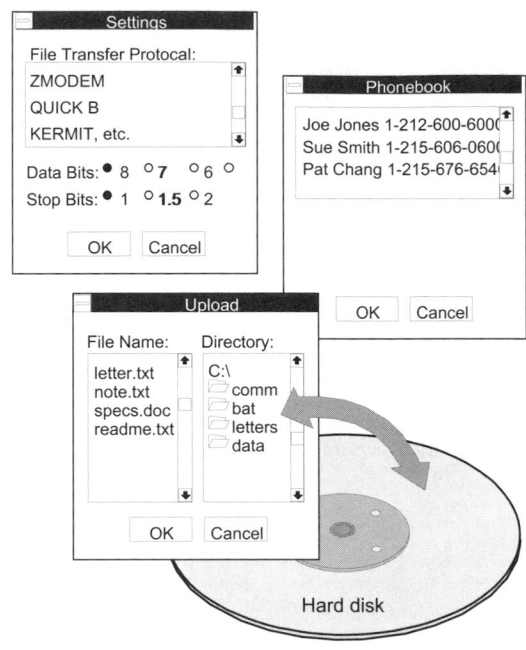

The Communications Program

All comm programs have facilities to (1) set the parameters for the transmission, (2) provide a phonebook for frequently dialed calls and (3) select appropriate files for uploading and downloading.

Communications Satellite

There are hundreds of commercial communications satellites in orbit providing services for both industry and consumers. By the 21st Century, it is expected that Internet access via satellite will be popular.

reside no more than 1,000 miles above the earth and revolve around the globe every couple of hours. They are only in view for a few minutes, and multiple LEOs are required to maintain continuous coverage. Medium-earth orbit (MEO) satellites are in the middle, taking about six hours to orbit the earth and in view for a couple of hours. See *Teledesic, Iridium, DSS* and *DirecPC*.

communications server

See *remote access server, modem server, terminal server* and *communications controller*.

Communicator

See *Netscape Communicator*.

COM object

A software component that conforms to Microsoft's Component Object Model (COM). See *COM*.

compact disc

See *CD*.

CompactFlash

A flash memory format from SanDisk Corporation, Sunnyvale, CA, (www.sandisk.com), that is about a third the size of a PC Card. It is electrically the same, but uses 50 pins instead of 68. It can plug into a CompactFlash socket, or with an adapter, into a standard Type II PC Card slot.

COMPACT II

A high-level numerical control programming language used to generate instructions for numerical control (machine tool) devices.

compandor

(COMpressor/exPANDOR) A device that improves the signal for AM radio transmission. On outgoing transmission, it raises the amplitude of weak signals and lowers the amplitude of strong signals. On incoming transmission, it restores the signal to its original form.

companies

See *hardware vendors, software vendors* and *online services*.

Compaq

(Compaq Computer Corporation, Houston, TX, www.compaq.com) The leading PC manufacturer founded in 1982 by Rod Canion, Jim Harris and Bill Murto. In 1983, it shipped 53,000 PC-compatible COMPAQ Portables, which resulted in $111 million in revenues and an American business record. The Portable's success was due to its rugged construction, ability to run all PC software and its semi-portability (it weighed 30 pounds!).

In 1984, it introduced its DESKPRO

Compaq's Founders
Canion, Harris and Murto (left to right) founded one of the most successful computer companies in the industry. *(Photo courtesy of Compaq Computer Corporation.)*

The Compaq Portable
The Compaq Portable was the first completely IBM-compatible PC. Its rugged construction and "luggability" made it a huge success. *(Photo courtesy of Compaq Computer Corporation.)*

desktop computers and achieved a computer-industry sales record in its second year. In 1986, it was the first to offer a 386-based machine. Throughout its history, Compaq has been well respected for its high-quality computer products and innovations. Maintaining this high profile kept it from initially competing with the mail order houses that were dramatically driving down prices in the 1990s. Compaq later became very competitive, and is now a leading vendor in the mass market chain stores.

In 1997, Compaq acquired Tandem Computers, the first company to build fault-tolerant computers from the ground up. Tandem brings Compaq a strong background in high-availability systems for mission critical applications. In 1998, Compaq acquired Digital Equipment Corporation, one of the oldest computer companies and pioneer of minicomputers in the 1960s. Digital's entree into major companies, plus its large service organization, adds a significant enterprise presence for Compaq.

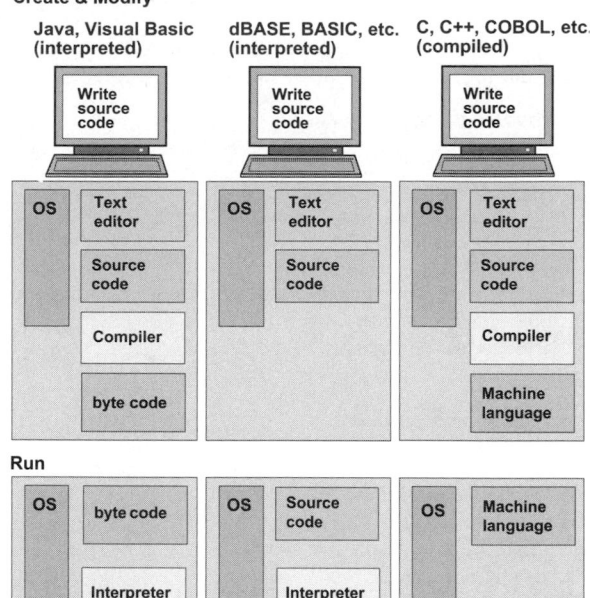

Compilers and Interpreters
Compiled programs (right) are translated into the machine language of the target computer. Interpreted programs (left and center) are either kept in their original source code or are precompiled into an intermediate form. In both cases, an interpreter is required to translate the program into machine language at runtime, whereas the compiled program is "ready to go."

comparator

A device that compares two quantities and determines their equality.

compare

A fundamental computer capability. By comparing one set of data with another, the computer can locate, analyze, select, reorder and make decisions. After comparing, the computer can indicate whether the data were equal or which set was numerically greater or less than the other. See *ASCII chart* and *computer*.

compatibility

See *standards*.

compatibility mode

A feature of a computer or operating system that allows it to run programs written for a different system. Programs often run slower in compatibility mode.

competitive access provider

See *CAP*.

compile

To translate a program written in a high-level programming language into machine language. See *compiler*.

compiler

(1) Software that translates a program written in a high-level programming language (COBOL, C, etc.) into machine language. A compiler usually generates assembly language first and then translates the assembly language into machine language.

The example on the next page compiles program statements into machine language.

```
Source code      Assembly Language    Machine language

IF COUNT=10      Compare A to B       Compare 3477 2883
  GOTO DONE      If equal go to C     If = go to 23883
   ELSE          Go to D              Go to 23343
  GOTO AGAIN
ENDIF
                 Actual machine code
                 10010101001010001010100
                 10101010010101001001010
                 10100101010001010010010
```

(2) Software that converts a set of high-level language statements into a lower-level representation. For example, a help compiler converts a text document embedded with appropriate commands into an online help system. A dictionary compiler converts terms and definitions into a dictionary lookup system.

compiler language
See *high-level language* and *compiler*.

compile time
The time it takes to translate a program from source language into machine language. Link editing time may also be included in compile time.

complement
The number derived by subtracting a number from a base number. For example, the tens complement of 8 is 2. In set theory, complement refers to all the objects in one set that are not in another set.

Complements are used in digital circuits, because it's faster to subtract by adding complements than by performing true subtraction. The binary complement of a number is created by reversing all bits and adding 1. The carry from the high-order position is eliminated. This example subtracts 5 from 8.

```
Decimal     Binary     Complement
   8         1000         1000
  -5        -0101        +1011
  ___       _____        _____
   3         0011         0011
```

complex data type
Any data that does not fall into the traditional field structure (alpha, numeric, dates) of a relational DBMS. Examples of complex data types are bills of materials, word processing documents, maps, time-series, images and video. In a relational DBMS, complex data types are stored in a LOB, but either the client application or some middleware is required to process the data. In an object DBMS or an object-relational DBMS, complex data types are stored as objects that are integrated into and activated by the DBMS.

complex instruction set computer
See *CISC*.

component
One element of a larger system. A hardware component can be a device as small as a transistor or as large as a disk drive as long as it is part of a larger system. Software components are routines or modules within a larger system. See *component software*.

component digital
The storage and transmission of digital video that keeps the red, green and blue data separate. Contrast with *composite digital*.

Component Object Model
See *COM*.

component software

Program modules that are designed to interoperate with each other at runtime. Components can be large or small. They can be written by different programmers using different development environments and they may or may not be platform independent. Components can be run in stand-alone machines, on a LAN, intranet or the Internet.

The terms component and object are used synonymously. Component architectures have risen out of object-oriented technologies, but the degree to which they comply to all the rules of object technology is often debated.

Component architectures may use a client/component model, in which the client application is designed as the container that holds the other components/objects. The client container is responsible for the user interface and coordinating mouse clicks and other inputs to all the components. A pure object model does not require a container. Any object can call any other without a prescribed hierarchy.

Component software implies the use of small modules that allow applications to be quickly customized. Rather than launch the huge, feature-rich applications in common use today, it is envisioned that users will run smaller, tighter applications in the future, calling in additional features (components) only when needed. See *COM, JavaBeans, CORBA* and *object technology*.

component video

The recording and transmission of video using separate red, green, blue and synchronization signals. Contrast with *composite video*.

COM port

A serial communications port on a PC. See *COM1* and *serial port*.

comport

See *COM port*.

composite black

The creation of black from cyan, magenta and yellow inks. Mixing inks is not a perfect operation, and composite black is often muddy. This is why a solid black fourth ink is used in professional printing (CMYK: Cyan, Magenta, Yellow, blacK).

composite digital

The storage and transmission of digital video that combines the red, green and blue data. Contrast with *component digital*.

composite video

The recording and transmission of video which mixes the red, green, blue and synchronization signals together. The RCA phono connector is commonly used for composite video on VCRs, camcorders and other consumer appliances. Contrast with *component video*.

STAND-ALONE MACHINE

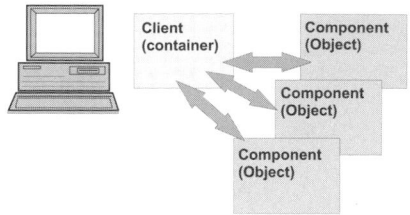

STORED REMOTELY, RUN LOCALLY

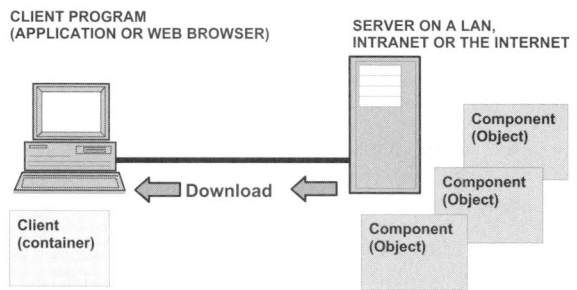

STORED REMOTELY, RUN REMOTELY

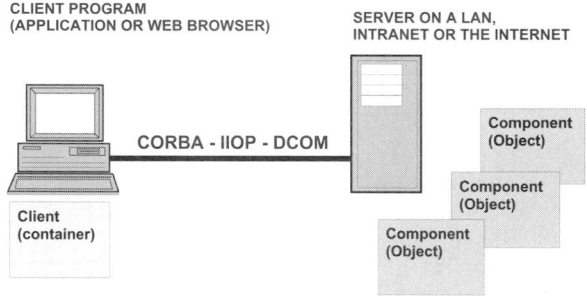

Where Components/Objects Are Run

compound document

A single document that contains a combination of data structures such as text, graphics, spreadsheets, sound and video clips. The document may embed the additional data types or reference external files by pointers of some kind. SGML and HTML are examples of compound document formats.

OLE and OpenDoc are examples of compound document architectures. They allow the user to edit each of the data objects by automatically calling in the application that created them.

compress

To compact data to save space. See *data compression*.

compression ratio

The measurement of compressed data. For example, a file compressed into 1/4th of its original size can be expressed as 4:1, 25%, 75% or 2 bits per byte. See *data compression*.

compression utility

A program such as PKZIP that compresses and decompresses files. See *data compression*.

compressor

(1) A device that diminishes the range between the strongest and weakest transmission signals. See *compandor*.

(2) A routine or program that compresses data. See *data compression*.

Compsurf

A NetWare utility that performs a high-level hard disk format. NetWare servers require their own proprietary format.

CompTIA

(Computing Technology Industry Association, Lombard, IL, www.comptia.org) Formerly ABCD:The Microcomputer Industry Association, it is a membership organization of resellers, distributors and manufacturers dedicated to business ethics and professionalism, founded in 1982. It sets voluntary guidelines and is involved with many issues including product returns, frieght and warranty claims and price protection.

CompTIA also provides certification for computer service technicians, known as A+, as well as for document imaging professionals with the Certified Document Imaging Architech (CDIA). Tests are administered worldwide. P.S. Architech is not a typo!

CompuServe

An online information service that provides access to the Internet, e-mail and a variety of databases. Access is via CompuServe's software, which is available for Windows and the Mac. Founded in 1980, CompuServe is one of the oldest online services. It developed the GIF graphics format, which is now widely used on the Internet. SPRYNET is CompuServe's Internet-only service. In 1998, CompuServe was acquired by America Online.

When sending e-mail to a CompuServe customer via the Internet, the comma in the CompuServe account number is turned into a dot; for example, account 71020,1560 becomes **71020.1560@compuserve.com**. See *online services*.

compute

To perform mathematical operations or general computer processing. For an explanation of "The 3 C's," or how the computer processes data, see *computer*.

compute bound

Same as *process bound*.

computer

A general-purpose machine that processes data according to a set of instructions that are stored internally either temporarily or permanently. The computer and all equipment attached to it are called *hardware*. The instructions that tell it what to do are called *software*. A set of instructions that perform a particular task is called a *program* or *software program*.

WHAT A COMPUTER DOES

The instructions in the program direct the computer to input, process and output as follows:

Input/Output

The computer can selectively retrieve data into its main memory (RAM) from any peripheral device (terminal, disk, tape, etc.) connected to it. After processing the data internally, the computer can send a copy of the results from its memory out to any peripheral device. The more memory it has, the more programs and data it can work with at the same time.

Storage

By outputting data onto a magnetic disk or tape, the computer is able to store data permanently and retrieve it when required. A system's size is based on how much disk storage it has. The more disk, the more data is immediately available.

PROCESSING
(The 3 C's*)

Once the data is in the computer's memory, the computer can process it by **calculating**, **comparing** and **copying** it.

Calculate

The computer can perform any mathematical operation on data by adding, subtracting, multiplying and dividing one set with another.

Compare

The computer can analyze and evaluate data by matching it with sets of known data that are included in the program or called in from storage.

Copy

The computer can move data around to create any kind of report or listing in any order.

By **calculating**, **comparing** and **copying**, the computer accomplishes all forms of data processing. For example, records are sorted into a new order by **comparing** two records at a time and **copying** the record with the lower value in front of the one with the higher value.

The computer finds one customer out of thousands by **comparing** the requested account number to each record in the file. The dBASE query statement: SUM SALARY FOR TITLE = "NURSE" causes the computer to **compare** the title field in each record for NURSE and then add (**calculate**) the salary field for each match.

In word processing, inserting and deleting text is accomplished by **copying** characters from one place to another.

Remember The 3 C's

If you wonder whether the computer can solve a problem, identify your data on paper. If it can be calculated, compared and copied on paper, it can be processed in the computer.

The 3 C's - Finding Things

This example counts all California records in the database by comparing each record with "CA." Every record in the database is read into memory. The memory locations that state is written into are compared with the letters "CA" in the program. If they are equal, a "1" is added to the California counter. The second record is written into the same memory bytes as the first record, and the field is compared again. This process is performed until the last record has been examined.

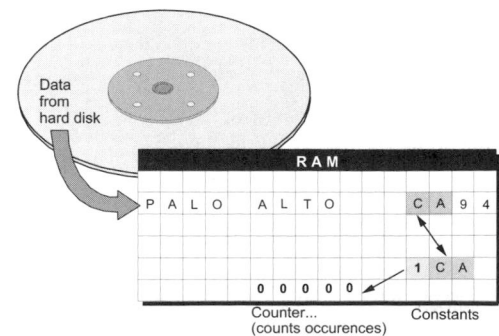

The 3 C's - Displaying and Printing

Data is stored as contiguous fields in the database. There are no blanks in between. The data is displayed and printed the way we like to see it by writing the data into memory and copying the characters into the desired order. The date in this example is printed through a "picture," which is a set of characters that acts as a filter. Each character in the date is compared to a corresponding character in the picture, and the one copied as output is determined by the rules. Pictures can be implemented in software or in hardware.

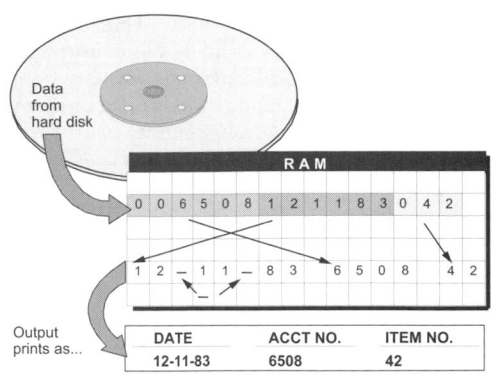

The 3 C's - Sorting

Sorting, or resequencing, data is accomplished by comparing each item of data with the others and copying it into the appropriate order. Of course, there's a ton of calculating going on to keep track of what's being compared. Years ago, when databases were stored on tape, the speed of a vendor's sort program was a powerful marketing feature. All transactions had to be sorted into account number sequence in order to be processed. In today's online systems, data is often indexed. Instead of sorting the actual data records themselves, the much smaller indexes are sorted.

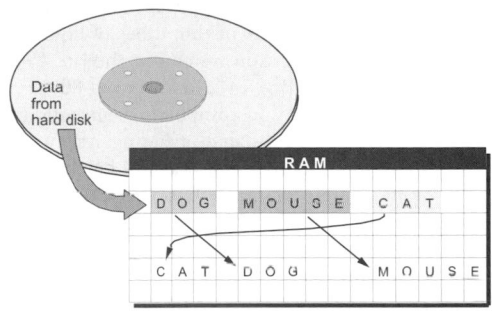

The 3 C's - Editing

The magic of word processing is really nothing more than copying the text in memory. In this example, if you want to insert a character into an existing line, the remaining characters are copied one memory location (byte) to the right so there is room for the additional letter. Deleting is just copying in reverse. As in all data processing, there is a whole lot of calculating and comparing going on to keep track of where the text is stored in memory.

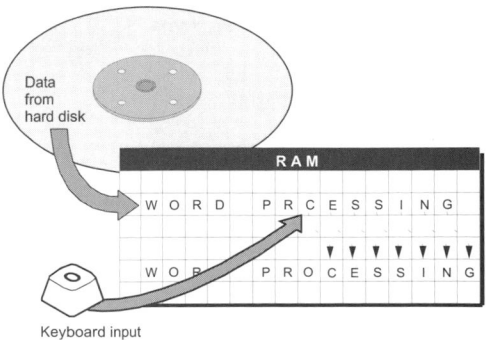

THE STORED PROGRAM CONCEPT

The computer's ability to call in instructions and follow them is known as the *stored program concept*. Instructions are copied into memory from a disk, tape or other source before any data can be processed. The computer is directed to start with the first instruction in the program. It copies the instruction from memory into its control unit circuit and matches it against its built-in set of instructions. If the instruction is valid, the processor carries it out. If not, the computer comes to an abnormal end (abend, crash).

The computer executes instructions sequentially until it finds a GOTO instruction that tells it to go to a different place in the program. It can execute millions of instructions per second tracing the logic of the program over and over again on each new set of data it brings in.

As computers get faster, operations can be made to overlap. While one program is waiting for input from one user, the operating system (master control program) directs the computer to process data in another program. Large computers are designed to allow inputs and outputs to occur simultaneously with processing. While one user's data is being processed, data from the next user can be retrieved into the computer.

It can take hundreds of thousands of discrete machine steps to perform very routine tasks. Your computer could easily execute a million instructions to put a requested record on screen for you.

GENERATIONS OF COMPUTERS

First-generation computers, starting with the UNIVAC I in 1951, used vacuum tubes, and their memories were made of thin tubes of liquid mercury and magnetic drums.

Second-generation systems in the late 1950s replaced tubes with transistors and used magnetic cores for memories (IBM 1401, Honeywell 800). Size was reduced and reliability was significantly improved.

Third-generation computers, beginning in the mid 1960s, used the first integrated circuits (IBM 360, CDC 6400) and the first operating systems and DBMSs. Online systems were widely developed, although most processing was still batch oriented using punched cards and magnetic tapes.

Starting in the mid 1970s, the fourth generation brought us computers made entirely of chips. It spawned the microprocessor and personal computer. It introduced distributed processing and office automation. Query languages, report writers and spreadsheets put large numbers of people in touch with the computer for the first time.

The fifth generation is becoming visible in the mid 1990s with more widespread use of voice recognition, natural and foreign language translation, optical disks and fiber optic networks. Higher-speed machines combined with more sophisticated software will enable the average computer to talk to us with reasonable intelligence sometime after the dawn of the 21st century.

TYPES OF COMPUTERS

Computers can be as small as a chip or as large as a truck. The difference is in the amount of work they do within the same time frame. Its power is based on many factors, including word size and the speed of its CPU, memory and peripherals. Following is a rough guide to system cost.

Computer system type	Approximate cost (US$)
Computer on a chip (4, 8, 32, 16-bit)	2 - 75
Microprocessor chip (4, 8, 16, 32, 64-bit)	5 - 1000
Personal computer client (16, 32, 64-bit)	800 - 15,000
Personal computer server (32, 64-bit)	6,000 - 30,000
Workstation (32, 64-bit)	6,000 - 100,000
Mini/midrange server (32, 64-bit)	25,000 - 1,000,000
Mainframe (32, 64-bit)	500,000 - 10,000,000
Supercomputer (64-bit)	1,000,000 - 10,000,000

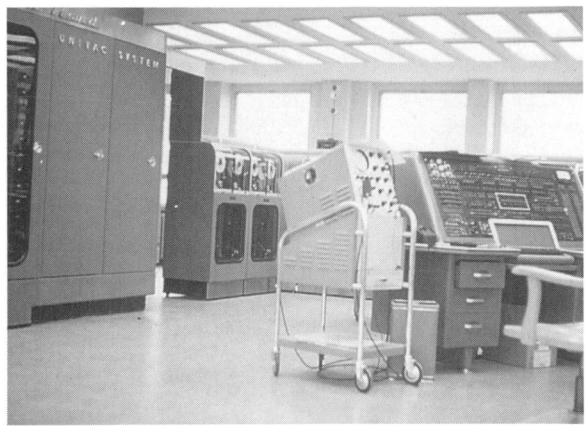

The Beginning of Commercial Computing

In the early 1950s, the Univac I ushered in the computer age. This picture was taken in Frankfurt, Germany in 1956 and shows the console on the right, a little more than half the CPU on the left and the tape drives in the background.

The Installation

This picture, taken in 1956, shows half the CPU of the UNIVAC I. Imagine yourself watching this awesome sight and someone says to you, "in 20 years, everything you see being wheeled up the ramp will fit on the tip of your finger." Would you have believed it?

computer-aided design
See *CAD*.

computer-aided engineering
See *CAE*.

computer-aided manufacturing
See *CAM*.

computer-aided software engineering
See *CASE*.

computer animation
The creation of animated sequences within the computer. Contrast with *stop-motion animation*.

computer architecture
The design of a computer system. It sets the standard for all devices that connect to it and all the software that runs on it. It is based on the type of programs that will run (business, scientific) and the number of them run concurrently.

It specifies how much memory is needed and how it is managed (memory protection, virtual memory, virtual machine). It specifies register size and bus width (16-, 32-, 64-bit) and how concurrency is handled (channels, bus mastering, parallel processing).

Its native language instruction set stipulates what functions the computer performs and how instructions are written to activate them. This determines how programs will communicate with it forever after.

The trend toward large, complicated instruction sets has been reversed with RISC computers, which use simpler instructions. The result is a leaner, faster computer, but requires that the compilers generate more code for complex functions that used to be handled in hardware.

Fault tolerant operation influences every aspect of computer architecture, and computers designed for single purposes, such as array processors and database machines, require special designs.

computer-assisted learning
See *CBT*.

Computer Associates
See *CA*.

computer books
See *how to find a good computer book*.

computer center
Same as *datacenter*.

computer conferencing
See *chat*, *videoconferencing* and *data conferencing*.

computercruiter
A recruiter that specializes in placing computer professionals. Same as *nerd rustler*.

computer designer
A person who designs the electronic structure of a computer.

computer-enhanced image
A picture that has been digitized and modified in the computer. For example, once a photograph has been scanned into the computer, it can be changed in numerous ways using an image editor. The brightness and contrast can be adjusted, colors can be changed and images can be superimposed. There is no end to the amount of alterations that can be applied to an image.

computer exchange
A commodity exchange through which the public can buy and sell used computers. After a match, the buyer sends a check to the exchange and the seller sends the equipment to the buyer. If the buyer accepts it, the money is sent to the seller less commission. Commissions usually range from 10 to 20%.

With the American Computer Exchange, equipment is first sent to the exchange, which inspects it and then sends it to the buyer.

```
American Computer Exchange (AmCoEx)
800/786-0717    FAX 404/250-1399
www.amcoex.com

Boston Computer Exchange (BoCoEx)
800/262-6399    FAX 617/542-8849
www.bocoex.com

National Computer Exchange (NaComEx)
212/808-3062    FAX 212/681-9211
www.nacomex.com

The Computer Exchange
800/304-4639    FAX 404/898-0304
www.compexch.com

United Computer Exchange
(Specializing in Macintosh)
800/755-3033    FAX 770/612-1239
www.uce.com
```

computer graphics
See *graphics*.

computer language
A programming language, machine language or the language of the computer industry.

computer literacy

Understanding computers and related systems. It includes a working vocabulary of computer and information system components, the fundamental principles of computer processing and a perspective for how non-technical people interact with technical people.

It does not deal with how the computer works (digital circuits), but does imply knowledge of how the computer does its work (calculate, compare and copy). It requires a conceptual understanding of systems analysis & design, application programming, systems programming and datacenter operations.

To be a computer literate manager, you must be able to define information requirements effectively and have an understanding of decision support tools, such as query languages, report writers, spreadsheets and financial planning systems. To be truly computer literate, you must understand all the entries under "standards" in this database. If you can't sleep at night, it's a guaranteed cure for insomnia!

Computer Museum

(The Computer Museum, Boston, MA, www.tcm.org) A museum that provides an historical display of computing devices as well as hands-on exhibits of a wide variety of applications geared to kids and adults. You can run the world's largest personal computer, and you can walk through its components.

The Computer Museum is funded by several computer companies as well as private individuals. The Museum Store sells a unique variety of computer games, books, jewelry and artifacts. Open daily in the summer from 10am to 6pm; winters from 10am to 5pm, Tuesday thru Sunday, holidays excluded. Call 800/370-CHIP for group rates and reservations.

computer on a chip

A single chip that contains the processor, RAM, ROM, clock and I/O control unit. Hundreds of millions of them are used each year for myriads of applications from automobiles to toys. A computer on a chip is also called a *microcontroller*, or *MCU*.

computerphile

A person that enjoys learning about and using computers. See *technophile, hacker* and *dweeb*.

computer power

The effective performance of a computer. It can be expressed in MIPS (millions of instructions per second), clock speed (10Mhz, 16Mhz) and in word or bus size, (16-bit, 32-bit). However, as with automobile horsepower, valves and cylinders, such specifications are only

Some Keyboard!
A boy has fun on the giant keyboard of the Museum's Walk-Through Computer 2000 exhibit that opened at the end of 1995 (top). *(Photo by FAYFOTO/John Rich; courtesy of The Computer Museum.)*

A Computer on a Chip
This is the Motorola 6801, one of the first complete computers on a chip. This category of chip is widely used in automobiles, appliances and toys. Such chips can cost as little as one dollar in quantity.

guidelines. Real power is whether it gets your job done quickly.

A software package is "powerful" if it has a large number of features.

computer readable

Same as *machine readable*.

Computer Recycling Center

(Computer Recycling Center, Inc., Santa Rosa, CA, www.computerrecycling.org) A non-profit organization that channels old computer equipment to schools and other non-profit organizations. It accepts incomplete systems, parts and pieces as well as software. See *how to donate old equipment*.

computer science

The field of computer hardware and software. It includes systems analysis & design, application and system software design and programming and datacenter operations. For young students, the emphasis in typically on learning a programming language or running a personal computer with little attention to information science, the study of information and its uses.

If students were introduced to data administration, DBMS concepts and transaction and master files, they would have a better grasp of an organization's typical information requirements.

computer security

See *security*.

Computer Select

A CD-ROM subscription service from Information Access Company, Foster City, CA, (www.iacnet.com), that provides articles and abstracts from more than 75,000 documents from major computer periodicals. It includes brief descriptions of roughly 21,000 hardware and 40,000 software products, profiles of 10,000 vendors and a glossary of 26,000 terms. Subscribers receive a CD-ROM every month with articles from the preceding 12 months.

Computer Select is an extraordinary resource that is a "must have" for every information systems department in the English-speaking world. Computer Select was originally developed by the Computer Library division of the Ziff-Davis Publishing Company.

computer services

Data processing (timesharing, batch processing), software development and consulting services. See *service bureau*.

computer shows

See *PC EXPO, COMDEX, Computex* and *CeBIT*.

computer system

The complete computer made up of the CPU, memory and related electronics (main cabinet), all the peripheral devices connected to it and its operating system. Computer systems fall into ranges called *microcomputers* (personal computers), *minicomputers* and *mainframes*, roughly small, medium and large.

Computer systems are sized for the total user workload based on (1) number of terminals required, (2) type of work performed (interactive processing, batch processing, CAD, engineering, scientific), and (3) amount of online data required.

Following are the components of a computer system and their significance.

Platform

The hardware platform and operating system determine which programs can run on the computer. Every application is written to run under a specific CPU and operating system environment. The most widely used platform means more software is available for it.

Clock Speed

The megahertz rate of the CPU determines is internal processing speed.

Number of Terminals/PCs

On a multiuser computer, such as a mainframe or minicomputer, the number of terminals or PCs that is can handle deterimines the number of users that can access its data.

Disk/Memory Capacity

A computer system's disk capacity determines the amount of online information that is immediately available to users. Its memory capacity determines how many applications can be run concurrently as well as the complexity of those applications.

Fault Tolerance

The use of UPS systems as well as redundant processors, peripherals and power supplies provide fault tolerance in the event of power loss or component failure.

computer telephony

See *CTI* and *IP telephony*.

computer trends

See *hot topics and trends*.

Computex

A Taiwanese trade show for PC manufacturers and PC component buyers promoted by the China External Trade Development Council. For information, call Taiwan 886-2-725-5200, FAX 886-2-757-6653.

COMSAT

(COMSAT Corporation, Clarksburg, MD, www.comsat.com) Formerly Communications Satellite Corporation, it is a private company that was created by the U.S. Congress in 1962 that provides satellite communications to major carriers and organizations. In 1965, it launched Early Bird, the first commercial satellite in geostationary orbit. COMSAT is the U.S. signatory for INTELSAT and Inmarsat, and its primary business is providing communications over the INTELSAT system.

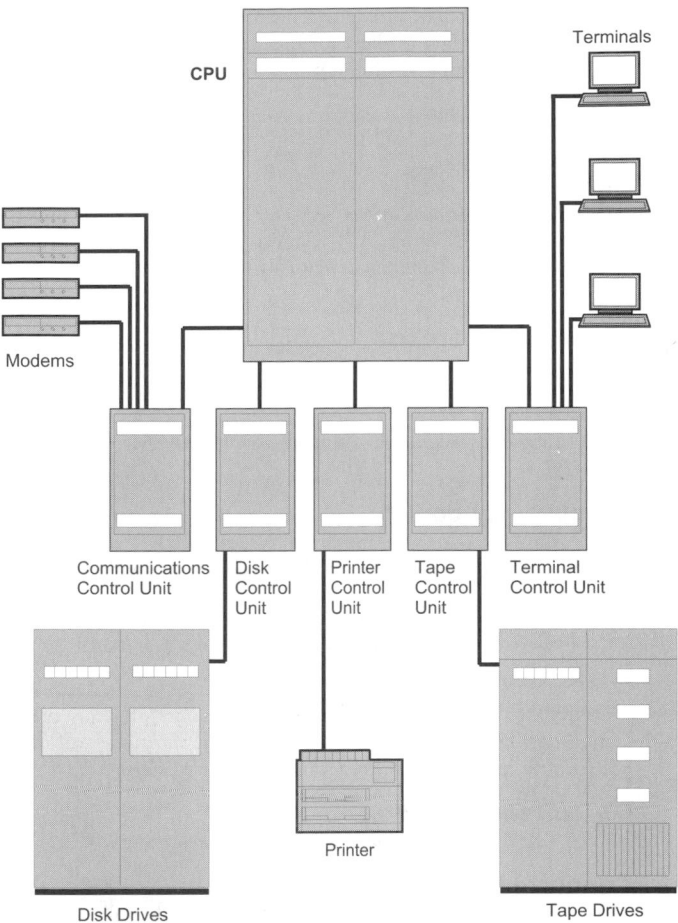

Multiuser Computer System

This diagram shows a multiuser computer, such as a mainframe or minicomputer. All computers contain the same components whether in multiple cabinets or in one. For vertical markets, PCs are also configured as multiuser systems that handle several terminals or readers. Such systems are often used for point of sale (POS) and generally run under UNIX.

concatenate

To link structures together. Concatenating files appends one file to another. In speech synthesis, units of speech called phonemes (k, sh, ch, etc.) are concatenated to produce meaningful sounds.

concentration

In communications, the combining of multiple channels into one.

concentrator

A device that combines several communications channels into one. It is often used to tie multiple terminals together into one line. It differs from a multiplexor, which also combines several lines into one, because the total bandwidth of a concentrator's inputs is not equal to its outputs. A concentrator may temporarily store data to allow for this discrepancy, whereas a multiplexor does not.

An Ethernet hub, which is a multiport repeater, is sometimes called a concentrator.

conceptual view
See *view*.

Concert
(Concert Communications Services, Reston, VA, www.concert.com) Founded as a joint venture of MCI and British Telecom (BT), Concert provides global communications services, including private, point-to-point voice and data circuits, Internet services and X.25 packet switching and frame relay. See *Tymnet*.

concrete superclass
See *superclass*.

concurrency
Simultaneous operation within the computer. See *multiprocessing, multitasking, multithreading, SMP* and *MPP*.

concurrency control
In a DBMS, managing the simultaneous access to a database. It prevents two users from editing the same record at the same time and is also concerned with serializing transactions for backup and recovery.

Concurrent DOS
An early multiuser DOS-compatible operating system from Digital Research. See *Multiuser DOS*.

concurrent licensing
Software licensing that is based on the number of simultaneous users accessing the program. Concurrent licensing is administered by the application itself or via independent software metering tools. See *software metering*. Contrast with *per seat licensing*.

concurrent operation
See *multitasking, multiprocessing* and *parallel processing*.

Concurrent PCI
An enhancement to the PCI bus architecture that allows PCI and ISA buses to transfer data simultaneously. For example, using Concurrent PCI, video performance would be improved with a PCI display adapter and an ISA sound card.

concurrent processing
See *multiprocessing*.

conditional branch
In programming, an instruction that directs the computer to another part of the program based on the results of a compare. In the following (simulated) assembly language example, the second line is the conditional branch.

```
COMPARE FIELDA with FIELDB
GOTO MATCHROUTINE if EQUAL.
```

High-level language statements, such as IF THEN ELSE and CASE, are used to express the compare and conditional branch.

conditioning
Extra cost options in a private telephone line that improve performance by reducing distortion and amplifying weak signals.

conductor
A material that can carry electrical current. Contrast with *insulator*.

Computer Desktop Encyclopedia

conferencing
See *teleconferencing*.

CONFIG.SYS
A DOS and OS/2 configuration file. It resides in the root directory and is used to load drivers and change settings at startup. Install programs often modify CONFIG.SYS in order to customize the computer for their particular use. Windows 95/98 executes the lines in CONFIG.SYS if it contains drivers that it found no counterpart for when it was installed.

configuration
The makeup of a system. To "configure" is to choose options in order to create a custom system. "Configurability" is a system's ability to be changed or customized.

configuration file
A file that contains information about a specific user, program, computer or file.

configuration management
(1) In a network, a system for gathering current configuration information from all nodes in a LAN.

(2) In software development, a system for keeping track of large projects. Although version control, which maintains a database of revisions, is part of the system, a full-blown software configuration management system (SCM system or CM system) automatically documents all components used to build executable programs. It is able to recreate each build as well as to recreate earlier environments in order to maintain previous versions of a product. It may also be used to prevent unauthorized access to files or to alert the appropriate users when a file has been altered.

Increasingly, parts of version control and configuration management are being added to application development systems.

Examples of stand-alone configuration management systems are PVCS, the CCC products from Softool and ClearCase.

connectionless
In communications, the inclusion of source and destination addresses within each packet so that a direct connection or established session between nodes is not required. Transmission within a local area network (LAN), such as Ethernet, Token Ring and FDDI, is connectionless. Each data packet sent contains the address of where it is going. Contrast with *connection oriented*.

Connection Machine
A family of parallel processing computers from former Thinking Machines Corporation, Cambridge, MA, that contained from 4K to 64K processors. Used in applications such as signal processing, simulation and database retrieval, they were set up as hypercubes and other topologies, which required another computer as a front end.

connection oriented
In communications, requiring a direct connection or established session or circuit between two nodes in order to transmit. Once set up, the circuit is dedicated to that single transmission until the session is completed. Then the circuit is "torn down." The most ubiquitous connection oriented network is the voice telephone system (POTS). ATM, which is used for both LANs and WANs is also connection oriented. Contrast with *connectionless*.

connectivity
(1) Generally, the term refers to communications networks or the act of communicating between computers and terminals.

(2) Specifically, the term refers to devices such as bridges, routers and gateways that link networks together.

connector
(1) Any plug, socket or wire that links two devices together.

(2) In database management, a link or pointer between two data structures.

(3) In flowcharting, a symbol used to break a sequence and resume the sequence elsewhere. It is often a small circle with a number in it.

connect time

The amount of time a user at a terminal is logged on to a computer system. See *online services* and *service bureau*.

console

(1) A terminal used to monitor and control a computer or network.

(2) Any display terminal.

constant

In programming, a fixed value in a program. Minimum and maximum amounts, dates, prices, headlines and error messages are examples.

constant bit rate

See *CBR*.

constant ratio code

A code that always contains the same ratio of 0s to 1s.

consultant

An independent specialist that may act as an advisor or perform detailed systems analysis and design. They often help users create functional specifications from which hardware or software vendors can respond.

consumer electronics

A broad field of electronics that includes devices such as TVs, VCRs, radios, walkie-talkies, hi-fi stereo, home theater, handheld and software-based games as well as Internet appliances and home computers.

contact

A metal strip in a switch or socket that touches a corresponding strip in order to make a connection for current to pass. Contacts may be made of precious metals to avoid corrosion.

contact manager

Software that holds names, addresses, appointments and notes. It is similar to a personal information manager (PIM), but is specialized for sales and service reps that make repetitive contact with prospects and customers.

container

See *OLE*.

container application

Same as *OLE container*. See *OLE*.

contention

A condition that arises when two devices attempt to use a single resource at the same time. See *CSMA/CD*.

contention resolution

Deciding which device gains access to a resource first when more than one wants it at the same time.

Consoles that Were Consoles!
Up until the late 1970s, computers were designed with panels of blinking lights, which added to their aura of science fiction. The designs gave each computer a personality that is sorely lacking in most of today's machines. *(Photos courtesy of International Business Machines Corporation and Unisys Corporation.)*

Computer Desktop Encyclopedia

content provider
An organization or individual that provides information, education or entertainment content for the Internet, CD-ROMs or other software-based products. A content provider generally does not provide the software used to access the material.

context
The current status, condition or mode of a system.

context sensitive help
Help screens that provide specific information about the condition or mode the program is in at the time help is sought.

context switching
Same as *task switching*.

contextual search
To search for records or documents based upon the text contained in any part of the file as opposed to searching on a pre-defined key field.

contiguous
Adjacent or touching. Contrast with *fragmentation*.

continuity check
A test of a line, channel or circuit to determine if the pathway exists from beginning to end and can transmit signals.

continuous carrier
In communications, a carrier frequency that is transmitted even when data is not being sent over the line.

continuous forms
A roll of paper forms with perforations for separation into individual sheets after printing. See *pin feed* and *burster*.

continuous tone
A printing process that produces photographic-like output. In a continuous tone image, pixel patterns (individual dots) are either not visible or are barely visible under a magnifying glass. Various dye sublimation, CYCOLOR and laser technologies can provide up to 256 intensities of color and even blend the inks. See *contone printer, dye sublimation printer* and *CYCOLOR*.

contone printer
A laser printer that begins to approach continuous tone quality by varying the dot size. However, unlike continuous tone, which can blend inks more thoroughly, contone has a limited number of dot sizes, and dithering is still used to make up shades. See *continuous tone*.

contrast
The difference between the lightest and darkest areas on a display screen. Contrast with *brightness*.

control
A program module that enhances the functionality of a program. A control is often a user interface function. In the Windows environment, OLE controls and ActiveX controls are examples. See *OCX* and *ActiveX control*.

control ball
Same as *trackball*.

control block
A segment of disk or memory that contains a group of codes used for identification and control purposes.

control break

(1) A change of category used to trigger a subtotal. For example, if data is subtotalled by state, a control break occurs when NJ changes to NM. See also *Ctrl-Break*.

control character

See *control code*.

control code

One or more characters used as a command to control a device. The first 32 characters in the ASCII character set are control codes for communications and printers. There are countless codes used to control electronic devices. See *escape character*.

Control Data

(Control Data Systems, Inc., Arden Hills, MN, www.cdc.com) Control Data Corporation (CDC) was one of the first computer companies. Founded in 1957, Bill Norris was its president and guiding force. Its first computer, the 1604, was introduced in 1957 and delivered to the U.S. Navy Bureau of Ships.

For more than 30 years, the company was widely respected for its high-speed computers used heavily in government and scientific installations. Using the CYBER trade name, Control Data produced a complete line from workstations to mainframes. It also manufactured supercomputers.

In 1992, it spun off its military involvement into an independent company called Ceridian Corporation, and Control Data Corporation became Control Data Systems. Soon after, it ceased R&D of its proprietary computers. While providing maintenance for its installed base, it currently specializes in systems integration of UNIX-based computers from HP, Sun and Silicon Graphics, which includes custom software, consulting services and facilities management.

William C. Norris
Norris founded and headed one of the most advanced computer companies in the industry. *(Photo courtesy of Control Data Corporation.)*

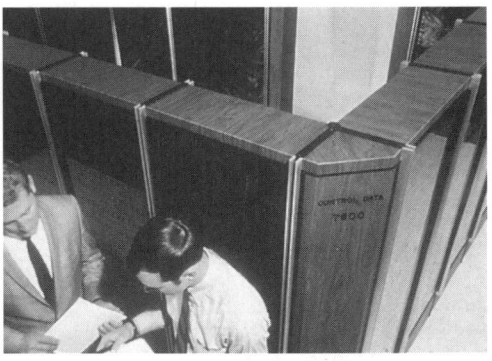

The 7600
Control Data's 7600 was open in the middle, and its sides were like walls. You could walk into it from the rear, which is visible in this picture. *(Photo courtesy of Control Data Corporation.)*

control field

Same as *key field*.

control key

Abbreviated "ctrl" or "ctl." A keyboard key that is pressed with a letter or digit key to command the computer; for example, holding down control and pressing U, turns on underline in some word processors. The caret (shift-6) symbol represents the control key: ^Y means control-Y.

controller

An electronic circuit board or system. In a personal computer, controllers contain the circuitry to run a peripheral device and are either contained on a plug-in expansion board or on the motherboard. Increasingly, plug-in boards for disk control, networking, sound, etc., are being replaced by built-in circuits (chips) on the motherboard.

In larger computers, a controller may be contained on one or more boards or in a stand-alone cabinet.

controller card

See *expansion board* and *control unit*.

control network

A network of sensors and actuators used for home automation and industrial control.

control panel

(1) A program used to change some setting in the operating system or computer. Control panels allow for changing keyboard and mouse sensitivity, speaker volume, display colors and resolution as well as modem, network and printer settings. Control panels are part of most operating systems, but also come with peripheral devices to allow fine tuning of particular features.

(2) A set of switches and dials used to operate a piece of equipment.

control parallel

Same as *MIMD*.

control program

Software that controls the operation of and has highest priority in a computer. Operating systems, network operating systems and network control programs are examples. Contrast with *application program*.

control signal

A pulse or frequency on a wire or fiber that is used to control something in a circuit. Control signals are often carried on dedicated lines that have a singular purpose such as starting or stopping a function.

control total

Same as *hash total*.

control unit

(1) Within the processor, the circuitry that locates, analyzes and executes each instruction in the program.

(2) Within the computer, hardware that performs the physical data transfers between memory and a peripheral device, such as a disk or screen. See *controller*.

control variable

In programming, a variable that keeps track of the number of iterations of a process. Its value is incremented or decremented with each iteration, and it is compared to a constant or other variable to test the end of the process or loop.

conventional memory

In a PC, the first 640K of memory. The next 384K is called the UMA (upper memory area). The term may also refer to the entire first megabyte (1024K) of RAM, which is the memory that DOS can directly manage without the use of additional memory managers. See *DOS memory manager*.

conventional programming

Writing a program in a traditional procedural language, such as assembly language or a high-level compiler language (C, Pascal, COBOL, FORTRAN, etc.).

convergence

(1) The intersection of red, green and blue electron beams on one CRT pixel. Poor convergence decreases resolution and muddies white pixels.

(2) See *digital convergence*.

conversational

An interactive dialogue between the user and the computer.

conversion

(1) Data conversion is changing data from one file or database format to another. It may also require code conversion between ASCII and EBCDIC.

(2) Media conversion is changing storage media such as from tape to disk.

(3) Program conversion is changing the programming source language from one dialect to another, or changing application programs to link to a new operating system or DBMS.

(4) Computer system conversion is changing the computer model and peripheral devices.

(5) Information system conversion requires data conversion and either program conversion or the installation of newly purchased or created application programs.

converter

(1) A device that changes one set of codes, modes, sequences or frequencies to a different set. See *A/D converter*.

(2) A device that changes current from 60Hz to 50Hz, and vice versa.

cookie

Data created by a Web server that is stored on a user's computer. It provides a way for the Web site to keep track of a user's patterns and preferences and, with the cooperation of the Web browser, to store them on the user's own hard disk.

The cookies contain a range of URLs (addresses) for which they are valid. When the browser encounters those URLs again, it sends those specific cookies to the Web server. For example, if a user's ID were stored as a cookie, it would save that person from typing in the same information all over again when accessing that service for the second and subsequent time.

You can have your browser warn you before accepting a cookie. Look for that option in Options/ Network Preferences/Protocols in Netscape or Options/Advanced in Internet Explorer. See *cookie file*.

cookie file

A file that contains cookies. Netscape saves cookies in a COOKIES.TXT file. Internet Explorer saves cookies in separate files in the Cookies folder. See *cookie* and *COOKIES.TXT*.

COOKIES.TXT

The name of the cookie file stored by Netscape Navigator in the Navigator folder (directory). See *cookie file*.

COOL (COOL:Gen, COOLBiz, COOLGen)

A family of tools from Sterling Software for modeling and developing enterprise applications for every major hardware platform. COOL:Biz is an extensive business and data modeling tool. COOL:Gen is a modeling tool and application generator that turns COOL:Biz and COOL:Gen models into working code. COOL:Jex provides object-oriented analysis and design and program generation as well as UML support, and COOL:Specs is used to define object interfaces. Support only for COOL:Enterprise is provided (see *Key:Enterprise*).

cooler

See *CPU cooler*.

CoolTalk

A set of data conferencing and telephony extensions for Netscape Navigator from Netscape. It includes an Internet phone, chat window, whiteboard and application sharing.

cooperative multitasking

Same as *non-preemptive multitasking*.

cooperative processing

Sharing a job among two or more computers such as a mainframe and a personal computer. It implies splitting the workload for the most efficiency.

coopetition

(COOPEration compeTITION) Cooperation between competing companies. In the information field, coopetition means settling on standards and then developing products that compete with each other using those standards.

coordinate

Belonging to a system of indexing by two or more terms. For example, points on a plane, cells in a spreadsheet and bits in dynamic RAM chips are identified by a pair of coordinates. Points in space are identified by sets of three coordinates.

Copland

The code name for a next generation Macintosh operating system that was expected to provide preemptive multitasking, multithreading, better crash protection and the ability to customize the user interface. Considerable effort went into Copland; however, only portions are expected to be used since Apple purchased NeXT Computer. See *Rhapsody*.

Computer Desktop Encyclopedia

copper

(Cu) A reddish-brown metal that is highly conductive and widely used for electrical wire. When a signal "runs over copper," it means that a metal wire is used rather than a glass wire (optical fiber). See *copper chip*.

copper chip

A chip that uses copper rather than aluminum in the top metalization layers, which interconnect all transistors and components together. Copper provides better performance, because it has less resistance than aluminum. Resistance increases as the lines (tracks) get smaller. In order to accomodate ever-decreasing die sizes, materials with inherent less resistance are required. Copper might have been used earlier, but it diffused into the silicon until IBM discovered a way to prevent that from happening. See *metalization layer*.

coprocessor

A secondary processor used to speed up operations by handling some of the workload of the main CPU. See *math coprocessor* and *graphics coprocessor*.

copy

To make a duplicate of the original. In digital electronics, all copies are identical, which is, of course, both a blessing and a curse. The blessing is that data can be maintained and remanufactured accurately forever. The curse is that anyone can duplicate copyrighted material and send it around the world in seconds.

The text in this database takes up approximately three megabytes. During the course of writing and updating it, the text has been copied hundreds of times, causing billions of bits to be transmitted between disk and memory. Just to show that things aren't entirely perfect, a character does get garbled every once in a while. We'll have to settle for 99.999999% instead of 100%!

copy & paste

To copy text or an image from one document to another. To perform the operation, do the following: (1) Highlight the text or graphics with the mouse and select Copy from the EDIT menu, (2) switch to the receiving document, (3) click in the location you want the information to go into, and (4) select Paste from the EDIT menu. See *cut & paste*.

copy buster

A program that bypasses the copy protection scheme in a software program and allows normal, unprotected copies to be made.

copyleft

See *GNU General Public License*.

copy protection

The ability to prevent unauthorized copying of software. Copy protection was never a serious issue with mainframes and minicomputers, since vendor support has always been vital in those environments. As personal computer software becomes more complex, technical support becomes just as crucial, requiring users to own valid copies of the product in order to obtain it.

In the early days of floppy-based personal computers, many copy protection methods were used. However, with each scheme introduced, a copy buster program was developed to get around it. When hard disks became the norm, copy protection was abolished. In order to manage a hard disk, files must be easily copied from one part of the disk to another.

This is a constant dilemma for software vendors as well as the publishing and broadcasting industries that transmit their content via digital means. Every recipient of a digitally-distributed medium has the ability to reproduce a perfect copy of the original.

The only copy protection system that works is the hardware key, which is a plug and socket that is attached to the computer's parallel port with a unique serial number that the software identifies. Hardware keys are used to protect high-priced software, but users are generally not fond of them, because it requires unplugging the printer cable, inserting the hardware key, and plugging back the printer.

A system similar to the hardware key designed into the personal computer from day one should have been established. Perhaps some day a solid state software capsule with a digital signature will plug into the computer. In the meantime, anyone who can figure out an economical way to prevent unauthorized duplication of digital material that does not interfere with managing a hard disk or the quality of the original transmission will become a zillionaire overnight!

CORBA

(Common Object Request Broker Architecture) A standard from The Object Management Group (OMG) for communicating between distributed objects.

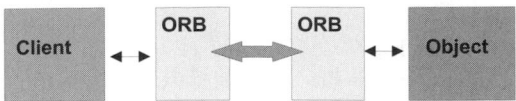

CORBA provides a way to execute programs written in any language no matter where they reside in the network or what platform they run on. It enables complex systems to be built across an entire enterprise. For example, three-tier client/server applications can be constructed using CORBA-compliant ORBs. CORBA is suited for widely disbursed networks, where an event occurring in one location requires services to be performed in another.

In CORBA, the client makes a request to a common interface known as the Object Request Broker or ORB. The ORB directs the request to the appropriate server that contains the object and redirects the results back to the client. The required object might also be located on the same machine as the client.

Technically, CORBA is the communications component of the Object Management Architecture (OMA). However, CORBA is the term that everybody uses to describe the OMG environment rather than OMA. CORBA is also often described as an "object bus," because it is a communications interface through which objects are located and accessed.

CORBA objects are defined by an interface definition language (IDL) that describes the services the object performs and the way data is passed to it. The IDL definitions are stored in an Interface Repository that can be queried by a client application to determine what functions (objects) are available on the object bus.

The first version of CORBA addressed source code portability across different platforms, and implementations such as IBM's SOM/DSOM, Sun's DOE and HP's DOMF were designed to this specification. In late 1994, CORBA 2 was introduced to support interoperability between ORBs, so that an ORB from one vendor can communicate directly to an ORB from another.

DCOM is Microsoft's standard for distributed objects. DCOM to CORBA interoperability is in the works. See *IIOP*.

core

(1) The heart, or central part, of something. The core of a network is its central backbone. The core of a microprocessor chip is its primary processing circuits. A core program would be the primary routines necessary for a larger application (see *kernel*).

(2) A round magnetic doughnut that represents one bit in a core storage system. A computer's main memory used to be referred to as core. See *core storage*.

core dump

Same as *memory dump*.

core frequency

The clock speed of the CPU, which is frequently higher than the speed of the buses that connect to it.

Corel

(Corel Corporation, Ottawa, Ontario, www.corel.com) Canada's leading software company, founded in 1985 by Dr. Michael Cowpland. For many years, it has been widely known for its award-winning CorelDRAW suite of graphics programs for Windows, Mac and UNIX. Corel offers a variety of business programs, including application suites that include WordPerfect and Quattro Pro. In 1996, it acquired the WordPerfect family of software from Novell. Corel also produces a complete line of publishing tools for the Internet.

Dr. Michael Cowpland
Cowpland founded Corel in 1985 and is currently CEO and president. Previous to Corel, he founded Mitel Corporation. *(Photo courtesy of Corel Corporation.)*

CorelDRAW

A suite of Windows graphics applications from Corel. CorelDRAW was originally a drawing program introduced in 1989, which became popular due to its speed and ease of use. As of CorelDRAW 5, it became a complete suite of applications for image editing, charting and presentations as well as desktop publishing with the inclusion of Corel VENTURA.

CorelFLOW

A flowcharting program for Windows from Corel that includes more than 2,000 shapes, photos and pieces of clip art as well as over 100 TrueType fonts.

Corel Office

A suite of applications for Windows from Corel that includes WordPerfect, Quattro Pro, Paradox, Presentations, CorelDRAW, CorelFLOW and a variety of additional applets. Corel Office was superseded by Corel Wordperfect Suite.

core logic

The primary processing logic of a component, function or system. For example, a PC chipset provides all the core logic on the motherboard except for the CPU. See *chipset*.

Corel Paradox

A relational database management (DBMS) and application development system for DOS and Windows from Corel. It includes the PAL programming language for writing complex business applications. When Paradox was originally released under DOS, it was noted for its visual query by example method, which made asking questions much easier than comparable products of the time. Originally developed by Ansa Corporation, it was later acquired by Borland and then Corel. See *relational query* for illustration.

Corel Quattro Pro

A Windows spreadsheet from Corel that provides advanced graphics and presentation capabilities, including goal seeking, 3-D graphing and the ability to create multi-layered slide shows. It is optionally keystroke compatible with Lotus 1-2-3. Quattro Pro was originally developed by Borland, then purchased by Novell in 1994 and Corel in 1996.

CorelRAID

Software from Corel that creates RAID arrays on a Novel 3.11 server using an ASPI-compatible SCSI host adapter and three or more SCSI disks.

CorelSCSI

A SCSI driver from Corel that supports a wide variety of SCSI devices, including removable media, juke boxes, digital cameras and WORM drives and translates them into the ASPI standard.

Corel VENTURA

A Windows desktop publishing program from Corel. It is a full-featured program suited for producing books and other long documents. It is designed to import data from other graphics and word processing programs and includes several graphics functions from CorelDRAW.

Corel VENTURA was formerly Ventura Publisher, developed by a company that was later acquired by Xerox. The early versions were available for DOS, Windows, OS/2 and the Mac. In 1993, Corel acquired it and enhanced it.

Corel WordPerfect

A full-featured word processing program for Windows from Corel. It is a sophisticated program that has been widely used on many platforms since its inception on the IBM PC in 1982. Under its original developer, WordPerfect became the leading word processor in the late 1980s. The company and product was acquired by Novell and later by Corel. See *WordPerfect Corporation*.

Corel WordPerfect Suite

A suite of office applications for Windows from Corel that includes Corel WordPerfect, Corel Quattro Pro, Corel Presentations, Corel Paradox, CorelCENTRAL (PIM, scheduling and integrated Netscape Communicator) and additional utilities. It is the successor to Corel Office.

co-resident

A program or module that resides in memory along with other programs.

core storage

A non-volatile memory that holds magnetic charges in ferrite cores about 1/16th" diameter. The direction of the flux determines the 0 or 1. Developed in the late 1940s by Jay W. Forrester and Dr. An Wang, it was used extensively in the 1950s and 1960s. Since it holds its content without power, it is still used in specialized applications in the military and in space vehicles.

In 1956, IBM paid Dr. Wang $500,000 for his patent on core memories, which he used to expand his company, Wang Laboratories.

Core System

The first proposed standard for computer graphics, developed by the Graphics Standards Planning Committee of SIGGRAPH and used in the late 1970s and early 1980s. Its objectives were portability of programs between computers and the separation of modeling graphics from viewing graphics. Almost all features of the Core System were incorporated into the ANSI-endorsed GKS standard.

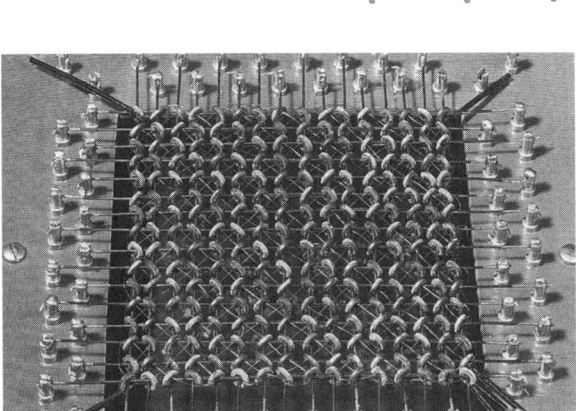

Cores from the WHIRLWIND
In 1952, this core plane from the WHIRLWIND I computer held 256 bits of memory. Today's memory chips occupying the same amount of space could easily hold more than a billion bits. *(Photo courtesy of The MITRE Corporation Archives.)*

corona wire

A charged wire in a laser printer that draws the toner off the drum onto the paper. It must be cleaned when the toner cartridge is replaced.

Corporation for Open Systems

An R&D consortium, founded in 1986, that was dedicated to assuring acceptance of worldwide standards. It closed 10 years later.

correlation

In statistics, a measure of the strength of the relationship between two variables. It is used to predict the value of one variable given the value of the other. For example, a correlation might relate distance from urban location to gasoline consumption. Expressed on a scale from -1.0 to +1.0, the strongest correlations are at both extremes and provide the best predictions. See *regression analysis*.

corrupted file

A data or program file that has been altered accidentally by hardware or software failure, causing the bits to be rearranged and rendering it unreadable.

corruption

Altering of data or programs due to viruses, hardware or software failure or power failure. See *data recovery*.

CorStream

A network operating system from Artisoft, Inc., Tucson, AZ, makers of LANtastic. CorStream is a version of Novell's NetWare 4.x combined with an Artisoft NLM, which turns a PC into a high-speed LANtastic server. LANtastic clients communicate with CorStream as if it was another LANtastic server.

COS

(Cray Operating System) An operating system used in Cray computers. See also *Corporation for Open Systems*.

COSE

(Common Open Software Environment) Pronounced "cozy." An alliance of major UNIX vendors dedicated to standardizing open systems. In 1993, its first specification was the CDE (Common Desktop Environment), a user interface based on Motif. COSE has since disbanded, and CDE is now governed by X/Open.

cosine

See *sine*.

cost-based query optimizer

Software that optimizes an SQL query for the fastest processing, based on the size of the file and other variables.

cost/benefits analysis

The study that projects the costs and benefits of a new information system. Costs include people and machine resources for development as well as running the system.

Tangible benefits are derived by estimating the cost savings of both human and machine resources to run the new system versus the old one. Intangible benefits, such as improved customer service and employee relations, may ultimately provide the largest payback, but are harder to quantify.

COTS

(Commercial Off-The-Shelf) Refers to ready-made merchandise that is available for sale.

counter

(1) In programming, a variable that is used to keep track of anything that must be counted. The programming language determines the number of counters (variables) that are available to a programmer.

(2) In electronics, a circuit that counts pulses and generates an output at a specified time.

counter-rotating ring

See *dual counter-rotating ring*.

country code

A two-character component of an e-mail or Web address that identifies a country. Computers read addresses from right to left. Thus, on encountering **sven@univ.oslo.net.se**, the message would first be sent to Sweden, since **se** is the country code for Sweden. Swedish routers would then send the message to **univ.oslo.net** where it will be waiting for Sven the next time he signs on.

Some search engines (AltaVista and Infoseek, among others) let you specify country codes in your search. This comes in handy when you want to locate (or avoid) sites that originate in a particular country. To find Web sites originating in France and devoted to French wines, for example, you might try an AltaVista search for **+wine +domain:fr**. To do the same thing with Infoseek, try **+wine +site:fr**.

If a particular search turns up many sites in a language you cannot understand, say Japanese for example, just do the search again and avoid all sites with the country code **jp**. On AltaVista, that would mean adding **-domain:jp** to your search request. On Infoseek, add **-site:jp**.

Courier

```
A monospaced typeface originating from the typewriter that is
commonly used for letters.  It is still considered by many to
be the "appropriate" typeface for business correspondence.
This paragraph is Courier.
```

Courier modem

A modem from U.S. Robotics that uses standard and proprietary protocols for communications. It is field upgradable and uses proprietary DSP chips made by U.S. Robotics. Over the years, Courier modems have gained a solid reputation for excellence and reliability.

courseware
Educational software. See *CBT*.

covert channel
A transfer of information that violates a computer's built-in security systems. A covert storage channel refers to depositing information in a memory or storage location that can be accessed by different security clearances. A covert timing channel is the manipulation of a system resource in such a way that it can be detected by another process.

CP
(1) (Copy Protected) See *copy protection*.

(2) (Central Processor) See *processor* and *CPU*.

(3) See *control program*.

CPA
(Computer Press Association, Landing, NJ, www.computerpress.org) An organization founded in 1983 that promotes excellence in computer journalism. Its annual awards honor outstanding examples in print, broadcast and electronic media.

CPE
(Customer Premises Equipment) Communications equipment that resides on the customer's premises.

CPF
(Control Program Facility) The IBM System/38 operating system that included an integrated relational DBMS.

CPGA
(Ceramic PGA) See *PGA*.

cpi
(1) (Characters Per Inch) The measurement of the density of characters per inch on tape or paper. A printer's CPI button switches character pitch.

(2) (Counts Per Inch) The measurement of the resolution of a mouse/trackball as flywheel notches per inch (horizontal and vertical flywheels rotate as the ball is moved). Notches are converted to cursor movement.

(3) (CPI) (Common Programming Interface) See *SAA* and *CPI-C*.

CPI-C
(Common Programming Interface for Communications) A general-purpose communications interface under IBM's SAA. Using APPC verbs as its foundation, it provides a common programming interface across IBM platforms. See *APPC*.

CPLD
(Complex PLD) A programmable logic device that includes a programmable interconnect between the logic blocks. See *SPLD, PLD* and *ASIC*.

CP/M
(Control Program for Microprocessors) A single user operating system for the 8080 and Z80 microprocessors from Caldera. Created by Gary Kildall of Digital Research, CP/M had its heyday in the early 1980s; however, as we enter the 21st century, it is still being used.

The Otrona Attache
Introduced in 1982, the Attache was the smallest CP/M portable computer on the market. Weighing 17 pounds and priced at $5000, the Attache became a kind of cult computer used by prominent people worldwide. *(Photo courtesy of Robin Bartlett.)*

CP/M was an unsophisticated program that didn't instill too much confidence in users, yet it was a major contributor to the personal computer revolution. Because the industry never standardized on a CP/M disk or video format, software publishers had to support dozens of screen displays and floppy disk versions. This chaos helped IBM set the standard with its PC in a very short time.

Although IBM asked Kildall to provide the operating system for its new PC, he didn't agree to certain demands. IBM went to Microsoft, which purchased QDOS from Seattle Computer Products and turned it into PC-DOS and MS-DOS. The rest is history. The irony is that DOS was modeled after CP/M. Digital Research was later acquired by Novell and then Caldera.

CPM

(1) (Critical Path Method) A project management planning and control technique implemented on computers. The critical path is the series of activities and tasks in the project that have no built-in slack time. Any task in the critical path that takes longer than expected will lengthen the total time of the project.

(2) (Cost Per Mille) Refers to the cost for a thousand (mille) of something.

cps

(1) (Characters Per Second) The measurement of the speed of a serial printer or the speed of a data transfer between hardware devices or over a communications channel. CPS is equivalent to bytes per second.

(2) (CPS) (Certified Product Specialist) See *Microsoft Certified Professional*.

CPU

(Central Processing Unit) The computing part of the computer. Also called the *processor*, it is made up of the control unit and ALU. Today, the CPUs of almost all computers are contained on a single chip.

The CPU, clock and main memory make up a computer. A complete computer system requires the addition of control units, input, output and storage devices and an operating system.

From the Mainframe Point of View
Computer professionals involved with mainframes and minicomputers often refer to the whole computer as the CPU, in which case, CPU refers to the processor, memory (RAM) and I/O architecture (channels or buses).

CPU bound
Same as *process bound*.

CP/M in Its Heyday
Hardly mentioned now, these news clips depict CP/M in its heyday. CP/M was the only non-proprietary operating system for microcomputers that was widely used. It was a major contributor to the personal computer revolution.

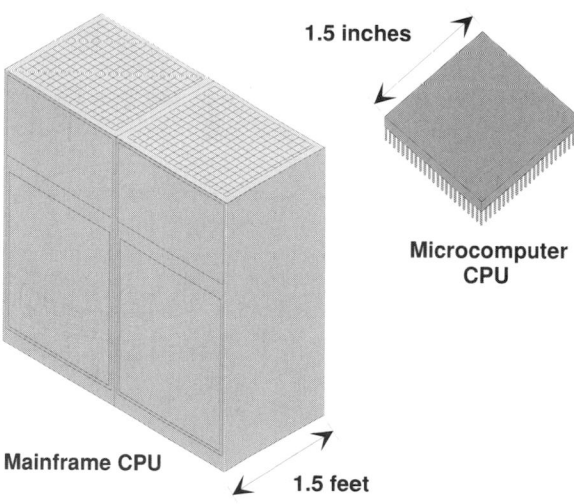

CPUs Come in Different Sizes
Depending on which end of the field you are in, a CPU can mean the processor, memory and everything inside the cabinet, or just the microprocessor itself.

CPU cache
See *cache*.

CPU chip
Same as *microprocessor*.

CPU clock
See *clock*.

CPU cooler
A device that keeps the CPU chip at a cooler temperature. The simplest type is a heat sink, which is a metal cover that provides a larger surface area for heat dissipation. A CPU fan is more effective than a heat sink, because it directs air movement over the chip. The most effective is a refrigeration system that can cause the chip to run at increased performance.

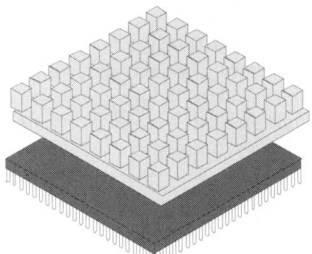

Heat Sink
The simplest CPU cooler is a heat sink, which provides a large surface area to dissipate heat.

CPU ID
The identification of a particular CPU. One of Intel's x86 instructions is CPU-ID, which is executed to find out what the capabilities and performance level of the current machine are.

CPUmark
See *Winbench*.

CPU speed
See *MHz*.

CPU time
The amount of time it takes for the CPU to execute a set of instructions and generally excludes the waiting time for input and output.

CQFP
See *QFP*.

CR
(Carriage Return) The character code generated when the return (enter) key is pressed. In ASCII and EBCDIC systems, it is a decimal 13 (hex 0D). See *return key*.

cracker
A person that breaks into a computer system without authorization, whose purpose is to do damage (destroy files, steal credit card numbers, plant viruses, etc.). See *hacker*.

CRAM
(Card Random Access Memory) A magnetic card mass storage device from NCR that was made available on its 315 computer systems in 1962. It offered reliable random access storage at a time when magnetic tapes were the primary storage medium. Up to 16 CRAM units could be online.

Each CRAM unit held one 5.5MB cartridge that contained 256 mylar, 3x14" cards with a magnetic recording surface. The cards were suspended from eight rods, which were selectively moved to release a specific card. The card was pulled out, wrapped around a rotating drum and read or written.

cramming
See *slamming*.

crapplet
A really terrible and useless Java applet. See *applet*.

crash
See *abend* and *head crash*.

crash recovery
The ability to automatically correct a hardware, software or line failure.

Computer Desktop Encyclopedia

crawler

Also known as a spider, ant, robot ("bot") and intelligent agent, a crawler is a program that searches for information on the World Wide Web. It is used to locate new documents and new sites by following hypertext links from server to server and indexing information based on search criteria.

Cray Computer

The Colorado Springs-based supercomputer company founded in 1989 by Seymour Cray after he left Cray Research. Cray developed the Cray-3, an incredibly fast gallium arsenide-based computer that ran at a 1GHz clock rate. With the Cray-4 sitting in the wings, the company was unable to attract customers for the new products and closed its doors in 1995.

Cray Research

(Cray Research, Inc., Eagan, MN, www.cray.com) A supercomputer manufacturer founded in 1972 by Seymour Cray, a leading designer of large-scale computers at Control Data. In 1976, it shipped its first computer to Los Alamos National Laboratory. The CRAY-1 was a 75MHz, 64-bit machine with a peak speed of 160 megaflops, making it the world's fastest vector processor.

The company has since launched the X-MP, Y-MP, C90, T90, J90 and T3E series, comprising models from entry-level to high-end supercomputers that are used in industrial, technical and commercial applications. Cray also incorporates its unique system architecture into its CS6400 line of SPARC and Alpha-based machines. All Cray computers use the UNIX operating system.

In 1989, Seymour Cray left Cray Research to found Cray Computer Corporation (see *Cray Computer*).

In 1996, Cray Research was acquired by Silicon Graphics, Inc. (SGI).

CRC

(Cyclical Redundancy Checking) An error checking technique used to ensure the accuracy of transmitting digital data. The transmitted messages are divided into predetermined lengths which, used as dividends, are divided by a fixed divisor. The remainder of the calculation is appended onto and sent with the message. At the receiving end, the computer recalculates the remainder. If it does not match the transmitted remainder, an error is detected.

CRC cards

(Class Responsibility Collaboration card) An object-oriented design method that uses ordinary 3x5 index cards. Developed by Ward Cunningham at Textronix, a card is made for each class containing responsibilities (knowledge and services) and collaborators (interactions with other objects). The cards provide an informal, intuitive way for group members to work on object design together.

For a book on CRC cards that provides a clear introduction to object concepts and modeling, read "Using CRC Cards" by Nancy Wilkinson, published by SIGS BOOKS, ISBN 1-884842-07-0.

Seymour Cray
Cray became world famous for his supercomputers. His passion for high-speed computing led to many innovative designs. *(Photo courtesy of Cray*

The Cray 1
The Cray 1 became synonymous with high-speed computing in the late 1970s. It was often photographed for "space-age" computer shots because of its science fiction silhouette. *(Photo courtesy of Cray Research, Inc.)*

Creative Labs

(Creative Labs, Inc., Milpitas, CA, www.creativelabs.com) A leading manufacturer of sound cards and products that was founded in 1988 by Sim Wong Hoo. It introduced the Sound Blaster card in 1989, which has become a de facto standard.

credit

A monetary amount that is added to an account balance. A credit to one account is a debit to another. See *debit*.

crippleware

Demonstration software with built-in limitations; for example, a database package that lets only 50 records be entered.

Cristina Foundation

See *National Cristina Foundation*.

criteria range

Conditions for selecting records; for example, "Illinois customers with balances over $10,000."

CR/LF

(Carriage Return/Line Feed) The end of line characters used in standard PC text files (ASCII decimal 13 10, hex 0D 0A). In the Mac, only the CR is used; in UNIX, the LF.

CromaClear monitor

A family of multiscan monitors from NECT that uses a combination shadow mask and aperture grille technology. See *slot mask*.

crop marks

Printed lines on paper used to cut the form into its intended size.

cross assembler

An assembler that generates machine language for a different type of computer than the one the assembler is running in. It is used to develop programs for computers on a chip or microprocessors used in specialized applications that are either too small or are otherwise incapable of handling the development software.

crossbar switch

See *crosspoint switch*.

cross compiler

A compiler that generates machine language for a different type of computer than the one the compiler is running in. See *cross assembler*.

crossfoot

A numerical error checking technique that compares the sum of the columns with the sum of the rows.

crosshatch

A criss-crossed pattern used to fill in sections of a drawing to distinguish them from each other.

cross memory services

The method used by MVS (OS/390) applications for linking to various operating system services. "Cross memory" means that the called routines reside in different address spaces than the calling program. They can even be in another computer. Rather than using a fixed address, cross memory services use a method of indirection whereby the calling program obtains a token that serves as a pointer to the actual routine. Cross memory services adds a more efficient approach than the supervisor call instruction that was initially the only method applications used to call the operating system.

crossover cable

Same as *null modem cable*.

cross platform

Refers to developing for and/or running on more than one type of hardware platform. It implies two different processes. The first is programming source code that is compiled into different machine environments, each of which has to be supported separately. For example, a software vendor may decide its application should run on a Windows NT and HP server, in which case it would compile once into Windows NT and again for HP/UX. Both environments would be tested separately. While a single set of source code might be the ideal, there are typically differences in the source code to optimize running in the target machine, requiring either two sets of source code or one set with alternate changes embedded within.

The second method is with the use of an interpreter such as the Java Virtual Machine. Java is said to be cross platform, because a program's source code is compiled into an intermediate "byte code" language. As long as a Java interpreter (Java Virtual Machine) is written for and installed on any computer, the Java byte code is expected to be executed in the same manner on that computer. The problems arise when the Java interpreter is not as up-to-date as the Java development system that created the program or the Java interpreters are not faithfully interpreting the byte code according to the same standard. See *multiple platforms*.

crosspoint switch

Also known as a crossbar or NxN switch, it is a switching device that provides for a fixed number of inputs and outputs. For example, a 32x32 switch is able to keep 32 nodes communicating at full speed to 32 other nodes.

cross post

To send the same message to several newsgroups.

cross software

Software that is developed on one type of computer, but used on another. See *cross assembler* and *cross compiler*.

Cross System Product

See *CSP*.

cross tabulate

To analyze and summarize data. A common example is summarizing the details from database records and placing them into a spreadsheet. The following example places the details of order records into summary form.

```
Transactions being cross tabbed
Date        Customer    Quantity
1- 7-93     Smith           7
1-13-93     Jones          12
2- 5-93     Gonzales        4
2-11-93     Fetzer          6
3-10-93     Smith          12
3-22-93     Gonzales       15


Results of cross tab
Customer    Jan   Feb   Mar   Total
Smith         7         12      19
Jones        12                 12
Gonzales            4   15      19
Fetzer              6            6

Total        19   10   27      56
```

crosstalk

(1) In communications, interference from an adjacent channel.

(2) (Crosstalk) A family of communications programs for DOS and Windows from Attachmate Corporation, Bellevue, WA, (www.attachmate.com). Crosstalk products were originally developed by

Microstuf, Inc., later merged with DCA and then Attachmate. It was one of the first personal computer communications programs, originating in the CP/M days. Crosstalk uses the Crosstalk Application Script Language (CASL).

crossware

Same as *cross platform*. Netscape coined the term for building Web-based applications using Java, JavaScript and JavaBeans, all of which run on multiple hardware platforms.

CRT

(**C**athode **R**ay **T**ube) A vacuum tube used as a display screen in a video terminal or TV. The term more often refers to the entire monitor rather than just the tube itself. Years ago, CRT was the popular term for the display screen. Today, monitor is the preferred term. See *VGA* and *monitor*.

crunch

(1) To process data. See *number crunching*.

(2) To compress data. See *data compression*.

cryogenics

Using materials that operate at very cold temperatures. See *superconductor*.

crypto

See *cryptography*.

cryptography

The conversion of data into a secret code for transmission over a public network. The original text, or plaintext, is converted into a coded equivalent called ciphertext via an encryption algorithm. The ciphertext is decoded (decrypted) at the receiving end and turned back into plaintext.

The encryption algorithm uses a key, which is a binary number that is typically from 40 to 128 bits in length. The data is "locked" for sending by combining the bits in the key mathematically with the data bits. At the receiving end, the key is used to "unlock" the code, restoring it to its original binary form.

Secret versus Public Key

There are two cryptographic methods. The traditional method uses a secret key, such as the DES standard. Both sender and receiver use the same key to encrypt and decrypt. This is the fastest method, but transmitting the secret key to the recipient in the first place is not secure.

The second method is public-key cryptography, such as RSA, which uses both a private and a public key. Each recipient has a private key that is kept secret and a public key that is published for everyone. The sender looks up the recipient's public key and uses it to encrypt the message. The recipient uses the private key to decrypt the message. Owners never have a need to transmit their private keys to anyone in order to have their messages decrypted, thus the private keys are not in transit and are not vulnerable.

Sometimes, both DES and RSA are used together. DES provides the fastest decryption, and RSA provides a convenient method for transmitting the secret key. Both the DES-encrypted text message and the secret key needed to decrypt it are sent via the RSA method. This is called a *digital envelope*.

Cryptography methods change as computers get faster. It has been said that any encryption code can

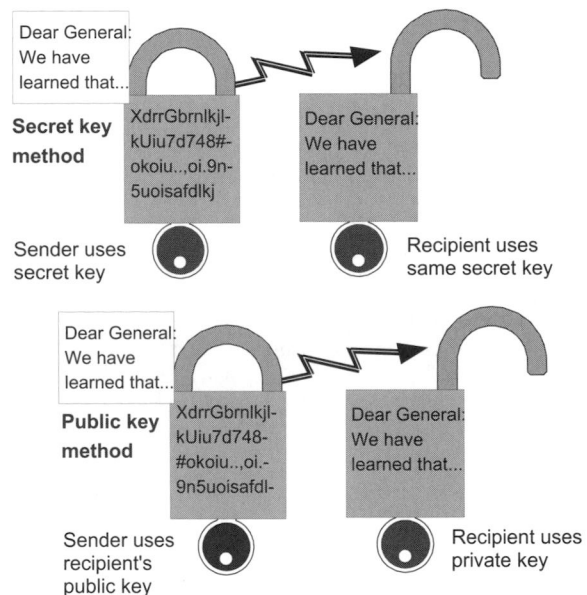

Secret Key vs Public Key

The secret method uses the same key to encrypt and decrypt. The problem is transmitting the key to the recipient in order to use it. The public key method uses two keys. One kept secret and never transmitted, and the other made public. Very often, the public key method is used to safely send the secret key to the recipient so that the message can be encrypted using the faster secret key algorithm.

Computer Desktop Encyclopedia

be broken given enough computer time to derive all of the permutations. However, if it takes months to break a code, the war could be won or lost, or the financial transaction has little meaning. As computers get faster, the keys get longer and the algorithms become more complex to stay ahead of the game. See *DES, RSA, digital signature* and *digital certificate.*

A Little History
The following is reprinted with permission from RSA Data Security, Inc.

In 1518, a Benedictine monk named Johannes Trithemius wrote Polygraphiae, the first published treatise on cryptography. Later, his text Steganographia described a cipher in which each letter is represented by words in successive columns of text, designed to hide inconspicuously inside a seemingly pious book of prayer.

Polygraphiae and Steganographia attracted a considerable amount of attention not only for their meticulous analysis of ciphers but more notable for the unexpected thesis of Steganographia's third and final section, which claimed that messages communicated secretly were aided in their transmission by a host of summoned spirits.

As might be expected, Trithemius' works were widely renounced as having magical content - by no means an unfamiliar theme in cryptographic history - and a century later fell victim to the zealous flames of the Inquisition during which they were banned as heretical sorcery.

crystal
A transparent quartz material that contains a uniform arrangement of molecules. See *crystalline* and *quartz crystal.*

crystalline
Like a crystal. It imples a uniform structure of molecules in all dimensions. For example, the crystalline state of a spot on a rewritable optical disk means that the laser beam will be reflected from it, in contrast to an amorphous state that will not reflect light. See *amorphous* and *nematic.*

c/s
See *client/server.*

CSA
(1) (Canadian Standards Association, Toronto, www.csa.ca) A standards-defining organization founded in 1919. It is involved in many industries, including electronics, communications and information technology.

(2) (Client Server Architecture) See *client/server.*

(3) (CallPath Services Architecture) An IBM standard that integrates applications with the telephone system, designed for use with AT&T, Northern Telecom and other PBX vendors.

CSE
(Certified Systems Engineer) See *Microsoft Certified Professional.*

C shell
A command line processor for UNIX. It provides more interactive control than the original Bourne shell, but is not available for all versions of UNIX. See *Bourne shell, Korn shell* and *UNIX.*

CSIC
(Customer Specific Integrated Circuit) Pronounced "C-sick." Another term for ASIC, which was coined by Motorola. Some feel this is a more accurate description of an ASIC chip, since ASICs can be used for a variety of purposes. See also *ASSP.*

CSID
(1) (Call Subscriber ID) A data field in a fax transmission that identifies the calling party. It can be entered at the fax machine or via software for fax/modems. The CSID can be used by the receiving system to route faxes to the appropriate workgroups and individuals.

(2) (Character Set ID) The number of a particular character set.

CSLIP
(Compressed SLIP) A version of SLIP that compresses the data for transmission.

CSMA/CD

(Carrier Sense Multiple Access/Collision Detection) The LAN access method used in Ethernet. When a device wants to gain access to the network, it checks to see if the network is free. If it is not, it waits a random amount of time before retrying. If the network is free and two devices access the line at exactly the same time, their signals collide. When the collision is detected, they both back off and each wait a random amount of time before retrying.

CSP

(1) (Cross System Product) An IBM application generator that runs in all SAA environments. CSP/AD (CSP/Application Development) programs provide the interactive development environment and generate a pseudo code that is interpreted by CSP/AE (CSP/Application Execution) software in the running computer. For AS/400 applications, CSP/AD generates compiled code. For the PS/2, EZ-PREP and EZ-RUN are the CSP/AD and CSP/AE counterparts.

(2) (Certified Systems Professional) An earlier award for successful completion of an ICCP examination in systems development. See *ICCP*.

CSS

(Cascading Style Sheet) The first specification for Web-based style sheets endorsed by the World Wide Web Consortium. CSS1 (Version 1.0) provides hundreds of layout settings that can be applied to all the subsequent HTML pages that are downloaded. CSS2 (Version 2.0) adds support for XML, oral presentations for the visually impaired, downloadable fonts and other enhancements. See *style sheet*.

CSS1, CSS2

The first and second specifications for Cascading Style Sheets on the Web. See *CSS*.

CSTA

(Computer Supported Telephony Application) An international standard interface between a network server and a telephone switch (PBX) established by the European Computer Manufacturers Association (ECMA).

CSTN

(Color STN) A color passive matrix screen technology developed by Sharp Electronics. CSTN displays have improved dramatically over the years and cost more than half that of an active matrix (TFT) display. See *passive matrix*.

CSU/DSU

See *DSU/CSU*.

CSV

(Comma Separated Value) Same as *comma delimited*.

CT

(1) (Certified Trainer) See *Microsoft Certified Professional*.

(2) (Computer Telephony) The integration of computers and telephones. See *CTI*.

CTFT

(Color TFT) See *TFT*.

CTI

(Computer Telephone Integration) Combining data with voice systems in order to enhance telephone services. For example, automatic number identification (ANI) allows a caller's records to be retrieved from the database while the call is routed to the appropriate party. Automatic telephone dialing from an address list is an outbound example.

CTIA

(1) See *CompTIA*.

(2) (Cellular Telecommunications Industry Association, Washington, DC, www.ctia.org) A membership organization founded in 1984 that is involved with regulatory and public affairs issues in the cellular phone industry.

Ctl
See *control key*.

CTO
(Chief Technical Officer) The executive responsible for the technical direction of an organization. See *CIO* and *salary survey*.

CTOS
An operating system that runs on Unisys' x86-based SuperGen series (formerly the B-series). It was originally developed by Convergent Technologies, which was acquired by Unisys. Designed for network use, its message-based approach allows program requests to be directed to any station in the network.

Ctrl
See *control key*.

Ctrl-Alt-Del
In a PC, holding down the CTRL and ALT keys and pressing the DEL key reboots the system.

Ctrl-Break
In a PC, holding down the CTRL key and pressing the BREAK key cancels the running program or batch file. Same as *Ctrl-C*.

Ctrl-C
In a PC under DOS, holding down the CTRL key and pressing the C key cancels the running program or batch file. Same as *Ctrl-Break*.

Ctrl-S
In a PC under DOS, holding down the CTRL key and pressing the S key pauses and continues the running program.

CTS
(1) (Clear To Send) The RS-232 signal sent from the receiving station to the transmitting station that indicates it is ready to accept data. Contrast with *RTS*. See also *carpal tunnel syndrome*.

CUA
(Common User Access) SAA specifications for user interfaces, which includes OS/2 PM and character-based formats of 3270 terminals. It is intended to provide a consistent look and feel across platforms and between applications.

CUI
(Character-based User Interface) A user interface that uses the character, or text, mode of the computer, such as DOS and UNIX. In order to instruct the computer, commands are typed in. Contrast with *GUI*.

CUL
Digispeak for "see you later."

Curie point
The temperature at which the molecules of a material can be altered when subjected to a magnetic field. In optical material, it is approximately 200 degrees Celsius. See *magneto-optic disk*.

current
(1) Present activities or the latest version or model.
(2) The flow of electrons within a wire or circuit, measured in amps.
(3) (Current) A Windows PIM from IBM that includes a calendar, address book, phone dialer, outliner, word processor and Gantt charts for project tracking. It was revised by its developer, Jensen-Jones Inc., Red Bank, NJ, into a new package called Commence.

current directory
The disk directory the system is presently working in. Unless otherwise specified, commands that deal with disk files refer to the current directory.

current loop

A serial transmission method originating with teletype machines that transmits 20 milliAmperes of current for a 1 bit and no current for a 0 bit. Today's circuit boards can't handle 20mA current and use optical isolators at the receiving end to detect lower current. Contrast with *RS-232*.

curses

A programming interface for character-based terminals. Curses provides a terminal-independent method of programming a terminal. It is part of the Single UNIX Specification governed by X/Open.

cursive writing

Handwriting.

cursor

(1) The symbol used to point to some element on screen. On DOS and other character-based screens, it is a blinking rectangle or underline. On Windows and other graphics-based screens, it is also called a *pointer*, and it changes shape as it is moved into different windows. For example, it may turn into an I-beam for editing text, an arrow for selecting menus or a pen for drawing. See *database cursor*.

(2) A pen-like or puck-like device used with a digitizer tablet. As the tablet cursor is moved across the tablet, the screen cursor moves correspondingly. See *digitizer tablet*.

cursor keys

The keys that move the cursor on screen, which include the up, down, left and right arrow, home, end, PgUp and PgDn keys. In addition to cursor keys, a mouse or tablet cursor also moves the cursor.

CU-SeeMe

Videoconferencing software for the Internet from White Pine Software Inc., Nashua, NH, (www.wpine.com). CU-SeeMe is available for Windows and Mac and allows point-to-point videoconferencing via modem over the Net. White Pine's Reflector software for UNIX and NT servers supports a group videoconference for up to 100 users.

custom ASIC

A redundant reference to an ASIC chip. ASICs are already customized for a specific use. See *ASIC*.

custom control

A software routine that adds some enhancement or feature to an application. Custom controls are written to provide as little as a few graphical interface improvements to as much as providing full imaging, spreadsheet and text editing extensions to the application. Depending on the development system, custom controls are either linked into the application when it is written or maintained as independent executable files that are called at runtime. DLLs, VBXs and OCXs are examples.

customer engineer

An IBM title for systems representative. See *systems representative*.

customizability

The ability for software to be changed by the user or programmer. See *application programmability*.

customized software

Same as *custom software*.

customized toolbar

A toolbar that can be custom configured by the user. Buttons can be added and deleted as required.

custom software

Software that is specifically designed and programmed for an individual customer. Contrast with *software package*.

cut & paste

To move text or an image from one document to another. To perform the operation, do the following: (1) Highlight the text or graphics with the mouse and select Cut from the EDIT menu, (2) switch to the receiving document, (3) click in the location you want the information to go into, and (4) select Paste from the EDIT menu. See *copy & paste*.

CUT mode

(Control Unit Terminal mode) A mode that allows a 3270 terminal to have a single session with the mainframe. Micro to mainframe software emulates this mode to communicate with the mainframe. Contrast with *DFT mode*.

cut-through switch

A switching device that begins to output an incoming data packet before the packet is completely received. Contrast with *store-and-forward switch*.

cyber

(1) From cybernetics, a prefix attached to everyday words to add a computer, electronic or online connotation.

(2) (CYBER) An early family of computers from Control Data that ranged from workstations to supercomputers.

cyberage

The high-tech era that we are living in today.

CyberAngels

(CyberAngels Internet Safety Organization, Los Angeles, CA, www.cyberangels.org) A Web site devoted to education and safety awareness on the Internet. It was founded in 1995 by Gabriel Hatcher along with Guardian Angels' founder Curtis Sliwa.

cybercafe

The high-tech equivalent of the coffee house. However, instead of playing chess or having heated political discussions, you browse the Internet and other online services and discuss the latest technology. CD-ROMs, games and other "cyber" stuff is available. They started in New York and are now to be found around the world.

CyberCash

A system of digital money from CyberCash, Inc. For credit card purchases, the merchant sends customers electronic invoices. Customers append their credit card numbers to the invoices which are encrypted via CyberCash software and sent back to the merchant. The merchants append their ID numbers to the invoices, encrypt them and send them to a CyberCash server for forwarding to the banking network.

Debit and cash transactions are handled by pre-establishing accounts with and making deposits into a participating bank. Encrypted messages are sent to the merchant to enable the funds transfer. See *digital money*.

cybercop

A criminal investigator of online fraud or harassment.

cybercrime

Crime on the information superhighway, typically having to do with online fraud.

cybercrook

A person who gains illegal entrance into a computer system or who diverts financial transfers into his or her own account. See *hacker*.

Cyberdog

A suite of Internet functions from Apple that are based on the OpenDoc technology.

cyberlibrarian

Librarians who do most of their research and information retrieval via the Internet and other online services. The title is often shortened to *cybrarian*.

cybermall

A shopping mall on the Internet. Cybermalls are online shopping centers that link a home page to hundreds or thousands of online storefronts. The cybermall generally handles the financial transactions for all the merchants so that a customer does not have to enter duplicate name and address information at each store. Items can literally be placed into an online shopping cart and paid for at once by credit card, ecash or other digital money method. See *digital money*.

cybernaut

An electronic astronaut. Avid Net surfers are cybernauts; however, anyone deeply involved in communications networks, online services, and computers in general can assume this handle.

cybernetics

The comparative study of human and machine processes in order to understand their similarities and differences. It often refers to machines that imitate human behavior. See *AI* and *robot*.

cyberpunk

A futuristic, online delinquent: breaking into computer systems; surviving by high-tech wits. The term comes from science fiction novels such as "Neuromancer" and "Shockwave Rider."

cyberspace

Coined by William Gibson in his novel "Neuromancer," it is a futuristic computer network that people use by plugging their minds into it! The term now refers to the Internet or to the online or digital world in general. See *Internet* and *virtual reality*. Contrast with *meatspace*.

cyberworld

The world of computers and communications. It implies today's fast-moving, high-technology world.

cyborg

(**CYB**ernetic **ORG**anism) A being that is part human and machine. See *cybernetics* and *bionic*.

cybrarian

See *cyberlibrarian*.

cycle

(1) A single event that is repeated. For example, in a carrier frequency, one cycle is one complete wave.

(2) A set of events that is repeated. For example, in a polling system, all of the attached terminals are tested in one cycle. See *machine cycle* and *memory cycle*.

cycles per second

The number of times an event or set of events is repeated in a second. See *Hertz*.

cycle stealing

A CPU design technique that periodically "grabs" machine cycles from the main processor usually by some peripheral control unit, such as a DMA (direct memory access) device. In this way, processing and peripheral operations can be performed concurrently or with some degree of overlap.

cycle time

The time interval between the start of one cycle and the start of the next cycle.

cyclical redundancy checking

See *CRC*.

CYCOLOR

(www.cycolor.com) A process for printing continuous-tone images that look just like photographs. Originally developed by Mead Imaging, the CYCOLOR process is very fast and quite amazing. It uses CYCOLOR DI FILM that contains billions of light-sensitive microcapsules, called *cyliths*. Resembling gel-caps, approximately 20,000 of them fit on the

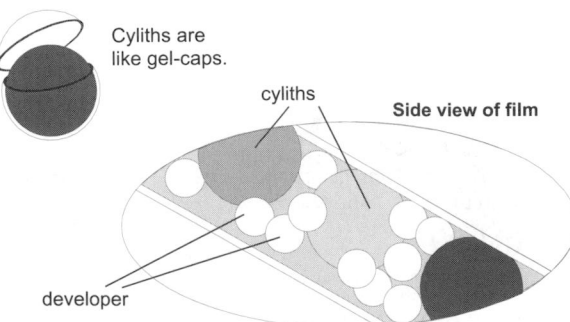

Cyliths are like gel-caps.

cyliths

Side view of film

developer

The CYCOLOR Process
CYCOLOR DI FILM contains billions of dye-filled, gel-cap-like cyliths that harden when exposed to a corresponding color of light. Then, the unhardened cyliths burst when pressed together, releasing their dye.

head of a pin. The cyliths contain either cyan, yellow or magenta-colored dyes that are sensitive to either red, green or blue light. The cylith hardens when exposed to its corresponding color, and the amount of hardness depends on the intensity of the light.

The exposed film is pressed under rollers to release the dyes. If an area was exposed heavily to all three colors, the cyliths become hard, do not release any dye and the white film shows. If an area was unexposed, all the cyliths burst under pressure and blend together to become black. All colors in between are based on the amount of hardness in the cyliths.

cylinder

The aggregate of all tracks that reside in the same location on every disk surface. On multiple-platter disks, the cylinder is the sum total of every track with the same track number on every surface. On a floppy disk, a cylinder comprises the top and corresponding bottom track.

When storing data, the operating system fills an entire cylinder before moving to the next one. The access arm remains stationary until all the tracks in the cylinder have been read or written.

cylinder skew

The offset distance from the start of the last track of the previous cylinder so that the head has time to seek from cylinder to cylinder and be at the start of the first track of the new cylinder. See *head skew*.

Cyrix

(Cyrix Corporation, Richardson, TX, www.cyrix.com) Founded in 1988, Cyrix is a manufacturer of x86-compatible CPU chips. Its first product was a math coprocessor. In 1992, it introduced a line of 486 CPUs, later followed by the 6x86 Pentium-class and 6x86MX Pentium II-class chips. Cyrix is expected to merge with and become a wholly-owned subsidiary of National Semiconductor. See also *Citrix*.

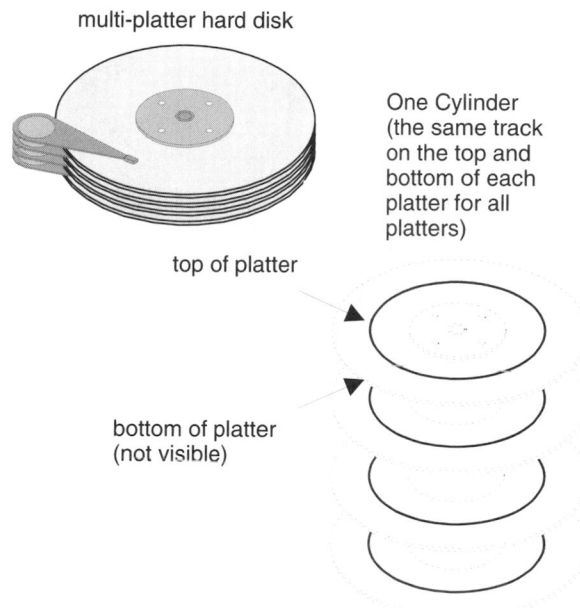

multi-platter hard disk

One Cylinder
(the same track
on the top and
bottom of each
platter for all
platters)

top of platter

bottom of platter
(not visible)

Cylinder
The cylinder is the aggregate of the same track number on every platter used for recording.

D

D1

A broadcast-quality digital video format that provides the highest quality recording, using expensive tape decks and metal-particle tape. D1 is a component format at 720x486 resolution and 24-bit color. It is raw, uncompressed digital video that uses 1MB of storage for each frame. At 30 frames per second, it requires a 30MB/sec transfer rate and nearly two gigabytes of storage per minute.

D2

A broadcast-quality digital video format that integrates well with analog equipment, because the equipment uses composite analog inputs and outputs.

D3

A broadcast-quality digital video format that provides a lower cost alternative to D1 recording. It is a composite format recorded on half-inch tape. See also *Pick System*.

D3D

See *Direct3D*.

D4

A framing format for T1 transmission that places 12 T1 frames into a superframe. See *ESF*.

D5

A broadcast-quality digital video format that provides a lower cost alternative to D1 recording. It is a component format recorded on half-inch tape.

DA

See *data administrator, desk accessory* and *data acquisition*.

DAC

(1) See *D/A converter*.

(2) (Discretionary Access Control) A security control that does not require clearance levels. See *NCSC*.

D/A converter

(Digital/Analog converter) A device that converts digital pulses into analog signals. Contrast with *A/D converter*. See *DSP* and *ladder DAC*.

DAD

(1) (Database Action Diagram) Documentation that describes the processing performed on data in a database.

(2) (Digital Audio Disc) Same as *CD*.

daemon

Pronounced "demon." A UNIX program that executes in the background ready to perform an operation when required. Functioning like an extension to the operating system, a daemon is usually an unattended process that is initiated at startup. Typical daemons are print spoolers and e-mail handlers or a scheduler that starts up another process at a designated time. The term comes from Greek mythology meaning "guardian spirit." See *agent*.

daisy chain

Connected in series, one after the other. Transmitted signals go to the first device, then to the second and so on.

daisy wheel

An earlier print mechanism that used a plastic or metal hub with spokes like an old-fashioned wagon wheel minus the outer rim. At the end of each spoke is the carved image of a type character. When the required character spins around to the print hammer, the image is banged into a ribbon and

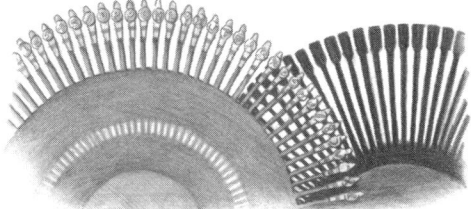

Daisy Wheel
In the early 1980s, daisy wheel printers cost $3,000 and more. They clicked and clacked to produce near typewriter-quality output. The technology was popular because you could change the fonts by changing wheels.

onto paper. The mechanism is then moved to the next location. Daisy wheel printers print typewriter-like quality from 10 to 75 cps and have been superseded by dot matrix and laser printers.

DAL

(Data Access Language) A database interface from Apple that allows the Mac to access DAL-supported databases on Macs or non-Apple computers. It is a superset of SQL. Database vendors license the specs and translate DAL calls to their database engines.

damping

A technique for stabilizing an electronic or mechanical device by eliminating unwanted or excessive oscillations.

D-AMPS

(Digital-Advanced Mobile Phone Service) The digital equivalent of the analog cellular phone service. Using the TDMA digital technology, analog cellphone systems can be upgraded to D-AMPS. See *AMPS* and *N-AMPS*.

dancing baloney

Small animated GIF images and other moving objects that are used to quickly and cheaply add "excitement" to a Web page. At best these images are harmless and not too distracting. At worst, they can make a given Web page look like the online equivalent of an animated ransom note.

DAO

(Data Access Objects) A programming interface for data access from Microsoft. DAO/Jet provides access to the Jet database, and DAO/ODBCDirect provides an interface to ODBC databases via RDO. DAO is a COM object. See *RDO, ADO, OLE DB* and *ODBC*.

DAP

(Directory Access Protocol) A protocol used to gain access to an X.500 directory listing. See *LDAP*.

dark current

The current that flows in a photodetector when it is not receiving any light. It may increase as the temperature rises.

darkened datacenter

Unattended datacenter operation. With printers distributed throughout the enterprise and the use of tape and optical libraries that automatically mount the appropriate disk and tape volume, the datacenter increasingly does not require human intervention.

dark fiber

Optical fiber that spans some geographic area. It is sold to carriers and businesses without any additional optics or electronics for providing the signalling paths. The customer is responsible for adding the transmission system at both ends.

Darlington circuit

An amplification circuit that uses two transistors coupled together.

DARPA

(Defense Advanced Research Projects Agency) The name given to the U.S. Advanced Research Projects Agency during the 1980s. It was later renamed back to ARPA. See *ARPAnet*.

DARS

(1) (Digital Audio Radio) A satellite-based digital radio service that provides CD-quality audio. It is expected that DARS-compliant radios will be used in the car and in portables in the future. Organizations such as CD Radio, Inc., and American Mobile Radio Corporation (AMRC) have assigned spectrum for this service.

(2) (Dow Aviation Reservation System) Dow Chemical's intranet-based reservations system. It lets employees reserve seats on corporate jets scheduled between company locations.

(3) (Disaster Assessment Recovery System) A disaster management application based on Domino from Corporate Workflow Solutions, Inc., Jupiter, FL. It is used to deploy equipment and personnel after natural disasters strike.

DASD

(Direct Access Storage Device) Pronounced "dazdee." A peripheral device that is directly addressable, such as a disk or drum. The term is used in the mainframe world.

Dashboard

A Windows utility from Starfish Software, Scotts Valley, CA, (www.starfishsoftware.com), that provides a centralized control panel for launching applications, finding files and viewing system resources. Dashboard was originally developed by HP, then acquired by Borland.

DAT

(1) (Digital Audio Tape) A magnetic tape technology used for backing up data. DAT uses 4mm cartridges that look like thick audio cassettes and conform to the DDS (Digital Data Storage) standard. DAT tape libraries hold from a handful to several hundred cassettes. DAT was initially a CD-quality audio format. It was thought to replace analog audiotapes for consumers, but wound up being used by professional musicians and sound studios. In 1988, Sony and HP defined the DDS format and quality level for computer storage. Like videotapes, DAT uses helical scan recording. For a summary of all storage technologies, see *storage*.

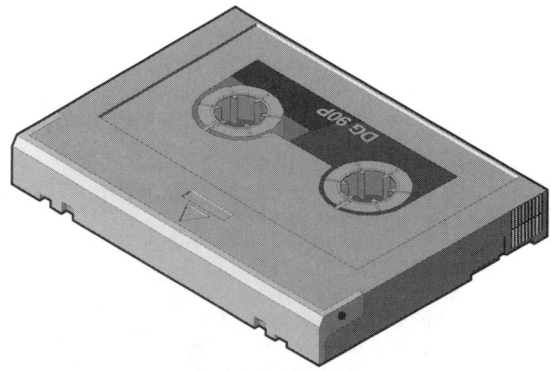

DAT Cartridge
DAT provides from one to 12GB of storage in a cartridge that is a little thicker, but smaller overall than an audio cassette.

Type	Native capacity
DDS-1	2GB
DDS-2	4GB
DDS-3	12GB

(2) (Dynamic Address Translator) A hardware circuit that converts a virtual memory address into a real address.

data

(1) Technically, raw facts and figures, such as orders and payments, which are processed into information, such as balance due and quantity on hand. However, in common usage, the terms data and information are used synonymously.

The amount of data versus information kept in the computer is a tradeoff. Data can be processed into different forms of information, but it takes time to sort and sum transactions. Up-to-date information can provide instant answers.

A common misconception is that software is also data. Software is executed, or run, by the computer. Data is "processed." Software is "run."

(2) Any form of information whether in paper or electronic form. In electronic form, data refers to files and databases, text documents, images and digitally-encoded voice and video.

(3) The plural form of datum.

data abstraction

See *abstraction*.

Data Access Language

See *DAL*.

data acquisition

(1) The automatic collection of data from sensors and readers in a factory, laboratory, medical or scientific environment.

(2) The gathering of source data for data entry into the computer.

data administration

The analysis, classification and maintenance of an organization's data and data relationships. It includes the development of data models and data dictionaries, which, combined with transaction volume, are the raw materials for database design.

The data administration organization often includes database administration. However, data administration functions provide the overall management of data as an organizational resource. Database administration is the technical design and management of the database.

Data Is Complex

The flow of data/information within a company is complex since the same data is viewed differently as it moves from one department to the other.

For example: When a customer places an order, the order becomes a commission for sales, a statistic for marketing, an order to keep track of in order processing, an effect on cash flow for financial officers, picking schedules for the warehouse, and production scheduling for manufacturing.

Users have different requirements for interrogating and updating data. Operations people need detail, management needs summaries. Database design must take this into consideration.

data administrator

A person who coordinates activities within the data administration department. Contrast with *database administrator*.

data aging

Adding years to a date to bring it into the year 2000 or beyond in order to test applications for Year 2000 compliance. See *Year 2000 problem*.

data analyst

See *data administrator*.

data bank

Any electronic depository of data.

database

A set of related files that is created and managed by a database management system (DBMS). Today, DBMSs can manage any form of data including text, images, sound and video. Database and file structures are always determined by the software. As far as the hardware is concerned, it's all bits and bytes.

database administrator

A person responsible for the physical design and management of the database and for the evaluation, selection and implementation of the DBMS.

In most organizations, the database administrator and data administrator are one in the same; however, when the two responsibilities are managed separately, the database administrator's function is more technical. See *salary survey*.

database analyst

See *data administrator, database administrator* and *salary survey*.

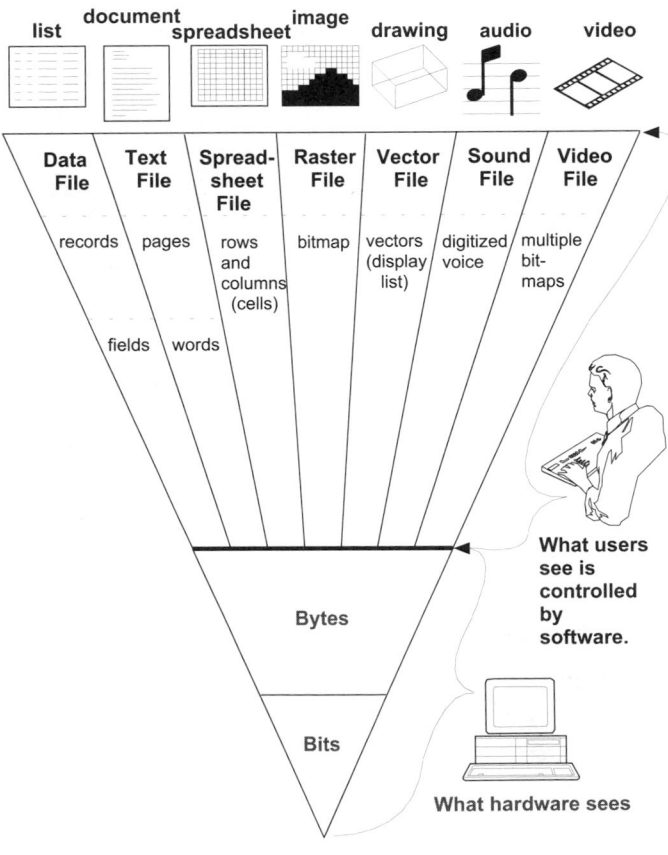

The Database
To better understand data and file concepts, learn the hierarchy and terms in this drawing.

database cursor

A record pointer in a database. When a database file is selected and the cursor is opened, the cursor points to the first record in the file. Using various commands, the cursor can be moved forward, backward, to top of file, bottom of file and so forth.

database designer

See *data administrator* and *database administrator*.

database driver

A software routine that accesses a database. It allows an application or compiler to access a particular database format.

database engine

Software that stores and retrieves data in a database. It may be a self-contained entity or part of a comprehensive database management system (DBMS). See *database manager*.

database machine

A computer system designed for database access. Database machines never caught on until the early 1990s when massively parallel processors (MPPs) from companies such as Teradata, now part of AT&T, nCube, Thinking Machines and Kendall Square Research, proved the concept. Using hundreds and even thousands of microprocessors with database software designed for parallelism, database machines can scan large files much faster than a mainframe.

Dramatic performance increases have been documented. For example, a large financial organization reduced 30 days worth of month-end analysis and reporting to a single day. In other cases, queries have been speeded up by a factor of 100. Database machines using MPP architecture are expected to grow in popularity for decision support systems in large organizations.

database management system

See *DBMS*.

database manager

(1) With personal computers, software that allows a user to manage multiple data files (same as *DBMS*). Contrast with *file manager*, which works with one file at a time.

(2) Software that provides database management capability for traditional programming languages, such as COBOL, BASIC and C, but without the interactive capabilities.

(3) The part of the DBMS that stores and retrieves the data.

database program

A software application that allows for the management of data and information structured as fields, records and files. Database programs provide a way of creating and manipulating the electronic equivalent of a name and address card that can hold large amounts of information.

Because all data is structured into a one record per subject or transaction format, it allows for powerful query capabilities, in which you can select records based on any of their content. A database program is the heart of a business information system and provides mainly file creation, data entry, update, query and reporting functions.

The traditional term for a database program is a database management system (DBMS). It is also called a *data management system*. For more details on the features of a DBMS, see *DBMS*. Also see *application software* for a breakdown of all major software applications.

User Interaction with a Database Program

The database programs available on personal computers let you perform all the following tasks interactively on one file at a time. However, as soon as you want data in one file to automatically update another, programming has to be done. That's where the faint of heart take their leave, and the hackers take over. Following are the common tasks you need to perform to create and work with a database file.

Create a File and Set Index Order

Each field in a record is defined by name, type and length. In order to keep the file in sequence, one or more fields are defined as key fields, upon which indexes are created and maintained. The index is updated whenever new records are added or existing records are deleted or any data in a key field changes.

Create Data Entry Forms
Data entry is accomplished by designing a form to display each record. Data entry forms contain field validation. You decide what data can go in and what must stay out of these fields.

Update/Edit
In a single-user, one-file-at-a-time application, there is nothing to predefine here. Changing data is just a matter of opening the file and selecting the EDIT mode. However, in a multiuser system, security must be administered and audit trails must be programmed.

View/Query
You can browse an entire file or just selected records. Selected records are usually created as a temporary file that can be saved or abandoned. The temporary file may be sorted into a new sequence if desired.

The ease with which a query can be composed determines how much users will ask their own questions or rely on their IS staff to create them. Getting data from two files; for example, customers and orders, or vendors and purchases, requires knowledge of how to link the files for the query. Most database programs have a JOIN function, which creates a new file with data from two existing files. Once a query description has been composed, it can be saved for use again.

Reporting
Reports provide details and summaries in a more elaborate fashion than queries. They have page and column headers and can be sorted into order by multiple fields; for example, county within city within state. Once a report description has been composed, it can be saved for use again.

Modify Structure
From time to time, it is necessary to add or delete fields, change their lengths or possibly their names. This function is similar to creating the record structure in the first place, except that you are editing the structure rather than defining it from scratch.

database publishing
Using desktop publishing to produce reports of database contents.

database server
A computer in a LAN dedicated to database storage and retrieval. The database server is a key component in a client/server environment. It holds the database management system (DBMS) and the databases. Upon requests from the client machines, it searches the database for selected records and passes them back over the network.

A database server and file server may be one in the same, because a file server often provides database services. However, the term implies that the system is dedicated for database use only and not a central storage facility for applications and files. See *client/server*.

data bits
The number of bits used to represent one character of data. When transmitting ASCII text via modem, either seven or eight bits may be used. Most other forms of data require eight bits.

DataBlade
A plug-in to Informix's Universal Server that extends its capability to work with a new type of data. See *Universal Server*.

DataBolts
Software components for Web sites from IBM. Available as JavaBeans or ActiveX controls, some of the first products are Cryptolope (encryption), Query and Retrieval (database access) and NewsTicker (scrolling news window). DataBolts are designed to provide all the enhancements necessary to keep visitors from straying off a Web site, such as the ability to search other sites for information and bring those results back to the site.

data broadcast
The one-way transmission of digital data directly to TVs and PCs. Using cable, satellite and the unused bandwidth in the VHF TV spectrum, data broadcast can deliver news, weather, stock prices, sports

scores, music, video and even Web pages. The user's set-top box functions as a tuner to the desired information.

data bus

An internal pathway across which data is transferred to and from the processor or to and from memory. See *local bus, system bus* and *peripheral bus*.

data carrier

(1) Any medium such as a disk or tape that can hold machine readable data.

(2) A carrier frequency into which data is modulated for transmission in a network.

data cartridge

(1) A cartridge used to hold computer data. See *cartridge*.

(2) (Data Cartridge) A 5.25" QIC-style magnetic tape technology that originally used the DC-6000 model designation. Tandberg Data has enhanced the technology in its MLR line for use in medium to high-end server markets with capacities up to 25MB. See *QIC*. For a summary of all storage technologies, see *storage*.

data cassette

A cassette used to hold computer data. See *cassette*.

Data Cell

An IBM mass storage device made in the 1960s that used 3 x 15" tape strips which were extracted out of a cartridge and wrapped around a rotating drum for reading. More than 100 of these units were installed worldwide, but the tapes were very susceptible to wear. See *CRAM*.

datacenter

The department that houses the computer systems and related equipment, including the data library. Data entry and systems programming may also come under its jurisdiction. A control section is usually provided that accepts work from and releases output to user departments.

The Datacenter
No matter how much computers are distributed into the organization, there always seems to be a need for a centralized datacenter in the large enterprise.

data circuit-terminating equipment

See *DCE*.

data code

(1) A digital coding system for data in a computer. See *ASCII* and *EBCDIC*.

(2) A coding system used to abbreviate data; for example, codes for regions, classes, products and status.

data collaboration

See *data conferencing*.

data collection

Acquiring source documents for the data entry department. It comes under the jurisdiction of the data control or data entry department. See *data acquisition*.

datacom

(**DATA COM**munications) See *communications* and *CA-DATACOM/DB*.

data communications

Transmitting text, voice and video in binary form. See *communications*.

data compression

Encoding data to take up less storage space. Digital data is compressed by finding repeatable patterns of binary 0s and 1s. The more patterns can be found, the more the data can be compressed. Text can generally be compressed to about 40% of its original size, and graphics files from 20% to 90%. Some files compress very little. It depends entirely on the type of file and compression algorithm used.

There are numerous compression methods in use. Two major technologies are Huffman coding and Lempel-Ziv-Welch (LZW), representing examples of the statistical and dictionary compression methods.

When a compression algorithm is packaged for use for a specific platform and file format, it is called a *codec* (compressor/decompressor). ADPCM, PCM and GSM are examples of codecs for sound, and Indeo, Cinepak and MPEG are examples of codecs for video.

In the DOS/Windows world, PKZIP is the most widely-used compression application. See *archive formats*.

Lossless versus Lossy

When text and financial data are compressed, they must be decompressed back to a perfect original, bit for bit. This is known as *lossless compression*. However, audio and video can be compressed to as little as 5% of its original size using *lossy compression*. Some of the data is actually lost, but the loss is not noticeable to the human ear and eye.

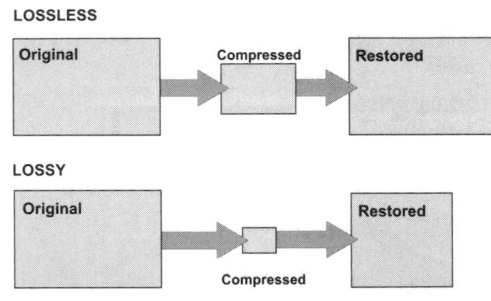

data conferencing

Sharing data interactively among several users in different locations. Data conferencing is made up of whiteboards and application sharing. A whiteboard is the electronic equivalent of the chalkboard or flip chart. Participants at different locations simultaneously write and draw on an on-screen notepad viewed by everyone.

Application sharing is the same as remote control software, in which multiple participants can interactively work in an application that is loaded on only one user's machine. Application viewing is similar to application sharing; however, although all users can see the document, only one person can actually edit it.

Whiteboards and application sharing are often used in conjunction with an audio or videoconferencing connection. An audio-only connection can be a separate telephone call or be transmitted with the data using simultaneous voice and data (SVD) modems. See *T.120*.

data control department

The function responsible for collecting data for input into a computer's batch processing operations as well as the dissemination of the finished reports. The data entry department may be under the jursidiction of the data control department or vice versa.

data conversion

Changing from one type of file format to another. See *conversion*.

DATA/DAT

(DATA/Digital Audio Tape) An earlier DAT format that allowed updating in place by dividing the tape into as many as 254 partitions. It gave way to the DDS formats. See *DAT*.

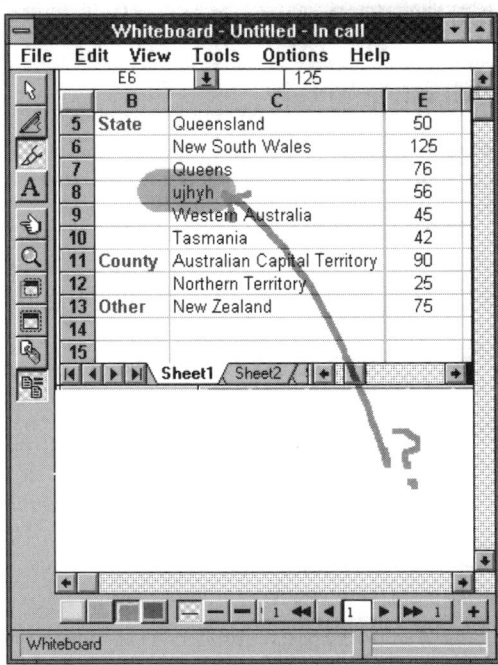

A Whiteboard
In this example, a screen shot of a spreadsheet was copied into the whiteboard. Using the whiteboard's marker, the user is querying another about the garbled text in the column. *(Example courtesy of PictureTel Corporation.)*

data declaration
Same as *data definition*.

data definition
(1) In a source language program, the definitions of data structures (variables, arrays, fields, records, etc.).

(2) A description of the record layout in a file system or DBMS.

data description language
See *DDL*.

data dictionary
A database about data and databases. It holds the name, type, range of values, source, and authorization for access for each data element in the organization's files and databases. It also indicates which application programs use that data so that when a change in a data structure is contemplated, a list of affected programs can be generated.

The data dictionary may be a stand-alone system or an integral part of the DBMS. Data integrity and accuracy is better ensured in the latter case.

data dipper
Software in a personal computer that queries a mainframe database.

data division
The part of a COBOL program that defines the data files and record layouts.

DataEase
A relational DBMS for DOS and Windows from MultiWare, Inc., Trumbull, CT (www.multi-ware.com). It provides a menu-driven interface for developing applications without programming and is noted for its ease of use. DataEase was one of the first products on the PC platform to offer an easier way to develop business applications.

data element
The fundamental data structure in a data processing system. Any unit of data defined for processing is a data element; for example, ACCOUNT NUMBER, NAME, ADDRESS and CITY. A data element is defined by size (in characters) and type (alphanumeric, numeric only, true/false, date, etc.). A specific set of values or range of values may also be part of the definition.

Technically, a data element is a logical definition of data, whereas a field is the physical unit of storage in a record. For example, the data element ACCOUNT NUMBER, which exists only once, is stored in the ACCOUNT NUMBER field in the customer record and in the ACCOUNT NUMBER field in the order records.

DATA ELEMENTS

Product description	Product number
FIELD	FIELD

DATA ITEMS

manilla folder	M004884
pencil	P3883
rubber band	RB45
copy paper	CP2300
paper clip	PC21-8
envelope	E7600

The Basic Unit of Storage
Technically, data elements describe the logical unit of data, fields are the actual storage units, and data items are the individual instances of the data elements as in this example. In everyday language, all three terms are used interchangeably. It's only when you read technical documentation on database management that you run across the proper use of these terms.

data encryption
See *cryptography*.

data entry
Entering data into the computer, which includes keyboard entry, scanning and voice recognition. When transactions are entered after the fact (batch data entry), they are just stacks of source documents to the keyboard operator. Deciphering poor handwriting from a source document is a judgment call that is often error prone. In online data entry operations, in which the operator takes information in person or by phone, there's interaction and involvement with the transaction and less chance for error. See *data loading*.

data entry department

The part of the datacenter where the data entry terminals and operators are located.

data entry operator

A person who enters data into the computer via keyboard or other reading or scanning device.

data entry program

An application program that accepts data from the keyboard or other input device and stores it in the computer. It may be part of an application that also provides updating, querying and reporting.

The data entry program establishes the data in the database and should test for all possible input errors. See *validity checking, table lookup, check digit* and *intelligent database.*

data error

Data on a digital medium has been corrupted. The error can be as little as one bit.

data file

A collection of data records. This term may refer specifically to a database file that contains records and fields in contrast to other files such as a word processing document or spreadsheet. Or, it may refer to a file that contains any type of information structure including documents and spreadsheets in contrast to a program file.

data flow

(1) In computers, the path of data from source document to data entry to processing to final reports. Data changes format and sequence (within a file) as it moves from program to program.

(2) In communications, the path taken by a message from origination to destination and includes all nodes through which the data travels.

data flow diagram

A description of data and the manual and machine processing performed on the data.

data fork

The part of a Macintosh file that contains data. For example, in a HyperCard stack, text, graphics and HyperTalk scripts reside in the data fork, while fonts, sounds, control information and external functions reside in the resource fork.

data format

Same as *file format.*

Data General

(Data General Corporation, Westboro, MA, www.dg.com) A computer manufacturer founded in 1968 by Edson de Castro. In 1969, it introduced the Nova, the first 16-bit mini with four accumulators, a leading technology at the time. During its early years, the company was successful in the scientific, academic and OEM markets. With its 32-bit ECLIPSE family of computers and its Comprehensive Electronic Office (CEO) software, Data General gained entry into the commercial marketplace in the early 1980s.

In 1989, the company introduced its AViiON line of UNIX-based servers that use the Motorola 88000 CPU, and more powerful models continue to be introduced. Data General's CLARiiON line of fault-tolerant (RAID) storage systems, introduced in 1992, are available for UNIX-based IBM and Sun computer systems.

The "Eagle project," DG's development of its ECLIPSE and first 32-bit computer, was chronicled in Tracy Kidder's Pulitzer-prize winning novel, "Soul of a New Machine," published by Little, Brown and Company, ISBN 0-316-49170-5.

Edson de Castro
De Castro founded Data General as the minicomputer market began to flourish. His line of Nova machines helped expand the market for low-priced (under $100,000) computers. This was a time when minicomputers were expected to make mainframes obsolete. *(Courtesy of Data General Corporation.)*

Computer Desktop Encyclopedia

data glove

A glove used to report the position of a user's hand and fingers to a computer. See *virtual reality*.

datagram

The unit of data, or packet, transmitted in a TCP/IP network. Each datagram contains source and destination addresses and data. See *UDP*.

DataHub

A database administration tool for DB2 and other database environments from IBM. It functions as a control center for accessing databases located throughout the enterprise.

data independence

Techniques that allow data to be changed without affecting the applications that process it. There are two kinds of data independence. The first type is data independence for data, which is accomplished in an database management system (DBMS). It allows the database to be structurally changed without affecting most existing programs. Programs access data in a DBMS by field and are concerned with only the data fields they use, not the format of the complete record. Thus, when the record layout is updated (fields added, deleted or changed in size), the only programs that must be changed are those that use those new fields.

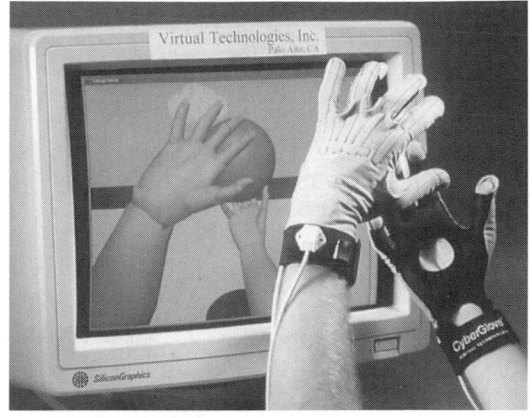

The Data Glove
This CyberGlove from Virtual Technologies is an example of a data glove. The wearer is playing a simulated ballgame. As he views the monitor, his hand movements are translated onto the screen via the data gloves. Each of the gloves in the picture contain 18 movement sensors. *(Photo courtesy of Virtual Technologies, Inc.)*

The second type is data independence for processing. This means that any data that can possibly be changed should be stored in a database and not "hard wired" into the code of the program. When values change, only the database item is altered, which is a simple task, rather than recompiling programs.

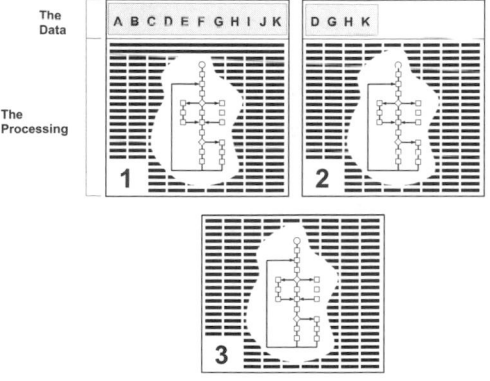

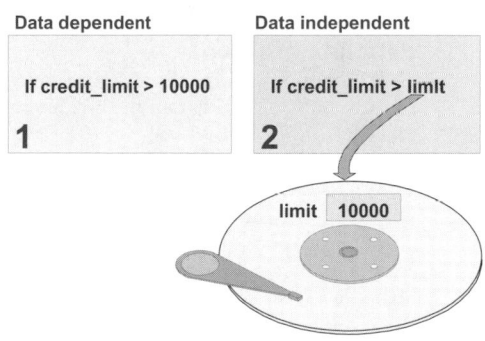

Data Independence for Data

Program #1 reserves space for the entire record (fields A to K). If the record format is changed, the space must be changed. Program #2 calls the DBMS to deliver just the fields it uses (D G H K). It still reserves space, but unless a field has been resized, it is not affected by other field changes. Program #3 is fully independent of the data structure. It calls for data by field name, and the DBMS allocates the space at runtime.

Data Independence for Processing

Program #1 uses a hard-coded value to test credit limit. To change the limit, the program must be recompiled. Program #2 retrieves the credit limit from a database. To change it, only the database must be updated, a simpler task.

data integrity
The process of preventing accidental erasure or adulteration in a database.

data item
A unit of data stored in a field. See *field*.

data legibility
The clear readability of data in a decision support system (DSS). One of the keys to a successful DSS is its ability to provide understandable answers to queries, which conform to the user's business model and use recognizable field and table names.

data library
(1) The section of the datacenter that houses offline disks and tapes. Data library personnel are responsible for cataloging and maintaining the media.

(2) A directory on a server that contains files for downloading. BBSs and online services sometimes call these sections data libraries.

data line
An individual circuit, or line, that carries data within a computer or communications channel.

data line monitor
In communications, a test instrument that analyzes the signals and timing of a communications line. It either visually displays the patterns or stores the activity for further analysis.

data link
In communications, the physical interconnection between two points (OSI layers 1 and 2). It may also refer to the modems, protocols and all required hardware and software to perform the transmission.

data link escape
A communications control character which indicates that the following character is not data, but a control code.

data link layer
The services in the OSI protocol stack (layer 2 of 7) that manage node-to-node transmission. See *data link protocol, OSI* and *MAC layer*.

data link protocol
In communications, the transmission of a unit of data from one node to another (OSI layer 2). It is responsible for ensuring that the bits received are the same as the bits sent. Following are the major categories:

Asynchronous Transmission
Originating from mechanical teletype machines, asynchronous transmission treats each character as a unit with start and stop bits appended to it. It is the common form of transmission between the serial port of a personal computer or terminal and a modem. ASCII, or teletype, protocols provide little or no error checking. File transfer protocols, such as Zmodem and Ymodem, provide data link services as well as higher-level services, collectively known as transport services.

Synchronous Transmission
Developed for mainframe networks using higher speeds than teletype terminals, synchronous transmission sends contiguous blocks of data, with both sending and receiving stations synchronized to each other. Synchronous protocols include error checking. Examples are IBM's SDLC, Digital's DDCMP, and the international HDLC.

LANs
Developed for medium to high transmission speeds between stations, LANs typically use collision detection (CSMA/CD) or token passing methods for transmitting data between nodes. Common examples are Ethernet, Token Ring and FDDI.

The IEEE 802 specification for LANs breaks the data link layer into two sublayers: the LLC (Logical Link Control) and MAC (Media Access Control). The LLC provides a common interface point to the

MAC layers, which specify the access method used. The following compares the data link layer in LANs to IBM's SNA and ISO's OSI model.

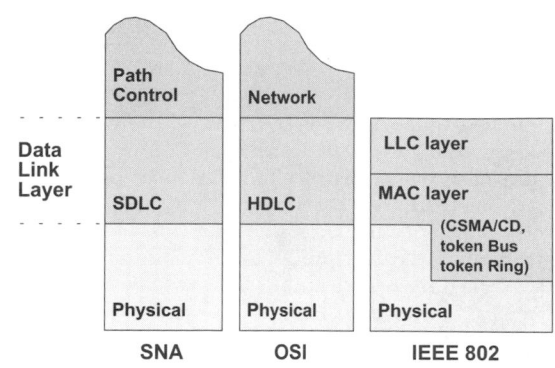

Data Link Switching

See *DLSw.*

data loading

Coping data from one electronic file or database into another. Data loading implies converting from one format into another; for example, from one type of production database into a decision support database from a different vendor. See *data entry.*

data management

Refers to several levels of managing data. From bottom to top, they are:

(1) The part of the operating system that manages the physical storage and retrieval of data on a disk or other device. See *access method.*

(2) Software that allows for the creation, storage, retrieval and manipulation of files interactively at a terminal or personal computer. See *file manager* and *DBMS.*

(3) The function that manages data as an organizational resource. See *data administration.*

(4) The management of all data/information in an organization. It includes data administration, the standards for defining data and the way in which people perceive and use it.

data management system

See *DBMS.*

data manipulation

Processing data.

data manipulation language

A language that requests data from a DBMS. It is coded within the application program such as COBOL or C.

data mart

A subset of a data warehouse for a single department or function. A data mart may have tens of gigabytes of data rather than hundreds of gigabytes for the entire enterprise. See *data warehouse.*

data migration

See *HSM.*

data mining

Exploring detailed business transactions. It implies "digging through tons of data"

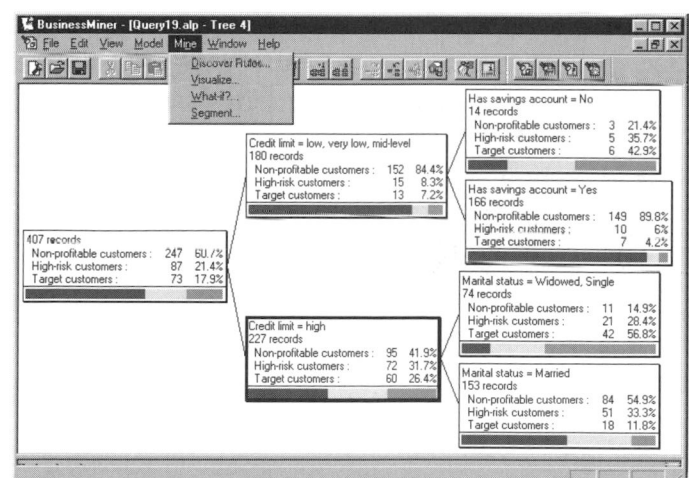

Data Mining

The goal of this credit card analysis is to determine the most influential factors common to non-profitable customers. In this case, BusinessMiner from Business Objects determined that the credit limit had the greatest effect on profitability and prioritized the results in graphical form. *(Screen shot courtesy of Business Objects.)*

to uncover patterns and relationships contained within the business activity and history. Data mining can be done manually by slicing and dicing the data until a pattern becomes obvious. Or, it can be done with programs that analyze the data automatically. See *OLAP, DSS, EIS, data warehouse* and *slice and dice.*

data mirroring

See *replication*.

data model

A description of the organization of a database. It is often created as an entity relationship diagram. Today's modeling tools allow the attributes and tables (fields and records) to be graphically created. The SQL code that defines the data structure (schema) in the database is automatically created from the visual representation.

data modem

A modem used for sending data and not faxes. See *modem* and *fax/modem*.

data module

A sealed, removable storage module containing magnetic disks and their associated access arms and read/write heads.

data name

The name assigned to a field or variable.

data network

A communications network that transmits data. See *communications*.

data packet

One frame in a packet-switched message. Most data communications is based on dividing the transmitted message into packets. For example, an Ethernet packet can be from 64 to 1518 bytes in length.

data parallel

Same as *SIMD*.

DataPhone

An AT&T trade name for various equipment and services. See *DDS*.

dataport

(1) An RJ-11 telephone socket that provides an outside line for sending data or a fax via modem. In the 1990s, hotels and motels throughout the U.S. started installing dataports in their rooms for customer use. See *RJ-11*.

(2) Any socket used for data communications, which can include infrared, serial and parallel ports.

data processing

(1) Processing information by machines. Data processing was the first name used for the information technology business, and it is still used as an umbrella title. In the early days, it meant feeding punched cards into tabulating machines. Then came computers.

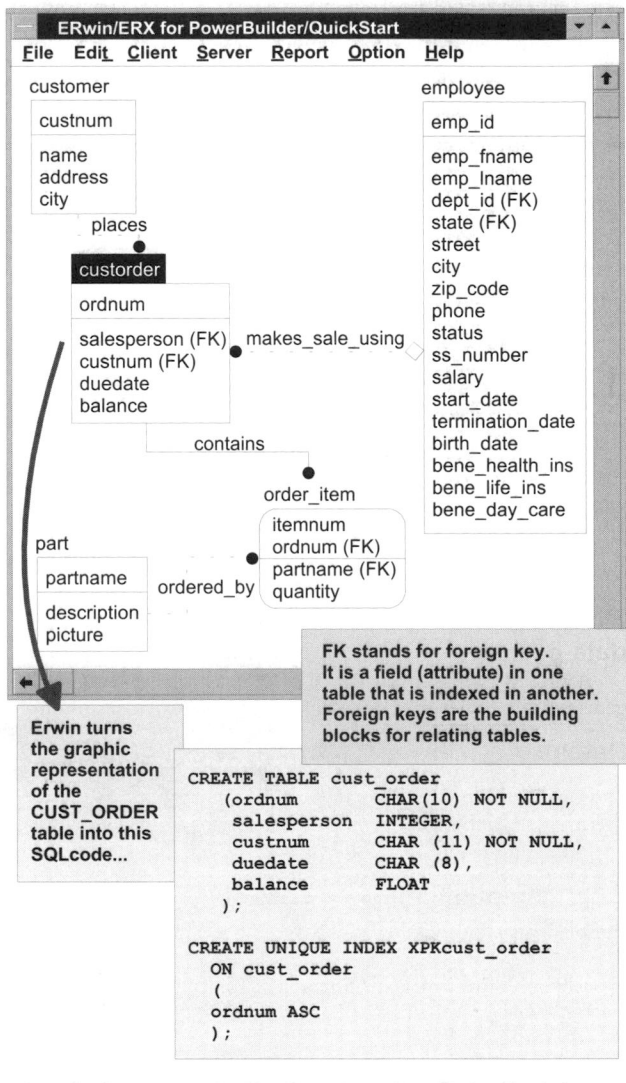

FK stands for foreign key. It is a field (attribute) in one table that is indexed in another. Foreign keys are the building blocks for relating tables.

Erwin turns the graphic representation of the CUST_ORDER table into this SQLcode...

```
CREATE TABLE cust_order
   (ordnum        CHAR(10) NOT NULL,
    salesperson   INTEGER,
    custnum       CHAR (11) NOT NULL,
    duedate       CHAR (8),
    balance       FLOAT
   );

CREATE UNIQUE INDEX XPKcust_order
   ON cust_order
   (
   ordnum ASC
   );
```

Building an Entity Relationship Data Model
The Erwin modeling program from Logic Works, Princeton, NJ, stands for Entity Relationship for Windows. In this order processing example, the tables for customers and orders are drawn graphically, and Erwin turns the graph into the appropriate SQL code for the target database. *(Example courtesy of Logic Works, Inc.)*

(2) Processing data/information. In this context, it refers specifically to processing the actual data of the business (raw number crunching) in contrast to the processing overhead of the operating system and networks. In many instances, the computer does very little data processing compared to the processing required by the operating system, graphical interface and other infrastructure components.

data processor

(1) A person who works in data processing.

(2) A computer that is processing data, in contrast with a computer performing another task, such as controlling a network.

data projector

A device that projects output from a computer onto a remote screen. The older-style data projectors are large and heavy and use tubes to create the image. Newer units weigh less than 20 pounds and combine an internal LCD panel with a light source that provides excellent viewing on large screens. Data projectors generally accept VGA output, and many support standard VCR/TV video. See *LCD panel* and *DLP*.

Data Propagator

An IBM query language that maintains consistency between DB2 and IMS/ESA DB databases. When data is changed in the IMS database, it is automatically changed in the DB2 database.

DataPropagator

A database administration tool for DB2 and other database environments from IBM. It is used to keep relational databases in sync throughout the enterprise.

data pump

A circuit that transmits pulses in a digital device. It typically refers to the chipset in a modem that generates the bits based on the modem's modulation techniques.

Dataquest

(Dataquest Inc., San Jose, CA, www.dataquest.com) A major market research and analysis firm in the information field. Dataquest offers market intelligence on more than 25 topics and provides conferences, annual subscriptions and custom research. Founded in 1971 as a unit of First Texas Inc., a Houston-based brokerage firm, it was spun off in 1976. In 1978, it was acquired by A.C. Nielsen Company, which itself was acquired by The Dun & Bradstreet Corporation in 1984. In 1995, Dataquest was acquired by the Gartner Group, Stamford, CT, also a leader in IT market research and analysis.

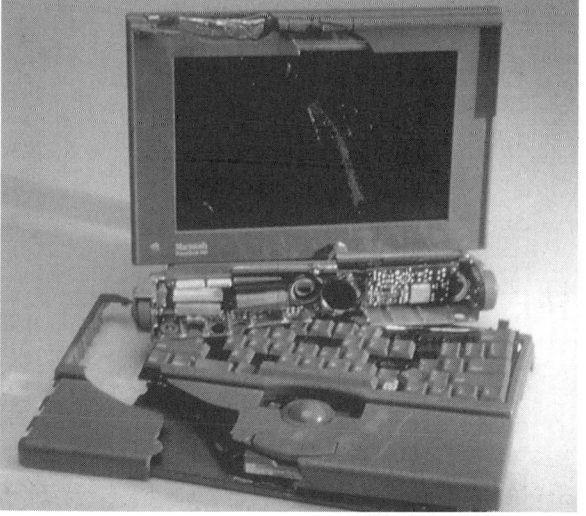

data rate

(1) The data transfer speed within the computer or between a peripheral and computer.

(2) The data transmission speed in a network.

data recovery

Restoring data that has been physically damaged or corrupted on a disk or tape. Disks and tapes can become corrupted due to viruses, bad software, hardware failure as well as from power failures that occur while the magnetic media is being written.

Recovered Data
Since 1985, the DriveSavers service bureau in Novato, CA, (www.drivesavers.com), has recovered data from damaged hard disks of all kinds. Even fires and natural disasters cannot keep them from successfully retrieving vital records from computers such as this. *(Photo courtesy of DriveSavers, Inc.)*

data repository
See *repository*.

data representation
How data types are structured; for example, how signs are represented in numerical values or how strings are formatted (enclosed in quotes, terminated with a null, etc.).

data resource management
Same as *data administration*.

data set
(1) A data file or collection of interrelated data. The term is used in the mainframe community, whereas file is used almost everywhere else.
(2) A modem in AT&T terminology.

data set ready
See *DSR*.

data sharing
See *data conferencing*.

data sheet
A page or two of detailed information about a product.

data signal
Physical data as it travels over a line or channel (pulses or vibrations of electricity or light).

data sink
A device or part of the computer that receives data.

data source
A device or part of the computer in which data is originated.

DataStage
A data extraction and transformation program for Windows NT servers from VMARK. It is used to pull data from legacy databases, flat files and relational databases and convert them into data marts and data warehouses.

data stream
The continuous flow of data from one place to another.

data striping
See *disk striping*.

data structure
The physical layout of data. Data fields, memo fields, fixed length fields, variable length fields, records, word processing documents, spreadsheets, data files, database files and indexes are all examples of data structures.

data switch
A switch box that routes one line to another; for example, to connect two computers to one printer. Manual switches have dials or buttons. Automatic switches test for signals and provide first-come, first-served switching.

data system
Same as *information system*.

data tablet
Same as *digitizer tablet*.

data terminating equipment
See *DTE*.

Computer Desktop Encyclopedia

data transfer

The movement of data within the computer system. Typically, data is said to be transferred within the computer, but it is "transmitted" over a communications network. A transfer is actually a copy function since the data is not automatically erased at the source.

data transfer rate

Same as *data rate*.

data transmission

Sending data over a communications network.

data transparency

The ability to easily access and work with data no matter where it is located or what application created it.

data type

A category of data. Typical data types are numeric, alphanumeric (character), dates and logical (true/false). Programming languages allow for the creation of different data types.

When data is assigned a type, it cannot be treated like another type. For example, alphanumeric data cannot be calculated, and digits within numeric data cannot be isolated. Date types can only contain valid dates.

data warehouse

A database designed to support decision making in an organization. It is batch updated and structured for fast online queries and summaries for managers. Data warehouses can contain enormous amounts of data. For example, large retail organizations can have 100GB or more of transaction history. When the database is organized for one department or function, it is often called a *data mart* rather than a data warehouse. See *OLAP, DSS* and *EIS*.

data word

See *word*.

date math

Calculations made upon dates. For example, March 30 + 5 yields April 4.

date windowing

Solving the Year 2000 problem without altering the database. The six-digit date remains in the database, but the programs convert it into an eight-digit date for computation, display and reporting.

datum

The singular form of data; for example, one datum. It is rarely used, and data, its plural form, is commonly used for both singular and plural.

daughterboard, daughtercard

A printed circuit board that plugs into another printed circuit board to augment its capabilities. Although Intel's Pentium II SEC modules are sometimes called daughterboards, it more typically refers to a small board that attaches to a removable expansion board such as a display adapter or sound card.

DAVID

(Digital Audio/Video Interactive Decoder) An operating system for set-top boxes from Microware Systems Corporation, Des Moines, IA, (www.microware.com). Based on Microware's OS-9 realtime operating system, it is used for interactive TV, video on demand and Internet applications. See *OS-9*.

dazdee

See *DASD*.

DB

See *database* and *decibel*.

DB2

(DATABASE 2) A relational DBMS from IBM that was originally developed for its mainframes. It is

a full-featured SQL language DBMS that has
become IBM's major database product. Known for
its industrial strength reliability, IBM has made DB/
2 available for all of its own platforms, including
OS/2, OS/400, AIX (RS/6000) and OS/390), as
well as for Solaris on Sun systems and HP-UX on
HP 9000 workstations and servers. See *DB2 UDB*.

DB2/2, DB2/400, DB2/6000
The OS/2, AS/400 and RS/6000 versions of
DB2. See *DB2*.

DB2 UDB
(DB2 **U**niversal **Da**ta**B**ase) An enhanced version
of DB2 that combines relational and object database
technology as well as various query optimization
techniques for parallel processing. Also geared for
electronic commerce, DB2 UDB provides graphical
administration, Java and JDBC support.

DB-9, DB-15, DB-25, DB-37, DB-50
A family of plugs and sockets widely used in
communications and computer devices. DB
connectors come in 9, 15, 25, 37 and 50-pin sizes.
The DB connector defines the physical structure of
the connector, not the purpose of each line.

A DB-9 connector is commonly used for the 1st
serial port (COM1) on a PC, which is typically
connected to the mouse. A DB-25 connector is used
for the 2nd serial port (COM2), often connected to
a modem, as well as the parallel port (see *printer
cable*). DB-25s are also used in a wide variety of
communications devices.

A high-density DB-15 connector is used for the
VGA port on a PC, which has 15 pins in the same
shell as the 9 pins in the DB-9 connector.

DBA
See *database administrator*.

dBASE
A relational database management (DBMS) and
application development system for DOS and
Windows from INPRISE. dBASE was the first
sophisticated database program for personal
computers and has been widely used since the early
1980s. dBASE file formats are de facto standards.

Starting with dBASE for Windows and then Visual dBASE, it became a client/server development
system with the inclusion of the Borland Database Engine. dBASE has automatic links to the Engine's
IDAPI interface, allowing dBASE applications to access remote database servers.

dBASE provides a Pascal-like, interpreted programming language and fourth-generation commands for
interactive use. The following dBASE 3GL example converts Fahrenheit to Celsius:

```
INPUT "Enter Fahrenheit  " TO FAHR
? "Celsius is ", (FAHR - 32) * 5 / 9
```

The following dBASE 4GL example opens the product file and displays green items:

```
use products
list for color ="GREEN"
```

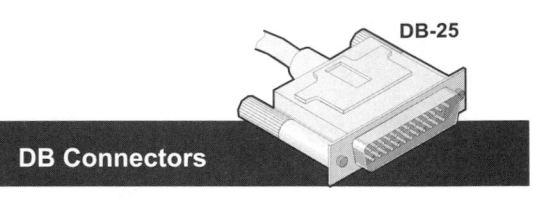

DB Connectors

DB-9 — Serial port (RS-232).

High-density DB-15 — VGA port.

DB-15 — Game port on PC, Thick Ethernet.

DB-25 — Parallel port on PC, Serial port (RS-232).

DB-37 — RS-423, 442, 449.

DB-50 — Dataproducts, Datapoint, etc.

DB Connectors
DB connectors are widely used to hook up computer
and communications devices.

EVOLUTION OF dBASE

dBASE II was the first comprehensive relational DBMS for personal computers. Originally named Vulcan, dBASE II was created by Wayne Ratliff to manage a company football pool. It was modeled after JPLDIS, the DBMS at Jet Propulsion Labs in Los Angeles.

Renamed dBASE II when Hal Lashlee and George Tate formed Ashton-Tate to market it (Ashton-Tate was acquired by Borland in 1991), dBASE became a huge success within a couple of years.

dBASE spawned the "Xbase" industry, which included Clipper, FoxBase, FoxPro and other products that provided a dBASE-like programming language and support for dBASE file formats.

dBASE compiler

Software that converts dBASE source language into machine language. The resulting programs execute on their own like COBOL or C programs and do not run under dBASE. See *CA-Clipper*.

DBCS

(Double Byte Character Set) See *Unicode*.

DB/DC

(DataBase/Data Communications) Refers to software that performs database and data communications functions.

C. Wayne Ratliff
Ratliff designed and programmed the first successful DBMS for personal computers, dBASE II. *(Photo courtesy Ratliff Software Productions.)*

DBEF

(Dual Brightness Enhancement Film) A film that increases the brightness of LCD screens from 3M. The film recycles most of the light that is normally lost in the rear polarizer.

DB EXPO

A trade show for IT professionals originally from the Blenheim Group and later Miller Freeman, Inc., that specialized in database and related products. It had become part of IT Forum, which was discontinued after its final show in April 1998.

DBMS

(DataBase Management System) Software that controls the organization, storage, retrieval, security and integrity of data in a database. It accepts requests from the application and instructs the operating system to transfer the appropriate data.

DBMSs may work with traditional programming languages (COBOL, C, etc.) or they may include their own programming language for application development.

DBMSs let information systems be changed more easily as the organization's requirements change. New categories of data can be added to the database without disruption to the existing system. Adding a field to a record does not require changing any of the programs that do not use the data in that new field.

MAJOR FEATURES OF A DBMS

Data Security

The DBMS can prevent unauthorized users from viewing or updating the database. Using passwords, users are allowed access to the entire database or subsets of it called *subschemas*. For example, in an employee database, some users may be able to view salaries while others may view only work history and medical data.

Data Integrity

The DBMS can ensure that no more than one user can update the same record at the same time. It can keep duplicate records out of the database; for example, no two customers with the same customer number can be entered.

Interactive Query

Most DBMSs provide query languages and report writers that let users interactively interrogate the database and analyze its data. This important feature gives users access to all management information as needed.

Interactive Data Entry and Updating

Many DBMSs provide a way to interactively enter and edit data, allowing you to manage your own files and databases. However, interactive operation does not leave an audit trail and does not provide the controls necessary in a large organization. These controls must be programmed into the data entry and update programs of the application.

This is a common misconception about personal computer DBMSs. Complex business systems can be developed in dBASE and Paradox, etc., but not without programming. This is not the same as creating lists of data for your own record keeping.

Data Independence

With DBMSs, the details of the data structure are not stated in each application program. The program asks the DBMS for data by field name; for example, a coded equivalent of "give me customer name and balance due" would be sent to the DBMS. Without a DBMS, the programmer must reserve space for the full structure of the record in the program. Any change in data structure requires changing all application programs.

DATABASE DESIGN

A business information system is made up of subjects (customers, employees, vendors, etc.) and activities (orders, payments, purchases, etc.). Database design is the process of organizing this data into related record types. The DBMS that is chosen is the one that can support the organization's data structure while efficiently processing the transaction volume.

Organizations may use one kind of DBMS for daily transaction processing and then move the detail to another DBMS better suited for random inquiries and analysis.

Overall systems design decisions are performed by data administrators and systems analysts. Detailed database design is performed by database administrators.

HIERARCHICAL, NETWORK AND RELATIONAL DATABASES

Information systems are made up of related files: customers and orders, vendors and purchases, etc. A key DBMS feature is its ability to manage these relationships.

Hierarchical databases link records like an organization chart. A record type can be owned by only one owner. In the following example, orders are owned by only one customer. Hierarchical structures were widely used with early mainframe systems; however, they are often restrictive in linking real-world structures.

In network databases, a record type can have multiple owners. In the example below, orders are owned by both customers and products, reflecting their natural relationship in business.

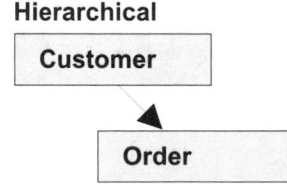

Relational databases do not link records together physically, but the design of the records must provide a common field, such as account number, to allow for matching. Often, the fields used for matching are indexed in order to speed up the process.

In the following example, customers, orders and products are linked by comparing data fields and/or indexes when information from more than one record type is needed. This method is more flexible for ad hoc inquiries. Many hierarchical and network DBMSs also provide this capability.

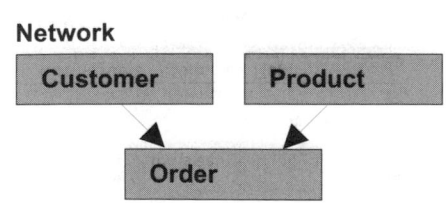

OBJECT DATABASES

Certain information systems may have complex data structures not easily modeled by traditional data structures. A newer type of database, known as the *object database*, can be employed when hierarchical, network and relational structures are too restrictive. Object databases can easily handle one-to-many relationships combined with many-to-one relationships.

Relational

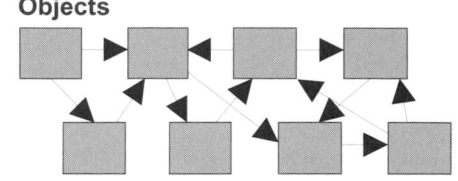

The world of information is also made up of data, text, pictures and voice. Many DBMSs manage text as well as data, but very few manage both with equal proficiency. Throughout the 1990s, DBMSs will begin to integrate all forms of information. Eventually, it will be common for a database to handle data, text, graphics, voice and video with the same ease as today's systems handle data.

The relational DBMS is not suited to storing multimedia data, because there are so many different types of sound and video formats. Although a relational DBMS may provide a LOB (large object) field that holds anything, extensive use of this field can strain the processing.

An object database is often better suited for multimedia. Using the object model, an object-oriented DBMS can store anything or refer to anything. For example, a video object can reference a video file stored elsewhere on some other hard disk and launch the video player software necessary to play it.

INTELLIGENT DATABASES

All DBMSs provide some data validation; for example, they can reject invalid dates or alphabetic data entered into money fields. But most validation is left up to the application programs.

Intelligent databases provide more validation; for example, table lookups can reject bad spelling or coding of items. Common algorithms can also be used such as one that computes sales tax for an order based on zip code.

When validation is left up to each application program, one program could allow an item to be entered while another program rejects it. Data integrity is better served when data validation is done in only one place. Mainframe DBMSs are increasingly becoming intelligent. Eventually all DBMSs will follow suit.

DBOMP

(DataBase Organization and Maintenance Processor) An early DBMS that was derived from BOMP.

DBQ

(DataBase for Quality) An RDBMS from Murphy Software, Southfield, MI, that runs on Windows clients and the AS/400. Specialized for quality management, it is used to promote ISO 9000 compliance.

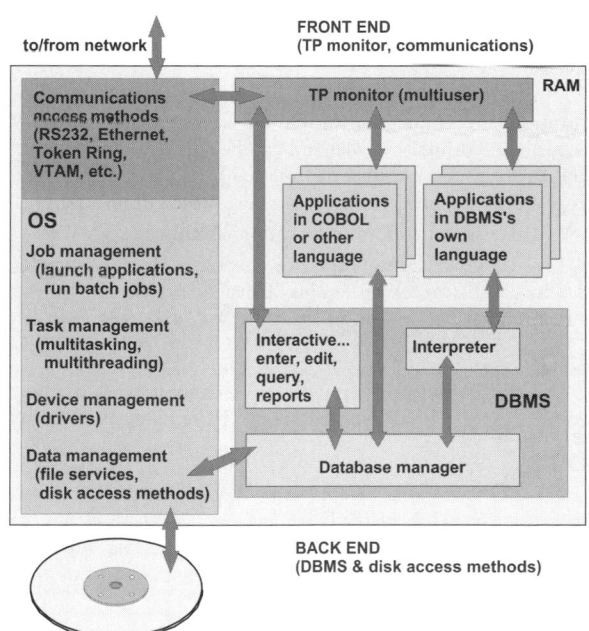

DBMS and OS Interaction

This diagram shows the interaction between the DBMS with other system and application software running in memory.

DBS

(Direct Broadcast Satellite) A one-way TV broadcast service from a satellite to a small 18" dish antenna. DBS offers every household in the country a cable-like TV service, using a highly-compressed digital signal. Prior to DBS, large dishes and costly equipment were required, and multiple satellites made viewing complicated.

Although DBS service existed in other countries, the first DBS satellite in the U.S. was launched in late 1993 by Hughes Communications (DirecTV) and Hubbard Broadcasting (USSB). DirecTV and USSB were offered in 1994 using the DSS standard, with equipment made by RCA and other manufacturers.

Soon after, Primestar introduced its DBS service, which includes installation of its own equipment that is leased along with the monthly programming. In 1995, EchoStar launched its first satellite and offers purchase, finance and lease options for its DISH (DIgital Sky Highway) network.

DB to DB adapter

A device that connects one type of DB connector to another. For example, a DB to DB adapter is used to connect a 9-pin mouse to a 25-pin serial port.

DC

(1) (Direct Current) An electrical current that travels in one direction and used within the computer's electronic circuits. Contrast with *AC*.

(2) (Data Communications) See *DB/DC*.

DC-2000

See *QIC*.

DCA

(1) (Document Content Architecture) IBM file formats for text documents. DCA/RFT (Revisable-Form Text) is the primary format and can be edited. DCA/FFT (Final-Form Text) has been formatted for a particular output device and cannot be changed. For example, page numbers, headers and footers are placed on every page.

(2) (Distributed Communications Architecture) A network architecture from Unisys.

(3) (Digital Communications Associates, Inc., Alpharetta, GA) A manufacturer of communications products, known for its famous "Irma" board. In late 1994, DCA merged with and became part of Attachmate Corporation of Bellevue, WA. See *Irma board*.

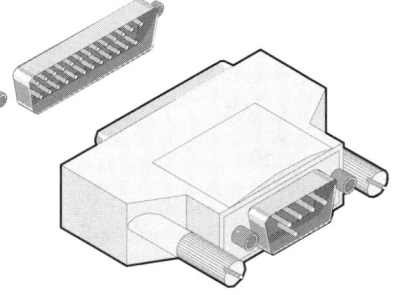

DB to DB Adapter
This male DB-9 to female DB-25 adapter is commonly used to attach a 9-pin plug on a mouse cable to a 25-pin serial port.

D/CAS

(Data/CASsette) A tape backup technology that uses an upgraded version of the common audio tape cassette. It can hold as much as 600MB of data.

DCC

(1) (Direct Cable Connection) A Windows 95/98 feature that allows PCs to be cabled together for data transfer. DCC actually sets up a network connection between the two machines. Even though it is not a dial-up situation, DCC requires that the Dial-Up Networking function be activated.

(2) (Digital Compact Cassette) A digital tape format that used a variation of the common analog audio cassette. DCC never caught on.

(3) (Digital Content Creation) The development of newsworthy, educational and entertainment material for distribution over the Internet or other digital media.

(4) (Distributed Call Center) An automatic call distribution (ACD) system from Teloquent Communications, Billerica, MA, (www.teloquent.com), that runs on standard PCs and uses public ISDN lines.

DCE

(1) (Data Communications Equipment or Data Circuit-terminating Equipment) A device that establishes, maintains and terminates a session on a network. It may also convert signals for transmission. It is typically the modem. Contrast with *DTE*.

(2) (Distributed Computing Environment) A set of programs from The Open Group that allows applications to be built across heterogeneous platforms in a network. DCE includes security, directory naming, time synchronization, file sharing, RPCs and multithreading services. DCE source code is licensed to major vendors, who sell the executable programs to their customers.

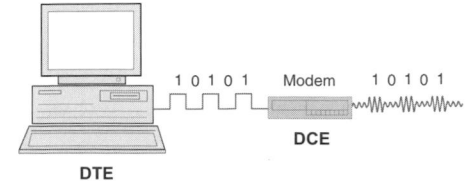

DCE and CORBA, the OMG's distributed, multi-platform implementation, are not mutually exclusive. For example, IBM uses DCE directory and time services in its CORBA-compliant SOM/DSOM implementation. CORBA can use DCE's RPC (remote procedure call) as its communications mechanism.

DCI

(Display Control Interface) An Intel/Microsoft programming interface for full-motion video and games in Windows. It allows applications to take advantage of video accelerator features built into the display adapter. DCI requires updated display drivers and the DCI DLL from Microsoft. DCI has been superseded by DirectDraw in Windows 95.

DCL

(1) (Digital Command Language) Digital's standard command language for the VMS operating system on its VAX series.

(2) (Data Compression Library) A set of compression routines that allow realtime compression and decompression of data.

(3) (Data Control Language) A language used to gain access to or manage a database.

DCOM

(Distributed Component Object Model) Formerly called *Network OLE*, it is Microsoft's technology for distributed objects. DCOM is based on COM, Microsoft's component software architecture, which defines the object interfaces. DCOM defines the remote procedure call which allows those objects to be run remotely over the network. DCOM began shipping with Windows NT 4.0 and is Microsoft's counterpart to CORBA. See *COM, component software* and *CORBA*.

DCS

(1) (Distributed Communications System) A telephone system that puts small switches close to subscribers making local loops shorter and maximizing long lines to the central office.

(2) (Digital Cross-connect System) See *digital cross-connect*.

(3) (Desktop Color Separation) A graphics format for color separation that uses five Encapsulated PostScript (EPS) files, one for each of the CMYK colors, and one master file, which links the other four and contains a preview image.

(4) (Distributed Control System) A process control system that uses disbursed computers throughout the manufacturing line for control.

DCT

(Discrete Cosine Transform) An algorithm, similar to Fast Fourier Transform, that converts data (pixels, waveforms, etc.) into sets of frequencies. The first frequencies in the set are the most meaningful; the latter, the least. For compression, latter frequencies are stripped away based on allowable resolution loss. The DCT method is used in the JPEG and MPEG compression.

DD

(Double Density) The designation for low-density diskettes, typically the 5.25" 360K and 3.5" 720K floppies. See *double density*. Contrast with *HD*.

D/DAT

See *DAT/DAT*.

DDBMS

(Distributed Database Management System) See *distributed database*.

DDC

See *VESA DDC*.

DDCMP

(Digital Data Communications Message Protocol) Digital's proprietary, synchronous data link protocol used in DECnet.

DDE

(Dynamic Data Exchange) A message protocol in Windows that allows application programs to request and exchange data between them automatically.

DDL

(1) (Data Description Language) A language used to define data and their relationships to other data. It is used to create the data structure in a database. Major database management systems (DBMSs) use a SQL data description language.

(2) (Document Description Language) A printer control language from Imagen that runs on the HP LaserJet series.

(3) (Direct Data Link) The ability of a supplier to directly interrogate a customer's inventory database in order to manage scheduling and shipping more efficiently. Pioneered by Ford Motor Co. in 1988, Ford lets suppliers check stock levels in assembly plants throughout North America.

DDM

(Distributed Data Management) Software in an IBM SNA environment that allows users to access data in remote files within the network. DDM works with IBM's LU 6.2 session to provide peer-to-peer communications and file sharing.

DDP

(Distributed Data Processing) See *distributed processing*.

DDR DRAM, DDR SDRAM

See *SDRAM*.

DDS

(1) (Dataphone Digital Service) An AT&T private line digital service with data rates from 2400 bps to 56Kbps. Private analog lines can be connected to DDS lines.

(2) (Digital Data Service) A private line digital service from a non-AT&T carrier.

(3) (Digital Data Storage) See *DAT*.

(4) (Data Dictionary System) See *OpenDDS*.

dead link

A World Wide Web link that turns up a "404 error" if the target page is deleted from the site or moved to another directory. See *404 error*.

deadlock, deadly embrace

A stalemate that occurs when two elements in a process are each waiting for the other to respond. For example, in a network, if one user is working on file A and needs file B to continue, but another user is working on file B and needs file A to continue, each one waits for the other. Both are temporarily locked out. The software must be able to deal with this.

dead tree

Paper. Any printed version of reference material or documentation. Contrast with *electronic publishing*.

deallocate

To release a computer resource that is currently assigned to a program or user, such as memory or a peripheral device.

debit

A monetary amount that is subtracted from an account balance. A debit from one account is a credit to another. See *credit*.

deblock

To separate records from a block.

debug

To correct a problem in hardware or software. Debugging software is finding the errors in the program logic. Debugging hardware is finding the errors in circuit design.

debugger

Software that helps a programmer debug a program by stopping at certain breakpoints and displaying various programming elements. The programmer can step through source code statements one at a time while the corresponding machine instructions are being executed.

DEC

(Digital Equipment Corporation) The trade name for Digital's products (DECmate, DECnet, etc.). Many people refer to the company as DEC.

decay

The reduction of strength of a signal or charge.

decentralized processing

Computer systems in different locations. Although data may be transmitted between the computers periodically, it implies limited daily communications. Contrast with *distributed computing* and *centralized processing*.

decibel

(dB) The unit that measures loudness or strength of a signal. dBs are a relative measurement derived from an initial reference level and a final observed level. A whisper is about 20 dB, a normal conversation about 60 dB, a noisy factory 90 dB and loud thunder 110 dB. 120 dB is the threshold of pain.

decimal

Meaning 10. The universal numbering system that uses 10 digits. Computers use binary numbers because it is easier to design electronic systems that can maintain two states rather than 10.

decipher

Same as *decrypt*.

decision box

A diamond-shaped symbol that is used to document a decision point in a flowchart. The decision is written in the decision box, and the results of the decision branch off from the points in the box.

decision instruction

In programming, an instruction that compares one set of data with another and branches to a different part of the program depending on the results.

decision making

Making choices. The proper balance of human and machine decision making is an important part of a system's design.

It is easy to think of automating tasks traditionally performed by people, but it is not that easy to analyze how decisions are made by an experienced, intuitive worker. If an improper analysis of human decision making is made, the wrong decision making may be placed into the machine, which can get buried in documentation that is rarely reviewed. This will become an important issue as AI applications proliferate.

From a programming point of view, decision making is performed two ways: algorithmic, a precise set of rules and conditions that never change, or heuristic, a set of rules that may change over time (self-modify) as conditions occur. Heuristic techniques are employed in AI systems.

decision support system

See *DSS, EIS* and *OLAP*.

decision table

A list of decisions and their criteria. Designed as a matrix, it lists criteria (inputs) and the results (outputs) of all possible combinations of the criteria. It can be placed into a program to direct its processing. By changing the decision table, the program is changed accordingly.

decision tree
A graphical representation of all alternatives in a decision making process.

deck
The part of a magnetic tape unit that holds and moves the tape reels. See also *DEC*.

declaration
In programming, an instruction or statement that defines data (fields, variables, arrays, etc.) and resources, but does not create executable code.

DECmate
A family of computer systems from Digital specialized for word processing. Introduced in 1981, DECmates use the PDP-8 architecture.

DECmcc
(DEC Managment Control Center) Digital's network management software for DECnet and TCP/IP. DECmcc Management Stations for VMS and ULTRIX support X Window and provide color-coded alarms.

DECnet
Digital's communications network, which supports Ethernet-style LANs and baseband and broadband WANs over private and public lines. It interconnects PDPs, VAXs, PCs, Macs and workstations. In DECnet philosophy, a node must be an intelligent machine and not simply a terminal as in other systems.

DECnet/DOS allows DOS machines to function as end nodes in DECnet networks, and DECnet/OSI is the implementation of DECnet Phase V that supports OSI and provides compatibility with DECnet Phase IV and TCP/IP.

decode
(1) To convert coded data back into its original form. Contrast with *encode*.
(2) Same as *decrypt*. See *cryptography*.

decoder
A hardware device or software that converts coded data back into its original form. See *decode* and *MPEG decoder*.

decollator
A device that separates multiple-part paper forms while removing the carbon paper.

decompiler
A program that converts machine language back into a high-level source language. The resulting code may be very difficult to maintain as variables and routines are named generically: A0001, A0002, etc. See *disassembler*.

decompress
To restore compressed data back to its original size.

decrement
To subtract a number from another number. Decrementing a counter means to subtract 1 or some other number from its current value.

decrypt
To convert encrypted data back into its original form. Contrast with encrypt. See cryptography.

DECstation
(1) A series of RISC-based single-user workstations from Digital, introduced in 1989, that run under ULTRIX.
(2) A PC series from Digital introduced in 1989.
(3) A small computer system from Digital, introduced in 1978, used primarily for word processing (DECstation 78).

Computer Desktop Encyclopedia

DECsystem

(1) A series of RISC-based, 32-bit computers from Digital that run under ULTRIX. Introduced in 1989, the 5400 model is a Q-bus system; the 5800 model uses the XMI bus.

(2) A series of mainframes from Digital that were introduced from 1974 through 1980 and were the successor to the 36-bit PDP-10 computers.

DECtalk

A voice synthesizing system from Digital that accepts serial ASCII text and converts it into audible speech. It is used in Touch-tone telephone response systems as well as for voice-output for visually handicapped users.

DECwindows

Digital's windowing architecture, based on X Window, Version 11. It is compatible with X Window while adding a variety of enhancements.

dedicated channel

A computer channel or communications line that is used for one purpose.

dedicated line

A phone or other communications line used for one purpose. Synonymous with *leased line* and *private line*.

dedicated service

A service that is not shared by other users or organizations.

de facto standard

A widely-used format or language not endorsed by a standards organization.

default

The current setting or action taken by hardware or software if the user has not specified otherwise.

default directory

Same as *current directory*.

default drive

The disk drive used if no other drive is specified.

default font

The typeface and type size used if none other is specified.

default gateway

The router used to forward all traffic that is not addressed to a station within the local subnet.

default profile

The normal default settings assigned to an application or system. See *user default profile*.

defragger

Also called an *optimizer* program, it is a software utility that defragments a disk. It rewrites the files and stores them in adjacent sectors. Sophisticated defraggers allow frequently-used files to be placed at the front of the disk for faster retrieval.

defragment

To reorganize the disk by putting files into contiguous order. Because the operating system stores new data in whatever free space is available, data files become spread out across the disk if they are updated often. This causes extra read/write head movement to read them back. Periodically, the hard disk should be defragmented to put files back into order. See *defragger*.

degausser

A device that removes unwanted magnetism from a monitor or the read/write head in a disk or tape drive. A monitor may have a built-in degaussing function with a degauss button on the front control panel. See *gauss*.

degrees of freedom

The amount of movement available in a robotics or virtual reality system. See *6DOF*.

Deja News

(www.dejanews.com) A search site on the Web that specializes in newsgroups. See *newsgroup, Usenet* and *Web search sites*.

de jure standard

A format or language endorsed by a standards organization.

delay equalization

Compensating for the late arrival of data in one or more channels when multiple channels are used in a transmission. Incoming data is buffered so all streams can be output sequentially when the most tardy channel is finally transmitting.

delay line

A communications or electronic circuit that has a built-in delay. Acoustic delay lines were used to create the earliest computer memories. For example, the UNIVAC I used tubes of liquid mercury that would slow down the digital pulses long enough (a fraction of a second) to serve as storage.

delete

To remove an item of data from a file or to remove a file from the disk. See *undelete*.

delimiter

A character or combination of characters used to separate one item or set of data from another. For example, in comma delimited records, a comma is used to separate each field of data.

deliverable

The measurable result or output of a process.

DEL key

(DELete key) The keyboard key used to delete the character under the screen cursor or some other currently-highlighted object.

Dell

(Dell Computer Corporation, Austin, TX, www.dell.com) A leading manufacturer of PCs founded in 1984 by Michael Dell. Originally selling under the "PCs Limited" brand, Dell was the first to legitimize mail-order PCs by providing quality telephone support. Dell was also the first major manufacturer to pre-load applications selected by the customer.

Dell's rise throughout the 1990s has been extraordinary. It made the Fortune 500 in 1991 with sales of 546 million. Six years later, sales were nearly eight billion. With more than 200 patents covering current and future computer systems and related technologies, Dell has become a major force in the industry.

Delphi

(1) An online information service that provides access to a wide variety of databases, files and shopping. It was the first major online service to provide full Internet access, not just for electronic mail. See *online services*.

(2) An application development system for Windows from INPRISE, introduced in 1995. Based on the object-oriented Object Pascal language, it includes visual programming tools and generates executable programs (.EXE files). It includes the Borland Database Engine, which allows access to dBASE, Paradox and ODBC databases. Delphi also uses Visual Basic controls (VBXs). The Delphi Client/Server upgrade supports major client/server databases such as Oracle, Sybase and INFORMIX.

(3) (Delphi Consulting Group, Boston, MA, www.delphigroup.com) The leading consulting organization that specializes in document management and workflow. Founded in 1987 by Thomas Koulopoulos, it provides consulting services, publications and inhouse and public seminars on the subjects.

delta

A incremental value between one number and another.

Computer Desktop Encyclopedia

delta backup

See *backup types*.

delta frame

In interframe coding, a frame that provides an incremental change from the key frame. See *interframe coding*.

delta modulation

A technique that is used to sample voice waves and convert them into digital code. Delta modulation typically samples the wave 32,000 times per second, but generates only one bit per sample. See *PCM*.

de-lurk

To finally type in a comment after "lurking" in a chat room for some time. See *lurk*.

DEMA

Founded in 1976 as the Data Entry Management Association, it later changed its name to the Association for Input Technology and Management. In 1993, it merged with TAWPI.

demand dial routing

The ability to establish a dial-up connection in order to forward data to a destination.

demand paging

Copying a program page from disk into memory when required by the program.

demand processing

Same as *transaction processing*.

demarcation point (demarc)

The location within a home or office where the lines from the telephone company connect to the customer's lines.

demodulate

To filter out the data signal from the carrier. See *modulate*.

demon

See *daemon*.

demoware

Demonstration software that shows some or all of the features of a commercial product. See *crippleware*.

demultiplex

To reconvert a transmission that contains several intermixed signals back into its original separate signals.

DEN

(Directory Enabled Networks) The management of a network from a central depository of information about users, applications and network resources. Originally an initiative from Microsoft and Cisco, DEN was turned over to the DMTF in 1998. A DEN schema is expected to be defined in 1998 for the CIM model. See *WBEM, CIM* and *DMTF*.

denial of service

A condition in which a system can no longer respond to normal requests. See *denial of service attack*.

denial of service attack

An assault on a network that floods it with so many additional requests that regular traffic is either slowed or completely interrupted. Unlike a virus or worm, which can cause severe damage to databases, a denial of service attack interrupts network service for some period. See *smurf attack, SYN flood attack* and *Ping of Death*.

density

See *packing density* and *bit density*.

departmental computing

Processing a department's data with its own computer system. See *distributed computing*.

dependent segment

In database management, data that depends on data in a higher level for its full meaning.

dequeue

Pronounced "d-q." To remove an item from a queue. Contrast with *enqueue*.

DES

(Data Encryption Standard) A NIST-standard secret key cryptography method that uses a 56-bit key. DES is based on an IBM algorithm which was further developed by the U.S. National Security Agency. It uses the block cipher method which breaks the text into 64-bit blocks before encrypting them. There are several DES encryption modes. The most popular mode exclusive ORs each plaintext block with the previous encrypted block.

DES decryption is very fast and widely used. The secret key may be kept a total secret and used over again. Or, a key can be randomly generated for each session, in which case the new key is transmitted to the recipient using a public key cryptography method such as RSA.

Triple DES is an enhancement to DES that provides considerably more security than standard DES, which uses only one 56-bit key. There are several Triple DES methods. EEE3 uses 3 keys and encrypts 3 times. EDE3 uses 3 keys to encrypt, decrypt and encrypt again. EEE2 and EDE2 are similar to EEE3 and EDE3, except that only 2 keys are used, and the first and third operations use the same key. See *cryptography, RSA* and *Fortezza*.

descender

The part of lower case characters g, j, p, q and y that fall below the line. Sometimes these characters are displayed and printed with shortened descenders in order to fit into a smaller character cell, making them difficult to read.

descending sort

Arranging data from high to low sequence; for example, from Z to A or from 9 to 0.

Deschutes

See *Pentium II*.

descriptor

(1) A word or phrase that identifies a document in an indexed information retrieval system.

(2) A category name used to identify data.

deserialize

To convert a serial stream of bits into parallel streams of bits.

DesignCAD

A family of 2-D and 3-D CAD programs from ViaGrafix, Pryor, OK, (www.viagrafix.com), for DOS, Windows and Mac, noted for their ease of use. DesignCAD 3-D for Windows includes such features as texture mapping, reflection mapping with up to eight light sources and keyframe animation.

Designer

See *Micrografx Designer*.

Designer/2000

See *Developer/2000*.

design optimization

See *automatic design optimization*.

desk accessory

In the Macintosh, a program that is always available from the Apple menu no matter what application is running. With System 7, all applications can be turned into desk accessories.

desk checking

Manually testing the logic of a program.

DeskJet

A family of popular desktop ink-jet printers for PCs from HP.

DESKPRO

A Compaq trade name for its PCs.

desktop

(1) An on-screen representation of a desktop, which is used in the Macintosh, Windows 95/98 and Windows NT.

(2) A buzzword attached to applications traditionally performed on more expensive machines that are now on a personal computer (desktop publishing, desktop mapping, etc.).

desktop accessory

Software that simulates an object normally found on an office desktop, such as a calculator, notepad and appointment calendar. See *TSR*.

desktop application

See *desktop accessory*.

desktop computer

A computer that is small enough to reside on a desktop. It either refers to personal computers (PCs, Macs, Amigas, PowerPCs, etc.) or to workstations from Sun, IBM, HP, Digital and others.

desktop conferencing

See *videoconferencing* and *data conferencing*.

desktop lockdown

The prevention of changes to configuration settings in a client machine. See *system policy*.

desktop manager

The part of a GUI that displays the desktop and icons, allows programs to be launched from the icon and files to be visually dragged & dropped (copied, deleted, etc.). The desktop manager combined with the window manager make up the GUI. The desktop manager is included with the Mac and Windows. In OSF/Motif and Open Look, products such as IXI's X.desktop and Visix Software's Looking Glass add this capability.

desktop mapping

Using a desktop computer to perform digital mapping functions.

desktop media

The integration of desktop presentations, desktop publishing and multimedia (coined by Apple).

desktop organizer

See *desktop accessory*.

desktop presentations

The creation of presentation materials on a personal computer, which includes charts, graphs and other graphics-oriented information. It implies a wide variety of special effects for both text and graphics that will produce output for use as handouts, overheads and slides as well as sequences that can be viewed on screen. Advanced systems generate animation and control multimedia devices.

desktop publishing

Abbreviated "DTP." Using a personal computer to produce high-quality printed output or camera-ready output for commercial printing. It requires a desktop publishing program, high-speed personal computer, large monitor and a laser printer.

A DTP program, also called a *page layout program*, provides complete page design capabilities, including magazine style columns, rules and borders, page, chapter and caption numbering as well as precise typographic aligment. A key feature is its ability to manage text and graphics on screen WYSIWYG style. The program can flow text around graphic objects in a variety of ways.

Text and graphics may be created in the DTP program, but graphics capability is usually very limited. Typically, the work is created in word processing, CAD, drawing and paint programs and then imported into the publishing system.

A laser printer may be used for final text output, but it cannot print line art and shaded drawings respectably unless its resolution is 1200 dpi or greater. For best results whether text or graphics, a high-resolution imagesetter at 1270 or 2540 dpi is top quality. For electronic transfer to a commercial printer, documents are generally saved as PostScript files, but printing houses are increasingly accepting native documents from popular page layout programs such as PageMaker and QuarkXPress.

DTP has dramatically brought down the cost of page layout, causing many projects to be done inhouse. Predefined style sheets for newsletters, brochures and other publishing tasks can help complete novices do respectable jobs. But, there is still no substitute for a graphics designer who knows which fonts to use and how to lay out the page artistically.

DeskWriter

A family of popular desktop ink-jet printers for the Macintosh from HP. Color models are also available.

DESQview

An earlier multitasking, windows environment for DOS from Quarterdeck. In the 1980s, DESQview was the first serious windows program for the DOS PC. Using the included QEMM memory manager, it ran multiple DOS text and graphics programs in resizable windows.

DESQview/X

A version of DESQview that adds X Windows to a PC network, allowing each DOS machine to run multiple applications on different PCs in the network. As an integration product, it allows DOS and Windows apps to run in an X Window network under UNIX or any other X-based environment.

destructive memory

Memory that loses its content when it is read, requiring that the circuitry regenerate the bits after the read operation.

detail file

Same as *transaction file*.

developer's toolkit

A set of software routines and utilities used to help programmers write an application. For graphical interfaces, it provides the tools and libraries for creating menus, dialog boxes, fonts and icons. It provides the means to link the application to libraries of software routines and to link it with the operating environment (OS, DBMS, protocol, etc.). See *API, development system, client/server development system* and *GUI builder*.

Developer/2000

A client/server application development system for Windows, Macintosh and Motif from Oracle. Formerly the Cooperative Development Environment, the core programs are Oracle Forms, Oracle Reports and Oracle Graphics. Oracle Procedure Builder provides drag and drop application partitioning. It also includes Discoverer/2000, which is an end user analysis suite made up of Oracle Data Query for reports and queries and Oracle Browser for viewing tables and data dictionaries.

Discoverer replaces Discoverer/2000 and combines several tools into one. Designer/2000 is Oracle's contrast w⁻data modeling and repository system.

development cycle

See *system development cycle*.

development system

(1) A programming language and related components. It includes the compiler, text editor, debugger, function library and any other supporting programs that enable a programmer to write a program. See *developer's toolkit* and *application development system*. For a list of popular client/server development tools, see *client/server development system*.

(2) A computer and related software for developing applications.

development tool

Software that assists in the creation of new software. Compilers, debuggers, visual programming tools, GUI builders, application generators are examples. See *developer's toolkit*. For a list of popular client/server development tools, see *client/server development system*.

Computer Desktop Encyclopedia

device

(1) Any electronic or electromechanical machine or component from a transistor to a disk drive. Device always refers to hardware.

(2) In semiconductor design, it is an active component, such as a transistor or diode, in contrast to a passive component, such as a resistor or capacitor.

device adapter

Same as *interface adapter*.

device address

See *address* and *I/O address*.

Device Bay

A specification from Compaq, Intel and Microsoft for a quick-change peripheral format that enables hard drives, CD-ROM drives and other devices to be easily hot swapped without opening the case. Using the USB and IEEE 1394 FireWire interfaces, it provides three form factors (DB13, DB20 and DB32), which are 13, 20 and 32mm in height. Visit www.device-bay.org. See *USB* and *FireWire*.

device context

A data structure in Windows programming that is used to define the attributes of text and images that are output to the screen or printer. The device context (DC) is maintained by GDI. A DC, which is a handle to the structure, is obtained before output is written and released after the elements have been written. See *GDI*.

device control character

A communications code that activates a function on a terminal. See *ASCII chart*.

device dependent

Refers to programs that address specific hardware features and work with only one type of peripheral device. Contrast with *device independent*. See *machine dependent*.

device driver

See *driver*.

device independent

Refers to programs that work with a variety of peripheral devices. The hardware-specific instructions are in some other program (OS, DBMS, etc.). Contrast with *device dependent*. See *machine independent*.

device level

(1) In circuit design, refers to working with individual transistors rather than complete circuits.

(2) Refers to communicating directly with the hardware at a machine language level.

device name

A name assigned to a hardware device that represents its physical address. For example, LPT1 is a DOS device name for the parallel port.

DFP port

(Digital Flat Panel port) A digital interface for a flat panel display as specified by the DFP Group (www.dfp-group.com). It uses a 20-pin mini-D ribbon (MDR) connector and TDMS transmission (Transition Minimized Differential Signaling).

The first round of flat panel displays for desktop use have provided the same VGA connector as CRTs. However, flat panels are digital devices, and by staying in the digital domain, the image quality can be improved. There is no need to convert to analog within the PC display adapter only to convert back to digital inside the flat panel. It is expected that flat panels will include both the analog VGA and digital DFP connectors.

Dfs

(Distributed File System) An enhancement to Windows NT and 95/98 that allows files scattered across multiple servers to be treated as a single group. With Dfs, a network administrator can build a hierarchical file system that spans the organization's LANs and WANs.

DFSMS

(Data Facility Storage Management System) Data management, backup and HSM software for MVS mainframes from IBM. Introduced in 1993, it combined separate backup, copy, HSM and device driver routines into one package, which provides all the I/O management for MVS. It has also been integrated into OS/390. See *SMS* and *ADSM*.

DFT mode

(Distributed Function Terminal mode) A mode that allows a 3270 terminal to have five concurrent sessions with the mainframe. Contrast with *CUT mode*.

DG

See *Data General*.

DG/UX

(Data General UNIX) A UNIX-based operating system developed by Data General. It supports symmetric multiprocessing and is generally used with the Tuxedo TP monitor for transaction processing.

DHCP

(Dynamic Host Configuration Protocol) Software that automatically assigns IP addresses to client stations logging onto a TCP/IP network. It eliminates having to manually assign IP addresses, and it allows a larger group of machines to share a limited pool of addresses, assuming not all users are logged on at the same time. DHCP can assign a new address to each machine at startup (dynamic) or permanent (static) addresses can be assigned. Newer DHCP servers dynamically update the DNS servers after making assignments. See *DNS* and *WINS*.

DHCP server

A server in the network dedicated to DHCP services or a file server that provides DHCP and other services. See *DHCP*.

Dhrystones

A benchmark program that tests a general mix of instructions. The results in Dhrystones per second are the number of times the program can be executed in one second. See *Whetstones* and *benchmark*.

DHTML

See *Dynamic HTML*.

DIA

(Document Interchange Architecture) An IBM SNA format used to exchange documents from dissimilar machines within an LU 6.2 session. It acts as an envelope to hold the document and does not set any standards for the content of the document, such as layout settings or graphics standards.

Diablo emulation

A printer that accepts the same commands as the Diablo printer.

diacritical

A small mark added to a letter that changes its pronunciation, such as the French cedilla, which is a small hook placed under the letter "c."

diagnostic board

An expansion board with built-in diagnostic tests that reports results via its own readout. Such boards typically have their own POST system and can test a malfunctioning computer that doesn't boot.

diagnostics

(1) Software routines that test hardware components (memory, keyboard, disks, etc.). In personal computers, they are often stored in ROM and activated on startup.

(2) Error messages in a programmer's source code that refer to statements or syntax that the compiler or assembler cannot understand.

diagnostic tracks

The spare tracks on a disk used by the drive or controller for testing purposes.

diagramming program

Software that allows the user to create flow charts, organization charts and similar diagrams. It is similar to a drawing program, but specialized for creating interconnected diagrams. It comes with a palette of predefined shapes and symbols and usually keeps the lines connected between them if they are edited and rearranged.

Examples of general flowcharting programs are Visio, FlowCharter, CorelFlow and allClear. Network diagram-specific programs that can link an equipment database to the objects in the diagram are ClickNet and netViz.

DIALOG

See *Knight-Ridder Information*.

dialog box

A small, on-screen window displayed in response to some request. It provides the options currently available to the user.

dial-up line

A two-wire line as used in the dial-up telephone network. Contrast with *leased line*.

dial-up network

(1) The switched telephone network regulated by government and administered by common carriers.

(2) A computer network that can be accessed remotely via modem. See *remote access server* and *Win 9x Dial-up Networking*.

dial-up networking

See *dial-up network* and *Win 9x Dial-up networking*.

diazo film

A film used to make microfilm or microfiche copies. It is exposed to the original film under ultraviolet light and is developed into identical copies. Copy color is typically blue, blue-black or purple.

DIB

(1) (Directory Information Base) Also called *white pages*, a database of names in an X.500 system.

(2) (Device Independent Bitmap) A BMP file when it resides in memory. See *BMP file*.

(3) (Dual Independent Bus) An enhanced bus architecture from Intel first implemented on the Pentium Pro chip. It provides two buses; one for connecting the CPU to system memory and another for the cache. The DIB enables Pentium II CPU bus speeds to jump from 66MHz to 100MHz.

dibit

Any one of four patterns from two consecutive bits: 00, 01, 10 and 11. Using phase modulation, a dibit can be modulated onto a carrier as a different shift in the phase of the wave.

DIBOL

(DIgital coBOL) A version of COBOL from Digital that runs on the PDP and VAX series.

dice

The plural of die. See *die*.

Dick Tracy watch

A wristwatch popularized in the 1940s by the Dick Tracy comics. Tracy was a detective that had radio communications to police headquarters via his famous watch.

dictionary method

See *LZW*.

DID

(Direct Inward Dialing) The ability to make a telephone call directly into an internal extension within an organization, without having to go through the operator.

die

The formal term for the square of silicon containing an integrated circuit. Die (singular) and dice (plural) are used by chip designers and engineers. The popular term is chip.

dielectric

An insulator (glass, rubber, plastic, etc.). Dielectric materials can be made to hold an electrostatic charge, but current cannot flow through them.

DIF

(1) (Data Interchange Format) A standard file format for spreadsheet and other data structured in row and column form. Originally developed for VisiCalc, DIF is now under Lotus' jurisdiction.

(2) (Display Information Facility) An IBM System/38 program that lets users build custom programs for online access to data.

(3) (Document Interchange Format) A file standard developed by the U.S. Navy in 1982.

(4) (Dual In-line Flatpack) A type of surface mount DIP with pins extending horizontally outward.

Difference Engine

An early calculator designed by Charles Babbage and subsidized by the British government. It used rods and wheels, which was tried before by other designers. It was started in 1821 and abandoned in 1833. Although never completed, it did improve the precision of Britain's machine-tool industry. Babbage later turned his attention to the Analytical Engine. In 1991, the National Museum of Science and Technology built a working model of the Difference Engine.

In 1879, Babbage's son reassembled a section of the Difference Engine from parts. In 1995, Christie's auction in London auctioned off the section to the Power House Museum in Sydney for $282,000. The other known sections are owned by Harvard and Cambridge Universities. See *Analytical Engine*.

The Difference Engine
(Photo courtesy of Smithsonian Institution.)

Differential Analyzer

An analog computational device built to solve differential equations by Vannevar Bush (MIT, 1930s). Less than a dozen were built, but they were effective in calculating ballistics tables in World War II. The machine took up an entire room and was programmed by changing camshaft-like gears with screwdriver and wrench. See illustration on next page.

differential backup

See *backup types*.

differential configuration

The use of individual wire pairs for each electrical signal for high immunity to noise and crosstalk. Contrast with *single-ended configuration*.

differential updating

Replacing only the files in a software application that have changed rather than replacing all the files.

differentiated services

Offerings that can be classified by type, or quality, of service. For example, a differentiated services network could prioritize realtime traffic for a higher fee.

Diffie-Hellman

A cryptographic technique that enables sending and receiving parties to exchange public keys in a manner that derives a shared, secret key at both ends. Using a common number, both sides use a different random number as a power to raise the common number. The results are sent to each other. The receiving party raises the received number to the same random power they used before, and the results are the same on both sides. See *ECC*.

Differential Analyzer
Programming with a screwdriver and wrench. A far cry from today's programmable machines. *(Photo courtesy of The MIT Museum.)*

It's Rather Clever

There's more computation in actual practice, but this example, which uses tiny numbers to illustrate the concept, shows a very clever mathematical approach. Each party raises the common number, which is 2 in this example (this has nothing to do with binary— it's just the number 2) to a random power and sends the result to the other. The received number is raised to the same random power. Note that both parties come up with the same secret key, which was never transmitted intact.

$$common\ number = 2$$

random number = 4	random number = 5
$2^4 = 16$	$2^5 = 32$
32	16
$32^4 = 1,048,576$	$16^5 = 1,048,576$

diffraction

Breaking up a signal into its constituent parts. For example, a light beam can be diffracted into the colors of the spectrum.

diffusion

A semiconductor manufacturing process that infuses tiny quantities of impurities into a base material, such as silicon, to change its electrical characteristics. See *chip* for illustration.

digerati

The "digital elite." People that are extremely knowledgeable about computers. It often refers to the movers and shakers in the industry. Digerati is the high-tech equivalent of "literati," which refers to scholars and highly-educated individuals.

DigiCash

See *ecash*.

digispeak

In online communications, the use of acronyms to make a shorthand out of common phrases. For example, BTW for "by the way" and IMHO for "in my humble opinion." People are doing so much typing these days that they welcome shortcuts, and the shortcuts are turning into a new language.

digit

A single character in a numbering system. In decimal, digits are 0 through 9. In binary, digits are 0 and 1.

digital

Traditionally, digital means the use of numbers and the term comes from digit, or finger. Today, digital is synonymous with computer. See also *Digital Equipment*.

Digital Means Original

The 0s and 1s of digital data mean more than than just on and off. They mean perfect copying. When information, music, voice and video are turned into binary digital form, they can be electronically manipulated, preserved and regenerated perfectly at high speed. The millionth copy of a computer file is exactly the same as the original. While this continually drives the software industry crazy protecting its copyrights, it is nevertheless a major advantage of digital processing.

digital audio

Sound waves that have been digitized and stored in the computer. The most common digital audio formats are music CDs and Windows WAV files. Music CDs are played in CD players as well as CD-ROM readers. WAV files are stored in the computer or on CD-ROMs and played by a media player software application. Although also in digital form and stored in the computer, MIDI music is not considered digital audio. MIDI files contain a coded version of the musical score, not the actual sound. See *MIDI*.

digital audio disc

Same as *CD*.

digital audio tape

See *DAT*.

digital camera

A video or still camera that records images in digital form. Unlike traditional analog cameras that convert light intensities into infinitely variable signals, digital cameras convert light intensities into discrete numbers for storage on a medium, such as a hard disk or flash disk. As with all digital devices, there is a fixed, maximum resolution and number of colors that can be represented.

Digital cameras record color images as intensities of red, green and blue, which are stored as variable charges in a CCD matrix. The size of the matrix determines the resolution, but the analog-to-digital converter (ADC), which converts the charges to digital data, determines the color depth.

TV studio cameras also use CCDs, but may generate traditional analog signals or digital signals depending on the application. Increasingly, TV is going digital, and is expected in time to be digital from end to end.

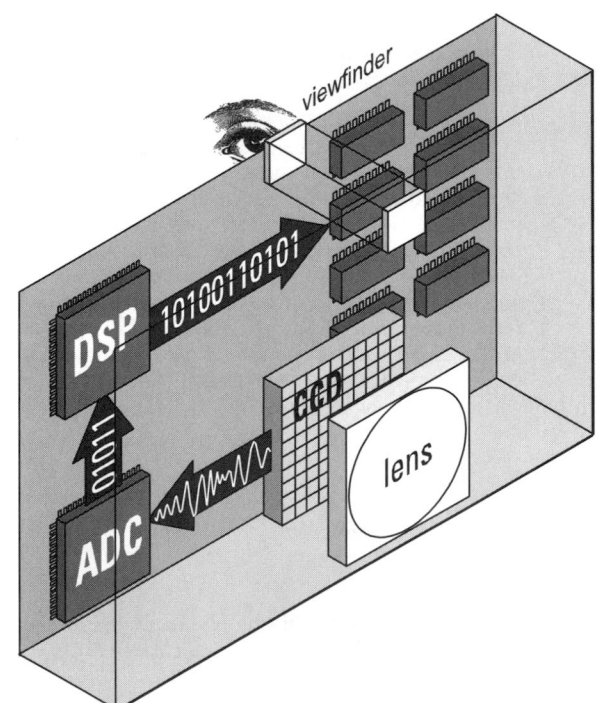

Digital Camera
Behind the lens, CCDs pick up the image as charges that are converted to digital data by an A/D converter chip (ADC). The DSP chip adjusts contrast and detail and compresses the digital data for storage.

digital cash, digital coins

See *digital money*.

digital cellphone

A cellular phone that uses a digital transmission technology. In the U.S., TDMA, CDMA and GSM are the digital cellular standards. See *TDMA, CDMA* and *GSM*.

digital certificate

The digital equivalent of an ID card used in conjunction with a public key encryption system. Also called *digital IDs*, digital certificates are issued by trusted third parties known as certification authorities (CAs) such as VeriSign, Inc., Mountain View, CA, (www.verisign.com), after verifying that a public key belongs to a certain owner. The certification process varies depending on the CA and the level of certification. Drivers licenses, notarization and fingerprints are examples of documentation required.

The digital certificate is actually the owner's public key that has been digitally signed by the CA. The digital certificate is sent along with an encrypted message to verify that the sender is truly the entity identifying itself in the transmission. The recipient uses the public key of the CA, which is widely publicized, to decrypt the sender's public key attached to the message. Then the sender's public key is used to decrypt the actual message.

The most vulnerable aspect of this method is the CA's private key, which is used to digitally sign a public key and create a certificate. If the CA's private key is uncovered, then false digital certificates can be created. See *digital signature* and *PKI*.

The digital certificate contains the following data:

```
owner name, company and address
owner public key
owner certificate serial number
owner validity dates
certifying company ID
certifying company digital signature
```

digital channel

A communications path that handles only digital signals. All voice and video signals have to be converted from analog to digital in order to be carried over a digital channel. Contrast with *analog channel*.

digital circuit

An electronic circuit that accepts and processes binary data (on/off) according to the rules of Boolean logic (AND, OR, NOT, etc.). See *chip* for illustration.

digital communications

Transmitting text, voice and video in binary form. See *communications*.

digital computer

A computer that accepts and processes data that has been converted into binary numbers. All common computers are digital. Contrast with *analog computer*.

digital convergence

The integration of computers, communications and consumer electronics. Data and text were converted into digital form for the very first computers years ago, however since the advent of audio CDs and, increasingly, digital video, it becomes apparent that all forms of information, both for business and entertainment, can be managed together.

Using cable TV coax, satellite dish, optical fiber or even the telephone line, music, movies, video games and other interactive programs can be requested on demand along with the Internet's inexhaustible array of offerings.

The DVD disc is expected to be a major convergence product. It is a video medium that is expected to replace LaserDiscs and VHS tapes for recorded movies as well as become the primary video vehicle for personal computers. As rewritable DVDs (DVD-RAM) become popular, they are expected to replace videotapes entirely and provide a single medium for home theater as well as computer storage. See *new media*.

In addition, the movement towards the IP protocol for not only data, but voice and video, is another major convergence technology. The Internet has upset the applecart from the get-go, and the telecom industry is spending billions to upgrade to IP as the core infrastructure of the future. See *IP on Everything*.

digital copy machine

A copy machine that duplicates the image to be copied by scanning the original into a digital memory and printing from the memory. Contrast with *analog copy machine*.

digital cross-connect

A network device used by telecom carriers and large enterprises to switch and multiplex low-speed voice and data signals onto high-speed lines and vice versa. It is typically used to aggregate several T1 lines into a higher-speed electrical or optical line as well as to distributed signals to various destinations; for example, voice and data traffic may arrive at the cross-connect on the same facility, but be destined for different carriers. Voice traffic would be transmitted out one port, while data traffic goes out another.

Digital cross-connects are widely used in conjunction with central office telephone switches and may be installed both before and/or after the switch. Cross-connections are established via an administrative process and are semi-permanent, whereas the telephone switch dynamically picks up dialing instructions and routes calls based on telephone number.

Cross-connects come large and small handling only a few ports up to a couple of thousand. Narrowband, wideband and broadband cross-connects support channels down to DS0, DS1 and DS3 respectively.

digital darkroom

Using digital hardware to create pictures. With digital cameras, scanners and computer printers, darkroom operations are performed in the light of day.

digital data

Data in digital form. All data in the computer is in digital form.

digital domain

The world of digital. When something is done in the digital domain, it implies that the original data (images, sounds, video, etc.) has been converted into a digital format and is manipulated inside the computer's memory.

digital effects

Special sounds and animations that have been created in the digital domain. Synthetic sounds and reverberation, morphing and transitions between video frames (fades, wipes, dissolves, etc.) are examples.

digital electronics

The field of electronics as it pertains to computers and other computer-controlled devices. See *digital circuit*.

digital envelope

(1) An encrypted message that uses both secret key and public key cryptography methods. The public key method is used to exchange the secret key, and the secret key is used to encrypt and decrypt the message. See *RSA*.

(2) A frame, or packet, of data that has been encrypted for transmission over a network.

(3) A term occasionally used to describe inserting data into a frame, or packet, for transmission over a network. The envelope metaphor implies a container.

Digital Equipment

(Digital Equipment Corporation, Maynard, MA, www.digital.com) Now merged into Compaq, Digital Equipment, commonly known as DEC or Digital, was founded in 1957 by Kenneth Olsen, who headed the company until he retired in 1992. Digital pioneered the minicomputer industry with its PDP series.

Kenneth H. Olsen
Olsen pioneered the minicomputer industry with his PDP computer series. He ran Digital for 35 years until his retirement in 1992. *(Photo courtesy of Digital Equipment Corporation.)*

Its early success came from the scientific, process control and academic communities; however, after the VAX was announced in 1977, Digital gained a strong foothold in commercial data processing. The VAX evolved into a complete line from desktop to mainframe, using the same VMS operating system in all models and causing Digital to achieve substantial growth in the 1980s.

Over the years, Digital was widely recognized for its high quality. Its strategy for the 1990s was to embrace open systems with its powerful, RISC-based Alpha architecture introduced in 1992. In addition, Digital has a large services business that provides full project life cycle support from installation to maintenance for Digital and non-Digital products.

In 1997, Digital sold its semiconductor manufacturing facilities to Intel, which will continue to make the Alpha chip for the next 10 years. In 1998, it was acquired by Compaq.

The First "Mini" Computer
This PDP-1 was Digital's first computer, which was a breakthrough in 1959. Digital spearheaded the minicomputer industry with its PDP series. *(Photo courtesy of Digital Equipment Corporation.)*

digital ID

Same as *digital certificate*.

digitally signed

Any message or key that has been encrypted with a digital signature. When a user's public key is digitally signed by a certification authority (CA), it is known as a *digital certificate* or *digital ID*. See *digital signature* and *digital certificate*.

digital mapping

Digitizing geographic information for a geographic information system (GIS).

digital money

Electronic money used on the Internet. In order to turn the Internet into a giant cybermall (online shopping center), companies have developed software that provides complete and secure order fulfillment over the Internet. These software packages support a variety of payment schemes, which mostly fall into two categories.

The first category is the traditional credit card. Most Web browsers and Internet Service Providers (ISPs) support one of the major security protocols such as Secure Socket Layer (SSL). For example, on Netscape's browser, if the transmission between browser and server is secure, the key icon at the lower left side of the screen is connected. Otherwise, it is split in half to signal an unsecure transmission. More elaborate methods, such as CyberCash's credit card system, prevent the merchant from seeing the credit card number.

The second type of digital money is like travelers checks and is being implemented and tested by several companies such as DigiCash (ecash) and CyberCash. This digital money is either downloaded as "digital coins" from a participating bank into the user's personal computer or a digital money account is set up within the bank. Either the digital coins or the transactions that debit the account are transmitted to the merchant for payment. All of these transactions are encrypted for security.

Many believe that if the cost for processing digital money can be kept down, it will fuel an entirely new online information industry that allows customers to pay for exactly what they use. For example, 5 cents for each information lookup or 10 cents for each applet download, perhaps even a fraction of a cent for certain transactions. Time will tell if the economics allow for this scenario.

In the meantime, although trillions of dollars are routinely transferred around the world via the private banking network, money traversing the public Internet would seem like easy pickings for the dishonest hacker. As with any new system, time, along with a few panics, will bring about the confidence necessary for everyday use. Surprises are definitely expected. See *ecash, CyberCash, First Virtual, cybermall* and *smart card.*

digital monitor

(1) A video monitor controlled by a computer circuit that retains settings and resolutions in memory. Subsequent changes in resolutions do not require adjustments. Most computer monitors today are digitally controlled, but still accept analog signals from the display adapter.

(2) A video monitor that accepts a digital signal from the computer and converts it into analog signals to illuminate the screen. Examples are the earlier MDA, CGA and EGA monitors used with PCs. Contrast with *analog monitor.*

digital nonlinear editing

See *nonlinear video editing.*

digital PABX

See *digital PBX.*

Digital Paper

See *Common Ground.*

DigitalPaper

The file format generated by the Common Ground document exchange software. The term implies that the computer file can be used to regenerate the style and format of the original paper form.

digital PBX

(digital **P**rivate **B**ranch E**x**change) A modern PBX that uses digital methods for switching in contrast to older PBXs that use analog methods.

Digital PC

(1) An Alpha PC that runs Windows applications. It runs a native Alpha version of Windows NT and uses the FX 32 emulator. See *FX 32.*

(2) An Intel-based PC made by Digital.

digital phone

A desktop or cellular phone that uses a digital transmission technology. Inhouse PBX-based and key telephone systems may use digital phones which convert sound into digital at the handset. Digital cellphones come in several varieties. See *digital cellphone* and *smart phone.*

Digital Printing

digital printing

Printing finished output on a computer printer. All printed output from a computer is technically digital printing. However, the term is increasingly used to refer to preparing finished manuals and booklets on a computer printer that would otherwise go to a printing house and be printed on a conventional offset printing press.

Digital printing eliminates numerous error-prone steps in the conventional printing process, including making films, color proofs, manually stripping the pieces together, making plates and running the paper through the press four or five times.

Software can sort pages in memory so that they can be printed in sequence (1,2,3... 1,2,3... etc.). Paper handling functions such as stapling and 3-hole punching are available on high-speed laser and LED printers so that a four-color booklet can be finished entirely on the printer.

Although digital printers cannot currently compete with the high-speed presses used by newspapers, magazines and major printers that can print millions of pages per day, it is expected that it is only a matter of time before these "analog" monsters will give way to all-digital devices.

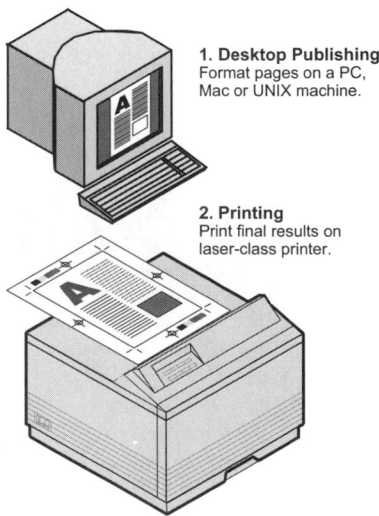

1. Desktop Publishing
Format pages on a PC, Mac or UNIX machine.

2. Printing
Print final results on laser-class printer.

Offset Printing

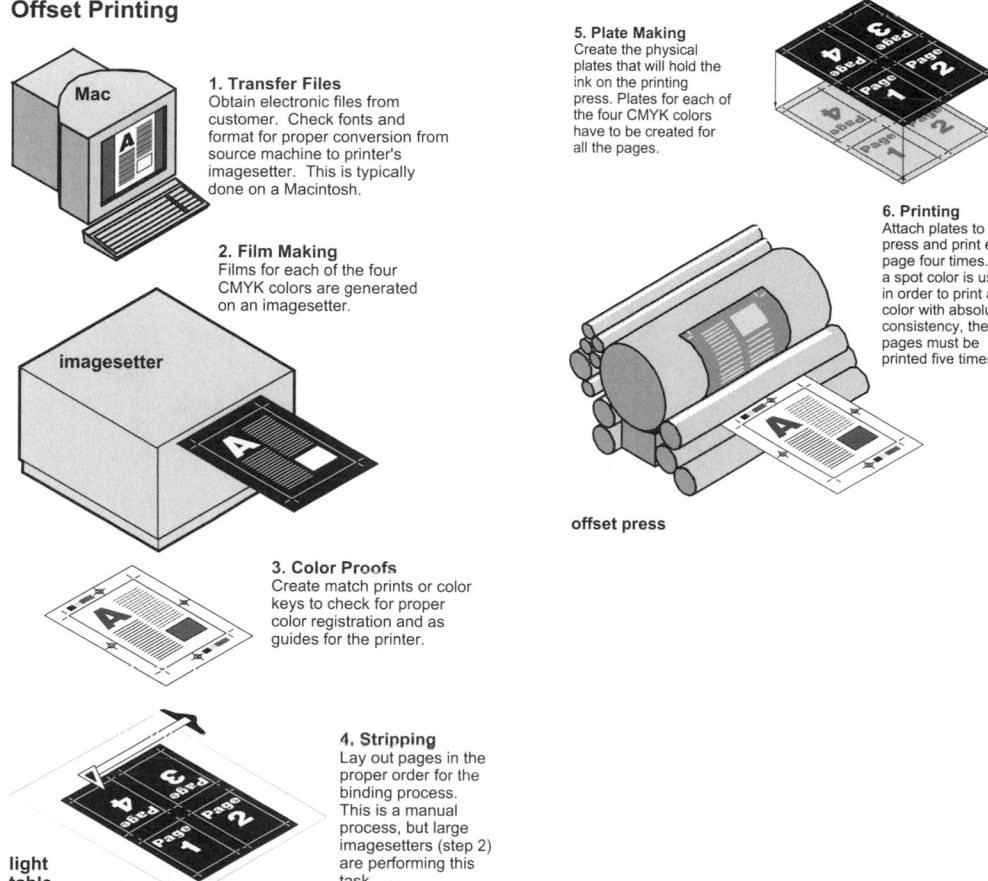

1. Transfer Files
Obtain electronic files from customer. Check fonts and format for proper conversion from source machine to printer's imagesetter. This is typically done on a Macintosh.

2. Film Making
Films for each of the four CMYK colors are generated on an imagesetter.

3. Color Proofs
Create match prints or color keys to check for proper color registration and as guides for the printer.

4. Stripping
Lay out pages in the proper order for the binding process. This is a manual process, but large imagesetters (step 2) are performing this task.

light table

5. Plate Making
Create the physical plates that will hold the ink on the printing press. Plates for each of the four CMYK colors have to be created for all the pages.

6. Printing
Attach plates to the press and print each page four times. If a spot color is used in order to print a color with absolute consistency, the pages must be printed five times.

offset press

digital radio
The microwave transmission of digital data via line of sight transmitters.

digital recording
See *digital video, digital nonlinear editing* and *magnetic recording*.

Digital Research
(Digital Research, Inc., Monterey, CA) A software company founded in 1976 by Gary Kildall that spearheaded the microcomputer revolution with its CP/M operating system. Other DRI products included the GEM windows environment, FlexOS realtime operating system and DR DOS, a DOS-compatible operating system with advanced features. In 1991, DRI was acquired by Novell.

digital signal
An electronic signal transmitted as binary code either as on/off pulses or as high and low voltages.

digital signal processing
See *DSP*.

digital signature
An electronic signature that cannot be forged. It is a computed digest of the text that is encrypted and sent with the text message. The recipient decrypts the signature and recomputes the digest from the received text. If the digests match, the message is authenticated and proved intact from the sender.

Signatures and Certificates

A digital signature ensures that the document originated with the person signing it and that it was not tampered with after the signature was applied. However, the sender could still be an impersonator and not the person he or she claims to be. To verify that the message was indeed sent by the person claiming to send it requires a digital certificate (digital ID) which is issued by a certification authority. See *digital certificate*.

The sender uses a one-way hash function to compute a small digest of her text message. Using her private key, she encrypts the digest, turning it into a digital signature. The signature and the message are then encrypted using the recipient's public key and transmitted. The recipient uses his private key to decrypt the text and derive the still-encrypted signature. Using his public key, he decrypts the signature back into the sender's digest and then recomputes a new digest from the text message. If the digests match, the message is authenticated. See *digital envelope* and *MAC*.

Digital TV

See *DTV*.

Digital Versatile Disc

An alternate name for DVD discs. See *DVD*.

digital video

Video recording in digital form. In order to edit video in the computer or to embed video clips into multimedia documents, a video source must originate as digital (digital camera) or be converted to digital. Frames from analog video cameras and VCRs are converted into digital frames (bitmaps) using frame grabbers or similar devices attached to a personal computer.

Uncompressed digital video signals require huge amounts of storage, and high-ratio realtime compression schemes, such as MPEG, are essential for handling digital video in today's computers. See *MPEG, DVD, digital nonlinear editing* and *HDTV*.

Digital VideoDisc

See *DVD*.

digital video effects

Visual effects performed by computer that create a more interesting transition from one scene to another rather than just switching scenes. They include fading or dissolving the frame, wiping one frame over another, flipping the frame and simulating a camera lens opening and closing (iris effect).

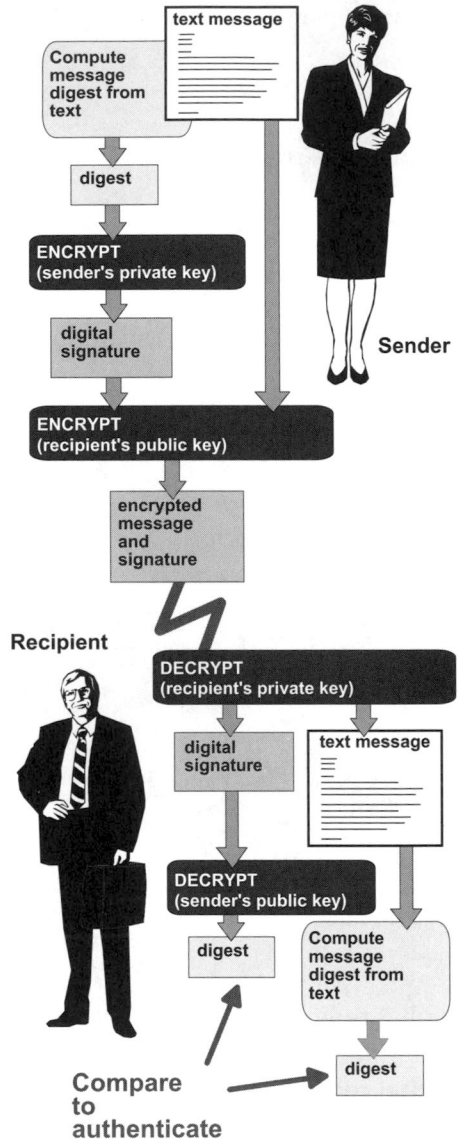

There Are Many Methods

This illustration uses one approach. There are others. For example, if the text message is small enough, only the signature needs to be sent. In addition, this illustration uses the public key method for encrypting the text itself. In practice, the public method is mostly used to send a secret key, and the text encryption and decryption are done with the secret key. This is called a *digital envelope*.

digital wallet

Software that provides the equivalent of a wallet for electronic commerce. A digital wallet, or e-wallet, holds digital money that you purchase similar to travelers checks. A wallet may also hold your credit card information along with a digital certificate that identifies you as the authorized card holder. See *digital money*.

digital watermark

A pattern of bits embedded into a file used to identify the source of illegal copies. For example, if a digital watermark is placed into a master copy of an audio CD, then all copies of that CD are uniquely identified. If a licensee were to manufacture and distribute them in areas outside of its authorized territory, the watermark provides a trace.

The watermark developer has to find creative ways of altering the file without disturbing it for the user. It is extremely difficult to embed a watermark within an ASCII file, which is just raw text. But it is somewhat easier to alter a few bits within digital audio samples without making a noticeable difference on playback.

digitize

To convert an image or signal into digital code by scanning, tracing on a graphics tablet or using an analog to digital conversion device. 3-D objects can be digitized by a device with a mechanical arm that is moved onto all the corners.

digitizer tablet

A graphics drawing tablet used for sketching new images or tracing old ones. The user makes contact with the tablet with a pen or puck (mistakenly called a mouse) that is either wireless or connected to the tablet by a wire. For sketching, the user draws with the pen or puck and the screen cursor "draws" a corresponding image.

The puck is generally preferred for tracing highly-detailed engineering drawings because the crosshairs, visible through a clear glass lens, let you precisely pinpoint ends and corners. Many tablets allow parts of the tablet surface to be customized into buttons that can be tapped to select menus and functions in the program.

When drawing or tracing on the tablet, a series of x-y coordinates (vector graphics) are created, either as a continuous stream of coordinates, or as end points.

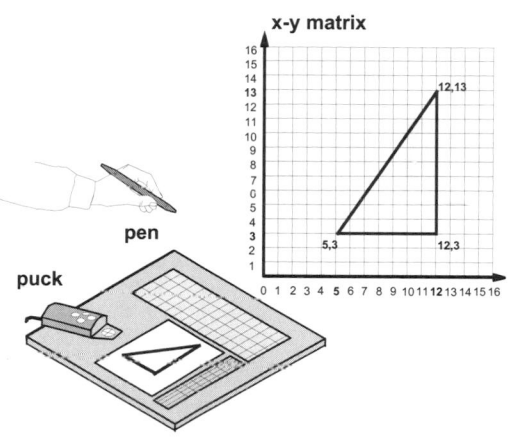

Digitizer Tablet

Digitzer tablets are also called *graphics tablets*. Objects are drawn using a pen or a puck. The puck is technically a tablet cursor, not a mouse. Drawings created on tablets are stored as mathematical line segments.

dimension

(1) One axis in an array. In programming, a dimension statement defines the array and sets up the number of elements within the dimensions.

(2) In a data warehouse, one side of the dimensional model set up for the department or organization. For example, the product dimension would be a list of the organization's products, the time dimension would be the calendar periods represented and so on.

dimensioning

In CAD programs, the management and display of the measurements of an object. There are various standards that determine such things as tolerances, sizes of arrowheads and orientation on the paper.

DIMM

(Dual In-line Memory Module) See *SIMM*.

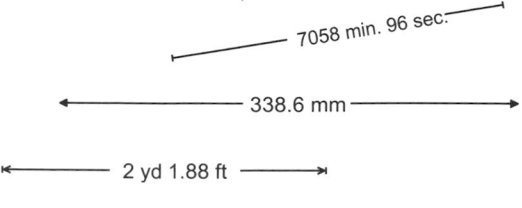

Dimensioning Examples

DIN connector

(Deutsches Institut fur Normung connector; German Standards Institute connector) A family of plugs and sockets used to connect a variety of devices. Earlier PC keyboards use a five-pin DIN. The PS/2 connector uses a smaller 6-pin Mini-DIN. See *PS/2 connector* for illustration.

Dingbats

A group of typesetting and desktop publishing symbols from International Typeface Corporation that include arrows, pointing hands, stars and circled numbers. They are formally called ITC Zapf Dingbats.

diode

An electronic component that acts primarily as a one-way valve. As a discrete component or built into a chip, it is used in a variety of functions. It is a key element in changing AC into DC. They are used as temperature and light sensors and light emitters (LEDs). In communications, they filter out analog and digital signals from carriers and modulate signals onto carriers. In digital logic, they're used as one-way valves and as switches similar to transistors.

DIP

(1) (Dual In-line Package) A common rectangular chip housing with leads (pins) on both long sides. Tiny wires bond the chip to metal leads that wind their way down into spider-like feet that are inserted into a socket or are soldered onto the board. See *CDIP, CERDIP* and *chip package.*

(2) (Document Image Processing) See *document imaging.*

DIP switch

(Dual In-line Package switch) A set of tiny toggle switches built into a DIP, which is mounted directly on a circuit board. The tip of a pen or pencil is required to flip the switch on or off.

Remember! Open is "off." Closed is "on."

Dir

(DIRectory) A CP/M, DOS and OS/2 command that lists the file names on the disk.

DirecPC

A satellite Internet service from Hughes Network Systems, (www.direcpc.com), that requires installation of a satellite dish cabled to an expansion board plugged into your PC. The uplink is made to the your own ISP through whatever medium you currently use, but the downlink is from the satellite to your dish at up to 400 Kbps.

Direct3D

A 3-D graphics programming interface (API) from Microsoft for Windows 95/98 and NT. It provides low-level access to the frame buffer and advanced features of the display adapter and allows game developers to write high-speed animated software. Game programs have stayed mostly in DOS throughout the Windows 3.x life cycle, because DOS programs can access the hardware directly to maximize speed. The Direct3D provides this capability for Windows 95/98 and NT. See *video accelerator* and *DirectDraw.*

Dingbats
Typing the alphabet in lower case produces these Dingbat symbols.

 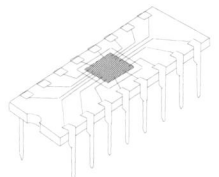

The DIP
The DIP package is commonly used to hold small chips, such as main memory, cache memory, A/D and D/A converters.

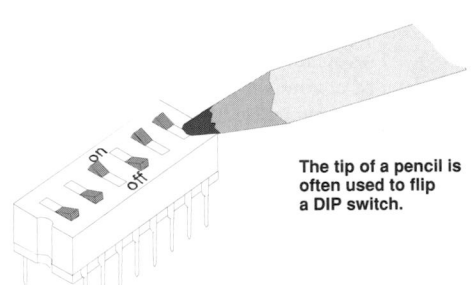

The tip of a pencil is often used to flip a DIP switch.

Switches on the DIP
DIP switches provide an inexpensive way to select options on a hardware device and will probably be used for years to come. However, as personal computers become more sophisticated, plug-in boards increasingly contain programmable chips. Instead of opening the case, pulling the board and figuring out which switch to flip, settings are changed using a software control panel.

direct access

The ability to go directly to a specific storage location without having to go through what's in front of it. Memories (RAMs, ROMs, PROMs, etc.) and disks are the major direct access devices.

direct access method

A technique for finding data on a disk by deriving its storage address from an identifying key in the record, such as account number. Using a formula, the account number is converted into a sector address. This is faster than comparing entries in an index, but it only works well when keys are numerically close: 100, 101, 102, etc.

direct access storage device

See *DASD*.

direct broadcast satellite

See *DBS*.

direct-connect modem

A modem that connects to a telephone line without the use of an acoustic coupler.

direct current

See *DC*.

direct data entry

Typing text into or drawing an image on the computer in contrast with copying or importing data from another source.

DirectDraw

A 2-D graphics programming interface (API) from Microsoft for Windows 95/98 and NT. DirectDraw provides low-level access to the frame buffer and advanced features of the display adapter. See *video accelerator* and *Direct3D*.

DirectInput

A programming interface (API) from Microsoft for Windows 95/98 and NT that provides controls for advanced digital input devices for games and virtual reality systems.

Director

A popular multimedia authoring program for Windows and Macintosh from Macromedia. Runtime versions can be run, edited and switched between Windows and Mac platforms. Shockwave is a browser plug-in that lets output from Macromedia's Director, Authorware and Freehand packages be viewed on the Web.

Director was initially introduced as MacroMind Director for the Mac in 1989, and it has been the de facto standard for Macintosh multimedia authoring. Before the Windows authoring version was introduced, a Windows player was available to run Director movies created on the Mac.

directory

A simulated file folder on disk. Programs and data for each application are typically kept in a separate directory (spreadsheets, word processing, etc.). Directories create the illusion of compartments, but are actually indexes to the files which may be scattered all over the disk. UNIX and DOS use the term directory, while the Mac and Windows use the term "folder."

directory enabled networks

See *DEN*.

directory listings

See *Web white pages* and *Web yellow pages*.

directory management

The maintenance and control of directories on a hard disk. Usually refers to menuing software that is easier to use than entering commands.

directory server

A network server that provides a directory, or naming service. See *directory service, naming service* and *ULS server.*

directory service

A directory of names, profile information and machine addresses of every user machine and resource on the network. When sent a user name, it either returns the logical address of that user; for example, Pat Smith = psmith@aol.com, or it may function like a naming service and return the physical address such as Pat Smith = 128.29.9.56. See *naming service* and *ULS server.*

directory tree

A graphic representation of a hierarchical directory. See *DOS Tree.*

direct overwrite

The ability to write a bit on a recording medium without having to erase it first. Magnetic disks and phase change optical disks provide direct overwrite capability. See *LIMDOW.*

DirectPlay

A programming interface (API) from Microsoft for Windows 95/98 and NT that provides the communications mechanism that allows multiple users to hook up and play a game with each other via modem, LAN or the Internet.

DirectSound

See *DirectX.*

direct thermal printer

A low- to medium resolution printer that uses a type of coated paper that darkens when heat is applied to it. The paper is passed by a line of heating elements that burn dots onto the paper. This is typically used in bar code printers and other small specialty printers. It was widely used in early fax machines. See *printer.*

direct view storage tube

See *DVST.*

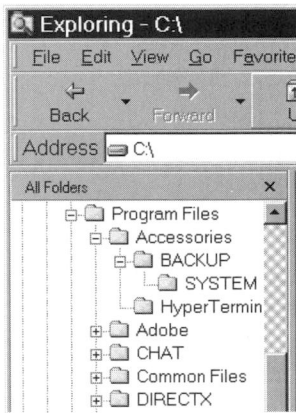

An Explorer Hierarchy
This Explorer example in Windows 95 shows various levels of the directory tree stemming from the Program Files folder. This graphical representation shows the folders within folders.

DirectX

A set of multimedia programming interfaces from Microsoft for Windows 95/98 and NT that provide low-level access to the hardware for improved performance. DirectDraw and Direct3D provide 2-D and 3-D graphics. DirectSound enables mixing multiple sound sources for sound cards. DirectPlay provides control for multiple users playing the same game via modem, LAN or the Internet. DirectInput provides control for advanced digital input devices for games and virtual reality.

dirty bit

A bit in a memory cache or virtual memory page that has been modified by the CPU, but not yet written back to storage.

dirty power

A non-uniform AC power (voltage fluctuations, noise and spikes), which comes from the electric utility or from electronic equipment in the office.

disable

To turn off a function. Contrast with *enable.*

disassembler

Software that converts machine language back into assembly language. Since there is no way to easily determine the human thinking behind the logic of the instructions, the resulting assembly language routines and variables are named and numbered generically (A001, A002, etc.). Disassembled code can be very difficult to maintain. See *decompiler.*

Computer Desktop Encyclopedia

disaster recovery

A plan for duplicating computer operations after a catastrophe occurs, such as a fire or earthquake. It includes routine off-site backup as well as a procedure for activating necessary information systems in a new location. See *data recovery*.

disc

An alternate spelling for disk. Some computer manufacturers use this spelling, but "disc" is usually used with read-only media, such as CDs and CD-ROMs. Rewritable disks are spelled with a "k." In this database, disc is used for CDs, CD-ROMs, CD-Rs and DVD-Rs, while disk is used for all other disk devices.

disc fixation (disc-at-once)

A process that ends the current recording session of a CD-R disc. The disc-at-once method finalizes the session and prevents future data from being appended. Track-at-once allows for more data to be appended, but the disc cannot be read until the final fixation. Multisession allows data to be read and appended at any time.

Discoverer/2000

See *Developer/2000*.

discrete

A component or device that is separate and distinct and treated as a singular unit.

discrete component

An elementary electronic device constructed as a single unit. Before integrated circuits (chips), all transistors, resistors and diodes were discrete. They are widely used in amplifiers and other devices that use large amounts of current. They are also still used on circuit boards intermingled with the chips.

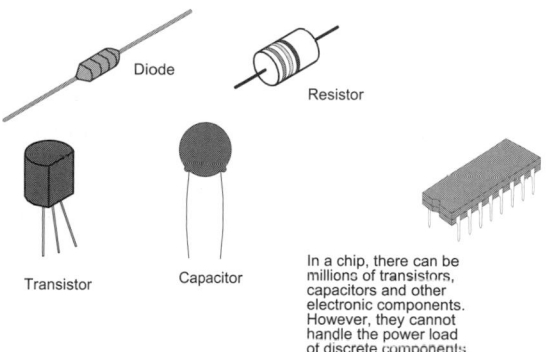

In a chip, there can be millions of transistors, capacitors and other electronic components. However, they cannot handle the power load of discrete components.

Discrete Components

discrete cosine transform

See *DCT*.

discrete manufacturing

Fabricating products by assembling ready-made components and subsystems into larger systems. The computer system, automobile and appliance industries are examples of discrete manufacturing. Contrast with *process manufacturing*.

discretionary hyphen

A user-designated place in a word for hyphenation. If the word goes over the margin, it will split in that location.

discussion thread

See *threaded discussion*.

dish

A saucer-shaped antenna that receives, or transmits and receives, signals from a satellite.

disintermediation

The elimination of the middleman. The term has been used to focus on the theoretical advantages of purchasing direct on the Web, such as convenience, cost savings and fast turnaround time. See *reintermediation*.

disk

A direct access storage device. See *floppy disk, hard disk, magnetic disk, optical disk* and *videodisc*.

disk access

Reading and writing the disk. It generally refers to the most time-consuming part of the operation, which is moving the read/write head. The disk access time is the average of the time it takes to position the head over the requested track. See *defragment* and *32-bit disk access*.

disk array

Two or more disk drives combined in a single unit for increased capacity, speed and/or fault tolerant operation. See *RAID*.

disk based

(1) A computer system that uses disks as its storage medium.

(2) An application that retrieves data from the disk as required. Contrast with *memory based*.

disk cache

See *cache*.

disk cartridge

A removable disk module that contains a single hard disk platter or a floppy disk. See *cartridge*.

disk compression

See *data compression*.

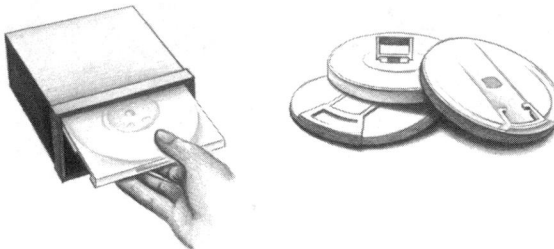

Old and New Disk Cartridges
The older cartridges (right) came in a variety of sizes as large as 16" in diameter. Today's cartridges (left) use much smaller 5.25" and 3.5" form factors. For the different kinds of cartridges currently in use, see *cartridge*.

disk controller

A circuit that controls transmission to and from the disk drive. In a personal computer, it is an expansion board that plugs into an expansion slot in the bus. See *hard disk*.

Diskcopy

A DOS and OS/2 utility used to copy entire floppy disks track by track.

disk crash

See *head crash*.

disk drive

A peripheral storage device that holds, spins, reads and writes magnetic or optical disks. It may be a receptacle for disk cartridges, disk packs or floppy disks, or it may contain non-removable disk platters like most personal computer hard disks. See *latest disk drives*.

disk dump

A printout of disk contents without report formatting.

disk duplexing

The recording of redundant data for fault tolerant operation. Data is written on two separate disks within the same system. Each disk drive is connected to its own controller. See *disk mirroring* for illustration. See also *RAID*.

disk duplicator

A device that formats and makes identical copies of floppy disks for software distribution. Simple units contain two floppy disks and require manual loading. Automated units have hoppers and stackers that can copy 50 or more diskettes without operator intervention. The most comprehensive machines can attach the diskette labels.

disk emulator

A solid state replication of a disk drive.

diskette

Same as *floppy disk*.

disk failure

See *head crash, data error* and *General failure reading drive x*.

disk farm

A very large number of hard disks. As more years of computer processing history pile up within the enterprise, databases are reaching staggering proportions. For example, thirty years of sales figures for companies with thousands of products in hundreds of locations result in multiple gigabytes of data. It is not uncommon to need a terabyte disk farm, which would require 250 four-gigabyte drives. See *server farm*.

disk file

A set of instructions or data that is recorded, cataloged and treated as a single unit on a disk. Source language programs, machine language programs, spreadsheets, data files, text documents, graphics files and batch files are examples.

disk format

The storage layout of a disk as determined by its physical medium and as initialized by a format program. For example, a 5.25" 360KB floppy vs a 3.5" 1.44MB floppy or a DOS disk vs a Mac disk. See *low-level format*, *high-level format*, *DOS/Windows disk format* and *file format*.

disk grooming

Deleting old and unnecessary files on a disk.

diskless workstation

A workstation without a disk. Programs and data are retrieved from the network server. The network computer (NC) is a diskless workstation.

disk management

The maintenance and control of a hard disk. Refers to a variety of utilities that provide format, copy, diagnostic, directory management and defragmenting functions.

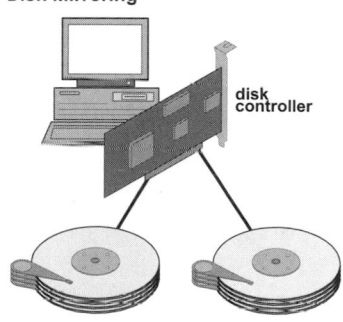

Disk Mirroring

disk controller

Disk Manager

A driver from Ontrack Data International, Inc., Eden Prarie, MN, (www.ontrack.com), that allows older PCs to support hard disks greater than 528MB. PCs made before 1994 may have a system BIOS that does not support the larger drives. The Disk Manager diskette and instructions are often bundled with new hard disks.

disk memory

Same as *disk*. In this lexicon, disks and tapes are called storage devices, not memory devices.

disk mirroring

The recording of redundant data for fault tolerant operation. Data is written on two partitions of the same disk or on two separate disks within the same system. Disk mirroring uses the same controller. See *RAID*.

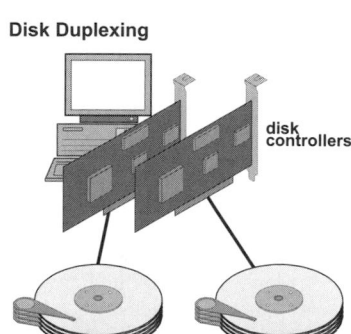

Disk Duplexing

disk controllers

disk operating system

See *DOS*.

disk optimizer

A utility program that defragments a hard disk. See *defragment*.

disk pack

An early removable hard disk module used in minis and mainframes that contained two or more platters housed in a dust-free container. For mounting, the bottom of the container was removed. After insertion, the top was removed. See illustration on next page.

disk parameters

See *hard disk parameters*.

disk partition

A subdivision of a hard disk. The maximum size of a disk partition depends on the operating system used. See *Fdisk*.

disk striping

The spreading of data over multiple disk drives to improve performance. Data is interleaved by bytes or by sectors across the drives. For example, with four drives and a controller designed to overlap reads and writes, four sectors could be read in the same time it normally takes to read one. Disk striping does not inherently provide fault tolerance or error checking. It is used in conjunction with various other methods. See *RAID*.

DISOSS

(DIStributed Office Support System) An IBM mainframe centralized document distribution and filing application that runs under MVS. Its counterpart under VM is PROFS. It allows for e-mail and the exchange of documents between a variety of IBM office devices, including word processors and PCs. DISOSS uses the SNADS messaging protocol.

Old Disk Packs
This picture taken in the 1970s shows the disk pack being loaded into the drive. Such disks held only a couple of hundred megabytes. *(Photo courtesy of Unisys Corporation.)*

dispatcher

Same as *scheduler*.

dispersed intelligence

Same as *distributed intelligence*.

displacement

Same as *offset*. See *base/displacement*.

display

(1) To show text and graphics on a CRT or flat panel screen.

(2) A screen or monitor.

display adapter

An expansion board that plugs into a desktop computer that converts the images created in the computer to the electronic signals required by the monitor. It determines the maximum resolution, maximum refresh rate and the number of colors that can be sent to the monitor. The monitor must be equally capable of handling its highest resolution and refresh. In a PC, the display adapter is known by many names (see below).

The display adapter converts the characters or graphic patterns (bitmaps) within the computer's memory into signals used to refresh the display screen. Display adapters also contain their own memory, which is used to build the images before they are displayed (see *frame buffer*).

In earlier digital systems (CGA, EGA, etc.), the display adapters generated digital signals for the monitor. The monitor then did the conversion from digital to analog. In today's analog systems (VGA, Macintosh, etc.), the display adapter creates the analog signals that are sent to the monitor. See *graphics accelerator* and *PC display modes*.

Take Your Pick

Graphics adapter, graphics board, graphics card, graphics controller, video display adapter, video display board, video display card, video display controller, video adapter, video board, video card, video controller, display board, display card, display controller, VGA adapter, VGA board, VGA card and VGA controller are other terms for the display adapter.

Computer Desktop Encyclopedia

By the way, a video graphics board is something different. It is a video capture board that accepts analog NTSC video from a videotape player (VCR) or camera. Increasingly, NTSC video is being integrated with computers, so the terminology might even get a tad more confusing! See *how to select a PC display system*.

display attribute
See *attribute*.

display board, display card
Same as *display adapter*.

display cycle
In computer graphics, the series of operations required to display an image.

display device
See *display screen* and *display adapter*.

display element
(1) In graphics, a basic graphic arts component, such as background, foreground, text or graphics image.

(2) In computer graphics, any component of an image.

display entity
In computer graphics, a collection of display elements that can be manipulated as a unit.

display font
Same as *screen font*.

display frame
In computer graphics, a single frame in a series of animation frames.

display list
In computer graphics, a collection of vectors that are used to display a vector graphic image on screen. The display list is generated from the drawing database.

display list processor
In computer graphics, an engine that generates graphic geometry (draws lines, circles, etc.) directly from the display list and independently of the CPU.

Display PostScript
The screen counterpart of the PostScript printer language that translates elementary commands in an application to graphics and text elements on screen. It is designed for inclusion in an operating system to provide a standard, device-independent display language.

display resolution
See *resolution*.

display screen
A surface area upon which text and graphics are temporarily made to appear for human viewing. It is typically a CRT or flat panel technology.

display terminal
See *video terminal*.

DisplayWrite
A full-featured IBM word processing program for PCs that stems from the typewriter-oriented DisplayWriter word processing system first introduced in 1980. DisplayWrite was widely used in organizations that were mostly IBM oriented.

distance learning
Obtaining education and training from a remote teaching site via TV or computer.

distance vector protocol

A simple routing protocol that uses distance or hop count as its primary metric for determining the best forwarding path. RIP, IGRP and EIGRP are examples. A distance vector protocol routinely sends its neigboring routers copies of its routing tables to keep them up-to-date. Contrast with *link state protocol* and *path vector protocol*. See *routing protocol*.

distributed computing

The use of multiple computers in an organization rather than one centralized system. Most all large organizations have computers dedicated to departmental use. Distributed computing implies that they are networked together, not just decentralized systems without any communications between them. In addition, client/server applications continue to disburse more and more computers throughout the enterprise. Distributed computing used to be called *distributed processing*. See *client/server*.

distributed database

A database physically stored in two or more computer systems. Although geographically dispersed, a distributed database system manages and controls the entire database as a single collection of data. If redundant data is stored in separate databases due to performance requirements, updates to one set of data will automatically update the additional sets in a timely manner. See *replication*.

distributed data processing

See *distributed processing*.

distributed file system

Software that keeps track of files stored across multiple networks. When the data is requested, it converts the file names into the physical location of the file so it can be found.

distributed function

The distribution of processing functions throughout the organization.

distributed intelligence

The placing processing capability in terminals and other peripheral devices. Intelligent terminals handle screen layouts, data entry validation and other pre-processing steps. Intelligence placed into disk drives and other peripherals relieves the central computer from routine tasks.

distributed logic

See *distributed intelligence*.

distributed objects

Software modules that are designed to work together but reside in multiple computer systems throughout the organization. A program in one machine sends a message to an object in a remote machine to perform some processing. The results are sent back to the calling machine. See *CORBA* and *DCOM*.

distributed printer

A computer printer that provides output in a range approximately from 25 to 60 ppm. It is generally considered a higher grade than a network printer and lower than a production printer. IBM typically uses this term. See *network printer* and *production printer*.

distributed processing

The first term used to describe the distribution of multiple computers throughout an organization in contrast to a centralized system. It started with the first minicomputers. Today, distributed processing is called *distributed computing*. See also *client/server*.

distribution disk

A floppy disk or CD-ROM used to disseminate files in a software package.

dithering

Simulating more colors and shades in a palette. In a monochrome system that displays or prints only black and white, shades of grays can be simulated by creating varying patterns of black dots. This is how halftones are created in a monochrome printer.

In color systems, additional colors can be simulated by varying patterns of dots of existing colors.

Dithering cannot produce the exact same results as having the necessary color depth (levels of gray or colors), but it can make shaded drawings and photographs appear much more realistic.

Dithering is also used to create a wide variety of patterns for use as backgrounds, fills and shading, as well as for creating anti-aliasing effects.

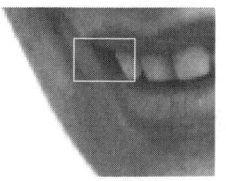 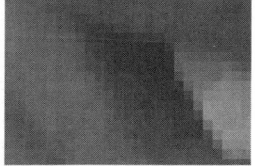

Dithering a Color Image
When there aren't enough colors in a display system to render an image properly, an infinite palette can be created by dithering. Quite often, a 24-bit color image is dithered to 256 colors. The right side is a magnification of the white box on the left.

DATABASE
DATABASE

DATABASE

DATABASE

Dithering Text
Text is also dithered. Notice how much softer the word DATABASE is at the top of this example, compared with the undithered word below it. The magnified view shows where lighter blue pixels filled in for the curves. When dithering is performed against the edges of an image, it is called *anti-aliasing*.

Ditto drive
A family of backup tape drives from Iomega. The original Easy 800 and Easy 3200 were Travan TR2 and TR3 drives with 400MB and 1.6GB native capacity. The subsequent 2GB and 3.7GB (stated in compressed 2x native capacities) models use proprietary formats, but can read QIC-80, QIC-Wide 80, QIC-3010 & 3020, TR1, TR2 and TR3 tapes.

Ditto Max drives use Verbatim's DM-EXtra cartridges in 3, 5 and 7GB capacities (compressed) and can read Ditto 2 and 3.7GB, TR3 and QIC-3020s. Ditto Max Professional units support a 10GB tape. Ditto Max cartridges have a 250MB Flash!File partition in the front of the tape that is reserved for frequently-used files. See *QIC*.

Divestiture
The breakup of AT&T. By federal court order, AT&T divested itself on January 1, 1984 of its 23 operating companies. Bell Labs was renamed AT&T Bell Labs, and its Western Electric manufacturing division became AT&T Technologies. See *RBOC, Bellcore* and *Trivestiture*.

divide overflow
A program error in which a number is accidentally divided by zero or by a number that creates a result too large for the computer to handle.

Divx
(DIgital Video EXpress) A DVD rental system that uses a specialized DVD machine that plays regular DVD movies as well as Divx discs. Consumers pay a rental charge for the Divx disc, which lasts for two days after the first viewing. Additional time can be ordered via modem from the Divx player. Rolled out in June 1998 in San Francisco, CA, and Richmond, VA, Divx is a joint venture of Circuit City and entertainment-law firm Zeffren, Brittenham, Branca & Fischer.

DIX standard
(DEC-Intel-Xerox standard) An earlier Ethernet standard which has been superseded by IEEE 802.3. Network protocols often use the Ethernet frame from this specification.

DL/1

(Data Language 1) An early database from IBM for its DOS/VSE mainframes. DL/1 is a modified version of IMS/DB. See *IMS*.

DLC

(1) (Data Link Control) See *data link* and *OSI*.

(2) (Data Link Control) The data link layer protocol (layer 2) that is used in IBM's SNA networking. See *SNA, data link protocol* and *Microsoft DLC*.

(3) (Digital Loop Carrier) See *loop carrier*.

DLL

(Dynamic Link Library) An executable program module that performs some function. DLLs are not launched directly by users. When needed, they are called for by a running application and loaded to perform a specific function. DLLs are generally written so that their routines are shared by more than one application at the same time (see *reentrant code*).

In the DOS world, there was never a solid way to dynamically link and share routines at runtime. ISRs and TSRs were created for this purpose, but they were not formally sanctioned by Microsoft and often caused conflict.

Windows, on the other hand, uses DLLs as a standard way of linking and sharing functionality. There are many DLLs that come with Windows that applications depend on and call for as required (look in your \WINDOWS\SYSTEM directory for the .DLL extension). Applications may also include their own DLLs, which are usually stored in the application directory.

Trouble in Windows City

A commonly-shared DLL, such as VBRUN400.DLL, which is the Visual Basic runtime module, may be placed into the \WINDOWS\SYSTEM directory by an application's install program. Some install programs simply overwrite their DLL on top of an existing one without checking file dates. This means the installation of a new application can foul up what you are already running, because your existing application depended on certain features in a newer DLL that was replaced with an older version.

On the other hand, even when the newer DLL is installed over the old one, the new version may not be compatible with the old version. Once again, your existing application may no longer run properly or run at all after installing another application. Although Microsoft has published guidelines, there is no way to enforce compliance, and Microsoft itself releases new versions of DLLs that are incompatible with older versions from time to time. The bottom line is that the shared DLL system in Windows is inherently flawed.

A method for monitoring these installation problems is expected in Windows 98, which may offer some assistance to this situation.

DLP

(Digital Light Processing) A data projection technology from TI that produces clear, readable images on screens in lit rooms. DLP is suitable for all ends of the projection spectrum, from units that weigh under 10 pounds to electronic cinema projectors that are expected to replace large-screen movie projectors some day. The technology uses a Digital Micromirror Device (DMD), a chip with from 400,000 to 1.2 million light switches that cancel or reflect light. Microelectromechanical mirrors, each 16 micrometers square, are built on top of a CMOS memory chip.

The state of each memory bit (0 or 1) rotates its mirror plus or minus 10 degrees. Gray scale is created by modulating

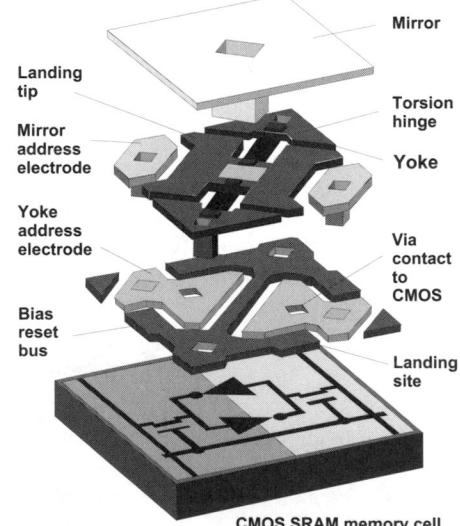

A Single DMD Pixel

More than a million of these light switches are on one CMOS chip. The state of the memory cell (0 or 1) rotates the mirror to cancel or reflect light. Gray scale is achieved by rotating the mirrors back and forth. (Redrawn from diagram courtesy of Texas Instruments, Inc.)

Computer Desktop Encyclopedia

the light, which is accomplished by rotating the mirrors back and forth some number of times within each 16 millisecond video frame. Color is achieved by using color filters with one, two or three DMD chips.

DLS server

See *ULS server*.

DLSw

(Data Link SWitching) A method for forwarding SNA traffic over all types of wide area networks by encapsulating the data in the TCP/IP protocol. DLSw is employed in the routers and adds significant overhead. RFC 1490 is a later technology designed to move SNA traffic over frame relay with greater performance.

DLT

(Digital Linear Tape) A magnetic tape technology originally developed by Digital for its VAX line. The technology was later sold to Quantum, which makes it available to other manufacturers. DLT uses half-inch, single-hub cartridges somewhat like IBM's 3480/3490/3590 line. It writes 128 or 208 linear tracks, depending on model, and provides capacities from 10 to 35GB. DLT usage started to grow rapidly in 1995 and has been widely used on medium to large-scale LANs. See *single-hub cartridge*. For a summary of all storage technologies, see *storage*.

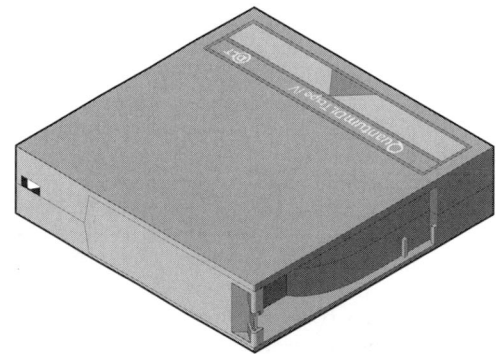

DLT Cartridge
Like IBM tapes, DLT use half-inch linear recording in a single-hub cartridge. After insertion, the tape is pulled from the cartridge onto the takeup reel inside the drive.

DLUR/DLUS

(Dependent LU Requester/Server) SNA enhancements that enable traditional host connections, such as host to terminal and host to printer, to run over an APPN network. It supports LU sessions other than 6.2. See *LU*.

DMA

(Direct Memory Access) Specialized circuitry or a dedicated microprocessor that transfers data from memory to memory without using the CPU. Although DMA may periodically steal cycles from the CPU, data is transferred much faster than using the CPU for every byte of transfer.

On PCs, there are eight DMA channels commonly used as follows. Most sound cards are set to use DMA channel 1.

```
DMA     Used for
0       8-bit transfer
1       8-bit transfer
2       Floppy disk controller
3       8-bit transfer
4       Cascaded from 0-3
5       16-bit transfer
6       16-bit transfer
7       16-bit transfer
```

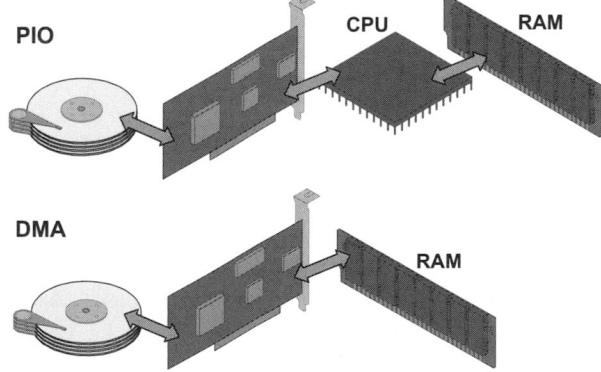

DMD

(Digital Micromirror Device) See *DLP*.

DMA Disk Transfers
There are verious modes of data transfer on IDE disk drives. The PIO modes use the CPU, and the DMA modes bypass the CPU.

DME

(Distributed Managment Environment) A network monitoring and control protocol defined by the Open Software Foundation (now The Open Group). DME was not widely used.

DMF

(Distribution Media Format) A floppy disk format that Microsoft uses to distribute its software. DMF floppies compress more data (1.7MB) onto the 3.5" diskette, and the files cannot be copied with normal DOS and Windows commands. A utility that supports the DMF format must be used.

DMI

(Desktop Managment Interface) A management system for PCs developed by the Desktop Management Task Force (DMTF). DMI provides a bi-directional path to interrogate all the hardware and software components within a PC. When PCs are DMI-enabled, their hardware and software configurations can be monitored from a central station in the network.

A memory-resident agent resides in the background. When queries are made to the agent, it responds by sending back data contained in MIFs (Management Information Files) and/or activating MIF routines. Static data in a MIF would contain items such as model ID, serial number, memory and port addresses. A MIF routine could report errors to the management console as they occur, or it could read ROM or RAM chips and report their contents, as well.

DMI LAYERS

Management Interface API	Calls to DMI from console software, such as Intel's LANdesk and Novell's NMS.
Service Layer	Actual DMI agent in each client machine (DLL, TSR, etc.)
Component Interface	Accesses the MIF and provides calls from component back to the console.

DMI is a complete management system but can co-exist with SNMP and other management protocols. For example, when an SNMP query arrives, DMI can fill out the SNMP MIB with data from its MIF. A single workstation or server can serve as a proxy agent that would contain the SNMP module and service an entire LAN segment of DMI machines.

Data-only MIFs can be created by anyone using a text editor, but it is expected that all hardware and software vendors will eventually include at least a data-only MIF with their products. See *CIM, WBEM* and *DTMF*.

DMPL

(Digital Microprocessor Plotter Language) A vector graphics file format from Houston Instruments that was developed for plotters. Most plotters support the DMPL or HPGL standards.

DMS

(1) (Document Management System) See *document management*.

(2) (Defense Messaging System) An X.500-compliant messaging system developed by the U.S. Dept. of Defense. It is used by all the branches of the armed forces as well as federal agencies involved with security.

(3) (Desktop Management Suite) A collection of software administration and backup programs for Windows from Seagate Software.

(4) (Digital Multiplex System) A telephone company central office computer. Northern Telecom makes a family of DMS-branded switches.

DMTF

(Desktop Management Task Force, Inc., Hillsboro, OR, www.dmtf.org) An industry consortium founded in 1992 that is involved with the development, support and maintenance of management standards for PCs. Its goal is to reduce the cost and complexity of PC management. Focusing initially on the DMI standard, the DMTF is involved with other management technologies, including CIM and DEN. See *DMI, CIM, WBEM* and *DEN*. See also *DTMF*.

DNA

(1) (Distributed interNet Architecture) Introduced in 1997, it is Microsoft's umbrella term for its enterprise network architecture based on COM and Windows NT 5.0.

(2) (Digital Network Architecture) Introduced in 1978, it is Digital's umbrella term for its enterprise network architecture based on DECnet.

DNS

(Domain Name System) Name resolution software that lets users locate computers on a UNIX network or the Internet (TCP/IP network) by domain name. The DNS server maintains a database of domain names (host names) and their corresponding IP addresses. In this hypothetical example, if **www.mycompany.com** were presented to a DNS server, the IP address **204.0.8.51** would be returned. DNS has replaced the manual task of updating HOSTS files in an inhouse UNIX network, and of course, it would be impossible to do this manually on the global Internet, given its size.

For Windows networks using TCP/IP, the counterpart to DNS is WINS. In a Windows-only network, only WINS needs to be used. In a mixed Windows/UNIX environment, the Microsoft DNS server integrates the two. When a UNIX station wants to resolve the name for a PC, it queries the Microsoft DNS server, which in turn queries the WINS server if it does not already have it. See *HOSTS file, ping, root server* and *WINS*.

docking station

A base station for a laptop that turns the portable computer into a desktop system. It uses a large plug and socket to quickly connect the laptop which duplicates all the cable lines for the monitor, printer, keyboard, mouse, etc. The docking station typically has one or two slots for expansion boards and may house speakers and other peripherals such as CD-ROM drive. See *port replicator*.

DocObjects

An extension to OLE that allows documents to be placed into OLE containers such as the Microsoft Office Binder or Internet Explorer. See *ActiveX Documents*.

docs

Short for documents or documentation.

DOCSIS

(Data Over Cable Service Interface Specification) A set of standards for transferring data via cable TV. DOCSIS is managed by Multimedia Cable Network System, an organization formed by four major cable operators.

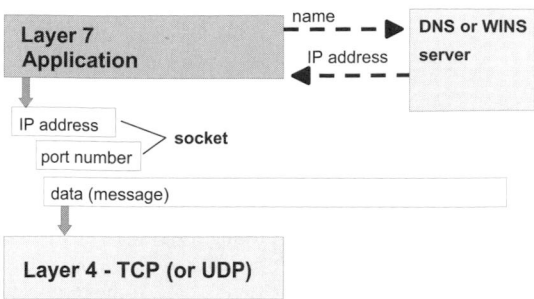

DNS Name Resolution
In an IP network, the application queries a DNS or WINS server to turn the name of the machine it wishes to communicate with into its IP address. See *TCP/IP abc's*.

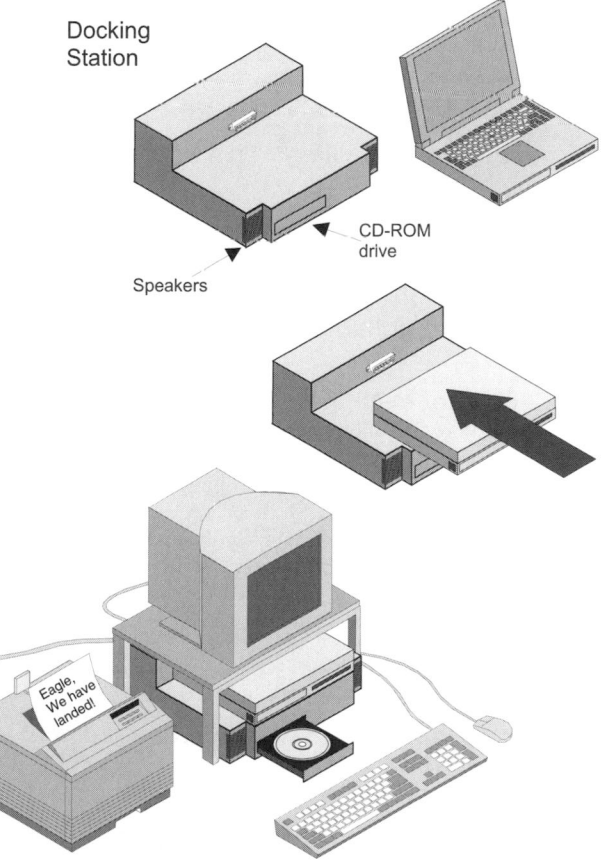

document

(1) Any paper form that has been filled in.

(2) A word processing text file.

(3) In the Macintosh, any text, data or graphics file created in the computer.

documentation

The narrative and graphical description of a system. Following are the kinds of documentation required to describe an information system for both users and systems staff. See also *technical writer* and *RTFM*.

Operating Procedures

1. Instructions for turning the system on and getting the programs initiated (loaded).
2. Instructions for obtaining source documents for data entry.
3. Instructions for entering data at the terminal, which includes a picture of each screen layout the user will encounter.
4. A description of error messages that can occur and the alternative methods for handling them.
5. A description of the defaults taken in the programs and the instructions for changing them.
6. Instructions for distributing the computer's output, which includes sample pages for each type of report.

System Documentation

1. Data dictionary - Description of the files and databases.
2. System flow chart - Description of the data as it flows from source document to report.
3. Application program documentation - Description of the inputs, processing and outputs for each data entry, query, update and report program in the system.

Technical Documentation

1. File structures and access methods
2. Program flow charts
3. Program source code listings
4. Machine procedures (JCL)

document centric

Focusing on the document as the foundation or starting point. In a document-centric system, the document is retrieved and automatically calls the appropriate software required to work with it. Contrast with *application centric*. See *component software*.

document collaboration

See *data conferencing*.

document exchange software

Software that allows document files to be viewed on other computers that do not have the original application that created it. The software comes in two parts. The first component converts the document into a proprietary format for distribution. The second is a viewer program that displays the files, and viewers are generally free.

Unlike file viewers that rely on the fonts installed in the computer to display file contents accurately, document exchange systems carry the fonts over within the file format to the viewing machine. The fonts are only used for displaying the document, however, not for general use by the system. The viewers may allow sections of the document to be copied to the clipboard. See *Acrobat*.

document handling

A procedure for transporting and handling paper documents for data entry and scanning.

document image management, document image processing

See *document imaging*.

document imaging

The online storage, retrieval and management of electronic images of documents. The main method of capturing images is by scanning paper documents.

Document imaging systems replace large paper-intensive operations. Documents can be shared by all users on a network and document routing can be controlled by the computer (workflow). The systems are often simpler to develop and implement than traditional data processing systems, because users are already familiar with the paper documents that appear on screen.

Document images are stored as bitmapped graphics, and although a small amount of text (keywords) may be associated with the document in order to index it, the meaning of the document content is known only to the human viewer, not the computer. Like microfilm, signatures and other original markings remain intact.

document management

The capture and management of documents within an organization. The term used to imply the management of documents after there were scanned into the computer. Today, the term has become an umbrella under which document imaging, workflow, text retrieval and multimedia fall.

The trend towards designing information systems as document centric, where the document becomes the focus, not the application that created it, is expected to bring document management to the forefront of computing. See illustration on next page.

document management system

Software that manages documents for electronic publishing. It generally supports a large variety of document formats and provides extensive access control and searching capabilities across LANs and WANs. A document management system may support multiple versions of a document. It may also be able to combine text fragments written by different authors. It often includes a workflow component that routes documents to the appropriate users. See *workflow*.

document mark

In micrographics, a small optical blip on each frame on a roll of microfilm that is used to automatically count the frames.

Document Objects

See *ActiveX Documents*.

document processing

Processing text documents, which includes indexing methods for text retrieval based on content. See *document imaging*.

document publishing software

See *document exchange software* and *desktop publishing*.

document sharing

See *data conferencing*.

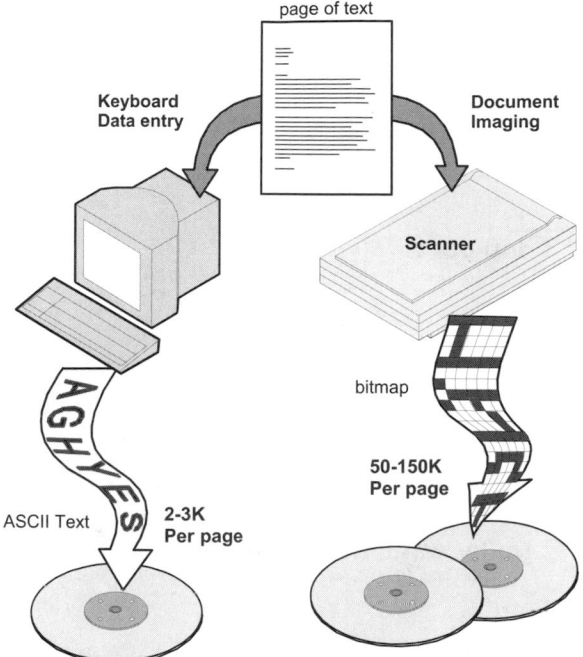

Document Imaging Takes Storage Space

When a page of text is scanned, it takes up much more storage space than if the individual characters were typed in. When data is entered on the keyboard, each character uses one byte of storage. When it is scanned, the piece of paper is turned into a digital picture, which is an image of dots. The white space on the paper also takes up storage. Depending on the resolution required for the printed text, a scanned page can take 50 times as much storage as the raw ASCII characters of typed-in data.

document viewer

See *file viewer* and *document exchange software*.

docuterm

A word or phrase in a text document that is used to identify the contents of the document.

DOF

See *6DOF*.

dog bone

The bone-shaped holographic stickers used to seal CD jewel cases.

DOJ

(Department Of Justice) The legal arm of the U.S. government which represents the public interest of the United States. It is headed by the Attorney General.

DOLAP

See *OLAP*.

Dolby AC-3, Dolby Digital

See *AC-3*.

Dolch

(Dolch Computer Systems, Fremont, CA, www.dolch.com) A manufacturer of high-end, ruggedized portable PCs for industrial use. It introduced the first portable active matrix PC, the first portable 386, 486, Pentium and dual Pentium, and in 1994, the first videoconferencing-equipped portable.

In 1976, Volker Dolch founded Dolch Logic Instruments, which became the largest supplier of logic analyzers in Europe. In 1987, he sold the company and arranged a management buy-out of its American division.

do loop

A high-level programming language structure that repeats instructions based on the results of a comparison. In a DO WHILE loop, the instructions within the loop are performed if the comparison is true. In a DO UNTIL loop, the instructions are bypassed if the comparison is true. The following DO WHILE loop prints 1 through 10 and stops.

```
counter = 0
do while counter < 10
  counter = counter + 1
  ? counter
enddo
```

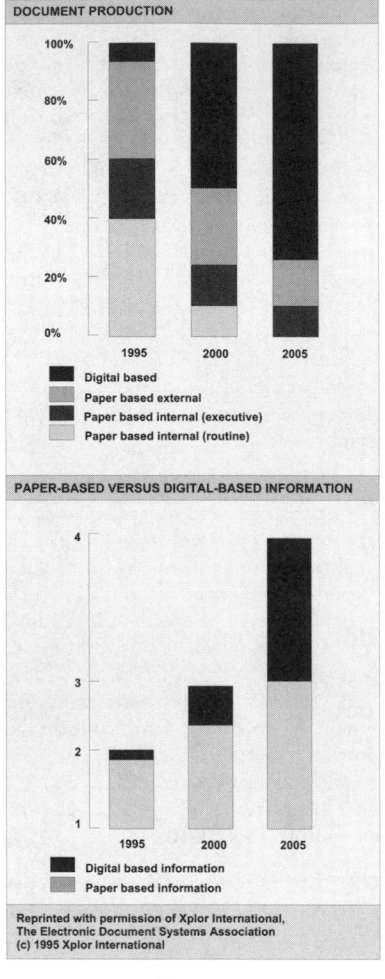

DOCUMENT PRODUCTION

- Digital based
- Paper based external
- Paper based internal (executive)
- Paper based internal (routine)

PAPER-BASED VERSUS DIGITAL-BASED INFORMATION

- Digital based information
- Paper based information

Reprinted with permission of Xplor International, The Electronic Document Systems Association (c) 1995 Xplor International

DOM

(Document Object Model) The interface for Dynamic HTML, which lets programs and scripts access HTML tags and modify them. See *Dynamic HTML*.

domain

(1) In a LAN, a subnetwork comprised of a group of clients and servers under the control of one security database. Dividing LANs into domains improves performance and security.

(2) In a communications network, all resources under the control of a single computer system.

(3) On the Internet, a registration category. See *domain name* and *Internet domain names*.

(4) In database management, all possible values contained in a particular field for every record in the file.

(5) In magnetic storage devices, a group of molecules that makes up one bit.

(6) In a hierarchy, a named group that has control over the groups under it, which may be domains themselves.

domain name

The term may refer to any type of domain within the computer field, since there are several types of domains (see above). However, today, it often refers to the address of an Internet site. See *Internet domain names, Internet address* and *InterNIC*.

Is a Name Already Taken?

To find out if a domain name is taken, visit www.internic.net. Select Registration Services, then Whois. Type in the name and press Enter.

domain namespace

See *namespace*.

domain name system

See *DNS*.

dominant carrier

A telecommunications services provider that has control over a large segment of a particular market.

Domino

See *Lotus Notes*.

donating old equipment

See *how to donate old equipment*.

dongle

Same as *hardware key*.

do nothing instruction

Same as *no-op*.

door

(1) In a BBS system, a programming interface that lets an online user run an application program in the BBS.

(2) See *drive door*.

doorway mode

In a communications program, a mode that passes function, cursor, ctrl and alt keystrokes to the BBS computer in order to use the remote application as if it were on the local machine.

dopant

An element diffused into pure silicon in order to alter its electrical characteristics.

doping

Altering the electrical conductivity of a semiconductor material, such as silicon, by chemically combining it with foreign elements. It results in an excess of electrons (n-type) or a lack of electrons (p-type) in the silicon.

DOS

(1) (Disk Operating System) Pronounced "dahss." A generic term for operating system.

(2) (Disk Operating System) A single-user operating system from Microsoft for the PC. It was the first OS for the PC and is still the underlying control program for Windows 3.1. Windows 95/98 and Windows NT build in their own version of DOS to support existing DOS applications.

The DOS version that Microsoft developed for IBM is PC-DOS, and the version that all other vendors have used is MS-DOS. However, except for DOS 6, which contain different versions of various utilities, PC-DOS and MS-DOS commands and system functions are the same. All releases of PC-DOS and MS-DOS are generally called *DOS*.

(3) See *DOS/VSE*.

(4) (DoS) See *denial of service*.

DOS 5

A major DOS upgrade in 1991 that included an enhanced user interface (DOS Shell) with task swapping, undelete commands, a full-screen text editor, online help and an improved memory manager. Support for 2GB hard disks and 2.88MB floppies was added. DOS 5 included QBasic, which superseded GW-BASIC in the MS-DOS version and accompanied BASICA in the IBM version.

DOS 6

An upgrade introduced in 1993 that includes built-in realtime compression and new utilities for memory management, backup, file transfer, disk optimization, antivirus and for managing multiple startup configurations.

IBM's DOS 6, which was formally introduced as PC-DOS 6.1, is somewhat different than Microsoft's DOS 6. All the fundamental DOS commands are the same, but PC-DOS 6.1 includes direct support for pen-based computing and the PC Card. For the first time, PC-DOS became available from IBM as a retail product, not just for IBM systems.

For years, the terms MS-DOS and PC-DOS differentiated Microsoft's version from IBM's version, but the term DOS is generally used for both. Up until DOS 6, they had been identical for practical purposes. See *DOS 7*.

DOS 7

In early 1995, IBM released PC-DOS 7 with enhanced memory management and virus protection. It includes the Stacker data compression program as well as utilites to enhance mobile computing.

Novell, which was the first to release a DOS 7, is no longer planning new DOS versions.

The DOS included in Windows 95/98 is often called DOS 7, which is an enhanced version of DOS 6. It is unlikely that Microsoft will introduce a DOS 7 independently of Windows.

DOS batch file

A file of DOS commands that are "batch" processed. Each command in a batch file is executed by DOS until the end of the file is reached.

The following batch file switches to the E drive, goes to the PAT directory and runs the MYPROG program:

```
e:
cd \pat
myprog
```

DOS box

Slang for a DOS session in Windows or OS/2. The "box" is actually an instance of the Intel x86 Virtual 8086 Mode, which simulates an independent, fully functional PC environment. See *Virtual 8086 Mode*.

DOS command

An instruction that DOS executes from the command line or from a batch file. A variety of internal commands, such as Dir and Copy, are built into the COMMAND.COM program and are always available as long as DOS is running. Many external commands, such as Format and Xcopy, are individual programs that reside in the DOS directory.

DOS device names

DOS device names are reserved names for common input and output devices.

```
Reserved name    Device
AUX              First connected serial port
PRN              First connected parallel port
COM1 thru COM4   Serial ports (modem, mouse, etc.)
LPT1 thru LPT3   Parallel ports (printer)
CON              Keyboard and screen
NUL              Dummy (testing purposes)
```

DOS directories
Simulated file folders on a disk. In Windows 95/98, a directory is called a *folder*.

DOS editor
A text editor that runs under DOS.

DOS environment
A reserved area in DOS for holding values used by DOS and other applications. The values stored in this area are called "environment variables" and are created with the Set command.

DOS extender
Software that is combined with a DOS application to allow it to run in extended memory (beyond 1MB). To gain access to extended memory, it runs the application in Protected Mode. When the application requests DOS services, the DOS extender either handles them itself or, with functions such as disk accesses, resets the machine to Real Mode, lets DOS service the request and then switches back into Protected Mode. Windows 3.0 included a DOS extender, and although it may seem ridiculous today, by breaking the 1MB limit, Windows solved a very thorny issue and became very popular. See *VCPI* and *DPMI*.

DOS extensions
Names used to identify DOS and Windows file types. See *extension* and *DOS file names*.

DOS external command
A separate utility program that comes with DOS, such as Format, Diskcopy, XCopy, Tree, Backup and Restore, but is not resident within DOS, such as Copy and Dir. Contrast with *DOS internal command*.

DOS file
(1) Any computer file created under DOS.
(2) An ASCII text file. See *DOS batch file*.

DOS file names
A file name from one to eight characters in length followed by a file extension up to three characters long. All executable programs in DOS use a .COM or .EXE extension. DOS batch files use a .BAT extension. Executable programs in Windows have an .EXE or .DLL extension. Valid characters are A-Z, a-z, 0-9, ! @ # $ % & ( ) ` ` - { } and ~. Look up *extension* for a list of more than 300.

DOS and Windows 3.x file names are the same. Windows 95/98 supports longer file names. See *Win 9x Long file names*.

DOS high memory
The area between 640K and 1024K reserved for system use. Also may refer to the area between 1024K and 1088K (HMA). See *PC memory map*.

DOS internal command
A command capability within DOS at all times, such as Dir, Copy, Del, Ren, Type and Cls. The internal commands are part of DOS' COMMAND.COM file. If you delete COMMAND.COM, you can no longer command DOS to do anything at the command line.

The other kind of commands DOS can execute are external commands. Each external command, such as Format, Xcopy and Backup, resides in its own file in the DOS directory. If any of those files are deleted accidentally or purposefully, you can still execute all of DOS' internal commands and any external commands that are still left on disk.

DOSmark
A unit of measurement of DOS benchmarks from Ziff-Davis. Its Windows counterpart is the Winmark. See *ZDBOp*.

DOS memory manager
Software that allows DOS to manage more than one megabyte of memory or to manage its first megabyte more effectively. Since the early days of DOS, third party memory managers, such as QEMM and 386MAX, have used every trick in the book to move TSRs and drivers out of the lower 640K and into the 384K upper memory area (UMA). Starting with DOS 5, DOS includes its own memory managers. HIMEM.SYS manages extended memory, and EMM386.EXE manages expanded memory.

DOS prompt

The message DOS displays when ready to accept user input. The default prompt for the root directory in the C drive is **C:\>**.

DOS shell

An optional, menu driven user interface that accompanied DOS 4 and 5.

DOS switch

A parameter that modifies a DOS command. DOS switches use a forward slash. For example, in the command **dir /w**, the /W is the switch that causes file names to be listed "wide" across the screen instead of in a column.

DOS system file

A DOS file that contains the fundamental part of DOS (the kernel). See *MSDOS.SYS*.

DOS text file

A text file that does not contain any proprietary coding schemes. Batch files and source language programs are examples. It contains only ASCII characters with CR/LFs (carriage return/line feed) at the end of each line. Text files are read by text editors as well as word processors with "ASCII" or "text" input options.

DOS/V

A Japanese version of DOS that supports two-byte-long characters for handling the Kanji character set. It can switch between English and Japanese and is geared for 286s and up with VGA graphics. Backed by IBM Japan and the OADG. In Japan, NEC is the major personal computer vendor with its PC-9801 series.

DOS/VS

(Disk Operating System/Virtual Storage) One of two operating systems offered on the IBM System/ 360. The other was OS/360. DOS/VS later evolved into DOS/VSE.

DOS/VSE

(Disk Operating System/Virtual Storage Extended) An IBM multiuser, multitasking operating system that was widely used on IBM's 43xx series. It used to be called DOS, but due to the abundance of DOS PCs, it is now referred to as VSE.

DOS wild cards

See *wild cards*.

DOS window

Generally refers to a DOS session under Windows. Windows can run DOS programs full screen or in a resizable windows similar to other Windows applications. See *DOS box*.

DOS/Windows

(1) Refers to a PC computer environment that uses DOS or Windows in contrast with Mac or UNIX.

(2) Refers specifically to a DOS and Windows 3.1 environment, in contrast with Windows 95/98.

DOS/Windows disk format

DOS and Windows use a file system known as the File Allocation Table (FAT) to keep track of data on a disk. All floppy disks and hard disks must be initialized with the FAT before use. This is known as a high-level format. Windows NT can optionally use its own native format (see *NTFS*).

There is also a low-level format required on every disk. The low-level format creates the original sectors on the disk that hold everything, including the FAT and the data. IDE and SCSI hard disks are low-level formatted at the factory. Floppy disks are not. Thus, when you format a floppy, you are putting both a low-level and high-level format on the diskette at the same time. When you format a hard disk, you are doing only a high-level format.

dot

(1) A tiny round, rectangular or square spot that is one element in a matrix, which is used to display or print a graphics or text image. See *dot matrix* .

(2) A period; for example, V dot 22 is the same as V.22.

(3) The dot, or period, is used as a name separator. For example, file names are separated from their extensions with a dot (CDE.ABC, CDE.NDX, etc.). It is used to separate the components of Web addresses, such as WWW.HOTSTUFF.COM.

dot addressable

The ability to program each individual dot on a video display, dot matrix printer or laser printer.

dot com

Refers to a commercial Internet address, which ends with a period and the word "com" (.com). See *Internet address*.

dot gain

An increase in size of each dot of ink when printed due to temperature, ink and paper type.

dot matrix

A pattern of dots that forms character and graphic images on printers. Although ink jet and laser printers print in dots, and monitors display dots as well, the term generally refers to images created with serial dot matrix printers. See *dot matrix printer*.

dot matrix printer

A printer that uses hammers and a ribbon to form images out of dots. The common desktop dot matrix printer, also known as a *serial dot matrix printer*, uses one or two columns of dot hammers that are moved across the paper. The more dot hammers used, the higher the resolution of the printed image. For example, nine pins produces draft quality, and 24-pin heads produce typewriter quality output. Speeds range from 200 to 400 cps, which is about 90 to 180 lpm.

A line matrix printer is a type of dot matrix printer that attains speeds up to 1,400 lpm and is used in datacenters and industrial environments (see *line matrix printer*).

Dot matrix printers are widely used to print multipart forms, address and diskette labels. The tractor and sproket mechanisms used in these printers handle thick media much better than laser and ink jet printers.

7 Pin   9 Pin   18 Pin   24 Pin

Dot Matrix Mechanism
Dot matrix printers print columns of dots in a serial fashion. The more dot hammers (pins), the better looking the printed results.

dot pitch

The distance between a red (or green or blue) dot and the closest red (or green or blue) dot on a color monitor (typically from .28 to .51mm; large presentation monitors may go up to 1.0mm). The smaller the dot pitch, the crisper the image. A .28 dot pitch means dots are 28/100ths of a millimeter apart. A dot pitch of .31 or less provides a sharp image, especially on text. See *slot pitch*.

double buffering

A programming technique that uses two buffers to speed up a computer that can overlap I/O with processing. For example, data in one buffer is being processed while the next set of data is read into the second buffer.

When video is displayed on screen, the data in one buffer is being filled while the data in the other is being displayed. Full-motion video is speeded up when the function of moving the data between buffers is implemented in a hardware circuit rather than being performed by software. See *video accelerator*.

Data is being read into this buffer

▶ 488598932938200320

while data in this buffer is being processed.

754399488000048804840MR88900032342

Double Buffers
Two buffers are commonly used to speed up program execution. Data is processed in one buffer while data is written into or read out of the other.

double byte characters

See *Unicode*.

double click

To press the mouse button twice in rapid succession.

double density

Twice the capacity of the prior format. Yesterday's double density can be today's low density (see *DD*).

double precision

Using two computer words instead of one to hold a number used for calculations, thus allowing twice as large a number for more arithmetic precision. Contrast with *single precision*.

double sided disk

A floppy disk that is recorded on both of its sides. See *DS/DD* and *DS/HD*.

DoubleSpace

A realtime compression technique built into DOS 6 and removed in 6.21.

double strike

Printing a character twice in order to darken the image.

double twist

Same as *supertwist*.

double word

Twice the length of a single computer word. A double word is typically 32 bits long. See *word*.

DOW

(Direct OverWrite) See *magneto-optic disk*.

down

Refers to a computer that ceases to operate due to hardware or software failure. A communications line is down when it is unable to transfer data.

downlink

A communications channel from a satellite to an earth station. Contrast with *uplink*.

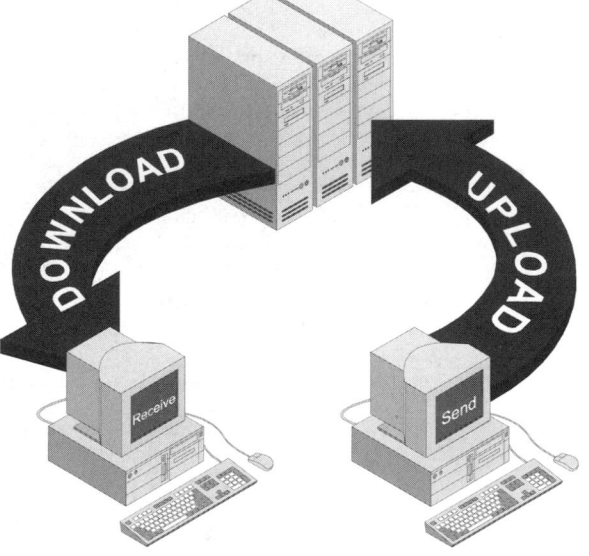

download

To receive a file transmitted over a network. In a communications session, download means receive, upload means transmit. Downloads depend on file size and network speed. Via a 28800 bps modem, small Web pages take seconds when everything is running smoothly, but a 10MB video file takes at least an hour. LAN downloads are much faster. That same 10MB file can fly across a high-speed LAN in one second.

Downloading files from the Internet has become a snap with "click here to download this file" messages on Web pages. The Web browser prompts you where to save the file. Downloading from an online service requires following the menu prompts to find the topics and files of interest. See *download protocol*.

On a network server, downloadable files are placed in public directories (folders) that can be copied using the normal file management procedures of the operating system. On a Windows LAN for example, files are selected by drive letter, directory (folder) and file name. The user could select the J: drive, \PUBLIC directory and NEWDRIVR.SYS file by clicking on the appropriate references to them in File Manager or Explorer.

downloadable font

Same as *soft font*.

download protocol

The communications protocol used to transmit a file, also known as a file transfer protocol. For example, the Internet uses FTP. UNIX systems use FTP and UUCP. Connections via modem to online services use protocols such as Zmodem and CompuServe's CIS B; however, a default protocol is set for downloads so the user is generally not aware of them. Using a general-purpose comm program to download from a BBS or private site does require selecting a common protocol. Zmodem is a good choice.

downsizing

Converting mainframe and mini-based systems to personal computer LANs.

downstream

From the provider to the customer. Downloading files and Web pages from the Internet is the downstream side. The upstream link is from the customer to the provider such as when requesting the Web page. In cable TV, the downstream signals are the network programs, movies and sports events transmitted over the cable. Unless the cable is used for the Internet, cable TV does not have an upstream. Pay-per-view cable requires an upstream link for requesting an event, which is usually the telephone.

downtime

The time during which a computer is not functioning due to hardware or system software failure. That's when you truly understand how important it is to have reliable hardware.

downward compatible

Also called *backward compatible*, it refers to hardware or software that is compatible with earlier versions. Contrast with *upward compatible*.

DP

See *data processing* and *dot pitch*.

DPCM

(Differential PCM) An audio digitization technique that codes the difference between samples rather than coding an absolute measurement at each sample point. See *ADPCM*.

dpi

(Dots Per Inch) The measurement of printer resolution. A 300 dpi printer means 90,000 dots are printable in one square inch (300x300). 400 dpi generates 160,000 dots; 500 dpi yields 250,000 dots.

DPM

(Documents Per Minute) The number of paper documents that can be processed in one minute.

DPMA

(1) (Dynamic Power Management Architecture) Power management features built into Intel chipsets. By monitoring system activity and turning itself off when not required, DPMA chipsets use up to 75% less power than previous chipsets. DPMA supports the ACPI interface. The 430TX was the first DPMA-compliant chipset. See *Intel chipsets* and *ACPI*.

(2) (Data Processing Management Association) See *AITP*.

DPMI

(DOS Protected Mode Interface) A programming interface from Microsoft that allows a DOS-extended program to run cooperatively under Windows 3.x. It is not compatible with VCPI, the first DOS extender standard, but Windows 3.1 is more tolerant of VCPI applications than Windows 3.0.

XMS, VCPI and DPMI all deal with extended memory. However, XMS allows data and programs to be stored in and retrieved from extended memory, whereas VCPI and DPMI allow programs to "run" in extended memory.

DPMS

See *VESA DPMS*.

DPPX

(Distributed Processing Programming EXecutive) The operating system used on the IBM 8100 minicomputer.

DPS

Minicomputer series from Bull HN.

DPSK

(Differential Phase Shift Keying) A common form of phase modulation used in modems. It does not require complex demodulation circuitry and is not susceptible to random phase changes in the transmitted waveform. Contrast with *FSK*.

DQDB

(Distributed Queue Dual Bus) The protocol used to control access to an IEEE 802.6 queued packet synchronous exchange (QPSX) network, used for metropolitan area networks (MANs). This architecture allows for both circuit and packet switching and supports data, voice and video traffic. Using fixed length cell relay technology, DQDB is suited to volatile network traffic.

Drafix CAD

A family of 2-D and 3-D CAD packages for Windows from Autodesk Personal Solutions, Kansas City, MO, that features professional functions. It provides constant on-screen information during drawing.

draft mode

The highest-speed, lowest-quality printing mode.

drag

To move an object on screen in which its complete movement is visible from starting location to destination. The movement may be activated with a stylus, mouse or keyboard keys.

To drag an object with the mouse, point to it. Press the mouse button and hold the button down while moving the mouse. When the object is at its new location, release the mouse button.

drag & drop

A graphical user interface (GUI) capability that lets you perform operations by moving the icon of an object or function with the mouse into another window or onto another icon. For example, files can be copied or moved by dragging them from one folder to another. Programs can be executed by dragging and dropping. To print a document, an icon of the document is dragged on top of the icon for the printer.

drag lock

The ability to lock onto a screen object so that it can be dragged with the mouse without continuously holding down the mouse (or trackball) button.

drain

One side of a field effect transistor. When the gate is pulsed, current flows from the source to the drain, or vice versa depending on the design. See *collector*.

DRAM

See *dynamic RAM*.

DRAW

(Direct Read After Write) Reading data immediately after it has been written to check for recording errors.

drawing program

A graphics program used for creating illustrations. It maintains an image in vector graphics format, which allows all elements of the picture to be isolated, moved and scaled independently from the others.

Drawing programs and CAD programs are similar; however, drawing programs usually provide a large number of special effects for fancy illustrations, while CAD programs provide precise dimensioning and positioning of each graphic element in order that the objects can be transferred to other systems for engineering analysis and manufacturing.

Examples of popular drawing programs for Windows are Adobe Illustrator, Macromedia Freehand, Designer and CorelDRAW. Adobe Illustrator and Macromedia Freehand are also available for the Macintosh. Contrast with *paint program*. See *diagramming program*.

DRDA

(Distributed Relational Database Architecture) An IBM architecture for distributing data across multiple heterogeneous platforms. It also serves as a protocol for access to these databases from IBM and non-IBM platforms. DRDA uses LU 6.2 as its transport protocol.

DRDBMS

(Distributed Relational DBMS) A relational DBMS that manages distributed databases. See *distributed database*.

DR-DOS

A multitasking DOS-compatible operating system from Caldera. It is used in embedded systems, thin clients and bootable disks for antivirus recovery programs. The embedded version includes display antialiasing so that it can be used in set-top boxes attached to TV sets. DR-DOS also breathes life into older PCs, because it is Y2K compliant and adds a driver that brings old ROM BIOSs up to Y2K compliance. Caldera's DR-WebSpyder provides a graphical browser that makes older 386s usable on the Internet.

DR-DOS was originally developed by Digital Research, the creators of CP/M, as the single-user version of Concurrent DOS. The operating system was extremely popular during the late 1980s and early 1990s, because it added many features lacking in MS-DOS, including memory management and disk compression. In addition, DR-DOS Version 5 was the first retail version of DOS that could be purchased in a computer store.

DR-DOS inspired Microsoft to improve subsequent versions of MS-DOS and to make major efforts to market against it. In 1991, Digital Research was acquired by Novell, which later sold it to Caldera. See *Caldera*.

DRI

See *Digital Research*.

dribbleware

(1) Software that is publicly displayed and previewed well in advance of its actual release. Dribbleware is one stage beyond vaporware.

(2) Software that is released in small increments, especially due to the ease with which updates can be downloaded from a Web site today.

drift

Change in frequency or time synchronization of a signal that occurs slowly.

drill down

To move from summary information to the detailed data that created it.

drive

(1) An electromechanical device that spins disks and tapes at a specified speed. Also refers to the entire peripheral unit such as *disk drive* or *tape drive*.

(2) To provide power and signals to a device. For example, "this control unit can drive up to 15 terminals."

drive bay

A cavity for a disk drive in a computer cabinet.

drive door

A panel, gate or lever used to lock a disk in a disk drive. In a 5.25" floppy drive, the drive door is the lever that is turned down over the slot after inserting the disk.

drive mapping

A letter or name assigned to a disk or tape drive. In a PC, the basic drive mappings are A: and B: for the floppy disk and C: for the primary hard disk. Additional drive mappings are assigned by the operating system based on the next available letter (D:, E:, etc.).

In a network, drive mappings reference remote drives and directories. For example, on your local machine, you might assign drive K: to be the root directory of drive C: on another machine in the network. Each time K: is referenced locally, the actual drive and directory on the remote machine is substituted behind the scenes for the K:. See *redirector* and *UNC*.

driver

(1) Also called a *device driver*, a program routine that links a peripheral device to the operating system. It is written by programmers who understand the detailed knowledge of the device's command language and characteristics and contains the precise machine language necessary to perform the functions requested by the application.

When a new hardware device is added to the computer, such as a display adapter, sound card or CD-ROM drive, its driver must be installed in order to run it. The operating system calls the driver, and the driver "drives" the device. Routines that perform internal functions, such as memory managers and disk caches, are also called drivers.

In a PC, fundamental drivers that manage such components as the keyboard, floppy and non-SCSI hard disks, are included in the system BIOS chip. Additional drivers are loaded at boot time by the operating system.

Drivers Can Drive You Crazy!

If it seems that the solution to every problem is to update a driver, that is often the case. The driver is the link between the operating system and the peripheral device. If the peripheral is changed, the driver must also be changed. If a bug is found in the driver, a new version is often released to solve it. New drivers are constantly made available on vendors' Web sites and bulletin boards for downloading.

In Windows, everything you see on screen is the result of the display driver (video driver) drawing the screen according to the commands that Windows issues to it. A display driver is extremely difficult to program and is error prone simply due to its complex nature. Display drivers cause much erratic behavior in Windows.

The Windows Display Driver
This diagram shows the part the driver plays when an application wants to display something on the screen. The application calls the GDI (Graphics Device Interface) in Windows and tells it to do something. GDI in turn sends commands to the driver supplied with the display adapter to actually draw the image. The display driver draws the image in the display adapter's memory, which is simultaneously being sent to the monitor.

There Used to Be Even More Drivers

The effort required to support different brands of peripheral devices was one of the major reasons DOS gave way to Windows. For example, in the DOS world, in order to provide complete control over the printing of a document, each application provides its own printer drivers for the most popular printers.

With Windows and the Macintosh, the printer driver is installed by the operating system, not by each application. From then on, all applications gain access to the printer through the operating system and its one driver for that printer.

(2) A driver is also a hardware device (typically a transistor) that provides signals or electrical current to activate a transmission line or display screen pixel. See *line driver*.

DriveSpace

Microsoft's disk compression that replaced the DoubleSpace technology previously used. It is included in DOS starting with Version 6.22 and in Windows 95/98. DriveSpace reduces cluster size from 32K to 512 bytes on 1 and 2GB drives under FAT16 partitions. See *cluster*.

drive type

See *hard disk*.

drop cap

In typography, a large first letter that drops below the first line.

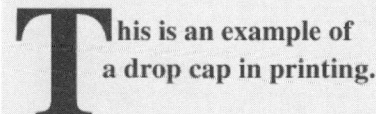

T his is an example of a drop cap in printing.

drop-down menu

See *pull-down menu*.

drop in

An extraneous bit on a magnetic medium that was not intentionally written, due to a surface defect or recording malfunction.

drop out

(1) On magnetic media, a bit that has lost its strength due to a surface defect or recording malfunction.

(2) In data transmission, a momentary loss of signal that is due to system malfunction or excessive noise.

droupie

(Data gROUPIE) A person who enjoys being with technical people.

DRP

(**D**istribution and **R**eplication **P**rotocol) A W3C protocol for downloading only updated Web information (differential downloads). The Web site maintains an index of its files, including HTML pages, images and applications. The browser downloads the DRP index which serves as a roadmap to the updated files when compared to the current index.

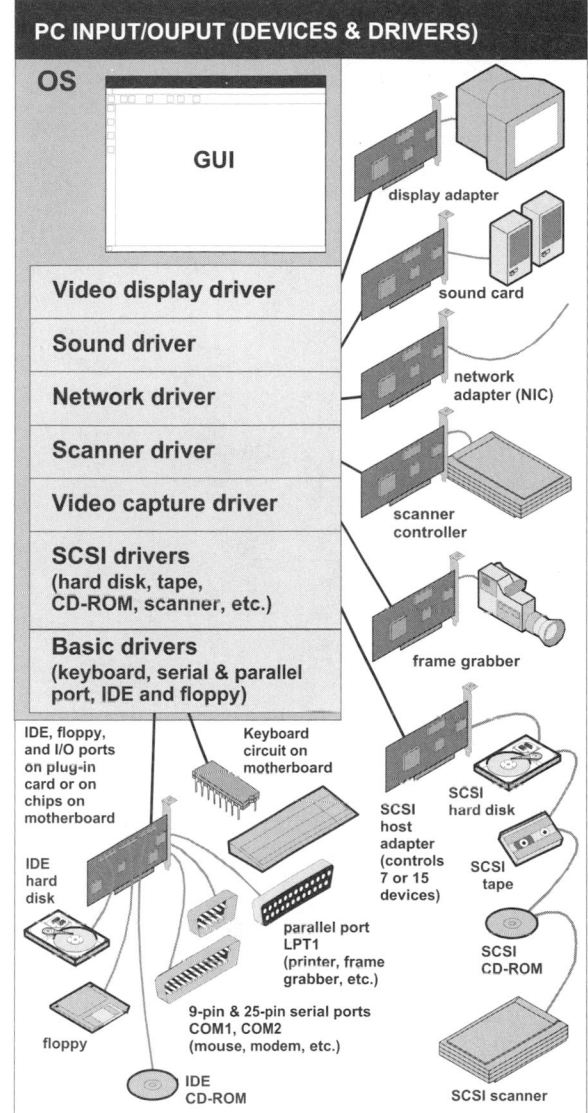

PC Drivers

Every peripheral device requires a driver. The drivers provide the detailed instructions necessary to activate and control the device.

drum plotter

A type of pen plotter that wraps the paper around a drum with a pin feed attachment. The drum turns to produce one direction of the plot, and the pens move to provide the other. The plotter was the first output device to print graphics and large engineering drawings. Using different colored pens, it could draw in color long before color ink jet printers became viable. Contrast with *flatbed plotter*.

drum printer

(1) A wide-format ink jet printer. The paper is taped onto a drum for precise alignment to the nozzles.

(2) An old line printer technology that used formed character images around a cylindrical drum as its printing mechanism. When the desired character for the selected position rotated around to the hammer line, the hammer hit the paper from behind and pushed it into the ribbon and onto the character.

drum scanner

A type of scanner used to capture the highest resolution from an image. Photographs and transparencies are taped, clamped or fitted into a clear cylinder (drum) that is spun at speeds exceeding 1,000 rpm during the scanning operation. A light source that focuses on one pixel is beamed onto the drum and moves down the drum a line at a time.

For transparencies, light is directed from the center of the cylinder. For opaque items, a reflective light source is used. Mirrors filter out the RGB values and send them to the drum scanner's photomultiplier tube (PMT), which is more sensitive than the CCDs used in flatbed and sheet-fed scanners and can produce resolutions exceeding 12,000 dpi. If one PMT is used, three passes across the image are required. When three PMTs are used, a faster single-pass scan is performed. Contrast with *flatbed scanner, sheet-fed scanner* and *hand-held scanner*.

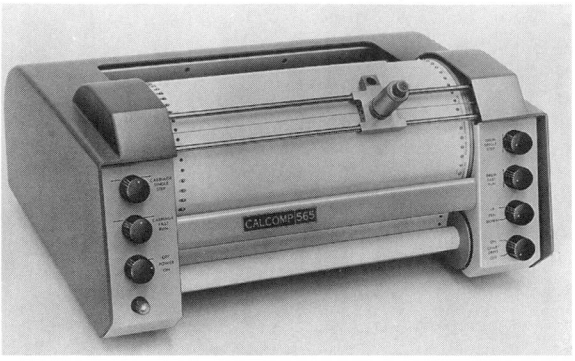

The First Drum Plotter
In 1959, the CalComp Model 565 was the world's first drum plotter. It had one pen and could handle media up to 11" wide. *(Photo courtesy of CalComp, Inc.)*

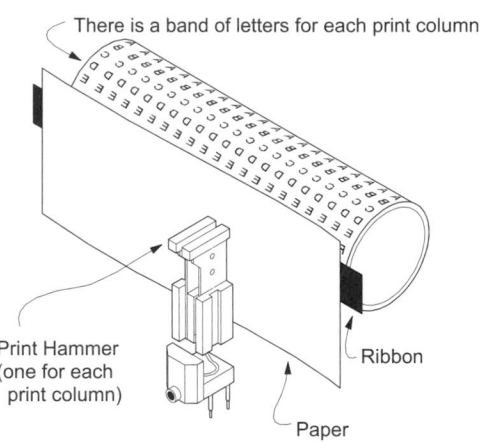

There is a band of letters for each print column

Print Hammer (one for each print column)

Ribbon

Paper

Drum Printer Mechanism
The hammer pushes the paper into the type slug when it rotated around to the proper position. Such printer technologies seem ridiculous compared to the quiet, high-speed workings of today's laser printers.

DRV-04

A 3-D model viewset of the Viewperf benchmark, which is used to test OpenGL performance. See *OPC*.

Dr. Watson

A Windows utility that reports extensive details about a crash. It sits in the background and captures the current status of the system at the moment of the abend.

dry copper

Unadulterated copper lines that have no processing, equalization or intelligence applied to them.

Drum Scanner

This SCREEN USA DT-S 1030 drum scanner provides resolution up to 5,200 dpi. Drum scanners provide the ultimate in scanning quality and resolution and are widely used for commercial graphics production as well as applications that turn photos into posters and wall-sized images. *(Photo courtesy of SCREEN USA.)*

dry plasma etching

A method for inscribing a pattern on a wafer by shooting hot ions through a mask to evaporate the silicon dioxide insulation layer. Dry plasma etching replaces the wet processing method that uses film and acid for developing the pattern.

DS (DS0, DS1, DS2, DS3, DS4)

(Digital Signal) A classification of digital circuits. The DS technically refers to the rate and format of the signal, while the T designation refers to the equipment providing the signals. In practice, "DS" and "T" are used synonymously; for example, DS1 and T1, DS3 and T3.

NORTH AMERICA, JAPAN, KOREA, ETC.

Service	Voice Channels	Speed	
DS0	1	64 Kbps	
DS1	24	1.544 Mbps	(T1)
DS1C	48	3.152 Mbps	(T1C)
DS2	96	6.312 Mbps	(T2)
DS3	672	44.736 Mbps	(T3)
DS4	4032	274.176 Mbps	(T4)

EUROPE (ITU)

Service	Voice Channels	Speed (Mbps)
E1	30	2.048
E2	120	8.448
E3	480	34.368
E4	1920	139.264
E5	7680	565.148

SONET CIRCUITS

Service		Speed (Mbps)	
STS-1	OC1	51.84	(28 DS1s or 1 DS3)
STS-3	OC3	155.52	(3 STS-1s)
STS-3c	OC3c	155.52	(concatenated)
STS-12	OC12	622.08	(12 STS-1s, 4 STS-3s)
STS-12c	OC12c	622.08	(12 STS-1s, 4 STS-3c's)
STS-48	OC48	2488.32	(48 STS-1s, 16 STS-3s)

DSA

(1) (Directory Server Agent) An X.500 program that looks up the address of a recipient in a Directory Information Base (DIB), also known as white pages. It accepts requests from the Directory User Agent (DUA) counterpart in the workstation.

(2) (Digital Signature Algorithm) The algorithm used in the Digital Signature Standard (DSS) by the

U.S. government. The de facto standard RSA algorithm is more widely used than DSA.

(3) (Digital Storage Architecture) A disk controller standard from Digital.

(4) (Digital Signal Analyzer) A Tektronix oscilloscope that samples high-frequency signals.

(5) (Distributed Systems Architecture) A Bull HN network architecture.

DSD

(Direct Stream Digital) See *DVD-Audio.*

DS/DD

(Double Sided/Double Density) Refers to floppy disks, such as the 5.25" 360KB PC format and 3.5" 720KB PC and 800KB Mac formats.

DS/HD

(Double Sided/High Density) Refers to floppy disks, such as the 5.25" 1.2MB PC format and 3.5" 1.44MB PC and Mac formats.

DSL

(Digital Subscriber Line) A modem technology that increases the digital speed of ordinary telephone lines by a substantial factor over common V.34 (33600 bps) modems. DSL technologies are either asymmetric or symmetric. Asymmetric provides faster downstream speeds, which is suited for Internet usage and video on demand. Symmetric provides the same rate coming and going.

DSL uses packet switching technology that operates independent of the voice telephone system, allowing the telephone companies to provide the service and not lock up circuits for long calls. Because of this, DSL is not as well suited to videoconferencing as is ISDN. Circuit-switched ISDN keeps the line open and connected throughout the session. The transmission rate of DSL technologies is very much tied to the distance between the telephone company and the customer.

Although DSL technologies have barely gotten off the ground, there are more versions and alphabet soup than real implementations. The widely-touted Asymmetrical DSL (ADSL) comes in two forms: Discrete Multitone (DMT) or Carrierless Amplitude Phase (CAP). ADSL requires a splitter installed on the customer's premises which separates the analog telephone line into analog voice and digital data. Splitterless ADSL eliminates the service call to the customer. ADSL Lite is a slower version of ADSL, and Universal ADSL from the Universal ADSL Working Group (UAWG) is expected to combine Splitterless ADSL and ADSL Lite into a new standard.

Consumer DSL (CDSL) is an asymmetric flavor that provides a type of ADSL Lite as well as regular 56 Kbps V.90 modem access if the ADSL service is not available. Rate adaptive DSL (RADSL) adjusts speeds based on signal quality, and ISDN DSL (IDSL) uses in-place ISDN facilities. High bit rate DSL (HDSL) provides symmetric transmission, but requires two cable pairs. Single line DSL (SDSL) is also symmetric, but uses one cable pair.

ASYMMETRIC DSL

Type	Upstream	Downstream	Cable Pairs	Dist. (ft)
CAP ADSL	64-640 Kbps	.5-8 Mbps	1	12-18000
DMT ADSL	176-640 Kbps	.5-8 Mbps	1	12-18000
ADSL Lite	64-384 Kbps	1-1.5 Mbps	1	12-18000
CDSL	128 Kbps	1 Mbps	1	12-18000
RADSL	128-1024 Kbps	.6-7 Mbps	1	18-25000
VDSL	1.6-2.3 Mbps	13-52 Mbps	1	1000-4500

SYMMETRIC DSL

Type	Upstream & downstream	Cable Pairs	Distance (ft)
HDSL	1.544 Mbps	2	12000
	2.048 Mbps	3	12000
SDSL	1.544-2.048 Mbps	1	10000
IDSL	128 Kbps	1	18000

DSOM

See *SOM.*

DSP

(1) (**D**igital **S**ignal **P**rocessor) A special-purpose CPU used for digital signal processing. It provides ultra-fast instruction sequences, such as shift and add, and multiply and add, which are commonly used in math-intensive signal processing applications. DSP chips are widely used in myriads of devices, including sound cards, fax machines, modems, cellular phones, high-capacity hard disks and digital TVs (see definition 2 below). The first DSP chip used in a commercial product was believed to be from TI, which was used in its very popular Speak & Spell game in the late 1970s.

(2) (**D**igital **S**ignal **P**rocessing) A category of techniques that analyze signals from sources such as sound, weather satellites and earthquake monitors. Signals are converted into digital data and analyzed using various algorithms such as Fast Fourier Transform.

Once a signal has been reduced to numbers, its components can be isolated, analyzed and rearranged more easily than in analog form. DSP is used in many fields including biomedicine, sonar, radar, seismology, speech and music processing, imaging and communications.

DSP chips are used in sound cards for recording and playback, compressing and decompressing and speech synthesis. Other audio uses are in amplifiers that simulate concert halls and surround sound effects for music and home theater.

DSR

(**D**ata **S**et **R**eady) An RS-232 signal sent from the modem to the computer or terminal indicating that it is able to accept data. Contrast with *DTR*.

DSS

(1) (**D**ecision **S**upport **S**ystem) An information and planning system that provides the ability to interrogate computers on an ad hoc basis, analyze information and predict the impact of decisions before they are made.

DBMSs let you select data and derive information for reporting and analysis. Spreadsheets and modeling programs provide both analysis and "what if?" planning. However, any single application that supports decision making is not a DSS. A DSS is a cohesive and integrated set of programs that share data and information. A DSS might also retrieve industry data from external sources that can be compared and used for historical and statistical purposes.

An integrated DSS directly impacts management's decision-making process and can be a very cost-beneficial computer application. See *EIS* and *OLAP*.

(2) (**D**igital **S**ignature **S**tandard) A National Security Administration standard for authenticating an electronic message. See *RSA* and *digital signature*.

(3) (**D**igital **S**atellite **S**ystem) A direct broadcast satellite (DBS) system from Hughes Electronics Corporation that delivers more than 175 TV channels. DSS receivers and dishes are made by RCA and other manufacturers. USSB and DirecTV provide the content. See *DBS*.

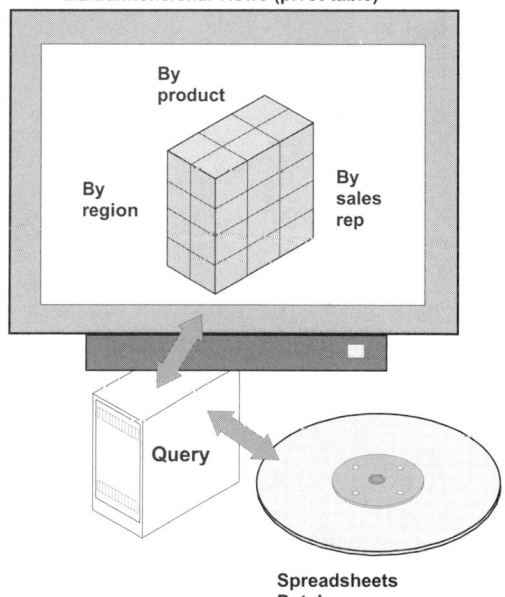

Multidimensional views (pivot table)

By product

By region

By sales rep

Query

Spreadsheets
Database programs
OLAP databases

Decision Support

Decision support systems increasingly use OLAP databases, which provide rapid access to multidimensional views of the data. A user can quickly flip from "by product" to "by region" with a multidimensional database.

DSTN

(1) (**D**ual-**s**can **STN**) An enhanced STN passive matrix LCD display. The screen is divided into halves, and each half is scanned simultaneously, thereby doubling the number of lines refreshed per second and providing a sharper appearance. DSTN is widely used on laptops. See *STN* and *LCD*.

(2) (Double layer **STN**) An earlier passive matrix LCD technology that used an extra compensating layer to provide a sharper image.

DSU/CSU

(Digital (or Data) Service Unit/Channel Service Unit) A pair of communications devices that connect an inhouse line to an external digital circuit (T1, DDS, etc.). It is similar to a modem, but connects a digital circuit rather than an analog one.

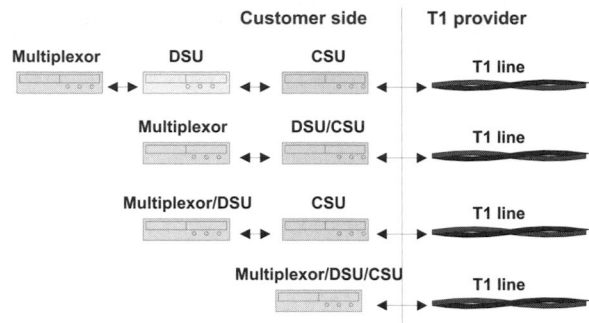

The CSU terminates the external line at the customer's premises. It also provides diagnostics and allows for remote testing. If the customer's communications devices are T1 ready and have the proper interface, then the CSU is not required, only the DSU.

The DSU does the actual transmission and receiving of the signal and provides buffering and flow control. The DSU and CSU are often in the same unit. The DSU may also be built into the multiplexor, commonly used to combine digital signals for high-speed lines.

DSVD

(Digital Simultaneous Voice and Data) An all-digital technology for concurrent voice and data (SVD) transmission over a single analog telephone line. DSVD is endorsed by Intel, Hayes, U.S. Robotics and others and has been submitted to the ITU for possible standardization. DSVD modems became available in the first half of 1995. See *SVD*.

DSX-1

(Digital Signal Cross-connect Level 1) A standard that defines the voltage, pulse width and plug and socket for connecting DS-1 (T1) signals.

DTA

(Design and Test Alliance) A group of ATE and EDA vendors, chip makers and systems houses dedicated to improving testing of complicated electronic systems.

DTD

(Document Type Definition) A file that defines the format codes in an SGML document. DTD files are optional with XML documents. See *SGML*.

DTE

(Data Terminating Equipment) A communications device that is the source or destination of signals on a network. It is typically a terminal or computer. Contrast with *DCE*. See *DCE* for illustration.

DTMF

(Dual-Tone MultiFrequency) The type of audio signals that are generated when you press the buttons on a touch-tone telephone. See also *DMTF*.

DTP

See *desktop publishing*.

DTR

(Data Terminal Ready) An RS-232 signal sent from the computer or terminal to the modem indicating that it is able to accept data. Contrast with *DSR*.

DTS

(1) (Digital Termination Service) A microwave-based, line-of-sight communications provided directly to the end user.

(2) (DeskTop Server) A motorola 68000-based network server from Banyan.

(3) (Developer Technical Support) The tech-support group for developers at Apple.

DTV

(**D**igital **TV**) A digital TV standard for the U.S. approved by the FCC in late 1996 and developed by the Advisory Committee on Advanced Television Service (ACATS). It offers 18 formats from SDTV (Standard TV), which is not much more than the digital counterpart of the current NTSC analog standard, except without snow and ghosts, all the way up to HDTV (High Definition TV), which uses a wide screen (16:9 aspect ratio) with up to 1080 lines of resolution and 5.1 Dolby Digital surround sound.

More SDTV channels can be transmitted within the same bandwidth than HDTV, so it will be up to the broadcasters, cable providers and satellite companies to determine the amount of content versus quality. DTV provides 14 progressive scan and four interlaced formats. For example, 480p defines a progressive scan format with 480 lines, while 1080i means 1080 interlaced lines.

In the fall of 1998, DTV is expected in some of the major U.S. cities, with the top 10 markets being covered by the summer of 1999 and half the U.S. households by the end of 1999. In order to receive DTV, you need a new Digital TV set or a set-top box for an existing TV. Digital TV sets will support analog TV, which is expected to be broadcast until at least 2006. See *HDTV, NTSC, interlaced* and *progressive scan*.

DUA

(**D**irectory **U**ser **A**gent) An X.500 routine that sends a request to the Directory Server Agent (DSA) to look up the location of a user on the network.

dual boot

A computer configuration that allows it to be started with either one of two different operating systems. The dual boot feature is contained in one of the operating systems. There are system programs that can be installed which let you boot from several operating systems. For example, System Commander from V Communications, San Jose, CA, lets you install all the operating systems you will ever need on one PC and choose which one you want at startup.

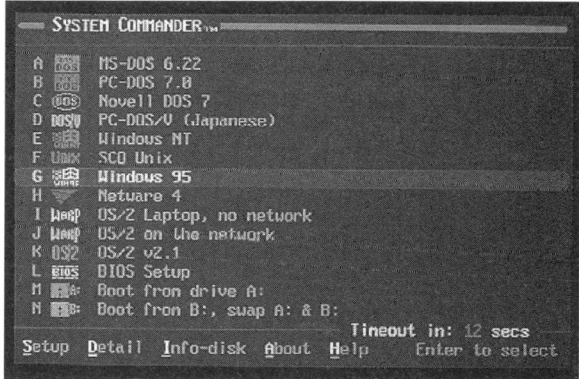

All the Boots You'll Ever Need
System Commander lets you install up to 100 different operating systems on your PC. On startup, this menu lets you choose your OS. *(Photo courtesy of V Communications, Inc.)*

dual counter-rotating ring

A network topology that uses two rings, with transmission in opposite directions in each ring. It is designed for fault tolerance and increased speed. If one of the rings breaks, the devices can reroute traffic on the other ring. Since traffic goes in both directions, packets travelling between two nodes can take the shortest distance between them. See *FDDI* and *Sebring ring*.

dual-homed

Connected to two networks or circuits. See *multihomed*.

dual Pentium

A PC with a motherboard that contains two Pentium CPUs. Such machines are designed for use with an operating system that supports symmetric multiprocessing (SMP), such as Windows NT. See *SMP*.

dual processors

Using two CPU chips in the same computer. See *SMP*.

dual-scan LCD

See *DSTN*.

dumb network

A network that provides raw wiring from one location to another and introduces either very little or no processing to support the types of signaling that may be used in transmission.

George Guilder, editor of the "Guilder Technology Report," has been calling the Internet a dumb network, and telecom consultant David Isenberg calls it a "stupid network." While the Internet does indeed contain intelligence, these phrases are used to contrast the Internet to the telephone system, which for years has been known as an "intelligent" network. Telephone switches must be programmed for any new type of service that is added, whereas the Internet serves as an oblivious transport, taking bits in and pushing them out the other side. New services and features are added at the periphery by installing new software in users' PCs and in the servers instead of revamping the network itself.

In order for the Internet to provide the quality of service necessary to effectively deal with interactive voice and video, its routers and switches will have to become even more intelligent in prioritizing traffic. Nevertheless, it is expected that all future networking will be based on Internet-like architectures (IP protocols) that can be upgraded by adding faster hardware as needed without major upgrades to the architecture, which should be kept as simple (dumb, stupid) as possible. As witness to the concept, both Qwest Communications and multibillion-dollar startup Level 3 Communications are building national voice and data networks based entirely on IP. AT&T has announced that its future infrastructure will be IP based. Times... they are a changin'. See *IP on Everything*.

dumb terminal

A display terminal without processing capability. It is entirely dependent on the main computer for processing. Although mainframe and minicomputer terminals (3270, 5150, etc.) are technically smart terminals, because they have a certain amount of built-in screen display capabilities, they are often called dumb terminals. Contrast with *smart terminal* and *intelligent terminal*.

dump

To print the contents of memory, disk or tape without any report formatting. See *memory dump*.

Dumpy

(Documentation User's MalPractice + Y) An award from InfoWorld magazine for the worst online documentation. See *RTFM*.

DUN

(DialUp Networking) The dial-up networking capability in Windows 95/98. See *Win 9x Dial-up Networking*.

duplex channel

See *full-duplex*.

duplexed system

Two systems that are functionally identical. They both may perform the same functions, or one may be standby, ready to take over if the other fails.

duplexing

See *duplex printing, duplexed system* and *full-duplex*.

duplex printing

The ability to print on both sides of the paper.

duplicate keys

Identical key data in a file. Primary keys, such as account number cannot be duplicated, since no two customers or employees should be assigned the same number. Secondary keys, such as date, product and city, may be duplicated in the file or database.

DVB

(Digital Video Broadcasting) An international digital broadcast standard for TV, audio and data. DVB can be broadcast via satellite, cable or terrestrial systems. It has been initially used in Europe and the Far East.

Computer Desktop Encyclopedia

DVD

A family of optical discs that are the same overall dimensions of a CD, but have significantly higher capacities. DVDs are also double sided, whereas CDs are single sided. Dual-layer versions are also planned. DVD drives read most CD media as well.

Both the computer and movie industries worked on DVD, and it is expected to become the next CD-ROM and primary digital movie medium, superseding Video CDs, analog LaserDiscs and eventually VHS tape.

There are several flavors of DVD. DVD-Video is the movie format. Players that attach to a TV or home theater system became available at the end of 1996. DVD-Video uses MPEG-2 compression providing approximately 133 minutes of LaserDisc-quality video per side. This is not a fixed length, because the compression rate is based upon the amount of motion taking place. DVD-Video supports AC-3 Dolby surround sound, which provides five discrete channels of CD-quality audio plus a subwoofer (5.1 channel).

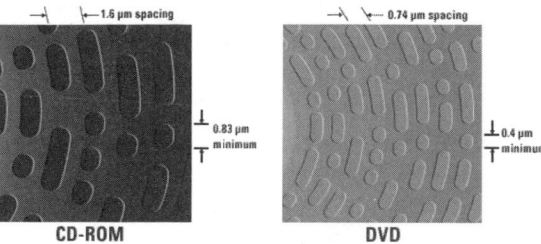

DVD Versus CD-ROM
At minimum, the capacity of a DVD is 750% that of a CD-ROM because its tracks, pits and lands are more than twice as dense, and it uses more efficient recording algorithms. *(Image courtesy of C-Cube Microsystems.)*

DVD-ROM is like a large CD-ROM, allowing for data and interactive material as well as audio and video. It requires a DVD-ROM drive installed in a computer. DVD-R is a write-once version used for creating masters, and DVD-RAM is the official rewritable DVD sanctioned by the DVD Forum. DVD+RW competes with DVD-RAM for the rewritable market, and MMVF is a rewritable version only available in Japan. DVD-R/W is also a rewritable version, but is more an extension to DVD-R than a competitor to DVD-RAM.

DVD-Audio is a next-generation music format that provides higher sampling rates than music CDs. There are currently two competing standards. One is the WG-4 specification from the DVD Consortium, and the other is Super Audio CD from Sony and Philips. Many audio purists believe that higher digital sampling of audio material is necessary to truly recreate the total sound spectrum. See *DVD-Audio*. For a summary of all storage technologies, see *storage*.

So What Does DVD Really Mean?

DVD originally stood for Digital VideoDisc. Since it spanned both the movie video and computer worlds, it was later called Digital Versatile Disc. Today, the acronym has become its name. DVD stands for D-V-D.

Specifications

Following are the various types of DVDs and their capacities. DVD-ROM, DVD-Video and DVD-Audio use the same physical format and capacity, but have different logical formats due to the differences in their content.

Type	Sides or layers used	Capacity
DVD-ROM	Read-only 1 side, 1 layer	4.7GB
DVD-ROM	Read-only 1 side, 2 layers	8.5GB
DVD-ROM	Read-only 2 sides, 1 layer	9.4GB
DVD-ROM	Read-only 2 sides, 2 layers	17.0GB
DVD-R	Write-once 1 side	3.95GB
DVD-R	Write-once 2 sides	7.90GB
DVD-R/W	Rewritable 1 side	3.95GB
DVD-RAM	Rewritable 1 side	2.6GB
DVD-RAM	Rewritable 2 sides	5.2GB
DVD+RW	Rewritable 1 side	3.0GB
DVD+RW	Rewritable 2 sides	6.0GB
MMVF	Rewritable 1 side	5.2GB
MMVF	Rewritable 2 sides	10.4GB

DVD+RW

A rewritable DVD disk from Sony, HP, Philips and others. Using phase change technology, DVD+RW disks hold 3GB per side instead of the 2.6GB of DVD-RAM. DVD+RW disks can be rewritten 100,000 times. See *DVD-RAM* and *DVD*.

DVD-Audio

The next-generation music format. The DVD Consortium introduced its WG-4 specification in late 1997, which provides for sampling rates up to 192KHz and sample sizes up to 24 bits, compared to 44.1KHz and 16 bits for CDs. A two-channel PCM track is mandatory, but up to six tracks may be used with other home theater coding systems such as Dolby Digital or Digital Theater Systems (DTS). WG-4 discs can also contain music videos, graphics and other information.

Sony and Philips are promoting their Super Audio CD format, which includes a standard PCM layer that can be read by CD players and a higher-quality Direct Stream Digital (DSD) layer. DSD recording generates one-bit samples at 2.8224MHz. The resulting one or zero indicates whether the sample is higher or lower on the scale than the previous one, creating a pulse train similar to the analog wave it is converting.

DVD-ROM, DVD-R, DVD-RAM

DVD-ROM

DVDs look like CDs, but hold from 4 to 28 times as much data. There is a DVD counterpart for every CD type.

DVD-ROMs are silver, read only discs. DVD-Rs are write once and have a pink cast. Rewritable DVD-RAMs can be double sided, so a cartridge is used to protect the surfaces and provide a label area.

DVD-R

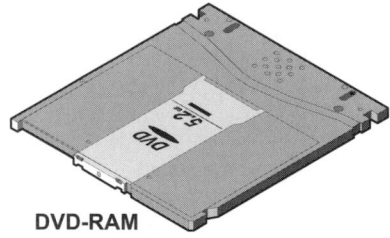

DVD-RAM

DVD-R

(DVD Recordable) A write-once optical disk used to master DVD-Video and DVD-ROM discs. Pioneer was the first company to introduce a DVD-R drive. DVD-R is not expected to compete with DVD-RAM, which is the rewritable DVD. DVD-Rs are the DVD counterpart to CD-Rs and use the same dye-layer recording technology to "burn" the disc. See *DVD, DVD-R/W* and *CD-R*. For a summary of all storage technologies, see *storage*.

DVD-RAM

A rewritable DVD disk. Using phase change technology, DVD-RAMs are expected to have significant impact on the VHS tape market by the turn of the century, since they provide an erasable, high-capacity optical disk that should become widely accepted. The first DVD-RAM drives with a capacity of 2.6GB (single sided) or 5.2GB (double sided) became available in the spring of 1998. DVD+RW, a competing rewritable DVD standard, is currently fragmenting a market that is just getting off the ground. See *DVD+RW, DVD-R/W* and *DVD*. For a summary of all storage technologies, see *storage*.

DVD-ROM

A read-only DVD disk used for storing data, interactive sequences as well as audio and video. Expected to become the CD-ROM of the 21st century, DVD-ROMs run in DVD-ROM or DVD-RAM drives, not DVD-Video players connected to TVs and home theaters. See *DVD*. For a summary of all storage technologies, see *storage*.

DVD-R/W

(DVD Read Write) A proposed standard for a rewritable DVD disk from Pioneer. Using phase change technology, it holds 3.95GB per side and can be rewritten up to 100,000 times. DVD-R/W is expected to be used for DVD-Video and DVD-ROM mastering, as it is more a rewritable version of DVD-R than a competing version of DVD-RAM. See *DVD-RAM, DVD+RW* and *DVD*. For a summary of all storage technologies, see *storage*.

DVD-Video

A read-only DVD disc used for full-length movies. DVD-Video discs hold approximately 133 minutes of full-motion video per side using MPEG-2 compression. The first DVD-Video players became available at the end of 1996. See *DVD*.

D-VHS

(Data-VHS) A VHS videocassette recorder that is able to store data from a digital satellite system (DSS). A D-VHS machine is a modified S-VHS VCR. See *DVCR*.

DVI

(Digital Video Interactive) A compression technique for data, audio and full-motion video from Intel. It provided up to 72 minutes of full-screen video on a CD-ROM with up to 100:1 compression ratio. Intel acquired DVI in 1988 from RCA's Sarnoff Research labs in Princeton, New Jersey. DVI never caught on.

Dvorak keyboard

A keyboard layout designed in the 1930s by August Dvorak, University of Washington, and his brother-in-law, William Dealey. 70% of words are typed on the home row compared to 32% with qwerty, and, more words are typed using both hands. In eight hours, fingers of a qwerty typist travel 16 miles, but only one for the Dvorak typist.

```
Qwerty

52%    Q W E R T Y U I O P
32%     A S D F G H J K L ; `
16%       Z X C V B N M , . /


Dvorak

22%    ` , . P Y F G C R L ?
70%     A O E U I D H T N S -
 8%       ; Q J K X B M W V Z
```

DVST

(Direct View Storage Tube) An early graphics screen that maintained an image without refreshing. The entire screen had to be redrawn for any change.

DVx chip

A microprocessor specialized for encoding and decoding MPEG-2 video from C-Cube Microsystems, Inc., Milpitas, CA, (www.c-cube.com). The single chip contains a SPARC processor, Motion Estimation engine (analyzes frames) and a Video DSP unit that handles low-level computations. For HDTV and other high-resolution formats, multiple DVx chips can be strung together via interprocess channels.

DWDM

(Dense WDM) See *WDM*.

dweeb

A very technical person. Dweebs sometimes call sales people "slime," anybody interested in technology for profit rather than the art of it.

DX

When referencing an Intel 386 CPU, the DX or 386DX is the full 386 with a 32-bit data path, in contrast to the 386SX, which uses a 16-bit data path. In an Intel 486 CPU, the DX or 486DX designation has a different meaning. It refers to the full 486, which contains the math coprocessor, in contrast to the 486SX, which does not.

DX-03

A visualization viewset of the Viewperf benchmark, which is used to test OpenGL performance. See *OPC*.

DX2

A 486 with a clock-doubled CPU. Clock doubling doubles the internal speed of the CPU without requiring any changes in the chip's external connections. For example, the 486DX2/66 has an internal speed of 66MHz, while its external bus from the CPU to RAM runs at 33MHz.

DX4

A 486 with a clock-tripled CPU. Clock tripling triples the internal speed of the CPU without requiring any changes in the chip's external connections. DX4s come in 75MHz and 100MHz versions that access RAM at 25MHz and 33MHz respectively.

DXF file

(Document EXchange Format file) An AutoCAD 2-D graphics file format. Many CAD systems import and export the DXF format for graphics interchange.

dyadic

Two. Refers to two components being used.

dye diffusion

See *dye sublimation printer*.

dye polymer recording

An optical recording technique that uses dyed plastic layers as the recording medium. WORM disks typically use a single layer, and erasable disks use two layers: a top retention layer and a bottom expansion layer. A bit is written by shining a laser through the retention layer onto the expansion layer, which heats the area and forms a bump that expands into the retention layer. The retention layer bumps are the actual bits read by the unit. To erase a bit, another laser (different wavelength) strikes the retention layer and the bump subsides.

dye sublimation printer

A printer that produces continuous-tone images that look like photographic film. It uses a ribbon containing an equivalent panel of dye for each page to be printed. Color printers have either three (CMY) or four (CMYK) consecutive panels for each page, thus the same amount of ribbon is used to print a full-page image as it is to print a tenth of the page. Special dye-receptive paper is used, and consumables (ribbon and paper) cost more than other printer technologies.

The paper and ribbon are passed together over the printhead, which contains thousands of heating elements that can produce varying amounts of heat. The hotter the element, the more dye is released. By varying the temperature, shades of each color can be overlaid on top of each other. The dyes are transparent and blend into continuous-tone color.

Thermal wax transfer uses the same transport mechanism as dye sublimation, but uses a wax-based ink, not a transparent dye. Like other color printers, it puts down a solid dot of ink and produces shades of colors by placing color dots side by side (dithering). Wax transfer prints faster than dye sub and consumables (ribbon and paper) are less expensive, but it does not produce photorealistic quality.

Some printers allow swapping of both ribbons so that thermal wax can be used for draft quality and dye sublimation for final output. See *printer*.

Dye Sublimation/Thermal Wax Transfer
The paper and ribbon are passed by the printhead. The ribbon is heated, and shaded dots of dye or solid dots of ink are transferred to the paper. The ribbon contains a panel equivalent in size to the page being printed, with three (CMY) or four (CMYK) panels for each color page to be printed.

dye transfer

See *dye sublimation printer*.

Dylan

(**DY**namic **LAN**guage) An object-oriented version of the Lisp programming language developed by Apple and used in the late 1980s.

dynamic

Refers to operations performed while the program is running. The expression, "buffers are dynamically created," means that space was created when actually needed, not reserved beforehand. Contrast with *static*.

dynamic address translation

In a virtual memory system, the ability to determine what the real address is at the time of execution.

dynamic binding

Also called *late binding*, it is the linking of a routine or object at runtime based on the conditions at that moment. Contrast with *early binding*. See *binding time* and *polymorphism*.

dynamic compression

The ability to compress and decompress data in realtime; for example, as it's being written to or read from the disk.

Dynamic Data Exchange

See *DDE*.

dynamic HTML

(1) A general term for Web pages that are customized for each user; for example, returning values from a search. Contrast with a *static HTML* page, which never changes.

(2) Specific enhancements to HTML tags that allow Web pages to function more like regular software. For example, fonts could be changed or images could be selected without having to jump to another page. Dynamnic HTML (DHTML) is based on the Document Object Model (DOM) interface that allows HTML tags to be dynamically changed via JavaScript or some other scripting language. Netscape Communicator and Internet Explorer 4.0 use different methods to implement DHTML.

dynamic invocation

See *dynamic method invocation*.

dynamic IP address

An IP address that is automatically assigned to a client station in a TCP/IP network, typically by a DHCP server. Network devices that serve multiple users, such as servers and printers, are usually assigned static IP addresses. See *static IP address, IP address* and *DHCP*.

dynamic link

The connection established at runtime from one program to another.

dynamic link library

A set of program routines that can be called at runtime as needed. See *DLL*.

dynamic memory allocation

Allocating memory as needed without having to specify a fixed amount beforehand. All advanced operating systems perform dynamic memory allocation to some extent.

dynamic method invocation

In object technology, the activation of a process (method) within an object at runtime.

dynamic network services

Realtime networking capabilities, such as adaptive routing, automatically reconfiguring the network when a node is added or deleted and the ability to locate any user on the network.

dynamic node addressing

A network technology that dynamically assigns machine addresses to nodes upon startup. For example, when a station is turned on in an AppleTalk network, it identifies itself to the network. If its number has been taken in the meantime by another node, it creates a new one using a random number generator.

dynamic RAM

The most common type of computer memory, also called *D-RAM* ("dee-RAM") and DRAM. It usually uses one transistor and a capacitor to represent a bit. The capacitors must be energized hundreds of times per second in order to maintain the charges. Unlike firmware chips (ROMs, PROMs, etc.) both major varieties of RAM (dynamic and static) lose their content when the power is turned off. Contrast with *static RAM*.

In memory advertising, dynamic RAM is often erroneously stated as a package type; for example, "DRAMs, SIMMs and SIPs on sale." It should be "DIPs, SIMMs and SIPs," as all three packages typically

E

See *exponent*.

e-

(Electronic-) The "e-dash" prefix may be attached to anything that has moved from paper to its electronic alternative, such as e-mail, e-cash, etc.

E1

The European counterpart to T1, which transmits at 2.048 Mbits/sec. See *DS* for chart.

EAM

(Electronic Accounting Machine) Another name for punched card tabulating equipment. EAM equipment (tabulating machines) was the mainstay of data processing for more than 70 years following the advent of Hollerith's card system for the 1890 census.

early binding

In programming, the assignment of types to variables and expressions at compilation time. Also called *static binding* and *static typing*. Contrast with *dynamic binding*. See *binding time*.

EAROM

(Electrically Alterable ROM) Same as *EEPROM*.

earth station

A transmitting/receiving station for satellite communications. It uses a dish-shaped antenna for microwave transmission. See *base station*.

Easel

(Easel Corporation) A Burlington, Massachusetts software tools company founded in 1981. It was acquired by VMARK Software in 1995. Easel developed client/server tools based on its ESL technology and its Smalltalk-based ObjectStudio.

Easel Workbench

See *ESL Workbench*.

Easter Egg

An undocumented function hidden in a program. Easter Eggs are secret "goodies" that are found by accident or word of mouth. For example, in Windows 3.1, to see the names of the people who worked on the project, open the About Program Manager dialog box (Help, About) and double click on the Windows icon at the upper left while holding down Ctrl and Shift. Click OK, then open the box again. Ctrl-Shift Double click again and note the dedication. Click OK and repeat once more.

The EAM Room
This was a typical EAM room in a medium-sized business. Huge rooms full of tabuling machines were common in large companies. *(Photo courtesy of IBM Corporation.)*

Earth Station
The earth station is no longer only the domain of commercial enterprises, now that millions of homes use small dishes to receive TV signals.

EasyCAD

Full-featured CAD programs for DOS and Windows from Evolution Computing, Tempe, AZ, (www.evcomp.com/evcomp), that are noted for their ease of use. EasyCAD users can migrate to FastCAD, which is almost identical on screen, but provides multiple windows and is designed for high-speed operations.

Easytrieve

See *CA-Easytrieve*.

EBCDIC

(Extended Binary Coded Decimal Interchange Code) Pronounced "eb-suh-dick." The binary code for text as well as communications and printer control from IBM. This data code originated with the System/360 and is still used in IBM mainframes and most IBM midrange computers. It is an 8-bit code (256 combinations) that stores one alphanumeric character or two decimal digits in a byte.

EBCDIC and ASCII are the two codes most widely used to represent data.

e-beam

See *electron beam*.

EBI

See *electron beam imaging*.

EBL

(Extended Batch Language) A shareware programming language by Frank Canova that allows for more complex programming in DOS batch files.

e-business

See *electronic commerce*.

EC

See *electronic commerce*.

ecash

A system of digital money from Amsterdam-based DigiCash. The concept of ecash can be likened to travelers checks, which are purchased from a bank and then spent at merchants who accept them. Customers purchase ecash by downloading "digital coins" from a participating bank into their personal computers. Payment is made by uploading a certain amount of ecash to a participating vendor. The transactions are encrypted to provide the necessary security for online transfer. See *smart card* and *digital money*.

ECC

(Elliptic Curve Cryptography) A public key cryptography method that provides fast decryption and digital signature processing. ECC uses points on an elliptic curve to derive a 163-bit public key that is equivalent in strength to a 1024-bit RSA key. The public key is created by agreeing on a standard generator point in an elliptic curve group (elliptic curve mathematics is a branch of number theory) and multiplying that point by a random number (the private key). Although the starting point and public key are known, it is extremely difficult to backtrack and derive the private key.

Once the public key is computed by ECC, it can be used in various ways to encrypt and decrypt. One way is to encrypt with the public key and decrypt with the private one. Another is to use the Diffie-Hellman method which uses a key exchange to create a shared secret key by both parties. Finally, ECC allows a digital signature to be signed with a private key and verified with the public key. For an in-depth look at elliptic curve cryptography, visit Certicom's Web site at www.certicom.com. There are live examples that show the math and methods. See *Diffie-Hellman*. See also *ECC memory*.

ECC memory, ECC RAM

(Error-Correcting Code memory) A memory system that tests for and corrects errors on the fly. It uses circuitry that generates checksums to correct errors greater than one bit.

ECCO

A Windows PIM from NetManage, Inc., Bellevue, WA, (www.netmanage.com). ECCO provides a phone book, calendar, to-do list, outlining and notetaking. It is noted for its tightly integrated and sophisticated functions.

ECF
(Enhanced Connectivity Facilities) IBM software that allows DOS PCs to query and download data from mainframes as well as issue mainframe commands. It also allows printer output to be directed from the PC to the mainframe. It uses the SRPI interface and resides in the PC (client) and mainframe (server). Applications issue SRPI commands to request services.

echo
(1) A repetition of a signal in a communications line. The difference in electrical characteristics at opposite ends can cause the echo.

(2) In communications, to transmit received data back to the sending station allowing the user to visually inspect what was received. A local echo displays what you type on your screen.

(3) A DOS and OS/2 command that displays messages and turns off/on screen responses.

echo cancellation
The elimination of an echo in a two-way transmission. Echo is created in the telephone company's central office switch when two-wire lines from the customer are converted to four-wire lines for backbone trunks. The echo is exacerbated over longer distances. Echo cancellers are built into the long-distance telephone system to eliminate it.

Echo cancellation is built into high-speed modems. Since telephone system echo cancellation is optimized for voice, the modem emits a 2100Hz signal to cancel it, allowing the modem's own cancellers to be used, which are more effective.

Echo cancellation is built into a speakerphone to cancel the echo caused by the microphone picking up sound from the speaker. Since echo cancellation is not built into sound cards, making a PC-to-PC voice call using regular speakers and a microphone causes echo. Headsets help eliminate this problem.

Echo cancellation uses extremely sophisticated DSP circuits that are able to isolate the echo and transmit a reverse frequency to cancel it.

echo check
In communications, an error checking method that retransmits the data back to the sending device for comparison with the original.

echo suppressor
A device that turns off reverse transmission in a telephone line, thus effectively making the circuit one way. It has been used to reduce the annoying effects of echoes in certain communications such as satellite circuits. See *echo cancellation*.

ECL
(Emitter-Coupled Logic) A variety of bipolar transistor that is noted for its extremely fast switching speeds.

ECM
(Error Correcting Mode) A Group 3 fax capability that can test for errors within a row of pixels and request retransmission. It is defined in the T.30 standard.

ECMA
(European Computer Manufacturers Association, Geneva, Switzerland, www.ecma.ch) An international association founded in 1961 that is dedicated to establishing standards in the information and communications fields. ECMA is a liaison organization to ISO and is involved in JTC1 activities.

ECMA Script
A scripting language that combines Netscape's JavaScript and Microsoft's Jscript with server side extensions from Borland.

ECNE
See *NetWare certification*.

e-comm, e-commerce
See *electronic commerce*.

ECP

(Enhanced Capabilities Port) See *IEEE 1284.*

EDA

(Electronic Design Automation) Using the computer to design and simulate the performance of electronic circuits on a chip. See *ATE.*

EDA/SQL

(Enterprise Data Access/SQL) Software from Information Builders, Inc., New York, (www.ibi.com), that provides a common interface between a wide variety of SQL programs and SQL databases. It also allows queries on data from different types of databases at the same time.

EDFA

(Erbium-Doped Fiber Amplifier) See *optical amplifier.*

edge concentrator

A device that connects a LAN to a high-speed backbone or switch such as an ATM switch. See *edge device.*

edge connector

The protruding part of an expansion board that is inserted into an expansion slot. It contains a series of printed lines that go to and come from the circuits on the board. The number of lines (pins) and the width and depth of the lines are different on the various interfaces (ISA, EISA, PCI, Micro Channel, etc.).

The printed lines carry the electricity from the circuits to and from the pins of the edge connector.

edge connector

edge device

A network device used to convert LAN frames (Ethernet, Token Ring, FDDI) to ATM cells and vice versa. It is typically a switching device with one ATM port and multiple LAN ports. To legacy stations, ports on an edge device look like a router port.

Under MPOA (Multiprotocol Over ATM), the edge device queries a route server for address resolution when the destination station is outside of its attached LANs. It sets up a switched virtual circuit (SVC) in the ATM network, maps LAN frames into ATM frames and forwards the traffic to the ATM backbone. Thus, the edge device performs functions usually associated with a router and becomes a major component in a LAN environment with an ATM backbone. See *ATM* for illustration.

Edge Connector
Edge connectors are very popular because they are "printed" onto the outer layers of the board in the same process that creates the circuit lines.

EDI

(Electronic Data Interchange) The electronic communication of business transactions, such as orders, confirmations and invoices, between organizations. Third parties provide EDI services that enable organizations with different equipment to connect. Although interactive access may be a part of it, EDI implies direct computer to computer transactions into vendors' databases and ordering systems.

According to Dataquest, the EDI market is expected to grow from $937 million in 1996 to two billion by 2000. The Internet is expected to make it easier for small and medium-sized companies to implement EDI systems. See *X12, Tradacoms, EDIFACT* and *extranet.*

EDIFACT

(Electronic Data Interchange For Administration Commerce and Transport) An ISO standard for EDI that is proposed to supersede both X12 and Tradacoms standards to become the worldwide standard.

e-disk

(Emulated-disk) Same as *RAM disk.*

edit

To make a change to existing data. See *update.*

editable PostScript

A file of PostScript commands that can be edited by a word processor or other program. This allows PostScript documents to be changed without requiring the use of the application that originally created it.

edit checking

Same as *validity checking*.

edit instruction

A computer instruction that formats a field for display or printing. Using an edit mask, it inserts decimal points, commas and dollar signs into the data.

edit mask

A pattern of characters that represent formatting codes through which data is filtered for display or printing. See *picture*.

edit mode

An operational state in a program that allows existing data to be changed.

editor

See *text editor* and *linkage editor*.

edit program

(1) A data entry program that validates user input and stores the newly created records in the file.

(2) A program that allows users to change data that already exists in a file. See *update*.

edit routine

A routine in a program that tests for valid data. See *validity checking*.

EDL

See *nonlinear video editing*.

EDMS

(Electronic Document Management System) See *document management*.

EDO RAM

(Extended Data Out RAM) A type of dynamic RAM chip that improves the performance of fast page mode memory by about 10%. As a subset of fast page mode, it can be substituted for page mode chips. However, if the memory controller is not designed for the faster EDO chips, the performance will remain the same as fast page mode.

EDO eliminates wait states by keeping the output buffer active until the next cycle begins. BEDO (Burst EDO) is a faster type of EDO that gains speed by using an address counter for next addresses and a pipeline stage that overlaps operations.

EDP

(Electronic Data Processing) The first name used for the computer field.

EDRAM

(Enhanced DRAM) A high-speed DRAM chip developed by Ramtron International Corporation, Colorado Springs, CO. It allows overlap of a read at the trailing end of a write operation to obtain its speed.

EDS

(Electronic Data Systems, Plano, TX, www.eds.com) Founded in 1962 by H. Ross Perot (independent challenger for the President of the U.S. in 1992), EDS is the largest outsourcing and data processing services organization in the country. It is the leading services provider to the health care, insurance and banking industries. In 1984, EDS was acquired by General Motors. Within a couple of years, Perot left EDS and later formed Perot Systems Corporation. In 1996, GM spun off EDS as an independent company.

EDS is known for huge contracts. For example, in 1994, Xerox contracted with it for 10 years worth of outsourcing valued at more than three billion dollars.

EDSAC

(Electronic Delay Storage Automatic Calculator) Developed by Maurice Wilkes at Cambridge University in England and completed in 1949, it was one of the first stored program computers and one of the first to use binary digits. Its memory was 512 36-bit words of liquid mercury delay lines, and its input and output were provided by paper tape. The EDSAC could do about 700 additions per second and 200 multiplications per second. It was in routine use at the University until 1958.

edu

An Internet address domain name for an educational organization. See *Internet address*.

education

Teaching concepts and perspectives. Computer education includes computer systems and information systems. Contrast with *training*.

The EDSAC

Using liquid mercury memory, the EDSAC could perform a mind-boggling 700 additions per second. It was one of the first computers to perform calculations in binary. *(Photo courtesy of Science Museum, London.)*

education & training

See *CBT, aptitude tests, certification, distance learning* and *tutorial*.

edutainment

Educational material that is also entertaining.

EEPROM

(Electrically Erasable Programmable Read Only Memory) A memory chip that holds its content without power. It can be erased, either within the computer or externally and usually requires more voltage for erasure than the common +5 volts used in logic circuits. It functions like non-volatile RAM, but writing to EEPROM is slower than writing to RAM.

EEPROMs are used in devices that must keep data up-to-date without power. For example, a price list could be maintained in EEPROM chips in a point of sale terminal that is turned off at night. When prices change, the EEPROMs can be updated from a central computer during the day. EEPROMs have a lifespan of between 10K and 100K write cycles. See *flash memory*.

eesa

See *EISA* and *ESA/370*.

EFF

(Electronic Frontier Foundation, Cambridge, MA, www.eff.org) A non-profit civil liberties organization founded in 1990 by Mitchell Kapor and John Perry Barlow. It works in the public interest to protect privacy and provide free access to online information.

e-forms

(Electronic-FORMS) See *forms software*.

EFT

(Electronic Funds Transfer) The transfer of money from one account to another by computer.

EGA

(Enhanced Graphics Adapter) An early IBM video display standard that provided medium-resolution text and graphics. It required a digital RGB Enhanced Color Display or equivalent monitor and was superseded by VGA.

egosurfing

Using a search engine such as AltaVista or DejaNews to see how many times your own name is cited. This is a popular, quasi-competitive sport at Silicon Valley parties and at gatherings of writers, artists, musicians and others who have some expectation of being referred to on the Web or in a newsgroup.

EGP

(1) (Exterior Gateway Protocol) A broad category of routing protocols that are designed to span different autonomous systems. Contrast with *IGP*.

(2) (Exterior Gateway Protocol) The original exterior gateway routing protocol (see above), which has been widely used in the U.S. Data Defense Network (DDN) and National Science Foundation Network (NSFNet). EGP is a distance vector protocol that uses polling to retrieve routing information. EGP has been superseded by BGP. See *BGP* and *routing protocol*.

EIA

(Electronic Industries Association, Washington, DC, www.eia.org) A membership organization founded in 1924 as the Radio Manufacturing Association. It sets standards for consumer products and electronic components. In 1988, it spun off its Information & Telecommunications Technology Group into a separate organization called the TIA.

EIA-232, EIA-422...

See *RS-232, RS-422...*

EIA-568

An EIA standard for telecommunications wiring in a commercial building. See *cable categories*.

EIDE

(Enhanced IDE) See *IDE*.

Eiffel

An object-oriented programming language developed by Bertrand Meyer, Interactive Software Engineering Inc., Goleta, CA, (www.eiffel.com). It runs on DOS, OS/2 and most UNIX platforms. The Eiffel compiler generates C code, which can be modified and recompiled with a C compiler.

eight-way server

See *8-way*.

EIGRP

See *IGRP*.

EIO

(Enhanced I/O) A hardware interface for HP printers that is used for adding an internal print server and network adapter, a hard disk and other plug-in functionality. EIO cards are smaller than previous MIO cards and more energy efficient. They use the PCI bus. See *MIO*.

EIS

(Executive Information System) An information system that consolidates and summarizes ongoing transactions within the organization. It provides top management with all the information it requires at all times from internal as well as external sources. In the EIS provides "what if?" manipulation capabilities like that of a DSS (decision support system), they are one in the same. See *DSS*.

EISA

(Extended ISA) Pronounced "ee-suh." A PC bus standard that extends the 16-bit ISA bus (AT bus) to 32 bits and provides bus mastering. ISA cards can plug into an EISA slot. It was announced in 1988 as a 32-bit alternative to the Micro Channel that would preserve investment in existing boards. EISA is also used in various workstations from HP and others.

EISA still runs at the slow 8MHz speed of the ISA bus in order to accommodate all the ISA cards that may be plugged into it. PCI and VL-bus local buses provide independent data paths and higher speeds than EISA. See *ISA* for illustration.

ELAN

(Emulated LAN) A virtual LAN in the ATM world. See *LANE* and *virtual LAN*.

EL display

(ElectroLuminescent display) A flat panel display technology that provides a sharp, clear image and wide viewing angle. It contains a powdered or thin film phosphor layer sandwiched between an x-axis and a y-axis panel. When an x-y coordinate is charged, the phosphor in that vicinity emits visible light. The phosphors are more like semiconductor materials than those used in a CRT. Most EL displays are monochrome, typically yellow orange.

Although some of the first portable computers used EL displays, they are mostly used today on instrumentation in demanding industrial and medical applications that require long life and crisp images. EL screens range from 3/4" to 10" and larger, but are more cost effective in the smaller sizes. Planar Systems is the leader in this field.

Active matrix EL is an advanced EL technology that uses a transistor at each pixel. It is used to make small head mounted displays (HMDs) that require very sharp images.

ELEC

(Enterprise LEC) An organization that is large enough (about 2500 or more employees) to file for CLEC status and become its own customer. As a CLEC, it can purchase telephone service at wholesale rates that it can sell to itself as well as to others to further reduce costs. The Yankee Group coined the term. See *LEC, CLEC* and *ILEC*.

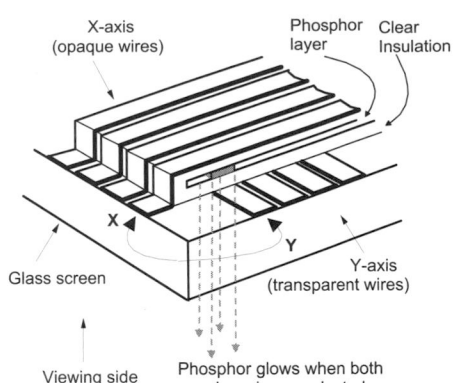

X-axis (opaque wires) — Phosphor layer — Clear Insulation

Glass screen — X — Y — Y-axis (transparent wires)

Viewing side — Phosphor glows when both x and y axis are selected.

Electroluminescent Technology

EL displays contain a powdered or thin film phosphor layer sandwiched between x and y axis panels. When an x-y coordinate is charged, the phosphor in that vicinity emits visible light. *(Diagram courtesy of Planar Systems, Inc.)*

electricity

The flow of electrons in a circuit. The speed of electricity is the speed of light (approximately 186,000 miles per second). In a wire, it is slowed due to the resistance in the material.

Its pressure, or force, is measured in *volts* and its flow, or current, is measured in *amperes*, or *amps*. The amount of work it produces is measured in *watts* (amps X volts).

electrode

A device that emits or controls the flow of electricity.

electroluminescent

See *EL display*.

electrolyte

In a battery, the material that allows electricity to flow from one plate to another (between positive and negative electrodes) by conducting ions. Electrolytes are typically liquid, but gelatinous and solid materials are also used. See *lithium polymer*.

electromagnet

A magnet that is energized by electricity. A coil of wire is wrapped around an iron core. When current flows in the wire, the core generates an energy called magnetic *flux*.

electromagnetic interference

Electromagnetic waves that eminate from an electrical device. It often refers to both low-frequency waves from electromechanical devices and high-frequency waves (RFI) from chips and other electronic devices. Allowable limits are governed by the FCC.

electromagnetic radiation

The energy that exists in all things, including humans, which incorporates cosmic rays, gamma rays, x-rays, ultraviolet light, visible light, infrared light and radar.

electromagnetic spectrum

The range of electromagnetic radiation in our known universe, which includes visible light as outlined below. Parts of the radio spectrum are still unassigned, but will eventually be used for some commercial communications purpose.

electromechanical

The use of electricity to run moving parts. Disk drives, printers and motors are examples. Electromechanical systems must be designed for the eventual deterioration of moving parts.

electromotive force

The pressure in an electric circuit measured in volts.

electron

An elementary particle that circles the nucleus of an atom. Electrons are considered to be negatively charged.

electron beam

A stream of electrons, or electricity, that is directed towards a receiving object.

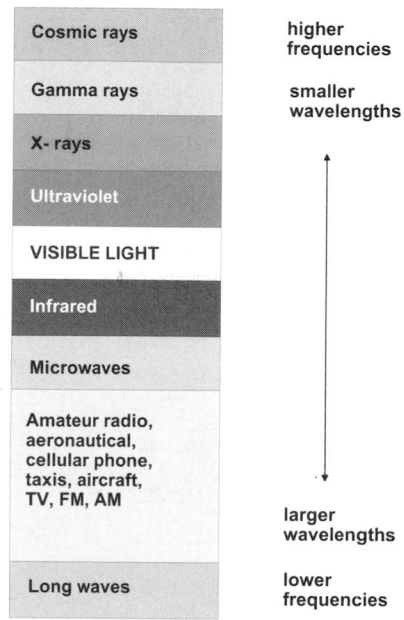

Electromagnetic Spectrum

electron beam imaging

A technology from Delphax Systems used in high-speed digital printing. It is similar to laser and LED printers in that toner is applied to a charged replica of the image to be printed and then the toned image is transferred to paper and fused. However, instead of using light to create the image, it uses electrons.

electron beam lithography

Using electron beams to create the mask patterns directly on a chip. The wavelength of an electron beam is only a few picometers compared to the 248 to 365 nanometer wavelengths of light used to create the traditional photomasks.

electron gun

A device which creates a fine beam of electrons that is focused on a phosphor screen in a CRT.

electronic

The use of electricity in intelligence-bearing devices, such as radios, TVs, instruments, computers and telecommunications. Electricity used as raw power for heat, light and motors is considered electrical, not electronic.

Although coined earlier, "Electronics" magazine (1930) popularized the term. The magazine subheading read "Electron Tubes - Their Radio, Audio, Visio and Industrial Applications." The term was derived from the electron (vacuum) tube.

electronic cash

See *ecash*.

electronic circuit

See *circuit* and *digital circuit*.

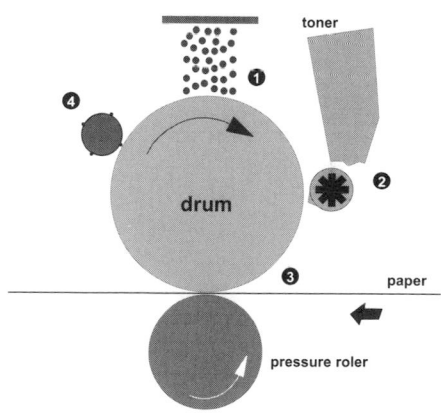

Electron Beam Imaging
The image is printed by (1) charging the drum, (2) adhering the toner to the drum, (3) transferring and fusing the toned image to the paper, and (4) cleaning the surface and erasing the residual charge.

electronic commerce

Doing business online. Also called *e-business* and *e-tailing*, it typically implies purchasing products via the Web. It also covers electronic data interchange (EDI), in which one company's computer queries and transmits purchase orders to another company's computer. See *microcommerce*.

Electronic Computer Glossary

The predecessor to the disk version of Computer Desktop Encyclopedia. First available for DOS in 1990 and then Windows in 1991, a Macintosh HyperCard stack was also introduced in 1990. All versions were superseded by the Windows-only version of Computer Desktop Encyclopedia in 1996.

electronic forms

See *forms software*.

Electronic Frontier Foundation

See *EFF*.

electronic mail, electronic messaging

See *e-mail* and *messaging system*.

electronic money

See *e-money*.

electronic prepress

The use of computers to prepare camera-ready materials up to the actual printing stage. It includes drawing, page makeup and typesetting, all performed electronically rather than by drafting or mechanical cut and paste methods.

electronic printer

A printer that uses electronics to control the printing mechanism, such as a laser printer and certain line printers.

electronic publishing

Providing information in electronic form to internal users or to subscribers via the Internet or an online service. The term also includes the publication of databases on floppy disk and CD-ROM. See *information utility, Internet* and *hot topics and trends*.

electronic switch

An on/off switch activated by electrical current.

electronic typewriter

See *memory typewriter* and *word processing*.

electronic wallet

The electronic equivalent of a checkbook or credit card for making online purchases. It may be software only or a combination of software and smart card.

electron tube

Same as *vacuum tube*.

electrophotographic

The printing technique used in copy machines, laser and LED printers. It uses electrostatic charges, light and dry ink (toner). A selenium-coated, photoconductive drum is positively charged. Using a laser or LEDs, a negative of the image is beamed onto the drum, cancelling the charge and leaving a positively-charged replica of the original image.

A negatively-charged toner is attracted to the positive image on the drum. The toner is then attracted to the paper, which is also positively charged. The final stage is fusing, which uses heat and pressure, pressure alone or light to cause the toner to permanently adhere to the paper.

Electrophotography was invented by Chester F. Carlson in his Queens, New York laboratory in 1938. His first of 28 patents on the subject was issued in 1940. By 1947, the Haloid Corporation in conjunction with Batelle Development Corporation were working with Carlson on his invention, and xerography was formally announced in 1948. Xerography replaced the messy liquid ink of the duplicating machines of the day with a dry, granular ink, which is how the name came about. In Greek, xerography means "dry writing." Xero means "dry," and graphy means "write."

electrosensitive printer

A dot matrix printer that burns away dots on the outer silver coating of a special black paper.

electrostatic

Stationary electrical charges in which no current flows. For example, laser printers and copier machines place a positive charge of the image on a drum, and negatively-charged toner is attracted onto the drum. The toner is then transferred to positively-charged paper and fused to the paper by heat.

electrostatic plotter, electrostatic printer

A plotter that uses an electrostatic method of printing. Liquid toner models use a postively-charged toner that is attracted to paper which is negatively charged by passing by a line of electrodes (tiny wires or nibs). Models print in in black and white or color, and some handle paper up to six feet wide.

Newer electrostatic plotters are really large-format laser printers and focus light onto a charged drum using lasers or LEDs.

elegant program

A program that is simple in design and uses the least amount of resources (memory, disk, etc.).

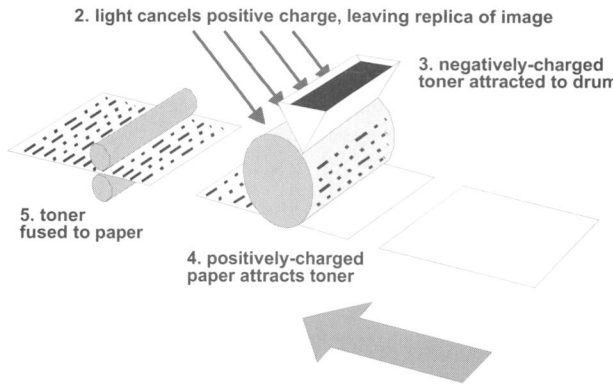

1. drum is positively charged
2. light cancels positive charge, leaving replica of image
3. negatively-charged toner attracted to drum
5. toner fused to paper
4. positively-charged paper attracts toner

Electrophotographic Process
Electrostatic charges are used to create a charged light image on the drum. The toner is attracted to the drum and then to the paper.

Chester Carlson

In this 1965 photo, Carlson enacts his 1938 experiment in which he wrote "10-22-38 ASTORIA" with india ink on a glass slide. The room was darkened, and a zinc plate, covered with sulphur, was rubbed vigorously with a handkerchief to apply an electrostatic charge. He put the slide on the plate, exposed it to light for a few seconds, removed the slide and sprinkled lycopodium powder on the plate. He gently blew off the loose powder and what remained was the first electrophotographic copy. After Xerox became very successful, Carlson was showered with honors and wealth. In 1968, he died of a stroke in a New York street after having left a fortune to charities. *(Photo courtesy of Xerox Corporation.)*

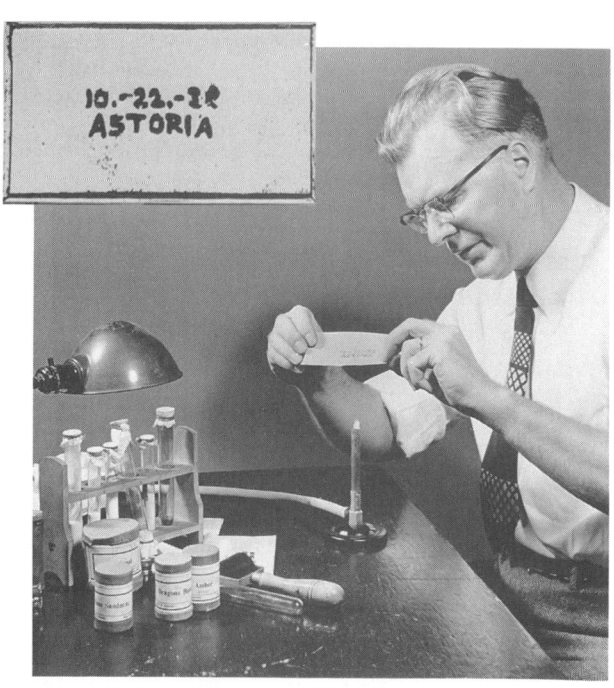

elevator

Also called a *thumb*, it is a square box that slides within a scroll bar. The elevator is dragged up and down to position the text or image on screen.

elevator seeking

A disk access technique that processes multiple requests in a priority based upon which ones are closest to the current position of the read/write head.

ELF

(Extemely Low Frequency) See *low radiation*.

em

In typography, a unit of measure equal to the width of the capital letter M in a particular font.

EMA

(1) (Enterprise Management Architecture) Digital's stategic plan for integrating network, system and application management. It provides the operating environment for managing a multi-vendor network.

(2) (Electronic Messaging Association, Arlington, VA, www.ema.org) A membership organization founded in 1983 devoted to promoting e-mail, voice mail, fax, EDI and other messaging technologies.

EMACS

(Editor **MAC**ro**S**) A UNIX text editor developed at MIT that is used for writing programs. It provides a wide variety of editing features including multiple windows.

e-mail

The transmission of memos and messages over a network. Users can send mail to a single recipient or broadcast it to multiple users. With multitasking workstations, mail can be delivered and announced while the user is working in an application. Otherwise, mail is sent to a simulated mailbox in the network server or host computer, which must be interrogated.

An e-mail system requires a messaging system, which provides the store and forward capability, and a mail program that provides the user interface with send and receive functions. See *messaging system, instant messaging* and *EDI*.

E-mail versus Fax

Fax documents are scanned images and are thus treated like pictures even if they contain only text. E-mail messages are raw ASCII text, which can be edited immediately in any text editor or word processor that imports ASCII text (most do).

In order to edit the text in a fax, the images of the characters have to be turned into ASCII text by an OCR (optical character recognition) program, which is error prone. If all you want to do is read a message, either method works well. However, if you are sending a text document that will be edited and used in a page layout program, e-mail will save your recipient from having to retype it all over again.

e-mail address

See *Internet address*.

e-mail address search sites

There are various Web sites that maintain directories of e-mail addresses. Examples of these sites are:

```
www.four11.com
www.bigfoot.com
www.whowhere.com
www.infospace.com
```

e-mail attachment

A file that rides along with an e-mail message. The attached file can be of any type. See *how to transfer a file over the Internet*.

e-mail client

Same as *mail client*.

Computer Desktop Encyclopedia

e-mail forwarding

Sending e-mail to its correct destination. There are Web sites that provide a name service either for a fee or at no cost because they are advertiser supported. These sites let you choose a permanent e-mail address, and all mail sent to that address is forwarded to your currently-active e-mail provider. If you ever change providers, you only have to update your forwarding information at these "name-only" sites. Two such sites are www.four11.com and www.bigfoot.com.

e-mail header

The beginning portion of an e-mail message that contains the To, From, Subject, Cc, Bcc and Attached fields. The header uses named fields so that the recipient's address can be quickly extracted by the e-mail system and the message subject can be easily identified by filters or the user. The rest of the message is unstructured text.

e-mail program

Same as *mail client*.

e-mail server

Same as *mail server*.

e-mail service

See *Internet e-mail service*.

e-mail virus

See *mail virus*.

embedded application

A program placed into a non-volatile memory such as ROM or flash memory. See *embedded system*.

embedded command

(1) A command inserted within text or other codes.

(2) In word processing, a command within the text that directs the printer to change fonts, print underline, boldface, etc. The command is inserted when the user selects a layout change. Commands are often invisible on screen, but can be revealed if required.

embedded controller

Controller circuitry built into a device or on the main system board in contrast with a removable card or module.

embedded SQL

SQL statements that are written into a high-level programming language such as C or Pascal. In a preprocessing stage, the SQL code is converted into function calls, which may be optimized to provide the fastest results. If the programmer knows exactly what the query is going to do, and the query does not change, it is called *static SQL*. If the query requires user input at runtime, it is called *dynamic SQL*. If the client program passes the SQL statements directly to the database server without any intermediate step, it is called *passthrough SQL*.

embedded system

A specialized computer used to control devices such as automobiles, home and office appliances, hand-held units of all kinds as well as machines as sophisticated as space vehicles. Operating system and application functions are often combined in the same program.

An embedded system implies a fixed set of functions programmed into a non-volatile memory (ROM, flash memory, etc.) in contrast to a general-purpose computing machine.

EMF

(1) (ElectroMagnetic Field) See *electromagnetic radiation*.

(2) (Enhanced MetaFile) The 32-bit version of the Windows Metafile (WMF) format. The original WMF format is simple and cannot completely replicate images created by sophisticated graphics programs. The EMF format enhances the structure and solves most of these deficiencies of the WMF format.

EMI

See *electromagnetic interference*.

emitter

One side of a bipolar transistor. See *collector*.

EMM

(Expanded Memory Manager) Software that manages expanded memory (EMS). In XTs and ATs, expanded memory boards must also be used. In 386s and up, the EMM converts extended memory into EMS.

EMM386.EXE

Starting with DOS 5 and Windows 3.0, EMM386.EXE is an expanded memory manager (EMM) for 386s and up, which is software that converts extended memory into EMS memory. It also allows drivers and TSRs to be stored in the upper memory area (UMA) between 640K and 1M.

E-Money

A merchant payment system from E-Money, Inc., Washington, DC, (www.emoney.net), that allows customers to purchase merchandise on the Internet via credit card or from their bank accounts. Transactions are sent from the merchant to E-Money servers, which access the bank card networks, and, for approved merchants, access the Automated Clearing House (ACH) to debit a customer's bank account. E-Money is the first to provide direct access to the ACH, which handles electronic funds transfer in the U.S. See *digital money*.

emotag

A pseudo-HTML tag used in chat rooms, e-mail, and newsgroup postings to express some feeling or emotion. They mimic the format of actual HTML tags; for example, someone might key in the following: <SMIRK>Wow! I'll bet that hurt a lot!</SMIRK>. See *emoticon*.

emoticon

(EMOTional ICON) Also called a *smiley*, it is an expression of emotion typed into a message using standard keyboard characters. The following examples are viewed sideways. Turn this book 90 degrees clockwise. See *emotag*.

Smiley	Meaning
:)	original smiley face
:-)	smile
:-(	frown
;-)	wink
:-D	big smile
:-O	mouth open in amazement
:-{}	smile (user has moustache)
:-{)}	moustache and beard
8-)	smile (user wears glasses)
:*)	red nosed smile, suggesting inebriation
@:{)===	sikh with turban and long beard

For an extensive list of more than 650 emoticons, read "Smileys" by David Sanderson, published by O'Reilly & Associates, Inc., ISBN 1-56592-041-4.

Santa Claus. Of Course!

EMS

(1) (Expanded Memory Specification) The first technique that allowed DOS to go beyond its one megabyte memory limit. It allowed access to 32MB of memory by bank switching it through a 64KB buffer (page frame) in the UMA. Either the application was written to use EMS (Lotus 1-2-3 Ver. 2.x, AutoCAD, etc.) or it was run in an environment that did such as DESQview. The first EMS memory in XTs and ATs required an EMS board and driver. When the 386 came out, it could create EMS memory from extended memory.

There used to be tremendous confusion over EMS. Not only did expanded memory (EMS) and extended memory sound alike, but in the early days, you had to allocate how much EMS you needed.

Today, EMS is practically unheard of. Windows manages all the memory in the computer and can allocate whatever EMS it needs on the fly for old DOS applications that require it. See *extended memory* for illustration.

(2) (Electronic Message Service) The part of the radio spectrum assigned to electronic messaging over digital satellite circuits.

(3) (Enterprise Messaging Server) Original name for Microsoft's Exchange Server. See *Microsoft Exchange*.

EMS emulator
Prior to the 386, it was a slow, low-cost software alternative to an EMS board. In XTs and ATs, it simulated EMS memory in extended memory or on disk. On 386s, it referred to a memory manager (EMM) that created EMS from extended memory. Technically, the 386 architecture does not emulate EMS, it maps extended memory into the page frame. See *EMS*.

EMU
(Economic and Monetary Union) The consolidation of European currencies into one monetary unit called the "Euro," which begins to phase in on January 1, 1999. Accounting systems that deal with the currencies of the participating countries have to deal with both native and Euro values. On January 1, 2002, Euro notes and coins must be available, with national currencies withdrawn by July of that year. It is expected that public and private companies will spend more than $150 billion modifying their information systems to accomodate the EMU.

emulation mode
An operational state of a computer when it is running a foreign program under emulation.

emulator
A device that is built to work like another. A computer can be designed to emulate another model and execute software that was written to run in the other machine. A terminal can be designed to emulate various communications protocols and connect to different networks. The emulator can be hardware, software or both.

enable
To turn on. Computer people and engineers prefer to say something is enabled rather than turned on. Of course! Contrast with *disable*.

Enable/OA
An earlier integrated software package for PCs from Enable Software, Inc., Ballston Lake, NY. It was a very comprehensive package rivaling many stand-alone programs. Version 4.0 also ran under UNIX.

Encapsulated PostScript
See *EPS*.

encapsulation
(1) In communications, a method for transmitting multiple protocols within the same network. The frames of one type of protocol are carried within the frames of another. For example, SNA's SDLC frames can be encapsulated within TCP/IP and transmitted over a TCP/IP network.

(2) In object technology, making the data and processing within the object private, which allows the internal implementation of the object to be modified without requring any change to the application that uses it. This is also known as *information hiding*. See *object technology*.

Encina
A UNIX-based TP monitor from Transarc Corporation, Pittsburgh, PA, (www.transarc.com), that is layered over OSF's Distributed Computing Environment (DCE). IBM's CICS/6000 TP monitor is based on Encina, and IBM acquired Transarc in 1994. Encina and BEA TUXEDO are the major TP monitors in the UNIX client/server environment.

encipher
Same as *encrypt*.

encode

(1) To assign a code to represent data, such as a parts code. Contrast with *decode*.

(2) Same as *encrypt*. See *cryptography*.

encoder

A hardware device or software that assigns a code to represent data. See *encode*.

Encore

(Encore Computer Corporation, Ft. Lauderdale, FL, www.encore.com) A computer company founded in 1983 that specializes in realtime systems and storage products. Its Infinity RT line is an SMP and Alpha-based realtime system that incorporates Encore's Reflective Memory channel, a high-speed memory to memory interconnect. Its Infinity SP disk products are SMP-based UNIX systems that emulate IBM mainframe storage controllers. They provide mainframe storage and also allow UNIX hosts and PC servers access to the same disks as if they were attached SCSI drives.

Encore's products stem back to Systems Engineering Labs, founded in 1961. SEL became a division of Gould, which was acquired by Encore in 1989.

encrypt, encryption

To encode data for security purposes. See *cryptography*.

encryption algorithm

The formula used to turn data into a secret code. See *cryptography* and *algorithm*.

endian

See *big endian*.

end key

A keyboard key commonly used to move the cursor to the bottom of the screen or file or to the next word or end of line.

endless loop

A series of instructions that are constantly repeated. It can be caused by an error in the program or it can be intentional; for example, a screen demo on continuous replay.

end points

In vector graphics, the two ends of a line (vector). In 2-D graphics, each end point is typically two numbers representing coordinates on x and y axes. In 3-D, each end point is made up of three numbers representing coordinates on x, y and z axes.

end user computing

Using personal computers. The end user is the user of the computer.

Energy Star

Power conservation requirements set forth by the Environmental Protection Agency of the U.S. Government. In order to display the Energy Star logo, devices (PCs, monitors, printers, etc.) must use less than 30 watts of power when inactive.

Enfin

A client/server development system based on the Smalltalk language. It is now part of the ObjectStudio environment. See *ObjectStudio*.

engine

(1) A specialized processor, such as a graphics processor. Like any engine, the faster it runs, the quicker the job gets done. See *graphics engine* and *printer engine*.

(2) Software that performs a primary and highly repetitive function such as a database engine, graphics engine or dictionary engine.

engineer

See *software engineer, systems engineer* and *network engineer*.

engineering cylinder

See *diagnostic tracks*.

engineering drawing sizes

```
A - 8 1/2 x 11
B - 11 x 17
C - 17 x 22
D - 22 x 34
E - 34 x 44
```

Enhanced BIOS
See *LBA*.

Enhanced IDE
See *IDE*.

Enhanced keyboard
A 101-key keyboard from IBM that superseded the PC and AT keyboards. It is the type commonly used on PCs today.

enhanced resolution
See *interpolated resolution*.

enhancement
Any improvement made to a software package or hardware device. Sometimes enhancements are really bug fixes in disguise.

ENIAC
(Electronic Numerical Integrator And Calculator) The first operational electronic digital computer developed for the U.S. Army by John Eckert and John Mauchly at the University of Pennsylvania in Philadelphia. Started in 1945 and completed in 1945, it was decimal-based, used 18,000 vacuum tubes, took up 1,800 square feet and performed 5,000 additions/second. Today, the equivalent technology fits in a wristwatch.

In 1946, The New York Times said "One of the war's top secrets, an amazing machine which applies electronic speeds for the first time to mathemaical tasks hitherto too difficult and cumbersome for solution, was announced here tonight."

The First Operational Digital Computer
What an awesome sight this must have been in 1946. The electrical power used could supply a thousand computers today. *(Photo courtesy The Moore School of Electrical Engineering, University of Pennsylvania.)*

enqueue
Pronounced "n-q." To place an item in a queue. Contrast with *dequeue*.

enquiry character
In communications, a control character that requests a response from the receiving station.

ENS
(Enterprise Networking Services) A variety of networking services from Banyan that have been separated from VINES and made available on other platforms such as NetWare, Windows NT and AIX. They include the Streettalk directory, network management and electronic mail services.

enter key
See *return key*.

enterprise
The entire organization. See *enterprise networking*.

enterprise data
Centralized data that is shared by many users throughout the organization.

Enterprise Developer
See *Team Enterprise Developer*.

enterprise model
A model of how an organization does business. Information systems are designed from this model.

enterprise network
A geographically-dispersed network under the jurisdiction of one organization. It often includes several different types of networks and computer systems from different vendors.

enterprise networking
The networking infrastructure in a large enterprise with multiple computer systems and networks of different types is extraordinarily complex. Due to the myriads of interfaces that are required, much of what goes on has little to do with the real data processing of the payroll and orders. An enormous amount of effort goes into planning the integration of disparate networks and systems and managing them, and, planning again for yet more interfaces as marketing pressures force vendors to develop new techniques that routinely change the ground rules.

Application Development and Configuration Management
There are a large number of programming languages and development tools for writing today's client/server applications. Each development system has its own visual programming interface for building GUI front ends and its own fourth-generation language (4GLs) for doing the business logic. Programmers are always learning new languages to meet the next generation.

Traditional programming has given way to programming for graphical user interfaces and object-oriented methods, two technologies with steep learning curves for the traditional programmer.

Programming managers are responsible for maintaining legacy systems in traditional languages while developing new ones in newer languages and tools for the client/server environment. They must also find ways to keep track of all the program modules and ancillary files that make up an application when several programmers work on a project. Stand-alone version control and configuration management programs handle this, and parts of these systems are increasingly being built into the development systems themselves (see *configuration management*).

Database Management
Like all software, a database management system (DBMS) must support the hardware platform and operating system it runs in. In order to move a DBMS to another platform, a version must be available for the new hardware and operating system. The common database language between client and server is SQL, but each DBMS vendor implements its own rendition of SQL, requiring a special SQL interface to most every DBMS.

For certain kinds of applications, relational databases (RDBMSs) are giving way to object-oriented databases (OODBMSs) or unified databases that are both relational and object oriented. This puts a new slant on learning about data structures and the way they are processed.

Database administrators must select the DBMS or DBMSs that efficiently process the daily transactions and also provide sufficient horsepower for decision support. They must decide when and how to split the operation into different databases, one for daily work, the other for ad hoc queries. They must also create the structure of the database by designing the record layouts and their relationships to each other.

Operating Systems/Network Operating Systems
Operating systems are the master control programs that run the computer system. Single-user operating systems, such as DOS, Windows and Mac, are used in the clients, and multiuser network operating systems, such as NetWare, Windows NT and all the variations of UNIX, are used in the servers. Windows is the clear winner on the desktop, and NT increasingly gains market share as a server OS.

The operating system sets the standard for the programs that run under it. The choice of operating system combined with the hardware platform determines which ready-made applications can be purchased to work on it.

Systems programmers and IS managers must determine when newer versions of operating systems make sense and plan how to integrate them into existing environments.

Communications Protocols

Communications protocols determine the format and rules for how the transmitted data is framed and managed from the sending station to the receiving station. IBM's SNA, Digital's DECnet, Apple's AppleTalk, Novell's IPX/SPX, Microsoft's NetBEUI and the UNIX/Internet's TCP/IP are the major ones. Exchanging data and messages between Macs, PCs, minis, mainframes and UNIX workstations means designing networks for a multiprotocol environment.

LANs

Transmission from station to station within a LAN is performed by the LAN access method, or data link protocol, such as Ethernet and Token Ring. As traffic expands within an organization, higher bandwidth is required, causing organizations to plan for Fast Ethernet, switched Ethernet, FDDI and CDDI. At the same time, ATM continues to make inroads, although not as fast as once predicted.

Repeaters, bridges, routers, gateways, hubs and switches are the devices used to extend, convert, route and manage traffic in an enterprise network. Increasingly, one device takes on the job of another (a router does bridging, a hub does routing). Vendor offerings are dizzying.

Network traffic is becoming as jammed as the Los Angeles freeways. Network administrators have to analyze current network traffic in light of future business plans and increasing use of Web pages, images, sound and video files. They have to determine when to increase network bandwidth while maintaining existing networks, which today have become the technical lifeblood of an enterprise.

WANs

Transmitting data to remote locations requires the use of private lines or public switched services offered by local and long distance carriers. Connections can be as simple as dialing up via modem or by leasing private lines, such as T1 and T3. Switched 56, frame relay, ISDN, SMDS and ATM offer a variety of switched services in which you pay for the digital traffic you use.

Laptop use has created a tremendous need for remote access to LANs. Network administrators have to design LANs with a combination of remote access and remote control capability to allow mobile workers access to their databases and processing functions.

Network Management

Network management is the monitoring and control of LANs and WANs from a central management console. It requires network management software, such as IBM's NetView and HP's OpenView. The Internet's SNMP has become the de facto standard management protocol, but there are many network management programs and options. For example, there are over 30 third-party add-ons for HP's popular OpenView software.

Systems and Storage Management

Systems management includes a variety of functions for managing computers in a networked environment, including software distribution, version control, backup & recovery, printer spooling, job scheduling, virus protection and performance and capacity planning. Network management may also fall under the systems management umbrella.

Storage management has become critical for two reasons. First, there is an ever-increasing demand for storage due to document management, data warehousing, multimedia and the World Wide Web as well as increasing daily transaction volume. Secondly, finding the time window in a 7x24 operation to copy huge databases for backup, archiving and disaster recovery is getting more difficult. To add to the burden, copies of live production databases are routinely required for Year 2000 testing.

Electronic Mail

Electronic mail requires a store and forward system so that mail can be safely kept in a "mailbox" until it is retrieved. Although messages and attached files are transmitted using standard transport protocols, the mail system is a high-level application with its own messaging protocols. The major ones are IBM's SNADS, the international X.400, Novell's MHS, Lotus' cc:mail, Microsoft Mail and the Internet's SMTP.

Formats
Word processors, DBMSs, spreadsheets, drawing and paint programs generate files in their own proprietary data format. For example, there are more than 75 graphics formats alone. Moving files from one application to another requires conversion (exporting and importing) from one format to another. Dealing with multiple formats and multimedia is why object-oriented databases are being evaluated. They can support any kind of text, picture, sound and video format that exists today or that comes tomorrow.

The Internet and Intranets
As everything mentioned above isn't enough to keep the technical staff busy, the World Wide Web comes along with a force of a nuclear bomb to turn everything in the computing world upside down. Now the Internet sets the standards. The browser becomes an alternate interface for accessing just about everything. Every component of system software from operating system to database management system as well as every application currently on the market has been or is being revamped in some manner to be Internet compliant. It's good. It keeps information professionals off the streets and gives them plenty to do! In summary... happy computing!

enterprise storage
The collection of online, nearline and offline storage within an organization. See *ESM*.

enterprise storage management
See *ESM*.

enterprise systems management
See *systems management*.

entity
In a database, anything about which information can be stored; for example, a person, concept, physical object or event. Typically refers to a record structure.

entity relationship model
A database model that describes the attributes of entities and the relationships among them. An entity is a file (table). Today, ER models are often created graphically, and software converts the graphical representations of the tables into the SQL code required to create the data structures in the database. See *data model* for example.

entity type
In a database, a particular kind of file; for example, a customer or product file.

entropy
In data compression, a measure of the amount of non-redundant, non-compressible information in an object.

entry
The input of an item or set of items at a terminal. See *data entry*.

entry point
In programming, the starting point of the instructions in a subroutine.

enumerate
To count or list one by one. For example, an enumerated data type defines a list of all possible values for a variable, and no other value can then be placed into it.

envelope
(1) A range of frequencies for a particular operation.
(2) A group of bits or items that is packaged and treated as a single unit.

environment
A particular configuration of hardware or software. "The environment" refers to a hardware platform and the operating system that is used in it. A programming environment would include the compiler and

associated development tools.

Environment is used in other ways to express a type of configuration, such as a networking environment, database environment, transaction processing environment, batch environment, interactive environment and so on. See *platform*.

environment variable

A stored value used by DOS as well as applications. Environment variables are set at startup. Path, Append, Comspec and Prompt are examples of DOS environment variables.

EOF, EOL, EOM, EOT

(End Of File, End Of Line, End Of Message, End Of Transmission)

EPIM

(Ethernet Port Interface Module) A plug-in module for a particular type of Ethernet port. Used in network devices such as hubs and switches, it enables different types of Ethernets (10BaseT, 10Base2, etc.) to be attached.

epitaxial layer

In chip making, a semiconductor layer that is created on top of the silicon base rather than below it. See *molecular beam epitaxy*.

epoch date

The starting point from which time is measured as the number of days, minutes, etc., from that time.

EPP

(1) (Enhanced Parallel Port) See *IEEE 1284*.

(2) (Ethernet Packet Processor) A chip from Kalpana, Inc., Santa, Clara, CA, that doubles speed of Ethernet transmission to 20Mbits/sec.

EPROM

(Erasable Programmable **ROM**) A programmable and reusable chip that holds its content until erased under ultraviolet light. EPROMS have a lifespan of a few hundred write cycles. EPROMS are expected to eventually give way to flash memory. See *EPROM programmer*.

EPROM programmer

A device that writes instructions and data into EPROM chips. Some earlier units were capable of programming both PROMs and EPROMs.

EPS

(Encapsulated PostScript) A PostScript file format used to transfer a graphic image between applications and platforms. EPS files contain PostScript code in ASCII text as well as an optional preview image in TIFF, WMF, PICT or EPSI format (EPSI is also ASCII). Adobe Illustrator has its own variation of EPS, therefore both Illustrator EPS and standard EPS files are in use.

The typical use of EPS would be to export an illustration created in a drawing program to an EPS file and to import it into a page layout program. Using the preview image, the illustration then could be scaled to fit the page design requirements. The document and embedded EPS images would be saved in the native format of the page layout program (PageMaker, QuarkXPress, etc.) and then printed on a local printer or "printed to disk" as a standard PostScript file for input to an imagesetter.

EPS files are considerably larger than most other graphics file formats; however, since they are text files, they will compress to about a quarter of their original size. See *EPSI*.

EPSF

(Encapsulated PostScript File) The full name of an EPS file. It is used for EPS file extensions in non-DOS and Windows platforms that can handle more than three characters. See *EPS*.

EPSI

(Encapsulated PostScript Interchange) A bitmap format used as a preview image in an EPS file. It contains only 7-bit ASCII data. It has been used in DOS applications that do not support TIFF, WMF and PICT formats. See *EPS*.

Epson emulation

Compatible with Epson dot matrix printers. The command set in the Epson MX, RX and FX printers has become an industry standard.

EPSS

(Electronic Performance Support System) A computer system that provides quick assistance and information without requiring prior training to use it. It may incorporate all forms of multimedia delivery as well as AI techniques such as expert systems and natural language recognition.

EQ

(EQual to) See *relational operator*.

equalization

In communications, techniques used to reduce distortion and compensate for signal loss (attenuation) over long distances.

equals sign

In programming, the equals sign (=) is used for equality and copying. For example, **if x = 0** means "if X is equal to zero;" however **x = 0** means "copy the value zero into the variable X." Double equals signs (==) means equals to in C. For example, **if (x == 0)** means if X is equal to zero. The unusual use of the double equals sign causes many errors in C programming.

equation

An arithmetic expression that equates one set of conditions to another; for example, **A = B + C**. In a programming language, assignment statements take the form of an equation. The above example would assign the sum of B and C to the variable A.

ERA

(Electrically Reconfigurable Array) A programmable logic chip (PLD) technology from Plessey Semiconductor that allows the chip to be reprogrammed electrically.

erase

See *delete*.

erase head

In a magnetic tape drive, the device that erases the tape before a new block of data is recorded.

erbium

A rare earth material used in optical amplifiers. See *optical amplifier*.

ergonomics

The science of people-machine relationships. An ergonomically-designed product implies that the device blends smoothly with a person's body or actions.

Erlang

A unit of traffic use that specifies the total capacity or average use of a telephone system. One Erlang is equivalent to the continuous usage of a telephone line. Traffic in Erlangs is the sum of the holding times of all lines divided by the period of measurement.

ER model

See *entity relationship model*.

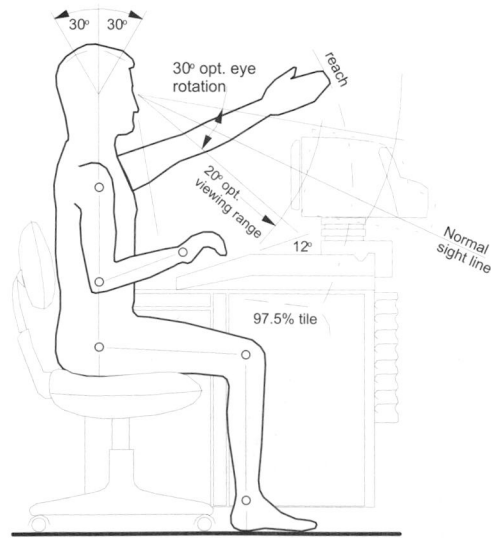

Ergonomics

Although ergonomically-designed seats, keyboards and mice are important, perhaps the most beneficial aspect of ergonomics is teaching people to get up periodically and stretch. *(Redrawn from illustration courtesy of Hewlett-Packard Company.)*

Computer Desktop Encyclopedia

ERP

(Enterprise Resource Planning) An integrated information system that servers all departments within an enterprise including manufacturing, financial and human resources. Evolving out of manufacturing, ERP implies the use of packaged software rather than inhouse or custom-developed software. ERP modules may be able to interface with an organization's proprietary software with varying degrees of effort. The major ERP vendors are SAP, PeopleSoft, Oracle, Baan and J.D. Edwards.

error checking

(1) Testing for accurate transmission of data over a communications network or internally within the computer system. See *parity checking* and *CRC*.

(2) Same as *validity checking*.

error control, error detection & correction

See *error checking* and *validity checking*.

error-free channel

An interface (wire, cable, etc.) between devices that is not subject to external interference; specifically not the dial-up telephone system.

error handling

Routines in a program that respond to errors. The measurement of quality in error handling is based on how the system informs the user and what alternatives it provides for dealing with them.

error message

The cryptic on-screen explantion you get when something goes wrong.

error rate

The measurement of the effectiveness of a communications channel. It is the ratio of the number of erroneous units of data to the total number of units of data transmitted.

Erwin

(Entity Relationship for WINdows) A data modeling program for Windows from Logic Works, Princeton, NJ, (www.logicworks.com). It allows the database schemas to be build graphically and turns the graphs into the appropriate SQL code for creating PowerBuilder, DB2, Oracle, Sybase and other databases. See *entity relationship model*.

ES/3090

A high-end IBM mainframe that incorporates the ESA/370 enhancements.

ES/9000

The IBM System/390 computer line introduced in late 1990 that uses 31-bit addressing with maximum memory capacities from 256MB to 9GB. It's 18 models (Model 120 to Model 960) offered the widest range of power in a single introduction at one time with prices ranging from $70K to $23M. Vector processing is optional on high-end water-cooled and certain air-cooled models. See *System/390*.

ESA/370

(Enterprise System Architecture/370) IBM enhancements that increase the performance of high-end 4381 and 3090 mainframes. Introduced in 1988, it increases virtual memory from 2GB to 16TB and adds techniques for managing it more effectively. This architecture is built into System/390 ES/9000 computers.

ES/9000 Model 900
The IBM mainframe in this photo is typical of the large centralized datacenter. The mainframe lives on despite predictions of its demise, because companies have a huge investment in mainframe applications and training. In addition, centralized processing is easier to manage and is more secure than distributing information systems all over the enterprise. *(Photo courtesy of IBM Corporation.)*

ESA/390

(Enterprise System Architecture/390) Extensions to ESA/370 for the System/390 series. It includes MVS/ESA, VM/ESA and VSE/ESA operating systems.

Esc

See *escape character* and *escape key*.

escape character

A control character often used to precede other characters to control a printer or other device. For example, escape, followed by &l10, sets the LaserJet to landscape mode. In ASCII, escape is decimal 27, hex 1B; in EBCDIC, it is hex 27.

escape key

A keyboard key commonly used to exit a mode or routine, or cancel some function.

escape sequence

(1) A machine command that starts with an escape character. Printers are often commanded by escape sequences. See *escape character*.

(2) In a modem, a unique sequence of characters that precedes a command. It allows modem commands (dial, hang up, etc.) to be transmitted with the data.

ESCD

(Extended System Configuration Data) A format for holding comprehensive data about the peripheral devices plugged into the computer, including ISA cards and Plug and Play cards. ESCD data can be stored in a disk file or non-volatile memory.

ESCON

(Enterprise Systems CONnection) An IBM S/390 fiber-optic channel that transfers 17 Mbytes/sec over distances up to 60 km depending on connection type. ESCON allows peripheral devices to be located across large campuses and metropolitan areas.

Compared to the copper-based, parallel bus and tag channels, ESCON provides greater speeds and uses a serial interface. An ESCON Director is a hub-and-spoke coupling device that provides 8-16 ports (Model 1) or 28-60 ports (Model 2). See *FICON*.

ESD

(1) (Electronic Software Distribution) Distributing new software and upgrades via the network rather than individual installations on each machine. See *ESL*.

(2) (ElectroStatic Discharge) Sparks (electrons) that jump from an electrically-charged object to an approaching conductive object.

(3) (Entry Systems Division) The IBM division that conceived and developed the original IBM PC.

ESDI

(Enhanced Small Device Interface) A hard disk interface that transfers data in the one to three MByte/sec range. ESDI was the high-speed interface for small computers for a while, but has been superseded by IDE and SCSI drives. See *hard disk*.

ESDL

(Electronic Software Distribution and Licensing) The combination of ESD and ESL.

ESDS

(Entry Sequence DataSet) A VSAM structure that stores records one after the other without regard to content. Records are retrieved by address. Contrast with *KSDS*.

ESF

(1) (Extended SuperFrame) An enhanced T1 format that allows a line to be monitored during normal operation. It uses 24 frames grouped together (instead of the 12-frame D4 superframe) and provides room for CRC bits and other diagnostic commands.

(2) (External Source Format) A specification language for defining an application in IBM's CSP/AD application generator.

ESL

(1) A family of client/server development tools for Windows and OS/2 from VMARK. It was originally developed by Easel Corporation, which was acquired by VMARK. ESL includes a screen scraper for turning character-based screens into GUI front ends and is often used to develop systems that incorporate the mainframe.

(2) (Electronic Software Licensing) Software that keeps track of the number of active users per application in order to comply with the multiuser licensing contracts that have been purchased.

ESL Renovator

A screen scraper from Easel Corporation that became part of the ESL development environment. See *ESL*.

ESL Workbench

An integrated component in the OS/2 version of ESL. The OS/2 version of ESL is commonly known as ESL Workbench. See *ESL*.

ESM

(1) (Enterprise Storage Management) Managing the online, nearline and offline storage within a large organization. It includes analysis of storage requirements as well as making routine copies of files and databases for backup, archiving, disaster recovery, hierarchical storage management (HSM) and testing purposes. See *SAN* and *HSM*.

(2) (Enterprise Systems Management) Systems management within a large enterprise. See *systems management*.

ESP

(1) (Enhanced Service Provider) An organization that adds value to basic telephone service by offering such features as call-forwarding, call-detailing and protocol conversion.

(2) (E-tech Speedy Protocol) A proprietary protocol of E-Tech Research used in its modems.

(3) (Electronic Still Photography) Digitizing and transmitting images over a telephone line. See *slow scan TV*.

(4) (Emulex SCSI Processor) A proprietary chip used in Emulex's SCSI disk controller.

ESS

(1) (Electronic Switching System) A large-scale computer used to route telephone calls in a central office. See *SS7* and *digital cross-connect*.

(2) (Executive Support System) See *EIS*.

(3) (Electronic SpreadSheet) See *spreadsheet*.

Essbase

A leading decision support tool from Arbor Software Corporation, Sunnyvale, CA, (www.arborsoft.com) that is optimized for business planning, analysis and management reporting. It provides an OLAP server that runs on Windows NT, OS/2, AS/400 and major UNIX platforms and supports Windows, Mac and UNIX clients. Data can be extracted from a variety of databases, data warehouses and spreadsheets into Essbase applications. Spreadsheet plug-ins for Lotus 1-2-3 and Excel are available, and the Application Manager is a Windows-based program for building analytical models and providing system management and data loading.

estimating a programming job

The hardest task in the computer business is estimating the time it takes to create a finished, working program. It always seems to take longer, and sometimes it seems to take forever.

Programmers are an extremely optimistic bunch, and unless they have written a very similar program before with the same programming tools, the new job inevitably takes longer for one reason. Application design is creative work. No matter how much a program is defined on paper, as soon as it starts to take shape, the design flaws become evident. It simply takes multiple iterations to get the design right.

Over the years, some programming estimates have been preposterous. What was thought to take three weeks takes a year. A one year job takes six. In order to improve the accuracy of any estimate, the functional requirements and user interfaces must be carefully designed before the programming begins, the programmers must be experienced, and the users must be involved throughout the project. See *to the recruiter*.

eSuite

A Java-based suite of applications from Lotus that includes word processing, spreadsheet, e-mail and presentation graphics. It runs in any NC or PC that has a Java Virtual Machine. Formerly code named Kona, the individual executable programs are considerably smaller than counterpart applications in Microsoft Office and other Windows-based software.

e-tailing

(Electronic-reTAILING) An online storefront. See *electronic commerce*.

EtherLoop

(ETHERnet Local LOOP) A transmission technology from Nortel that uses Ethernet packets at up to 10 Mbps over standard telephone lines between the customer and telco central office (CO). It does not use the regular Ethernet CSMA/CD collision method. EtherLoop is a last mile technology that is said to eliminate much of the crosstalk associated with DSL. See *last mile*.

Ethernet

The most widely-used LAN access method, which is defined by the IEEE 802.3 standard (Token Ring is the next most popular). Ethernet is normally a shared media LAN. All stations on the segment share the total bandwidth, which is either 10 Mbps (Ethernet), 100 Mbps (Fast Ethernet) or 1000 Mbps (Gigabit Ethernet). With switched Ethernet, each sender and receiver pair have the full bandwidth.

Standard Ethernet (10Base5), also called *Thick Ethernet* and *ThickNet*, uses a thick coax cable that can run as far as 1,640 feet without using repeaters. Attachment is made by clamping a transceiver onto the thick coax, which contains another cable that is connected to the adapter card via a 15-pin socket (AUI port).

Thin Ethernet (10Base2), also called *ThinNet* and *CheaperNet*, uses a thinner, less-expensive coax that is easier to connect but has a limitation of 607 feet per segment. ThinNet uses T-type BNC connectors, and the transceivers are built into the adapter cards.

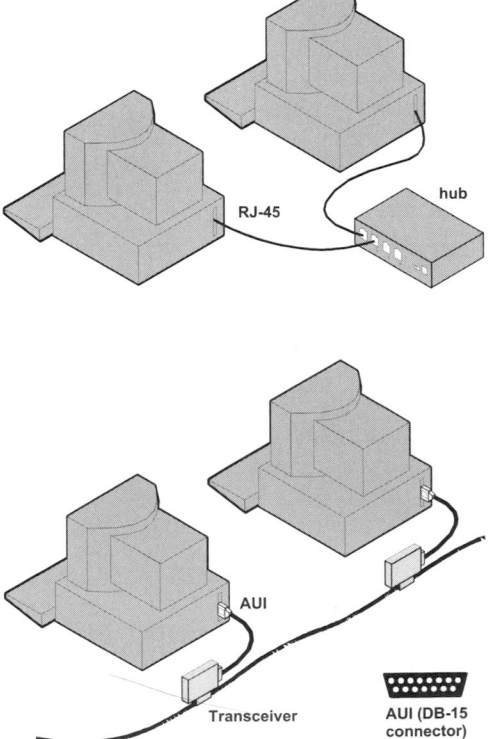

Twisted Pair Ethernet
10BaseT and 100BaseT are the most popular Ethernets. All nodes connect to a central hub using twisted pair wires and RJ-45 connectors.

The Original Ethernet
"Thick" Ethernet (10Base5) was the first Ethernet and uses a bus topology. Transceivers connect the network adapters to a common coaxial cable. They often use a vampire tap that "bites" into the coax.

Computer Desktop Encyclopedia

Thin Ethernet
"Thin" Ethernet (10Base2) is a variation of "thick" Ethernet and uses a thinner coaxial cable that is attached to each node using BNC T-connectors.

BNC
T-connector

BNC

Twisted pair Ethernet (10BaseT) uses economical telephone wiring and standard RJ-45 connectors, often taking advantage of installed wires in a building. It is wired in a star configuration and requires a hub. Fast Ethernet (100BaseT) is similar, but uses two different twisted pair configurations (see *100BaseT*).

Fiber Optic Ethernet (10BaseF and 100BaseFX) is impervious to external radiation and is often used to extend Ethernet segments up to 1.2 miles. Specifications exist for complete fiber optic networks as well as backbone implementations. FOIRL (Fiber Optic Repeater Link) was an earlier standard that is limited to .6 miles distance.

Ethernet transmits variable length frames from 72 to 1518 bytes in length, each containing a header with the addresses of the source and destination stations and a trailer that contains error correction data. Higher-level protocols, such as IP and IPX, fragment long messages into the frame size required by the Ethernet network being employed.

Ethernet uses the CSMA/CD technology to broadcast each frame onto the physical medium (wire, fiber, etc.). All stations attached to the Ethernet are "listening," and the station with the matching destination address accepts the frame and checks for errors. Ethernet is a data link protocol (MAC layer protocol) and functions at layers 1 and 2 of the OSI model.

Ethernet was invented by Robert Metcalfe and David Boggs at Xerox PARC in 1973, which first ran at 2.94 Mbps. Metcalfe later joined Digital where he facilitated a joint venture between Digital, Intel and Xerox to collaborate further on Ethernet. Version 1 was finalized in 1980, and products shipped in the following year. In 1983, the IEEE approved the Ethernet 802.3 standard. See *100BaseT, Gigabit Ethernet* and *switched Ethernet*.

ETHERNET LIMITATIONS

Type	Maximum Segment length		Maximum Devices
COAX (bus topology)			
10Base5 "thick"	1640 ft.	(500 m)	100
10Base2 "thin"	607 ft.	(185 m)	30
TWISTED PAIR (star topology)			
10BaseT	328 ft.	(100 m)	1
100BaseT	328 ft.	(100 m)	1
FIBER (star topology)			
FOIRL	.6 mi.	(1 km)	1
10BaseF	1.2 mi.	(2 km)	1
100BaseFX multimode	1.2 mi.	(2 km)	1
100BaseFX single-mode	6 mi.	(10 km)	1

Ethernet adapter, Ethernet card
The Ethernet hardware required to attach to an Ethernet network. It typically resides on an expansion board, but is sometimes built into the motherboard. An Ethernet adapter is required in each client and server. See *Ethernet* and *network adapter*.

Ethernet address

A unique number assigned to each Ethernet network adapter. It is a 48-bit number maintained by the IEEE. Hardware vendors obtain blocks of numbers that they can build into their cards.

Ethernet hub

A device that all lines on an Ethernet segment are plugged into. 10BaseT and 100BaseT Ethernets are star networks and require a hub for operation. The earlier 10Base5 and 10Base2 Ethernets are bus networks, but are often wired into a star configuration using a central hub for improved troubleshooting. A hub is also known as a multiport repeater and is sometimes called a concentrator. See *hub*.

Ethernet switch

See *switched Ethernet*.

EtherTalk

Macintosh software from Apple that accompanies its Ethernet Interface NB Card and adapts the Mac to Ethernet networks.

EtherWave

An Ethernet system from Farallon Communications, Alameda, CA, (www.farallon.com), that provides network adapters that daisy chain 10BaseT wire from machine to machine. Regular 10BaseT systems require a central hub that connects all machines. To add a station to the network when a hub is out of ports requires adding a hub. EtherWave allows connecting seven daisy-chained EtherWave PCs to a single hub port.

E-time

See *execution time*.

ETSI

(European Telecommunications Standards Institute, Sophia Antipolis technical park, Nice, France, www.etsi.fr) A non-profit membership organization founded in 1988, dedicated to standardizing telecommunications throughout Europe. It promotes worldwide standards, and its efforts are coordinated with the ITU. Any European organization proving an interest in promoting European standards may represent itself in ETSI.

Eudora

A very popular Internet mail program from Qualcomm Inc., San Diego, CA, (www.qualcomm.com). A light version is often provided by Internet service providers to its customers. Eudora started out on the Macintosh in 1988 and by 1996 had more than 10 million users. See *stationery*.

EULA

(End User License Agreement) The legal agreement between the manufacturer and purchaser of software. It is either printed somewhere on the packaging or displayed on screen at time of installation, the latter being the better method, because it cannot be avoided. The user must click "Accept" or "I Agree" and the license does stipulate the terms of usage, whether the user reads them or not.

The license disclaims all liabilities for what might happen in the user's computer when the software is running. It generally guarantees nothing except that the disk will be replaced if defective. If it sounds like a license to get away with making inferior software, one has to consider that it is impossible for even the largest vendor to test a program in every possible configuration in the PC world. Some combination of hardware and software can always cause a program to crash and cause the loss of whatever data is in the machine at that time.

Euro

See *EMU*.

Eurocard

A family of European-designed printed circuit boards that uses a 96-pin plug rather than edge connectors. The 3U is a 4x6" board with one plug; the 6U is a 6x12" board with two plugs; the 9U is a 14x18" board with three plugs.

European Computer Manufacturers Association

See *ECMA*.

Evans & Sutherland

(Evans & Sutherland Computer Corporation, Salt Lake City, UT, www.es.com) A computer graphics and simulation company founded in 1968 by David Evans and Ivan Sutherland. Sutherland's doctoral thesis on computer graphics in 1963 became a cult paper on the subject. They developed many of the first effects at the University of Utah.

In the mid 1970s, the company developed commercial flight simulators in conjunction with Rediffusion Simulation in England. More than a decade later, it dissolved this relationship and began to develop military simulations. The company makes the computer hardware and software, which is then integrated with domes and cockpits into the final product. The simulations are extremely realistic and are output at more than 100 frames per second to eliminate the subliminal flicker produced when scenes are projected inside a dome. The company later created a division that creates special effects for the education and entertainment fields.

even parity

See *parity checking*.

event driven

An application that responds to input from the user or other application at unregulated times. It's driven by choices users makes (select menu, press button, etc.). Contrast with *procedure oriented*.

EVGA

(Extended VGA) See *VGA*.

e-wallet

(Electronic-WALLET) See *digital wallet*.

exa

One quintillion (10^{18}). See *space/time*.

Evans & Sutherland Flight Simulator
This 20 foot dome has an actual cockpit inside. Inside, scenes such as the one below are projected onto the outer walls, and the hydraulics move the unit. *(Photos courtesy of Evans & Sutherland Computer Corporation.)*

Exabyte

(Exabyte Corporation, Boulder, CO, www.exabyte.com) The world's largest independent tape drive manufacturer. Its high-capacity 8mm tape drives, introduced in 1987, are sold direct and through OEMs. With acquisitions made in 1993, Exabyte also makes QIC and DAT drives.

examinations

See *CCP, NetWare certification* and *Microsoft Certified Professional*.

Excel

A full-featured spreadsheet for PCs and the Macintosh from Microsoft. It can link many spreadsheets for consolidation and provides a wide variety of business graphics and charts for creating presentation materials.

Exception error 12

A DOS error message that means DOS does not have enough room to handle hardware interrupts. Increase the number of stacks in the STACKS= command in the CONFIG.SYS file.

exception report

A listing of abnormal items or items that fall outside of a specified range.

Exchange

See *Microsoft Exchange*.

Excite

(www.excite.com) One of the major search sites on the Web. See *Web search sites*.

exclusive NOR, exclusive OR

See *NOR* and *OR*.

executable

A program in machine language that is ready to run in a particular computer environment.

execute

To run a program (follow instructions in the program). Same as *run*.

execution time

The time in which a single instruction is executed. It makes up the last half of the instruction cycle.

executive

Refers to an operating system or only to the operating system's kernel.

executive information system

See *EIS*.

EXE file

(EXEcutable file) A runnable program in DOS, OS/2 and VMS. In DOS, if a program fits within 64K, it may be a COM file.

exit

(1) To get out of the current mode or quit the program. Contrast with *launch*.

(2) In programming, to get out of the loop, routine or function that the computer is currently in.

expanded memory

See *EMS*, *EMM* and *expanded storage*.

expanded memory emulator

A memory manager for 386s and up that converts extended memory into EMS memory. See *EMM*.

expanded storage

Auxiliary memory in IBM mainframes. Data is usually transferred in 4K chunks from expanded storage to central storage (main memory).

expand the tree

To display the sublevels of a hierarchical tree.

expansion board

A printed circuit board that plugs into an expansion slot and extends the computer's ability to control another type of peripheral device. All the boards (cards) that plug into a personal computer's bus are expansion boards, such as display adapters, disk controllers and sound cards.

Support for additional peripherals can be built into the motherboard. For example, in the early days of the PC, the serial and parallel ports were always contained on an expansion board. Today, they may be built into the motherboard. Stereo sound and VGA display may also be built into the motherboard, eliminating the need to plug in separate expansion boards. See *ISA*. See also *bus extender*.

expansion bus

An input/output bus typically comprised of a series of slots on the motherboard. Expansion boards are plugged into the bus. ISA, EISA, PCI and VL-bus are examples of expansion buses used in a PC. See also *bus extender*.

expansion card

Same as *expansion board*.

expansion slot

A receptacle inside a computer or other electronic system that accepts printed circuit boards. The number of slots determines future expansion. In personal computers, the slots are connected to the bus.

ExperLogo

A Macintosh version of Logo developed by ExperTelligence, Inc., Goleta, CA. It contains more functions similar to LISP than most versions of Logo.

expert system

An AI application that uses a knowledge base of human expertise for problem solving. Its success is based on the quality of the data and rules obtained from the human expert. In practice, expert systems perform both below and above that of a human.

It derives its answers by running the knowledge base through an inference engine, which is software that interacts with the user and processes the results from the rules and data in the knowledge base.

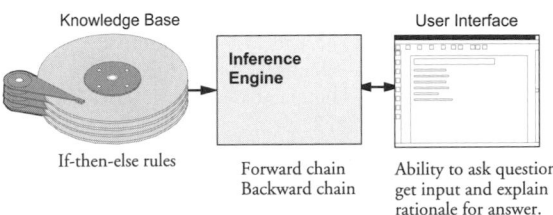

Expert System

Examples of uses are medical diagnosis, equipment repair, investment analysis, financial, estate and insurance planning, vehicle routing, contract bidding, production control and training. See *EPSS*.

expireware

Software with a built-in expiration date, either by date or number of uses.

explode

(1) To break down an assembly into its component pieces. Contrast with *implode*.

(2) To decompress data back to its original form.

Explorer

The file manager in Windows 95/98. See *Win 9x Explorer* and *Internet Explorer*.

exponent

The number written above the line and to the right of a number that indicates the power of a number, or how many zeros there are in it. For example 10 to the 3rd power indicates three zeros. The number 467,000 can be stated as 467 x 10 to the 3rd. On a screen or printout, the number is expressed as 467E3. See *floating point*.

exponential growth

Extremely fast growth. On a chart, the line curves up rather than being straight. Contrast with *linear*.

exponential smoothing

A widely-used technique in forecasting trends, seasonality and level change. Works well with data that has a lot of randomness.

export

To save a copy of the current document or database into the file format required by a different application. See *import, foreign format* and *Save as*.

expression

In programming, a statement that describes data and processing. For example, **value=2*cost** and **product="HAT" and color="GRAY"**.

extended application

A DOS application that runs in extended memory under the control of a DOS extender.

extended ASCII

The second half of the ASCII character set (characters 128 through 255). Extended ASCII symbols are different for each font. The standard font in DOS uses extended ASCII for foreign language letters as well as characters that make up simple charts and diagrams (see *ASCII chart*). The Macintosh allows extended ASCII characters to be user defined.

The extended ASCII characters in most Windows fonts are defined by ANSI for foreign languages, and the Character Map utility can be used to view them.

Extended Data Out RAM

See *EDO RAM*.

Extended Edition

The IBM version of OS/2 that includes communications and database management. The Communications Manager has built-in LU 6.2 and X.25 protocols. The Database Manager uses IBM's SQL.

Extended Error 53

A DOS error message that typically means a network connection has been broken between two stations.

extended maintenance

On-call service that is ordered for periods in addition to the primary period of maintenance.

extended memory

In Intel 286s and up, it is standard memory above one megabyte. Extended memory is used directly by Windows and OS/2 as well as DOS applications that run with DOS extenders. It is also used under DOS for RAM disks and disk caches. Contrast with expanded memory (EMS), which is specialized memory above one megabyte. Memory boards can usually be set up as a mix of the two. See *EMS*, *XMS* and *DOS extender*.

For more details on addressing and the UMA, see *PC memory map*

Extended Memory (1MB and up)

HMA (High Memory Area)

UMA (Upper Memory Area (640K to 1MB)

Page frame

Drivers & TSRs

Conventional Memory (0-640K)

Regular DOS Applications

DOS COMMAND.COM

RANGE OF DOS

Expanded Memory (EMS)

EMS memory is bank switched into the UMA through a reserved area called the page frame.

extender

See *bus extender*.

extensible

Capable of being expanded or customized. For example, with extensible programming languages, programmers can add new control structures, statements or data types.

Extensible Markup Language

See XML.

extension

A DOS, Windows and OS/2 file category. Extensions are file types, or file categories, that are added to the end of DOS, Windows 95/98 and OS/2 file names. The extension is separated from the file name with a dot such as LETTER.DOC.

An extension can have up to three letters or digits. Executable files use .EXE, .COM and .BAT extensions; for example, NOTEPAD.EXE is the text editor that comes with Windows. Following is a list of most file extensions. See *graphics formats*. See also *Macintosh extension*.

3DS	3D Studio		CLP	Windows clipboard
906	Calcomp plotter		CLS	Visual Basic class module
			CMF	Corel metafile
ABC	This program's master index		CMP	JPEG bitmap, LEAD bitmap
ABK	CorelDRAW auto backup		CMX	Corel clip art
ACL	CorelDRAW keyboard accelerator		CMV	Corel Presentation Exchange
AD	After Dark image		CNT	Windows help contents
ADM	After Dark MultiModule		COM	Executable program
ADR	After Dark Randomizer		CPD	Fax cover document
AFM	Adobe font metrics (Type 1)		CPE	Fax cover document
AG4	Access G4 document imaging		CPI	DOS code page
AI	Adobe Illustrator graphics,		CPL	Windows control panel applets
	Encapsulated PostScript header			Corel color palette
AIF	Digital audio (Macintosh)		CPP	C++ source code
ALB	JASC Image Commander		CPR	Knowledge Access bitmap
ANI	Animated cursor			Corel Presents presentation
ANN	Windows help annotations		CPT	Corel Photopaint image
ANS	ANSI text		CPX	Corel Presentation Exchange
ARC	ARC, ARC+ compressed archive		CRD	Cardfile file
ARJ	Compressed archive (Jung)		CRP	Corel Presents runtime presentation
ART	Xara Studio drawing		CSC	Corel script
ASC	ASCII file		CSV	Comma delimited
ASD	Word temporary document		CT	Scitex CT bitmap
ASM	Assembly source code		CUR	Cursor
ASP	Active Server Page		CUT	Dr. Halo bitmap
ATT	AT&T Group IV fax		CV5	Canvas 5 vector/bitmap
AU	Digital audio (Sun)			
AVI	Microsoft movie format		DAT	Data
				WordPerfect merge data
BAK	Backup		DB	Paradox table
BAS	BASIC source code		DBF	dBASE database
BAT	DOS, OS/2 batch file		DBT	dBASE text
BFC	Windows briefcase document		DBX	DATABEAM bitmap
BIN	Driver, overlay		DCA	IBM text
BM1	Apogee BioMenace file		DCS	Color separated EPS format
BML	Bookmark library (SyncURL)		DCX	Fax image
BMP	Windows & OS/2 bitmap		DCT	Dictionary
BMK	Windows help bookmarks		DEF	Definition
BS1	Apogee Blake Stone file		DG	Autotrol vector graphics
			DGN	Intergraph vector graphics
C	C source code		DID	Windows DIB bitmap
CAB	Microsoft distribution format		DIC	Dictionary
CAL	Windows calendar,		DIF	Spreadsheet
	SuperCalc spreadsheet,		DLG	Dialogue script
	CALS raster and vector formats		DLL	Dynamic link library
CAP	Ventura Pub. captions		DOC	Document (Word and others)
CAL	CALS raster and vector formats		DOT	Word template
CCB	Visual Basic animated button		DOX	MultiMate V4.0 document
CCH	Corel Chart		DPI	Pointline bitmap
CDA	CD audio track		DRV	Driver
CDR	CorelDRAW vector graphics		DRW	Designer vector graphics (Ver. 3.x)
CDT	CorelDRAW template		DS4	Designer vector graphics (Ver. 4.x)
CDX	CorelDRAW compressed drawing		DSF	Designer vector graphics (Ver. 6.x)
	FoxPro and Clipper index		DWG	AutoCAD vector format
CFG	Configuration		DX	Autotrol document imaging
CGM	CGM vector graphics		DXF	AutoCAD vector format
CH3	Harvard Graphics chart			
CHP	Ventura Pub. chapter		ED5	EDMICS bitmap (DOD)
CHK	DOS Chkdsk chained file		EMF	Enhanced Windows metafile
CIF	Ventura Pub. chapter info.		EPS	Encapsulated PostScript
CIT	Intergraph scanned image		ESI	Esri plot file (vector)
CK?	iD/Apogee Commander Keen ?		EVY	Envoy document
COB	COBOL source code,		EXE	Executable program
	Truespace 3-D file			

FAX	Various fax formats		IFF	Amiga bitmap
FDX	Force index		IGF	Inset Systems (Hijaak)
FH3	Freehand 3			raster & vector graphics
FLC	Autodesk animation		IL	Icon library (hDC Computer)
FLD	Hijaak thumbnail folder		IMG	GEM Paint bitmap
FLI	Autodesk animation		INF	Setup information
FLT	Graphics conversion filter		INI	Initialization
FMT	dBASE Screen format			
FMV	FrameMaker raster & vector		JFF	JPEG bitmap
FNT	Windows font		JIF	JPEG bitmap
FOG	Fontographer font		JPG	JPEG bitmap
FON	Windows bitmapped font,		JT	JT Fax
	Telephone file		JTF	JPEG bitmap
FOR	FORTRAN source code			
FOT	Windows TrueType font info.		KDC	Kodak Photo bitmap
FOX	FoxBase compiled program		KFX	Kofax Group IV fax
FM3	Format info for 1-2-3 Version 3		KYE	Kye game program data
FP1	Flying Pigs for Windows data			
FRM	dBASE report layout		LBL	dBASE label
FTG	Windows help file links		LBM	Deluxe Paint graphics
FTS	Windows help text search index		LEG	Legacy text
			LIB	Function library
G4	GTX RasterCAD (raster into vector)		LOG	Log file
GAL	Corel Multimedia Manager album		LNK	Windows 9x/NT shortcut
GCA	IBM MO:DCA - GOCA vector graphics		LST	List
GDF	GDDM format		LZH	LHARC compressed
GED	Arts & Letters graphics		LZS	Skyroads program data
GEM	GEM vector graphics			
GFI	Genigraphics presentation link		M3D	Corel Motion 3-D
GFX	Genigraphics presentation link		MAC	MacPaint bitmap
GID	Windows help global index		MAK	Visual Basic/MS C++ project
GIF	CompuServe bitmap		MAP	Linkage editor map
GIM	Genigraphics presentation link		MB1	Apogee Moster Bash file
GIX	Genigraphics presentation link		MCS	MathCAD format
GNA	Genigraphics presentation link		MCW	Word for Macintosh document
GNX	Genigraphics presentation link		MDB	Access database
GP4	CALS Group IV - ITU Group IV		MET	OS/2 Metafile
GRA	Microsoft graph		MEU	Menu items
GRF	Micrografx Charisma vector		MDX	dBASE IV multi-index
GRP	Windows ProgMan Group		MID	MIDI sound file,
GWX	Genigraphics presentation link			Eudora script file
GWZ	Genigraphics presentation link		MIL	Same as GP4
GX1	Show Partner bitmap		MME	MIME-encoded file
GX2	Show Partner bitmap		MMF	Microsoft mail file
GZ	UNIX Gzip		MMM	Macromind animation format
			MOD	Eudora script file
H	C header		MOV	QuickTime for Windows movie
HED	HighEdit document		MPE	MPEG file
HGL	HP Graphics language		MPG	MPEG file
HLP	Help text		MPP	Microsoft Project
HPJ	Visual Basic help project		MRK	Informative Graphics markup file
HPP	C++ program header		MSG	Message file
HPL	HP Graphics language		MSP	Microsoft Paint bitmap
HQX	BinHex format		MUS	Music
HT	HyperTerminal		MVB	Microsoft Multimedia Viewer
HTM	HTML document (Web page)			
HYC	WordPerfect hypen list		NAP	NAPLPS format
			NAV	Eudora script file
ICA	IBM MO:DCA - IOCA bitmap		NDX	dBASE index
ICB	Targa bitmap		NG	Norton Guides text
ICO	Windows icon		NLM	NetWare NLM program
IDD	MIDI instrument definition		NTZ	InVircible antivirus blueprint
IDE	Development environment config.			
IDX	FoxBase index			

Computer Desktop Encyclopedia

OAZ	OAZ Fax	PRS	WordPerfect printer driver,
OBD	Microsoft Office binder	PRT	Formatted text
OBJ	Object module,	PS	PostScript page description
	Wavefront 3-D file	PSD	Photoshop native format
OBZ	Microsoft Office wizard	PSR	Powersoft report
OLB	OLE object library	PTx	PageMaker template (x=ver.)
OLE	OLE object	PUB	Microsoft Publisher publication,
ORG	Organizer file		Ventura Publisher publication
OVL	Overlay module	PUZ	Across puzzle
OVR	Overlay module	P10	Tektronix Plot10 plotter
OZM	Sharp Organizer memo bank		
OZP	Sharp Organizer telephone bank	QBW	QuickBooks
OUT	Encyclopedia definitions	QLB	Quick programming library
		QLC	ATM font info.
P10	Tektronic Plot 10	QT	QuickTime movie
PAL	Windows palette	QTM	QuickTime movie
PAS	Pascal source code		
PAT	CorelDRAW pattern	RA	Real Audio file
PBD	PowerBuilder dynamic library	RAM	Real Audio file
PBK	Microsoft Phonebook	RAS	Sun bitmap
PBM	Portable Bitmap	RAW	3-D file (open standard)
PCL	HP LaserJet series	RC	Resource script
PCD	Photo CD bitmap	REC	Recorder file
PCM	LaserJet cartridge info.	REG	Registration file
PCS	PICS animation	RES	Programming resource
PCT	PC Paint bitmap,	RFT	DCA/RFT document
	Macintosh PICT bitmap & vector	RGB	SGI bitmap
PCW	PC Write document	RIA	Alpharel Group IV bitmap
PCX	PC Paintbrush bitmap	RIB	Renderman graphics
PDF	Acrobat format, Printer	RIC	Roch FaxNet
	driver, QuarkXpress	RIX	RIX virtual screen
	printer description	RLC	CAD Overlay ESP (Image Systems)
PDV	PC Paintbrush printer driver	RLE	Compressed (run length encoded)
PDW	HiJaak vector graphics	RMI	MIDI music
PFA	Type 1 font (ASCII)	RND	AutoShade rendering format
PFB	Type 1 font (encrypted)	RNL	GTX Runlength bitmap
PFM	Windows Type 1 font metrics	RTF	Microsoft text/graphics
PGL	HPGL 7475A plotter	R8P	LaserJet portrait font
PIC	Various vector formats:	R8L	LaserJet landscape font
	Lotus 1-2-3,	RV	Real Video file
	Micrografx Draw,		
	Mac PICT format,	SAM	Ami Pro document
	IBM Storyboard bitmap	SAT	ACIS 3-D model
PIF	Windows info. for DOS programs,	SAV	Saved file
	IBM Picture Interchange	SBP	IBM Storyboard graphics
PIN	Epic Pinball data		Superbase text
PIX	Inset Systems bitmap & vector	SC	Paradox source code
PLT	AutoCAD plotter file	SC?	ColoRIX raster (?=res.)
	HPGL plotter file	SC2	Microsoft Schedule+ 7
PM	PageMaker graphics/text	SCD	Microsoft Schedule+ 7
PMx	PageMaker document (x=ver.)	SCH	Microsoft Schedule+ 1
PML	PageMaker library	SCM	ScreenCam movie
PNG	PNG bitmap	SCP	Dial-up Networking script
POV	POV-Ray ray tracing	SCR	dBASE screen layout,
PP4	Picture Publisher 4		Generic script,
PPD	PostScript printer description		Windows screen saver,
PPM	Portable Pixelmap		Fax image
PPT	Microsoft PowerPoint	SCT	Lotus Manuscript text capture
PRD	Microsoft Word printer driver		Scitex bitmap
PRE	Lotus Freelance	SDL	SmartDraw library
PRG	dBASE source code	SDR	SmartDraw vector graphics
PRN	XyWrite printer driver,	SDT	SmartDraw template
	Temporary print file	SET	Setup parameters
	Harvard Graphics	SFP	LaserJet portrait font

SFL	LaserJet landscape font		WP?	WordPerfect document (?=ver)
SFS	PCL 5 scalable font		WPG	WordPerfect raster & vector
SGI	SGI bitmap		WPM	WordPerfect macro
SHB	Corel Show		WPT	WordPerfect template
SHG	HotSpot bitmap		WQ?	Quattro Pro for DOS (?=ver)
SHW	Corel Show		WPS	Microsoft Works document
SLD	AutoCAD slide		WRI	Windows Write document
SLK	SYLK format (spreadsheets)		WRK	Symphony spreadsheet
SMI	SMIL multimedia		WRL	VRML page
SND	Digital audio		WS?	WordStar for Windows (?=ver)
SPD	Speedo scalable font		WSD	WordStar 2000 document
STY	Ventura Pub. style sheet		WVL	Wavelet compressed file
SUN	Sun bitmap			
SVX	Amiga sound file		XAR	Corel Xara drawing
SY3	Harvard Graphics symbol		XBM	X Window bitmap
SYL	SYLK format (spreadsheets)		XFX	JetFax
SYS	DOS, OS/2 driver		XLA	Excel add-in
			XLB	Excel toolbar
TAL	Adobe Type Align shaped text		XLC	Excel chart
TAR	Tape archive		XLD	Excel dialogue
TAZ	UNIX Gzip archive		XLK	Excel backup
TDF	Speedo typeface definition		XLM	Excel macro
TFM	Intellifont font metrics		XLS	Excel spreadsheet
TGA	TARGA bitmap		XLT	Excel template
TGZ	UNIX Gzip archive		XLW	Excel project
TIF	TIFF bitmap		XPM	X Window pixelmap
TLB	OLE type library		XWD	X Window dump
TMP	Temporary		XY?	XyWrite document (?=version)
TRM	Terminal file		XYW	XyWrite for Windows document
TTC	TrueType font compressed			
TTF	TrueType font		Z	UNIX Gzip archive
TXT	ASCII text		ZIP	PKZIP compressed
			ZOO	Zoo compressed
USP	LaserJet portrait font			
USL	LaserJet landscape font		$$$	Temporary
VBP	Visual Basic project			
VBX	Visual Basic custom control			
VDA	Targa bitmap			
VGR	Ventura Pub. chapter info.			
VOC	Sound Blaster sound			
VOX	Voxware compressed audio			
VP	Ventural Publisher publication			
VST	Targa bitmap			
VUE	dBASE relational view			
WAV	Digital audio (Windows)			
WB?	Quattro Pro spreadsheet (?=ver)			
WBK	Microsoft Word backup			
WBT	WinBatch file			
WCM	WordPerfect macro			
WDB	Microsoft works data file			
WGP	Wild Board games data			
WID	Font width table			
WIF	Wavelet image			
WIZ	Microsoft Word wizard			
WKQ	Quattro spreadsheet			
WK1	Lotus ver. 2.x			
WK3	Lotus ver. 3.x & Windows			
WK4	Lotus ver. 4.x			
WKS	Lotus 1-2-3 ver. 1a spreadsheet			
WMF	Windows Metafile			
WPD	Corel WordPerfect, Windows printer description			

Computer Desktop Encyclopedia

extent
Contiguous space on a disk reserved for a file or application.

exterior gateway protocol
See *EGP*.

external bus
A data pathway between the CPU and peripheral devices that are housed either inside or outside of the computer cabinet. External buses in a PC are the ISA, EISA and PCI buses. Contrast with *internal bus*.

external cache
Same as *L2 cache*. See *cache*.

external command
(1) In DOS and OS/2, a function performed by a separate utility program that accompanies the operating system. Contrast with *internal command*. See *DOS external command*.
(2) A user-developed HyperCard command. See *XCMD*.

External Data Representation
See *XDR*.

external function
A subroutine that is created separately from the main program. See *XFCN*.

external interrupt
An interrupt caused by an external source such as the computer operator, external sensor or monitoring device, or another computer.

external modem
A self-contained modem that is connected via cable to the serial port of a computer. It draws power from a wall outlet. The advantage of an external modem is that a series of status lights on the outside of the case display the changing states of the modem (off-hook, carrier detect, transmitting, etc.). In varying degrees, the communications program informs the user as well. However, having the indicators on the unit itself is very helpful if a problem occurs. Contrast with *internal modem*.

external reference
In programming, a call to a program or function that resides in a separate, independent library.

external sort
A sort program that uses disk or tape as temporary workspace. Contrast with *internal sort*.

external storage
Storage outside of the CPU, such as disk and tape.

EXTRA!
Terminal emulation software from Attachmate Corporation, Bellevue, WA. It is used with 3270 and 5250 emulators to gain access to a mainframe or mini from a personal computer. Versions for Windows and Mac are available.

extranet
A Web site for existing customers rather than the general public. It can provide access to paid research, current inventories and internal databases, virtually any information that is private and not published for everyone. An extranet uses the public Internet as its transmission system, but requires passwords to gain access.

extremely low frequency
See *low radiation*.

eye candy
Images and animated graphics added to Web sites and interactive software that makes the information exciting. In other words, glitz, sizzle and pizzazz.

EZ135

A 135MB removable hard drive from SyQuest. It was superseded by the 230MB EZFlyer. EZ135 was the first departure from SyQuest's original 3.5" format. See *EZFlyer disk* and *SyQuest disk*.

EZ drive

See *EZ135* and *EZFlyer disk*.

EZFlyer disk

A 230MB removable hard drive from SyQuest. This 3.5" drive supersedes the EZ135, which was the first of a new family of economical drives geared to the home market in 1995. EZFlyer drives support EZ135 cartridges, but are not compatible with SyQuest's original 3.5" format. See *SyQuest disk*. For a summary of all storage technologies, see *storage*.

e-zine

(Electronic magaZINE) A magazine or newsletter published online. See *Webzine*.

EZFlyer Cartridge
Although EZFlyer cartridges resemble SyQuest's original 3.5" format, they are keyed differently and will not fit in the wrong drive.

Computer Desktop Encyclopedia

F

f

See *farad* and *femto*.

F1 key

Function key number one. There are 12 function keys on a PC keyboard. F1 is used for retrieving help in Windows and in most DOS applications.

F2F

Digispeak for "face-to-face." For example, "let's meet and work it out F2F."

fab

A manufacturing plant that makes semiconductor devices. Be the first on your block to start making chips. All it takes is a couple of billion dollars to build a state-of-the-art facility.

fabless

(FABricationLESS) A semiconductor vendor that does not have inhouse manufacturing facilities. Although it designs and tests the chips, it relies on external foundries for their actual fabrication. See *foundry*.

fabric

See *switch fabric*.

FaceLift

A font scaler for Windows and WordPerfect from Bitstream Inc., Cambridge, MA, (www.bitstream.com), that provides on-the-fly font scaling for Bitstream's own Speedo fonts. FaceLift for Windows also supports Type 1 fonts. FaceLift for WordPerfect lets users create a wide variety of custom fonts, including outlines, shadows and fill scaling, for the DOS version of WordPerfect.

face recognition

The ability to recognize people by their facial characteristics. The most successful methods use neural networks that learn from their experience and can distinguish the same person with different appearances, such as with and without glasses, changing hair styles and seasonal skin color.

facilities management

The management of a user's computer installation by an outside organization. All operations including systems, programming and the datacenter can be performed by the facilities management organization on the user's premises.

facsimile

See *fax*.

factorial

The number of sequences that can exist with a set of items, derived by multiplying the number of items by the next lowest number until 1 is reached. For example, three items have six sequences (3x2x1=6): 123, 132, 231, 213, 312 and 321.

failover

Maintaining an up-to-date copy of a database on an alternate computer system for backup. The alternate system takes over if the primary system becomes unusable. See *replication*.

fail safe

Same as *fault tolerant*.

fail soft

The ability to fail with minimum destruction. For example, a disk drive can be built to automatically park the heads when power fails. Although it doesn't correct the problem, it minimizes destruction.

fallback/fall forward

Features in a modem that allow it to negotiate a lower or higher speed with the other modem as line conditions change.

fallback system
Any system of hardware and/or software maintained as a backup to the main system. If a failure occurs in the primary system, the fallback system takes over.

false drops
Search results that meet your search criteria but have nothing to do with the information you were trying to find. For example, you want biographical details about Grover Cleveland, but you get information about Cleveland, Ohio. See *full-text search*.

FAMOS
(Floating gate Avalanche-injection Metal Oxide Semiconductor) A type of EPROM.

fan
A device that uses motor-driven blades to circulate the air in a computer or other electronic system. Today's CPUs run extremely hot, and large computer cabinets use two and three fans to reduce temperature.

fan-fold paper
Same as *continuous forms*.

fan in
To direct multiple signals into one receiver.

fan out
To direct one signal into multiple receivers. See *port multiplier*.

FAQ
(Frequently Asked Questions) A group of commonly-asked questions about a subject along with the answers. Vendors may use them to augment the description of their products. FAQs are very popular on the Internet.

farad
A unit of electrical charge that is used to measure the storage capacity of a capacitor. In microelectronics, measurements are usually in microfarads or picofarads.

far pointer
In an Intel x86 segmented address, a memory address that includes both segment and offset. Contrast with *near pointer*.

Fast ATA
The higher transfer rates used by the EIDE (Enhanced IDE) hardware interface. See *EIDE* and *IDE*.

FastCAD
A full-featured CAD program for DOS from Evolution Computing, Tempe, AZ, (www.evcomp.com/evcomp), that is known for its well-designed user interface. It requires a math coprocessor. Users with less sophisticated requirements can start out with FastCAD's baby brother, EasyCAD.

Fast Ethernet
See *100BaseT*.

Fast Fourier Transform
See *FFT*.

Fast IP
An IP switching technique from 3Com. The originating machine sends the first packet to the router, which forwards it to its destination. The destination machine sends back a response using the sender's layer 2 address. If the sending machine receives the response, it knows there is a direct connection without going through the router and forwards the remaining packets via layer 2. Fast IP uses a modified version of the NHRP protocol.

fast page mode
See *page mode memory*.

Fast SCSI

A SCSI interface that transfers at 10 Mbytes/sec rather than 5 Mbytes/sec. The maximum cable length is 9.8 feet. See *SCSI*.

FAT

(File Allocation Table) The part of the DOS, Windows and OS/2 file system that keeps track of where data is stored on disk. When the disk is high-level formatted, the FAT is recorded twice and contains a table with an entry for each disk cluster.

The directory list, which contains file name, extension, date, etc., points to the FAT entry where the file starts. If a file is larger than one cluster, the first FAT entry points to the next FAT entry where the second cluster of the file is stored and so on to the end of the file. If a cluster becomes damaged, its FAT entry is marked as such and that cluster is not used again. The original 16-bit version of the FAT, which is widely used, is limited to 2GB hard drives. The 32-bit version (FAT32) became available with Windows 95 in late 1996 and increases the limit to 2TB. See *VFAT* and *FAT32*.

Cluster 0	Cluster 2	RESUME.DOC
Cluster 1	Cluster 4	BUDGET.XLS
Cluster 2	Cluster 3	
Cluster 3	Cluster 7	
Cluster 4	Cluster 8	
Cluster 5	Damaged	
Cluster 6	Damaged	
Cluster 7	End	
Cluster 8	Cluster 9	
Cluster 9	End	

The FAT Table

The file RESUME.DOC is stored in clusters 0, 2, 3 and 7. The directory entry points to cluster 0 where the file begins. The entry for cluster 0 points to cluster 2 and so on. BUDGET.XLS is stored in clusters 1, 4, 8 and 9.

FAT16

Refers to the original FAT after FAT32 was introduced. See *FAT* and *FAT32*.

FAT32

The 32-bit version of the file allocation table (FAT) that was added to Windows 95 starting with OEM Service Release 2 (OSR2) in 1996. This version is only installed by PC vendors. FAT32 supports hard disks up to 2TB instead of 2GB. It is able to relocate the root directory on the disk and use the backup copy of the FAT table, providing more safeguards in the event of disk failure. It also reduces cluster waste. On drives up to 8GB, cluster size was reduced from 32K to 4K. See *cluster*.

fatal error

A condition that halts processing due to faulty hardware, program bugs, read errors or other anomalies. If you get a fatal error, you usually cannot recover from it. The computer typically locks up, and all data that you have changed that has not yet been saved to disk is lost.

There is no rule of thumb with fatal errors. You may never get one again, or it may manifest until you fix the problem. If you get a fatal error after just adding a new peripheral or installing a new software package, remove or uninstall it and try again.

fat binary

A Macintosh executable program that contains machine language in one file for both the Macintosh and PowerMac machines (680x0 and PowerPC CPUs). Software distributed in this format will run native on whichever Mac architecture it is loaded on.

fat client

A client machine in a client/server environment that performs most or all of the application processing with little or none performed in the server. Contrast with *thin client* and *fat server*. See *two-tier client/server*.

A Fat Client

father file

See *grandfather-father-son*.

fat pipe

A high-speed communications channel. Contrast with *thin pipe*.

fat server

A server in a client/server environment that performs most or all of the application processing with little or none performed in the client. The counterpart to a fat server is a thin client. Contrast with *fat client*. See *two-tier client/server*.

fault resilient

See *high availability*.

fault tolerant

The ability to continue non stop when a hardware failure occurs. A fault tolerant system is designed from the ground up for reliability by building multiples of all critical components, such as CPUs, memories, disks and power supplies into the same computer. In the event one component fails, another takes over without skipping a beat.

Many systems are designed to recover from a failure by detecting the failed component and switching to another computer system. These systems, although sometimes called fault tolerant, are more widely known as *high availability* systems, requiring that the software resubmits the job when the second system is available.

True fault tolerant systems are the most costly, because redundant hardware is wasted if there is no failure in the system. On the other hand, fault tolerant systems provide the same processing capacity after a failure as before, whereas high availability systems often provide reduced capacity.

Tandem and Stratus are the two major manufacturers of fault-tolerant computer systems for the transaction processing (OLTP) market. Stratus computers are used by long distance carriers for 800 routing and other out-of-band services.

fax

(**FACS**imile) Originally called telecopying, it is the communication of a printed page between remote locations. Fax machines scan a paper form and transmit a coded image over the telephone system. The receiving machine prints a facsimile of the original. A fax machine is made up of a scanner, printer and modem with fax signalling.

Fax standards were developed starting in 1968 and are classified by Groups. Groups 1 and 2, used until the late 1980s, transmitted a page in six and three minutes respectively. Group 3 transmits at less than one minute per page and uses data compression at 9,600 bps. The Group 3 speed increase led to the extraordinary rise in usage in the late 1980s. Group 3 resolution is 203x98 dpi in standard mode, 203x196 in fine mode and 203x392 in super fine mode.

Group 3 is still the standard today, but Group 4 machines can transmit a page in just a few seconds and provide up to 400x400 resolution. Group 4 requires 56 to 64 Kbps bandwidth and needs ISDN or Switched 56 circuits. See *fax/modem* and *e-mail*.

fax board

Fax capability built onto a printed circuit board. Today, most fax boards are fax/modems, which also provide data transmission. See *fax/modem*.

fax logging

Automatically storing copies of incoming and outgoing faxes onto some storage medium.

fax/modem

A combination fax board and data modem available as an external unit that plugs into the serial port of the computer or as an expansion board for internal installation. It includes a switch that routes the call to the fax or data modem. Incoming faxes are printed on the computer's printer. Most all modems today are fax/modems.

A fax/modem requires software that generates the fax transmission from typed-in text, a disk file or from a screen image. Fax/modems often transmit a sharper image than a fax machine, which obtains its source material by scanning the page.

Group 3 fax/modems provide various levels of processing based upon their service class. Class 1 devices perform basic handshaking and data conversion and are the most flexible, because much of the work is done by the computer's CPU. Class 2 devices establish and end the call and perform error checking. There are a variety of de facto Class 2 implementations and one Class 2.0 standard. As PCs have become more powerful, future service classes with more features are unlikely.

fax server

A computer in a network that provides a bank of fax/modems, allowing users to fax out and remote users to fax in over the next available modem. The fax server may be a dedicated machine or implemented on a file server that is providing other services.

fax switch

A device that tests a phone line for a fax signal and routes the call to the fax machine. When a fax machine dials a number and the line answers, it emits an 1,100Hz tone to identify itself. Some devices handle voice, fax and data modem switching and may require keying in an extension number to switch to the modem.

FC

See *Fibre Channel*.

FC-AL

(Fibre Channel-Arbitrated Loop) A topology for Fibre Channel in which all devices are linked together in a loop. Fibre Channel is also used point-to-point or in a switched fabric. See *Fibre Channel*.

FCB

(File Control Block) A method of handling files in DOS 1.0. Older applications that remain compatible with DOS 1.0 may use this method.

FCC

(Federal Communications Commission, Washington, DC, www.fcc.gov) The U.S. government agency that regulates interstate and international communications including wire, cable, radio, TV and satellite. The FCC was created under the U.S. Communications Act of 1934, and its board of commissioners is appointed by the president of the United States.

FCC Class

An FCC certification of radiation limits on digital devices. Class A certification is for business use. Class B, for residential use, is more stringent in order to avoid interference with TV and other home reception. See Part 15, Subpart B, of the Federal Register (CFR 47, Parts 0-19).

FCFS

First come, first served.

fci

(Flux Changes per Inch) The measurement of polarity reversals on a magnetic surface. In MFM, each flux change is equal to one bit. In RLL, a flux change generates more than one bit.

FCIF

See *CIF*.

F connector

A two-wire (signal and ground) coaxial cable connector used to connect antennas, TVs and VCRs. F connector cables typically carry NTSC TV signals (audio and video). The plug's shell and socket are threaded. See *RCA connector* for illustration.

FD

(Floppy Disk) For example, FD/HD refers to a floppy disk/hard disk device.

FDD

Abbreviation for floppy disk drive.

FDDI

(Fiber Distributed Data Interface) An ANSI standard token passing network that uses optical fiber cabling and transmits at 100 Mbits/sec up to two kilometers. FDDI provides network services at the same level as Ethernet and Token Ring (OSI layers 1 and 2).

FDDI is used for MANs and LANs and includes its own Station Management (STM) network management standard. The TP-PMD (CDDI) version runs over copper (UTP), although typically limited to distances up to 100 meters.

FDDI provides an optional dual counter-rotating ring topology that contains primary and secondary rings with data flowing in opposite directions. If the line breaks, the ends of the primary and secondary rings are bridged together at the closest node to create a single ring again.

SAS or DAS

Stations can be configured as Single Attached Stations (SAS) connected to concentrators, or as Dual Attached Stations (DAS), connected to both rings. Groups of stations are typically wired to concentrators connected in a hierarchical tree to the main ring. Large networks may be configured as a "dual ring of trees," in which the dual ring provides the backbone to which multiple hierarchies of concentrators are attached.

FDDI II adds circuit-switched service to this normally packet-switched technology in order to support isochronous traffic such as realtime voice and video.

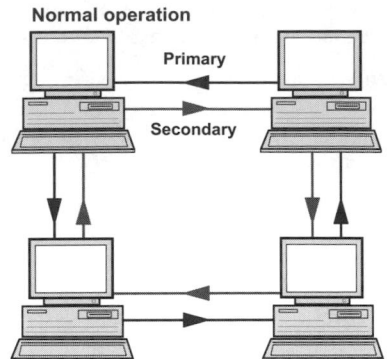

Normal operation

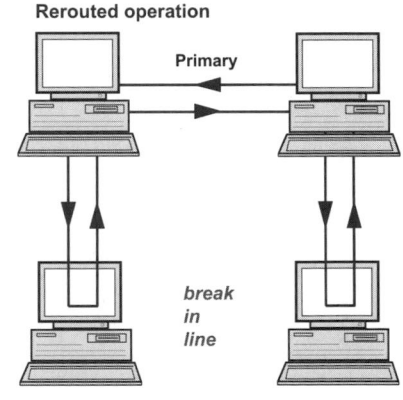

Rerouted operation

FDISK

A DOS and Windows utility that is used to partition a hard disk, which is necessary before high-level formatting.

FDM

(Frequency Division Multiplexing) A technology that transmits multiple signals simultaneously over a single transmission path, such as a cable or wireless system. Each signal travels within its own unique frequency range (carrier), which is modulated by the data (text, voice, video, etc.). Television uses FDM and transmits several TV channels from the same antenna. The TV tuner locks onto a particular frequency (channel) and filters out the video signal. Contrast with *TDM*. See also *WDM*.

FDMA

(Frequency Division Multiple Access) The technology used in the analog cellular telephone network that divides the spectrum into 30KHz channels. See *TDMA, CDMA* and *CDPD*.

FD:OCA

(Formatted Data:Object Content Architecture) An SAA-compliant (CCS) specification for formatting data in fields.

FDSE

(Full-Duplex Switched Ethernet) See *full-duplex Ethernet*.

FDX

See *full-duplex*.

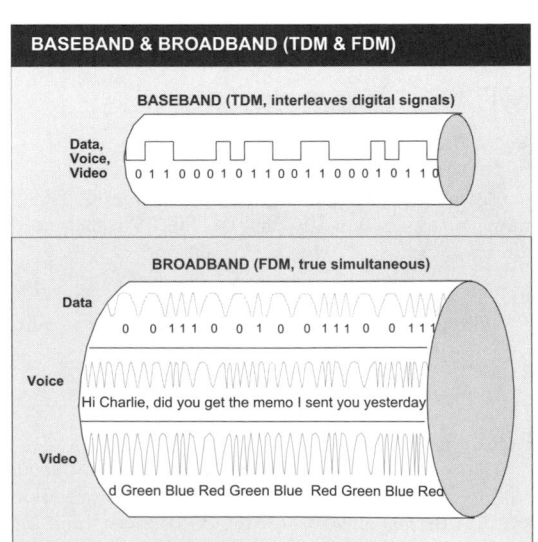

FEA

(Finite Element Analysis) A mathematical technique for analyzing stress, which breaks down a physical structure into substructures, called finite elements. The finite elements and their interrelationships are converted into equation form and solved mathematically.

Graphics-based FEA software can display the model on screen as it is being built and, after analysis, display the object's reactions under load conditions. Models created in popular CAD packages can often be accepted by FEA software.

feasibility study

The analysis of a problem to determine if it can be solved effectively. The operational (will it work?), economical (costs and benefits) and technical (can it be built?) aspects are part of the study. Results of the study determine whether the solution should be implemented.

feature connector

See *VGA feature connector*.

feature negotiation

See *automatic feature negotiation*.

FEC

See *forward error correction*.

FECN

(Forward Explicit Congestion Notification) A frame relay message that notifies the receiving device that there is a congestion problem.

FED

(Field Emission Display) A flat panel display that provides an image quality equal to or better than a CRT. FED displays provide wide viewing angles and can survive in very harsh temperature environments. Their ultra-fast switching speeds also enables them to support full-motion video.

FEDs are like a thin CRT, using a vacuum-filled chamber and phosphor-coated glass. However, instead of illuminating phosphors with three "guns" that scan the entire screen, FEDs use hundreds of millions of stationary cone-shaped emitters, with some 1600 of them per pixel. Some FED designs use low voltage emission and high current while others use high voltage and low current, which is more like a standard CRT.

Although the FED concept was invented in the 1970s, it took more than 20 years to realize it. With more than 300 patents on the technology, PixTech is the pioneer in this with 5" monochrome displays in production in 1998 and 8" mono and color units in 1999. Larger sizes are expected in the future.

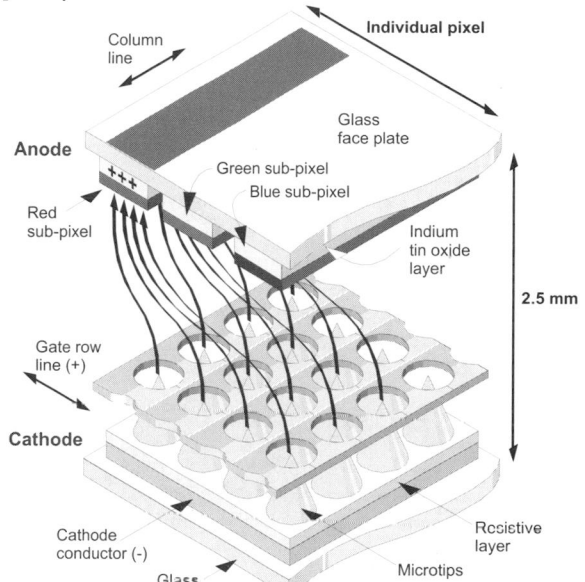

The FED Technology

This illustration, which is somewhat conceptual, shows how the energy flows from the microtips to the phosphors (anode). Electrons from the negatively-charged (-) cone column are emitted when the gate row is positively charged (+). The electrons then flow to the phosphors that are momentarily given a larger positive charge (+++), which, in this diagram, are the red ones. The pixels are addressed 180 times per second, providing a very high refresh rate. *(Redrawn from illustration courtesy of PixTech.)*

feeware

Commercial software that is sold. Contrast with *freeware*.

female connector

A plug or socket that contains receptacles. The male counterpart contains pins.

femto

Quadrillionth (10^{-15}). See *space/time*.

femtosecond

One quadrillionth of a second. See *space/time* and *ohnosecond*.

FEP

See *front end processor*.

ferric oxide

(Fe_2O_3) An oxidation of iron used in the coating of magnetic disks and tapes.

ferromagnetic

The capability of a material, such as iron and nickel, to be highly magnetized. See *FRAM*.

ferromagnetic RAM

See *FRAM*.

FET

(Field Effect Transistor) The type of transistor used in CMOS and other types of MOS circuits. The transistor works by pulsing a line called the *gate*, which allows current to flow from the *source* to the *drain*, or vice versa depending on the design.

fetch

To locate the next instruction in memory for execution by the CPU.

FF

See *form feed*.

FFS

(Flash File System) See *flash memory*.

FFT

(Fast Fourier Transform) A class of algorithms used in digital signal processing that break down complex signals into elementary components.

fiber bundle

(1) A set of adjacent optical fibers running in parallel and adhered together. It is used for transmitting light to brighten an area as well as transmitting whole images, but not for digital communications.

(2) A collection of optical fibers.

Fiber Channel

See *Fibre Channel*.

Fiber Distributed Data Interface

See *FDDI*.

fiber loss

The amount of attenuation of signal in an optical fiber transmission.

fiber optic

Communications systems that use optical fibers for transmission. Fiber-optic transmission became widely used in the 1980s when the long-distance carriers created nationwide systems for carrying voice conversations digitally over optical fibers.

Eventually, all transmission systems may become fiber optic-based. Also, in time, the internals of computers may be partially or even fully made of light circuits rather than electrical circuits. See *FDDI, Fibre Channel* and *optical fiber*.

Fiber-optic Connectors

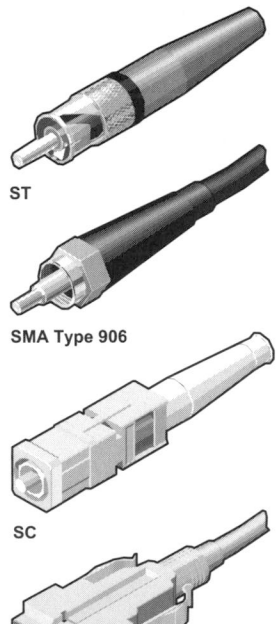

ST

SMA Type 906

SC

MIC

ST is widely used in the U.S. and SMA is used in Europe.

SC is used for Fibre Channel, cable splices and other network transmissions, while MIC is the FDDI standard connector.

fiber-optic connectors

There are several types of connectors used to connect pairs of optical fibers. The most popular are the ST and SMA connectors. The ST connector uses a bayonet mount, and the SMA connector uses a threaded mount. ST is popular in the U.S., and SMA is popular in Europe.

The MIC connector is the FDDI standard, and the SC connector is used in Fibre Channel and various other network applications.

Attaching a fiber-optic connector to an optical fiber is a bit of an art. The end has to be cut in a special way and carefully polished in order to let the maximum light pass through. Most class time on the subject is "hands on." See illustration on opposite page.

Fibonacci numbers

A series of whole numbers in which each number is the sum of the two preceding ones: 1, 1, 2, 3, 5, 8, 13, etc. It is used to speed up binary searches by dividing the search into the two lower numbers; for example, 13 items would be divided into 5 and 8 items; 8 items would be divided into 5 and 3.

Fibre Channel

A high-speed transmission technology that can be used as a front-end communications network, a back-end storage network, or both at the same time. Fibre Channel is a driving force in the storage area network (SAN) arena for connecting multiple hosts to dedicated storage systems. With Fibre Channel, the hosts can not only talk to the storage system via SCSI, but the hosts can talk to each other via IP over the same network. Fibre Channel supports existing peripheral interfaces and communications protocols, including SCSI, IPI, HiPPI, IP and ATM. Its name is somewhat misleading as Fibre Channel not only supports singlemode and multimode fiber connections, but coaxial cable and twisted pair as well.

Fibre Channel can be configured point-to-point, in an arbitrated loop (FC-AL) or via a switched topology. It supports data rates of of 12.5, 25, 50 and 100 Mbytes/sec in each direction and uses the same FC-0 physical layer as Gigabit Ethernet. The actual bit rate is greater, because there is framing and encoding overhead (IBM's 8B/10B encoding method adds two bits to every byte).

Fibre Channel provides both connection-oriented and connectionless modes. Class 1 Fibre Channel provides a dedicated connection, and Class 4 provides virtual connections. Classes 2 and 3 are connectionless. Following are the functional levels of the Fibre Channel architecture.

Node levels
FC-4 Translation between Fibre Channel and command sets that use it: HiPPI, SCSI, IPI, IP, ATM, etc.
FC-3 Common services across multiple ports.

Port levels (FC-PH standard)
FC-2 Signaling and framing.
FC-1 Transmission (8B/10B encoding, error detection).
FC-0 Electrical and optical characteristics.

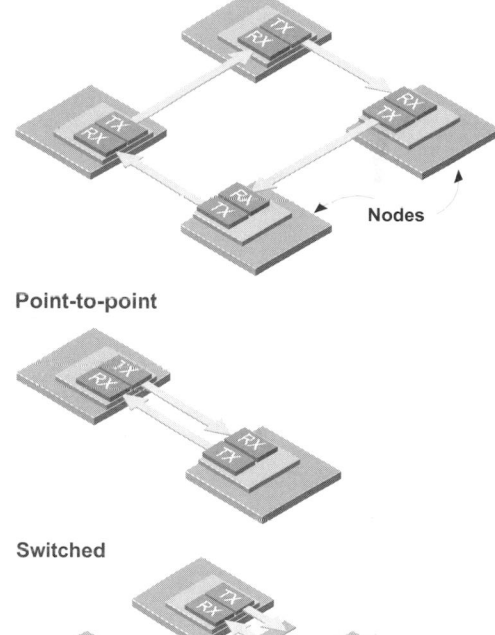

Fibre Channel Topologies
Fibre Channel can fit into the network structure best suited for the application. Each port uses a pair of fibers for two-way communications. The transmitter (TX) is connected to a receiver (RX) on the opposite end. A node can be a computer or a storage system.

fiche

Same as *microfiche*.

FICON

(FIber CONnector) An IBM mainframe channel introduced with its G5 servers in 1998. Based on the Fibre Channel standard, it boosts the transfer rate of ESCON's half-duplex 17MB/sec to a full-duplex 100MB/sec. Each FICON channel can support up to 4,000 I/O operations per second and is equivalent to eight ESCON channels. See *ESCON* and *Parallel Enterprise Server*.

FidoNet

An e-mail system developed in 1984 by Tom Jennings, creator of the Fido BBS. It was the first popular method of providing e-mail and file transfer across multiple BBSs. FidoNet, as well as all BBS use, has declined dramatically in the U.S., but FidoNet has also grown in other countries. Today, there are more than 25,000 FidoNet nodes in use around the world, many of which are used to provide an e-mail connection to the Internet.

field

A physical unit of data that is one or more bytes in size. A collection of fields make up a record. A field also defines a unit of data on a source document, screen or report. Examples of fields are NAME, ADDRESS, QUANTITY and AMOUNT DUE.

The field is the common denominator between the user and the computer. When you interactively query and update your database, you reference your data by field name.

There are several terms that refer to the same unit of storage as a field. A *data element* is the logical definition of the field, and a *data item* is the actual data stored in the field. For each data element, there are many fields in the database that hold the data items. See *data element* for illustration.

field engineer

A person who is responsible for hardware installation, maintentance and repair. Formal training is in electronics, although many people have learned on the job.

field name

An assigned name for a field (NAME, ADDRESS, CITY, STATE, etc.) that will be the same in every record.

field separator

A character used to mark the separation of fields in a record. See *comma delimited* and *tab delimited*.

field service

See *field engineer*.

field squeeze

In a mail merge, a function that eliminates extra blank spaces between words when fixed-length fields are inserted into the document text. See *line squeeze*.

field template

See *picture*.

Fiery engine

A raster image processor (RIP) from Electronics for Imaging, Inc., San Mateo, CA, (www.efi.com), that is noted for its high quality color processing and speed. Since 1991, the Fiery Color Server, which is a combination of hardware and software, has been used to transform digital color copiers into color printers. Toward the end of the 1990s, the Fiery components were added to lower-cost color devices such as laser printers and wide format ink jet printers.

FIF

(Fractal Image Format) A graphics file format from Iterated Systems, Inc., Norcross, GA, that stores fractal images with compression ratios as high as 2,500:1.

FIFO

(First In-First Out) A storage method that retrieves the item stored for the longest time. Contrast with *LIFO*.

Computer Desktop Encyclopedia

fifth-generation computer

A computer designed for AI applications. Appearing after the turn of the century, these systems will represent the next technology leap.

FIGS

(1) (French, Italian, German, Spanish) The major European languages. This acronym is commonly found in localization circles. See *localization*.

(2) (figs.) Abbreviation of figures; for example, "this process is explained in figs. 3 and 4.

file

A collection of bytes stored as an individual entity. All data on disk is stored as a file with an assigned file name that is unique within the directory it resides in.

To the computer, a file is nothing more than a string of bytes. The structure of a file is known to the software that manipulates it. For example, database files are made up of a series of records. Word processing files contain a continuous flow of text.

Following are the major file types. Except for ASCII text files, most files contain proprietary information contained in a header or interspersed throughout the file.

Type	Contents
data file (table)	data records
document	text
spreadsheet	rows and columns of cells
image	rows and columns of bits
drawing	list of vectors
audio	digitized sound waves
MIDI	MIDI instructions
video	digital video frames
Web page	text
batch file	text
source program	text
executable program	machine language

file and record locking

A first-come, first-served technique for managing data in a multiuser environment. The first user to access the file or record prevents, or locks out, other users from accessing it. After the file or record is updated, it is unlocked and available.

file association

(1) The relationship between the file and the application that created it. In Windows, the association is made by the file extension, which are the last letters of the name preceded by a period, such as .DOC, .GIF and so forth. When a document is double clicked, the extension identifies which application should be launched to open it.

(2) The relationship of one file to another based on the data it contains.

file attribute

A file access classification that allows a file to be retrieved or erased. Typical attributes are read/write, read only, archive and hidden.

file compression

See *data compression*.

file conversion

See *conversion*.

file extension

See *extension*.

file extent

See *extent*.

file find
A utility that searches all directories for matching file names. See *how to find a file.*

file format
The structure of a file. There are hundreds of proprietary formats for database, word processing and graphics files. See *native format, foreign format, graphics formats* and *record layout.*

file grooming
Cleaning up the files on a computer system. It includes deleting temporary and backup files as well as defragmenting the disk.

file handle
A temporary reference assigned by the operating system to a file that has been opened. The handle is used to access the file throughout the session.

file layout
Same as *record layout.*

file maintenance
(1) The periodic updating of master files. For example, adding/deleting employees and customers, making address changes and changing product prices. It does not refer to daily transaction processing and batch processing (order processing, billing, etc.).

(2) The periodic reorganization of the disk drives. Data that is continuously updated becomes physically fragmented over the disk space and requires regrouping. An optimizing program is run (daily, weekly, etc.) that rewrites all files contiguously.

FileMaker
(1) A database management system (DBMS) for the Macintosh and Windows NT from FileMaker. Originally a file manager from Claris Corporation, it has been a popular program for general data management. It provides a variety of statistical functions, fast search capabilities and extensive reporting features.

(2) (FileMaker, Inc., Santa Clara, CA, www.filemaker.com) A software subsidiary of Apple. Originally Claris Corporation, FileMaker was formed in 1998, retaining the FileMaker Pro line of database software and Claris Home Page for Web development.

FileMan
(1) Public-domain MUMPS software that provides a stand-alone, interactive DBMS as well as a set of utilities for the MUMPS programmer.

(2) Nickname for Windows' file manager, which is precisely named "File Manager."

file manager
(1) Software used to manage files on a disk. It provides functions to delete, copy, move, rename and view files as well as create and manage directories. The file managers in Windows 3.x and Windows 95/98 are File Manager and Explorer.

(2) Software that manages data files. Often erroneously called database managers, file managers provide the ability to create, enter, change, query and produce reports on one file at a time. They have no relational capabilty and usually don't include a programming language.

file name
A name assigned by the user or programmer that is used to identify a file.

FileNet
A document imaging system from FileNet Corporation, Costa Mesa, CA, (www.filenet.com). Introduced in 1985, FileNet is the most widely-used high-end workflow system. It runs on PCs and a variety of UNIX workstations.

File Not Found
A DOS error message that means DOS cannot locate the file you have specified. Use the Dir command to check its spelling. It may be also be in another directory.

Computer Desktop Encyclopedia

file protection

Preventing accidental erasing of data. Physical file protection is provided on the storage medium by turning a switch, moving a lever or covering a notch. Writing is prohibited even if the software directs the computer to do so. For example, on half-inch tape, a plastic ring in the center of the reel is removed (no ring-no write).

Logical file protection is provided by the operating system which can designate files as read only. This allows both regular (read/write) and read only files to be stored on the same disk volume. Files can also be designated as hidden files, which makes them invisible to most software programs.

file protect ring

A plastic ring inserted into a reel of magnetic tape for file protection.

file recovery program

Software that recovers disk files that have been accidentally deleted or damaged.

If You're Holey, You're Protected!
On a 3.5" diskette, your data is protected when both holes are showing.

file server

A high-speed computer in a network that stores the programs and data files shared by users. It acts like a remote disk drive. The difference between a file server and an application server is that the file server stores the programs and data, while the application server runs the programs and processes the data. See *database server*.

file sharing protocol

A communications protocol that provides a structure for file requests (open, read, write, close, etc.) between stations in a network. If file sharing is strictly between workstation and server, it is also called a *client/server protocol*. It refers to layer 7 of the OSI model.

file size

The length of a file in bytes. See "Byte Specifications" in the term *byte*.

file spec

(file **SPEC**ification) A reference to the location of a file on a disk, which includes disk drive, directory name and file name. For example, in DOS, Windows and OS/2, **c:\wordstar\books\chapter** is a file spec for the file CHAPTER in the BOOKS subdirectory in the WORDSTAR directory on drive C.

file system

(1) A method for cataloging files in a computer system. HPS, FAT, FAT32, NTFS and HPFS are common file systems used on personal computers. See *hierarchical file system*.

(2) A data processing application that manages individual files. Files are related by customized programming. Contrast with *relational database*.

file transfer program

A program that transmits files from one computer to another such as Travelling Software's LapLink or the Direct Cable Connection utility that comes with Windows 95/98. The computers can be cabled together via the serial or parallel ports or be in different locations. See *FTP, null modem cable* and *how to transfer a file*.

file transfer protocol

A communications protocol used to transmit files without loss of data. A file transfer protocol can handle all types of files including binary files and ASCII text files. Common examples are Xmodem, Ymodem, Zmodem and Kermit. See *FTP*.

file viewer

Software that displays the contents of a file as it would be normally displayed by the application that created it. A single file viewer program is generally capable of displaying a wide variety of document, database and spreadsheet formats. Examples of file viewers for Windows are Symantec's Norton File Viewer, Phoenix Technologies' Eclipse Find and Systems Compatibility's Outside In. See *document exchange software*.

fill

(1) In a graphics program, to apply color to a graphics objects such as a rectangle, circle or polygon. In a paint program, the fill function is depicted as a paint bucket icon. It is used to "paint" objects or the entire canvas.

(2) In a spreadsheet, to enter common or repetitive values into a group of cells.

fill pattern

(1) A color, shade or pattern used to fill an area of an image.

(2) Signals transmitted by a LAN station when not receiving or transmitting data in order to maintain synchronization.

fill scaling

The ability to change a fill pattern from light to dense. For example, if polka dots were used, the fill pattern could range from thick dots widely separated to very thin dots tightly packed together.

film recorder

A device that takes a 35mm slide picture from a graphics file, which has been created in a CAD, paint or business graphics package. It generates very high resolution, generally from 2,000 to 4,000 lines.

It typically works by recreating the image on a built-in CRT that shines through a color wheel onto the film in a standard 35mm camera. Some units provide optional Polaroid camera backs for instant previewing. Film recorders can be connected to personal computers by plugging in a controller board cabled to the recorder.

filter

(1) A process that changes data, such as a sort routine that changes the sequence of items or a conversion routine (import or export filter) that changes one data, text or graphics format into another. See also *image filter*.

(2) A pattern or mask through which only selected data is passed. For example, certain e-mail systems can be programmed to filter out important messages and alert the user. In dBASE, **set filter to file overdue**, compares all data to the matching conditions stored in OVERDUE.

financial planning language

A language used to create data models and command a financial planning system.

financial planning system

Software that helps the user evaluate alternatives. It allows for the creation of a data model, which is a series of data elements in equation form; for example, **gross profit = gross sales - cost of goods sold**. Different values can be plugged into the elements, and the impact of various options can be assessed (what if?).

A financial planning system is a step above a spreadsheet by providing additional analysis tools; however, increasingly, these capabilities are being built into spreadsheets. For example, sensitivity analysis assigns a range of values to a data element, which causes that data to be highlighted if it ever exceeds that range.

Goal seeking provides automatic calculation. For example, by entering **gross margin = 50%** as well as the minimums and maximums of the various inputs, the program will calculate an optimum mix of inputs to achieve the goal (output).

financial software

A broad category of software that deals with accounting and monetary transactions. It includes payroll, accounts receivables and payables, general ledger, spreadsheets, financial planning, check writing and portfolio management.

Finder

The part of early Macintosh operating systems that keeps track of icons, controls the Clipboard and

Computer Desktop Encyclopedia

Scrapbook and allows files to be copied. Finder manages one application at a time, while MultiFinder, its successor, manages multiple apps. MultiFinder is now an inherent part of the Mac OS.

find file
See *file find* and *how to find a file*.

finger
A UNIX command widely used on the Internet to find out information about a particular user, such as telephone number, whether currently logged on or the last time logged on. The person being "fingered" must have placed his or her profile on the system. Profiles can be very elaborate either as a method of social introduction or to state particular job responsibilities. Fingering requires entering the full **user@domain** address.

finger mouse
Same as *touchpad*.

fingerprint reader
A scanner used to identify a person's fingerprint for security purposes. After a sample is taken, access to a computer or other system is granted if the fingerprint matches the stored sample. A PIN may also be used with the fingerprint sample.

finite element
See *FEA*.

finite state machine
See *state machine*.

firewall
A method for keeping a network secure. It can be implemented in a single router that filters out unwanted packets, or it may use a combination of technologies in routers and hosts. Firewalls are widely used to give users access to the Internet in a secure fashion as well as to separate a company's public Web server from its internal network. They are also used to keep internal network segments secure. For example, a research or accounting subnet might be vulnerable to snooping from within.

Following are the types of techniques used individually or in combination to provide firewall protection.

Packet Filter
Blocks traffic based on IP address and/or port numbers. Also known as a "screening router."

Fingerprint Reader
Fingerprint readers such as this machine from Identix provide significantly more security than an ID and password. It is extremely difficult to fake a fingerprint. *(Photo courtesy of Identix, Inc.)*

Firewall Management
Elron Firewall, which runs under NT as well as its own proprietary OS, uses Elron's Stateful MultiLayer Inspection (SMLI) technology, which combines stateful inspection, multilayer analysis of IP and IPX packets and network address translation to secure a network. The window on the left can scroll down to more than 70 user services, including Telnet, Lotus Notes and CU-SeeMe. *(Screen example courtesy of Elron Software, www.elron.com.)*

Proxy Server

Serves as a relay between two networks, breaking the connection between the two. Also typically caches Web pages (see *proxy server*).

Network Address Translation (NAT)

Hides the IP addresses of client stations in an internal network by presenting one IP address to the outside world. Performs the translation back and forth.

Stateful Inspection

Tracks the transaction in order to verify that the destination of an inbound packet matches the source of a previous outbound request. Generally can examine multiple layers of the protocol stack, including the data, if required, so blocking can be made at any layer or depth.

FireWire

A high-speed serial bus developed by Apple and Texas Instruments that allows for the connection of up to 63 devices. Also known as the IEEE 1394 standard, the original spec calls for 100, 200 and 400 Mbits/sec transfer rates. IEEE 1394b provides 800, 1600 and 3200 Mbps. FireWire supports hot swapping, multiple speeds on the same bus and isochronous data transfer, which guarantees bandwidth for multimedia operations. It is expected to be widely used for attaching video devices to the computer. See *Tailgate*.

Firey engine

See *Fiery engine*.

firmware

A category of memory chips that hold their content without electrical power and include ROM, PROM, EPROM and EEPROM technologies. Firmware becomes "hard software" when holding program code.

first-generation computer

A computer that used vacuum tubes as switching elements; for example, the UNIVAC I.

first-level cache

Same as *L1 cache*. See *cache*.

First Virtual

A system of digital money from First Virtual Holdings, Inc., San Diego, CA, (www.fv.com). Customers have to establish an account with First Virtual using a credit card. When they want to purchase something online, they send their First Virtual ID number to the participating vendor, who in turn e-mails First Virtual and the customer for confirmation. Money is then transferred to the vendor via the Automated Clearing House (ACH).

fixation

See *disc fixation*.

fixed disk

A non-removable hard disk such as is found in most personal computers. Programs and data are copied to and from the fixed disk. For a summary of all storage technologies, see *storage*.

fixed-frequency monitor

A monitor that accepts one type of video signal, such as VGA only. Contrast with *multiscan monitor*.

fixed head disk

A direct access storage device, such as a disk or drum, that has a read/write head for each track. Since there is no access arm movement, access times are significantly improved.

fixed length field

A constant field size; for example, a 25-byte name field takes up 25 bytes in each record. It is easier to program, but wastes disk space and restricts file design. Description and comment fields are always a dilemma. Short fields allow only abbreviated remarks, while long fields waste space if lengthy comments are not required in every record. Contrast with *variable length field*.

fixed length record
A data record that contains fixed length fields.

fixed point
A method for storing and calculating numbers in which the decimal point is always in the same location. Contrast with *floating point*.

FK
See *foreign key*.

Fkey
(Function **key**) A Macintosh command sequence using command, shift and option key combinations. For example, Fkey 1 (command-shift 1) ejects the internal floppy. See also *function keys*.

flag
(1) In communications, a code in the transmitted message which indicates that the following characters are a control code and not data.

(2) In programming, a "yes/no" indicator built into certain hardware or created and controlled by the programmer.

(3) A UNIX command line argument. The symbol is a dash. For example, in the command **head -15 filex**, which prints the first 15 lines of the file FILEX, the **-15** flag modifies the Head command.

flame
To communicate emotionally and/or excessively via electronic mail. In other words, "online cursing." See *netiquette* and *holy war*.

flame bait
A subject posted to an Internet newsgroup that is designed to produce an emotional reaction and start a flame war.

flame war
In an Internet newsgroup, an ongoing tirade of contrasting opinions about a topic.

flash BIOS
A PC BIOS that is stored in flash memory rather than in a ROM. A flash BIOS chip can be updated in place, whereas a ROM BIOS must be replaced with a newer chip. See *BIOS*.

flash card
A flash memory or flash disk module housed in a PC Card format. Contrast with *socket flash*. See *flash memory*.

flash disk
A solid state disk made of flash memory chips. It emulates a standard disk drive in contrast with flash memory cards, which require proprietary software to make them function. See *flash memory*.

flash fusing
See *fusing*.

flash memory
A memory chip that holds its content without power. Derived from the EEPROM chip technology, which can be erased in place, flash memory is less expensive and more dense. Unlike DRAM and SRAM memory chips, in which a single byte can be written, flash memory must be erased and written in fixed blocks, typically ranging from 512 bytes up to 256KB. The term was coined by Toshiba for its ability to be erased "in a flash.

Flash chips have been used in various communications and industrial products as well as to replace ROM BIOS chips so that the BIOS could be updated. Flash chips generally have lifespans from 100K to 300K write cycles.

Flash memory chips are conveniently packaged as "flash cards," using the PCMCIA PC Card format. They are becoming more visible as solid state disks in palmtops, digital cameras and, increasingly, in consumer products.

There are two types of flash disks. The earlier linear flash, which is also used to execute a program directly from the chip (XIP), requires Flash Translation Layer (FTL) or Flash File System (FFS) software to make it look like a disk drive. There are various implementations of FTL and FFS.

The second newer type is the ATA flash disk, which uses the same 512-byte block size as a hard disk. Since the ATA interface is a common standard, all ATA flash disks are interchangeable. See *CompactFlash*.

flash RAM, flash ROM

See *flash memory*.

flat address space

A memory that is addressed starting with 0. Each susequent byte is referenced by the next sequential number (0, 1, 2, 3, etc.) all the way to the end of memory. Except for PCs, which are based on the Intel CPU architecture, most computers use a flat address space.

A PC running in 16-bit mode (Real Mode) uses a segmented address space. Memory is broken up into 64KB segments, and a segment register always points to the base of the segment that is currently being addressed. The PC's 32-bit mode is considered a flat address space, but it too uses segments. Since one 32-bit segment addresses 4GB, one segment covers all of memory.

flatbed plotter

A graphics plotter that contains a flat surface that the paper is placed on. The size of this surface (bed) determines the maximum size of the drawing. Contrast with *drum plotter*.

flatbed scanner

A scanner that provides a flat, glass surface to hold pages of paper, books and other objects for scanning. The scan head is moved under the glass across the page. Sheet feeders are usually optionally available that allow multiple sheets to be fed automatically. Contrast with *sheet-fed scanner, hand-held scanner* and *drum scanner*.

flat file

A data file that is not related to or does not contain any linkages to another file. It is generally used for stand-alone lists. When files must be related (customers to orders, vendors to purchases, etc.), a relational database manager is used, not a flat file manager. Flat files can be related, but only if the applications are programmed to do so.

Years ago, flat files were the very type used in a relational database. Before relational databases, files were related with built-in pointers that could not be dynamically changed. The relational database eliminated the hardwired linkages, resulting in "flat files." Today, flat files do not relate; just the opposite. Another example of how the terminology in this industry can drive you nuts.

An 85MB Flash Disk
Flash disks are used in portable devices such as digital cameras, palmtops and PDAs. They are considerably more expensive than hard disks, but are much more rugged and are not volatile. *(Photo courtesy of SanDisk)*

An Early Flatbed Plotter
In the 1970s, this CalComp Model 738 large-format, flatbed plotter was an offline device. Data was delivered to it via magnetic tape. *(Photo courtesy of CalComp, Inc.)*

flat network

A network in which all stations can reach other without going through any intermediary hardware devices, such as a bridge or router. A flat nework is one network segment. Large networks are segmented to contain broadcast traffic and to improve traffic within a workgroup. Contrast with *segmented network*. See *broadcast traffic* and *LAN segment*.

flatpack

A plastic, square surface mount chip package that contains leads (pins) on all four sides that extend straight outward. The leads are bent and cut for the specific application. See *QFP* and *chip package*.

flat panel display

A thin display screen that uses any of a number of technologies, such as LCD, plasma, EL and FED. Traditionally used in laptops, flat panel displays are slowly beginning to replace desktop CRTs for specialized applications. However, in time, flat panels are expected to replace all CRTs. See *LCD, plasma display, EL display* and *FED*.

flat screen

(1) A CRT in which the viewing surface is flatter than earlier CRTs, which are slightly rounded. The flat screen provides less distortion at the edges.

(2) See *flat panel display*.

flat shading

In computer graphics, a technique for computing a one-tone shaded surface to simulate simple lighting.

FLC file

An animation file format from Autodesk, Inc., Sausalito, CA, that is commonly known as a "flick" file. It uses the .FLC file extension and provides a 640x480 resolution. An earlier .FLI format provides 320x200 resolution. Both FLC and FLI files provide animated sequences, but not sound. FLI and FLC formats were introduced respectively with Autodesk's Animator and Animator Pro programs for DOS.

flexible disk

Same as *floppy disk* and *diskette*.

flicker

A fluctuating image on a video screen. See *interlaced*.

flick file

See *FLC file*.

FLI file

See *FLC file*.

Flat Panel Display
This PageMaster LCD 15" display pivots horizontally or vertically. When viewing an 8.5x11" document in vertical mode as shown above, it is equivalent to a 21" screen. *(Photo courtesy of Portrait Displays, Inc.)*

flip-flop

An electronic circuit that alternates between two states. When current is applied, it changes to its opposite state (0 to 1 or 1 to 0). Made of several transistors, it is used in the design of static memories and hardware registers.

flippy board

A PC expansion board that connects to both ISA/EISA and Micro Channel buses. ISA/EISA connectors are on one edge of the board; MCA on the other.

float

In programming, a declaration of a floating point number.

floating point

A method for storing and calculating numbers in which the decimal points do not line up as in fixed point numbers. The significant digits are stored as a unit called the mantissa, and the location of the radix point (decimal point in base 10) is stored in a separate unit called the exponent. Floating point methods are used for calculating a large range of numbers quickly.

Floating point operations can be implemented in hardware (math coprocessor), or they can be done in software. In large sysems, they can also be performed in a separate floating point processor that is connected to the main processor via a channel. See *numbers* for illustration.

FLOATING POINT EXAMPLES

Mantissa	Exponent	Value
71	0	71
71	1	710
71	2	7100
71	-1	7.1

floating point processor

An arithmetic unit designed to perform floating point operations. It may be a coprocessor chip in a personal computer, a CPU designed with built-in floating point capabilities or a separate machine, often called an *array processor*, which is connected to the main computer.

floppy disk

A reusable magnetic storage medium introduced by IBM in 1971. The floppy has been the primary method for distributing personal computer software until the mid to late 1990s when CD-ROMs became the preferred medium. Floppies are still widely used for backup and to transfer data between users that are not attached to a network.

Also called a *diskette*, the floppy is a flexible circle of magnetic material similar to magnetic tape, except that both surfaces are used for recording. The drive grabs the floppy's center and spins it inside its housing. The read/write head contacts the surface through an opening in the plastic shell or envelope.

Floppies spin at 300 rpm, which is from 10 to 30 times slower than a hard disk. They are also at rest until a data transfer is requested. The following list shows floppy sizes, from newest to oldest. Today, the common 3.5" format holds 1.44MB.

External format	Capacity	Creator
3.5" rigid case	400KB - 2.8MB	Sony
5.25" flexible envelope	100KB - 1.2MB	Shugart
8" flexible envelope	100 - 500KB	IBM

Although floppy disks look the same, what's recorded on them determines their capacity and compatibility. Every new floppy must be "formatted," which records the sectors on the disk that hold the data. See *format program, magnetic disk* and *high-capacity floppy*. For a summary of all storage technologies, see *storage*.

FLOPS

(FLoating point Operations Per Second) The measurement of floating point calculations. For example, 100 megaflops (mflops) is 100 million floating point operations per second.

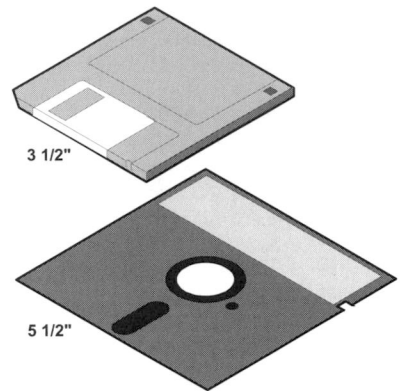

3 1/2"

5 1/2"

Floppy Formats
Although quite ubiquitous in its heyday, the 5.25" diskette gave way to the 3.5" format in the mid 1990s. Although costing less than a quarter, the 3.5" floppy is woefully undersized for today's applications.

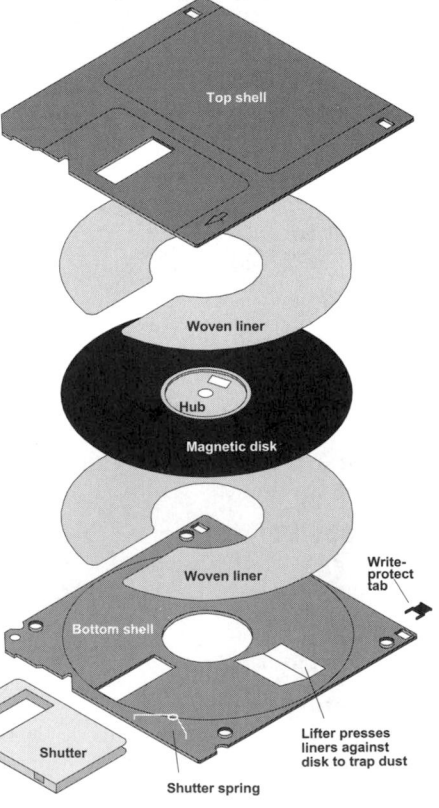

Top shell

Woven liner

Hub

Magnetic disk

Woven liner

Write-protect tab

Bottom shell

Shutter

Shutter spring

Lifter presses liners against disk to trap dust

Anatomy of a Floppy

Floptical

(FLoppy OPTICAL) An earlier type of floppy disk that stored 21MB and used optical alignment and magnetic recording. Introduced in 1989 by Insite Peripherals of San Jose, it did not become popular most likely because it did not offer a substantial enough increase in storage capacity. Similar technology is used in the LS-120 drive that was introduced in 1996 with 120MB. See *LS-120*.

flowchart

A graphical representation of the sequence of operations in an information system or program. Information system flowcharts show how data flows from source documents through the computer to final distribution to users. Program flowcharts show the sequence of instructions in a single program or subroutine. Different symbols are used to draw each type of flowchart.

FlowCharter

A Windows 95/98 and NT flowcharting program from Micrografx that includes more than 400 shapes prearranged by application. It includes a set of pre-defined templates for popular chart designs that can be quickly filled with shapes. The previous Windows 3.1 versions were called ABC FlowCharter. See *diagramming program*.

flowcharting program

See *diagramming program*.

flow control

(1) In communications, the management of transmission between two devices. It is concerned with the timing of signals and enables slower-speed devices to communicate with higher-speed ones. There are various techniques, but all are designed to ensure that the receiving station is able to accept the next block of data before the sending station sends it. See *xon-xoff*.

(2) In programming, the if-then and loop statements that make up the program's logic.

flush

To empty the contents of a memory buffer onto disk.

flush left, center, right

Flush left aligns text to the left margin. In this book, the first line of body text paragraphs are indented.

Flush center is the centering
of text uniformly between
the left and right margins.

Flush right aligns text uniformly
to the right margin while
the left margin is set ragged left.

flux

The energy field generated by a magnet.

flux transition

The change of magnetic polarity from 0 to 1 or 1 to 0 on a magnetic disk or tape.

flying head

A read/write head that "flies" over a magnetic disk. The heads are attached to a slider, which is a block of material that acts as an airfoil. The slider's shape and contour, which is designed for a particular disk speed, determine how high it flies. See *flying height*.

flying height

The distance between the surface of a disk platter and the read/write head. See *flying head*.

FM

(1) (Frequency Modulation) A transmission technique that blends the data signal into a carrier by varying (modulating) the frequency of the carrier. See *modulate*.

(2) (Frequency Modulation) An earlier magnetic disk encoding method that places clock bits onto the medium along with the data bits. It has been superseded by MFM and RLL.

FM synthesis

A MIDI technique that simulates the sound of musical instruments. It uses operators, typically four of them, which create wave forms or modulate the wave forms. FM synthesis does not create sound as faithfully as wave table synthesis, which uses actual samples of the instruments.

Fn key

(FuNction key) A keyboard key that works like a shift key to activate the second function on a dual-purpose key, typically found on laptops to reduce keyboard size. It is different than the function keys F1, F2, etc.

FOAF

Digispeak for "friend of a friend."

FOCA

(Font Object Content Architecture) See *MO:DCA*.

FOCUS

(1) A DBMS from Information Builders, Inc., New York, (www.ibi.com), that runs on PCs, mainframes and minis. It allows relational, hierarchical and network data structures and can access a variety of databases, including standard IBM mainframe files, DB2, IMS, IDMS and others. It includes a fourth-generation language and a variety of decision support facilities.

(2) (Federation On Computing in the United States, www.acm.org/focus) The U.S. representative of the International Federation of Information Processing (IFIP). FOCUS was founded in 1991 by the ACM and the IEEE Computing Society (IEEE-CS) and alternately sponsor its Secretariat.

FOIA

(Freedom Of Information Act) A U.S. Government rule that states that public information shall be delivered within 10 days of request.

FOIRL

(Fiber Optic Inter Repeater Link) An IEEE standard for fiber optic Ethernet. FOIRL and 10BaseF are compatible, but FOIRL is an earlier standard generally used to extend a backbone beyond the 328 foot limitation of 10BaseT. FOIRL is limited to .6 miles distance per segment, whereas 10BaseF segments can extend to 1.2 miles. 10BaseF is a more comprehensive standard for complete fiber-based installations.

folder

In the Macintosh and Windows 95/98, a simulated file folder that holds data, applications and other folders. A folder is the same as a DOS or Windows 3.1 directory, and a folder within a folder (subfolder) is the same as a DOS or Windows 3.1 subdirectory. Folders were popularized on the Mac and later adapted to UNIX and Windows.

foldering

Using folders to store and manipulate documents on screen.

Folio

(1) Text management software for PCs from the Folio division of Open Market, Inc., Cambridge, MA, (www.folio.com). It provides storage, retrieval and hypertext capability for text databases. It can import text from over 40 file formats. Folio files are called *Infobases*. Open Market acquired Provo, Utah-based Folio Corporation in 1997.

(2) (folio) In typography, a printed page number. For example, folio 3 could be the 27th physical page in a book.

FON file

(**FON**t file) In Windows 3.1 and 95/98, a file that contains a font used for on-screen displays (menus, buttons, etc.) by Windows and Windows applications as well as by DOS applications running under Windows. Most .FON files contain bitmapped fonts. Contrast with *TTF file*.

font

A set of type characters of a particular typeface design and size. Usually, each typeface (Times Roman, Helvetica, Arial, etc.) is made available in four variations: normal weight, bold, italic and bold italic. Thus, for bitmapped fonts, which are fully generated ahead of time, four fonts would be required for each point size used in each typeface. For scalable fonts, which are generated in any point size on the fly, only four fonts would be required for each typeface.

Fonts come built into the printer, as plug-in cartridges or as soft fonts, which reside on the computer's hard disk or a hard disk built into the printer. See *bitmapped font* and *scalable font*.

font cartridge

A set of bitmapped or outline fonts for one or more typefaces contained in a plug-in module for the printer. The fonts are stored in a ROM chip within the cartridge. Contrast with *soft font* and *internal font*.

font characteristics

The attributes and properties of a font. In HP LaserJet, font selection is made by sending a coded command to the printer with the following criteria:

```
Code             Characteristic
Typeface         Courier, Times Roman, etc.
Orientation      Portrait or landscape
Symbol set       Country or special characters
Spacing          Proportional or fixed
Pitch            Characters per inch (fixed)
Point size       Height
Style            Upright or italic
Stroke weight    Light, medium, bold
```

font compiler

Same as *font generator*.

font editor

Software that allows fonts to be designed and modified.

font family

A set of fonts of the same typeface in assorted sizes, including bold, italic and bold italic variations.

font generator

Software that converts an outline font into a bitmap (dot pattern required for a particular font size). Font generation is not linear, simply expanding a letter to any size. As fonts get bigger, their characteristics must change in order to make them attractive.

Font generation is used to create bitmapped fonts, which are fully generated and stored on disk before use. Contrast with *font scaler*, which generates the font in any point size the instant it is needed for display or printing.

font manager

See *font scaler*.

font metric

Typographic information (width, height, kerning) for each character in a font.

font number

An identification number assigned to a font. A program references the font by this number.

font rasterizer

See *font scaler*.

font scaler

Software that converts scalable fonts into bitmaps on the fly as required for display or printing. Examples are TrueType, Adobe Type Manager and Bitstream's Facelift. See *scalable font* and *font generator*.

font style

A typeface variation (normal, bold, italic, bold italic).

font utility

Software that provides functions for managing fonts, including the ability to download, install, design and modify fonts.

Fontware

A font generator for various DOS applications from Bitstream Inc., Cambridge, MA, (www.bitstream.com), which includes a library of typeface outlines in normal, italic, bold and bold italic weights. FontWare has been discontinued in favor of newer scalable font technogies. See *font scaler*.

font weight

The thickness of characters (light, medium or bold).

foo

A popular name for a temporary file, function or variable, or example of same. Often used with "bar" to create "foobar," which also comes from Fouled Up Beyond All Recognition (FUBAR).

footer

In a document or report, common text that appears at the bottom of every page. It usually contains the page number.

footnote

Text that appears at the bottom of a page, which adds explanation. It is often used to give credit to the source of information. When accumulated and printed at the end of a document, they are called *endnotes*.

footprint

The amount of geographic space covered by an object. A computer footprint is the desk or floor surface it occupies. A satellite's footprint is the earth area covered by its downlink.

foreground/background

The priority assigned to programs running in a multitasking environment. In a multiuser environment, foreground programs have highest priority, and background programs have lowest. Online users are given the foreground, and batch processing activities (sorts, updates, etc.) are given the background. If batch activities are given a higher priority, terminal response times may slow down considerably.

In a personal computer, the foreground program is the one the user is currently working with, and the background program might be a print spooler or communications program.

foreign exchange service

A telephone service that provides a local telephone number to a location outside of the customer's calling area. The telephone company creates a private line between the local telephone central office and the remote central office (foreign exchange). When customers dial the local number, they get a dial tone in the foreign exchange.

foreign file, foreign format

A file format that is different than the native format used by an application. Contrast with *native format*. See *import, export* and *file format*.

foreign key

In relational database, it is a field in one table that is indexed in another. Foreign keys provide the building blocks for relating tables. For example, in a customer order table, the salesperson field might contain an employee number. That field would be a foreign key in the table, because the employee table would be indexed on employee number. See *data model* for illustration.

foreign language characters

See *unicode*.

ForeRunner

A family of ATM adapters from Fore Systems, Warrendale, PA.

Forest & Trees

A data analysis program for Windows from Platinum Technology, Inc., Oakbrook Terrace, IL, (www.platinum.com), that integrates data from a variety of applications. It provides a control room interface that lets users monitor important business information.

FORE Systems

(FORE Systems, Inc., Warrendale, PA, www.fore.com) A leading manufacturer of ATM switches and networking equipment. Founded in 1990 by four Carnegie Mellon University faculty members, the company name was derived from its founders' first names: Francois, Onat, Robert and Eric. FORE commercialized the ATM market and offers a comprehensive line of ATM switches and related equipment. FORE's products are widely deployed in enterprise internets as well as the Internet. See *ATM*.

fork

(1) In UNIX, to make a copy of a process for execution.

(2) In the Macintosh, a part of a file. See *data fork* and *resource fork*.

form

(1) A paper form used for printing.

(2) A formatted screen display designed for a particular application. See *forms software*.

formant information

The structure of speech formation. It deals with how the mouth and vocal tract move to make sounds. See *phoneme*.

format

The structure, or layout, of an item.

Screen formats are the layout of fields on the screen.

Report formats are the columns, headers and footers on a page.

Record formats are the fields within a record.

File formats are the structure of data and program files, word processing documents and graphics files (vectors and bitmaps) with all their proprietary headers and codes. See *format program, disk format, DOS/ Windows disk format* and *style sheet*.

FORE's Founding Four
The founders of FORE start with Onat Menzilcioglu at the top left and go clockwise to Eric Cooper, Robert Sansom and Francois Bitz. *(Photo courtesy of FORE Systems, Inc.)*

Far Out
Everyone does a double take when they arrive at FORE headquarters, thinking that an earthquake just hit Western Pennsylvania. Having been used as the set for TV spots and movies, the architecture is just as far out on the inside. *(Photo courtesy of FORE Systems, Inc.)*

format program

Software that initializes a disk. There are two formatting levels. The low-level format initializes the disk surface by creating the physical tracks and storing sector identification in them as required by the particular drive technology used. Today's IDE and SCSI drives are all low-level formatted at the factory.

The high-level format creates the indexes used by the operating system's file system to keep track of data stored on the disk. HFS, FAT, FAT32, NTFS and HPFS are examples of such file systems used on personal computers.

Floppy disk format programs perform both levels of formatting on the diskette at the same time.

formatted text

Text that contains codes for font changes, headers, footers, boldface, italics and other page and document attributes. Word processors create formatted text, but all the major ones use their own coding systems. See *ASCII file*.

form factor

The physical size of a device as measured by outside dimensions. With regard to a disk drive, the form factor is the overall diameter of the platters and case, such as 3.5" or 5.25", not the size in terms of storage capacity.

form feed

Advancing a printer form to the top of the next page. It is done by pressing the printer's form feed (FF) button or by sending the form feed code (ASCII 12) to the printer from the computer.

forms software

(1) Workflow software used to create on-screen data entry forms and provide e-mail routing and tracking of the resulting electronic documents.

(2) Program development tools that build applications by designing the on-screen forms for data entry, update and so on. The forms are generally designed with visual programming tools that allow fields, buttons and logos to be drawn directly on screen. The business logic is either selected via menus and/or written in behind each field or button with lines of 4GL or 3GL programming code.

formula

(1) An arithmetic expression that solves a problem. For example, **(fahrenheit-32)*5/9** is the formula for converting Fahrenheit to Celsius.

(2) In spreadsheets, an algorithm that identifies how the data in a specific number of cells is to be calculated. For example, **+C3*D8** means that the contents of cell C3 are to be multipled by the contents of cell D8 and the results are to be placed where the formula is located.

form view

A screen display showing one item or record arranged like a preprinted form. Contrast with *table view*.

for statement

A high-level programming language structure that repeats a series of instructions a specified number of times. It creates a loop that includes its own control information. The following BASIC and C examples print "Hello" 10 times:

```
BASIC              C

for x = 1 to 10    for (x = 0;  x < 10;  x++)
 print "hello"      printf ("hello\n");
next x
```

Forte

An application development system for enterprise client/server environments from Forte Software, Inc., Oakland, CA, (www.forte.com). Introduced in 1994, it is a repository-driven system that supports Windows, Mac and Motif clients and all the major UNIX servers as well as VMS. It supports Oracle, Sybase and Rdb databases and provides partitioning for creating three-tier applications. Testing and debugging is done in an interpreted mode while production programs are compiled into C++ code.

Fortezza

An authentication system endorsed by the National Security Agency that uses a PC Card as the authentication token. Fortezza is part of the U.S. Government's GOSIP policy, and vendors must supply Fortezza-compliant products in order to win contracts. Fortezza uses a 56-bit key based on the DES encryption method. The term means "fortress" in Italian.

FORTH

(FOuRTH-generation language) A high-level programming language created by Charles Moore in the late 1960s as a way of providing direct control of the computer. Its syntax resembles LISP, it uses reverse

Computer Desktop Encyclopedia

polish notation for calculations, and it is noted for its extensibility.

It is both compiler and interpreter. The source program is compiled first and then executed by its operating system/interpreter. It is used in process control applications that must quickly process data acquired from instruments and sensors. It is also used in arcade game programming as well as robotics and other AI applications. The following polyFORTH example converts Fahrenheit to Celsius:

```
: CONV ( n) 32 - 5 9 * / . ." Celsius
: USER_INPUT   ." Enter Fahrenheit " CONV ;
```

FORTRAN

(FORmula TRANslator) The first high-level programming language and compiler, developed in 1954 by IBM. It was originally designed to express mathematical formulas, and although it is used occasionally for business applications, it is still the most widely used language for scientific, engineering and mathematical problems.

FORTRAN IV is an ANSI standard, but FORTRAN V has various proprietary versions. The following FORTRAN example converts Fahrenheit to Celsius:

```
WRITE(6,*) 'Enter Fahrenheit '
READ(5,*) XFAHR
XCENT = (XFAHR - 32) * 5 / 9
WRITE(6,*) 'Celsius is ',XCENT
STOP
END
```

forum

An information interchange regarding a specific topic or product that is hosted on an Internet newsgroup, online service or BBS. It can include the latest news on the subject, a conferencing capability for questions and answers by participants as well as files for downloading fixes, demos and other related material.

forward chaining

In AI, a form of reasoning that starts with what is known and works toward a solution. Known as bottom-up approach. Contrast with *backward chaining*.

forward compatible

Same as *upward compatible*.

forward error correction

A communications technique that can correct bad data on the receiving end. Before transmission, the data is processed through an algorithm that adds extra bits for error correction. If the transmitted message is received in error, the correction bits are used to repair it.

FOT file

(FOnt TrueType file) In Windows 3.1, a TrueType font file that points to the location of the TTF file, which contains the actual mathematical outlines of the font. See *TTF file*.

foundry

A semiconductor manufacturer that makes chips for third parties. It may be a large chip maker that sells its excess manufacturing capacity or one that makes chips exclusively for other companies. As of 1995, it costs at least a billion dollars to construct a high-production semiconductor manufacturing plant that produces standard chips. See *fabless*.

fountain fill

In computer graphics, a painted area that smoothly changes its color or pattern density. A radial fountain fill starts at the center of an area and radiates outward.

Four11

See *Web white pages*.

fourth-generation computer

A computer made up almost entirely of chips with limited amounts of discrete components. We are currently in the fourth generation.

fourth-generation language

Also known as a *4GL*, it is a computer language that is more advanced than traditional high-level programming languages. For example, in dBASE, the command **List** displays all the records in a data file. In second- and third-generation languages, instructions would have to be written to read each record, test for end of file, place each item of data on screen and go back and repeat the operation until there are no more records to process.

First-generation languages are machine languages; second-generation are machine dependent assembly languages; third-generation are high-level programming languages, such as FORTRAN, COBOL, BASIC, Pascal, and C.

Although many languages, such as dBASE, are called fourth-generation languages, they are actually a mix of third and fourth. The dBASE List command is a fourth-generation command, but applications programmed in dBASE are third-generation. The following example shows the difference between dBASE third- and fourth-generation syntax to open a customer file and display all names and addresses on screen.

```
dBASE 3GL                 dBASE 4GL

use customer              use customer
do while .not. eof()      list name, address
  ? name, address
  skip
enddo
```

Query language and report writers are also fourth-generation languages. Any computer language with English-like commands that doesn't require traditional input-process-output logic falls into this category.

Many fourth-generation language functions are also built into graphical interfaces and activated by clicking and dragging. The commands are embedded into menus and buttons that are selected in an appropriate sequence.

four-way server

See *4-way*.

FoxBASE

An earlier Xbase development system for the Macintosh from Microsoft. It was succeeded by FoxPro. Originally developed by Fox Software for DOS, FoxBASE gained a reputation early on for its speed and compatibility with dBASE. See *Visual FoxPro*.

FoxPro

See *Visual FoxPro*.

FPD

(1) (Flat Panel Display) See *LCD, plasma display, EL display, FED* and *flat panel display*.
(2) (Field Programmable Device) See *PLD*.

FPGA

(Field Programmable Gate Array) A programmable logic chip (PLD) with a high density of gates. There are a variety of FPGA architectures, some of which can be very sophisticated, including not only programmable logic blocks, but programmable interconnects and switches between the blocks. See *gate array* and *ASIC*.

FPM RAM

See *page mode memory*.

FPO

(For Position Only) A low-resolution image that is printed to mark the placement of a picture. It is commonly used when publishing on standard laser printers. Before printing the finished product, the FPOs are replaced with high-quality images created from high-resolution scanners or by photographing the picture through a halftone screen.

fps

(Frames Per Second) The measurement of full-motion video performance. See *frame*.

FPU

(Floating Point Unit) A computer circuit that handles floating point operations.

FQDN

(Fully Qualified Domain Name) The complete domain name for a specific computer (host) on the Internet. It provides enough information so that it can be converted into a physical IP address. The FQDN consists of host name and domain name. For example, **www.computerlanguage.com** is the FQDN on the Web for the publisher of this database. The WWW is the host. That's right. There are hundreds of thousands of hosts named WWW in order to maintain uniformity. COMPUTERLANGUAGE.COM is the domain name with .COM being the top level domain (TLD) name. See *DNS* and *Internet domain names*.

FR4

(Flame Retardant 4) A widely-used insulating material for making printed circuit boards. It is constructed of woven glass fibers (fiberglass) that are epoxied together.

Fractal Design Painter

See *Painter*.

fractals

A lossy compression method used for color images. It provides ratios of 100:1 or greater and is especially suited to natural objects, such as trees, clouds and rivers. It turns an image into a set of data and an algorithm for expanding it back to the original.

The term comes from "fractus," which is Latin for broken or fragmented. It was coined by IBM Fellow and doctor of mathematics Benoit Mandelbrot, who expanded on ideas from earlier mathematicians and discovered similarities in chaotic and random events and shapes.

fractional T1

A service that provides less than full T1 capacity. Increments of 64 Kbps are provided.

fractional T3

A service that provides less than full T3 capacity. Increments of 3 Mbps are typically provided.

FRAD

(Frame Relay Assembler/Disassembler) A communications device that formats outgoing data into the format required by a frame relay network. It strips the data back out at the other end. It is the frame relay counterpart to the X.25 PAD.

fragmentation

(1) Storing data in non-contiguous areas on disk. As files are updated, new data is stored in available free space, which may not be contiguous. Fragmented files cause extra head movement, slowing disk accesses. A defragger program is used to rewrite and reorder all the files.

(2) In an IP network, breaking a data packet into smaller pieces in order to accomodate the maximum transmission unit of the network. See *MTU*.

fragments

The pieces into which a packet is broken when the packet is too large to be sent over a particular network as a single unit. See *fragmentation* and *MTU*.

FRAM

(1) (Ferroelectronic **RAM**) A non-volatile semiconductor memory that retains its content without power for up to 10 years.

(2) (Ferromagnetic **RAM**) A non-volatile memory that records microscopic bits on a magnetic surface.

frame

(1) In computer graphics, one screenful of data or its equivalent storage space. In full-motion video, it requires approximately 24 consecutive frames in one second (24 fps) to simulate real, continuous motion.

(2) In communications, a fixed block of data transmitted as a single entity. In local area networks (LANs), the terms frame and packet are used synonymously. See *packet* and *Ethernet*.

(3) In a Web browser, a separate, scrollable window on screen. See *frames*.

(4) In desktop publishing, a movable, resizable box that holds a graphic image.

(5) In AI, a data structure that holds a general description of an object, which is derived from basic concepts and experience.

frame buffer

An area of memory used to hold a frame of data. A frame buffer is typically used for screen display and is the size of the maximum image area on screen. It is a separate memory bank on the display adapter that holds the bitmapped image while it is being "painted" on screen. Sophisticated graphics systems are built with several memory planes, each holding one or more bits of the pixel.

frame grabber

A device that accepts standard TV signals and digitizes the current video frame into a bitmap image. Frame grabbers can be stand-alone units or a function built into video graphics boards.

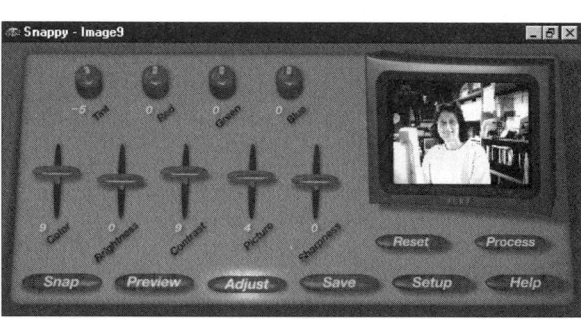

FrameMaker

A desktop publishing program from Adobe that runs on UNIX platforms, Macintosh and Windows. It is noted for its large number of advanced features, including full text and graphics editing capabilities. Optional viewers let documents run on machines without FrameMaker, providing a way to distribute hypertext-based help systems.

The Snappy Frame Grabber

Snappy is a device from Play Inc. that plugs into the parallel port of the PC and accepts a video cable from a camcorder or VCR. This is Snappy's Windows-based control panel, which allows you to adjust the image and preview the results. You take the picture by clicking "snap." *(Screen shot courtesy of Play Inc.)*

frame relay

A high-speed packet switching protocol used in wide area networks (WANs). It has become popular for LAN to LAN connections across remote distances, and services are provided by all the major carriers. Frame relay is faster than traditional X.25 networks, because it was designed for today's reliable circuits and performs less rigorous error detection.

Frame relay provides for a granular service up to DS3 rates of 44.736 Mbps and is suited for data and image transfer. Because of its variable-length packet architecture, it is not the most efficient technology for realtime voice and video.

frames

A Web browser feature that enables a Web page to be displayed in a separate scrollable window on screen. Older browsers do not support the frames feature, and many Web sites have a frames and non-frames version of the site to accomodate them.

frame switch

A network device that switches variable-length packets from sender to receiver. Ethernet, Token Ring and FDDI switches are examples. Contrast with *cell switching*. See *LAN switch* and *frame switching*.

frame switching

Using frame switches to speed up network traffic. For example, when a 10BaseT Ethernet hub is replaced with an Ethernet frame switch, each sending and receiving pair of stations obtains the full bandwidth of the network. See *frame switch*.

framework

(1) See *application framework*.

(2) (FrameWork) One of the first integrated software packages for PCs that included a programming language. It was developed by Ashton-Tate, later acquired by Borland.

framing bit
Same as *start bit* and *stop bit*.

FRED
(Friendly Rollabout Engineered for Doctors) A mobile medical conferencing unit. See *videoconferencing*.

Freedman's law
"Every 18 months, more novices are programming." By Alan Freedman, author of "The Computer Glossary" and "Computer Desktop Encyclopedia." The job of programming is very misunderstood. It is actually easier to write a program than most people would think. However, the lack of experience causes programmers to create a maze that cannot easily be traversed later. For more details, see *programmer*. See also *user interface* and *laws*.

free-form database
A database system that allows entry of text without regard to length or order. Although it accepts data as does a word processor, it differs by providing better methods for searching, retrieving and organizing the data. See *PIM* for illustration.

free-form language
A language in which statements can reside anywhere on a line or even cross over lines. It does not imply less syntax structure, just more freedom in placing statements. For example, any number of blank spaces are allowed between symbols. Most high-level programming languages are free-form.

FreeHand
See *Macromedia FreeHand*.

Freelance Graphics
A presentation graphics program for Windows from Lotus that is also part of Lotus' SmartSuite set of applications.

Freeman Reports
A series of technical reports on data storage devices from Ray Freeman of Freeman Associates, Inc., Santa Barbara, CA. They provide exhaustive detail about the disk and tape industry and include up-to-date data on the technology, capacities, purposes, market share and future trends.

Free Software Foundation
(Free Software Foundation, Inc., Boston, MA, www.gnu.org) A non-profit organization founded in 1985 by Richard Stallman, dedicated to eliminating restrictions on copying and modifying programs by promoting the development and use of freely redistributable software. Its GNU computing environment, X Windows and other programs are available for a transaction charge. See *League for Programming Freedom*.

freeware
Software distributed without charge. Ownership is retained by the developer who has control over its redistribution, including the ability to change the next release of the freeware to payware. See *shareware* and *public domain software*. Contrast with *feeware*.

freeze-frame video
Video transmission in which the image is changed once every couple of seconds rather than 30 times per second as is required in full-motion video.

frequency
The number of oscillations (vibrations) in an alternating current within one second. See *frequency response, audio* and *carrier*.

frequency division multiplexing
See *FDM*.

frequency hopping
A wireless modulation method that rapidly changes the center frequency of a transmission. See *802.11*.

frequency modulation
See *FM*.

frequency range
In a communications system, the range of frequencies from the lowest to the highest. In a high-fidelity audio system, this would be typically from 20Hz to 20,000Hz.

frequency response
In an audio system, the accuracy of sound reproduction. A totally flat response means that there is no increase or decrease in volume level across the frequency range. Measured in decibels (dB), this would be plus or minus 0 dB from 20Hz to 20,000Hz. A high-end audio system can deviate by +/- 0.5 dB, but a CD-ROM drive should not be off by more than +/- 3 dB.

frequency shift
See *FSK*.

friction feed
A mechanism that allows cut paper forms to be used in a printer. The paper is passed between the platen and a roller that presses tightly against it. Contrast with *tractor feed*.

frob
To manipulate and adjust dials and buttons for fun. From the term "frobnicate," of course.

front end
The head, starting point or input side in a system. For example, it may refer to the graphical interface on a user's workstation where all data is entered or to a communications system, such as a front end processor or TP monitor that accepts incoming transactions and messages. See *back end*.

front-end CASE
CASE tools that aid in systems analysis and design. Contrast with *back-end CASE*.

front end processor
A computer that handles communications processing for a mainframe. It connects to the communications lines on one end and the mainframe on the other. It transmits and receives messages, assembles and disassembles packets and detects and corrects errors. It is sometimes synonymous with a communications controller, although the latter is usually not as flexible.

FrontPage
A popular Web authoring program from Microsoft for Windows and the Mac. FrontPage Editor is the graphical editor for designing the pages and FrontPage Explorer is the management tool that lets you construct and maintain the entire site. It also includes WebBots, which generate code for complex functions such as searching and password protection.

frontware
Same as *screen scraper*.

FS
See *flat screen*.

FSK
(Frequency Shift Keying) A simple modulation technique that merges binary data into a carrier. It creates only two changes in frequency: one for 0, another for 1.

FSN
(Full-Service Network) A communications network that provides shopping, movies on demand and access to databases and a variety of online, interactive services. Telephone, cable and TV companies are positioning themselves to provide FSN services that are expected to evolve throughout the 1990s.

FSR
(Free System Resource) In Windows 3.x, the amount of unused memory in various 64K blocks reserved for managing current applications. Every open window takes some space in this area. See *Windows memory limitation*.

FSTN

(Film Compensated STN) A passive matrix LCD technology that uses a film compensating layer between the STN display and rear polarizer for added sharpness. It was used in laptops before the DSTN method became popular. See *DSTN* and *LCD*.

FT1

See *fractional T1*.

FTAM

(File Transfer Access and Management) A communications protocol for the transfer of files between systems of different vendors.

FTG file

See *Windows help system*.

FTL

(Flash Translation Layer) See *flash memory*.

FTP

(File Transfer Protocol) A protocol used to transfer files over a TCP/IP network (Internet, UNIX, etc.). It includes functions to log onto the network, list directories and copy files. It can also convert between the ASCII and EBCDIC character codes. FTP operations can be performed by typing commands at a command prompt or via an FTP utility running under a graphical interface such as Windows. FTP transfers can also be initiated from within a Web browser by entering the URL preceded with **ftp://**.

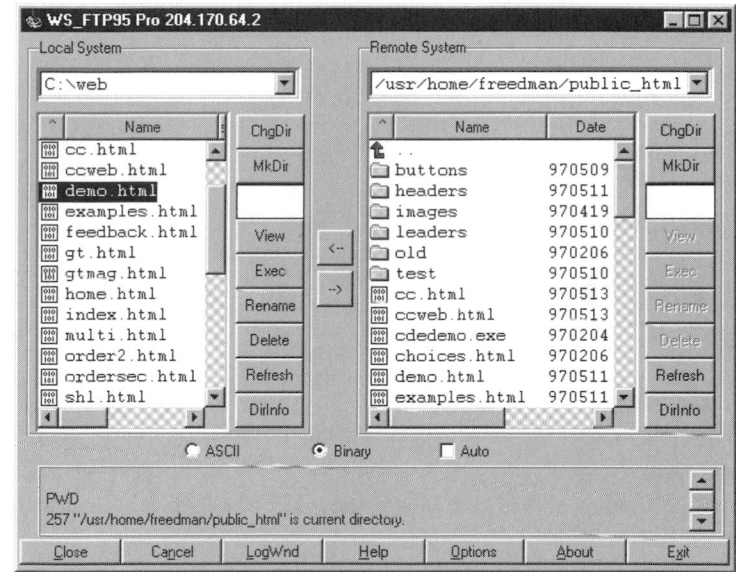

FTP Utility

Ipswitch's WS_FTP Pro makes FTP'ing easy under Windows. After logging on and switching to the appropriate folders on the local and remote systems, transferring files requires only highlighting, dragging and dropping.

Unlike e-mail programs in which graphics and program files have to be "attached," FTP is designed to handle binary files directly and does not add the overhead of encoding and decoding the data.

The term is also used as a verb; for example, "let's FTP them the file." See *anonymous FTP* and *TFTP*.

FTP site

A computer system on the Internet that maintains files for downloading. See *anonymous FTP*.

FTS 2000

(Federal Telecommunications System 2000) A digital fiber-optic network providing voice, video, e-mail and high-speed data communications for the U.S. government. AT&T and Sprint are the major equipment providers. FTS 2000 expires in 1998 and will be superseded by FTS 2001.

FTS file

See *Windows help system*.

FTTC

(Fiber To The Curb) The installation of optical fiber to within a thousand feet of the home or office. See *FTTH*.

FTTH

(Fiber To The Home) The installation of optical fiber from the carrier directly into the home or office. See *FTTC*.

FTX

(Fault Tolerant UNIX) Stratus Computer's version of UNIX System V for its XA/R fault tolerant computer systems.

FUBAR

(Fouled Up Beyond All Recognition) See *foo*.

FUD factor

(Fear Uncertainty Doubt factor) A marketing strategy used by a dominant or privileged organization that restrains competition by not revealing future plans.

full backup

See *backup types*.

full bleed

See *bleed*.

full-duplex

Transmitting and receiving simultaneously. In pure digital networks, this is achieved with two pairs of wires. In analog networks or in digital networks using carriers, it is achieved by dividing the bandwidth of the line into two frequencies, one for sending, the other for receiving.

full-duplex Ethernet

An extension to 10BaseT Ethernet that is implemented in a switched Ethernet environment, which has a dedicated line between the station and switch. It is built into the network adapter (NIC) and switch, providing bi-directional transmission that boosts bandwidth from 10 to 20 Mbps.

full featured

Hardware or software that provides capabilities and functions comparable to the most advanced models or programs of that category.

full-height drive

A 5.25" disk drive that measures 3.25" in height. It was the size of first-generation drives in desktop computers, but high-capacity hard drives are still made in this size. A full-height drive bay allows for the installation of one full-height drive or two half-height drives. Contrast with *half-height drive*.

full-motion video

Video transmission that changes the image 30 frames per second (30 fps). Motion pictures are run at 24 fps, which is the minimum frequency required to eliminate the perception of moving frames and make the images appear visually fluid to the eye.

TV video generates 30 interlaced frames per second, which is actually transmitted as 60 half frames per second.

Video that has been digitized and stored in the computer can be displayed at varying frame rates, depending on the speed of the computer. The slower the computer, the more jerky the movement. Contrast with *freeze-frame video*.

full path

A path name that includes the drive (if required), starting or root directory, all attached subdirectories and ending with the file or object name. Contrast with *relative path*. See *path*.

full project life cycle

A project from inception to completion.

full-screen mode

A programming capability that allows data to be displayed in any row, column or pixel location on screen. Contrast with *teletype mode*.

Computer Desktop Encyclopedia

full-text search

A search that compares every word in a document, as opposed to searching an abstract or a set of keywords associated with the document. Full-text searching is the type performed by most Web search engines. Although it is very thorough, it often results in too many false drops. See *false drops*.

fully populated

A circuit board whose sockets are completely filled with chips.

fully qualified domain name

See *FQDN*.

function

In programming, a self-contained software routine that peforms a job for the program it is written in or for some other program. The function performs the operation and returns control to the instruction following the calling instruction or to the calling program. Programming languages provide a set of standard functions and may allow programmers to define others. For example, the C language is built entirely of functions.

functional decomposition

Breaking down a process into non-redundant operations. In structured programming, it provides a hierarchical breakdown of the program into the individual operations, or routines, that are required.

functional specification

The blueprint for the design of an information system. It provides documentation for the database, human and machine procedures, and all the input, processing and output detail for each data entry, query, update and report program in the system. See *system development cycle* for illustration.

function call

A request by a program to use a subroutine. The subroutine can be large and perform a significant amount of processing, or it can be as small as computing two numbers and returning the result. When applications are running, they make millions of function calls to the operating system.

A function call written in a program states the name of the function followed by any values or parameters that have to be passed to it. When the function is called, the operation is performed, and the results are returned as variables or pointers with new values.

The function may be written within the program, be part of an external library that is combined with the program when it is compiled or be contained in another program, such as the operating system or DBMS.

Functional Decomposition of a Program

This example is ultra simplistic, but shows the hierarchical breakdown of the program into its constituent components.

function keys

A set of keyboard keys used to command the computer (F1, F2, etc.). F1 is often the help key, but the purpose of any function key is determined by the software currently running.

function library

A collection of program routines. See *function*.

function overloading

In programming, using the same name for two or more functions. The compiler determines which function to use based on the type of function, arguments passed to it and type of values returned.

function prototyping

In programming, formally defining each function in the program with the number and types of parameters passed to it and its return values. The compiler can then report an error if a function is not written to conform to the prototype.

fuse

(1) A protective device that is designed to melt, or blow, when a specified amount of current is passed through it. PROM chips are created as a series of fuses that are selectively blown in order to create the binary patterns of the data or machine language.

(2) To bond together.

fusible link

A line in a PROM or PLD chip that is designed to be blown apart to program the circuit. It functions like a fuse, which, when blown, does not conduct current. See *PROM programmer* and *PLD*.

fusing

In electrophotography, making the toner adhere permanently to the paper. Heat fusing melts the toner, which is pressed into the paper. Cold fusing presses the toner into the paper without applying any heat. Flash fusing melts the toner with light, and no heat or pressure is used. The latter is more flexible with all types of media.

Fusion

See *Cold Fusion* and *NetObjects Fusion*.

Fusion FTMS

(Fusion File Transfer Management System) A mainframe to LAN file transfer program from Proginet Corporation, Garden City, NY, (www.proginet.com). It provides file transfer between MVS and Windows desktops and servers. Part of the software resides in the mainframe, another part in the Windows server and client. Support for additional server platforms is expected.

Futurebus+

An IEEE standard multisegment bus that can transfer data at 32, 64, 128 and 256-bits and can address up to 64 bits. Clock speeeds range from 25 to 100MHz. At 100MHz and 256 bits, it transfers 3.2 Gbytes/sec.

future Intel chips

Following are the CPU chips expected from Intel in the future.

Katmai - Expected in early 1999 with 70 more MMX instructions, code named Katmai New Instructions, that provide floating point operations on parallel sets of data.

Willamette - Expected in 1999 with increased speed. Enhanced 3-D geometry and parallel capabilities are also expected.

Merced - Next-generation Intel architecture aimed at workstations and servers. Expected in 2000, it introduces the 64-bit IA-64 instruction set jointly designed by Intel and HP. See *Merced* and *IA-64*.

Flagstaff - Expected in 2000, using two chips for the processor and first Intel chips to use .18 micron technology.

future proof

Not obsolete in the future. As much as the computer field drives the future, there are very few future-proof products within it. One exception might be optical fiber, which seems capable of handling more bandwidth than we can ever imagine. However, we also said 640K would be all the memory we would ever need in a desktop computer.

fuzzy computer

A specially-designed computer that employs fuzzy logic. Using such architectural components as analog circuits and parallel processing, fuzzy computers are designed for AI applications. See illustration on next page.

fuzzy logic

A mathematical technique for dealing with imprecise data and problems that have many solutions rather than one. Although it is implemented in digital computers which ultimately make only yes-no decisions, fuzzy logic works with ranges of values, solving problems in a way that more resembles human logic.

Fuzzy logic is used for solving problems with expert systems and realtime systems that must react to an imperfect environment of highly variable, volatile or unpredictable conditions. It "smoothes the edges" so to speak, circumventing abrupt changes in operation that could result from relying on traditional either-or and all-or-nothing logic.

Fuzzy logic was conceived by Lotfi Zadeh, former chairman of the electrical engineering and computer science department at the University of California at Berkeley. In 1964, while contemplating how computers could be programmed for handwriting recognition, Zadeh expanded on traditional set theory by making membership in a set a matter of degree rather than a yes-no situation.

Fuzzy Computer
Since the whole computer industry seems fuzzy much of of the time, how about a really fuzzy computer!

fuzzy logician

An individual who is involved in developing fuzzy logic algorithms.

fuzzy search

An inexact search for data that finds answers that come close to the desired data. It can get results when the exact spelling is not known or help users obtain information that is loosely related to a topic.

FWIW

Digispeak for "for what it's worth."

FX

See *foreign exchange service*.

FX 32

An emulator from Digital that allows 32-bit Windows programs to run on Alpha machines. It emulates x86 machine language instructions. It also performs a translation of a program the first time it is run so that it will run faster the second and subsequent times.

FYI

Digispeak for "for your information."

G

G

See *giga*.

G3

(1) The third generation of IBM's CMOS-based mainframes (Parallel Enterprise Servers). There were no G1 or G2 designations. See *Parallel Enterprise Server*.

(2) A series of Macintosh desktop machines and PowerBook portables that use the PowerPC 750, an enhanced version of the PowerPC chip. Models were introduced in 1997, running at 233MHz and 266MHz.

G4

(1) The fourth generation of IBM's CMOS-based mainframes (Parallel Enterprise Servers). There were no G1 or G2 designations. See *Parallel Enterprise Server*.

(2) The successor to the G3 series of PowerPC chips expected in the 1999 timeframe. See *G3*.

G5

The fifth generation of IBM's CMOS-based mainframes (Parallel Enterprise Servers). Introduced in 1998, G5 doubles the performance of G4 servers, debuts the FICON channel and adds hardware-based Triple DES cryptography and numerous internal improvements. Memory was increased to 24GB. See *Parallel Enterprise Server* and *FICON*.

G.711

An ITU standard for speech codecs that provides toll quality audio at 64 Kbps, using either A-Law or mu-Law PCM methods. This uncompressed digital format is a required codec for H.323 audio and videoconferencing in order to allow easy connections to legacy telephone networks.

G.721

An ITU standard for speech codecs that provides toll quality audio at 32 Kbps using the ADPCM method.

G.722

An ITU standard for speech codecs that provides high-quality audio at 64 Kbps, using the ADPCM method.

G.723

An ITU standard for speech codecs that provides toll quality audio at 20 or 40 Kbps, using the ADPCM method.

G.723.1

An ITU standard for speech codecs optimized for modems. It provides toll quality audio at 5.3 or 6.4 Kbps using the LD-CELP method. The higher rate requires less processing power. It also provides a mode where one person speaks at a time and uses the extra bandwidth for the talking party.

G.728

An ITU standard for speech codecs that provides near toll quality audio at 16 Kbps, using the LD-CELP method.

G.729

An ITU standard for speech codecs that provides toll quality audio at 8 Kbps using the CELP method.

G.729.A

An ITU standard for speech codecs that is less complex than G.729 and is designed for simultaneous voice and data.

gain

The amount of increase that an amplifier provides on the output side of the circuit.

GAL

(Generic Array Logic) A programmable logic chip (PLD) technology from Lattice Semiconductor.

gallium arsenide

An alloy of gallium and arsenic compound (GaAs) that is used as the base material for chips. It is several times faster than silicon.

game port

An I/O connector used to attach a joy stick. It is typically a 15-pin socket on the back of a PC. See *serial port*.

gamma

The relationship between the input and output of a device, expressed as a number, with 1.0 being a perfect linear plot (the output is increased in the exact same proportion as the input).

gamma correction

An adjustment to the light intensity of a scanner, monitor or printer. It generally refers to the adjustment of the brightness of a display screen in order to compensate for a CRT's irregularity. A gamma correction plot is a curve, not a straight line as is the standard brightness control. Gamma correction is also used to make the monitor display images more closely in appearance with the laser printer that creates the output.

gamut

See *color gamut*.

gang punch

To punch an identical set of holes into a deck of punched cards.

Gantt chart

A type of floating bar chart usually used in project management to show resources or tasks over time.

gap

(1) The space between blocks of data on magnetic tape.

(2) The space in a read/write head over which magnetic flux (energy) flows causing the underlying magnetic tape or disk surface to become magnetized in the corresponding direction.

gapless

A magnetic tape that is recorded in a continuous stream without interblock gaps.

garbage collection

A routine that searches memory for program segments or data that are no longer active in order to reclaim that space.

garbage in...

See *GIGO*.

Garoud shading

See *Gouraud shading*.

GARP

(General Attributes Registration Protocol) A standard for registering a client station into a multicast domain. See *802.1p*.

GAS

See *gallium arsenide*.

gas discharge display, gas plasma

See *plasma display*.

gate

(1) An open/closed switch.

(2) A pattern of transistors that makes up an AND, OR or NOT Boolean logic gate. See *gate array*.

(3) In a field effect transistor (CMOS), the line that activates the switch. Same as *base* in a bipolar transistor.

gate array

An unfinished chip with electronic components that have not been connected. The chip is completed by designing and adhering the top metal layers which provide the interconnecting pathways. This final masking stage is less costly than designing the chip from scratch.

The gate array is made up of basic cells, each cell containing some number of transistors and resistors depending on the vendor. Using a cell library (gates, registers, etc.) and a macro library (more complex functions), the customer designs the chip, and the vendor's software generates the masks that connect the transistors. See *hard macro* and *soft macro*.

gated

Switched "on" or capable of being switched on and off.

gatekeeper

A server that translates user names into physical addresses for H.323 conferencing. It can also be used to provide call authorization and accounting information.

gateway

(1) A computer that performs protocol conversion between different types of networks or applications. For example, a gateway can convert a TCP/IP packet to a NetWare IPX packet and vice versa, or from AppleTalk to DECnet, from SNA to AppleTalk and so on.

Gateways function at layer 4 and above in the OSI model. They perform complete conversions from one protocol to another rather than simply support one protocol from within another, such as IP tunneling. Sometimes routers can implement gateway functions.

An electronic mail, or messaging, gateway converts messages between two different messaging protocols. See also *IP gateway*. See *LAN* for illustration.

(2) An earlier name for router. Many people still use the term for a layer 3 device. See *router* and *layer 3 switch*.

Gateway 2000

(Gateway 2000, N. Sioux City, SD, www.gw2k.com) A major PC manufacturer founded in 1985 by Ted Waitt and Mike Hammond. Gateway first sold peripherals to owners of Texas Instrument computers. In 1987, it began to offer complete systems and has continued to drive down the cost of quality PCs by mail.

gateway address

The default address of a network or Web site. It provides a single domain name and point of entry to the site. See *proxy server*.

gather write

To output data from two or more noncontiguous memory locations with one write operation. See *scatter read*.

gauss

A unit of measurement of magnetic intensity named after Karl F. Gauss (1777-1855), considered to be one of the greatest mathematicians of all time. See *degausser*.

Gaussian distribution

A random distribution of events that is often graphed as a bell-shaped curve. It is used to represent a normal or statistically probable outcome.

Gaussian noise

In communications, a random interference generated by the movement of electricity in the line. Also called *white noise*.

Gb, Gbit; GB, Gbyte

See *gigabit* and *gigabyte*.

Gbits/sec, Gbps, Gb/s; Gbytes/sec, GBps, GB/s

(GigaBits Per Second; GigaBytes Per Second) One billion bits per second; one billion bytes per second. Using lower case "b" for bit and upper case "B" for byte is not always followed and often misprinted. See *space/time*.

GCOS

(General Comprehensive OS) An operating system from Bull used in its minis and mainframes. GCOS was orginally developed by GE in the early 1970s as GECOS (GE Comprehensive OS), then changed to General Comprehensive OS when Honeywell took over GE's computer division. Later, Bull acquired Honeywell's computer products.

GCR

(1) (Group Code Recording) An encoding method used on magnetic tapes and Apple II and Mac 400K and 800K floppy disks.

(2) (Gray Component Replacement) A method for reducing the amount of printing ink used. It substitutes black for the amount of gray contained in a color, thus black ink is used instead of the three CMY inks. See *UCR* and *dot gain*.

GD&R

Digispeak for "grinning, ducking and running," said after a snide remark. Another variation is GD&WVVF, which stands for "grinning, ducking and walking very, very fast."

GDDM

(Graphical Data Display Manager) Software that generates graphics images in the IBM mainframe environment. It contains routines to generate graphics on terminals, printers and plotters as well as accepting input from scanners. Programmers use it for creating graphics, but users can employ its Interactive Chart Utility (ICU) to create business graphics without programming.

GDDM/graPHIGS is a programming environment that combines graphics capability with a user interface similar to the Presentation Manager in OS/2.

GDI

(Graphics Device Interface) The graphics display system in Microsoft Windows. When an application needs to display or print, it makes a call to a GDI function and sends it the parameters for the object that must be created. GDI in turn "draws" the object by sending commands to the screen and printer drivers, which actually render the images. See *DirectX* and *device context*.

GDI printer

A printer designed to work only from Windows. It uses Windows' internal graphics display system (GDI) to rasterize the image. GDI printers are lower-cost printers that place a greater demand on the host processor than traditional printers.

GDM

(Global DOS Memory) The first megabyte of memory that DOS supports. It consists of conventional memory (0-640K), the UMA (640-1024K) and the HMA (1024-1088K).

GDMO

(Guidelines for the Definition of Managed Objects) An ISO standard for defining objects, which supports a strict inheritance hierarchy for object classes and a tree structure for object names.

GE

(Greater than or Equal to) See *relational operators*.

geek

Another term for nerd. Both words are used interchangeably; however, geek often refers to the most glaring stereotype. Take your pick.

geekspeak

Technical language. Same as *nerdspeak*.

GEM

(Graphics Environment Manager) A graphical user interface from Digital Research that was similar to the Mac/Windows environment. It was built into ROM in several Atari computers. The DOS version of Ventura Publisher came with a runtime version of GEM.

GEMBASE

A client/server application development system from Ross Systems, Inc., Atlanta, GA, (www.rossinc.com), that is noted for its high transaction performance and scalability. It runs on Windows NT, OpenVMS and UNIX servers that support dumb terminals and Windows clients. Its proprietary 4GL programming language can access Oracle, Rdb and Sybase databases as well as provide application partitioning.

GEMBASE's largest customer is Ross Systems itself, which develops the Renaissance CS applications for the process manufacturing industry. GEMBASE was originally developed by Pioneer Computing.

GEMMS

(Global Enterprise Manufacturing Management System) An ERP system from Oracle that runs on a variety of UNIX-based computers. It provides more than a dozen integrated modules for research & development, manufacturing, distribution, customer service and financial activities. GEMMS was developed by Datalogix, which was acquired by Oracle in 1997.

gender changer

A coupler that reverses the gender of one of the connectors in order that two male connectors or two female connectors can be joined together.

gene chip

A chip that is used to detect the DNA makeup of a cell. The chip contains hundreds of thousands of tiny squares designed to mate with a particular gene. They react to the liquified human cells poured over it and are detectable by a laser. Gene chips are expected to revolutionize medicine by being able to pinpoint a very specific disease or the susceptibility to it.

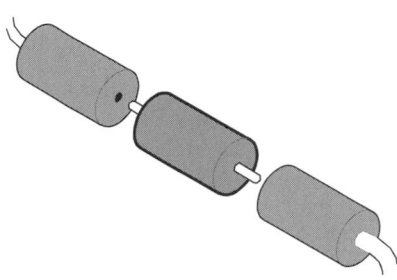

Gender Changer
The unit in the middle is the gender changer.

General failure reading drive x

A DOS error message. The full message is

```
General failure reading drive X
Abort, Retry, Fail?
```

This usually means that an unformatted floppy is being used. Press A to Abort, format the floppy and try again.

General Fault

See *GPF*.

generalized program

Software that serves a changing environment. By allowing variable data to be introduced, the program can solve the same problem for different users or situations. For example, the electronic versions of this database could be programmed to read in a different title and thus be used for any type of dictionary.

General Magic

(General Magic, Inc., Sunnyvale, CA, www.genmagic.com) A company founded in 1990 as a spinoff of Apple Computer. It was established to create personal communications products and services by developing and licensing technology to a wide variety of manufacturers and service providers. See *Telescript* and *Magic Cap*.

General MIDI

A standard set of 128 sounds for MIDI sound cards and devices (synthesizers, sound modules, etc.). By assigning instruments to specific MIDI patch locations, General MIDI provides a standard way of communicating MIDI sound.

MIDI's small storage requirement makes it very desirable as a musical sound source for multimedia applications compared to digitizing actual music. For example, a three-minute MIDI file may take only 20 to 30K, whereas a WAV file (digital audio) could consume up to several megabytes depending on sound quality.

General Protection Fault

See *GPF.*

general-purpose computer

Refers to computers that follow instructions, thus virtually all computers from micro to mainframe are general purpose. Even computers in toys, games and single-function devices follow instructions in their built-in program. In contrast, computational devices can be designed from scratch for special purposes (see *ASIC*).

general-purpose controller

A peripheral control unit that can service more than one type of peripheral device; for example, a printer and a communications line.

general-purpose language

A programming language used to solve a wide variety of problems. All common programming languages (FORTRAN, COBOL, BASIC, C, Pascal, etc.) are examples. Contrast with *special-purpose language.*

generator

(1) Software that creates software. See *application generator* and *macro generator.*

(2) A device that creates electrical power or synchonization signals.

Generic CADD

A full-featured CADD package for DOS from Autodesk, Inc., Sausalito, CA, (www.autodesk.com), that offers levels for beginner, intermediate and advanced users. It was originally developed by Generic Software of Bothell, WA.

generic top-level domain

See *Internet domain names.*

Genie

An online information service from IDT, Hackensack, NJ, that provides Internet access, chat lines, roundtable discussions and games. It was originally the General Electric Network for Information Exchange. See *online services.*

genlock

(**gen**erator **lock**) Circuitry that synchronizes video signals for mixing. In personal computers, a genlock display adapter converts screen output into an NTSC video signal, which it synchronizes with an external video source.

GEO

(**G**eostationary or **G**eosynchronous **E**arth **O**rbit) A communications satellite in orbit 22,282 miles above the equator. At this orbit, it travels at the same speed as the earth's rotation, thus appearing stationary. GEOs are excellent for TV broadcasting, but produce distracting, half-second delays in interactive voice conversations, because of the long round trip from earth and back. LEOs and MEOs, which are closer to the earth, are being deployed for interactive services. See *LEO* and *MEO.*

geographic information system

See *GIS.*

geometry accelerator

A high-performance graphics engine that performs geometry calculations. See *geometry calculations.*

geometry calculations

In 3-D graphics rendering, the computation of the base properties for each point (vertex) of the triangles forming the objects in the 3-D world. These properties include x-y-z coordinates, RGB values, alpha translucency, reflectivity and others. The geometry calculations involve transformation from 3-D world coordinates into corresponding 2-D screen coordinates, clipping off any parts not visible on screen and lighting. See *geometry accelerator.* See *graphics accelerator* for illustration.

geometry transformation

In 3-D graphics rendering, the translation of the x-y-z coordinates for each point (vertex) of the triangles forming the objects in the 3-D world into their corresponding 2-D screen coordinates. Animating 3-D objects requires enormous numbers of calculations. See *geometry calculations.*

GeoPort

A serial port from Apple designed for voice and video applications. With an adapter, it can be used to dial an analog phone. Standard on various Macintosh models, GeoPort provides a 2 Mbps bandwidth, suitable for very high-quality videoconferencing. The GeoPort is endorsed by Versit.

GEOS

An operating system that provides a graphical interface for PDAs and consumer-oriented devices from Geoworks, Inc., Alameda, CA, (www.geoworks.com).

geostationary, geosynchronous

Earth aligned. See *GEO.*

Geoworks Ensemble

An earlier graphical environment for DOS from Geoworks, Inc., Alameda, CA, (www.geoworks.com), that included a basic suite of applications and provided a launching pad for all other applications.

germanium

(Ge) The material used in making the first transistors. Although still used in very limited applications, germanium was replaced by silicon years ago.

gesture recognition

The ability to interpret simple hand-written symbols such as check marks and slashes.

get

(1) In programming, a request for the next record in an input file. Contrast with *put.*

(2) An FTP command to copy a file or to display the contents of a text file.

Gflops

See *gigaflops.*

ghost

(1) A faint second image that appears close to the primary image on a display or printout. On a printer, it is caused by bouncing print elements as the paper passes by.

(2) In transmission, a secondary signal that arrives ahead of or later than the primary signal.

(3) To display the text of a menu option or the elements on a toolbar button in a grayed or fuzzy manner, indicating that the operation is not currently selectable.

GHz

(GigaHertZ) One billion cycles per second. High-speed radio frequency applications transmit in the gigahertz range. See *RF.*

giant magnetoresistive

See *magnetoresistive.*

A Ghosted Button
The button on the left is ghosted, indicating that the function is not available at that moment. When it is usable, the elements are restored as in the example on the right.

GIF

(Graphics Interchange Format) A popular bitmapped graphics file format developed by CompuServe. It supports 8-bit color (256 colors) and is widely used on the Web, because the files compress well. GIFs include a color table that includes the most representative 256 colors used. For example, a picture of the forest would include mostly greens. This method provides excellent realism in an 8-bit image.

GIF89 allows one of the colors to be made transparent and take on the background color of the underlying page or window. GIF89a supports animated GIFs, which are sequences of images displayed one after the other to simulate movement.

Macintosh users call GIF files "giff" files, while PC users call them "jiff" files. See *PNG*.

GIFSCII

(1) **(GIF ASCII)** A program that converts images into ASCII art or the image that was created in such a manner. See *ASCII art*.

(2) Converting ASCII text into a GIF image for the Web in order to preserve the original fonts and formatting.

gig, giga

Billion. Abreviated "G." It often refers to the precise value 1,073,741,824 since computer specifications are usually binary numbers. See *binary values* and *space/time*.

gigabit

One billion bits. Also Gb, Gbit and G-bit. See *giga* and *space/time*.

Gigabit Ethernet

An Ethernet technology that raises transmission speed to 1 Gbps. It is used primarily for backbones. The first IEEE standard (802.3z) for Gigabit Ethernet defined its use over multimode optical fiber (see below) and provides full-duplex operation from switch to end station or to another switch and half-duplex using CSMA/CD in a shared environment. The 1000BaseTX copper cable alternative (802.3ab) is expected to be a formal standard in 1999.

Fiber Diameter (microns)	Modal Bandwidth (MHz-km)	Range (meters)
1000BaseSX		
62.5	160	220
62.5	200	275
50	400	500
50	500	550
1000BaseLX		
62.5	500	550
50	400	550
50	500	550
9	—	5000

gigabyte

One billion bytes. Also GB, Gbyte and G-byte. See *giga* and *space/time*.

gigaflops

(GIGA FLoating point OPerations per Second) One billio floating point operations per second. See *FLOPS*.

gigahertz

See *GHz*.

GigaPOP

(GIGAbit Point Of Presence) A high-speed switching point being developed by universities across the U.S. as part of the Internet2 project. See *Internet2*.

Gig E

See *Gigabit Ethernet*.

GIGO

(Garbage In Garbage Out) "Bad input produces bad output." Data entry is critical. All possible tests should be made on data entered into a computer.

"Garbage In, Gospel Out"
An alternate meaning. Many people have complete faith in computer output!

GIOP

(General Inter-Orb Protocol) The protocol used by CORBA to communicate between ORBs. GIOP defines the messages and format that are passed over the ORB between the client and the object. GIOP is a high-level protocol that rides on top of a transport protocol such as TCP/IP. The combination of GIOP running on TCP/IP is IIOP. See *IIOP* and *CORBA*.

GIS

(1) (Geographic Information System) A digital mapping system used for exploration, demographics, dispatching and tracking.

(2) (Generalized Information System) An early IBM mainframe query and data manipulation language.

GKS

(Graphical Kernel System) A device-independent graphics language for 2-D, 3-D and bitmapped graphics images. It allows graphics applications to be developed on one system and easily moved to another with minimal or no change. It was the first true standard for graphics applications programmers and has been adopted by both ANSI and ISO.

glare filter

A fine mesh screen that is placed over a CRT screen to reduce glare from overhead and ambient light.

glass house

The large datacenter, which typically contains one or more mainframes and is often constructed with windows to the inside. Glass houses may contain raised floors for underground wiring and are generally very well air conditioned.

GLINT

A family of 2-D and 3-D processors from 3D Labs, Inc., San Jose, CA, (www.3dlabs.com), that are widely used in high-end display adapters.

glitch

A temporary or random hardware malfunction. It is possible that a bug in a program may cause the hardware to appear as if it had a glitch in it and vice versa. At times it can be extremely difficult to determine whether a problem lies within the hardware or the software.

global

Pertaining to an entire file, database, volume, program or system.

The Big Glass House
Mainframes have typically resided in the "glass house" due to stringent air conditioning requirements. Although newer machines dissipate less heat than older models, many units in one room still require substantial cooling. *(Photo courtesy of IBM Corporation.)*

global variable

In programming, a variable that is used by all modules in a program.

global village

(1) A term coined by Marshall McLuhan who envisioned the world interconnected via electronic communications.

(2) (Global Village Communications, Inc., Sunnyvale, CA, www.globalvillage.com) A manufacturer of communications products for the Macintosh and Windows PCs founded in 1989.

Global Virtual Private Network

See *GVPN*.

GLperf

(OpenGL PERFormance) A benchmark developed by the OPC group for measuring the raw performance of an OpenGL system. See *OPC*.

glue chip

A support chip that adds functionality to a microprocessor, for example, an I/O processor or extra memory.

glue logic

A small amount of digital circuitry (logic gates) used to interconnect ready-made circuits. See *standard cell*.

GM

See *General MIDI*.

GMR

(Giant Magnetoresistive) See *magnetoresistive*.

GMTA

Digispeak for "great minds thing alike."

GNU

(Gnu's Not UNIX) A project sponsored by the Free Software Foundation that is developing a complete software environment including operating system kernel and utilities, editor, compiler and debugger. Many consultants and organizations provide support for GNU software. See *Linux* and *GNU General Public License*.

GNU General Public License

The license that accompanies the GNU software. Also known as a "copyleft," it gives everyone the right to use and modify the material as long as they make it available to everyone else with the same licensing stipulation.

go

A command used on a BBS or online service to switch the user to a particular forum or section. For example, typing **go macintosh** would switch you to a section specializing in Macintosh computers. Like any command language, you have to know what words to enter.

goal seeking

The ability to calculate a formula backward to obtain a desired input. For example, given the goal **gross margin = 50%** as well as the range of possible inputs, goal seeking attempts to obtain the optimum input.

GOCA

(Graphics Object Content Architecture) See *MO:DCA*.

gold code

Programming source code that is finalized for commercial duplication. See *build*.

good books

See *how to find a good computer book*.

gooey

See *GUI*.

gooey builder

See *GUI builder*.

Gopher

A program that searches for file names and resources on the Internet and presents hierarchical menus to the user. As users select options, they are moved to different Gopher servers on the Internet. Where links have been established, Usenet news and other information can be read directly from Gopher. There are more than 7,000 Gopher servers on the Internet. See *Veronica, Archie, Jughead, WAIS* and *World Wide Web*.

Gopherspace

The collective information made available on Gopher servers throughout the Internet.

GOPS

(Giga <billion> Operations Per Second) The measurement of instructional performance of a chip or system. It typically refers to DSP operations. See *MOPS*.

Goraud shading

See *Gouraud shading*.

Gorizont

A Russian satellite that was placed in a geostationary orbit for communications purposes.

GOSIP

(Government Open Systems Interconnection Profile) A U.S. government mandate that after August 15, 1990, all new network procurements must comply with OSI. Testing is performed at the NIST, which maintains a database of OSI-compliant commercial products. GOSIP also allows TCP/IP protocols to be used.

Since broad adoption of OSI standards never came to fruition, GOSIP evolved into POSIT (Profiles for Open Systems Internetworking Technologies), which is a set of non-mandatory standards that acknowledge the widespread use of TCP/IP.

goto

(1) In a high-level programming language, a statement that directs the computer to go to some other part of the program. Low-level language equivalents are *branch* and *jump*.

(2) In dBASE, a command that directs the user to a specific record in the file.

(3) In word processing, a command that directs the user to a specific page number.

goto-less programming

Writing a program without using goto instructions, an important rule in structured programming. A goto instruction points to a different part of the program without a guarantee of returning. Instead of using goto's, structures called subroutines or functions are used, which automatically return to the next instruction after the calling instruction when completed.

Gouraud shading

In 3-D graphics, a technique developed by Henri Gouraud that computes a shaded surface based on the color and illumination at the corners of every triangle. The surface normals at the triangle's points are used to create RGB values, which are averaged across the triangle's surface. Gouraud shading is computed faster than Phong shading. See *Phong shading*.

gov

An Internet address domain name for a governmental agency. See *Internet address*.

GPC

(GPC Group) Originally the Graphics Performance Characterization committee of the NCGA, the GPC Group is now part of Standard Performance Evaluation Corporation (SPEC) and oversees the following graphics performance benchmarks: APC, OPC, PLB and XPC. APC tests applications, MBC tests multimedia, OPC tests OpenGL, XPC tests X Window, and PLB tests wireframe and surface modeling. See *APC, MBC, OPC, XPC, PLB* and *SPEC*.

GPCmark

See *PLB*.

GPEG

See *JPEG*.

GPF

(1) (General Protection Fault) The name of an abend, or crash, in a Windows application, starting with Version 3.1. When the GPF occurs, an error message is displayed, and the program is generally unable to continue. See *Application Error* and *abend*.

(2) (GUI Programming Facility) An OS/2 application generator from GPF Systems, Inc., Moodus, CT.

GPI

(Graphical Programming Interface) A graphics language in OS/2 Presentation Manager. It is a derivative of the GDDM mainframe interface and includes Bezier curves.

GPIB

(General Purpose Interface Bus) An IEEE 488 standard parallel interface used for attaching sensors and programmable instruments to a computer. It uses a 24-pin connector. HP's version is the HPIB.

gppm

(Graphics Pages Per Minute) The measurement of printer speed based on printing graphics, which takes considerably longer to print than text. A gppm rating is more meaningful to the graphics designer than ppm (pages per minute), which usually rates the speed of printing text.

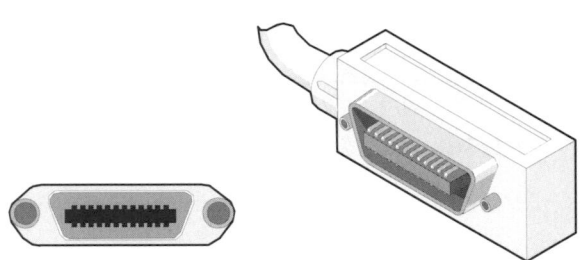

GPIB (IEEE-488) Connectors
GPIC connectors are used to attach sensors and programmable instruments to computer systems.

GPS

(Global Positioning System) A system of 24 satellites for identifying earth locations, launched by the U.S. Department of Defense. By triangulation of signals from three of the satellites, a receiving unit can pinpoint its current location anywhere on earth to within a few meters.

With GPS, the "James Bond" style of on-screen mobile map reading is a reality. Units combined with CD players that read the map data are widely available for automobile installation. These systems guide you to your destination via screen display and voice instructions.

GPSS

(General Purpose Simulation System) A programming language for discrete event simulation, which is used to build models of operations such as manufacturing environments, communications systems and traffic patterns. Originally developed by IBM for mainframes, PC versions are available, such as GPSS/PC by Minuteman Software and GPSS/H by Wolverine Software.

GPS in the Car
Sony's NVX-F160 was one of the first automobile GPS systems. It can direct you to the nearest restaurant, hotel or other points of interest. *(Photo courtesy of Sony Corporation.)*

GQL

(Graphical Query Language) A family of query and reporting tools used to access databases on client/server systems from Andyne Computing, Ltd., Ottawa, Ontario, (www.andyne.com).

Computer Desktop Encyclopedia

grabber

See *frame grabber, screen grabber* and *grabber hand*.

grabber hand

A screen tool that is shaped like a hand and is used to move objects within a window. For example, if the image is larger than the current window size, the grabber hand lets you scroll the image. When the tool is selected, the screen pointer turns into the hand. When clicked on an image, it "grabs" it so it can be moved.

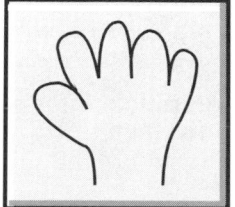

The Grabber Hand
This tool was widely used on the Macintosh before it found its way into the Windows world.

graceful degradation

A system that continues to perform at some reduced level of performance after one of its components fails.

graceful exit

The ability to get out of a problem situation in a program without having to turn the computer off.

grade

The transmission capacity of a line. It refers to a range or class of frequencies that it can handle; for example, telegraph grade, voice grade and broadband.

gradient

A smooth blending of shades from light to dark or from one color to another. In 2-D drawing programs and paint programs, gradients are used to create colorful backgrounds and special effects as well as to simulate lights and shadows. In 3-D graphics programs, lighting can be rendered automatically by the software. See *3-D graphics*.

A Gradient
The software generates the gradient automatically as in this example created in Photoshop.

GRAFCET

(GRAPHe de Commande Etape-Transition - stage transition command graph) A PLC specification and programming language.

gram

See *metric system*.

grammar checker

Software that checks the grammar of a sentence. It can check for and highlight incomplete sentences, awkward phrases, wordiness and poor grammar.

Grammatik

A popular grammar checking program for DOS, Windows, Macintosh and UNIX that was developed by Reference Software, San Francisco, and acquired by WordPerfect Corporation in 1993. Novell later acquired WordPerfect, then sold it to Corel. U.S. Government versions check for usage according to the Government Printing Office and other military and civilian guides.

grandfather-father-son

A method for storing previous generations of master file data that are continuously updated. The son is the current file, the father is a copy of the file from the previous cycle, and the grandfather is a copy of the file from the cycle before that one.

granularity

The degree of modularity of a system. The more granularity (grains or granules), the more customizable or flexible the system.

graph

A pictorial representation of information. See *business graphics*.

graphical interface, graphical user interface

See *GUI*.

graphic character

See *character graphics*.

graphics

Called *computer graphics*, it is the creation and manipulation of picture images in the computer. It is defined in this database under "graphics" to keep the term next to other entries that begin with "graphics."

A fast desktop computer is required for graphics work, and although a mouse can be used for drawing, graphics tablets are widely used for CAD (computer-aided design) applications. A scanner is also typically used.

Vector Graphics and Bitmapped Graphics

Two methods are used for storing and maintaining pictures in a computer. The first method, called *vector graphics*, maintains the image as a series of points, lines, arcs and other geometric shapes.

The second method, called *bitmapped graphics* and also known as raster graphics, resembles television, where the picture image is made up of dots. Understanding these two methods and how they intertwine is essential.

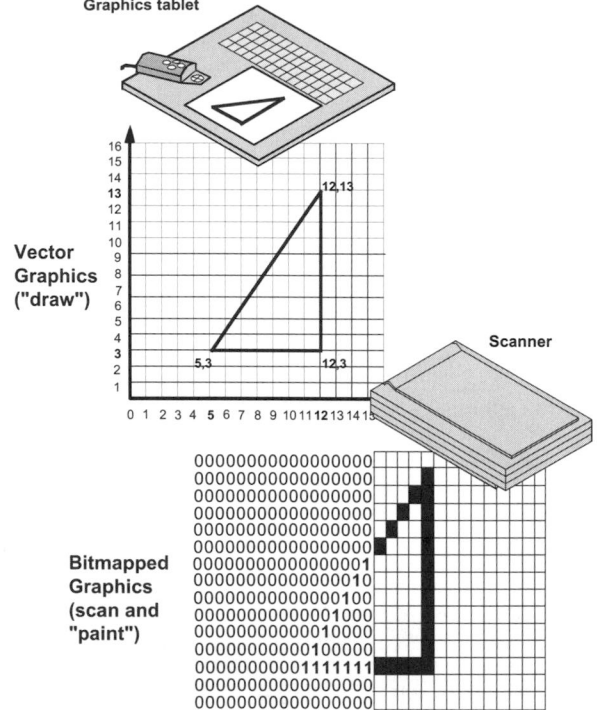

Drawing, Scanning and Painting

Pictures are "drawn" into vector graphics images using a digitizer tablet or mouse. Pictures are turned into bitmaps with scanners and digital cameras. Using a paint program, bitmaps can also be "painted" freehand, using the screen as a canvas.

Vector Graphics for CAD and Drawing

Vector graphics is the method employed by computer-aided design (CAD) and drawing packages. As you draw, each line of the image is stored as a vector, which is two end points on an x-y matrix. For example, a square becomes four vectors, one for each side. A circle is turned into dozens or hundreds of tiny straight lines, the number of which is determined by the resolution of the drawing. The entire image is commonly stored in the computer as a list of vectors.

A vector graphics image is a collection of graphic elements, such as lines, squares, rectangles and circles. Although grouped together, each element maintains its own integrity and identity and can always be selected and erased or resized independent of all the others.

Vector graphics can be transmitted directly to x-y plotters that "draw" the images from the list of vectors. Older CAD systems used vector screens that also drew the vectors. Today, all monitors are raster displays made up of dots, and the vectors are "rasterized" into the required dot patterns by hardware or software. In addition, most plotters have given way to ink jet printers.

3-D Graphics

3-D images use vector graphics, but 3-D CAD and drawing programs are significantly different than 2-D programs. Objects are created in 3-D form in a 3-dimensional workspace. They can be viewed at any angle by simply rotating them, whereas in 2-D programs, the object would have to be redrawn entirely. 3-D programs can render the drawing with lights and shadows, and camera angles and light sources are used to depict the objects as real-world elements. See *3-D graphics* for illustration.

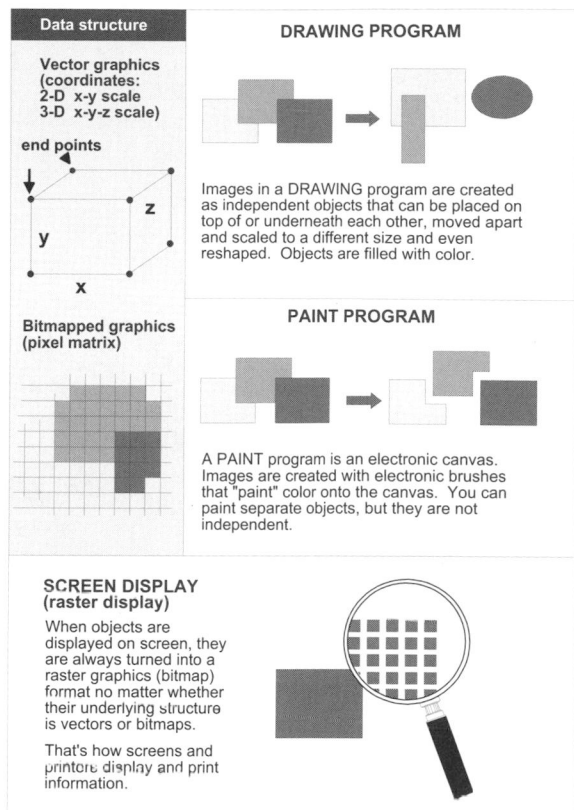

Drawing vs Painting

Although more painting tools are added to drawing programs and more drawing tools are added to paint programs, their inherent structure is different. Drawing programs (vector graphics) allow for the creation of objects that can be manipulated independently. Paint programs (bitmapped graphics) provide a canvas that can be covered with electronic paint.

Canvas Specializes in Both

Deneba Software's Canvas combines extensive drawing and imaging tools in one program. The PC drawing on top is a vector graphics rendering and the "first mouse" below is a bitmap. The open menus show image editing tools that are not normally found in a drawing program.

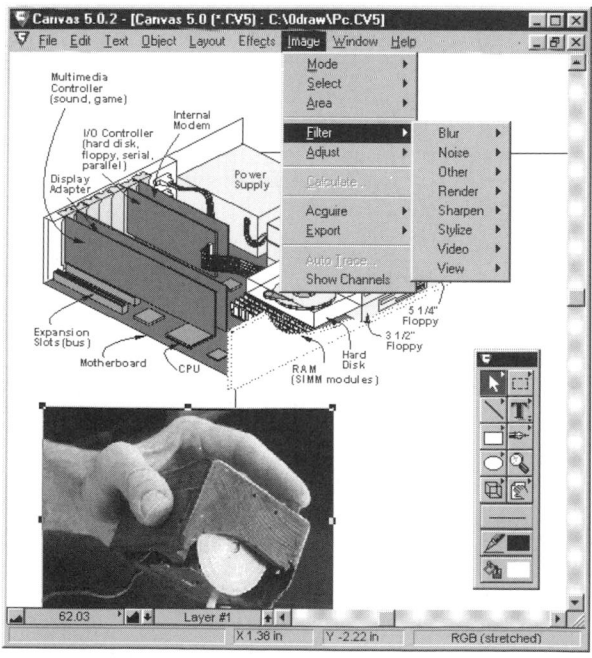

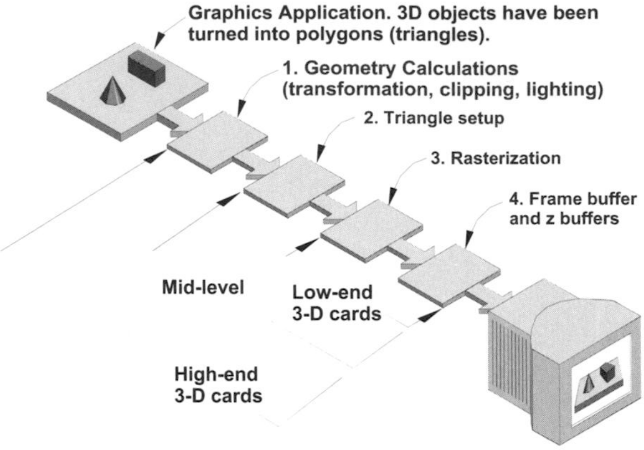

Bitmapped Graphics for Imaging and Painting

Bitmapped graphics is the TV-like method that uses dots to display an image on screen. Bitmapped images are created by scanners and cameras and are also generated by paint packages. A picture frame is divided into hundreds of horizontal rows, with each row containing hundreds of dots, called pixels.

Unlike TV, which uses one standard (NTSC) for the country, there are dozens of bitmapped graphics standards. Also, unlike TV, which records and displays the dots as infinitely variable shades and colors (analog), computer graphics have a finite number of shades and colors (digital).

When you scan an image or paint an object into the computer, the image is created in a reserved area of memory called a *bitmap*, with some number of bits corresponding to each dot (pixel). The simplest monochrome bitmap uses one bit (on/off) for each dot. Gray scale bitmaps (monochrome shades) hold a number for each dot large enough to hold all the gray levels. Color bitmaps require three times as much storage in order to hold the intensity of red, green and blue.

The image in the bitmap is continuously transmitted to the video screen, dot for dot, a line at a time, over and over again. Any changes made to the bitmap are instantly reflected on the screen.

Since colors are designated with numbers, changing red to green is simply searching for the red number and replacing it with the green number. Animation is accomplished by continuously copying new sequences from other areas in memory into the bitmap, one after the other.

Bitmapped images may take up more space on disk than their vector graphics counterpart, because storage for each pixel is required even if it's part of the background. A small object in vector graphics format will take up only a few vectors in the graphics database.

Graphics Application. 3D objects have been turned into polygons (triangles).

1. Geometry Calculations (transformation, clipping, lighting)
2. Triangle setup
3. Rasterization
4. Frame buffer and z buffers

Mid-level

Low-end 3-D cards

High-end 3-D cards

3-D Graphics Generation

Rendering an image requires each of the four stages above. The more work done in hardware, the faster the results. *(Illustration courtesy of Intergraph Computer Systems.)*

graphics accelerator

A high-performance display adapter that provides hardware functions to speed up 2-D, 3-D or video operations or all three. When functions are built into the chips on the display adapter, there is less work for the host CPU to do to render the images on screen.

There are many functions that can be built into hardware, including line draw and pixel block moves (bitblt) for 2-D operations, texture mapping and Gouraud shading for 3-D and color space conversion and hardware scaling for video. Much of the performance improvements on new PCs and workstations are due to speeding up the display systems. See *geometry accelerator* and *triangle setup*.

graphics adapter

Same as *display adapter*.

graphics based

The display of text and pictures as graphics images; typically bitmapped images. Contrast with *text based*.

graphics board, graphics card

Same as *display adapter*.

graphics character

See *character graphics*.

graphics coprocessor

Graphics hardware that performs various 2-D and 3-D geometry and rendering functions, offloading the main CPU from performing such tasks. This typically refers to a very high-end graphics subsystem, but may also refer to a graphics accelerator. See *graphics accelerator* and *geometry accelerator*.

Graphics Device Interface
See *GDI*.

graphics engine
(1) Hardware that performs graphics processing tasks independently of the computer's CPU. See *graphics accelerator* and *graphics coprocessor*.

(2) Software that accepts commands from an application and builds images and text that are directed to the graphics driver and hardware. Macintosh's QuickDraw and Windows' GDI are examples.

graphics file
A file that contains only graphics data. Contrast with *text file* and *binary file*.

graphics formats
There is a wide variety of graphics formats in use today. The following list contains most of them. The formats are in order by extension name under bitmapped or vector category. Some formats appear in both categories because they can hold both raster and vector images.

BITMAPPED FORMATS (RASTER GRAPHICS)

AG4	Access G4 document imaging		JFF	JPEG (JFIF)
ATT	AT&T Group IV		JPG	JPEG
BMP	Windows & OS/2		KFX	Kofax Group IV
CAL	CALS Group IV			
CIT	Intergraph scanned images		MAC	MacPaint
CLP	Windows Clipboard		MIL	Same as GP4 extension
CMP	Photomatrix G3/G4 scanner format		MSP	Microsoft Paint
CMP	LEAD Technologies			
			NIF	Navy Image File
CPR	Knowledge Access			
CT	Scitex Continuous Tone		PBM	Portable bitmap
CUT	Dr. Halo		PCD	PhotoCD
			PCX	PC Paintbrush
DBX	DATABEAM		PIX	Inset Systems (HiJaak)
DX	Autotrol document imaging		PNG	Portable Network Graphics
			PSD	Photoshop native format
ED5	EDMICS (U.S. DOD)			
ED6	EDMICS (U.S. DOD)		RAS	Sun
EPS	Encapsulated PostScript		RGB	SGI
			RIA	Alpharel Group IV document imaging
FAX	Fax		RLC	Image Systems
FMV	FrameMaker		RLE	Various RLE-compressed formats
			RNL	GTX Runlength
GED	Arts & Letters			
GDF	IBM GDDM format		SBP	IBM StoryBoard
GIF	CompuServe		SGI	Silicon Graphics RGB
GP4	CALS Group IV - ITU Group IV		SUN	Sun
GX1	Show Partner			
GX2	Show Partner		TGA	Targa
			TIF	TIFF
ICA	IBM IOCA (see *MO:DCA*)			
ICO	Windows icon		WPG	WordPerfect image
IFF	Amiga ILBM			
IGF	Inset Systems (HiJaak)		XBM	X Window bitmap
IMG	GEM Paint		XPM	X Window pixelmap
			XWD	X Window dump

VECTOR GRAPHICS FORMATS

3DS	3D Studio	IGF	Inset Systems (HiJaak)
906	Calcomp plotter	IGS	IGES
AI	Adobe Illustrator	MCS	MathCAD
		MET	OS/2 metafile
CAL	CALS subset of CGM	MRK	Informative Graphics markup file
CDR	CorelDRAW		
CGM	Computer Graphics Metafile	P10	Tektronix plotter (PLOT10)
CH3	Harvard Graphics chart	PCL	HP LaserJet
CLP	Windows clipboard	PCT	Macintosh PICT drawings
CMX	Corel Metafile Exchange	PDW	HiJaak
		PGL	HP plotter
DG	Autotrol	PIC	Variety of picture formats
DGN	Intergraph drawing format	PIX	Inset Systems (HiJaak)
DRW	Micrografx Designer 2.x, 3.x	PLT	HPGL Plot File
DS4	Micrografx Designer 4.x		(HPGL2 has raster format)
DSF	Micrografx Designer 6.x	PS	PostScript Level 2
DXF	AutoCAD		
DWG	AutoCAD	RLC	Image Systems "CAD Overlay ESP"
			vector overlaid onto raster
EMF	Enhanced metafile		
EPS	Encapsulated PostScript	SSK	SmartSketch
ESI	Esri plot file (GIS mapping)		
		WMF	Windows Metafile
FMV	FrameMaker	WPG	WordPerfect graphics
		WRL	VRML
GCA	IBM GOCA		
GEM	GEM proprietary		
G4	GTX RasterCAD - scanned images into		
	vectors for AutoCAD		

graphics interface
See *graphics language* and *GUI*.

graphics language
A high-level language used to create graphics images. The language is translated into images by software or specialized hardware. See *graphics engine*.

graphics mode
A screen display mode that displays graphics. Contrast with *text mode* and *character mode*.

graphics port
(1) A socket on the computer for connecting a graphics monitor.

(2) Also called *GrafPort*, it is a Macintosh graphics structure that defines all the characteristics of a graphics window.

graphics primitive
An elementary graphics building block, such as a point, line or arc. In a solid modeling system, a cylinder, cube and sphere are examples.

graphics processor
Same as *graphics engine*.

graphics program
See *paint program, drawing program, presentation graphics, image editor* and *image processing*.

graphics tablet
Same as *digitizer tablet*.

graphics terminal
A terminal or personal computer that displays graphics.

graPHIGS

See *GDDM*.

Graybar

(Graybar, Clayton, MO, www.graybar.com) An international distributor of electrical and voice and data communications equipment. In 1869, the company was founded in Cleveland as Gray and Barton by Elisha Gray and Enos Barton. It initially manufactured Gray's telegraph equipment, the most successful of which was his printing telegraph.

Gray and Barton was later renamed Western Electric Company when Western Union, its major customer, became an investor. Although Elisha Gray and Alexander Graham Bell had battled in the courts over patent rights to the telephone, and Bell had won, Western Electric became the manufacturer of Bell's telephones. Western Electric also supplied electrical products to the telephone companies as well as to other organizations as the electrical business flourished in the country.

In 1926, Western Electric spun off its electrical distribution as Graybar Electric Company. In 1929, Graybar was the first large company to be bought out by its own employees.

In the mid 1980s, after the breakup of AT&T, Graybar added more voice communications suppliers and got heavily involved in data communications. Today, it handles tens of thousands of products from more than 250 major suppliers.

Gray's Printing Telegraph
The printing telegraph was Gray's most successful invention in the late 1800s. Imagine the excitement this machine caused because it was no longer necessary for a telegraph operator to interpret the code and write the text. *(Photo courtesy of Graybar.)*

gray scale

A series of shades from white to black. The more shades, or levels, the more realistic an image can be recorded and displayed, especially a scanned photo. Scanners differentiate typically from 16 to 256 gray levels.

Although compression techiques help reduce the size of graphics files, high-resolution gray scale requires huge amounts of storage. At a printer resolution of 300 dpi, each square inch is made up of 90,000 pixels. At 256 levels, it takes one byte per pixel, or 90,000 bytes per square inch of image. See *halftone*.

greek

In desktop publishing, to display text in a representative form in which the actual letters are not discernible, because the screen resolution isn't high enough to display them properly. The software lets you set which font sizes should be greeked.

The term comes from typography and graphics design, in which Greek or Latin letters and words are placed into layouts to hold the position for and represent the real text that was forthcoming. Foreign words and letters were used to quickly identify them as a mockup.

Green Book

See *CD-I*.

green PC

An energy-saving personal computer or peripheral device. Green computers, printers and monitors go into a low-voltage "suspend mode" if

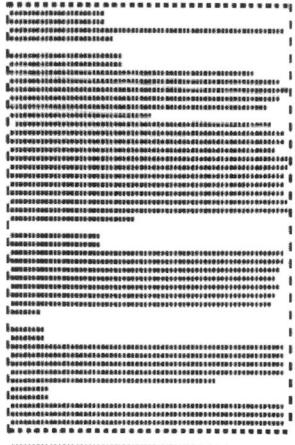

Greeking
This is the type of greeking that would occur when the amount of space available for text is too small to display or print the individual letters.

not used after a certain period of time. Laser printers especially waste a lot of energy when not in use, because of their heat-induced fusing mechanism.

Many contemporary CPUs can run at variable clock rates and can idle at very low speeds, to save current. When input is detected, they revert to full-power.

The green concept includes using less packaging materials, recycling toner cartridges, providing a return location for used batteries, distributing multi-disk software on a CD-ROM and sending e-mail rather than paper mail.

grep
(Global Regular Expression and Print) A UNIX pattern matching utility that searches for a string of text and outputs any line that contains the pattern.

ground
An electrically conductive body, such as the earth, which maintains a zero potential (not positively or negatively charged) for connecting to an electrical circuit.

ground current
The current found in a ground line. It may be caused by imbalanced electrical sources; for example, the ground line in a communications channel between two computers deriving power separately.

ground fault
The temporary current in the ground line, caused by a failing electrical component or interference from an external electrical source such as a thunderstorm.

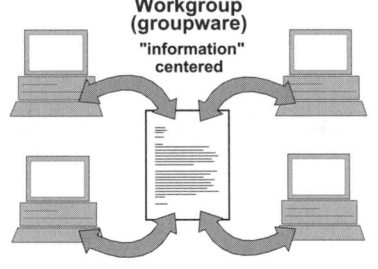

ground loop
An unwanted ground current flowing back and forth between two devices that are grounded at two or more points.

ground noise injection
An intentional insertion of unwanted noise by a power supply into the ground line.

group collaboration products
See *e-mail, groupware, data conferencing* and *videoconferencing*.

group scheduling
See *calendaring*.

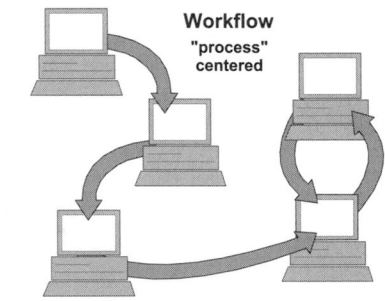

groupware
Software that is designed to support multiple users that work on related tasks. Groupware is an evolving concept that is more than just multiuser software which allows access to the same data. Groupware provides a mechanism that helps users coordinate and keep track of on-going projects together.

The heart of groupware is a messaging system, because e-mail is used to notify team members, obtain responses and send alerts. E-mail messages increasingly include live links to databases, intranets and the Internet. Other applications include document sharing and document

Groupware and Workflow
Groupware focuses on the information being processed and enabling users to share it. Workflow emphasizes the process, which acts as a container for the information. Groupware is "information centered." Workflow is "process centered." *(Illustration courtesy of Delphi Consulting Group, Inc.)*

management, group calendaring and scheduling, group contact and task management, threaded discussions, text chat, data conferencing and audio and videoconferencing. Workflow, which allows messages and documents to be routed to the appropriate users, is often part of a groupware system.

Lotus Notes is often considered the father of groupware, because it was the first to popularize a multifunction groupware system and development environment. There are myriads of programs that provide a single groupware function; however, Lotus Notes, GroupWise and Microsoft Exchange are examples of products that provide multiple groupware functions. Communicator and Internet Explorer/ NetMeeting are also examples.

The Internet/intranet explosion has focused attention on groupware, because of the ease with which HTML pages can be created and shared. However, as documents become widely used and distributed throughout the enterprise, security and synchronization problems surface. Document management becomes a problem, and access control and replication become issues. Thus, what starts out as a simple way to electronically publish information, winds up becoming as strategic as the client/server systems that have been distributed throughout the enterprise. Groupware is becoming a critical issue in computing.

GroupWise

Messaging and groupware software from Novell that provides a universal inbox for calendaring, group scheduling, task management, document sharing, workflow and threaded discussions. Whiteboards and application sharing are available through third-parties. GroupWise clients run on Windows, Mac and UNIX, and the GroupWise server runs on NetWare, NT and UNIX. GroupWise supports a wide variety of mail systems as well as Novell's NDS directory. Text-to-speech and speech-to-wave files lets mobile users hear and create e-mail by telephone. Although entirely revamped, GroupWise stems back to WordPerfect Office, which was acquired by Novell in 1994.

GSM

(Global System for Mobile Communications) A digital cellular phone technology based on TDMA that is widely deployed in Europe and throughout the world. GSM coverage is increasing in the U.S. Most PCS phones use GSM and operate in the 1.8 to 1.9GHz band, compared to 800-900MHz for other cellular systems. Higher frequencies extend battery life. See *TDMA, CDMA* and *PCS*.

GSMP

(General Switch Management Protocol) The call setup protocol used in the IP Switch. See *IP Switch*.

GSOS

(GS Operating System) A graphical operating system for the Apple IIGS that also accepts ProDOS applications.

GSTN

(General Switched Telephone Network) Same as *PSTN*.

GT

(Greater Than) See *relational operator*.

gTLD

(Generic Top-Level Domain) A general-purpose domain name on the Internet. The IAHC created seven new gTLDs in early 1997 (.firm, .store, .web, .arts, .rec, .info & .nom). It has recommended that the international TLDs .com, .net & .org be redefined as gTLDs.

guard band

A frequency that insulates one signal from another. In an analog telephone line, the low band is 0-300; the high band is 3300-4000Hz.

guest

A person that logs into a network or service that does not have a user account. Guests are given a default set of privileges until they formally register to the service. See *guest account, guest privileges* and *user account*.

guest account

A default set of permissions and privileges given to non-registered users of a system or service. See *guest* and *guest privileges*.

guest privileges

The rights and permissions given to a non-registered user of a system or service. See *guest*.

GUI

(Graphical User Interface) A graphics-based user interface that incorporates icons, pull-down menus and a mouse. The GUI has become the standard way users interact with a computer. The three major GUIs are Windows, Macintosh and Motif. In a client/server environment, the GUI resides in the user's client machine. See *drag & drop, desktop manager, window manager* and *Star*. Contrast with *CUI*.

GUI accelerator

See *graphics accelerator*.

GUI builder

Visual programming software that lets a user build a graphical user interface by dragging and dropping elements from a toolbar onto the screen. It may be a stand-alone program or part of an application development system or client/server development system. See *application development system* and *client/server development system*.

guiltware

Shareware that makes a poignant plea to the user to purchase the product and support the developers.

GUI painter

Same as *GUI builder*.

The First Commercial GUI
Xerox's Star workstation was the first commercial implementation of the graphical user interface. The Star was introduced in 1981 and was the inspiration for the Mac and all the other GUIs that followed. *(Photo courtesy of Xerox Corporation.)*

GUI widget

A small element used in a graphical user interface (GUI) such as a button or scroll bar.

gull-wing lead

A pin on a chip package that extends slightly out, down and then out again. Gull wing leads are used on surface mount chips such as QFPs and SOICs. See *QFP, SOIC* and *J-lead*.

gulp

An unspecified number of bytes.

Gupta

See *Centura*.

gutter

In typography, the space between two columns.

GVPN

(Global Virtual Private Network) A service from cooperating carriers that provides international digital communications for multinational companies.

GVRP

(GARP VLAN Registration Protocol) A standard for registering a client station into a VLAN. See *802.1p*

GW-BASIC

(Gee Whiz-BASIC) A BASIC interpreter that accompanied MS-DOS prior to 5.0. See *QBasic*.

H

h

(Hexadecimal) A symbol that refers to a hex number. For example, 09h has a numeric value of 9, whereas 0Ah has a value of 10. See *hex chart*. See also *henry*.

H&J

(Hyphenation and Justification) The alignment of the right margin in a document. Hyphenation breaks up words that exceed the margin. Justification aligns text uniformly at the right margin while spacing text evenly between both margins.

H.221

An ITU standard for the framing structure of a videoconferencing transmission over a 64 to 1920 Kbits/sec channel. See *H.230*.

H.230

An ITU standard for controlling the synchronization of videoconferencing frames. See *H.221*.

H.231

An ITU standard for multipoint control units for videoconferencing. See *MCU*.

H.245

An ITU standard protocol for making an audio and videoconferencing call. It defines flow control, encryption and jitter management as well as the signals for initiating the call, negotiating which features are to be used and terminating the call. It also determines which side is the master for issuing various commands.

H.261

An ITU standard for compressing an H.320 videoconferencing transmission. The algorithm can be implemented in hardware or software and uses intraframe and interframe compression. It uses one or more 64 Kbps ISDN channels (Px64). H.261 supports CIF and QCIF resolutions. See *CIF*.

H.262

An ITU standard for compressing a videoconferencing transmission. It uses the MPEG-2 compression algorithm.

H.263

An ITU standard for compressing a videoconferencing transmission. It is based on H.261 with enhancements that improve video quality over modems. H.263 supports CIF, QCIF, SQCIF, 4CIF and 16CIF resolutions. See *CIF*.

H.310

An ITU standard for videoconferencing over ATM and Broadband ISDN networks using MPEG compression.

H.320

An ITU standard for videoconferencing over digital lines. Using the H.261 compression method, it allows H.320-compliant videoconferencing room and desktop systems to communicate with each other over ISDN, switched digital and leased lines. A counterpart standard for data conferencing is T.120.

H.321

An ITU standard for videoconferencing over ATM and Broadband ISDN networks.

H.322

An ITU standard for videoconferencing over local area networks (LANs) that can guarantee bandwidth, such as Isochronous Ethernet.

H.323

An ITU standard for videoconferencing over packet-switched networks such as local area networks (LANs) and the Internet. It allows any combination of voice, video and data to be transported. H.323 specifies several video codecs, including H.261 and H.263, and audio codecs, including G.711 and G.723.1. Gateways, gatekeepers and multipoint control units (MCUs) are also covered. H.323 is widely supported for Internet telephony.

H.324

An ITU standard for videoconferencing over analog telephone lines (POTS) using modems.

H5

Refers to models of IBM's water-cooled mainframes that use the bipolar chip technology.

hack

Program source code. You might hear a phrase like "nobody has a package to do that, so it must be done through some sort of hack." This means someone has to write programming code to solve the problem, because there is no pre-written routine or function that does it.

The purist would say that doing a hack means writing in languages such as assembly language and C, which are low level and highly detailed. The more liberal person would say that writing any programming language counts as hacking.

hacker

A person who writes programs in assembly language or in system-level languages, such as C. Although it may refer to any programmer, it implies very tedious "hacking away" at the bits and bytes.

The term has become widely used for people that gain illegal entrance into a computer system. This use of the term is not appreciated by the vast majority of honest hackers. See *hack* and *cracker*.

HAL

(1) (Hardware Abstraction Layer) The translation layer in Windows NT that resides between the kernel and I/O system and the hardware itself. Its purpose is to be able to port NT to another platform by designing a new HAL layer for it. In practice, parts of the kernel may have to be optimized.

(2) (Heuristic/**AL**gorithmic) The computer in the film "2001," which takes over command of the spaceship. Each of the letters in H-A-L coincidentally precede the letters I-B-M.

half-adder

An elementary electronic circuit in the ALU that adds one bit to another, deriving a result bit and a carry bit.

half-duplex

The transmission of data in both directions, but only one direction at a time. Two-way radio was the first to use half-duplex, for example, while one party spoke, the other party listened. Contrast with *full-duplex*.

half-height drive

A 5.25" disk drive that takes up half the vertical space of first-generation drives in desktop computers. Measuring 1 5/8" in height, it is commonly used for 5.25" floppy disks and hard disks. Contrast with *full-height drive*.

half-inch tape

A magnetic tape format that has been in use for half a century. Second-generation computers used 7-track, half-inch tape in open reels that were threaded by hand. Third-generation computers used 9-track open reels. Although the maximum storage is little more than 250MB per reel, open reels and drives are still being made.

Half-inch reels evolved into half-inch, self-threading tape cartridges, including IBM's 3490/3490/3590 line, Quantum's DLT and StorageTek's Redwood, which hold from 800MB to 50GB. See *Magstar, DLT* and *Redwood*. For a summary of all tape technologies, see *storage device*.

halftone

In printing, the simulation of a continuous-tone image (shaded drawing, photograph) with dots. All printing processes, except for Cycolor, print dots. In photographically-generated halftones, a

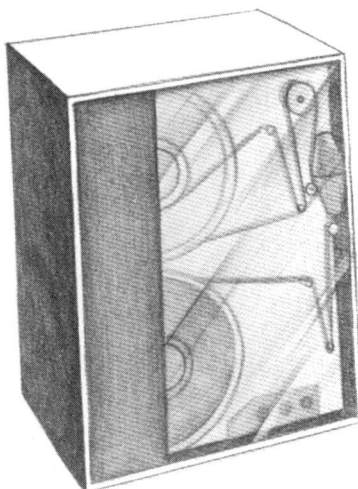

Open Reel Tape
Although organizations have migrated to cartridge formats, legacy applications remain that still use open reels.

camera shoots the image through a halftone screen, creating smaller dots for lighter areas and larger dots for darker areas. Digitally-composed printing prints only one size of dot.

In order to simulate variable-sized halftone dots in computer printers, dithering is used, which creates clusters of dots in a "halftone cell." The more dots printed in the cell, the darker the gray. As the screen frequency gets higher (more cells per inch), there is less room for dots in the cell, reducing the number of shades of gray or color that can be generated.

In low-resolution printers, there is always a compromise between printer resolution (dpi) and screen frequency (lpi), which is the number of rows of halftone cells per inch. For example, in a 300 dpi printer, the 8x8 halftone cell required to create 64 shades of grays results in a very coarse 38 lines per inch of screen frequency (300 dpi divided by 8). However, a high-resolution, 2400 dpi imagesetter can easily handle 256 shades of gray at 150 lpi (2400 / 16).

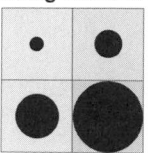
Analog halftone dots

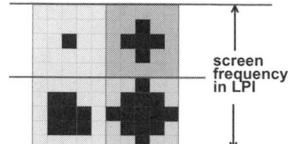
Digital halftone cells

screen frequency in LPI

Analog versus Digital
The analog world of commercial printing prints dots in varying sizes. The digital world prints in grids of dots. Increasingly, digital printers use techniques that overlap dots to achieve greater variability in dot sizes.

PRINTER RESOLUTION & MAXIMUM SCREEN FREQUENCY

Cell size	Shades of gray or cols	At printer resolutions: 300 dpi	1200 dpi	2400 dpi
4x4	16	150 lpi	300 lpi	600 lpi
8x8	64	38 lpi	130 lpi	300 lpi
16x16	256	19 lpi	75 lpi	150 lpi

hammer

In a printer, the mechanism that pushes the typeface onto the ribbon and paper or pushes the paper into the ribbon and typeface.

Hamming code

An error correction method that intersperses three check bits at the end of each four data bits. At the receiving station, the check bits are used to detect and correct one-bit errors automatically.

hand coding

Writing in a programming language. Hand coding in assembly language or in a third-generation language, such as COBOL or C, is the traditional way programs have been developed. In contrast, visual programming tools allow full applications or parts of an application to be developed without writing lines of programming code.

hand-held computer

See *palmtop*.

hand-held scanner

A scanner that is moved across the image to be scanned by hand. Hand-held scanners are small and less expensive than their desktop counterparts, but rely on the dexterity of the user to move the unit across the paper. Trays are available that keep the scanner moving in a straight line. Contrast with *flatbed scanner, sheet-fed scanner* and *drum scanner*.

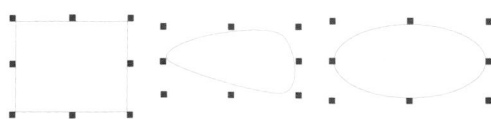
Graphics Handles
The handles are the tiny (blue) squares that are displayed when you select an object.

handle

(1) In computer graphics, a tiny, square block on an image that can be grabbed for reshaping.

(2) A temporary name or number assigned to a file, font or other object. For example, an operating

system may assign a sequential number to each file that it opens as a way of identifying it.

(3) A nickname used when conferencing like a "CB handle" used by a truck driver.

handler
A software routine that performs a particular task. For example, upon detection of an error, an error handler is called to recover from the error condition.

handoff
Switching a cellular phone transmission from one cell to another as a mobile user moves into a new cellular area. The switch takes place in about a quarter of a second so that the caller is generally unaware of it.

handset
The part of the telephone that contains the speaker and the microphone.

handshaking
Signals transmitted back and forth over a communications network that establish a valid connection between two stations.

hang
To have the computer freeze or lock up. When a personal computer hangs, there is often no indication of what caused the problem. The computer could have crashed, or it could be something simple such as the printer running out of paper.

hanging indent, hanging paragraph
In a hanging indent, the first line of the paragraph
    is set to the left margin, and all
    subsequent lines are indented
    as is this paragraph.

haptic interface
Communicating with the computer via some tactile method. Haptic devices sense some form of finger, hand, head or body movement.

haptics
Dealing with the sense of touch. See *haptic interface*.

hard boot
Same as *cold boot*.

hard coded
Software that is programmed to perform a fixed number of tasks, use a fixed set of values, work with a fixed number of devices or any combination thereof. Hard coded solutions to problems are usually the fastest to program and may even run the fastest, but they are not as easy to change. See *data independence*.

hard copy
Printed output. Contrast with *soft copy*.

Internal Hard Disk
Hard disks use one or more metal or glass platters covered with a magnetic coating.

hard disk
The primary computer storage medium, which is made of one or more aluminum or glass platters, coated with a ferromagnetic material. Most hard disks are fixed disks, which are permanently sealed in the drive. Removable cartridge disks are gaining in popularity and are increasingly available in more varieties.

Most desktop hard disks are either IDE or SCSI. The advantage of SCSI is that up to seven or more devices can be attached to the same controller board. Hard disks provide fast retrieval because they rotate constantly at high speed, from 3,000 to 10,000 rpm. In laptops, they can be turned off when idle to preserve battery life.

First Microcomputer Hard Disk
Seagate introduced the first hard for personal computers in 1979. At 5MB, the ST506 drive was a big improvement over the floppy-based machines of the time. *(Photo courtesy of Seagate Technology, Inc.)*

What Four Decades Hath Wrought
Introduced in 1998, Seagate's Elite 47 holds a whopping 47GB. Four decades have enabled us to store more than 100,000 times as much on the same platter surface. *(Photo courtesy of Seagate Technology, Inc.)*

Older hard disks held as little as five megabytes and used platters up to 12" in diameter. Today's hard disks can hold several gigabytes and generally use 3.5" platters for desktop computers and 2.5" platters for notebooks.

Hard disks arc usually low-level formatted from the factory, which records the original sector identification on them. See *floppy disk, magnetic disk* and *format program*. For a summary of all disk technologies, see *storage device*.

TYPES OF HARD DISKS

Interface Type	Encoding Method*	Transfer rate (Per sec)	Capacities
ST506	MFM	625KB	5MB – 100MB
ST506 RLL	RLL	937KB	30MB – 200MB
IDE	RLL	3-8MB	40MB – 1GB
EIDE**	RLL	3-33MB	500MB – 16GB
ESDI	RLL	1-3MB	80MB – 2GB
SCSI***	RLL	5-80MB	20MB – 47GB
SMD	RLL	1-4MB	200MB – 2GB
IPI	RLL	10-25MB	200MB – 3GB

```
  * Most disks use RLL, but encoding methods are
      not prescribed by all interfaces.
 ** For details on EIDE (ATA) modes, see IDE.
*** For details on SCSI rates, see SCSI.
```

Hard Disk Measurements

Capacity is measured in bytes, and speed is measured in bytes per second (see above) and in milliseconds (access time). Hard disk access times range from 5ms to about 20ms, whereas CDs and DVDs are from 80ms to 120ms.

hard disk configuration, hard disk parameters

Following are the parameters stored in a PC's CMOS memory that describe the configuration of the hard disks in the system. SCSI hard disks are usually not identified in the CMOS setup memory.

```
TYPE       There are 46 hard disk types, numbered 1
           to 46, that include all the required
           parameters below.  Since they cover
           earlier drives that only go up to 152MB,
           the user-configurable Type 47 is usually
           chosen and the remaining parameters are
           entered manually.

CYLINDERS  Number of cylinders.
HEADS      Number of read/write heads.
WPCOM      Write precomensation starting track.
LANDING
    ZONE   Cylinder used for parking heads.
SECTORS    Number of sectors per track.
CAPACITY   Total capacity derived from above
           parameters:
           (heads X cylinders X sectors X 512)
```

hard disk references

Following are some sources for obtaining hard disk parameters. Most new drives have the number of cylinders, heads and sectors printed directly on their housing. Many earlier drives do not. Listings of hard drive parameters are available from many bulletin boards as well. On the Internet, visit www.blue-planet.com/tech.

"Pocket PCRef" is a handy pocket reference that also contains DOS commands, printer commands and other useful references and specifications for the support person.

"Pocket PCRef" by Thomas Glover & Millie Young
```
Sequoia Publishing, Inc., Littleton, CO, ISBN 0-9622359-7-0
```

"Hard Drive Bible"
```
Corporate Systems Center, Sunnyvale, CA, 408/737-7312
```

"Hard Disk Technical Guide"
"Hard Disk Encyclopedia" (3 volumes)
```
Micro House, Boulder, CO, 800/926-8299
```

"DrivePro"
```
Hard disk installation and setup utility includes hard disk and
controller information. Micro House, Boulder, CO, 800/926-8299
```

hard drive

The mechanism that reads and writes a hard disk. The terms hard drive and hard disk are used interchangeably.

hard error

(1) A permanent, unrecoverable error such as a disk read error. Contrast with *soft error*.

(2) A group of errors that requires user intervention and includes disk read errors, disk not ready (no disk in drive) and printer not ready (out of paper).

hard hyphen

A hyphen that always prints. Contrast with *soft hyphen*.

hard macro

The design of a logic function that specifies how the required logic elements are interconnected and specifies the physical pathways and wiring patterns between the components. Also called a "macro cell." Contrast with *soft macro*.

hard return

A code inserted into a text document by pressing the enter key. If the hard return does not display as a symbol on screen, it can usually be revealed along with other layout codes in an expanded mode. DOS, Windows and OS/2 insert a CR/LF combo: Carriage Return and Line Feed. Mac uses only a CR, and UNIX only an LF. Contrast with *soft return*.

hard sectored

A sector identification technique that uses a physical mark. For example, hard sectored floppy disks have a hole in the disk that marks the beginning of each sector. Contrast with *soft sectored*.

hard space

A special space character that acts like a letter or digit, used to prevent multiple-word, proper names from breaking between lines.

hardware

Machinery and equipment (CPU, disks, tapes, modem, cables, etc.). In operation, a computer is both hardware and software. One is useless without the other. The hardware design specifies the commands it can follow, and the instructions tell it what to do. See *instruction set*.

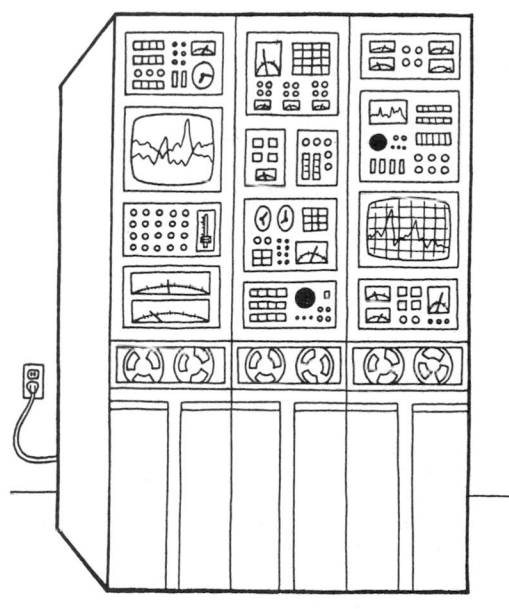

Hardware Is "Storage and Transmission"

The more memory and disk storage a computer has, the more work it can do. The faster the memory and disks transmit data and instructions to the CPU, the faster it gets done. A hardware requirement is based on the size of the databases that will be created and the number of users or applications that will be served at the same time. How much? How fast?

Software Is "Logic and Language"

Software deals with the details of an ever-changing business and must process transactions in a logical fashion. Languages are used to program the software. The "logic and language" involved in analysis and programming is generally far more complicated than specifying a storage and transmission requirement.

If you bump into it... it's hardware!

hardware circuit

A system made up of electronic components such as transistors, resistors and capacitors. For computers and other digital devices, almost all hardware circuits are built into a chip, with a single chip containing an entire subsystem such as a CPU, controller or codec. The exceptions are power supplies and other devices that use transformers and discrete components too large for chip fabrication.

hardware dependent

See *machine dependent*.

hardware engineer

A person involved with the design, implementation and testing of hardware (circuits, components, systems, etc.). See *software engineer*.

hardware failure

A malfunction within the electronic circuits or electromechanical components (disks, tapes) of a computer system. Contrast with *software failure*.

hardware independent

Same as *machine independent*.

hardware interface

An architecture used to interconnect two pieces of equipment. It includes the design of the plug and socket, the type, number and purpose of the wires and the electrical signals that are passed across them. See *bus, local bus, ISA, VL-bus, RS-232, PCI, IDE, SCSI* and *channel*.

hardware interrupt

An interrupt caused by some action of a hardware device, such as the depression of a key or mouse movement. See *IRQ* and *interrupt*.

hardware key

Also called a *dongle*, it is a copy protection device supplied with software that plugs into a computer port, often the parallel port on a PC. The software sends a code to that port, and the key responds by reading out its serial number, which verifies its presence to the program. The key hinders software duplication, because each copy of the program is tied to a unique number, which is difficult to obtain, and the key has to be programmed with that number.

The key also acts as a pass-through to the printer or other peripheral. Multiple hardware keys can be used, each plugged in one after the other.

hardware monitor

A device attached to the hardware circuits of a computer that reads electronic signals directly in order to analyze system performance.

hardware platforms

Each hardware platform, or CPU family, has a unique machine language. All software presented to the computer for execution must be in the binary coded machine language of that CPU. Following is a list of the major hardware platforms in existence today.

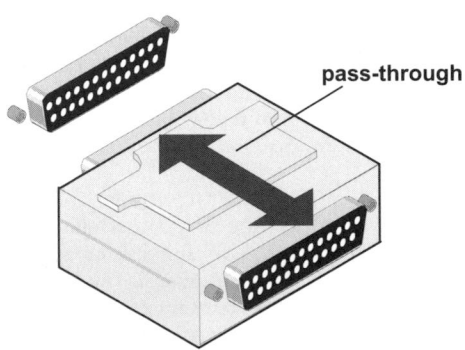

pass-through

The Hardware Key
Hardware keys provide a pass-through so that a peripheral cable can be plugged into the key just as if it were plugged into the back of the computer. Multiple keys can be plugged together as well.

```
CISC chips
Platform   Developed by and usage
x86        Intel, AMD, Cyrix (all PCs)
680x0      Motorola, mostly earlier Macintoshes
VAX        Digital's mini series, VMS OS
S/370      IBM mainframes
S/390      IBM mainframes
AS/400     IBM midrange, formerly System/38
S/36       old IBM mini, System/36
Tandem     fault tolerant systems, Non-Stop
Unisys     Unisys mainframes
PDP/11     Digital's 1st mini

RISC chips
Platform   Developed by and usage
88000      Motorola, DG, Encore
MIPS       SGI, Pyramid, Tandem, NEC, Siemens
SPARC      Sun and SPARC-licened clones
PA-RISC    HP workstations, servers
Alpha      Digital workstations, servers
PowerPC    Apple, IBM, Motorola
i860       Intel, Stratus systems
ARM        Arm, Ltd., embedded systems, NCs
```

Computer Desktop Encyclopedia

hardware profile

Settings that define a specific configuration of peripherals and drivers. Multiple profiles let you set up more than one hardware configuration, which is commonly done when a laptop also serves as a desktop computer. The desktop profile activates one set of peripherals, the laptop profile another.

A separate hardware profile is also used as a last resort when an application conflicts with one of the drivers that is routinely loaded. A special profile is created that boots the computer without the problem driver so the application can run. In order to run the rest of the programs, the machine must be rebooted with the regular profile.

hardware scaling

Enlarging a video frame by performing the operation within the circuits of the display adapter. Putting the function in a chip speeds up the process. See *video accelerator*.

hardware vendors

Following are annual revenues from the major hardware manufacturers in the computer industry over the past several years. See also *software vendors*.

Year	Company	Sales (000,000)	Profit (000)	Employees (000)	Year	Company	Sales (000,000)	Profit (000)	Employees (000)
Computer System Manufacturers									
1997	IBM	78,508	6,093	269	1997	Sun	8,598	762	22
1996		75,947	5,429	269	1996		7,095	476	17
1995		71,940	4,178	252	1995		5,902	336	14
1994		64,052	3,021	243	1994		4,690	196	13
1993		62,716	(8,101)	267	1993		4,309	157	13
1992		65,096	(4,965)	308	1992		3,628	173	13
1991		64,792	(2,827)	345	1991		3,260	190	12
1997	HP	42,895	3,119	122	1997	Apple	7,081	(1,045)	9
1996		38,420	2,586	112	1996		9,833	(816)	12
1995		31,519	2,433	102	1995		11,062	424	15
1994		24,991	1,599	98	1994		9,189	310	15
1993		20,317	1,177	96	1993		7,977	87	15
1992		16,427	549	93	1992		7,087	530	15
1991		14,541	755	89	1991		6,309	310	14
1997	Compaq	24,584	1,855	37	1997	Unisys	6,636	(853)	32
1996		18,109	1,313	19	1996		6,371	50	33
1995		14,755	789	20	1995		6,460	(625)	50
1994		10,866	867	14	1994		7,400	101	46
1993		7,191	462	11	1993		7,743	565	49
1992		4,132	213	10	1992		8,422	(361)	54
1991		3,260	190	12	1991		8,696	(1,393)	60
1997	DEC	13,047	141	55	1997	Gateway	6,294	110	13
1996		14,563	(112)	59	1996	2000	5,035	251	10
1995		13,813	122	62	1995		3,676	173	9
1994		13,451	(2,156)	78	1994		2,701	96	5
1993		14,371	(251)	94	1993		1,732	66	4
1992		14,027	(2,796)	114	1992		1,107	70	2
1991		14,024	(617)	121					
					1997	Silicon	3,663	79	11
1997	Dell	12,327	944	16	1996	Graphics	2,921	115	10
1996		7,759	518	10	1995		2,228	225	6
1995		5,296	272	8	1994		1,482	141	4
1994		3,475	149	6	1993		1,091	95	4
1993		2,014	102	5	1992		867	(118)	4
1992		890	51	3	1991		557	33	3
1991		546	27	2					

Year	Company	Sales (000,000)	Profit	Employees (000)
1997	Data	1,533	56	5
1996	General	1,322	28	5
1995		1,056	(47)	5
1994		1,121	(88)	6
1993		1,078	(60)	7
1992		1,127	(63)	7
1997	Intergraph	1,124	(70)	8
1996		1,095	(69)	8
1995		1,098	(45)	8
1994		1,041	(70)	9
1993		1,050	(116)	10
1992		1,182	8	10
1991		1,205	71	10

Drive Manufacturers

Year	Company	Sales (000,000)	Profit	Employees (000)
1997	Seagate	8,940	658	111
1996		8,588	213	87
1995		4,540	260	65
1994		3,500	225	53
1993		3,044	195	43
1992		2,889	63	43
1991		2,691	67	43
1997	Quantum	5,319	149	6
1996		4,423	(90)	7
1995		3,368	82	7
1994		2,131	3	3
1993		1,697	94	2
1992		1,128	47	2
1991		878	74	1
1997	Western	4,178	268	13
1996	Digital	2,865	97	10
1995		2,131	123	8
1994		1,540	73	7
1993		1,225	(25)	7
1992		940	(73)	7
1991		986	(134)	7
1997	EMC	2,938	539	6
1997	StorageTek	2,145	232	8
1996		2,040	180	8
1995		1,929	(142)	10
1994		1,625	41	10
1993		1,405	(78)	10
1992		1,521	15	10
1991		1,653	93	10
1997	Iomega	1,740	115	5

Semiconductor Manufacturers

Year	Company	Sales (000,000)	Profit	Employees (000)
1997	Motorola	29,794	1,180	150
1996		27,973	1,154	139
1995		27,037	1,781	142
1994		22,245	1,560	132
1993		16,983	1,022	120
1992		13,341	453	107
1991		11,341	454	102
1997	Intel	25,070	6,945	64
1996		20,847	5,157	49
1995		16,202	3,566	42
1994		11,521	2,288	33
1993		8,782	2,295	30
1992		5,922	1,067	26
1991		4,779	819	25
1997	Rockwell	11,759	644	45
1996	Int'l.	14,343	726	59
1995		13,009	742	83
1994		11,205	634	72
1993		10,840	562	77
1992		10,995	(1,036)	79
1991		12,028	601	87
1997	Texas	10,562	1,805	44
1996	Inst.	11,713	63	63
1995		13,128	1,088	60
1994		10,315	691	56
1993		8,523	472	59
1992		7,470	247	61
1991		6,812	(409)	63
1997	National	2,507	28	12
1996	Semi.	2,623	185	
1995		2,379	264	22
1994		2,295	264	22
1993		2,014	130	23
1992		1,726	(120)	27
1991		1,711	(151)	30
1997	AMD	2,356	(21)	13
1995		2,430	301	13
1994		2,135	305	12
1993		1,648	229	12
1992		1,531	245	12
1991		1,227	145	11

hardware virtual memory

Virtual memory management built into a chip. Although virtual memory can be performed by software only, it is far more efficient to do it in hardware. See *DAT* and *PMMU*.

hardwired

(1) Electronic circuitry that is designed to perform a specific task. See *hard coded*.

(2) Devices that are closely or tightly coupled. For example, a hardwired terminal is directly connected to a computer without going through a switched network.

harmonic distortion

In communications, frequencies that are generated as multiples of the original frequency due to irregularities in the transmission line.

Harvard Graphics

Popular presentation graphics programs for DOS and Windows from Software Publishing Corporation, Fairfield, NJ, (www.spco.com). Its DOS version was one of the first business graphics packages to allow for the creation of columnar and free form text charts.

hash function

An algorithm that turns a variable-sized amount of text into a fixed-sized output (hash value). Hash functions are used in creating digital signatures. See *digital signature* and *one-way hash function*.

hash total

A method for ensuring the accuracy of processed data. It is a total of several fields of data in a file, including fields not normally used in calculations, such as account number. At various stages in the processing, the hash total is recalculated and compared with the original. If any data has been lost or changed, a mismatch signals an error.

hash value

The fixed-length result of a one-way hash function. See *hash function* and *hash total*.

HASP

(Houston Automatic Spooling Program) A mainframe spooling program that provides task, job and data management functions.

Hayes

(Hayes Corporation, Atlanta, GA, www.hayes.com) A communications company specializing in modems and remote access products. Founded in 1977 by Dennis Hayes, the company pioneered personal computer communications with the design of its Smartmodem and shipped its first 300 baud model in 1978. Initially Hayes Microcomputer Products, Inc., it became Hayes Corporation in 1997 when it merged with Access Beyond, a spin-off of Penril Data Communications. See *Hayes Smartmodem* and *AT command set*.

Hayes compatible

Refers to modems controlled by the Hayes command language. See *AT command set*.

Hayes Smartmodem

A family of intelligent modems for personal computers from Hayes. Hayes developed the intelligent modem for first-generation personal computers in 1978, and its command language (Hayes Standard AT Command Set) for modem control has become an industry-standard.

The Intelligent Modem

An intelligent modem has a command state and an online state. In the command state, it accepts instructions. In the online state, it dials, answers, transmits and receives.

Once connected, it performs the handshaking with the remote modem, which is similar to the opening exchange of a telephone call. The called party says "hello," the calling party says "hello, this is..." After this, the real conversation begins. If the modem's speaker is on, you can hear the whistles and tones used in the handshake.

Once the handshake is completed, you are online with the other computer, and data can be transmitted back and forth.

An important part of the Hayes standard is the escape sequence, which tells the modem to switch from online to the command state. It usually consists of three plus signs in sequence (+++) with a Hayes-patented, one-second guard time interval before and after it, which prevents the modem from mistaking a random occurrence of the escape sequence. The escape sequence and guard time interval can be programmed in the modem's Status registers.

To issue an escape sequence, hold down the shift key and press + + +. Pause one second before and after the sequence. The modem will return the OK result code, indicating it is ready to accept commands.

HBL

(Hue Brightness Luminosity) A color model that is similar to HSV. See *HSV*.

HC

See *high color*.

HD

(1) (High Density) The designation for high-density diskettes such as the 3.5" 1.44MB floppy.

(2) (Hard Disk) For example, FD/HD refers to a floppy disk/hard disk device such as a controller.

(3) (High Definition) See *HDTV*.

HDA

(Head Disk Assembly) The mechanical components of a disk drive (minus the electronics), which includes the actuators, access arms, read/write heads and platters.

HDD

Abbreviation for hard disk drive.

HDF

(Hierarchical Data Format) A file format for scientific data that is developed and maintained by NCSA. Governments and research organizations around the world use HDF for archiving and distributing collected data.

HDL

(Hardware Description Language) A language used to describe the functions of an electronic circuit for documentation, simulation or logic synthesis (or all three). Although many proprietary HDLs have been developed, Verilog and VHDL are the major standards. The first book to provide side-by-side examples of subsets of both languages that can be simulated and synthesized is "HDL Chip Design" by Douglas J. Smith, published by Doone Publications, (www.doone.com), ISBN 0-9651934-3-8. See *Verilog* and *VHDL*.

HDLC

(High-level Data Link Control) An ISO communications protocol used in X.25 packet switching networks. It provides error correction at the data link layer. SDLC, LAP and LAPB are subsets of HDLC. See *SDLC*.

HDML

(Hand-held Device Markup Language) An abbreviated version of HTML designed to enable wireless pagers, cellphones and other hand-held devices to obtain Web pages. See *WAP*.

HD-ROM, HD-ROSETTA

An archival storage technology from Norsam Technologies, Inc., Los Alamos, NM, (www.norsam.com). A two-inch disc holds up to 90K pages in analog form similar to microfilm, except that the images are "chiseled" into metal instead of on film. The discs, which are created at the Norsam plant, are extremely durable.

HD-ROM (High-Density ROM) is the digital version of HD-ROSETTA. It is expected to store 200GB and more on a CD-sized platter using charged particle technology. HD-ROM writers are expected to be installed at the customer's site where payment is based upon the amount of data recorded.

HDS

(Hitachi Data Systems, Santa Clara, CA, www.hdshq.com) A provider of IBM-compatible mainframes, open systems hardware and software, storage products and consulting services. It was founded in 1989 when Hitachi, Ltd. and EDS acquired NAS (National Advanced Systems) from National Semiconductor and renamed it. NAS was formed in 1979 when National Semiconductor took over Itel's Computer Products Group, which had been selling National's IBM-compatible mainframes. Later, NAS ceased manufacturing and marketed systems from Hitachi, Ltd.

HDSL

See *DSL*.

HDTV

(High Definition TV) A high-resolution TV standard. Japan was the first to develop HDTV and currently broadcasts an 1125-line signal picked up on 36" to 50" TV sets that cost about $10,000. Both Japan and Europe's HDTV use traditional analog signalling.

The HDTV Format
Intergraph was the first to develop a 28" HDTV-format monitor for computer use. The 16:9 aspect ratio on the HDTV unit (right) is wider than the standard 4:3 monitor on the left. *(Photo courtesy of Intergraph Computer Systems.)*

For several years in the U.S., high definition formats (HD) in both analog and digital form have been used for creating videos that are superior to regular TV/video (NTSC). HD is used to shoot videos for closed circuit presentations in corporate theaters and board rooms, trade shows and similar events. It was expected that this would naturally evolve into the next TV standard.

In late 1996, the FCC approved the DTV standard for the U.S., which offers a variety of higher-quality all-digital signals for TV transmission. See *DTV*.

HDX

See *half-duplex*.

head

See *read/write head* and *HDA*.

head crash

The physical destruction of a hard disk. Misalignment or contamination with dust can cause the read/write head to collide with the disk's recording surface. The data is destroyed, and both the disk platter and head have to be replaced.

The read/write head touches the surface of a floppy disk, but on a hard disk, it hovers above its surface at a distance that is less than the diameter of a human hair. It has been said that the read/write head flying over the disk surface is like trying to fly a jet plane six inches above the earth's surface.

Read/Write Head and Disk Surface
Head crashes used to be much more common years ago. When you realize the distance between the head and platter is about 20 millionths of an inch, today's reliability is truly a feat of engineering. However, it can happen, and when it does, it is a literal crash. The head collides into and destroys the magnetic coating of the disk. Your bits go bye-bye.

head end

The originating point in a communications system. In cable TV, the head end is where the cable company has its satellite dish and TV antenna for receiving incoming programming. In online services, the head end is the service company's computer system and databases.

header

(1) The first record in a disk or tape file. It may be used for identification only (name, date of last update, etc.), or it may describe the structural layout of the contents, as is common with many document and database formats.

(2) In a document or report, common text printed at the top of every page.

(3) In communications, the first part of the message, which contains controlling data, such as originating and destination stations, message type and priority level.

(4) Any caption or description used as a headline.

header label

A record used for file identification that is recorded at the beginning of the file.

head mounted display

See *HMD.*

head-per-track disk

Same as *fixed head disk.*

head skew

The offset distance from the start of the previous track so that the head has time to switch from top of platter to bottom of platter and be at the start of the new track. See *cylinder skew.*

heap

In programming, the common pool of free memory available to the program.

heartbeat

See *MHz.*

heat fusing

See *fusing.*

heat sink

A material that absorbs heat. It is usually made of aluminum or some other metal. Heat sinks are commonly used in amplifiers and other electronic devices that build up heat. A heat sink is often glued to the top of a CPU chip to keep it cooler. See *CPU cooler* for illustration.

helical scan

A tape recording method that runs the tracks diagonally in order to increase storage capacity. Helical scan uses a rather complex transport mechanism. After the cassette is inserted into the drive, the tape is pulled out and wrapped around the read/write head. Helical scan is used in various tape formats, including VHS videotapes, Exabyte's 8mm, Sony's SDX, 4mm DAT (DDS) and StorageTek's Redwood.

Hello, World

The classic first program a programmer writes in a new programming language. It came from the C and UNIX world, and all it does is display "Hello, World" on screen. The "Hello, World" example is often used as a tutorial for starting to learn a programming language, since it demonstrates the framework necessary to do a simple function.

help

On-screen instruction regarding the use of a program. On PCs, pressing F1 is the de facto standard for getting help. With graphics-based interfaces (Mac, Windows, etc.), clicking a "?" or HELP button gets help. See *context sensitive help.*

help compiler

Software that translates text and compiler instructions into an online help system. See *Windows help system.*

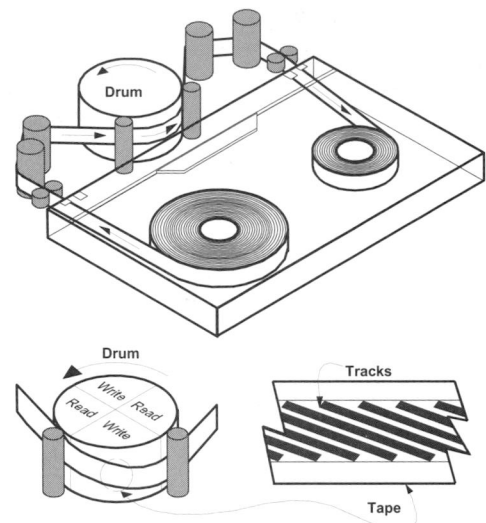

Helical Scan

Helical scan records tracks on the diagonal, which uses up more of the tape surface than linear recording along the length. The tape is pulled out of the cartridge and wrapped around the read/write head.

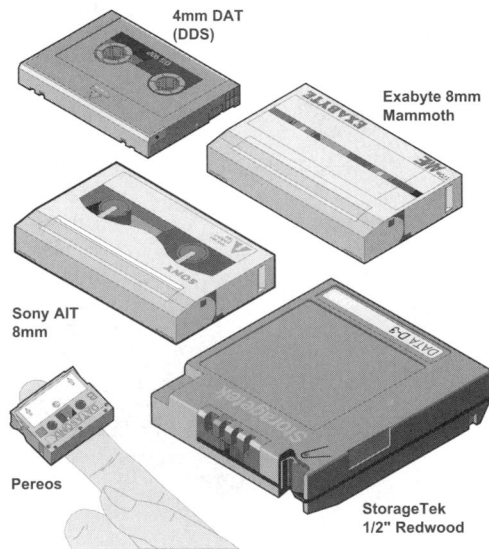

Helical Scan Formats

These are the helical scan tape formats used for computer storage.

help desk
A source of technical support for hardware or software. Help desks are staffed by people that can either solve the problem directly or forward the problem to someone else. Help desk software provides the means to log in problems and track them until solved. It also provides the management information regarding support activities.

helper application
An application that adds additional capabilities to the program that is running. See *Netscape plug-in*.

help key
The keyboard key that is pressed in order to obtain help when working in an application. In the DOS/Windows environment, the help key is the function key F1.

henry
A unit of measurement of the strength of a magnetic field in an inductor. See *inductor*.

Hercules Graphics
The de facto standard monochrome display adapter for PCs, which provides a graphics and text resolution of 720x348 pixels. IBM's monochrome display adapter displayed only text, and Hercules Computer Technology introduced its product in 1982 to fill the void.

Hertz
The frequency of electrical vibrations (cycles) per second. Abbreviated "Hz," one Hz is equal to one cycle per second. In 1883, Heinrich Hertz detected electromagnetic waves. See *MHz*.

heterogeneous
Not the same. Contrast with *homogeneous*.

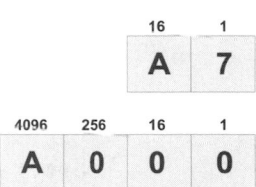

heterogeneous environment
Using hardware and system software from different vendors. Organizations often use computers, operating systems and databases from a variety of vendors. Contrast with *homogeneous environment*.

heuristic
A method of problem solving using exploration and trial and error methods. Heuristic program design provides a framework for solving the problem in contrast with a fixed set of rules (algorithmic) that cannot vary.

Hewlett-Packard
See *HP*.

hex, hexadecimal
Hexadecimal means 16. The base 16 numbering system is used as a shorthand for representing binary numbers. Each half byte (four bits) is assigned a hex digit as shown in the following chart with its decimal and binary equivalents. Hex values are identified with an "h" or dollar sign, thus $3E0, 3E0h and 3E0H all stand for the hex number 3E0. See *hex chart*.

Base			Base		
16	10	2	16	10	2
Hex	Dec	Binary	Hex	Dec	Binary
0	0	0000	A	10	1010
1	1	0001	B	11	1011
2	2	0010	C	12	1100
3	3	0011	D	13	1101
4	4	0100	E	14	1110
5	5	0101	F	15	1111
6	6	0110			
7	7	0111			
8	8	1000			

How to Interpret the Hex
As decimal digits increment by 10, hex digits increment by 16. Two hex digits make up one byte; for example, A7 is equivalent to one byte containing the binary number 10100111, or 167 in decimal. A is 10, thus 160 (10x16) plus 7 (7x1).

The hex number A000 (pronounced "A thousand") is 40,960 in decimal (10x4096); however, for PC addressing, hex addresses are interpreted uniquely (see *paragraph*).

hex chart

```
┌─────────────────────────────────────────┬──────────────────────────┐
│          Standard ASCII                  │     Extended ASCII       │
│  The first 32 characters are             │        (DOS)             │
│          control codes.                  │                          │
└─────────────────────────────────────────┴──────────────────────────┘
```

	Standard ASCII				Extended ASCII (DOS)			
00	Null	21	!	51	Q	80	Ç	AE	«	DC
01	Start of heading	22	"	52	R	81	ü	AF	»	DD
02	Start of text	23	#	53	S	82	é	B0		DE
03	End of text	24	$	54	T	83	â	B1		DF
04	End of transmit	25	%	55	U	84	ä	B2		E0	α
05	Enquiry	26	&	56	V	85	à	B3		E1	β
06	Acknowledge	27	'	57	W	86	å	B4	┤	E2	Γ
07	Audible bell	28	(	58	X	87	ç	B5	╡	E3	π
08	Backspace	29	)	59	Y	88	ê	B6	╢	E4	Σ
09	Horizontal tab	2A	*	5A	Z	89	ë	B7	╖	E5	σ
0A	Line feed	2B	+	5B	[	8A	è	B8	╕	E6	µ
0B	Vertical tab	2C	,	5C	\	8B	ï	B9	╣	E7	τ
0C	Form feed	2D	-	5D	]	8C	î	BA	║	E8	Φ
0D	Carriage return	2E	.	5E	^	8D	ì	BB	╗	E9	θ
0E	Shift out	2F	/	5F	_	8E	Ä	BC	╝	EA	Ω
0F	Shift in	30	0	60	`	8F	Å	BD	╜	EB	δ
10	Data link escape	31	1	61	a	90	É	BE	╛	EC	∞
11	Device control 1	32	2	62	b	91	æ	BF	┐	ED	ø
12	Device control 2	33	3	63	c	92	Æ	C0	└	EE	∈
13	Device control 3	34	4	64	d	93	ô	C1	┴	EF	∩
14	Device control 4	35	5	65	e	94	ö	C2	┬	F0	≡
15	Neg. acknowledge	36	6	66	f	95	ò	C3	├	F1	±
16	Synchronous idle	37	7	67	g	96	û	C4	─	F2	≥
17	End trans. block	38	8	68	h	97	ù	C5	┼	F3	≤
18	Cancel	39	9	69	i	98	ÿ	C6	╞	F4	⌠
19	End of medium	3A	:	6A	j	99	Ö	C7	╟	F5	⌡
1A	Substitution	3B	;	6B	k	9A	Ü	C8	╚	F6	÷
1B	Escape	3C	<	6C	l	9B	¢	C9	╔	F7	≈
1C	File separator	3D	=	6D	m	9C	£	CA	╩	F8	°
1D	Group separator	3E	>	6E	n	9D	¥	CB	╦	F9	·
1E	Record separator	3F	?	6F	o	9E	₧	CC	╠	FA	·
1F	Unit separator	40	@	70	p	9F	ƒ	CD	═	FB	√
20	Blank space	41	A	71	q	A0	á	CE	╬	FC	ⁿ
		42	B	72	r	A1	í	CF	╧	FD	²
		43	C	73	s	A2	ó	D0	╨	FE	■
		44	D	74	t	A3	ú	D1	╤	FF	
		45	E	75	u	A4	ñ	D2	╥	
		46	F	76	v	A5	Ñ	D3	╙	
		47	G	77	w	A6	ª	D4	╘	
		48	H	78	x	A7	º	D5	╒	
		49	I	79	y	A8	¿	D6	╓	
		4A	J	7A	z	A9	⌐	D7	╫	
		4B	K	7B	{	AA	¬	D8	╪	
		4C	L	7C	|	AB	½	D9	┘	
		4D	M	7D	}	AC	¼	DA	┌	
		4E	N	7E	~	AD	¡	DB	█	
		4F	O	7F	△					
		50	P							

ASCII Characters (Hexadecimal)

These are the standard ASCII characters (0-127), plus the extended ASCII characters as implemented in the DOS PC. This chart shows the values in hexadecimal (00-FF).

.HFC network

(Hybrid Fiber-Coax network) A communications network (typically a cable TV network) that uses a combination of optical fibers and coaxial cable. The fiber provides the high-speed backbone, and the coax is used to connect end users to the backbone.

HFS

(Hierarchical File System) The file system used in the Macintosh. See *hierarchical file system*.

HGC

See *Hercules Graphics*.

HHOK

Digispeak for "ha ha only kidding."

Hi-8

A video recording and playback system that uses 8mm video cassettes and the S-video technology.

hidden file

A file classification that prevents a file from being accessed. It is usually an operating system file; however, utility programs let users hide files to prevent unauthorized access.

hierarchical

A structure made up of different levels like a company organization chart. The higher levels have control or precedence over the lower levels. Hierarchical structures are a one to many relationship; each item having one or more items below it.

hierarchical communications

A network controlled by a host computer that is responsible for managing all connections. Contrast with *peer-to-peer communications*.

hierarchical database

A database organization method that is structured in a hierarchy. All access to data starts at the top of the hierarchy and moves downward; for example, from customer to orders, vendor to purchases, etc. Contrast with *relational database* and *network database*.

hierarchical data format

See *HDF*.

hierarchical file system

A file organization method that stores data in a top-to-bottom organization structure. All internal access to the data starts at the top and proceeds throughout the levels of the hierarchy.

Most all operating systems use hierarchical file systems to store data and programs, including DOS, OS/2, Windows NT and 95/98, UNIX and the Macintosh. See *root directory, path* and *HFS*.

hierarchical storage management

See *HSM*.

hierarchy

A structure that has a predetermined ordering from high to low. In object technology, the hierarchy is a ordering of objects.

HiFD disk

(HIgh Capacity Floppy Disk) A 3.5" diskette from Sony and Fuji Photo Film Company that holds 200MB. HiFD drives read and write standard 1.44MB floppy disk. See *latest disk drives*. For a summary of all storage technologies, see *storage*.

HiFD Cartridge
HiFD disks hold 138 times as much data as a standard floppy, but the drives also support the 3.5" diskettes as well.

high availability

Also called *RAS* (reliability, availability, serviceability) or *fault resilient*, it refers to a multiprocessing system that can quickly recover from a failure. It also implies servicing a component in the system without shutting down the entire operation. This is not the same as fault tolerant, in which redundant components are designed for continuous processing without skipping a heartbeat. See *hot fix*.

high-capacity floppy

Removable disks that use a technology similar to floppy disks, but provide a considerable increase in capacity over the standard 1.44MB medium. See *Zip disk, LS-120* and *HiFD disk*.

high color

The ability to generate 32,768 colors (15 bits) or 65,536 colors (16-bit). 15-bit color uses five bits for each red, green and blue pixel. The 16th bit may be a color, such as XGA with 5-red, 6-green and 5-blue, or be an overlay bit that selects pixels to display over video input. See *true color*.

high definition TV

See *HDTV*.

high density

Refers to increased storage capacity of bits and/or tracks per square inch. See *HD*.

high-density CD-ROM

See *DVD*.

high DOS memory

Same as *UMA*.

high-level format

A set of indexes on the disk that the operating system uses to keep track of the data stored on the disk. See *format program*.

high-level language

A machine-independent programming language, such as FORTRAN, COBOL, BASIC, Pascal and C. It lets the programmer concentrate on the logic of the problem to be solved rather than the intricacies of the machine architecture such as is required with low-level assembly languages.

There are dramatic differences between high-level languages. Look up the terms C, BASIC and COBOL, and review the sample code. What is considered high level depends on the era. There were assembly languages thirty years ago that were easier to understand than C.

highlight

To identify an area on screen in order to select, move, delete or change it in some manner.

highlight bar

The currently-highlighted menu item. Choice is made by moving the bar to the desired item and pressing enter or clicking the mouse. The bar is a different color on color screens or reverse video on monochrome screens.

high memory

(1) The uppermost end of memory.

(2) In PCs, it may refer to three areas of memory: (1) the upper part of the first megabyte (between 640K and 1M), called the *Upper Memory Area*, or *UMA*, (2) the memory above 1M, called *extended memory*, or (3) the 64K area between 1024K and 1088K, called the *High Memory Area*, or *HMA*. Real straightforward, isn't it? See *PC memory, UMA, HMA* and *extended memory*.

high-performance computing

High-speed computing, which typically refers to supercomputers used in scientific research.

High-Performance Routing

See *HPR*.

high resolution

A high-quality image on a display screen or printed form. The more dots used per square inch, the higher the quality. To display totally realistic images including the shades of human skin requires about 1,000x1,000 pixels on a 12" diagonal screen.

Desktop laser printers print respectable text and graphics at 300 dpi, but typesetting machines print 1,270 and 2,540 dpi. At 600 dpi, laser printers can produce excellent text for camera-ready reproduction. Going beyond 600 dpi does not generally make much improvement with text unless the text is very small (6-8 points). On the other hand, photographs and shaded drawings require more than 600 dpi resolution for quality reproduction in a book or journal.

High Sierra

The first CD-ROM file format, named for an area near Lake Tahoe where it was developed in 1985. High Sierra evolved into ISO 9660.

high tech, high technology

Refers to the latest advancements in computers and electronics as well as to the social and political environment and consequences created by such machines.

HiJaak

A popular Windows graphics file conversion and screen capture program from IMSI, San Rafael, CA, (www.imsisoft.com). It supports a wide variety of raster and vector graphics formats as well as fax boards. It also handles conversion between PC and Mac formats.

HIMEM.SYS

An extended memory manager that is included with DOS and Windows, starting with DOS 5 and Windows 3.0. It allows programs to cooperatively allocate extended memory in 286 and higher PCs. HIMEM.SYS is an XMS driver. In Windows 95, HIMEM.SYS is automatically loaded at startup. See *XMS*.

hints

Font instructions that make a character uniform and legible at small point sizes and lower resolutions. They also ensure that serifs and accents appear in proper proportion. When there are not enough pixels in the print or display image, smaller fonts can sometimes translate into patterns that are not recognizable as the characters they represent. Hints ensure that both sides of an H, for example, must be of uniform width and that certain elements of the character cannot be left out.

Hints are not necessary when printing at 600 dpi or more, but are required when printing characters 13 points or less at 300 dpi. When displaying those same characters on a screen with a 96 dpi or lower resolution, hints are also needed.

HiPerMOS

(HIgh PERformance MOS) A CMOS chip technology from Motorola used for high-performance microprocessors and memories. HiPerMOS chips contain a high density of components and use copper for the metalization layer instead of aluminum.

HIPO

(Hierarchy plus Input-Process-Output) Pronounced "hy-po." An IBM flow-charting technique that provides a graphical method for designing and documenting programs.

HiPPI

(HIgh Performance Parallel Interface) An ANSI-standard high-speed communications channel that uses a 32-bit or 64-bit cable and transmits at 100 or 200 Mbytes/sec. It is used as a point-to-point supercomputer channel or, with a crosspoint switch, as a high-speed LAN.

hi res

Same as *high resolution*.

histogram

A chart displaying horizontal or vertical bars. The length of the bars are in proportion to the values of the data items they represent.

history

A user's input and keystrokes entered within the current session. A history feature keeps track of user commands and/or retrieved items so that they can be quickly reused or reviewed. Web browsers maintain a list of downloaded pages in the current session so that you can quickly review everything that you have retrieved.

Hitachi Data Systems

See *HDS*.

hit rate

The chief measurement of a cache, which is the percentage of all accesses that are satisfied by the data in the cache. See *cache* and *hits*.

hits

The number of times a program or item of data has been accessed or matches some condition. For example, each time you download a home page on the Web, that is considered one hit to that Web site. If a search yields 100 items that match the searching criteria, those 100 items could be called 100 hits. See *hit rate*.

HKEY

See *Win 9x Registry*.

HLLAPI

(High Level Language Application Program Interface) An IBM programming interface that allows a PC application to communicate with a mainframe application. The hardware hookup is handled via normal micro to mainframe 3270 emulation. An extended version of the interface (EHLLAPI) has also been defined.

HLS

(Hue Lightness Saturation) A color model that is closely related to HSV, except that Lightness replaces Value and is measured differently (0=black, 0.5=pure hues, 1=white). See *HSV*.

HMA

(High Memory Area) In PCs, the first 64K of extended memory from 1024K to 1088K, which can be accessed by DOS. It is managed by the HIMEM.SYS driver. It was discovered by accident that this area could be used by DOS, even though it was beyond the traditional one-megabyte barrier.

HMD

(Head Mounted Display) A display system built and worn like goggles that gives the illusion of a floating monitor in front of the user's face. Single-eye units are used to display hands-free instructional material, and dual-eye, or stereoscopic, units are used for virtual reality applications. See also *CAVE*.

HMOS

(High-density MOS) A chip with a high density of NMOS transistors.

hog

A program that uses an excessive amount of computer resources, such as memory or disk, or takes a long time to execute.

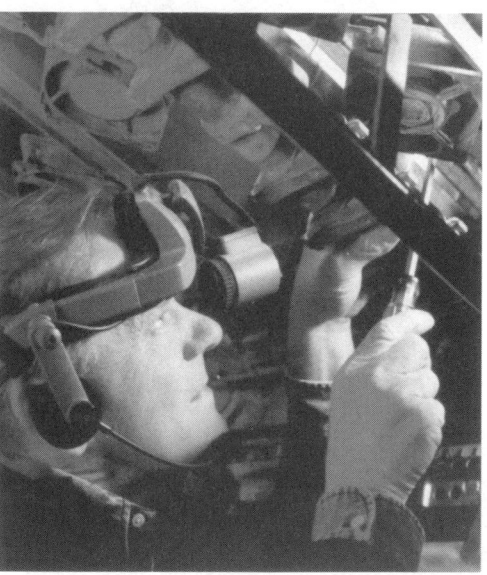

Single-Eye HMD
When repairing equipment requires the use of both hands, a head-mounted display such as this Xybernatu 133P is invaluable. Connected to a voice-activated, body-worn computer, it allows the technician to read instructions and do the work at the same time. *(Photo courtesy of Xybernaut Corporation.)*

Hollerith machine

The first automatic data processing system. It was used to count the 1890 U.S. census. Developed by Herman Hollerith, a statistician who had worked for the Census Bureau, the system used a hand punch to record the data in dollar-bill-sized punched cards and a tabulating machine to count them.

It was estimated that, with manual methods, the 1890 census wouldn't be completed until after 1900. With Hollerith's machines, it took two years and saved five million dollars.

Hollerith formed the Tabulating Machine Company and sold his machines throughout the world for a variety of accounting functions. In 1911, his company was merged into the company that was later renamed IBM.

Herman Hollerith
A rather dapper young man for the father of modern data processing. *(Photo courtesy of Library of Congress.)*

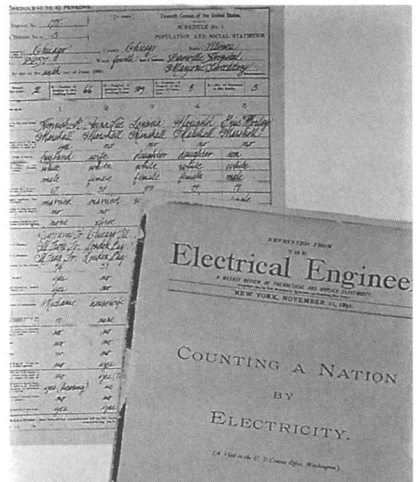

What a Novel Concept!
Imagine. Using electricity to count. The date on this issue of "Electrical Engineer" was November 11, 1891. The page at the top is a census form filled out by one of the census takers. *(Photo courtesy of Library of Congress.)*

Hollerith's Keypunch Machine
All 60 million Americans were counted by punching holes into a card from the census forms. *(Photo courtesy of IBM Corporation.)*

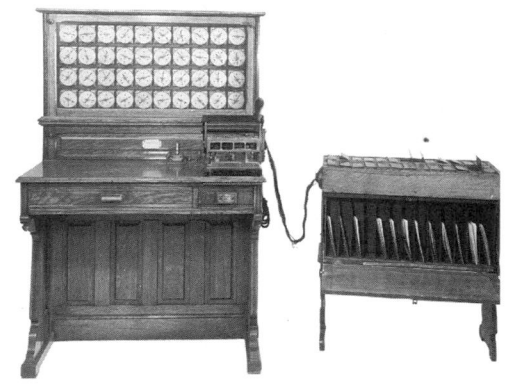

Hollerith's Tabulating Machine

The card was placed in the press, the handle was pushed down, and the data was tabulated on the dials. Then the appropriate lid opened up on the sorting box, and the punched card was dropped in. *(Photo courtesy of Smithsonian Institution.)*

High Tech, 1890 Style

The beginning of data processing made the August 30, 1890 cover of Scientific American. The binary concept. A hole or no hole! *(Photo courtesy of Scientic American Magazine.)*

holographic storage

A future technology that records data as holograms that fill up the entire volume of a small optical cylinder no larger than one millimeter by one centimeter. The hologram is created by two lasers. One laser is beamed into the lithium niobate optical material through a matrix of LCD shutters, called a *spatial light modulator*. The shutters are opened or closed based on the binary pattern of the page of data being stored. For example, using a matrix of 1,024 pixels on each side, the page could hold a million bits.

A reference laser is angled into and intersects with the data laser at the storage unit. If the angle and/or frequency is changed, another hologram can be created overlapping and filling the same space as the first hologram. In fact, 10,000 holograms (pages) can overlap each other.

The page is read by directing just the reference laser back into the hologram. The light is diffracted into an original copy of the data which is sensed by a matrix of CCD sensors.

Although research in this area stems back to the 1960s, it is expected that holographic storage will begin to make inroads after the turn of the century. Such devices could hold 50 million images or 10 billion pages of text and deliver them instantaneously. It is expected that holographic storage will be first used for high-speed imaging and video requirements. See *PRISM*. For a summary of all storage technologies, see *storage*.

Holy Grail

A very desired object or outcome that borders on a sacred quest. There are several Holy Grails in the computer business. Standards tend to be high on the list; for example, having "one" standard that everybody uses and is happy with for each required area. Writing software once and having it run on every computer platform is also desired by many. Another is a software component architecture that allows software modules to "plug together" like hardware components, no matter the platform they run on or which programming language they were written in.

The term's original meaning is the chalice that Joseph of Arimathea used to collect drops of Jesus' blood at the Crucifixion. Legends of the quest for the Holy Grail, which would bring healing and eternal life, have been recounted in various ancient treatises.

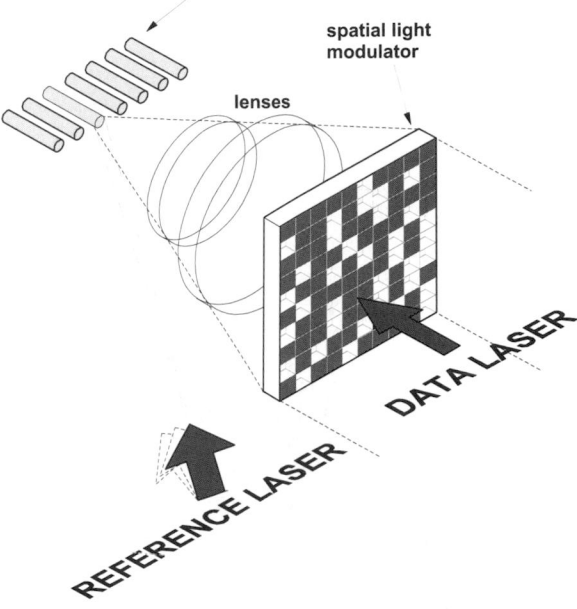

Conceptual Diagram
This simplistic drawing shows the data and reference lasers intersecting at the optical material, creating the holographic page. The spatial light modulator creates the data pattern. The reference laser determines the optical location of the page.

holy war

An ongoing dialogue on an Internet newsgroup about some controversial subject. See *flame*.

home brew

Products that are developed at home by hobbyists.

home button

An icon that represents the beginning of a file or a set of basic or starting functions.

home computer

In the 1980s, a home computer was the lowest-priced computer of the time, such as an Apple II, Commodore 64 or 128, Tandy Color Computer or Atari ST. Today, the term generally refers to a PC or Mac used in the home.

home directory

A disk directory assigned to each user on a UNIX system attached to the Internet. It is the directory you start out in when you log on. It can be used to store temporary or permanent files, a user profile that can be "fingered," as well as lists of newsgroups that have been subscribed to.

home key

A keyboard key used to move the cursor to the top of the screen or file or to the previous word or beginning of line. See *home button*.

home page

The first page retrieved when accessing a Web site. It serves as a table of contents to the rest of the pages on the site or to other Web sites. See *World Wide Web* and *URL*.

HomePort

Netscape's name for a user's desktop that can be customized and accessed from any location. It is expected in future browsers.

home run

A cable that begins at a central distribution point, such as a hub or PBX, and runs to its destination station without connecting to anything else. Home runs are used in star topologies.

home theater

An audio/video entertainment center that has a large-screen TV and hi-fi system with three speakers in the front (left, right and center) and left and right speakers in the rear. Starting in the early 1990s, video inputs were added to stereo receivers and preamplifiers. Today, almost all vendors make a combination audio/video control center for home theater listening and viewing. See *AC-3*.

homogeneous

The same. Contrast with *heterogeneous*.

homogeneous environment

Hardware and system software from one vendor; for example, an all-IBM or all-Digital shop. Contrast with *heterogeneous environment*.

homologation

Certification, confirmation or approval. Data communications equipment is often subject to the homologation requirements of various countries.

Honeywell

In 1927, the Minneapolis Honeywell Regulator Company was formed as a merger of Alfred Butz' temperature control company (1885) and Mark Honeywell's water heater company (1906). In 1957, Honeywell, along with Ratheon, introduced one of the first computers in the U.S., the Datamatic 1000. Two years later, Honeywell's 800 and 400 models earned a solid reputation for advanced features.

In the mid 1960s, Honeywell's 200 series gave IBM serious competition. It outperformed IBM's very successful 1401 computer, which it emulated, causing IBM to accelerate its introduction of its System/360. In 1966, Honeywell acquired Computer Control Company's minicomputer line, and in 1970, it acquired the assets of GE's computer business. The computer division was renamed Honeywell Information Systems, Inc.

The Datamatic 1000

Introduced in 1957, the Datamatic 1000 was a monstrous, tube-driven computer that was very sophisticated for its time. One of them was still in commercial use up until the late 1960s. *(Photo courtesy of Honeywell Inc.)*

Through Honeywell's association with Groupe Bull in Europe and Bull's association with NEC in Japan, research and development were mutually explored and products were jointly developed. In the late 1980s, the three companies formed Honeywell Bull, and later Bull acquired the majority interest, renaming the organization Bull HN. The famous Honeywell name, having been identified with the most advanced computers, remained only as the "H" in Bull HN.

Computer Desktop Encyclopedia

hook

In programming, instructions that provide breakpoints for future expansion. Hooks may be changed to call some outside routine or function or may be places where additional processing is added.

hooked vector

A trapped interrupt in a PC. The pointer for a particular interrupt in the interrupt vector table has been modified to jump to a new routine to service that interrupt.

hookemware

Free software that contains a limited number of features designed to entice the user into purchasing the more comprehensive version.

hop

The link between two network nodes. Each link requires processing.

hop count

The number of links in a transmission path. Each hop adds overhead to the transmission since the gateway or router must analyze or convert the packet of data before forwarding it to its destination.

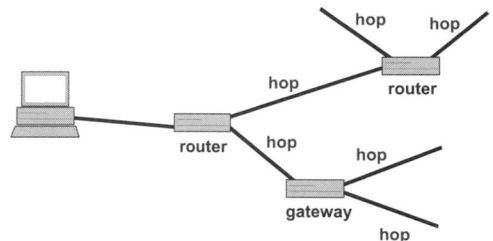

Hops in a Network
Electrical signals may travel near the speed of light in a wire, but each junction point (router, gateway, etc.) adds processing overhead.

hopper

A tray, or chute, that accepts input to a mechanical device, such as a disk duplicator or printer. The term was widely used in the days of punched cards, when hundreds of thousands of cards were sorted routinely by placing them on the hopper, taking them out of the stackers and putting them back in the hopper for the next card column.

horizontal market software

Software packages, such as word processors and spreadsheets, that are used in all industries (banking, insurance, etc.). Such products are also called *productivity software*. Contrast with *vertical market software*.

horizontal resolution

The number of elements, or dots, on a horizontal line (columns in a matrix). Contrast with *vertical resolution*.

horizontal retrace

See *raster scan*.

horizontal scaling

In multiprocessing, adding more computer systems to the environment. Contrast with *vertical scaling*.

horizontal scan frequency

The number of lines illuminated on a video screen in one second. For example, a resolution of 400 lines refreshed 60 times per second requires a scan rate of 24KHz plus overhead (time to bring the beam back to the beginning of the next line). Same as horizontal sync frequency in TV. Contrast with *vertical scan frequency*.

Sorter Hopper
Punched cards were placed into the hopper at the top right of this IBM sorter, which was widely used in the 1960s. Most hoppers were fitted with two-foot extensions that held more cards. *(Photo courtesy of IBM Corporation.)*

horizontal scan rate, horizontal sync
Same as *horizontal scan frequency*.

horizontal software
See *horizontal market software*.

HOS
(Higher Order Software) A design and documentation technique used to break down an information system into a set of functions that are mathematically correct and error free. It uses a rigid set of rules for the decomposition of the total system into its elementary components. The resulting specifications are complete enough to have machine language programs generated directly from them.

host
A computer that acts as a source of information or signals. The term can refer to almost any kind of computer, from a centralized mainframe that is a host to its terminals, to a server that is host to its clients, to a desktop PC that is host to its peripherals. In network architectures, a client station (user's machine) is also considered a host, because it is a source of information to the network in contrast to a device such as a router or switch that directs traffic. See *host adapter* and *host name*.

host adapter
Also called a *controller*, it is a device that connects one or more peripheral units to a computer. It is typically an expansion card that plugs into the bus. IDE and SCSI are examples of peripheral interfaces that call their controllers host adapters. See *host*.

host address
The physical address of a computer in a network. On the Internet, a host address is the IP address of the machine. See *IP address* and *host name*.

host attached
Connected directly to the computer using a peripheral interface such as SCSI, IDE, SSA or ESCON.

host based
A system controlled by a central or main computer. A host-based system typically refers to a hierarchical communications system controlled by a central computer.

host-based printer
A printer that relies on the computer's CPU to do the rasterization of the pages. Non-host-based printers accept a command language from the computer, such as PostScript and PCL, and perform the rasterization internally. GDI printers are an example of host-based printers, which rely on the CPU's processing power to do the work.

hostid
See *IP address*.

host mode
A communications mode that allows a computer to answer an incoming telephone call and receive data without human assistance.

host name
The logical name assigned to a computer. On the Web, most hosts are named WWW; for example, **www.mycompany.com**. If a site is composed of several hosts, they might be given different names such as **support.mycompany.com** and **sales.mycompany.com**. SUPPORT and SALES are the host names, MYCOMPANY the subdomain name, and COM is the top-level domain name. See *HOSTS file, IP address* and *TLD*.

hostname
See *host name*.

HOSTS file
A text file in a UNIX network that provides name resolution of host names to IP addresses. HOSTS files, which contain host names and IP addresses, are manually updated and replicated onto all the servers

in the enterprise. Except in small networks, HOSTS files have given way to the DNS system. See *DNS* and *LMHOSTS file*.

hoteling

Using office space on an as-needed basis like a hotel room. Telecommuters reserve office space ahead of time for trips to the office. See *virtual company* and *telecommuter*.

hot fix

(1) To make a repair during normal operation. It often refers to marking sectors in poor condition as bad and remapping the data to spare sectors. Some SCSI drives can automatically move the data in sectors that are becoming hard to read to spare sectors without the user, operating system or even the SCSI host adapter being aware of it. See *hot swap*.

(2) Microsoft's term for a bug fix, which is accomplished by replacing certain existing files in the application with revised versions.

HotJava

A Web browser from Sun that supports the Java programming language, which was also developed by Sun. HotJava executes Java programs embedded directly within Web documents.

hotkey

The key or key combination that causes some function to occur in the computer, no matter what else is currently running. It is commonly used to activate a memory resident (TSR) program.

hot link

A predefined connection between programs so that when information in one database or file is changed, related information in other databases and files are also updated. See *hypertext, hypergraphic, compound document* and *OLE*.

hotlist

A listing of the best of something. It typically refers to the most popular Web sites.

Hotmail

(Hotmail Corporation, www.hotmail.com) A free, advertiser-supported e-mail service that provides you with a permanent Internet e-mail address. Your mail can be accessed from any Web browser. See *Internet e-mail services*.

hot plug

See *hot swap*.

hot potato routing

(1) In communications, rerouting a message as soon as it arrives.

(2) On the Internet, routing a message from one backbone to another at the nearest exchange point (NAP) to eliminate as much traffic as possible. See *NAP*.

hot spot

(1) An icon or part of a larger image used as a hyperlink to another document or file. When the hot spot is clicked, the linked material is searched for and displayed.

(2) The exact part of an icon or screen pointer that is sensitive to selection. A hot spot may be part of a larger image. For example, an image may have several hot spots, one for each of its components. When clicked, a greater explanation of the component is produced. Where hot spots begin and end determine how easy they are to select.

The screen pointer also has a hot spot, which is a small number of pixels that make contact with the icon's hot spot. For example, the tip of an arrow or finger pointer or the crosspoint of an X-shaped pointer may be the pointer's hot spot.

(3) A network node that is processing at its maximum or is backlogged due to an excessive number of transactions.

(4) The instructions in a program that are executed the most in actual operation. To improve execution performance, the hot spots are the routines that should be refined.

HotSpot

A Java compiler from Sun that optimizes the parts of the program that are executed most frequently (the hot spots). See *hot spot*.

hot swap

To pull out a component from a system and plug in a new one while the power is still on and the unit is still operating. Redundant systems can be designed to swap drives, circuit boards, power supplies, virtually anything that is duplexed within the computer. See *warm swap* and *hot fix*.

Hot topics and trends

This entry summarizes the major topics that are constantly driving this industry. It is intended to help the novice or person getting back into the field to obtain an overview of these subjects.

The Information Superhighway

The Internet has exploded into the consciousness of every country in the world. Nothing in the computer and communications industries ever came onto the scene with more momentum than the World Wide Web. The Clinton/Gore administration had been touting the "information superhighway" for some time and had pointed to the Internet as a model for such a future system, but the excitement over the World Wide Web turned the Internet into the superhighway whether it was ready for it or not. The simplicity of the Web's hypertext link, an address that points to another Web page on the same server or on any server in the world, spread like wildfire.

As a result, there is hardly a single software product that hasn't been affected. Every application is being reworked to deal with the Internet in some manner. This Encyclopedia now contains hundreds of Web terms and products that were not here a couple of years ago.

Even with its growing pains, which grow larger each day, the Internet has managed to become the global superhighway which has changed the lives of millions. That it works as well as it does is indeed quite miraculous. With less than 500 Web sites in 1994 to more than two million today, the Web has become the information melting pot for the planet. It provides a marketplace and meeting ground for every subject known to the human race.

The real superhighway was meant to modernize the telecommunications infrastructure in the U.S. so that everyone has access to information and educational materials no matter what their station in life. Right now, there is a monthly service fee for the Internet, and you have to have a personal computer or set-top box. Although Internet access is available in libraries and other public venues, the Internet is still not a service for everyone at home.

In addition, "surfing the Net" via modem is often an experiment in patience. High-speed access is necessary to keep up this extraordinary momentum. The delivery of the superhighway is now in the hands of the telephone and cable companies, because they are already wired into every home and office and are capable of delivering content at much higher speed with communications technologies such as ISDN, ADSL and cable modems. Internet backbone providers, regional providers and local Internet service providers (ISPs) are upgrading their facilities at a furious pace. The information superhighway is transfiguring itself almost daily.

Entertainment is as much a driving force as information and education as games, video-on-demand and all variety of interactive services converge into this new frontier of online delivery. With deals made daily between cable and telephone companies, video providers, Internet service providers and TV networks, major companies are positioning themselves for the marketplace of the 21st century.

The frenzy has died down a little, because the Internet has already become mainstream. But, making it profitable is another story. One thing is certain. Organizations are making huge investments hoping they know what the business world as well as mom, pop and the kids want to see and purchase, and perhaps more to the point, how much they will pay for it. See *World Wide Web, cable Internet, WorldGate* and *IP on Everything*.

The Intranet

The Internet spawned the World Wide Web, and the Web gave birth to the intranet, an inhouse, private Web site that uses the same protocols and browsers as the external Web. The intranet is protected from the Internet via a firewall. Users have access to internal documents and applications, and they can access the Internet, but Internet users cannot get into the intranet.

In addition to using Web-style pages and links, the Java programming language is enabling the intranet to host full-blown client/server applications with the advantage that, once programmed, they can run in a variety of different desktop computers, including Windows, Mac, UNIX and network computers.

The Internet declared a world standard for document distribution. It only made sense to bring it inhouse.

NCs and Internet Appliances

The Internet and intranet have spawned new hardware platforms called *network computers* and *Internet appliances*. These are slimmed-down client machines that have no local disk storage and obtain everything from the Internet or intranet.

The network computer (NC) is a business-oriented model used with an intranet. It includes a compact operating system, a Web browser and the Java Virtual Machine, which is an interpreter that runs Java applications. The NC is being positioned as a low-cost replacement for the desktop PC as well as an alternative to replacing mini and mainframe terminals. Sun and Oracle are its major promoters.

The Internet appliance, also called the *Internet PC, Internet box, Web PC, Web appliance* or *Web box* lets home users surf the Net. These set-top boxes use a modem for connection to a specific Web service, such as WebTV, and display the output on the TV set. There are no standards for these devices, although some vendors have announced compliance with the NC Reference Profile.

While the Internet appliance seems viable for the home market, there is controversy over the NC as a business model. Proponents believe the NC offers an alternative to the ever increasing Wintel (Windows-Intel) monopoly. It is also believed that a fresh platform will allow new, streamlined programs to be developed and alleviate the tech support and overhead of today's massive desktop applications with features most people never use.

Others feel the NC is a return to the past, to centralized processing where the IS department ruled with an iron hand and users had no choice. NCs mean that users work with what is on the server and nothing else. Plus, downloading everything from the server impacts network traffic. The savings of the cheaper NCs may be offset by the cost of faster networks.

The NC has been hyped up the kazoo by its proponents, who have even proclaimed that it will replace Windows. However, with continuing lower prices for a Windows PC, which can do everything the NC can do, NCs have not set the world on fire, at least not yet. According to Dataquest, 144,000 units were shipped in 1997 and 482,000 were projected for 1998.

Multimedia

Multimedia is the use of pictures, voice and video along with traditional text. It is a major catalyst that forces hardware vendors to make faster and more capacious hardware. And when they don't, it makes software vendors develop innovative algorithms that compress the bits even more. Typing a page of text uses three to five thousand bytes of storage, but scanning that same page and treating it as an image can take 50 thousand bytes or more. Color pages can take megabytes.

The World Wide Web took off because it could display graphics, not just text. Now, we're turning the Internet into a multimedia delivery system for audio, video, telephone, fax and videoconferencing. Multimedia excites us. We're bored with plain text. We want pictures and animation.

A high-quality digital video movie takes about 5GB even when compressed (MPEG-2). Emerging DVD discs can hold this much data and future formats even more. By the turn of the century, DVD drives will obsolete shipments of CD-ROM drives, since they read both DVDs and CD-ROMs. Today's multi-gigabyte hard disks will be strained as more graphics and video are stored on them. Multimedia pushes every platform to its extreme.

Client/Server and Downsizing

For nearly a decade, new information systems have been developed for PCs connected by local area networks (LANs) rather than the central computer architecture of mainframes and minicomputers. Although mainframes and minis perform an enormous amount of daily processing in organizations, the trend has been to migrate older systems and develop new ones to client/server architectures. Client/server primarily means storing the database management systems (DBMSs) on the server and using the client workstations to access them (see *client/server*).

A major incentive for downsizing to LANs has been the wide availability of client/server applications and sources for purchasing both client and server hardware, which continue to decline in cost every year. The client workstations have typically been PCs, and the servers have typically been PCs running NetWare or SCO Open Server or a UNIX server made by Sun, HP, IBM and others. Increasingly, Pentium PCs running Windows NT are gaining market share as servers. Dual and quad-CPU Pentium Pro servers are exploiting the symmetric multiprocessing capability of NT, allowing them to handle workloads that previously only high-end UNIX servers would support.

Although hardware costs may have been less than minis and mainframes, many organizations have discovered that maintenance costs for client/server architectures are considerably higher than expected. Nevertheless, the increased horsepower and lower prices of Intel-based CPUs still makes PC-based client/server networks the largest segment of the computer industry.

Networking

Networking is the backbone of an organization's high-tech infrastructure. The combined demands of client/server applications, multimedia, e-mail and intranets and the Internet just continue to push the envelope. In addition, tying together heterogeneous networks from different departments, subsidiaries and divisions is a daunting task for network administrators and IS managers.

Three trends in networking are to replace shared media networks with switches, to develop high-speed backbones and to switch to TCP/IP as the standard protocol. Shared media networks (Ethernet, Token Ring, FDDI) share all the bandwidth among attached stations. Switches dramatically increase capacity by giving each pair of users sending and receiving to each other the total bandwidth of the line. They also allow for virtual LANs, which make network administration simpler in some cases.

Network backbones are being revamped with high-speed (100 Mbps and above) technologies such as Fast Ethernet and ATM. ATM supports variable speeds up into the multi-gigabit range. Although ATM is currently the only scalable technology that supports realtime voice and video, it's growth has not been as dramatic as predicted due to problems integrating existing LANs and protocols. Now, Gigabit Ethernet is giving ATM a run for its money. Gigabit Ethernet offers 100 times the bandwidth of standard Ethernet and uses connections and technologies network administrators are familiar with.

The Internet has brought us another trend. Since the advent of the Web, the Internet's TCP/IP protocol has become accepted worldwide, and many organizations are adopting it as a standard. For sure, change is the only constant in this field. The network is the lifeblood of enterprise information systems and continues to be the most complex of all operations. See *enterprise networking*.

Groupware

Groupware is software that lets users share and collaborate. The heart of a groupware system is e-mail, since e-mail is used to notify and alert team members on a daily basis. The primary data collaboration tools are electronic whiteboards, which is a shared "chalkboard," and application sharing, which lets remote users work in the same application together. Some form of human communication is also necessary, so either text chat, audio or videoconferencing becomes part of the total system.

Groupware vendors are trying to consolidate a host of collaboration and conferencing features into one client front end that they hope you will use all day for everything. Products such as Lotus Notes, GroupWise, Microsoft Exchange, Netscape Communicator and Internet Explorer/NetMeeting are being positioned as universal front ends to groupware activities. They include e-mail and some combination of the collaboration tools mentioned above as well as document sharing, group calendaring and scheduling and personal information management. Needless to say, all these products are now or will be Internet compliant.

The Internet has brought groupware into focus. Fueled by the ease with which HTML pages can be created and shared, organizations are publishing millions of intranet pages. However, the data placed on these pages is increasingly being extracted from corporate databases.

As the data becomes more integral to the daily operation of the business, problems surface. What happens when the documents are distributed to remote servers? Which ones are the latest? Who keeps them up-to-date? What starts out as a simple method of electronically publishing internal documents winds up becoming a strategic information system requiring the same care and attention as the data processing systems that have been deployed for decades.

Groupware is poised to become another abused buzzword, but its timing is logical. We've been building our networks for years. We're globalizing and standardizing them with the Internet. We're simply trying to harness the power of our computers and networks to collaborate more efficiently.

Objects and Components

Just like plugging an expansion board into an expansion slot, objects and components are software modules that are designed to work with each other at runtime. The ability to plug together software routines that can be purchased from a wide variety of sources holds enormous promise for software developers, especially if those routines can run on all popular platforms locally as well as remotely on LANs, intranets and on the Internet.

The terms objects and components are used interchangeably. Objects are self-contained program modules created by object-oriented programming languages. Objects have spawned component architectures such as Microsoft's ActiveX technologies, which are based on its COM architecture for Windows and Sun's JavaBeans. JavaBeans is the newest component architecture on the block for the Java environment.

Component technologies have a container/object relationship. The container is the client application that holds the objects. It provides the user interface and distributes mouse movement and keyboard input to all the objects it communicates with. Component/object technologies are considered important for application development, and the subject often generates heated debate as to which architecture more closely follows the rules of object-oriented programming. However, the component technologies that survive will be those that are marketed the best, not which ones are more object oriented. See *object technology*.

In order to run objects remotely in the network, there are two distributed object technologies currently competing for prime time: the industry standard CORBA from the Object Management Group and DCOM from Microsoft. CORBA allows objects to run no matter where they reside, and DCOM allows most of Microsoft's COM-based components to do the same. JavaBeans can be run remotely under CORBA or via Sun's own RMI protocol. Netscape has built in IIOP into its browsers, which is the CORBA message protocol designed for the Web. Thus, it boils down once again to Microsoft versus the rest of the world. However, we convert from one method to another all the time in this business, so CORBA to DCOM and DCOM to CORBA conversion should allow both of these distributed object technologies to interoperate. See *component software, CORBA, COM, DCOM* and *JavaBeans*.

One rather irksome outcome of objects and components is the names themselves. These common English language words are so useful that they conflict with the specific uses of these technologies.

Hardware Costs

The price of hardware continues to plummet. Each year, we get more computer per dollar than we did the year before. Over the past couple of years, memory chip prices have dropped through the roof. When compared to just a few years ago, technology seems to be a huge bargain. However, hardware costs are misleading, because our requirements continue to increase as rapidly as costs decrease.

In addition, we focus on CPU speed, and although it's marvelous that a 300MHz Pentium system costs as little as $1,500 these days, add a really nice 21" monitor and display adapter, and the price more than doubles. Add more goodies, and a fully-configured power user's PC can easily cost $5,000. The real irony is that much of this great new speed goes up in smoke as more novice programmers are hired by software vendors, which is often why the next version of your favorite application is slower than the current one. Switching to object-oriented languages may also add significant overhead. While it is impossible to add functionality ad infinitum without paying some performance penalty, it takes experienced programmers to keep new features from slowing everything to a crawl. Veteran programmers are increasingly harder to find due to the worldwide demand for this expertise.

In almost every organization, a user is attached to an internal network that is ever expanding. More Internet usage requires faster connections. The general complexity of this entire business means more inhouse expertise and third-party consulting. Certain hardware is also going up. Larger monitors are replacing smaller ones. Flat panel displays are emerging on the desktop at four times the cost of a CRT. Our mobile workforce uses laptops at an ever-increasing rate, which command a huge premium over desktop machines.

There is a vast amount of off-the-shelf software that solves a lot of requirements, but even the smallest organizations often have special needs.

> If the auto industry had done what the computer industry has done in the last 30 years, a Rolls-Royce would cost $2.50 and get 2,000,000 miles per gallon.

Half the Equation

This slogan has been used in the computer field for years, but it tells only one side of the story. Hardware may be cheap by comparison, but people costs are not, and worldwide computing requirements are increasing rapidly.

Custom programming is more expensive today because labor rates are higher. The bottom line is that there are more demands for technology and more money being spent on it than ever before.

housekeeping

A set of instructions that are executed at the beginning of a program. It sets all counters and flags to their starting values and generally readies the program for execution.

how to access the Internet

There are three ingredients needed to access the Internet. First is an access provider, which can be a major online service such as America Online, CompuServe or Prodigy, an Internet service provider (ISP) such as UUNET or NetCom or any of hundreds of smaller ISPs throughout the country. The ISPs generally offer unlimited access for a fixed rate per month.

The second thing you need is a modem, and the third is the software, which is normally supplied by your service. The software usually consists of an e-mail program, a Web browser and possibly an Internet Relay Chat (IRC) program. E-mail lets you send a message to anybody in the world that subscribes to an Internet provider, an online service or an e-mail service. The Web browser lets you access the World Wide Web and newsgroups. Internet Relay Chat lets you keyboard conference globally to people via hundreds of IRC channels on countless subjects.

When you sign up with an ISP, you are given instructions on how to download the software, how to install it and get started. The physical process for gaining access is to dial up your service, launch your browser and/or e-mail program and go to it. Since the Internet explosion, the online services are trying to distinguish themselves from the ISPs by offering all-in-one interfaces that make dial-up, e-mail, newsgroups, chat and Web browsing easier, combined with whatever specialized databases they might offer.

The Coolest Web Sites

The company that is setting the standards for the World Wide Web is Netscape Communications. It is continually designing new capabilities that can be programmed into Web pages and releases new versions of its Web browser to support them.

Since there is considerable competition to have the "coolest" Web site, Web pages are reprogrammed with the new functions as fast as Netscape comes up with them. As a result, if you don't use the Netscape browser, or, in fact, do not have the latest release of it, you may get Web pages that do not display as the designer intended. Such extras are usually bypassed by the browser, but they can also cause older browsers to crash if not implemented carefully.

New versions of Internet Explorer (IE), Microsoft's Web browser, generally follow the Netscape versions and support all new enhancements as well. IE continues to gain market share, because it is free and because of Microsoft's power in the business. Microsoft also implements proprietary features on the Web, such as ActiveX controls.

The Right Provider

If you only browse the Web, there is little lost in starting with one service and switching to another. However, switching your e-mail address is not like switching your street address. The post office will forward your mail for a while, but if you close your account with an online service or ISP, they are usually not as accomodating. It would be a good idea to find out, if you plan on promoting your e-mail address heavily.

There are two ways around this problem. First is to register your own domain name with the InterNIC and use an ISP that supports unique domain names. Most of them do and will even handle the InterNIC registration for you. Then, if you ever change ISPs, you can transfer your name to the new ISP. There is an annual charge for domain registration from the InterNIC and additional charges from your ISP for hosting your private domain name.

Second is to establish an account with an Internet e-mail provider. There are sites on the Web and off the Web that provide free e-mail and e-mail forwarding. See *Internet e-mail service*.

how to buy a new computer

See *how to select a personal computer*.

how to buy a used computer

See *computer exchange*.

how to check out a domain name

See *InterNIC*.

how to convert files

There are dozens of file formats for word processing documents, database files, graphics, spreadsheets and so on. If a file was created in one application and you want to use it in another, you can either import the file or use a conversion program.

Converting Text Files

Most word processing programs provide an Import function, which provides built-in conversion for various document formats. Simply select Import from the File or Import menu and choose the document type you want to input.

If your word processor does not import the document type you need, you can usually use the ASCII file format as a common denominator; however, you will need the word processing program that created the original document.

If both word processing programs import and export ASCII files, convert your original document into an ASCII file using the source word processor. Look for Export in the File or Export menu. Select ASCII file or Text File. After creating an ASCII file of the source document, use the destination word processor and import that file using the Import option, again for an ASCII file or Text File. Note that all format commands (bold, italics, headers, footers, etc.) will generally be lost between conversion.

Converting Database Files

Most database programs provide an Import function, which provides built-in conversion for various record formats. Simply select Import from the File or Import menu and choose the database type you want to input.

If your database program does not import the file type you need, you can usually use the ASCII file format as a common denominator; however, you will need the database program that created the original file.

If both database programs import and export ASCII files, convert your original file into an ASCII file using the source database program. Look for Export in the File or Export menu. Select ASCII file or Text File. There are generally two types of ASCII files that can be created: comma delimited and SDF.

Comma delimited separates each field with a comma and puts quotes around text fields, for example:

```
"Harry Bacon","123 Main","El Paso","TX"
"Mary Katz",4 W. 3rd St.","New York","NY"
```

The SDF, or standard data format, creates contiguous fixed fields:

```
Harry Bacon     123 Main        El Paso    TX
Mary Katz       4 W. 3rd St.    New York   NY
```

Each field in a comma delimited or SDF format follows in the order of its original placement. In your destination database program, create a new database file with the same structure as the original, using the same order as the original. Then import the ASCII file into that structure. You can always modify the structure after you have imported the data into it.

Converting Images and Drawings

Most paint, drawing, word processing, desktop publishing and presentation graphics programs provide an Import function, which provides built-in conversion for various image and drawing formats. Simply select Import from the File or Import menu and choose the graphics file type you want to input.

If your program does not import the file type you need, you can convert one image or drawing format into another using an independent graphics conversion program, such as Inset System's popular HiJaak.

Note that image formats, or bitmapped graphics (raster graphics) formats, such as PCX, BMP, TIFF, GIF, etc. cannot be converted into drawing formats, or vector graphics formats, such as WMF, DXF, DRW, CGM, etc., but vector formats can be turned into bitmapped images (for more on bitmaps and vectors, see *graphics* and *graphics formats*).

Windows programs can usually import BMP and WMF files, which are the standard Windows graphics formats. BMP is a bitmapped graphics format (image) and WMF is a vector graphics format (drawing).

how to copy a file

Windows 3.1 File Manager

In Windows 3.1, File Manager is used to copy files. File Manager contains one or more directory windows. Clicking a directory on the left pane of a directory window displays the directory's contents in the right pane. To copy a file from the right pane into a directory in the left pane, hold Control down and drag and drop the icon of the file you want to copy. To copy multiple files, hold the Control key down while selecting the file icons. Then hold Control down and drag and drop from any highlighted line.

If you want to view the contents of the destination directory that you are copying into, you can open a second window by selecting NEW WINDOW from the Window menu. You can then drag and drop from the right pane of one window into the right pane of the second window.

Windows 95/98

In Windows 95/98, there are two ways to copy files. If the files are in folders on the desktop, the folders can be double clicked to open them into windows. To copy a file from one window into another, hold Control down and drag and drop the icon of the file you want to copy. To copy multiple files, hold the Control key down while selecting the file icons. Then hold Control down and drag and drop from any highlighted line.

EXPLORER

If a file is not in a folder on the desktop, launch the Explorer by right clicking the Start button and clicking Explore.

Clicking a folder in the left pane of an Explorer window displays its contents in the right pane. To copy a file from the right pane into a folder in the left pane, hold Control down and drag and drop the icon of the file you want to copy. To copy multiple files, hold Control down while selecting the file icons. Then hold Control down and drag and drop from any highlighted line.

If the destination folder is out of view on the left side, you can highlight the files in the right pane and select Edit/Copy, then scroll the left pane to the right folder, highlight it and select Edit/Paste.

You can also launch multiple instances of Explorer and drag and drop from the right pane of one Explorer window into the right pane of the other.

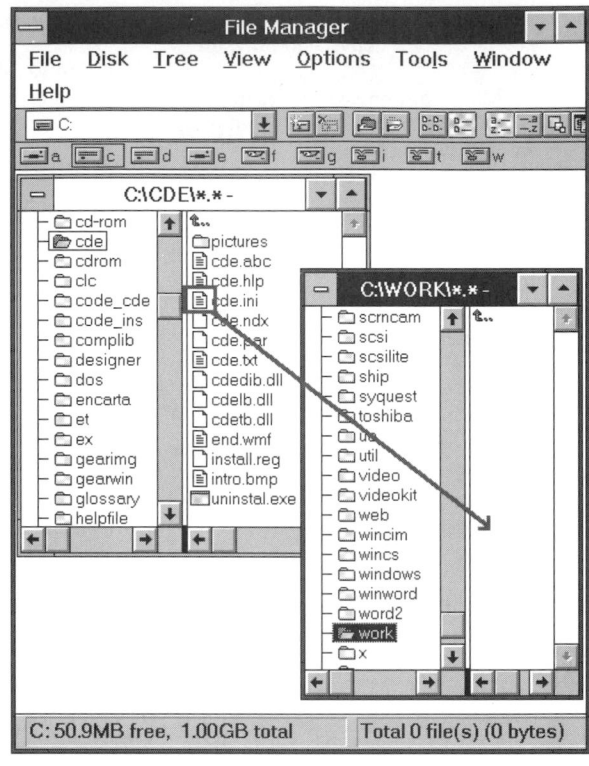

File Manager Windows
To copy the CDE.INI file from the CDE directory into the WORK directory, the icon of the file is dragged and dropped into the open WORK window while the Control key is held down.

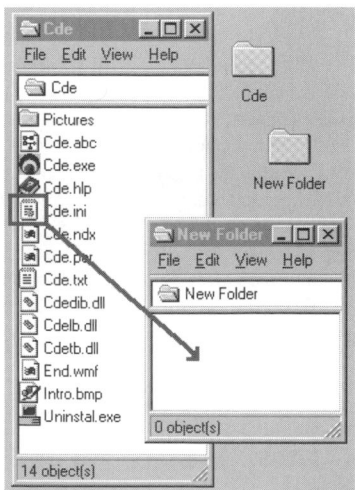

Copying From Folders
This example shows the CDE folder and a new folder both present on the desktop. When the folders are opened, files can be dragged and dropped from one folder into another.

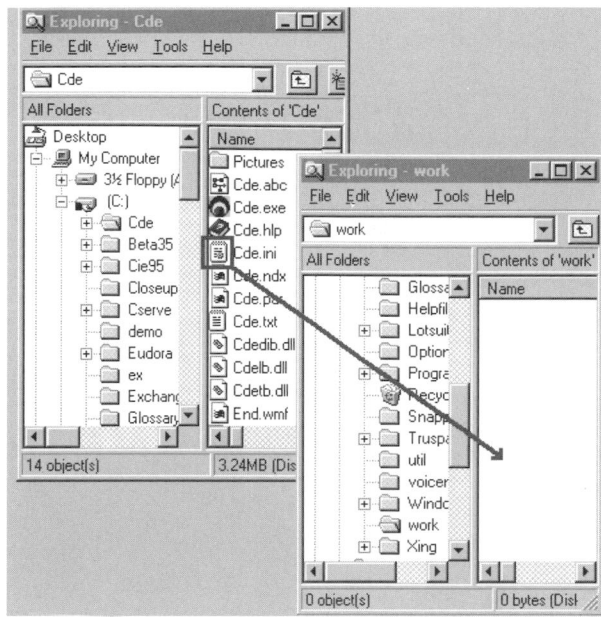

Explorer Windows
The CDE.INI file is being dragged between two Explorer sessions. However, you do not need to launch Explorer twice to do this. For example, using only the Explorer on the left, you would highlight CDE.INI and select Edit/Copy. Then, scroll the left pane to the WORK folder, highlight it and select Edit/Paste.

how to donate old equipment

There are organizations that channel old computer equipment to the less fortunate. The National Cristina Foundation maintains a database of organizations that support the handicapped. The East-West foundation provides a warehouse and support for equipment sent to schools and other public service organizations in the U.S. and around the world. The Computer Recycling Center maintains a warehouse and support for machines intended for schools and non-profit organizations.

Millions of devices become "obsolete" every day in our high-tech society. Don't throw them out! They might be very useful for those less fortunate. Contact:

National Cristina Foundation
591 West Putnam Ave.
Greenwich, CT 06830
800/274-7846
(www.cristina.org)

Computer Recycling Center, Inc.
1245 Terra Bella Ave.
Mountain View, CA 94043
415/428-3700
(www.computerrecycling.org)

how to download a file

See *download*.

how to find a file

It is easy to forget which directory/folder you saved a file in. A file find utility searches directories for a file or category of files.

WINDOWS 95/98
Select FIND from the Start menu. Select FILES OR FOLDERS. Type in the drive letter (C:, D:, etc.) you want to search into "Look in." Type in the name of the file you want to find into "Named." Use wild cards to select a group of files; for example, *.**exe** finds all the .EXE files. Click FIND NOW, and all matches are displayed in a results window.

WINDOWS 3.1

In File Manager, select SEARCH from the FILE menu. Type in the drive letter (C:, D:, etc.) you want to search into "Start From." Type in the name of the file you want to find into "Search For." Use wild cards to select a group of files; for example, *.exe finds all the .EXE files. Click OK, and all matches are displayed in a results window.

DOS

Starting as of DOS 5, the /s switch used with the Dir command searches for file names in all directories. For example, to find the X.BAT file starting from the root directory, you would type:

```
C:\>dir x.bat /s
```

how to find a good computer book

Good computer books are worth their weight in gold, because the online help in most applications leaves a lot to be desired. Unfortunately, while millions are spent programming software, considerably less money is allocated to documenting it. Worse yet, the documentation is usually last minute, rushed and never read by anyone but the unfortunate user of the software. That's why having auxiliary documentation in the form of books is extremely helpful.

How to find a good book is simple. Get two or three on the same subject. Today, software applications are often the culmination of decades worth of functions and features that includes everything everyone ever wanted in the program. It is rare to find a single author equally competent in all areas of the program, and you won't know that when you browse the book in the bookstore, only when you're stuck later on. If you have more than one book, your chances are greater that your question will be answered.

In lieu of direct technical support from the software vendor or from your organization's help desk or IS department, several books on the subject is your best bet.

how to find some business on the Net

See *Web yellow pages*.

how to find someone on the Net

See *Web white pages*.

how to find things on the Net

See *Web search sites* and *how to access the Internet*.

how to format a disk

See *Win 9x Format a disk*.

how to get a domain name

See *how to register a domain name*.

how to import a file

See *how to transfer a file*.

how to impress your friends

See *online*.

how to make backups

Backups are copies of documents, spreadsheets, databases and images on the hard disk that have been placed onto an external storage medium such as floppy disk or tape. Backups should be made routinely because the hard disk can self destruct (see *head crash*). There is definitely more paranoia about this than the number of incidents, but they do happen, so it is wise to make backups.

Using a Copy Command or Function

There are two ways to back up files onto external storage media. The first is to copy the individual files using a copy command or function. In DOS, you would use the Copy or Xcopy commands. In Windows or the Mac, you would dragg the file icon with a mouse from the graphical representation of the hard disk to that of the desired floppy. Copying files works best for copying a small number of files or if you are sure that the all the required files fit on the target storage medium. To fit more files onto a single diskette, you can compress files before you copy.

Using a Backup Command or Utility

The second way to back up files is to use a backup program or backup command. The advantage of this method is that you can copy any number of files as long as you have enough blank floppy disks. When a floppy disk is full and only a part of the file has been copied, the backup program copies the remaining part of the file to the next disk. When restoring files, the backup program deals with these overlapping files, which normal copy commands cannot.

In addition, backup programs support tape backup units, something that copy commands do not generally do. They also compress files automatically to save space.

DOS provides its own Backup and Restore commands, but if you use Backup to back up your files onto floppies and then switch to a different computer, the Restore command from a different DOS version won't restore your files. As of DOS 6, separate backup utilities (MSbackup) are included that make the job easier. However, third-party backup utilities provide more versatility than both the commands and utilities included with DOS.

Another advantage of using a backup utility is that you can make a full copy of your entire disk directory, not just your data files, but the software too. This is especially helpful as you add more and more applications to your system. If your disk crashed, reinstalling everything would take quite some time. However this works best when you use high-capacity tapes or optical disks for backup. Routine copying onto multiple floppies is a nuisance.

Remember, it's your data (documents, spreadsheets, databases, images, etc.) that is most critical. As long as it is still popular, you can always obtain another copy of the software. But you cannot purchase copies of your data from anybody. See *backup types*.

how to register a domain name

If you are setting up your own Web server, you will have to register directly with the InterNIC. If you are putting a Web site onto the server of your Internet service provider (ISP), that organization will generally handle the registration for you, typically for an additional fee. To find out more about the InterNIC visit www.internic.net.

Is a Name Already Taken?

To find out if a domain name is taken, visit www.internic.net. Select Registration Services, then Whois. Type in the name and press Enter.

how to search the Web

See *Web search sites*.

how to select a personal computer

The most important thing in selecting a personal computer is that you obtain the performance and storage capacity from your system that you need as well as the technical support from your dealer that you require. The primary decision criteria are:

1. PC versus Mac
2. Windows versus DOS
3. Ergonomics
4. Desktop versus Laptop
5. Where to buy

PC VERSUS MAC

The first decision is whether to purchase a PC or a Macintosh. It is, after all, a PC and Mac personal computer world. Although Apple has only about 4% of the business, it is also only one company. The rest of the market is made up of thousands of PC vendors from mom and pop shops to the big companies such as Compaq, IBM, Dell and Gateway. Apple continues to hang on, due to its fiercely loyal customer base and its superior technology.

The Mac is easier to use compared to Windows and DOS machines, because the Mac was designed from the ground up to be a graphics-based machine. Windows inherits much of its complexity because it remains compatible with the DOS world. With the Mac, you can spend more time learning your application and less time configuring your computer. Since applications are becoming more feature laden and more complicated for both platforms, this is a decided advantage.

It is also considerably easier to upgrade a Mac than a PC. Adding a second or third peripheral to a PC can be difficult. Adding one to a Mac usually means "just plug in it." Although Windows 95/98's Plug and Play works much better than the previous Windows 3.x, the Mac is still easier to upgrade.

The main disadvantage of the Mac is compatibility. Although, major applications, such as Word, Excel and PageMaker, run on both Mac and Windows, there are many applications that are not available on both platforms. Processing data created on the other platform may require conversion. If your company supports PCs and Macs, support personnel have most likely determined the appropriate applications and utilities that make file transfer between both platforms straightforward. If not, you may have problems.

Another disadvantage is that there are decidedly more applications for Windows than there are for the Mac. Using SoftWindows, the Mac can run most Windows applications, but generally not as fast as a native Windows machine.

WINDOWS VERSUS DOS

If you've settled on a PC, then the type of applications you will run determines the system size. If you are only running older vertical market applications (doctor, dentist, retailer, etc.) that are still DOS based, you can get by with a minimal PC (see requirements below). However, all new applications are Windows, and almost all DOS productivity programs (spreadsheets, word processors, etc.) have long since had their last revision as a DOS program.

Windows requires a fast and large machine. Windows applications take enormous amounts of disk space these days, from 20 to 50 megabytes. In some cases as much as 100. You may not be entering a lot of data, but you could use up 200 to 400 megabytes of disk just by installing a dozen applications. In addition, if you want to keep a half dozen or more applications open at the same time, you need plenty of memory (RAM).

If this is your first Windows machine, start with Windows 95 or Windows 98, not Windows 3.1. If you learn on 3.1 first, you will have to relearn it over again later on. In addition, newer applications only run under Windows 95/98 and not 3.1.

Future Windows applications will be even more demanding than current ones. If you can afford it, get the faster machine. Following are recommended PC configurations.

RECOMMENDED SYSTEM FOR DOS

CPU	486/66
Bus	ISA
RAM	4MB
Hard disk	340MB
Monitor	15"
Resolution	640x480

RECOMMENDED SYSTEM FOR WINDOWS

	Word processing, database, spreadsheets	CAD, imaging, multimedia, desktop publishing
CPU	Pentium/266	Pentium II/400
Bus	ISA/PCI	ISA/PCI
RAM	64MB	128MB
Hard disk	4GB	6-9GB
Display System:		
Screen	17"	21"
Res	800x600	1024x768, 1280x1024 1600x1200
Refresh	72Hz +	72Hz +
CD-ROM	12x	24x
Sound	16 bit	16 bit

Yes, It Can Be Slower

You can always get by with a slower machine. It's all a matter of patience while you wait for the computer to respond when you click a button. Your experience level has nothing to do with the power of the machine you deserve. You will get used to the fastest PC on the market in 10 minutes. Then, if you go to a slower machine, you will understand why speed is so much of an issue in this business.

ERGONOMICS

The most important parts of your PC are the keyboard, mouse and screen. In the highly-competitive PC world, these are the areas where vendors skimp. Keyboards cost from $15 to $200. There is a difference. After eight hours of typing, you'll understand what it is. Check out the newer angled keyboards. They offer a more natural position for your hands if you do a lot of typing.

The mouse is another device that can vary widely in cost and design. One can be far more comfortable than another. Trackballs are an alternative that some prefer.

Lastly, display systems, which are made up of the display adapter (the card that plugs into the PC) and the monitor, vary widely in cost and quality.

The Windows desktop simulates an office desktop, but when is the last time you worked at a desk one foot wide? Running Windows on a 14" monitor is limiting. You cannot see an entire document unless you run at a resolution that makes everything very small. A 17" monitor is much better, and a 21" monitor is even better yet.

A small, inexpensive monitor can cost as little as $200. A 21" monitor can cost from $1000 to $2000 and more. A low-end display adapter for $35 is not the same as the $300 to $800 high-end card used for CAD, desktop publishing and imaging work. There is a difference in image quality and speed.

DESKTOP VERSUS LAPTOP

If you have a requirement for a computer in more than one location, a laptop can be an economical alternative. It can function as a desktop computer by attaching a full-size monitor and keyboard.

The caveat with laptops is that they are not as expandable as desktops. On a destop PC, if you need more hard disk, you can add another or swap your current one for a larger one. On laptops, the hard disk may not be upgradable at all. If it is, there may be a limited number of options, and it will usually cost at least twice that of a desktop drive, so plan ahead.

A docking station may provide one or two expansion slots for expandability, but you will have to duplicate docking stations and peripherals if you need them in both locations. Laptops with PC Card slots also offer flexibility for expansion.

In addition, the display resolution on a laptop is built into the motherboard. Even if you attach a large monitor, you cannot upgrade to a higher resolution unless you have a docking station with another VGA adapter installed in it and the laptop is built to switch to an external adapter. For a list of laptop features, see *laptop computer*.

WHERE TO BUY

The best price to pay for a personal computer and the best place to buy it often has more to do with the support you need than the equipment you purchase. If you don't need support, shop for the best price from local dealers, superstores and the mail-order houses.

Most components in PCs are highly reliable, but there are always exceptions. Hard and floppy drives come from a handful of vendors, but there are dozens of motherboard manufacturers. Look for OS/2 and Novell certification, a good sign of compatibility. If the motherboard (not just the chip) is made by Intel, you are assured of compatibility. Get customer referrals.

If you use your computer all day, or if you keep it on 24 hours as some do, opt for the brand name. The power supply in the no-name clone might give way in a year or so. An option is to buy the no-name clone and put in a better power supply, such as one from PC Power and Cooling, Carlsbad, CA.

If you're new to computers, look for local dealers that specialize in hand holding for the novice. There is usually a dealer nearby that caters to the beginner. You may pay a few hundred dollars more for your system, but it may be well worth it, saving you time and frustration later.

The superstores are also a good source for computers, but the amount of support you get will vary. Remember, you can always pay a consultant by the hour to help you if you don't know any sympathetic hackers.

The mail-order houses are another good source with quality machines, but you will have to rely on technical support by phone. Ironically, the more successful the direct sales organization, the worse its phone support becomes, if only temporarily. A disadvantage of mail order is that you will have to ship back your unit if you can't fix it by phone. Look for mail-order firms with on-site support administered by a national repair organization.

how to spoof your technical friend

how to spoof your technical friend

Caution # 1 - The Small Business

The small business looking to automate its accounting is going to need more help. Don't be fooled by the prices of hardware and off-the-shelf software. The small company often has information requirements as complicated as a much larger one. There are countless custom-designed applications that have cost $5,000 to $25,000, running on $1,500 PCs, because no off-the-shelf software package could fit the bill.

It's tempting to think a $100 software package can do the accounting for your entire company, and the fact is, in many cases, it very well can. But, even if you understand your detailed information requirements, matching them with the marketing blurbs on a package cover is not simple. You generally do not find the software's limitations until after you are up and running.

Determining the best accounting software for your particular needs is not something most PC vendors want to get involved with. To do the job right, it can take hours, days or weeks of analysis depending on your business and what you want to computerize. You may want to use the services of a software consulting firm or an independent consultant.

Caution #2 - The Bleeding Edge

Even if you can easily afford the newest technology, it's not always a good idea to be the first on the block to have it. Wait a bit. Ask around. When the bugs are finally fixed, and that can take several months, you may be a lot better off. Good luck and happy computing.

how to spoof your technical friend

To have a light-hearted joke with your technical colleagues, take the highest clock rate of an Intel CPU chip and double or triple it. Then, simply say "did you hear about Intel's 800MHz Pentium? They've kept it a secret, but they're shipping it now!" Expect a "wow" reaction, or "that's impossible!"

Be careful. You have to stay on top of the numbers. Years ago, a 100MHz chip sounded unbelievable. Today, workstation chips have already reached 600MHz speeds, and 1GHz clocks will eventually be here. See also *buffer flush* and *Stringy Floppy*.

how to surf the Net

See *how to access the Internet* and *Web search sites*.

how to transfer a file

Within the Same Machine From one Application to Another

The ability to transfer a file from one application to another within the same machine depends on the import and export capabilities of the application. All full-featured applications accept a variety of foreign files.

Graphics applications (drawing programs, desktop publishing, image editing, etc.) are typically designed to import and export a wide variety of file formats. Just look at the import/export menus.

Some word processing and database programs can detect different file types by merely opening the file. Others have to be explicity told the type of file it is. Look for Import, Export and Place functions in the menus. See *ASCII file*.

From One Computer to Another Using a File Transfer Program

File transfer programs provide a way to transfer only one or many files between two computers cabled together or in different locations. Programs such as the DOS Interlink utility, Windows 95/98's Direct Cable Connection (DCC) and LapLink, a veteran file transfer product, are examples of these utilities.

For remote transfer, you need a modem and the file transfer program on both machines. The modems do not have to come from the same vendor, but the file transfer programs do. However, if the remote computer does not already have the program installed, the transfer program can usually install itself on the remote computer after you connect to it, using its remote install procedure. If you are connected to the Internet, attaching files via e-mail is an easy way to send a limited number of files to a remote user (see *how to transfer a file over the Internet*).

Since a file transfer program is dedicated to this single purpose, the transfer protocol is typically built in and hidden from the user rather than being selectable as it is in a general-purpose communications program. You can also view on screen the directories of both the local and remote machines.

Third-party transfer programs come with special cables to connect both computers via the serial or parallel ports. See *null modem cable*, *LapLink cable*, *DCC* and *LapLink*.

From One Computer to Another Using a Communications Program

General-purpose communications programs used to be very popular for file transfer and general access to a BBS before the days of the Internet. The programs in both machines do not have to be from the same vendor as they all support a selection of popular transfer protocols. In order to transfer a file remotely, both machines need modems, which can come from different vendors.

The user in the receiving computer sets the communications program to Auto Answer. The user in the sending computer uses the communications program to dial up the modem of the receiving machine. Both users must agree on a file transfer protocol, the best one generally being Zmodem. When a connection is made, the sending computer selects Upload and identifies the file or files to be sent. The receiving computer selects Download. When the transfer is complete, each user selects "hang up."

If the machines are side by side, instead of using a modem, connect a null modem cable between the serial ports of both machines. Since there are no modems and telephone lines to dial, the transfer is made by selecting Upload and Download (send and receive) in the respective communications programs.

how to transfer a file over the Internet

There are two ways to transfer files over the Internet. One is to send a file along with an e-mail message, and the other is to use an FTP program.

Via E-mail

E-mail programs have the ability to "attach a file" to a message, which means that any type of file (program, graphics, spreadsheet, etc.) can be transmitted along with the text message. This is the simplest way to send a file via the Internet. However, although widely used, it can be problematic. Old e-mail programs, light versions of e-mail programs and some mail gateways can cause problems.

The standard Internet mail protocol supports only text. In order to transmit non-text files, an encoding method such as MIME, UUencoding or BinHex is used by the e-mail program to convert 8-bit bytes into the 7-bit ASCII characters that are supported. The files are decoded by the receiving mail program. The most widely supported method today is MIME; however, older e-mail clients may use an encoding scheme such as UUencoding that a light version of an e-mail client may not be able to decipher. In such cases, you can ask the sender to encode in MIME, or you may want to upgrade to the full version of the e-mail program.

Occasionally, a mail gateway is set up to limit the total length of an e-mail message. If attached files exceed this limit, they can be broken up into several files that are delivered to you. These files can be manually combined and decoded; however, this is a technical chore beyond the scope of most e-mail users.

Via FTP and the Web

The protocol on the Internet that was designed to handle file transfers is FTP (file transfer protocol). It supports large files and the full 8-bit byte structure. With a Web browser, you can download from an FTP site, but not upload. You would use the **ftp://** prefix and address (URL), which includes the domain name and directories.

In order to upload to an FTP site, you generally need an ID and password. If you have such privilege, you can use a terminal program and type in the raw UNIX commands, or use a graphical FTP program with menus and buttons. There are always shareware or freeware FTP programs available on the Web.

HP

(Hewlett-Packard Company, Palo Alto, CA, www.hp.com) The second largest computer company in the U.S. HP was founded in 1939 by William Hewlett and David Packard in a garage behind the Packard's California home. Its first product, an audio oscillator for measuring sound, was the beginning of a line of electronics that made HP an international supplier of electronic test and measurement instruments. Walt Disney Studios, HP's first big customer, purchased eight oscillators to develop and test a new sound system for the movie "Fantasia."

HP entered the computer field in 1966 with the 2116A, the first of the HP 1000 series designed to gather and analyze the data produced by HP instruments. HP 1000 computers are used for CIM applications, such as process monitoring and control, alarm management and machine monitoring.

In 1972, HP branched into business computing with the 3000 series, a multiuser system that became well known for its high reliability, especially for that time. The successful 3000 family has continued to be one of HP's major computer series. Also in 1972, HP introduced the first scientific handheld calculator, the HP-35, obsoleting the slide rule and ushering in a new age of pocket-sized calculators. In 1982, the first HP 9000 workstation was introduced.

HP's first personal computer was the Touchscreen 150, a non-standard MS-DOS personal computer that gained only modest acceptance. In 1985, it introduced its first completely IBM-compatible PC, the 286-based Vectra. As of the 1990s, the Vectra has become a very successful part of HP's business.

In 1984, HP revolutionized the printer market with its desktop LaserJet printer, which has set the standard for the industry. HP continues its leadership in this area with routine advances in resolution, speed and price.

In 1986, it introduced Precision Architecture, a RISC-based architecture for its 3000 and 9000 series product lines, which has proven very successful. In 1989, HP acquired Apollo Computer, a workstation manufacturer, and combined technologies to become a formidable contender in this field. In 1994, HP was the second largest workstation vendor after Sun.

HP sells over 10,000 different products in the electronics and computer field and has gained a worldwide reputation for its quality engineering.

Hewlett and Packard

Dave Packard (left) and Bill Hewlett (right) develop their innovative audio oscillator in Packard's Palo Alto garage in 1939. Perhaps they didn't realize they were starting one of the largest and most-respected high-technology companies in the world. *(Photo courtesy of Hewlett-Packard Company.)*

Hewlett and Packard 50 Years Later

Nearly 50 years after the picture above, this photo was taken in 1988 at an awards ceremony at corporate headquarters. *(Photo courtesy of Hewlett-Packard Company.)*

HP's First Product

This is the advertisement for the original audio oscillator, HP's first product in 1939. *(Photo courtesy of Hewlett-Packard Company.)*

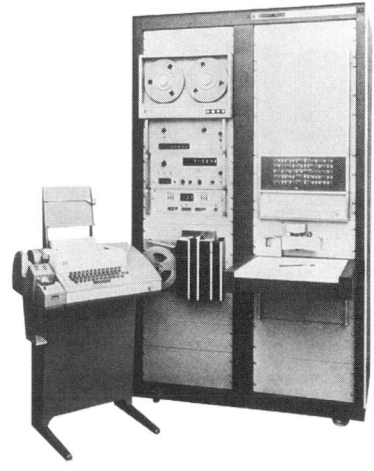

The 2116A
The 2116A was HP's first computer designed for the process control industry. It was the beginning of a long line of computers for this niche as well as for scientific and commercial applications. *(Photo courtesy of Hewlett-Packard Company.)*

HP 1000
A family of realtime computers from HP introduced in 1966. They are sensor-based computers used extensively in laboratory and manufacturing environments for collecting and analyzing data.

HP 3000
A family of business-oriented servers from HP that run under the MPE/iX operating system. Models are available from entry level to mainframe class. Introduced in 1972, the HP3000A was HP's first business computer. With 128KB of RAM and costing about $250,000, it set a standard for reliability that was unmatched for that era.

In 1986, the line began to migrate to HP's PA-RISC chips, while maintaining compatibility with the original CPUs. Over the years, HP 3000s have migrated from the central minicomputer architecture to client/server, in which intelligent workstations and PCs have replaced the dumb terminal.

HP 9000
A family of high-performance workstations and servers from HP that are based on HP's PA-RISC architecture and run under the HP/UX operating system. Both workstations and servers are available in a wide range of machines from entry level to supercomputer class. HP VISUALIZE models are workstations with high-performance graphics capabilities. Back in the 1980s, the first HP 9000s used Motorola 680x0 CPUs.

HPA
(High Performance Addressing) A type of active addressing technology that improves the quality of a passive matrix (LCD) screen.

HPC
(Handheld **PC**) A palmtop computer that weighs less than one pound and runs specialized versions of popular applications. Microsoft coined the term for its Windows CE operating system, which is an abbreviated version of Windows 95/98. See also *High-Performance Computing.*

HP-compatible printer
A printer that accepts the PCL printer commands used in HP LaserJet printers. Most non-HP laser printers support PCL. However, PCL capabilities evolve over the years, and an HP-compatible printer may not support the latest version of PCL.

HP EIO printer
An HP printer that uses the EIO hardware interface for adding functionality. See *EIO.*

HPFS
(High Performance File System) The file system introduced with OS/2 Version 1.2 that handles large disks (2TB volumes; 2GB files) and long file names (256 bytes). It coexists with the existing FAT system.

HPGL

(Hewlett-Packard Graphics Language) A vector graphics file format from HP that was developed as a standard plotter language. Most plotters support the HPGL and DMPL standards.

HPIB

(Hewlett-Packard Interface Bus) HP's version of the IEEE 488 standard GPIB.

HP PA-RISC

See *PA-RISC*.

HPR

(High-Performance Routing) Extensions to IBM's APPN networking that improve routing performance and reliability. HPR is designed to eliminate congestion on network backbones.

HPS

See *Seer*HPS*.

HP-UX

HP's version of UNIX that runs on its 9000 family. It is based on SVID and incorporates features from BSD UNIX along with several HP innovations.

HP-VUE

A Motif-based graphical user interface used in HP workstations. Parts of HP-VUE are used in COSE's CDE (Common Desktop Environment).

HREF

(Hypertext REFerence) The mnemonic used to assign a hypertext address to an HTML document. The **HREF=** is followed by the name or URL of the target document. The HREF resides within a hypertext anchor. See *hypertext anchor*.

HS

(High Speed) See *modem*.

HSB

(Hue Saturation Brightness) Same as *HSV*.

HSI

(Hue Saturation Intensity) A color model similar to HSV. See *HSV*.

HSL

(Hue Saturation Luminosity) A color model similar to HSV. See *HSV*.

HSM

(Hierarchical Storage Management) The automatic movement of files from hard disk to slower, less-expensive storage media. The typical hierarchy is from magnetic disk to optical disk to tape. HSM software constantly monitors hard disk capacity and moves data from one storage level to the next based on age, category and other criteria as specified by the network or system administrator. HSM often includes a system for routine backup as well.

When a file is moved off the hard disk, it is replaced with a small stub file that indicates where the original file is located.

magnetic disk

optical disk

magnetic tape

Data Migration

A data migration path in an HSM system might be from high-speed hard disk to slower speed optical disk to offline tape. In time, optical disks will almost surely replace magnetic media, but there will still be a need to take data off premises for protection against fire and accidents.

HSRP

(Hot Standby Router Protocol) A protocol from Cisco for switching to a backup router in the event of failure.

Computer Desktop Encyclopedia

HSSI

(High-Speed Serial Interface) A serial interface with transmission rates up to 52 Mbps. It is often used to connect one or more LAN routers and network devices to a T3 line, which provides 44.736 Mbps. A T3 multiplexor using HSSI can divide the T3 bandwidth into the appropriate speeds of the various devices.

HST

(1) An asymetrical modem protocol from U.S. Robotics that includes error control and compression and transmits from 4800 to 14400 bps in one direction and from 300 to 400 bps in the other. HST was the first reliable, high-speed modem protocol before the V.32bis and V.42 standards became widely used.

(2) (Hubble Space Telescope) Launched in April 1990, it views star material some 10 to 12 billion light years from earth.

HSV

(Hue Saturation Value) A color model that is similar to the way an artist mixes colors by adding white and black to pure pigments. HSV adds saturation (white) and value (black) to colors in order to derive new colors. HSV is often illustrated as an inverted, six-sided pyramid (hexcone).

The hue is measured around the vertical axis from 0 to 359 degrees (0=red, 60=yellow, 120=green, 180=cyan, 240=blue, 300=magenta). Saturation and value (white and black) are measured from 0 to 1 (or 0-100%), with 0 being the most amount of white, and black and 1 being the least, yielding pure hues.

HTML

(HyperText Markup Language) The document format used on the World Wide Web. Web pages are built with HTML tags, or codes, embedded in the text. HTML defines the page layout, fonts and graphic elements as well as the hypertext links to other documents on the Web. Each link contains the URL, or address, of a Web page residing on the same server or any server worldwide, hence "World Wide" Web.

HTML 2.0 was defined by the Internet Engineering Task Force (IETF) with a basic set of features including interactive forms capability. Subsequent versions added more features such as blinking text, custom backgrounds and tables of contents. However, each new version requires agreement on the tags (codes) used and browsers must be modified to implement those tags.

Although programming-like statements are being added to HTML, it is not a full-blown programming language such as Java or JavaScript. Rather it could be considered a "presentation language." HTML is derived from SGML, the Standard Generalized Markup Language, which is widely used to publish documents. HTML is an SGML document with a fixed set of tags that, although change with each new revision, are not flexible. XML is a subset of SGML that includes some of SGML's flexibility for structuring and coding Web pages. See *dynamic HTML, CGI script, VRML* and *XML*.

HTML editor

A low-level Web site authoring tool that is essentially a text editor, specialized for writing HTML code. It assists the HTML author by cataloging all HTML tags and common structures in menus and by being able to catch certain syntax errors. It often displays tags and contents in colors so they pop out for easy reference. See *Web authoring software*.

HTML tag

A code used in HTML to define a format change or hypertext link. HTML tags are surrounded by the angle brackets < and >. For example, <TITLE> is the tag that is placed in front of text used as a title, and </TITLE> is the code at the end.

HTTP

(HyperText Transport Protocol) The communications protocol used to connect to servers on the World Wide Web. Its primary function is to establish a connection with a Web server and transmit HTML pages to the client browser. Addresses of Web sites begin with an **http://** prefix; however, Web browsers typically default to the HTTP protocol. For example, typing **www.yahoo.com** is the same as typing **http://www.yahoo.com**.

Version 1.0 of HTTP adds considerable overhead to a Web download. Each time a graphic on the same page or another page on the same site is requested, a new protocol connection is established between the browser and the server. In HTTP Version 1.1, a persistent connection allows multiple downloads with less overhead. Version 1.1 also improves caching and makes it easier to create virtual hosts (multiple Web sites on the same server). In order to obtain these advantages, both browser and server must be upgraded to the new version.

It is expected that the HTTP protocol will undergo several revisions in an attempt to manage the escalating traffic on the Internet. However, many believe that only entirely new protocols will be able to meet the demand. Stay tuned!

HTTP proxy

A proxy server that specializes in HTML (Web page) transactions. See *proxy server*.

HTTPS

(1) (HyperText Transport Protocol Secure) The protocol for accessing a secure Web server. Using HTTPS in the URL instead of HTTP directs the message to a secure port number rather than the default Web port number of 80. The session is then managed by a security protocol. See *security protocol*.

(2) (HyperText Transport Protocol Server) A Web server that runs under Windows NT, developed by the European Microsoft Windows Academic Centre.

hub

A central connecting device in a network that joins communications lines together in a star configuration. Passive hubs are just connecting units that add nothing to the data passing through them. Active hubs, also sometimes called *multiport repeaters*, regenerate the data bits in order to maintain a strong signal, and intelligent hubs provide added functionality.

Hubs are mandatory in 10BaseT twisted pair Ethernet as well as Token Ring networks. They are also used to replace the daisy chain cabling in 10Base5 and 10Base2 coaxial Ethernets in order to improve network management.

In Token Rings, the hub is called a MAU (Multi-station Access Unit). Multiple media hubs interconnect different types of Ethernets (twisted pair, coax and optical fiber) and can bridge between Ethernet, Token Ring, FDDI and ATM topologies. Switching hubs provide Ethernet and ATM switching.

Hubs have become very intelligent, modular and customizable, allowing for the insertion of bridging, routing and switching modules all within the same unit. A hub can even host a CPU board and network operating system, turning the hub into a file server or some type of network control processor that performs LAN emulation or other complex function as networks grow.

hub ring

A flat ring pressed around the hole in a 5.25" floppy disk for rigidity. The drive's clamping ring presses the hub ring onto the spindle.

hue

The dominant wavelength of a color. A color system, or model, measures color by hue, saturation and luminance. The hue is the predominant color, the saturation is the color intensity, and the luminance is the brightness. See *HLS* and *HSV*.

Huffman coding

A statistical compression method that converts characters into variable length bit strings. Most-frequently-ocurring characters are converted to shortest bit strings; least frequent, the longest. Compression takes two passes. The first pass analyzes a block of data and creates a tree model based on its contents. The second pass compresses the data via the model. Decompression decodes the variable length strings via the tree. See *LZW*.

Intelligent Hub
Cabletron's MMAC PLUS is an example of a highly scalable and flexible multiple media hub. It supports all types of Ethernets as well as Token Ring, FDDI, ATM and WAN connections and provides bridging and routing between them. It also supports Ethernet and ATM switching. This type of device provides a backbone and centralized management for a heterogeneous network. *(Photo courtesy of Cabletron Systems.)*

Hungarian notation
In programming, the use of standard prefixes in naming variables. For example, "p" means pointer, hence, pTEXTBUF is a pointer to a buffer called TEXTBUF.

h/w
See *hardware*.

HX chipset
See *Intel chipsets*.

hybrid circuit
A circuit that contains different types of circuitry or chips. See *mixed signal* and *hybrid microcircuit*.

hybrid computer
A digital computer that accepts analog signals, converts them to digital and processes them in digital form. It is used in process control and robotics.

hybrid file
Sometimes refers to a graphics file that contains vector graphics and bitmaps. See *metafile*.

hybrid microcircuit
An electronic circuit composed of different types of integrated circuits and discrete components, mounted on a ceramic base. Used in military and communications applications, it is especially suited for building custom analog circuits including A/D and D/A converters, amplifiers and modulators. See *MCM* and *chip package*.

hybrid network
In communications, a network made up of equipment from multiple vendors.

Hydra
(1) See *Windows Terminal Server*.

(2) (Hybrid Document Reproduction Apparatus) A printer, photocopier, scanner and fax built into one machine.

(3) A device that converts analog signals to ISDN Basic Rate Interface (BRI).

(4) A utility from the Austin Mac Developer's Association that tests Macintosh graphics card performance.

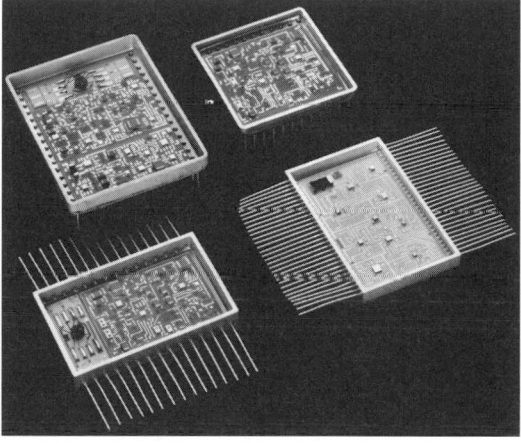

Hybrid Microcircuits
The picture shows a variety of hybrid circuits. The tiny, square white spots are the actual chips. *(Photo courtesy of Circuit Technology, Inc.)*

HyperCard
A Macintosh application development system from Apple that was one of the first visual tools for building hyperlinked applications. "Stacks" of "cards" are built that hold text, graphics, sound and video with links between them. Complex routines can be embedded in the cards using the HyperTalk programming language.

Until HyperCard 2.1, the HyperCard program had to be resident in the computer to run the stack. Although HyperCard compilers have been available from third parties, as of HyperCard 2.1, a runtime engine is included in the stack so that HyperCard does not have to be on the target machine.

hypercube
A parallel processing architecture made up of binary multiples of computers (4, 8, 16, etc.). The computers are interconnected so that data travel is kept to a minimum. For example, in two eight-node cubes, each node in one cube would be connected to the counterpart node in the other.

hypergraphic
A linkage between related information by means of a graphic image. It is the graphics counterpart of

hypertext. Instead of clicking on a word, you click on an icon to jump to the related section, document or file. See *hypertext* and *hot spot*.

hyperlink

A predefined linkage between one object and another. The link is displayed either as text or as an icon. On World Wide Web pages, a text hyperlink displays as underlined text typically in blue, while a graphical hyperlink is a small graphics image. See *hypertext* and *hypergraphic*.

hypermedia

The use of data, text, graphics, video and voice as elements in a hypertext system. All the various forms of information are linked together so that a user can easily move from one to another.

HyperPAD

An earlier application development system from Brightbill-Roberts & Company, that followed the HyperCard paradigm to PCs.

HyperTalk

The programming language used in HyperCard.

hypertext

A linkage between related text. For example, by selecting a word in a sentence, information about that word is retrieved if it exists, or the next occurrence of the word is found. In this software, you can hypertext to the definition of any term you encounter by clicking on the word or highlighting the phrase.

Hypertext is the foundation of the World Wide Web. Links embedded within Web pages are addresses to other Web pages either stored locally or in a Web server anywhere in the world. Links can be text only, in which case they are underlined, or they can be represented as an icon of any size or shape.

The hypertext concept was originally coined by Ted Nelson as a method for making the computer respond to the way humans think and require information.

hypertext anchor

In an HTML document, the codes used to define a hypertext link to another page or to a location elsewhere in the document. The following anchor points to the EXAMPLES.HTML Web page located in the same directory on the same server. The word "Examples" is the link text, the text the user sees and clicks on. In the following example, the full path to the page is implied.

```
<a href = examples.html>Examples</a>
```

hyperware

Hypertext products.

hyphenation

Breaking words that extend beyond the right margin. Software hyphenates words by matching them against a hyphenation dictionary or by using a built-in set of rules, or both. See *discretionary hyphen*.

hyphenation dictionary

A word file with predefined hyphen locations.

hyphenation zone

The distance from the right margin within which a word may be hyphenated.

hypotenuse

In a right triangle, the side opposite the right angle. See *sine*.

hysteresis

The lag between making a change, such as increasing or decreasing power, and the response or effect of that change.

Hz

(HertZ) See *Hertz*.

I

I18N

(I + 18 letters + N) See *internationalization* and *L10N*.

I₂O

(Intelligent I/O) A standard for offloading input and output to an auxiliary processor. The auxiliary processor (I/O processor) manages the data transfer while the CPU does something else. Although I_2O is being implemented in small systems, it embodies the principle behind mainframe channels, which can have several hundred data transfers occurring simultaneously.

i386

A folder on the Windows NT distribution CD-ROM that contains files for PC (Intel x86) use. There is also an Alpha directory for Digital Alpha files. See also *386*.

i750

A programmable compression chip from Intel that supports a variety of techniques including DVI, MPEG and JPEG.

i860

A 64-bit RISC-based microprocessor from Intel that included floating-point applications. Although it could serve as a general-purpose CPU, it was used mostly in DSP and 3-D graphics applications. The i860 had its heyday in the early 1990s.

i960

A general-purpose 32-bit RISC-based microprocessor from Intel that is used in a variety of devices including laser printers and networking equipment. The first i960s were the KA/KB models introduced in 1988.

IA-32

(Intel Architecture-32) The 32-bit architecture used in Intel's Pentium chips. See *IA-64* and *future Intel chips*.

IA-64

(Intel Architecture-64) The 64-bit architecture used in Intel's upcoming Merced chip. Instead of the variable-length instructions of the x86, which are from one to 14 bytes in length, IA-64 uses four-byte, fixed-length instructions bundled in sets of three (long instruction words). IA-64 chips use 256 registers for integer and floating point operations compared to 16 in the x86.

It also employs a technique called *predication*, where both sides of a branch instruction are executed in parallel. When the correct branch is determined, the results for the incorrect side are discarded. With IA-64, compilers have to be much more intelligent, placing codes into the instruction bundles that tell the CPU how to execute instructions in parallel. They also have to place instructions in interleaved order for predication.

If predication is not set up, the CPU will perform traditional branch prediction, whereby it attempts to guess the outcome of a branch and executes those instructions in parallel. IA-64 also supports speculative loading, which loads data into its registers before the instructions actually need to process it. See *Merced* and *future Intel chips*.

IAB

See *Internet Architecture Board*.

IAC

(1) (InterApplication Communications) The interprocess communications capability in the Macintosh starting with System 7.0. Many IAC events take place behind the scenes. For example, when you drag and drop an object onto an icon, the Finder may send an IAC message to the application, or an application may send a message to another application, to perform a function.

(2) (Internet Access Coalition) A consortium of vendors including Microsoft, Intel and IBM, whose mission is to keep the Internet affordable and promote high-speed access. They oppose any regulations that would enable a telephone company to charge a customer more for a data call than a voice call.

IAHC

See *Internet Ad Hoc Committee*.

IANA

See *Internet Assigned Numbers Authority*.

IANAL

Digispeak for "I am not a lawyer, but..."

IAP

(Internet Access Provider) See *internet service provider*.

IAW

Digispeak for "in accordance with."

IBI

(Information Builders, Inc., New York, www.ibi.com) IBI is the creator of the FOCUS database management system and the EDA/SQL middleware. See *FOCUS* and *EDA/SQL*.

IBIS

(I/O Buffer Information Specification) A format for defining the analog characteristics of the input and output of integrated circuits. IBIS models are ASCII files that provide the behavioral information required to model the device without divulging the proprietary design of the circuit. IBIS supports increasingly complex devices such as SIMM modules and MCMs.

IBM

(International Business Machines Corporation, Armonk, NY, www.ibm.com) The world's largest computer company. It started in New York in 1911 when the Computing-Tabulating-Recording Company. (CTR) was created by a merger of The Tabulating Machine Company (Hollerith's punched card company in Washington, DC), International Time Recording Company (time clock maker in NY state), Computing Scale Company (maker of scales and food slicers in Dayton, Ohio), and Bundy Manufacturing (time clock maker in Poughkeepsie, NY). CTR started out with 1,200 employees and a capital value of $17.5 million.

The Man that Built an Empire
This photo of Thomas J. Watson, Sr., was taken in 1920, four years before he renamed the company IBM. *(Photo courtesy of IBM Corporation.)*

In 1914, Thomas J. Watson, Sr., became general manager. During the next 10 years, he dispensed with all non-tabulating business and turned it into an international enterprise renamed IBM in 1924. Watson instilled a strict, professional demeanor in his employees that set IBMers apart from the rest of the crowd.

IBM achieved spectacular success with its tabulating machines and the punched cards that were fed them. From the 1920s through the 1960s, it developed a huge customer base that was ideal for conversion to computers.

IBM launched its computer business in 1953 with the 701 and introduced the 650 a year later. By the end of the 1950s, the 650 was the most widely used computer in the world with 1,800 systems installed. The 1401, announced in 1959, was its second computer winner, and by the mid 1960s, an estimated 18,000 were in use.

In 1964, it announced the System/360, the first family of compatible computers ever developed. The 360s were enormously successful and set a standard underlying IBM mainframes to this day.

During the 1970s and 1980s, IBM made a variety of incompatible minicomputer systems, including the System/36 and System/38. Its highly-successful AS/400, introduced in 1988, provides a broad family of compatible machines in this segment.

In 1981, IBM introduced the PC into a chaotic personal computer field and set the standard almost overnight. IBM is still one of the largest PC manufacturers, but the majority of PC sales come from the PC industry at large, from companies such as Compaq, Dell and HP to mom and pop shops by the thousands.

Although like everyone else, IBM includes Windows on its PCs, but it still maintains its OS/2 operating system for PC desktops and servers. OS/2 is highly praised, but has not gained significant market share.

Although IBM is a company with over 70 billion dollars in sales, the early 1990s were gut-wrenching years. IBM experienced major losses in 1992 and 1993, due mainly to slowing sales of high-profit mainframes as companies worldwide began to implement client/server systems with smaller computers. IBM also reduced PC prices to become competitive, further reducing margins. To meet the challenges of the 1990s, IBM reduced its staff by more than 150,000 employees.

In 1991, IBM startled the industry by teaming up with Apple and Motorola to produce the PowerPC chip, a single-chip version of IBM's RS/6000 workstations. Although PowerPC systems introduced in 1995 had no impact as stand-alone PCs, the PowerPC chips are breathing new blood into IBM's RS/6000 and AS/400 lines.

IBM Office, London, 1935
"Dayton Money Making Machines" were sold all across the world. IBM became an international enterprise in the late 1930s. *(Photo courtesy of IBM Corporation.)*

In 1995, IBM surprised us once again with the purchase of Lotus Development Corporation, publishers of Lotus 1-2-3 and the popular Notes groupware.

As to the future, IBM is not a company to be underestimated. Although it does not control the PC market, it has rebounded in general, returning to the huge profits it has been accustomed to. IBM sells an enormous number of mainframes, minicomputers, workstations and PCs, and more dollar value of software than anybody else in the world.

In addition, with all the push to distributed client/server systems, the bulk of the data in most large enterprises still resides in IBM mainframes. As each year goes by, more electronic history piles up, creating massive databases that mainframes handle with ease. The universe runs in cycles. More surprises are in store.

IBMBIO.COM
See *IBMDOS.COM*.

IBM-compatible mainframe
A mainframe that is compatible with an IBM mainframe and which runs mainframe operating systems, such as OS/390. In the late 1960s, RCA's computer division produced the Spectra 70, the first line of machines compatible with the System/360. Later, Amdahl, National Semiconductor (marketed through Itel) and Hitachi entered this segment. Today, Hitachi Data Systems and Amdahl are the major IBM-compatible mainframe vendors. See *HDS* and *Amdahl*.

IBM-compatible PC
A personal computer that is compatible with the IBM PC and PS/2 standards. Although this term is still used, it had validity in the early days when PC makers were trying to copy the IBM PC, and many

Hitachi's Skyline
Used in large companies, Hitachi's Skyline offers fast IBM-compatible mainframe processing. Up to 512 channels per system and 16 ports into main memory provide enormous transaction throughput. *(Photo courtesy of Hitachi Data Systems.)*

PCs were not compatible. Today, PCs conform to standards set by Intel, Microsoft and the PC industry at large.

IBMDOS.COM

One of two hidden system files that make up IBM's PC-DOS. The other is IBMBIO.COM. These two system files are loaded into memory when the computer is booted. They process the instructions in CONFIG.SYS, then load COMMAND.COM and finally process the instructions in AUTOEXEC.BAT. The MS-DOS counterparts of these system files are IO.SYS and MSDOS.SYS.

IBM format

Generally refers to applications and files for a PC.

IBM mainframes

Following is a list of the different series of mainframes IBM has offered over the years. All of the series in this list stem from the original System/360 architecture introduced in 1964. For information about a series, look up the individual term.

IBM Mainframe
This S/390 G4 model is an example of IBM's CMOS-based mainframes. Although more powerful than older bi-polar units, they take up only a fraction of the floorspace. *(Photo courtesy of IBM Corporation.)*

Year Intro.	Series name	(model numbers)
1964	System/360	(20 to 195)
1970	System/370	(115 to 168)
1977	303x series	(3031, 3032, 3033)
1979	43xx series	(4300 to 4381, ES/4381)
1980	308x series	(3081, 3083, 3084)
1986	3090 series	(120 to 600, ES/3090)
1986	9370 series	(9370, ES/9370)
1990	System/390	(ES/9000, 120 to 9X2)
1994	S/390	(Parallel Enterprise Server)
1996	S/390	(Multiprise Server)
1998	S/390	(G5 series)

IBM minicomputers

Following is a list of the different series of minicomputers IBM has offered over the years. For information about a series, look up the individual term.

Year Intro.	Series name
1969	System/3
1975	System/32
1976	Series/1
1977	System/34
1978	System/38
1978	8100
1983	System/36
1985	System/88
1988	AS/400
1990	RS/6000
1993	RS/6000 (PowerPC based)
1995	AS/400 (PowerPC based)

IBM PC

A PC made by IBM. IBM created the PC industry and is still one of its largest vendors. Introduced in 1981, IBM's first PCs were named PC, XT, etc., while subsequent PS/2 machines were given model numbers

IBM PC
The computer that launced the PC industry. *(Photo courtesy of IBM Corporation.)*

that did not reflect the CPU type. Later, IBM adopted the same convention as other vendors, which includes the processor type and speed somewhere in the designation. See *PC, IBM-compatible PC* and *personal computer*. For details on ThinkPad laptops, see *ThinkPad*.

IBM workstation
See *RS/6000*.

IC
See *integrated circuit* and *information center*.

ICA
(Intelligent Console Architecture) The presentation services protocol from Citrix that governs input/output between the client and the server. See *WinFrame, Windows Terminal Server* and *T.share*.

ICAP
(Internet Calendar Access Protocol) An interface for group calendaring and scheduling over the Internet that is expected to be endorsed by the IETF.

I-CASE
(Integrated CASE) CASE systems that generate applications code directly from design specifications. Features include support for rapid prototyping, modeling the data and processing and drawing logic diagrams.

ICCA
(Independent Computer Consultants Association, St. Louis, MO, www.icca.org) A membership organization of independent consultants in the information technology field. It is devoted to helping members improve their professional services capabilities. Chapters are in major metropolitan areas throughout the U.S.

ICCP
(Institute for Certification of Computer Professionals, Des Plaines, IL, www.iccp.org). An organization founded in 1973 that offers industry certification and worldwide test centers. The Associate Computer Professional (ACP) exam is open to all, but the Certified Computing Professional (CCP) requires four years of experience, although academic credit may substitute for two.

The CCP combines the former Certified Computer Programmer (CCP), Certified Data Processor (CDP) and Certified Systems Professional (CSP)

ICE
(1) (In-Circuit Emulator) A chip used for testing and debugging logic circuits typically in embedded systems. The chip emulates a particular microprocessor and contains breakpoints and other debugging functions. See *ROM emulator*.

(2) (Information and Content Exchange) A data sharing specification that allows one Web site to obtain data from another Web site. Using meta tags, ICE provides a standard way of defining a company's data. ICE is based on XML and OPS. See *XML, OPS* and *meta tag*.

(3) (Ice) A Lotus 1-2-3 add-on program from Baler Software Corporation, Rolling Meadows, IL, that adds extensions to Lotus macros. It is used for developing customized macro-driven 1-2-3 programs.

ICL
(International Computers Ltd., London, www.icl.com) A leading European computer systems and services organization. ICL was formed in 1968, following a decade of frantic mergers by major British electronics firms, largely in response to increasing U.S. dominance of global IT markets (primarily IBM) and by the lack of funding at home for competitive R&D. The dominant survivor of the 10-year scramble was International Computers and Tabulators (ICT), which later merged with Elliott-Automation, English Electric (EE), Lyons Electronic Office (LEO), and Marconi, to become ICL.

ICMP
(Internet Control Message Protocol) A TCP/IP protocol used to send error and control messages. For example, a router uses ICMP to notify the sender that its destination node is not available. A ping utility sends ICMP echo requests to verify the existence of an IP address.

ICMP storm attack

See *smurf attack*.

iCOMP

(Intel COmparative Microprocessor Performance) An index of CPU performance from Intel. It tests a mix of 16-bit and 32-bit integer, floating point, graphics and video operations. The second version of iCOMP (iCOMP 2.0) is not compatible with the first release of the benchmark.

icon

In a graphical user interface (GUI), a small, pictorial, on-screen representation of an object, such as a document, program, folder or disk drive.

iconic interface

A user interface that uses icons.

ICP

(1) (Internet Cache Protocol) A protocol used by one proxy server to query another for a cached Web page without having to go to the Internet to retrieve it. See *CARP* and *proxy server*.

(2) (Internet Content Provider) An organization that provides news, reference, audio or video content for Web sites.

IC package

See *chip package*.

ICQ

("I Seek You") A conferencing program for the Internet from Mirabilis, Tel Aviv, Israel, (www.mirabilis.com). It provides interactive chat, e-mail and file transfer and can alert you when someone on your predefined list has also come online. The chat rooms and alerts are managed by the Mirabilis servers.

ICR

(Intelligent Character Recognition or Image Character Recognition) The machine recognition of hand-printed characters as well as machine printing that is difficult to recognize.

ICSA

(International Computer Security Association, Carlisle, PA, www.icsa.net) A membership organization founded in 1989 with the purpose of providing education and a clearing house for computer security issues. Formerly NCSA (National Computer Security Association) and renamed ICSA in 1998, it sells all the major books written on the subject. An annual conference is hosted in Washington, DC.

ICT

(International Computers and Tabulators) See ICL.

IDA

(Intelligent Drive Array) A high-performance hard disk interface from Compaq that controls a disk array via the EISA bus.

IDAPI

(Independent Database API) The programming interface to the Borland Database Engine. IDAPI calls are made from dBASE, Paradox and C++ applications to access data in one of the supported databases. See *Borland Database Engine*.

IDC

(International Data Corporation, Framingham, MA, www.idcresearch.com) A major market research, analysis and consulting firm in the information field. Founded in 1964, it provides annual briefings and in-depth reports on all aspects of the industry.

i.d.Centric

A family of programs for UNIX and Windows platforms from Firstlogic, Inc., La Crosse, WI (www.idcentric.com) that enhances data quality in existing databases. It includes programs that standardize address conventions and make names and addresses consistent across databases as well as add demographic information to customer records and other databases. See *Postalsoft*.

IDE

(1) (Integrated Drive Electronics)

(2) (Integrated Development Environment)

(1) (Integrated Drive Electronics) A type of hardware interface widely used to connect hard disks, CD-ROMs and tape drives to a PC. IDE is very popular because it is currently the least expensive way to connect peripherals. Starting out with 40MB capacities years ago, 2GB and 4GB IDE disk drives have become entry level, costing less than five cents per megabyte.

With IDE, the controller electronics are built into the drive itself, requiring a simple circuit in the PC for connection. IDE drives were attached to earlier PCs using an IDE host adapter card. Today, two Enhanced IDE (EIDE) sockets are built onto the motherboard, and each socket connects to two devices via a 40-pin ribbon cable.

The IDE interface is formally known as the ATA (AT Attachment) specification. ATA-2, or Fast ATA, defines the faster transfer rates used in Enhanced IDE. ATA-3 added improvements to the interface, including the ability to report potential problems (see *S.M.A.R.T.*). ATA-3 is widely used under PIO Mode 4. ATA-4 (Ultra ATA) boosts speed under DMA to 33MB.

ATAPI (ATA Packet Interface) defines the IDE standard for CD-ROMs and tape drives. Following are the transfer rates for the various ATA modes.

Type	PIO Mode	Transfer rate MBytes/sec	DMA Mode	Transfer rate MBytes/sec
ATA	0	3.3	0	4.2
ATA	1	5.2		
ATA	2	8.3		
ATA-2, 3	3	11.1	1	13.3
ATA-2, 3	4	16.6	2	16.6
ATA-4			2	33.3

(2) (Integrated Development Environment) A set of programs run from a single user interface. For example, programming languages often include a text editor, compiler and debugger, which are all activated and function from a common menu.

IDEA

(International Data Encryption Algorithm) A secret key cryptography method that uses a 128-bit key. Introduced in 1992, its European patent is held by Ascom Tech AG, Solothurn, Switzerland. It uses the block cipher method which breaks the text into 64-bit blocks before encrypting them.

IDE controller

(1) The controlling electronics built into an IDE drive.

(2) The adapter on the plug-in card or motherboard that connects to the IDE controller. This is technically the IDE host adapter, but is often called the IDE controller.

IDE host adapter

An earlier expansion board that plugs into a PC and contains the connection for up to four IDE hard disks. It generally also provides control for two floppyies, two serial, one parallel and one game port. Today, all of this is built into the motherboard. See *IDE*.

IDL

(Interface Definition Language) A language used to describe the interface to a routine or function. For example, objects in the CORBA distributed object environment are defined by an IDL, which describes the services performed by the object and how the data is to be passed to it.

idle character

In data communications, a character transmitted to keep the line synchronized when there is no data being sent.

idle interrupt

An interrupt generated when a device changes from an operational state to an idle state.

idle time

The duration of time a device is in an idle state, which means that it is operational, but not being used.

IDMS

See *CA-IDMS* and *IDMSX*.

IDMSX

(Integrated Data Management System Extended) A database management system (DBMS) from ICL that is widely used on its VME mainframes. It supports journaling, recovery and locking options. A single IDMSX database can contain up to a terabyte of data. See *TPMS*.

IDSL

See *DSL*.

IE

See *Microsoft Internet Explorer* and *information engineering*.

IEC

(International Electrotechnical Commission, Geneva, Switzerland, www.iet.ch) An organization that sets international electrical and electronics standards founded in 1906. It is made up of national committees from over 40 countries.

IEEE

(Institute of Electrical and Electronics Engineers, New York, www.ieee.org) A membership organization that includes engineers, scientists and students in electronics and allied fields. Founded in 1963, it has more than 300,000 members and is involved with setting standards for computers and communications.

The Computer Society of the IEEE is a separate entity that has more than 100,000 members. It holds meetings and technical conferences on computers (visit www.computer.org).

IEEE 1284

An IEEE standard for an enhanced parallel port that is compatible with the Centronics port commonly used on PCs. Instead of just data, it can send addresses, allowing individual components in a multifunction device (printer, scanner, fax, etc.) to be addressed independently. IEEE 1284 also defines the required cable type that increases distance to 32 feet.

EPP (Enhanced Parallel Port) mode increases bi-directional transfer from the Centronics 150 Kbytes/sec to between 600 Kbytes/sec and 1.5 Mbytes/sec. Nibble and byte modes provide slower rates. ECP (Enhanced Capabilities Port) mode is designed for printers. It uses DMA channels, which reduces CPU overhead, and also provides a FIFO buffer. The peripheral driver determines which mode to use.

IEEE 1394

See *FireWire*.

IEEE 488

See *GPIB*.

IEEE 802

IEEE standards for local area networks (LANs) and metropolitan area networks (MANs). The IEEE specification for LANs breaks the data link layer into two sublayers: the LLC (Logical Link Control) and MAC (Media Access Control). The LLC provides a common interface to the MAC layers, which specify the access method used.

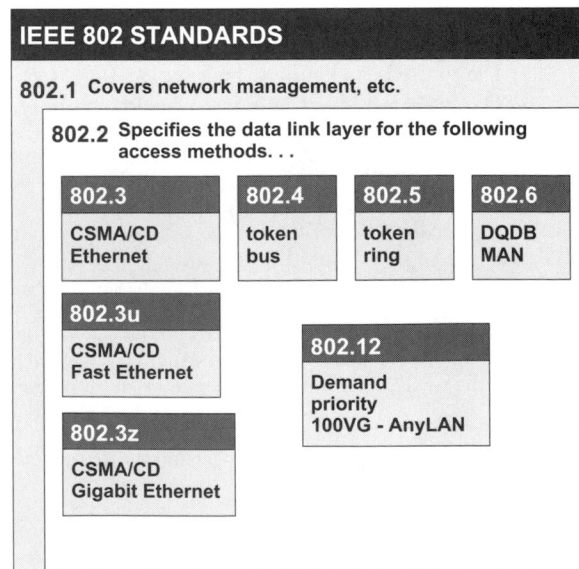

IEEE 802 STANDARDS

802.1 Covers network management, etc.

802.2 Specifies the data link layer for the following access methods. . .

802.3	802.4	802.5	802.6
CSMA/CD Ethernet	token bus	token ring	DQDB MAN

802.3u
CSMA/CD Fast Ethernet

802.3z
CSMA/CD Gigabit Ethernet

802.12
Demand priority 100VG - AnyLAN

Computer Desktop Encyclopedia

IEF

(Information Engineering Facility) A fully-integrated set of CASE tools from Sterling Software that runs on PCs and MVS mainframes. It generates COBOL code for PCs, MVS mainframes, VMS, Tandem, AIX, HP-UX and other UNIX platforms. IEF was developed by TI and later renamed Composer. It was acquired by Sterling Software in 1997, which renamed it COOL:Gen. See *COOL*.

IESG

See *Internet Engineering Task Force*.

IETF

See *Internet Engineering Task Force*.

I/E time

See *instruction cycle*.

IEW

(Information Engineering Workbench) CASE software from Sterling Software that runs on DOS PCs and generates COBOL, CICS and IMS code for MVS mainframes. IEW was developed by Knowledgeware, which Sterling acquired in 1984. IEW migrated to ADW for OS/2, which was then renamed Key:Enterprise and later COOL:Enterprise. See *COOL*.

IFC

(Internet Foundation Classes) A class library from Netscape that provides an application framework and graphical user interface (GUI) routines for Java programmers. IFC was later made part of the Java Foundation Classes (JFC). See *JFC, AFC* and *AWT*.

IFIP

(International Federation of Information Processing, Geneva, Switzerland) A multinational affiliation of professional groups concerned with information processing, founded in 1960. There is one voting representative from each country, and the U.S. representative is FOCUS. See *FOCUS*.

IFMP

(Ipsilon Flow Management Protocol) The protocol used in Nokia Telecommunication's IP Switch for flow redirection. IFMP is also used in third party devices, and interoperability is supported by many vendors. See *IP Switch*.

I-frame

A key frame used in MPEG compression. See *MPEG*.

IFS

(Installable File System) An OS/2 feature that supports multiple file systems. Different systems can be installed (UNIX, CD-ROM, etc.) just like drivers are installed for new peripherals.

IFSHLP.SYS

See *IFSMgr*.

IFSMgr

(Installable File System ManaGeR) The driver that provides the 32-bit file system for Windows for Workgroups and Windows 95/98. It also uses a "helper" file called IFSHLP.SYS which, among other things, translates 16-bit to 32-bit calls. See *installable file system*.

if-then-else

A high-level programming language statement that compares two or more sets of data and tests the results. If the results are true, the THEN instructions are taken; if not, the ELSE instructions are taken. The following is a BASIC example:

```
10   IF ANSWER = "Y"   THEN PRINT "Yes"
20   ELSE PRINT "No"
```

In certain languages, THEN is implied. All statements between IF and ELSE are carried out if the condition is true. All instructions between ELSE and ENDIF are carried out if not true. The following dBASE example produces the same results as above:

```
IF ANSWER = "Y"
    ? "Yes"
  ELSE
    ? "No"
ENDIF
```

IGES

(Initial Graphics Exchange Specification) An ANSI graphics file format that is system independent and also intended for human interpretation. It evolved out of the Air Force's Integrated Computer Automated Manufacturing (ICAM) program in 1979. See *PDES.*

IGP

(Interior Gateway Protocol) A broad category of routing protocols that support a single, confined geographic area such as a local area network (LAN). Contrast with *EGP.* See *routing protocol.*

IGRP

(Interior Gateway Routing Protocol) A proprietary routing protocol from Cisco that was developed in 1988 to overcome the shortcomings of RIP. IGRP takes bandwidth, latency, reliability and current traffic load into consideration. It is typically used within an autonomous system, such as an Internet domain. IGRP was superseded by Enhanced IGRP (EIGRP), which provides enhancements such as the ability to detect a loop in the network.

IHV

(Independent Hardware Vendor) An organization that makes electronic equipment. It implies a company that specializes in a niche area, such as display adapters or disk controllers, rather than a computer systems manufacturer. Contrast with *ISV.* See *VAR* and *systems integrator.*

IIA

(1) (Information Industry Association, Washington, DC, www.infoindustry.org) A trade organization that includes members from all aspects of the information field. Its purpose is to conduct active government relations that safeguard the interests of a healthy, competitive information industry. IIA sponsors seminars and conferences and provides newsletters, newspapers and books.

(2) (Information Interchange Architecture) IBM formats for exchanging documents between different systems.

IIOP

(Internet Inter-ORB Protocol) The CORBA message protocol used on a TCP/IP network (Internet, intranet, etc.). CORBA is an industry standard for distributed objects, which allows programs (objects) to be run remotely in a network. IIOP links CORBA's General Inter-ORB protocol (GIOP), which specifies how CORBA's Object Request Brokers (ORBs) communicate with each other, to TCP/IP.

IIOP is built into Netscape 4.0, which is expected to give a tremendous boost to the use of CORBA objects over the Internet. When a user accesses a Web page that uses a CORBA object, a small Java applet is downloaded into Netscape, which invokes the ORB to pass data to the object, execute the object and get the results back. See *CORBA.*

IIS

See *Microsoft Internet Information Server.*

ILEC

(Incumbent Local Exchange Carrier) A traditional local telephone company such as one of the Regional Bell companies (RBOCs). Contrast with *CLEC.* See *ELEC* and *TELRIC.*

ill-behaved

See *well-behaved.*

illegal operation

An operation that is not authorized or understood. The Windows 95/98 error message that reports an illegal operation means the application crashed. See *abend.*

illustration program
Same as *drawing program*.

Illustrator
See *Adobe Illustrator*.

ILS server
See *ULS server*.

IM
See *information management* and *Intelligent Messaging*.

IMA
(Interactive Multimedia Association, Annapolis, MD, www.ima.org) A trade association founded in 1988 originally as the Interactive Video Industry Association. The IMA provides an open process for adopting existing technologies and is involved in subjects such as networked services, scripting languages, data formats and intellectual property rights.

iMac
A Macintosh computer from Apple introduced in 1998. It is a low-priced, Internet-ready Mac with a new look aimed at the consumer. In its first incarnation, the iMac comes with 32MB RAM, 4GB hard disk, CD-ROM drive and 33.6 Kbps modem. Only the memory can be upgraded. It is also the first personal computer to not have a floppy disk drive. The CD-ROM is used for software installation.

image
(1) A picture (graphic).
(2) See *system image*.

image editing
Changing or improving graphics images either interactively using a paint program or by using software routines that alter contrast, smooth lines or filter out unwanted data. See *image filter* and *anti-aliasing*.

image editing program
See *image editor*.

image editor
Software that allows scanned images to be altered and enhanced. They are designed to read and convert a wide variety of graphics formats and may include a native file format for special features. Image editors include many image filters, but run the gamut from just a few to an abundance of painting tools. They allow images to be scaled and altered in many different ways and may allow plug-ins for infinite expansion. Examples of full-featured image editors are Adobe Photoshop, Picture Publisher and Fractal Design Painter. High-end image editors are sometimes called *photo illustration programs*. See *image filter*.

image enhancement
See *image editing*.

image filter
A routine that changes the appearance of an image or part of an image by altering the shades and colors of the pixels in some manner. Filters are used to increase brightness and contrast as well as to add a wide variety of textures, tones and special effects to a picture.

image map
A picture that is logically separated into areas, each of which is used to select a different option or display a different message when clicked. It is widely used on the Web to provide links to other pages.

The Original Picture
This photograph was scanned into the computer and edited in Adobe Photoshop.

Lens Flare
The Lens Flare filter lets you simulate a flare from three types of lenses at any point in the image. The amount of brightness can also be adjusted.

image processing

(1) The analysis of a picture using techniques that can identify shades, colors and relationships that cannot be perceived by the human eye. It is used to solve identification problems, such as in forensic medicine or in creating weather maps from satellite pictures and deals with images in bitmapped graphics format that have been scanned in or captured with digital cameras.

(2) Any image improvement, such as refining a picture in a paint program that has been scanned or entered from a video source.

(3) Same as *imaging*.

imagesetter

A machine that generates output for the printing process, which is either a film-based paper that is photographed or the actual film for making the printing plates. Input comes from the keyboard, or via disk, tape or modem. Earlier machines handled only text and were called *phototypesetters*. Most imagesetters today support the PostScript language.

Modern imagesetters use lasers to generate the image directly onto the film. Older machines passed light through a spinning font photomask, then through lenses that created the point size and onto film. Others created images on CRTs and exposed the film.

The typesetter was originally the only machine that could handle multiple fonts and text composition such as kerning. Today, desktop laser printers are used for many typesetting jobs and are quickly advancing in resolution, although the 1270 and 2540 dpi resolutions of the imagesetter combined with the high-quality of film still provide the finest printing for photographs and halftones.

mage viewer

See *viewer*.

imaging

Creating a film or electronic image of any picture or paper form. It is accomplished by scanning or photographing an object and turning it into a matrix of dots (bitmap), the meaning of which is unknown to the computer, only to the human viewer. Scanned images of text may be encoded into computer data (ASCII or EBCDIC) with page recognition software (OCR). See *micrographics, image processing* and *document imaging*.

imaging model

A set of rules for representing images.

imaging system

See *document imaging, image processing* and *image enhancement*.

IMAP

(Internet Messaging Access Protocol) A standard mail server expected to be widely used on the Internet. It provides a message store that holds incoming e-mail until users log on and download it. IMAP4 is the latest version.

IMAP is more sophisticated than the Post Office Protocol (POP3) mail server. Messages can be archived in folders, mailboxes can be shared, and a user can access multiple mail servers. There is also better integration with MIME, which is used to attach files. For example, users can read only the headers in the message without having to automatically accept and wait for attached files to download that they don't want.

Both IMAP and POP accept SMTP-formatted messages that have been routed across the Internet. See *POP3, SMTP* and *messaging system*.

IMAP4

See *IMAP*.

IMCO

Digispeak for "in my considered opinion."

IMHO

Digispeak for "in my humble opinion." See *IMO*.

immediate access

Same as *direct access*.

IMO

Digispeak for "in my opinion." See *IMHO*.

impact printer

A printer that uses a printing mechanism that bangs the character image into the ribbon and onto the paper. See *printer* for examples.

impedance

The resistance to the flow of current in a circuit.

implementation

The carrying out or physical realization of something. The phrase "there are various implementations of the protocol" means that there are several software products that execute that protocol. A computer system implementation would be the installation of new hardware and system software. An information system implementation would be the installation of new databases and application programs and the adoption of new manual procedures.

implode

To link component pieces to a major assembly. It may also refer to compressing data using a particular technique. Contrast with *explode*.

import

To insert a foreign file into a document, which is not native to the application. An import filter provides either a conversion capability to change the foreign format into the native format, or it provides the ability to insert and deal with the foreign file in the foreign file's native format. Contrast with *export*.

Improv

A multidimensional Windows spreadsheet from Lotus that allows for easy switching to different views of the data. Data is referenced by name as in a database rather than the typical spreadsheet row and column coordinates. Improv was originally developed for the NeXt computer.

IMS

(Information Management System) An IBM hierarchical DBMS for IBM mainframes running under MVS. It was widely implemented throughout the 1970s and continues to be used. IMS/DB (IMS/DataBase) is the database, which functions in a batch processing environment. IMS/DC (IMS/Data Communications) is the component required when running in an online environment such as CICS. IMS/DC is also used to access DB2 databases.

IMTC

(International Multimedia Teleconferencing Association, San Ramon, CA, www.imtc.org) An international membership organization founded in 1993 as Consortium for Audiographics Teleconferencing Standards (CATS). IMTC contributes to the development of and implements the standards recommendations of the ITU for data and videoconferencing.

imux

See *inverse multiplexor*.

in band

Inside the primary frequency or system. See *signaling in/out of band*.

incident light

In computer graphics, light that strikes an object. The color of the object is based on how the light is absorbed or reflected by the object.

in-circuit emulator

See *ICE*.

Incorrect DOS version

A DOS error message that means the command you are using belongs to another version of DOS. Somehow an earlier or later version of a command is on your hard disk. Commands from one DOS version often do not work in other versions.

increment

To add a number to another number. Incrementing a counter means adding 1 to its current value.

incremental backup

See *backup types*.

incremental spacing

See *microspacing*.

IND$FILE

An IBM mainframe program that transfers files between the mainframe and a PC functioning as a 3270 terminal.

indent

To align text some number of spaces to the right of the left margin. See *hanging paragraph*.

Indeo

A video compression/decompression algorithm from Intel that is used to compress movie files.

index

(1) In data management, the most common method for keeping track of data on a disk. Indexes are directory listings maintained by the OS, DBMS or the application.

An index of files contains an entry for each file name and the location of the file. An index of records has an entry for each key field (account no., name, etc.) and the location of the record.

(2) In programming, a method for keeping track of data in a table. See *indexed addressing* and *color palette*.

indexed addressing

A technique for referencing memory that automatically increments the address with the value stored in an index register. See *subscript*.

indexed color

See *color palette*.

indexed sequential access method

See *ISAM*.

index hole

A small hole punched into a hard sectored floppy disk that serves to mark the start of the sectors on each track.

indexing

(1) Creating indexes based on key data fields or keywords.

(2) Creating timing signals based on detecting a mark, slot or hole in a moving medium.

index map

See *index* and *color palette*.

index mark

A physical hole or notch, or a recorded code or mark, that is used to identify a starting point for each track on a disk.

index register

A high-speed circuit used to hold the current, relative position of an item in a table (array). At execution time, its stored value is added to the instructions that reference it.

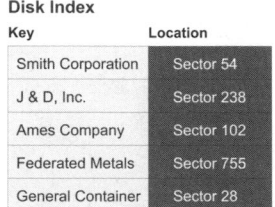

Disk Index

Key	Location
Smith Corporation	Sector 54
J & D, Inc.	Sector 238
Ames Company	Sector 102
Federated Metals	Sector 755
General Container	Sector 28

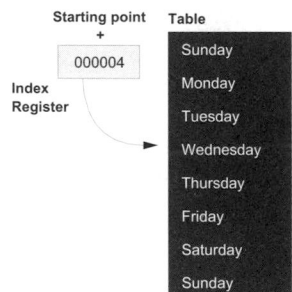

Programming Index

Starting point + [000004] Index Register

Table: Sunday, Monday, Tuesday, Wednesday, Thursday, Friday, Saturday, Sunday

Types of Indexes

An index is a data table that points to some location just like an index in a book. Indexes are widely used to keep track of the physical location of data on the disk as well as the logical location of data within a database.

On the other hand, an index register is a hardware circuit whose contents is combined with a value in the program to point to a position in a table.

Indigo

A family of desktop graphics computers from SGI. The low end are the Indy machines, which include their own digital video camera. The high end includes a variety of Indigo workstations, with models specialized for graphics functions such as accelerated texture mapping and image procesing. See *SGI*.

indirect addressing

An address mode that points to another pointer rather than the actual data. This mode is prohibited in RISC architecture. See *indirection*.

indirection

Not direct. Indirection provides a way of accessing instructions, routines and objects where their physical location may constantly be changing. The initial routine points to some place, and, using hardware and/or software, that place points to some other place. There can be multiple levels of indirection. For example, point to A, which points to B, which points to C. See *indirect addressing*.

inductance

The magnetic field that is generated when a current is passed through an inductor.

induction

The process of generating an electric current in a circuit from the magnetic influence of an adjacent circuit as in a transformer or capacitor.

Electrical induction is also the principle behind read/write heads on magnetic disks. To create (write) the bit, current is sent through a coil that creates a magnetic field which is discharged at the gap of the head onto the disk surface as it spins by. To read the bit, the magnetic field of the bit "induces" an electrical charge in the head as it passes by the gap.

inductor

A coil of wire that generates a magnetic field when current is passed through it. The strength of the magnetic field is measured in henrys. When the current is removed, as the magnetic field disintegrates, it generates a brief current in the opposite direction of the original.

industrial strength

Refers to software that is designed for high-volume, multiuser operation. It implies that the software is robust and that there are built-in safeguards against system failures. For example, an industrial-strength operating system runs its applications in protected address spaces and does not lock up or stop if one of them crashes. Industrial-strength features in a DBMS are referential integrity and two-phase commit.

The term is used to refer to any solid, sound program that has been thoroughly tested in live user environments for extensive periods, whether system software (OS, DBMS, etc.) or application software (order entry, desktop publishing, etc.).

industry analyst

An individual that follows the computer industry and writes about on-going topics and trends. Analysts are made up of individuals in the trade press as well as in market research organizations such as Dataquest and IDC.

I-net

See *Internet*.

inetd

(INternET Daemon) A UNIX function that manages many common TCP/IP services. It is activated at startup and waits for various connection requests (FTP, Telnet, etc.) and launches the appropriate server components. See *daemon*.

inference engine

The processing program in an expert system. It derives a conclusion from the facts and rules contained in the knowledge base using various artificial intelligence techniques.

INF file

(INFormation file) A Windows file that contains installation information. The SETUP.INF file is used to install Windows itself, and other INF files are used for installing other programs and hardware devices.

infix notation

The common way arithmetic operators are used to reference numeric values. For example, **A+B/C** is infix notation. Contrast with *Polish notation* and *reverse Polish notation.*

infobahn

(INFOrmation **BAHN**) A nickname for the information superhighway. It comes from the German "Autobahn," or automobile superhighway.

Infobase

A database created in Folio. See *Folio.*

infomediary

(INFOrmation interMEDIARY) An information provider that gathers content from several sources and functions as a data aggregator for a target audience.

infopreneur

A person who is in business to gather and disseminate electronic information.

InfoPump

Software from Trinzic Corporation, Palo Alto, CA, that is used to synchronize data in different types of databases by moving the data and converting it to the destination format. It supports Lotus Notes documents, ASCII files, mainframe file formats and most of the popular databases. A Windows-based client component controls the InfoPump Server. Data movement can be performed on a scheduled or event-driven basis.

informate

To dispense information, as coined by Harvard Professor Shoshana Zuboff.

informatics

Same as information technology and information systems. The term is more widely used in Europe.

information

The summarization of data. Technically, data are raw facts and figures that are processed into information, such as summaries and totals. But since information can also be raw data for the next job or person, the two terms cannot be precisely defined. Both terms are used synonymously and interchangeably.

It may be helpful to view information the way it is structured and used, namely: data, text, spreadsheets, pictures, voice and video. Data are discretely defined fields. Text is a collection of words. Spreadsheets are data in matrix (row and column) form. Pictures are lists of vectors or frames of bits. Voice is a continuous stream of sound waves. Video is a sequence of frames.

Increasingly, databases are capable of storing all kinds of information. See *universal server.*

information appliance

A type of future home or office device that can transmit to or plug into common public or private networks. Envisioned is a "digital highway," like telephone and electrical power networks.

information center

The division within the IS department that supports end-user computing. Responsible for training users in applications and solving related personal computer problems.

information collaboration

See *data conferencing.*

information engineering

An integrated set of methodologies and products used to guide and develop information processing within an organization. It starts with enterprise-wide strategic planning and ends with running applications.

information hiding

Keeping details of a routine private. Programmers only know what input is required and what outputs are expected. See *encapsulation* and *abstraction.*

information highway

See *information superhighway*.

information industry

(1) Organizations that publish information via online services or through distribution by diskette or CD-ROM.

(2) All computer, communications and electronics-related organizations, including hardware, software and services.

Information Industry Association

See *IIA*.

information management

The discipline that analyzes information as an organizational resource. It covers the definitions, uses, value and distribution of all data and information within an organization whether processed by computer or not. It evaluates the kinds of data/information an organization requires in order to function and progress effectively.

Information is complex because business transactions are complex. It must be analyzed and understood before effective computer solutions can be developed. See *data administration*.

information processing

Same as *data processing*.

information requirements

The information needed to support a business or other activity. Requirements are typically defined as lists of detailed items as well as summarized data from business transactions, such as orders and purchases, and master records, such as customers and vendors. How frequently this information must be made available is also part of the requirement.

Information requirements (the what and when) are turned into functional specs (the how) of an information system by systems analysts. The information is defined as a collection of data elements that are obtained by running query and report programs against a particular database or group of databases. The data and information that is stored in the databases in the first place is also derived from the information requirements. See *functional specification*.

information resource management

See *Information Systems* and *information management*.

information science

See *information management*.

information service

Any information retrieval, publishing, timesharing or BBS facility. See *online services*.

Information Services

See *Information Systems*.

information sharing

See *data conferencing*.

Laying Optical Fiber
The ultimate information superhighway requires high-speed lines nearby every building and home. In time, all copper wires will be replaced with optical fibers, but the job is a daunting one that takes "financial muscle" as well as real muscle. *(Photo courtesy of Corning Incorporated.)*

information superhighway

A proposed high-speed communications system that was touted by the Clinton/Gore administration to enhance education in America in the 21st century. Its purpose was to help all citizens regardless of their income level. The Internet was originally cited as a model for this superhighway; however, with the explosion of the World Wide Web, the Internet became the information superhighway whether it was ready for it or not.

information system

A business application of the computer. It is made up of the database, application programs, manual and machine procedures and encompasses the computer systems that do the processing.

The database stores the subjects of the business (master files) and its activities (transaction files). The application programs provide the data entry, updating, query and report processing. The manual procedures document how data is obtained for input and how the system's output is distributed. Machine procedures instruct the computer how to perform the batch processing activities, in which the output of one program is automaticaly fed into another program.

The daily processing is the interactive, realtime processing of the transactions. At the end of the day or other period, the batch processing programs update the master files that have not been updated since the last cycle. Reports are printed for the cycle's activities.

The periodic processing of an information system is the updating of the master files, which adds, deletes and changes the information about customers, employees, vendors and products.

RELATIONSHIP BETWEEN SYSTEMS

structure (is)	function (does)
Management System	
1. People	Sets organization's goals
2. Machines	and objectives, strategies
	and tactics, plans,
	schedule and controls.
Information System	
1. Database	Defines data structures
2. Application	Data entry, updating,
programs	queries and reporting.
3. Procedures	Defines data flow
Computer System	
1. CPU	Processes (the 3 C's)
2. Peripherals	Store and retrieve
3. Operating system	Manages computer system

Information Systems

The formal title for a data processing, MIS, or IS department. Other titles are Data Processing, Information Processing, Information Services, Management Information Systems, Management Information Services and Information Technology.

information technology

Processing information by computer.

information theory

The study of encoding and transmitting information. From Claude Shannon's 1938 paper, "A Mathematical Theory of Communication," which proposed the use of binary digits for coding information.

information utility

(1) A service bureau that maintains up-to-date databases for public access.

(2) A central source of information for an organization or group.

information visualization

Representing data in 3-D images in order to navigate through it more quickly and access it in a more natural manner. Although the term was coined at Xerox's Palo Alto Research Center, which has developed very advanced techniques, multidimentional cubes, or pivot tables, are a simpler form of information visualization that is widely used today. See *OLAP* and *slice and dice*.

information warehouse

The collection of all databases in an enterprise across all platforms and departments.

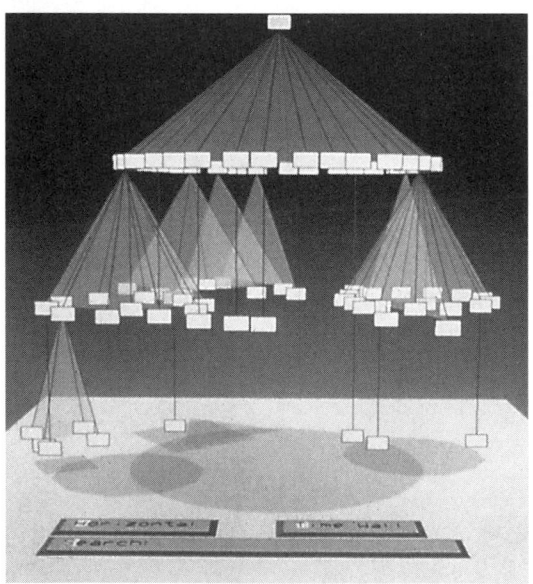

A 3-D Cone Tree

Data representated in this form provides faster navigation and allows more information to be seen at one time. The Cone Tree shows the structure of an entire hierarchy all at once, and the cones spin around to retrieve occluded data. *(Photo courtesy of Xerox Palo Alto Research Center; Brian Tramontana, photographer.)*

information warfare
(www.infowar.com) Creating havoc by disrupting the computers that manage stock exchanges, power grids, air traffic control and telecommunications. While the term often refers to warring nations, it also refers to the disruption of individual organizations.

INFORMIX
A relational database management system (DBMS) from Informix Software, Inc., Menlo Park, CA, (www.informix.com), that runs on most UNIX platforms, including SCO UNIX for x86 machines and NetWare. Development tools from Informix include INFORMIX-4GL, a fourth-generation language, and INFORMIX-New Era, a client/server development system for Windows clients that supports INFORMIX and non-INFORMIX databases.

InfoSeek
(www.infoseek.com) One of the major search sites on the Web. See *Web search sites*.

Info Select
A personal information manager for DOS and Windows from Micro Logic Corporation, Hackensack, NJ, (www.miclog.com), that provides an unstructured method for organizing information. Unlike most PIMs, which provide many fixed fields for data, Info Select lets you place names, addresses and random notes into windows and retrieve them based on any text contained in the window.

infowar
See *information warfare*.

infoware
Information sold electronically, such as the electronic versions of this database.

infrared
An invisible band of radiation at the lower end of the electromagnetic spectrum. It starts at the middle of the microwave spectrum and goes up to the beginning of visible light. Infrared transmission requires an unobstructed line of sight between transmitter and receiver. It is used for wireless transmission between computer devices as well as most all hand-held remotes for TVs, video and stereo equipment. Contrast with *ultraviolet*. See *IrDA*.

infrared port
A transmitter/receiver for infrared signals. See *IrDA*.

infrastructure
The fundamental structure of a system or organization. The basic, fundamental architecture of any system (electronic, mechanical, social, political, etc.) determines how it functions and how flexible it is to meet future requirements.

Ingres
See *CA-OpenIngres*.

in hardware
Refers to logic that has been placed into the electronic circuits of the computer.

inheritance
In object technology, the ability of one class of objects to inherit properties from a higher class.

inhouse
An operation that takes place on the user's premises.

INI file
(INItialization file) A file that contains startup information required to launch a program or operating system. Same as *CFG file*. See *WIN.INI* and *SYSTEM.INI*.

INIT
(INITiate) A Macintosh routine that is run when the computer is started or restarted. It is used to load and activate drivers and system routines. Many INITs are memory resident and may conflict with each other like TSRs in the PC environment.

initialization string

Same as *setup string*.

initialize

To start anew, which typically involves clearing all or some part of memory or disk.

ink jet cartridge

A replaceable unit that holds ink and the print nozzles for ink jet printers. A separate cartridge for each of the four CMYK colors is the most efficient. Low-cost printers include cyan, magenta and yellow inks in one cartridge, requiring the entire unit be replaced when one color is empty. The least efficient is a single cartridge that contains all four colors.

ink jet printer

A printer that propels droplets of ink directly onto paper. Today, almost all ink jet printers produce color, or at least, have a color option. Low-end ink jets use three ink colors (cyan, magenta and yellow), but produce a composite black that is often muddy. Four-color ink jets (CMYK) use black ink for pure black printing.

Ink jet printers are affordable, quiet and popular, but they do not provide the color quality or text resolution of color laser printers. Notable exceptions are high-end ink jets, such as Tektronix's laser-class solid ink printer and the IRIS printers, which produce extraordinary color quality.

The cost for ink cartridges in some low-priced ink jets can make the less-expensive model more costly in the long run. For example, if the black ink does not come in a separate cartridge, you have to replace the entire four-color unit when you run out of black. Also, for resolution quality, look at text, not graphics. For color quality, be sure that samples from different models are printed on the same kind of paper. Clay-coated and other specialty papers greatly improve the printed results, because they do not absorb the ink as does paper. You may want to use them. Ink and paper costs are on-going expenses.

Large-format ink jet printers are used to produce final output for commercial posters and banners. Using special coated paper, their output is quite extraordinary. Such devices have almost entirely replaced the older pen plotters used to "draw" engineering and architectural renderings.

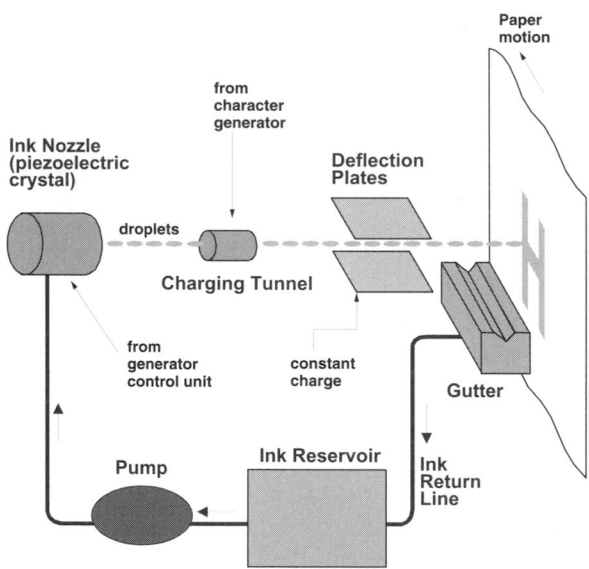

Continuous Ink versus Drop on Demand

The first ink jet mechanism that was developed sprays a continuous stream of droplets that are aimed onto the paper. Although still used, most ink jets use the drop on demand method, which forces a drop of ink out of a chamber by heat or electricity. The thermal method used by HP, Canon and others heats a resistor that forces the a droplet of ink out of the

Continuous Ink Jet Technology

This method sprays continuous droplets of ink that either reach the paper or wind up in the return gutter. The nozzle uses a piezoelectric crystal to synchronize the chaotic droplets that arrive from the pump. The charging tunnel selectively charges the drops that are deflected into the gutter. The uncharged droplets make it to the paper. The diagram depicts a single nozzle.

nozzle by creating an air bubble in the ink chamber. Epson and others use a piezoelectric technique that charges crystals which expand and "jet" the ink. See *solid ink printer, IRIS printer* and *printer*.

Computer Desktop Encyclopedia

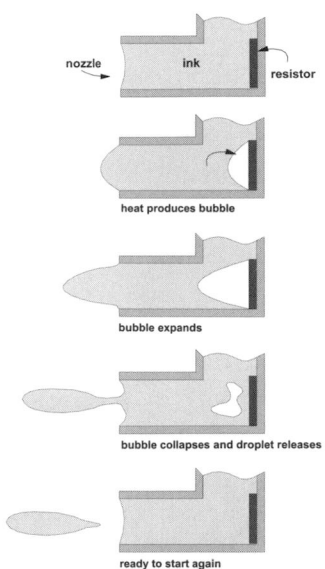

Thermal Drop on Demand Method

The thermal drop on demand ink jet technology is very popular. Used by HP, Canon and others, droplets of ink are forced out of the nozzle by heating a resistor, which causes an air bubble to expand. When the bubble collapses, the droplet breaks off and the system returns to its original state.

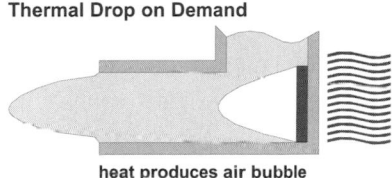

Thermal Drop on Demand

heat produces air bubble

Drop on Demand Printheads

There are two ways to "jet" the ink in drop on demand systems. The thermal method heats a resistor and expands an air bubble. The piezoelectric method charges crystals that expand.

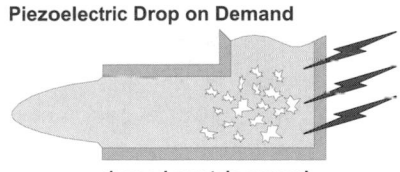

Piezoelectric Drop on Demand

charged crystals expand

inline cache

A memory cache that resides next to the CPU, but shares the same system bus as other subsystems in the computer. It is faster than lookaside cache, but slower than a backside cache. See *backside cache* and *lookaside cache*.

inline code

Source code of a different type that is written into the body of a program. For example, assembly language instructions can be embedded within a C program.

inline graphics

Graphics images that are embedded within a text document. Inline graphics on the Web are actually HTML pages with links to graphics files stored on the Web server. The browser displays the text and images as if they were physically on the same page.

inline routine

A routine that is written into the program rather than being called externally as a separate subroutine or program module. Inline routines run faster, but add more size to the executable file.

Inmarsat

(Inmarsat, London, www.inmarsat.org) Formerly International Maritime Satellite, it is an international organization founded in 1979 to provide global satellite communications to the maritime industry. Today, it provides satellite service to ships, planes, trains, offshore rigs and mobile phones. COMSAT is the U.S. signatory to Inmarsat.

innoculate

To store characteristics of an executable program in order to detect a possible unknown virus if the file is changed.

i-node

(Identification **NODE**) An individual entry in a directory system that contains the name of and pointer to a file or other object.

INPRISE

(INPRISE Corporation, Scotts Valley, CA, www.inprise.com) A software company founded as Borland International in 1983 by Philippe Kahn. The company is noted for its language and development products. It also popularized the desktop accessory for PCs with its DOS-based Sidekick program. Its Turbo Pascal moved Pascal out of the academic halls into a commercial product, and its Turbo C became an industry standard for DOS. Borland C++ and Delphi are widly used for developing Windows applications.

The company acquired the Paradox database in 1987 and dBASE in 1991, making it the leader in PC database software in the early 1990s. It later sold Paradox to Corel. In 1995, Kahn resigned as president, but remained as chairman. In 1998, Borland changed its name to INPRISE in recognition of its focus on "integrating the enterprise."

Philippe Kahn
INPRISE's founder (then Borland) was a notable personality in the early days of personal computing and led the company into some very successful ventures. *(Photo courtesy of INPRISE Corporation.)*

input

(1) Data that is ready for entry into the computer.
(2) To enter data into the computer.

input area

A reserved segment of memory that is used to accept data from a peripheral device. Same as *buffer*.

input device

A peripheral device that generates input for the computer such as a keyboard, scanner, mouse or digitizer tablet.

input/output

See *I/O*.

input program

Same as *data entry program*.

input queue

A reserved segment of disk or memory that holds messages that have been received or job control statements describing work to be done.

input stream

A collection of job control statements entered in the computer that describe the work to be done.

inquiry program

Same as *query program*.

insert mode

A data entry mode that causes new data typed on the keyboard to be inserted at the current cursor location on screen. Contrast with *overwrite*.

Ins key

(INSert key) A keyboard key that is used to switch between insert and overwrite mode or to insert an object at the current cursor location.

in software

Refers to logic in a program. For example, "that routine is done in software."

installable file system

A file system that can be added to an operating system that is designed to handle multiple file systems. Multiple file systems allow different types of file structures to be accessed. See *IFSMgr*.

installation spec

Documentation from an equipment manufacturer that describes how a product should be properly installed within a physical environment.

installed base

The number of people using a software package or hardware device.

install program

Also called a *setup program*, it is a program that prepares an application (software package) to run in the computer. It creates a default directory or folder on the hard disk and copies the files from the distribution CD-ROM or diskettes to the hard disk. It decompresses them if they are distributed in a compressed format.

Install programs may analyze the computer's current environment and/or ask the user to identify components in order to link in the appropriate software drivers required to display and print properly.

An install program may also be used to activate new hardware by setting or resetting parameters in an updatable memory (flash memory, EEPROM, etc.) on the expansion board. It is often used to identify resource requirements when installing a new peripheral, such as IRQs and I/O addresses.

During installation, a component of the install, or setup, program is often copied to and left on the hard disk to allow the user to make additional changes to the application or hardware at a later time.

instance

(1) A single copy of a running program. Multiple instances of a program mean that the program has been loaded into memory several times.

(2) In object technology, a member of a class; for example, "Lassie" is an instance of the class "dog." When an instance is created, the initial values of its instance variables are assigned.

instance variable

In object-oriented programming, a variable used by an instance of a class. It holds data for a particular object. Contrast with *class variable*. See *class*.

instantiate

In object technology, to create an object of a specific class. See *instance*.

instant messaging

Alerting the user as soon as an e-mail has been delivered. E-mail systems typically require that users check their mailboxes. With instant messaging, a dialog box pops up immediately on the user's screen.

instant print

The ability to use the computer as a typewriter. Each keystroke is transferred to the printer.

instruction

(1) A statement in a programming language.

(2) A machine instruction.

instruction cycle

The time in which a single instruction is fetched from memory, decoded and executed. The first half of the cycle transfers the instruction from memory to the instruction register and decodes it. The second half executes the instruction.

instruction mix

The blend of instruction types in a program. It often refers to writing generalized benchmarks, which requires that the amount of I/O versus processing versus math instructions, etc., reflects the type of application the benchmark is written for.

instruction register

A high-speed circuit that holds an instruction for decoding and execution.

instruction repertoire

Same as *instruction set*.

instruction set

The repertoire of machine language instructions that a computer can follow (from a handful to several hundred). It is a major architectural component and is either built into the CPU or into microcode. Instructions are generally from one to four bytes long.

instruction time

The time in which an instruction is fetched from memory and stored in the instruction register. It is the first half of the instruction cycle.

insulator

A material that does not conduct electricity. Contrast with *conductor*.

int

A programming statement that specifies an interrupt or that declares an integer variable. See *interrupt* and *integer*. For example, int 13 is a DOS interrupt used to activate disk functions, such as seek, read, write and format. Int 14 is a DOS interrupt used to activate functions on the serial port. Int 21 is a multipurpose DOS interrupt used for various functions including reading the keyboard and writing to the console and printer. It was also used to read and write disks using the earlier File Control Block (FCB) method.

integer

A whole number. In programming, sending the number 123.898 to an integer function would return 123. See *integer arithmetic*.

integer arithmetic

Arithmetic without fractions. A computer performing integer arithmetic ignores any fractions that are derived. For example, 8 divided by 3 would yield the whole number 2. See *integer*.

Integer BASIC

Apple's version of BASIC for the Apple II that handles only fixed point numbers (non-floating point). Due to its speed, many games are written in it.

integrated

A collection of distinct elements or components that have been built into one unit.

integrated CASE

See *I-CASE*.

integrated circuit

The formal name for the chip. In 1958, TI inventor Jack Kilby demonstrated the first electronic circuit in which more than one transistor was fabricated on a single piece of semiconductor material. It was about half the size of a paper clip.

integrated injection logic

A type of bipolar transistor design known for its fast switching speeds.

The First Integrated Circuit
Only 7/16" wide and containing two transistors, this unassuming integrated circuit was nevertheless the first. It was mounted on a bar of germanium and was demonstrated by TI on September 12, 1958. *(Photo courtesy of Texas Instruments, Inc.)*

Computer Desktop Encyclopedia

integrated software package

Software that combines several applications in one program, typically database management, word processing, spreadsheet, business graphics and communications. Such programs (Microsoft Works, AppleWorks, etc.) provide a common user interface for their applications plus the ability to cut and paste data from one to the other.

User interfaces, such as found on the Macintosh and Windows, provide this capability with all applications written for their environments.

integrator

In electronics, a device that combines an input with a variable, such as time, and provides an analog output; for example, a watt-hour meter.

integrity

See *data integrity*.

Intel

(Intel Corporation, Santa Clara, CA, www.intel.com) The predominant manufacturer of the CPU chips for the PC world. It was founded in 1968 by Robert Noyce, Gordon Moore and Andy Grove in Mountain View, CA. A year later it introduced its first product, a 64-bit bipolar static RAM chip. By 1971, its very successful memory chips began to obsolete magnetic core storage.

In that same year, Intel developed the microprocessor. In response to a calculator chip order from Japanese manufacturer Busicom, Intel engineer Marcian E. "Ted" Hoff decided it would make more sense to design a general-purpose machine. The resulting 4004 chip was the world's first microprocessor.

Although known for its x86 family of chips, over the years, Intel has developed a wide variety of chips and board-level products, including the MULTIBUS bus used in industrial applications. Intel started with 12 people and its first year revenues were less than three thousand dollars. In 1996, it had 49,000 employees with revenues of more than 21 billion. See *future Intel chips*.

Intel Founders
The founders of Intel posing with a rubylith of the 8080 CPU in 1978. From left to right: Andy Grove, Robert Noyce and Gordon Moore. *(Photo courtesy of Intel Corporation.)*

Inside the Plant
Chip making is performed in clean rooms, where the air is exchanged seven times each minute and the workers wear "bunny suits" to keep themselves from contaminating the process. *(Photo courtesy of Intel Corporation.)*

Intel chips
See *x86*.

Intel chipsets
A set of chips that provides the interfaces between all of the PC's subsystems. It provides the buses and electronics to allow the CPU, memory and input/output devices to interact. Most Intel chipsets, which are contained on two to four chips, also include built-in EIDE support. Intel's trade name for its PCI-based chipsets is PCIset.

Intel uses 420 designations for its 486 chipsets (420EX, 420TX and 420ZX) and 430, 440 and 450 for Pentiums. Intel used to call its chipsets "Triton," but has since discontinued that branding. Following is a brief summary of the most popular Pentium PCIsets.

430LX - Mercury - 1st Pentium chipset ('93) for 60-66MHz models. Supports PCI and FPM RAM.
430NX - Neptune - Supports 90 and 100MHz Pentiums.
430FX, (formerly Triton) - Supports EDO RAM, Plug and Play.
430MX - Version of 430FX designed for portable computers.
430TX - Desktop and mobile use. 1st mobile chipset to support Concurrent PCI.
    Supports USB, DPMA, Ultra DMA, SMBus.
430HX (formerly Triton II) - Geared for business market. Supports EDO RAM,
    Concurrent PCI, BGA packaging.
430VX (formerly Triton VX) - Geared for home market. Supports USB, SDRAM, Concurrent PCI.
440FX - Optimized for Pentium Pro and II. Supports USB, EDO & ECC memory, two CPUs.
440LX - Optimized for Pentium II. Supports LS-120, 33MHz Ultra DMA, AGP, USB, SDRAM,
    ECC RAM, PC 97 power management, Concurrent PCI.
440LXR - Low-end version of 440LX.
440BX - Optimized for Pentium II. Supports 100MHz bus, FireWire, ACPI, Concurrent PCI.
440GX - For midrange workstations. Supports two CPUs, 2GB SDRAM, dual AGP.
450GX, 450KX - Optimized for Pentium Pro. Supports FPM memory only. KX supports dual
    processors, 1GB RAM. GX supports quad processors, 8GB RAM.
450NX - For high-end workstations and servers. Supports four CPUs, 2MB L2 cache,
    Intelligent I/O, 8GB EDO memory, two 32-bit or one 64-bit PCI.

Intellect
A natural language query program for IBM mainframes developed by Artificial Intelligence Corporation, which was later acquired by Trinzic Corporation.

intellectual property
See *IP*.

Intellifont
A scalable font technology from Agfa CompuGraphic. Intellifont typefaces are built into LaserJet IIIs and 4s (see *LaserJet*). The Intellifont for Windows font scaler creates matching screen fonts for Windows from Intellifont and compatible typefaces.

intelligence
Processing capability. Every computer is intelligent, which is more than can be said for all humans!

intelligent agent
See *agent*.

intelligent cable
Same as *smart cable*.

intelligent controller
A peripheral control unit that uses a built-in microprocessor for controlling its operation.

intelligent database
A database that contains knowledge about the content of its data. A set of validation criteria are stored with each field of data, such as the minimum and maximum values that can be entered or a list of all possible entries. See *DBMS*.

intelligent form, intelligent paper

A data entry application that provides help screens and low levels of AI in aiding the user to enter the correct data.

intelligent hub

A central connecting device in a network that performs a variety of processing functions such as network management, bridging, routing and switching. Contrast with *passive hub* and *active hub*. See *hub*.

Intelligent Messaging

A messaging system from Banyan Systems Inc., Westboro, MA, (www.banyan.com), that runs on NetWare and VINES servers and incorporates Banyan's popular Streettalk directory service. It includes a basic mail program, which can be upgraded to Banyan's more advanced BeyondMail system.

intelligent modem

A modem that responds to commands and can accept new instructions during online transmission. It was originally developed by Hayes.

intelligent network

A network that is not passive. It contains built-in diagnostics, management, fault tolerance and other capabilities that keep it running smoothly. Contrast with *dumb network*.

intelligent terminal

A terminal with built-in processing capability, but no local disk or tape storage. It may use a general-purpose CPU or may have specialized circuitry as part of a distributed intelligence system. Contrast with *dumb terminal*.

IntelliMirror

A feature of Windows NT 5.0 that stores fundamental configuration data about a user's machine on the server, including a copy of the user's desktop. It allows a crashed PC to be more easily restored and also enables mobile users to access their applications from a different client machine.

IntelliMouse

A mouse from Microsoft that adds a rubber wheel at the top of the unit between the two buttons. Moving the wheel causes scrolling in applications that are IntelliMouse aware.

IntelliSense

Features in Microsoft applications that help the user by making decisions automatically. By analyzing activity patterns, the software can derive the next step without the user having to explicitly state it. Automatic typo correction and suggesting shortcuts also fall under the IntelliSense umbrella.

INTELSAT

(INTELSAT, Washington, DC, www.intelsat.int) An international cooperative of more than 135 member nations. It is the world's largest supplier of commercial satellite services with more than 20 satellites in orbit. It was created in 1964 with 11 countries participating. COMSAT is the U.S. signatory of INTELSAT.

interactive

Back-and-forth dialog between the user and a computer.

interactive fiction

An adventure game that has been created or modified for the computer. It has multiple story lines, environments and endings, all of which are determined by choices the player makes at various times.

interactive session

Back-and-forth dialogue between user and computer. Contrast with *batch session*.

interactive TV

Two-way communications between the TV viewer and service providers. Although various experiments have taken place throughout the 1980s, interactive TV has yet to take off. The closest thing to it on a widescale basis is pay TV, which dedicates an entire channel to the same movie so that the viewer can begin to watch it with reasonably short notice.

Internet TV, which began in 1996 with WebTV, is a new attempt at interaction between the home user and the provider. With the Internet's momentum and the vast amounts of information and interaction available on it, Internet TV may succeed where interactive TV did not. Stay tuned! See *Internet TV* and *digital convergence*.

Interactive UNIX

A UNIX-based operating system from SunSoft that runs on x86 machines. It has been widely used to connect character-based terminals or process control devices, such as bar code readers in a supermarket, to a central computer.

interactive video

The use of CD-ROM and videodisc controlled by computer for an interactive education or entertainment program. See *CD-ROM* and *videodisc*.

InterBase

A relational DBMS from InterBase Software Corporation (a subidiary of INPRISE), Scotts Valley, CA, www.interbase.com, that runs on UNIX workstations and VAXes. Designed to handle online complex processing (OLCP), InterBase is used in centralized, small to medium-size businesses. It is also the database engine in various third-party packages from independent vendors.

interblock gap

Same as *interrecord gap*.

Intercast

Broadcasting Web pages and other information via TV, using the unused portion of the video signal known as the vertical blanking interval (VBI). Developed by Intel, Intercast data is transmitted in 10 of the 45 lines of the VBI and can provide up to 10.5KBytes/sec of data. Requirements are a TV channel that transmits Intercast data and an Intercast-compliant TV board for the PC or set-top box for the TV. See *TV board*.

interexchange carrier

See *IXC*.

interface

The connection and interaction between hardware, software and the user.

Hardware interfaces are the plugs, sockets, wires and the electrical pulses travelling through them in a particular pattern. Also included are electrical timing considerations. Examples are RS-232 transmission, the Ethernet and Token Ring network topologies and the IDE, ESDI, SCSI, ISA, EISA and Micro Channel interfaces.

Software, or programming, interfaces are the languages, codes and messages programs use to communicate with each other and to the hardware. Examples are the applications that run under the Mac, DOS and Windows operating systems as well as the SMTP e-mail and LU 6.2 communications protocols.

User interfaces are the keyboards, mice, commands and menus used for communication between you and the computer. Examples are the command lines in DOS and UNIX and the Mac, Windows and Motif graphical interfaces.

Interfacing is a major part of what engineers, programmers and consultants do. Users "talk to" the software. The software "talks to" the hardware and other software. Hardware "talks to" other hardware. All this is interfacing. It has to be designed, developed, tested and redesigned, and with each incarnation, a new specification is born that may become yet one more de facto or regulated standard.

Format & Function

Every interface implies a structure. Electrical signals are made up of voltage levels, frequencies and duration. The data passed from one device or program to another has a precise format (header, body, trailer, etc.).

Every interface implies a function. At the hardware level, electronic signals activate functions; data is read, written, transmitted, received, analyzed for error, etc. At the software level, instructions activate the hardware (access methods, data link protocols, etc.). At higher levels, the data transferred or transmitted may itself request functions to be performed (client/server, program to program, etc.).

Language & Programming

An interface is activated by programming language commands. The complexity of the functions and the design of the language determine how difficult it is to program.

User Interface, Protocol, API and ABI

The design of the interaction between the user and the computer is called a *user interface*. The rules, formats and functions between components in a communications system or network is called a *protocol*. The language and message formats between routines within a program or between software components is called an *API*. The specification for an operating system working in a specific machine environment is called an *ABI*.

All the above interactions are interfaces. Regardless of what they're called, they all create rules that must be precisely followed in a digital world.

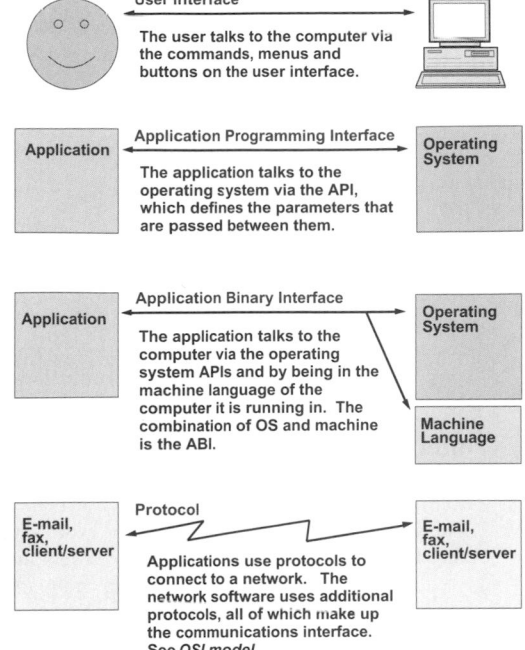

User Interface
The user talks to the computer via the commands, menus and buttons on the user interface.

Application Programming Interface
The application talks to the operating system via the API, which defines the parameters that are passed between them.

Application Binary Interface
The application talks to the computer via the operating system APIs and by being in the machine language of the computer it is running in. The combination of OS and machine is the ABI.

Protocol
Applications use protocols to connect to a network. The network software uses additional protocols, all of which make up the communications interface. See *OSI model*

interface adapter

In communications, a device that connects the computer or terminal to a network.

interface designer

See *GUI builder*.

interframe coding

In video compression, the coding of only the differences between frames. A video sequence is made up of key frames, which contain the entire image and subsequent delta frames, which encode only the incremental differences from the key frame. When a certain amount of image material changes in the sequence, a new key frame is generated.

Interframe coding allows very high compression ratios to be achieved, but the compression varies according to the amount of changes in the video content. See *intraframe coding*.

Intergraph

(Intergraph Corporation, Huntsville, AL, www.intergraph.com) A graphics computer systems company founded in 1969 as M&S Computing by Jim and Nancy Meadlock, Keith Schonrock, Bob Thurber and Terry Schansman. Initially a computer consulting firm to government agencies, it specialized in computer graphics and changed its name to Intergraph in 1980.

Intergraph developed expertise on Digital PDP and VAX computers and later developed proprietary UNIX workstations based on its own Clipper chip technology. In 1992, it migrated to Windows NT and became the world's leader in NT-based graphics workstations. In 1996, it introduced the first 28" HDTV-format computer monitor. The company's hardware and software is divided into Intergraph Computer Systems and Intergraph Software Solutions.

Interactive Graphics
Realistic flight simulation is an example of the interactive graphics provided by Intergraph's workstations and graphics subsystems. *(Photo courtesy of Intergraph Computer Systems.)*

interlaced

Illuminating a CRT by displaying odd lines first and then the even lines. Interlacing provides a way of displaying more information on screen using a less-sophisticated circuit, but at a penalty of producing an annoying flutter visible on small elements such as icons and buttons. It is less noticeable with motion than a still image, which is why traditional analog television, which uses an interlaced signal, is fine until you have to read still text (see *NTSC*).

Today, most computer displays are non-interlaced. However, earlier displays were often interlaced at the highest resolution. For example, 640x480 and 800x600 might be non-interlaced, but 1024x768 was interlaced.

A related issue is the vertical scan frequency, or the number of times the entire screen is refreshed per second. For a solid image, 70 times per second (70 Hz) is required. The higher the refresh rate, the more pixels have to be redisplayed each second. Most monitors are not designed for the highest resolution working with the highest refresh rate, so there is typically a compromise. The higher the resolution, the lower the refresh rate. The combination of interlacing and low refresh rate can produce headaches and eye strain.

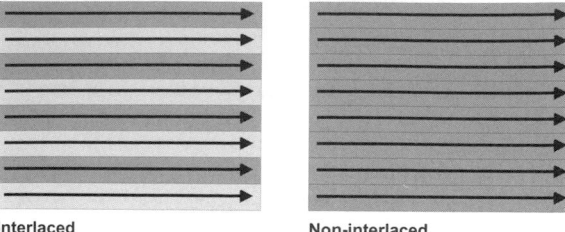

Interlaced   Non-interlaced

Interleaf

Desktop publishing software for DOS, Windows 95/98, NT and a variety of UNIX-based computers from Interleaf, Inc., Waltham, MA, (www.interleaf.com). Interleaf is a full-featured program that supports a large number of document and image types. It is used for creating compound documents as well as extremely long documents (hundreds of thousands of pages).

It includes built-in word processing and graphics tools and provides a number of optional components for enhanced document control and workgroup operation. Interleaf used to be known as Interleaf TPS (Technical Publishing Software). In 1990, it became Interleaf5, later Interleaf6, etc.

Interleaf RDM (Relational Document Manager) is another product that provides distribution and tracking of documents. Interleaf WorldView provides runtime viewing with customizable searches for Interleaf and other document types.

interleave

See *sector interleave* and *memory interleaving*.

interlock

A device that prohibits an action from taking place.

intermediate language

A language that is generated from a programming source language, but that is not directly executable by a CPU. The intermediate language, also called *p-code, pseudo code, pseudo language* or *byte code*, must be interpreted or compiled into machine language for execution. This method allows the same source language to be used for different types of computers.

An intermediate language supports architecture neutrality as does an interpreted language. However, the intermediate language is usually faster, because some of the program has been precompiled, whereas the interpreted language remains in source code and must be fully converted to machine code at runtime.

Visual Basic and Java are notable examples of programming languages that generate an intermediate language. They are compiled into byte code, which is then converted into machine code at runtime.

intermediate node routing

Routing a message to non-adjacent nodes; for example, if three computers are connected in series A—B—C, data transmitted from A to C can be routed through B.

intermittent error

An error that occurs sporadically, not consistently. It is the most difficult type of problem to diagnose and repair.

internal bus

A pathway between the CPU and memory. Contrast with *external bus*. See *local bus*.

internal command

In DOS and OS/2, a command, such as Copy, Dir and Rename, which may be used at all times. Internal commands are executed by the command processor programs COMMAND.COM in DOS and

CMD.EXE in OS/2. The command processor is always loaded when the operating system is loaded. Contrast with *external command*.

internal font

A set of characters for a particular typeface that is built into a printer. Contrast with *font cartridge* and *soft font*.

internal interrupt

An interrupt that is caused by processing, for example, a request for input or output or an arithmetic overflow error. Contrast with *external interrupt*.

internal modem

A modem that plugs into an expansion slot within the computer. Unlike an external modem, an internal modem does not provide a series of display lights that inform the user of the changing modem states. The user must rely entirely on the communications program. Contrast with *external modem*.

internal sort

Sorting that is accomplished entirely in memory without using disks or tapes for temporary files.

Internal stack failure

A DOS error message that means DOS has gotten completely confused. Turn off the computer and restart.

internal storage

Same as *memory*.

International Business Machines

See *IBM*.

internationalization

Sometimes abbreviated "I18N," it is support for the display of monetary values, time and date for many countries. See *localization*.

Internaut

A person that uses the Internet.

internet

(1) A large network made up of a number of smaller networks.

(2) (Internet) "The" Internet is made up of more than 100,000 interconnected networks in over 100 countries, comprised of commercial, academic and government networks. Originally developed for the military, the Internet became widely used for academic and commercial research. Users had access to unpublished data and journals on a huge variety of subjects. Today, the Internet has become commercialized into a worldwide information highway, providing information on every subject known to humankind.

The Internet's surge in growth was twofold. As the major online services (America Online, CompuServe, etc.) connected to the Internet for e-mail exchange, the Internet began to function as a central hub for e-mail outside of the Internet community. A member of one online service could send mail to a member of another using the Internet as a gateway. The Internet glued the world together for electronic mail.

Secondly, World Wide Web servers on the Internet link documents around the world, providing an information exchange of unprecedented proportion that is growing exponentially. With the advent of graphics-based Web browsers such as Mosaic and Netscape, this wealth of information became easily available to users with PCs and Macs rather than only scientists and hackers at UNIX workstations. The Web has also become "the" storehouse for drivers, updates and demos that are downloaded via the browser.

Daily news and information is also available on the Net. Usenet (User Network) newsgroups have been delivering timely information on myriads of subjects long before the Web was created. The news can be selected and read directly from your Web browser.

Chat rooms provide another popular Internet service. Internet Relay Chat (IRC) offers multiuser text conferencing on diverse topics. Dozens of IRC servers provide hundreds of channels that anyone can log onto and participate in via the keyboard.

Internet Access

Today, all the major online services provide full Internet access. DELPHI was the first, and all the others followed suit. In addition, thousands of Internet service providers (ISPs) have risen out of the woodwork to offer individuals and organizations access.

The Original Internet

The backbone of the Internet was originally a series of high-speed links between major supercomputer sites and educational and research institutions within the U.S. and throughout the world. A major part of it was the NFSNet, managed by the U.S. National Science Foundation. In 1995, large commercial Internet providers (ISPs), such as MCI, Sprint and UUNET, took responsibility for the Internet backbones and have increasingly enhanced their capacities. Regional ISPs link into these backbones to provide lines for their subscribers, and smaller ISPs hook either directly into the national backbones or into the regional ISPs.

Internet computers use the TCP/IP communications protocol. There are more than 20 million hosts on the Internet, a host being a mainframe, mini, workstation or high-end PC that is online via TCP/IP. The Internet is also connected to all types of computer networks worldwide through gateways that convert TCP/IP into other protocols.

Although most new users interact with the Internet via their Web browsers, for years, command-line UNIX utilities have been used. For example, an FTP (File Transfer Protocol) program allows files to be downloaded, and the Archie utility provides listings of these files. Telnet is a terminal emulation program that lets you log onto a computer in the Internet and run a program. Gopher provides hierarchical menus describing Internet files (not just file names), and Veronica lets you make more sophisticated searches on Gopher sites. See *FTP, Archie, Telnet, Gopher* and *Veronica*.

Ironically, some of the original academic and scientific users of the Internet are developing their own network once again. The Internet is so jammed these days that they no longer enjoy the quick access they were used to (see *Internet2*).

See *World Wide Web, how to search the Web, intranet, hot topics and trends, IAB, information superhighway* and *online services.*

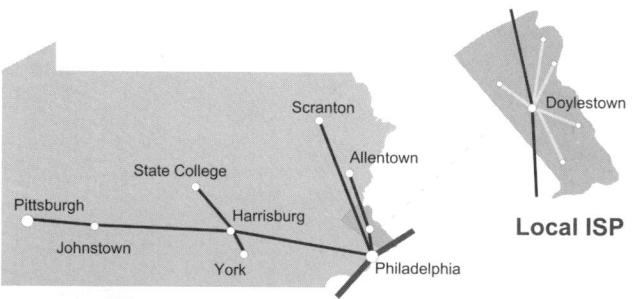

Local ISP

Regional ISP

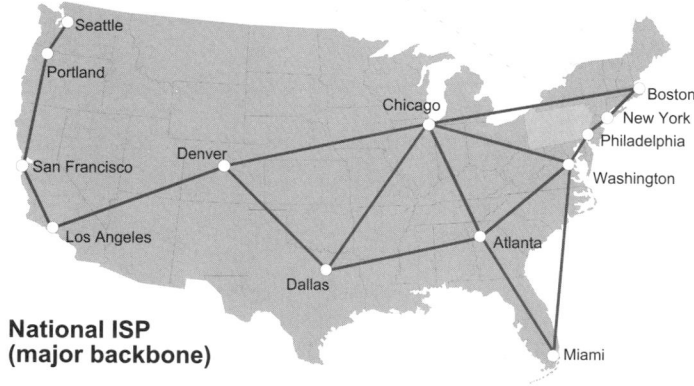

**National ISP
(major backbone)**

How the Internet Is Connected

Small Internet service providers (ISPs) hook into regional ISPs, which themselves link into major backbones that traverse the U.S. connecting major metropolitan areas. This diagram shows what a typical national backbone might look like as well as a county and state provider. While local ISPs may offer services only within their county, regional providers often span state lines.

It Has Gone Commercial

There has been more activity, excitement and hype over the Internet than any other computer or communications topic. Using the World Wide Web, thousands of companies, from conglomerates to mom and pop shops, are trying to figure out how to make the Internet a worldwide shopping mall. Will it become "the" model for commerce in the 21st century? Will traffic bog down like the Los Angeles freeway? Or, will it just become one more option for doing business in a world rich with choices? Stay tuned!

Internet2

A high-speed network for government, academic and research use administered by UCAID and being developed by more than 100 universities with assistance from private companies and the U.S. government. It is not intended for commercial use or to replace the Internet, but is, in fact, the reincarnation of it. However, whereas the first Internet was designed to primarily exchange text, Internet2 is being developed to exchange realtime, multimedia data at high speed, something today's commercial Internet does not do well. Resulting technological advancements should eventually migrate to the global Internet.

Universities are developing different techniques for providing high-speed points of presence known as "GigaPOPs," which serve as switching points for the network. The first GigaPOP was deployed in Research Triangle Park, North Carolina in late 1997. High-bandwidth applications, such as full-motion video and 3-D animations, are being developed and tested to determine the transport designs necessary to carry them in realtime.

UCAID works closely with Clinton's Next-Generation Internet (NGI), which is funding research on high-speed networks for federal agencies. Internet2 uses existing networks such as the vBNS backbone of the National Science Foundation. The Abilene network is expected to provide another backbone. Related Web sites are www.ucaid.org, www.ngi.gov, www.ccic.gov and www.vbns.net. See *vBNS* and *Abilene*.

Internet access

See *how to access the Internet*.

Internet access provider

Same as *Internet service provider*.

Internet access router

A router that provides access to the Internet. It is typically connected to the LAN and forwards IP packets destined for the Internet to the WAN ports (modem, ISDN, T1, etc.).

Internet address

There are two kinds of addresses that are widely used on the Internet. One is a person's e-mail address, and the other is the address of a Web site, which is known as its URL. Following is an explanation of Internet e-mail addresses. For more on URLs, see *URL* and *Internet domain names*.

The format for addressing a message to an Internet user is USER NAME @ DOMAIN NAME. For example, the address of the author of this database is **freedman@computerlanguage.com**. There are no spaces between any of the words. FREEDMAN is the user name and COMPUTERLANGUAGE.COM is the domain name. The .COM stands for the commercial top level domain category (see *Internet domain names*).

Sending to Online Services

You can send e-mail via the Internet directly to the mailboxes of users of all the major online services such as America Online and CompuServe. If you have an old account name or number of someone you wish to reach, that can be translated into an Internet address of the online service.

To reach CompuServe users, change the comma in their CompuServe account numbers to a period. For example, 71020,1560 becomes 71020.1560@compuserve.com.

The following examples show how the name "jmorrison" would be used in addresses to other online services. If the account name were "j morrison," you would remove the blank space.

```
jmorrison@aol.com          America Online
jmorrison@genie.geis.com   GEnie
jmorrison@mcimail.com       MCI Mail
jmorrison@prodigy.com       PRODIGY
jmorrison@delphi.com        DELPHI
```

How to Get Your Own Address

You get your e-mail address from your Internet service provider (ISP) or from your online service. However, if you change your service, your Internet address changes. To obtain a permanent e-mail address, you can register your own domain name with the InterNIC or you can use an e-mail service, such as one of the following. See *InterNIC*.

```
www.bigfoot.com
www.four11.com
www.whowhere.com
www.infospace.com
```

How to Find Someone Else's Address

There are Web sites that maintain directories, or white pages, of e-mail addresses. New sites are coming online all the time. You may have to try several sites to find someone, and there's no guarantee. In the meantime, check out:

```
www.bigfoot.com
www.four11.com
www.whowhere.com
www.switchboard.com
www.infospace.com
```

For the actual structure of an Internet address, see *IP address*.

Internet Ad Hoc Committee

(www.iahc.org) A coalition of participants from the Internet community that was formed to generate new top level domain names. See *Internet domain names*.

Internet appliance

A device designed for accessing the World Wide Web on the Internet. Internet TV services, such as WebTV, are designed for home use, whereas network computers (NCs) are designed for business use. PDAs and specialized hand-held devices with wireless connection to the Internet are also expected. See *Internet TV, network computer* and *smart phone*.

Internet Architecture Board

(www.iab.org) Founded in 1983 as the Internet Activities Board, it is a mostly volunteer organization that provides architectural guidance to and adjudicates conflicts for the Internet Engineering Task Force (IETF). It appoints the IETF Chair and all other Internet Engineering Steering Group (IESG) candidates. It also advises the Internet Society (ISOC) relating to technical and procedural matters.

Internet Assigned Numbers Authority

(www.iana.org) An Internet body chartered by the Internet Society (ISOC) and Federal Network Council (FNC) that maintains a central registry of Internet protocol parameters. Internet protocols require unique names and numbers in Internet addresses, domain names, protocol ports, private enterprise numbers, etc. IANA is located at and operated by the Information Sciences Institute at the University of Southern California.

Internet backbones

A group of communications networks managed by several commercial companies that provide the major high-speed links across the country. ISPs are either connected directly to these backbones or to a larger regional ISP that is connected to one. The backbones themselves are interconnected at various access points known as *NAPs*. The major backbone providers are MCI, Sprint, UUNET, AGIS and BBN. See *NAP*.

Internet box

See *Internet appliance*.

Internet computer

See *Internet appliance* and *network computer*.

Internet content provider

See *content provider*.

internet daemon
See *inetd*.

Internet directories
See *Web white pages* and *Web yellow pages*.

Internet domain names
An Internet domain name is an organization's unique name combined with a top level domain name (TLD). For example, **computerlanguage.com** is the domain name of the publisher of this software. Following are the top level domains. The .edu, .mil and .gov domains are traditionally U.S. domains. See *DNS, IP address* and *FQDN*.

```
.com    commercial
.net    gateway or host
.org    non-profit organization
.edu    educational and research
.gov    government
.mil    military agency
.int    international intergovernmental
```

The **.int** domain name is not widely used. Outside of the U.S., the top level domains are typically the country code; for example, **uk** for United Kingdom.

In early 1997, the Internet Ad Hoc Committee (IAHC) introduced a category called a *generic top-level domain*, or *gTLD*, which included the following entries. The IAHC also recommended that the top level domains (TLDs) .com, .net and .org, which have been considered international TLDs, be redefined as generic TLDs.

```
.firm    a business
.store   goods for sale
.web     WWW activities
.arts    culture/entertainment
.rec     recreation/entertainment
.info    information service
.nom     individual/personal
```

Internet e-mail service
An organization that provides you with an Internet e-mail address either for free, because it is advertiser supported, or for a fee. Some organizations manage your e-mail and maintain their own mail servers, while others simply forward your mail to the e-mail address you have with your current online service or Internet service provider (ISP). In some cases, you may be able to choose from a variety of domain names. Access to your e-mail may be through your Web browser or off the Net via special software and a separate dial-up connection.

The concept behind these services is a lifetime e-mail address so that if you are not entirely satisfied with your ISP, you don't lose your e-mail address if you switch to another one. Of course, the e-mail service has to stay in business as well. Some of these sites are:

```
www.hotmail.com
www.juno.com
www.four11.com    (forwarding)
www.bigfoot.com   (forwarding)
```

Internet Engineering Task Force (Steering Group)
(c/o Corporation for National Research Initiatives, Reston, VA, www.ietf.org) Founded in 1986, the IETF is a mostly volunteer organization of working groups dedicated to identifying problems and proposing technical solutions for the Internet. It facilitates transfer of ideas from the Internet Research Task Force (IRTF) to the Internet community and is supported by efforts of the Internet Society (ISOC). The Internet Architecture Board (IAB) provides architectural guidelines for the IETF, and the Internet Engineering Steering Group (IESG) provides overall direction.

Internet Explorer
See *Microsoft Internet Explorer*.

Internet fax
Using the Internet to send faxes. Fax servers accept an incoming fax message and route it to a fax server in the same locality as the destination fax machine. The fax server then makes a local telephone call to send the fax.

Internet filter
See *Web filtering* and *firewall*.

Internet gateway
A computer system that converts messages back and forth between TCP/IP and other protocols. Internet gateways connect the Internet to all the other communications networks in the world.

Internet PC
See *network computer*.

Internet phone
(1) A device or software application that provides the client part of an Internet telephone call.

(2) (Internet Phone) An Internet telephony client program for Windows from VocalTec Communications, Ltd., Northvale, NJ, (www.vocaltec.com). It allows voice calls to be placed over the Internet or to a standard telephone via an ITSP in the destination city. Video capability is also included. Introduced in early 1995, Internet Phone was the first IP telephony software on the market. See *IP telephony* and *ITSP*.

Internet Protocol
See *Internet* and *TCP/IP*.

Internet Relay Chat
Computer conferencing on the Internet. There are hundreds of IRC channels on numerous subjects that are hosted on IRC servers around the world. After joining a channel, your messages are broadcast to everyone listening to that channel. IRC client programs, such as mIRC, provide a graphical interface for all functions, including logging onto popular servers and obtaining a list of their active channels. See *MUD*.

Internet Research Task Force
(www.irtf.org) An organization of working groups involved in researching future Internet tecnologies. The IRTF is managed by the IRTF Chair in conjunction with the Internet Research Steering Group (IRSG). The IRTF Chair is appointed by the Internet Architecture Board (IAB). When the technologies are deemed ready for development, they are transferred to the Internet Engineering Task Force (IETF). See *Internet Engineering Task Force*.

Internet roaming
Accessing your own ISP locally when travelling abroad. Organizations such as GRIC and iPass have alliances with ISPs around the world that enable international travellers to obtain their e-mail without making long distance calls.

Internet Router
(1) A router in the Internet that forwards packets of Internet traffic between local, regional and national providers.

(2) (InterNet Router) Macintosh software from Apple that internetworks different access methods (LocalTalk, EtherTalk, TokenTalk, etc.) and can reside in any network station. Each Router can connect up to eight networks with a maximum of 1,024 networks and 16 million nodes.

Internet service provider
An organization that provides access to the Internet. Small Internet service providers (ISPs) provide service via modem and ISDN while the larger ones also offer private line hookups (T1, fractional T1, etc.). Customers are generally billed a fixed rate per month, but other charges may apply. For a fee, a Web site can be created and maintained on the ISP's server, allowing the smaller organization to have a

presence on the Web with its own domain name.

The major online services, such as America Online and CompuServe, provide Internet access but are still known as "online services," not ISPs. They generally offer the databases, forums and services that they originated over the years in addition to Internet access. While they may host a customer's home page, they typically do not host Web sites with unique domain names. All this is changing rapidly, however. To keep up-to-date, look for Boardwatch Magazine's "Internet Service Providers" bimonthly directory at your local bookstore or visit www.boardwatch.com.

Internet Society

(Internet Society, Reston, VA, www.isoc.org) An international membership organization dedicated to extending and enhancing the Internet, founded in 1992. It supports Internet bodies such as the IETF and works with governments, organizations and the general public to promote Internet research, information, education and standards. It also helps developing nations design their Internet infrastructure.

Internet Talk Radio

Audio coverage of news events digitized into Internet files at the National Press Building in Washington, DC. ITR files are distributed to FTP sites for users with computers that have sound capabilities.

Internet telephony

Using the Internet for a voice call. See *IP telephony*.

Internet TV

An Internet service for home TV use. It uses a set-top box that connects the TV to a modem and telephone line. The user interface has been specialized for viewing on an interlaced TV screen rather than a computer monitor. WebTV was the first such service to obtain widespread distribution. See *WebTV*.

Internet utility

Software used to search the Internet. See *Archie, Gopher, Veronica, WAIS* and *Web browser*.

internetwork

(1) To go between one network and another.

(2) A large network made up of a number of smaller networks. Same as *internet* (small "i," not the Internet). See *internet*.

InterNIC

(Internet Network Information Center, www.internic.net) The organization that handles Internet domain name registration. It is currently managed by Network Solutions, Inc. (NSI), Herndon, VA, and was formed in 1993 by agreements between it, the National Science Foundation, General Atomics and AT&T. See *ARIN*.

Is a Name Already Taken?

To find out if a domain name is taken, visit www.internic.net. Select Registration Services, then Whois. Type in the name and press Enter.

interoperable

The ability for one system to communicate or work with another.

interpolate

To estimate values that lie between known values.

interpolated resolution

An enhanced resolution of a scanning device that is computed using a software algorithm. It makes an image appear as if it were scanned at a higher resolution. An interpolated resolution is considerably greater than the optical resolution, which is the inherent physical resolution of the device. Depending on the contents of the image and the scanning algorithm, an interpolated, or enhanced, resolution can improve or degrade the original. See *optical resolution* and *scanner*.

Interpress

A page description language from Xerox used on the 2700 and 9700 page printers (medium to large-scale laser printers). Ventura Publisher provides output in Interpress.

interpret

To run a program one line at a time. Each line of source language is translated into machine language and then executed.

interpreter

A high-level programming language translator that translate and runs the program at the same time. It translates one program statement into machine language, executes it, then proceeds to the next statement. This differs from regular executable programs that are presented to the computer as binary-coded instructions. Interpreted programs remain in the same source language format the programmer wrote in: as text files, not machine language files.

Interpreted programs run slower than their compiler counterparts. Whereas the compiler translates the entire program before it is run, interpreters translate a line at a time while the program is run. However, it is very convenient to write an interpreted program, since a single line of code can be tested interactively.

Interpreted programs must always be run with the interpreter. For example, in order to run a BASIC or dBASE program, the BASIC or dBASE interpreter must be in the target computer.

If a language can be both interpreted and compiled, a program may be developed with the interpreter for ease of testing and debugging and later compiled for production use. See *compiler* for illustration.

interpretive language

A programming language that requires an interpreter to run it.

interprocess communication

See *IPC*.

interrecord gap

The empty space generated between blocks of data on older magnetic tapes, which is created by the starting and stopping of the reel. Today's drives do not use erase heads, and the stop-start areas are filled with padded blocks of data or special frequencies.

interrogate

(1) To search, sum or count records in a file. See *query*.

(2) To test the condition or status of a terminal or computer system.

interrupt

A signal that gets the attention of the CPU and is usually generated when I/O is required. For example, hardware interrupts are generated when a key is pressed or when the mouse is moved. Software interrupts are generated by a program requiring disk input or output.

An internal timer may continually interrupt the computer several times per second to keep the time of day current or for timesharing purposes.

When an interrupt occurs, control is transferred to the operating system, which determines the action to be taken. Interrupts are prioritized; the higher the priority, the faster the interrupt will be serviced.

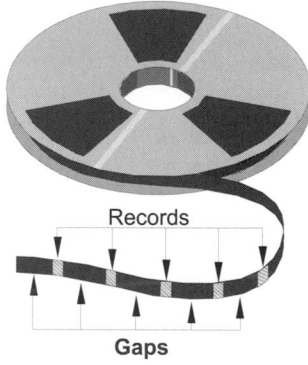

Records

Gaps

Interrecord Gaps
In the old days, the gaps between the records were often larger than the blocks of data.

interrupt-driven

A computer or communications network that uses interrupts.

interrupt latency

The time it take to service an interrupt. It becomes a critical factor when servicing realtime functions such as a communications line. See *UART overrun*.

interrupt mask

An internal switch setting that controls whether an interrupt can be processed or not. The mask is a bit that is turned on and off by the program.

Computer Desktop Encyclopedia

interrupt priorities

The sequence of importance assigned to interrupts. If two interrupts occur simultaneously, the interrupt with the highest priority is serviced first. In some systems, a higher-priority interrupt can gain control of the computer while it's processing a lower-priority interrupt.

Interrupt Request

See *IRQ*.

interrupt vector

In the PC, one of 256 pointers that reside in the first 1KB of memory. Each vector points to a routine in the BIOS or elsewhere in memory, which handles the interrupt.

intersect

In a relational database, to match two files and produce a third file with records that are common in both. For example, intersecting an American file and a programmer file would yield American programmers.

interstitial ad

An advertisement on a Web site that is more like a TV commercial, which takes center stage. Interstitial ads display while you're downloading the next Web page. Contrast with a banner ad, which is a more passive form of advertising. See *banner ad*.

intraframe coding

Compressing redundant areas within a video frame. See *interframe coding*.

intranet

(1) An inhouse Web site that serves the employees of the enterprise. Although intranet pages may link to the Internet, an intranet is not a site accessed by the general public.

Using programming languages such as Java, client/server applications can be built on intranets. Since Web browsers that support Java run under Windows, Mac and UNIX, such programs also provide cross-platform capability.

Intranets use the same communications protocols and hypertext links as the Web and thus provide a standard way of disseminating information internally and extending the application worldwide at the same time. See *network computer* and *extranet*.

(2) The term as originally coined in the definition above has become so popular that it is often used to refer to any inhouse LAN and client/server system.

intranet computer

A computer dedicated for intranet use only. See *network computer*.

intranet server

A computer dedicated to providing intranet services to users on the network. See *intranet*.

IntranetWare

A network operating system and intranet server from Novell. In late 1996, Novell combined NetWare 4.11, its Web server, TCP/IP support and the Netscape browser into a single package named IntranetWare. NetWare still retained its name, but became part of the IntranetWare package. In NetWare 5.0, the IntranetWare branding was dropped. See *NetWare*.

Invalid directory

A DOS error message that means you entered the name of a directory that does not exist.

Invalid drive specification

A DOS error message. If you get this message on a valid drive such as C:, it may mean that your hard disk has become corrupted.

Invalid file name or file not found

A DOS error message. You have probably used an invalid character in a DOS file name, or you have used wild cards when they are not applicable. For example, **type** *.* will produce this error, because you cannot Type more than one file at a time.

Invalid media type

A DOS error message that means DOS doesn't recognize the format of the drive being referenced. The disk has been corrupted in some manner and is not readable. You will also get this message if you low-level formatted a new disk, performed the Fdisk procedure, but forgot to high-level format it with the Format command.

inverse addressing

To perform the opposite of the normal addressing function. For example, inverse addressing in DNS servers converts the IP address into the URL, instead of the URL into the IP address.

inverse kinematics

In 3-D animation, a technique that provides automatic movement of objects. It allows elements of an object to be linked, such as the parts of an arm or leg, and causes them to move in a prescribed, realistic manner.

inverse multiplexor

In communications, a device that breaks up a high-speed transmission into several low-speed transmissions and vice versa. It is used to transmit LAN and videoconferencing traffic over lower-speed digital channels. For example, to transmit Ethernet over a T3 link, the 10 Mbps Ethernet channel would be inverse multiplexed into multiple 64 Kbps channels of the T3 line. A 336 Kbps videoconferencing transmission could be split into six 56 Kbps channels to transmit over a Switched 56 service. Contrast with *multiplexor*.

inverse video

Same as *reverse video*.

inverted file

In data management, a file that is indexed on many of the attributes of the data itself. For example, in an employee file, an index could be maintained for all secretaries, another for managers. It's faster to search the indexes than every record. Inverted file indexes use lots of disk space; searching is fast, updating is slower.

inverted list

Same as *inverted file*.

inverter

(1) A logic gate that converts the input to the opposite state for output. If the input is true, the output is false, and vice versa. An inverter performs the Boolean logic NOT operation.

(2) A circuit that converts DC current into AC current. Contrast with *rectifier*.

InVircible

An antivirus program from NetZ Computing Ltd., Israel, that can detect known and unknown viruses. It records the patterns of existing executable programs and analyzes whether they have been tampered with later. It also includes a data recovery capability for damaged disks.

invoke

To activate a program, routine, function or process.

I/O

(Input/Output) Transferring data between the CPU and a peripheral device. Every transfer is an output from one device and an input into another.

I/O address

(1) On PCs, a three-digit hexadecimal number (2AB, 2A0, etc.) used to identify and signal a peripheral device (serial port, parallel port, sound card, etc.). Address assignments must be unique, otherwise conflicts will occur. There are usually a small number of selectable addresses on each controller card. See *PC I/O addressing*.

(2) The identifying address of a peripheral device.

I/O area

A reserved segment of memory used to accept data from an input device or to accumulate data for transfer to an output device. See *buffer*.

I/O bound

Refers to an excessive amount of time getting data in and out of the computer in relation to the time it takes for processing it. Faster channels and disk drives improve the performance of I/O bound computers. See *I/O intensive*.

IOCA

(Image Object Content Architecture) See *MO:DCA*.

I/O card

See *expansion board* and *PC card*.

I/O channel

See *channel*.

IOCS

(Input Output Control System) An early, rudimentary IBM operating system (1950s). It was a set of I/O routines for tapes and disks. Today's counterpart in the PC is the BIOS.

I/O device

Any peripheral device (keyboard, disk, etc.).

I/O intensive

Refers to an application that reads and/or writes a large amount of data. The performance of such an application depends on the speed of the computer's peripheral devices and can cause a computer to become I/O bound. See *I/O bound*.

I/O interface

See *port* and *expansion slot*.

Iomega

(Iomega Corporation, Roy, Utah, www.iomega.com) A mass storage company founded in 1980 that made the Bernoulli Box famous. More recently, it introduced the Zip and Jaz drives, which have become very popular. See *Zip disk, Jaz disk, Ditto drive, click! disk* and *Bernoulli Box*.

ion deposition

A printing technology used in high-speed page printers. It is similar to laser printing, except instead of using light to create a charged image on a drum, it uses a printhead that deposits ions. After toner is attracted to the ions on the drum, the paper is pressed directly against the drum fusing toner to paper.

Quality approaches that of a laser printer; however, the ink has not been embedded as deeply, and the paper can smear more easily.

I/O port

(Input/Output port) See *port*.

I/O processor

Circuitry specialized for I/O operations. See *front end processor*.

IOS

(1) (Internetwork Operating System) An operating system from Cisco that is the primary control program used in its routers. IOS is widely-used, robust system software that supports the common functions of all products under Cisco's CiscoFusion architecture.

(2) (Integrated Office System) See *office automation*.

I/O statement

A programming instruction that requests I/O.

IO.SYS

See *MSDOS.SYS*.

IOW

Digispeak for "in other words."

IP

(1) (Internet Protocol) The IP part of the TCP/IP communications protocol. IP implements the network layer (layer 3) of the protocol, which contains a network address and is used to route a message to a different network or subnetwork. IP accepts "packets" from the layer 4 transport protocol (TCP or UDP), adds its own header to it and delivers a "datagram" to the layer 2 data link protocol. It may also break the packet into fragments to support the maximum transmission unit (MTU) of the network. See *TCP/IP, TCP/IP abc's, datagram, IP address* and *IP on Everything*.

(2) See *image processing*.

(3) (Intellectual Property) A broad category of intangible materials that are legally recognized as proprietary to an organization. In the computer field, software and text is copyrighted, certain algorithms used within the software may be patentable and brand names can be trademarked. However, IP covers more than just copyrights, trademarks and patents; for example, customer databases, mailing lists, trade secrets and other business information are also included.

IP address

(Internet Protocol address) The address of a computer attached to a TCP/IP network. Every client and server station must have a unique IP address. Client workstations have either a permanent address or one that is dynamically assigned to them each dial-up session. IP addresses are written as four sets of numbers separated by periods; for example, 204.171.64.2.

The TCP/IP packet uses 32 bits to contain the IP address, which is made up of a network and host address (netid and hostid). The more bits used for network address, the fewer remain for hosts. Certain high-order bits identify class types and some numbers are reserved. The following table shows how the bits are divided. The Class Number is the decimal value of the high-order eight bits, which identifies the class type.

Class	Class Number	Maximum Networks	Maximum Hosts	bits in— NetID	HostID
A	1-127	127	16,777,214	7	24
B	129-191	16,383	65,534	14	16
C	192-223	2,097,151	254	21	8

Class C addresses have been expanded using the CIDR addressing scheme, which uses a variable network ID instead of the fixed numbers shown above. Network addresses are supplied to organizations by the InterNIC Registration Service. See *CIDR, InterNIC, IPv6, TCP/IP abc's* and *IP on Everything*.

Logical or Physical?

An IP address is somewhat of a hybrid, which can be thought of as either logical or physical depending on how you view it. It is a unique number assigned to a node, which makes it seem physical, especially because there is so much name to IP address resolution going on in the network. Yet, there is also the Ethernet address that is built into the network adapter. That is indeed physical, and it does not change, which is very typical of physical device names. However, since IP addresses can be dynamically assigned, causing the same client workstation to have a different IP address every day, the IP address seems more like a logical address. Regardless of what it is, it would make a great debate in a computer science class. See *logical vs physical*.

IPC

(InterProcess Communication) The exchange of data between one program and another either within the same computer or over a network. It implies a protocol that guarantees a response to a request. Examples are OS/2's Named Pipes, Windows' DDE, Novell's SPX and Macintosh's IAC.

IPCs are performed automatically by the programs. For example, a spreadsheet program could query a database program and retrieve data from one of its databases. A manual example of an IPC function is performed when users cut and paste data from one file to another using the clipboard.

IPCS

See *AS/400 Integrated PC Server*.

IPDC

(Internet Protocol Device Control) A protocol for controlling media gateways developed by the Technical Advisory Committee, which was convened by Level 3 and others. It analyzes incoming data signals, in band control signals and tones and sets up and controls the appropriate gateways. It also handles management and reporting. See *media gateway controller*.

IPDS

(Intelligent Printer Data Stream) The native format built into IBM laser printers, which accepts fonts and formatted raster images. One of its major functions is its communications protocol that negotiates printer transfers from servers in the network that perform the rasterization. IBM used to make only IPDS printers. Today, many of its printers natively support PostScript and PCL (LaserJet) as well. See *PSF* and *AFP*.

IP gateway

A device that converts data into the IP protocol. It often refers to a voice-to-IP device that converts an analog voice stream, or a digitized version of the voice, into IP packets. See *ITSP, ITXC, H.323* and *Nacchio's law*.

IPI

(Intelligent Peripheral Interface) A high-speed hard disk interface used with minis and mainframes that transfers data in the 10 to 25 MBytes/sec range. IPI-2 and IPI-3 refer to differences in the command set that they execute. See *hard disk*.

IPL

(Initial Program Load) Same as *boot*.

ipm

(1) (Impressions Per Minute) See *ppm*.

(2) (IPM) (Intel Power Monitor) A utility from Intel that monitors power usage in notebook computers.

IP multicast

Transmitting data to a group of selected users at the same time on a TCP/IP network (internal, intranet or Internet). It is used for streaming audio and video over the network, but is also good for downloading a file to multiple users. IP multicast saves network bandwidth, because the files are transmitted as one data stream over the backbone and only split apart to the target stations by the router at the end of the path.

IP network

A network that uses the TCP/IP protocol, which includes the Internet, intranets and private UNIX networks. See *TCP/IP*.

IPng

(IP Next Generation) See *IPv6*.

I-PNNI

(Integrated PNNI) An extension to the PNNI routing protocol used by ATM switches. I-PNNI has been implemented in edge devices and legacy routers, but was not widely used.

IPO

(Initial Public Offering) The first time a company offers shares of stock to the public. While not a computer term per se, many founders, employees and insiders of computer companies have found this acronymn more exciting than any tech term they ever heard.

IP on Everything

A while back, Vinton Cerf, Senior VP at MCI, who is often called the "Father of the Internet," introduced the raucous T-shirt "IP on Everything!" Meant as a tongue-in-cheek forecast of the future, IP is indeed turning the telecommunications industry upside down.

We've spent the past three years trying to turn the Internet into one global communications system. However, until the Internet's infrastructure can handle quality of service (QoS), which allows traffic to be prioritized, it cannot support voice and video like a dedicated telephone connection. Reducing a $25 international phone call to zero might justify the jerks and blips, but for routine communications, we still want to hear a pin drop.

What makes the Internet most attractive is that, once upgraded for QoS, all future innovations come at the edge of the network. In contrast to the telephone company network, which must be reprogrammed for each type of new service that is offered, all that is necessary to launch an Internet service is to install the software in the servers, add the client piece to the user's machine and let 'er rip. If it works, more users put the stuff in their PCs, it becomes a "happening," and another Netscape is born. If not, the Internet keeps on transporting the bits and bytes, and nobody knows any different (see *dumb network*). What's more, the packet switching nature of IP maximizes every microsecond of bandwidth. Circuit-switched voice does not. The tiny pauses between speech go wasted in dedicated channels. Half the time, only one person is talking.

IP has become the new religion of the telecom industry. Qwest Communications' optical fiber network is IP based. Spanning more than 16,000 miles in the U.S, Qwest claims its available bandwidth will be larger than AT&T, MCI/WorldCom and Sprint put together by the end of 1999. Multi-billion dollar startup Level 3 Communications is designing another IP-based, nationwide fiber network for data and voice. AT&T is offering IP telephony and has announced its future infrastructure will be IP based. All the major carriers are determining how IP fits into their future. See *Qwest* and *Level 3*.

The Internet has not only affected every business, information systems department and software publisher, but it is changing world communications forever.

IP over SONET

See *packet over SONET*.

ips

(Inches Per Second) The measurement of the speed of tape passing by a read/write head or paper passing through a pen plotter.

IPSec

(IP SECurity) A security protocol from the IETF that provides authentication and encryption over the Internet. Unlike SSL, which provides services at layer 4, IPSec works at layer 3. IPSec is supported by IPv6. See *IPv6* and *security protocol*.

IP space

A group of IP addresses. See *namespace*.

IP spoofing

Inserting the IP address of an authorized user into the transmission of an unauthorized user in order to gain illegal access to a computer system. Routers and other firewall implementations can be programmed to identify this discrepancy. See *firewall*.

IP Switch

A high-speed routing and switching system from Nokia IP Routing, a business unit of Nokia Telecommunications, Inc., Sunnyvale, CA (www.ipsilon.com). Originally developed by Ipsilon Networks of Palo Alto, CA, the IP switch routes IP traffic over ATM switches using a proprietary control protocol.

The IP Switch Controller analyzes the first frame of a message and lets short-lived traffic, such as DNS and SNMP queries, flow through the Controller back to the switch. When long-duration traffic is encountered, it sets up a virtual circuit in an ATM switch, and remaining packets flow at high speed. IP Switch uses the General Switch Management Protocol (GSMP) for call setup and the Ipsilon Flow Management Protocol (IFMP) for flow redirection. See *IP switching*.

IP switching

Switching TCP/IP packets at high speed. Ipsilon's IP Switch started the trend and various organizations have followed suit with different approaches, including Cisco's tag switching and 3Com's Fast IP. The goal is to switch IP packets faster than traditional router-based layer 3 forwarding. See *layer 3 switch, IP Switch* and *tag switching*.

IP telephony

The two-way transmission of audio over an IP network. Also called *voice over IP*, IP telephony allows telephone conversations to travel over the Internet, intranets or private LANs and WANs that use the

TCP/IP protocol. Intranets and private networks can provide from good to excellent quality, matching that of the PSTN.

Over the Internet, voice quality varies considerably. The Internet cannot provide the same quality as a private network or the PSTN; however, protocols that support quality of service (QoS) are expected to improve this condition in time. Nevertheless, IP telephony over the Internet (Internet telephony) means free voice calls as long as sending and receiving users have identical software that uses proprietary techniques or compatible software that uses the H.323 standard. They must also be willing to talk from their PCs and to prearrange the times to talk. When users go online and launch their IP telephony client software, the session and current IP address is registered on a directory server on the Internet so that others may contact them.

Using Internet telephony service providers (ITSPs), users can make PC-to-phone or phone-to-phone calls, using the Internet as the network backbone. ITSPs have been initially popular for international calls (see *ITSP*).

Although, Internet voice quality can be erratic, the underlying IP protocol is either being used or being considered for future network backbones by all the major telecom carriers (see *IP on Everything*). See *Internet phone, gatekeeper* and *RSVP*.

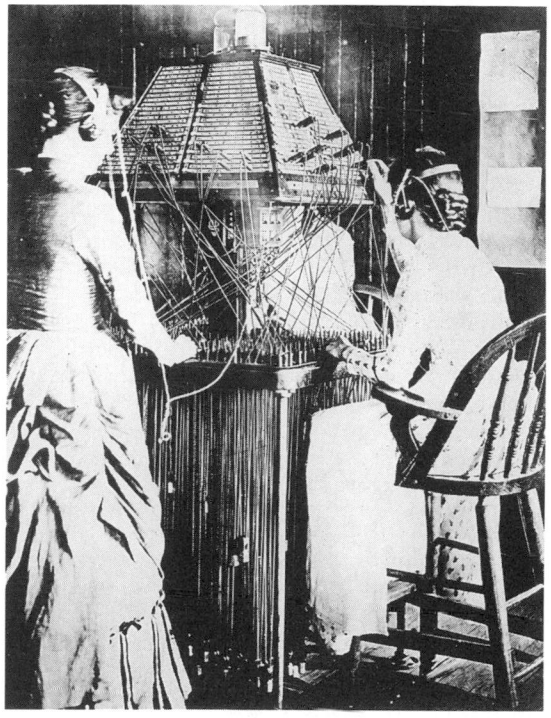

Not Quite IP Telephony
We can be certain that they didn't have the IP protocol in mind when they set up this telephone switchboard in 1882. It was used to switch phone calls for all the lawyers in Richmond, Virginia. *(Photo courtesy of AT&T.)*

IP tunneling
Carrying a foreign protocol within a TCP/IP packet. For example, IPX can be encapsulated and transmitted via TCP/IP.

IPv4
(Internet Protocol Version 4) The current version of the IP protocol. See *IPv6*.

IPv6
(Internet Protocol Version 6) The next generation IP protocol. Started in 1991, the specification was completed in 1997 by the Internet Engineering Task Force (IETF). IPv6 is backward compatible with and is designed to fix the shortcomings of IPv4, such as data security and maximum number of user addresses.

IPv6 increases the address space from 32 to 128 bits, providing for an unlimited number of networks and systems. It also supports quality of service (QoS) parameters for realtime audio and video. The draft version of IPv6 was originally called IP Next Generation, or IPng.

IP voice
See *IP telephony*.

IPX
(Internetwork Packet EXchange) A NetWare communications protocol used to route messages from one node to another. IPX packets include network addresses and can be routed from one network to another. An IPX packet can occasionally get lost when crossing networks, thus IPX does not guarantee delivery of a complete message. Either the application has to provide that control or NetWare's SPX protocol must be used.

IPX provides services at layers 3 and 4 of the OSI model (network and transport layers). See *SPX*.

IR

(1) (Industry Remarketer) Same as *VAR* or *VAD*.

(2) See *infrared*.

IRC

See *Internet Relay Chat*.

IrDA

(Infrared Data Association, Walnut Creek, CA, www.irda.org) A membership organization founded in 1993 and dedicated to developing standards for wireless, infrared transmission systems between computers. With IrDA ports, a laptop or PDA can exchange data with a desktop computer or use a printer without a cable connection. IrDA requires line-of-sight transmission like a TV remote control. IrDA products began to appear in 1995. The LaserJet 5P was one of the first printers with an IrDA port.

IrDA is comprised of the IrDA Serial IR physical layer (IrDA-SIR), which provides a half-duplex connection of up to 115.2 Kbps. This speed allows the use of a low-cost UART chip; however, higher non-UART extensions for 1.15 and 4 Mbps have also been defined. IrDA uses the Infrared Link Access Protocol (IrLAP), an adaptation of HDLC, as its data link protocol. The Infrared Link Management Protocol (IrLMP) is also used to provide a mechanism for handshaking and multiplexing of two or more different data streams simultaneously.

IrDA port

A transmitter/receiver for infrared signals. See *IrDA*.

IRG

(InterRecord Gap) See *interrecord gap*.

Iridium

(Iridium LLC, Washington, DC, www.iridium.com) A communications company that offers voice, data, fax and pager service anywhere in the world. Using a combination of low-earth orbit (LEO) satellites along with cellular and landline partners, Iridium phones access the satellites directly as well as local cellular facilities. Iridium was announced in 1990 and completed in 1998 at a cost of more than $5 billion. It was the first commercial system based on LEO satellites and the first to offer a handheld satellite phone. See *LEO*.

IRIS

The name of Silicon Graphic's first graphics terminals and workstations. The name was later used for SGI's high-availability software for its servers (IRIS FailSafe).

IRIS printer

A large-format color printer from IRIS Graphics, Inc., Bedford, MA, (www.iris.com). IRIS printers use a patented continuous ink jet technology to produce consistent, continuous-tone, photorealistic output on several varieties of paper, canvas, silk, linen and other low-fiber textiles.

The IRIS is able to "jet" variable droplets of ink. Although its addressable resolution is only 300 dpi, the perceived resolution is up to 1800 dpi, providing extraordinary results.

Although IRIS printers cost from $25,000 to $100,000, they are often easily cost justified in commercial applications, because their cost of consumables is low. For example, a 21x28" matte proof costs less than two dollars, which is very inexpensive for this kind of output.

In addition, IRIS prints are noted for their color consistency. When multiple proofs are distributed for review or when nuances of color play an important role in shaded maps and other critical output, IRIS prints provide the necessary uniformity.

IRIX

A UNIX-based operating system from Silicon Graphics (SGI) that is used in its computer systems from desktop to supercomputer. It is an enhanced version of UNIX System V Release 4. IRIX integrates the X Window system with OpenGL, creating the first realtime 3-D X environment.

IRM

(1) (Information Resource Management) See *Information Systems* and *information management*.

(2) (Inherited Rights Mask) In NetWare 3.x and 4.x, a filter that defines the access rights that have been passed down from the parent directory.

Irma

Attachmate's trade name for a variety of host connectivity hardware and software products. The Irma board was the first 3270 emulator, which allowed a PC to function as an IBM mainframe terminal. Irma is not an acronym, rather it is the lady's name.

Irma board

The first 3270 emulator for PCs. Introduced in 1982, it was the first product to provide PC to IBM host connectivity. Irma was originally spelled all caps (IRMA) and was developed by Digital Communications Associates (DCA), which later merged with and became part of Attachmate Corporation.

Irmalan

An earlier family of gateway programs from Attachmate Corporation, Bellevue, WA, (www.attachmate.com), that allowed PCs to connect to NetWare, NetBIOS and VINES networks to access an SNA host. Irmalan gateways supported IEEE 802.2, SDLC (via modem) and DFT environments.

Irma software

A family of terminal emulation software products from Attachmate Corporation, Bellevue, WA, (www.attachmate.com), that provide desktop to host connectivity. Irma for the Mainframe provides Windows, Mac, DOS, NT and OS/2 client connectivity to IBM mainframes via modem, LAN and 3270 emulator.

Irma for the AS/400 provides Windows client connectivity to the AS/400 via modem, LAN and twinax card. Irma for Open Systems provides Telnet and LAT support on a Windows client to VAX, HP and UNIX hosts as well as online services via LAN and modem. See *Irma board*.

iron oxide

The material used to coat the surfaces of magnetic tapes and lower-capacity disks.

IRQ

(Interrupt ReQuest) A hardware interrupt on a PC. There are 16 IRQ lines used to signal the CPU that a peripheral event has started or terminated. Except for PCI devices, two devices cannot use the same line. If a new expansion board is preset to the IRQ used by an existing board, one of them must be changed. This was an enormous headache in earlier machines.

Starting with the 286, two 8259A controller chips are cascaded together for a total of 16 IRQs (the first PCs had only one chip and eight IRQs). However, IRQ 2 is lost because it is used to connect to the second chip. All the IRQs except for 10, 11, 12 and 15 are preassigned.

If a second parallel port is not used, IRQ 5 is available. IRQ 9 is also often available as most VGA cards do not require an IRQ. Thus IRQs 5, 9, 10, 11, 12 and 15 are arbitrarily used for scanners, SCSI boards, CD-ROM controllers, sound boards and any other peripheral that can be attached to a PC. They become the "IRQ battleground."

PCI to the Rescue

The PCI bus allows IRQs to be shared, which helps to solve the problem of limited IRQs available on a PC. For example, if there were only one IRQ left over after ISA devices were given their required IRQs, all PCI devices could share it. In a PCI-only machine, there cannot be insufficient IRQs, as all can be shared.

```
IRQ   Assignment            11    **
0     System timer          12    **
1     Keyboard              13    Math coprocessor
2     Connects to IRQ 9     14    Hard disk
3     COM2, COM4            15    **
4     COM1, COM3
5     LPT2**
6     Floppy disk
7     LPT1
8     Realtime clock
9     VGA, 3270 emulation**     ** For general use.  "The battleground."
10    **
```

IRQ steering

See *PCI steering*.

IRTF

See *Internet Research Task Force*.

IS

See *Information Systems*.

ISA

(1) (Industry Standard Architecture) Pronounced "eye-suh." An expansion bus commonly used in PCs. It accepts the plug-in boards that control the video display, disks and other peripherals. Most PCs today use the ISA and PCI buses and have a combination of ISA and PCI slots.

ISA was originally called the *AT bus*, because it was first used in the IBM AT, extending the original bus from eight to 16 bits. Earlier ISA PCs provided a mix of 8-bit and 16-bit expansion slots. Today most PCs have only 16-bit ISA slots. Contrast with *EISA* and *Micro Channel*. See *local bus*.

(2) (Interactive Services Association, Silver Spring, MD, www.isa.net) A trade group for the online industry originally founded in 1981 as the Videotex Industry Association (VIA). Members are online services, service bureaus and hardware and software companies, all providing products for users with a computer and modem. See *motherboard* for illustration.

ISAM

(Indexed Sequential Access Method) A common disk access method that stores data sequentially, while maintaining an index of key fields to all the records in the file for direct access. The sequential order would be the one most commonly used for batch processing and printing (account number, name, etc.).

ISAPI

(Internet Server API) A programming interface on Internet Information Server (IIS), Microsoft's Web server. Using ISAPI function calls, Web pages can invoke programs that are written as DLLs on the server, typically to access data in a database. IIS comes with a DLL that allows embedded queries to access ODBC-compliant databases. ISAPI is an alternative to using CGI scripts on Microsoft Web servers.

ISDN

(Integrated Services Digital Network) An international telecommunications standard for transmitting voice, video and data over digital lines running at 64 Kbps. The telephone companies commonly use a 64 Kbps channel for digitized, two-way voice conversations. ISDN service is becoming widely available in the U.S. It is expected to be fully nationwide in a couple of years.

ISDN uses 64 Kbps circuit-switched channels, called B channels, or "bearer" channels, to carry voice and data. It uses a separate D channel, or "delta," channel for control signals. The D channel is used to signal the telephone company computer to make calls, put them on hold and activate features such as

PC BUSES	Bandwidth	
	Bits	Speed
ISA	8 16	8-10MHz
EISA	32	8-10MHz
PCI	32 64	33MHz
AGP	32	66MHz
Micro Channel	32	5-20MHz
VL-bus	32	40MHz

Types of Expansion Boards
ISA boards are still widely used, but they are giving way to the PCI bus. The AGP bus is used for the display adapter, and EISA, Micro Channel and VL-bus have all but disappeared.

conference calling and call forwarding. It also receives information about incoming calls, such as the identity of the caller.

ISDN's basic service is Basic Rate Interface (BRI), which is made up of two 64 Kbps B channels and one 16 Kbps D channel (2B+D). If both channels are combined into one, called *bonding*, the total data rate becomes 128 Kbps and is four and a half times the bandwidth of a V.34 modem (28.8 Kbps).

ISDN's high-speed service is Primary Rate Interface (PRI). It provides 23 B channels and one 64 Kbps D channel (23B+D), which is equivalent to the 24 channels of a T1 line. When several channels are bonded together, high data rates can be achieved. For example, it is common to bond six channels for quality videoconferencing at 384 Kbps. In Europe, PRI includes 30 B channels and one D channel, equivalent to an E1 line.

ISDN SERVICES

Basic Rate Interface (BRI)
Two 64 Kbps B Channels, one 16 Kbps D Channel

(B) 64 Kbps (B) 64 Kbps (D) 16 Kbps

Bonded (B) + (B) = 128 Kbps

Primary Rate Interface (PRI)
23 64 Kbps B Channels, 1 64 Kbps D Channel

(D)(B)(B)(B) (B)(B)(B)(B) (B)(B)(B)(B)
(B)(B)(B)(B) (B)(B)(B)(B) (B)(B)(B)

Connecting an ISDN Device

Connecting ISDN to a personal computer requires a network terminator (NT1) and ISDN terminal adapter. The NT1 plugs into the two-wire line from the telephone company and provides four-wire output to the terminal adapter. The NT1 is typically built into the terminal adapter.

The terminal adapter is often called an *ISDN modem*, but it is technically not a modem. It provides a digital to digital connection, not a conversion to audio tones. The terminal adapter plugs into the serial port or into an expansion slot in the computer. Some adapters hook into the parallel port for higher speed. ISDN adapters may also include an analog modem and automatically switch between analog and digital depending on the type of call.

For Internet hookup, although the ISDN terminal adapter may support bonding, the Internet service provider must also support the Multilink PPP protocol (MP or MPPP), which supports multiple channels from the software side. See *BISDN*.

ISDN adapter
See *ISDN terminal adapter*.

ISDN bonding
The bridging of two or more ISDN channels to achieve higher data rates. See *ISDN*.

ISDN modem
An alternate name for ISDN terminal adapter. The term is widely used, because the unit looks like a modem and connects to the same serial port as a modem. It is also easier to say. However, since ISDN is digital, the device does not MODulate or DEModulate any signal. See *ISDN terminal adapter*.

ISDN TA, ISDN terminal adapter
A device that adapts a computer to a digital ISDN line. Like a modem, it plugs into the serial port of the computer or into an expansion slot. Some terminal adapters use the parallel port for higher speed. The adapter may also include a regular data or fax/modem and switch automatically between analog and digital depending on the type of call.

I Seek You
See *ICQ*.

IS-IS
(Intermediate System to Intermediate System) An ISO protocol that provides dynamic routing between routers.

ISO

(International Standards Organization, Geneva, www.iso.ch) An organization that sets international standards, founded in 1946. The U.S. member body is ANSI. ISO deals with all fields except electrical and electronics, which is governed by the older International Electrotechnical Commission (IEC). With regard to information processing, ISO and IEC created JTC1, the Joint Technical Committee for information technology.

It carries out its work through more than 160 technical committees and 2,300 subcommittees and working groups and is made up of standards organizations from more than 75 countries, some of them serving as secretariats for these technical bodies.

ISO 13346

A standard format for a rewritable optical disk from the International Standards Association. It specifies the logical format of the disk so that removable cartridges can be interchanged among different platforms.

ISO 9000

A standard for quality in the manufacturing and service industries from the International Standards Association. ISO 9000 defines the criteria for what should be measured. ISO 9001 covers design and development. ISO 9002 covers production, installation and service, and ISO 9003 covers final testing and inspection. ISO 9000 certification does not guarantee product quality. It ensures that the processes that develop the product are performed in a quality manner.

Initially popular in Europe, ISO 9000 certification began to increase in the U.S. in 1993. In the computer field, hardware vendors were the first to seek certification. Certification requires exacting documentation and demonstrations in practice over time. The process can take up to a year.

ISO 9660

A standard CD-ROM file format from the International Standards Association. Evolving from the High Sierra format, ISO 9660 specifies the directory format of the disc. The physical format is defined in the Yellow Book. ISO 9660 provides for read-only interoperability between different computer systems. Subsequently, the UDF format was created for read-write interoperability. See *UDF*.

ISOC

See *Internet Society*.

isochronous

Time dependent. Realtime voice, video and telemetry are examples of isochronous data.

Isochronous Ethernet

National Semiconductor's enhancement to Ethernet for handling realtime voice and video. It adds 96 ISDN channels to standard 10 Mbps Ethernet and runs over the same Category 3 UTP that most 10BaseT networks use. Each ISDN B channel is 64 Kbps, providing a total bandwidth of 6.144 Mbps that can be used for videoconferencing. A D channel and maintenance channel are also provided.

Isochronous Ethernet can be integrated into an existing network by adding an Isochronous Ethernet hub in the wiring closet and replacing standard Ethernet with Isochronous Ethernet adapters.

IsoENET, IsoEthernet

See *Isochronous Ethernet*.

isometric view

In computer graphics, a rendering of a 3-D object that eliminates the distortion of shape created by true perspective. In isometric views, all lines on each axis are parallel to each other, and the lines do not converge. Such drawings are commonly used in technical illustrations because of their clarity, simplicity and speed of creation.

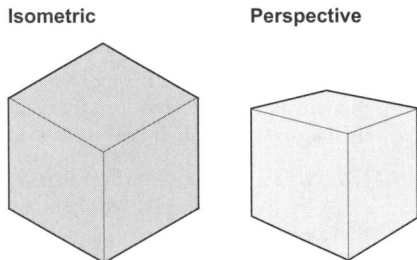

Isometric   **Perspective**

Isometric View

Isometric views of objects are made to show as much detail as possible, typically with technical drawings. In the normal perspective, all lines converge in a vanishing point, and detail at the farthest ends can be difficult to see.

isotropic

Refers to properties, such as transmission speed, that are the same regardless of the direction that is measured. Contrast with *anisotropic*.

ISP

See *Internet service provider*.

ISPF

(Interactive System Productivity Facility) A full-screen editor from IBM for writing application programs. It is also used to develop dialogs for interactive terminal sessions. Program Development Facility (PDF) provides enhancements to ISPF, including interfaces to languages such as REXX.

ISR

(Interrupt Service Routine) Software routine that is executed in response to an interrupt.

ISV

(Independent Software Vendor) A person or company that develops software. It implies an organization that specializes in software only and is not part of a computer systems or hardware manufacturer. Contrast with *IHV*.

IT

(Information Technology) Processing information by computer. The latest title for the information processing industry.

ITAA

(Information Technology Association of America, Arlington, VA, www.itaa.org) Formerly the Association of Data Processing Service Organizations (ADAPSO). A membership organization founded in 1960 that defines performance standards, improves management methods and monitors government regulations in the computer services field.

item

One unit or member of a group. See *data item*.

iteration

One repetition of a sequence of instructions or events. For example, in a program loop, one iteration is once through the instructions in the loop.

iterative operation

An operation that requires successive executions of instructions or processes.

ITI

(Information Technology Industry Council, Washington, DC, www.itic.org) Formerly the Computer and Business Equipment Manufacturers Association (CBEMA), founded in 1916. ITI is a membership organization composed of approximately 30 large companies. Its mission is to produce market-driven voluntary standards for information technology in the U.S. and abroad. It sponsors several dozen committees which used to be given alphabetic names such as X3J4, but now fall under the NCITS (National Committee for Information Technology Standards) umbrella.

I-time

See *instruction time*.

ITMS (AICPA)

(Information Technology Membership Section, American Institute of Certified Public Accountants, New York, www.aicpa.org) A membership group of the AICPA whose mission is to provide value to their clients and employers through effective application of information technologies. Volunteers serve on committees supported by the Information Technology Team professional staff.

The ITMS provides a forum for all AICPA members, including public practice, industry, education and government, to exchange ideas and benefit from each other's experiences. It helps CPAs improve their competency in technology and keep abreast of the latest changes.

ITSEC

See *NCSC.*

ITSP

(Internet Telephony Service Provider) An organization, such as an ISP or telephone company (CLEC, LEC, etc.), that supports IP telephony. Using the Internet as the primary backbone, it allows customers to make phone-to-phone calls or PC-to-phone calls. The majority of customers use an ITSP to save money on international calls, and the quality can vary substantially due to the inconsistency of the Internet. The ITSP uses IP gateways to convert between voice and IP packets. See *IP gateway* and *ITXC.*

ITU

(International Telecommunications Union, Geneva, Switzerland, www.itu.ch) Formerly the CCITT (Consultative Committee for International Telephony and Telegraphy), it is an international organization founded in 1865 and headquartered in Geneva that sets communications standards. The ITU is comprised of over 150 member countries. The Telecommunications Standards Section (TSS) is one of four organs of the ITU. An ITU-T or ITU-TSS designation refers to the TSS organ.

ITXC

(Internet Telephony Exchange Carrier Corporation, Princeton, NJ, www.itxc.net) An Internet telephony communications organization that provides routing, authorization and settlement (billing) services to ITSPs (Internet Telephony Service Providers) throughout the world. It provides routing information to ITSPs that enable the call to be received by a cooperating ITSP at the other end. The majority of traffic handled by ITXC is international phone calls. See *ITSP.*

IV

See *interactive video.*

IVDS

(Interactive Video and Data Services) The wireless implementation of interactive TV. In 1994, an additional part of the VHF television spectrum (218-219 MHz), which was divided into 1450 licenses, was auctioned to the highest bidders by the U.S. government. Organizations that own these licenses will be able to provide interactive television services to subscribers in their jurisdictions. See *interactive TV.*

Iverson notation

A set of symbols developed by Kenneth Iverson for writing statements in APL.

IVR

(Interactive Voice Response) An automated telephone answering system that responds with a voice menu and allows the user to make choices and enter information via the keypad. IVR systems are widely used in call centers as well as a replacement for human switchboard operators. The system may also integrate database access and fax response. See *ACD* and *CTI.*

I-way

(Information SuperhighWAY) Slang for the *Internet.*

IX

(Internet eXchange) See *NAP* and *CIX.*

IXC

(1) (IntereXchange Carrier) An organization that provides interstate communications services, such as AT&T, MCI and Sprint.

(2) (IXC Communications Inc., Austin, TX, www.ixc-comm.com) A wholesale telecommunications provider that offers private line, long-distance, frame relay and ATM services over its nationwide fiber-optic network. IXC is an IXC.

J

J

A high-level mathematical programming language developed by Kenneth Iverson, the author of APL. J is the successor to APL and runs on a variety of platforms, including DOS, Windows, OS/2 and the Macintosh. The Windows version can be used as a calculating engine for Visual Basic, in which Visual Basic is used to write the file handling and user interface portions, and J is used to program the math.

J++

See *Visual J++*.

jack

A receptacle into which a plug is inserted.

jacket

A plastic housing that contains a floppy disk. The 5.25" disk is built into a flexible jacket; the 3.25" disk uses a rigid jacket.

Jacquard loom

An automated loom that transformed the 19th century textile industry and became the inspiration for future calculating and tabulating machines. Developed by the French silk-weaver, Joseph-Marie Jacquard (1752-1834), it used punched cards to control its operation.

Although punched cards were used in earlier looms and music boxes, Jacquard's loom was a vast improvement and allowed complex patterns to be created swiftly. The loom was inspiration to Charles Babbage and, later, to Herman Hollerith.

JAD

(Joint Application Development) An approach to systems analysis and design introduced by IBM in 1977 that emphasizes teamwork between user and technician. Small groups meet to determine system objectives and the business transactions to be supported. They are run by a neutral facilitator who can move the group toward well-defined goals. Results include a prototype of the proposed system.

jaggies

The stairstepped appearance of diagonal lines on a low-resolution graphics screen.

The Jaggies
A low-resolution image with the jaggies is on the left. A higher-resolution image on the right.

JAM

(JYACC Application Manager) An application development system for client/server environments from JYACC, Inc., New York, (www.jyacc.com). It supports Windows, Mac and Motif clients and most all UNIX servers and VMS. It supports over 20 databases and includes its own database (JDB) for prototyping. JAM/CASE allows CASE information to be moved into JAM. JAM/TPi integrates JAM with the Tuxedo and Encina TP monitors.

Japanese PC market

NEC has over half the market with its PC-98 series. Apple has the next largest share with approximately 14%. The remainder is divided among Fujitsu, IBM, Epson, Toshiba and others. Japanese versions of Windows are widely used.

The Jacquard Loom
The binary principle embodied in the punched-card operation of the loom was inspiration for future computing machines. *(Photo courtesy of Smithsonian Institution.)*

JAR

(1) (Java ARchive) A file format used to distribute a Java application. It contains all the resources required to install and run a Java program in a single compressed file. JARs are also used to distribute JavaBeans.

(2) A compression program for backup archiving from ARJ Software, Inc., Norwood, MA, (www.arjsoftware.com). JAR is similar to ARJ, but files are not compatible. See *ARJ*.

Java

A programming language for Internet (World Wide Web) and intranet applications from Sun. Java was modeled after C++, and Java programs can be called from within HTML documents or launched stand alone. The first Web browsers to run Java applications were Sun's HotJava and Netscape's Navigator 2.0. Java was designed to run in small amounts of memory and provides its own memory management.

Java is an interpreted language that uses an intermediate language. The source code of a Java program is compiled into "byte code," which cannot be run by itself. The byte code must be converted into machine code at runtime. Upon finding a Java applet, the Web browser switches to its Java interpreter (Java Virtual Machine) which translates the byte code into machine code and runs it. This means Java programs are not dependent on any specific hardware and will run in any computer with the Java Virtual Machine. On the server side, Java programs can also be compiled into machine language for fastest performance, but they lose their hardware independence as a result.

Like other programming languages, Java is royalty free to developers for writing applications. However, the Java Virtual Machine, which executes Java applications, is licensed to the companies that incorporate it in their browsers and servers.

Java is a full-blown and difficult programming language not intended for the casual programmer and certainly not the end user. JavaScript, on the other hand, is a script language from Netscape that is somewhat easier to use, but not as powerful. JavaScript uses the HTML page as its user interface, whereas Java can display a completely customized interface like C and C++.

PC CLIENT

PC

OS (DOS, Win, Mac)

Web browser with JVM

Web page

Java "byte code" program

OS

Web browser with JVM

NC CLIENT

NC

OS and JVM and browser

Java "byte code" program

No local hard disk.

WEB SERVER or INTRANET SERVER

OS (UNIX, NT, Mac)

Server program (Java, C++, JavaScript, VB, etc.)

Web pages that reference Java programs.

Server program (Java, C++ JavaScript, VB, etc.)

Java "byte code" programs

Java Runs on PCs and NCs

Java programs can be stored on a Web server on the Internet or on an internal intranet. On a PC, they must be run from a Web page under control of a browser. On NCs, they can be run the same way, or they can be run directly by the operating system. For client/server systems, server-side programs can also be written in Java, but would be compiled into machine code for best performance.

Java: A Revolution?

Java was originally developed in 1991 as a language for embedded applications such as those used in set-top boxes and other consumer-oriented devices. It became the fuel to ignite a revolution in thinking when Sun transitioned it to the Web in 1994. Unlike HTML, which is a document display format that is continually beefed up to make it do more, Java is a full-blown programming language like C and C++. It allows for the creation of sophisticated client/server applications to be developed for the Web and for intranets. See *JFC, network computer, CaffeineMark* and *caffeine based.* See *compiler* for illustration of interpreters and compilers.

The following Java example of changing Farhenheit to Celsius is rather wordy compared to the C example in this database. Java is designed for GUI-based applications, and several extra lines of code are necessary here to allow input from a terminal.

```
import java.io.*;
class Convert {
 public static void main(String[]args)
  throws IOException {
   float fahr;
   StreamTokenizer in = new StreamTokenizer (new InputStreamReader(System.in));
   System.out.print("Enter Fahrenheit ");
   in.nextToken();
   fahr = (float) in.nval;
   System.out.println ("Celsius is " + (fahr-32)*5/9);
 }
}
```

JavaBeans

A component software architecture from Sun that runs in the Java environment. JavaBeans are independent Java program modules that can be called up and executed. JavaBeans components can be run remotely in a distributed computing environment using Sun's Remote Method Invocation (RMI) or the OMG's CORBA. JavaBeans is the Java counterpart of Microsoft's COM. See *component software.*

Java chip

A CPU chip from Sun that executes Java byte code natively. It is based on Sun's picoJava architecture and is expected to be used in a wide range of devices from small, hand-held appliances to desktop network computers. See *microJava.*

Java compiler

A compiler for the Java language that converts source code into native machine code. Although this makes the program platform dependent since it only runs in one CPU family, it also runs the fastest when compiled into native machine language. The term may also refer to a Java just-in-time compiler (JIT compiler), which compiles all the Java byte code downloaded from the server just before running the application. This is faster than interpreting the byte code one line at a time, but it also takes time to compile the program. See *Java.*

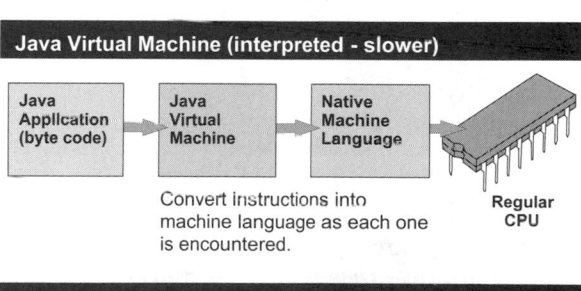

Java Virtual Machine (interpreted - slower)

Convert instructions into machine language as each one is encountered.

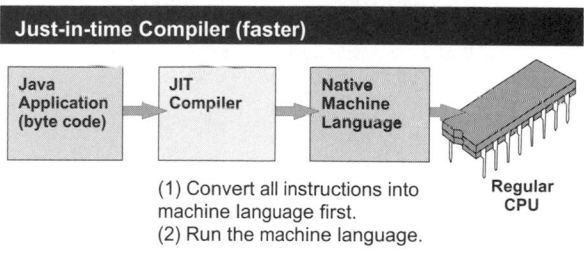

Just-in-time Compiler (faster)

(1) Convert all instructions into machine language first.
(2) Run the machine language.

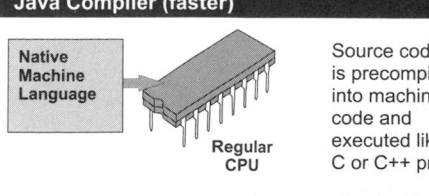

Java Compiler (faster)

Source code is precompiled into machine code and executed like a C or C++ program.

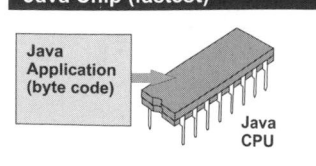

Java Chip (fastest)

The Java chip executes Java byte code just like other CPUs execute their native machine code.

JavaOS

A Java operating system from Sun that requires minimal hardware requirements and is intended for network computers and embedded systems. It includes the Java Virtual Machine, which combined with the kernel, are written in the native machine language of the target CPU. Network and graphical user interface components are mostly written in Java.

Java sandbox

The constrained arena within which Java applications run, preventing for example, access to the local hard disk or to the network. While this restricts the program's capabilities, it provides security for downloading Java apps from the Internet. See *object signing*.

JavaScript

A script language from Netscape that is supported in Netscape Navigator as of Version 2.0. It is easier to use than Java, but not as powerful. JavaScript uses the HTML page as its user interface, whereas Java can generate a completely custom interface. On the client, JavaScript applets are maintained in source code. On the server, they are compiled into byte code (intermediate language), similar to Java programs.

JavaScript evolved from Netscape's LiveScript language and was made more compatible with Java. JavaScript does not have the programming overhead of Java, but can be used in conjunction with it. For example, a JavaScript applet could be used to display a data entry form and validate the input, while a Java program processes the information. JavaScript is also used to tie Java applets together. See *Java*.

JavaSoft

The division within Sun that supports the Java programming language and licenses the Java Virtual Machine.

JavaStation

A family of network computers from Sun that comply with the NC Reference Profile. Introduced with the same 100MHz MicroSPARC CPU used in Sun's SPARC 4 and 5 workstations, JavaStations are expected to migrate to the Java chip. JavaStations can also run Windows applications on an NT server using software from Insignia Solutions or Citrix that turns NT into a timeshared central computer.

Java Virtual Machine

A Java interpreter from the JavaSoft division of Sun. It converts the Java intermediate language (byte code) into machine language one line at a time and then executes it. The Java Virtual Machine is licensed to software companies that incorporate it into their browsers and server software. Since it is used on all major platforms, Java programs run in "virtually" every computer. Microsoft also calls its Java interpreter a Java Virtual Machine. See *Java*.

Javelin Plus

A spreadsheet for DOS that can simulate multidimensional views of data. Introduced in 1985 by Javelin Software, it was more a modeling program than a spreadsheet and was the forerunner of today's OLAP databases, which are inherently designed for multiple dimensions. It was later acquired by Information Resources, Inc. and Javelin Plus 3.5 in 1993 was the last version marketed. The technology, along with IRI's Express software, was acquired by Oracle in 1995.

jaybod

See *JBOD*.

Jaz disk

A high-capacity removable hard disk system from Iomega. Introduced in late 1995, Iomega startled the industry with its breakthrough price of $99 for a 1GB removable disk cartridge. The Jaz has been very popular. In 1997, 2GB drives were introduced, which support 1GB and 2GB cartridges. See *latest disk drives*. For a summary of all storage technologies, see *storage*.

Jaz Cartridge
Iomega introduced its 1GB cartridge at 10 cents per megabyte in late 1995, which was a breakthrough price for that year.

JBOD

(Just a Bunch Of Disks) A group of hard disks in a computer that are not set up as any type of RAID configuration. They are just a bunch of disks.

JCL

(Job Control Language) A command language for mini and mainframe operating systems that launches applications. It specifies priority, program size and running sequence, as well as the files and databases used.

JDBC

(Java DataBase Connectivity) A programming interface that lets Java applications access a database via the SQL language. Since Java interpreters (Java Virtual Machines) are available for all major client platforms, this allows a platform-independent database application to be written. JDBC is the Java counterpart of Microsoft's ODBC.

J/Direct

(Java/Direct) An extension to Microsoft's Java Virtual Machine that lets Java programs access Windows routines directly. Java programs talk to the Win32 API.

JDK

(Java Development Kit) A software development environment from JavaSoft for writing Java applications. Each new version of the JDK adds features and enhancements to the language. When Java programs are developed under the new version, the Java interpreter (Java Virtual Machine) that executes them must also be updated to that same version.

JEDEC

(Joint Electronic Device Engineering Council) An international body that sets integrated circuit standards.

JEIDA

(Japanese Electronic Industry Development Association) A Japanese trade and standards organization. JEIDA joined with PCMCIA to standardize the PC card in 1991. The PC card specifications JEIDA 4.1 and PCMCIA 2.0 are the same.

JES

(Job Entry Subsystem) Software that provides batch communications for IBM's MVS operating system. It accepts data from remote batch terminals, executes them on a priority basis and transmits the results back to the terminals. The JES counterpart in VM is called RSCS.

Jet

(Joint Engine Technology) The database engine used in Microsoft Access and which accompanies Visual Basic and C++. Jet is typically used for storing data in the client machine. Developers using Access and Visual Basic access Jet via the DAO/Jet interface, which is a COM object. See *DAO*.

JetSend

A technology from HP that provides direct communications between network devices, such as cameras, scanners and printers, that is independent of any servers or applications. JetSend uses IP addressing over the Internet or an intranet.

jewel box, jewel case

The plastic container used to package an audio CD or CD-ROM disc. See *tray card*.

JFC

(Java Foundation Classes) A class library from Sun that provides an application framework and graphical user interface (GUI) routines for Java programmers. Sun, Netscape, IBM and others contributed to JFC, which combines Sun's Abstract Windowing Toolkit (AWT) and Netscape's Foundation Classes (IFC). See *AFC, IFC* and *AWT*.

JFIF

See *JPEG*.

JFS
See *journaled file system* and *Joliet file system*.

jiff
See *GIF*.

JIT compiler
(Just-In-Time compiler) A compiler that converts all the source code into machine code just before the program is run. In the case of Java, JIT compilers convert Java's intermediate language (byte code) into native code. See *Java* for illustration.

jitter
A flickering transmission signal or display image.

J-lead
A pin on a chip package that extends down and around under the housing like a reverse "J." J-leads are used on SOJs chips. See *SOJ* and *gull-wing lead*.

JMAPI
(Java Management API) A programming interface from Sun for managing network and systems via the Web. It uses the Common Information Model (CIM) schema for storing information about the node. See *WBEM*.

JNI
(Java Native Interface) A programming interface (API) in Sun's Java Virtual machine used for calling native platform elements such as GUI routines. RNI (Raw Native Interface) is the JNI counterpart in Microsoft's Java Virtual Machine.

job
A unit of work running in the computer. A job may be a single program or a group of programs that work together.

job categories
See *salary survey*. Also review the Job categories lesson.

job class
The descriptive category of a job that is based on the computer resources it requires when running.

job control language, job management language
See *JCL*.

job processing
Handling and processing jobs in the computer.

job queue
The lineup of programs ready to be executed.

job scheduling
In a large computer, establishing a job queue to run a sequence of programs over any period of time such as a single shift, a full day, etc.

job stream
A series of related programs that are run in a prescribed order. The output of one program is the input to the next program and so on.

Joe
(Java Objects Everywhere) A CORBA-compliant ORB from Sun. It allows a Java-compliant Web browser or network computer running a Java operating system to have access to CORBA objects in a network. See *CORBA* and *RMI*.

join

In relational database management, to match one table (file) against another based on some condition creating a third table with data from the matching tables. For example, a customer table can be joined with an order table creating a table for all customers who purchased a particular product.

The default type of join is known as an "inner" join. It produces a resulting record if there is a matching condition. For example, matching shipments with receipts would produce only those shipments that have been received. On the other hand, an "outer" join using that example would create a record for every shipment whether or not it was received. The data for received items would be attached to the shipments, and empty, or null, fields would be attached to shipments without receipts.

Joliet file system

An extension to the ISO 9660 file format used on CD-ROMs that supports Windows long file names. CD-ROMs using this format cannot be read by DOS, Windows 3.x and Mac machines.

Josephson junction

An ultra-fast switching technology that uses superconductor materials, originally conceived by Brian Josephson. Circuits are immersed in liquid helium to obtain near-absolute zero degrees required for operation. Switching takes place in a few picoseconds. Although Josephson junctions have not materialized for computer circuits, they have been used thus far in medical instruments that sense brain waves.

joule

A unit of energy equal to 10,000,000 ergs. Surge protectors are often given joule ratings, but this refers only to the amount of energy they can absorb, not what gets through.

journal

Same as *log*.

journaled file system

A file system that contains its own backup and recovery capability. Before indexes on disk are updated, the information about the changes is recorded in a log. If a power or other system failure corrupts the indexes as they are being rewritten, the operating system can use the log to repair them when the system is restarted.

journaling

Keeping track of events by recording them in a journal, or log.

JOVIAL

(Jules' Own Version of the International Algebraic Language) An ALGOL-like programming language developed by Systems Development Corp. in the early 1960s and widely used in the military. Its key architect was Jules Schwartz.

joy stick

A pointing device used to move an object on screen in any direction. It employs a vertical rod mounted on a base with one or two buttons. Joy sticks are used extensively in video games and in some CAD systems.

PRODUCT FILE

A006	Suit
A050	Suit
B205	Hat
C200	Coat
D300	Shoes

SALES FILE

05-23-95 004543 B205
07-30-95 004543 A050
10-01-95 004543 D300

RESULT

05-23-95 004543 B205	Hat
07-30-95 004543 A050	Suit
10-01-95 004543 D300	Shoes

A Simple Join
This example matches the sales table against the product table based on product number to derive the product description.

JPEG

(Joint Photographic Experts Group) Pronounced "jay-peg." An ISO/ITU standard for compressing still images that is becoming very popular due to its high compression capability. Using discrete cosine transform, it provides lossy compression (you lose some data from the original image) with ratios up to 100:1 and higher.

It depends on the image, but ratios of 10:1 to 20:1 may provide little noticeable loss. The more the loss can be tolerated, the more the image can be compressed. Compression is achieved by dividing the picture into tiny pixel blocks, which are halved over and over until the ratio is achieved.

JPEG is implemented in software and hardware, with the latter providing sufficient speed for realtime, on-the-fly compression. C-Cube Microsystems introduced the first JPEG chip.

JPEG++ is an extension to JPEG from Storm Technology, Mountain View, CA, that allows picture areas to be selectable for different ratios. For example, the background could be compressed higher than the foreground image.

JPEG uses the JPEG File Interchange Format, or JFIF. File extensions are .JPG or .JFF. M-JPEG and MPEG are variations of JPEG used for full-motion digital video. See *MPEG*.

JRMI

(Java RMI) See *RMI*.

JRP

(Joint Requirements Planning) Systems planning performed cooperatively by a team of users and technicians. Functions should be prioritized and related to the organization's goals and business opportunities.

Jscript

(JavaSCRIPT) Microsoft's implementation of JavaScript. Jscript is built into Internet Explorer. See *VB Script*.

JSQL

(Java SQL) An implementation of the SQL query language for database applications written in Java. It provides a common way of using SQL from within Java to access a database.

JTAG

(Joint Test Action Group) An IEEE standard for boundary scan technology. See *scan technology*.

JTC1

(Joint Technical Committee 1) See *ISO*.

Jughead

An Internet utility used to search for a keyword throughout all levels of a Gopher menu. With Jughead, you do not have to jump from one menu level to the next.

jukebox

A storage device for multiple sets of CD-ROMs, tape cartridges or disk modules. Using carousels, robot arms and other methods, a jukebox physically moves the storage medium from its assigned location to an optical or magnetic station for reading and writing. Access between modules usually takes several seconds.

Julian date

The representation of month and day by a consecutive number starting with Jan. 1. For example, Feb. 1 is Julian 32. Dates are converted into Julian dates for calculation.

jump

Same as *goto*.

jumper

The simplest form of an on/off switch. It is just a tiny, plastic-covered metal block, which is pushed onto two pins to close that circuit. It is used to select myriads of functions on a printed circuit board or on a peripheral device. For example, on a PC, jumpers are used to select I/O addresses and IRQs. On an IDE drive, a jumper selects between master and slave. A jumper can be used in place of a more costly DIP switch. See *jumperless*. See illustration on next page.

Computer Desktop Encyclopedia

jumperless

Without the use of jumpers. It means that configuration settings on the hardware are done via software rather than by setting jumpers. See *jumper*.

junction

The point at which two elements make contact. In a transistor, a junction is the point where an N-type material makes contact with a P-type material.

junk e-mail

Transmitting e-mail to unsolicited recipients. U.S. federal law 47USC227 prohibits broadcasting junk faxes and e-mail, allowing recipients to sue the sender in Small Claims Court for $500 per copy.

junk faxes

Transmitting faxes to unsolicited recipients. U.S. federal law 47USC227 prohibits broadcasting junk faxes and e-mail, allowing recipients to sue the sender in Small Claims Court for $500 per copy.

junk mail

See *junk e-mail* and *junk faxes*.

Juno

(Juno Online Services, L.P., www.juno.com, 800 654-JUNO) A free, advertiser-supported e-mail service that provides you with an Internet e-mail address. Your mail must be accessed with the Juno software via a dial-up connection to the Juno computer. See *Internet e-mail services*.

justification

In typography, the alignment of text evenly between left and right margins. Contrast with *ragged right*.

justify

(1) To shift the contents of a field or register to the right or left.

(2) To align text evenly between left and right margins.

just-in-time compiler

See *JIT compiler*.

JVM

See *Java Virtual Machine*.

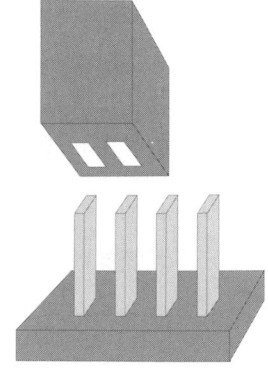

Jumper
Jumpers are used to select options on countless printed circuit boards. The more sophisticated the board, the fewer the jumpers. Having no jumpers is best if changes have to be made by the user, otherwise the board has to be pulled out of the case.

K

K

See *kilo*.

K&R C

(**K**ernighan and **R**itchie **C**) A version of C defined by Brian Kernighan and Dennis Ritchie that preceded the ANSI standard.

K5

A Pentium-class CPU chip from AMD. K5 chips are available in models that rival a 166MHz Pentium chip.

K56Flex

See *V.90*.

K6

A Pentium II-class CPU chip from AMD. The first models were introduced in 1997 at 166MHz, 200MHz and 233MHz clock speeds. The K6 chip contains the MMX instruction set used in Pentium MMX and Pentium II CPUs and plugs into the Socket 7 processor socket on Pentium motherboards. The K6 was originally engineered by NexGen, which AMD acquired in 1966.

Katmai

See *future Intel chips* and *MMX*.

Kb, Kbit; KB, KByte

See *kilobit* and *kilobyte*.

Kbits/sec, Kbps, Kb/s; Kbytes/sec, KBps, KB/s

(**K**ilo**B**its **P**er **S**econd; **K**ilo**B**ytes **P**er **S**econd) One thousand bits per second; one thousand bytes per second. Using lower case "b" for bit and upper case "B" for byte is not always followed and often misprinted. See *kilo* and *space/time*.

Kensington lock

A security system from Kensington Microware, Ltd, San Mateo, CA, (www.kensington, com) that discourages the theft of portable computers and other devices. Formally known as the Universal Notebook Security Cable, the locking slot for this cable is built into many notebook computers. The cable is looped through some permanent object in the room, then looped through itself and locked into the slot.

Kerberos

A security system developed at MIT that authenticates users. It does not provide authorization to services or databases; it establishes identity at logon, which is used throughout the session.

Kermit

An asynchronous file transfer protocol developed at Columbia University, noted for its accuracy over noisy lines. Several extensions exist, including SuperKermit, a full-duplex, sliding window version. Kermit is popular on minis and mainframes and can also handle byte-oriented transfers over 7-bit ASCII systems.

kernel

The fundamental part of a program, typically an operating system, that resides in memory at all times and provides the basic services. It is the part of the operating system that is closest to the machine and may activate the hardware directly or interface to another software layer that drives the hardware. See *microkernel*.

kerning

In proportional spacing, the tightening of space between letters to create a visually appealing flow to the text. Letter combinations, such as WA, MW and TA, are routinely kerned for better appearance. See *tracking*.

Kerr effect

A change in rotation of light reflected off a magnetic field. The polarity of a magneto-optic bit causes the laser to shift one degree clockwise or counterclockwise.

Computer Desktop Encyclopedia 493

key

(1) A keyboard button.

(2) In *cryptography*, a numeric code that is combined in some manner with the text to encrypt it for security purposes. See *cryptography*.

(3) See *key field* and *sort key*.

KEY:Assemble

A Windows-based client/server application development system from Byteback Computer Solutions Ltd., Lower Earley, Reading, England. KEY:Assemble applications can access multiple databases, including Oracle and Sybase. Business graphics and spreadsheet capabilities can be included. KEY:Assemble was originally ObjectView from Knowledgeware, which was acquired by Sterling Software. Byteback acquired KEY:Assemble in 1998.

keyboard

A set of input keys. On terminals and personal computers, it includes the standard typewriter keys, several specialized keys and the features outlined below.

All Keyboards Are Not Equal

Keyboards feel different, and touch typists should spend a few hours with any keyboard, especially on a laptop, before purchasing it. Key placement is also important. Laptop keyboards often have awkward cursor, page up/down, home and end key placements.

keyboard buffer

A memory bank or reserved memory area that stores keystrokes until the program can accept them. It lets fast typists continue typing while the program catches up.

keyboard connector

On a PC, there are two types of keyboard connectors. The standard PC uses a 5-pin DIN plug and socket. PS/2s and laptops use a smaller 6-pin mini DIN plug and socket. See *PS/2 connector* for illustration.

keyboard controller

A circuit that monitors keystrokes and generates the required data bits when pressed.

keyboard enhancer

Same as *macro processor*.

keyboard interrupt

A signal that gets the attention of the CPU each time a key is pressed. See *interrupt*.

keyboard macro processor

See *macro processor*.

keyboard processor

See *keyboard controller* and *keyboard enhancer*.

keyboard template

A plastic card that fits over the function keys to identify each key's purpose in a particular software program.

key cap

A replaceable, top part of a keyboard key. To identify commonly-used codes, it can be replaced with a custom-printed key cap.

key click

An audible feedback provided when a key is pressed. It may be adjustable by the user.

key command

A key combination (Alt-G, Ctrl-B, Command-M, etc.) used as a command to the computer.

key driven

Any device that is activated by pressing keys.

KEY:Enterprise

Formerly Application Development Workbench (ADW) it is an integrated CASE-based application development system that runs under OS/2 from Sterling Software. It includes a variety of tools for designing and developing client/server, AS/400 and IBM mainframe applications. KEY:Enterprise was renamed COOL:Enterprise. See *COOL*.

key entry

Data entry using a keyboard.

key escrow

A security technique that places a cryptographic key into the hands of a trusted third party.

key field

A field in a record that holds unique data which identifies that record from all the other records in the file or database. Account number, product code and customer name are typical key fields. As an identifier, each key value must be unique in each record. See *sort key*.

key frame

In video compression, a frame with a complete image. See *interframe coding*.

keyframe

In computer graphics animation, a frame that indicates the beginning or end of an object in motion.

keyframe animation

Animating a graphics object by creating smooth transitions between various keyframes.

key in

To enter data by typing on a keyboard.

key management

In cryptography, the creation, transmission and maintenance of a secret key.

keypad

A small keyboard or supplementary keyboard keys; for example, the keys on a calculator or the number/cursor cluster on a computer keyboard.

keypunch

To punch holes in a punched card. Although punched cards are obsolete, some people still say "keys are punched" on a keyboard.

keypunch department

Same as *data entry department*.

keypunch machine

A punched-card data entry machine. A deck of blank cards is placed into a hopper, and, upon operator command, the machine feeds one card to a punch station. As characters are typed, a series of dies at the punch station punch the appropriate holes in the selected card column.

key recovery

The ability to uncover the secret key to a cryptographic message. See *key escrow*.

key system

See *key telephone system*.

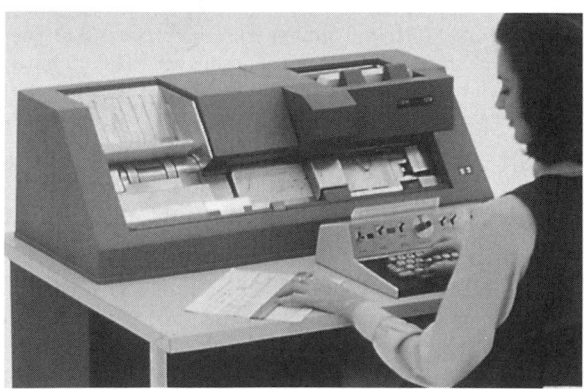

IBM Keypunch Machine
This is the type of keypunch machine that was used in the 1960s and 1970s. Tens of thousands of keypunch operators would spend a full shift keypunching orders, time cards and a host of other transactions. *(Photo courtesy of IBM Corporation.)*

key telephone system

An inhouse telephone system that is not centrally connected to a PBX. Each telephone has buttons for outside lines that can be dialed directly without having to "dial 9."

key-to-disk machine

A stand-alone data entry machine that stores data on magnetic disk for computer entry.

key-to-tape machine

A stand-alone data entry machine that stores data on magnetic tape for computer entry. Introduced by Mohawk Data Sciences in the mid 1960s, it was the first advancement in data entry since the card keypunch. Mohawk's stock went from $2 to $200 in a couple of years.

key word

See *keyword*.

keyword

(1) A word used in a text search.

(2) A word in a text document that is used in an index to best describe the contents of the document.

(3) A reserved word in a programming or command language.

Khornerstones

A benchmark program that tests CPU, I/O and floating point performance. See *benchmark*.

KHz

(KiloHertZ) One thousand cycles per second. See *horizontal scan frequency*.

kicks

See *CICS* and *CIX*.

killer app

An application that is exceptionally useful or exciting. When new operating systems are on the horizon, people wish for one or two killer apps that run under the new system in order to justify the migration effort and expense. Otherwise known as rationale.

killer bit stream

A demanding section of compressed video data. Interframe compression codes only the differences between frames, thus when there is a lot of moving objects in view, it takes more computing power to decompress the video stream.

kilo

Thousand (10 to the 3rd power). Abbreviated "K." For technical specifications, it refers to the precise value 1,024 since computer specifications are based on binary numbers. For example, 64K means 65,536 bytes when referring to memory or storage (64x1024), but a 64K salary means $64,000. The IEEE uses "K" for 1,024, and "k" for 1,000. See *binary values* and *space/time*.

kilobit

(**thousand bits**). For technical specifications, it refers to 1,024 bits. In general usage, it sometimes refers to an even one thousand bits (see *kilo*). Also Kb, Kbit and K-bit. See *space/time*.

kilobyte

(**thousand bytes**). For technical specifications, it refers to 1,024 bytes. In general usage, it sometimes refers to an even one thousand bytes (see *kilo*). Also KB, Kbyte and K-byte. See *space/time*.

kilogram

See *metric system*.

kiosk

A small, self-standing structure such as a newstand or ticket booth. Unattended multimedia kiosks dispense public information via computer screens. Either a keyboard, touch screen or both are used for input. See *self-service application*. See illustration on next page.

Klamath

The code name for the Intel *Pentium II* chip.

KLOC

(Kilo Lines Of Code) One thousand lines of programming source code. See *lines of code*.

kludge

Also spelled "kluge" and pronounced "klooj." A crude, inelegant system, component or program. It may refer to a makeshift, temporary solution to a problem as well as to any product that is poorly designed or that becomes unwieldy over time.

Knight-Ridder Information

Formerly DIALOG, an online information service that contains the world's largest collection of databases. See *online services*.

knowledge acquisition

The process of acquiring knowledge from a human expert for an expert system, which must be carefully organized into IF-THEN rules or some other form of knowledge representation.

knowledge base

A database of rules about a subject used in AI applications. See *expert system*.

knowledge based system

An AI application that uses a database of knowledge about a subject. In time, it is expected that everyday information systems will increasingly become knowledge based and provide users with more assistance than they do today. See *expert system*.

knowledge domain

A specific area of expertise of an expert system.

knowledge-driven process management

The automation of process management using a rule-based expert system that invokes the appropriate tools and supplies necessary information, checklists, examples and status reports to the user.

knowledge engineer

A person who translates the knowledge of an expert into the knowledge base of an expert system.

KnowledgeMan

An application development system for DOS, OS/2, VMS and UNIX environments from Micro Data Base Systems, Inc., Lafayette, IN, (www.mdbs.com). It includes an RDBMS, object-based 4GL programming and integrated functions, allowing, for example, database queries to update spreadsheets or results to be embedded in text documents.

knowledge representation

A method used to code knowledge in an expert system, typically a series of IF-THEN rules (IF this condition occurs, THEN take this action).

Korn shell

A command line processor for UNIX that adds extensions to the Bourne shell. It includes many C shell functions, but is supported by more versions of UNIX than C shell. See *Bourne shell, C shell* and *UNIX*.

Kovar

An inert metal alloy that does not oxidize.

Kruegerapp

A term for a downloaded application that, instead of enhancing performance, "kills" your system. The reference is to Freddy Krueger, the gruesome character from the horror series "Nightmare on Elm Street."

The Kiosk
The software in kiosks must be designed for ease of use. Touch screens make the interface simple and straightforward.

KSDS

(Keyed Sequence DataSet) A VSAM structure that uses an index to store records in available free space. Retrieval is by key field or by address. Contrast with *ESDS*.

KSR terminal

(Keyboard Send Receive terminal) Same as *teleprinter*. Contrast with *RO terminal*.

L

L10N
(L + 10 letters + N) See *localization* and *I18N*.

L1 cache, L2 cache
The internal and external memory caches. L1 caches are built into the CPU chip or packaged within the same module as the chip. L2 caches are memory chips that are external to the CPU chip. See *cache*.

L2F
(Layer 2 Forwarding) A protocol from Cisco for creating virtual private dial-up networks over the Internet. It has been combined with PPTP in the L2TP protocol. See *L2TP*.

L2TP
(Layer 2 Tunneling Protocol) A protocol from the IETF for creating virtual private networks (VPNs) over the Internet. It supports non-IP protocols such as AppleTalk and IPX as well as the IPSec security protocol. It is a combination of Microsoft's Point-to-Point Tunneling Protocol and Cisco's Layer 2 Forwarding (L2F) technology. See *VPN, PPTP* and *IPSec*.

label
(1) In data management, a made-up name that is assigned to a file, field or other data structure.

(2) In a spreadsheet, any descriptive text that is entered into a cell as a page, column or row heading.

(3) In programming, a made-up name used to identify a variable or a subroutine.

(4) In computer operations, a self-sticking form attached to the outside of a disk or tape in order to identify it.

(5) In magnetic tape files, a record used for identification at the beginning or end of the file.

label prefix
In a spreadsheet, a character typed at the beginning of a cell entry. For example, in 1-2-3, a single quote (') identifies what follows as a descriptive label even if it's a number.

ladder DAC
(ladder Digital to Analog Converter) Circuitry used to convert digital sound back into analog form for amplification. An individual resistor is associated with each bit of the digital sample, typically 16 bits. The resistors are weighted to the mathematical value of the bit they represent. The 16-bit sample is read, passed to all 16 resistors at the same time, and the sum total of the current passing through the resistors represents the analog value of the digital sample.

Ladder DACs represent a parallel conversion of the sample. See *1-bit DAC*.

LADDIS test
See *SPEC*.

lamer
A technophobic person or neophyte to computers and technology, as viewed by the technically competent who have little empathy for the novice. See *technophobic*.

LAN
(Local Area Network) A communications network that serves users within a confined geographical area. It is made up of servers, workstations, a network operating system and a communications link.

Servers are high-speed machines that hold programs and data shared by network users. The workstations (clients) are the users' personal computers, which perform stand-alone processing and access the network servers as required (see *client/server*).

Diskless and floppy-only workstations are sometimes used, which retrieve all software and data from the server. Increasingly, "thin client" network computers (NCs) and Windows terminals are also used. A printer can be attached to a workstation or to a server and be shared by network users.

Small LANs can allow certain workstations to function as a server, allowing users access to data on another user's machine. These peer-to-peer networks are often simpler to install and manage, but dedicated servers provide better performance and can handle higher transaction volume. Multiple servers are used in large networks.

The controlling software in a LAN is the network operating system (NetWare, UNIX, Windows NT, etc.) that resides in the server. A component part of the software resides in each client and allows the application to read and write data from the server as if it were on the local machine.

The message transfer is managed by a transport protocol such as TCP/IP and IPX. The physical transmission of data is performed by the access method (Ethernet, Token Ring, etc.) which is implemented in the network adapters that are plugged into the machines. The actual communications path is the cable (twisted pair, coax, optical fiber) that interconnects each network adapter. See *WAN*. See *bandwidth* for LAN transmission speeds.

LAN adapter
Same as *network adapter*.

LAN administrator
See *network administrator*.

LAN analyzer
See *network analyzer*.

land
A non-indented area on an optical medium such as a CD-ROM or DVD. Contrast with *pit*.

LANDA
(**LAN D**ealers **A**ssociation) An association that merged with NOMDA to become the Business Technology Association. See *BTA*.

landing zone
A safe non-data area on a hard disk used for parking the read/write head.

landline
Land based. Refers to standard telephone and data communications systems that use in-ground and telephone pole cables in contrast to wireless cellular and satellite services.

Landmark rating
An earlier PC performance test from Landmark Research International, Clearwater, FL, that measured CPU, video and coprocessor speed. It ran under DOS and was widely used. In 1995, Landmark was acquired by Quarterdeck.

landscape
A printing orientation that prints data across the wider side of the form. Contrast with *portrait*.

landscape monitor
A monitor that is used to display facing text pages. It is wider than it is high.

LANE, LAN emulation
The ability to connect Ethernet and Token Ring networks together via ATM. LANE makes the process transparent, requiring no modification to Ethernet and Token Ring stations. LANE allows common protocols, such

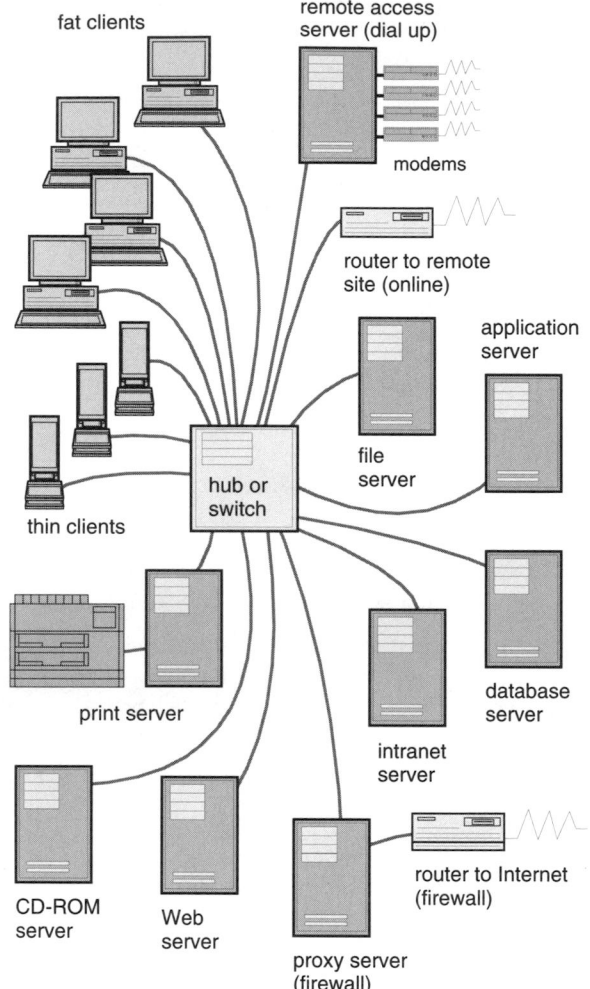

Clients and Servers in a LAN

This illustration shows one server for each type of service on a LAN. In practice, several functions can be combined in one machine and, for large volumes, multiple machines can be used to balance the traffic for the same service. For example, a large Internet Web site is often comprised of several computer systems (servers).

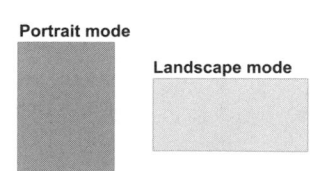

as IP, IPX, AppleTalk and DECnet, to ride over an ATM backbone.

The LANE driver provides the encapsulation of Ethernet and Token Ring packets into LANE packets and then converts them into ATM cells, reversing the function at the other end. The driver resides in an edge device which sits between the LAN and the ATM switch. The driver is also required in each ATM client station that communicates with Ethernet and Token Ring.

LANE is also used to create emulated LANs (ELANs) that logically combine users by workgroup traffic (ELANs are the same as VLANs). With LANE, broadcast domains can be larger than with other network technologies, because LANE can manage broadcast traffic within ELANs and keep it under control.

LANE is implemented in an ATM switch or stand-alone server and is made up of two software components: the LANE Configuration Server (LECS), which provides address resolution, and the Broadcast and Unknown Server (BUS), which manages multicast and broadcast traffic within the ELAN.

The ATM Forum governs the LANE User-to-Network Interface (LUNI), which defines how an end station communicates with the ATM network.

With LANE, in order to communicate between one subnet and another, a router is required. This is eliminated with MPOA. See *MPOA*.

LAN Hardware

OSI LAYER 4 (Transport layer) and higher

GATEWAY Convert from one protocol to another.

SNA to TCP/IP
IPX/SPX to TCP/IP
SNA to DECnet, etc.

OSI LAYER 3 (Network layer)

ROUTER IP IPX SNA DECnet AppleTalk

LAN

LAN

LAN

OSI LAYERS 1 & 2 (Data link layers)

HUB
Shared
E thernet, Token Ring

SWITCH
Dedicated
Switched E thernet, Switched Token Ring, ATM

BRIDGE Segment LANs or convert between E thernet & Token Ring.

LAN segment

LAN segment

REPEATER Regenerate signals to span longer distances.

LAN segment

LAN segment

LAN fax

A fax service provided in a local area network (LAN). The LAN fax software is installed on a server and turns it into a LAN fax server. It provides a centralized service for network users to send and receive faxes.

language

A set of symbols and rules used to convey information. See *machine language, programming language, graphics language, page description language, fourth-generation language, standards* and *user interface.*

language processor

Language translation software. Programming languages, command languages, query languages, natural languages and foreign languages are all translated by software.

LAN Manager

A network operating system from Microsoft that runs as a server application under OS/2. It supports both DOS, Windows and OS/2 clients. LAN Manager was superseded by Windows NT Server, and many parts of LAN Manager are used in NT. See *LAN Server.* See also *network administrator.*

LAN Network Manager

IBM Token Ring network management software. LAN Station Manager is the workstation counterpart that collects data for LAN Network Manager.

LAN Requester

The client part of LAN Server.

LANRover

A remote access server from Shiva that provides modem and ISDN access to remote users on a network. The LANRover is a proprietary device that connects to the LAN and supports the PPP protocol as well as standard dial-up ANSI terminal connections.

LAN segment

A section of a local area network that is used by a particular workgroup or department and separated from the rest of the LAN by a bridge, router or switch. Networks are divided into multiple segments for security and to improve traffic flow by filtering out packets that are not destined for the segment. See *subnet mask*.

LAN Server

(1) A network operating system from IBM that runs as a server application under OS/2 and supports both DOS, Windows and OS/2 clients. Originally based on LAN Manager when OS/2 was jointly developed by IBM and Microsoft, starting with LAN Server 3.0, it runs only under IBM's OS/2.

LAN Server provides disk mirroring, CID capability and Network Transport Services/2 (NTS/2) for concurrent access to NetWare servers. Options are LAN Server for the Macintosh for Mac client access and System Performance/2 (SP/2), a series of network management utilities.

(2) (LAN server) Generically, a file server in a network.

LAN station

(1) A workstation in a local area network.
(2) See *LAN Network Manager*.

LAN switch

A network device that cross connects stations or LAN segments. LAN switches are available for Ethernet, Fast Ethernet, Token Ring and FDDI. A LAN switch is also known as a frame switch. ATM switches are generally considered a category by themselves.

Network switches are increasingly replacing shared media hubs in order to increase bandwidth. For example, a 16-port 10BaseT hub shares the total 10 Mbps bandwidth with all 16 attached nodes. By replacing the hub with a switch, each sender/receiver pair has the full 10 Mbps capacity. Each port on the switch can give full bandwidth to a single server or client station or it can be connected to a hub with several stations.

LANtastic

A peer-to-peer LAN operating system for DOS, Windows and OS/2 from Artisoft, Inc., Tucson, AZ, (www.artisoft.com). It supports Ethernet, ARCNET and Token Ring adapaters as well as its own twisted-pair adapater at two Mbits/sec. LANtastic was very popular in the days of DOS.

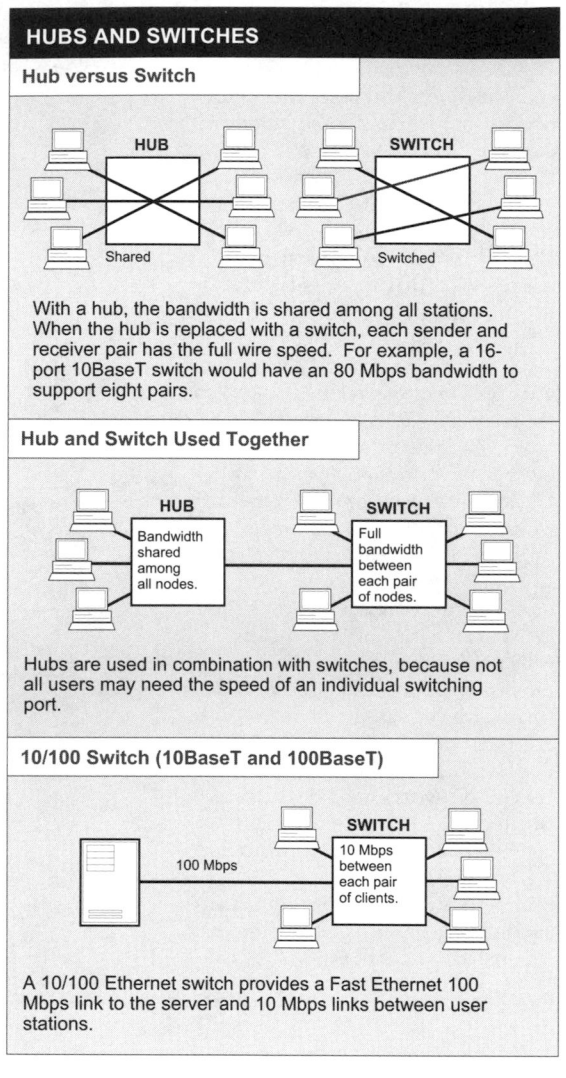

HUBS AND SWITCHES

Hub versus Switch

With a hub, the bandwidth is shared among all stations. When the hub is replaced with a switch, each sender and receiver pair has the full wire speed. For example, a 16-port 10BaseT switch would have an 80 Mbps bandwidth to support eight pairs.

Hub and Switch Used Together

HUB — Bandwidth shared among all nodes.

SWITCH — Full bandwidth between each pair of nodes.

Hubs are used in combination with switches, because not all users may need the speed of an individual switching port.

10/100 Switch (10BaseT and 100BaseT)

100 Mbps

SWITCH — 10 Mbps between each pair of clients.

A 10/100 Ethernet switch provides a Fast Ethernet 100 Mbps link to the server and 10 Mbps links between user stations.

LAN Workplace

A family of software products from Novell that allows DOS, Windows, Macintosh and OS/2 clients in a NetWare environment to access resources on a TCP/IP network. LAN Workplace for DOS can also encapsulate NetWare protocols and run NetWare-dependent applications entirely within a TCP/IP network.

LAP

(Link Access Procedure) An ITU family of error correction protocols originally derived from the HDLC standard.

```
LAP-B (Balanced)      Used in X-25 networks.
LAP-D (D channel)     Used in ISDN data channel.
LAP-M (Modem)         V.42 (uses some LAP-D methods and adds additional ones)
LAP-X (Half-dupleX)   Used in ship to shore transmission.
```

LapLink

A file transfer program for DOS, Windows and the Mac from Traveling Software, Inc., Bothell, WA, (www.travsoft.com). This veteran product has been so widely used that people often refer to "laplinking" as a general term for file transfer. LapLink Mac transfers files between PCs and Macs. See *LapLink cable* and *how to transfer a file*.

LapLink cable

A serial cable used to connect two computers together for file transfer. This type of cable is technically a *null modem cable*, but is often called a LapLink cable due to the popularity of the LapLink program. The LapLink cable simulates two modems using the telephone system. It crosses the receiving line with the sending line. A special parallel port cable is also available for higher transfer speeds.

laptop computer

A portable computer that has a flat screen and usually weighs less than a dozen pounds. It uses AC power and/or batteries. Most have connectors for an external monitor and keyboard transforming them into desktop computers. Most laptop computers today fall in the notebook computer category (see list below). Following are the major features of a laptop.

Keyboard
Keyboard layout is often sacrificed. The Home, End, PageUp and PageDn keys may not be dedicated keys, requiring that you hold down the Fn key in conjunction with them. This is cumbersome.

Function keys and cursor keys are often made smaller. There's only one rule— test drive the keyboard carefully.

Screen Quality
Active matrix LCD screens (TFT) provide a sharper image and wider viewing angle than dual scan or HPA passive matrix.

Screen Resolution & Acceleration
Unlike a desktop computer, you cannot replace the display adapter for one with a higher resolution. The built-in display system also feeds an external monitor, so be sure it has the maximum resolution you require.

External Display & Keyboard Connectors
Connect a full-size CRT and keyboard for home/office. Even if you like your laptop keyboard, you may want to use an external keyboard with your external monitor, because the laptop screen usually doesn't lie back flat to get out of the way from straight-on viewing of the external monitor.

A full-size keyboard can be connected through the external keyboard connector on most laptops. Keyboards can be attached to earlier laptops with an adapter via the serial or parallel port.

Built-in Pointing Device
There are a wide variety of pointing devices built into laptops, including trackballs and tracksticks,

but each one has a different feel. Try it first. The best option is always an external mouse port that lets you connect your favorite desktop mouse if the built-in device becomes cumbersome.

Expansion

Expansion is critical on a laptop. All laptops have PC Card (PCMCIA) slots, and newer laptops have USB ports. For desktop use, a docking station may provide ISA or PCI slots.

Auto Resume

Lets you return to the computer and pick up where you left off without having to reload your applications.

Batteries

Nickel hydride and lithium ion batteries do not suffer from the "memory effect" of older nickel cadmium batteries. Check out battery life and weight.

Removable Hard Disk

A removable hard drive is the best bet. If you run out of space, you can replace the old disk with a larger one.

One of the First Laptops

In 1983, Tandy's Radio Shack division launched the Model 100 Micro Executive Workstation. It weighed only four pounds and included a built-in word processor, name and address list as well as a modem. The Model 100 was inspiration for the huge portable market that followed. *(Photo courtesy of Tandy Corporation.)*

Multimedia

All laptops today have built-in sound, speakers and CD-ROMs that are either built in or swappable with the floppy drive.

Weight

Seven pounds doesn't sound like much until you lug it around all day. Some subnotebooks use an external floppy disk to reduce poundage. Also, check the transformer weight (also called the AC adapter or power adapter). They never mention this, but it can add one or two pounds, and it is an item you will always carry with you for emergency. Following is a rough guide to current-day weights:

Type	Weight (in pounds without transformer)
Laptop	4-18
Notebook	4-7
Subnotebook	2-4
Pocket	1

large-format printer

See *wide-format printer*.

laser

(Light Amplification from the Stimulated Emission of Radiation) A device that creates a very uniform light that can be precisely focused. It generates a single wavelength or narrow band of wavelengths and is used in applications such as communications, printing and disk storage. Unlike the transmission of electricity, transmission of light pulses over optical fibers is not affected by nearby electrical interferences. See *LED*.

The Laser Discovery

In 1957, the laser was conceived by Gordon Gould, a graduate student in physics at Columbia University. When Gould filed for patents in 1959, he found that Columbia professor Charles Townes and Arthur Schawlow of Bell Labs had already filed for them. The year before, AT&T had, in fact, demonstrated a working laser at Bell Labs. In 1977, after years of litigation, a court awarded Gould rights to the first of three patents and later to all of them. He finally reaped millions in royalties.

laser-class printer

A category of computer printers that produces output with the same resolution and color quality of a laser printer. Output from LED, solid ink, dye sublimation and Iris printers is in the same class as laser printers.

LaserDisc

An optical disk used for full-motion video. In the 1970s, various videodisc systems were introduced, but only the Philips LaserVision survived. LaserDiscs have been used for interactive training as well as for home theater, where its higher resolution is noticeable on larger screens.

For the most part, CD-ROMs have replaced LaserDiscs for training, and it is expected that DVDs will replace the LaserDisc as well as VHS tape for movies. Most LaserDiscs are 12" in diameter, and an 8" version is also used.

Movies use the CLV (constant linear velocity) format, which records the signal on a continuous, spiraling track. Each side contains 108,000 frames for one hour of video. For interactive training and games, the CAV (constant angular velocity) format is used, similar to hard disks. Tracks are concentric circles, each containing one video frame. There are 54,000 frames for 30 minutes of video per side.

Early LaserDiscs recorded analog sound. Today, most LaserDiscs contain analog and digital soundtracks, and newer players default to the digital sound if available. Some players let the user select the soundtrack, allowing multiple languages and other annotations to be included on the same disc.

LaserJet

A family of desktop laser printers from HP. Introduced in 1984 at $3,495, the first LaserJet revolutionized the desktop laser printer market. LaserJets print at 600 dpi, and PCL is the printer command language.

LaserJets accept bitmapped fonts from the computer (soft fonts) and from plug-in cartridges, which were popular on the earlier models. Built-in Intellifont scalable fonts were included starting with the LaserJet III (PCL Version 5).

PostScript capability became available starting with the Series II in the form of plug-in cartridges from HP and others. Native PostScript models were introduced with the LaserJet 4.

In 1994, HP launched its first LaserJet in color at $7295. It prints color at 2 ppm and 10 ppm in black and white. In 1996, the second color model, the HP Color LaserJet 5, raised the speed to 3

The First LaserJet
In 1984, the first LaserJet was introduced at a retail price of $3,495. Although noisier than today's models, its ruggedness and reliability launched a revolution in desktop laser printing. *(Photo courtesy of Hewlett-Packard Company.)*

ppm and dropped the price to $5995, which was subsequently lowered to $3995. The Color printer uses an enhanced PCL 5 language, and PostScript Level 2 is optional.

laser printer

A printer that uses a laser and the electrophotographic method to print a full page at a time. Laser printers are often called *page printers* or *electronic printers*. The laser is used to "paint" a charged drum with light, to which toner is applied and then transferred onto paper (see *electrophotographic* for more details). Desktop laser printers use cut sheets like a copy machine. Large machines use cut sheets or paper rolls that are cut after printing.

In 1975, IBM introduced the first laser printer, the model 3800. Later, Siemens introduced the ND 2 and Xerox came out with the 9700. These self-contained printing presses were online to a mainframe or offline, accepting print image data on tape or disk.

In 1984, HP introduced the LaserJet, the first desktop laser printer, which rapidly became a huge success and a major part of the company's business. Desktop lasers obsoleted the clackety daisy wheel printers, but they did not eliminate dot matrix printers, which are still widely used for labels and multipart forms.

Low-end, personal laser printers print in the 4 to 8 ppm range, and prices have fallen below $200 for entry-level units. Typical office or workgroup units print 12 to 24 ppm, and models run from $1,000 to $6,000 and more. HP is the major vendor, and many quality companies compete aggressively such as Lexmark, IBM and Okidata.

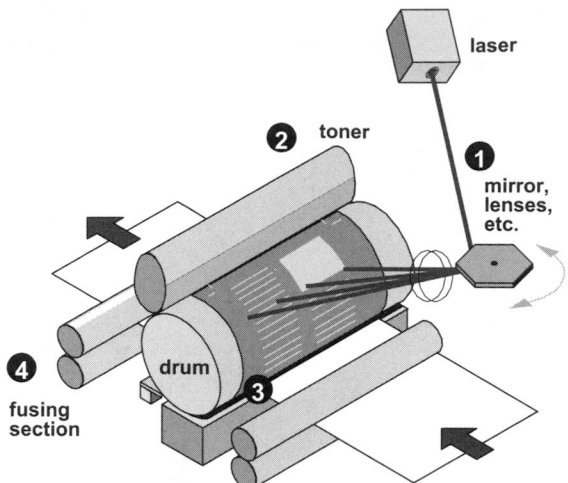

The Laser Mechanism
The laser printer uses electrostatic charges to (1) create an image on the drum, (2) adhere toner to the image, (3) transfer the toned image to the paper, and (4) fuse the toner to the paper. The laser creates the image by "painting" a negative of the page to be printed on the charged drum. Where light falls, the charge is dissipated, leaving a positive image to be printed.

Mid-range units print in the 40-60 ppm range, with a large jump to high-end printers that print from 150 to more than 700 ppm and can cost $100,000 and up.

The resolution of laser printers is from 300 to 1200 dpi, although 600 dpi has pretty much become the low side. Specialty printers can go as high as imagesetters in the 2400 dpi range.

Color laser printers are considerably slower than monochrome lasers, typically in the 2 to 6 ppm range. In 1997, desktop color lasers broke the $3000 level, and prices are expected to be $2000 within a couple of years. IBM's high-end 3170 printer jumps in speed to 70 duplexed color pages per minute. Such "digital printing presses" produce finished booklets and manuals and cost upwards of $250,000. See *digital printing*.

Laser printers are increasingly offering paper handling functions found on copy machines such as collation, stapling and 3-hole punching. Some models can accomodate wide paper.

There are several printer technologies that fall into a "laser-class printer" category, which produce the same quality as a laser printer, but do not actually use a laser. For example, LED printers use an array of LEDs to beam the image onto the drum. Electron beam imaging (ion deposition) beams the image with electricity rather than light, and solid ink printers propel a waxlike ink onto the drum.

LaserWriter

A family of desktop laser printers from Apple, introduced in 1985. Most models support PostScript and built-in networking.

last mile

The connection between the customer and the telephone or cable company. The last mile is made of copper-based telephone wire or coaxial cable. See *local loop*.

LAT

(Local Area Transport) A communications protocol from Digital for controlling terminal traffic in a DECnet environment.

LATA

(Local Access and Transport Area) The geographic region set up to differentiate local and long distance telephone calls. Any telephone call between parties within a LATA is handled by the local telephone company.

latch

An electronic circuit that maintains one of two states. See *flip-flop*.

late binding

Same as *dynamic binding*.

latency

The time between initiating a request for data and the beginning of the actual data transfer. On a disk, latency is the time it takes for the selected sector to come around and be positioned under the read/write head. Channel latency is the time it takes for a computer channel to become unoccupied in order to transfer data. Network latency is the delay introduced when a packet is momentarily stored, analyzed and then forwarded.

latent image

An invisible image typically of electrical charges. For example, in a copy machine, a latent image of the page to be copied is created on a plate or drum as an electrical charge.

latest disk drives

New disk storage technologies appear all the time. The latest ones follow.

```
Quest disk       ORB disk       Jaz disk
SparQ disk       Click! disk    Zip disk
HiFD disk        a:drive        SyJet disk
Shark disk       SuperDisk      EZFlyer disk
```

On the Horizon

Terastor, Inc., and the Quinta Division of Seagate are developing next-generation disk technologies. Terastor's Near Field Recording (NFR) and Quinta's Optically Assisted Winchester (OAW) are combination magnetic and optical drives that are expected to provide a quantum leap in storage density at hard disk speeds and provide the technology that will take us well into the next century.

Terastor and Quinta both use concepts that are similar to a magneto-optic (MO) disk, which has been a very robust storage technology for the past several years. Like MO, both systems employ a laser for reading the bit and assisting in writing the bit. For writing, the laser heats the magnetic bit to the Curie point so that its polarity can be changed. For reading, the laser is reflected through the bit, which rotates the beam based on its polarity. Also like MO, the bits are recorded vertically rather than longitudinally.

Unlike MO, which places the laser and magnet on opposite sides of the platter, Terastor and Quinta are putting optical and magnetic elements together on a flying head similar to a magnetic disk. But, the heads fly higher over the platter, allowing cheaper, less-precise plastic media to be used instead of alumunum and glass, which is common on hard disks.

The actual optical technologies differ quite a bit between the two companies. Terastor uses a patented Solid Immersion Lens (SIL) from Stanford University that focuses the laser beam down to a tiny spot, while Quinta uses a fiber to direct the light to a rotating, microelectromechanical (MEMS) mirror. Quinta claims the MEMS mirror allows track densities of 100,000 tpi rather than the 10,000 tpi of today's hard disks (DVD-RAM disks exceed 32,000 tpi).

There are other differences, too. For details, visit www.terastor.com and www.seagate.com/quinta.html. As far as product goes, Terastor claims to have a removable, 5.25" 20GB drive in production by early 1999 that costs the same as a 2GB Jaz disk. It can be used stand-alone or as an MO drive replacement in jukeboxes, in which case it would give an 8-times storage boost to a library's capacity. Quinta is aimed at the fixed disk market with a product expected by the end of 1998.

LaTeX

(LAmport TeX) A document preparation system based on the TeX language developed by Leslie Lamport at SRI International. LaTex lets the user concentrate on the logical structure of the document rather than the format codes.

launch

To cause a program to load and run. Contrast with *exit*.

laws

See *Amdahl's law, Brook's law, Freedman's law, Metcalfe's law, Moore's law* and *Nacchio's law*.

layer

(1) In computer graphics, one of several on-screen "drawing boards" for creating elements within a picture. Layers can be manipulated independently, and the sum of all layers make up the total image.

(2) In communications, a protocol that interacts with other protocols to provide all the necessary transmission services. See *OSI*.

layer 2

In networking, the communications protocol that contains the physical address of a client or server station. It is called the *data link layer* or *MAC layer* and contains the address inspected by a bridge or switch. Layer 2 processing is faster than layer 3 processing, because less analysis of the packet is required. See *MAC layer* and *OSI*.

layer 2 switch

A network device that forwards traffic based on MAC layer (Ethernet or Token Ring) addresses. See *LAN switch* and *layer 3 switch*.

layer 3

In networking, the communications protocol that contains the logical address of a client or server station. It is called the network layer and contains the address (IP, IPX, etc.) inspected by a router that forwards it through the network. Layer 3 contains a type field so that traffic can be prioritized and forwarded based on message type as well as network destination. Since layer 3 provides more filtering capabilities, it also adds more overhead than layer 2 processing. See *layer 3 switch, router* and *OSI*.

layer 3 switch

A network device that forwards traffic based on layer 3 information at very high speeds. Traditionally, routers, which inspect layer 3, have been considerably slower than layer 2 switches. In order to increase routing speeds, many "cut-through" techniques have been used, which perform an "inspect the first packet at layer 3 and send the rest at layer 2" type of processing. Ipsilon's IP Switch and Cabletron's SecureFast switches were pioneers in cut-through switching; however, the MPLS protocol is expected to standardize this technique.

As more routing lookup functions are moved from software into the ASIC chips, layer 3 switches can inspect each packet just like a router at high speed without using proprietary cut-through methods. If a layer 3 switch supports packet-by-packet inspection and supports routing protocols, it is called a *routing switch* or *switch router*, which simply means "fast router."

The more deeply a packet is examined, the more forwarding decisions can be made based upon type of traffic, quality of service and so on. To get to this information means digging into the packet's headers to ferret out the data, which takes processing time. To understand how the packets are formed, see *TCP/IP abc's*. The following shows what is examined at each layer. See *layer 3, layer 2 switch* and *virtual LAN*.

```
               Forwarding decision
     Layer     Based on            Examples
       2       MAC address         Ethernet, Token Ring, etc.
       3       Network address     IP, IPX, etc.
       3       Service quality     IP, IPX, etc.
       3       Application         IPX socket
       4       Application         IP socket
```

layer 4

See *transport protocol*.

layer 4 switch

A network device that integrates routing and switching by forwarding traffic at layer 2 speed using layer 4 and layer 3 information. When packets are inspected at layer 4, the sockets can be analyzed and decisions can be made based on the type of application being serviced. See *layer 3 switch*.

layers

In a CAD, drawing or image editing program, the ability to maintain elements on separate "canvases" for greater control and enhanced editing. Layers provide different capabilities depending on the program. For example, paint and image editing programs deal with bitmapped images, which are matrices of pixels. When one element is finally placed on top of another, it cannot be removed without leaving a blank space in its stead. When such programs use layers, elements can be freely moved under and over each other, because each complete, original element is maintained within its own layer. A composite of the layers is used as a final image, but the original layered images can always be maintained for further editing.

CAD and drawing programs automatically allow any number of graphic elements to be placed on top of or below others. However, such programs also use layers to separate groups of related elements so that elements in one layer can be easily worked on together. For example, all the elements in a layer can be quickly selected and changed without affecting the rest of the drawing.

lazy write

Refers to the effect caused by using a write back cache. Data is written to the cache first and, later, during idle machine cycles, is written to disk if it is a disk cache or to memory if it is a CPU cache.

LBA

(Logical Block Addressing) A method used to support IDE hard disks larger than 504MB (528,482,304 bytes) on PCs. LBA provides the necessary address conversion in the BIOS to support drives up to 8GB. BIOSs after mid 1994, which are sometimes called Enhanced BIOSs, generally provide LBA conversion. LBA support is required for compatibility with the FAT32 directory.

LBRV

(Low Bit Rate Voice) A voice sampling technique that analyzes each 15-30 millisecond speech segment independently and converts it into a 30-byte frame.

LCC

See *leadless chip carrier, CLCC* and *PLCC*.

LCD

(Liquid Crystal Display) A display technology that uses rod-shaped molecules (liquid crystals) that flow like liquid and bend light. Unenergized, the crystals direct light through two polarizing filters, allowing a natural background color to show. When energized, they redirect the light to be absorbed in one of the polarizers, causing the dark appearance of crossed polarizers to show. The more the molecules are twisted, the better the contrast and viewing angle.

Because it takes less power to move molecules than to energize a light-emitting device, LCDs replaced LEDs in digital watches years ago. The LCD was developed in 1963 at RCA's Sarnoff Research Center in Princeton, NJ. The different types of LCDs follow.

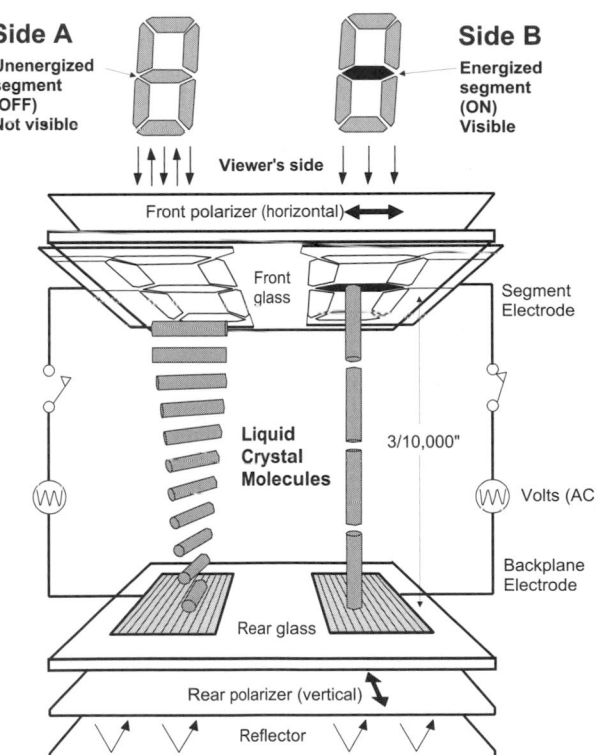

Twisted-Nematic Liquid Crystal Display

On side A, the unenergized segment causes the crystals to line up with the front and rear polarizers. The segment appears light gray, which is actually the light travelling down and reflected back up the crystals.

On side B, the energized segment causes the crystals to become perpendicular to the polarizers. The segment appears dark, which is the effect of crossed polarizers. Most LCDs use a translucent reflector with light behind it, which makes the background brighter and the characters sharper. *(Redrawn from illustration courtesy of LXD, Inc.)*

Passive Display (TN and STN)

Called "passive matrix" when used for computer screens and "passive display" when used for small readouts, all the active electronics (transistors) are outside of the display screen. Passive displays have improved immensely, but do not provide a wide viewing angle, and submarining is noticeable. The passive display types are:

TN - Twisted Nematic - 90° twist
Low-cost displays for consumer products and instruments. Black on gray/silver background.

STN - Supertwisted Nematic- 180-270° twist
Used extensively on laptops for mono and color displays. DSTN and FSTN provide improvements over straight STN.

> 180 ° - green/blue on yellow background
> 270 ° - blue on white/blue background

Dual Scan STN
Improves STN display by dividing the screen into two halves and scanning each half simultaneously, doubling the number of lines refreshed. Not as sharp as active matrix.

Active Display (TFT)

Typically used for laptop color screens and, increasingly, for flat desktop screens. Known as "active matrix" displays, transistors are built into each pixel within the screen. For example, 640x480 color VGA screen requires 921,600 transistors; one for each red, green and blue dot. Provides a sharp, clear image with good contrast and eliminates submarining, but fabrication costs are high. Uses a 90° (TN) twist. Also called *TFT LCD* (thin film transistor LCD).

Reflective vs Backlit

Reflective screens used in many consumer appliances and some lightweight laptops require external light and only work well in a bright room or with a desk lamp. Backlit and sidelit screens have their own light source and work well in dim lighting.

LCD panel, LCD projector

Also called a *projection panel*, it is a data projector that accepts computer output and displays it on a see-through liquid crystal screen that is placed on top of an overhead projector. See *data projector*.

LCD printer

An electrophotographic printer that uses a single light source directed by liquid crystal shutters.

LD

See *LaserDisc*.

LDAP

(**L**ightweight **D**irectory **A**ccess **P**rotocol) A protocol used to access a directory listing. LDAP support is being implemented in Web browsers and e-mail programs, which can query an LDAP-compliant directory. It is expected that LDAP will provide a common method for searching e-mail addresses on the Internet, eventually leading to a global white pages.

LDAP is a simplified version of the DAP protocol, which is used to gain access to X.500 directories. It is easier to code the query in LDAP than in DAP, but LDAP is less comprehensive. For example, DAP can initiate searches on other servers if an address is not found, while LDAP cannot in its initial specification.

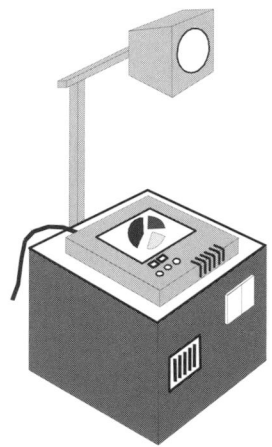

LCD Panel
An LCD panel requires an overhead projector. LCD systems are also available with their own light source. Such units generally provide the best quality, because the light and lenses are fine tuned to the built-in LCD screen.

LE

(Less than or Equal to) See *relational operator*.

lead

A pin that extends out from a chip which is plugs into a socket or is soldered onto a circuit board. See *pin, socket mount* and *surface mount*.

lead acid

A rechargeable battery technology widely used in portable gardening tools, but has been used in some portable computers. It uses lead plates and an acid electrolyte. It provides the least amount of charge per pound of the rechargeable technologies. See *nickel cadmium, nickel hydride* and *zinc air*.

leaded chip carrier

A surface mount chip package that uses pins that extend out of the chip. Contrast with *leadless chip carrier*. See *PLCC*.

leader

(1) A length of unrecorded tape used to thread the tape onto the tape drive.

(2) A dot or dash used to draw the eye across the printed page, such as in a table of contents.

leading

In typography, the vertical spacing between lines of type (between baselines). The name comes from the early days of typesetting when the space was achieved with thin bars of lead. See *typeface* for illustration.

leading edge

(1) The edge of a punched card or document that enters the reading station first.

(2) In digital electronics, a pulse as it changes from a 0 to a 1.

(3) In programming, a loop that tests a condition before the loop is entered.

(4) (Leading Edge Products, Inc., Westborough, MA) A PC manufacturer founded in 1980. Its Model M (for Mitsubishi) in 1982 was the first PC from overseas. Korean Daewoo Corporation supplied it with products since 1984 and acquired it in 1989. Leading Edge computers are no longer sold in the U.S.

leading zeros

Zeros used to fill a field that do not increase the numerical value of the data. For example, all the zeros in 0000006588 are leading zeros.

leadless chip carrier

A chip package that uses flat metal pads that make contact with the socket or circuit board. Contrast with *leaded chip carrier*. See *CLCC*.

leaf

In database management, the last node of a tree.

League for Programming Freedom

(League for Programming Freedom, Cambridge, MA, www.lpf.org) An organization founded in 1989 that is dedicated to preventing software monopolies. Its major tenet is that software copyrights and patents jeopardize the industry, specifically when they pertain to user interfaces.

leapfrog test

A storage diagnostic routine that replicates itself throughout the storage medium.

leased line

A private communications channel leased from a common carrier. It can be ordered in pairs, providing a four-wire channel for full-duplex transmission (dial-up system provides only two-wire lines). To improve line quality, it can also be conditioned.

Leased lines are a huge business. According to Vertical Systems Group, Dedham, MA, worldwide 1994 leased line revenues were $35 billion. In that same year, frame relay revenues were $250 million and ATM was $35 million, although both of these technologies are expected to grow rapidly.

leased line modem

A high-speed modem used in private lines. It may have built-in lower speeds for alternate use in dial-up lines.

least significant digit

The rightmost digit in a number.

LEC

(1) (Local Exchange Carrier) An organization that provides local telephone service, which includes the RBOCs, large companies such as GTE and hundreds of small, rural telephone companies. A LEC controls the service from its central office (CO) to subscribers within a local geographic area. See *CLEC* and *ILEC*.

(2) (LAN Emulation Client) A software driver that provides LAN emulation (LANE) in an ATM network. It resides in an ATM end station or in computer system that provides the LAN to ATM conversion, often known as a LAN access device. See *LANE*.

LED

(Light Emitting Diode) A display technology that uses a semiconductor diode that emits light when charged. It usually gives off a red glow, although other colors can be generated. It is used in readouts and on/off lights in myriads of electronic appliances. It was the first digital watch display, but was superseded by LCD, which uses less power.

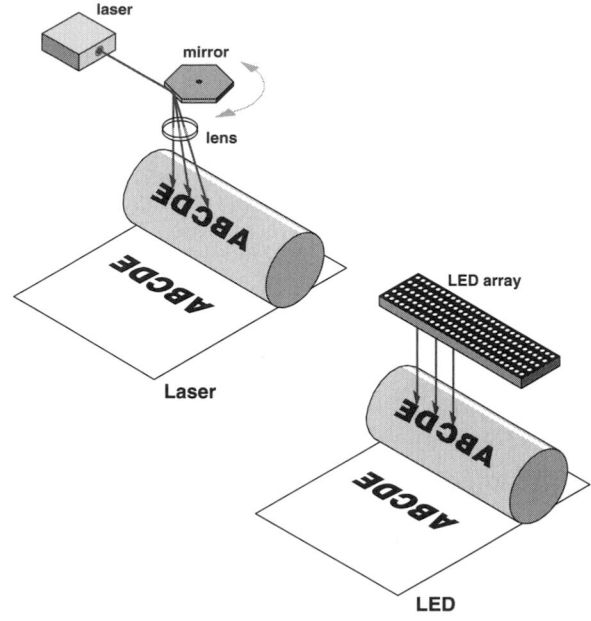

LED Versus Laser Printing

The LED mechanism is much simpler, because it is a stationary array of light emitting diodes (LEDs) rather than a number of moving parts.

LED printer

An electrophotographic printer that uses a matrix of LEDs as its light source. The LED mechanism is much simpler than its laser printer counterpart. A stationary array of LEDs is used instead of numerous moving parts, and the LEDs are selectively beamed onto the drum. LED printers are available from very low-end 4 ppm personal printers to huge digital printing presses that can print more than 700 ppm.

left click

To press the left button on the mouse.

left justify

Same as *flush left*.

legacy application

An application that has been in existence for some time. It often refers to mainframe and minicomputer applications; however, increasingly, as users migrate to Windows 95/98 and NT, it refers to DOS and Windows 3.1 applications.

legacy card

In a PC, an expansion card that does not have the ISA Plug and Play capability built into it. Up until late 1994, all cards were legacy cards.

legacy data

Critical organizational data stored in mainframes and minis (legacy systems). See *legacy system*.

legacy LAN

A LAN topology, such as Ethernet or Token Ring, that has a large installed base.

legacy protocol

A proprietary communications protocol such as DECnet, AppleTalk or SNA. With IP having become the universal protocol, everything but IP is often said to be a legacy protocol.

legacy system

A mainframe or minicomputer information system that has been in existence for a long time.

Lempel Ziv

A data compression algorithm that uses an adaptive compression technique. See *LZW*.

LEN

(Low Entry Networking) In SNA, peer-to-peer connectivity between adjacent Type 2.1 nodes, such as PCs, workstations and minicomputers. LU 6.2 sessions are supported across LEN connections.

LEO

(Low-Earth Orbit) A communications satellite in orbit some 500 to 600 miles above the earth.

The Legacy
A lot of data still exists on half-inch open reel tapes. Each standard that is widely used in the computer field hangs around for many years after it is no longer popular.

Being much closer than 22,282 mile-high geosynchronous satellites (GEOs), LEO signals make the round trip from earth much faster. Thus, low-powered pizza dishes and hand-held devices can be used. LEOs are also better suited to interactive conferencing. Unlike GEOs, which travel at earth speed, LEOs revolve around the globe every couple of hours, and any single LEO is in view for only a few minutes. In order to maintain continuous communications, multiple LEOs must be used.

Iridium, the world's first commercial LEO system, was completed in 1998. Using 66 LEOs that orbit 485 miles above the earth, Iridium offers voice, data, fax and pager services worldwide. See *Iridium, GEO* and *MEO*.

letter bomb

An e-mail or word processing document that contains active code intended to cause damage to the recipient's computer such as erasing the hard disk. See *macro virus* and *mail bomb*.

letterbox format

See *16:9*.

letter quality

The print quality of an electric typewriter. Laser printers, ink jet printers and daisy wheel printers provide letter quality printing. 24-pin dot matrix printers provide near letter quality (NLQ), but the characters are not as dark and crisp.

level 1 cache, level 2 cache

See *L1 cache* and *L2 cache*.

Level 3

(Level 3 Communications, Louisville, CO, www.l3.com) A telecommunications carrier founded in 1985 as Kiewit Diversified Group (KDG). KDG was a wholly owned subsidiary of Peter Kiewit Sons', Inc., a prominent construction company that was founded in 1884. KDG changed its name to Level 3 and spun itself off as a public company.

Level 3 is building a nationwide, optical fiber network based on IP with eventual links to networks in Europe and Asia. Its intentions are to provide fiber access directly into office buildings and provide businesses with end to end voice and data services. With nearly three billion in capital from Pieter Kiewit Sons' and expertise from many people who previously worked for MFS (created under Kiewit and later sold to WorldCom), Level 3 packs a huge wallop as a startup. Initial service is expected in serveral cities by the end of 1998.

lexicographic sort

Arranging items in alphabetic order like a dictionary. Numbers are located by their alphabetic spelling.

LEXIS-NEXIS

A service that provides online legal and business information. LEXIS was the first full-text information service for the legal profession. NEXIS provides the archives of The New York Times as well as Wall Street industry analysis, public records, tax information, political analysis, SEC filings and more. See *online services*.

Lexmark

(Lexmark International, Inc., Lexington, KY, www.lexmark.com) A manufacturer of desktop and network printers that was spun off from IBM in 1991. For five years, IBM and Lexmark agreed not to compete with each other, and IBM continued to market printers to its own mainframe and minicomputer customers. During those five years, Lexmark built itself into a two-billion dollar company selling quality printers at affordable prices. Lexmark makes its own printer engines and was the first to bring a 600 dpi laser printer to market as well as a true 1,200 dpi printer.

LF

See *line feed*.

LHA, LHARC

A popular freeware compression program developed by Haruyasu Yoshizaki that uses a variant of the LZW (LZ77) dictionary method followed by a Huffman coding stage. It runs on PCs, UNIX and other platforms as its source code is also free.

librarian

(1) A person who works in the data library.

(2) See *CA-Librarian*.

library

(1) A collection of programs or data files.

(2) A set of ready-made software routines (functions) for programmers. The routines are linked into the program when it is compiled. See *class library*.

(3) A storage device that handles multiple units of media and provides one or more drives for reading and writing them. For example, a tape library holds multiple tape cartridges and includes a robotic mechanism that moves them in and out of the drive(s).

(4) See *data library*.

library function

A subroutine that is part of a function library. Same as *library routine*.

library management

See *version control*.

library routine

A subroutine that is part of a macro or function library.

license agreement

See *EULA*.

life cycle

See *system life cycle*.

LIFO

(Last In First Out) A queueing method in which the next item to be retrieved is the item most recently placed in the queue. Contrast with *FIFO*.

ligature

Two or more typeface characters that are designed as a single unit (physically touch). Fi, ffi, ae and oe are common ligatures.

light guide

A transmission channel that contains a number of optical fibers packaged together.

light pen

A light-sensitive stylus wired to a video terminal used to draw pictures or select menu options. The user brings the pen to the desired point on screen and presses the pen button to make contact. Contrary to what it looks like, the pen does not shine light onto the screen, rather the screen beams into the pen. Screen pixels are constantly being refreshed. When the user presses the button, the pen senses light, and the pixel being illuminated at that instant identifies the screen location.

LightShip

A family of client/server tools for analyzing data from multidimensional databases from Pilot Software, Cambridge, MA, (www.pilotsw.com), a pioneer in the OLAP database field. LightShip includes tools for financial modeling, budgeting and consolidation of large databases. It provides Windows-based point-and-click reporting, a full programming language for advanced users, and support for all the popular databases.

light source

In computer graphics, the implied location of a light source in order to simulate the visual effect of a light on a 3-D object. Some programs can compute multiple light sources.

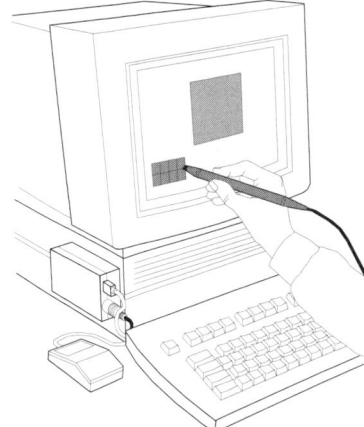

Light Pen
Light pens provide a very precise pointing capability directly on the screen.

light version

An abbreviated version of an application that is either given away free or bundled with other software. It is a marketing approach used to gain market share and entice users to upgrade to the full version, which has more features. In most cases, light versions are very usable products.

lightwave

Light in the infrared, visible and ultraviolet ranges, which falls between x-rays and microwaves. Wavelengths are between 10 nanometers and one millimeter.

lightwave system

A device that transmits light pulses over optical fibers at extremely high speeds (Gbits/sec range). Many intercity telephone trunks have been converted to lightwave systems.

lightweight protocol

A communications protocol designed with less complexity in order to reduce overhead. For example, it uses fixed-length headers because they are faster to parse than variable-length headers. To ensure compatibility, it eliminates optional subsets of the standard so that both sides are always equipped to deal with each other.

li-ion

See *lithium ion*.

LIMDOW

(Light Intensity Modulation Direct OverWrite) An enhancement of the magneto-optic technology that improves writing speed by allowing a bit to be written in one pass instead of two. The LIMDOW media is more costly than standard non-direct overwrite MO media. Many MO drives support both types. See *direct overwrite*.

limited distance modem

Same as *short-haul modem*.

Linda

A set of parallel processing functions added to languages, such as C and C++, that allows data to be created and transferred between processes. It was developed by Yale professor David Gelernter, when he was a 23-year old graduate student.

line

(1) A communications channel.

(2) A row of text characterts.

(3) A row of pixels (graphics).

line adapter

In communications, a device similar to a modem, that converts a digital signal into a form suitable for transmission over a communications line and vice versa. It provides parallel/serial and serial/parallel conversion, modulation and demodulation.

line analyzer

A device that monitors the transmission of a communications line.

linear

Sequential or having a graph that is a straight line.

linear address space

See *flat address space*.

linear editing

See *linear video editing*.

linear programming

A mathematical technique used to obtain an optimum solution in resource allocation problems, such as production planning.

line art

A graphic image drawn only as lines without any color filling or shading.

The First Lines

This photo, taken at Broadway and Courtlandt Streets in New York in 1883, shows a nation exploding with its first communications. The very same thing is happening today with the Internet, only the infrastructure is not visible. *(Photo courtesy of AT&T.)*

linear video

Continuous playback of videotape or videodisc. It typically refers to analog video technology.

linear video editing

Editing analog videotape. Before digital editing (nonlinear video editing), video sequences were edited by inserting new frames and reconstructing the balance of the tape by adding the remainder of the frames. Contrast with *nonlinear video editing*.

line bonding

See *channel bonding*.

line break

A code that signifies the end of the line. When word processing documents are saved as ASCII text files, some word processors insert a hard return at the end of each line. If the text file is opened up in a word processor or text editor with different margins than the original document, the text will not wrap like the original paragraphs.

line concentration, line conditioning

See *concentrator* and *conditioning*.

line drawing

A graphic image outlined by solid lines. The mass of the drawing is imagined by the viewer. See *wireframe modeling*.

line driver

A device that extends the transmission distance between terminals and computers that are connected via private lines or networks. Line drivers can extend distance limitations of a few dozen or a few hundred feet up to several miles.

line editor

An outmoded editing program that allows text to be created and changed one line at a time. The Edlin editor included with DOS is an example.

line feed

(1) A character code that advances the screen cursor or printer to the next line. The line feed is used as an end of line code in UNIX. In DOS and OS/2 text files, the return/line feed pair (ASCII 13 10) is the standard end of line code.

(2) A printer button that advances paper one line when depressed.

line frequency

The number of times each second that a wave or some repeatable set of signals is transmitted over a line. See *horizontal scan frequency*.

line level

In communications, the signal strength within a transmission channel, measured in decibels or nepers.

line load

(1) In communications, the percentage of time a communications channel is used.

(2) In electronics, the amount of current that is carried in a circuit.

line matrix printer

An impact printer that prints a line at a time. Printronix pioneered this technology in 1974. Line matrix and band printers are the surviving line printer technologies, but line matrix can print graphics, whereas band printers cannot. Line matrix resolution is in the 70 to 140 dpi range and speeds range from 400 to 1,400 lpm.

Line matrix printers offer medium resolution, monochrome printing with a very low ribbon cost. They also provide high speed; for example, printing a 3-part form at 1,200 lpm is equivalent to a 65 ppm page printer. Line matrix printers can exist in harsh conditions and are often found in warehouses and other industrial environments.

The print mechanism is a row of dot hammers that is almost as wide as the page. The hammers are mounted on a shuttle that oscillates back and forth approximately two inches in a track. The hammers are magnetically released at the appropriate time and bang into a ribbon and onto the paper. See *printer*.

line number

(1) A specific line of programming language source code.

(2) On display screens, a specific row of text or row of dots.

(3) In communications, a specific communications channel.

line of sight

An unobstructed view from transmitter to receiver.

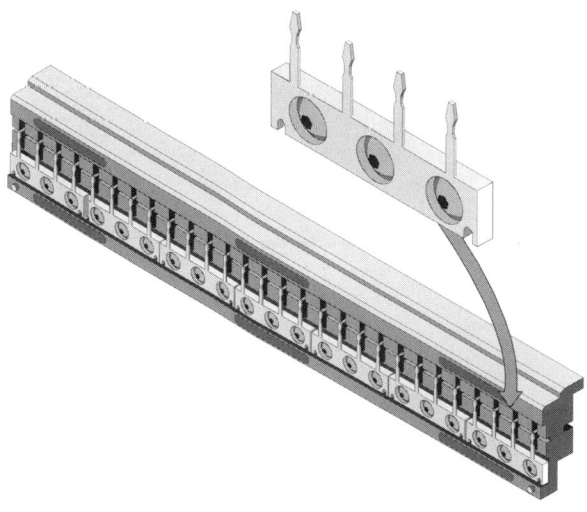

Printronix Printhead
This printhead contains seven sets of print hammers that oscillate back and forth to cover 16" wide paper. The hammers are held back by magnets. The hammer is demagnetized and springs forward onto the ribbon. As it recoils, it is remagnetized back in place. *(Original drawing courtesy of Printronix, Inc.)*

line printer

An impact printer that prints one line at a time. The two surviving line printer technologies are band printers and line matrix printers. Line printers are still widely used in datacenters and in industrial environments and can print multipart forms at a very rapid rate. For example, a 1,000 lpm line printer printing on 3-part forms is the equivalent of a 50 ppm laser printer. See *band printer, line matrix printer* and *printer*.

line segment

In vector graphics, same as *vector*.

lines of code

The statements and instructions that a programmer writes when creating a program. One line of this "source code" may generate one machine instruction or several depending on the programming language. A line of code in assembly language is typically one instruction, which is turned into one machine instruction. In a high-level language, such as C or COBOL, one line of code may generate a series of assembly language instructions, which result in multiple machine instructions.

One line of code in any language may call for the inclusion of a subroutine that can be of any size, so while used to measure the overall complexity of a program, they are not an absolute. Comparisons can also be misleading if the programs are not in the same language or category. For example, 20 lines of code in COBOL might require 200 lines of code in assembly language.

In addition, a measurement in lines of code says nothing about the quality of the code. A thousand lines of code written by one programmer can be equal to three thousand lines by another. See *KLOC*.

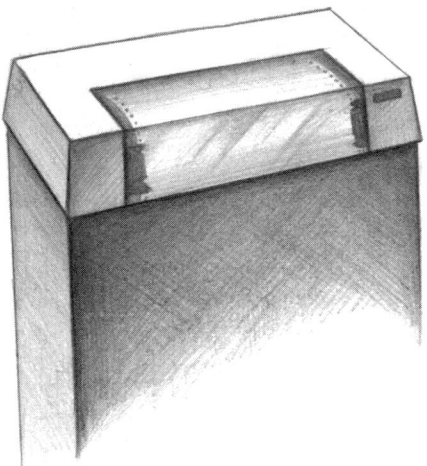

Line Printer
The line printer is typically enclosed in a cabinet that completely seals the unit from the outside world. This used to be essential when line printers were extremely noisy. Today's line printers are even quieter than laser printers.

line speed

See *data rate*.

line squeeze

In a mail merge, the elimination of blank lines when printing names and addresses that contain no data in certain fields, such as title, company and second address line. See *field squeeze*.

```
Without line squeeze        With line squeeze

Pat Smith                   Pat Smith
                            10 South Main
                            Bearcat, OR 80901
10 South Main
Bearcat, OR 80901
```

link

(1) In communications, a line, channel or circuit over which data is transmitted.

(2) On the World Wide Web, an address (URL) to another document on the same server or on any remote server. See *hypertext*.

(3) In data management, a pointer embedded within a record that refers to data or the location of data in another record.

(4) In programming, a call to another program or subroutine.

linkage editor

A utility program that links a compiled or assembled program to a particular environment. It formally unites references between program modules and libraries of subroutines. Its output is a load module, a program ready to run in the computer.

Computer Desktop Encyclopedia

link edit
To use a linkage editor to prepare a program for running.

linked list
In data management, a group of items, each of which points to the next item. It allows for the organization of a sequential set of data in noncontiguous storage locations.

linker
See *linkage editor*.

link rot
An outdated link on a Web site. See *404 error*.

link state protocol
A complex routing protocol that shares information with other routers in order to determine the best path. OSPF, NLSP and IS-IS are examples. Rather than continuously broadcast its routing tables as in a distance vector protocol, a link state protocol router only notifies its neighboring routers when it detects a change. Contrast with *distance vector protocol* and *path vector protocol*. See *routing protocol, OSPF, NLSP* and *IS-IS*.

link text
A word or short phrase on a Web page that provides the visual hypertext link to another page or to somewhere else on that same page. Link text is typically underlined. See *hypertext anchor*.

Linpack
A package of FORTRAN programs for numerical linear algebra that is commonly used to create benchmark programs for testing a computer's floating point performance. See *benchmark*.

Linux
A version of UNIX that runs on x86, Alpha and PowerPC machines. Linux is freeware, and the full distribution of Linux is available on CD-ROM, which includes the complete source code as well as hundreds of tools, applets and utilities.

In 1990, Finnish computer science student Linus Torvalds turned Minix, a popular classroom teaching tool, into Linux, which is closer to the real UNIX. Torvalds created the kernel, and most of the supporting applications and utilities came from the GNU project of the Free Software Foundation. Many programmers have contributed to the Linux/GNU system. See *GNU*.

LIPS
(Logical Inferences Per Second) The unit of measurement of the thinking speed of an AI application. Humans do about 2 LIPS. In the computer, one LIPS equals from 100 to 1,000 instructions.

liquid crystal shutters
A method of directing light onto the drum in an electrophotographic printer. A matrix of liquid crystal dots function as shutters that are opened and closed. See *LCD*.

Lisa
The first personal computer to include integrated software and use a graphical interface. Modeled after the Xerox Star and introduced in 1983 by Apple, it was ahead of its time, but never caught on due to its $10,000 price and slow speed. It gave way to the Macintosh, which was developed by a separate group within Apple. In fact, the final production units of the Lisa were modified into a somewhat-compatible version of the Macintosh.

The Lisa
It was as slow as molasses, but users were entranced by its graphical interface and ability to cut and paste between applications. *(Photo courtesy of Apple Computer, Inc.)*

LISP

(**LIS**t Processing) A high-level programming language used for developing AI applications. Developed in 1960 by John McCarthy, its syntax and structure is very different than traditional programming languages. For example, there is no syntactic difference between data and instructions.

LISP is available in both interpreter and compiler versions and can be modified and expanded by the programmer. Many varieties have been developed, including versions that perform calculations efficiently. The following Common LISP example converts Fahrenheit to Celsius:

```
(defun convert ()
  (format t "Enter Fahrenheit ")
  (let ((fahr (read)))
   (format t "Celsius is <126>D"
    (truncate (*(-fahr 32)
       (/ 5 9)))))))
```

list

(1) An arranged set of data, often in row and column format.

(2) In fourth-generation languages, a command that displays/prints selected records. For example, in dBASE, **list name address** displays all names and addresses in the current file.

list box

An on-screen display of text items in a scrollable window. For example, in the Windows version of this database, the index on the left side of the screen is a list box.

listproc

See *mailing list*.

list processing

Processing non-numeric data.

list processing language

A programming language, such as LISP, Prolog and Logo, used to process lists of data (names, words, objects). Although operations such as selecting the next to first, or next to last element, or reversing all elements in a list, can be programmed in any language, list processing languages provide commands to do them. Recursion is also provided, allowing a subroutine to call itself over again in order to repetitively analyze a group of elements.

LISTSERV

Mailing list management software from L-Soft international, Inc., Landover, MD, (www.lsoft.com), that runs on mainframes, VMS, NT and various UNIX machines. LISTSERV scans e-mail messages for the words "subscribe" and "unsubscribe" to automatically update the list. See *mailing list*.

literal

In programming, any data typed in by the programmer that remains unchanged when translated into machine language. Examples are a constant value used for calculation purposes as well as text messages displayed on screen. In the following lines of code, the literals are 1 and VALUE IS ONE.

```
if x = 1
  print "value is one"
endif
```

lit fiber

Optical fiber that is regularly being used to transmit data. Contrast with *dark fiber*.

lithium ion

A rechargeable battery technology that provides more than twice the charge per pound as nickel hydride. Although used in camcorders and other devices, Toshiba introduced the first lithium ion notebook in the U.S. in late 1993. See *lithium polymer*.

lithium polymer

A rechargeable battery technology introduced in 1998 that is similar to lithium ion in power rating. The difference is that lithium polymer uses a gelatinous electrolyte rather than liquid. Thus, instead of requiring a steel can, lithium polymer cells can be manufactured in various shapes and sizes for custom requirements.

little endian

See *big endian*.

live link

A reference to a document or image that is active. Clicking on the icon or text that symbolizes the link causes the document to be displayed. Web pages contain hypertext links to other Web pages, this feature being the one that made the World Wide Web explode onto the scene. Live links are also placed into e-mail, allowing users to quickly open an attached document, access a database or go to a Web site.

liveware

People.

LiveWire

See *Netscape LiveWire*.

LiveWire Professional

A DOS program from CableSoft, Inc., Ojai, CA, that is used for online analysis of the stock market by brokers and financial analysts. It accesses live data feeds, tracks invidivual securities and monitors portfolios. See also *Netscape LiveWire*.

LIW

See *VLIW*.

LLC

(Logical Link Control) See "LANs" under *data link protocol*.

LLCC

See *leadless chip carrier*.

LMDS

(Local Multipoint Distribution Service) A digital wireless cable system that provides two-way transmission in the 28GHz range. It uses line of sight and requires a transmitter every couple of miles. LMDS provides greater upstream bandwidth than MMDS and other wireless services. It is expected to be used for wireless data services and Internet access. See *MMDS*.

LMHOSTS file

A text file in a Windows network (NetBIOS protocol) that provides name resolution of host names to IP addresses. LMHOSTS files, which contain host names and IP addresses, are manually updated and replicated onto all the servers in the enterprise. Except in small networks, LMHOSTS files have given way to the WINS system. The LM in LMHOSTS came from LAN Manager, Microsoft's earlier network operating system (NOS). See *WINS* and *HOSTS file*.

load

(1) To copy a program from some source, such as a disk or tape, into memory for execution. In the early days, programs were loaded first and then run. Today, "launching" a program and "running" a program mean load and run.

(2) To fill up a disk with data or programs.

(3) To insert a disk or tape into a drive.

(4) In programming, to store data in a register.

(5) In performance measurement, the current use of a system as a percentage of total capacity.

(6) In electronics, the flow of current through a circuit.

(7) In a network, the amount of current traffic.

load balancing

The fine tuning of a computer system, network or disk subsystem in order to more evenly distribute the data and/or processing across available resouces. For example, in clustering, load balancing might distribute the incoming transactions evenly to all servers, or it might redirect them to the next available server.

loaded

Brought into the computer and ready to go. See *load*.

loaded line

A telephone line from customer to central office that uses loading coils to reduce distortion.

loader

A program routine that copies a program into memory for execution.

loader routine

Same as *loader*.

load high

To load programs into high memory. See *high Loadhigh*.

loading coil

A device used in local telephone loops (exceeding 18,000 ft.) that boosts voice-grade transmission. It often adds noise to high-speed data transmission and must be removed for such traffic.

load module

A program in machine language form ready to run in the computer. It is the output of a link editor.

load sharing

Sharing the workload in two or more computers.

LOB

(Large OBject) A database field that holds any digitized information including text, images, audio and video.

lobe length

In a Token Ring network, the length of cable between the MAU and the workstation.

local access

Retrieving something from a nearby source. See *LEC, CLEC, local loop* and *local drive*.

local access carrier

See *LEC* and *CLEC*.

local area network

See *LAN*.

local bus

Also called the *system bus*, it is the pathway between the CPU, memory and peripheral devices. When the higher-speed VL-bus and PCI bus were introduced, they were called local buses, because they ran at the then-current speed of the local bus. Since then, local buses have gone beyond the speeds of VL-bus and PCI. For example, the local bus in many Pentium PCs is 66MHz, twice as fast as the PCI's 33MHz.

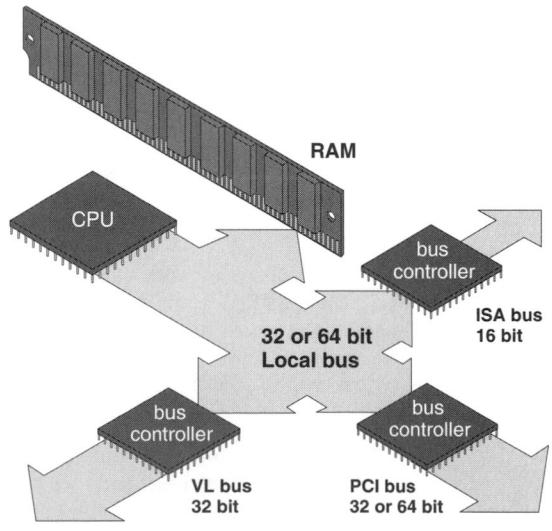

Local Bus
The peripheral controller cards plug into slots on the ISA, PCI and VLbus buses.

Computer Desktop Encyclopedia

```
Bus Speed Comparisons

Type     Width     Speed    Total rate
ISA      16 bits   8MHz     16MB
EISA     32 bits   8MHz     32MB
VL-bus   32 bits   25MHz    100MB
VL-bus   32 bits   33MHz    132MB
PCI      32 bits   33MHz    132MB
PCI      64 bits   33MHz    264MB
```

local bypass
An interconnection between two facilities without the use of the local telephone company.

local console
A terminal or workstation directly connected to the computer or other device that it is monitoring and controlling.

local drive
A disk or tape drive connected to the user's computer. Contrast with *network drive*.

local echo
In communications, to display on screen what is being transmitted.

local exchange carrier
See *LEC*.

localization
Customizing software for a particular country. It includes the translation of menus and messages into the native spoken language as well as changes in the user interface to accomodate different alphabets and culture. See *internationalization*.

local loop
The lines between a customer and the telephone company's central office, often called the "last mile." Local loops use copper-based telephone wire. See *last mile, loop carrier* and *FTTH*.

local memory
The memory used by a single CPU or allocated to a single program or function.

local resource
A peripheral device, such as a disk, modem or printer, that is directly connected to a user's personal computer. Contrast with *remote resource*.

local storage
The disk storage used by a single CPU.

LocalTalk
A LAN access method from Apple that uses twisted pair wires and transmits at 230,400 bps. It runs under AppleTalk and uses a daisy chain topology that can connect up to 32 devices within a distance of 1,000 feet. Third party products allow it to hook up with bus, passive star and active star topologies.
Apple's LocalTalk PC Card lets a PC gain access to an AppleTalk network.

local variable
In programming, a variable used only within the routine or function it is defined in.

lock down
To restrict the functionality of a system. For example, network administrators can lock down client desktops so that users can perform only certain operations.

lock manager
Software that provides file and record locking for multiple computer systems or processors that share a single database.

lockup

Refers to a computer's inability to respond to user input. See *abend* and *hang*.

log

A record of computer activity used for statistical purposes as well as backup and recovery. Log files are created for such purposes as storing incoming text dialog, error and status messages and transaction detail.

logic

The sequence of operations performed by hardware or software. Hardware logic is made up of circuits that perform an operations. Software logic (program logic) is the sequence of instructions in a program. See *algorithm*.

Note: Logic is not the same as logical. See *logical vs physical* and *logical expression*.

logical

(1) A reasonable solution to a problem.

(2) A higher level view of an object; for example, the user's view versus the computer's view. See *logical vs physical*.

logical data group

Data derived from several sources. Same as *view*.

logical drive

An allocated part of a physical disk drive that is designated and managed as an independent unit. For example, drives C:, D: and E: could represent three physical drives or one physical drive partitioned into three logical drives. Contrast with *physical drive*.

logical expression

An expression that results in true or false. Same as *Boolean expression*.

logical field

A data field that contains a yes/no, true/false condition.

logical lock

The prevention of user access to data that is provided by marking the file or record through the use of software. Contrast with *physical lock*.

logical operator

One of the Boolean logical operators (AND, OR and NOT).

logical record

A reference to a data record that is independent of its physical location. It may be physically stored in two or more locations.

Logical Unit

See *LU, LU 6.2* and *LUN*.

logical vs physical

High-level versus low-level. Logical implies a higher view than the physical. Users relate to data logically by data element name; however, the actual fields of data are physically located in sectors on a disk. For example, if you want to know which customers ordered how many of a particular product, your logical view is customer name and quantity. Its physical organization might have customer name in a customer file and quantity in an order file cross referenced by customer number. The physical sequence of the customer file could be indexed, while the sequence of the order file could be sequential.

A message transmitted from Phoenix to Boston logically goes between two cities; however, the physical circuit could be Phoenix to Chicago to Philadelphia to Boston.

When you command your program to change the output from the video screen to the printer, that's a logical request. The program will perform the physical change of address from, say, device number 02 to device number 04.

logic analyzer

(1) A device that monitors computer performance by timing various segments of the running

programs. The total running time and the time spent in selected progam modules is displayed in order to isolate the the least efficient code.

(2) A device used to test and diagnose an electronic system, which includes an oscilloscope for displaying various digital states.

logic array
Same as *gate array* or *PLA*.

logic board
A printed circuit board that contains logic circuits. Apple calls the motherboard in its Macintoshes the main logic board. See *logic circuit* and *logic gate*.

logic bomb
A program routine that destroys data; for example, it may reformat the hard disk or insert random bits into data files. It may be brought into a personal computer by downloading a corrupt public-domain program. Once executed, it does its damage right away, whereas a virus keeps on destroying.

logic chip
A processor or controller chip. Contrast with *memory chip*.

logic circuit
A circuit that performs some processing or controlling function. Contrast with *memory*.

logic controller
See *PLC*.

logic diagram
A flow chart of hardware circuits or program logic.

logic error
A program bug due to an incorrect sequence of instructions.

logic function
An elementary processing function in a digital circuit. Logic function and logic circuit are used synonymously. See *logic circuit* and *digital circuit*.

logic gate
A collection of transistors and resistors that implement Boolean logic operations on a circuit board. Transistors make up logic gates. Logic gates make up circuits. Circuits make up electronic systems. The truth tables for logic gates follow. See *Boolean logic*.

logic operation
An operation that analyzes one or more inputs and generates a particular output based on a set of rules. See *Boolean logic*.

logic-seeking printer
A printer that analyzes line content and skips over blank spaces at high speeds.

logic synthesis
The conversion of a high-level electronic circuit description into a list of logic gates and their interconnections, called the *netlist*. Every logic synthesis program understands some subset of Verilog and VHDL. The market leader in logic synthesis software is Synopsis, Mountain View, CA, (www.synopsis.com). See *silicon compiler*.

login
Same as *logon*.

Logo
A high-level programming language noted for its ease of use and graphics capabilities. It is a recursive language that contains many list processing functions that are in LISP, although Logo's syntax is more understandable for novices.

Logo's graphics language is called Turtle Graphics, which allows complex graphics images to be created with a minimum of coding. The turtle is a triangular-shaped cursor, which is moved on screen with commands that activate the turtle as if you were driving it, for example, go forward 100 units, turn right 45 degrees, turn left 20 degrees.

Stemming from a National Science Foundation project, Logo was created by Seymour Papert in the mid 1960s along with colleagues at MIT and members of Bolt Beranek & Newman. Originally developed on large computers, it has been adapted to most personal computers.

The following Object Logo example converts Fahrenheit to Celsius:

```
convert
local [fahr]
print "|Enter Fahrenheit |
make "fahr ReadWord
print "|Celsius is |
print (:fahr - 32) * 5 / 9
end
```

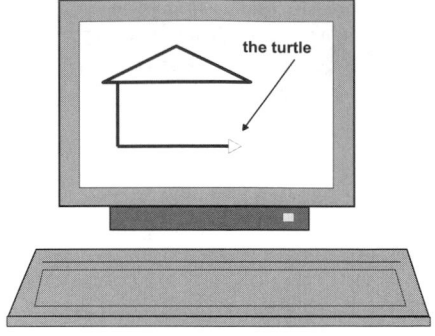

The Logo Turtle
Logo's Turtle Graphics provides a simple, intuitive way to learn about and program graphics. The commands cause the triangular pointer (the turtle) to draw the image on screen.

log off
To quit, or sign off, a computer system.

logoff
The process of quitting, or signing off, a computer system. To *log off* is the verb.

log on
To gain access, or sign in, to a computer system. If access is restricted, it requires users to identify themselves by entering an ID number and/or password. Service bureaus often base their charges for the time between logon and logoff.

logon
The process of gaining access, or signing in, to a computer system. To *log on* is the verb. If access is restricted, it requires users to identify themselves by entering an ID number and/or password. Service bureaus often base their charges for the time between logon and logoff.

logout
Same as *logoff*.

LOL
Digispeak for "laughing out loud."

long
In programming, an integer variable. In C, a long is four bytes and can be signed (-2G to +2G) or unsigned (4G). Contrast with *short*.

long card
In PCs, a full-length controller board that plugs into an expansion slot. Contrast with *short card*.

Short card

Long card

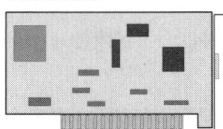

long file names
File names that exceed the common eight plus three (8.3) character limitation used in DOS and Windows 3.1. UNIX, Mac and Windows 95/98 support long file names. See *DOS file names*.

Computer Desktop Encyclopedia

long-haul

In communications, modems or communications devices that are capable of transmitting over long distances.

longitudinal redundancy check

See *LRC*.

long lines

In communications, circuits that are capable of handling transmissions over long distances.

LonWorks

A control network from Echelon Corporation, Palo Alto, CA, (www.lonworks.echelon.com), that uses the Echelon's LonTalk protocol and Neuron chip, made by Motorola and Toshiba. Each chip uses a 48-bit number for identification. Modules containing the chip and transceivers for RS-485, twisted pair, coax and AC power lines are available on credit card-sized boards. The LonWorks Interoperability Association was formed to maintain open standards for LonWorks products.

look and feel

Generally refers to the user interface of a program, especially with regard to its similarity to other programs. This issue has been and will continue to be hotly contested in the courts, because some programs look and function like others, and the original developer sometimes gets upset about it.

Oddly enough, programming languages have never been copyrighted or patented, which allows a developer to write a compiler that translates an language identical to one already in use. However, when a vendor sells a software package that looks and feels like another, it is subject to litigation, and look and feel cases have been won in the U.S. courts.

lookaside cache

A memory cache that shares the system bus with main memory and other subsystems. It is slower than inline caches and backside caches. See *inline cache* and *backside cache*.

lookup

A data search performed within a predefined table of values (array, matrix, etc.) or within a data file.

lookup table

An array or matrix of data that contains values that are searched. See *index* and *color palette*.

loop

In programming, a repetition within a program. Whenever a process must be repeated, a loop is set up to handle it. A program has a main loop and a series of minor loops, which are nested within the main loop. Learning how to set up loops is what programming technique is all about.

The following example prints an invoice. The main loop reads the order record and prints the invoice until there are no more orders to read. After printing date and name and addresses, the program prints a variable number of line items. The code that prints the line items is contained in a loop and repeated as many times as required.

Loops are accomplished by various programming structures that have a beginning, body and end. The beginning generally tests the condition that keeps the loop going. The body comprises the repeating statements, and the end is a GOTO that points back to the beginning. In assembly language, the programmer writes the GOTO, as in the example on the following page that counts to 10.

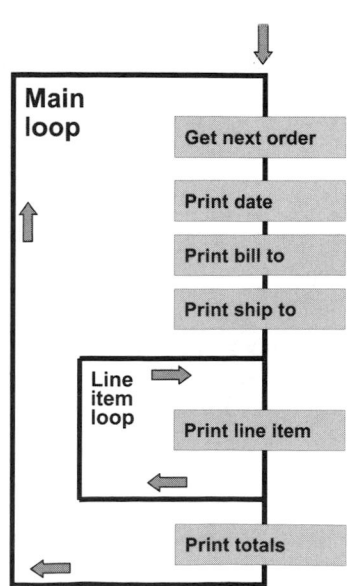

```
            MOVE      "0" TO COUNTER
   LOOP     ADD       "1" TO COUNTER
            COMPARE   COUNTER TO "10"
            GOTO      LOOP IF UNEQUAL
            STOP
```

In high-level languages, the GOTO is generated by the interpreter or compiler; for example, the same routine as above using a WHILE loop.

```
   COUNTER = 0
   DO WHILE COUNTER  10
       COUNTER = COUNTER + 1
   ENDDO
   STOP
```

For a more detailed look at a loop, look at the end of the C definition. The main event loop of the DOS version of this database is presented.

loopback plug

A connector used for diagnosing transmission problems. It plugs into a port, such as a serial or parallel port, and crosses over the transmit line to the receive line so that outgoing signals can be redirected back into the computer for testing.

loop carrier

In telephone communications, a system that concentrates a number of analog or digital lines from a remote termination station into the central office. It normally converts analog voice into digital at the remote station; however, it can be adapted to provide ISDN service to a customer.

loosely coupled

Refers to stand-alone computers connected via a network. Loosely coupled computers process on their own and exchange data on demand. Contrast with *tightly coupled*.

lo-res

See *low resolution*.

lossless compression

A compression technique that decompresses data back to its original form without any loss. The decompressed file and the original are identical. Contrast with *lossy compression*.

lossy compression

A compression technique that does not decompress data 100% back to original. Lossy compression provides high degrees of compression and results in very small compressed files, but there is a certain amount of loss when they are restored.

Audio, video and some imaging applications can tolerate some loss, and in many cases, it may not be very noticeable to the human eye. In other cases, it may be noticeable, but it is not that critical to the application. The more tolerance for loss, the smaller the file can be compressed.

Lossy compression is never used for business data and text, which demand a perfect restoration, or lossless compression.

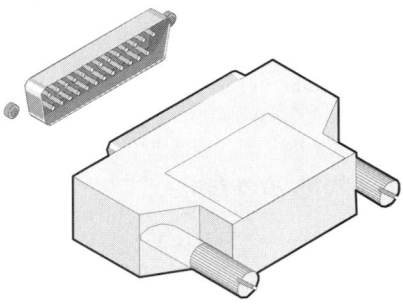

Looping Back
This loopback plug is designed for a 25-pin serial port. It crosses the sending pin over to the receiving pin so that outgoing signals come right back in.

LOSSLESS

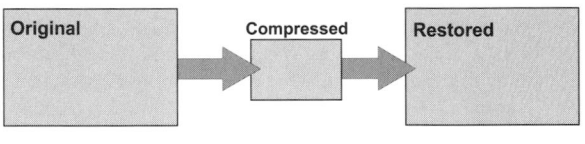

LOSSY

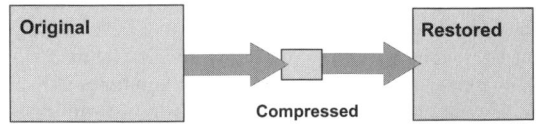

Lossless Versus Lossy Compression
Business data requires lossless compression, while audio and video applications can tolerate some loss, which may not be very noticeable.

Computer Desktop Encyclopedia

lost cluster

Disk records that have lost their identification with a file name. This can happen if a file is not closed properly, which can sometimes occur if the computer is turned off without formally quitting an application.

lost packet

A packet of data that never reaches its destination. For example, if the network becomes congested and the traffic exceeds the momentary holding capacity (buffer space) of the router, packets will be lost.

Lotus

(Lotus Development Corporation, Cambridge, MA, subsidiary of IBM, www.lotus.com) A major software company founded in 1981 by Mitch Kapor. It achieved outstanding success by introducing Lotus 1-2-3, the first spreadsheet for the IBM PC. Over the years, it developed a variety of applications and helped set industry standards. In 1989, it introduced Lotus Notes, the first major groupware product, which continues to be a strong contender in this arena. In 1990, it acquired Samna Corporation, developers of the popular, Windows-based Ami word processors. Lotus was acquired by IBM in 1995.

Lotus 1-2-3

A popular spreadsheet for Windows and OS/2, which is part of the Lotus SmartSuite package. 1-2-3 was introduced for DOS in 1983 and later on many other platforms, including minis and mainframes.

The 1-2-3 name was chosen, because it integrated spreadsheet, database and graphics. It was the first innovative spreadsheet for the PC and was launched with a superior marketing campaign. Its ability to function like a simple database was unique, and turning data into a chart with a single keystroke was dazzling for its time. The Lotus macro language was the first to be widely used in a spreadsheet. It has since been supplemented with LotusScript, a BASIC-like language that supports Notes manipulation.

Mitchell D. Kapor
Mitch Kapor was the founder of Lotus and co-programmer of Lotus 1-2-3. The Lotus spreadsheet helped make the IBM PC an outstanding success within a few years of its introduction. *(Photo courtesy of ON Technology, Inc.)*

Lotus Notes

Messaging and groupware software from Lotus that was introduced in 1989 for OS/2 and later expanded to Windows, Mac, UNIX, NetWare, AS/400 and S/390. Notes provides e-mail, document sharing, workflow, group discussions and calendaring and scheduling. It also accepts plug-ins for other functions. The heart of Notes, and what makes it different from other groupware, is its document database. Everything, including mail and group discussions, are maintained in a Notes database, which can hold data fields, text, audio and video.

Notes provides strong replication capability, which synchronizes databases distributed in multiple locations and to mobile users. The Notes Name & Address Book provides a central directory for all resources. Many applications have been built with Notes using its macro language and LotusScript, a Visual Basic-like programming language.

In 1996, the Notes client was decoupled from the Notes server, which was renamed Domino. Domino is Internet compliant and can

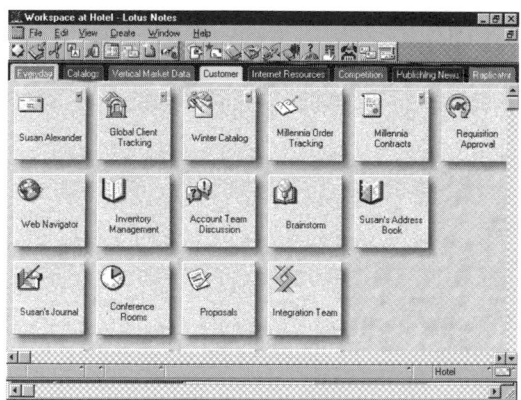

The Notes Client
The Notes interface can be customized according to users' individual needs. The square blocks are the databases which are organized by the tabs. The "Workspace at" on the title bar (top left) indicates the location of the user for synchronization purposes. *(Screen shot courtesy of Lotus Development Corporation.)*

be accessed by a Web browser, converting Notes database contents into HTML pages on the fly. The Notes client also contains a browser, which can download Web pages and maintain them as Notes documents.

Notes is often considered the father of groupware, because it was the first to popularize a development environment around groupware functions.

low density

Refers to an earlier version of a storage device with less bits per inch than today's version. See *DD* and *double density*.

low frequency

An electromagnetic wave that vibrates in the range from 30 to 300,000 Hertz.

low-level access

Close to the hardware. It refers to writing software that drives the hardware directly without going through a software translation layer and its associated overhead. An operating system can provide both low- and high-level APIs, the high-level ones being capable of very elaborate processing. The low-level APIs make programmers do more work, but allows them access to hardware features. For example, Microsoft's DirectDraw and Direct3D APIs allow directly manipulation of the frame buffer in the display adapter.

low-level format

The sector identification on a disk that the drive uses to locate sectors for reading and writing. Today's IDE and SCSI hard disks are low-level formatted at the factory. See *format program*.

low-level language

A programming language that is very close to machine language. All assembly languages are low-level languages. Contrast with *high-level language*.

low radiation

Refers to video terminals that emit less VLF (Very Low Frequency) and ELF (Extremely Low Frequency) radiation. This level of radiation cannot be shielded by office partitions. It must be cancelled out from the CRT. Health studies on this are not conclusive and are very controversial. See *MPR II*.

low resolution

A low-grade display or printing quality due to a lower number of dots or lines per inch.

lpi

(Lines Per Inch) The number of lines printed in a vertical inch.

lpm

(Lines Per Minute) The number of lines a printer can print or a scanner can scan in a minute.

LPT1

In a PC, the logical name assigned to parallel port #1. The parallel port is typically used for the printer. A second parallel port, if installed, is assigned to LPT2. Contrast with *COM1*.

LPX

An Intel motherboard used for low-profile (space-saving) PCs. It provides more space on the motherboard for I/O ports, because expansion cards are plugged into a riser card.

LQ

See *letter quality*.

LRC

(Longitudinal Redundancy Check) An error checking method that generates a parity bit from a specified string of bits on a longitudinal track. In a row and column format, such as on magnetic tape, LRC is often used with VRC, which creates a parity bit for each character.

LS-120

(Laser Servo-120) A floppy disk technology that holds 120MB, developed by 3M, Compaq,

Matsushita and O.R. Technology. LS-120 drives use a dual-gap head which reads and writes 120MB disks as well as standard 3.5" 1.44MB and 720KB floppies. The technology records data magnetically, but uses optical tracks in the disk to align the heads. LS-120 disks have 2,490 tracks per inch, compared to 135 tpi for the 1.44MB floppy. See *SuperDisk*. For a summary of all storage technologies, see *storage*.

LSAPI

(Licensing Service **API**) A programming interface from Microsoft that allows a licensing server to track applications in use for managing multiuser software licenses.

LSI

(Large Scale Integration) Between 3,000 and 100,000 transistors on a chip. See *SSI, MSI, VLSI* and *ULSI*.

LSI-11

A family of board-level computers from Digital that uses the micro version of the PDP-11. Introduced in 1974, it was the first to use the Q-bus.

LSL

(Link Support Layer) A common interface for network drivers. It provides a common language between the transport layer and the data link layer and allows different transport protocols to run over one network adapter or one transport protocol to run on different network adapters.

Instead of directly calling a particular data link protocol, the transport protocol calls the LSL library. Thus, any LSL-compliant network driver can provide data link services in that protocol stack. LSL is part of UNIX System V. It is also the basis of Novell and Apple's ODI specification. See *ODI* and *STREAMS*.

LT

(Less Than) See *relational operator*.

LU

(Logical Unit) In SNA, one end of a communications session. The complete LU to LU session is defined by session type. Common types are:

```
  1   Host to 3770 RJE terminal
  2   Host to 3270 mainframe terminal
  3   Host to 3270 printer
6.2   Program-to-program
  7   Host to 5250 midrange terminal
```

LU 6.2

An SNA protocol that establishes a session between two programs. It allows peer-to-peer communications as well as interaction between programs running in the host with PCs, Macs and midrange computers.

Before LU 6.2, processing was done only in the mainframe. LU 6.2 allows processing to take place at both ends of the communications, necessary for today's distributed computing and client/server environment. See *APPC* and *CPI-C*.

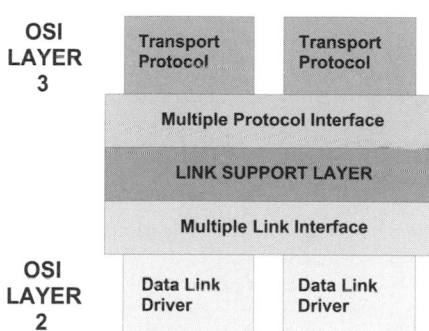

LS-120 Cartridge
LS-120 media look very similar to floppy disks, but hold more than 80 times as much.

Lucent

(Lucent Technologies, Murray Hill, NJ, www.lucent.com) A major manufacturer of telecommunications equipment. Lucent makes telephones and telephone systems, large telephone switching computers and integrated circuits and optoelectronics components for communications and computer applications.

The company has a long history in the telecom arena. Its roots go back to 1869 when Elisha Gray and Enos Barton founded Gray and Barton in Cleveland, Ohio, a company that provided parts and models for inventors such as Gray himself. Gray and Barton was later renamed Western Electric Company when Western Union, its major customer, became an investor.

In 1881, American Bell Telephone purchased controlling interest in Western Electric, which became the manufacturing arm of the Bell companies. In 1899, AT&T, which was created 14 years earlier, took over American Bell and Western Electric. In 1925, the already-combined engineering departments of Western Electric and AT&T were turned into Bell Labs, which has become world famous for its research.

Lucent Has History
Although a new company in 1996, Lucent goes way back, spawning Bell Labs and Graybar Electric and inventing and/or developing some of the most important technologies in the western world. *(Photo courtesy of Lucent Technologies.)*

A year later, Western Electric spun off its electrical distribution operations as Graybar Electric Company, which became the first large company to be bought out by its own employees.

Over the years, the company ushered in the electronic age by developing the vacuum tube. It also invented the loudspeaker, brought sound to motion pictures and introduced mobile communications, the forerunner of today's cellular system. When AT&T was divested of its Bell operating companies in 1984, Western Electric remained with AT&T, but was soon split up into a variety of divisions, including Network Systems, which builds the major switching and telecom equipment. When spun off from AT&T in 1996, Lucent retained all of AT&T's manufacturing units as well as Bell Labs.

lumen

A unit of measurement of the flow (rate of emission) of light. A wax candle generates 13 lumens; a 100 watt bulb generates 1,200. See *candela*.

Lumena

A paint and animation program from Western Imaging, Inc., Cloverdale, CA, (www.lumena.com) that runs on DOS, Mac, OS/2 and UNIX. Lumena provides very sophisticated special effects combining analog and digital video and is often used in TV production applications. Lumena was originally developed by Time Arts.

luminance

The amount of brightness, measured in lumens, that is given off by a pixel or area on a screen. It is the black/gray/white information in a video signal.

LUN

(Logical Unit Number) The physical number of a device in a daisy chain of drives. See *SCSI*.

lurk

To view the interaction in a chat room or online forum without participating by typing in any comments. See *de-lurk*.

LUT

(LookUp Table) An array or matrix of values that contains data that is searched. See *index* and *color palette*.

lux

A unit of measurement of the intensity of light. It is equal to the illumination of a surface one meter away from a single candle. See *candela*.

LVD

(Low Voltage Differential) A type of SCSI signalling that supports cable lengths up to 39.4 feet. See *SCSI*

LX chipset

See *Intel chipsets*.

Lycos

(www.lycos.com) One of the major search sites on the Web. See *Web search sites*.

Lynx

A text-based Web browser created at the University of Kansas. Though largely supplanted by graphical browsers such as Netscape Navigator and Internet Explorer, Lynx is still popular among people with visual disabilities and those with very slow modem connections.

LZW

(Lempel-Ziv-Welch) A compression method that stems from two techniques introduced by Jacob Ziv and Abraham Lempel. LZ77 creates pointers back to repeating data, and LZ78 creates a dictionary of repeating phrases with pointers to those phrases. Unisys researcher Terry Welch created an enhanced version of these methods, and Unisys holds a patent on the algorithm. LZW is widely used in many hardware and software products, including V.42bis modems, GIF and TIF files and PostScript Level 2. See *PNG*.

M

M

(1) See *mega*.

(2) Formerly known as MUMPS, it is a high-level programming language and integrated database that is widely used in the health-care field. Its extensive string handling capabilities make it suitable for storing vast amounts of free text. It was originally developed in 1966 at Massachusetts General Hospital as the Massachusetts Utility MultiProgramming System. The MUMPS Development Committee has maintained the language since 1973, and it became an ANSI standard in 1977.

M has unique features including the ability to store both data and program statements in its database, a fundamental property of object-oriented programming. In addition, formulas written in a program can be stored and used by other programs. See *M Technology Association*.

The following M example converts Fahrenheit to Celsius:

```
READ "Enter Fahrenheit ",FAHR
SET CENT=(FAHR-32)*5/9
WRITE "Celsius is", CENT
```

MAC

(1) (Message Authentication Code) A number computed from the contents of a text message that is used to authenticate the message. The MAC is a checksum that is computed using an algorithm and secret key and then sent with the message. The recipient recomputes the MAC at the other end using the same algorithm and secret key and compares it to the one that is sent. If they are the same, the message has not been tampered with. A MAC is like a digital signature, except that a secret key was used in its creation rather than a private key. See *digital signature* and *cryptography*.

(2) (Mandatory Access Control) A security control that requires clearance levels. See *NCSC*.

(3) See *Macintosh* and *MAC layer*.

MacAPPC

LU 6.2-compliant software from Apple that allows a Macintosh to be a peer to an IBM APPC application.

MacBench

A benchmark from Ziff-Davis that tests the graphics, disk, processor, video and CD-ROM performance of a Macintosh system. See *ZDBOp*.

Mac clone

See *Macintosh clone*.

MacDFT

Software that provides 3270 emulation for the Macintosh from Apple. It accompanies Apple's TwinAx/Coax board and supports CUT and DFT modes and DFT multiple sessions under SNA.

MacDraw Pro

A Macintosh drawing program from Claris that is an enhanced version of the original MacDraw from Apple and includes full on-screen slide presentation capability. It is used for illustrations and elementary CAD work. MacDraw files are a subset of the Claris CAD file format.

Mach

A UNIX-like operating system developed at Carnegie-Mellon University. It is designed with a microkernel architecture that makes it easily portable to different platforms.

machine

Any electronic or electromechanical unit of equipment. A machine is always hardware; however, "engine" refers to hardware or software.

machine address

Same as *absolute address*.

machine code

Same as *machine language*.

machine cycle

The shortest interval in which an elementary operation can take place within the processor. It is made up of some number of clock cycles.

machine dependent

Also called *platform dependent* or *hardware dependent*, it refers to software that is designed to run in only one computer or family of computers derived from the same architecture. Machine-dependent software has been compiled into the machine language of that specific hardware platform. Contrast with *machine independent*. See *device dependent*.

machine independent

Also called *platform independent* and *hardware independent*, it refers to software that runs in a variety of computers. The hardware-specific instructions are in some other program (operating system, DBMS, interpreter, etc.). For example, interpreted programs are machine independent, providing there are interpreters for more than one machine. Contrast with *machine dependent*. See *device independent* and *interpreter*.

machine instruction

An instruction in machine language. Its anatomy is a verb followed by one or more nouns:

```
OP CODE      OPERANDS (one or more)
(verb)       (nouns)
```

The op code is the operation to be performed (add, copy, etc.), while the operands are the data to be acted upon (add a to b). There are always machine instructions to INPUT and OUTPUT, to process data by CALCULATING, COMPARING and COPYING it, and to go to some other part of the program with a GOTO instruction. See *hardware platforms* and *computer*.

machine language

The native language of the computer. In order for a program to run, it must be presented to the computer as binary-coded machine instructions that are specific to that CPU model or family. Although programmers are sometimes able to modify machine language in order to fix a running program, they do not create it. Machine language is created by programs called *assemblers, compilers* and *interpreters*, which convert the lines of programming code a human writes into the machine language the computer understands.

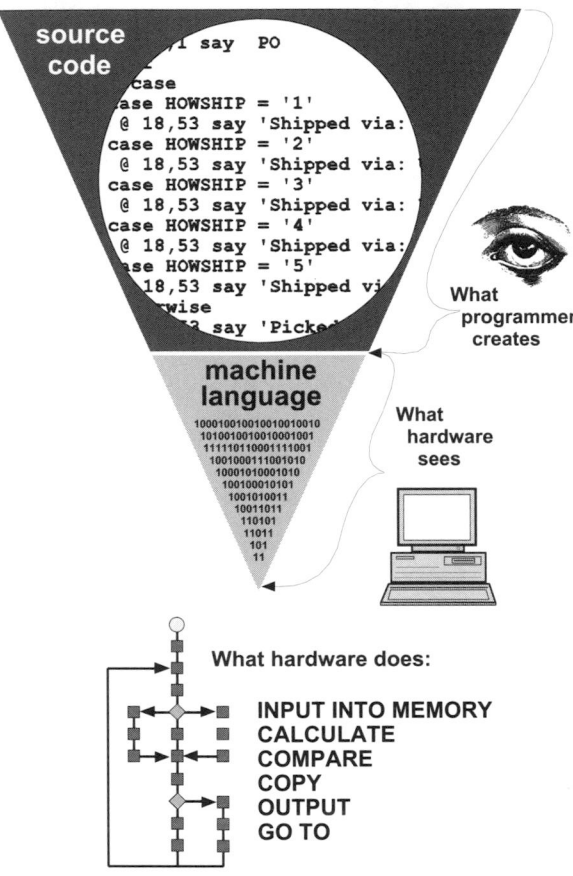

SOURCE CODE TO MACHINE LANGUAGE

What programmer creates

What hardware sees

What hardware does:

INPUT INTO MEMORY
CALCULATE
COMPARE
COPY
OUTPUT
GO TO

A computer only understands machine language, which is a set of instructions built into its circuits and is specific to that CPU model or family. The programs that it executes are made up of binary-coded instructions in that machine language, which were generated by software translators called assemblers, compilers and interpreters. Every program, whether it is a business application programmed inhouse or a commercial program purchased outside, must be available in the machine language of the computer you want to run it on, or you can't use it.

Programmers write in a programming language, which may be close to the machine or many levels removed from it. For years, the goal of the business organization has been to describe the problem and have that description turned into machine language. The goal is achieved somewhat in the form of application generators and CASE (computer aided-software engineering) tools, but the great majority of programs are written in exacting detail by the programmer.

Machine language tells the computer what to do and where to do it. When a programmer writes: **total = total + subtotal**, that statement is converted into a machine instruction that tells the computer to add the contents of two areas of memory (where TOTAL and SUBTOTAL are stored).

A programmer deals with data logically, "add this, subtract that," but the computer must be told precisely where this and that are located.

Machine languages differ substantially. What may take one instruction in one machine can take 10 instructions in another. See *hardware platforms, assembly language* and *interpreter*.

machine readable

Data in a form that can be read by the computer, which includes disks, tapes and punched cards. Printed fonts that can be scanned and recognized by the computer are also machine readable.

Macintosh

A family of personal computers from Apple, introduced in 1984. It was the first computer to popularize the graphical user interface (GUI), which, along with its hardware architecture, has provided a measure of consistency and ease of use that is unmatched. The Macintosh family is the largest non-IBM compatible personal computer series in use in what is essentially a PC versus Mac world.

The first Mac had only a floppy disk and 128K of memory. Its "high-rise" cabinet and built-in 9" monochrome screen were unique. Maintained for a number of years and streamlined in its Classic model, the high-rise machine has long since given way to more traditional cabinetry.

The first Macs were powered by Motorola's 32-bit 680x0 family of CPUs. In 1994, Apple introduced the PowerMacs, the next generation of Macintoshes, which use the PowerPC CPU chip. PowerMacs run native PowerPC applications and emulate traditional Mac 680x0 applications. DOS and Windows applications can be run with Insignia Solution's SoftWindows. See *Apple*.

The Macintosh User Interface

The Macintosh popularized the graphical user interface (GUI) and simulated desktop. It was the first widespread system that enabled users to simulate file management by dragging

The First Macintosh
The first Macintosh had a shape and size that made it quite unique compared to the machines of the era. Its graphical interface was revolutionary for a personal computer. *(Photo courtesy of Apple Computer, Inc.)*

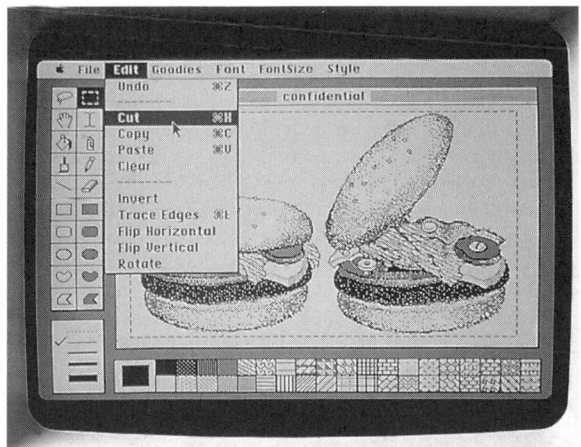

The First Mac GUI
This is a screen shot of MacPaint on the first Macintosh. The Mac's graphical ability made it a natural for graphics shops and desktop publishing. It might have been sluggish, but it was far more affordable than the workstations used for such purposes in the 1980s. *(Photo courtesy of Apple Computer, Inc.)*

icons of documents from one folder to another and literally dumping them into an on-screen trashcan for deletion. When introduced, it was immediately favored by non-technical people who avoided DOS commands or for non-typists.

The Mac interface used consistent menus on screen and Apple provided guidelines for application design, all of which was absent in the DOS world. In operation, the operating system and applications were almost indistinguishable, and Apple kept technical jargon to a minimum.

The graphical user interface was actually developed by Xerox and introduced on its Star workstation in 1981. Apple borrowed heavily from the Star and popularized the interface on the Macintosh. The Macintosh style has been adapted to many environments, including Windows, OS/2 and Motif. Windows 95/98 is more like the Mac than Windows 3.1, but is still much more complicated.

Why Aren't There More Macs?

The Macintosh has gained a following of millions of loyal users that would do almost anything to avoid switching to Windows. Just ask them. The Mac has always been easier to use. If you need more storage on a Mac, just plug in a second hard disk. There are no IRQ, I/O address and upper memory block settings to deal with as there have been with the PC for so many years. With the Mac, it's "plug it in and go" versus a technical quagmire. Windows 95/98 Plug & Play, a giant effort to change the situation, has helped considerably, but is still problematic. The Mac was introduced only a couple of years after the PC. Why then didn't the Mac take the world by storm?

There are several reasons. DOS PCs had definite advantages, especially in the corporate world. The first was speed. Text-based DOS programs were much faster than the Macintosh's graphical equivalents. It takes much more computation to display graphics than text. Secondly, professional programmers enjoy using commands such as found in DOS and UNIX. The batch languages and command sequences that can automate myriads of tasks were woefully absent in the Mac's early days, and in many cases still are. There was sound reason for the early expression, "real programmers don't use mice."

Thirdly, intensive keyboard users laughed at the Mac replacing their word processor. Apple emphasized the mouse so much in the early days that it gave little thought to sensible keyboard alternates for text entry. This was hardly a way to gain market share in a world where word processing was the single largest application.

In time, of course, smart keyboard commands were added and CPU speeds increased dramatically, but for the most part, the DOS world was simply too entrenched by the time these improvements came about. Windows 3.0 and 3.1, which offered a graphical interface with some of the Mac's advantages, was a natural successor to DOS, since it ran as an extention to DOS. Windows 95 added almost all of the graphical attributes of the Mac, and by this time, it was no contest. The world was buying Windows.

Fourthly, for many years the Mac was pricier than a PC. Purchasing agents found this hard to justify. Although many corporate users even purchased their own Macs due to their aversion to PCs, IS personnel were not fond of supporting them. They sweated bullets dealing with DOS and Windows. Supporting yet another environment, simple or otherwise, was not met with enthusiasm.

Last, but perhaps most important, until recently, Apple kept its technology proprietary and discouraged attempts by others to develop a clone industry. Apple maintained its sole source vendor status, which was not an advantage when compared to the choices from countless PC makers.

As a result, the Macintosh followed its natural bent and became popular in desktop publishing and graphics design, literally pioneering the use of personal computers for these applications. The Mac is the de facto standard in the graphics arts industry. Macs became widely used in small businesses and eventually made inroads into major companies. However, with about 5% of the desktop market today, they still remain, as Apple put it in its early ad campaigns, "the computer for the rest of us."

Perhaps "the rest" do have the advantage!

Macintosh clone

A Power Macintosh from a company other than Apple. In late 1994, Apple began to license its operating system and hardware technologies to third-parties. The first models appeared in the spring of 1995 from Radius, Power Computing and DayStar Digital. In late 1996, Apple ceased all future licensing, and the clone business was soon to become history.

Macintosh extension

Additional software functions for the Macintosh, which include drivers and other enhancements to the operating system. In System 7, system extensions reside in the Extensions folder. Mac extensions are the counterpart to the CONFIG.SYS file for DOS.

Macintosh Toolbox

Software routines that perform the graphical user interface functions in the Macintosh. Apple has licensed the Mac Toolbox to vendors developing a version of PowerOpen. This is the first time Apple has licensed the Toolbox. See *MAS*.

MacIRMA

A 3270 emulator board for the Macintosh from Attachmate Corporation, Bellevue, WA, (www.attachmate.com). It is the Macintosh counterpart of the IRMA board, the first 3270 emulator for PCs. See *Irma software*.

MAC layer

(Media Access Control layer) The protocol that controls access to the physical transmission medium on a LAN. The MAC layer is built into the network adapter. Common MAC layer standards are the CSMA/CD architecture used in Ethernet and the token passing methods used in Token Ring, FDDI and MAP. The MAC layer is synonymous with the data link layer in the OSI model. See *data link protocol* for illustration.

MacLink Plus

A Macintosh file transfer program from DataViz Corporation, Trumbull, CT, (www.dataviz.com), that provides document conversion for a wide variety of Mac and PC formats. Versions are also available for Sun, NeXT and Wang systems.

Mac OS

(**MAC**intosh **O**perating **S**ystem) In late 1994, Apple formally renamed its System 7 operating system Mac OS and introduced the Mac OS logo. However, the term has been used for years to refer to all versions of Mac operating systems.

Mac OS X

The next-generation operating system for the Mac from Apple. It is expected to include memory protection, multiprocessing and multithreading and use parts of the Rhapsody operating system Apple has been developing. The X is the Roman numeral 10, not "x."

MacPaint

A full-featured Macintosh paint program from Claris that was originally developed by Apple and bundled with every Mac up until the Mac Plus. MacPaint's PICT file format is used for printing the screen. By pressing Command-shift-3, the current screen is stored in a PICT file for printing either in MacPaint or other program.

macro

(1) A series of menu selections, keystrokes and/or commands that have been recorded and assigned a name or key combination. When the macro name is called or the macro key combination is pressed, the steps in the macro are executed from beginning to end.

Macros are used to shorten long menu sequences as well as to create miniature programs within an application. Macro languages often include programming controls (IF THEN, GOTO, WHILE, etc.) that automate sequences like any programming language. See *macro recorder*, *batch file* and *shell script*.

(2) In assembly language, a prewritten subroutine that is called for throughout the program. At assembly time, the macro calls are substituted with the actual subroutine or instructions that branch to it. The high-level language equivalent is a function.

(3) See *hard macro* and *soft macro*.

macro assembler

An assembly language that allows macros to be defined and used.

macro call

Same as *macro instruction*.

macro cell

See *hard macro*.

macro generator

See *macro recorder*.

macro instruction

An instruction that defines a macro. In assembly language, MACRO and ENDM are examples that define the beginning and end of a macro. In C, the #DEFINE statement is used.

macro language

(1) Commands used by a macro processor. Same as *script*.

(2) An assembly language that uses macros.

Macromedia

(Macromedia, Inc., San Francisco, CA, www.macromedia.com) A software company specializing in multimedia authoring tools. It was founded in 1992 by the merger of Aurhorware, Inc., which was founded in 1984, and MacroMind-Paracomp. Macromind was founded in 1984 and merged with Paracomp in 1991. Its primary products are Authorware Professional and Macromedia Director, both for Macintosh and Windows.

Macromedia Freehand

A full-featured drawing program for Windows and Macintosh from Macromedia. It combines a wide range of drawing tools with special effects. FreeHand was first available on the Mac and was originally Aldus Freehand from Aldus Corporation.

macro processor

(1) Software that creates and executes macros from the keyboard.

(2) The part of an assembler that substitutes the macro subroutines for the macro calls.

macro recorder

A program routine that converts menu selections and keystrokes into a macro. A user turns on the recorder, calls up a menu, selects a variety of options, turns the recorder off and assigns a key command to the macro. When the key command is pressed, the selections are executed.

macro virus

A virus that is written in a macro language and placed within a document. Viruses have to be "run" in order to do things. When the document is opened and the macro is executed, commands in the macro language do the destruction or the prank. Thankfully, the overwhelming majority of viruses are harmless. Let's pray they stay that way! See *Word macro virus, letter bomb* and *virus*.

MacTerminal

Macintosh terminal emulation software from Apple that allows a Mac to function as an IBM 3278 Model 2 (when used with an AppleLine Protocol Converter) or Digital VT 52 or VT 100 terminal.

Mac to midrange

Using the Macintosh as the terminal to IBM S/3x and AS/400 computers. Apple and third party connectivity products add local processing and a friendly interface to IBM midrange computers.

MacWrite

A full-featured Macintosh word processing program from Claris Corporation. MacWrite was originally packaged with every Mac.

MAE

(1) (Macintosh Application Environment) Software from Apple that allows Macintosh programs to run on UNIX workstations under the X Window system. MAE supports AppleTalk and MacTCP, allowing UNIX users to share printers, files and e-mail with other Macintosh users on the network.

(2) (Metropolitan Area Exchange) Originally known as Metropolitan Area Ethernets, MAEs are major network access points (NAPs) on the Internet. See *NAP*.

Maestro

(1) (Maesto NT) Scheduling software for Windows NT from Tivoli Systems, Inc., Austin, TX, (www.tivoli.com).

(2) (Business Maestro) Business planning and analysis software for Windows from Planet Corporation, Worcester, MA, (www.planet-corp.com).

(3) (NFS Maestro Gateway) Software from Hummingbird Communications, Ltd., North York, Ontario, (www.hummingbird.com), that lets Windows clients access files on UNIX servers via NFS.

mag

Abbreviation for "magnetic."

magazine style columns

Text that is displayed in side-by-side columns. The text flows from the bottom of one column to the top of the next column on the same page.

Magellan

A disk management utility for PCs from Lotus that searches for file names and contents. It popularized the file viewer, which lets you look into various data files as if you were using the applications that created them.

Magic Cap

(**M**agic **C**ommunicating **A**pplications **P**latform) An object-oriented control program from General Magic for personal intelligent communicating devices (PDAs, hand-held units, etc.) that includes the Telescript language. See *Telescript*.

Magic Link

A PDA from Sony that uses the Magic Cap operating system and includes an infrared port, fax/modem and PC Card slot. It has a built-in PIM and direct connection to AT&T's PersonaLink service, which requires a phone jack for communication.

magnetic card

(1) See *magnetic stripe*.

(2) Magnetic tape strips used in early data storage devices and word processors. See *CRAM* and *Data Cell*.

magnetic coercivity

The amount of energy required to alter the state of a magnet. The higher a magnetic disk's coercivity index, the more data it can store.

magnetic disk

The primary computer storage device. Like tape, it is magnetically recorded and can be re-recorded over and over. Disks are rotating platters with a mechanical arm that moves a read/write head between the outer and inner edges of the platter's surface. It can take as long as one second to find a location on a floppy disk to as little as a couple of milliseconds on a fast hard disk. See *floppy disk* and *hard disk*.

Tracks and Sectors

The disk surface is divided into concentric tracks (circles within circles). The thinner the tracks, the more storage. The data bits are recorded as tiny magnetic spots on the tracks. The tinier the spot, the more bits per inch and the greater the storage. Most disks hold the same number of bits on each track, even though the outer tracks are physically longer than the inner ones. Some disks pack the bits as tightly as possible within each track.

Tracks are further divided into sectors, which hold the least amount of data that can be read or written at one time; for example,

Magazine Style Columns

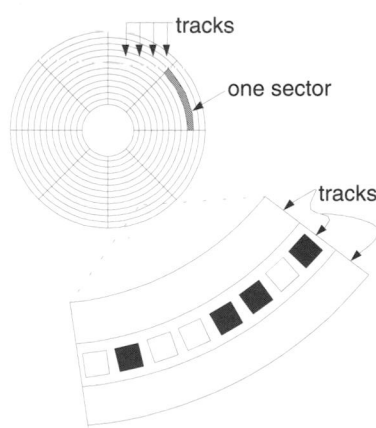

Tracks and Sectors

Tracks are concentric circles on the disk, broken up into storage units called *sectors*. The sector, which is typically 512 bytes, is the smallest unit that can be read or written.

READ TRACK 7 SECTOR 24. In order to update the disk, one or more sectors are read into the computer, changed and written back to disk. The operating system figures out how to fit data into these fixed spaces. For a summary of magnetic disk and all other storage technologies, see *storage*.

magnetic disk & tape

The primary computer storage media. The choice depends on accessing requirements. Disk is direct access; tape is sequential access. Locating a program or data on disk can take a fraction of a second. On tape, it can take seconds or minutes.

On minis and mainframes, disks are used for daily transaction processing, and tapes are used for backup and history. Tapes have traditionally been more economical for archival storage and easier to transport than disk packs.

For personal computers, hard disks are used for all interactive processing, and both floppy disks and tapes are used for backup. Bernoulli disks and removable hard disks are increasingly becoming backup alternatives.

In time, magnetic disks may be as obsolete as punched cards. Optical disks are getting faster and cheaper, and optical technologies that employ no moving parts may supersede them all. Compared to the magical technology within the chip, whirling chunks of metal around is rather old fashioned, don't you think? For a summary of all storage technologies, see *storage*.

magnetic drum

An early high-speed, direct access storage device that used a magnetic-coated cylinder with tracks around its circumference. Each track had its own read/write head.

magnetic field

An invisible energy emitted by a magnet. Same as *flux*.

magnetic ink

A magnetically detectable ink used to print the MICR characters that encode account numbers on bank checks.

magnetic oxide

See *ferric oxide*.

magnetic recording

With regard to computers, the technique used to record, or write, digital data in the form of tiny spots (bits) of negative or positive polarity on tapes and disks. A read/write head discharges electrical impulses onto the moving ferromagnetic surface. Reading is accomplished by sensing the polarity of the bit with the read/write head.

magnetic stripe

A small length of magnetic tape adhered to ledger cards, badges and credit cards. It is read by specialized readers that may be incorporated into accounting machines and terminals. Due to heavy wear, the data on the stripe is in a low-density format that may be duplicated several times.

magnetic tape

A sequential storage medium used for data collection, backup and historical purposes. Like videotape, computer tape is made of flexible plastic with one side coated with a ferromagnetic material. Tapes come in reels and cartridges of many sizes and shapes. Although still used in legacy systems, open reels have been mostly superseded by cartridges with enhanced storage capacities. For a summary of magnetic tape and all other storage technologies, see *storage*.

Locating a specific record on tape requires reading every record in front of it or searching for markers that identify predefined partitions. Although most tapes are used for archiving rather than routine updating, some drives can allow rewriting in place if the byte count does not change.

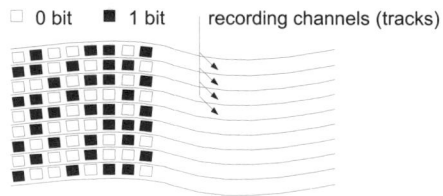

Tracks on Magnetic Tape
Except for helical scan recording, most tracks on magnetic tape run parallel to the length of the tape.

Otherwise, updating requires copying files from one tape to a scratch tape.

Tracks either run parallel to the edge of the tape (linear recording) or diagonally (helical scan). A variation of linear recording is serpentine recording, where sets of tracks are duplicated and the data "snakes" back and forth from the end to the beginning.

Open reel tapes use nine linear tracks (8 bits plus parity), while modern cartridges use up to 128 or more (Magstar). Data is recorded in blocks of contiguous bytes, separated by a space called an interrecord or interblock gap. Tape drive speed is measured in inches per second (ips). Over the years, storage density has increased from 200 to 38,000 bpi.

Tape is more economical than disks for archival data. However, if tapes are stored for the duration, they must be periodically recopied or the tightly coiled magnetic surfaces may contaminate each other.

magnetographic

A non-impact printer technology that prints up to 90 ppm. A magnetic image is created by a set of recording heads across a magnetic drum. A toner is applied to the drum to develop the image, which is transferred to paper by light pressure and an electrostatic field. The toner is then fused by heat. The print quality is not as good as a laser printer, but the machines require less maintenance.

magneto-optic disk

A rewritable optical disk that uses a combination of magnetic and optical methods. MO disks use removable cartridges and come in two form factors. The 3.5" disks hold 128MB, 230MB and 640MB, and the 5.25" disks hold 650MB, 1.3GB, 2.6GB and 5.2GB. The latter are double sided, but must be removed and flipped over to use the other side. Pinnacle Micro introduced a proprietary 4.6GB drive in 1995 that also supports 2.6GB cartridges.

MO disks disks are very robust and are typically used in high-end disk libraries. They have a 30-year shelf life and can withstand a million rewrites. MO access times are in the sub-25ms range, compared to more than 100ms for phase change disks, the pure optical technology used in CD-RW, DVD-RAM and PD disks.

Data is written on an MO disk by both a laser and a magnet. The laser heats the bit to the Curie point, which is the temperature at which molecules can be realigned when subjected to a magnetic field. Then, a magnet changes the bit's polarity. The laser is focused on one side of the platter, and the magnet is used on the opposite side, which is why double sided media must be flipped over to access the other side.

Reading is accomplished with a lower-power laser that reflects light from the bits. The light is rotated differently depending on the polarity of the bit, and the difference in rotation is sensed. Writing takes two passes. The existing bits are set to zero in

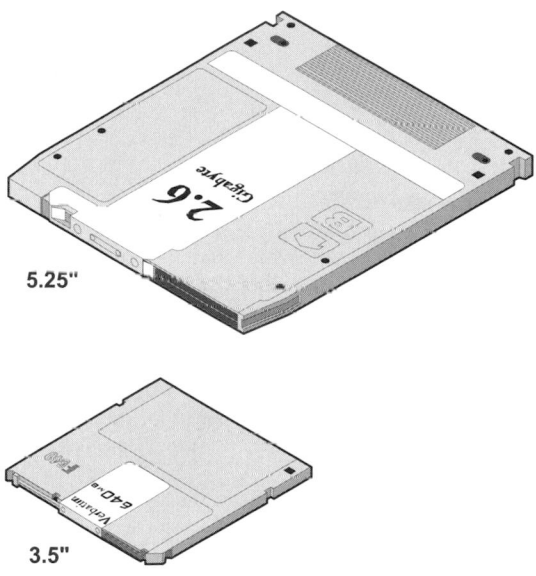

5.25"

3.5"

MO Cartridges
The 5.25" cartridges are double sided and must be flipped to reach the other side. The 3.5" cartridges are single sided.

one pass, and data is written on the second pass. A direct overwrite method (LIMDOW) was later added that erases and writes in one rotation. Many drives support the LIMDOW disks, which is more costly than standard MO media. See *Kerr effect* and *optical disk*. For a summary of all storage technologies, see *storage*.

magnetoresistive

A technology used for the read element of a read/write head on a high-density magnetic disk. As storage capacity increases, the bit gets smaller and its magnetic field becomes weaker. MR heads are more sensitive to weaker fields than the earlier inductive read coils.

Magnetoresistive means that a material's electrical resistance changes when brought in contact with a magnetic field. Unlike inductive heads in which the bit on the medium induces the current across a gap, the MR mechanism is an active element with current flowing through it. The magnetic orientation of the bit increases the resistance in a thin-film, nickel-iron layer, and the difference in current is detected by the read electronics. MR heads use the traditional inductive coil for writing.

Although this technology was used earlier in analog tape recorders, in 1991, IBM was the first to use it in computer disk drives. In 1998, IBM introduced drives with giant magnetoresistive (GMR) heads, which are sensitive to even weaker fields. GMR heads use additional thin film layers in the sensing element to boost the change in resistance. MR disks are expected to reach 5 Gbits/sq.in., while GMR is expected to go beyond 10 Gbits/sq.in.

Magstar

A high-performance magnetic tape technology from IBM. The Magstar is the latest model in the half-inch, single-hub cartridge line that comprises the 3480, 3490 and 3490e. Designated the 3590, the Magstar boosts capacity to 10GB and provides ESCON and SCSI connectivity to IBM mainframes and midrange systems. By the end of 1998, a 20GB cartridge is expected with an increase in transfer rate from 9 to 14MB/sec. Tape libraries are available that hold from a handful to thousands of cartridges. For a summary of all storage technologies, see *storage*. See also *Magstar MP*.

Type	Year	Tracks	Length	Raw Capacity	Raw tfr Rate
3480	'84	18	160 m	200MB	3MB/sec
3490	'89,	18	160 m	400MB	3MB/sec
3490e	'91,	36	300 m	800MB	3MB/sec
3590	'95,	128	300 m	10GB	9MB/sec

Magstar MP

(Magstar MultiPurpose) A magnetic tape technology from IBM for midrange systems. Except for the use of linear recording, Magstar MP is completely different than the Magstar line. It uses a 5GB cassette-style cartridge rather than a single-hub unit, and it uses 8mm tape rather than half inch. The Magstar MP cartridge was especially designed for picking in a robotic library. Instead of at the beginning, the starting

point is in the middle of the tape for faster retrieval. For a summary of all storage technologies, see *storage*.

mail API

See *messaging API* and *MAPI*.

mail bomb

A huge number of e-mail messages sent to one destination. Mail bombs are sent to antagonize their recipients and/or to cause them problems by filling up their disks and overloading the system. See *spam* and *letter bomb*.

mailbot

(MAIL roBOT) An e-mail server that automatically returns to the sender a fixed e-mail message, typically a description about a service or product or the status of some situation.

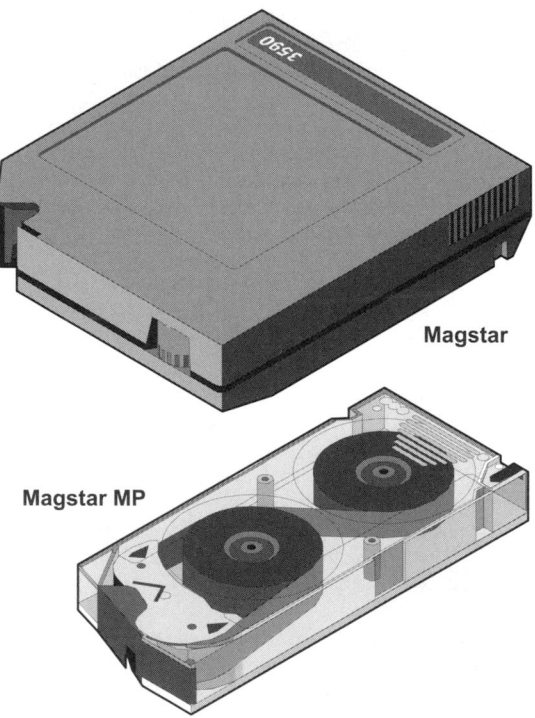

Magstar

Magstar MP

Magstar Cartridges
Magstar and Magstar MP are very different tape technologies. Magstar uses a half-inch, single-hub cartridge, while Magstar MP uses an 8mm cassette-style cartridge that starts in the middle for faster retrieval. Both use linear recording.

mailbox

A simulated mailbox on disk that holds incoming electronic mail.

mail client

An e-mail program that resides in the user's computer and has access to mail servers on the network. See *universal client*.

mail enabled

Refers to an application that has built-in, although typically very limited, mail capabilities. For example, it can send or send and receive a file that it has created over one or more messaging systems. See *messaging API*.

mailer

(1) An e-mail program. See *mail client*.

(2) A message sent by an e-mail program.

(3) A person or organization sending e-mail.

mailing list

An automated e-mail system on the Internet, which is maintained by subject matter. There are more than 10,000 such lists. New users generally subscribe by sending an e-mail with the word "subscribe" in it and subsequently receive all new postings made to the list automatically. Mailing lists are also called *listprocs* and *listservs*, the latter coming from the popular LISTSERV package. Majordomo is a popular public domain mailing list program.

mail merge

Printing customized form letters. A common feature of a word processor, it uses a letter and a name and address list. In the letter, Dear A: Thank you for ordering B from our C store..., A, B and C are merge points into which data is inserted from the list. See *field squeeze* and *line squeeze*.

Letter

Dear A:
Thank you for
ordering B
at our C store.
Sincerely,
The Management

Database

A	B	C
Mr. Smith	1 Widgit	New York
Ms. Gomez	2 Dingits	Chicago
Mr. Jones	1 Frabbits	Los Angeles
Mr. Gold	3 Widgits	Atlanta
Ms. Chang	2 Frabbits	Philadelphia
Mr. Russo	4 Dingits	Boston

The Mail Merge
The mail merge inserts the fields from the database into the predefined merge points in the form letter.

mail program

See *mail client*.

mail protocol

See *messaging protocol* and *messaging system*.

mail proxy

A proxy server that specializes in e-mail transactions. See *proxy server*.

mail server

A computer in a network that provides "post office" facilities. It stores incoming mail for distribution to users and forwards outgoing mail through the appropriate channel. The term may refer to just the software that performs this service, which can reside on a machine with other services. See *messaging system*.

mail system

See *e-mail* and *messaging system*.

mail virus

A macro virus in a document attached to an e-mail message. See *macro virus*.

mainboard

Same as *motherboard*.

main distribution frame

See *MDF*.

mainframe

A large computer. In the "ancient" mid 1960s, all computers were called mainframes, since the term referred to the main CPU cabinet. Today, it refers to a large computer system.

There are small, medium and large-scale mainframes, handling from a handful to tens of thousands of online terminals. Large-scale mainframes support multiple gigabytes of main memory and terabytes of disk storage. Large mainframes use smaller computers as front end processors that connect to the communications networks.

The original mainframe vendors were Burroughs, Control Data, GE, Honeywell, IBM, NCR, RCA and Univac, otherwise known as "IBM and the Seven Dwarfs." After GE and RCA's computer divisions were absorbed by Honeywell and Univac respectively, the mainframers were known as "IBM and the BUNCH."

IBM has the lion's share of the mainframe business, and Hitachi Data Systems and Amdahl are its major competitors, making System/390-compatible computers (see *IBM-compatible mainframe*). Unisys, Sun, Digital and others make mainframes or mainframe-class machines, but run under proprietary or UNIX-based operating systems, not IBM's OS/390.

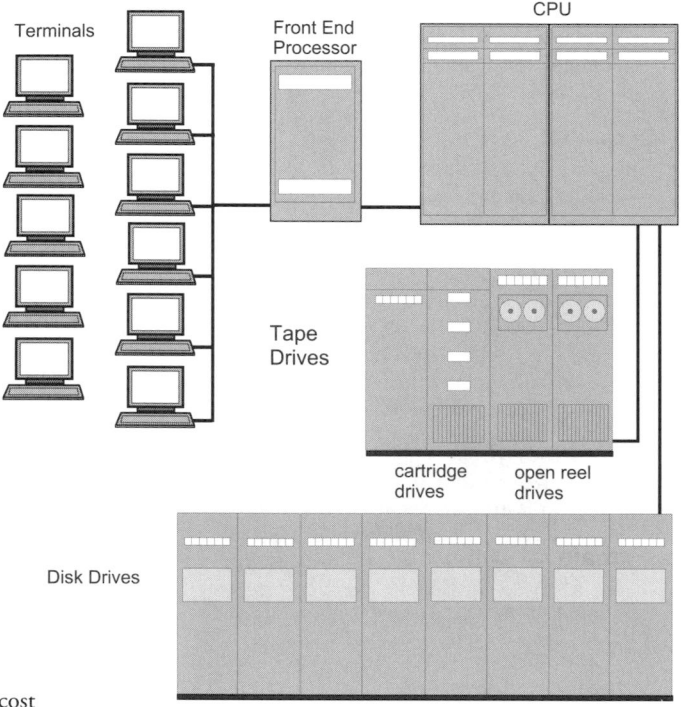

Mainframe System

There Is a Difference!

One might wonder why mainframes cost up to several millions of dollars when their raw megahertz (MHz) or MIPS rates are no higher than a PC costing 1,000 times less. There are reasons. Firstly, in a small computer such as a PC, the CPU does almost all the processing. Unless direct memory transfer (DMA) is used, the CPU is also involved with getting data to and from the peripherals, the most time-consuming part of the whole operation.

A mainframe provides enormous amounts of throughput by offloading its input/output processing to a peripheral channel, which is a computer in itself. Mainframes can support hundreds of channels, up to 512 in some models. Mainframes also have multiple ports into memory and especially into high-speed caches, which can be 10 times faster than main memory. Additional computers may act as I/O traffic cops between the CPU and the channels and handle the processing of exceptions (what happens if the channel is busy, if it fails, etc.). All these subsystems handle the transaction overhead, freeing the CPU to do real "data processing" such as computing balances in customer records and subtracting amounts from inventories, the purpose of the computer in the first place.

Secondly, the internal bus transfer rates of mainframes are also higher than small computers. A 200MHz Pentium has a data bus that runs at 66MHz, but a 200MHz mainframe may have a data bus that also runs at 200MHz, three times as fast. The multipliers add up. Three times the bus speed, 10 times the cache speed, perhaps 32 or 64 overlapped data transfers. Multiply one times the other, and the combination of fast buses, fast caches, multiple memory ports and independent channels and subsystems makes a processing machine unlike anything else.

Thirdly, much of the hardware circuitry in a mainframe is designed to detect and correct errors. Every subsystem is continuously monitored for potential failure, in some cases even triggering a list of parts to be replaced at the next scheduled downtime. As a result, mainframes are incredibly reliable. The mean time between failure (MTBF) is generally 20 years!

In addition, mainframes are highly scalable. Based on symmetric multiprocessing (SMP), mainframes can be expanded by adding CPUs to a system or by adding systems in clusters.

They're Here to Stay

Once upon a time, mainframes meant "complicated" and required the most programming and operations expertise. That is no longer. Networks of client/server-based PCs make mainframes look easy. Nothing is more complicated than the DOS/Windows environment. Add NetWare, throw in a little UNIX for good measure, and you have enterprise computing at its most complex ever. With more than two trillion dollars worth of mainframe applications in place, mainframes are here to stay, and their centralized architecture, which is easiest to manage, may just be the wave of the future!

UNIVAC Mainframe
Mainframes have provided the computing power for major corporations for more than 40 years. Sperry Rand (Univac), IBM, GE, RCA, NCR, Burroughs, Honeywell and Control Data were the first companies that made mainframes in the U.S. This picture was taken in the mid 1970s. *(Photo courtesy of Unisys Corporation.)*

main line
See *main loop*.

main loop
The primary logic in a program. It contains the instructions that are repeated after each event or transaction has been processed. See *loop*.

main memory, main storage
Same as *memory*.

main processor
Same as CPU.

maintenance
(1) Hardware maintenance is the testing and cleaning of equipment.

(2) Information system maintenance is the routine updating of master files, such as adding and deleting employees and customers and changing credit limits and product prices.

(3) Software, or program, maintenance is the updating of application programs in order to meet changing information requirements, such as adding new functions and changing data formats. It also includes fixing bugs and adapting the software to new hardware devices.

(4) Disk or file maintenance is the periodic reorganizing of disk files that have become fragmented due to continuous updating.

maintenance credits
Monetary credits issued to a customer by the vendor for qualified periods during which the vendor's products are not functioning properly.

maintenance service
A service provided to keep a product in good operating condition.

Majordomo
A mailing list program on the Internet made up of a series of Perl scripts and C source code. It runs in most all UNIX environments. See *mailing list*.

major key
The primary key used to identify a record, such as account number or name.

make

To compile a program made up of several independent software modules. The make utility recompiles only those modules that have been updated since the last compilation.

male connector

A plug or socket that contains pins. The female counterpart contains receptacles.

Maltron keyboard

A keyboard that uses independent left- and right-hand modules shaped to conform to the natural position of the hands, designed to prevent strain (RSI).

MAN

(Metropolitan Area Network) A communications network that covers a geographic area such as a city or suburb. See *LAN* and *WAN*.

management console

A terminal or workstation used to monitor and control a network.

management information system

See *MIS*.

management science

The study of statistical methods, such as linear programming and simulation, in order to analyze and solve organizational problems. Same as *operations research*.

management support

See *DSS* and *EIS*.

management system

The leadership and control within an organization. It is made up of people interacting with other people and machines that, together, set the goals and objectives, outline the strategies and tactics, and develop the plans, schedules and necessary controls to run an organization.

ManageWise

Network management software from Novell that manages NetWare and Windows NT servers and all supported clients.

Manchester Code

A self-clocking data encoding method that divides the time required to define the bit into two cycles. The first cycle is the data value (0 or 1) and the second cylce provides the timing by shifting to the opposite state.

ManMan

See *CA-ManMan/X*.

man page

(MANual Page) A page of online documentation in a UNIX system. The command **man** followed by the command name retrieves the appropriate page from the online manual.

MANTIS

An application development language from Cincom Systems, Inc., Cincinnati, OH, (www.cincom.com), that runs on IBM mainframes, VAXs and other mainframes. It provides procedural and non-procedural languages for developing prototypes and applications and works with Cincom's SUPRA database, DB2 and IMS.

mantissa

The numeric value in a floating point number. See *floating point*.

map

(1) A set of data that has a corresponding relationship to another set of data.

(2) A list of data or objects as they are currently stored in memory or disk.

(3) To assign a path or drive letter to a disk drive. See *drive mapping*.

(4) To transfer a set of objects from one place to another. For example, program modules on disk are mapped into memory. A graphic image in memory is mapped onto the video screen. An address is mapped to another address. A logical database structure is mapped to the physical database. Mapping typically requires a conversion of one format to another.

(5) To relate one set of objects with another. For example, a vendor's protocol stack is mapped to the OSI model.

(6) (MAP) (Manufacturing Automation Protocol) A communications protocol introduced by General Motors in 1982. MAP provides common standards for interconnecting computers and programmable machine tools used in factory automation. At the lowest physical level, it uses the IEEE 802.4 token bus protocol.

MAP is often used in conjunction with *TOP*, an office protocol developed by Boeing Computer Services. TOP is used in the front office and MAP is used on the factory floor.

MAPI

(Mail **API**) A programming interface that enables an application to send and receive mail over the Microsoft Mail messaging system. Simple MAPI is a subset of MAPI that includes a dozen functions for sending and retrieving mail.

MAPICS

(Manufacturing Accounting and Production Information Control System) A comprehensive and widely-used ERP system from Marcam Corporation, Newton, MA, (www.marcam.com), that includes more than 45 different software modules. Originally developed by IBM in 1978 and purchased by Marcam in 1993, MAPICS runs on Windows clients and AS/400 servers.

MAPI method

Procedures for equipment replacement analysis and capital investment analysis from the Machinery and Allied Products Institute.

MAPPER

(MAintaining, Preparing and Processing Executive Reports) A Unisys mainframe fourth-generation language. In 1980, it was introduced as a high-level report writer and was later turned into a full-featured development system used successfully by non-technical users.

mapping

See *map* and *digital mapping*.

marginal test

A system test that introduces values far above and far below the expected values.

Marimba

(Marimba, Inc., Palo Alto, CA, www.marimba.com) A software company founded in 1996 by four key members of Sun's original Java development team. In 1996, it introduced Castanet, a family of Java-based delivery systems for publishing and automatically distributing application updates and other published materials via the Internet and intranets.

mark

(1) A small blip printed on or notched into various storage media used for timing or counting purposes.

(2) To identify a block of text in order to perform some task on it such as deletion, copying and moving.

(3) To identify an item for future reference.

(4) In digital electronics, a 1 bit. Contrast with *space*.

(5) On magnetic disk, a recorded character used to identify the beginning of a track.

(6) In optical recognition and mark sensing, a pencil line in a preprinted box.

(7) On magnetic tape, a *tape mark* is a special character that is recorded after the last character of data.

Mark I

An electromechanical calculator designed by professor Howard Aiken, built by IBM and installed at Harvard in 1944. It strung 78 adding machines together to perform three calculations per second. It was 51 feet long, weighed five tons and used punched cards and typewriters for I/O. Made of 765,000 parts, it sounded like a thousand knitting needles according to Admiral Grace Hopper. The experience helped IBM develop its own computers a few years later.

The Mark I
Five tons of mechanical calculator and 51 feet long, the Mark I could perform three calculations a second in 1944. *(Photo courtesy of Smithsonian Institution.)*

marking engine

See *printer engine*.

MARK IX

An application generator from Sterling Software's Answer Systems Division, Woodland Hills, CA, that runs on IBM mainframes and personal computers. It stems from MARK IV, the first report writer to use fill-in-the-blanks forms. MARK V was a subsequent online version.

mark sensing

Detecting pencil lines in predefined boxes on paper forms. The form is designed with boundaries for each pencil stroke that represents a yes, no, single digit or letter, providing all possible answers to each question. A mark sense reader detects the marks and converts them into digital code.

markup language

See *SGML* and *HTML*.

MAS

(1) (Multiple Address System) A radio service in the 932-932.5 and 941-941.5Mhz frequency that covers a 25-mile radius from the antenna. It is used for sensor-based and transaction systems (ATMs, reservations, alarms, traffic control, etc.).

(2) (Multiple Award Schedule) A list of approved products available for purchase by U.S. government agencies.

(3) (Macintosh Application System) Software that allows a Macintosh 680x0 application to run in a PowerPC. It includes a 680x0 emulator and the Macintosh Toolbox, which contains the Mac's graphical functions. The Macintosh graphical user interface runs native in the PowerPC while only the Motorola 680x0 instructions are emulated.

mask

(1) A pattern used to transfer a design onto an object. See *photomask*.

(2) A pattern of bits used to accept or reject bit patterns in another set of data. For example, the Boolean AND operation can be used to match a mask of 0s and 1s with a string of data bits. When a 1 occurs in both the mask and the data, the resulting bit will contain a 1 in that position.

Hardware interrupts are often enabled and disabled in this manner with each interrupt assigned a bit position in a mask register.

maskable interrupts

Hardware interrupts that can be enabled and disabled by software.

mask bit
A 1 bit in a mask used to control the corresponding bit found in data.

MASM
See *macro assembler*.

massage
To process data.

massively parallel
See *MPP*.

mass storage
High-capacity, external storage such as disk or tape.

master boot record
The first sector on the hard disk, which directs the computer to the location of the operating system. See *boot sector*.

master clock
A clock that provides the primary source of internal timing for a processor or stand-alone control unit.

master console
The main terminal used by the computer operator or systems programmer to command the computer.

master control program
The program in control of the machine. See *operating system*.

master file
A collection of records pertaining to one of the main subjects of an information system, such as customers, employees, products and vendors. Master files contain descriptive data, such as name and address, as well as summary information, such as amount due and year-to-date sales. Contrast with *transaction file*.

Following are the kinds of fields that make up a typical master record in a business information system. There can be many more fields depending on the organization. The "key" fields below are the ones that are generally indexed for matching against the transaction records as well as fast retrieval for queries. The account number is usually the primary key, but name may also be primary. There can be secondary indexes; for example, in an inverted file structure, almost all the fields could be indexed. See *transaction file* for examples of typical transaction records.

```
      EMPLOYEE MASTER RECORD              VENDOR MASTER RECORD
key   Employee account number      key   Vendor account number
key   Name (last)                  key   Name
      Name (first)                       Address, city, state, zip
      Address, city, state, zip          Terms
      Hire date                          Quality rating
      Birth date                         Shipping method
      Title
      Job class                          PRODUCT MASTER RECORD
      Pay rate                     key   Product number
      Year-to-date gross pay       key   Name
                                         Description
      CUSTOMER MASTER RECORD             Quantity on hand
key   Customer account number            Location
key   Name                               Primary vendor
      Bill-to address, city, state, zip  Secondary vendor
      Ship-to address, city, state, zip
      Credit limit
      Date of first order
      Sales-to-date
      Balance due
```

master record

A set of data for an individual subject, such as a customer, employee or vendor. See *master file*.

master-slave communications

Communications in which one side, called the master, initiates and controls the session. The other side (slave) responds to the master's commands.

match print

In prepress, a high-quality sample of printed output that is used as a comp for the customer and a guide for the printer. It is made by exposing the CMYK negatives onto four acetate films which are developed and laminated together. See *color key*.

Mathcad

Mathematical software for PCs and Macs from Mathsoft, Inc., Cambridge, MA, (www.mathsoft.com). It allows complicated mathematical equations to be expressed, performed and displayed.

math coprocessor

A mathematical circuit that performs high-speed floating point operations. It is generally built into the CPU chip. In older PCs, such as the 386 and 486SX, the math coprocessor was an optional and separate chip. Floating point capability is very important to computation-intensive CAD work, and many CAD programs will not operate without it. A spreadsheet may use it if available, but it is not mandatory. See *array processor* and *vector processor*.

Mathematica

Mathematical software for the Macintosh, DOS, Windows, OS/2 and various UNIX platforms from Wolfram Research, Inc., Champaign, IL, (www.wolfram.com). It includes numerical, graphical and symbolic computation capabilities, all linked to the Mathematica programming language. Its use requires a math coprocessor.

mathematical expression

A group of characters or symbols representing a quantity or an operation. See *arithmetic expression*.

mathematical function

A rule for creating a set of new values from an existing set; for example, the function $f(x) = 2x$ creates a set of even numbers (if x is a whole number).

matrix

An array of elements in row and column form. See *x-y matrix*.

matrix printer

See *dot matrix* and *printer*.

MAU

(Multi-station Access Unit) A central hub in a Token Ring local area network. See *hub*.

maximize

In a graphical environment, to enlarge a window to full size. Contrast with *minimize*.

MB

(1) (MegaByte or MotherBoard) MB mostly stands for megabyte, but on ads for raw components, it may refer to motherboard.

(2) (Mb) (MegaBit) A lower case "b" in Mb should stand for megabit, but using "b" for bit and "B" for byte is not always followed and often misprinted. Thus, Mb may refer to megabyte. See *space/time* for common usage.

Mbits/sec, Mbps, Mb/s; Mbytes/sec, MBps, MB/s

(MegaBits Per Second; MegaBytes Per Second) One million bits per second; one million bytes per second. Using lower case "b" for bit and upper case "B" for byte is not always followed and often misprinted. See *space/time*.

Mbone

(Multicast backBONE) A collection of sites on the Internet that support the IP multicast protocol (one-to-many) and allow for live audio and videoconferencing.

MBR

(Master Boot Record) See *boot sector*.

MCA

See *Micro Channel*.

MCC

(The Microelectronics and Computer Technology Corporation, Austin, TX, www.mcc.com) An industrial research and development consortium chartered in 1982. Its membership comes from a wide variety of companies, and its hardware and software projects are just as wide ranging. MCC services include newsletters, seminars and workshops.

MCI

(Media Control Interface) A high-level programming interface from Microsort and IBM for controlling multimedia devices. It provides commands and functions to open, play and close the device.

MCI decision

An FCC decree in 1969 that granted MCI the right to compete with the Bell System by providing private, intercity telecommunications services.

MCIS

(Microsoft Commercial Internet System) A family of Web server software products from Microsoft that runs on Windows NT and works with Internet Information Server (IIS). Intended for ISPs and other online services, it includes Web, chat, news and search servers and a variety of development tools. It also includes support for NetMeeting and provides an Internet-based messaging system that is different than Microsoft Exchange. MCIS was originally code named Normandy.

MCM

(MultiChip Module or MicroChip Module) A chip housing that uses a ceramic base and contains two or more raw chips closely connected with high-density lines. This packaging method saves space and speeds processing due to short leads between chips.

MCMs were originally called *microcircuits* or *hybrid microcircuits*, since this technique was suited for mixing analog and digital components together. MCMs offer a more workable solution to wafer scale integration, in essence, building the "superchip," which has been very difficult to implement. See *hybrid microcircuit, chip package* and *Trilogy*.

MCPS

See *Microsoft Certified Professional*.

MCS

(1) See *Microsoft Cluster Server*.

(2) (Microsoft Consulting Services) The consulting arm of Microsoft which offers support for installation and maintenance of Microsoft applications and operating systems.

(3) (Multivendor Customer Service) The consulting arm of Digital Equipment that was founded in 1993. It provides hardware, software and network services for a variety of platforms.

(4) (Multimedia Conference Server) A family of videoconferencing servers from VideoServer, Inc., Lexington, MA. The MCS was the first multipoint control unit to comply with H.320.

(5) A family of microcontroller units (MCUs) from Intel. In 1995, Intel introduced its 8-bit MCS 251 chips which are binary compatible with its older MCS 51 series.

MCSD, MCSE, MCT

See *Microsoft Certified Professional*.

MCU

(1) (MicroController Unit) A computer on a single chip. See *computer on a chip*.

(2) (Multipoint Control Unit) A device that connects multiple sites and stations for videoconferencing. The MCU joins the lines and switches the video either automatically depending on who is speaking or manually under the direction of a moderator.

MD

See *MiniDisc*.

MD5 (MD2, MD4)

(Message Digest 5) A popular one-way hash function developed by Ronald Rivest (the "R" in RSA) which is used to create a message digest for digital signatures. MD5 is faster than SHA-1, but is considered less secure. MD5 is similar to the previous MD4 method as both were designed for 32-bit computers, but MD5 adds more security since MD4 has been broken. The earlier MD2 function was designed for 8-bit computers. See *one-way hash function*.

MDA

(1) (Monochrome Display Adapter) The first IBM PC monochrome video display standard for text only. Due to its lack of graphics, MDA cards were often replaced with Hercules cards, which provided both text and graphics. See *PC display modes*.

(2) (Modular Digital Architecture) A snap-together, building-block approach for adding peripherals to a PC from NeoSystems, Inc.

(3) (Mechanical Design Automation) Refers to applications that help automate the design and engineering processes from concept to manufacturing. Automotive, aerospace and discrete manufacturing are examples of industries that use MDA.

MDBS IV

A DBMS from that runs on DOS, OS/2, UNIX, MPE and VMS servers from Micro Data Base Systems, Inc., Lafayette, IN, (www.mdbs.com). Noted for its performance and maturity (in 1984, MDBS III was the first client/server DBMS), it provides a superset of hierarchical, network and relational storage concepts. M/4 for Windows is a single-user Windows version.

MD DATA

The data storage counterpart of Sony's MiniDisc drive. See *MiniDisc*.

MDDB

(MultiDimensional DataBase) See *OLAP*.

MDF

(Main Distribution Frame) A connecting unit between external and internal lines. It allows for public or private lines coming into the building to connect to internal networks. See *CDF*.

MDI

(1) (Multiple Document Interface) A Windows function that allows an application to display and lets the user work with more than one document at the same time. If the application is not programmed for MDI and you want to work with multiple documents of the same type concurrently, you must load the application again for each subsequent document. Contrast with *SDI*.

(2) (Medium Dependent Interface) Refers to an Ethernet port connection. The MDI-X port on an Ethernet hub is used to connect to a workstation (the X stands for crossing the transmit and recieve lines). An MDI port (not crossed) is used to connect to the MDI-X port of another hub.

(3) (Manual Data Input) Refers to entering data using the keyboard rather than by disk, tape or communications link.

MDIS

See *Metadata Coalition*.

MDRAM

(Multibank DRAM) A type of dynamic RAM chip from MoSys, Inc., Sunnyvale, CA, (www.mosys.com), that is available in 256KB increments. It enables embedded applications with fixed memory requirements to have exactly the amount of RAM they need. MDRAM uses an internal bus connected to independent 32KB banks of DRAM, which provides a bandwidth of 666 MBytes/sec.

meatspace
The physical world. Contrast with *cyberspace*.

mechanical mouse
A mouse that uses a rubber ball that rolls against wheels inside the unit. Contrast with *optical mouse*.

media
Materials that hold data in any form or that allow data to pass through them, including paper, transparencies, multipart forms, hard, floppy and optical disks, magnetic tape, wire, cable and fiber. Media is the plural of "medium."

media access method
See "LANs" under *data link protocol*.

media bus
A high-speed channel designed for transferring audio and video data. See *VESA Media Channel*.

media control
Also called *media processing*, in computer telephony it refers to some processing or altering of the call; for example, digitizing the content. Contrast with *call control*.

Media Control Interface
See *MCI*.

media conversion
See *data conversion* and *conversion*.

media failure
A condition of not being able to read from or write to a storage device, such as a disk or tape, due to a defect in the recording surface.

media gateway
A device that converts multimedia input into a backbone network and vice versa. A media gateway can be an IP gateway, a circuit switch (telephone switch) or a modem bank. See *media gateway controller* and *IP gateway*.

media gateway controller
A device that controls media gateways. It analyzes incoming signals and determines the appropriate backbone network and services required to route the data. See *media gateway* and *IPDC*.

Media GX
A CPU from Cyrix that includes sound, display, memory control and PCI circuits on the same chip.

Media Player
A Windows multimedia utility that is used to play sound and video files.

media processing
See *media control*.

media processor
A controller or chip that is used to build a multimedia subsystem that processes any combination of audio, video, graphics, fax and modem operations.

medium frequency
An electromagnetic wave that oscillates in the range from 300,000 to 3,000,000 Hz. See *electromagnetic spectrum*.

MEDLINE
The online database of the U.S. National Library of Medicine (NLM). The data is available for a fee on the Internet, CompuServe and directly from the NLM. MEDLINE contains millions of articles from thousands of medical publications.

meg, mega

(1) Million (10 to the 6th power). Abreviated "M." It often refers to the precise value 1,048,576 since computer specifications are based on binary numbers. See *binary values* and *space/time.*

(2) (MEGA) A personal computer series from Atari that was Motorola 68000 based, ran under GEM and the TOS operating system and included a MIDI interface. It was ST compatible.

megabit

One million bits. Also Mb, Mbit and M-bit. See *mega* and *space/time.*

megabyte

One million bytes. Also MB, Mbyte and M-byte. See *mega* and *space/time.*

megaflops

(mega **FL**oating point **OP**erations per Second) One million floating point operations per second. See *FLOPS.*

megahertz

One million cycles per second. See *MHz.*

megapel display

In computer graphics, a display system that handles a million or more pixels. A resolution of 1,000 lines by 1,000 dots requires a million pixels for the full screen image.

membrane keyboard

A dust and dirtproof keyboard widely used with restaurant cash registers and factory floor machines. It is constructed of two thin plastic sheets (membranes) that contain flexible printed circuits made of electrically conductive ink. The top membrane is the printed keyboard and a spacer sheet with holes is in the middle. When a user presses a simulated key, the top membrane is pushed through the spacer hole and makes contact with the bottom membrane, completing the circuit.

Memmaker

A DOS utility that is used to optimize the first megabyte of memory.

memo field

A data field that holds a variable amount of text. The text may be stored in a companion file, but it is treated as if it were part of the data record. For example, in the dBASE command **list name, biography,** name is in the data file (DBF file) and biography could be a memo field in the text file (DBT file).

memory

The computer's workspace (physically, a collection of RAM chips). It is an important resource, since it determines the size and number of programs that can be run at the same time, as well as the amount of data that can be processed instantly.

All program execution and data processing takes place in memory. The program's instructions are copied into memory from disk or tape and then extracted from memory into the control unit circuit for analysis and execution. The instructions direct the computer to input data into memory from a keyboard, disk, tape or communications channel.

As data is entered into memory, the previous contents of that space are lost. Once

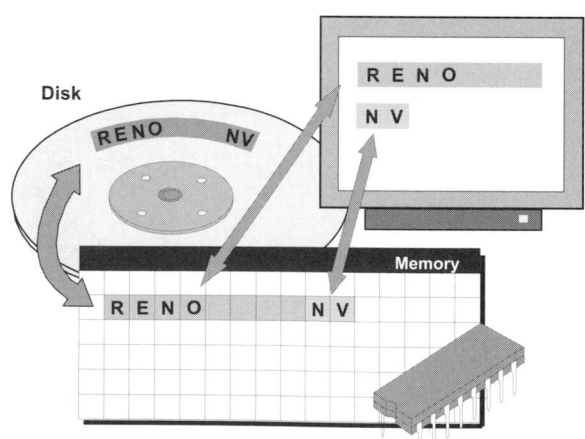

Memory Is an Electronic Checkerboard
Each checkerboard square of memory holds one byte. The contents of any single byte or group of bytes can be calculated, compared and copied independently. That's how fields are put together to form records and broken apart when read back in. On the disk, data is stored in sectors, which hold a chunk of data (typically 512 bytes) and are the smallest unit that can be read or written.

the data is in memory, it can be processed (calculated, compared and copied). The results are sent to a screen, printer, disk, tape or communications channel.

Memory is like an electronic checkerboard, with each square holding one byte of data or instruction. Each square has a separate address like a post office box and can be manipulated independently. As a result, the computer can break apart programs into instructions for execution and data records into fields for processing.

Memory Doesn't Usually Remember

Oddly enough, the computer's memory doesn't remember anything when the power is turned off. That's why you have to save your files before you quit your program. Although there are memory chips that do hold their content permanently (ROMs, PROMs, EPROMs, etc.), they're used for internal control purposes and not for the user's data.

"Remembering" memory in a computer system is its disks and tapes, and although they are also called memory devices, many prefer to call them storage devices (as we do) in order to differentiate them from internal memory. Perhaps in time, memory will refer to disks exclusively and RAM will refer to working memory. Until then, its usage for both RAM and disk only adds confusion to the most confusing industry on earth.

Memory Can Get Clobbered!

Memory is such an important resource that it cannot be wasted. It must be allocated by the operating system as well as applications and then released when not needed. Errant programs can grab memory and not let go of it even when they are closed, which results in less and less memory available as you load and use more programs.

In addition, if the operating system is not advanced, a malfunctioning application can write into memory used by another program, causing all kinds of unspecified behavior. You discover it when the system freezes or something wierd happens all of a sudden. If you were to really look into memory and watch how much and how fast data and instructions are written into and out of it in the course of a day, it's truly a miracle that it works.

Other terms for memory are *RAM, main memory, main storage, primary storage, read/write memory, core* and *core storage*. See also *SIMM*.

memory allocation

Reserving memory for specific purposes. Operating systems and applications generally reserve fixed amounts of memory at startup and allocate more when additional functions must be executed. If there is not enough free memory to load the core kernel of an application, it cannot be launched. Although a virtual memory function will simulate an almost unlimited amount of memory, there is always a certain amount of "real" memory that is needed.

When an application is programmed, the programmer must typically allocate additional memory as needed and release that memory when that function is no longer used. This is tedious and error prone, as it is easy to forget to deallocate the memory which can remain unusable after the program is closed and until the computer is turned off and back on. Some operating systems perform "garbage collection," whereby they release memory automatically when a program is closed or when the contents of the memory have not been used for some period of time. One of the advantages of the Java environment is that memory allocation and deallocation is handled automatically by the Java Virtual Machine.

On a personal computer, additional memory can be allocated by the operating system or by the user for a disk cache, which retains large chunks of data from the disk in faster RAM. However, a large disk cache that speeds up one application may slow down another because there is less normal memory available.

On PCs before DOS 6, users were expected to allocate the right mix of expanded memory (EMS) and extended memory, causing third-party memory managers such as QEMM and 386MAX to become popular because they did it automatically. DOS 6 provided automatic allocation, and Windows 95 included even more dynamic memory allocations. Users should never have had to make such technical decisions in the first place. After all, that's what a computer is supposed to do.

memory bank

(1) A physical section of memory. See *memory interleaving*.

(2) Refers generically to a computer system that holds data.

memory based

Programs that hold all data in memory for processing. Almost all spreadsheets are memory based so that a change in data at one end of the spreadsheet can be instantly reflected at the other end.

memory cache
See *cache.*

memory card
A credit-card-sized memory module used as an additional disk or disk alternative in laptops and palmtops. Called IC cards, ROM cards and RAM cards, they use a variety of chip types, including RAM, ROM, EEPROM and flash memory. RAM cards used in this manner contain a battery to keep the cells charged.

Note that when you add more memory in a laptop, the plug-in cards may also be called memory cards or RAM cards, but these are not substitutes for disk. They extend the computer's normal RAM memory and are typically contained on proprietary plug-in modules. The memory card that functions as a disk typically uses the PCMCIA architecture and requires special software that accompanies the computer. See *solid state disk* and *flash memory.*

memory cell
One bit of memory. In dynamic RAM memory, a cell is made up of one transistor and one capacitor. In static RAM memory, a cell is made up of about five transistors.

memory chip
A chip that holds programs and data either temporarily (RAM), permanently (ROM, PROM) or permanently until changed (EPROM, EEPROM, flash memory).

memory cycle
A series of operations that take place to read or write a byte of memory. For destructive memories, it includes the regeneration of the bits.

memory cycle time
The time it takes to perform one memory cycle.

memory dump
A display or printout of the contents of memory. When a program abends, a memory dump can be taken in order to examine the status of the program at the time of the crash. The programmer looks into the buffers to see which data items were being worked on when it failed. Counters, variables, switches and flags are also inspected.

memory effect
See *nickel cadmium* and *nickel hydride.*

memory interleaving
A category of techniques for increasing memory speed. For example, with separate memory banks for odd and even addresses, the next byte of memory can be accessed while the current byte is being refreshed.

memory leak
A program that does not free up the extra memory it allocates. In some programming languages, such as C and C++, the programmer must specifically allocate additional chunks of memory to hold data and variables as required. When the routine is exited, it is supposed to deallocate the memory. A serious memory leak will eventually usurp all the memory, bringing everything to a halt. In other environments, such as Java, the operating system allocates and deallocates memory automatically, which is the way it should work. See *garbage collection.*

memory management
Refers to a variety of methods used to store data and programs in memory, keep track of them and reclaim the memory space when they are no longer needed. In also includes virtual memory, bank switching and memory protection techniques.

Memory management was a major issue in DOS-based PCs, because the PC has more different types of memory regions than any computer in history. In a PC, memory management refers to managing conventional memory, the upper memory area (UMA), the high memory area (HMA), extended memory and expanded memory.

Because of DOS' original limitation of one megabyte of memory, expanding a DOS PC has been difficult, often requiring manual editing of configuration files, which is not a task for the casual user. For

Computer Desktop Encyclopedia

technicians, countless books have been written on this problem that never should have existed in the first place. There have even been two-day courses on the subject. Subsequent versions of DOS, and especially Windows, added the necessary memory management functions to eliminate this frustration with most PCs. However, machines with older peripherals and drivers may still require manual tweaking to get everything working together, and this is still sometimes required to solve some problems in Windows 3.1 and 95/98. See *virtual memory, garbage collection, memory protection, EMS, EMM* and *DOS memory manager*. See *PC memory map* for an illustration of memory regions in a PC.

memory manager
Software that manages memory in a computer. See *memory management*.

memory map
The location of instructions and data in memory. See *PC memory map* for a digaram of the PC's upper memory area.

memory mapped I/O
A peripheral device that assigns specific memory locations to input and output. For example, in a memory mapped display, each pixel or text character derives its data from a specific memory byte or bytes. The instant this memory is updated by software, the screen is displaying the new data.

memory module
A printed circuit board with memory chips that plugs into the motherboard or some other type of backplane. See *SIMM* and *DIMM*.

memory protection
A technique that prohibits one program from accidentally clobbering another active program. Using various different techniques, a protective boundary is created around the program, and instructions within the program are prohibited from referencing data outside of that boundary.

When a program does go outside of its boundary, DOS, Windows 3.x and earlier personal computer operating systems simply lock up (crash, bomb, abend, etc.). Operating systems such as UNIX, OS/2 and Windows NT are more robust and generally allow the errant program to be closed without affecting the remaining active programs.

memory resident
A program that remains in memory at all times. See *TSR*.

memory sniffing
Coined by Data General, a diagnostic routine that tests memory during normal processing. The processor uses cycle stealing techniques that allow it to test memory during unused machine cycles. A memory bank can be "sniffed" every few minutes.

memory typewriter
A typewriter that holds a few pages of text in its memory and provides limited word processing functions. With a display screen of only one or two lines, editing is tedious.

Memory Sniffing
Sniffing a memory bank may not look exactly like this, but it does the job of testing memory while the computer is running the daily work.

MEMS
(MicroElectroMechanical Systems) Semiconductor chips that have a top layer of mechanical devices such as mirrors or fluid sensors. They are used as pressure sensors, chemical sensors and light reflectors and switches. MEMS devices have been in the research labs since the 1980s and began to materialize as commercial products in the mid 1990s. See *DLP*.

menu
An on-screen list of available functions, or operations, that can be performed currently. Depending on the type of menu, selection is accomplished by (1) highlighting the menu option with a mouse and

releasing the mouse, (2) pointing to the option name with the mouse and clicking on it, (3) highlighting the option with the cursor keys and pressing Enter, or (4) pressing the first letter of the option name or some designated letter within the name. See *pull-down menu*.

menu-driven
Using menus to command the computer. Contrast with *command-driven*.

menuing software
Software that provides a menu for launching applications and running operating system commands.

MEO
(Medium-Earth Orbit) A communications satellite in orbit some 6,000 miles above the earth, which is higher than a LEO and lower than a GEO. MEOs take six hours to orbit the earth and are in view for a couple of hours. See *LEO* and *GEO*.

Merced
Intel's next-generation CPU architecture, also known as the P7. Expected in 2000, it is jointly designed by Intel and HP. Although it uses a new instruction architecture (IA-64), Merced is also expected to run x86 and PA-RISC software natively with clock speeds at 600MHz and beyond.

Merced chips should contain more than 10 million transistors using .18 micron technology, and its IA-64 architecture is designed for fast parallel instruction execution. The bottom line is that Merced was designed at the end of the 20th century, whereas x86 chips hark back to an architecture from the early 1970s, which was based on a fraction of the number of transistors available today. The Merced should be a formidable product. In addition, not only will HP-UX and Windows NT run on Merced, but Digital Unix, SCO UnixWare and Solaris are expected to be ported to the new chip family. See *IA-64* and *future Intel chips*.

merchant server
A server in a network that handles online purchases and credit card transactions. It implements an electronic commerce protocol that ensures a secure transmission between the clients and cooperating banks. The term may refer to the entire computer system or just the software that provides this service. A merchant server is also called a *commerce server*.

merge
See *mail merge* and *concatenate*.

merge purge
To merge two or more lists together and eliminate unwanted items. For example, a new name and address list can be added to an old list while deleting duplicate names or names that meet certain criteria.

mesa
A semiconductor process used in the 1960s for creating the sublayers in a transistor. Its deep etching gave way to the planar process.

mesh
A term often used to describe an interconnect architecture that cross connects several devices. It is synonymous with *fabric*. Contrast with *point-to-point*.

mesh network
A net-like communications network in which there are at least two pathways to each node. Since the term network means net-like as well as communications network, the term mesh is used to avoid saying network communications network.

message
(1) In communications, a set of data that is transmitted over a communications line. Just as a program becomes a job when it's running in the computer, data becomes a message when it's transmitted over a network.

(2) In object technology, communicating between objects, similar to a function call in traditional programming.

message based

An interface that is based on a set of commands. A message-based system is a type of client/server relationship, in which requests are made by a client component, and the results are provided by a server component. It implies greater flexibility and interoperability in contrast with a hard coded operation, which would have to be modified by reprogramming the source code.

message digest

A condensed text string that has been distilled from the contents of a text message. Its value is derived using a one-way hash function and is used to create a digital signature. See *digital signature* and *MD5*.

message handling

(1) An electronic mail system. See *messaging system*.

(2) In communications, the lower level protocols that transfer data over a network, which assemble and disassemble the data into the appropriate codes for transmission.

message handling system

Same as *messaging system*.

message header

The identification lines at the beginning of an e-mail message, such as To:, From:, Subject: and Date:.

MessagePad

A family of PDAs from Apple that use the Newton operating system. See *Newton*.

message queue

A storage space in memory or on disk that holds incoming transmissions until the computer can process them. See *messaging middleware*.

message switch

A computer system used to switch data between various points. Computers have always been ideal switches due to their input/output and compare capabilities. It inputs the data, compares its destination with a set of stored destinations and routes it accordingly. Note: A message switch is a generic term for a data routing device, but a messaging switch converts mail and messaging protocols.

message thread

A running commentary by one user in a threaded discussion.

message transfer agent

The store and forward capability in a messaging system. See *messaging system*.

messaging API

A programming interface that enables an application to send and receive messages and attached files over a messaging system. VIM, MAPI and CMC are examples. Novell's SMF-71, although also called an API, is actually the message format that mail must be placed into for submission to Novell's MHS. There are no functions associated with it.

messaging gateway

A computer system that converts one messaging protocol to another. It provides an interface between two store and forward nodes, or message transfer agents (MTAs).

messaging middleware

Software that provides an interface between applications, allowing them to send data back and forth to each other asynchronously. Data sent by one program can be stored and then forwarded to the receiving program when it becomes available to process it. For example, messaging middleware is used to queue up transactions in a transaction processing system.

Messaging middleware and e-mail messaging systems provide similar functionality. The primary difference is that messaging middleware deals with transactions between programs, whereas e-mail messaging deals with messages between people. See *messaging system*.

messaging protocol

The rules, formats and functions for exchanging messages between the components of a messaging system. The major industry messaging protocols are the international X.400, SMTP (Internet), IBM's SNADS and Novell's MHS. Widely-used messaging products such as cc:Mail and Microsoft Mail use proprietary messaging protocols. See *messaging system*.

messaging switch

A messaging hub that provides protocol conversion between several messaging systems. Examples of switches include Soft-Switch's EMX, HP's OpenMail and Digital's MAILbus. A messaging switch differs from a messaging gateway in that it supports more than two protocols and connections as well as providing management and directory integration.

messaging system

Software that provides an electronic mail delivery system. It is comprised of three functional areas, which are either packaged together or are modularized as independent components. (1) The user agent, or UA, submits and receives the message. (2) The message transfer agent, or MTA, stores and forwards the message. (3) The message store, or MS, holds the mail and allows it to be selectively retrieved and deleted. It also provides a list of its contents.

Messaging products such as cc:Mail, Microsoft Mail, PROFS, DISOSS and ALL-IN-1 implement the entire messaging system. Other products must use components of other systems; for example, DaVinci Mail uses Novell's MHS. See *messaging middleware*.

meta

One definition of this Greek word is transcending, or going above and beyond. In the computer field, it defines things that embrace more than the usual. For example, a metafile contains all types of data. Metadata describes other data. See *metafile, metadata* and *meta tag*.

MetaCrawler

(www.metacrawler.com) A search site on the Web that searches other search sites. It reports the number of hits from each of the sites it investigated and displays the titles of all the matching documents. See *Web search sites*.

metadata

(1) Data that describes other data. Data dictionaries and repositories are examples of metadata. The meta tag that describes the content of a Web page is called metadata. The term may also refer to any file or database that holds information about another database's structure, attributes, processing or changes. See *data dictionary, repository* and *meta tag*.

(2) (Metadata) A trade name of Metadata Information Partners, Long Beach, CA. a consulting firm providing custom information systems to the health care industry.

Metadata Coalition

An organization of database and data warehouse vendors founded in 1995. Within a year, it introduced the Metadata Interchange Specification (MDIS) as a standard for defining metadata.

metafile

A file that contains other files. It generally refers to graphics files that can hold vector drawings and bitmaps. For example, a Windows Metafile (WMF) can store pictures in vector graphics and bitmap formats as well as text. A Computer Graphics Metafile (CGM) also stores both types of graphics.

MetaFrame

The server component from Citrix that allows Windows Terminal Server to interact with client stations running the ICA protocol. Windows Terminal Server normally supports Windows-only clients, using the T.share protocol. With MetaFrame (originally named pICAsso), ICA terminals and DOS, Mac and UNIX clients can also run Windows applications on the server. See *Windows Terminal Server* and *WinFrame*.

metalanguage

A language used to describe another language.

metalization layer

The top layers of a chip that interconnect the transistors and resistors. There are usually two to four such layers made of aluminum that are separated by a silicon dioxide insulation layer. See *copper chip*.

Computer Desktop Encyclopedia

metamail
A public-domain UNIX utility that composes and decomposes a MIME message on the Internet.

metamerism
The quality of some colors that causes them to appear differently under different light sources. For example, two color samples might appear the same in natural light, but not in artifical light.

metaphor
The derivation of metaphor means "to carry over." Thus the "desktop metaphor" as so often described means that the office desktop has been brought over and simulated on computers.

metasite
(1) A Web search site that searches other search sites. See *MetaCrawler*.

(2) A Web site that functions as a directory to other Web sites.

meta tag
An HTML tag that identifies the contents of a Web page. Using a <meta name=" " content=" "> format, meta tags contain such things as a general description of the page, keywords for search engines and copyright information.

Metcalfe's law
"The value of a network increases exponentially with the number of nodes." By Bob Metcalfe, founder of 3Com Corporation and major designer of Ethernet. A network becomes more useful as more users are connected. A primary example is the Internet. It fostered global e-mail, which becomes more valuable as more users are connected. See *laws*.

meter
The basic unit of the metric system (39.37 inches). A yard is about 9/10ths of a meter (0.9144 meter).

method
In object technology, a method is the processing that an object performs. When a message is sent to an object, the method is implemented.

methodology
The specific way of performing an operation that implies precise deliverables at the end of each stage.

metric
Measurement. Although metric generally refers to the decimal-based metric system of weights and measures, software engineers often use the term as simply "measurement." For example, "is there a metric for this process?" See *software metrics*.

metric system
A system of weights and measures that uses the gram, meter and liter as its primary units of weight, distance and capacity.

```
Metric                      English
1 gram                      .0022046 lb. (.03527 oz.)
1 decagram (10 gr)          .022046 lb. (.3527 oz.)
1 hectogram (100 gr)        .22046 lb. (3.527 oz.)
1 kilogram (1000 gr)        2.2046 lbs. (35.27 oz.)

1 meter                         39.37 in.
1 decameter (10 m)              32.8 ft.
1 hectometer (100 m)           328.08 ft.
1 kilometer (1000 m)          3280.8 ft.
1 decimeter (1/10 m)             3.937 in.
1 centimeter (1/100 m)           .3937 in.
1 millimeter (1/1000 m)          .03937 in.

1 liter                      1.0567 liquid quart
```

MFC

See *Microsoft C* and *Visual C++*.

MF-COBOL

See *Micro Focus*.

MFD

(MultiFunction Device) Hardware that combines several functions into one unit; for example, the combination fax, copier, printer and scanner. Such devices save money and room on crowded desktops.

Mflops

See *megaflops*.

MFM

(Modified Frequency Modulation) A magnetic disk encoding method used on most floppy disks and most hard disks under 40MB. It has twice the capacity of the earlier FM method, transfers data at 625 Kbytes per second and uses the ST506 interface. See *hard disk*.

MFP

(MultiFunction Product, MultiFunction Peripheral) Same as *MFD*.

MGA

(1) (Monochrome Graphics Adapter) A display adapter that employs Hercules Graphics, combining graphics and text on a monochrome monitor.

(2) (Matrox Graphics Accelerator) A trade name used by Matrox Graphics Inc., Dorval, Quebec, on its graphics adapters; for example, the MGA Millennium.

MGP

(Monochrome Graphics Printer port) A display adapter that employs Hercules Graphics and a parallel printer port on the same expansion board.

MHS

(1) (Message Handling Service) A messaging system from Novell that supports multiple operating systems and other messaging protocols, including SMTP, SNADS and X.400. It uses the SMF-71 messaging format. Standard MHS runs on a DOS machine attached to the server. Global MHS runs as a NetWare NLM. Under NetWare, MHS runs on top of IPX. MHS has been superseded by GroupWise.

(2) See *messaging system*.

MHz

(MegaHertZ) One million cycles per second. It is used to measure the transmission speed of electronic devices, including channels, buses and the computer's internal clock. Megahertz is generally equivalent to one million bits per second or to one million times some number of bits per second.

When it refers to the computer's clock, it is used to measure the speed of the CPU. For example, a 133MHz Pentium processes data internally (calculates, compares, copies) twice as fast as a 66MHz Pentium. However, this does not mean twice as much finished work gets done in the same time frame, because cache design, disk speed and software design all contribute to the computer's actual performance, not just CPU speed. See *MIPS* and *Hertz*.

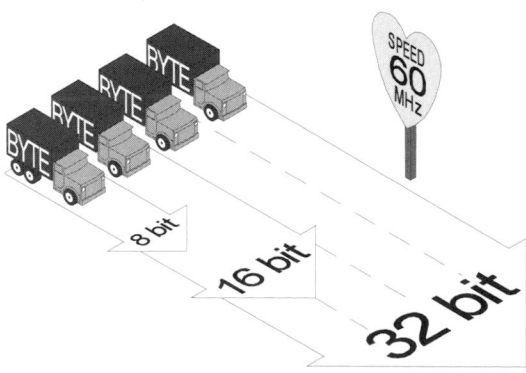

The MegaHertz Speed Limit
MegaHertz is analogous to a highway speed limit. The higher the speed, the faster the traffic moves. In a CPU, the higher the clock rate, the quicker data gets processed. The 8-, 16- and 32 bit designation is the CPU's word size and can be thought of as the number of lanes on the highway. The more lanes, the more traffic. The combination of speed and number of paths determines the total processing speed or channel bandwidth.

Computer Desktop Encyclopedia

MHz Is the Heartbeat

When referencing CPU speed, the megahertz rating is really the heartbeat of the computer, providing the raw, steady pulses that energize the circuits. If you know any German, it's easy to remember this. The word "Herz," pronounced "hayrtz," means heart.

MIB

(Management Information Base) An SNMP structure that describes the particular device being monitored. See *SNMP.*

MIC connector

(Medium Interface Connector) A fiber-optic cable connector that handles a pair of cables. The design of the plug and socket ensures that the polarity is maintained (transmit and receive cables are in correct order). It is used in FDDI and a variety of LANs and wiring hubs. See *fiber-optic connectors.*

mickey

A unit of mouse movement typically set at 1/200th of an inch.

MICR

(Magnetic Ink Character Recognition) The machine recognition of numeric data printed with magnetically-charged ink. It is used on bank checks and deposit slips. MICR readers detect the characters and convert them into digital data. Although optical methods (OCR) became as sophisticated as the early MICR technology, magnetic ink is still used. It serves as a deterrent to fraud, because a photocopied check will not be printed with magnetic ink.

MICR Font
The E13B standard font is used for MICR digits and symbols on bank checks and deposit slips. There are only 14 characters in the font.

micro

(1) A microcomputer or personal computer.
(2) Millionth (10 to the -6th power). See *space/time.*
(3) Microscopic or tiny.

Micro Channel

Also known as MCA (Micro Channel Architecture), it is a proprietary 32-bit bus from IBM that was used in PS/2, RS/6000 and certain ES/9370 models. It supports 15 levels of bus mastering and transfers data from 20 to 80MBytes/sec. The boards have a unique, built-in ID that allows for easier installation than ISA devices. In late 1996, IBM discontinued its use in favor of the PCI bus. See *ISA* for illustration.

microchip

Same as *chip.*

microchip module

See *MCM.*

microcircuit

A miniaturized, electronic circuit, such as is found on an integrated circuit. See *chip* and *MCM.*

microcode

A permanent memory that holds the elementary circuit operations a computer must perform for each instruction in its instruction set. It acts as a translation layer between the instruction and the electronic level of the computer and enables the computer architect to more easily add new types of machine instructions without having to design electronic circuits. Microcode is used in CISC architecture. See *microprogramming.*

microcommerce

Low-value transactions in electronic commerce. The ability to charge pennies for a transaction enables the selling of single articles from a newspaper or invidivual lookups from a dictionary or encyclopedia.

microcomputer

Generally synonymous with personal computer, such as a Windows PC or Macintosh, but it can refer to any kind of small computer. When the term was first introduced, it meant a computer with a single microprocessor chip as its CPU, namely, the personal computer. Today, most every computer uses a microprocessor CPU, including workstations, minicomputers and even mainframes.

microcontroller

See *computer on a chip*.

microelectomechanical systems

See *MEMS*.

microelectronic

The miniaturization of electronic circuits. See *chip*.

microfiche

Pronounced "micro-feesh." A 4x6" sheet of film that holds several hundred miniaturized document pages. See *micrographics*.

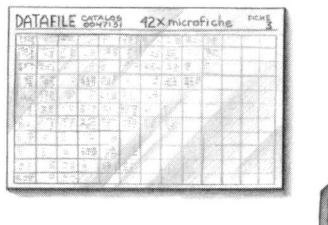 

Microfilm and Microfiche
Billions of pages have been recorded on film and fiche, but optical methods are replacing this old imaging method.

microfilm

A continuous film strip that holds several thousand miniaturized document pages. See *micrographics*.

microfloppy

The formal name for the standard 3.5" floppy disk, which was developed by Sony.

Micro Focus

(Micro Focus Inc., Palo Alto, CA, www,microfocus.com) A software company founded in 1976 that specializes in COBOL application development for a variety of platforms. It is known for its COBOL programming tools. Micro Focus products are used to develop applications on personal computers and workstations that are intended for execution on mainframes, as well as to move COBOL, CICS and IMS applications from the mainframe to client/server environments.

microform

In micrographics, a medium that contains microminiaturized images such as microfiche and microfilm.

Micrografx

(Micrografx, Inc., Richardson, TX, www.micrografx.com) A software company founded in 1982 by Paul and George Grayson that specializes in graphics software. With its award-winning Designer drawing program, Microfgrafx was the first company to bring the graphics tools commonly found on the Macintosh to the Windows platform. Micrografx provides very full-featured and sophisticated graphics products.

Micrografx Designer

A full-featured Windows drawing program that is part of the Micrografx Graphics Suite. Designer is a very sophisticated vector graphics program providing many features of a CAD program, including layers and dimensioning. It creates its own file formats (DRW, DS4 and DSF) and supports PIC files compatible with other Micrografx products. See illustration on next page.

Micrografx Graphics Suite

A suite of graphics applications for Windows 95/98 and NT from Micrografx. It includes the Designer drawing program, Picture Publisher image editor, FlowCharter diagramming tool and Simply 3D 3-D modeling and animation program. See *Micrografx Designer*.

micrographics

The production, handling and use of microfilm and microfiche. Images are created by cameras or by COM units that accept computer output directly. The documents are magnified for human viewing by readers, some of which can automatically locate a page using indexing techniques.

Microfiche and microfilm have always been an economical alternative for high-volume data and picture storage. However, optical disks are quickly superseding fiche and film for archival storage. See *COLD*.

microimage

In micrographics, any photographic image of information that is too small to be read without magnification.

microinstruction

A microcode instruction. It is the most elementary computer operation that can take place; for example, moving a bit from one register to another. It takes several microinstructions to carry out one machine instruction.

microjacket

In micrographics, two sheets of transparent plastic that are bonded together to create channels into which strips of microfilm are inserted and stored.

microJava

Sun's implementation of its Java chip, based on the picoJava core architecture. The microJava 701 is the first model expected in 1998. It executes an extended set of byte codes that enable low-level access to the chip. Operating systems compiled from languages such as C and C++ into this byte code can use the additional instructions to control registers and perform cache management and other necessary OS functions.

Micrografx Designer

Most of the illustrations in this book were drawn in Micrografx Designer, which offers a huge assortment of drawing tools for the illustrator. This picture is one of the elements in the drawing under "transistor" in this book.

microkernel

(1) The part of an operating system that is specialized for the hardware it is running in. The other components of the OS interact with the microkernel in a message-based relationship and do not have to be rewritten when the OS is ported to a new platform. Only the hardware-dependent microkernel has to be reprogrammed. See *kernel*.

(2) A small control program that is designed to perform a limited set of functions in one type of computer.

microlithography

Using x rays instead of light rays to form the patterns of elements on a chip. This technology is expected to emerge by the 21st century. AT&T Bell Labs has speculated that by the year 2001, a dynamic RAM chip with one billion bits (1 gigabit) will be built using .18 micron microlithography.

micromainframe

A personal computer with mainframe or near mainframe speed.

micro manager

A person who manages personal computer operations within an organization and is responsible for the analysis, selection, installation, training and maintenance of personal computer hardware and software. See *information center* and *MMA*.

micromechanics

The microminiaturization of mechanical devices (gears, motors, rotors, etc.) using similar photomasking techniques as in chip making.

micromini

A personal computer with minicomputer or near minicomputer speed.

micron

One millionth of a meter. Approximately 1/25,000 of an inch. The tiny elements that make up a transistor on a chip are measured in microns. For example, the 486 started out with 1.0 micron technology. The first Pentiums were .8 micron. The current state-of-the-art is .25 micron with .18 expected in 1999. It may not seem like much, but each improvement (.35 to .25, .25 to .18, etc.) is a major breakthrough. Going from 1.0 micron to .18 micron, one fifth the size, has taken thousands of man years and billions of dollars worth of research and development.

micropayment

An electronic commerce transaction of very low value. See *microcommerce*.

Micro PDP-11

The microcomputer version of the PDP-11 from Digital introduced in 1975. Uses the Q-bus and serves as a stand-alone computer or is built into other equipment.

Micropolis

A manufacturer of disk drives that was known for its high-quality products. Founded in 1976 and based in Chatsworth, CA, it produced its first floppy drive in 1977 and its first hard drive in 1981. Acquired by Singapore Technologies in 1996, Micropolis closed its doors in 1997.

microprocessor

A CPU on a single chip. In order to function as a computer, it requires a power supply, clock and memory. The first-generation microprocessors were Intel's 8080, Zilog's Z80, Motorola's 6800 and Rockwell's 6502. The first microprocessor was created by Intel. Today's popular microprocessor families are the x86, PowerPC, Alpha, MIPS and SPARC.

microprocessor based

A computer that uses a single microprocessor chip as its CPU.

microprogram

Same as *microcode*.

microprogramming

Programming microcode.

micropublishing

In micrographics, the issuing of new or reformatted information on microfilm for sale or distribution.

microrepublishing

In micrographics, the issuing of microfilm that has been previously or is simultaneously published in hardcopy for sale or distribution.

microsecond

One millionth of a second. See *space/time* and *ohnosecond*.

microsegmentation

In networking, the ability to manage a smaller number of nodes as a single segment or domain. Total microsegmentation is accomplished with a switch, which treats each node as a segment.

Computer Desktop Encyclopedia

Microsoft

(Microsoft Corporation, Redmond, WA, www.microsoft.com) The world's largest independent software company. Microsoft was founded in 1975 by Paul Allen and Bill Gates, two college students who wrote the first BASIC interpreter for the Intel 8080 microprocessor. Allen now runs Asymetrix Corporation.

MBASIC was licensed to Micro Instrumentation and Telemetry Systems to accompany its Altair 8800 kit. By the end of 1976, more than 10,000 Altairs were sold with MBASIC. Versions were licensed to Radio Shack, Apple and other vendors. Later, Gee Whiz BASIC (GW-BASIC) was developed for 16-bit personal computers.

Although Microsoft became a leader in microcomputer programming languages, its outstanding success was caused by fitting PCs with DOS and Windows. Windows has become the clear winner on desktops, and Windows NT is a major contender in the server market. Microsoft has also become the leader in the applications market, and its application business is the largest part of the company today. The Microsoft Office suite, which includes Excel, Word, PowerPoint and Access, has been extremely successful.

Microsoft's position as the supplier of the major operating systems and applications to the world's largest computer base gives it considerable power, influence and advantage. Since the explosion of the World Wide Web, Microsoft has worked hard to get a strong foothold on the Internet. It gives away its Web browser and server along with Windows, and has fully integrated the browser into the Windows 98 desktop.

William H. Gates, III
Bill Gates has become the most widely-known business entrepreneur in the world, regardless of industry. It all started by supplying IBM with DOS. The rest is history. *(Photo courtesy of Microsoft Corporation.)*

Microsoft Access

A database program for Windows, available separately or included in the Microsoft Office suite. Access is programmable using Visual Basic for Applications (VBA). Access can read Paradox, dBASE and Btrieve files, and using ODBC, Microsoft SQL Server, SYBASE SQL Server and Oracle data.

Microsoft BackOffice

See *BackOffice*.

Microsoft Bob

An alternate Windows interface from Microsoft that was introduced in early 1996, but never caught on. It let you decorate your own "rooms" with familiar objects, and various animated guides, such as Rover the dog, provided online help. It also came with a word processor, checkbook and other home-oriented utilities.

Microsoft C

A C compiler and development system for DOS and Windows applications from Microsoft. Windows programming requires the Windows Software Development Kit (SDK), which is included.

Version 7.0 includes C++ capability and Version 1.0 of the Microsoft Foundation Class Library (MFC), which provide a base framework of object-oriented code to build an application upon. See *Visual C++*.

Microsoft Certified Professional

A training program that provides certification of competency in Microsoft products. Administered throughout the world at Microsoft centers as well as colleges and universities, it provides the following certification levels.

The Microsoft Certified Systems Engineer (MCSE) is for the technical specialist involved with advanced Microsoft products. Candidates are required to pass exams on NT Workstation and Server, networking and either Windows 3.1, Worgroups or 95/98. They must choose two electives from a variety of SQL, SNA and TCP/IP subjects.

The Microsoft Certified Product Specialist (MCPS) is for the user and reseller who supports Windows-based PCs. Candidates must pass one operating system exam and may elect to take additional exams in their area of specialization.

The Microsoft Certified Solution Developer (MCSD) is for the VAR or software developer. Candidates must pass two exams on Windows architecture and services and two exams on programming languages of their choice.

The Microsoft Certified Trainer (MCT) exam is for the person that wants to train others in these subjects through Microsoft authorized education sites. For information, visit www.microsoft.com/train_cert.

Microsoft Cluster Server

Clustering software from Microsoft for Windows NT. It provides rudimentary load balancing and two-node failover, which allows a second server to take over if the first one fails. More sophisticated load balancing is expected in 1998. Cluster Server was formerly code named Wolfpack.

Microsoft Consulting Services

The consulting arm of Microsoft which offers support for installation and maintenance of Microsoft applications and operating systems.

Microsoft DLC

(Microsoft Data Link Control) A communications protocol for Windows clients that supports terminal connections to IBM mainframes and AS/400s. HP printers that are attached via the network using HP's JetDirect internal print servers may optionally use or even require this protocol. See *SDLC, DLC* and *3270 emulator*.

Microsoft Exchange

Messaging and groupware software for Windows from Microsoft. Microsoft Exchange Server is an Internet-compliant messaging system that runs under Windows NT and can be accessed by Web browsers, the Windows Inbox, Exchange client or Outlook.

The Exchange client includes an e-mail client with server based rules, forms design, threaded discussions and group calendaring and scheduling. The Inbox is a limited version of the Exchange client that comes on Windows 95 and NT desktops.

Outlook 97 can be used as the Exchange client, adding features such as richer forms design, group contact and task management, journaling (tracking hourly billing), message recall (unread messages can be pulled back), shared folders and freeform notes.

Microsoft Internet Explorer

A Web browser from Microsoft that runs under Windows 95, NT, Mac and UNIX. Also known as "IE," it continues to gain serious market share, because, thus far, Microsoft gives it away at no charge. In Windows 98, Internet Explorer is fully integrated into the desktop.

Microsoft Internet Information Server

Web server software from Microsoft that runs under Windows NT. It supports Netscape's SSL security protocol and turns an NT-based PC into a Web site. Microsoft's Web browser, Internet Explorer, is also included.

Microsoft Mail

A messaging system from Microsoft that runs on PC and AppleTalk networks. Gateways are available to a variety of mail systems including X.400, PROFS, Novell's MHS and MCI Mail. Microsoft Mail-enabled applications are written to the MAPI programming interface. See *Microsoft Exchange*.

Microsoft Message Queue Server

Messaging middleware for Windows NT from Microsoft. Code named Falcon, and abbreviated MSMQ, it allows programs to send messages to other programs. It can be used to queue up transactions in a transaction processing system, for example. MSMQ is optionally used with Microsoft Transaction Server, Microsoft's COM-based TP monitor. See *messaging middleware* and *Microsoft Transaction Server*.

Microsoft Network

An online service from Microsoft that was launched with Windows 95. Windows 95 enabled a user to register online, initially causing much furor in the industry, believing Microsoft was taking undue advantage of its position. Originally intended as a general-purpose service similar to America Online and CompuServe, MSN has evolved into an Internet provider (ISP) with added functions. See also *Windows network*.

Microsoft Office

A suite of Microsoft's primary desktop applications for Windows and Macintoshes. Depending on the package, it includes some combination of Word, Excel, PowerPoint, Access and Schedule along with a host of Internet and other related utilities. The applications share common functions such as spell checking and graphing, and objects can be dragged and dropped between applications. Microsoft Office is the leading application suite on the market.

Office 4.x is the last 16-bit version. The 32-bit Office 95 was introduced after Windows 95 was released in 1995. Office 97 (1997) adds Internet integration and Outlook, a personal information manager (PIM) and e-mail client. Excel 97, PowerPoint 97 and Word 97 file formats changed from Office 95. An Office 97 option allows saving files in a dual 95/97 format for backward compatibility. A new Access 97 file format is not backward compatible. See *Binder*.

Microsoft Plus!

A set of utilities from Microsoft that augment the Windows 95/98 operating system, including visual enhancements for the desktop, improved disk compression and the ability to dial up your computer from a remote location.

Microsoft SQL Server

A relational DBMS from Microsoft that runs on Windows NT servers. It is Microsoft's high-end client/server database and a key component in its BackOffice suite of server products. SQL Server was originally developed by Sybase and also sold by Microsoft for OS/2 and NT. In 1992, Microsoft began development of its own version. Today, Microsoft SQL Server and Sybase SQL Server are independent products with some compatibility.

Microsoft TechNet

A CD-ROM subscription service from Microsoft that contains technical documentation, drivers and patches for all of Microsoft's products. It includes two updated CD-ROMs every month and contains the Microsoft Knowledge Base with more than 30,000 questions and answers.

Microsoft Transaction Server

A TP monitor for Windows NT servers from Microsoft that supports transaction-based applications on LANs, the Internet and intranets. It also serves as the infrastructure for a multitier system. It is used in the middle tier between the client and the database server. Microsoft Transaction Server (MTS) supports two-phase commit with its included Distributed Transaction Coordinator (DTC).

Based on Microsoft's component software architecture (COM), MTS hosts business logic written as ActiveX Server Components. A component is written for a single user, and MTS scales the process for many users. The server components access the required data via any of several interfaces including ADO, OLE DB and ODBC. See *Microsoft Message Queue Server*.

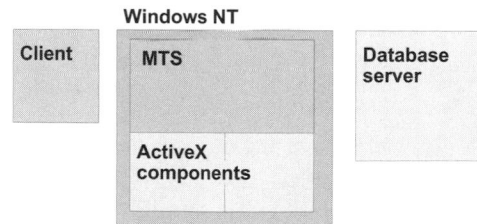

Middle Tier Processing
Microsoft Transaction Server provides the infrastructure for the middle tier in a transaction environment. It serves as the container for ActiveX components.

Microsoft Windows

See *Windows*.

Microsoft Windows network

See *Windows network*.

Microsoft Word

A full-featured word processing program for Windows and the Macintosh from Microsoft. It is a sophisticated program with rudimentary desktop publishing capabilities that has become the most widely-used word processing application on the market. The first versions of Word came out under DOS and provided both graphics-based and text-based interfaces for working with a document.

Microsoft Works

An integrated software package for Windows and the Macintosh from Microsoft. It provides file management with relational-like capabilities, word processing, spreadsheet, business graphics and communications capabilities in one package.

microspacing

Positioning characters for printing by making very small horizontal and vertical movements. Many dot matrix printers and all laser printers have this ability.

MicroStation

A full-featured 2-D and 3-D CAD program for DOS, Windows, Mac and UNIX workstations from Bentley Systems, Inc., Exton, PA, (www.bentley.com). Created in 1984, MicroStation is a high-end package used worldwide in environments where many designers work on large, complex projects. MicroStation Modeler is a superset of MicroStation that provides solid modeling, and MasterPiece is MicroStation's rendering and animation program.

MicroStation has also been marketed by Intergraph as the software for its proprietary workstations. See *solid modeling*.

micro to mainframe

An interconnection of personal computers to mainframes. See *3270 emulator*.

MicroVAX

A series of entry-level VAXs introduced in 1983 that run under VMS or ULTRIX. Some models use the Q-bus architecture.

microwave

An electromagnetic wave that vibrates at 1GHz and above. Microwaves are the transmission frequencies used in communications satellites as well as in line-of-sight systems on earth.

middleware

Software that functions as a conversion or translation layer. The term is used to describe a diverse group of products. It may refer to software that sits between an application and a control program (operating system, network control program, DBMS, etc.) that provides a single programming interface for the applications to be written to. The application will run in as many different computer environments as the middleware runs in.

TP monitors are called *middleware*, because they reside between the client applications and the servers. Information Builder's EDA/SQL is called middleware, because it translates various query languages to different database programs. Microsoft's ODBC interface is also called middleware, because it provides a common API to many different databases.

Early Microwave Tower
This microwave radio relay station was installed in 1968 at Boulder Junction, Colorado. *(Photo courtesy of AT&T.)*

MIDI

(Musical Instrument Digital Interface) A standard protocol for the interchange of musical information between musical instruments, synthesizers and computers. It defines the codes for a musical event, which includes the start of a note, its pitch, length, volume and musical attributes, such as vibrato. It also defines codes for various button, dial and pedal adjustments used on synthesizers.

MIDI is commonly used to synchronize notes produced on several synthesizers. Its control messages can orchestrate a series of synthesizers, each playing a part of the musical score.

A computer with a MIDI interface can be used to record a musical session, but instead of recording the analog sound waves as in a tape recorder, the computer stores the music as keystroke and control codes. The recording can be edited in an entirely different manner than with conventional recording; for example, the rhythm can be changed by editing the timing codes in the MIDI messages. In addition, the computer can easily transpose a performance from B major into D major. MIDI files also take up much less disk space than sound files that contain the actual digitized music.

The objective of MIDI was to allow the keyboard of one synthesizer to play notes generated by another. However, since Version 1.0 in 1983, MIDI has brought electronic control of music to virtually everybody, benefiting musicians and teachers alike.

MIDI makes an ideal system for storing music on digital media due to its small storage requirement compared with digitizing actual music. Since the advent of General MIDI, a standard for defining MIDI instruments, MIDI has become widely used for musical backgrounds in multimedia applications. See *General MIDI, MIDI sequencer, MIDI patch, MIDI voices, MPU-401, wave table synthesis, FM synthesis* and *sound card*.

MIDI (digital notes)

10011101 10010011 10010010 00110010 1001010C

Digital Audio (digitized sound waves)

100111001010001110110110011010110010110101011100110
00101110001010111010001010110111000110011110101101
01011101011101010100001001010111010001010110101
10001011101110101010110100010010100101011110101000
10100101100100010110101101011000101010100100011101
00101101110110100010101001010111010101011011110100
01011101001011010110101101001001001011001000010101

MIDI Versus Digitized Sound

This shows musical notes stored in MIDI compared to digital audio. MIDI is musical notation, whereas digital audio is a sample of the actual waveforms. This is a conceptual example. The binary coding is not accurate.

midicomputer

A computer with performance and capacity between a minicomputer and a mainframe.

MIDI file

A MIDI sound file that contains MIDI messages. MIDI files used in DOS and Windows have a .MID extension. A variation of this format is the RIFF MIDI file, which uses the .RMI extension.

The format for MIDI files, or Standard MIDI File (SMF), contains a header "chunk" at the beginning of the file, which defines the format type, followed by one or more track chunks. Type 0 files store all tracks in one track chunk. Type 1 files use a separate chunk for each track, with the first chunk storing the tempo.

Type 0 files use less memory and run faster than type 1. Thus, original MIDI music is maintained in type 1 format and frequently distributed in type 0. MIDI files distributed for editing are usually in type 1 format, since it is difficult to convert from type 0 to type 1 using a MIDI sequencer.

A less-widely used type 2 file can contain several type 0 files.

MIDI Mapper

A Windows application that converts MIDI sound sequences (MIDI messages) to conform to a particular MIDI sound card or module. The keyboard map is used to assign values to non-standard keyboard keys. The patch map assigns sounds to an instrument number (see *MIDI patch*). The channel map assigns input channels to output channels.

MIDI messages

A series of MIDI notes for a musical sequence. Since MIDI data is a set of musical note definitions rather than the actual sound of the music, the contents of a MIDI file are called MIDI messages.

MIDI patch

One of 16 channels in a MIDI device. Many keyboard synthesizers and MIDI sound modules can handle several waveforms per patch, mixing different instruments together to create synthetic sounds. Each waveform counts as a MIDI voice. Some sound cards can support two or more waveforms per patch.

Before General MIDI, which standardized patches, MIDI vendors assigned patch numbers to their synthesizer products in an arbitrary manner. See *MIDI voices*.

MIDI sequencer

A hardware device or software application that allows for the composition, editing and playback of MIDI sound sequences. Media player applications can play MIDI sound files, but creating and modifying MIDI files requires a sequencer.

MIDI sound module

A stand-alone device that generates MIDI sound. Other MIDI sound-generating devices are synthesizers with keyboards and sound cards for personal computers.

MIDI voices

The number of musical notes that can be played back simultaneously in a MIDI sound device. MIDI provides up to 16 channels of simultaneous playback. The number of voices is the total number of notes from all the instruments played back through all the channels.

For example, if one of the channels (patches) is a piano, up to 10 fingers could strike the keyboard at the same time, generating 10 notes, assuming that particular piano patch triggers only one waveform (see *MIDI patch*). Typically, a MIDI sound card will support from 24 to 32 voices. Keyboard synthesizers and sound modules can handle up to 64.

midrange computer

A medium-sized computer system or server. Midrange computers encompass a very broad range between high-end PCs and mainframes and cost from $25,000 to more than a million dollars. IBM's AS/400s, HP's 3000s and Digital's Alpha families are examples. Formerly called *minicomputers*, which used dumb terminals connected to centralized systems, most midrange computers today function as servers in a client/server configuration.

MIF

(1) (Maker Interchange Format) An alternate file format for a FrameMaker document. A MIF file is ASCII text, which can be created in another program and imported into FrameMaker.

(2) (Management Information File) A DMI file format that describes a hardware or software component used in a PC. It can contain data, code or both. See *DMI*.

migration

A change from one hardware or software technology to another. Migration is a way of life in the computer industry. For example, once known only to those in the glass-enclosed datacenter, users today understand the meaning of migrating from one operating system to another.

migration path

A series of conversion steps that allow an organization to evolve smoothly to newer hardware and software in order to keep pace with changing technology.

mil

An Internet address domain name for a military agency. See *Internet address*.

mill

A very old term for processor (number crunching!).

Millenium Bug

See *Year 2000 Problem*.

Miller Freeman

(Miller Freeman, Inc., San Francisco, CA, www.mfi.com, wholly owned by United News & Media plc) The world's largest trade show organizer that serves a variety of industries including information technology, jewelry, sports, fashion, food, medical, building and travel. It is also a major publisher of magazines and digital media. In late 1996, Miller Freeman acquired the Blenheim Group, producers of PC EXPO, a prominent trade show for corporate buyers of IT.

milli

Thousandth (10 to the -3rd power). See *space/time*.

Millicent

(MILLI CENT) A microcommerce application from Digital that allows transactions of very small monetary value to be contracted on the Internet. The term stands for "one thousandth of a cent." See *microcommerce*.

millimeter

One thousandth of a meter, or 1/25th of an inch.

million

One thousand times one thousand (10 to the 6th power). See *space/time*.

millisecond

One thousandth of a second. See *space/time* and *ohnosecond*.

MIL STD

(MILitary STandarD) A detailed technical specification for a product that is purchased by a U.S. military agency.

MIMD

(Multiple Instruction stream Multiple Data stream) A computer architecture that uses multiple processors, each processing its own set of instructions simultaneously and independently of the others. Contrast with *SIMD*.

MIME

(Multipurpose Internet Mail Extensions) A common method for transmitting non-text files via Internet e-mail, which was originally designed for ASCII text. MIME encodes the files using one of two encoding methods and decodes it back to its original format at the receiving end. A MIME header is added to the file which includes the type of data contained and the encoding method used. S/MIME (Secure MIME) is a version of MIME that adds RSA encryption for secure transmission. See *base64*, *UUcoding*, *BinHex* and *Wincode*.

MIME type

An identification code used in the MIME encoding system. MIME codes are embedded within HTML pages in order to identify audio, video and other data structures to the browser so that it can launch the required plug-in to handle the content.

mini

See *minicomputer*.

minicartridge

See *QIC*.

minicomputer

A medium-scale computer that functions as a multiuser system for up to several hundred users. The minicomputer industry was launched in 1959 after Digital introduced its PDP-1 for $20,000, an unheard-of low price for a computer in those days. Subsequently, a variety of systems became available from HP, Data General, Wang,

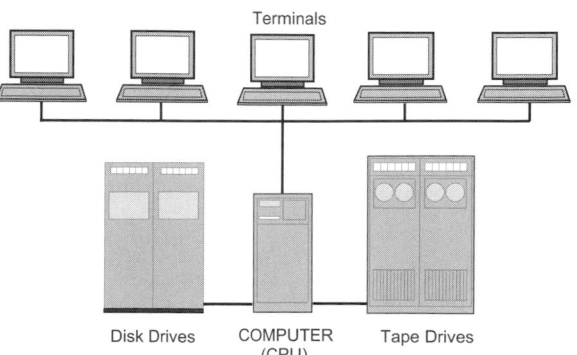

Terminals

Disk Drives   COMPUTER   Tape Drives
(CPU)

Minicomputer System

Tandem, Datapoint and Prime. The minicomputer evolved into a centralized system with dumb terminals. The term was also used for high-end, single-user workstations. Today, *midrange computer* and *server* are more popular terms for medium-sized systems. See *midrange computer*.

MiniDisc

A compact digital audio disc from Sony that comes in read-only and rewritable versions. Introduced in late 1993, the MiniDisc has been popular in Japan. The read-only 2.5" disc stores 140MB compared to 650MB on a CD, but holds the same 74 minutes worth of music due to Sony's Adaptive Transform Acoustic Coding (ATRAC) compression scheme, which eliminates inaudible portions of the signal. MD discs store disc and track titles that the player can display.

Used for music recording, rewritable MiniDiscs employ magneto-optic technology and come in 60 and 74-minute cartridges. The MiniDisc drive for computers (MD DATA) never caught on.

minifloppy

The formal name for the once-ubiquitous, black floppy disk encased in a 5.25"-wide plastic jacket. Introduced by Shugart in 1978, it superseded IBM's 8" floppy. Although used extensively, the 5.25" minifloppy gave way to the 3.5" disk in the mid 1990s. See *microfloppy*.

minimize

In a graphical environment, to hide an application that is currently displayed on screen. The window is removed and represented with an icon on the desktop or taskbar.

mining

See *data mining*.

mini-phone connector

A plug and socket widely used for audio connections. Walkmans, headphones, CD players, speakers and all variety of audio equipment use stereo (three wire) and monoaural (two wire) mini-phone connectors. See *RCA connector* for illustration.

Minitel

An online service of the French government that is used to look up phone numbers, pay bills, purchase merchandise and chat. Introduced in the early 1980s, the videotex-based terminals have been freely distributed by France Telecom. Access to the services, known as the Teletel network, is free except for telephone charges. Because it was quite advanced for the 1980s and widely used, Minitel has slowed France's acceptance of the Web.

MINIX

A version of UNIX for the PC, Mac, Amiga and Atari ST developed by Andrew Tannenbaum and published by Prentice-Hall. It comes with complete source code.

minor key

A secondary key used to identify a record. For example, if transactions are sorted by account number and date, account number is the major key and date is the minor key.

MIO

(Modular I/O) A hardware interface for HP printers that is primarily used to plug in an internal print server and network adapter. MIO has been superseded by EIO. See *EIO*.

MIP mapping

A texture mapping technique that uses multiple texture maps, or MIP maps. Each MIP map is half the size of the first one, providing several texture maps for various levels of depth.

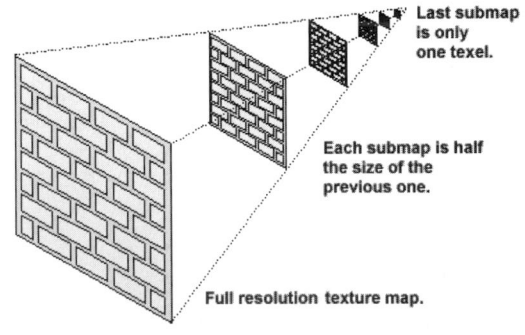

MIP Maps

MIP maps provide more depth realism to objects, because texture maps for varying levels of depth have been prepared. *(Illustration courtesy of Intergraph Computer Systems.)*

MIP mapping is combined with various other techniques to produce different amounts of realism. It is typically used with bilinear interpolation and always used with trilinear interpolation. MIP stands for "multum in parvo," which is Latin for "many in a small place." See *bilinear interpolation, trilinear interpolation, texture map* and *point sampling*.

MIPS

(Million Instructions Per Second) The execution speed of a computer. For example, .5 MIPS is 500,000 instructions per second. High-speed personal computers and workstations perform at 200 MIPS and higher. Digital's Alpha chip has a peak rate of over 1,200 MIPS (that's 1.2 BIPS!). Inexpensive microprocessors used in toys and games may be in the .05-.1 MIPS range.

MIPS rates are not uniform. Some are best-case mixes while others are averages. In addition, it takes more instructions in one machine to do the same thing as another (RISC vs CISC, mainframe vs micro). As a result, MIPS has been called "MisInformation to Promote Sales" as well as "Meaningless Interpretation of Processor Speed."

MIPS rate is just one factor in overall performance. Bus and channel speed and bandwidth, memory speed, memory management techniques and system software also determine total throughput. See also *MIPS Computer*.

MIPS and MHz

There is a mathematical relationship between MIPS and MHz. You can derive MIPS from MHz if you know how many machine cycles it takes to execute an instruction in the CPU. For example, a 486 takes 1.9 cycles on average. To obtain MIPS on a 50MHz 486, you would divide 50 by 1.9, yielding 26 MIPS.

MIPS Computer

(MIPS Technologies, Inc., Sunnyvale, CA, subsidiary of SGI). Founded in 1984 as MIPS Computer Systems Inc., the company merged with Silicon Graphics in 1992. MIPS is the designer of RISC-based microprocessors, which are made under license by NEC, Toshiba, Philips and others. They are widely used in the industry. SGI computers are all powered by MIPS CPUs as well as computers from Pyramid, Tandem, NEC and Siemens/Nixdorf.

The MIPS 32-bit R3000 family of CPUs has been used in a variety of desktop systems as well as in embedded and consumer applications. The R3000 has been followed by 64-bit R4000, R5000, R8000 and R10000 families, each increasing performance and pushing the envelope further. MIPS also licenses its compilers and RISC/OS system software. See *SGI*.

mIRC

A popular Internet Relay Chat program developed by Khaled Mardam-Bey. mIRC runs under Windows and provides a graphical interface for logging onto IRC servers and listing, joining and leaving channels.

mirrored

Duplicated. See *mirroring* and *disk mirroring*.

mirroring

Duplicating data onto another computer at another location. Mirroring is performed for backup purposes or to be in closer proximity to the user. See *disk mirroring* and *replication*.

mirror site

An alternate site that contains the same information. Many software vendors have mirror sites on the Web due to the high volume of requests they get for drivers and beta copies of programs.

MIS

(1) (Management Information System) An information system that integrates data from all the departments it serves and provides operations and management with the information they require.

It was "the" buzzword of the mid to late 1970s, when online systems were implemented in all large organizations. See *DSS*.

(2) (Management Information Services) See *Information Systems*.

mission critical

Vital to the operation of an organization. In the past, mission critical information systems were implemented on mainframes and minicomputers. Increasingly, they are being designed for and installed on personal computer networks. See *client/server*.

Mixed Mode CD

A compact disc format that contains both data and audio. Data is stored in track 1, and audio is stored in the remaining tracks. Some audio CD players will skip the first track upon encountering the data, while earlier players will attempt to play the non-audio data, causing a loud, raucous sound in the speakers. This method has been improved with CD Plus. See *CD Plus*.

mixed object

Same as *compound document*.

mixed signal

The combination of analog and digital processing. It typically refers to the capabilities of a chip.

M-JPEG

See *MPEG*.

MKS

(Mortice Kern Systems Inc., Waterloo, Ontario, www.mks.com) A software company that specializes in programming tools and utilities for a variety of platforms. For example, its RCS system for Windows, OS/2 and UNIX is a version control software package.

ML

A symbolic programming language developed in the 1970s at the University of Edinburgh, Scotland. Although similar to LISP, its commands and structures are like Pascal.

MLPPP

See *MPPP*.

MM

(1) See *Multiple Master*.
(2) (mm) (MilliMeter) One thousandth of a meter.

MMA

(Microcomputer Managers Association, Inc.) A membership organization with chapters throughout the U.S. that was devoted to educating personnel responsible for personal computers. It disbanded in 1996.

MMCD

(MultiMedia CD) A high-capacity CD specification from Sony and Philips that was merged with the Super Density (SD) format to become DVD. See *DVD*.

MMDS

(Multichannel Multipoint Distribution Service) A wireless cable system that provides 33 analog channels or from five to 10 times as many digital channels. Working in the 26 GHz range, it requires line of sight between the transmitter and receiving antenna. With its flat terrain, Phoenix, Arizona is a perfect MMDS site. A single mountaintop transmitter can reach 95% of its population. In cities such as Houston and St. Louis, up to 80% can be reached.

Digital signals let MMDS support more channels and also deal better with the topography. Signals can be beamed to a high building, which can serve as one or more cell sites transmitting in various directions. Digital signals can be regenerated many times without ever a loss of quality. See *LMDS*.

MME

See *Multimedia Extensions*.

MMF

See *multimode fiber*.

MMI

(Man Machine Interface) Same as *user interface*.

MMU

(Memory Management Unit) A virtual memory circuit that translates logical addresses into physical addresses.

MMVF

(MultiMedia Video File) A proposed rewritable DVD format from NECT. It holds 5.2GB per side. MMVF is initially only available in Japan and is not expected to be a branded product in the U.S. See *DVD*.

MMX

(MultiMedia EXtensions) A set of 57 additional instructions built into Intel CPU chips that are used for faster audio, video, graphics and modem operations. MMX is found in Pentium MMX and Pentium II chips, but not in Pentiums and Pentium Pros. MMX instructions allow operations to be performed simultaneously on multiple units of data; for example, eight 8-bit units or four 16-bit units can be added or multiplied at the same time. In addition, MMX includes a multiply-add instruction that allows most of the capabilities of a DSP chip to be provided at very high speed. MMX provides these capabilities on integer data only.

Intel's competitors (AMD, Cyrix and Centaur) have extended their MMX-compliant chips with proprietary floating point instructions for performing the geometry calculations required to move 3-D objects on screen. In order to allow 3-D applications to run on computers with different instruction sets, the chip vendors have helped Microsoft modify its Direct3D graphics system to support their variations. Similar to the way 3-D accelerator cards work that have specialized functions built in, if Direct3D finds special instructions in the CPU, it uses them. If not, it uses regular instructions.

Intel is expected to provide floating point capability on its Katmai chips with an additional 70 MMX instructions known as the Katmai New Instructions. See *future Intel chips, DSP* and *SIMD*.

mnemonic

Pronounced "nuh-monic." Means memory aid. A name assigned to a machine function. For example, in DOS, COM1 is the mnemonic assigned to serial port #1. Programming languages are almost entirely mnemonics.

MNP

(Microcom Networking Protocol) A family of communications protocols from Microcom, Inc., Norwood, MA, that have become de facto standards for error correction (classes 2 though 4) and data compression (class 5).

```
Class and Features
1   Half-duplex asynchronous transmission. Early mode, no longer used.)
2   Full-duplex asynchronous transmission.
3   Full-duplex synchronous transmission using HDLC framing with 64-byte
    blocks.  Start/stop bits stripped.
4   Increased throughput. Shorter headers, frames up to 256 bytes.  Some
    vendors adjust frame size based on line quality.
5   Compresses data up to two times.
6   Starts at V.22bis modulation and switches to V.29 if possible.  Uses
    pseudo-duplexing ping-pong for faster turnaround of V.29 transmission.
7   Compresses data up to three times.
8   Not in use.
9   Adds Piggy-back Acknowledgement** and selective retransmission for more
    efficient transport.  Provides better performance over variety of links.
10  Adds Adverse Channel Enhancements** for efficient operation on noisy lines.

    ** Proprietary Microcom techniques.
```

M-O, MO

See *magneto-optic disk*.

Mobile IP

An IP enhancement that provides forwarding of traffic to moving users. It uses agents in the user's home network and in all foreign networks. When logging on to a remote network, users register their presence with the foreign agent, and the home agent forwards the packets to the remote network.

Mobitex
A packet radio service from RAM Mobile Data (joint venture of RAM Broadcasting and BellSouth). Base stations serve major cities throughout the U.S.

mod
See *modulo*.

modal
Mode oriented. A modal operation switches from one mode to another. Contrast with *non-modal*.

modal bandwidth
The capacity of an optical fiber measured in MHz-km (megahertz over one kilometer). One MHz-km equals approximately .7 to .8 Mbps. Thus, a 100 MHz-km fiber can carry about 70 to 80 Mbps of data.

modal dispersion
A signal distortion in an optical fiber in which the light pulses spread out, and the receiving device cannot detect the beginnings and ends of pulses.

MO:DCA
(Mixed Object:Document Content Architecure) An IBM compound document format for text and graphics elements in a document. It supports Revisable Documents, which are editable like revisable-form DCA, Presentation Documents, which provide specific output formatting similar to DCA final-form, and Resource Documents, which hold control information such as fonts.

Formats for specific objects are specified in OCAs (Object Content Architectures): PTOCA for Presentation and Text that has been formatted for output, GOCA for vector Graphics objects, IOCA for bitmapped Images and FOCA for Fonts. MO:DCA is implemented as IBM's AFP page description language.

mode
An operational state that a system has been switched to. It implies at least two possible conditions. There are countless modes for hardware and software. See *Real Mode, Protected Mode, burst mode, insert mode, supervisor state* and *program state*.

model
(1) A style or type of hardware device.

(2) A mathematical representation of a device or process used for analysis and planning. See *data model, data administration, financial planning system* and *scientific applications*.

model-based expert system
An expert system based on fundamental knowledge of the design and function of an object. Such systems are used to diagnose equipment problems, for example. Contrast with *rule-based expert system*.

modeling
Simulating a condition or activity by performing a set of equations on a set of data. See *data model, data administration, financial planning system* and *scientific applications*.

modem
(MOdulator-DEModulator) A device that adapts a terminal or computer to a telephone line. It converts the computer's digital pulses into audio frequencies (analog) for the telephone system and converts the frequencies back into pulses at the receiving side. The modem also dials the line, answers the call and controls transmission speed. Although modems have come in speeds of 300, 1200, 2400, 9600, 14400, 28800, 33300 and 56000 bits per second, only the latter, higher speeds are typically used (see *V.34* and *V.90*).

For hookup to a personal computer, an internal modem needs a free expansion slot, while an external modem requires a free serial port. The software required to use a modem depends on what service you want. A connection to an Internet service provider (ISP) requires a Web browser and TCP/IP stack, both of which are either provided by the ISP or are included with the operating system such as Windows 95/98 and NT. The online services (America Online, CompuServe, etc.) generally give you the required software and dial-up utilities. To connect to a BBS or private computer, a communications program (comm program) is required.

All new modems have built-in error correction (V.42) and data compression (V.42bis, MNP 5). On files that are already compressed, the hardware data compression adds little value, because it cannot make compressed files smaller. Modems also have automatic feature negotiation, which adjusts to the other modem's speed and hardware protocols.

Most personal computer modems use the Hayes AT command set, which is the series of machine instructions that control the modem. The term modem is also used as a verb; for example, "I'll modem you later."

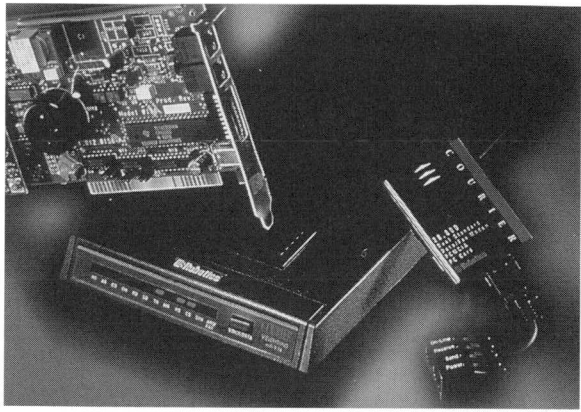

Modem Housings

Modems are built on internal plug-in cards (left), as external units (middle) and on PC Cards for laptops (right). *(Photo courtesy of 3Com Corporation.)*

Modem Status Signals

The following acronyms are used with the display lights on the modem to identify the unit's current status. There are several acronyms used for certain operations.

Acronym	Meaning
AA	Auto answer mode
CA	Compression active
CD	Carrier detect
CTR	Clear to send
DTR	Data terminal ready (terminal ready)
EC	Error control active
HS	High speed (typically 4,800 bps and up)
LB	Low battery
MR	Modem ready (data set ready)
OH	Off hook
PWR	Power on
RI	Ringing
RNG	Ringing
RTS	Request to send
RXD	Receiving data
RD	Receiving data
SD	Transmitting (sending) data
TM	Test mode
TD	Transmitting (sending) data
TR	Terminal ready
TXD	Transmitting (sending) data

modem eliminator

A device that allows two close computers to be connected without modems. For personal computers, it is the same as a null modem cable. In synchronous systems, it provides active intelligence for synchronization.

modem pool

A collection of modems and software that let users dial out and remote users dial in on the next available modem. The modem pool may be internal or external to the remote access server. See *remote access server*.

modem server

Same as *modem pool*.

moderated newsgroup

A newsgroup that is managed by a human referee who keeps the discussion focused and prevents it from getting out of hand.

modify structure

A database command that changes a file's structure. Field lengths and field names can be changed, and fields can be added or deleted. It may convert the old data file into the new structure without data loss, unless fields have been truncated or deleted.

MODKA

See *MO:DCA*.

Modula-2, Modula-3

(MODUlar LAnguage-2) An enhanced version of Pascal introduced in 1979 by Swiss professor Nicklaus Wirth, creator of Pascal. It supports separate compilation of modules, allowing it to be used for large projects. Modula-3 , developed by Digital and Olivetti, adds object-oriented extensions, automatic garbage collection and improved exception handling. It is considered an excellent teaching language. The following Modula example changes Fahrenheit to Celsius:

```
    MODULE FahrToCent;
FROM InOut IMPORT ReadReal,WriteReal,
WriteString,WriteLn;
VAR Fahr:REAL;
BEGIN
WriteString("Enter Fahrenheit ");
ReadReal(Fahr);
WriteLn;
WriteString("Celsius is ");
WriteReal((Fahr - 32) * 5 / 9);
    END   FahrToCent
```

modular hub

A network hub that is configured by adding different modules, each supporting a topology, such as Ethernet, Token Ring, FDDI, etc. See *hub*.

modularity

The characteristic of a system that has been divided into smaller subsystems which interact with each other.

modular programming

Breaking down the design of a program into individual components (modules) that can be programmed and tested independently. It is a requirement for effective development and maintenance of large programs and projects.

Modular programming has evolved into object-oriented programming, which provides formal rules for developing self-contained software modules. See *object-oriented programming*.

modulate

To vary a carrier wave. Modulation blends a data signal (text, voice, etc.) into a carrier for transmission over a network. The most common methods are (1) amplitude modulation (AM), which modulates the height of the carrier wave, (2) frequency modulation (FM), which modulates the

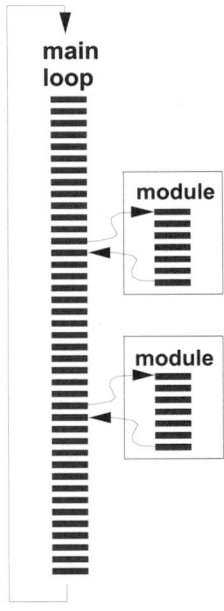

Modular Programming

Building a program in modules, or independent routines, is common practice. The module performs a function and then returns control back to the program or instruction that called it. Modular programming has evolved into object-oriented programming, which provides stricter rules for developing self-contained routines.

frequency of the wave, and (3) phase modulation (PM), which modulates the polarity of the wave. Contrast with *demodulate*. See *carrier*.

module

A self-contained hardware or software component that interacts with a larger system. Hardware modules are often made to plug into a main system. Program modules are designed to handle a specific task within a larger program. See *memory module, ROM card, MCM* and *modular programming*.

modulo

A mathematical operation (modulus arithmetic) in which the result is the remainder of the division. For example, 20 MOD 3 results in 2 (20/3 = 6 with a remainder of 2).

MOF

(1) (Managed Object Format) An ASCII file that contains the formal definition of a CIM schema. See *CIM*.

(2) (Meta Object Facility) An object model from the Object Management Group (OMG) for defining metadata in a distributed CORBA environment. Its four levels define the meta-meta model, meta model, model and instance data. See *CORBA* and *OMG*.

moire

Pronounced "mor-ray" and spelled "moiré." In computer graphics, a visible distortion. It results from a variety of conditions; for example, when scanning halftones at a resolution not consistent with the printed resolution or when superimposing curved patterns on one another. Internal monitor misalignment can also be a cause.

MOLAP

See *OLAP*.

molecular beam epitaxy

A technique that "grows" atomic-sized layers on a chip rather than creating layers by diffusion.

molecular memory

A potential future memory technology that stores data at the molecular level. Using lasers and the bacteriorhodopsin protein molecule, the W. M. Keck Center for Molecular Electronics has built a molecular memory device holding several hundred megabytes. The advantage of such a memory is its small size and stability. It holds its content without power.

MOM

(Messaging-Oriented Middleware) See *messaging middleware*.

monadic

One. A single item or operation that deals with one item or operand.

monaural

Same as *monophonic*.

moniker

A COM object that is used to create instances of other objects. Monikers save programmers time when coding various types of COM-based functions such as linking one document to another (OLE). See *COM* and *OLE*.

monitor

(1) A display screen used to present output from a computer, camera, VCR or other video generator. A monitor's clarity is based on video bandwidth, dot pitch, refresh rate and convergence. See *VGA, analog monitor* and *digital monitor*.

(2) Software that provides utility and control functions such as setting communications parameters. It typically resides in a ROM chip and contains startup and diagnostic routines.

(3) Software that monitors the progress of activities within a computer system.

(4) A device that gathers performance statistics of a running system via direct attachment to the CPU's circuit boards.

monitor calibrator
A hand-held device that is placed over the screen of a monitor and "reads" the colors.

monitor profile
A file of attributes about a specific monitor, which includes information about its gamma, white point and phosphors. It is used to produce accurate color conversion from the display to some other destination such as a printer.

monitor size
Monitor size is measured by the distance from one corner of the screen's viewable area to the diagonally-opposite corner. With CRTs, the number is generally about an inch greater than the actual area. Starting in the late 1990s, the real number is included in the specs. For example, you might see a 17" monitor state 16.1" viewable. See *resolution*.

mono, monochrome
The display of one foreground color and one background color; for example, black on white, white on black and green on black. Monochrome screens have been widely used on mini and mainframe terminals. Non-color laptop screens on PCs are often said to be "monochrome VGA" screens, but they are actually gray-scale screens, not monochrome. See also *monophonic*.

monolithic integrated circuit
The common form of chip design, in which the base material (substrate) contains the pathways as well as the active elements that take part in its operation.

monophonic
Also called *mono* and *monaural*. Sound reproduction using a single channel. Contrast with *stereophonic*.

monospaced font
A font in which each character is the same width. For example, the word `mini` in a monospaced Courier font takes up more room than **mini** in proportional spacing. Contrast with *proportional spacing*.

Monte Carlo method
A technique that provides approximate solutions to problems expressed mathematically. Using random numbers and trial and error, it repeatedly calculates the equations to arrive at a solution.

MOO
(MultiUser Dimension Object-Oriented Technology) Same as *MUD*.

Moore's law
"The number of transistors on a chip doubles every 18 months." By Intel co-founder Gordon Moore regarding the pace of semiconductor technology. It has proven fairly accurate. See *laws*.

mopier
A machine that makes mopies. See *mopy*.

MOPS
(Mega <million> Operations Per Second) The measurement of instructional performance of a system. It typically refers to DSP operations. See *GOPS*.

mopy
(Multiple Original Prints + Y) To print multiple copies of a document on a computer printer. As more information is created digitally and printers become faster, it is increasingly easier to print multiple originals than to use a copy machine later. In other words, "mopy... don't copy!"

morphing
Transforming one image into another; for example, a car into a tiger. The term comes from metamorphosis. Morphing programs work by marking prominent points, such as tips and corners, of the before and after images. The points are used to mathematically compute the movements from one object to the other. See *tweening*. See illustration on next page.

morray

See *moire*.

Morse code

A character code represented by dots and dashes, developed by Samuel Morse in the mid-19th century. A dot can be a voltage, carrier wave or light beam of one duration, while a dash is a longer duration. It was used to send telegraph messages before the telephone and was used in World War II for signalling by light.

Mortice Kern

See *MKS*.

MOS

(Metal Oxide Semiconductor) Pronounced "moss." One of two major categories of chip design (the other is bipolar). It derives its name from its use of metal, oxide and semiconductor layers. There are several varieties of MOS technologies, including PMOS, NMOS and CMOS.

Mosaic

A Web browser created by the University of Illinois National Center for Supercomputing Applications (NCSA) and released on the Internet in early 1993. Mosaic was "the" application that caused interest in the World Wide Web to explode. Originally developed for UNIX, it was soon ported to Windows. An enhanced version of NCSA Mosaic is offered by Spyglass, Inc., Naperville, IL. See *Netscape Navigator*.

MOSFET

(Metal Oxide Semiconductor Field Effect Transistor) A common type of transistor fabricated as a discrete component or into MOS integrated circuits.

most significant digit

The leftmost, non-zero digit in a number. It is the digit with the greatest value in the number.

motherboard

The main printed circuit board in an electronic device, which contains sockets that accept additional boards. In a personal computer, the motherboard contains the bus, CPU

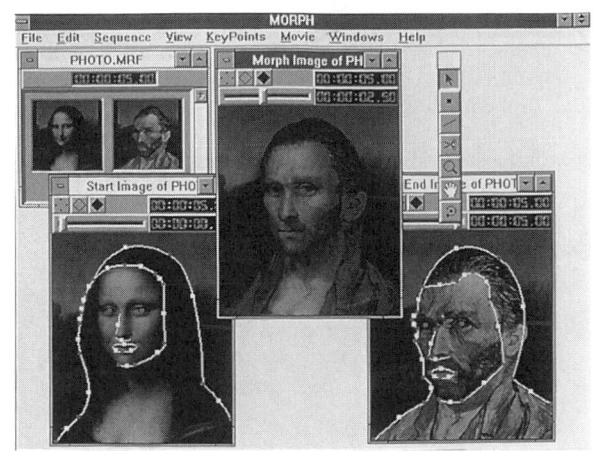

Plotting the Points

The prominent points of both the before and after images are marked in Gryphon's Morph software, which computes all the in-between stages. *(Photo courtesy of Gryphon Software Corporation.)*

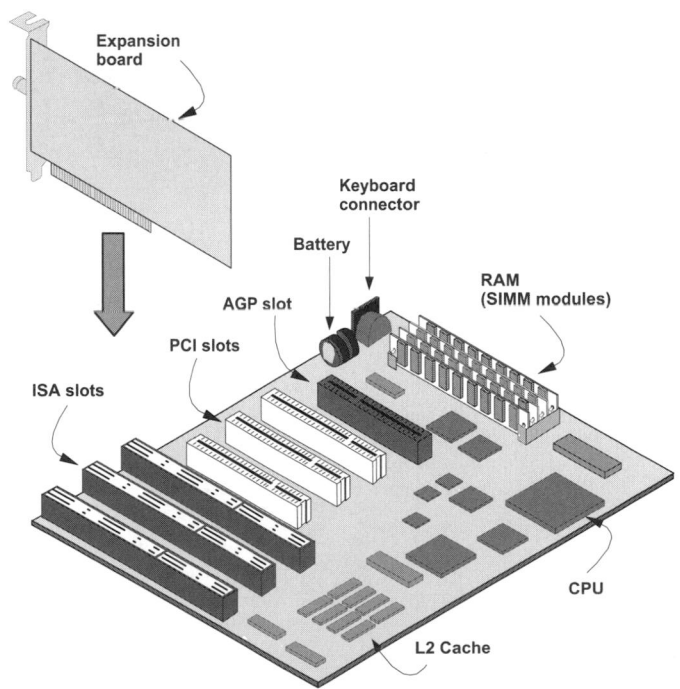

Motherboard

This is a Baby AT style motherboard for a PC. The adapter cards (expansion boards) plug into the expansion slots on the motherboard.

and coprocessor sockets, memory sockets, keyboard controller and supporting chips.

Chips that control the video display, serial and parallel ports, mouse and disk drives may or may not be present on the motherboard. If not, they are independent controllers that are plugged into an expansion slot on the motherboard.

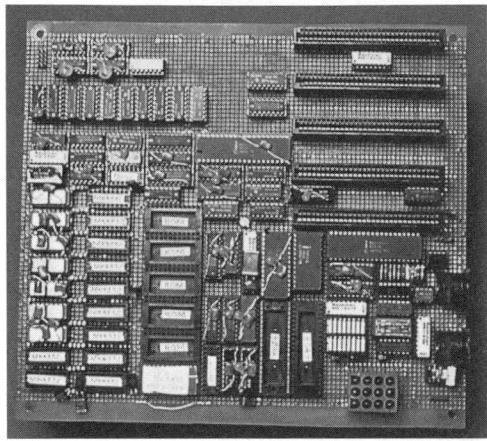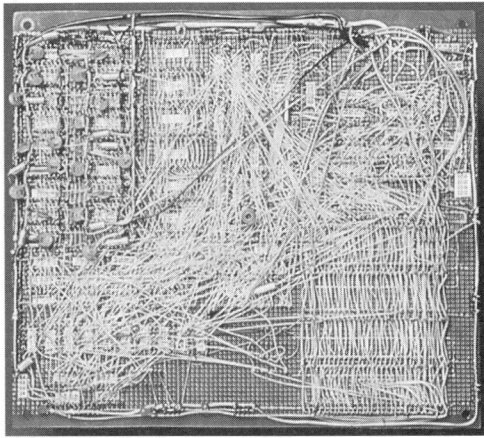

The Mother of All Motherboards

This is the front and back of the prototype of the first IBM PC motherboard in 1981. The chips are wired together on a "breadboard" designed for making new system boards. *(Photos courtesy of IBM Corporation.)*

Motif

The graphical user interface (GUI) endorsed by the Open Software Foundation. It has become the standard graphical interface for UNIX. Motif, Windows and Mac are the three major GUIs. See *Open Group*.

motion capture

The entering of a movement pattern into the computer. For example, if a person, hooked up to sensors, goes through the act of batting a ball, that motion trail can be used to simulate a more realistic baseball player in the computer.

Motion JPEG

See *MPEG*.

motion path

In computer graphics, the path to be followed by an animated object.

motion video

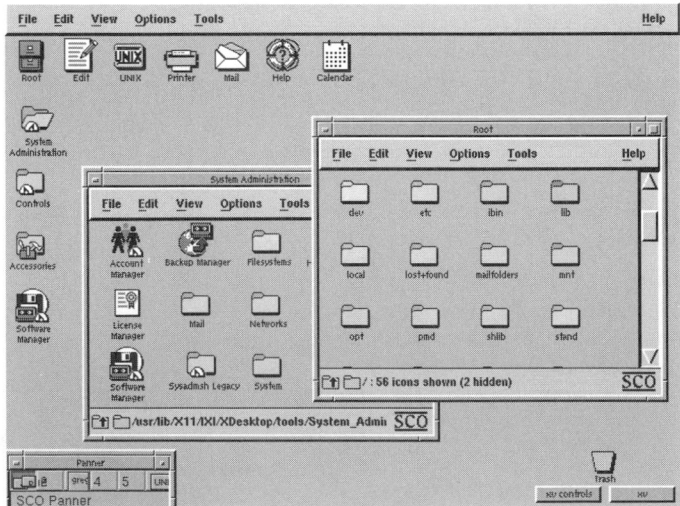

The Motif GUI

Motif is the de facto standard graphical interface for the UNIX world today. (Zoom in to see the full image.) *(Screen shot courtesy of The Santa Cruz Operation, Inc.)*

Refers to moving video images, but does not imply a frame rate. Full-motion video refers to fluid, TV-like images displayed at a rate of 24 to 30 frames per second.

Motorola

(Motorola, Inc., Schaumburg, IL, www.motorola.com) A leading manufacturer of semiconductor devices founded in Chicago in 1928 by Paul V. Galvin as the Galvin Manufacturing Corporation. Its first product allowed radios to operate from household current instead of batteries. In the 1930s, the company commercialized car radios under the Motorola brand suggesting "sound in motion." In 1937, it introduced a line of home radios and its first two-way radio products. By 1947, the Motorola name became so popular that the company changed its name to match.

Motorola's first semiconductor plant was operating in 1953, and by the 1960s, the company was a leader in semiconductors, communications and consumer electronics. It produced its first integrated circuits in 1960 and its first microprocessor in 1974, the same year that it sold its color TV business as it migrated away from the consumer side.

In the computer industry, Motorola is widely known for its 680x0 and PowerPC microprocessor families. It is also one of the world's largest suppliers of microcontrollers (computers on a single chip). The company has more than 50,000 semiconductor items in its product line that are used in myriads of radio, communications, automotive and industrial applications.

mount

To cause a file on a remote workstation or server to be available for access locally. For example, in NFS (Network File System), a server maintains a list of its directories that are available to clients. When a client mounts a directory on the server, that directory and its subdirectories become part of the client's directory hierarchy. See *automounting*.

mouse

The most popular pointing device. It was called a mouse because it more or less resembled one, with the cord being the mouse's tail. Graphical interfaces (GUIs) are designed to be used with pointing devices, but key commands may be substituted. However, graphics applications, such as CAD and image editing, demand a mouse-like device. On a PC, the mouse generally connects to a serial port via a 9-pin DB or PS/2 connector.

Mouse movement is relative. The screen cursor moves from its existing location. The mouse could be moved over anything, not just the desktop. The mouse-like object on a graphics tablet, which is correctly called the *tablet cursor* or *puck* is not relative. It contacts the tablet with absolute reference. Placing it on the upper left part of the tablet moves the screen cursor to the corresponding location.

After years of use by millions of users, it is now widely known that mice can be hazardous to your health. Many applications require endless clicking and dragging to accomplish tasks. Continuous use puts enormous stress on the wrist, and constant double clicking can be the most strenuous function. See *pointing device, mechanical mouse, optical mouse, serial mouse, bus mouse, mickey* and *carpal tunnel syndrome*. See illustrations on next page.

The Galvin Brothers
This picture was taken around 1930 of Paul Galvin (left) and his brother Joseph. *(Photo courtesy of Motorola Museum of Electronics.)*

America Was Driving to Music
In 1930, Motorola produced the first affordable and commercially successful car radio. In the beginning, it had to be installed by the dealer. By the early 1940s, Motorola was becoming a household word. *(Photo courtesy of Motorola Museum of Electronics.)*

The First Mouse
Invented by Doug Engelbart in the early 1960s while at Stanford Research Institute (now SRI), the device employed two moving wheels 90 degrees apart. This is how most mice are still made except that the wheels are inside, and the ball moves the wheels. *(Photo courtesy of The Bootstrap Institute.)*

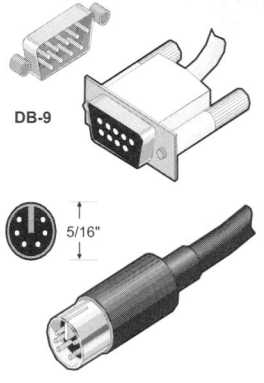

PC Mouse Connectors

DB-9

5/16"

6-pin Mini-DIN (PS/2 connector)

Mice are generally attached to PCs via the serial port using a 9-pin DB connector or via the PS/2 port, which uses a 6-pin Mini-DIN connector.

mouse pad
A fabric-covered rubber pad roughly 9" square that provides a smooth surface for rolling a mouse. There are also mouse pads than provide a better surface; for example, 3M makes the Precise Mousing Surface, an ultra-thin mouse pad that is engineered to reduce friction.

mouse port
A socket in the computer into which a mouse is plugged. The mouse port on a laptop PC uses a PS/2 connector, which is a 6-pin Mini-DIN socket. On desktop PCs, the serial port is typically used for the mouse, not a mouse port. On a Macintosh, the ADB connector is used.

mouse potato
See *click potato*.

mouse trails
The creation of repeating, trailing images of the pointer when it moves across the screen in order to make it more visible on passive matrix screens. See *submarining*.

MOV
(1) (Metal Oxide Varistor) A discrete electronic component that diverts excessive voltage to the ground and/or neutral lines. See *MOV surge suppression*.

(2) An assembly language instruction that moves (copies) data from one location to another.

Mouse Trails
On a passive matrix screen, mouse trails are left when an object, such as this pointer, is moved quickly across the screen.

move
(1) In programming, to copy data from one place in memory to another. At the end of the move, source and destination data are identical.

(2) In word processing and graphics, to relocate text and images to another part of the document or drawing.

moves-adds-changes
Typically refers to the network administration necessary when users or network components are added to, removed from or change their location in the network.

movie file
A file that contains full-motion, digital video, such as an AVI file.

MOV surge suppression
The most common type of surge suppression technology in which the surge energy is diverted to neutral and/or ground. The metal oxide varistor (MOV) is the component that shunts the surge to the neutral and ground lines. Contrast with *series mode surge suppression*.

Mozart
A screen scraper from Mozart Systems Corporation, Burlingame, CA, (www.mozart.com), that is used to turn a character-based mainframe screen into a Windows or DOS front end via 3270 emulation. It is noted for being able to easily combine multiple terminal screens into one. Mozart was originally named Enter 3270.

Mozilla
The code name for Netscape Navigator and Netscape's first alligator-like mascot. It stood for "Mosaic Killer." Mosaic was the Web browser that caused the Web to become popular, which was created by the same people that later founded Netscape.

In early 1998, Netscape Communicator was made free of charge, and its source code was also made available to the developer world. An internal group within Netscape, entitled "mozilla.org," was created to act as a central clearing house for improvements made to Communicator by third parties. For more information, visit www.mozilla.org.

MP
See *multiprocessing* and *PPP*.

MP3
See *MPEG Audio Layer 3*.

MPC
(Multimedia PC Working Group, Washington, DC, subsidiary of Software Publishers Association, www.spa.org/mpc) An organization that has set minimum standards for multimedia PCs. PC vendors and multimedia component vendors certified by MPC may display the MPC2 and MPC3 insignias on their products.

The following chart shows a brief summary of minimum requirements for Level 3. The minimums for levels 1 and 2 required a 3MB 386SX and a 4MB 486SX, which is not relevant today. Also, do not be mislead by Level 3, which seems to have rather elementary specs. There are more details to it, and the complete specification, which is available from MPC's Web site, is very demanding. It was not until January 1997 that the first PC vendor, namely Dell Computer, became MPC3 compliant.

```
MPC Level 3 (1996)

RAM           8MB
Processor     75MHz Pentium
Input         2-button mouse, 101 key keyboard
Hard disk     540MB
CD-ROM        4x, 250 ms, CD-ROM XA multisession
Sound         16-bit, wavetable MIDI playback
Graphics      color space conversion & scaling direct access to frame buffer
Video         OM1-compliant MPEG1 (hardware or software)
```

MPEG
(Moving Pictures Experts Group) Pronounced "em-peg." An ISO/ITU standard for compressing video. MPEG is a lossy compression method, which means that some of the original image is lost. MPEG-1, which is used in CD-ROMs and Video CDs, provides a resolution of 352x240 at 30 fps with 24-bit color and CD-quality sound. Most MPEG boards also provide hardware scaling that boosts the image to full screen. MPEG-2 is a broadcast-quality standard that provides better resolution than VHS tapes. MPEG-2 is used in DVD movies. An MPEG-3 specification was under development but was combined with MPEG-2.

true

true

true

true

false

For the best playback, MPEG-encoded material requires an MPEG board, and the decoding is done in the board's hardware. It is expected that MPEG circuits will be built into future computers. If the computer is fast enough (200MHz Pentium, PowerPC, etc.), the CPU can decompress the material using software.

MPEG uses the same intraframe coding as JPEG for individual frames, but also uses interframe coding, which further compresses the video data by encoding only the differences between periodic key frames, known as I-frames.

A variation of MPEG, known as Motion JPEG, or M-JPEG, does not use interframe coding and is thus easier to edit in a nonlinear editing system than full MPEG. MPEG-1 uses bandwidth from 500 Kbps to 4 Mbps, averaging about 1.25 Mbps. MPEG-2 uses from 4 to 16 Mbps. See *MPEG Audio Layer 3, JPEG* and *DVx chip*.

MPEG Audio Layer 3

An audio compression technology that is part of the MPEG-1 and MPEG-2 specifications. It compresses CD-quality sound by a factor of 12, while maintaining the same high-fidelity. Greater compression ratios are also obtainable that provide reasonable sound quality.

MPEG decoder

Software or hardware that decompresses MPEG data into viewable form. The results are not exactly the same as the orginal video image, because MPEG is a lossy compression method. See *MPEG*.

MPE/iX

(MultiProgramming Executive/POSIX) A POSIX-compliant multitasking operating system that runs on the HP 3000 series. The earlier non-POSIX version was called MPE.

MPG

The extension used on the MPEG file format. See *MPEG*.

MPLS

(MultiProtocol Label Switching) A specification for layer 3 switching from the IETF. Similar to Cisco's tag switching, MPLS uses labels, or tags, that contain forwarding information, which are attached to packets by the initial router. The switches and routers down the road examine the label more quickly than if they had to look up destination addresses in a routing table.

MPOA

(MultiProtocol Over ATM) An ATM Forum standard that provides routing of legacy protocols (IP, IPX, etc.) over ATM networks. MPOA separates the routing processing from the actual forwarding. A route server performs the routing calculations and sends its results to the ATM switches and edge devices which perform high-speed forwarding of the packets. See *virtual routing, I-PNNI* and *IP Switch*.

MPP

(Massively Parallel Processing or Massively Parallel Processor) A multiprocessing architecture that uses up to thousands of processors. Some might contend that a computer system with 64 or more CPUs is a massively parallel processor. However, the number of CPUs is not as much the issue as the architecture. MPP systems use a different programming paradigm than the more common symmetric multiprocessing (SMP) systems used as servers.

In an MPP system, each CPU contains its own memory and copy of the operating system and application. Each subsystem communicates with the others via a high-speed interconnect. In order to use MPP effectively, an information processing problem must be breakable into pieces that can all be solved simultaneously. In scientific environments, certain simulations and mathematical problems can be split apart and each part processed at the same time. In the business world, a parallel

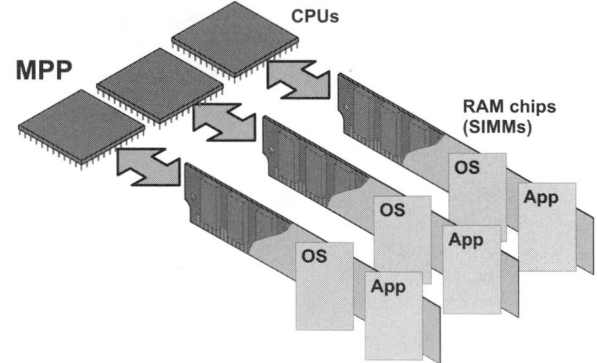

data query (PDQ) divides a large database into pieces. For example, 26 CPUs could be used to perform a sequential search, each one searching one letter of the alphabet.

To take advantage of more CPUs in an MPP system means that the specific problem has to be broken down further into more parallel groups. However, adding CPUs in an SMP system increases performance in a more general manner. Applications that support parallel operations (multithreading) immediately take advantage of SMP, but performance gains are available to all applications, simply because there are more processors. For example, four CPUs can be running four different applications. See *SMP*.

MPPP
(MultiLink PPP) An extension to the point-to-point protocol that enables two channels to be linked together to double the throughput. It is used for ISDN transmission and channel bonding. See *PPP, ISDN* and *channel bonding*.

MPR
(MultiProtocol Router) Software from Novell that provides router capabilities for its NetWare servers. It supports IPX, IP, AppleTalk and OSI protocols as well as all the major LANs and WANs.

MPR II
The Swedish government standard for maximum video terminal radiation. The earlier MPR I is less stringent. See *TCO*.

MPS
(MultiProcessing Specification) A specification from Intel for designing SMP-based PCs using its Pentium processors. It defines how memory and interrupts are shared.

MPU
(MicroProcessor Unit) Same as *microprocessor*.

MPU-401
A MIDI standard from Roland Corporation that has become the de facto interface for connecting a personal computer to a MIDI device.

MQSeries
Messaging middleware from IBM that allows programs to communicate with each other across all IBM platforms, Windows, VMS and a variety of UNIX platforms. Introduced in 1994, it provides a common interface (API) that programs are written to. The MQ was derived from Message Queue. See *messaging middleware*.

MR
See *magnetoresistive*.

MRCI
(Microsoft Realtime Compression Interface) The programming interface for Microsoft's DoubleSpace technology used in DOS 6.

MRP
(Material Requirements Planning) An information system that determines what assemblies must be built and what materials must be procured in order to build a unit of equipment by a certain date. It queries the bill of materials and inventory databases to derive the necessary elements. See *MRP II*.

MRP II
(Manufacturing Resource Planning II) An information system that integrates all manufacturing and related applications, including decision support, material requirements planning (MRP), accounting and distribution. See *MRP* and *ERP*.

ms
(1) (MilliSecond) See *space/time*.
(2) (MS) See *Microsoft* and *messaging system*.

MS Access
See *Microsoft Access*.

MSa/s

(MegaSAmples per Second) A measurement of sampling rate in millions of samples per second.

MSCDEX

(MicroSoft CD-ROM EXtensions) See *CD-ROM Extensions*.

MSCS

See *Microsoft Cluster Server*.

MSD

(MicroSoft Diagnostics) A utility that accompanies Windows 3.1 and DOS 6 that reports on the internal configuration of the PC. A variety of information on disks, video, drivers, IRQs and port addresses is provided.

MS-DOS

(MicroSoft-Disk Operating System) A single user operating system for PCs from Microsoft. It is functionaly identical to IBM's PC-DOS version, except that starting with DOS 6, MS-DOS and PC-DOS each provide different sets of auxiliary utility programs. Both MS-DOS and PC-DOS are called DOS.

MSDOS.SYS

One of two hidden system files that make up Microsoft's MS-DOS. The other is IO.SYS. These two system files are loaded into memory when the computer is booted. They process the instructions in CONFIG.SYS, then load COMMAND.COM and finally process the instructions in AUTOEXEC.BAT. The PC-DOS counterparts of these system files are IBMBIO.COM and IBMDOS.COM.

In Windows 95/98, MSDOS.SYS is a text configuration file rather than an executable program. It determines among other things whether the computer boots into DOS or into Windows 95/98. IO.SYS is still a binary executable that is loaded when the computer is booted.

MSI

(Medium Scale Integration) Between 100 and 3,000 transistors on a chip. See *SSI, LSI, VLSI* and *ULSI*.

MSIE

See *Microsoft Internet Explorer*.

MSMQ

See *Microsoft Message Queue Server*.

MSN

See *Microsoft Network*.

MS-Net

(MicroSoft Network) Microsoft's version of PC-Network introduced in 1985. It was not widely used. See *PC Network*.

MSO

(Multiple System Operator) A major cable TV organization that has franchises in multiple locations.

MSP

(1) A Microsoft Paint graphics file format.

(2) (Microsoft Solution Provider) A Microsoft certification for qualifying resellers that sell and provide training and support on Microsoft products. A certain number of employees must be Microsoft Certified Professionals.

(3) (Multi-Tech Supervisory Protocol) A simultaneous voice and data (SVD) protocol from Multi-Tech Systems, Inc., Mounds View, MN. When a telephone handset is picked up, the modem switches to packet mode, digitizes the voice and interleaves the voice packets with the data packets. See *SVD*.

(4) (Media Suite Pro) A popular Macintosh-based nonlinear video editing system from Avid Technologies, Tewksbury, MA.

(5) An operating system used in Fujitsu IBM-compatible mainframes.

(6) (Multiprocessing Server Pack) A utility that enables LAN Manager to utilize a computer's multiprocessing capabilities.

MS-Windows, MS-Word, MS-Works

See *Windows, Microsoft Word* and *Microsoft Works.*

MTA

(1) (Message Transfer Agent) The store and forward part of a messaging system. See *messaging system.*

(2) See *M Technology Association.*

MTBF

(Mean Time Between Failure) The average time a component works without failure. It is the number of failures divided by the hours under observation.

M Technology Association

(M Technology Association, Silver Spring, MD, www.mtechnology.org) Formerly the MUMPS Users Group, it is an organization that supports the M community through training, meetings and distribution of publications and software.

MTF

(1) (Modulation Transfer Function) A measurement of monitor sharpness. MTF compares the contrast ratio between alternating black and green lines that are one pixel thick.

(2) (Microsoft Tape Format) A backup tape format developed by Seagate Software and Microsoft. It is able to identify operating system-specific data.

MTS

(1) See *Microsoft Transaction Server.*

(2) (Modular TV System) The stereo channel added to the NTSC standard, which includes the SAP audio channel for special use.

MTTR

(Mean Time To Repair) The average time it takes to repair a failed component.

MTU

(Maximum Transmission Unit, Maximum Transfer Unit) The largest packet size that can be transmitted over the network. Messages longer than the MTU must be divided into smaller packets by the communications protocol.

MUD (MOO, MUCK, MUSE, MUSH)

(MultiUser Dungeon, MultiUser Dimension, MultiUser Dialogue) Interactive games played by several people on the Internet. Originally dungeons and dragon games with demons, elves and magicians, MUDs have been created for science fiction themes, cartoon characters and other types of games. MUDs have also evolved into 3-D virtual reality sites.

There are many variations and permutations of MUDs. MOOs are object-oriented MUDs, and MUSEs (Multiuser Shared Environments) are generally designed for elementary and secondary students. A MUSH (MultiUser Shared Hallucination) allows new rooms and situations to be created. A MUCK (MultiUser Chat Kingdom) is a text-based MUD system similar to MUSH, and there is yet another MUCK (MultiUser Construction Kit), heavy on fantasy and myth. See *avatar* and *VRML.*

MUG

(Macintosh User Group) There are many Macintosh user groups throughout the world.

mu-Law

A North American standard for converting analog data into digital form using pulse code modulation (PCM). North America and Japan use mu-Law, while Europe uses A-Law. Mu-Law comes from μ-Law, which uses the Greek letter μ, pronounced "myoo." See *PCM* and *A-Law.*

MULTIBUS

An advanced bus architecture from Intel used in industrial, military and aerospace applications. It includes message passing, auto configuration and software interrupts. MULTIBUS I is 16-bits; MULTIBUS II is 32-bits.

multicast

(1) In data communications networks, to transmit a message to multiple recipients at the same time.

Multicast is a one-to-many transmission similar to broadcasting, except that multicasting implies sending to a list of specific users, whereas broadcasting implies sending to everybody. Contrast with *unicast*. See *IP multicast*.

(2) In digital television broadcasting, to send multiple channels of programming over the allotted bandwidth for digital transmission rather than one high-definition TV (HDTV) signal.

multicast backbone
See *Mbone*.

multichip module
See *MCM*.

multicomputer
A computer made up of several computers. The term generally refers to an architecture in which each processor has its own memory rather than multiple processors with a shared memory. See *parallel computing*.

MULTICS
(MULTiplexed Information and Computing Service) Developed at MIT and Bell Labs in the mid 1960s, MULTICS was the first timesharing operating system. It was used on GE's mainframes, which were absorbed into the Honeywell product line, later acquired by Bull.

multidimensional database
See *OLAP*.

multidimensional query
Asking for a multidimensional view of data.

multidimensional spreadsheet
See *spreadsheet*.

multidimensional views
Looking at data in several dimensions; for example, sales by region, sales by sales rep, sales by product category, sales by month, etc. See *OLAP*.

multidrop line
See *multipoint line*.

MultiFinder
See *Finder*.

multifrequency monitor
A monitor that adjusts to all frequencies within a range (multiscan) or to a set of specific frequencies, such as VGA and Super VGA.

multifunction drive
A storage drive that reads and writes more than one type of storage medium. For example, a magneto-optic disk drive can be used for rewritable disks as well as write once disks. A Floptical drive can read and write floppy disks as well as Floptical disks.

multifunction printer
See *MFD*.

multihomed
Connected to two or more networks or having two or more network addresses. For example, a network server may be connected to a serial line and a LAN or to muliple LANs.

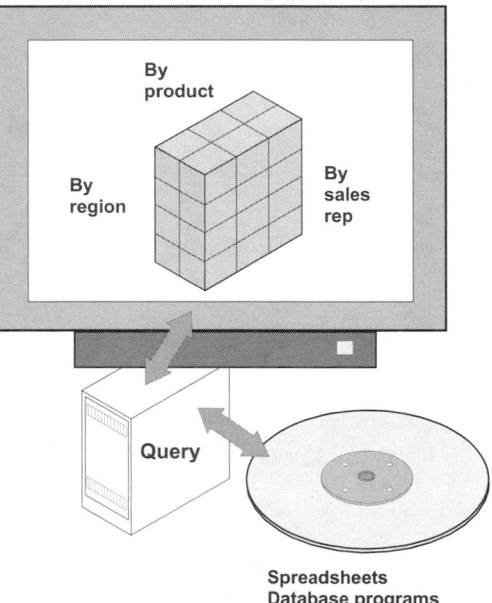

Multidimensional views (pivot table)

By product

By region

By sales rep

Query

Spreadsheets
Database programs
OLAP databases

Multidimensional Views
The ability to quickly switch between one slice of data and another allows users to analyze their information in small palatable chunks instead of a giant report that is confusing.

multilaunch
To open the same application that is stored in a server simultaneously in two or more clients.

multilayer optical disk
See *multilevel optical disk*.

multilayer switch
See *layer 3 switch*.

multilevel optical disk
An optical disk technology that uses multiple platters sandwiched together with a tiny spacer between them. The different layers are accessed by moving the lens up and down and focusing on one of the disk surfaces. IBM demonstrated this technology in 1994 at its Almaden Research Center in San Jose, CA, and showed its feasibility with various optical technologies. It is expected that, in time, all optical disks, including audio CDs and CD-ROMs, will employ multilevel technology to increase storage capacity.

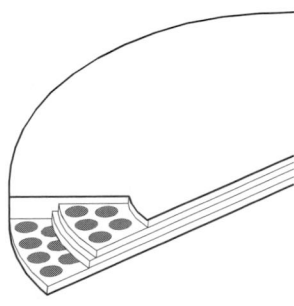

Multilevel Optical Disk
Using multiple layers of recording within the disc's surface yields higher capacities. Using two layers, the DVD disc provides the equivalent storage of 14 CD-ROMs per side.

multiline
A cable, channel or bus that contains two or more transmission paths (wires or optical fibers).

multimastering
See *bus mastering*.

MultiMate
A DOS word processing program that was popular during the 1980s. It was noted for its similarity to the Wang word processing system. Developed by MultiMate International Corporation, it was acquired by Ashton-Tate in 1985.

multimedia
Disseminating information in more than one form. It includes the use of text, audio, graphics, animated graphics and full-motion video. Multimedia programs are typically games, encyclopedias and training courses on CD-ROM. However, any application with sound and/or video can be called a multimedia program. See *hot topics and trends* and *MPC*.

multimedia conferencing
See *videoconferencing* and *data conferencing*.

Multimedia Extensions
Windows routines that support audio recording and playback, animation playback, joysticks, MIDI, the MCI interface for CD-ROM, videodiscs, videotapes, etc., and the RIFF file format. See also *MMX*. See *MPC*.

multimedia monitor
A monitor that contains built-in speakers. In time, multimedia monitors are expected to contain a built-in camera for videoconferencing.

multimedia PC
A PC that includes stereo sound and a CD-ROM drive. PCs that are sold with the MPC label meet the stringent requirements of the Multimedia PC Marketing Council. To upgrade an older system to multimedia requires installing a CD-ROM drive, a sound card and shielded speakers, which can be purchased separately or together in a multimedia upgrade kit. See *MPC* and *multimedia upgrade kit*.

multimedia upgrade kit
The hardware and software necessary to turn a standard PC into a multimedia PC (MPC). The package includes a CD-ROM drive, sound card and speakers. Some combination of bundled software and/or CD-ROMs may also be included. The advantage of the kit is that the CD-ROM controller card

and sound card have been preset to avoid potential conflicts with each other, and the correct cables are included. See *CD-ROM audio cable*.

multimode fiber

An optical fiber with a core diameter of from 50 to 100 microns. It is the most commonly used optical fiber for short distances such as LANs. Light can enter the core at different angles, making it easier to connect the light source. However, light rays bounce around within the core causing some distortion and providing less bandwidth than singlemode fiber. Contrast with *singlemode fiber*. See *chromatic dispersion*.

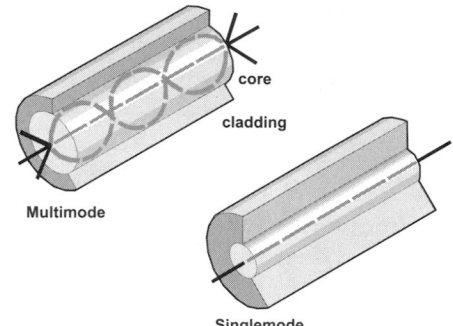

core

cladding

Multimode

Singlemode

MultiPlan

An early spreadsheet for CP/M machines and PCs from Microsoft. It was one of the first spreadsheets.

multiple inheritance

In object-oriented programming, a class that can contain more than one parent. Contrast with *single inheritance*.

Multiple Master

A font technology from Adobe that allows a typeface to be generated in different styles, from condensed to expanded and from light to heavy. Multiple Master can generate fonts that are more optically correct at both extremes in size from very small to very large than standard Type 1 fonts.

multiple platforms

Two or more operating environments, which typically include the CPU family and operating system. For example, if versions of a program run on Windows and the Macintosh, the software is said to support multiple platforms. That application is also known as a cross platform application.

A program that runs on all versions of Windows (3.1, 95, 98 and NT) is sometimes said to support multiple platforms. Although Windows operating systems all stem from the same core, 32-bit Windows programs (95, 98 and NT) will not run under Windows 3.1, and many Windows 3.1 programs behave poorly under 95, 98 and NT. See *cross platform*.

multiplexing

Transmitting multiple signals over a single communications line or computer channel. The two common multiplexing techniques are FDM, which separates signals by modulating the data onto different carrier frequencies, and TDM, which separates signals by interleaving bits one after the other.

multiplexor

In communications, a device that merges several low-speed transmissions into one high-speed transmission and vice versa. Contrast with *inverse multiplexor*.

multiplexor channel

A computer channel that transfers data between the CPU and several low-speed peripherals (terminals, printers, etc.) simultaneously. It may have an optional burst mode that allows a high-speed transfer to only one peripheral at a time.

multiple zone recording

See *ZBR*.

multiplier-accumulator

A general-purpose floating point processor that multiplies and accumulates the results of the multiplication. Newer versions also perform division and square roots.

multipoint conferencing

Same as *teleconferencing*. This is a redudant phrase, because conferencing implies three or more participants, rather than point to point between two people.

Computer Desktop Encyclopedia

multipoint control unit
See *MCU*.

multipoint line
In communications, a single line that interconnects three or more devices.

multiport bridge
A bridge with more than two ports. There is little difference between a multiport bridge and a switch, such as used to switch Ethernet packets, except that the multiport bridge may introduce some overhead. The switch must be able to maintain the full wire speed of the medium between any two ports.

multiported memory
A type of memory that provides more than one access path to its contents. It allows the same bank of memory to be read and written simultaneously. See *video RAM*.

multiport repeater
A hub in a 10BaseT network is often known as a multiport repeater, because it sends any input signal to all outputs. See *10BaseT*.

multiport serial card
A circuit board that contains multiple serial ports for connection to modems or other serial devices. The serial port is used as an interface by a many different kinds of sensors and data collection terminals in a variety of industrial and medical applications.

Multiprise
A family of System/390 entry-level to medium-scale mainframes from IBM that use microprocessor-based CMOS technology. They house the control units, channels and hard disks in the same cabinet similar to midrange servers. The first Multiprise models were introduced in 1996. See *IBM mainframes*.

multiprocessing
Simultaneous processing with two or more processors in one computer, or two or more computers processing together. When two or more computers are used, they are tied together with a high-speed channel and share the general workload between them. If one fails, the other takes over.

It is also accomplished in special-purpose computers, such as array processors, which provide concurrent processing on sets of data. Although computers are built with various overlapping features, such as executing instructions while inputting and outputting data, multiprocessing refers specifically to concurrent instruction executions. See *parallel processing, SMP, MPP, bus mastering* and *fault tolerant*.

multiprocessor
Multiple processors. A multiprocessor machine uses two or more CPUs for routine processing. See *multiprocessing*.

multiprogramming
Same as *multitasking*.

multiprotocol router
A router that supports two or more communications protocols, such as IPX, TCP/IP and DECnet. It is used to switch network traffic between different LANs located throughout the enterprise as well as to switch LAN traffic to WANs.

MultiRead CD-ROM drive
A drive that can read CD-DA, CD-ROM, CD-R and CD-RW disks.

multiscan monitor
A monitor that adjusts to all frequencies within a range. See *multifrequency monitor*.

multisession
A compact disc capability in which data is recorded in more than one session. Each subsequent recording session can be linked to the previous so that they all appear as one. See *multisession drive* and *CD Plus*.

multisession drive

A CD-ROM drive that can read a multisession compact disc. All current CD-ROM drives have this capability. See *multisession*.

MultiSync monitor

A family of multiscan monitors from NECT. NECT popularized the multiscan monitor.

multitasking

The running of two or more programs in one computer at the same time. The number of programs that can be effectively multitasked depends on the type of multitasking performed (preemptive vs cooperative), CPU speed and memory and disk capacity.

Programs can be run simultaneously in the computer because of the differences between I/O and processing speed. While one program is waiting for input, instructions in another can be executed. During the milliseconds one program waits for data to be read from a disk, millions of instructions in another program can be executed. In interactive programs, thousands of instructions can be executed between each keystroke on the keyboard.

In large computers, multiple I/O channels also allow for simultaneous I/O operations to take place. Multiple streams of data are being read and written at the exact same time.

In the days of mainframes only, multitasking was called *multiprogramming*, and multitasking meant *multithreading*.

multithreading

Multitasking within a single program. It allows multiple streams of execution to take place concurrently within the same program, each stream processing a different transaction or message. In order for a multithreaded program to be of any value, it must be run in a multitasking or multiprocessing environment, which allows multiple operations to take place.

Certain types of applications lend themselves to multithreading. For example, in an order processing system, each order can be entered independently of the other orders. In an image editing program, a calculation-intensive filter can be performed on one image, while the user works on another. In a symmetric multiprocessing (SMP) operating system, its multithreading allows multiple CPUs to be controlled at the same time. It is also used to create synchronized audio and video applications.

Multithreading generally uses reentrant code, which cannot be modified when executing, so that the same code can be shared by multiple programs.

multitier application

An application, in which one part runs on one server and another part runs on another. See *three-tier client/server*.

multi-timbral

The ability to play multiple instrument sounds (patches) simultaneously. See *MIDI patch* and *timbre*.

multiuser

Two or more users.

Multiuser DOS

(1) A multiuser DOS-compatible operating system from Caldera that supports multiple terminals from a single PC (386 and up). It is distributed mainly through VARs that have modified it for their own purposes. Multiuser DOS evolved out of Concurrent DOS from Digital Research, which was acquired by Novell and later sold to Caldera.

(2) (multiuser DOS - generic) A DOS-compatible operating system that supports multiple terminals from a single PC.

multiuser NT

Using Windows NT like a central, timeshared computer. Citrix developed this method with its WinFrame software and subsequently worked with Microsoft to create Windows Terminal Server. Since NT is a network operating system (NOS), it already services multiple users (file server, Web server, etc.); however, multiuser NT refers to Windows Terminal Server and Winframe. See *Windows Terminal Server* and *WinFrame*.

multivariate

The use of multiple variables in a forecasting model.

MultiWin

See *WinFrame*.

MUMPS

See *M*.

MUSE, MUSH

See *MUD*.

Musicam

See *5.1 channel*.

music CD

Generally refers to an audio CD, otherwise known as "Red Book audio." However, the term could refer to a CD-ROM that contains sound files, such as WAV and MID files.

mutex

(1) (MUTually EXclusive) A programming flag used to grab and release an object. When data is acquired that cannot be shared or processing is started that cannot be performed simultaneously elsewhere in the system, the mutex is set to "lock," which blocks other attempts to use it. The mutex is set to "unlock" when the data is no longer needed or the routine is finished. See *flag*.

(2) (MUsic TEX) A package of macros for the TeX typesetting system that supports musical notation.

MUX

(MUltipleXor) See *multiplexor*.

MVGA

(Monochrome VGA) The designation is sometimes used for a non-color laptop screen. It should more accurately be called "gray scale VGA," since monochrome means two colors; for example, black and white and no shades in between.

MVIP

(MultiVendor Integration Protocol) A voice bus and switching protocol for PCs originated by a number of companies, including Natural Microsystems of Natick, MA, its major supporter. It provides a second communications bus within the PC that is used to multiplex up to 256 full-duplex voice channels from one voice card to another.

Digital voice, fax, video (any digital data) is bussed over a ribbon cable connected at the top of each ISA, EISA or Micro Channel card. For example, several fax boards could be cabled to a board that multiplexes their lines onto a T1 channel. Using the high bandwidth of this second bus, video conferencing systems are built around MVIP.

MVIP products can make the PC perform like a small-scale PBX. For example, an interactive voice response system on one card could pass incoming voice conversations to a card that switches the lines to live agents in a call center.

The ability to plug a card into a standard AT bus and perform voice and video processing is opening up a whole new world to vendors. It allows far more flexible and affordable systems to be built, and it helps solve worldwide interface problems. A variety of interface cards from different countries can be plugged in, allowing MVIP products to connect to telephone systems all around the world.

MVP

(Multimedia Video Processor) A high-speed DSP chip from TI introduced in 1994. Formally the TMS320C80, it combines RISC technology with the functionality of four DSPs on one chip.

MVS

(Multiple Virtual Storage) Introduced in 1974, the primary operating system used on IBM mainframes (the others are VM and DOS/VSE). MVS is a batch processing-oriented operating system that manages large amounts of memory and disk space. Online operations are provided with CICS, TSO and other system software.

MVS/XA (MVS/eXtended Architecture) manages the enhancements, including 2GB of virtual memory, introduced in 1981 with IBM's 370/XA architecture.

MVS/ESA (MVS/Enterprise Systems Architecture) manages the enhancements made to large scale mainframes, including 16TB of virtual memory, introduced in 1988 with IBM's ESA/370 architecture. MVS/ESA runs on all models of the System/390 ES/9000 product line introduced in 1990.

In 1996, MVS/ESA was packaged with an extensive set of utilities and renamed OS/390. The name MVS is still used to refer to the base control program in OS/390. See *OS/390*.

MVS/ESA, MVS/XA

See *MVS*.

MYOB

Digispeak for "mind your own business."

NACCB

(National Association of Computer Consultant Businesses, Greensboro, NC, www.naccb.resourcecenter.com) An organization representing companies that provide temporary, high-level professional help in the information technology field. Founded in 1987, it is concerned with legislation that affects computer consultants.

Nacchio's law

"The number of ports and price per port of an IP gateway (analog voice to digital IP) improve by two orders of magnitude every 18 months." By Joseph Nacchio, president and CEO of Qwest Communications and former head of long distance service at AT&T. Economical IP gateways are essential to enable voice over IP to become commonplace. See *Qwest*.

NAEC

See *NetWare certification*.

nag screen

An advertisement in a shareware program that routinely asks the user to register and pay for the software. Although it generally pops up at the beginning or end of the program, it can appear at certain intervals as it is being used. See *nagware*.

nagware

Software that periodically prompts the user to register the product. Similar to a nag screen for shareware, nagware is built into a commercial product. See *nag screen*.

nailed up

In communications, it refers to a permanent connection rather than one that is dynamically created and released. For example, a leased, private, point-to-point line is a nailed-up connection.

NAK

(Negative AcKnowledgement) A communications code used to indicate that a message was not received, or that a terminal does not wish to transmit. Contrast with *ACK*.

Named Pipes

An IPC facility in LAN Manager that allows data to be exchanged from one application to another either over a network or running within the same computer. The use of the term pipes for interprocess communication was coined in UNIX.

name resolution

Converting a name into the address required by a machine or network. In a TCP/IP network, HOSTS and LMHOSTS files are examples of manually keeping host names and IP addresses updated. DNS and WINS are examples of systems that automatically update the names. See *naming service, DNS, WINS, HOSTS file* and *LMHOSTS file*.

name server

A network server that provides a naming, or directory, service. See *naming service* and *directory service*.

name service

See *naming service*.

namespace

A name or group of names that are defined according to some naming convention. A flat namespace uses a single, unique name for every device. For example, a small Windows (NetBIOS) network requires a different, made-up name for each computer and printer. The Internet uses a hierarchical namespace that partitions the names into categories known as top level domains such as .com, .edu and .gov, etc., which are at the top of the hierarchy. See *Internet domain names*.

naming service

Software that converts a name into a physical address on a network, providing logical to physical conversion. Names can be user names, computers, printers, services or files. The transmitting station sends a name to the server containing the naming service software, which sends back the actual address of the user or resource. The process is known as name resolution.

A naming service functions as a Yellow Pages for the network, which is precisely what Sun's NIS system was originally called. Novell's naming service starting with NetWare 4.0 is called NDS (NetWare Directory Service). In AppleTalk, the naming service is embedded within the protocol. In the case of the Internet or other IP network, a DNS server returns the IP address for the submitted name. See *directory service.*

N-AMPS

(Narrow-bandwidth **AMPS**) A version of the analog cellular mobile phone system that uses a narrower bandwidth. See *AMPS* and *D-AMPS.*

NAND

(Not **AND**) A Boolean logic operation that is true if any single input is false. Two-input NAND gates are often used as the sole logic element on gate array chips, because all Boolean operations can be created from NAND gates.

NAND		
IN	IN	OUT
0	0	1
0	1	1
1	0	1
1	1	0

nanny software

See *parental control software.*

nano

Billionth (10^{-9}). See *space/time.*

nanometer

One billionth of a meter. One nanometer is equal to 10 angstroms. Nanometers are used to measure the wavelengths of light.

nanosecond

(1) One billionth of a second. Used to measure the speed of logic and memory chips, a nanosecond can be visualized by converting it to distance. In one nanosecond, electricity travels about nine inches in a wire.

Even at 186,000 miles per second, electricity is never fast enough for the hardware designer who worries over a few inches of circuit path. The slightest delay is multiplied millions of times, since millions of pulses are sent through a wire in a single second. See *space/time* and *ohnosecond.*

(2) The time between a traffic light turning green and a New York City cab driver blowing his horn.

nanotechnology

A science that experiments with building devices at the molecular and atomic level. For example, a bit might be represented by only one atom some time in the future. Nanotechnology could be used to build anything, not just computers and communications devices.

NAP

(Network Access Point) A junction point where major Internet service providers interconnect with each other. Also known as Internet Exchanges (IXs), connection at one or more of these NAPs means "connected to the Internet."

When the Net went commercial in 1995, four official NAPs were created: three run by the telephone companies in San Francisco, Chicago and New York (actually Pennsauken, NJ), and the fourth in Washington, D.C. run by Metropolitan Fiber Systems (MFS) and known as MAE-East (Metropolitan Area Exchange-East). Four more MAEs have become de facto NAPs, plus three historical exchanges (two Federal plus CIX) add up to about a dozen major

All About NAPs and ISPs
Boardwatch Magazine's directory of ISPs includes a lot of well-written and detailed information about how the Internet is connected. Visit their Web site at www.boardwatch.com for more information and related articles.

exchange points within the U.S. National ISPs generally connect at all four of the original ones and all MAEs. This is known as public peering.

In addition, due to the congestion at these exchanges, large ISPs peer privately and interconnect with each other at many other points throughout the country where equipment at both companies is conveniently located. Dropping the packet off earlier to the destination backbone eliminates considerable traffic. Private peering enables larger ISPs to move traffic more efficiently than smaller ones. See *peering* and *CIX*.

NAPLPS

(North American Presentation-Level Protocol Syntax) An ANSI-standard protocol for videotex and teletext. It compresses data for transmission over narrow-bandwidth lines and requires decompression on the receiving end. PRODIGY uses this format for transmitting and displaying some of its graphics.

narrowband

In communications, transmission rates from 50 bps to 64 Kbps. Earlier uses of the term referred to 2,400 bps or less or to sub-voice grade transmission from 50 to 150 bps. Contrast with *wideband* and *broadband*.

narrowcast

To transmit data to selected individuals. Contrast with *broadcast*.

NAS

(1) (Network Attached Storage) A specialized file server that connects to the network. It uses traditional LAN protocols such as Ethernet and TCP/IP and processes only file I/O requests such as NFS (UNIX) and SMB (DOS/Windows). See *SAN* for details on storage networks.

(2) (Network Application Support) Digital's implementation of open systems, which provides standards-based software that allows a variety of workstations (VMS, ULTRIX, Sun, DOS, Windows, OS/2, Mac, etc.) to interface via VAX and ULTRIX servers.

NASI

(1) (NetWare Asynchronous Service Interface) A protocol from Novell for connecting to modems in a communications server. It was derived from the NCSI protocol. NASI provides more advanced features than the common int 14 (interrupt 14) method. It allows a specific modem or line to be chosen. It frees the call more quickly, and it transfers data more efficiently.

(2) (National Association of Systems Integrators, Walpole, MA, www.nasi-info.com) An organization of more than 10,000 members founded in 1991, dedicated to exchanging up-to-date information on members' products and services. Its annual Computer Industry Buying Guide in print and on disk includes suppliers and services.

NAT

(Network Address Translation) An IETF standard that allows an organization to present itself to the Internet with one address. NAT converts the address of each LAN node into one IP address for the Internet and vice versa. It also serves as a firewall by keeping individual IP addresses hidden from the outside world.

National Cristina Foundation

(National Cristina Foudation, Stamford, CT, www.cristina.org) A not-for-profit public charity that seeks donations of used or excess computers. Founded in 1984 by Yvette Marrin and Bruce McMahan, it was named in honor of McMahan's daughter, Cristina, who has cerebral palsy. Donations are directed to programs that rehabilitate people with disabilities, students at risk of failing and the economically disadvantaged. The foundation has helped hundreds of thousands of individuals in the U.S. and abroad. See *how to donate old equipment*.

National Semiconductor

(National Semiconductor Corporation, Santa Clara, CA, www.national.com) A major semiconductor manufacturer that provides system-level products for telecommunications, desktop computers, automobiles, consumer products and the military. Founded in 1959 in Danbury, CT, National Semiconductor was in the forefront of the first transistors and integrated circuits. Over the years, it has become known for its analog and mixed mode signalling devices. In 1987, it acquired Fairchild Semiconductor, which it sold in 1997, the same year it merged with Cyrix Corporation.

native application

An application designed to run in the computer environment (machine language and OS) being referenced. The term is used to contrast a native application with an interpreted one such as a Java application, which is not native to a single platform. The term may also be used to contrast a native application with an emulated application, which was originally written for a different platform.

native capacity

The raw capacity of a device. The storage capacity of many backup tapes is published as compressed storage in order to sound larger. It is typically expressed as twice the native capacity. The actual capacity may be less than or exceed the published figure, because different data compress at different rates. Text files generally compresses to about 40% of their original size, but other files may not compress nearly as well.

native file, native format

The file format that an application normally reads and writes. The native format of a Microsoft word document is different than a WordPerfect document, etc., etc. The problem is that there are tons of et ceteras. Even image editing programs, which are designed to read and convert a raft of different graphics file types, have their own built-in native format. For example, in order to build an image in layers, Photoshop converts foreign images into its native, layered file format (.PSD extension). Contrast with *foreign format* and *file format*.

native language

Same as *machine language*. See *native mode*.

native mode

(1) The normal running mode of a computer, executing programs from its built-in instruction set. Contrast with *emulation mode*.

(2) The highest performance state of a computer, such as a 486 or Pentium running in Protected Mode.

NATURAL

A fourth-generation language from Software AG, Reston, VA, that runs on a variety of computers from micro to mainframe.

natural language

English, Spanish, French, German, Japanese, Russian, etc.

natural language query

A query expressed by typing English, French or any other spoken language in a normal manner. For example, "how many sales reps sold more than a million dollars in any eastern state in January?" In order to allow for spoken queries, both a voice recognition system and natural language query software are required.

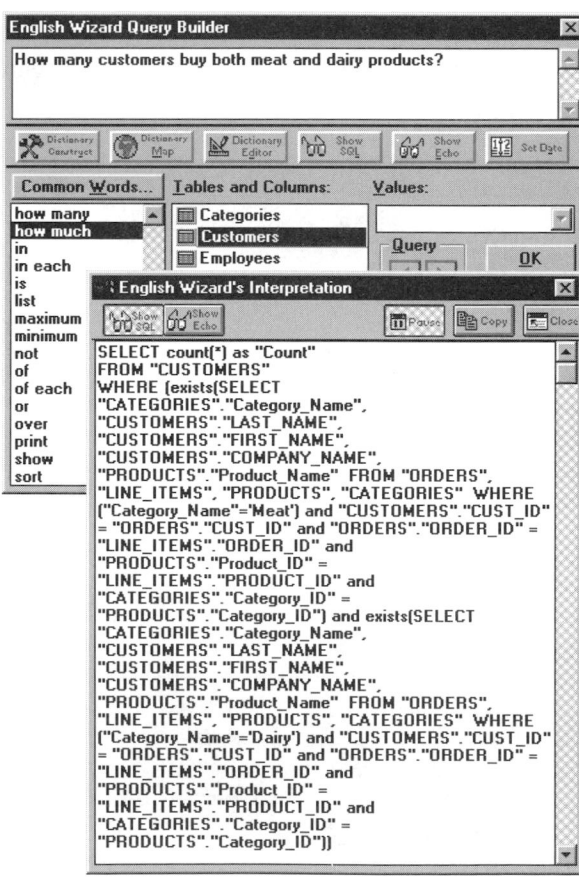

A Natural Language Example
Linguistic Technology's English Wizard generated the SQL code in the window at the bottom from the English sentence at the top. It is amazing how much SQL is necessary to ask what looks like a simple question. *(Screen shot courtesy of Linguistic Technology Corporation.)*

natural language recognition

Same as *voice recognition*.

NAU

(1) (Network Access Unit) An interface card that adapts a computer to a local area network.

(2) (Network Addressable Unit) An SNA component that can be referenced by name and address, which includes the SSCP, LU and PU.

navigate

"Surfing the Web." To move from page to page on the Web.

Navigator

See *Netscape Navigator* and *Norton Navigator*.

Naviken

A format used for geographic databases that originated in Japan. Naviken CD-ROMs have become a de facto standard for car navigation maps. See *GPS*.

NB card

(NuBus card) See *NuBus*.

NBS

(National Bureau of Standards) See *NIST*.

NC

See *network computer* and *numerical control*.

NCA

(1) (Network Computing Architecture) An architecture from Oracle for developing applications within a networked computing environment. It provides a three-tier distributed environment based on CORBA that uses program components known as "cartridges." NCA is managed by Oracle Enterprise Manager software that integrates clients with processes running in application and database servers.

(2) (National Computer Association, Clearwater, FL, www.nca-net.com) A membership association of independent consultants, developers, resellers and service technicians in the computer field. Founded in 1995, NCA benefits include discounts on business services, training seminars and quarterly publications. Members pool each other's resources to enhance their capabilities and knowledge.

NCB

(Network Control Block) A packet structure used by the NetBIOS communications protocol.

NCF file

(NetWare Command File) A file of NetWare commands that are executed one at a time, similar to a DOS batch (.BAT) file. The NetWare AUTOEXEC.NCF file is executed in the server at startup, just like the DOS AUTOEXEC.BAT file.

NCGA

(National Computer Graphics Association) A Fairfax, Virginia-based organization dedicated to developing and promoting the computer graphics industry. It maintained a clearinghouse for industry information. NCGA closed its doors in 1996.

NCI

(Network Computer, Inc., Redwood Shores, CA, subsidiary of Oracle Corporation, www.nc.com) A software company that specializes in the network computer field. It initially promoted the NC Reference Profile specification, which was later turned over to The Open Group. NCI provides the software for the Network in a Box, a complete turnkey solution sold through VARs. It also offers software that adds NC capability to existing UNIX and NT servers. See *network computer*.

NC machine

See *network computer* and *numerical control*.

NCP

(1) (Network Control Program) See *SNA* and *network control program*.

(2) (NetWare Core Protocol) The application layer protocol in NetWare. It is the internal NetWare language used to communicate between client and server and provides functions such as opening, closing, reading and writing files and obtaining access to the NetWare bindery and NDS naming service databases.

The counterpart of NCP in the UNIX world is NFS (Network File System), which is known as a *distributed file system*. DOS, Windows and OS/2 use the SMB (Server Message Block) protocol to perform these functions. NCP, SMB and NFS are all high-level protocols that ride above the transport protocols (IPX/SPX, NetBEUI and TCP/IP), which manage the transfer. See *NFS* and *SMB*.

(3) (Not Copy Protected) Software that can be easily copied.

NCR

(NCR Corporation, Dayton, OH, www.ncr.com) A major manufacturer of computers and financial terminals. It was founded in 1884 when John Henry Patterson purchased National Manufacturing Company of Dayton, Ohio, and renamed it National Cash Register. It became the leading cash register company and, by 1911, had sold its one millionth machine.

Starting in the 1930s, NCR made accounting machines that posted customer accounts and became successful in the banking and retail industries, in which it has remained ever since.

In 1957, it introduced the "304" transistorized computer. It accepted data from NCR cash registers and banking terminals via paper tape. The 304 was very reliabile and widely accepted.

NCR computer lines have included the Century series (1960s), Criterion series (1970s) and the V and I series (1980s). Starting in 1982 with the UNIX- and Motorola 68000-based Tower series, NCR embraced open systems and industry standards. In 1990, the x86-based System 3000 series was introduced, a complete line from desktops to massively parallel machines running DOS, Windows and OS/2 at the low end and UNIX at the high end. The desktop line was later dropped.

In 1991, AT&T acquired the company and ran it as a wholly-owned subsidiary, renaming it AT&T Global Information Systems (AT&T GIS) in early 1994. The NCR name did remain on ATM and POS terminals as well as microelectronics and business forms. In 1996, AT&T GIS was spun off of AT&T,

John H. Patterson
Patterson was the consumate salesman and built a small empire as machinery was first introduced into the commercial world at the end of the 19th Century. *(Photo courtesy of NCR Corporation.)*

An Early Cash Register
These were marvelous machines when first introduced, because they could tally the days receipts automatically. *(Photo courtesy of NCR Corporation.)*

The NCR 304
Introduced in 1957, the 304 was NCR's first computer. Using paper tape from NCR cash registers as input, it was very reliable and widely accepted. *(Photo courtesy of NCR Corporation.)*

renamed NCR, and it became an independent company once again.

NC Reference Profile, NCRP

(Network Computer Reference Profile) The specification for network computer compliance established by Oracle and endorsed by Sun, IBM and others. The first version of this specification is known as the NC1 Reference Profile. See *NCI* and *network computer*.

NCR paper

(No Carbon Required paper) A multiple-part paper form that does not use carbon paper. The ink is adhered to the reverse side of the previous sheet.

NCSA

(1) (National Center for Supercomputer Applications, Urbana-Champaign, IL, www.ncsa.uiuc.edu) A high-performance computing facility located at the University of Illinois at Urbana-Champaign. Founded in 1985 by a National Science Foundation grant, the NCSA provides supercomputer resources to hundreds of universities and organizations engaged in scientific research.

(2) (National Computer Security Association) See *ICSA*.

NCSC

(National Computer Security Center) The arm of the U.S. National Security Agency that defines criteria for trusted computer products. Following are the Trusted Computer Systems Evaluation Criteria (TCSEC), DOD Standard 5200.28, also known as the Orange Book, and the European equivalent. The Red Book is the Orange Book counterpart for networks. Level D is a non-secure system. Level C provides discretionary access control (DAC). The owner of the data can determine who has access to it.

```
C1   Requires user log-on, but allows group ID.

C2   Requires individual user log-on with password and an audit mechanism.
```

Levels B and A provide mandatory access control (MAC). Access is based on standard DOD clearances. Each data structure contains a sensitivity level, such as top secret, secret and unclassified, and is available only to users with that level of clearance.

```
B1   DOD clearance levels.

B2   Guarantees path between user and the security system.  Provides assurances
     that system can be tested and clearances cannot be downgraded.

B3   System is characterized by a mathematical model that must be viable.

A1   System is characterized by a mathematical model that can be proven.
```

Highest security. Used in military computers.

European Ratings

The European Information Technology Security Evaluation Criteria (ITSEC) is similar to TCSEC, but rates functionality (F) and effectiveness (E) separately.

```
Orange Book
TCSEC          ITSEC
D              E0
C1             F-C1, E1
C2             F-C2, E2
B1             F-B1, E3
B2             F-B2, E4
B3             F-B3, E5
A1             F-B3, E6
```

NCSI

(Network Communications Services Interface) Also called "nixie," it is a protocol used to handle serial port communications on a network. NCSI applications talk to the NCSI driver rather than directly to the COM port, which allows redirection of the data to a communications server on the network. See *NASI*.

n-dimensional

Some number of dimensions. See *multidimensional views*.

NDIS

(Network Driver Interface Specification) A network driver interface from Microsoft. See *network driver interface*.

NDS

See *NetWare Directory Service*.

NE

(Not Equal to) See *relational operator*.

near field optics

An optical recording technology in which the distance between the read/write head and the bit (spot, pit, etc.) is less than the diameter of the bit (wavelength of light). See *Terastor*.

nearline, near online

Available within a short amount of time, but not instantly. Tape and disk libraries are considered nearline devices, because it takes several seconds to retrieve the appropriate cartridge before it can be read. Contrast with *online*.

near pointer

In an x86 segmented address, a memory address within a single segment (the offset). Contrast with *far pointer*.

NEBS compliant

(Network Equipment Building Systems compliant) Adhering to standards from Bellcore for equipment used in telco central offices (COs). It provides stringent specifications for durability, grounding, cables and hardware interfaces.

NEC, NECT

(NEC Technologies, Inc., Itasca, IL, www.nec.com) The North American subsidiary of NEC that specializes in imaging peripherals, including monitors, data projectors, printers and CD-ROM drives. In 1986, NECT introduced its MultiSync line, the first multifrequency monitors, which have become very popular. In 1996, the CromaClear line of monitors was introduced that combines the aperture grille and shadow mask into a new CRT technology for improved resolution.

NECT's parent company was founded in Tokyo in 1899 as Nippon Electric Company, Ltd., which was renamed NEC Corporation in 1983. NEC was the first Japanese company to joint venture with a foreign enterprise, which was Western Electric Company, then part of AT&T. Throughout the 20th century, NEC has been involved with electrical, communications, electronics and computer products worldwide.

negative logic

The use of high voltage for a 0 bit and low voltage for a 1 bit. Contrast with *positive logic*.

nematic

The stage between a crystal and a liquid that has a threadlike nature; for example, a liquid crystal. See *crystalline* and *LCD*.

neper

The unit of measurement based on Napierian logarithms that represents the ratio between two values, such as current or voltage.

nerd

A person typically thought of as dull socially. Nerds often like technical work and are generally introspective. Contrast with *hacker*, a technical person that may or may not be a nerd.

nerd rustler

A recruiter that specializes in placing computer people. Same as *computercruiter*.

nerdspeak

Same as *geekspeak*.

nesting

In programming, the positioning of a loop within a loop. The number of loops that can be nested may be limited by the programming language. See *loop*.

net

Abbreviation of network. "The Net" generally refers to the Internet.

NetBench

A benchmark from Ziff-Davis that tests the performance of a file server handling requests from any mix of DOS, Windows or Mac client stations, one of which must be Windows. NetBench computes the average throughput based on all the client requests.

NetBEUI

(**Net**BIOS **E**xtended **U**ser **I**nterface) Pronounced "net-booey." The transport layer for NetBIOS. NetBIOS and NetBEUI were originally part of a single protocol suite that was later separated. NetBIOS sessions can be transported over NetBEUI, TCP/IP and SPX/IPX protocols. See *NetBIOS*.

NetBIOS

The native networking protocol in DOS and Windows networks. Although originally combined with its transport layer protocol (NetBEUI), NetBIOS today provides a programming interface for applications at the session layer (layer 5). NetBIOS can ride over NetBEUI, its native

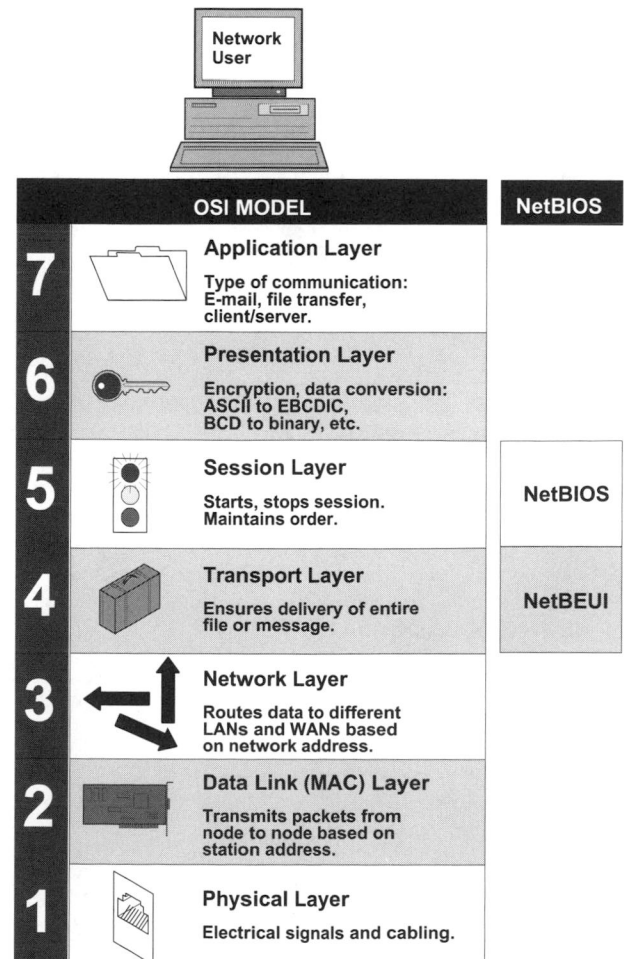

transport, which is not routable, or over TCP/IP and SPX/IPX, which are routable protocols.

NetBIOS computers are identified by a unique 15-character name, and Windows machines (NetBIOS machines) periodically broadcast their names over the network so that Network Neighborhood can catalog them. For TCP/IP networks, NetBIOS names are turned into IP addresses via manual configuration in an LMHOSTS file or a WINS server.

There are two NetBIOS modes. The Datagram mode is the fastest, but does not guarantee delivery. It uses a self-contained packet with send and receive name, usually limited to 512 bytes. If the recipient device is not listening for messages, the datagram is lost. The Session mode establishes a connection until broken. It guarantees delivery of messages up to 64KB long. See *WINS* and *LMHOSTS file*.

netbooey
See *NetBEUI*.

netcast, Netcaster
See *Webcast* and *Netscape Netcaster*.

Netcenter
(www.netcenter.com) Netscape's home page and Web portal. It provides Web search facilities, news, white and yellow pages directories, classified ads and a variety of features. There were so many visitors to Netscape's home page that it was later turned into a full-service Web portal.

netfilter
See *Web filtering*.

netid
See *IP address*.

netiquette
(NETwork etIQUETTE) Proper manners when conferencing between two or more users on an online service or the Internet. Emily Post may not have told you to curtail your cussing via modem, but netiquette has been established to remind you that profanity is not in good form over the network.

Using UPPER CASE TO MAKE A POINT all the time and interjecting emoticons throughout a message is also not good netiquette. See *flame*.

Netizen
A user of the Internet. A Net "citizen."

netlist
A list of logic gate and their interconnections which make up a circuit. See *logic synthesis*.

netmask
See *subnet mask*.

NetMeeting
A set of collaboration and conferencing functions that come with and add groupware capabilities to Internet Explorer, Microsoft's Web browser. It includes a whiteboard and application sharing, a text chat window as well as audioconferencing (Internet phone) and videoconferencing. Starting with Version 2.0, NetMeeting supports the H.323 standard.

NetNews
See *Usenet*.

NetObjects Fusion
A popular Windows-based Web authoring system from NetObjects, Inc., Redwood City, CA, (www.netobjects.com). It provides a visual environment for designing Web pages and can import an existing site. It was one of the first Web authoring programs to apply desktop publishing tools to an entire site. It is also noted for its ability to generate a complex site without writing any lines of code.

NetPC
(NETwork PC) A Windows-based computer that is designed to be centrally managed in a network. It is typically configured as a fat client, but can alternatively be used as a thin client. As a fat client, a NetPC

is similar to a PC, except that it obtains its initial and all subsequent installations of Windows and applications from the server. The software remains installed on the hard disk just like a PC, but program versions are monitored by a management server each time the NetPC is turned on. Floppy and/or CD-ROM drives are optional, but may, if included, be locked down by network administrators for restricted use only.

NetPCs can alternatively be configured as thin clients, in which case the operating system is booted from the network each time the NetPC is turned on, and all applications and data are obtained from the server. The difference between this NetPC scenario and an NC is that NetPCs are Windows based only, and their local hard disks are used for caching parts of the application during the day to improve performance. NCs typically do not use a hard disk.

NetPCs must conform to the NetPC Design Guidelines, which include the management capabilities of Intel's Wired for Management Baseline Specification (see *WfM*).

Intel's LANDesk Configuration Manager was the first management server to support NetPCs. Subsequently, Computer Associates and others provide management software for NetPCs and WfM-enabled PCs. These capabilities are partially supported by Microsoft's Zero Administration Kit (ZAK) and more thoroughly supported in Windows 98 and NT 5.0. NetPCs were announced near the end of 1996, and the first models were introduced in the last half of 1997. See *ZAW, ZAK* and *WfM*. See *network computer* for illustration.

Net phone
See *Internet phone*.

Netscape
(Netscape Communications Corporation, Mountain View, CA, www.netscape.com) A company that specializes in World Wide Web software, including the Netscape Navigator Web browser and SoftSuite, a collection of Web server applications. Founded in 1994 by James Clark, former patriarch of Silicon Graphics (SGI) and Marc Andreessen, who, along with Eric Bina, created the Mosaic browser while at the University of Illinois, Netscape quickly became the number one topic of conversation as Internet and Web fever enveloped the nation in the mid 1990s.

Netscape seriously impacted the status quo. Its stock was catapulted to a market cap of more than two billion before the company ever made a dime, making it one of the most successful public offerings in stock market history. Netscape forced software giant Microsoft into restructuring its entire product line to become Internet compliant. Microsoft reacted so strongly to Netscape's position that it developed a browser and Web server that it has literally given away free. Stay tuned!

Netscape Collabra
See *Netscape Communicator*.

Netscape color palette
A palette of 216 colors that Netscape displays the same on its Windows and Mac browsers. If other colors are used in images, Netscape will dither them, and the results will differ between the platforms.

Netscape Communicator
A suite of Web browsing and groupware tools from Netscape. It includes the Netscape Navigator 4.0 browser, Netscape Messenger e-mail client, Netscape Collabra threaded discussions, Netscape Composer HTML editor and Netscape Conference, which provides audio and videoconferencing, whiteboard, text chat and collaborative browsing. The Professional version adds group calendaring and scheduling, remote administration and 3270 emulation. See *Netscape Netcaster*.

Netscape Composer, Netscape Conference
See *Netscape Communicator*.

Netscape Constellation
See *Netscape Netcaster*.

Netscape LiveWire
A suite of management and development tools from Netscape for Netscape Web sites. It includes a site manager for maintaining HTML links, a compiler for developing JavaScript applications and a library that provides SQL connectivity to a variety of databases. LiveWire Pro includes an Informix database and the Crystal Reports report and analysis program.

Netscape Messenger

See *Netscape Communicator.*

Netscape Navigator

A Web browser for Windows, Macintosh and X Windows from Netscape. It provides secure transmission over the Internet, and Netscape server software provides encryption based on the RSA method. Navigator has become the most popular Web browser. As of Version 2.0, Navigator supports Java applications and provides a formal method for hosting plug-in applications from third parties. See *Netscape Communicator.*

Netscape Netcaster

A component of Netscape Communicator that provides a push model delivery system based on Marimba's Castanet Tuner. Users can subscribe to content channels on the Internet and receive information updates in the background while working on other applications. See *Netscape Communicator.*

Netscape palette

See *Netscape color palette.*

The Navigator Interface
Navigator is displaying the home page that was retrieved by typing **www.computerlanguage.com** into the URL field and pressing Enter. The buttons on the left are links to other pages on the site.

Netscape plug-in

A third-party software product, such as a multimedia viewer, that extends Netscape Navigator's capabilities while browsing the Web. A Netscape helper application provides similar capabilities but runs as an external application and typically launches another window for viewing.

NetShow

Client and server software from Microsoft for streaming audio and video over the Internet. It uses the Active Streaming Format (ASF) and provides utilities for translating common audio, video and image formats into ASF. Using IP multicast, NetShow provides ActiveX extensions to NT Server. NetShow On-Demand provides transmission of static data. NetShow Live handles live broadcasts. See *RTSP.*

netspeak

The vocabulary associated with the concepts, functions and features of the Internet.

Net surfer

An individual that regularly accesses the Internet.

Net TV

See *Internet TV.*

NetView

IBM SNA network management software that provides centralized monitoring and control for SNA, non-SNA and non-IBM devices. NetView/PC interconnects NetView with Token Ring LANs, Rolm CBXs and non-IBM modems, while maintaining control in the host.

NetWare

A family of network operating systems from Novell that support DOS, Windows, OS/2 and Mac clients. UNIX client support is available from third parties. NetWare is the most widely-used LAN control program.

Except for Personal NetWare and previous Lite versions, NetWare is a stand-alone operating system that runs in the server. The server hard disks are formatted with a Novell format. The NetWare Administrator utility is included for system administration.

Introduced in 1993, NetWare 4.0 was the first version of NetWare to use NDS, Novell's NetWare Directory Service, which provides directory services for a global enterprise. A NetWare 4.x server supports up to 1,000 concurrent users, includes realtime disk compression and SMP support for up to 32 processors. NetWare 4.x is backward compatible with NetWare 2.x and 3.x versions.

In late 1996, NetWare 4.11 was combined with Novell's Web server and related components in a package entitled IntranetWare. Novell also introduced IntranetWare for Small Business, designed for simplified administration of networks of up to 25 users. Within IntranetWare, the NetWare name is still retained as the core operating system. The NetWare brand returns in NetWare 5.0, and IntranetWare has been dropped.

NetWare 3.12 (originally NetWare 386) was the last release of the first 32-bit version of NetWare, which supports up to 250 concurrent users. NetWare 3.12 is still sold and supported. It uses the Novell bindery which provides directory services for a single server unlike the global NDS directory in NetWare 4.x and IntranetWare. NetWare 2.x (originally Advanced NetWare 286) runs in a 286 and supports up to 100 concurrent users.

Personal NetWare is a peer-to-peer network operating system, which allows any client workstation to be a server. It supersedes earlier peer-to-peer versions known as NetWare Lite and NetWare ELS (Entry Level System).

Fault tolerant capability can (NetWare SFT) can be added to NetWare 4.11 and IntranetWare, which provides automatic recovery from network malfunctions. See *IPX, SPX* and *MHS*.

OSI MODEL		NETWARE
7	**Application Layer** Type of communication: E-mail, file transfer, client/server.	**NCP (NetWare Core Protocol)**
6	**Presentation Layer** Encryption, data conversion: ASCII to EBCDIC, BCD to binary, etc.	
5	**Session Layer** Starts, stops session. Maintains order.	**Named Pipes, NetBIOS**
4	**Transport Layer** Ensures delivery of entire file or message.	**SPX**
3	**Network Layer** Routes data to different LANs and WANs based on network address.	**IPX**
2	**Data Link (MAC) Layer** Transmits packets from node to node based on station address.	**LSL (ODI, NDIS)** **LAN Driver**
1	**Physical Layer** Electrical signals and cabling.	**Physical**

NetWare Protocols

This chart compares the NetWare protocol stack with the OSI model. One difference is the LSL layer, which provides a common interface to network drivers. ODI and NDIS are the two most commonly used LSL implementations.

NetWare certification

Novell provides certification for technical competence with self-study tests and courses given at National Authorized Education Centers (NAECs). Certificates include CNA (Certified NetWare Administrator), CNE (Certified NetWare Engineer), ECNE (Enterprise CNE, which includes WAN expertise) and CNI (Certified NetWare Instructor).

The ECNE program has been replaced with a Master CNE, which includes an area of specialization. ECNEs can become Master CNEs by passing a single examination.

NetWare Core Protocol
Application layer protocols in the NetWare network operating system. It is the internal NetWare language used to communicate between client and server and provides functions such as opening, closing, reading and writing files and obtaining access to the naming service databases (bindery and NDS).

NetWare Directory Service
Also known as *NDS*, it is Novell's flagship directory service (naming service) that is included with NetWare 4.x and IntranetWare. It is also available for Windows NT. NDS maintains a hierarchical database of information about the network resources within a global enterprise, including networks, users, subgroups, servers, volumes and printers. Unlike the bindery, which was the directory service in NetWare 3.x, NDS users log onto the network as a whole, not a specific server, and NDS determines their access rights.

NDS is based on the X.500 directory standard and is LDAP compliant. Novell provides the NDS source code free of charge to developers that wish to integrate it into their products. In NDS, every network resouce is called an object, and each object contains properties (fields). For example, a user object would contain login ID, password, name, address, telephone and node address.

NetWare Global Messaging
E-mail software from Novell for NetWare 3.x that includes directory synchronization across distributed servers and provides optional interfaces to X.400, SMTP and SNADS. See *SMF*.

NetWare Loadable Module
Known as an *NLM*, it is software that enhances or provides additional functions in a NetWare 3.x or higher server. Support for database engines, workstations, network protocols, fax and print servers are examples. The NetWare 2.x counterpart is a VAP.

NetWare Management System
Also known as *NMS*, it is an SNMP-based network management software from Novell for monitoring and controlling NetWare networks. NMS was superseded by ManageWise.

NetWare NFS
Software from Novell that implements the NFS distributed file system on NetWare servers. It allows UNIX and other NFS client machines to access files on a NetWare server. See *LAN Workplace*.

NetWare Users International
(www.novell.com/nui) A voluntary organization of more than 250 NetWare user groups worldwide.

NetWire
Novell's BBS on CompuServe, which provides technical support for its NetWare products.

network
(1) An arrangement of objects that are interconnected. See *LAN* and *network database*.

(2) In communications, the transmission channels interconnecting all client and server stations as well as all supporting hardware and software.

network accounting
The reporting of network usage. It gathers details about user activity including the number of logons and resources used (disk accesses and space used, CPU time, etc.).

network adapter
A printed circuit board that plugs into both the clients (personal computers or workstations) and servers and controls the exchange of data between them. The network adapter provides services at the data link level of the network, which is also known as the *access method* (OSI layers 1 and 2).

The most common network adapters are Ethernet and Token Ring. Sometimes, the Ethernet adapter is built into the motherboard. LocalTalk, which provides the data link services of Apple's AppleTalk network, is built into all Macintoshes.

A transmission medium, such as twisted pair, coax or fiber optic, interconnects all the adapters in the network. A network adapter is also called a *NIC*, or network interface card.

network administrator

A person who manages a communications network within an organization. Responsibilities include network security, installing new applications, distributing software upgrades, monitoring daily activity, enforcing licensing agreements, developing a storage management program and providing for routine backups. See *system administrator* and *salary survey*.

network analyzer

Software only or a combination of hardware and software that monitors traffic on a network. It can also read unencrypted text transmitted over the network.

network architecture

(1) The design of a communications system, which includes the hardware, software, access methods and protocols used. It also defines the method of control; for example, whether computers can act independently or are controlled by other computers monitoring the network.

(2) The access method in a LAN, such as Ethernet and Token Ring.

network-attached storage

See *NAS*.

network card

See *network adapter*.

network cloud

A cloud-like symbol in a network diagram used to reduce an entire communications network into points of entry and exit. It infers that although there may be any number of switches, routers, trunks, and other network devices within the cloud, the point of interconnection to the cloud (network) is the only technical issue in the diagram. Clouds are often used to depict a WAN (wide area network).

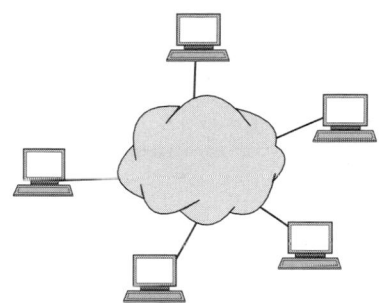

Network Cloud
The cloud symbol represents communications services without specific details of the network architecture. The user is only responsible for getting data into and out of the network.

network computer

(1) A computer in the network.

(2) A desktop computer that provides connectivity to intranets and/or the Internet. It is designed as a "thin client" that downloads all applications from the network server and obtains all of its data from and stores all changes back to the server. The network computer (NC) is similar to a diskless workstation and does not have floppy or hard disk storage.

The attraction of NCs is twofold. Since everything is maintained at the server side, software is installed and upgraded in one place rather than at each client station. NCs are thus being touted as "the way" to lower the cost of computer maintenance. NCs are designed to run Java applications, which are interpreted programs. The goal is that once a Java application is written, it can be run in any NC with a Java interpreter (Java Virtual Machine), regardless of the NC's CPU type (x86, Macintosh, SPARC, etc.).

There are numerous varieties of NCs being developed, but they mostly run a compact operating system that can be booted from the server. The operating system hosts a Web browser, which launches the Java Virtual Machine when a Java application is downloaded. The browser also downloads HTML pages from the intranet or Internet as does any browser in a PC or Mac. NCs may include slots for smart cards for user login verification.

In order to support existing Windows applications, NCs may use software from Citrix or other licensees of Citrix, which turns a Windows NT server into a timeshared central computer. In this mode, the NCs function similar to dumb terminals connected to a centralized system.

Oracle subsidiary, Network Computer, Inc. (NCI), has established a specification for ensuring compliance with a minimum set of capabilities. Vendors that license its Network Computer Reference Profile (NCRP) and build compliant machines are able to brand them with the NC logo. The NCRP has been turned over to The Open Group.

Network computers are designed for business use and have standard computer monitors, whereas Web set-top boxes connect to a TV set. Such devices are aimed at the home user and may or may not conform to the NC standard. See *NetPC*.

Are NCs a Panacea?

NCs may lower the cost of ownership compared to a PC, but control is placed squarely in the hands of the IS department, and all new software must be implemented by the IS staff. Users can no longer experiment with new software on their own.

Java is an interpreted language, and interpreted programs take longer to run than compiled programs, which have been translated into machine language ahead of time. In addition, initial results show that vendors are tweaking their Java programs to run faster on specific CPU families. This age-old tendency to make software run faster by specializing it for a specific machine obviates the "write-once-run-anywhere" advantage of Java.

network control program

Software that manages the traffic between terminals and the host mini or mainframe. It resides in the communications controller or front end processor. In a personal computer LAN, it is called a *network operating system* and resides in the server and manages requests from the workstations. IBM's SNA network control program is called *NCP*.

network database

(1) A database that runs in a network. It implies that the DBMS was designed with a client/server architecture.

(2) A database that holds addresses of other users in the network.

(3) A database organization method that allows for data relationships in a net-like form. A single data element can point to multiple data elements and can itself be pointed to by other data elements. Contrast with *relational database* and *hierarchical database*.

network drive

A disk or tape drive connected to a server in the network that is shared by multiple users. Contrast with *local drive*.

network driver

Software that activates the actual transmission and receipt of data over the network. It provides the data link protocol (Ethernet, Token Ring, etc.) that controls the specific brand of network adapter installed in the computer.

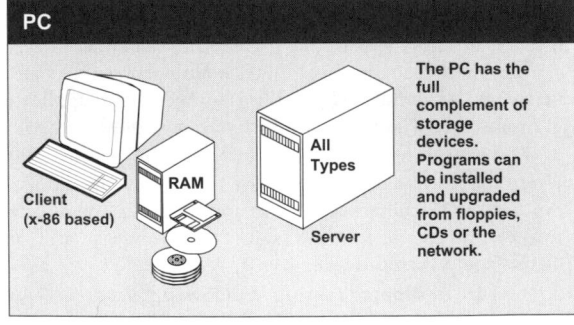

NETWORK COMPUTER (NC)

An NC runs Java programs locally just as a PC runs DOS and Windows programs, but NCs get their programs and their data only from the network server.

Client / RAM / All Types / Server

WINDOWS TERMINAL

Like a mini or mainframe terminal, a Windows terminal provides only input and output. All data processing is done in the server.

Client / RAM / Windows NT / Server

NETPC

Client (x-86 based) / RAM / Windows NT / Server

NetPCs can be configured as fully-loaded PCs (fat clients) or as network computers (thin clients).

As fat clients, the installation of Windows and applications and all subsequent software upgrades are obtained from the server.

As thin clients, they function like a network computer (NC) and obtain OS, apps and data from the server. The difference is that parts of the application may be cached on the local hard disk during the day to improve performance.

PC

The PC has the full complement of storage devices. Programs can be installed and upgraded from floppies, CDs or the network.

Client (x-86 based) / RAM / All Types / Server

network driver interface

A software interface between the transport protocol and the data link protocol (network driver). The interface provides a protocol manager that accepts requests from the transport layer and activates the network adapter. Network adapters with compliant network drivers can be freely interchanged.

This method allows multiple protocol stacks to run over one network adapter. For example, a PC can connect to a NetWare network running SPX/IPX and a UNIX network running TCP/IP. It also allows one transport protocol to run over different network adapters; for example, SPX/IPX over Ethernet and Token Ring.

In PC LANs, the two primary network driver interfaces are Novell's ODI and Microsoft's NDIS. Novell provides an ODI interface utility that allows NDIS and ODI protocols to work in the same computer.

network engineer

A person who designs, implements and supports local area and wide area networks within an organization. Network engineers are high-level technical analysts specializing in networks. See *network administrator* and *salary survey*.

Network in a Box

A turnkey network computer (NC) solution from NCI that includes an x86-based server with the NCOS operating system, Oracle Web server, Oracle Interoffice messaging and various bundled applications. Two or more x86-based client machines are also included. Network in a Box is sold through VARs.

network interface card

Same as *network adapter*.

network layer

The services in the OSI protocol stack (layer 3 of 7) that provide internetworking for the communications session. See *OSI*.

network management

Monitoring an active communications network in order to diagnose problems and gather statistics for administration and fine tuning. Examples of network management products are IBM's NetView, HP's OpenView, Sun's SunNet Manager and Novell's NMS. Almost all network management software supports the SNMP network management protocol. Other management protocols are CMIP and DME. See *systems management* and *configuration management*.

network management console

The client component of network management software that provides the user interface and "control room" view of the network.

network manager

See *network administrator*.

network meltdown

A condition in which the network barely ceases to function due to excessive traffic. It can be caused by a legitimate overload of valid traffic or by malicious or erroneous conditions. See *broadcast storm*.

network modem

A modem shared by all users in a network. See *remote access server*.

network operating system

Also called a *NOS*, it is an operating system that manages network resources. It manages multiple requests (inputs) concurrently and provides the security necessary in a multiuser environment. It may be a completely self-contained operating system, such as NetWare, UNIX and Windows NT, or it may require an existing operating system in order to function (LAN Server requires OS/2; LANtastic requires DOS, etc.).

One piece of the network operating system resides in each client machine and another resides in each server. It allows the remote drives on the server to be accessed as if they were local drives on the client machine. It allows the server to handle requests from the client to share files and applications as well as network devices such as printers, faxes and modems.

In a peer-to-peer network, the network operating system allows each station to be both client and server. In a non-peer-to-peer network, dedicated servers are used, and files on a client machine cannot be retrieved by other users.

In networks of PCs, NetWare is the most widely used network operating system. Windows NT, Windows for Workgroups, Windows 95/98, VINES, LAN Server, LAN Manager and LANtastic are also examples.

UNIX, combined with TCP/IP and NFS, VMS combined with DECnet, the Mac OS combined with AppleTalk, and SNA, combined with VTAM and NCP, also provide network operating system services.

Along with file and print services, a network operating system may also include directory services and a messaging system as well as network management and multiprotocol routing capabilities.

network PC

See *NetPC* and *network computer*.

network printer

A computer printer connected to the network. Network printers are typically in the range of 25 ppm and under. See *distributed printer* and *production printer*.

network protocol

A communications protocol used by the network. There are many layers of network protocols. See *OSI*.

network ready

Software designed to run in a network. It implies that multiple users can share databases without conflict.

network security

The authorization of access to files and directories in a network. Users are assigned an ID number and password that allows them access to information and programs within their authority. Network security is controlled by the network administrator.

network segment

See *LAN segment*.

network server

See *file server*.

network switch

See *LAN switch*.

neural network

A modeling technique based on the observed behavior of biological neurons and used to mimic the performance of a system. It consists of a set of elements that start out connected in a random pattern, and, based

CLIENT SOFTWARE

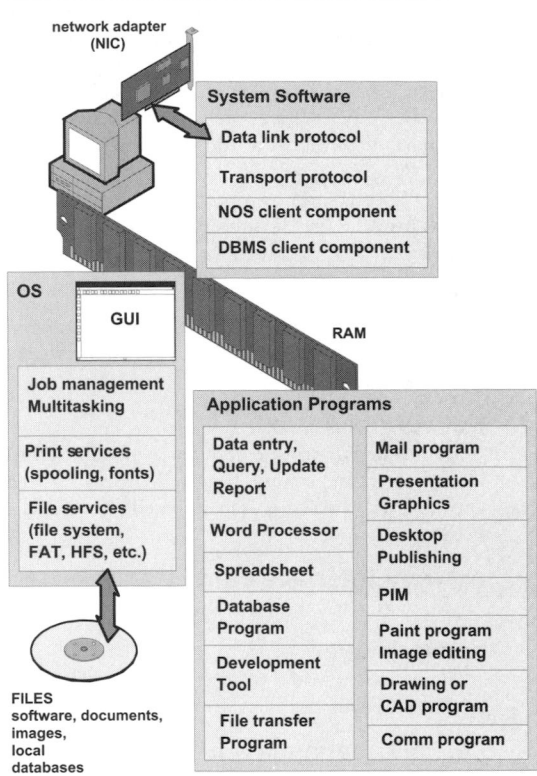

SERVER SOFTWARE

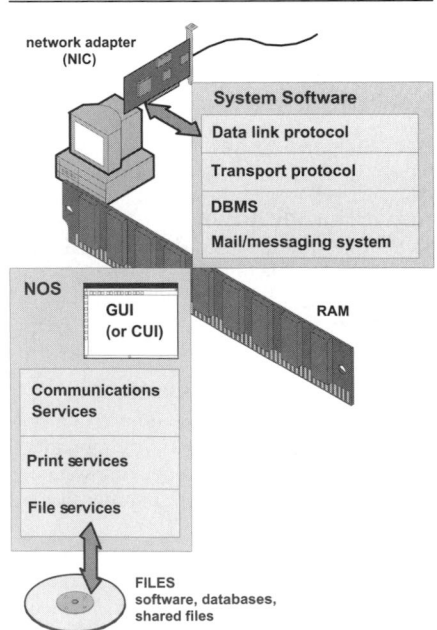

upon operational feedback, are molded into the pattern required to generate the required results. It is used in applications such as robotics, diagnosing, forecasting, image processing and pattern recognition.

newbie

The first-time user of computers or of a particular environment, such as Windows or UNIX. The term is often used for newcomers to the Internet.

new disk drives

See *latest disk drives*.

New Era

See *INFORMIX*.

newline

End of line code. See *CR/LF*.

new media

The forms of communicating in the digital world, which includes electronic publishing on floppy disk, CD-ROM, DVD and perhaps, most significantly, the Internet. It implies the use of desktop and portable computers as well as wireless, handheld devices. Most every company in the computer industry is involved with new media in some manner. See *digital convergence*.

NeWS

(Network Extensible Windowing Support) A networked windowing system (similar to X Windows) from SunSoft that renders PostScript fonts on screen the way they print on a PostScript printer.

news and weather

See *Usenet* and *online services*.

newsfeed

The actual news being routed from its sources to news servers or end users.

newsgroup

A message board on the Internet. Also known as Internet discussion groups, they are like player-piano rolls of messages devoted to a particular topic. It all starts by someone posting an initial query or comment, and other members reply. Still others reply to the replies, and so the "discussion" forms a chain of related postings called a *message thread*.

Newsgroups were popular long before the World Wide Web exploded onto the scene. By the end of 1997, there were more than 50,000. Some are moderated; some are not, and no single server or online service hosts them. They originate from many sources and are hosted on many systems, known collectively as the Usenet network, the original name given to this service. It is the system administrator at any given ISP or online service such as AOL or CompuServe that decides which newsgroups will be offered and how long postings will be available, typically about two weeks.

Newsgroups are organized into topical hierarchies, which include alt (alternative), biz (business), comp (computing), misc (miscellaneous), rec (recreational), and others. As you move to the right in a newsgroup name, the subject focus becomes more limited. For example, the group **alt.music** might discuss every aspect of music, while **alt.music.baroque** and **alt.music.jazz** are more specific.

Newsgroup postings amount to what noted computer author Alfred Glossbrenner has called the "collective consciousness." Newsgroup postings represent the wisdom, experiences, and opinions of millions of people around the world on just about any topic imaginable. Unlike a Web site, which is owned by someone or some organization, nobody controls or filters what appears in a newsgroup. Although everything should be taken with a grain of salt, newsgroups can nevertheless be extremely valuable.

In the early days, Internet users would hear about a group of interest and then "subscribe" to it with a UNIX-based newsreader program. This made it possible to automatically retrieve all the postings you had not yet seen whenever you accessed a group. You could read postings and prepare queries and replies to given messages offline and then upload them to your favorite groups in a batch.

That can still be done today with the newsreaders built into Netscape Navigator and Internet Explorer. But the feeling of community within most groups no longer exists, and many are clogged with spam. However, if newsgroups are treated as a vast database of potentially useful information on a subject, they can be quite worthwhile. Try Deja News (www.dejanews.com), a search engine devoted to newsgroups that not only archives years worth of postings, it also aggressively filters out spam.

newsreader

An Internet utility, such as nn, rn or tin, that is used to read the messages in a newsgroup.

news server

A Usenet server on the Internet that hosts newsgroups.

Newton

A set of mobile computing technologies from Apple used in its MessagePad personal digital assistant (PDA), which was introduced in 1993. In 1997, Apple spun off the Newton into a wholly owned subsidiary (Newton, Inc.), but folded it back in early 1998, when it announced that the Newton OS would no longer be enhanced. Newton functionality is expected in future versions of the Mac OS.

NeXT

A computer company that became a software company and then merged into Apple. NeXT Computer was founded in Redwood City, California in 1985 by Steven Jobs, co-founder of Apple. In 1988, it introduced a high-resolution workstation housed in a black cube that ran under the NextStep operating system.

The computer was discontinued in 1993, at which time NeXT became NeXT Software and focused on OpenStep, the object-oriented development components within NextStep, which were made available on x86, Sun and HP machines. In 1996, NeXT Software was acquired by Apple and Steve Jobs was returned to the company he helped create.

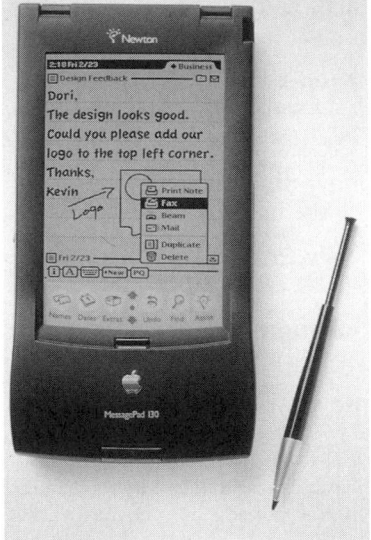

Apple's MessagePad
More commonly known as the "Newton," which is the technology behind the MessagePad, this hand-held unit helped popularize the PDA. The first models didn't take the world by storm, but subseqent generations became much more powerful and usable. *(Photo courtesy of Apple Computer, Inc.)*

NextStep

A UNIX-based operating system and development environment originally designed for the NeXT computer. It was also ported to x86, Sun and HP workstations. NextStep evolved into OpenStep. See *NeXT* and *Rhapsody*.

NFR

(Near Field Recording) See *near field optics* and *Terastor*.

NFS

(Network File System) The UNIX networking protocol that allows files and printers to be shared across the network. This de facto UNIX standard, which is widely known as a *distributed file system*, was developed by Sun. NFS services are also available on Windows NT servers, which enables UNIX workstations to gain access to its files and printers.

The counterpart of NFS in the DOS, Windows and OS/2 world is SMB (Server Message Block), and in NetWare, NCP (NetWare Core Protocol). NFS, SMB and NCP are all high-level protocols (layers 5 to 7) that provide open and close file and read and write functions as well as access control. They ride on top of the transport protocols (TCP/IP, NetBEUI, IPX/SPX), which manage the transfer. See *WebNFS*, *SMB* and *NCP*.

NGI

(Next Generation Internet) A project of the U.S. government for researching high-speed network technologies for use by federal agencies. See *Internet2*.

NGM

See *NetWare Global Messaging*.

Computer Desktop Encyclopedia

NHRP

(Next Hop Resolution Protocol) A protocol for layer 3 switching that routes a request through traditional routers to obtain the destination address and sends the data packets via layer 2 switches. An NHRP request is dropped if it is not recognized by an intermediate router.

NI

See *non-interlaced*.

nibble

Half a byte (four bits).

nibble mode memory

A type of dynamic RAM that outputs four consecutive bits (nibble) at one time.

NIC

(Network Interface Card) Same as *network adapter*. See also *InterNIC*.

NICAD

A trademark of SAFT America Inc., Valdosta, GA, for nickel cadmium products. See *nickel cadmium*.

nickel cadmium

(NiCd) A rechargeable battery technology that has been widely used in portable applications, including portable computers. It provides more charge per pound than lead acid batteries, but less than nickel hydride or zinc air. Its major problem is a so-called "memory effect," in which the battery seems to remember how full it was when you last charged it, and it doesn't go past that point the next time. Nickel cadmium batteries should be completely drained periodically to maintain the longest charge. It uses a nickel and cadmium plate and potassium hydroxide as the electrolyte. See *lead acid, nickel hydride* and *zinc air*.

nickel hydride

A rechargeable battery technology that provides more charge per pound than lead acid and nickel cadmium, but less than zinc air. It does not suffer from the nickel cadmium memory effect. It uses nickel and metal hydride plates with potassium hydroxide as the electrolyte. See *lead acid, nickel cadmium* and *zinc air*.

nickname

(1) An alternate name used to identify yourself in a chat room.

(2) A shortcut for identifying a recipient in an e-mail address book.

Nifty Serve

A Japanese online service. Nifty Serve and PC-VAN are the major online services in Japan.

NII

(National Information Infrastructure) The proposal by the Clinton/Gore administration to provide universal high-bandwidth telecommunications throughout the U.S. Highlights are:

```
1 - network funded by private industry
2 - supports two-way communications of data, images, voice and video
3 - services available to rich and poor alike
4 - legislation overhauls Telecommunications Act of 1934 and the Modified
    Final Judgment that broke up AT&T
5 - any service provider will be able to buy access to the network
```

NIS

(Network Information Services) A naming service from SunSoft that allows resources to be easily added, deleted or relocated. Formerly called Yellow Pages, NIS is a de facto UNIX standard. NIS+ is a redesigned NIS for Solaris 2.0 products. The combination of TCP/IP, NFS and NIS comprise the primary networking components of UNIX.

NIST

(National Institute of Standards & Technology, Washington, DC, www.nist.gov) The standards-defining agency of the U.S. government, formerly called the National Bureau of Standards.

nixie

See *NCSI*.

NJE

(Network Job Entry) An IBM mainframe protocol that allows two JES devices to communicate with each other.

N-key rollover

An essential keyboard circuit built into most keyboards, which is vital for fast typing. To test this capability, press four adjacent keys in sequence without removing any finger from any of the keys. If all four letters appear on screen, it has this feature.

NLM

See *NetWare Loadable Module*.

NLQ

(Near Letter Quality) The print quality that is almost as sharp as an electric typewriter. The slowest speed of a dot matrix printer often provides NLQ.

NLSP

(NetWare Link Services Protocol) A routing protocol from Novell that is used in NetWare networks. NLSP is a link state protocol that was designed to reduce the wasted bandwidth associated with the RIP routing protocol. See *routing protocol, link state protocol* and *distance vector protocol*.

NLX motherboard

An Intel motherboard used for NetPCs and other low-profile (space-saving) systems. Introduced in 1997, NLX supports the AGP and uses a riser card for expansion boards.

nm

See *nanometer*.

NMI

(NonMaskable Interrupt) A high-priority interrupt that cannot be disabled by another interrupt. It is used to report malfunctions such as parity, bus and math coprocessor errors.

NMOS

(N-Channel **MOS**) Pronounced "N moss." A type of microelectronic circuit used for logic and memory chips. NMOS transistors are faster than their PMOS counterpart and more of them can be put on a single chip. It is also used in CMOS design.

NMS

See *NetWare Management System*.

nn

(NetNews) A newsreader for Usenet newsgroups that maintains a database of article headers for keeping track of subjects. Nn was developed in Denmark. See *Usenet*.

NNI

(Network-to-Network Interface) An interface between networks. See *UNI*.

NNTP

(Network News Transfer Protocol) The protocol used to connect to Usenet groups on the Internet. Usenet newsreaders support the NNTP protocol.

NNTP client

A Usenet newsreader that connects to a news server via the NNTP protocol. NNTP clients include command-line UNIX newsreaders such as rn and trn to GUI-based newsreaders built into Web browsers.

Computer Desktop Encyclopedia

NOC

(Network Operations Center) A central location for network management. If functions as a control center for network monitoring, analysis and accounting.

node

(1) In communications, a node is a network junction or connection point. For example, a personal computer in a LAN is a node. A terminal connected to a minicomputer or mainframe is a node.

(2) In database management, a node is an item of data that can be accessed by two or more routes.

(3) In computer graphics, a node is an endpoint of a graphical element.

(4) In multiprocessing systems, a node can be a single processor or system. In MPP, it is one processor. In SMP, it is one computer system with two or more processors and shared memory.

noise

An extraneous signal that invades an electrical transmission. It can come from strong electrical or magnetic signals in nearby lines, from poorly fitting electrical contacts, and from power line spikes.

NOMAD

A relational DBMS for IBM mainframes, PCs and VAXes from Thomson Software Products, Norwalk, CT, (www.thomsoft.com). Introduced in the mid 1970s, it was one of the first database systems to provide a non-procedural language for data manipulation. NOMAD can also access data on Oracle, Sybase, DB2 and other databases.

NOMDA

(National Office Machine Dealers Association) An association that merged with LANDA to become the Business Technology Association. See *BTA*.

non-blocking

The ability of a signal to reach its destination without interference or delay. In a non-blocking switch, all ports can run at full wire speed without any loss of packets or cells.

non-breaking space

See *hard space*.

non-document mode

A word processing mode used for creating source language programs, batch files and other text files that contain only text and no proprietary headers and format codes. All text editors output this format.

non-impact printer

A printer that prints without banging a ribbon onto paper. Laser, LED, ink jet, solid ink, thermal wax transfer and dye sublimation printers are examples of non-impact printers. See *printer*.

non-interlaced

Illuminating a CRT by displaying lines sequentially from top to bottom. Non-interlaced monitors eliminate annoying flicker found in interlaced monitors, which illuminate half the lines in the screen in the first cycle and the remaining half in the second cycle. Contrast with and see *interlaced* for a diagram.

nonlinear

A system in which the output is not a uniform relationship to the input.

nonlinear video editing

Storing video in the computer for editing. It is much easier to edit video in the computer than with earlier analog editing systems. Today's digital nonlinear editing systems provide high-quality post-production editing on a personal computer. However, lossy compression is used to store digital images, and some detail will be lost.

Depending on the purpose for the video presentation, output is either the final video turned back into analog or an edit decision list (EDL) that describes frame sources and time codes in order to quickly convert the original material into the final video in an editing room. For commercial production, the latter allows editing to be done offline rather than in a studio that costs several hundred dollars per hour.

Prior to digital, a system using several analog tape decks was considered a nonlinear video editing system. Contrast with *linear video editing*.

non-modal

Not mode oriented. A non-modal operation moves from one situation to another without apparent mode switching.

non-numeric programming

Programming that deals with objects, such as words, board game pieces and people, rather than numbers. Same as *list processing*.

non-parity memory

Memory chips that do not have a ninth bit used for parity checking. See *parity checking*.

non-preemptive multitasking

A multitasking environment in which an application is able to give up control of the CPU to another application only at certain points, such as when it is ready to accept input from the keyboard. Under this method, one program performing a large number of calculations for example, can dominate the machine and cause other applications to have limited access to the CPU.

Non-preemptive multitasking is also called *cooperative multitasking*, because programs must be designed to cooperate with each other in order to work together effectively in this environment.

A non-preemptive multitasking operating system cannot guarantee service to a communications program running in the background. If another application has usurped the CPU, the CPU cannot process the interrupts from the communications program quickly enough to capture the incoming data, and data can be lost. Contrast with *preemptive multitasking*.

non-procedural language

A computer language that does not require traditional programming logic to be stated. For example, a command, such as LIST, might display all the records in a file on screen, separating fields with a blank space. In a procedural language, such as COBOL, all the logic for inputting each record, testing for end of file and formatting the screen has to be explicitly programmed.

Query languages, report writers, interactive database programs, spreadsheets and application generators provide non-procedural languages for user operation. Contrast with and see *procedural language* for an example.

non-repudiation

Unable to deny the validity of a document.

non-routable protocol

A communications protocol that contains only a device address and not a network address. It does not incorporate an addressing scheme for sending data from one network to another. Examples of non-routable protocols are NetBIOS and DEC's LAT protocols. Contrast with *routable protocol*.

Non-system disk error or disk error

A DOS error message. The full message is

```
Non-system disk or disk error
Replace and press any key when ready
```

This usually means there's a non-bootable floppy in drive A. The computer looks for DOS on a floppy before it looks for DOS on the hard disk. If an ordinary floppy is in drive A at startup, it causes this error. Remove the disk and press any key.

non-text file

A file that contains more than simple text. See *binary file*.

non trivial

A favorite word used among programmers for any task that isn't simple.

non-volatile memory

Memory that holds its content without power. ROMs, PROMs, EPROMs and flash memory are examples. Disks and tapes may be called non-volatile memory, but they are usually considered storage devices. Sometimes the term refers to memory that is inherently volatile, but maintains its content because it is connected to a battery at all times. See *solid state disk*.

Computer Desktop Encyclopedia

no-op, NOP

(NO OPeration) An instruction that does nothing but hold the place for a future machine instruction or fill up the space of a very large instruction word (VLIW). See *VLIW*.

no parity

Not using a parity bit to check for errors. For example, an 8-N-1 communications setting means each character transmitted contains (8) eight bits, (N) "no" ninth parity bit and (1) one additional stop bit to mark the end. See *non-parity memory*.

NOR

(Not OR) A Boolean logical operation that is true if all inputs are false, and false if any input is true. An exclusive NOR (XNOR) is true if both inputs are the same.

NOR			EXCLUSIVE NOR		
IN	IN	OUT	IN	IN	OUT
0	0	1	0	0	1
0	1	0	0	1	0
1	0	0	1	0	0
1	1	0	1	1	1

normalization

In relational database management, a process which breaks down data into record groups for efficient processi There are six stages. By the third stage (third normal forr data is identified only by the key field in the record. For example, ordering information is identified by order number, customer information, by customer number.

normal wear

Deterioration due to natural forces that act upon a product under average, everyday use.

Northgate

(Northgate Computers, Inc., Eden Prarie, MN) A PC manufacturer founded in 1987 by Arthur Lazere that was known for its quality systems and keyboards. Its PCs were sold through direct marketing, and its highly-praised line of OmniKey keyboards were also sold through dealers.

Norton Desktop for Windows

A popular Windows 3.x shell from Symantec. It includes a comprehensive package of utilities and provides a large amount of customizability. Norton Desktop for Windows was preceded by Norton Desktop, which was a DOS shell.

Norton Navigator

A Windows 95 file management and desktop utility from Symantec. It is the successor to Norton Desktop for Windows 3.x and provides multiple desktops and enhanced file manipulation, but omits the backup and antivirus functions.

Norton SI

(Norton System Information) A early Norton utility that measured computer performance. It provided a computing index (CI) for CPU speed, a disk index (DI) for disk speed and a performance index (PI) that blended CI and DI. The IBM XT was used as a reference of 1.0.

Norton Utilities

Widely-used utility programs for DOS, Windows and Macintosh from Symantec. It includes programs to search, edit and undelete files, restore damaged files, defragment the disk and more. Originally from Peter Norton Computing, these programs were the first to popularize disk utilities for the PC.

NOS

See *network operating system*.

NOS/VE

(Network Operating System/Virtual Environment) A multitasking, virtual memory operating system from Control Data that runs on its medium to large-scale mainframes.

NOT

A Boolean logic operation that reverses the input. If a 0 is input, a 1 is output, and vice versa. See *AND-OR-NOT*.

notation

How a system of numbers, phrases, words or quantities is written or expressed. Positional notation is the location and value of digits in a numbering system, such as the decimal or binary system.

notebook computer

A laptop computer that weighs from approximately five to seven pounds. A notebook that weighs under five pounds is usually called a *subnotebook*. For features of a portable computer, see *laptop computer*.

Notes

See *Lotus Notes*.

Not ready error reading drive x

A DOS error message. The full message is

```
Not ready reading drive x
Abort, Retry, Fail?
```

This means the drive door is left open, or the floppy disk is not in the drive. Either put the appropriate floppy disk in the drive or close the drive door (turn lever) and press R.

To switch to another drive, press F, and type in the drive letter you want to go back to when you get the "Current drive is no longer valid>" message. In DOS versions prior to 4.0, type I for Ignore rather than F for Fail.

Not ready writing device PRN

A DOS error message. The full message is

```
Not ready writing device PRN
Abort, Retry, Fail?
```

This means the printer is turned off or unavailable. Press A to cancel, or turn the printer on and press R. You might also check the cable connection to the printer.

Nova

A minicomputer series from Data General. When introduced in 1969, it was the first 16-bit mini to use four CPU accumulators, quite advanced for its time. Novas and its RDOS operating system were used extensively in the OEM marketplace.

NovaNET

A satellite-based network for educational services created by the Education Research Lab of the University of Illinois. It includes over 10,000 hours of lesson material from third grade to post graduate work in over a hundred subject areas.

Novell

(Novell Inc., Provo, UT, www.novell.com) Novell was founded as Novell Data Systems in 1981 by Jack Davis and George Canova. It initially manufactured terminals for IBM mainframes. In 1983, Ray Noorda became CEO and president of a restructured Novell, Inc., which would concentrate on the development of its NetWare operating system. NetWare has grown into the most widely used network operating system in the world.

With the acquisition of AT&T's UNIX in 1993 and WordPerfect and Quattro Pro in 1994, Novell extended its system software products and branched into applications. It planned to integrate UnixWare and NetWare into a "super" network operating system, but instead sold UNIX to the Santa Cruz Operation (SCO) in 1995 and WordPerfect and Quattro Pro to Corel Corporation in 1996.

Novell DOS

The name Novell gave to DR-DOS after it acquired it from Digital Research in 1991. Novell added NetWare client support to the product and released it as Novell DOS 7 in 1994. It was later dropped from the product line and then sold to Caldera. See *DR-DOS* and *Caldera*.

Novell network

A LAN controlled by one of Novell's NetWare operating systems. See *NetWare*.

no wait state memory

Memory fast enough to meet the demands of the CPU. Idle wait states do not have to be introduced.

nroff

(Nontypesetting RunOFF) A UNIX utility that formats documents for terminals and dot matrix printers. Using a text editor, troff codes are embedded into the text and the nroff command converts the document into the required output. Complex troff codes are ignored. See *troff.*

NRZ

(Non-Return-to-Zero) A data transmission method in which the 0s and 1s are represented by different polarities, typically positive for 0 and negative for 1. See *NRZI.*

NRZI

(Non-Return-to-Zero Inverted) A magnetic recording and data transmission method in which the polarity of the bit is reversed when a 1 bit is encountered. All subsequent 0s following the 1 are recorded at the same polarity.

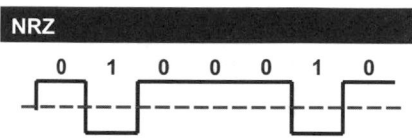

ns

(NanoSecond) See *space/time.*

NSAPI

(NetScape API) A programming interface on Netscape's Web Server. Using NSAPI function calls, Web pages can invoke programs on the server, typically to access data in a database. NSAPI is an alternative to using CGI scripts on Netscape Web servers.

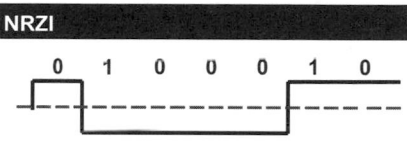

NSFnet

(National Science Foundation NETwork) The network funded by the U.S. National Science Foundation, which linked five supercomputer sites across the country in the mid 1980s. Universities were also allowed to connect to it. In 1988, it was upgraded from its original 56 Kbps lines to T1 circuits. By the early 1990s, NSFnet was using a T3 backbone and served as the primary Internet backbone until 1995, when the Net became commercialized. See *ARPAnet.*

NSI

(Network Solutions, Inc.) See *InterNIC.*

NSP

(1) (Network Service Provider) A high-level Internet provider that offers high-speed backbone services. ISPs hook into NSPs. See *Internet backbones.*

(2) (Native Signal Processing) Enhancements to Pentium CPUs proposed by Intel that later evolved into the MMX CPU. See *MMX.*

NSTL

(National Software Testing Lab, Philadelphia) An independent organization that evaluates computer hardware and software. It adheres to controlled testing methods to ensure objective results and publishes its findings in Software Digest Ratings Report and PC Digest.

NT

See *Windows NT.*

NT1

(Network Terminator 1) A device that terminates an ISDN line at the customer's premises. See *ISDN.*

NT Cluster Server

See *Microsoft Cluster Server.*

NT File System

See *NTFS.*

NTFS

(NT File System) A file system used in Windows NT which uses the Unicode character set and allows file names up to 255 characters in length. The NTFS is designed to recover on the fly from hard disk crashes. Windows NT supports multiple file systems. It can run with a DOS/Windows FAT, an OS/2 HPFS and a native NTFS, each in a different partition on the hard disk. NT's security features require that the NTFS be used.

NTFSDOS

A redirector that enables DOS/Windows clients to access drives on UNIX servers (NTFS drives). NTFS drives can be accessed via the DOS command line, File Manager or Explorer. For more information, visit http://www.ntinternals.com.

n-tier

Some number of tiers. See *two tier client/server* and *three tier client/server*.

NT multiuser

See *multiuser NT*.

NTSC

(National TV Standards Committee) A color TV standard that was developed in the U.S. Administered by the FCC, NTSC broadcasts 30 interlaced frames per second (60 half frames per second, or 60 "fields" per second in TV jargon) at 525 lines of resolution. The signal is a composite of red, green and blue and includes an audio FM frequency and an MTS signal for stereo. NTSC is used throughout the world including the U.S., Canada, Japan, South Korea and several Central and South American countries. See *PAL* and *SECAM*.

NTSC port

An analog video connection. An NTSC port on a computer is typically an input connector for an analog video source such as a standard VCR or camcorder.

NTTP

See *NNTP*.

NuBus

A bus architecture (32-bits) originally developed at MIT and defined as a Eurocard (9U). Apple has changed its electrical and physical specs for its Macintosh series. Many Macs have one or more NuBus slots for peripheral expansion.

NUI

(1) (Network User Interface) A user interface for a computer attached to the network. The NUI is designed to work with remote applications and files as easily as local files.

(2) (Notebook User Interface) A term coined by Go Corporation for its PenPoint pen-based interface.

(3) (Network User Identifier) A code used to gain access into local European packed-switched networks.

(4) See *NetWare Users International*.

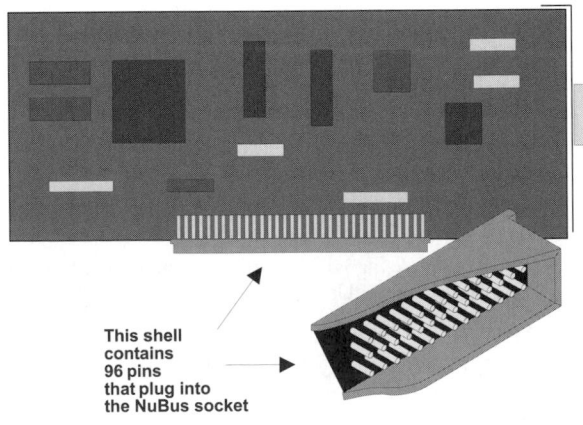

This shell contains 96 pins that plug into the NuBus socket

The NuBus Card
The plugs on NuBus cards use pins rather than the edge connectors found on ISA, EISA and PCI cards.

null

The first character in ASCII and EBCDIC, also known as the "NUL" character. In hex, it prints as 00; in decimal, it prints as a blank. It is naturally found in binary numbers when a byte contains no 1 bits. It is also used to pad fields and act as a delimiter; for example, in C, it specifies the end of a character string.

null modem cable

An RS-232 cable used to connect two personal computers together in close proximity for file transfer. It attaches to the serial ports of both machines and simulates what would occur naturally if modems and the phone system were used. It crosses the sending wire with the receiving wire. A counterpart special cable is also available that uses the parallel port for higher transfer speed. See *LapLink cable*.

null pointer

In programming, a reference to zero. It may be the starting value in the pointer, or may be used as the response to an unsuccessful search function.

null string

In programming, a character string that contains no data.

null value

A value in a field or variable that indicates nothing was ever derived and stored in it. For example, in a decimal-based amount field, a null value might be all binary 0s (null characters), but not a decimal 0. The decimal 0 would imply no dollars and cents, which could in fact be a valid derived value. See *null*.

NUMA

(Non-Uniform Memory Access) A multiprocessing architecture in which memory is separated into close and distant banks. NUMA is similar to SMP, in which multiple CPUs share a single memory. However, in SMP, all CPUs access a common memory at the same speed. In NUMA, memory on the same processor board as the CPU is accessed faster than memory on other processor boards.

number crunching

Refers to computers running mathematical, scientific or CAD applications, which perform large amounts of calculations.

Number Nine

(Number Nine Visual Technology Corporation, Lexington, MA, www.nine.com) A manufacturer of PC display adapters founded in 1982 as Number Nine Computer Corporation by Andrew Najda and Stan Bialek. Over the years, Number Nine display adapters have been highly praised for advancing the state of the art. Products often begin with a #9, such as #9GXe and #9FX.

numbers

In a computer, numbers can be stored in several forms. Although they are all coded as binary digits (bits), BCD and packed decimal numbers retain the decimal relationship of a number, whereas fixed and floating point do not.

Binary Coded Decimal (BCD)

BCD encodes each decimal digit in a single byte. The number 7100 would take four bytes. A variation, called *packed decimal*, encodes two digits in one byte.

Binary Fixed Point

This method converts the entire decimal number into a binary number, placing it in a fixed unit of storage. The number 7100 would require at least two bytes. Binary numbers are calculated faster than decimal (BCD) numbers.

Bytes	Bits	Values
1	8	0 to 255
2	16	0 to 65,535
4	32	0 to 4,294,967,295

Binary Floating Point

Floating point allows very small fractions and very large numbers to be maintained and calculated quickly. Both the mantissa (significant digits) and the exponent (power to which the base is raised) are converted into binary numbers. See *floating point*.

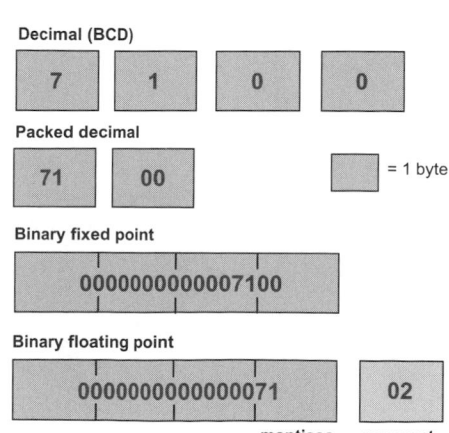

Decimal (BCD)

| 7 | 1 | 0 | 0 |

Packed decimal

| 71 | 00 |

☐ = 1 byte

Binary fixed point

0000000000007100

Binary floating point

0000000000000071   02

mantissa   exponent

number sign

In some programming languages, the number sign (#), also called the *pound sign*, is used as a not-equals symbol. For example, the expression **if amount # 500** means "if amount not equal to 500."

numerical aperture

The amount of light that can be coupled to an optical fiber. The greater the aperture, the easier it is to connect the light source to the fiber.

numerical control

A category of automated machine tools, such as drills and lathes, that operate from instructions in a program. Numerical control (NC) machines are used in manufacturing tasks, such as milling, turning, punching and drilling.

First-generation machines were hardwired to perform specific tasks or programmed in a very low-level machine language. Today, they are controlled by their own microcomputers and programmed in high-level languages, such as APT and COMPACT II, which automatically generate the tool path (physical motions required to perform the operation).

The term was coined in the 1950s when the instructions to the tool were numeric codes. Just like the computer industry, symbolic languages were soon developed, but the original term remained.

numeric data

Refers to quantities and money amounts used in calculations. Contrast with *string* or *character data*.

numeric field

A data field that holds only numbers to be calculated. Contrast with *character field*.

Num Lock

(NUMeric Lock) A keyboard key used to toggle a combination number/cursor keypad between number keys and cursor keys.

NURB

(NonUniform Rational B-spline) A type of b-spline that is very flexible. NURB curves can represent any shape from a straight line to a circle or ellipse with very little data. They can also be used for guiding animation paths, for approximating data and for controlling the shapes of 3-D surfaces. NURBs are known for their ability to control the smoothness of a curve. See *spline* and *b-spline*.

NutCRACKER

A software porting tool for converting UNIX applications to Windows 95 and Windows NT from DataFocus, Inc., Fairfax, VA, (www.datafocus.com). It includes MKS Toolkit, which is a comprehensive set of UNIX utilities from Mortice Kern that can be used in the Windows environment.

NVRAM

(Non-Volatile **RAM**) See *non-volatile memory*.

Nx586, Nx686

Families of Pentium-class and Pentium-Pro class CPUs from NexGen, Inc. After AMD acquired NexGen, the Nx586 line was dropped, and the Nx686 became the K6.

NxN switch

See *crosspoint switch*.

nybble

See *nibble*.

NZ

(Non Zero) A value greater or less than 0.

OA

See *office automation*.

OADG

(**O**pen **A**rchitecture **D**evelopment **G**roup) An organization founded by IBM Japan in 1991 to promote PC standards in Japan. See *DOS/V*.

OAI

(**O**pen **A**pplication **I**nterface) A computer to telephone interface that lets a computer control and customize PBX and ACD operations.

OAW

(**O**ptically **A**ssisted **W**inchester) See *Quinta*.

object

(1) A self-contained module of data and its associated processing. Objects are the software building blocks of object technology. See *object technology* and *object-oriented programming*.

(2) In a compound document, an independent block of data, text or graphics that was created by a separate application.

object bus

The communications interface through which objects are located and accessed. An object bus is a high-level protocol which rides on top of a lower-level transport protocol. See *CORBA* and *DCOM*.

object code

Same as *machine language*. This is an early term that has no relationship to object technology.

object computer

Same as *target computer*. This is an early term that has no relationship to object technology.

object database

See *object-oriented database*.

Object Database Management Group

(Object Database Management Group, Burnsville, MN, www.odmg.org) An organization founded in 1991 to promote standards for object databases. The ODMG standard adds programming extensions to C++ and Smalltalk for accessing an object-oriented database. It also includes a superset of SQL 92 Entry Level, the most widely supported version of SQL.

The Object Database Management Group (ODMG) defines an interface to the database, whereas the Object Management Group (OMG) defines an interface for using objects in a distributed environment. The ODMG object model complies with the core model of the Object Management Architecture (OMA) of the OMG. See *OMA* and *CORBA*.

Objective-C

The first commercial object-oriented version of the C programming language. It runs on PCs, Macs and various UNIX workstations. Originally developed by the Stepstone Corporation, it was acquired by NeXT Computer.

object language

(1) A language defined by a metalanguage.

(2) An object-oriented programming language.

(3) Same as *machine language* or *target language*.

Object Linking and Embedding

See *OLE*.

Object Management Architecture

A definition of a standard object model from the Object Management Group. It defines the behavior of objects in a distributed environment. The communications component of the Object Management Architecture, or OMA, is the Common Object Request Broker, or CORBA. CORBA is often referenced more than OMA, but it is part of OMA and thus implies OMA. See *CORBA*.

Object Management Group

(Object Management Group, Framingham, MA, www.omg.org) An international organization founded in 1989 to endorse technologies as open standards for object-oriented applications. The OMG specifies the Object Management Architecture (OMA), a definition of a standard object model for distributed environments, more commonly known as CORBA. See *CORBA*. Also see *Object Database Management Group*.

object model

(1) A description of an object architecture, including the details of the object structure, interfaces between objects and other object-oriented features and functions.

(2) An object-oriented description of an application.

object module

The output of an assembler or compiler, which must be linked with other modules before it can be executed. This is an early term that has no relationship to object technology.

object oriented

See *object technology* and *object-oriented programming*.

object-oriented analysis

The examination of a problem by modeling it as a group of interacting objects. An object is defined by its class, data elements and behavior. For example; in an order processing system, an invoice is a class, and printing, viewing and totalling are examples of its behavior. Objects (individual invoices) inherit this behavior and combine it with their own data elements.

object-oriented database

A database that holds abstract data types (objects) and is managed by an object-oriented database management system (DBMS). See *object-oriented DBMS*.

object-oriented DBMS

A database management system (DBMS) that manages objects, which are abstract data types. An object-oriented DBMS (ODBMS) is suited for data with complex relationships that are difficult to model and process in a relational DBMS. It is also capable of handling multimedia data types (images, audio and video).

A relational DBMS is designed to handle numbers, alphanumeric text and dates. It may also support a LOB field, which holds any binary data (image, video, etc.), but the database program does not manipulate the LOB directly. Another application has to be written or some middleware has to be used to process the LOB. In an object database, a picture or video clip object can include the routine to display it which is dynamically invoked by the DBMS.

Some ODBMSs are entirely object oriented and are accessed from an application program written in an object-oriented programming language. Others allow access via an SQL-like language or derivative.

Examples of pure object-oriented DBMSs are Servio Corporation's Gemstone, Object Design's Object Store and Ontos' ONTOS DB. Increasingly, object databases (ODBMSs) are being merged with

Objects

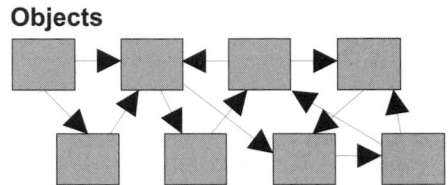

Object Databases Handle Complex Structures

An object-oriented database can handle data structures that cannot easily be modeled with hierarchical, network or relational databases.

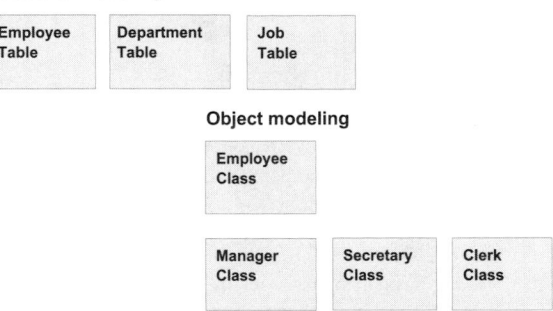

A New Paradigm for System Design

When information systems are modeled as objects, they can employ the powerful inheritance capability. Instead of building a table of employees with department and job information in separate tables, the type of employee is modeled. The employee class contains the data and the processing for all employees. Each subclass (manager, secretary, etc.) contains the data and processing unique to that person's job. Changes can be made globally or individually by modifying the class in question.

relational databases (RDBMSs), providing a single environment for traditional business transactions, multimedia data and complex structures. UniSQL was one of the first vendors to provide both capabilities in one product, and all major RDBMS vendors eventually followed suit. See *universal server* and *ODMG*.

object-oriented design

Transforming an object-oriented model into the specifications required to create the system. Moving from object-oriented analysis to object-oriented design is accomplished by expanding the model into more and more detail.

object-oriented graphics

Same as *vector graphics*.

object-oriented interface

A graphical interface that uses icons and a mouse, such as Mac, Windows and Motif.

object-oriented operating system

An operating system that is based on objects.

object-oriented programming

Abbreviated "OOP," programming that supports object technology. It is an evolutionary form of modular programming with more formal rules that allow pieces of software to be reused and interchanged between programs. Major concepts are (1) encapsulation, (2) inheritance, and (3) polymorphism.

Encapsulation is the creation of self-sufficient modules that contain the data and the processing (data structure and functions that manipulate that data). These user-defined, or abstract, data types are called classes. One instance of a class is called an object. For example, in a payroll system, a class could be defined as Manager, and Pat and Jan, the actual objects, are instances of that class.

Classes are created in hierarchies, and **inheritance** allows the knowledge in one class to be passed down the hierarchy. That means less programming is required when adding functions to complex systems. If a step is added at the bottom of a hierarchy, then only the processing and data associated with that unique step needs to be added. Everything else about that step is inherited.

Object-oriented programming allows procedures about objects to be created whose exact type is not known until runtime. For example, a screen cursor may change its shape from an arrow to a line depending on the program mode. The routine to move the cursor on screen in response to mouse movement would be written for "cursor," and **polymorphism** would allow that cursor to be whatever shape is required at runtime. It would also allow a new shape to be easily integrated into the program.

The SIMULA simulation language was the original object-oriented language. It was used to model the behavior of complex systems. Xerox's Smalltalk was the first object-oriented programming language and was used to create the graphical user interface whose derivations are so popular today. C++ has become the major commercial OOP language, because it combines traditional C programming with object-oriented capabilities. ACTOR and Eiffel are also meaningful OOP languages.

The following list compares some fundamental object-oriented programming terms with traditional programming terms and concepts. See *object technology*.

```
Object-oriented      Traditional
programming          programming
class                data type + characteristics
instance             variable
instantiate          declare a variable
method               processing code
message              call
object               data type + processing
```

object-oriented technology

Same as *object technology*.

Object Packager

A Windows utility that embeds a document as an icon inside another document. It is part of Windows' OLE (object linking and embedding). It also allows objects created by non-OLE-compliant applications to be embedded. When the icon is double clicked, the application that created it is opened to view and edit it. See *OLE*.

ObjectPro

An object-oriented client/server development system from Platinum Technology, Inc., Oakbrook Terrace, IL, (www.platinum.com). It includes its own programming language and generates executable programs for Windows, HP/UX and Solaris. It supports the major databases and also provides an interpreted mode for development.

object program

A machine language program ready to run in a particular operating environment. It has been assembled, or compiled, and link edited. This is an early term that has no relationship to object technology.

object references

To learn about object technology, two excellent easy-to-read books on the subject are David Taylor's "Object-Oriented Technology: A Manager's Guide" (Addison-Wesley ISBN 0-201-56358-4) and "Business Engineering with Object Technology" (Wiley ISBN 0-471-04521-7). These are excellent starter books.

For more in-depth analysis, also read "Object-Oriented Analysis and Design" by Grady Booch (Benjamin Cummings ISBN 0-8053-5340-2) and "Object-Oriented Modeling and Design" by James Rumbaugh, et al (Prentice-Hall, ISBN 0-13-629841-0).

object-relational database

See *universal server*.

object-relational DBMS

See *universal server*.

Object Request Broker

See *ORB*.

objects

See *object technology* and *object-oriented programming*.

object signing

The ability to assign access privileges to Java applications that lets them work outside of their normally-constrained arena. See *Java sandbox*.

ObjectStudio

An object-oriented client/server development system that supports Windows, OS/2, UNIX and the major databases from Cincom Systems, Inc., Cincinnati, OH, (www.cincom.com). Its Synchronicity module is used to graphically diagram the data and business logic and generate Enfin Smalltalk code. A visual programming tool is used to create the user interfaces. ObjectStudio was originally developed by Easel Corporation, which was acquired by VMARK Software. ObjectStudio was then sold to Cincom.

object technology

The use of objects as the building blocks for applications. Objects are independent program modules written in object-oriented programming languages. Just as hardware components are routinely designed as modules to plug into and work with each other, objects are software components designed to work together at runtime without any prior linking or precompilation as a group.

The ultimate goal of objects is that it should not matter which source language they were programmed in or which computer on the network they are running in. They are designed to interoperate strictly through the messages passed between them.

Objects as building blocks are an

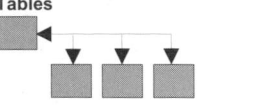

Tables

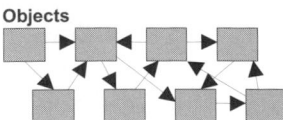

Objects

Structural Flexibility

Object-oriented information systems provide more flexibility than systems designed for relational databases. While relational databases easily provide one-to-many and many-to-one relationships, object databases allow for many to many. Information systems that require complex relationships can be more easily modeled with object technology, rather than being "shoehorned" into the row and column format of relational tables.

Multimedia Ready
Relational databases store everything in rows and columns. Although they may support large binary object (LOB) fields that can hold anything, an object database can support any type of data combined with the processing to display it.

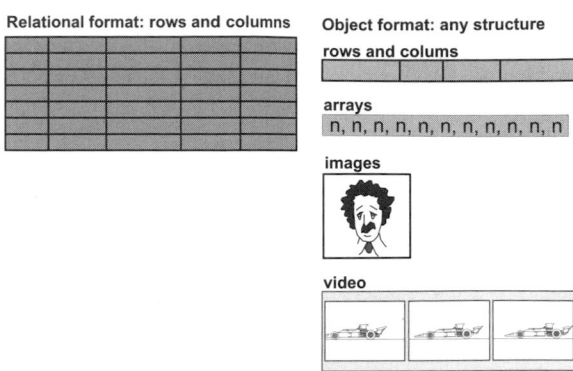

New Modeling Paradigms
When information systems are modeled as objects, they can employ the powerful inheritance capability. Instead of building a table of employees with department and job information in separate tables, the type of employee is modeled. The employee class contains the data and the processing for all employees. Each subclass (manager, secretary, etc.) contains the data and processing unique to that person's job. Changes can be made globally or individually by modifying the class in question.

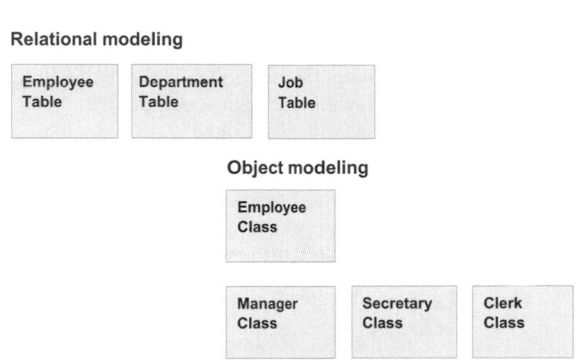

evolutionary architecture, being a more formalized approach to modular programming, which has been around for years. What is revolutionary about objects is that they provide a new way of modeling applications, and this is expected to have a significant impact on application development. With objects, a system can be designed as familiar business functions, and the design can be carried all the way down to the programming level. In traditional systems analysis, the programs are decomposed into procedures that are more alien to the business model. Thus, object technology assists business process reengineering (BPR) by providing an implementation method that more closely supports the business processes being designed.

However, in order to design object-oriented applications, programmers, and especially systems designers, must undergo a major paradigm shift. It has often been said that object technology is easier to comprehend by non-computer professionals that have not been steeped in procedural logic.

There are countless applications of objects in use today, but most objects are generally created in and used in their own programming environments. What has arisen out of object technology is today's component software, which could be considered "objects in practice." Component architectures such as COM/ActiveX and JavaBeans do not necessarily embody all the concepts of object technology, but they do provide interfaces that let independent program modules communicate with each other at runtime. As a result, the terms object and component are often used synonymously. See *object references, object-oriented programming* and *component software*.

object technology references
See *object references*.

ObjectView
See *KEY:Assemble*.

ObjectVision

An earlier development package from Borland for creating Windows and OS/2 2.0 applications. It used visual techniques for user interface design and programming logic. It also provided links to spreadsheets and databases.

ObjectWindows

See *OWL*.

Obsydian

See *Synon/2E*.

OC-1, OC-3, OC-12, OC-48, OC-192

SONET transmission rates of 51.84, 155.52, 622.08, 2488.32 and 9953.28 Mbps repsectively. See *SONET*.

occam

A parallel processing language designed to handle concurrent operations. The INMOS Transputer executes occam almost directly. In the following statements, two items of data are read and incremented at the same time. PAR specifies that following statements are to be executed concurrently, and SEQ indicates that the following statements are executed sequentially.

```
PAR
  SEQ
    chan1 ? item1
    item1 := item1 + 1
  SEQ
    chan2 ? item2
    item2 := item2 + 1
```

OCF

(OpenCard Framework) A smart card specification from the OpenCard Consortium. Introduced in early 1998, it is designed to standardize smart cards for use in ATM machines, set-top boxes and merchant readers.

OCR

(Optical Character Recognition) The machine recognition of printed characters. OCR systems can recognize many different OCR fonts, as well as typewriter and computer-printed characters. Advanced OCR systems can recognize hand printing.

When a text document is scanned into the computer, it is turned into a bitmap, which is a picture of the text. OCR software analyzes the light and dark areas of the bitmap in order to indentify each alphabetic letter and numeric digit. When it recognizes a character, it converts it into ASCII text. Hand printing is much more difficult to analyze than machine-printed characters. Old, worn and smudged documents are also difficult. Scanning documents and processing them with OCR is sometimes as much an art as it is a science.

octal

A numbering system that uses eight digits. It is used as a shorthand method for representing binary

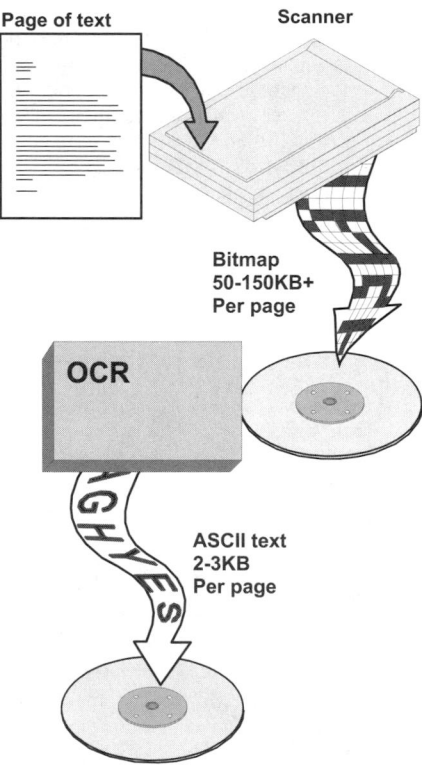

Page of text   **Scanner**

Bitmap
50-150KB+
Per page

OCR

ASCII text
2-3KB
Per page

OCR Processing
When text documents are scanned, they are "photographed" and stored as pictures in the computer. OCR software converts the pictures into actual text characters, which take up considerably less room on disk.

characters that use six-bits. Each three bits (half a character) is converted into a single octal digit. Okta is Greek for 8.

Decimal	Binary	Octal
0	000	0
1	001	1
2	010	2
3	011	3
4	100	4
5	101	5
6	110	6
7	111	7

octet

An eight-bit storage unit. In the international community, octet is often used instead of byte.

octopus cable

A cable that is spliced into several branches. There is one connector on one end and multiple connectors on the other.

OCX

(OLE Control EXtension) A component software technology from Microsoft that enables a Windows program to add funtionality by calling ready-made components. Generally called *OLE controls* or *OLE custom controls*, they appear to the end user as just another part of the program.

OCXs are Microsoft's second-generation component architecture. Unlike first-generation 16-bit Visual Basic controls (VBXs), which were only written in Visual Basic, OCXs can be written in several languages and come in 16-bit and 32-bit versions. The interface requirements for OCXs were reduced to speed up interaction via the Web, and they turned into ActiveX controls. See *VBX* and *ActiveX control*.

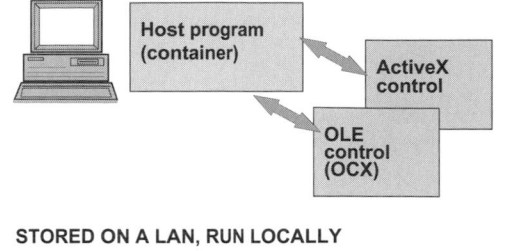

STAND-ALONE MACHINE (CLIENT or SERVER)

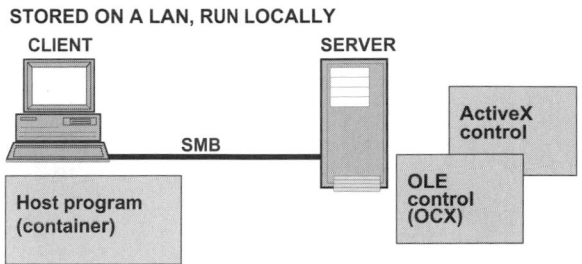

STORED ON A LAN, RUN LOCALLY

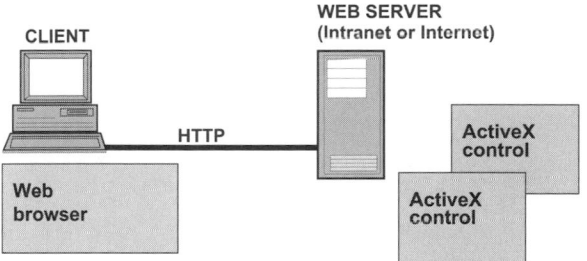

STORED ON A WEB SITE, RUN LOCALLY

OCXs and ActiveX Controls

OCXs evolved into ActiveX controls when their interface requirements were reduced to speed up interaction via the Web.

ODAPI

(Open Data API) A database programming interface from Borland that was rewritten and turned into the IDAPI interface. See *Borland Database Engine*.

ODBC

(Open DataBase Connectivity) A database programming interface from Microsoft that provides a common language for Windows applications to access databases on a network. ODBC is made up of the function calls programmers write into their applications and the ODBC drivers themselves.

For client/server database systems such as Oracle and SQL Server, the ODBC driver provides links to their database engines to access the database. For desktop database systems such as dBASE and FoxPro, the ODBC drivers actually manipulate the data. ODBC supports SQL and non-SQL databases. Although the application always uses SQL to communicate with ODBC, ODBC will communicate with non-SQL databases in its native language.

ODBCDirect

See *DAO*.

ODBMS

See *object-oriented DBMS*.

odd parity

See *parity checking*.

ODI

(Open Data-Link Interface) A network driver interface from Novell. ODI is based on the LSL interface developed by AT&T for its UNIX System V operating system. See *network driver interface* and *LSL*.

ODMA

(1) (Open Document Management API) A programming interface used to allow client programs to communicate with document management systems on a server.

(2) (Optical Disc Manufacturing Association, Milford, PA, www.odma.com) A membership organization that addresses various issues in the manufacturing, testing, labeling and packaging of CD and DVD media.

ODMG

See *Object Database Management Group*.

ODSI

(Open Directory Services Interface) A programming interface from Microsoft for gaining access to network naming services and directory services. A driver that translates ODSI calls to NetWare's NDS is expected from Microsoft.

ODT

See *SCO Open Desktop*.

Oe

See *Oersted*.

OEM

(Original Equipment Manufacturer) A manufacturer that sells equipment to a reseller. Also refers to the reseller itself. OEM customers either add value to the product before reselling it, private label it, or bundle it with their own products. See *VAR*.

OEM font

A font that uses the extended ASCII characters as defined by IBM for the original PC. The OEM, or DOS/OEM character set contains line draw and other symbols commonly used by DOS programs to create charts and simple graphics. Also known as the PC-8 symbol set as well as Code Page 437, the OEM character set is built into every display adapter. It is also the character set used by Windows in order to display DOS applications properly. See *ASCII chart* for the actual characters.

OEMI

(OEM Information) An IBM publication that describes the parallel channel interface. See *parallel channel*.

OEM Service Release 2

See *OSR2*.

Oersted

Pronounced "ers-ted." The measurement of magnetic energy. The higher the Oe rating in a material, the more current is required to changes its magnetic polarity. Named after the Danish scientist, Hans Cristian Oersted (1777-1851), it is used, for example, to measure the coercivity point on magnetic media. See *coercivity*.

offboard

Refers to a chip or other hardware component that is not directly attached to the printed circuit board (motherboard). Contrast with *offboard*.

off-hook

The state of a telephone line that allows dialing and transmission but prohibits incoming calls from being answered. The term stems from the days when a telephone handset was lifted off of a hook. Contrast with *on-hook*.

Office

See *Microsoft Office*.

office application

Any of the typical applications that come bundled in a suite of applications, such as word processing, spreadsheet and database management. See *application suite*.

office automation

The integration of office information functions, including word processing, data processing, graphics, desktop publishing and e-mail.

The backbone of office automation is a LAN, which allows users to transmit data, mail and even voice across the network. All office functions, including dictation, typing, filing, copying, fax, Telex, microfilm and records management, telephone and telephone switchboard operations, are candidates for integration.

Office document

(1) Any file created in a Microsoft Office application, such as a Word text document or an Excel spreadsheet.

(2) (office document) A document created in a business environment. See *application suite*.

OfficeJet

A combination ink jet printer, copier and fax machine from HP. The first OfficeJet was introduced in 1994.

office suite

See *application suite*.

Office Vision

Integrated office automation applications from IBM that run in all IBM computer families. Introduced in 1989, it includes e-mail, scheduling, document creation and distribution as well as decision support and graphics capabilities. It was the first major implementation of SAA and incorporates the Presentation Manager interface across OS/2 networks, AS/400s and mainframes.

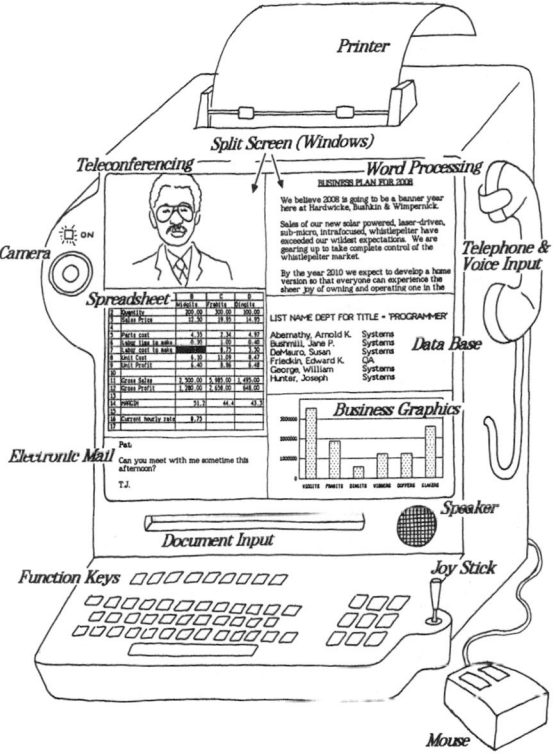

Office Automation

This drawing was made by the author in 1981 to depict an integrated terminal in the office of the future. Most of the features have been incorporated into today's desktop computers, except for the telephone, which still remains a separate device in most cases.

offline

Not connected to or not installed in the computer. If a terminal, printer or other device is physically connected to the computer, but is not turned on or in ready mode, it is still considered offline.

Disks and tapes that have been demounted and stored in the data library are considered offline. Contrast with *online*.

offline browser, offline navigator

See *offline reader*.

offline reader

Software that downloads e-mail and selected data from an online service or the Internet, allowing the user to browse the captured material after disconnecting. It automates retrieving routine data and saves online fees by shortening the connect time.

offline storage

Disks and tapes that are kept in a data library.

offload

To remove work from one computer and do it on another. See *cooperative processing*.

offset

(1) The distance from a starting point, either the start of a file or the start of a memory address. Its value is added to a base value to derive the actual value. An offset into a file is simply the character location within that file, usually starting with 0; thus "offset 240" is actually the 241st byte of the file. See *relative address*.

(2) In word processing, the amount of space a document is printed from the left margin.

off site

In another location. It is common practice to store copies of important data off site as part of a disaster recovery program. See *disaster recovery*.

off-the-shelf

Refers to products that are packaged and available for sale.

OH

See *off-hook* and *modem*.

ohm

A unit of measurement for electrical resistance. One ohm is the resistance in a circuit when one volt maintains a current of one amp.

ohnosecond

(**Oh No! second**) That tiny fraction of a second it takes for you to realize you've just made a big mistake on the computer. For example, you just clicked "No" when prompted to save the document you've been composing all day. Or, you just clicked "Send," and forgot to delete the profanity you wrote at the bottom of the e-mail message to your boss.

OIC

Digispeak for "oh, I see."

Oil Change

A software update service for Windows 95/98 from CyberMedia, Inc., Santa Monica, CA, (www.cybermedia.com). The Oil Change software analyzes the applications in your PC and, after connection to the CyberMedia Web site, alerts you to bug fixes, free enhancements and other "goodies" you might want to download from the Internet.

Okidata

(Okidata, Mount Laurel, NJ, www.okidata.com) A manufacturer of fax machines and dot matrix, laser-class and ink jet printers, founded in 1972. Okidata's printers are known for their durability. For years, its dot matrix line has been considered the workhorse of desktop impact printers. Starting in 1982, it introduced the first of its LED-based, laser-quality printers, which are widely used.

The company is a division of Oki America, Inc., which is a subsidiary of Tokyo-based Oki Electric Industry Company, Ltd. Oki Electric began making telephones in 1881 and developed the first thermal fax machine in 1976.

OLAP

(OnLine Analytical Processing) Decision support software that allows the user to quickly analyze information that has been summarized into multidimensional views and hierarchies. For example, OLAP tools are used to perform trend analysis on sales and financial information. They can enable users to drill down into masses of sales statistics in order to isolate the products that are the most volatile.

Traditional OLAP products, also known as multidimensional OLAP, or MOLAP, summarize transactions into multidimensional views ahead of time. User queries on these types of databases are extremely fast, because most of the consolidation has already been done.

A relational OLAP, or ROLAP, tool extracts data from a traditional relational database. Using complex SQL statements against relational tables, it is able to create the multidimensional views on the fly.

A database OLAP, or DOLAP, refers to a relational DBMS that is designed to host OLAP structures and perform OLAP calculations.

A Web OLAP, or WOLAP, refers to OLAP data that is accessible from a Web browser.

OLAP cube

A multidimensional database that holds data more like a 3-D spreadsheet rather than a relational database. The cube allows different views of the data to be quickly displayed. See *OLAP* and *multidimensional views*.

olay

See *OLE*.

OLCP

(OnLine Complex Processing) Processing complex queries, long transactions and simultaneous reads and writes to the same record. Contrast with *OLTP*, in which records are updated in a more predictable manner.

OLE

A compound document technology from Microsoft that is based on its Component Object Model (COM). OLE allows an object such as a spreadsheet or video clip to be embedded into a document, called the *container application*. When the object is double clicked, the application that created it, called the *server application*, is launched in order to edit it.

An object can be linked instead of embedded, in which case the container application does not physically hold the object, but provides a pointer to it. If a change is made to a linked object, all the documents that contain that same link are automatically updated the next time you open them. An application can be both client and server. See *Object Packager*.

OLE was originally known as "Object Linking and Embedding." However, with version 2.0, OLE's infrastructure was built on a new component architecture known as COM (Component Object Model) that went beyond compound documents. New capabilities such as OLE automation and Network OLE were widely promoted. Later, Microsoft dropped the term OLE for all COM operations except compound documents; however, the old usage still lingers. See *ActiveX Documents* and *COM*.

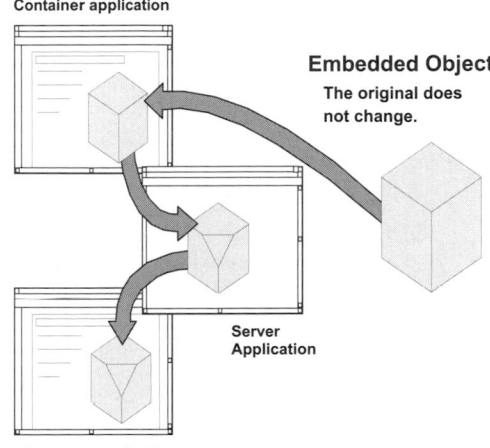

Embedded Object
The original does not change.

OLE Embedding
If an object is embedded, the document contains a copy of it. Changes made to the object affect only the document that contains it.

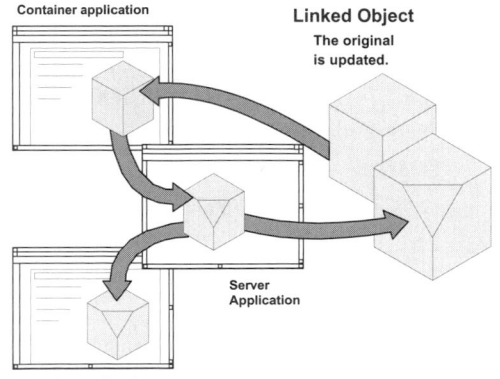

Linked Object
The original is updated.

OLE Linking
If an object is linked, the document contains a pointer to the original file. When you change a linked object, you are changing the original, and all the documents that link to that object are automatically updated.

OLE automation client, OLE automation server

See *COM automation*.

OLE container

In OLE compound document technology, it is the OLE client application, which holds the linked or embedded objects. See *OLE*.

OLE control, OLE custom control

See *OCX*.

OLE Database, OLE DB

A programming interface for data access from Microsoft. It functions in a similar manner as ODBC, but for every type of data source not just SQL databases. Applications can use OLE DB to access ODBC databases as well. OLE DB for OLAP is used to access OLAP databases. OLE DB is a COM object. See *ODBC, DAO, RDO* and *ADO*.

OLE server

In OLE compound document technology, it is the application that is called upon to display and process a linked or embedded object. See *OLE*.

OLR

See *offline reader*.

OLTP

(OnLine Transaction Processing) See *transaction processing* and *OLCP*.

OM1

(Open MPEG-1) A programming interface developed by the Open PC MPEG Consortium for interactive MPEG-1 titles. It provides a common set of commands for programming interactive games that are compressed under MPEG. OM1 is based on Sigma Design's RealMagic MPEG-1 board and has become a de facto standard.

OMA

See *Object Management Architecture*.

OME

(Open Messaging Environment) An open messaging system from Novell. It is based on Microsoft's MAPI and is a superset of Novell's MHS and WordPerfect Office's messaging systems.

OMEGAMON

A family of performance tools for S/390 environments from Candle that monitor processing activities of major systems programs such as MVS, CICS and DB2. OMEGAMON was the first realtime performance monitor for MVS.

OMG

See *Object Management Group*.

omnidirectional

In all directions. For example, an omnidirectional antenna can pick up signals in all directions.

OmniPage

Character recognition software for PCs and the Macintosh from Caere Corporation, Los Gatos, CA, (www.caere.com). It was the first personal computer software that could distinguish text from graphics and convert a wide variety of fonts into text.

OMNIS 7

A client/server development system for creating Windows and Mac applications from Blyth Software, Foster City, CA, (www.blyth.com). It includes its own database manager for local and laptop use and supports a wide variety of databases. OMNIS includes visual programming tools and a 4GL for application development.

OMR

(Optical Mark Reader) A scanner that reads marks on specific areas of the page. See *mark sensing*.

OMT

(Object Modeling Technique) An object-oriented analysis and design method developed by James Rumbaugh. See *object references*.

ONA

(Open Network Architecture) An FCC plan that allows users and competing enhanced service providers (ESPs) equal access to unbundled, basic telephone services. The Open Network Provision (ONP) is the European counterpart.

onboard

Refers to a chip or other hardware component that is directly attached to the printed circuit board (motherboard). Contrast with *offboard*.

ONC

(Open Network Computing) A family of networking products from SunSoft for implementing distributed computing in a multivendor environment. Includes TCP/IP and OSI protocols, NFS distributed file system, NIS naming service and TI-RPC remote procedure call library. ONC+ adds Federated Services, which is an interface for third-parties to connect network services into the Solaris environment.

one-chip computer

See *computer on a chip*.

one-off

One at a time. CD-ROM recorders (CD-R drives) are commonly called one-off machines because they write one CD-ROM at a time.

one-way hash function

In cryptography, an algorithm that generates a fixed string of numbers from a text message. The "one-way" means that is extremely difficult to turn the fixed string back into the text message. One-way hash functions are used for creating digital signatures for message authentication. See *digital signature*.

on-hook

The state of a telephone line that can receive an incoming call. Contrast with *off-hook*.

onion diagram

A graphical representation of a system that is made up of concentric circles. The innermost circle is the core, and all outer layers are dependent on the core.

online

Available for immediate use. If your data is on disk attached to your computer, the data is online. If it is on a disk in your desk drawer, it is offline. If you use the Internet or an online service, such as AOL or Prodigy, you are online when you have made the connection via modem and logged on with your account number. When you log off, you are offline.

A peripheral device (terminal, printer, etc.) that is turned on and connected to the computer is said to be online. However, a printer can be taken offline by simply pressing the ONLINE or SEL button. It is still attached and connected, but is internally cut off from receiving data from the computer. Pressing the ONLINE or SEL button will turn it back online.

online means happiness!

In the 1960s and 70s, the ancient days of computers, systems were designed as either online or batch. Online meant terminals were connected to a central computer, and batch meant entering batches of transactions (from punched cards or tape) on a second or third shift. Other terms, such as *realtime* and *transaction processing* evolved from online processing. See also *nearline*.

Want to impress your friends?

Although somewhat overkill, it is not incorrect to say that one has an online, realtime, transaction processing system (that is, providing you do). In this day and age of buzzwords such as modems and hard disks, this phrase still sounds pretty high tech. But if you say this at your next cocktail party, watch out. Your friends will start asking you how to get their printers to work right and their programs not to crash. An experienced systems analyst will probably chuckle!

online complex processing

See *OLCP*.

online help

On-screen instruction that is immediately available. See *user interface* and *RTFM*.

online industry

The collection of service organizations that provide dial-up access to databases, shopping, news, weather, sports, e-mail, etc. See *online services*.

online services

Following are the major online service providers and their primary offerings. This is not a list of ISPs, of which there are thousands. Although many of the following provide access to the Internet, these services existed before the Internet became mainstream, and they offer databases and forums that are not on the Internet.

```
America Online, Inc.
Internet access, various databases
 800/827-6364
 www.aol.com

BIX (Byte Magazine)
Personal computer technical
 800/695-4775
 www.bix.com

CompuServe Information Service, Inc.
Internet access, various databases
 800/848-8990
 www.compuserve.com

DataTimes Corporation
Newspapers, magazines, financial
 800/642-2525
 www.datatimes.com

Delphi Internet Services
Internet access, various databases
 Cambridge, MA 02138
 www.delphi.com

Dow Jones Interactive
Finance, news & news searching
 800/522-3567
 http://bis.dowjones.com

EasyLink (AT&T)
Messaging services (e-mail, EDI)
 800/242-6005
 www.att.com/easycommerce/easylink
```

```
Genie
Internet access, BBSs, roundtables
 800/638-9636
 www.genie.com

Knight-Ridder Information Inc.
More than 600 DIALOG databases
 800/334-2564
 www.krinfo.com

LEXIS-NEXIS
Legal and news information
 800/227-4908
 www.lexis-nexis.com

National Library of Medicine
MEDLINE and MEDLARS databases
 800/638-8480
 www.nlm.nih.gov

MCI Mail
E-mail, fax, Telex, Dow Jones access
 800/444-6245
 www.mcimail.com

Microsoft Network
Internet access, various databases
 800/386-5550
 www.msn.com

NewsNet, Inc.
Business news and analysis
 800/952-0122
 www.newsnet.com
```

```
Prodigy                                West Publishing/WESTLAW
Internet access, various databases     Legal databases
 800/776-3449                           800/WESTLAW
 www.prodigy.com                        www.westpub.com

Questel - Orbit
Patent, trademark, scientific,
chemical, business news/info
 800/456-7248
 www.questel.orbit.com
```

online storefront
A store on the Internet that offers items for sale and is capable of handling the financial transaction online. See *cybermall* and *digital money*.

online transaction processing
See *transaction processing* and *OLCP*.

OnNow
A feature that allows a PC to be turned on by external devices. Implementing the Advanced Configuration and Power Interface (ACPI) that is expected in new PC motherboards, the PC can be placed into a sleep mode that uses virtually no power until it is "awakened." See *ACPI*.

on the fly
As needed. It implies little or no degradation in performance to accomplish the task. See *realtime* and *realtime compression*.

OO
Object oriented.

OOA
See *object-oriented analysis*.

OOAD
(Object-Oriented Analysis & Design) See *object-oriented analysis* and *object-oriented design*.

OOBE, "oobie"
(Out Of Box Experience) The experience of setting up and using a new computer or software package.

OOD
See *object-oriented design*.

OODB
See *object-oriented database*.

OODBMS
See *object-oriented DBMS*.

OOOS
See *object-oriented operating system*.

OOP
See *object-oriented programming*.

OOPL
(OOP Language) An object-oriented programming language.

OOPS
(Object-Oriented Programming System) See *object-oriented programming*.

OORDBMS
(Object-Oriented Relational DBMS) A relational database management system that has object-oriented capabilities.

OOT

(Object-Oriented Technology) See *objects* and *object-oriented programming*.

op amp

(Operational Amplifier) A device that amplifies analog signals. It uses two inputs; one for power and one for data. It is used in myriads of applications from communications to stereo.

OPC

(OpenGL Performance Characterization) A project group within GPC that manages OpenGL benchmarks. OPC endorses the Viewperf and GLperf benchmarks. Viewperf was created by IBM and OPC provides viewsets for it, which are combinations of tests using specific applications to test OpenGL performance. Parametric Technology's CDRS (CDRS-03) is used for modeling and rendering. IBM's Data Explorer (DX-03) is used for visualization. Intergraph's DesignReview (DRV-04) is used for 3-D models. Alias/Wavefront's Advanced Visualizer (AWadvs-01) is used for animation, and Lightscape Technology's Lightscape Visualization System (Light-01) is used for radiosity visualization.

Developed by the OPC, the GLperf benchmark measures low-level OpenGL 2-D and 3-D graphics primitives. The results are the raw performance of a system rather than the application performance as provided by the Viewperf benchmarks. Viewperf results are in frames per second, and GLperf results are in primitives per second. See *GPC*.

op code

See *operation code*.

open

(1) To engage a disk or tape file for reading and writing. The open procedure "locks on" to an existing file. Contrast with *close*.

(2) With regard to a switch, open is "off."

(3) Made to operate with other products. See *open architecture* and *open systems*.

open architecture

A system in which the specifications are made public in order to encourage third-party vendors to develop add-on products. Much of Apple's early success was due to the Apple II's open architecture. The PC is open architecture.

open computing

See *open systems*.

OpenDDS

(OpenVME Data Dictionary System) A central repository for administering databases and systems from ICL for its OpenVME environment. OpenDDS provides an enhanced interface to DDS and supports the CDIF format for data interchange with CASE tools.

Open Desktop

See *SCO OpenServer*.

OpenDoc

An object-oriented compound document and component architecture. Documents and images can be embedded within or linked to documents set up as containers. OpenDoc is a superset of OLE, and OLE objects can be placed into OpenDoc documents and behave like OLE objects. OpenDoc components (Live Objects) are CORBA compliant and can be called up on a remote computer. OpenDoc was governed by Component Integration Labs (CI Labs), a vendor consortium in Sunnyvale, CA. In June 1997, CI Labs dissolved, and OpenDoc became history.

open file

A file, typically a disk file, that has been made available to the application by the operating system for reading and/or writing. All files must be "opened" before they can be accessed and "closed" when no longer required.

OpenGL

(OPEN Graphics Language) A 3-D graphics language developed by Silicon Graphics, which has become a de facto standard endorsed by many vendors. OpenGL can be implemented as an extension to an operating system or a window system and is supported by most UNIX-based workstations, Windows and X Window. Most high-end 3-D accelerators support OpenGL. See *OPC*. See *graphics accelerator*.

Open Group

(The Open Group, Cambridge, MA, www.opengroup.org) Formed in 1966 as the merger of the Open Software Foundation (OSF) and X/Open organizations, The Open Group is dedicated to promoting open standards. The OSF side is responsible for research and development and licensing of source code, while X/Open is responsible for certification and registration.

Founded in 1988, OSF is a coalition of worldwide vendors and users that delivers technology innovations in all areas of open systems. Founded in 1984, X/Open is dedicated to developing specifications and tests for open system compliance. X/Open also manages the UNIX trademark on behalf of the industry. Following are the major products that have come out of the OSF side. See also *ANDF*.

OSF/1

The OSF/1 operating system uses Carnegie Mellon's Mach kernel. It is a B1-secure, symmetric multiprocessing system that is compliant with POSIX, XPG4 and SVID base and kernel extensions. IBM, HP, DEC and Hitachi use OSF/1 in full or in part.

Motif

Motif is a graphical user interface (GUI) for applications running on any system with X Window Version 11. Compliant with POSIX, ANSI C and XPG, Motif is the de facto standard graphical interface for UNIX.

DCE

The Distributed Computing Environment is a set of programs that allows applications to be built across heterogeneous platforms in a network. DCE has been adopted by many organizations.

DME

The Distributed Management Environment is a set of programs for system and network management. DME was not widely used.

OPEN LOOK

An X Window-based graphical user interface for UNIX developed by Sun. It has been widely used by Sun and was defined and distributed by AT&T when it was still involved with UNIX. OPEN LOOK has given way to Motif, which has become the standard user interface in the UNIX world.

OpenMail

An electronic mail system from HP that runs on UNIX servers. It complies with the X.400 messaging and X.500 directory standards and supports all major mail programs that run on the client.

OpenNT

A software subsystem that adds UNIX capability to Windows NT from Softway Systems, Inc., San Francisco, CA. A developer's kit allows UNIX applications to be recompiled into POSIX and X/Open-compliant applications that can run under NT.

OpenPIC

(OPEN Programmable Interrupt Controller) An SMP chip architecture endorsed by AMD and Cyrix Corporation that provides symmetric multiprocessing (SMP) for x86 and PowerPC systems It can support up to 32 processors. See *APIC*.

open pipe

A continuous path from sender to receiver, such as found in a circuit-switching network or leased line. Transmitted data is not broken up into packets.

open reel

A reel of magnetic tape. It typically refers to half-inch open reels that still remain in the archives of many data libraries. In the 1950s, before the 8-bit byte, 7-track tapes (seven parallel tracks) were used to accomodate a 6-bit character plus parity. Starting in the 1960s, 9-track tapes were used to support the byte. See *half-inch tape*. For a summary of all storage technologies, see *storage*.

Open Server

See *SCO OpenServer*.

open shop

A computing environment that allows users to program and run their own programs. Contrast with *closed shop*.

Open Software Foundation

See *Open Group*.

open source

Free source code of a program, which is made available to the development community at large. The rationale is that a broader group of programmers will utlimately produce a more useful product for everyone. For example, Netscape Communicator was made open source (see *Mozilla*) in 1998. For more information, visit www.opensource.org.

open standard

See *open system*.

OpenStep

An object-oriented development environment from Apple, which runs on Windows, Sun and HP machines. OpenStep was originally developed by NeXT Computer as part of its NextStep operating system. OpenStep has been incorporated into Rhapsody. See *NeXT* and *Rhapsody*.

open storage

Disk and tape systems that connect via standard interfaces such as SCSI and IDE.

open systems

For years, open systems and UNIX-based computing have been synonymous, because UNIX runs on more different kinds of computers than any other operating system. The goal of open systems is interoperability between hardware and software that is defined by the industry at large and not one or two vendors.

Open systems includes database management systems (DBMSs) that run on many different platforms as well and any other tools that are used across multiple platforms. While this provides a certain freedom for future changes, it is by no means a problem free environment and never will be. Whenever several hardware platforms are used, a version of each software product must be available for that platform.

For example, in order to migrate an application from one UNIX system to another, all the system software components (DBMSs, TP monitors, compilers, etc.) that are currently linked to that application must also be available for the new system. Otherwise, custom conversion programs must be developed and more conversion effort is required.

The goal of open systems is a beautiful one, very much akin to world peace. Everyone pledges allegiance to it, but getting there seems to take forever.

Increasingly, the term also refers to the Wintel PC. Technically, the PC is an open architecture, not an open system, since Intel and Microsoft control the primary hardware and software standards. However, countless third-party vendors have been encouraged to write software for the platform as well as make hardware add-ons and interoperable products, which is why the PC became the largest segment of the computer industry.

Many in the industry also use the term to refer to everything other than proprietary IBM S/390, AS/400 and RS/6000 environments. Contrast with *closed system*. See *OSI, Open Group* and *X/Open*.

OpenType

A font technology from Microsoft and Adobe that maintains typeface fidelity in the receiving system by sending the fonts along with the documents. It supports both TrueType and Type 1 fonts. OpenType is expected to be used on the Web to give site designers their choice of fonts. Without such a system, they rely on the fonts installed in the user's computer.

OpenView

Network management software from HP. It supports SNMP and CMIP protocols, and third-party products that run under OpenView support SNA and DECnet network management protocols. OpenView is an enterprise-wide network management solution.

OpenVME

An operating system from ICL that was introduced in 1994 for its Series 39 mainframes and carried forth on its Trimetra systems. OpenVME is the open systems version of the VME operating system, which includes all the open interfaces previously available as an option. In late 1992, VME had already achieved XPG4 branding for its conformance to open systems standards. See *VME*.

OpenVMS

A later version of the VMS operating system from Digital that is POSIX and XPG3-compliant and runs on VAX and Alpha systems.

operand

The part of a machine instruction that references data or a peripheral device. In the instruction, **ADD A to B**, A and B are the operands (nouns), and ADD is the operation code (verb). In the instruction **READ TRACK 9, SECTOR 32,** track and sector are the operands.

operating system

The master control program that runs the computer. It is the first program loaded when the computer is turned on, and its main part, called the kernel, resides in memory at all times. It may be developed by the vendor of the computer it's running in or by a third party.

It is an important component of the computer system, because it sets the standards for the application programs that run in it. All programs must "talk to" the operating system.

The main difference between an operating system and a network operating system is its multiuser capability. Operating systems, such as Macintosh System 7, DOS and Windows, are single user, designed for one person at a desktop computer. Windows NT and UNIX on the other hand are network operating systems, because they are designed to manage multiple user requests at the same time.

An operating system is also called an *executive* or *supervisor*. Operating systems perform the following functions.

User Interface

The user interface, or shell, provides the interaction between the user and the operating system. Operating systems may allow for different shells; for example, DOS and UNIX provide command-driven interfaces but can host other shells that provide a menu-driven or graphical interface. Even Windows, which is graphics based to begin with, allows other shells to provide an interface to the user.

Job Management

Job management controls the running of programs. Which one gets executed first, then next. In small computers, the operating system responds to interactive commands from the user and loads the requested application program into memory for execution. Larger computers are more oriented to accepting a batch of instructions. For example, job control language (JCL) may describe the programs that must be run for an entire shift. In some cases, the output of one program may then be input into another and so on.

Task Management

Task management controls the simultaneous execution of programs. In single tasking computers, the operating system has virtually no task management to do, but in multitasking computers, it is responsible for the concurrent operation of one or more programs (jobs). Advanced operating systems have the ability to prioritize programs so that one job gets done before the other.

In order to provide users at terminals with the fastest response time, batch programs can be put on lowest priority and interactive programs can be given highest priority. Advanced operating systems can be fine tuned by the computer operator so that a specific job can be speeded up or slowed down.

Multitasking is accomplished by executing instructions for one function while data is coming into or going out of the computer for another. Large computers are designed to overlap these operations, and data can move simultaneously in and out of the computer through separate channels with the operating system governing these actions.

In small computers, the operating system can monitor idle time when a user is interactively working with a program to execute another program in the background. Even the milliseconds between keystrokes can be used for something else. A user, pausing at the keyboard for just a couple of seconds, is light years to the computer, which can use that time to execute hundreds of thousands of instructions.

Data Management

Data management keeps track of data on the disk; hence the term DOS, or disk operating system. The application program does not know where the data is actually stored or how to get it. That knowledge is contained in the operating system's access method, or device driver, routines. When a program is ready to accept data, it signals the operating system with a message. The operating system finds the data and delivers it to the program. Conversely, when the program is ready to output, the operating system transfers the data from the program onto the available space on disk.

Device Management

Device management controls the input and output of data to and from the peripheral devices. The operating system is responsible for providing central management of all devices, not just disk drives. When a new type of peripheral is added to the computer, the operating system is updated with a new driver for that device. The driver contains the specific instructions necessary to run it. The operating system calls the drivers for input and output, and the drivers talk to the hardware.

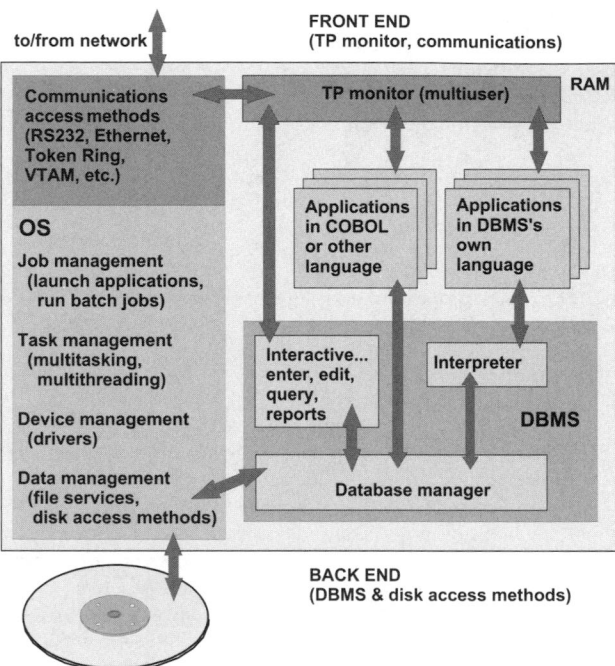

System and Application Software
This diagram shows how the major system software interacts with applications in memory. System software comprises the programs that support the running of applications (operating system, DBMS, TP monitor and access methods).

In the DOS world, software developers often bypassed the operating system and addressed the hardware directly to improve performance. In addition, DOS does not support device management for all peripheral devices, requiring application developers to support myriads of brands of hardware. This is a major reason why DOS gave way to Windows, which provides centralized device management.

Security

Multiuser operating systems maintain a list of authorized users and provide password protection to unauthorized users who may try to gain access to the system. Large operating systems also maintain activity logs and accounting of the user's time for billing purposes. They also provide backup and recovery routines to start over again in the event of a system failure.

History

The earliest operating systems were developed in the late 1950s to manage tape storage, but programmers mostly wrote their own I/O routines. In the mid 1960s, operating systems became essential to manage disks, complex timesharing and multitasking systems.

Today, all multi-purpose computers from micro to mainframe use an operating system. Special-purpose devices (appliances, games, toys, etc.) generally do not. They usually employ a single program that performs all the required I/O and processing tasks.

Common Operating Systems

PCs primarily use DOS, Windows 3.x, Windows 95/98, Windows NT and OS/2 with all the various Windows versions being the most popular. Macintoshes use the Mac OS (System 7, System 8, etc.). Minicomputers and workstations use a variety of UNIX operating systems, and IBM mainframes primarily use OS/390 (formerly MVS).

In the past, when a vendor introduced a new operating system, users had little understanding of this behind-the-glass-enclosed-datacenter phenomenon. Today, it is squarely in their hands.

operation code

The part of a machine instruction that tells the computer what to do, such as input, add or branch. The operation code is the verb; the operands are the nouns.

operations

See *datacenter*.

operations research

See *management science*.

operator

(1) A person who operates the computer and performs such activities as commanding the operating system, mounting disks and tapes and placing paper in the printer. Operators may also write the job control language (JCL), which schedules the daily work for the computer. See *salary survey*.

(2) In programming and logic, a symbol used to perform an operation on some value. See *arithmetic operators* and *Boolean operator*.

operator overloading

In programming, the ability to use the same operator to perform different operations. For example, arithmetic operators such as +, -, * and / could be defined to perform differently on certain kinds of data.

OPI

(Open Prepress Interface) An extension to PostScript that provides color separations. It was developed by Aldus Corporation, which was later acquired by Adobe.

OPROM

(Option **ROM**) Firmware on adapter cards that control bootable peripherals. The system BIOS interrogates the option ROMs to determine which devices can be booted. See *BBS*.

OPS

(Open Profiling Standard) A specification for sharing data and ensuring privacy of a user's data. The OPS provides a standard way of identifying which data can be transferred from the user to a Web site and how it can and cannot be used. See *ICE*.

optical amplifier

A device that boosts light signals in an optical fiber. Unlike regenerators, which have to convert the light signal to electricity in order to amplify it and then convert it back to light, the optical amplifier amplifies the light signal itself. The rare earth material, erbium, is used for creating the first successful optical amplifiers.

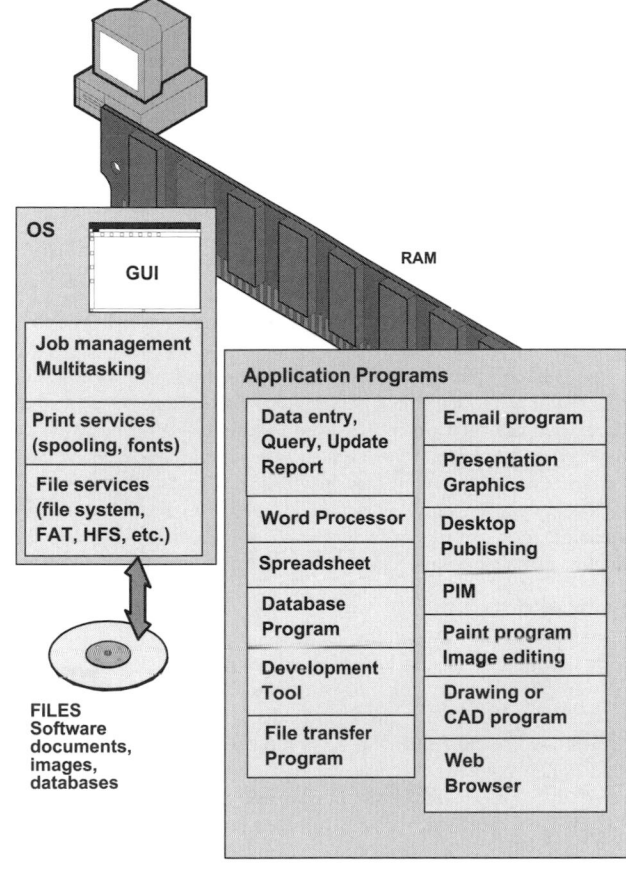

Operating System and Application Software
This diagram shows the components of the operating system and typical application programs that run in a desktop computer.

The optical amplifier gave a tremendous boost to fiber-optic transmission systems. Instead of requiring a regenerator every 20-25 miles, an optical amplifier is placed 75 miles apart, and a regenerator is required only once in several hundred miles. In addition, an optical amplifier can amplify all of the channels in a DWDM signal, whereas regenerators are required for each channel. See *WDM*.

optical disk

A direct access disk written and read by light. CD, CD-ROM, DVD-ROM and DVD-Video disks are optical disks that are recorded at the time of manufacture and cannot be erased. WORM, CD-R and DVD-R disks are recorded in the user's environment, but cannot be erased.

Erasable, or rewritable, optical disks function like magnetic disks and can be rewritten over and over. Rewritable disks use either magneto-optic or phase change technology. MO disks are very robust and are geared to business applications, typically in high-capacity disk libraries. Phase change disks (CD-RW, DVD-RAM and PD) are lower cost consumer-oriented products. DVD-RAM is expected to become very popular.

It is likely that optical disks will replace magnetic disks some time in the future. Although some argue this will not happen, there are significant advantages to optical disks. They have greater removable storage capacities and they are approaching magnetic disk speeds. In addition, optical disks are not subject to head crashes or corruption from stray magnetic fields. They have a 30-year life and are less vulnerable to extremes of hot and cold than magnetic disks.

New optical technologies are expected from Terastor and Quinta. Similar to magneto-optic (MO) in concept, they employ more advanced technologies to increase storage capacity. For details, see *latest disk drives*. For a summary of all storage technologies, see *storage*.

optical disk library

Also called an *optical jukebox*, it is an optical disk storage system that houses multiple disk platters. It is similar to a music jukebox, except that instead of "playing one tune," more than one drive can be used to read and write several disks simultaneously. Such devices are made for rewritable optical disks, write once disks and CD-ROMs, and can hold from a handful to several thousand disks or cartridges.

optical fiber

A thin glass wire designed for light transmission, capable of transmitting billions of bits per second. Unlike electrical pulses, light pulses are not affected by random radiation in the environment.

The telephone companies have used fibers extensively to rebuild their communications infrastructure. For example, by 1995 in the U.S., more than eight million miles of fiber had been laid. Copper cable is increasingly being replaced with fibers for LAN backbones as well, and this usage is expected to increase substantially over the years.

An optical fiber is constructed of a transparent core made of pure silicon dioxide ($SiO2$), through which the light travels. This core is so transparent that you could see through a three-mile thick window made out of it. The core is surrounded by a cladding layer that reflects light, keeping it in the core. The cladding is surrounded by a plastic layer, a layer of kevlar fibers for strength and an outer sheath of plastic or Teflon.

Multimode fiber is the most commonly used, which has a core diameter of from 50 to 100 microns. For intercity cabling and highest speed,

Fiber Versus Copper
Not only does optical fiber provide enormous transmission bandwidth, but it takes a lot less room. The single strand of fiber in the center is equivalent in capacity to any one of the copper bundles in the picture. *(Photo courtesy of Corning Incorporated.)*

Computer Desktop Encyclopedia

singlemode fiber with a core diameter of less than 10 microns is used. See *multimode fiber, singlemode fiber, FDDI* and *cable categories*.

optical isolator

A device used with current loop transmission that uses an LED and photoresistor to detect current in the line.

optical jukebox, optical library

See *optical disk library*.

optical mouse

A mouse that uses light to get its bearings. It is rolled over a small desktop pad that contains a reflective grid. The mouse emits a light and senses its reflection as it is moved. Contrast with *mechanical mouse*.

optical reader

An input device that recognizes typewritten or printed characters and bar codes and converts them into their corresponding digital codes.

optical recognition

See *OCR*.

optical resolution

The built-in resolution of a scanning device. Contrast with *interpolated resolution*, which enhances an image by software. Both resolutions are given as dots per inch (dpi), thus a 2,400 dpi scanner can be the true resolution of the machine or a computed resolution. See *interpolated resolution* and *scanner*.

optical scanner

See *scanner*.

optical storage

See *optical disk* and *optical disk library*.

optical switch

An all-optical fiber optic switching device that maintains the signal as light from input to output.

optimizer

Hardware or software that improves performance. See *defragger* and *disk management*.

opt-in

To purposefully accept some situation or condition ahead of time. For example, to opt-in to an e-mail campaign means that you want to receive the specific information being sent.

option ROM

See *OPROM*.

optoelectronics

Merging light and electronics technologies, such as in optical fiber communications systems.

opt-out

To cancel some situation or condition.

OQL

(Object Query Language) A query language that supports complex data types (multimedia, spatial, compound documents, etc.) that are stored as objects. Defined by the ODMG, it is a superset of the SQL-92 query language. Standard SQL queries can still be used, and the OQL server process converts the objects into relational views.

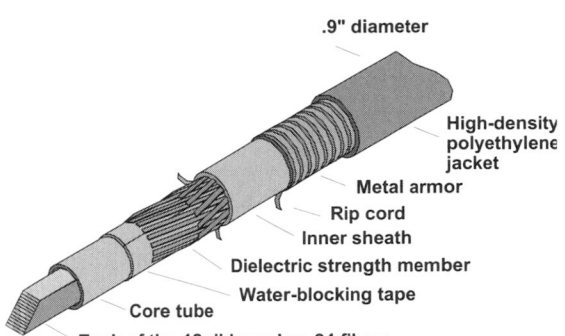

288 Fibers in One Cable

With the assistance of Antec Corporation, Lucent developed this record high-fiber-count, singlemode cable with 288 fibers. In 1996, Time Warner Cable in New York purchased 50 miles of it for transporting high-bandwidth video, voice and data to its Manhattan subscribers.

OQL also supports the OMG's object model (OM), allowing queries to be made against CORBA objects. In addition, OQL commands can be embedded in URL links that are sent to an OQL gateway by the HTTP server. The results are converted back into Web pages for the user.

OR			EXCLUSIVE OR		
IN	IN	OUT	IN	IN	OUT
0	0	0	0	0	0
0	1	1	0	1	1
1	0	1	1	0	1
1	1	1	1	1	0

OR

A Boolean logic operation that is true if any of the inputs is true. An exclusive OR (XOR) is true if only one of the inputs is true, but not both. See *AND-OR-NOT*.

Oracle

(Oracle Corporation, Redwood Shores, CA, www.oracle.com) The world's largest database and application development software vendor founded in 1977 by Larry Ellison. The Oracle database was the first DBMS to incorporate the SQL language and to be ported to a wide variety of platforms. Oracle offers a variety of application development tools and is a major promoter of the network computer. Its Network Computer subsidiary defines the specifications for a compliant platform.

Oracle8

Oracle's relational database managment system (DBMS). This is the current version of Oracle's flagship product, which includes such features as replication and high availability. Oracle8 runs on more than 80 platforms and includes object-oriented extensions.

Oracle Browser

See *Developer/2000*.

Oracle Data Query

The query function in Discoverer/2000. See *Developer/2000*.

Oracle Documents

An earlier name for a variety of Oracle software products, including a messaging system, text database and document management system. Each of the products was later offered separately.

Oracle Forms

See *Developer/2000*.

Oracle Media Server

An multimedia system for interactive TV delivery from Oracle Corporation that runs on nCUBE, HP and other hardware platforms. The client software runs on Macs, PCs and set-top boxes. It is designed to store and disseminate multiple streams of text (news), images, audio and video on demand.

Oracle Parallel Server

A version of the Oracle database system designed for massively parallel processors (MPPs). It allows multiple CPUs to access a single database.

Oracle Rdb

(Oracle Relational DataBase) A relational DBMS that runs under OpenVMS on Digital's VAX and Alpha systems. Rdb was originally developed by Digital and widely used on VAX systems. Oracle acquired it in 1994 and has enhanced the product.

Oracle Reports

See *Developer/2000*.

Oracle Universal Server

Oracle's object-relational version of the Oracle7 DBMS. Object-relational databases store multimedia data as well as the traditional row and column tables of relational data.

Orange Book

See *NCSC* and *CD*.

ORB

(**O**bject **R**equest **B**roker) Software that handles the communication of messages from the requesting program (client) to the object as well as any return values from the object back to the calling program. See *CORBA* and *DCOM*. See also *Orb disk*.

ORB disk

A high-capacity removable hard disk system from Castlewood Systems, Inc., Pleasanton, CA, (www.castlewoodsystems.com). Expected in 1998 with a capacity of 2.1GB and a 12MB transfer rate, ORB drives use magnetoresistive (MR) read/write head technology. The drive is expected at $199 with the cartridges at a breakthrough price of $29.95. Castlewood is a private company founded by Syed Iftikar, the founder of SyQuest and co-founder of Seagate. See *latest disk drives*.

ORB Cartridge
Castlewood is pushing the envelope of affordable, removable disks with its 2.2GB cartridges.

ORB gateway

Software that translates messages between two different ORBs.

Orbix

A CORBA-compliant ORB from IONA Technologies Inc., Dublin, Ireland (U.S. office, Marlboro, MA). Founded in 1991, IONA is a leading member of the OMG, and Orbix has become a popular CORBA-based system due to its multi-platform support and OLE integration. This combination made it the first distributed solution for OLE automation.

OrbixWeb is IONA's Java implementation of Orbix. When users retrieve OrbixWeb-based Java applets, OrbixWeb is downloaded into their machines, providing them with CORBA connectivity.

ORDBMS

(**O**bject **R**elational **DBMS**) A relational database that supports object structures. ORDBMSs are now called *universal servers*.

order

See *precedence* and *big endian*.

ordering upgrades

The Encyclopedia is available in several options for individuals and organizations. To find out about them, press F1 and click "Ordering upgrades and licenses."

order of magnitude

A change in quantity or volume as measured by the decimal point. For example, from tens to hundreds is one order of magnitude. Tens to thousands is two orders of magnitude; tens to millions is three orders of magnitude, etc.

ordinal number

The number that identifies the sequence of an item, for example, record #34. Contrast with *cardinal number*.

org

An Internet address domain name for a non-profit organization. See *Internet address*.

organizer

See *PIM* and *PDA*.

orientation

In typography, the direction of print across a page. See *portrait*.

original equipment manufacturer

See *OEM*.

OROM

(Optical **ROM**) An optical storage technology from Ioptics, Inc., Bellevue, WA, (www.ioptics.com), that is expected in 1999. Designed for portable devices, OROM provides 10 ms access to 128MB in a thin, plastic 2.25x1.75" data card that connects via PC Card or USB. It uses stationary organic LEDs (OLEDs) that shine through 5000 "data patches" on the card, which are 2-D images that each hold 32KB of data. OROM cards are pressed in a manner similar to CDs. Write-once OROM writers are also expected for desktop PCs. For a summary of all storage technologies, see *storage*.

orphan

See *widow & orphan*.

OS

See *operating system*.

OS/2

A single user, multitasking operating system for PCs from IBM that runs OS/2, DOS and Windows applications. It provides both a graphical user interface as well as a command line interface similar to DOS. Many OS/2 and DOS commands are the same. OS/2 is highly regarded as a robust operating system.

OS/2's graphical user interface, called *Presentation Manager* (PM) in Versions 1.x and *Workplace Shell*, starting with Version 2.0, is similar to Windows and the Macintosh. The term Presentation Manager however still refers to the programming interface used to write OS/2 graphical applications. OS/2 includes a dual boot feature, allowing you to boot to either OS/2 or DOS. Also included is Adobe Type Manager for rendering Type 1 fonts on screen and providing PostScript output on non-PostScript printers. See *OS/2 Warp*.

OS/2 PM

(OS/2 Presentation Manager) The graphical user interface in OS/2 Version 1.x. It is now called *Workplace Shell* in Versions 2.x. See *OS/2*.

OS/2 Warp

Introduced in late 1994 and officially known as OS/2 Warp, Version 3, it is the successor to OS/2 for Windows and OS/2 Version 2.1. It is an enhanced version that can run in 4MB of memory, but 8MB is more realistic. It includes a simpler installation, improved multimedia support, Internet utilities with access via IBM's Global Network and a variety of bundled applications. The applications include IBM Works, a productivity suite, a fax program, PIM, comm program and others.

There are two versions of OS/2 Warp. One requires Windows 3.1 to be installed, the other includes a modified version of Windows 3.1.

OS/2 Warp Connect

The networking version of OS/2 Warp. It includes peer-to-peer networking to OS/2 and Windows for Workgroup machines as well as to Windows NT servers. See *Warp Server*.

OS/8

A single user, multitasking operating system from Digital for its PDP-8 computers. Variants run on DECstation and DECmate systems.

OS-9

A UNIX-like realtime operating system from Microware Systems Corporation, Des Moines, IA, (www.microware.com) that is widely used in embedded systems such as pagers and cellular phones. OS-9 runs on Motorola 68000 and PowerPC CPUs. Originally developed for the 6809 chip, a version of OS-9 was created for CD-I players. See *DAVID*.

OS/360

The operating system for the IBM System/360, which was introduced in 1964. It was later released in two versions. OS/MFT (Multiple Fixed Transactions) supported multiple programs that used fixed memory regions, and OS/MVT (Multiple Variable Transactions) supported varying program sizes. OS/MFT and OS/MVT were later enhanced for virtual storage and became OS/VS1 and OS/VS2. OS/VS2 evolved into MVS.

OS/390

The primary operating system used in IBM mainframes. OS/390 was originally the MVS/ESA operating system renamed and repackaged in 1996 with an extensive set of utilities. Although the name MVS is still used to refer to the base control program of OS/390, enhancements in usability and workload balancing have made OS/390 stand apart from its MVS heritage. OS/390 is upward compatible from MVS/ESA 5.2.2, but downward compatibility is not ensured.

OS/400

The operating system designed for the AS/400 minicomputer from IBM.

OS/9000

A portable version of OS-9, written in C, which runs on x86 and Motorola 68000 CPUs.

oscillate

To swing back and forth between the minimum and maximum values. An oscillation is one cycle, typically one complete wave in an alternating frequency.

oscillator

An electronic circuit used to generate high-frequency pulses. See *clock*.

oscilloscope

A test instrument that displays electronic signals (waves and pulses) on a screen. It creates its own time base against which signals can be measured, and display frames can be frozen for visual inspection.

OSD

(1) (On-Screen Display) An on-screen control panel for adjusting monitors and TVs. The OSD is used for contrast, brightness, horizontal and vertical positioning and other monitor adjustments.

(2) (Open Software Description) A data format for describing a software package, module or component. Based on XML, OSD is designed for distributing and updating software via push technology. Initially introduced for Windows, it is expected to be adopted for other platforms.

OSF

See *Open Group*.

OSF/Motif

See *Motif* and *Open Group*.

OSI

(Open System Interconnection) An ISO standard for worldwide communications that defines a framework for implementing protocols in seven layers. Control is passed from one layer to the next, starting at the application layer in one station, proceeding to the bottom layer, over the channel to the next station and back up the hierarchy.

At one time, most vendors agreed to support OSI in one form or another, but OSI was too loosely defined and proprietary standards were too entrenched. Except for the OSI-compliant X.400 and X.500 e-mail and directory standards, which are widely used, what was once thought to become the universal communications standard now serves as the teaching model for all other protocols.

Most of the functionality in the OSI model exists in all communications systems, although two or three OSI layers may be incorporated into one. See *OSI model*.

OSI model

Application - Layer 7

This top layer defines the language and syntax that programs use to communicate with other programs. The application layer represents the purpose of communicating in the first place. For example, a program in a client workstation uses commands to request data from a program in the server. Common functions at this layer are opening, closing, reading and writing files, transferring files and e-mail messages, executing remote jobs and obtaining directory information about network resouces.

Presentation - Layer 6

When data is transmitted between different types of computer systems, the presentation layer negotiates and manages the way data is represented and encoded. For example, it provides a common denominator between ASCII and EBCDIC machines as well as between different floating point and binary formats. Sun's XDR and OSI's ASN.1 are two protocols used for this purpose. This layer is also used for encryption and decryption.

Session - Layer 5

Provides coordination of the communications in an orderly manner. It determines one-way or two-way communications and manages the dialogue between both parties; for example, making sure that the previous request has been fulfilled before the next one is sent. It also marks significant parts of the transmitted data with checkpoints to allow for fast recovery in the event of a connection failure.

In practice, this layer is often not used or services within this layer are sometimes incorporated into the transport layer.

Transport - Layer 4

The transport layer is responsible for overall end to end validity and integrity of the transmission. The lower data link layer (layer 2) is only responsible for delivering packets from one node to another. Thus, if a packet gets lost in a router somewhere in the enterprise internet, the transport layer will detect that. It ensures that if a 12MB file is sent, the full 12MB is received.

"OSI transport services" include layers 1 through 4, collectively responsible for delivering a complete message or file from sending to receiving station without error.

Network - Layer 3

The network layer establishes the route between the sending and receiving stations. The node to node function of the data link layer (layer 2) is extended across the entire internetwork, because a routable protocol contains a network address in addition to a station addresses.

This layer is the switching function of the dial-up telephone system as well as the functions performed by routable protocols such as IP, IPX, SNA and AppleTalk. If all stations are contained within a single network segment, then the routing capability in this layer is not required. See *layer 3 switch*.

Data Link - Layer 2

The data link is responsible for node to node validity and integrity of the transmission. The transmitted bits are divided into frames; for example, an Ethernet, Token Ring or FDDI frame in local

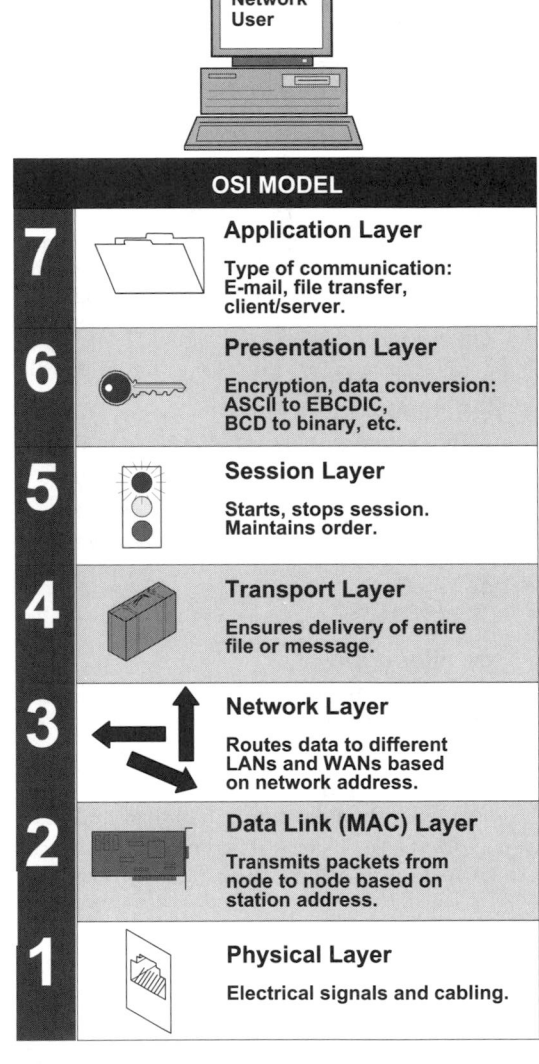

area networks (LANs). Layers 1 and 2 are required for every type of communications. For more on this layer, see *data link protocol*.

Physical - Layer 1
The physical layer is responsible for passing bits onto and receiving them from the connecting medium. This layer has no understanding of the meaning of the bits, but deals with the electrical and mechanical characteristics of the signals and signalling methods. For example, it comprises the RTS and CTS signals in an RS-232 environment, as well as TDM and FDM techniques for multiplexing data on a line. SONET also provides layer 1 capability.

OSI stack
The protocol stack in the OSI model. See *OSI*.

OSP
(Online Service Provider) See *online services*.

OSPF
(Open Shortest Path First) A routing protocol that determines the best path for routing IP traffic over a TCP/IP network. OSPF is an interior gateway protocol (IGP), which is designed to work within an autonomous system. It is also a link state protocol that provides less router to router update traffic than the RIP protocol (distance vector protocol) that it was designed to replace. See *RIP* and *routing protocol*.

OSR2
(OEM Service Release 2) Also known as Win95B, it is a version of Windows 95 released to PC vendors in late 1996 that included a variety of bug fixes as well as support for enhanced power management, FAT32, IDE bus mastering, 32-bit CardBus and Version 1.1 of DMI. See *Win 95 Version number*.

OSTA
(Optical Storage Technology Association, Santa Barbara, CA, www.osta.org) A membership organization composed of major optical drive manufacturers. Its purpose is to endorse standards and promote the use of optical media in computing.

OSX
See *Mac OS X*.

OT
(Object Technology) The use of objects.

OTOH
Digispeak for "on the other hand."

OTP
(1) (One Time Programmable) Refers to programming the content into chips such as ROMs and EEPROMs, which cannot be altered.

(2) (One Time Pad) A cryptography method that uses a random number to generate a unique encryption key, which is stored on a smart card. See *SwapCrypt*.

(3) (Open Trading Protocol) A framework for Internet commerce that provides a consistent purchasing experience regardless of the hardware and software used.

OTPROM
(One Time PROM) A PROM chip that can be programmed only once.

outdent
Same as *hanging paragraph*.

outline font
A type of font made from basic outlines of each character. The outlines are scaled into actual characters (bitmaps) before printing. See *scalable font*.

outline processor
Software that allows the user to type in thoughts and organize them into an outline form.

Outlook 97

A mail client and personal information manager (PIM) with groupware functions that comes with Office 97. It includes an e-mail client, forms design, calendaring, contact and task management (to-do lists), shared folders and freeform notes. It also provides a journaling capability for keeping track of hourly billing. Outlook can be used as the client end to Microsoft's Exchange Server, offering more features than the Exchange client. See *Microsoft Office* and *Microsoft Exchange*.

out of band

Outside the primary frequency or system. See *signaling in/out of band*.

out of memory

See *Windows memory limitation*.

output

(1) Any computer-generated information displayed on screen, printed on paper or in machine readable form, such as disk and tape.

(2) To transfer or transmit from the computer to a peripheral device or communications line.

output area

A reserved segment of memory used to collect data to be transferred out of the computer. Same as *buffer*.

output bound

Excessive overall slowness due to moving data out of the computer to low-speed lines or devices. See *printer buffer*.

output device

Any peripheral that presents output from the computer, such as a screen or printer. Although disks and tapes receive output, they are called storage devices.

outsourcing

Contracting with outside consultants, software houses or service bureaus to perform systems analysis, programming and datacenter operations. See *facilities management*.

overclock

To speed up the computer beyond the manufacturer's specifications in order to it run faster. This is accomplished by changing a jumper on the motherboard or by changing the clock crystal. The motherboard and CPU may or may not be able to handle the increased speed.

OverDrive CPU

Intel's trade name for its CPU upgrade chips. For the 486, there are 486 and Pentium OverDrives. Depending on the motherboard, the old chip is either replaced or the new one is installed in the upgrade socket, leaving the old chip intact or removing it. Pentium Overdrive chips install in the original socket.

overflow error

An error that occurs when calculated data cannot fit within the designated field. The result field is usually left blank or is filled with some symbol to flag the error condition.

overhead

(1) The amount of processing time used by system software, such as the operating system, TP monitor or database manager.

(2) In communications, the additional codes transmitted for control and error checking, which take more time to process.

overlay

(1) A preprinted, precut form placed over a screen, key or tablet for indentification purposes. See *keyboard template*.

(2) A program segment called into memory when required. When a program is larger than the memory capacity of the machine, parts of the program not in constant use can be set up as overlays. Each overlay called in overwrites the existing overlay in memory. Virtual memory provides for automatic overlays. See *virtual memory*.

overlay card

A controller that digitizes NTSC signals from a video source for display in the computer.

overloading

In programming, the ability to use the same name for more than one variable or procedure, requiring the compiler to differentiate them based on context.

oversampling

Creating a more accurate digital representation of an analog signal. In order to work with real-world signals in the computer, analog signals are sampled some number of times per second (frequency) and converted into digital code. Using averaging and different algorithms, samples can be generated between existing samples, creating more digital information for complex signals, "smoothing out the curve" so to speak.

Sampling requires at least twice the bandwidth of the frequency being sampled. For example, with regard to sound, 20KHz is the highest frequency perceptible to the human ear, and sampling is done at 44.1KHz for high quality audio playback. A 2x oversampling means that the CD player runs at twice the rate, or 88.2KHz, and inserts a made-up sample in between each real sample on the disc. An 8x oversampling runs eight times faster and so on. See *sampling rate*.

overscan

Outside of the normal rectangular viewing area on a display screen. Contrast with *underscan*.

overstrike

(1) To type over an existing character.

(2) A character with a line through it.

overwrite

(1) A data entry mode that writes over existing characters on screen when new characters are typed in. Contrast with *insert mode*.

(2) To record new data on top of existing data such as when a disk record or file is updated.

OWL

(ObjectWindows Library) A class library of Windows objects from Borland that serves as application frameworks for developing Windows applications in C++. It is the Borland counterpart of the Microsoft Foundation Class Library (MFC).

P

P2

See *Pentium II*.

P6

The Intel code name for the Pentium Pro, which is optimized for 32-bit applications. The P6 generation includes the Pentium Pro and Pentium II.

P6 class

Refers to a Pentium Pro or Pentium II CPU chip or to a PC that uses the chip. See *P6*.

P7

Intel's next-generation CPU architecture. See *Merced*.

P75, P90, P100, etc.

Generally refers to Pentium CPUs or Pentium systems running at 75, 90, 100MHz, etc.

P1394

See *FireWire*.

PABX

(Private Automatic Branch eXchange) Same as *PBX*.

PACBASE

Integrated CASE software for mainframes and UNIX systems from CGI Systems, Malvern, PA, subsidiary of IBM, (www.cgisystems.com). It supports a wide variety of databases including DB2 and Oracle. PACLAN is the version for PC servers running OS/2 and Windows NT. PACBASE generates COBOL code for the servers. Visual Age for PACBASE is used to create the client side.

pack

(1) To compress data in order to save space. Unpack refers to decompressing data. See *data compression*.

(2) An instruction that converts a decimal number into a packed decimal format. Unpack converts a packed decimal number into decimal.

(3) In database programs, a command that removes records that have been marked for deletion.

Packard Bell NEC

(Packard Bell NEC, Inc., Westlake Village, CA, www.packardbell.com) A major PC manufacturer that pioneered sales into the mass-market retail chains in the late 1980s. The first to offer toll-free support to end users, it is a major supplier of PCs to the retail channel.

The original Packard Bell was founded in 1926 as a consumer radio manufacturer and later entered the defense electronics industry. It was acquired by Teledyne in 1968. In 1986, Beny Alagem and a group of partners acquired the Packard Bell name from Teledyne and formed Packard Bell Electronics.

In 1995, Packard Bell acquired Zenith Data Systems and, in 1996, merged with NEC's personal computer operations to become Packard Bell NEC.

packed decimal

A storage mode that places two decimal digits into one byte, each digit occupying four bits. The sign occupies four bits in the least significant byte.

packet

A block of data used for transmission in packet switched systems. The terms frame, packet and datagram are often used synonymously. See *TCP/IP abc's*.

packet cellular

The transmission of data over the cellular network. Data is divided into packets, or frames, for error checking. Contrast with *circuit cellular*. See *CDPD* and *wireless*.

packet filtering

Discarding unwanted network traffic based on its originating address or range of addresses or its type (e-mail, file transfer, etc.). Packet filtering is generally performed in a router. See *firewall, Web filtering* and *router*.

packetized voice

The transmission of realtime voice in a packet switching network.

packet overhead

Refers to the time it takes to transmit data on a packet-switched network. Each packet requires extra bytes of format information, which, combined with the assembly and dissassembly of packets, reduces the overall transmission speed of the raw data.

packet over SONET

A metropolitan area network (MAN) or wide area network (WAN) transport technology that carries IP packets directly over SONET transmission without any data link facility such as ATM in between. Packet over SONET is intended to transmit data at the highest rates possible, because SONET has a smaller packet header overhead than ATM (28 bytes out of an 810-byte frame compared with 5 out of a 53-byte ATM cell). However, ATM has traditionally provided proven management and quality of service (QoS) for long haul transport.

packet radio

The wireless transmission of data, which is divided into packets, or frames, for error checking. See *Ardis* and *Mobitex*.

packet switching

A networking technology used in wide area networks (WANs) that breaks up a message into smaller packets for transmission and switches them to their required destination. Unlike circuit switching, which requires a constant point-to-point circuit to be established, each packet in a packet switched network contains a destination address. Thus all packets in a single message do not have to travel the same path. They can be dynamically routed over the network as pathways become available or unavailable. The destination computer reassembles the packets back into their proper sequence.

Packet switching efficiently handles messages of different lengths and priorities. By accounting for packets sent, a public network can charge customers for only the data they transmit. Packet switching is suitable for data, but not realtime voice and video.

The first international standard for wide area packet switching networks was X.25, which was defined when all circuits were analog and very susceptible to noise. Subsequent technologies, such as frame relay and SMDS were designed for today's almost-error-free digital lines. The Internet's TCP/IP protocol is also packet switched.

ATM uses a cell-switching technology that provides the bandwidth-sharing efficiency of packet switching with the guaranteed bandwith of circuit switching.

Higher-level protocols, such as TCP/IP, IPX/SPX and NetBIOS, are also packet based and designed to ride over packet-switched topologies.

Public packet switching networks may provide value added services, such as protocol conversion and electronic mail. Contrast with *circuit switching*.

packing density

The number of bits or tracks per inch of recording surface. Also refers to the number of memory bits or other electronic components on a chip.

pad

(1) To fill a data structure with padding characters.

(2) (PAD) (Packet Assembler/Disassembler) A communications device that formats outgoing data into packets of the required length for transmission in an X.25 packet switching network. It also strips the data out of incoming packets.

padding

Characters used to fill up unused portions of a data structure, such as a field or communications message. A field may be padded with blanks, zeros or nulls.

paddle

An input device that moves the screen cursor in a back-and-forth motion. It has a dial and one or more buttons and is typically used in games to hit balls and steer objects. See *joy stick*.

page

(1) In virtual memory systems, a segment of the program that is transferred into memory.

(2) In videotex systems, a transmitted frame.

(3) In word processing, a printed page.

(4) On the Web, a single HTML document. See *HTML*.

page break

In printing, a code that marks the end of a page. A "hard" page break, inserted by the user, breaks the page at that location. "Soft" page breaks are created by word processing and report programs based on the current page length setting.

page description language

A device-independent, high-level language for defining printer output. If an application generates output in a page description language, such as PostScript, the output can be printed on any printer that supports it.

Much of the character and graphics shaping is done within the printer rather than in the user's computer. Instead of downloading an entire font from the computer to the printer, which includes the design of each character, a command to build a particular font is sent, and the printer creates the characters from font outlines. Likewise, a command to draw a circle is sent to the printer rather than sending the actual bits of the circle image.

page fault

A virtual memory interrupt that signals that the next instruction or item of data is not in physical memory and must be swapped back in from the disk. If the required page on disk cannot be found, then a page fault error occurs, which means that either the operating system or an application has corrupted the virtual memory. If such an error occurs, the user has to reload the application.

page frame

See *EMS*.

page header

Common text that is printed at the top of every page. It generally includes the page number and headings above each column.

page layout program

A desktop publishing program such as PageMaker and QuarkXPress. See *desktop publishing*.

PageMaker

A full-featured desktop publishing program for Windows and Macintosh from Adobe. PageMaker is the de facto standard in the graphics arts industry. It is used to create ads, brochures, newsletters and books of all sizes and kinds. Originally introduced for the Mac in 1985 by Aldus Corporation, it set the standard for desktop publishing. In fact, Paul Brainerd, president of Aldus, coined the term. The PC version was introduced in 1987 for Windows 1.0 and was the first non-Microsoft Windows application.

page makeup

Formatting a printed page, which includes the layout of headers, footers, columns, page numbers, graphics, rules and borders.

PageMill

Web authoring software for Windows and Macintosh from Adobe. It provides a visual environment for creating Web pages. SiteMill is an additional program that works with PageMill for managing the entire site.

page mode memory

The common dynamic RAM chip design. Memory bits are accessed by row and column coordinates. Prior to page mode, each bit was accessed by pulsing the row and column select lines. With page mode, the row is selected only once for all the columns (bits) within the row, resulting in faster access. Page mode memory is also called *fast page mode* memory (also FPM memory, FPM RAM, FPM DRAM). The "fast" designation was added back when newer chips ran at 100 nanoseconds and faster.

page on demand

Also called *byte serving*, it is the ability to retrieve a specific page or set of pages rather than the entire document.

page printer

A printer that prints a page at a time. Laser, LED and solid ink printers are examples. The first page printers were huge, floor-standing devices, and although such "digital printing presses" today print much faster and even in color, the ubiquitous page printer is the desktop laser printer. See *laser printer, LED printer, solid ink printer, digital printing* and *printer*.

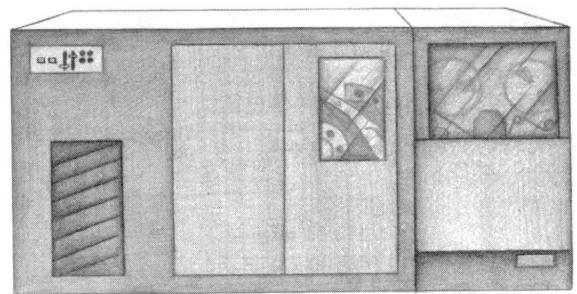

The Page Printer
Whenever you need to print a million forms in a hurry, use a high-speed page printer.

page recognition

Software that recognizes the content of a printed page which has been scanned into the computer. It uses OCR to convert the printed words into computer text and should be able to differentiate text from other elements on the page, such as pictures and captions.

page view

A Web page, which can be of any length.

pagination

(1) Page numbering.

(2) Laying out printed pages, which includes setting up and printing columns, rules and borders. Although pagination is used synonymously with *page makeup*, the term often refers to the printing of long manuscripts rather than ads and brochures.

paging

(1) In a virtual memory computer, paging is the transfer of program segments (pages) into and out of memory. Although paging is the primary mechanism for virtual memory, excessive paging is not desired. See *thrashing*.

(2) A communications service that is evolving from a one-way beeper service to a one-way text service, and eventually, to a two-way text and voice service. It is expected that the paging industry will undergo several changes as new hand-held devices and wireless services mature. See *PCS*.

paint

(1) In computer graphics, to "paint" the screen using a tablet stylus or mouse to simulate a paintbrush.

(2) To transfer a dot matrix image as in the phrase "the laser printer paints the image onto a photosensitive drum."

(3) To create a screen form by typing anywhere on screen. To "paint" the screen with text.

Painter

A full-featured paint program for Macintosh and Windows from MetaCreations Corporation, Carpinteria, CA, (www.metacreations.com), formerly Fractal Design Corporation. Painter is noted for its sophisticated image editing capabilities as well as its ability to simulate natural painting styles, such as oil, watercolor and charcoal, on almost every kind of paper texture. The disks and manuals have come appropriately packaged... in a paint can! See illustration on next page.

paint program

A graphics program that allows the user to simulate painting on screen with the use of a mouse or graphics tablet. The images that are generated in a paint program, which are made up of dots, are called *bitmapped graphics* or just plain *bitmaps*. Full-featured paint programs are called *image editors*. They include a variety of image editing capabilities for enhancing scanned images, which are also created as bitmaps.

Unlike drawing programs, which generate vector graphics images, the picture objects created in a paint program cannot be easily isolated and scaled independently. Bitmapped graphics are much like a painted canvas: objects are "painted" together. However, colors can be changed and parts or all of an image can be run through image filters to create a wide variety of special effects. See *image editor* and *Painter*.

PAL

(1) (Programmable Array Logic) A type of programmable logic chip (PLD) that contains arrays of programmable AND gates and predefined OR gates. See *PLA* and *PLD*.

(2) (Phase Alternating Line) A color TV standard that was developed in Germany. It broadcasts 25 interlaced frames per second (50 half frames per second) at 625 lines of resolution. Brazil uses PAL M, which broadcasts 30 fps. PAL is used throughout Europe and China as well as in various African, South American and Middle Eastern countries. PAL's color signals are maintained automatically, and the TV set does not have a user-adjustable hue control. See *NTSC* and *SECAM*.

(3) (Paradox Application Language) Paradox's programming language.

palette

(1) In computer graphics, a range of colors used for display and printing. See *color palette*.

(2) A collection of on-screen painting tools.

(3) A toolbar that contains a set of functions for any kind of application.

palmtop

A computer small enough to hold in one hand and operate with the other. Palmtops may have specialized keyboards or keypads for data entry applications or have small qwerty keyboards.

pan

(1) In computer graphics, to move (while viewing) to a different part of an image without changing magnification.

(2) To move (while viewing) horizontally across a text record.

(3) (PAN) (Personal Area Network) A transmission technology developed at IBM's Almaden Research Center, San Jose, CA, that lets people transfer information by touch. For example, you could exchange electronic business cards by shaking hands. By touching your pager in one hand, you could send the calling telephone number

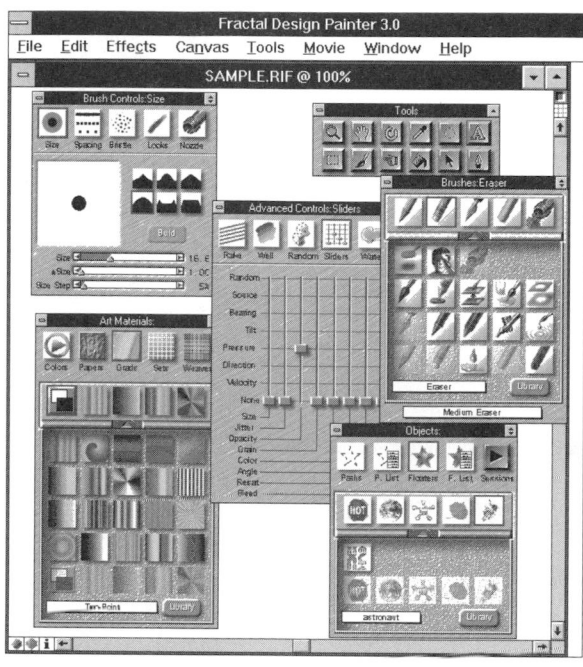

An Electronic Paintbox
Painter offers the most amazing variety of painting tools on the market. You can fine tune your brushes, felt pens, ink pens and chalk and even simulate different types of paper. The number of settings is staggering, and the tools shown in this screen shot are merely a small sampling of all that are available.

One of the First Palmtops
This was one of the first fully-functional 486 palmtops. Weighing less than a pound and a half, it used a CompactFlash card (shown on right) and a PC Card (not visible) for storage. *(Photo courtesy of SanDisk Corporation.)*

to your cell phone in the other. A PAN-enabled unit worn on the wrist could transmit a user's ID to all variety of check-in or check-out machines (ATMs, security checkpoints, hospital admittance, etc.). The miniscule amount of current is a thousand times less than the electricity generated by combing your hair and is easily conducted through the body.

panacea

Some antidote or remedy that completely solves a problem. Most so called panaceas in this industry, if they survive at all, wind up sitting alongside and working with the products they were supposed to replace. In addition, nothing solves a problem without introducing its own new set of problems. See *Systemantics*.

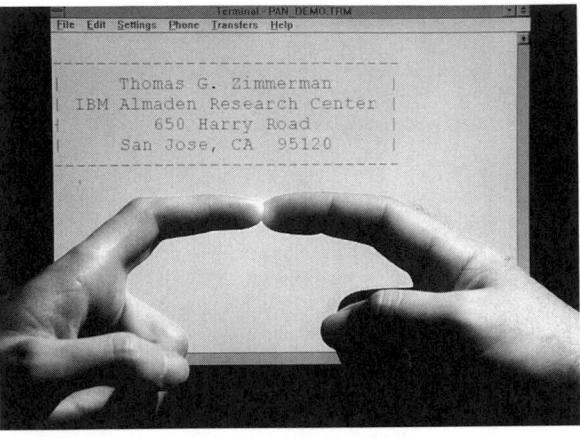

Touch and Transfer
Reminiscent of the movie E.T., this photo depicts the transfer of business card information by touching fingers. *(Photo courtesy of IBM Almaden Research Center.)*

Panvalet

See *CA-Panvalet*.

PAP

(Password Authentication Protocol) The most basic access control protocol for logging onto a network. A table of usernames and passwords is stored on a server. When users log on, their usernames and passwords are sent to the server for verification. Contrast with *CHAP*, which encrypts the username and password before transmitting it.

paperless office

Long predicted, the paperless office is still a myth. Although paper usage has been reduced in some organizations, it has increased in others. Today's PCs make it easy to churn out documents.

As one technology eliminates paper, another comes along to increase its usage. While laptops with gigabyte hard disks help replace paper on the road, the Internet comes along with tons of interesting Web pages that beg to be printed.

Color laser printers, which are slowly being implemented now in the corporate world, are expected to increase dramatically as prices fall over the next several years. This alone will increase paper usage. Perhaps the only thing that could ever bring about a paperless office is if paper costs went through the roof.

Xplor International predicts that by 2005, 30% of all documents will still be printed with the rest created and maintained electronically. That compares with 90% of all documents being printed in the mid 1990s. However, the amount of information is doubling every three to four years. Therefore, in 2005, there will still be more than twice as much printed output as in the 1990s. As Keith Davidson, Executive Director of Xplor International, succinctly put it, "the paperless office is as about as realistic as the paperless toilet!"

paper tape

(1) A slow, low-capacity, sequential storage medium used in the first half of the 20th century to hold data as patterns of punched holes.

(2) A paper roll printed by a calculator or cash register.

paradigm

Pronounced "para-dime." A model, example or pattern.

Paradox

See *Corel Paradox*.

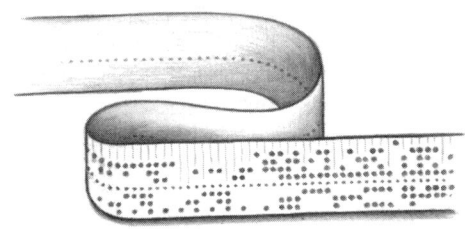

Paper Tape
Paper tape was widely used in the early years of computing as a storage medium. Its capacity of only a handful of characters per inch seems pitiful by today's storage standards.

paragraph

(1) In DOS programming, a 16 byte block. Memory addresses are generated as "segment:offset," where the segment is expressed in paragraphs. To compute an address, the segment register is shifted left four bits, which effectively multiplies it by 16. For example, in the address A000:0100, the A000 becomes A0000, as follows:

```
Segment   A0000    655,360
Offset     0100        256
Result    A0100    655,616
```

This means there are 4,096 possibilities for expressing each memory byte, a situation that has helped generate confusion.

(2) In word processing and desktop publishing, a collection of words and sentences that contains an end-of-line character (return, line feed or both) at the end of it. From the viewpoint of the software, even a single word followed by a return is a paragraph.

paragraph tag

In desktop publishing, a code embedded in the text that defines a style for the paragraph that follows it. It defines typeface, tab, indent, letter spacing, alignment and other settings. See *character tag*.

parallel channel

(1) A channel that transmits data over several wires simultaneously, typically in increments of a byte (8-bit channel, 16-bit, etc.).

(2) A parallel channel for IBM mainframes that transmits up to 4.5MB/sec. In byte multiplexing mode, bytes are interleaved from several low speed devices. In block multiplexing mode, the channel provides full bandwidth to the device, but can disconnect when the device does not require a data transfer such as when a disk is performing a seek. IBM's parallel channel is also known as a bus and tag channel, OEMI channel and block multiplexor channel.

parallel computer

A computer that can perform multiple processes simultaneously. See *parallel computing*.

parallel computing

Solving a problem with multiple computers or computers made up of multiple processors. It is an umbrella term for a variety of architectures, including symmetric multiprocessing (SMP), clusters of SMP systems and massively parallel processors (MPPs). See *SMP, MPP, pipeline processing, array processor, vector processor* and *hypercube*.

Parallel Enterprise Server

A family of S/390 (System/390) mainframes from IBM that are air cooled and use CMOS-based microprocessor technology (the CPU is on one chip). Introduced in 1994 as the 9672 series, Parallel Enterprise Servers are rapidly replacing the earlier water-cooled, bipolar machines that are considerably larger and consume significantly more power.

Parallel Enterprise Servers employ symmetric multiprocessing (SMP) and can support up to 10 CPUs per server. Up to 32 servers can be tied together in a Parallel Sysplex cluster.

Parallel Enterprise Server model designations do not jive with the generations. Generation 1 used Rx1 model numbers. Generation 2 used Rx2 and Rx3. G3 is Rx4, G4 is Rx5, and G5 is Rx6. The G5 product line was introduced in May of 1998.

See *IBM mainframes, Parallel Sysplex* and *G5*.

parallel interface

A multiline channel that transfers one or more bytes simultaneously. Personal computers generally connect printers via a Centronics 36-wire parallel interface, which transfers one byte at a time over eight wires, the remaining ones being used for control signals. Large computer parallel interfaces transfer more than one byte at a time. It is faster than a serial interface, because it transfers several bits concurrently. Contrast with *serial interface*. See *Centronics*.

parallelism

An overlapping of processing, input/output (I/O) or both.

parallelizing

To generate instructions for a parallel processing computer.

parallel port

A socket on a computer used to connect a printer or other peripheral device. It may also be used to attach a portable hard disk, tape backup or CD-ROM. Transferring files between two PCs can be accomplished by cabling the parallel ports of both machines together and using a file transfer program such as LapLink.

On the back of a PC, the parallel port is a 25-pin female DB-25 connector. In a PC, the parallel port circuit is built into the motherboard. On earlier PCs, it was contained on a small expansion card along with serial ports and a game port, or it was included on the IDE host adapter card, which contained the serial ports and game port as well as floppy disk control.

The IEEE 1284 parallel port provides bi-directional transfer at increased speed and cable length up to 32 feet. See *IEEE 1284*.

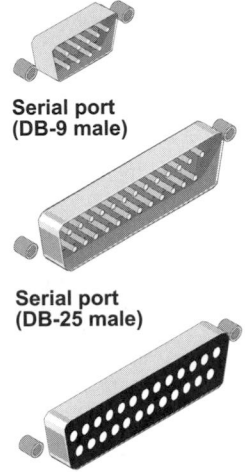

Serial & Parallel Ports on a PC

Serial port
(DB-9 male)

Serial port
(DB-25 male)

Parallel port
(DB-25 female)

A PC usually comes with two serial ports (COM1, COM2) and one parallel port (LPT1).

On the back of the PC, the serial ports are either two male DB-9 connectors or one DB-9 and one DB-25. The parallel port is a DB-25 female connector.

parallel processing

(1) An architecture within a single computer that performs more than one operation at the same time. See *pipeline processing, array processor* and *vector processor*.

(2) An architecture using multiple computers. See *parallel computing*.

Parallel Query Server

An early CMOS-based mainframe from IBM, specialized for decision support. It was later replaced by the Parallel Enterprise Server. See *Parallel Enterprise Server*.

parallel server

A computer system used as a server that provides various degrees of simultaneous processing. See *SMP, MPP* and *multiprocessing*.

Parallel Sysplex

IBM's umbrella name for its System/390 multiprocessing architecture. It includes a variety of features that allow multiple System/390 computers to be clustered together as a single system with data sharing and workload balancing. For example, the Sysplex Timer external clock is used to synchronize time-of-day clocks in multiple processors. If failure occurs in a multiprocessor complex, precise transaction time stamps are required for accurate rollback and recovery.

Parallel Transaction Server

An early CMOS-based mainframe from IBM, specialized for transaction processing. It was later replaced by the Parallel Enterprise Server. See *Parallel Enterprise Server*.

parallel transmission

Transmitting one or more bytes at a time using a cable with multiple lines dedicated to data (8, 16, 32 lines, etc.). Contrast with *serial transmission*.

parameter

(1) Any value passed to a program by the user or by another program in order to customize the program for a particular purpose. A parameter may be anything; for example, a file name, a coordinate, a range of values, a money amount or a code of some kind. Parameters may be required as in parameter-driven software (see below) or they may be optional. Parameters are often entered as a series of values

Computer Desktop Encyclopedia

following the program name when the program is loaded.

A DOS switch is a parameter. For example, in the DOS Dir command **dir /p** the DOS switch **/p** (pause after every screenful) is a parameter.

(2) In programming, a value passed to a subroutine or function for processing. Programming today's graphical applications with languages such as C, C++ and Pascal requires knowledge of hundreds, if not thousands, of parameters.

In the following C function, which creates the text window for the Windows version of this database, there are 11 parameters passed to the CreateWindow routine. Some of them call yet other functions for necessary information. In order to call this routine in a program, the programmer must decide what the values are for every parameter.

```
hWndText = CreateWindow      (
    "TextWClass",
    NULL,
    WS_CHILD|WS_BORDER|WS_VSCROLL|WS_TABSTOP,
    xChar*23+GetSystemMetrics(SM_CXVSCROLL)+8,
    yChar*4,
    Rect.right-Rect.left+1-xChar*23-2*GetSystemMetrics(SM_CXVSCROLL)+5,
    yChar*(Lines+1)+2,
    hWnd,
    IDC_TEXTLIST,
    (HANDLE)hInstance,
    NULL                     ) ;
```

parameter-driven

Software that requires external values expressed at runtime. A parameter-driven program solves a problem that is partially or entirely described by the values (parameters) that are entered at the time the program is loaded. For example, typing **bio 6-20-36** might load a program that calculates biorhythms for someone born on June 20, 1936. In this case, the date is a required parameter. The more user-friendly approach is a menu-driven program that would have you select a menu option and present you with a data entry box to type in date of birth.

Parameter-driven software is widely used when a program is called for and loaded by another program rather than by the user. Since the parameters are generated by one program and used by another, any number of parameters can be passed no matter how obscure the codes.

parameter RAM

See *PRAM*.

parametric modeling

In a CAD system, the ability to maintain consistent relationships between elements even though the object is scaled to different dimensions. For example, it would ensure that two holes are always one inch apart, or that one hole is always offset two inches from the edge, or that one lever is always half the size of another, etc.

PARC

(Palo Alto Research Center, Palo Alto, CA, www.parc.xerox.com) Founded in 1970, PARC is Xerox Corporation's research and development center. Although Xerox headquarters are in Stamford, Connecticut, and manufacturing and marketing are in Rochester, New York, PARC is located in the heart of Silicon Valley.

Over the years, PARC has made significant contributions to the computer industry, including the development of the Smalltalk programming language, the mouse and graphical user interface (GUI) and Ethernet. It continues to be on the cutting edge of high technology. See *Xerox*.

parental control software

A special browser or filtering program designed to reject Web sites not suited for children. Such programs may screen pages by word content, site rating or by URL, using an updated database of objectionable sites, or any combination of these techniques. Visit the sites mentioned on the next page. See *PICS* and *RSAC*.

Information	www.netparents.org
ChiBrow	www.chibrow.com
Cyber Patrol	www.cyberpatrol.com
CYBERsitter	www.solidoak.com
Net Nanny	www.netnanny.com
Net Shepherd	www.netshepherd.com
Surfin' Annette	www.spycatcher.com
SurfWatch	www.surfwatch.com
WebChaperone	www.webchaperone.com
WizGuard	www.wizguard.com

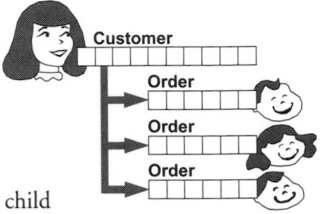

parent-child

In database management, a relationship between two files. The parent contains required data about a subject, such as employees and customers. The child is the offspring; for example, an order is the child to the customer, who is the parent.

parent directory

A disk directory that is one level up from the current directory. In DOS and Windows, two dots (..) refer to the preceding directory level, or parent directory.

parent program

The main, or primary, program or first program loaded into memory. See *child program*.

PA-RISC

(Precision Architecture-**RISC**) A proprietary RISC-based CPU architecture from HP that was introduced in 1986. It is the foundation of HP's 3000 and 9000 computer families.

parity

See *parity checking* and *RAID*.

parity bit

An extra bit attached to the byte, character or word used to detect errors in transmission.

parity checking

An error detection technique that tests the integrity of digital data within the computer system or over a network. Parity checking uses an extra ninth bit that holds a 0 or 1 depending on the data content of the byte. Each time a byte is transferred or transmitted, the parity bit is tested.

Even parity systems make the parity bit 1 when there is an even number of 1 bits in the byte. Odd parity systems make it 1 when there is an odd number of 1 bits.

There are 12% more memory cells in nine-bit parity memory than there are in eight-bit non-parity memory. To shave costs, many desktop computers are built with non-parity memory; however, sometimes you can choose to use either type.

parity drive

A separate disk drive that holds parity bits in a disk array. See *RAID*.

parity error

An error condition that occurs when the parity bit of a character is found to be incorrect.

parity memory, parity RAM

Memory that uses a ninth bit for parity checking. See *parity checking*.

park

To retract the read/write head on a hard disk to its home location before the unit is physically moved in order to prevent damage. Most modern drives park themselves when the power is turned off.

parse

To analyze a sentence or language statement. Parsing breaks down words into functional units that can be converted into machine language. For example, to parse the dBASE expression **sum salary for title = "MANAGER"** SUM must be identified as the primary command, FOR as a conditional search, TITLE as a field name and MANAGER as the data to be searched.

Parsing breaks down a natural language request, such as "**What's the total of all the managers' salaries**" into the commands required by a high-level language, such as in the example above.

parser
A routine that performs parsing operations on a computer or natural language.

partition
A reserved part of disk or memory that is set aside for some purpose. On a PC, new hard disks must be partitioned before they can be formatted for the operating system, and the Fdisk utility is used for this task. It can make one partition, creating one drive letter for the entire disk, or it can make several partitions sized to your requirements. For example, drives C:, D: and E: could be the same physical disk, but they would act like three separate drives to the operating system and user. See *Fdisk*.

partitioning
To divide a resource or application into smaller pieces. See *partition, application partitioning* and *PDQ*.

Pascal
A high-level programming language developed by Swiss professor Niklaus Wirth in the early 1970s and named after the French mathematician, Blaise Pascal. It is noted for its structured programming, which caused it to achieve popularity initially in academic circles. Pascal has had strong influence on subsequent languages, such as Ada, dBASE and PAL. See *Turbo Pascal*.

Pascal is available in both interpreter and compiler form and has unique ways of defining variables. For example, a set of values can be stated for a variable, and if any other value is stored in it, the program generates an error at runtime. A Pascal set is an array-like structure that can hold a varying number of predefined values. Sets can be matched and manipulated providing powerful non-numeric programming capabilities. The following Turbo Pascal example converts Fahrenheit to Celsius:

```
program convert;
var
fahr, cent : integer;
begin
 write('Enter Fahrenheit ');
 readln(fahr);
 cent := (fahr - 32) * 5 / 9;
 writeln('Celsius is ',cent)
end.
```

Pascaline
A calculating machine developed in 1642 by French mathematician Blaise Pascal. It could only add and subtract, but gained attention because 50 units were placed in prominent locations throughout Europe. Accountants expressed grave concern that they might be replaced by technology!

passive backplane
A backplane that adds no processing in the circuit. See *backplane*.

passive component
A device that does not have any impact on the electrical signals or the data that passes through it. See *active component*.

passive hub
A central connecting device in a network that joins wires from several stations in a star configuration. It does not provide any processing or regeneration of signals. Contrast with *active hub* and *intelligent hub*. See *hub*.

The Pascaline
We're always worried about technology taking over our jobs! *(Photo courtesy of Pascal Institute.)*

passive matrix

A common LCD technology used in laptops. Passive matrix displays (DSTN, CSTN, etc.) are not quite as sharp and do not have as broad a viewing angle as active matrix (TFT) displays, but they have improved dramatically over the years. Looking head on into a passive matrix screen is not all that different than looking at an active matrix (TFT) screen. The difference is more noticeable with the viewing angle. A person looking from the side sees a dimmer image with passive matrix. See *LCD*.

passive star

See *passive hub*.

password

A word or code used to serve as a security measure against unauthorized access to data. It is normally managed by the operating system or DBMS. However, the computer can only verify the legitimacy of the password, not the legitimacy of the user. See *NCSC*.

paste

See *cut & paste*.

patch

A temporary or quick fix to a program. Too many patches in a program make it difficult to maintain. The term may also refer to changing the actual machine code when it is not convenient to recompile the source program. See *MIDI patch*.

patch cable, patch cord

A short length of cable used to connect ports in patch panels or in expansion boards and systems that are in close proximity. It is typically a telephone, data communications, audio or video cable that is generally no longer than 10 feet in length.

patch panel

A group of sockets that function as a manual switching center between incoming and outgoing lines in a communications or other electronic or electrical system.

path

(1) In communications, the route between any two nodes. Same as line, channel, link or circuit.

(2) In database management, the route from one set of data to another, for example, from customers to orders.

(3) The route to a file on a disk. In DOS, Windows and OS/2, the path for file MYLIFE located in subdirectory STORIES within directory JOE on drive C: looks like:

```
c:\joe\stories\mylife
```

The equivalent UNIX path follows. UNIX knows which drive is used:

```
/joe/stories/mylife
```

Although not common, the Macintosh can also use a path in certain command sequences; for example, with "hard disk" as the drive, the same path is:

```
hard disk:joe:stories:mylife
```

path determination

In a network router or switch, the processing that determines which output port the incoming packet or frame is diverted to.

Path not found

A DOS error message that means you entered an invalid path name.

path vector protocol

A routing protocol, sometimes known as a policy routing protocol, that is used to span different autonomous systems. EGP and BGP are examples. The routing table maintains the autonomous systems that are traversed in order to reach the destination system. Contrast with *distance vector protocol* and *link state protocol*. See *autonomous system, routing protocol, EGP* and *BGP*.

PATHWORKS

A network operating system from Digital that lets a VAX minicomputer function as a server for DOS, Windows, Windows NT, OS/2 and Macintosh clients. DECnet, TCP/IP, AppleTalk and NetWare protocols are supported.

PAX

(1) (Private Automatic Exchange) An inhouse intercom system.

(2) (Parallel Architecture Extended) A parallel processing environment standard based on Intel's i860 RISC chip, UNIX System V and Alliant Computer's parallel and 3-D graphics technologies.

payload

The data-carrying capacity of some structure. It typically refers to a part of a packet or frame in a communications system that holds the message data in contrast to the headers, which are considered overhead.

payware

Software distributed for money. Contrast with *freeware*.

PBX

(Private Branch eXchange) An inhouse telephone switching system that interconnects telephone extensions to each other, as well as to the outside telephone network. It may include functions such as least cost routing for outside calls, call forwarding, conference calling and call accounting.

Modern PBXs use all-digital methods for switching and can often handle digital terminals and telephones along with analog telephones.

PC

(1) Also see *printed circuit board*.

(2) (Personal Computer) Although the term PC is sometimes used to refer to any kind of personal computer (Mac, Amiga, etc.), in this database and in general, PC refers to

An Early PBX
This PBX began operation in Bangor, Maine in 1883.
(Photo courtesy of AT&T.)

computers that conform to the PC standard originally developed by IBM. Today, PC hardware is governed by Intel, and PC operating systems by Microsoft. The PC is the world's largest computer base.

PCs are used as stand-alone personal computers or as workstations and file servers in a LAN (local area network). They predominantly run under Windows although many DOS systems still linger. If an Intel-based PC is used as a server running UNIX or other operating system, it is typically called an Intel-based server, or x86-based server, not a PC.

Although there are literally thousands of PC vendors, from mom and pop shops to large mail order houses (Dell, Gateway, etc.) to the major computer companies (Compaq, HP, etc.), and of course IBM, still one of the world's largest PC makers, all PCs use an Intel x86 or compatible CPU.

After IBM introduced the PC in 1981, the first attempts at cloning it were not all successful. From 1982 to 1985, there were a lot of "almost compatible" PCs. However, as soon as the part of the operating system known as the BIOS was successfully cloned and made commercially available, true compatibles appeared in abundance.

Today, you can replace floppies, hard disks and video displays, as well as add a scanner, CD-ROM or other device without too much difficulty. In general, PC components are interchangeable. Expansion cards are easily plugged in and out, and an entire motherboard can be replaced with one (from a different vendor) in about a half hour.

The problems come when you add a second or third device and run into a conflict with an existing one. Before Windows 95, having to modify DOS's infamous AUTOEXEC.BAT and CONFIG.SYS configuration files has caused every novice to flinch in the beginning.

Conflicts aside, the PC has become a commodity item, winding its way onto the shelves of a wide variety of retail outlets. This is a testimonial to the power of a computer standard, even one fraught with loopholes and inconsistencies.

Today, most PCs run most software and work with most plug-in boards, but there are always exceptions. With the myriads of adapters and applications available for the PC, one device, application or utility can always conflict with another. The way to guarantee that something works is to try it. This has been true since day one in the computer business.

What's Inside a PC

PC-8

A symbol set that contains the extended ASCII characters of the IBM PC.

PC 9x

Specifications from Microsoft and Intel that define minimum system requirements for Windows-based PCs. Thus far, the PC 95, PC 97, PC 98 and PC 99 specs have been defined, and details change

PC 66

A specification from Intel for designing memory chips that support the 66MHz system bus in Pentium CPUs. See *PC 100*.

PC 95

The first PC 9x specification, which required that ISA cards be Plug and Play compliant. See *PC 9x*.

PC 97

The second PC 9x specification, which was aimed at Windows 97 (now Win 98) and NT 5.0. It defines three categories (Basic, Workstation and Entertainment), retains the ISA bus and adds USB and FireWire buses. The minimum requirements are a 120MHz CPU and 16MB of RAM. See *PC 9x*.

PC 98

(1) The third PC 9x specification, which defines six categories (Consumer, Office, Mobile, NetPC, Entertainment and Workstation). It eliminates the ISA bus and pushes the minimum requirements to a 200MHz CPU with 32MB of RAM. See *PC 9x*.

(2) (PC-98) A personal computer series from NEC. It is the most popular PC in Japan.

PC 99

The fourth PC 9x specification, which defines the minimum system as a 300MHz machine with 128KB of L2 cache and two USB ports. Consumer PCs must have 32MB of RAM, and office machines must have 64MB. The ISA bus is eliminated.

PC 100

A specification from Intel for designing memory chips that support the 100MHz system bus expected in Pentium II CPUs in 1998. See *PC 66*.

PC/104

A PC bus architecture that uses 3.5" square modules that snap together. This "stack through" bus provides a modular, compact and rugged design for building process control and embedded systems.frequently. See *PC 99*.

PCB, PC board

See *printed circuit board.*

PC bus

The bus architecture used in first-generation IBM PCs and XTs. It refers to the original 8-bit bus, which accepted only 8-bit expansion boards. In 286s and up, it was superseded by the 16-bit AT bus, later known as the ISA bus. Contrast with *ISA, EISA* and *Micro Channel.*

PC Card

A credit-card sized, removable module for portable computers standardized by PCMCIA. PC Cards are also known as "PCMCIA cards." PC Cards are 16-bit devices that are used to attach modems, network adapters, sound cards, radio transceivers, solid state disks and hard disks to a portable computer. The PC Card is a "plug and play" device, which is configured automatically by the Card Services software (see below).

All PC Cards are 85.6 mm long by 54 mm wide (3.37" x 2.126") and use a 68-pin connector. The original Type I card is 3.3 mm thick and is typically used to hold memory.

Type II cards (5.0 mm thick) are commonly used for memory, modems and LAN adapters in laptops. Type III cards (10.5 mm thick) are used to hold a hard disk, wireless transceiver or other peripheral that needs more space. The Type III slot can hold two Type II cards.

Toshiba introduced a 16 mm Type IV card, but this has not been officially adopted by the PCMCIA. Smaller cards will work in a Type IV slot.

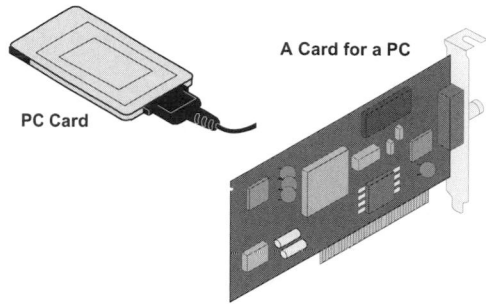

The PC Card

The PC Card (left) on laptops is the equivalent expansion mechanism as the printed circuit board (right) is on desktop computers.

Card and Socket Services

In order to use a PC Card slot in the computer, Card and Socket services must be loaded, typically at system startup. Card and Socket Services software is generally included with laptops that have PC Card slots. It also comes packaged with PC Cards.

Card Services manage system resources required by the PC Card, and, on PCs, determines which IRQs and memory and I/O addresses are assigned. They also manage hot swapping and pass changes in events to higher-level drivers written for specific cards.

Card Services talk to Socket Services, which is the lowest level of software that communicates directly with the PC Card controller chips. Socket Services can be built into the system BIOS or added via software.

CardBus

In early 1995, PCMCIA introduced the 32-bit CardBus standard. Although electrically different, the CardBus is architecturally identical to the PCI bus. The CardBus supports bus mastering and accommodates cards operating at different voltages. Its advanced power managment features allows the computer to take advantage of CardBus cards designed to idle or turn off in order to increase battery life. The CardBus specification allows data transfer up to 132 Mbytes/sec over a 33MHz, 32-bit data path. For more information, visit www.pc-card.com. See *PCMCIA.*

PC chipset

A set of chips that provides the interfaces between all of the PC's subsystems. It provides the buses and electronics to allow the CPU, memory and input/output devices to interact. Most PC chipsets, which are contained on from one to four chips, also include built-in EIDE support. The PC chipset, CPU, memory, clock, buses, keyboard circuit and BIOS make up the PC motherboard.

PC compatible

A misguided reference to a PC. The term IBM compatible is more accurate, because IBM made the first PC. Even that has little meaning today, because Intel and Microsoft set PC standards. The correct way to refer to a PC is to call it a "PC."

PC CPU models

The brains of the PC is a CPU, or processor, from the Intel 8086 family (x86) of microprocessors or from a company that makes x86-compatible CPUs, such as AMD (Advanced Micro Devices) and Cyrix Corporation. IBM also makes its own x86-compatible chips. Following are the major classes of PCs, starting with the very first models

XT CLASS - 8086, 8088

The original PC launched by IBM in 1981 used the 16-bit 8088 CPU. This chip family was designed so that the major installed base of CP/M applications could be easily ported to the new architecture.

Unfortunately, it was limited to one megabyte of memory and was designed with limited flexibility. Nobody knew this would become the world's greatest hardware standard. Although more advanced CPUs (386, 486, Pentium, etc.) came later, they had to build in 16-bit operating modes to conform to the original standard and run all the DOS and Windows 3.x applications on the market.

These first PCs, known as XT-class machines, are sold only at computer flea markets. They are still usable with older DOS software.

AT CLASS - 286

First used in the IBM AT in 1984, the 286's 16-bit CPU can address up to 16 megabytes of memory. ATs were just faster XTs, and memory above one megabyte was rarely used for applications until Windows 3.0 became popular. By then, 386s and 486s were widely available. AT-class machines were used under DOS, but were extremely sluggish under Windows.

386, 486 & Pentium

First used by Compaq in 1986, the 386 introduced an advanced architecture that has been carrier forth in all subsequent chips, including the 486 and Pentium models. The 386 brought a 32-bit mode of operation and the ability to address four gigabytes of memory, although even today, most PC motherboards cannot hold anywhere near that amount of memory. The 32-bit mode was rarely used until Windows 95 was introduced.

The 486 came out in late 1989 and offered faster speed and a built-in math coprocessor, which is required by CAD programs. In 1993, the Pentium was introduced and is now the entry level CPU in desktop and laptop PCs. The Pentium Pro, introduced in 1995, is optimized for 32-bit operating systems and applications. Users running Windows 3.1 are better off with the straight Pentium. The Pentium MMX and the Pentium II are Pentium and Pentium Pro CPUs respectively with additional instructions for speeding up multimedia applications. Programs must be written to execute the new instructions in order to take advantage of it. See *PC operating environments*.

PC data buses

The bus in a PC is the common pathway between the CPU and the peripheral devices. Controller boards for the video, disks and other devices plug directly into slots in the bus.

ISA

The original PC used an 8-bit bus known as the PC or XT bus. When the AT came out, the bus was extended to 16-bits, and motherboards became available with a mix of 8- and 16-bit slots. The 8-bit cards fit in both slots, but 16-bit cards require 16-bit slots. The 16-bit bus has become known as the ISA ("i-suh") bus, or Industry Standard Architecture bus.

Micro Channel

When IBM introduced the PS/2 line, it switched from ISA to the high-speed 32-bit Micro Channel (MCA) bus. MCA provided bus mastering, but it was rarely used. Later, IBM introduced ISA-based PS/2 models for greater compatibility with the rest of the world and eventually abandoned Micro Channel in favor of PCI.

EISA

To counter IBM's Micro Channel and extend the ISA bus from 16 to 32 bits, EISA ("e-suh") was conceived by major PC vendors in 1988. The EISA bus accepts both EISA and ISA boards, but still runs at the same slow ISA clock speeds in order to accommodate ISA boards.

VL-bus & PCI (Local Bus)

The VL-bus and PCI bus improve performance by providing a higher-speed channel to the CPU than the slower ISA and EISA buses. These two buses were known as local buses when they were originally introduced. Today, the PCI bus has become the de facto standard for Pentium PCs, and the local bus nomenclature is no longer used.

AGP

The most recent addition to the bus line is the Accelerated Graphics Port (AGP). Running at twice the speed of the PCI bus, there is typically one AGP port used only for the display adapter.

PCD file

See *Photo CD*.

PC display modes

The screen resolution on a PC is determined by an expansion board, called a *display adapter* or *graphics adapter*, which is plugged into one of the computer's expansion slots. The monitor must also be able to adjust to the resolutions of the display adapter. The common display adapter is the VGA card.

All display adapters come with their own drivers for Windows, which is installed after the adapter is plugged in. The driver lets Windows display its output at a certain number of resolutions and colors. In Windows 3.1, users switch resolutions in the software control panel supplied by the card vendor. Windows 95/98 and NT have a built-in control panel for the display.

The display adapter may also come with drivers for the DOS version of AutoCAD or other specialized graphics program under DOS. Such drivers have no effect on Windows or other DOS applications and are used only by that specific application.

When the computer boots up in DOS, the display is in text mode with an on-screen resolution of 720x400 pixels and 16 colors. When Windows is loaded, the PC is switched to the graphics mode last set in the control panel. Graphics applications that run in a DOS-only machine do the same thing. They switch the PC to the graphics mode that was previously set.

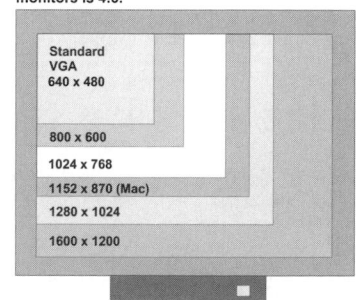

The aspect ratio of most computer monitors is 4:3.

Screen Resolutions
At higher resolutions, more of the document is visible, but the text and images will appear smaller.

The primary screen resolutions are 640x480, 800x600, 1024x768 and 1280x1024. At higher resolutions, more of the document is visible, but the text and images appear smaller. On smaller monitors, 640x480 is used. On 17" monitors, 800x600 is often used, and 1024x768 and above is common on 20 and 21" monitors. Display adapters may also provide a 1600x1200 mode, and adapters with higher resolutions are available for demanding applications.

The number of colors that can be displayed jump in large increments from 256, to 65K to 16 million. Although high-end adapters can provide maximum colors at maximum resolution, it is typically a tradeoff. The higher the resolution, the fewer the colors. Following is a summary of PC display modes.

```
VESA STANDARDS - SUPER VGA
640x480 text & graphics (256-16M colors)
800x600 text & graphics (16-16M colors)
1024x768 text & graphics (16-16M colors)
1280x1024 text & graphics (16-16M colors)


IBM STANDARDS
MDA   720x350 text only, monochrome
CGA   320x200 text & graphics (4 colors)
EGA   640x350 text & graphics (16 colors)
MCGA  640x400 text; 320x200 graphics (256 cols)
VGA   720x400 text; 640x480 graphics (16 colors)
8514  1024x768 text & graphics (256 colors)
XGA   1024x768 text & graphics (256 colors)


HERCULES STANDARD
720x348 text & graphics (monochrome)
```

REQUIRED DISPLAY ADAPTER MEMORY (MB)

RESOLUTION	NUMBER OF COLORS			
	16 (4 bit)	256 (8 bit)	65K (16 bit)	16M (24 bit)
640 x 480	.5	.5	1	2
800 x 600	.5	1	2	2
1024 x 768	1	1	2	4
1152 x 870	1	2	2	4
1280 x 1024	1	2	4	4
1600 x 1200	2	2	4	8

Memory Requirements
More memory is required on the display adapter for higher resolutions and more colors.

PC-DOS

The DOS operating system originally developed by Microsoft and supplied by IBM on its PCs before Windows 95 became the norm. Up until DOS 6, PC-DOS was almost identical to Microsoft's MS-DOS for non-IBM PCs, and both versions are called *DOS*. See "IBM's DOS 6" under *DOS 6*.

PC EXPO

A trade show for resellers and corporate PC buyers from Miller Freeman. It is held in New York in the summer and in Chicago in the fall. It started in New York in 1983 with 120 exhibitors and 9,600 attendees. In 1997, 500 exhibitors drew 90,000 attendees.

PC floppy disks

Until 1995, there were two kinds of floppy disks routinely used in a PC: the 5.25" disk, housed in a square, flexible envelope, and the 3.5" disk in its rigid plastic case. Today, 5.25" disks are obsolete, and the 3.5" floppy is the standard.

5.25" DISKETTES

The first floppy, the low-density 360KB 5.25" diskette, was widely used as the distribution medium for software even after the high-density 1.2MB drive came out in 1984. The high-density drive also reads and writes the low-density format.

3.5" DISKETTES

The 3.5" diskettes were introduced in a low-density 720KB version on IBM's Convertible laptop. Capacity was doubled to 1.44MB with the PS/2 line. The high-density drive also reads and writes the low-density format. You can tell the difference between the 720KB and 1.44MB disks. Looking at it from the label side with the aluminum slider at the bottom, the 1.44MB disk has a hole in the upper left corner, while the 720KB disk does not.

IBM included its extra-high density 2.88MB floppy drives on selected models. It was compatible with 1.44MB diskettes, but the format never caught on.

```
Floppy Disk Formats

 720KB   3.5"   DS/DD   Low density (Double Density)     DS = double sided
1.44MB   3.5"   DS/HD   High density
2.88MB   3.5"   DS/ED   Extra-high density (IBM)

 360KB   5.25"  DS/DD   Low density (Double Density)
 1.2MB   5.25"  DS/HD   High density
```

PC hard disks

The primary storage medium in a PC is a non-removable hard disk. Hard disks are available with storage capacities up to 9GB and above. Most systems today come with at least 1GB. Today, applications use enormous amounts of disk space compared with a few years ago.

There have been several types of hard disks used on PCs over the years including MFM, RLL, ESDI, IDE and SCSI. Today, most hard disks are either IDE or SCSI. Both types can co-exist within the same computer, in which case the IDE disk is generally the boot disk. The IDE host adapter, which is generally built into the motherboard, can control up to four IDE disks. SCSI adapters can support seven or 15 peripherals.

Since most hard disks are not removable, the low-level physical format of one drive has no bearing on a disk in a different machine. Two computers can be cabled together and files can be transferred from the IDE hard disk of one to the SCSI disk of another. The hard disk controllers are reading and writing their disks according to their own technology.

Removable disk drives provide the convenience of transportability and unlimited storage, although only one disk is in the drive at a time. Removable drives are proprietary, and the cartridges are not interchangeable with other types. Cartridge capacities are up to 1GB and higher.

PCI

(Peripheral Component Interconnect) A peripheral bus commonly used in PCs, Macintoshes and workstations. It was designed primarily by Intel and first appeared on PCs in late 1993. PCI provides a high-speed data path between the CPU and peripheral devices (video, disk, network, etc.). There are typically three or four PCI slots on the motherboard. In a Pentium PC, there is generally a mix of PCI and ISA slots or PCI and EISA slots. Early on, the PCI bus was known as a "local bus."

PCI provides "plug and play" capability, automatically configuring the PCI cards at startup. When PCI is used with the ISA bus, the only thing that is generally required is to indicate in the CMOS memory which IRQs are already in use by ISA cards. PCI takes care of the rest.

PCI allows IRQs to be shared, which helps to solve the problem of limited IRQs available on a PC. For example, if there were only one IRQ left over after ISA devices were given their required IRQs, all PCI devices could share it. In a PCI-only machine, there cannot be insufficient IRQs, as all can be shared.

PCI runs at 33MHz, supports 32- and 64-bit data paths and bus mastering. The number of peripheral devices the bus can handle is based on loads, which have to do with inductance, capacitance and other electrical characteristics. Normally there are 10 loads per bus. The PCI chipset uses three, leaving seven for peripherals. Controllers built onto the motherboard use one load, whereas controllers that plug into an expansion slot use 1.5 loads. See *Concurrent PCI* and *Sebring ring*.

PC input/output

There are three ways of getting data into and out of the PC. The first is via the keyboard, which plugs into a keyboard connector built into the motherboard. The keyboard plugs into a 5-pin DIN or 6-pin mini-DIN socket.

The second is via the data bus, or expansion bus, which is a set of slots on the motherboard. Expansion boards (cards) are plugged into the slots and contain cables to their respective devices. These cards are control circuits for disk drives, the video display, CD-ROM reader and network adapter for example. Scanners often come with their own cards.

The third way is through serial and parallel ports which are input/output pathways built into the motherboard or contained on a separate expansion board. On the back of the PC, there are typically two serial ports, one 9-pin male and one 25-pin male. The first port is named COM1, and the second is COM2. The parallel port (LPT1) uses a 25-pin female connector on the PC.

The serial ports are typically used for modems, mice and digitizer tablets, and the parallel port is generally used for the printer. Both serial and parallel ports can be used for file transfer between two computers cabled together. See *driver* for illustration of PC input/output.

PC BUSES		Bandwidth	
		Bits	Speed
ISA		8 16	8-10MHz
EISA		32	8-10MHz
PCI		32 64	33MHz
AGP		32	66MHz
Micro Channel		32	5-20MHz
VL-bus		32	40MHz

Types of Expansion Boards

Except for ISA and AGP, all the other boards in this illustration have given way to PCI. Although most PC motherboards still have ISA slots, they too will give way to PCI.

PC I/O addressing

This is a method for passing signals from the CPU to the controller boards of peripheral devices on x86 machines. An I/O address, also called a *port address*, references a separate memory space on peripheral boards. This is often confused with memory-mapped peripherals, such as video cards, which use a block of upper memory (UMB) in the upper memory area (UMA). Peripheral devices often use both methods: an I/O address for passing control signals and an upper memory block (UMB) for transferring and buffering data to and from the CPU.

There is a 64K address space for I/O addresses, although typically less than 1K is used. Each board that uses an I/O address contains a few bytes of memory (16, 32, etc.) set to a default address range. One or more alternate addresses is also provided to resolve conflicts with other boards. These I/O spaces are a bunch of tiny memory banks scattered over different devices. As long as each one is set to a different address, the CPU can transmit signals to the appropriate boards without conflict.

An I/O address operation takes place as follows. If a program needs to send a byte to the serial port, it issues an OUT instruction to the CPU with the address of that serial port. The CPU notifies the address bus to activate the I/O space, not regular memory, and the address bus signals the appropriate byte location on the board. The CPU then sends the data character over the data bus to that memory location.

Following are the default I/O addresses for the serial and parallel ports in a PC.

Port	PC	PS/2
COM1	3F8h	
COM2	2F8h	
COM3	2E8h	
COM4	2E0h	
LPT1	378h	3BCh
LPT2	278h	378h
LPT3	3BCh	278h

PCIset
A chipset that supports the PCI bus. See *Intel chipsets*.

PCI steering
Directing PCI interrupts to an IRQ in the PC. There are four PCI interrupts used by PCI plug-in cards or onboard devices such as the USB. These are directed to one of the available IRQs by the BIOS or operating system. See *PCI*.

PCjr
(PC JunioR) IBM's first home computer introduced in 1983. It was discontinued two years later, because there was not enough compelling software for the family at that time. In addition, the PCjr was introduced with a chiclet keyboard that was not suitable for touch typing. By the time IBM added a better keyboard, the handwriting was on the wall. It took another decade before the PC became widely used in the home.

PC keyboard
(1) The keyboard introduced with the IBM PC that provides a dual-function keypad for numeric entry and cursor movement. It was severely criticized for its non-standard shift key placement, which was corrected with the AT keyboard. Regardless of key placement, users love the feel of IBM keyboards.

(2) Any keyboard made for the PC, including the PC keyboard, AT keyboard and Enhanced keyboard.

PC keyboards
IBM introduced three generations of keyboards that drove touch typists batty. The original PC keyboard used an awkward return and left shift key placement. Finally corrected on the AT keyboard, the backspace key was made harder to reach. The Enhanced keyboard fixed the backspace key and relocated a host of other keys. At that point, it became impossible to assign function keys intelligently. What was easy to reach on one keyboard was hard to reach on the other.

Most manufacturers follow the herd and make the same keyboards. Only a few have dared to be different. Keyboards on laptops are even worse. Often-used Alt and Ctrl keys may be in hard-to-reach places, and users may be forced to press an additional Fn key for common functions. There are excellent keyboards, too. Touch typists beware!

There are few compatibility problems with PC keyboards. Most work well on all desktop PCs and as an alternate laptop keyboard. Older keyboards may have a manual XT-AT switch that changes internal electronics from the first PC keyboard used with XTs to the later AT and subsequent keyboards. Keyboards plug into either a 5-pin DIN or a 6-pin mini-DIN socket on the motherboard. Adapters connect a 5-pin plug to a 6-pin socket. See *PS/2 connector* for illustration.

PCL
(Printer Control Language) The command language for the HP LaserJet printers. It has become a de facto standard used in many printers and typesetters. PCL Level 5, introduced with the LaserJet III in

1990, also supports Compugraphic's Intellifont scalable fonts. Starting with the LaserJet 5 in 1996, PCL Level 6 streamlines the graphics and font commands, reducing the amount of information that has to be sent to the printer. See *PJL*.

PC LAN

(1) A network of IBM or IBM-compatible PCs.

(2) A network of any variety of personal computers.

PCM

(1) (Pulse Code Modulation) A technique for converting analog signals into digital form that is widely used by the telephone companies in their T1 circuits. Every minute of the day, millions of telephone conversations, as well as data transmissions via modem, are converted into digital via PCM for transport over high-speed intercity trunks. In North America and Japan, PCM samples the analog waves 8,000 times per second and converts each sample into an 8-bit number, resulting in a 64 Kbps data stream. The sampling rate is twice the 4KHz bandwidth required for a toll-quality conversation. See *ADPCM, A-Law, mu-Law* and *sampling rate*.

(2) (Plug Compatible Manufacturer) An organization that makes a computer or electronic device that is compatible with an existing machine.

PCMCIA

(Personal Computer Memory Card International Association, San Jose, CA, www.pc-card.com) An international standards body that was founded in 1989 to establish the PC Card. See *PC Card*.

PC memory

The original PC design was constrained to one megabyte of memory. In addition, certain parts of the operating system were placed into fixed locations in the upper part of memory without any method for cooperatively storing additional drivers and programs. This design gave rise to the most confusing platform in history. Windows 3.0 became very popular because it handled all of the memory types much better than DOS.

Following are the different types of memory in a PC. In other computers, there is just plain memory. In mainframes and supercomputers, there are also large, auxiliary memory banks that function as caches between disk and RAM. See *PC memory map*.

```
Conventional Memory        First 640K
UMA (Upper Memory Area)    Next 384K
HMA (High Memory Area)     Next 64K
Extended Memory            From 1MB up
EMS (Expanded Memory)      Bank switched
                             into the UMA
```

PC memory map

The chart on the right shows how the first megabyte of RAM is used in a PC.

PCM modem

See *V.90*.

PC network

(1) A network of PCs or of any variety of personal computers.

(2) (PC Network) The first PC LAN from IBM introduced in 1984. It inaugurated the NetBIOS interface and used the CSMA/CD access method. Token Ring support was later added. See *MS-Net*.

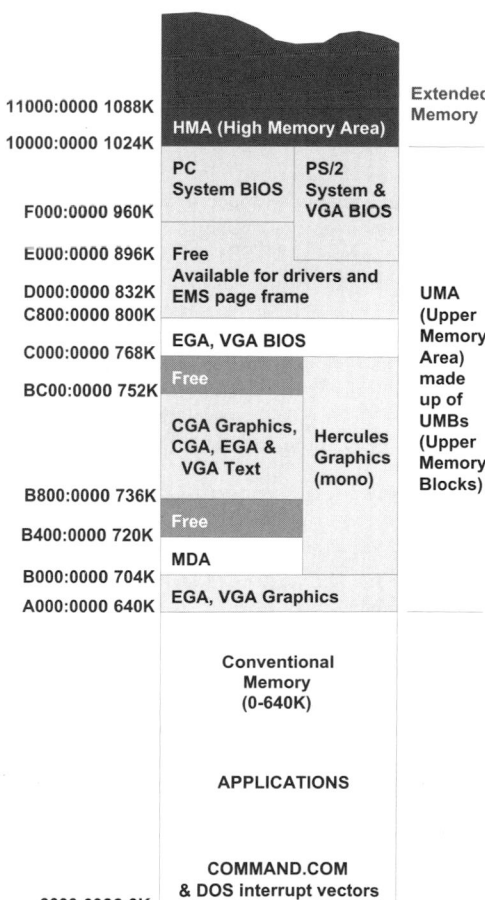

Memory Allocation in a PC

p-code

See *intermediate language*.

PC operating environments

Almost all PCs use the DOS or Windows operating systems. With Windows 3.1, DOS is loaded first, then Windows is loaded. Windows 95/98 boots up with DOS for compatibility purposes and immediately switches to Windows. At startup, Windows 95/98 can also be booted into DOS without Windows. Although Windows 95/98 has become the de facto standard on new PCs, Windows 3.1 is still widely used. Many 3.1 users have simply waited until they have to upgrade their favorite application, and the newer version does not run under Windows 3.1.

OS/2, highly regarded as a robust and stable operating system, has its loyal followers but continues to suffer from limited application support and driver support for new peripherals.

Windows in all of its incarnations (3.1, 95/98 and NT) is the clear winner on the desktop. Windows NT is gaining market share as a client operating system, but is also gaining serious market share as a server product.

The History of PC Operating Systems

The PC was created without a glimmer of its future potential. As it became mainstream, its flaws surfaced. For example, its 8088 CPU was limited to one megabyte of memory, the first 640K of which was used for applications, with the remaining 384K set aside for the operating system and drivers (see *PC memory map*). That upper 384K, known as the UMA, or Upper Memory Area, gave rise to countless techniques for squeezing more drivers into it so there would be room for applications in the precious 640K below. This limitation is still a problem in Windows machines that run many older applications.

DOS was designed to run only one program at a time, and users eventually wanted more than one program active so they could switch back and forth. In order to get around DOS' single task nature and the PC's 640K limit, a variety of add-ons, techniques and remedies were created to solve this dilemma. Following is a synopsis.

TSRs

In 1984, Borland introduced Sidekick and popularized the TSR, or popup, program. Sidekick stayed in memory but swapped in and out of view by pressing a hotkey. Users could instantly switch to a handy phone directory or notepad. However, keeping many TSRs in memory may not leave room for bigger applications, and TSRs are known to cause conflicts. TSRs can still run under Windows, but generally must be popped up within a DOS window.

EXPANDED MEMORY

In 1984, expanded memory (EMS) was created to break the one megabyte barrier. An EMS board with multiple megabytes of RAM could be plugged in, and its memory used directly by EMS applications. Lotus 1-2-3 quickly took advantage of it and hundreds of other applications were written to use it. Windows supports EMS for older DOS applications that require it. See *EMS*.

TASK SWITCHERS & MULTITASKERS

Programs such as Software Carousel extended DOS's capabilities by allowing the user to keep a variety of programs open at the same time and switch back and forth between them. These "task switchers" used EMS memory, extended memory and/or the hard disk to swap applications in and out of conventional memory.

Combining multitasking with task switching, Quarterdeck's popular DESQview was the first control program to use expanded (EMS) memory to allow programs to run in, not just reside in, the background.

MEMORY MANAGERS

Memory managers were developed to store TSRs and other memory-resident software (drivers) in the Upper Memory Area. Memory managers manage both extended and EMS memory, and products, such as QEMM, 386MAX and DOS 6's EMM386.EXE, can allocate both types on demand. See *DOS memory manager* and *memory allocation*.

EXTENDED MEMORY & WINDOWS

By the late 1980s, the DOS extender was introduced, which is software that allows DOS applications to run in, not just reside in, extended memory. Paradox 386 and Lotus 1-2-3 Version 3.0 were some of the first programs to use it.

Windows uses its own equivalent DOS extender technologies to manage all the memory in the PC. It lets users launch, keep active and switch between several Windows and DOS applications. Windows' ability to finally use large amounts of memory in the PC contributed to its success. Windows 95/98, which utilizes the 32-bit architecture of the x86 chip, inherently uses all of extended memory, but still has to deal with conventional memory for legacy applications.

DOS 5 & 6

DOS 5 added a task switching capability that ran multiple DOS applications, swapping inactive ones to disk. It improved memory management, freeing up more conventional memory by loading operating system components into upper memory.

DOS 6 improved memory management and added realtime compression. It can allocate extended memory and EMS memory on demand, making it more flexible for running a mix of old DOS and new Windows programs. Its DoubleSpace or DriveSpace compression can double the capacity of a hard disk. In DOS 6, for the first time, a variety of stand-alone utility programs were included.

DR DOS

DR DOS is a DOS-compatible operating system with advanced memory management and other features that always inspired Microsoft to include similar functionality in its subsequent DOS releases. Novell acquired DR DOS, added NetWare functionality to it, and then sold it to Caldera.

PC Paintbrush

A DOS paint program developed by the ZSoft Corporation, Marietta, GA. It was the first popular paint program for the PC, and its PCX bitmapped graphics format became a de facto standard for bitmapped images. See *PCX* and *graphics formats.*

PC printers

There are hundreds of printer models that work with PCs. The printer typically plugs into the PC's parallel port. The most popular printers are ink jet and laser-class printers. Dot matrix printers are still used for mailing and diskette labels on continuous forms and for applications requiring multipart forms. The dot matrix resolution is more course than ink jet or laser class.

Ink jet printers provide reasonable text quality. They are slower than laser-class printers, but provide the most affordable color printing. Monochrome laser-class printers, which are made up of laser printers and LED printers, provide finer text quality and are suited to business applications. GDI printers are laser-class Windows printers that are the most affordable, because they do not process as much data internally. They rely on Windows to send the finished page to the printer.

Color laser-class printers are slower than their monochrome counterparts and more expensive. Color lasers are broke the $3,000 barrier in 1997.

Windows provides centralized management of printers and fonts. After the printer is installed, it is available to all Windows applications. Whenever new fonts are installed, they are available to all Windows applications. DOS provides no centralized management. DOS applications that deal with page layout have to support the printer directly, and the fonts used in one DOS application may not be usable in another. This is one reason why DOS gave way to Windows. See *printer.*

PCradio

An IBM laptop designed for mobile use. It is a ruggedized machine that provides cellular, wireless data radio (Ardis) and modem communications.

PCS

(1) (Personal Communications Services) Refers to a variety of wireless services emerging after the U.S. Government auctioned commercial licenses in late 1994 and early 1995. This radio spectrum in the 2GHz range is used for digital transmission services that compete with analog cellular (AMPS), digital cellular and other wireless services.

(2) (Personal Conferencing Specification) A videoconferencing technology that uses Intel's Indeo compression method. It is endorsed by the Intel-backed Personal Conferencing Working Group (PCWG). Initially competing against H.320, Intel subsequently announced its videoconferencing products will also be H.320 compliant.

PCT

(Private Communications Technology) A protocol from Microsoft that provides secure transactions over the World Wide Web. See *security protocol*.

PC-to-host

Refers to desktop computers (PCs) communicating with minis and mainframes (hosts). The connections may be direct cabling from the PC to the host or via the network.

PC Tools

A popular and comprehensive packages of utilities for DOS and Windows from Symantec (originally Central Point Software). They include a DOS or Windows shell as well as antivirus, file management, caching, backup, compression and data recovery utilities.

PC/TV

A PC with a built-in TV tuner. TV boards that plug into a personal computer typically have standard RCA phono inputs to connect a VCR or camera. Some also have S-VHS inputs.

PCX

A popular bitmapped graphics file format that handles monochrome, 2-bit, 4-bit, 8-bit and 24-bit color and uses RLE to achieve compression ratios of approximately 1.1:1 to 1.5:1. Images with large blocks of solid colors compress best under the RLE method. See *PC Paintbrush*.

PDA

(Personal Digital Assistant) A handheld computer that serves as an organizer for personal information. It generally includes at least a name and address database, to-do list and note taker. PDAs are pen based and use a stylus to tap selections on menus and to enter printed characters. The unit may also include a small on-screen keyboard which is tapped with the pen. Data is synchronized between the PDA and desktop computer via cable or wireless transmission. Apple's MessagePad, more commonly known as the "Newton," was the first to popularize the concept. The difference between a PDA and palmtop computer is that the PDA uses a pen, the palmtop uses a small keyboard.

PDC

(Primary Domain Controller) A Windows NT service that manages security for its local domain. Every domain has one PDC, which contains a database of usernames, passwords and permissions. See *BDC*.

PD disk

(Phase change Dual disk) A rewritable optical disk from Panasonic that uses phase change technology. Introduced in 1995, it uses 5.25" cartridges that hold 650MB and can withstand 500,000 rewrites. The PD drive also reads CD-ROMs, and the drive tray accomodates both PD cartridges and CD-ROM discs. The drive does not support Panasonic's earlier 5.25" phase change (PCR) cartridges. Panasonic's DVD-RAM drives also read and write PD disks. See *phase change*. For a summary of all storage technologies, see *storage*.

PDES

(Product Data Exchange Specification) A standard format for exchanging data between advanced CAD and CAM programs. It describes a complete product, including the geometric aspects of the images as well as manufacturing features, tolerance specifications, material properties and finish specifications. See *IGES*.

PDF417

A two-dimensional bar code developed by Symbol Technology, Inc., Bohemia, NY. The bar code is read horizontally and vertically and can hold 1,800 characters in the area the size of a

PD Cartridge
The PD cartridges look like and use the same technology as DVD-RAM disks. Panasonic's DVD-RAM drives read and write PD cartridges.

postage stamp. Symbol Technologies and other companies make PDF417 readers. See *bar code* for illustration.

PDF file

(Portable Document Format file) The file format used by the Acrobat document exchange system. See *Acrobat*.

PDIAL

(Public Dialup Internet Access List) A list of Internet service providers (ISPs) maintained by Peter Kaminsky. The last available PDIAL list is on various Web sites.

PDIP

(Plastic DIP) See *DIP*.

PDL

See *page description language*.

PDM, PDMS

(Product Data Management System) An information system used to manage product development from inception to manufacturing and maintenance. It handles all the data necessary at all stages including plans, geometric models, CAD drawings, images, NC programs as well as all related project data, notes and documents. PDMs are developed for workgroups as well as the entire enterprise.

PDN

(1) (Packet Data Network) See *packet switching*.

(2) (Premises Distribution Network) The network that connects a customer's ADSL transceiver (ATU-R) to the Service Modules (PCs, routers, set-top boxes, etc.). See *DSL*.

PDP

(1) (Programmed Data Processor) A minicomputer family from Digital that started with the 18-bit PDP-1 in 1959. Its $120,000 price was much less than the million dollar machines of the time and 50 units were built.

In 1965, Digital legitimized the minicomputer industry with the PDP-8, which sold for about $20,000. By the late 1970s, the PDP-8 processor was put on a single chip and used in DECmate workstations. Other PDPs were built, including 12-bit, 18-bit and 36-bit machines, the larger ones evolving into DECsystem models.

In 1970, Digital introduced the 16-bit PDP-11, which became the most widely used minicomputer with more than 50,000 systems sold. The VAX series was introduced in 1977, but PDP machines lingered on for many years.

(2) (Plasma Display Panel) See *plasma display*.

PDQ

(Parallel Data Query) A query optimized for massively parallel processors (MPPs). The software breaks down the query into pieces so that several parts of the database can be searched simultaneously. See *SMP*.

PDP-8
In 1965, this $20,000 computer legitimized the minicomputer industry. *(Photo courtesy of Digital Equipment Corporation.)*

PDS

(1) (Processor Direct Slot) In the Macintosh, an expansion socket used to connect high-speed peripherals as well as additional CPUs. It is equivalent to the local bus in the PC. There are different types of PDSs for various Macintosh models and types. Some Macs do not have a PDS, others have both PDS and NuBus slots.

(2) (Premises Distribution System) The cabling, racks and adapters that connect telephone wires within a building or group of buildings to each other and to external lines of the telephone company.

PD software

See *public domain software.*

PDU

(Protocol Data Unit) The technical name of a frame of data transmitted over a local area network.

PE

(1) (Phase Encoding) An early magnetic encoding method used on 1600 bpi tapes in which a 1 is an up transition and a 0 is a down transition in the center of the bit cell.

(2) (Processing Element) One of multiple CPUs in a parallel processing system.

(3) (Professional Engineer) An engineering degree.

Pearl

See *Perl.*

PEBCAK

Digispeak for a person that does something stupid. It stands for "problem exists between chair and keyboard."

peek/poke

Instructions that view and alter a byte of memory by referencing a specific memory address. Peek displays the contents; poke changes it.

peer

In communications, a functional unit that is on the same protocol layer as another.

peering

The act of one national Internet backbone provider accepting and passing traffic from another national provider. See *NAP.*

peer protocol

A protocol at the same protocol layer; for example, a layer 2 protocol talking to another layer 2 protocol, layer 3 with layer 3, etc. See also *peer-to-peer communications* and *peer-to-peer network.*

peer-to-peer communications

Communications in which both sides have equal responsibility for initiating, maintaining and terminating the session. Contrast with *master-slave communications,* in which the host determines which users can initiate which sessions. If the host were programmed to allow all users to initiate all sessions, it would look like a peer-to-peer system to the user.

peer-to-peer network

A communications network that allows all workstations and computers in the network to act as servers to all other users on the network. Dedicated file servers may be used, but are not required as in a *client/ server network.*

Do not confuse this term with "peer-to-peer communications." A peer-to-peer network implies peer-to-peer communications, but peer-to-peer communications does not imply a peer-to-peer network. Don't you love the extensive thought and analysis that goes into naming things in this business in order to make the terms perfectly clear and understandable!

PE format

(Portable Executable format) A Win32 file format for executable programs (EXEs and DLLs) supported under Windows 3.1 Enhanced Mode (Win32s) and Windows NT.

pel

Same as *pixel*.

PEM

(Privacy Enhanced Mail) A standard for secure e-mail on the Internet. It supports encryption, digital signatures and digital certificates as well as both private and public key methods.

pen-based computing

Using a stylus to enter hand writing and marks into a computer. See *gesture recognition*.

Pentium

The fifth generation of the Intel x86 family of CPU chips. The term may refer to the chip or to a PC that uses it. Introduced in 1993, it is the successor to the 486, and depending on clock speed, can be up to 10 times as fast. Although integer performance of Pentium chips rivals RISC-based CPUs (Alpha, HP-PA, SPARC, etc.), their floating point performance is generally slower.

Variations of the Pentium were later introduced, including the Pentium Pro, Pentium MMX and Pentium II. The Pentium Pro is optimized for 32-bit operating systems and applications. The Pentium MMX and Pentium II are counterparts of the Pentium and Pentium Pro that contain additional instructions for multimedia operations (MMX instructions). See *Pentium Pro, Pentium MMX* and *Pentium II*.

Pentium CPU Technical Specs

It is a 32-bit multitasking microprocessor that uses the same registers and operational modes as the 386. The chip is housed in a PGA package using from 273 to 321 pins. The Pentium uses RISC design techniques and obtains its speed by using two internal 8K caches (one for code, the other for data) and a "superscaler" dual pipeline architecture, which executes two instructions in the same clock cycle when it determines that the next instruction is not dependent on the outcome of the current one.

The Pentium uses a 64-bit internal bus compared to 32-bits on the 486. PC makers use a variety of high-speed bus and cache controllers to enhance performance; for example, a 128-bit memory bus can be used to extract data 128 bits at a time into the external cache, which feeds it to the CPU 64 bits at a time.

The first Pentium models had clock rates of 60 and 66MHz, ran on 5 volts and used .8 micron technology. Subsequent models run faster, use less voltage (3.3, 2.9, etc.) and are built with ever-decreasing semiconductor elements (.035 and smaller). The chip contains 3.1 million transistors.

The following list contains the bus speeds of most Pentium chips.

Model	System bus (local bus)
60MHz	60Mhz
66MHz	66Mhz
75MHz	50Mhz
90MHz	60Mhz
100MHz	66Mhz
120MHz	60Mhz
133MHz	66Mhz
150MHz	60MHz
166MHz	66MHz
200MHz	66MHz

Pentium class

Refers to a Pentium CPU chip or to a PC that uses the chip. The term is also used for non-Intel CPUs that are Pentium compatible, such as the K5 from AMD and the 6x86 from Cyrix. See *P6 class*.

Pentium clone

Refers to a Pentium-based computer system that is not made by a top-tier vendor or to a Pentium CPU chip that is not made by Intel.

Pentium II

The successor to the Pentium Pro from Intel. Pentium II refers to the Pentium II CPU chip or to the PC that uses it. Code named "Klamath," the Pentium II is a Pentium Pro with MMX instructions. Introduced in 1997 at clock rates of 233MHz and 266MHz, it uses a 66MHz system bus and houses the chip in a cartridge, called the Single Edge Connector (SEC). It holds the CPU and separate L2 cache and plugs into Slot 1 on the motherboard. The chip also requires variable power voltages.

In January 1998, Intel introduced a new model of the Pentium II (code named Deschutes) that is built with .25 micron technology (rather than .35), thereby reducing the chip size from 202 to 131 square millimeters. The first model runs at 333MHz and uses a 66MHz bus with many variations coming (see chart below). See *future Intel chips*.

```
PENTIUM II CONFIGURATIONS

          CPU     System  L2 cache
          Speed   Bus     Bus     L1/L2
Slot      (MHz)   (MHz)   (MHz)   Cache     Chipset

Mid-level PCs (Klamath - .35µ)
Slot 1    233      66     116.5   16/512K   440FX, LX
Slot 1    266      66     133     16/512K   440BX
Slot 1    300      66     150     16/512K   440BX

High-end PCs (Deschutes - .25µ)
Slot 1    333      66     166.5   32/512K   440FX, LX
Slot 1    350     100     175     32/512K   440BX
Slot 1    400     100     200     32/512K   440BX
Slot 1    450     100     225     32/512K   440BX

Consumer PCs (Celeron - .25µ)
Slot 1    266      66     N/A     32/None   440LXR
Slot 1    300      66     N/A     32/None   440LXR
Slot 1    300      66     150     32/128K   440LXR
Slot 1    333      66     166.5   32/128K   440LXR
Slot 1    366      66     183     32/128K   440LXR

Servers (Xeon - .25µ)
Slot 2    400     100     400     32/.5-2MB 450NX
Slot 2    450     100     450     32/.5-2MB 450NX

Laptops - .25µ)
Mobile 233        66     116.5   32/512KB  440BX
Mobile 266        66     133     32/512KB  440BX
Mobile 300        66     150     32/512KB  440BX
```

Pentium II class

Refers to a Pentium II CPU chip or to a PC that uses the chip. The term is also used for non-Intel CPUs that are Pentium II compatible, such as the K6 from AMD and the 6x86MX from Cyrix. See *P6 class*.

Pentium MMX

A Pentium CPU that contains additional instructions for improved multimedia performance. The term refers to the CPU chip or to the PC that uses it. The MMX instructions are also found in the Pentium II chip. See *MMX*.

Pentium Pro

The sixth generation of the Intel x86 family of CPU chips. The term may refer to the chip or to a PC that uses it. Introduced in 1995, it is the successor to the Pentium, and models from 150MHz to 200MHz were released. The Pentium Pro is better suited to running 32-bit operating systems and applications than the Pentium. Using the first generation of Intel's Extended Server Memory Architecture, Pentium Pro CPUs can address 64GB of memory rather than 4GB.

The Pentium Pro is used in servers and high-end workstations, which can employ SMP multiprocessing to increase performance. The Pentium Pro was succeeded by the Pentium II, which is a Pentium Pro with MMX instructions. However, since MMX instructions are not often used in a server environment, the Pentium Pro still serves as an effective server. See *Pentium* and *Pentium II*.

Pentium Pro class

Refers to a Pentium Pro CPU chip or to a PC that uses the chip. The term is also used for non-Intel CPUs that are Pentium Pro compatible, such as the K6 from AMD. See *P6 class*.

Pentium upgradable

The ability to be upgraded to a Pentium CPU. 486 motherboards designed for Pentium upgrades contain a ZIF socket to make chip changing easy and are, in theory, designed to support the higher speeds of the Pentium chip.

Pen Windows

An extension to Windows that allows pen-based computing.

PeopleSoft

(PeopleSoft, Inc., Walnut Creek, CA, www.peoplesoft.com) A software company that specializes in human resource and accounting packages for client/server environments. All major databases are supported. The products are known for their ease of modification and custom development using the PeopleTools development system.

PEP

(1) (Packet Exchange Protocol) A Xerox protocol used internally by NetWare to transport internal Netware NCP commands (NetWare Core Protocols). It uses PEP and IPX for this purpose. Application programs use SPX and IPX.

(2) A high-speed modem protocol suited for cellular phone use from Telebit Corporation, Sunnyvale, CA, (www.telebit.com).

PEPPER board

An earlier family of high-resolution display adapters for PCs from Number Nine Visual Technology Corporation, Lexington, MA.

per clock

For each clock cycle. The phrase "the CPU does four instructions per clock" means that four machine instructions have been executed within one cycle of the CPU clock, the master clock that synchronizes everything in the computer. For example, in a 200MHz computer, each clock cycle is 5ns long (one billion nanoseconds divided by 200 million). See *clock*.

Pereos

The world's smallest magnetic tape technology. The drive, which is about the size of a bar of soap, weighs 10 ounces, runs on AA batteries and connects via the parallel port. Using helical scan technology, the tiny cartridges hold more than 1.25GB compressed. Originally developed by Datasonix and manufactured by Sony, Pereos products later became available from J&J Peripherals, Broomfield, CO, (www.jj-peripherals.com).

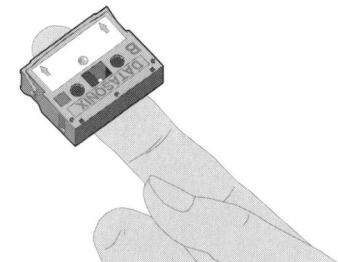

It Doesn't Get Much Smaller
Helical scan technology crams more than a gigabyte (compressed) on the tiny Pereos cartridges.

PerfectOffice

A suite of applications for Windows from Novell that includes WordPerfect, Quattro Pro, Presentations (presentation graphics), InfoCentral PIM, Envoy document exchange software and GroupWise e-mail and calendar. PerfectOffice Professional also includes Paradox and AppWare.

performance ratings

See *benchmark*.

peripheral

Any hardware device connected to a computer, such as a monitor, keyboard, printer, disk, tape, graphics tablet, scanner, joy stick, paddle and mouse.

peripheral bus

An input/output bus that connects peripherals to the computer. ISA, EISA, PCI and VL-bus are examples of peripheral buses used in a PC.

peripheral card
See *expansion board*.

peripheral controller
See *control unit*.

Perl
(Practical Extraction Report Language) A programming language written by Larry Wall that combines syntax from several UNIX utilities and languages. Perl is designed to handle a variety of system administrator functions. Because of its comprehensive string handling capabilities, it is widely used on Web servers. Stemming from the UNIX world, Perl has been adapted to other platforms. See also *PURL*.

permanent font
(1) A soft font that is kept in the printer's memory until the printer is turned off.

(2) Same as *internal font*.

permanent memory
Same as *non-volatile memory*.

permutation
One possible combination of items out of a larger set of items. For example, with the set of numbers 1, 2 and 3, there are six possible permutations: **12, 21, 13, 31, 23** and **32.**

perpendicular recording
See *vertical recording*.

per seat licensing
Software licensing based on a per user basis. For example, a 100-user license means that up to 100 specifically-named users have access to the program. Per seat licensing is administered by providing user-level security to the directory containing the program. Contrast with *concurrent licensing*.

persistence
(1) In a CRT, the time a phosphor dot remains illuminated after being energized. Long-persistence phosphors reduce flicker, but generate ghost-like images that linger on screen for a fraction of a second.

(2) In object technology, the storage of an object on a disk or other permanent storage device.

persistent data
Data that exists from session to session. Persistent data is stored in a database on disk or tape. Contrast with *transient data*.

persistent link
See *hot link*.

persistent object
An object that continues to exist after the program that created it has been unloaded. An object's class and current state must be saved for use in subsequent sessions. In object technology, persistence means storing the object for later use.

personal communicator
See *PDA*.

personal computer
Synonymous with microcomputer, a computer that serves one user in the office or at home. With the addition of a modem, the personal computer becomes a terminal capable of retrieving information from other computers, online services and the Internet.

There are a variety of personal computers on the market priced from $800 to well over $10,000. Size is based on memory and disk capacity. Speed is based on the CPU that runs it, and output quality is based on the resolution of its display screen and printer.

The personal computer world is dominated by Windows-based PCs. There are thousands of vendors that make them, from mom and pop shops to huge companies such as Compaq, HP and IBM. The alternate personal computer standard is Apple's Macintosh, which is made by Apple and a handful of others. Atari and Commodore once carved out their respective niches, but Atari is no longer in the business and Commodore has since closed its doors.

The History of Personal Computers

The industry began in 1977, when Apple, Radio Shack and Commodore introduced the first off-the-shelf computers as consumer products. The first machines used an 8-bit microprocessor with a maximum of 64K of memory and floppy disks for storage. The Apple II, Atari 500, and Commodore 64 became popular home computers, and Apple was successful in companies after the VisiCalc spreadsheet was introduced. However, the business world was soon dominated by the Z80 processor and CP/M operating system, used by countless vendors in the early 1980s, such as Vector Graphic, NorthStar, Osborne and Kaypro. By 1983, hard disks began to show up on these machines, but CP/M was soon to be history.

In 1981, IBM introduced the PC, an Intel 8088-based machine, slightly faster than the genre, but with 10 times the memory. It was floppy-based, and its DOS operating system from Microsoft was also available for the clone makers (MS-DOS). The 8088 was cleverly chosen so that CP/M software vendors could convert to it easily. They did!

dBASE II was introduced in 1981 bringing mainframe database functions to the personal computer level and launching an entire industry of compatible products and add-ons. Lotus 1-2-3 was introduced in 1982, and its refined interface and combined graphics helped spur sales of the new standard.

The IBM PC was successfully cloned by Compaq and unsuccessfully by others. However, by the time IBM announced the AT in 1984, vendors were effectively cloning the PC and, as a group, eventually grabbed the majority of the PC market.

In 1983, Apple introduced the Lisa, a graphics-based machine that simulated the user's desktop. Although ahead of its time, Lisa was abandoned for the Macintosh in 1984. The graphics-based desktop environment caught on with the Mac, especially in desktop publishing, and the graphical interface, or "gooey," (GUI) worked its way to the PC world with Microsoft Windows, and, eventually Ventura Publisher with its GEM interface.

In 1986, the Compaq 386 ushered in the first Intel 386-based machine. In 1987, IBM introduced the PS/2, its next generation of personal computers, which added improved graphics, 3.5" floppy disks and an incompatible bus to help fend off the cloners. OS/2, jointly developed by IBM and Microsoft, was also introduced to handle the new machines, but the early versions didn't catch on.

In the same year, more powerful Macintoshes were introduced, including the Mac SE and Mac II, which opened new doors for Apple.

In 1989, the PC makers introduced 486-based computers, and Apple gave us faster Macs, which it has continued to do each year since.

In 1990, Microsoft introduced Windows 3.0, which became a huge success within a couple of years. Software publishers developed Windows versions of all their products.

In 1991, Microsoft and IBM decided to go it alone each working on their own version of the future PC operating system (IBM's OS/2 and Microsoft's Windows NT). Today, NT has gained significant market share, but OS/2 has not.

1992 was the year of PC price cuts with all major suppliers slashing prices to keep in line with mail-order vendors, such as Gateway 2000, who along with others, had dramatically driven down the cost.

In 1993, Intel introduced its Pentium CPU, and then its Pentium Pro two years later to keep pace with the multimedia explosion that has been going on

The First Personal Computer
In the mid 1970s, Xerox developed the Alto, which was the forerunner of its Star workstation and inspiration for Apple's Lisa and Macintosh. *(Photo courtesy of Xerox Corporation.)*

throughout the 1990s. The once text-based PC has become a graphics workstation competing with machines that cost 100 times as much only a few years ago. Within a couple of years, the home market would explode with low-cost, high-performance PCs.

In 1995, the personal computer became a window into the Internet for global e-mail and access to the fastest growing information bank the world has ever witnessed. Although graphical Web browsers such as Mosaic and Netscape were the catalyst, had the desktop personal computer not been in place, the World Wide Web in all of its glory would have never exploded onto the scene.

Inspired by Radio Shack's Model 100 over a decade ago and ignited by companies such as Toshiba and Zenith, the laptop market has had explosive growth throughout the 1990s. More circuits are being stuffed into less space, providing computing power on the go that few would have imagined back in 1977, the dawn of the personal computer era.

Summary

The personal computer industry sprang up without any planning. All of a sudden, it was there. Machines were bought to solve individual problems, such as automating a budget or typing a letter.

The personal computer has become the desktop appliance in every office throughout the developed world. It has been networked together with the organization's mainframes and minis and is an integral part of the technology infrastructure of every company, small, medium and large. Within the past two decades, no single device has had more impact on more people and more businesses than the personal computer.

As stand-alone machines, personal computers have placed creative capacity into the hands of an individual that would have cost millions of dollars less than 25 years ago. They slowly but surely are shifting the balance of power from the large company to the small, from the elite to the masses, from the wealthy to individuals of modest means. The personal computer has revolutionized the computer industry and the world.

peta

Quadrillion (10 to the 15th power). See *space/time*.

PET computer

(Personal Electronic Transactor computer) A CP/M and floppy disk-based personal computer introduced in 1977 by Commodore. It was one of the first personal computers along with the Apple II and Radio Shack's TRS-80. See *Commodore*.

PFA file, PFB file

(Printer Font ASCII file, Printer Font Binary file) Type 1 font files that contain the mathematical outlines of each character in the font. The codes in this file are in ASCII (raw text). PFB files are an encrypted version of the PFA format. See *Type 1 font* and *PostScript*.

PFM file

(Printer Font Metrics file) A Type 1 font file that contains the measurements of each character in the font. In a PC, both PFM and PFB files are required. The PFB files are located in the \PSFONTS folder, and the PFM files are in the \PSFONTS\PFM folder. Sometimes \PSFONTS is in the \WINDOWS folder. See *Type 1 font, PFB file* and *PostScript*.

PFQ

(Per-Flow Queuing) A queuing method that forwards traffic based on priority, not the order of arrival into the queue as with first in-first out. See *FIFO*.

PGA

(1) (Pin Grid Array) A ceramic, square chip package with a high density of pins (200 pins can fit in 1.5" square). Used for large amounts of I/O, its underside looks like a "bed of nails." In an SPGA (Staggered PGA), the pins are staggered and do not line up in perfect rows and columns.

(2) (Programmable Gate Array) See *gate array* and *FPGA*.

(3) (Professional Graphics Adapter) An early IBM PC display standard for 3-D processing with 640x480x256 resolution. It was not widely used.

PGP

(Pretty Good Privacy) Public key cryptography software from Pretty Good Privacy, Inc., San Mateo, CA, (www.pgp.com). It was developed by Phil Zimmermann, founder of the company, and it is based on the RSA cryptographic method. A version for personal, non-business use is available on various BBSs and Internet hosts. See *cryptography*.

PgUp/PgDn keys

The Page Up and Page Down keys are typically used to move text up and down one screenful, but they can be programmed to do anything.

phase change

A rewritable optical disk technology developed by Panasonic (Matsushita). Phase change was used in a line of optical drives in the early 1990s. It was later used in Panasonic's PD drive and is also the technology used for writing CD-RWs and DVD-RAMs.

Phase change is a pure optical technology and does not rely on any magnetic influence as does magneto-optic and its progeny. A short, high-intensity laser pulse turns a bit in the recording layer from its natural crystalline state (reflective) to an amorphous one (dull), which does not reflect light as well. A medium-intensity pulse restores the crystalline structure, and a low-intensity pulse reads the bit. See *optical disk* and *PD disk*.

phase change disk

A rewritable optical disk that uses phase change technology originally developed by Panasonic. Panasonic's earlier PCR disks and its subsequent PD disks as well as CD-R and DVD-RAM disks all use phase change technology. See *phase change*.

phase change printer

See *solid ink printer*.

phase encoding

See *PE*.

phase locked

A technique for maintaining synchronization in an electronic circuit. The circuit receives its timing from input signals, but also provides a feedback circuit for synchronization.

phase modulation

A transmission technique that blends a data signal into a carrier by varying (modulating) the phase of the carrier. See *modulate*.

phase-shift keying

See *DPSK*.

PHIGS

(Programmer's Hierarchical Interactive Graphics Standard) A graphics system and language used to create 2-D and 3-D images. Like the GKS standard, PHIGS is a device independent interface between the application program and the graphics subsystem.

It manages graphics objects in a hierarchical manner so that a complete assembly can be specified with all of its subassemblies. It is a very comprehensive standard requiring high-performance workstations and host processing.

Phoenix BIOS

A popular PC BIOS from Phoenix Technolgies Ltd., San Jose, CA, (www.phoenix.com). Phoenix was the first company to successfully mass produce the ROM BIOS for the PC, which made the PC industry possible.

phone connector

(1) A plug and socket widely used to connect microphones to amplifiers and for other audio applications. Phone connectors come in stereo (three wire) and monaural (two wire) versions. The prong is .25" thick by 1.25" long. See *RCA connector* for illustration.

(2) A plug and socket for a telephone line, typically the RJ-11 modular connector.

phone hawk

A person who calls up a computer via modem and either copies or destroys data.

phoneme

A speech utterance, such as "k," "ch," and "sh," that is used in synthetic speech systems to compose words for audio output. See *formant information*.

PhoneNET

Communications products from Farallon Communications, Inc., Emeryville, CA, (www.farallon.com), that extend LocalTalk distances to 3,000 feet and use unshielded twisted phone lines instead of shielded twisted pair. Configurations include daisy chain, passive star as well as active star topologies for both EtherTalk and LocalTalk. Optional Traffic Watch software provides network management and administration.

Phong shading

In 3-D graphics, a technique developed by Phong Bui Tuong that computes a shaded surface based on the color and illumination at each pixel. The surface normals at the triangle's points are used to compute a surface normal for each pixel, which in turn creates a more accurate RGB value for each pixel. Phong shading is more realistic than Gouraud shading, but requires much more computation. See *Gouraud shading*.

phono connector

See *RCA connector*.

phosphor

A rare earth material used to coat the inside face of a CRT. When struck by an electron beam, the phosphor emits a visible light for a few milliseconds. In color displays, red, green and blue phosphor dots are grouped as a cluster.

Photo CD

A CD imaging system from Kodak that digitizes 35mm slides or negatives onto a CD-ROM disc. The Photo CD is created by photo finishers that have a Kodak Picture Imaging Workstation. It takes about a half hour to put 100 photos (the maximum per disc) onto the CD. Each photographic-quality image (2048x3072x24) compresses into six megabytes. A replica of each image in the form of contact prints is also included.

Hardware requirements for Photo CD are 10MB of RAM in order to display an image in full resolution and a current-day CD-ROM drive that has multisession capability, which can read images that were added after the original set.

Other formats include the Photo CD Portfolio, which holds up to 800 TV-quality images (512x768), the Pro Photo CD, which stores images from professional format film (120, 4x5, etc.), the Photo CD Catalog, which holds thousands of pictures and the Photo CD Medical disk for storing film-based images.

Many software packages can access Photo CD images, and many paint, drawing and image enhancement programs support Photo CD's PCD file format. A Kodak Photo CD player is available that lets you view the Photo CDs on your TV and also play audio CDs.

photocomposition

Laying out a printed page using electrophotographic machines, such as imagesetters and laser printers. See *page makeup* and *pagination*.

photoconductor

The type of material typically used in a photodetector. It increases its electrical conductivity when exposed to light.

PhotoDeluxe

A consumer version of Photoshop that is bundled with a variety of scanners, digital cameras and other software. Although it lacks the myriad of sophisticated features found in Photoshop, it is widely used to add basic enhancements to scanned images. See *Photoshop*.

photodetector

A device that senses the light pulses in an optical fiber and converts them into electrical pulses. It uses the principle of photoconductivity, which is exhibited in certain materials that change their electrical conductivity when exposed to light.

photo editing
See *image editing*.

photo illustration program
See *image editor*.

photolithography
A lithographic technique used to transfer the design of the circuit paths and electronic elements on a chip onto a wafer's surface. A photomask is created with the design for each layer of the chip. The wafer is coated with a light-sensitive film (photoresist) that is hardened when exposed to light shining through the photomask. The wafer is then exposed to an acid bath (wet processing) or hot ions (dry processing), and the unhardened areas are etched away.

photomask
An opaque image on a transluscent plate that is used as a light filter to transfer an image from one device to another. See *chip*.

photomicrography
Photographing microscopic images.

photomultiplier tube
A vacuum tube that converts light into electrical energy and amplifies it. Photomultiplier tubes are used in high-end drum scanners, because they are more sensitive to light than the CCD elements used in lower-cost devices.

photon
A unit of energy. Elementary particle of electromagnetic radiation (light, radio waves, X-rays, etc.).

photonics
The science of building machine circuits that use light instead of electricity.

photooptic memory
A storage device that uses a laser beam to record data onto a photosensitive film.

photo printer
A photograph printer that uses dye sublimation or CYCOLOR technology to provide photorealistic quality output, typically no larger than 4x6". The images may be created in or scanned into the computer or taken from a digital camera. See *photo scanner*.

photorealistic
Having the image quality of a photograph.

photorealistic image synthesis
In computer graphics, a format for describing a picture that depicts the realism of the actual image. It includes such attributes as surface texture, light sources, motion blur and reflectivity.

photoresist
A film used in photolithography that temporarily holds the pattern of a circuit path or microscopic element of a chip. When exposed to light, it hardens and is resistant to the acid bath that washes away the unexposed areas.

One of the First
The FARGO FotoFUN! printer was one of the first photo printers on the market. It was introduced in 1995 at a breakthrough price of $595 for a dye sublimation printer. *(Photo courtesy of FARGO Electronics, Inc.)*

photo scanner
A scanner specialized for reading photographs up to 4x6". It uses the same principles as a larger desktop scanner, but is generally a low-cost, consumer-oriented device geared for digitizing home photos into the computer. See *scanner* and *photo printer*.

photosensitive
A material that changes when exposed to light.

photosensor
A light-sensitive device that is used in optical scanning machinery.

Photoshop
A popular high-end image editor for the Macintosh and Windows from Adobe. The original Mac versions were the first to bring affordable image editing down to the personal computer level in the late 1980s. Since then, Photoshop has become the de facto standard in image editing. Although it contains a large variety of image editing features, one of Photoshop's most powerful capabilities is layers, which allows images to be rearranged under and over each other for placement. Photoshop is designed to read and convert a raft of graphics images, but it provides its own native file format for layers (.PSD extension). See *image editor* and *layers*.

Photoshop plug-in
A third-party software product that extends Photoshop's capabilities. There are countless plug-ins that provide ways to enhance and change an image beyond the already-comprehensive set of tools that comes with Photoshop.

phototypesetter
See *imagesetter*.

phreaker
A person who makes free long distance phone calls using illegal methods.

physical
Refers to devices at the electronic, or machine, level. Contrast with *logical*. See *logical vs physical*.

physical address
The actual, machine address of an item or device.

physical drive
Refers to the actual unit of hardware of a disk or tape drive. Contrast with *logical drive*.

physical format
See *record layout* and *low-level format*.

physical layer
The services in the OSI protocol stack (layer 1 of 7) that provide the transmission of bits over the network medium. See *OSI*.

physical link
(1) An electronic connection between two devices.

(2) In data management, a pointer in an index or record that refers to the physical location of data in another file.

physical lock
A device that prevents access to data, such as a key lock switch on a computer or a file protection mechanism on a floppy disk. Contrast with *logical lock*.

Physical Unit
See *PU*.

PIC
(1) (PICture) A file extension used for graphics formats. Lotus PIC is a vector format for 1-2-3 charts and graphs. Videoshow PIC is a vector format that is a subset of the NAPLPS standard.

(2) (Programmable Interrupt Controller) An Intel 8259A chip that controls interrupts. Starting with the 286-based AT, there are two PICs in a PC, providing a total of 15 usable IRQs. The PIC has been superseded by an Advanced Programmable Interrupt Controller, or 82489DX chip, that is enhanced for multiprocessing. See *IRQ*.

pica

(1) In word processing, a monospaced font that prints 10 characters per inch.

(2) In typography, about 1/6th of an inch (0.166") or 12 points.

Pick System

A multiuser operating environment and database management system (DBMS) from Pick Systems, Inc., Irvine, CA, (www.picksys.com), that runs on x86, PowerPC and UNIX platforms. It has been highly praised for its ease of use, flexibility and advanced features. The DBMS portion of the Pick System is widely used in third-party products. R83 is the original Pick System. R93 and Advanced Pick are later versions. D3 is the DBMS, and D3 Pro Plus is a Linux/DBMS package.

The Pick System was originally developed by Richard Pick, who created a system for the U.S. Army while working at TRW Corporation. He later transformed it into the Reality operating system for Microdata and then obtained the right to license it to other vendors.

pico

Trillionth (10^{-12}). See *space/time*.

picoJava

The core architecture in Sun's Java chip. See *microJava*.

picometer

One trillionth of a meter. Pronounced "pee-co-meter." See *nanometer*.

picosecond

One trillionth of a second. Pronounced "pee-co-second." See *space/time* and *ohnosecond*.

PICS

(1) (Pantone Internet Color System) The Pantone implementation of the Netscape color palette. See *Netscape color palette*.

(2) (Platform for Internet Content Selection) A system for rating the content of Web sites that has been endorsed by the World Wide Web Consortium. PICS is promoted worldwide in order to encourage self regulation and avoid governmental censorship. For information, visit www.w3.org.

PICT

(PICTure) The primary Macintosh graphics file format. It holds QuickDraw vector images, bitmapped images and text and is the Mac counterpart to the Windows Metafile (WMF) format. When PICT files are converted to the PC, they use the .PCT file extension.

picture

In programming, a pattern that describes the type of data allowed in a field or how it will print. The pattern is made up of a character code for each character in the field; for example, 9999 is a picture for four numeric digits. A picture for a telephone number could be (999) 999-9999. XXX999 represents three alphanumerics followed by three numerics. Pictures are similar but not identical in all programming languages.

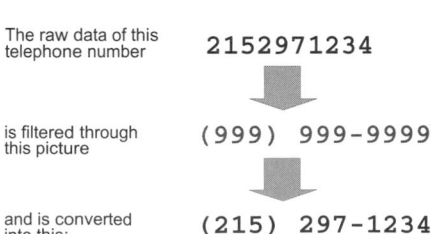

The raw data of this telephone number

2152971234

is filtered through this picture

(999) 999-9999

and is converted into this:

(215) 297-1234

picture element

See *pixel*.

Picturephone

The proposed video/telephone introduced by AT&T at the 1964 World's Fair in New York. Many thought it would flourish by the end of the 1980s. Realtime video is expected to be widely used after the turn of the century.

Picture Publisher

A full-featured image editing program for Windows from Micrografx. It includes a customizable user interface and provides layers for building composite pictures. In Version 5.0, every user action is recorded in a command list that can be edited and used as a macro.

PID

(1) (Process IDentifier) A temporary number assigned by the operating system to a process or service.

(2) (Proportional Integral Derivative) A controller used to regulate a continuous process such as grinding or cooking.

pie chart

A graphical representation of information in which each unit of data is represented as a pie-shaped piece of a circle. See *business graphics*.

piezoelectric

The property of certain crystals that causes them to oscillate when subjected to electrical pressure (voltage). See *ink jet printer* for a diagram of the piezoelectric drop on demand ink jet technology.

PIF

(Program Information File) A Windows data file used to hold requirements for DOS applications running under Windows. Windows comes with a variety of PIFs, but users can edit them and new ones can be created with the PIF editor if a DOS application doesn't work properly. An application can be launched by clicking on its PIF.

piggyback board

A small printed circuit board that plugs into another circuit board in order to enhance its capabilities. It does not plug into the motherboard, but would plug into the boards that plug into the motherboard.

PII

See *Pentium II*.

PIL

(Publishing Interchange Language) A standard for document interchange that defines the placement of text and graphics objects on the page. It does not address the content of the objects.

PILOT

(Programmed Inquiry Learning Or Teaching) A high-level programming language used to generate question-and-answer courseware. A version that incorporated turtle graphics ran on Atari computers.

PIM

(Personal Information Manager) Software that organizes names and addresses and random notes for fast retrieval. It provides a combination of features such as a telephone list with automatic dialing, calendar, scheduler and tickler. A PIM lets you jot down text for any purpose and retrieve it based on any of the words you typed in. PIMs vary widely, but all of them attempt to provide methods for managing information the way you use it on a daily basis.

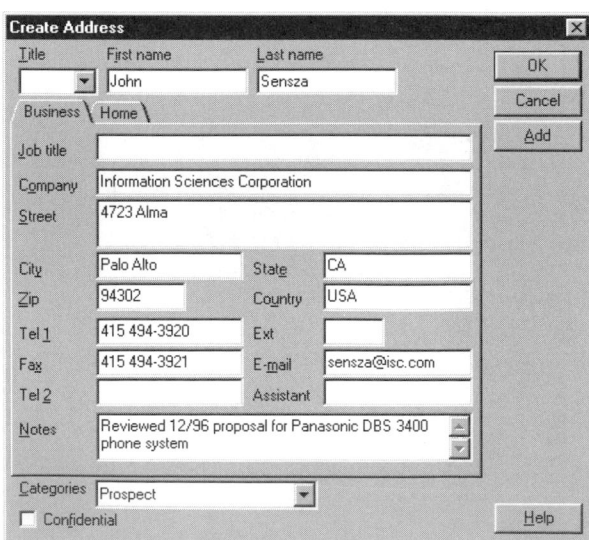

pin

(1) The male lead on a connector (serial port, VGA cable, keyboard, etc.) or the spiderlike foot on a chip. Each pin is plugged into a socket to complete the circuit. The number of pins on a

Two Schools of Thought
While both PIMs (opposite page and right) provide the ability to generate fixed forms, Lotus Organizer (opposite page) provides a structured way to record addresses. The Info Select window (right) provides a free-form area where you can place text anywhere you wish. The best method is the one that suits your personality. Usually, people strongly prefer one method over the other.

connector determines the maximum number of wires that can carry signals in the cable. The number of pins on a chip determines the maximum number of signal paths that may be used.

(2) (PIN) (Personal Identification Number) A personal password used for identification purposes.

(3) (PIN) (Processor Independent NetWare) A version of NetWare 4.1 designed for portability to multiple platforms. Development was stopped in early 1995.

pinch roller
A small, freely-turning wheel in a tape drive that pushes the tape against a motor-driven wheel in order to move it.

pin compatible
Refers to a chip or other electronic module that can be plugged into the same socket as the chip or module it is replacing.

pincushioning
A screen distortion in which the sides bow in. Contrast with *barrel distortion*.

pin feed
A method for moving continuous paper forms. Pins at both ends of a rotating platen or tractor engage the forms through pre-punched holes at both sides. See *tractor feed*.

ping
(1) (Packet INternet Groper) An Internet utility u to determine whether a particular IP address is online. used to test and debug a network by sending out a packet and waiting for a response.

Ping also functions like a domain name (DNS) server, because "pinging" a domain name will return its IP address. See *ICMP*.

(2) See also PNG.

Pin Feed Platen
This platen has pins on both ends that engage the continous forms. Pin feed platens and tractors are widely used on dot matrix printers.

Ping of Death
A ping request that crashes the target computer. It is caused by an invalid packet size value in the packet header. There are patches for most operating systems that get around it. See *denial of service attack*.

ping pong
(1) A half-duplex communications method in which data is transmitted in one direction and acknowledgement is returned at the same speed in the other. The line is alternately switched from transmit to receive in each direction. Contrast with *asymmetric modem*.

(2) To go in one direction and then in the other.

ping-pong buffer
See *double buffering*.

pinouts
The description and purpose of each pin in a multiline connector.

PIO mode
(Programmed Input/Output mode) The data transfer mode used by IDE drives. These modes use the CPU's registers for data transfer in contrast with DMA, which transfers directly between main memory and the peripheral device. For transfer rates, see *IDE*. See *DMA* for illustration.

pipe
A shared space that accepts the output of one program for input into another. In DOS, OS/2 and UNIX, the pipe command is a vertical line (|). For example, in DOS and OS/2, the statement, **dir | sort** directs the output of the directory list to the sort utility.

pipeline burst cache
A common type of static RAM chip used for memory caches. Access to subsequent memory locations after the first byte is accessed takes fewer machine cycles than previous designs. See *L2 cache* and *static RAM*.

pipeline processing
A category of techniques that provide simultaneous, or parallel, processing within the computer It refers to overlapping operations by moving data or instructions into a conceptual pipe with all stages of the pipe processing simultaneously. For example, while one instruction is being executed, the computer is decoding the next instruction. In vector processors, several steps in a floating point operation can be processed simultaneously.

piracy
See *software piracy*.

pit
An indentation in an optical medium such as a CD-ROM or DVD. The laser beam is either absorbed in the pit or reflects off the non-indented areas, which are called *lands*. Using various algorithms, the reflections are converted into 0 and 1 bits.

pitch
The number of printed characters per inch. With proportionally spaced characters, the pitch is variable and must be measured as an average. See *dot pitch* and *pitch-yaw-roll*.

pitch-yaw-roll
Movements of an object that are measured as angles. Pitch is up and down like a box lid. Yaw is left and right like a door on hinges, and roll is rotation.

pivot table
A multidimensional data structure which allows the user to quickly switch to different views of the data. Pivot tables are created in spreadsheets and database programs. See *multidimensional views* for illustration.

pixel
(**PIX** [picture] **EL**ement) The smallest addressable unit on a display screen. The higher the pixel resolution (the more rows and columns of pixels), the more information can be displayed.

In storage, pixels are made up of one or more bits. The greater this "bit depth," the more shades or colors can be represented. The most economical

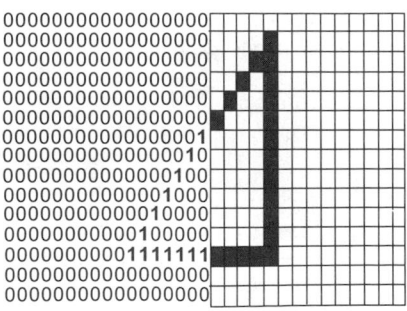

A Monochrome Bitmap
The simplest pixel representation is a monochrome image in which one bit represents a dark or light pixel (black or white, black or amber, etc.).

system is monochrome, which uses one bit per pixel (on/off). Gray scale and color displays typically use from 4 to 24 bits per pixel, providing from 16 to 16 million colors. See *bit depth*.

On screen, pixels are made up of one or more dots of color. Monochrome and gray scale systems use one dot per pixel. For monochrome, the dark pixel is energized light. For gray scale, the pixel is energized with different intensities, creating a range from dark to light. Color systems use a red, green and blue dot per pixel, each of which is energized to different intensities, creating a range of colors perceived as the mixture of these dots. Black is all three dots dark, white is all dots light.

pixelated

The appearance of pixels in a bitmapped image. For example, when an image is displayed or printed too large, the individual, square pixels are discernible to the naked eye where one color or shade of gray blends into another. Sometimes, images are pixelated purposefully for special effects.

A Pixelated Picture

pixel depth

Same as *bit depth*.

pixel graphics

Same as *bitmapped graphics*.

PJL

(Printer Job Language) A printer command language from HP that adds control for individual print jobs and also includes the ability to set printer default settings. See *PCL*.

PKI

(Public Key Infrastructure) A policy for establishing a secure method for exchanging information within an organization, an industry or a nation. It includes the cryptographic methods, the use of digital certificates and certificate authorities (CAs) and the system for managing the process. See *digital certificate*.

PKZIP, PKUNZIP

Popular compression programs for DOS, Windows, OS/2 and VMS/VAX from PKWARE Inc., Brown Deer, WI, (www.pkware.com). PK stands for Phil Katz. PKZIP compresses files into a ZIP file and PKUNZIP decompresses them. PKWARE also provides its data compression library (DCL) to developers that want to include realtime compression and decompression of data in their applications.

The PKZIP programs are also available on other platforms from a third party. PKARC and PKXARC were previous compression programs that are no longer supported.

PL1

See *PL/I*.

PLA

(Programmable Logic Array) A type of programmable logic chip (PLD) that contains arrays of programmable AND and OR gates. See *PAL* and *PLD*.

Placeable Metafile

See *Windows Metafile*.

plaintext

Normal text that has not been encrypted and is readable by text editors and word processors. Contrast with *ciphertext*.

plain vanilla

Refers to the bare minimum of functions that are known to be available in an application or system. Contrast with *bells and whistles*.

planar

A technique developed by Fairchild Instruments that creates transistor sublayers by forcing chemicals under pressure into exposed areas. Planar superseded the mesa process and was a major step toward creating the chip.

planar area

In computer graphics, an object that has boundaries, such as a square or polygon.

planning system

See *spreadsheet* and *financial planning system*.

plasma display

Also called *gas discharge display*, a flat-screen technology that contains an inert ionized gas sandwiched between x- and y-axis panels. A pixel is selected by charging one x- and one y-wire, causing the gas in that vicinity to glow. Plasma displays were initially monochrome, typically orange, but color displays are increasingly being used for large screens. Models 40 inches diagonal and greater have been developed. Color plasma technology is expected to be widely used.

plastic LCC

See *PLCC*.

plastic quad flat package

See *PQFP*.

platen

A long, thin cylinder in a typewriter or printer that guides the paper through it and serves as a backstop for the printing mechanism to bang into.

platform

A hardware or software architecture. The term originally dealt with only hardware, and it is still used to refer to a CPU model or computer family. For example, "the x86, or PC, is the world's largest hardware platform." VAX, AS/400 and SPARC are other examples of hardware platforms (see *hardware platforms* for a complete list).

Platform also refers to an operating system, in which case the hardware may or may not be implied. For example, when a program is said to "run on the Windows platform," it means that the program has been compiled into the Intel x86 machine language and that it communicates with the Windows operating system. If for example Windows were to become extremely popular on Alpha hardware, then "it runs on the Windows platform" would be ambiguous. In order to differentiate, one would have to say "Windows for Alpha" or "Windows for Intel."

This is especially true for UNIX. Since some variation of UNIX runs on almost every hardware platform, the phrase "the program runs on the UNIX platform" is not precise. It generally means that the application runs on the most popular UNIX workstations, but you would have to find out which ones to be sure.

The term also refers to software-only environments. For example, a messaging platform or groupware platform implies one or more programming interfaces that e-mail, calendaring and other client programs are written to in order to communicate with the services provided by the server.

The terms platform and environment are often used interchangeably. See *environment*.

platform dependent, platform independent

See *machine dependent* and *machine independent*.

platter

One of the disks in a hard disk drive. Each platter provides a top and bottom recording surface. See *magnetic disk*.

PLB, PLBmark, PLBsurf, PLBwire

(Picture Level Benchmark) A benchmark for measuring graphics performance on workstations. The Benchmark Interface Format (BIF) defines the format, the Benchmark Timing Methodology (BTM) performs the test, and the Benchmark Reporting Format (BRF) generates results in PLBmarks (formerly GPCmarks), which are divided into PLBwire93 (wireframe modeling) and PLBsurf93 (surface modeling) ratings. Image quality is not rated. See *GPC*.

PLC

(Programmable Logic Controller) A computer used in process control applications. PLC microprocessors are typically RISC-based and are designed for high-speed, realtime and rugged industrial environments.

PLCC

(Plastic Leaded Chip Carrier) A plastic, square, surface mount chip package that contains leads on all four sides. The leads (pins) extend down and back under and into tiny indentations in the housing. See *chip package*.

PLD

(Programmable Logic Device) A logic chip that is programmed at the customer's site. It uses either fusible links, which are "blown" to open the lines or Actel's Antifuse technology to fuse them together. There are a wide variety of PLD techniques; however, most PLDs are of the PLA (Programmable Logic Array) or PAL (Programmable Array Logic) variety, which provide different configurations of AND and OR gates.

Unlike gate arrays, which require the final masking fabrication process, PLDs are easily programmable in the field. PLDs are always used for logical functions, but programmable storage chips such as PROMs and EPROMs may also be considered as PLDs if they contain program code rather than just data. See *SPLD, CPLD* and *ASIC*.

plenum

In a building, the space between the real ceiling and the dropped ceiling, which is often used as an air duct for heating and air conditioning. It is also filled with electrical, telephone and network wires. See *plenum cable*.

plenum cable

Cable that is suitable for running in air ducts and spaces between the floor and ceiling. It uses a fire retardant coating that must comply with local building codes. See *plenum*.

PL/I

(Programming Language 1) A high-level IBM programming language introduced in 1964 with the System/360 series. It was designed to combine features of and eventually supplant COBOL and FORTRAN, which never happened. A PL/I program is made up of procedures (modules) that can be compiled independently. There is always a main procedure and zero or more additional ones. Functions, which pass arguments back and forth, are also provided.

PL/M

(Programming Language for Microprocessors) A dialect of PL/I developed by Intel as a high-level language for its microprocessors. PL/M+ is an extended version of PL/M, developed by National Semiconductor for its microprocessors.

plot

To create an image by drawing a series of lines. In programming, a plot statement creates a single vector (line) or a complete circle or box that is made up of several vectors.

plotter

A graphics printer that draws images with ink pens. It actually draws point-to-point lines directly from vector graphics files. The plotter was the first computer output device that could print graphics as well as accomodate full-size

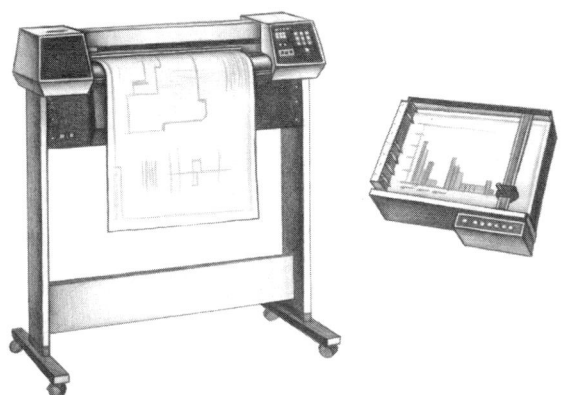

Drum and Flatbed Plotters
Both types of plotters actually "draw" the images. The drum plotter (left) wraps the paper around a drum with pin feeds. It moves the paper back and forth for one direction of the plot. The pens move across the paper, creating the other axis. The bed of the flatbed unit (right) determines the maximum size of the total drawing.

engineering and architectural drawings. Using different colored pens, it was also able to print in color long before ink jet printers became an alternative.

Pen plotters are still the most affordable printing device for CAD use and offer resolution unlike any other printer. The lines are not made up of dots. They are actually drawn, providing infinite resolution. See *drum plotter, flatbed plotter, electrostatic plotter* and *ink jet printer*.

PL/SQL

(Procedural Language/SQL) A superset of the SQL language from Oracle that is used to write triggers and stored procedures that are executed by the database management system. It is also used to include additional processing in SQL commands. A PL/SQL program is structured as a "block," which is comprised of a declaration, executable commands and exception handling section. See *SQL, trigger* and *stored procedure.*

plug and hope

Refers to the frustration of installing additional peripheral devices on a PC.

plug and play

(1) The ability to add a new component and have it work without having to perform any technical analysis or procedure.

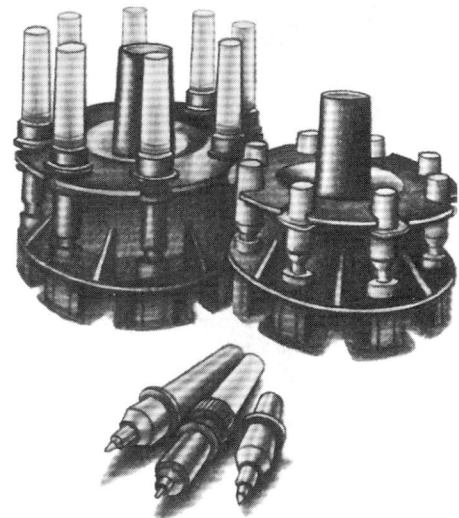

Drawing Pens
Pen plotters use drawing pens that provide infinite resolution, because the lines are actually drawn. All other printing devices print dots.

(2) (Plug and Play) Also known as *PnP*, it is an Intel standard for the design of PC expansion boards. Plug and Play is supported directly in Windows 95/98. It eliminates the frustration of configuring the system when adding new peripherals. IRQ and DMA settings and I/O and memory addresses self configure on startup.

Implementing Plug and Play requires a system BIOS on the motherboard that supports Plug and Play as well as Plug and Play expansion cards. Plug and Play can also be retrofitted to older systems by installing the DWCFGMG.SYS driver and using new Plug and Play cards.

A Plug and Play system will also assist with older non-Plug and Play cards. When a non-Plug and Play card is installed, the ISA Configuration Utility, or ICU, will check its list of known card requirements and recommend the appropriate settings. If the card is not in the list, it will also help the user determine the correct settings, providing a "plug and tell" capability.

In time, when all systems and cards are Plug and Play, we can forget the "plug and hope" days of installing PC peripherals.

Plug and Play BIOS

A system BIOS in a PC that supports Plug and Play. Although it ensures effective operation of Plug and Play under all circumstances, it is not vital for general Plug and Play operation.

plug and pray

What some people call Plug and Play on the PC. Plug and Play goes a long way to solving the frustration of adding peripherals to a PC, but it is not perfect.

plug and tell

Refers to installing new peripheral devices in a PC and using a utility program that helps to configure the device properly. Micro Channel and EISA bus installations, as well as installing a non-Plug and Play card in a Plug and Play machine, are plug and tell because they analyze the system and recommend which settings should be made.

Plug and tell is between the "plug and hope" of installing a legacy ISA card in a PC and the "plug and play" of installing an ISA Plug and Play card in a Plug and Play machine.

plugboard

A board containing a matrix of sockets used to program early tabulating machines and computers.

Alan Freedman, 1962
In the "good 'ole days," you learned data processing by carrying the data on your back. Trays of punched cards were heavy, and tons of cards were moved from one machine to the other. The plugboard, which was used to program the machines, is on the desk.

Each wire either directs a column of data from source to destination or it functions as a switch by closing a circuit. Complicated programs looked like "mounds of spaghetti."

plug compatible
Hardware that is designed to perform exactly like another vendor's product. A plug compatible CPU runs the same software as the machine it's compatible with. A plug compatible peripheral works the same as the device it's replacing.

plug-in
An auxiliary program that works with a major software package to enhance its capability. For example, plug-ins are widely used in image editing programs such as Photoshop to add a filter for some special effect. Plug-ins are added to Web browsers such as Netscape to enable them to support new types of content (audio, video, etc.). The term is widely used for software, but could also be used to refer to a plug-in module for hardware.

plugs & sockets
The physical connectors used to link together all variety of electronic devices. Following are illustrations of all the plugs and sockets described in this database.

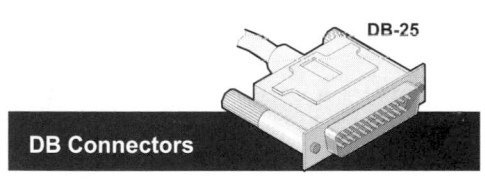

DB Connectors

DB-9
Serial port (RS-232).

High-density DB-15
VGA port.

DB-15
Game port on PC, Thick Ethernet.

DB-25
Parallel port on PC, Serial port (RS-232).

DB-37
RS-423, 442, 449.

DB-50
Dataproducts, Datapoint, etc.

Centronics Connector

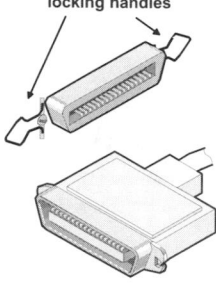

locking handles

A 36-pin Centronics connector is used on PC printers. A 50-pin variation is used for SCSI-1 devices. After insertion, the locking handles on the socket are snapped into the catches on the plug.

RJ-11 Connector (telephone)

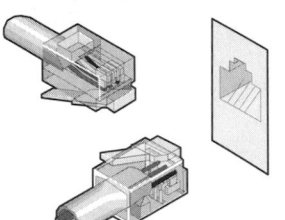

Four-wire RJ-11 connectors are used for telephone handsets and wall outlets.

There is also a six-wire variation.

RJ-45 Connector (Ethernet, Token Ring)

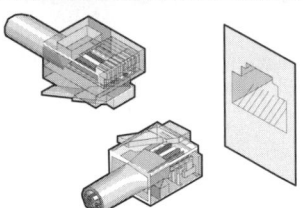

Eight-wire RJ-45 connectors are used with 10BaseT Ethernet and Type 3 Token Ring networks.

DIN Connector (keyboard, mouse)

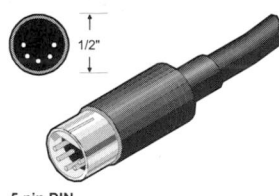

**5-pin DIN
(PC keyboard)**

1/2"

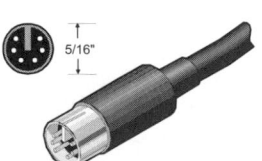

**6-pin Mini-DIN
(PS/2 connector)**

5/16"

The larger 5-pin DIN connector is used for earlier PC keyboards and various audio devices, including microphones.

The PS/2 connector uses the 6-pin mini version for mice and keyboards.

Bus Mouse Connector

5/16"

Bus mice were used in earlier PCs when a serial port was unavailable. The interface was also included on some display adapters.

Audio-Video Connectors

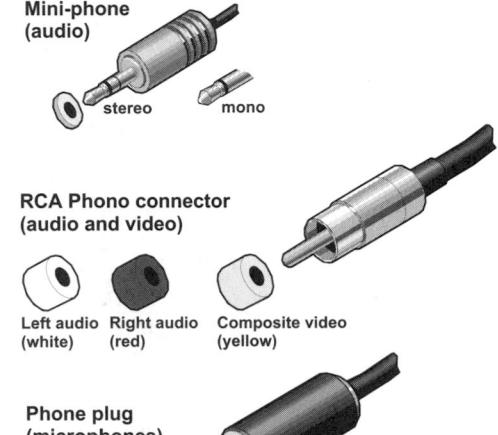

**Mini-phone
(audio)**

stereo   mono

**RCA Phono connector
(audio and video)**

Left audio   Right audio   Composite video
(white)   (red)   (yellow)

**Phone plug
(microphones)**

stereo   mono

**F Connector
(NTSC video)**

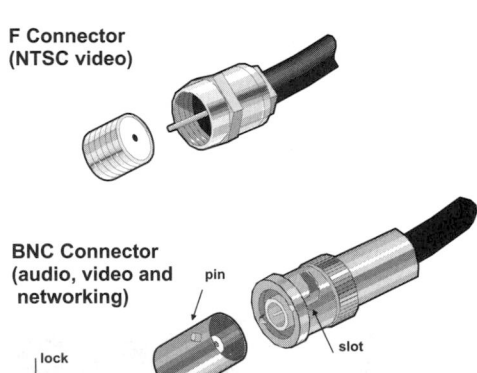

**BNC Connector
(audio, video and
networking)**

pin

lock   slot

Type 1 IBM Connector

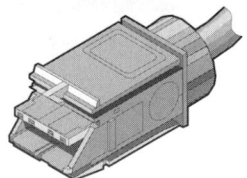

Type 1 connectors are used in Token Ring networks. The same connector is both plug and socket just by flipping one 180 degrees with the other.

USB Connector

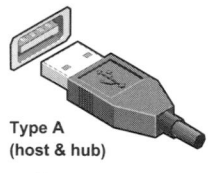

Type A (host & hub)

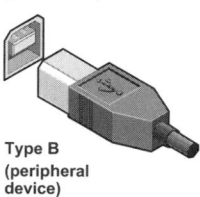

Type B (peripheral device)

Type A sockets are found on the host computer as well as the hub. All cables that are permanently attached to the peripheral device have a rectangular Type A plug.

Devices that use a separate cable have a square Type B socket, and the cable that connects them has both a Type A and a Type B plug.

SCSI-1 External Connectors

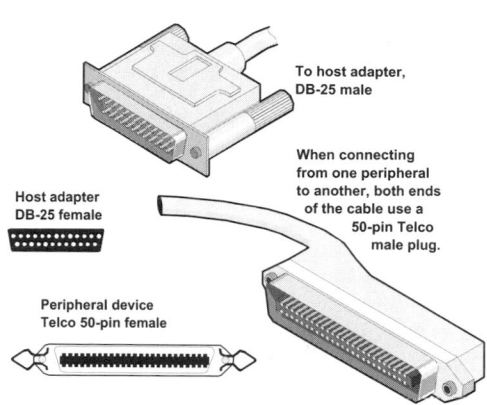

To host adapter, DB-25 male

Host adapter DB-25 female

When connecting from one peripheral to another, both ends of the cable use a 50-pin Telco male plug.

Peripheral device Telco 50-pin female

Apple Desktop Bus Connector (ADB)

5/16"

The Apple Desktop Bus (ADB) is used to connect keyboards, mice, trackballs, tablets and other devices to the computer.

SCSI-2 External Connectors

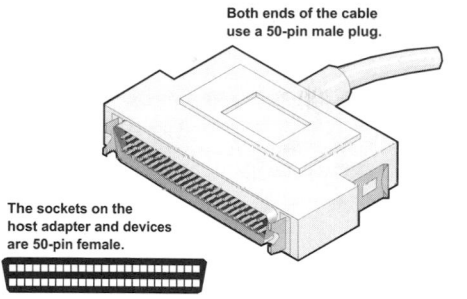

Both ends of the cable use a 50-pin male plug.

The sockets on the host adapter and devices are 50-pin female.

Twinaxial Connector

Twinaxial connectors are used on IBM System 3x and AS/400 systems.

SCSI-3 External Connectors

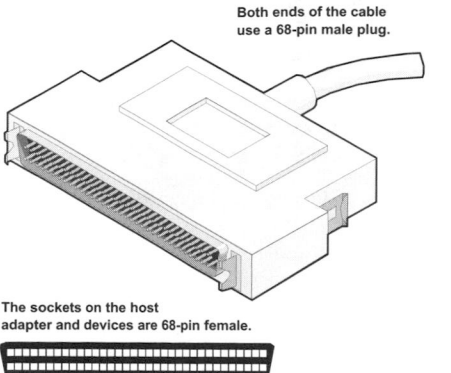

Both ends of the cable use a 68-pin male plug.

The sockets on the host adapter and devices are 68-pin female.

IEEE-488 Connector (GPIB, HPIB)

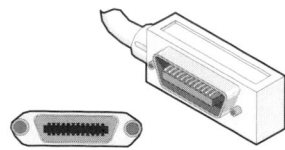

IEEE-488 connectors are used to attach sensors and programmable instruments to a computer.

PM

V.35 Connector

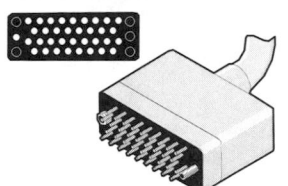

V.35 connectors are used for high-speed transmissions that combine various telephone circuits.

Fiber-optic Connectors

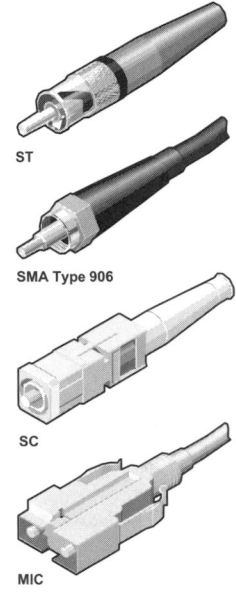

ST

SMA Type 906

SC

MIC

ST is widely used in the U.S. and SMA is used in Europe.

SC is used for Fibre Channel, cable splices and other network transmissions, while MIC is the FDDI standard connector.

PM

See *preventive maintenance, Presentation Manager, Program Manager* and *phase modulation.*

PMJI

Digispeak for "pardon my jumping in."

PMMU

(Paged Memory Management Unit) A virtual memory chip for the 68020 processor (it is built in on the 68030), which is required to run A/UX on the Mac or any 68020 platform running hardware virtual memory.

PMOS

(Positive channel **MOS**) Pronounced "P moss." A type of microelectronic circuit in which the base material is positively charged. PMOS transistors were used in the first microprocessors and are still used in CMOS. They are also used in low-cost products (calculators, watches, etc.).

PMS

(Pantone Matching System) A color matching system that has a number assigned to over 500 different colors and shades. This standard for the printing industry has been built into many graphics and desktop publishing programs to ensure color accuracy.

PMT

See *photomultiplier tube.*

PNG

(Portable Network Graphics) A bitmapped graphics file format endorsed by the World Wide Web Consortium. It is expected to eventually replace the GIF format, because there are lingering legal problems with GIFs. CompuServe owns the format, and Unisys owns the compression method. In addition, GIF is a very basic graphics format that is limited to 256 colors (8-bit color).

PNG provides advanced graphics features such as 48-bit color, including an alpha channel, built-in gamma and color correction, tight compression and the ability to display at one resolution and print at another.

PNNI

(Private Network-to-Network Interface) A routing protocol used between ATM switches in an ATM network. It lets the switches inform each other about network topology so they can make appropriate forwarding decisions. PNNI is based on the OSPF protocol, but also measures line capacities and delays rather than just simple cost metrics. Thus, ATM switches can dynamically reroute packets based on current line conditions.

PnP

See *Plug and Play*.

pocket computer

A hand-held, calculator-sized computer that runs on batteries. It can be plugged into a personal computer for data transfer.

Pocket Excel, Pocket Word

Versions of Microsoft Excel and Word for the Windows CE operating system.

POD

(Print On Demand) The ability to print a pamphlet or manual in small quantities as required. It implies printing from a computer rather than the traditional offset printing process.

point

(1) To move the cursor onto a line or image on screen by rolling a mouse across the desk or by pressing the arrow keys.

(2) In typography, a unit equal to 1/72nd of an inch, used to measure the vertical height of a printed character.

point and shoot

To select a menu option or activate a function by moving the cursor onto a line or object and pressing the return key or mouse button.

PointCast

An Internet news system from PointCast, Inc., Cupertino, CA, (www.pointcast.com). It is a free service that transmits selected news and stock quotes from the Internet to your computer. Supported by ad revenues, it displays the information as a screen saver. Users permanently connected to the Net can request downloads at regular intervals. Dial-up users can download on demand. The PointCast software can be downloaded from PointCast's Web site.

pointer

(1) In database management, an address embedded within the data that specifies the location of data in another record or file.

(2) In programming, a variable that is used as a reference to the current item in a table (array) or to some other object, such as the current row or column on screen.

(3) A symbol used to point to some element on screen. See *cursor*.

pointing device

An input device used to move the pointer (cursor) on screen. The major pointing devices are the mouse, trackball, pointing stick and touchpad.

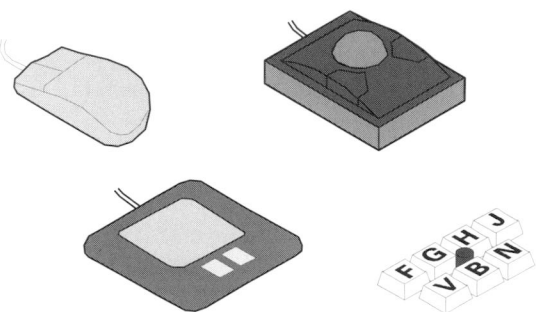

The Major Pointing Devices
The mouse, trackball, touchpad and pointing stick are the four major pointing devices.

pointing stick

A pointing device that looks like a pencil eraser between the G, H and B keys. It is moved with the forefinger, while the thumb is used to press related keys located in front of the space bar. IBM popularized this device by introducing the TrackPoint on its ThinkPad notebooks. See *mouse, trackball* and *touchpad*.

point of sale

Capturing data at the time and place of sale. Point of sale systems use personal computers or specialized terminals that are combined with cash registers, bar code readers, optical scanners and magnetic stripe readers for accurately and instantly capturing the transaction.

Point of sale systems may be online to a central computer for credit checking and inventory updating, or they may be stand-alone machines that store the daily transactions until they can be delivered or transmitted to the main computer for processing.

Point of Sale
Busy supermarkets would be hard pressed to keep up with the traffic if it were not for bar code readers and point of sale systems. Do we even remember the days without them? *(Photo courtesy of Sweda International AB.)*

point sampling

Also called *nearest neighbor*, it is the simplest form of texture mapping, which is often associated with low-end games and applications that do not demand much realism. An algorithm is used to map a screen pixel to the corresponding point on the texture map. The attributes (color, alpha, etc.) of the nearest texel are then directly applied to the screen pixel. The process in repeated for each pixel forming the object being textured. See *texture map, bilinear interpolation, trilinear interpolation* and *MIP mapping*.

point-to-multipoint

A communications network that provides a path from one location to multiple locations (from one to many).

point-to-point

A communications network that provides a path from one location to another (point A to point B).

Point-to-Point Protocol

See *PPP*.

Poisson distribution

A statistical method developed by the 18th century French mathematician S. D. Poisson, which is used for predicting the probable distribution of a series of events. For example, when the average transaction volume in a communications system can be estimated, Poisson distribution is used to determine the probable minimum and maximum number of transactions that can occur within a given time period.

poke

See *peek/poke*.

polarity

(1) The direction of charged particles, which may determine the binary status of a bit.

(2) In micrographics, the change in the light to dark relationship of an image when copies are made. Positive polarity is dark characters on a light background; negative polarity is light characters on a dark background.

polarized

A one-way direction of a signal or the molecules within a material pointing in one direction.

policy management

Enforcing the rules and regulations of the organization that pertain to information and computing. It includes the types of internal and external information that employees have permission to view while on the job as well as the kinds of software they may install on their own desktop machines. See *security*.

policy routing protocol

See *path vector protocol*.

Polish notation

A method for expressing a sequence of calculations developed by the Polish logician Jan Lukasiewicz in 1929. For example, **a(b+c)** would be expressed as ***a+bc**. In reverse Polish, it would be **abc+***.

polling

A communications technique that determines when a terminal is ready to send data. The computer continually interrogates its connected terminals in a round robin sequence. If a terminal has data to send, it sends back an acknowledgement and the transmission begins. Contrast with *interrupt-driven*, in which the terminal generates a signal when it has data to send.

polling cycle

One round in which each and every terminal connected to the computer or controller has been polled once.

polycarbonate

A category of plastic materials used to make myriads of products, including CDs and CD-ROMs.

polygon

In computer graphics, a multi-sided object that can be filled with color or moved around as a single entity. See *triangle*.

polyhedron

A six- or more-sided object. A group of connected polygons.

polyline

In computer graphics, a single entity that is made up of a series of connected lines.

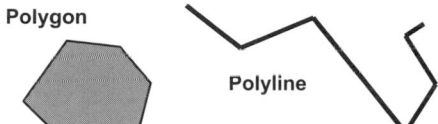

polymorphic tweening

See *tweening*.

polymorphic virus

A virus that changes its binary pattern each time it infects a new file to keep it from being identified. See *stealth virus*.

polymorphism

Meaning many shapes. In object technology, the ability of a generalized request (message) to produce different results based on the object that it is sent to. See *polymorphic virus*.

polyphonic

The ability to play back some number of musical notes simultaneously. For example, 16-voice polyphony means a total of 16 notes, or waveforms, can be played concurrently.

POP

(Point of Presence) The point at which a line from a long distance carrier (IXC) connects to the line of the local telephone company or to the user if the local company is not involved. For online services and Internet providers, the POP is the local exchange users dial into via modem. See *POP3, POP-1* and *push/pop*.

POP-1

(Package for Online Programming) The first of a family of programming languages introduced in England in the mid 1960s. It used reverse polish notation. Successors were POP-2, POP-9X, POP-10, POP-11, POPCORN, POP++, POPLOG and POPLER.

POP3

(Post Office Protocol 3) A standard mail server commonly used on the Internet. It provides a message store that holds incoming e-mail until users log on and download it. POP3 is a simple system with little selectivity. All pending messages and attachments are downloaded at the same time. POP3 uses the SMTP messaging protocol. See *IMAP* and *messaging system*.

POP server

A server that implements the Post Office Protocol. See *POP3*.

populate

To plug in chips or components into a printed circuit board. A fully populated board is one that contains all the devices it can hold.

popup

(1) A type of menu called for and displayed on top of the existing text or image. When the item is selected, the menu disappears and the screen is restored.

(2) Same as *TSR*.

port

(1) A pathway into and out of the computer. The serial and parallel ports on a personal computer are external sockets for plugging in communications lines, modems and printers. On a front end processor, serial ports connect to communications lines and modems. See *serial port, parallel port* and *PC input/ output*.

(2) To convert software to run in a different computer environment. The phrase "to port the program to UNIX," means to make the necessary changes in the application to enable it to run under UNIX.

(3) A number assigned to an application running in a server. See *port number*.

port 80

The default port address used to link incoming Web traffic to the appropriate application program. See *port number*.

portable

Refers to software that can be easily moved from one type of machine to another. It implies a product that has a version for several hardware platforms or has built-in capabilities for switching between them. However, a program that can be easily converted from one machine type to another is also considered portable.

portable computer

A personal computer that can be transported. In 1981, Adam Osborne pioneered the portable personal computer business with his Osborne I, a CP/M machine that came bundled with a variety of software. The Osborne I was soon followed by Kaypro, Hyperion, Otrona and many others. In the following year, Compaq introduced the first MS-DOS portable. See *laptop computer, notebook computer* and *pocket computer*.

port address

See *I/O address* and *port number*.

portal

See *Web portal*.

port configuration hub

See *port switching hub*.

port density

The number of ports on a device, such as a network switch, router or hub. The more ports (the greater the port density), the more devices or lines can be supported by the unit.

port expander

A device that connects several lines to one port in the computer. The port may be one interface type that is expanded into several by this device (see *port multiplier*), or it may contain multiple interfaces. For example, a port expander may provide additional serial and parallel ports on a laptop.

porting

See *port*.

port multiplier

Also called a *fan-out*, it is a device that expands one port into several. For example, an Ethernet port multiplier allows multiple stations to be connected to a 10Base5 cable via one transceiver tap. Otherwise, each station requires its own transceiver.

port number

In a TCP/IP-based network such as the Internet, it is a number assigned to an application program running in the computer. The number is used to link the incoming data to the correct service. Well-known ports are standard port numbers used by everyone; for example, port 80 is used for HTTP traffic (Web traffic). See *UNIX socket*.

portrait

An orientation in which the data is printed across the narrow side of the form. Contrast with *landscape*.

Portrait mode

Landscape mode

port replicator

A device used to connect multiple peripherals to a laptop. The desktop devices are permanently plugged into the port replicator, which connects to the laptop via a large plug and socket that duplicates all the cable lines for the monitor, printer, keyboard, mouse, etc. It serves a similar purpose as a docking station, but does not contain any slots for expansion or speakers or peripherals. See *docking station*.

Laptop

Expansion Port

Port Replicator

port switching hub

An intelligent network hub that attaches to multiple LAN segments. Via software, it allows the station ports to be connected to one of the segments. This is a type of virtual LAN, because one LAN segment can be located on different floors or geographic locations.

POS

See *point of sale* and *packet over SONET*.

POSIT

(Profiles for Open Systems Internetworking Technolgoies) A set of voluntary standards published by the National Institute of Standards and Technology (NIST) for network equipment purchased by the U.S. government. It is the successor to GOSIP.

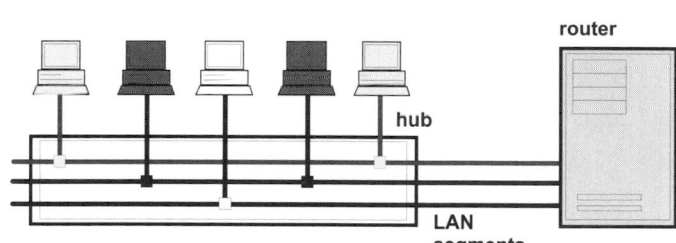

router

hub

LAN segments

Port Switching Hub

Each station attached to a port switching hub can be linked to a different LAN segment via software. In order to forward traffic from one LAN segment to another, a router is required.

positive logic

The use of low voltage for a 0 bit and high voltage for a 1 bit. Contrast with *negative logic*.

POSIX

(Portable Operating System Interface for UNIX) An IEEE 1003.1 standard that defines the language interface between application programs and the UNIX operating system. Adherence to the standard ensures compatibility when programs are moved from one UNIX computer to another. POSIX is primarily composed of features from UNIX System V and BSD UNIX.

POST

(1) (Power On Self Test) A series of built-in diagnostics that are performed when the computer is first started. Proprietary codes are generated (POST codes) that indicate test results. See *diagnostic board*.

(2) (post) To send a message to an Internet newsgroup or to place an HTML page on the Web or on an intranet. See *Usenet*.

Postalsoft

A family of programs for UNIX and Windows platforms from Firstlogic, Inc., La Crosse, WI (www.postalsoft.com) that provides mail automation and management. Since 1984, Postalsoft programs have been used to create mailing labels, correct addresses, assign postal codes and consolidate mailing lists (merge purge). Firstlogic was originally Postalsoft, Inc. See *i.d.Centric*.

posterization

The effect produced when a photographic image is displayed or printed with a small number of colors or shades of gray. For example, displaying color photographs or video with 16 colors produces a visible posterization, but the images are discernible. At 256 colors, the flesh tones on color images are still mildly posterized. For realistic flesh tones, it takes 65K colors. For absolute realism, it requires 16M colors.

postfix notation

See *reverse Polish notation*.

postprocessor

Software that provides some final processing to data, such as formatting it for display or printing.

PostScript

A page description language (PDL) from Adobe that is used extensively on all computer platforms. It is the de facto standard in commercial typesetting and printing houses. Most all accept and may even require PostScript files as electronic input.

PostScript commands do not drive the printer directly. They are language statements in ASCII text that are translated into the printer's machine language by a PostScript interpreter built into the printer. Fonts are scaled to size by the interpreter, thus eliminating the need to store a variety of font sizes on disk. PostScript Level 2, downward compatible with original PostScript, adds data compression and enhancements, especially for color printing. Level 3 adds more enhancements and native fonts and the ability to directly support more formats, including HTML, PDF, GIF and JPEG.

Encapsulated PostScript (EPS) is a subset of PostScript used to exchange a single graphic image in the PostScript format. See *EPS* and *Adobe Type Manager*.

8 colors

From 128 to 8 Colors
These examples show how an image posterizes as fewer colors are used to display it. The top picture is displayed with 128 colors, and the bottom one contains only eight.

PostScript Fonts

PostScript fonts come in Type 1 and Type 3 formats. Type 1 fonts are widely used and are made by Adobe and other companies. Type 1 fonts are encrypted and compressed and also allow for hints, which improve the appearance of text at 300 dpi and lower resolutions. Type 1 fonts use a simpler, more efficient command language than Type 3. With Adobe Type Manager, Type 1 fonts can also be used on non-PostScript printers.

Type 3 fonts do not use encryption or hints, but can use the entire PostScript language to create complex designs. They can also be bitmaps. Type 3 fonts are not widely used; however, in order to speed up printing small fonts on PostScript printers, Windows 3.1 creates Type 3 bitmaps from its TrueType outlines.

Type 1 Font Files

Type 1 fonts are distributed by Adobe as two files. One contains the outlines, and the other contains the font metrics, which includes character widths and heights and kerning values.

Type 1 font distribution disks for Windows contain PFB, AFM and INF files. The PFB (Printer Font Binary) outline files are copied to the hard disk, and the AFM (Adobe Font Metric) files are converted into PFM (Printer Font Metric) files on the hard disk. INF files contain information that the font installer requires.

Type 1 font distribution disks for the Mac contain outline and metric files that are copied onto the hard disk. For example, a Helvetica font would have an outline file named "Helve" and a font metrics file named "Helvetica." The icon for the font metrics file looks like a suitcase, and is often called the "suitcase file." A Helve.AFM file may also be included on the distribution disk.

PostScript font distribution disks for UNIX contain both AFM and PFA (Printer Font ASCII) files. The PFA files contain the PostScript ASCII code of the outline.

PostScript emulation

Using a PostScript interpreter that is not from Adobe.

pot

See *potentiometer*.

potentiometer

A device that controls the amount of current that flows through a circuit, such as a volume switch on a radio.

POTS

(Plain Old Telephone Service) See *PSTN* and *AMPS*.

POV-Ray

(Persistance Of Vision Raytracer) A popular freeware ray tracing program for DOS, Windows, Mac and various UNIX platforms from the Persistance of Vision development team. The program and source code are available at www.povray.org.

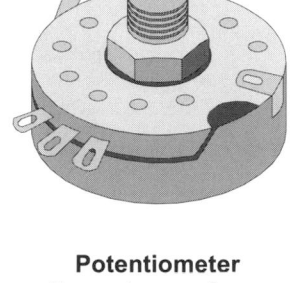

Potentiometer
It may have a fancy name, but it is quite often nothing more than the volume control on your radio or hi-fi.

power

(1) See *computer power*.

(2) (POWER) (Performance Optimization With Enhanced RISC) A RISC-based CPU architecture from IBM used in its RS/6000 workstation and parallel computer line. The PowerPC, enhanced by Motorola and Apple, is a single-chip version of the POWER architecture.

power adapter

A transformer that converts AC power from a wall outlet into the DC power required by an electronic device.

PowerBook

Apple's trade name for its portable computers, which are widely used and very popular. See *Macintosh* for specifications of earlier models.

PowerBuilder

A popular application development system for Windows client/server environments from Powersoft. It supports various databases, including DB2 and Oracle, and is also packaged with the Watcom SQL database. PowerBuilder provides visual programming tools as well as a BASIC-like programming language called PowerScript. Macintosh, Windows NT and UNIX support is also provided.

PowerMaker is a subset of PowerBuilder with a simplified interface for non-programmers and departmental use. PowerViewer is the query, reporting and business graphics generator for both products.

The PowerBook
At first glance, this model 5300ce looks like any notebook computer, except it's a Mac, not a PC. *(Photo courtesy of Apple Computer, Inc.)*

power down

To turn off the computer in an orderly manner by making sure all applications have been closed normally and then shutting the power.

power good

A signal transmitted from the power supply to the circuit board indicating that the power is stable. For various power supply definitions, see *power supply*.

PowerHouse

A fourth-generation language from Cognos that was introduced in the late 1970s for midrange computers. It supports both character-oriented, terminal-based applications as well as Windows clients. Applications developed under PowerHouse can be imported into Cognos' Axiant client/server environment.

Power Macintosh, PowerMac

A PowerPC-based Macintosh, officially known as the "Power Macintosh." PowerMacs were introduced in 1994 along with more than 100 applications that were ported to the new architecture. Since then, Apple has migrated all of its Macintosh line from the Motorola 680x0 CPU family to the PowerPC RISC chip.

In order to accommodate both platforms, Apple created a "fat binary" disk that allows software to be distributed in both 680x0 and PowerPC formats. Although PowerMacs emulate 680x0 applications, they can run faster on a PowerMac, because Apple's QuickDraw graphics engine runs native. Applications call the graphics engine extensively for screen display.

Using the SoftWindows emulator, Windows applications can also be run on PowerMacs and, with the latest PowerPC models, at respectable speeds.

The first PowerMacs came with 8MB of RAM and used the 601 CPU chip with clock speeds of 60, 66 and 80MHz versions (the 6100/60, 7100/66 and 8100/80). Subsequent 603 and 604 models are substantially faster.

power management

Maximizing battery power by using low-voltage CPUs and slowing down components when they are inactive. See *SMM*.

power margin

The excess capacity in a UPS system. For example, if a PC uses 400 watts and the UPS provides 600 watts, there is 200 watts of power margin.

PowerPC

A family of CPU chips designed by Apple, IBM and Motorola, introduced in 1993. Both IBM and Motorola offer the chips for sale, but IBM owns the architecture. The PowerPC is designed to span a range of computing devices from hand-held machines to supercomputers.

To date, PowerPC chips have been used as the CPUs in Apple's PowerMacs, IBM's RS/6000 and AS/400 models as well as in embedded systems. IBM originally offered the PowerPC as a stand-alone AIX or Windows NT machine, but since dropped the models.

PowerPC CPU Technical Specs

The PowerPC is a refined version of IBM's RS/6000 single-chip CPU. It is a RISC-based 32-bit multitasking microprocessor that has an internal 64-bit data path to memory similar to the Pentium.

The first PowerPC chip was the 601 (MPC601), which was introduced with clock speeds of 50 and 66MHz. Subsequent models include the 602, 603, 603e, 604 and 604e. The 602 is designed for consumer products, while the 603s are geared for notebooks. The 604 and 604e provide higher speeds, mostly due to increased amounts of built-in cache and higher clock speeds.

In 1977, the PowerPC 750 was introduced, providing a significant increase in performance. Also known as the G3 series, the first chips arrived with clock speeds of 233MHz and 266MHz. See *CHRP*.

power platform

Refers to a mature, high-speed computer system.

PowerPlay

A decision support system from Cognos that summarizes information for management. It combines EIS and DSS features in an integrated environment, and its Transformer creates multidimensional views of information. It runs on Windows clients and VMS and UNIX servers.

PowerPoint

A presentation graphics program from Microsoft for Macintosh and Windows. It was the first desktop presentation program for the Mac and provides the ability to create output for overheads, handouts, speaker notes and film recorders.

PowerShare

Software from Apple that resides in a Macintosh server and provides messaging store and forward, authentication of network users, encryption of messages and other workgroup/enterprise services.

Powersoft

(Powersoft Corporation, Concord, MA, www.powersoft.com) The developer of the popular PowerBuilder application development system. In 1995, the company was acquired by Sybase, creating a software vendor with 4,400 employees and revenues of 700 million. The Powersoft brand has been maintained as a separate tools division of the company.

power supply

An electrical system that converts AC current from the wall outlet into the DC currents required by the computer circuitry. In a personal computer, +5, -5, +12 and -12 voltages are generated. The 5 volts are used for the electronic circuitry, and the 12 volts are required for the drives.

The following power supply definitions are reprinted with permission from PC Power & Cooling, Inc., Carlsbad, CA 92008, a manufacturer of exceptionally high-quality power supplies.

agency approval
UL, CSA and TUV are safety agencies that test specifications such as component spacing, hi-pot isolation, leakage currents, circuit board flammability and temperature rating. Hi-pot (high-potential) isolation is the ability to accept voltage surges with safety.

efficiency
Ratio of output power to input power expresses as a percentage.

EMI
(ElectroMagnetic Interference) Noise generated by the switching action of the power supply and other system components. Conducted EMI is radiation reflected back into the power line, which is normally controlled with a line filter. Radiated EMI is that portion that would radiate into free space, but is suppressed by enclosing a power supply's circuitry in a metal case. The FCC governs conducted and radiated emission levels in the U.S.

fan rating
Airflow rated in cubic feet per minute. A 100% increase in airflow will reduce system operating temperatures by 50% relative to ambient temperature. For each 18 degrees (Fahrenheit) of reduction, the life of the system is doubled (Arrhenius equation).

hold-up time
Time period that a power supply's output will remain within specified limits, following power disturbances or a loss of input power. Adequate hold-up time keeps the computer running until a standby UPS takes over within a few milliseconds.

load regulation
Change in output voltage due to a varying load. Expressed as a percent of the normal output voltage, a power supply with tight load regulation delivers optimum voltages regardless of system configuration. This is tested by measuring the difference in output voltage when applying a light load and a heavy load.

line regulation
Change in output voltage due to varying input voltage. Expressed as a percent of the normal ouput voltage, a power supply with tight line regulation delivers optimum voltages throughout the operating range. This is tested by measuring the difference in output voltages while varying the input voltage from minimum to maximum, i.e., from 85 to 135 volts.

MTBF
(Mean Time Between Failure) Measurement of the relative reliability of a power supply based upon actual operating data or calculated according to MIL-HDBK-217.

noise (loudness)
Issues include fan blade pitch and speed, hub size, venturi depth, bearing quality and layout of power supply components. Acoustical noise is measured logarithmically; each 3 db reduction represents 50% less noise.

operating range
Minimum and maximum input voltage limits within which a power supply will operate to specifications. A power supply with a wide input range is recommended when the line voltage is subject to brownouts and surges.

operating temperature
Range of ambient temperatures within which a power supply can be safely operated.

output current
Maximum current that can be continuously drawn from the output of a power supply. PC motherboards and expansion cards draw 5 volt current. Drive motors draw 12 volts.

overcurrent protection
Circuit that shuts down the power supply from excessive current, inluding short circuits.

overvoltage protection
Circuit that shuts down the power supply if the output voltage exceeds a specified limit.

power good signal
Signal used to prevent the computer from starting until the power has stabilized. The power good line switches from 0 to +5 volts within one tenth to one half second after the power supply reaches normal voltage levels. Whenever low input voltage causes the output voltage to fall below operating levels, the power good signal goes back to zero.

ripple
AC voltage superimposed onto the DC output, expressed as a percent of the normal output voltage or as peak to peak volts. A power supply with clean DC output is essential for computers with high-speed CPUs and memory.

transient response
Time required for the output voltage to return within the regulation envelope following a 50% load change. A power supply with quick transient response will reduce the risk of read/write errors.

power surge
An oversupply of voltage from the power company that can last up to several seconds. Power surges are the most common cause of loss to computers and electronic equipment. See *spike* and *sag*.

PowerTalk
Secure messaging software from Apple that is included in the System 7 operating system (starting with Mac System 7 Pro). PowerTalk provides a unified mail box that holds different types of communications, including e-mail, fax, voice mail and pager. It provides for RSA digital signatures, which guarantees the authenticity of documents electronically signed by other users.

PowerTalk uses the AppleTalk transport protocol for network transmission. PowerTalk runs on individual Macs, while PowerShare runs on Mac servers.

PowerToys
A set of utilities from Microsoft that enhance the Windows 95/98 operating system for the power user. They provide shortcuts for executing functions and various options. However, although written by the Microsoft development team and available from the Microsoft Web site, they are not supported functions.

power up
To turn the computer on in an orderly manner.

power user

A person who is very proficient with personal computers. It implies knowledge of a variety of software packages.

PPC, PPCP

(PowerPC Platform) A term used for CHRP for a while. See *CHRP*.

PPD file

(PostScript Printer Description file) A file that contains detailed information about a particular printer. Although PostScript is a device-independent language, the PostScript driver uses information in the PPD file to take advantage of special features in the target printer or imagesetter. The PPD file is an ASCII file that can be transferred between PCs and Macs.

PPGA

(Plastic PGA) See *PGA*.

pph

(Pages Per Hour) Measures printing speed.

ppi

(1) (Pixels Per Inch) The measurement of the display or print elements.
(2) (Points Per Inch, Pulses Per Inch) The measurement of mouse movement.

ppm

(Pages Per Minute) The measurement of printer speed. See *gppm*.

PPP

(Point-to-Point Protocol) A data link protocol that provides dial-up access over serial lines. It can run on any full-duplex link from POTS to ISDN to high-speed lines (T1, T3, etc.). Developed by the Internet Engineering Task Force in 1991, it has become popular for Internet access as well as a method for carrying higher level protocols.

Over ISDN, PPP uses one 64 Kbps B channel for transmission. The Multilink PPP protocol (MP, MPPP or MLPPP) bridges two or more B channels for higher-speed operation. For example, using ISDN's Basic Rate service (BRI), you can obtain 128 Kbps with Multilink PPP.

PPP encapsulates protocols in specialized Network Control Protocol packets; for example, IPCP (IP over PPP) and IPXCP (IPX over PPP). It can be used to replace a network adapter driver, allowing remote users to log on to the network as if they were inhouse. PPP can hang up and redial on a low-quality call.

PPP also provides password protection using the Password Authentication Protocol (PAP) and the more rigorous Challenge Handshake Authentication Protocol (CHAP). See *PPTP* and *SLIP*.

pps

(Packets Per Second) The measurement of transmission speed in a local area network (LAN). In LANs such as Ethernet, Token Ring and FDDI, data is broken up and transmitted in packets (frames), each with a source and destination address. Network devices, such as hubs, bridges, routers and switches are rated for performance by the number of packets they can forward in one second.

PPTP

(Point-to-Point Tunneling Protocol) A protocol that encapsulates other protocols for transmission over an IP network. For example, it can be used to send NetWare IPX packets over the Internet. Due to its RSA encryption, PPTP is also used to create a private network (VPN) within the public Internet. Remote users can access their corporate networks via any ISP that supports PPTP on its servers.

PQFP

(Plastic Quad Flat Package) A surface mount chip housing with flat leads on all four sides. The PQFP is widely used.

prairie dogging

A phenomenon that occurs in cubicle-filled office buildings. Whenever there's a loud sound or other unusual occurrence, everyone pops up to look over the walls to see what's happening. Co-worker conversations and team meetings may also take place via prairie dogging as an alternative to the water cooler or conference room.

PRAM

(**P**arameter **RAM**) Pronounced "P RAM." A battery-backed part of the Macintosh's memory that holds Control Panel settings and the settings for the hidden desktop file. If the command and option keys are held down at startup, the desktop settings are cleared and a dialog to rebuild the desktop is initiated.

precedence

The order in which an expression is processed. Mathematical precedence is normally:

```
1. unary + and - signs
2. exponentiation
3. multiplication and division
4. addition and subtraction
```

In order to properly compute the formula that converts Fahrenheit to Celsius, which is **fahrenheit-32*5/9**, the expression

```
(fahrenheit-32)*5/9
```

must be used with parentheses separating the fahrenheit-32 from the multiplication. Since multiplication is evaluated before subtraction, 32 would be multiplied by 5 first, which is not what is wanted.

Logical precedence is normally:

```
1. NOT
2. AND
3. OR
```

In the dBASE query

```
list for item = "TIE" .and. color = "GRAY" .or. color = "RED"
```

all gray ties and anything red will be selected, since ANDs are evaluated before ORs. Grouping the colors in parentheses as in the example below yields only gray and red ties.

```
(color= "GRAY" .or. color= "RED")
```

precision

The number of digits used to express the fractional part of a number. The more digits, the more precision. See *single precision* and *double precision*. See also *accuracy*.

precompile

To do a preliminary conversion before doing the final conversion. The precompile phase sets up the source code, database, etc., in such a way that the final phase is performed faster.

predicate

In programming, a statement that evaluates an expression and provides a true or false answer based on the condition of the data.

predication

In CPU instruction execution, executing all outcomes of a branch in parallel. When the correct branch is finally known, the results of the incorrect branch sequences are discarded. See *branch prediction*.

predictive branching

See *branch prediction*.

preemptive multitasking

A multitasking method that shares processing time with all running programs. Preemptive multitasking creates a true timesharing environment in which all running programs get a recurring slice of time from the CPU. Depending on the operating system, the time slice may be the same for all programs or it may be adjustable to meet the current mix of programs and users. For example, background

Computer Desktop Encyclopedia

programs can be given more CPU time no matter how heavy the foreground load and vice versa.

Preemptive multitasking is vital in a mainframe, but is also useful in a desktop operating system. For example, it ensures that data will not be lost if a transmission is taking place in the background. The OS is able to grab the machine cycles that the modem or network program needs to keep processing the incoming data stream. Contrast with *non-preemptive multitasking*.

preferences
Options in a program that can be changed by the user. Preferences usually control the user interface, letting users customize the way they view their data. They may also control routine actions taken by the program. If preferences are not modified by the user, the default settings are used. See *default*.

prefetch
To bring data or instructions into a higher-speed storage or memory before it is actually processed. See *cache*.

prefix notation
See *Polish notation*.

PReP
(PowerPC REference Platform) A common specification for PowerPCs from IBM and Apple that allows them to run a variety of operating systems. PReP was superseded by CHRP. See *CHRP*.

prepress
In typography and printing, the preparation of camera-ready materials up to the actual printing stage, which includes typesetting and page makeup.

preprocessor
Software that performs some preliminary processing on the input before it is processed by the main program.

presentation graphics
Business graphics, charts and diagrams used in a presentation. Presentation graphics software provides predefined backgrounds and sample page layouts to assist in the creation of complete computer-driven slide shows, which in combination with a data projector, are obsoleting the 35mm slide presentation.

The software also provides a variety of special effects that can be used to fade and wipe one frame into another such as commonly found in the video world. Sound and video can also be merged into the presentation. Examples of Windows presentation graphics programs are Harvard Graphics, Freelance Graphics, PowerPoint and Charisma.

presentation layer
The services in the OSI protocol stack (layer 6 of 7) that provide conversion of codes and formats for the communications session. See *OSI*.

Presentation Manager
A graphical user interface (GUI) library used to develop OS/2 applications. Character-based OS/2 applications can be developed similar to DOS applications, but OS/2 PM applications are graphics based like Macintosh, Windows and Motif applications. The term used to be the name of the interface itself, which is now called *Workplace Shell*.

presentation services protocol
A protocol that provides graphical interface screen updates to a client station from an application executing in a multiuser computer system. ICA and T.share are examples for the WinFrame and Windows-based Terminal Server systems. See *WinFrame, Windows Terminal Server, ICA* and *T.share*.

preventive maintenance
The routine checking of hardware that is performed by a field engineer on a regularly scheduled basis. See *remedial maintenance*.

primary index
The index that controls the current processing order of a file. It maintains an index on the primary key. See *secondary index*.

primary key
An indexed field that maintains the primary sequence of the file/table.

primary storage
The computer's internal memory (RAM). Contrast with *secondary storage*.

primitive
(1) In computer graphics, a graphics element that is used as a building block for creating images, such as a point, line, arc, cone or sphere.

(2) In programming, a fundamental instruction, statement or operation.

(3) In microprogramming, a microinstruction, or elementary machine operation.

print column
A column of data on a printed report that may be subtotalled or totalled. Print columns are the heart of a report writer's description.

printed circuit board
A flat board that holds chips and other electronic components. The board is made of reinforced fiberglass or plastic and interconnects components via copper pathways. The main printed circuit board in a system is called a system board or motherboard, while smaller ones that plug into the slots in the main board are called *boards* or *cards*.

The printed circuit board of the 1960s connected discrete components together. The circuit board of the 1990s interconnects chips, each containing hundreds of thousands and millions of elementary components.

The "printed" circuit is really an etched circuit. A copper foil is placed over the glass or plastic base and covered with a photoresist. Light is shined through a negative image of the circuit paths onto the photoresist, hardening the areas that will remain after etching. When passed through an acid bath, the unhardened areas are washed away. A similar process creates the microminiaturized circuits on a chip (see *chip*).

printer
A device that converts computer output into printed images. Following is an overview of the various technologies.

For more details, look up the individual entries.

GENERAL CATEGORIES

Serial Printers (Character Printers)

Serial printers print one character at a time moving across the paper. Electrosensitive, direct thermal, older daisy wheel and even ink jet printers could be cataloged in this group; however, the primary desktop serial printer is the serial dot matrix printer, with speeds ranging from 200 to 400 cps, which is about 90 to 180 lines per minute (lpm).

Line Printers

Line printers print a line at a time from approximately 400 to 2,000 lpm and are commonly found in datacenters and industrial environments. Earlier technologies included drum, chain, train and dot band matrix technologies. The surviving technologies use band and line matrix mechanisms.

Page Printers

Page printers print a page at a time from four to more than 800 ppm. Laser, LED, solid ink and electron beam imaging printers fall into this category. All of these printers adhere toner or ink onto a drum which is transferred to the entire page in one cycle.

IMPACT PRINTERS

Serial Dot Matrix

A desktop printer that uses a moving printhead of wire hammers. It forms characters and graphics by impacting a ribbon and transferring dots of ink onto the paper. See *dot matrix printer*.

Line Matrix

A type of line printer that uses an oscillating row of print hammers. The hammers form characters and graphics by impacting a ribbon and transferring dots of ink onto the paper. See *line matrix printer*.

Band

A type of line printer that uses a fixed set of characters attached to a continuously-revolving metal band. A set of hammers (one for each column) hit the paper, pushing it into the ribbon and against the character image on the band. See *band printer*.

Earlier Impact Technologies

Impact printers were developed for the first computers, and several earlier technologies have gone by the wayside. Chain, train and drum printers were precursors to band printers. They all used actual shaped characters, or type slugs, to print a fixed size and style of letter and digit. Daisy wheel printers were desktop impact printers used in the 1970s and 1980s. Dot band matrix printers used a combination of band printer and dot matrix methods. See *chain printer, train printer, drum printer, daisy wheel* and *dot band matrix printer*.

NON-IMPACT PRINTERS

Laser & LED

Laser printers and LED printers employ the electrophotographic method used in copy machines. Both technologies are available from small desktop units to high-speed digital printing presses, ranging in speed from four to more than 700 ppm, and color units from three to 75 ppm. See *laser printer, LED printer* and *electrophotographic*.

Ink Jet

Ink jets have become the most popular form of desktop, personal printer. Most all units can print in color or have a color option. Ink jets propels droplets of ink directly onto the paper. See *ink jet printer*.

IRIS

IRIS printers use ink jet technology, but are in a class by themselves. They achieve a perceived 1,800 dpi resolution and can print on fabric as well as paper. See *IRIS printer*.

Solid Ink

Solid ink printers use sticks of wax ink that are melted into a liquid. The ink is directed onto a drum, similar to a laser printer, and then transferred onto paper for high-quality output. See *solid ink printer*.

Electron Beam Imaging

A technology somewhat similar to a laser printer, except that electricity is used to create the image instead of light. This evolved from ion deposition and is used in very high-speed page printers exceeding 800 ppm. See *electron beam imaging*.

Thermal Wax Transfer & Dye Sublimation

Dots of ink or dye are transferred from a ribbon onto paper by passing the ribbon and the paper across a line of heating elements. Thermal wax is used for bar code and other types of labels as well as medium-resolution graphics. Dye sublimation is used for photorealistic color output. See *thermal wax transfer printer* and *dye sublimation printer*.

Electrosensitive

A dot matrix printhead charges dots on aluminum-coated silver paper, usually in a serial fashion. The charge removes the coating, leaving a black image. See *electrosensitive printer*.

Direct Thermal

Used in bar code and other specialty printers as well in earlier fax machines, dots are burned onto a type of coated paper that darkens when heat is applied to it. See *direct thermal printer*.

Electrostatic

Dots are charged onto a coated paper, typically a line at a time. A toner is attracted to the paper and made permanent by pressure or heat. See *electrostatic plotter*.

printer buffer

A memory device that accepts printer output from one or more computers and transmits it to the printer. It lets the computer dispose of its printer output at full speed without waiting for each page to print. Printer buffers with automatic switching are connected to two or more computers and accept their output on a first-come, first-served basis.

printer cable

A cable that connects a printer to a computer. On a PC, the cable has a 25-pin DB-25 male connector to plug into the computer and a 36-pin Centronics male connector to plug into the printer.

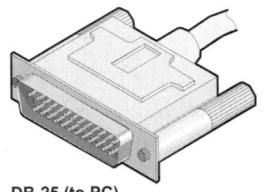 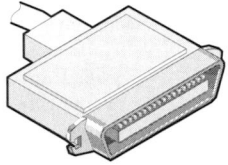

DB-25 (to PC)   **Centronics (to printer)**

printer description file

A configuration file that contains information about a specific printer. See *PPD file*.

printer driver

A software routine that converts an application program's printing request into the language the printer understands. For example, PostScript printer drivers create a file that is accepted by PostScript printers. HP printer drivers create PCL files and so on. Drivers for Windows-only printers rasterize the pages (RIP function) and send the actual bit patterns to the printer, which are applied to the drum by the laser or LED array.

printer engine

The unit within a printer that does the actual printing. In a laser printer, it includes the laser and mechanism to transfer the toner onto the paper. A printer engine is specified by its resolution and speed. See *electrophotographic*.

printer file

(1) A document in print image format ready to be printed. See *print to disk*.

(2) Same as *printer driver*.

printer font

A font used for printing. Printer and screen resolutions are not the same, thus fonts generated for the printer will not display accurately on screen. Contrast with *screen font*.

print head

A mechanism that deposits ink onto paper in a character printer.

print image

A text or graphics document that has been prepared for the printer. Format codes for the required printer have been embedded in the document at the appropriate places. With text files, headers, footers and page numbers have been created and inserted in every page.

print image format

See *print image*.

Print Manager

In Windows 3.x, the software that prints documents in the background. It is also used if the computer is connected to a network and the printer is shared with other users. Print Manager is the Windows print spooler, which accepts the incoming print jobs, stores them and prints them in the background.

printout

(**PRINT**er **OUT**put) Same as *hard copy*.

print queue

Disk space that holds output designated for the printer until the printer can receive it.

print screen

The ability to print the current on-screen image. See *screen dump*.

print server

A computer in a network that controls one or more printers. It stores the print-image output from all users of the system and feeds it to the printer one job at a time. The print server function may be software that is part of the network operating system or an add-on utility. It may also be contained on a network card that is plugged into the printer.

print spooler

Software that manages printing in the computer. When an application is requested to print a document, it quickly generates the output on disk and sends it to the print spooler, which feeds the print images to the printer at slower printing speeds. The printing is then done in the background while the user interacts with other applications in the foreground. See *spooling* and *Print Manager*.

print to disk

To redirect output from the printer to the disk. The resulting file contains text and graphics with all the codes required to direct the printer to print it. The file can be printed later or at a remote location without requiring the word processor, DTP or drawing program that was originally used to create it. This is actually the first stage of a print spooling operation. See *print spooler*.

PRISM

(1) (Photorefractive Information Storage Materials Consortium) A collaboration of IBM, Stanford University, GTE, Hughes Research Labs, Optitek, SRI International and Rockwell Science Center that is funded by the U.S. Government's Advanced Research Projects Agency for the purpose of researching holographic storage.

(2) (PRogrammable Integrated Scripts for Mirror) The programming language for the Mirror communications programs.

privacy

The authorized distribution of information (who has a right to know?). Contrast with *security*, which deals with unauthorized access to data.

Private Eye

A headband-mounted LED display system that plugs into a PC from Reflection Technology, Waltham, MA, (www.reflection.com). Its 1x1" screen gives the appearance of a 12" monitor floating in space. See *virtual display*.

private file

A file made available only to the user that created it. Contrast with *public file*.

private key

The private part of a two-part, public key cryptography system. The private key is kept secret and never transmitted over a network. See *RSA* and *cryptography*.

private key cryptography

Same as *secret key cryptography*.

private line

(1) A dedicated line leased from a common carrier.

(2) A line owned and installed by the user.

private peering

Peering between two ISPs rather than at a national exchange point. See *NAP*.

privileged mode

An operational state of hardware or software that has the highest priority. Also called the *supervisor mode* or *supervisor state*, it is typically the mode in which the operating system runs.

PRMD

(PRivate Management Domain) An inhouse e-mail service. See *X.400*.

PRML

(Partial Response Maximum Likelihood) A technique used to differentiate a valid signal from noise by measuring the rate of change at various intervals of the rising waveform. Bits generated by a modem or by reading a hard disk have uniform characteristics, whereas random noise does not. PRML uses digital signal processing (DSP) to reconstruct the data.

On magnetic disks, PRML increases the number of bits that can be recorded over earlier methods. It uses an RLL encoding sequence of 0,4,4 and provides an 8:9 ratio of user data to recorded data. See *RLL*.

PRN
(PRiNter) The DOS name for the first connected parallel port. See *DOS device names*.

Pro*COBOL
A precompiler for Windows from Oracle that converts SQL and PL/SQL statements embedded within a COBOL program to normal COBOL statements that can be compiled.

problem-oriented language
A computer language designed to handle a particular class of problem. For example, COBOL was designed for business, FORTRAN for scientific and GPSS for simulation.

procedural language
A programming language that requires programming discipline, such as COBOL, FORTRAN, BASIC, C, Pascal and dBASE. Programmers writing in such languages must develop a proper order of actions in order to solve the problem, based on a knowledge of data processing and programming. Contrast with *non-procedural language*.

The following dBASE examples show procedural and non-procedural ways to list a file. Procedural and non-procedural languages are also considered third and fourth-generation languages.

```
Procedural (3GL)        Non-procedural (4GL)
USE FILEX               USE FILEX
DO WHILE .NOT. EOF      LIST NAME, AMOUNTDUE
  ? NAME, AMOUNTDUE
  SKIP
ENDDO
```

procedure
(1) Manual *procedures* are human tasks.

(2) Machine *procedures* are lists of routines or programs to be executed, such as described by the job control language (JCL) in a mini or mainframe, or the batch processing language in a personal computer.

(3) In programming, another term for a subroutine or function.

procedure oriented
An application that forces the user to follow a predefined path from step A to step B. Data entry programs are typical examples. Contrast with *event driven*.

process
To manipulate data in the computer. The computer is said to be processing no matter what action is taken upon the data. It may be updated or simply displayed on screen.

In order to evaluate a computer system's performance, the time it takes to process data internally is analyzed separately from the time it takes to get it in and out of the computer. I/O is usually more time consuming than processing. For an explanation of "The 3 C's," or how the computer processes data, see computer.

process bound
An excessive amount of processing in the CPU that causes an imbalance between I/O and processing. In a multitasking system, process-bound applications may slow down other applications and other users depending on how the operating system slices time (see *preemptive multitasking*). A personal computer can become process bound when it is recalculating a spreadsheet, for example.

Process Charter
A flowcharting and simulation program for Windows from Scitor Corporation, Menlo Park, CA,

(www.scitor.com). It provides the ability to model and simulate a process based on the resources required for each step.

process color

A color printed from four separate printing plates. Four-color process printing uses cyan, magenta, yellow and black (CMYK) inks to produce full color reproduction. Contrast with *spot color*.

process control

The automated control of a process, such as a manufacturing process or assembly line. It is used extensively in industrial operations, such as oil refining, chemical processing and electrical generation. It uses analog devices to monitor real-world signals and digital computers to do the analysis and controlling. It makes extensive use of analog/digital, digital/analog conversion.

process identifier

See *PID*.

processing

Manipulating data within the computer. The term is used to define a variety of computer functions and methods. See *centralized processing, distributed processing, batch processing, transaction processing* and *multiprocessing*. For an explanation of "The 3 C's," or how the computer processes data, see *computer*.

process management

The execution and monitoring of repeatable business processes that have been defined by a set of formal procedures. See *knowledge-driven process management*.

process manufacturing

Fabricating products from materials that come directly from the earth. The integrated circuit, pharmaceutical and food & beverage industries are examples of process manufacturing. Contrast with *discrete manufacturing*.

processor

(1) Same as *CPU*.

(2) May refer to software. See *language processor* and *word processor*.

processor unit

Same as *computer*.

process printing

See *process color*.

Procomm Plus

A communications program for Windows from Quarterdeck that supports a wide number of protocols and terminals. Procomm was originally developed for DOS by Datastorm Technologies and was also available as a shareware program, which was very popular.

Prodigy

An online information service that provides access to the Internet, e-mail and a variety of databases. Launched in 1988, Prodigy was the first consumer-oriented online service in the U.S. The original service, which uses proprietary software, is now Prodigy Classic, and Prodigy Internet is a newer all-Internet service that uses a Web browser. Prodigy was founded as a partnership of IBM and Sears. It was acquired by International Wireless in 1996. See *online services*.

ProDOS

(PROfessional Disk Operating System) An operating system for the Apple II family that superseded Apple's DOS 3.3. It provided a hierarchical file system and file names up to 15 characters.

production database

A central database containing an organization's master files and daily transaction files.

production printer

A high-speed computer printer used for volume printing, manuals and booklets. Production printers start around 60 ppm, although some vendors claim that printers must produce 100 or 150 ppm to qualify for this designation. See *network printer* and *distributed printer*.

production system

A computer system used to process an organization's daily work. Contrast with a system used only for development and testing or for ad hoc inquiries and analysis.

productivity software

Refers to word processors, spreadsheets, database management systems, PIMs, schedulers and other software packages that are designed for individual use. Contrast with custom-designed, multiuser information systems which provide the primary data processing in an organization.

productivity suite

A suite of applications that generally includes a word processor, spreadsheet, database program, comm program and perhaps a presentation graphics or charting program.

Professional Write

A word processing program for Windows from Software Publishing Corporation, Fairfield, NJ (www.spco.com). It is the successor to PFS:Write, one of the earliest word processors for personal computers.

Professional YAM

(Professional Yet Another Modem) A communications program for DOS, Windows, OS/2 and various UNIX platforms from Omen Technology, Inc., Portland, OR, (www.omen.com). It is a flexible, full-featured program for the advanced communications user.

proficiency tests

See *aptitude tests*.

PROFS

(PRofessional OFfice System) IBM office automation software for the VM mainframe environment. It provides an e-mail facility for text and graphics, a library service for centrally storing text, electronic calendars and appointment scheduling, and it allows document interchange with DISOSS users. PROFS uses IBM's proprietary ZIP messaging protocol.

ProgMan

See *Program Manager*.

PROGMAN.INI

A Windows configuration file that describes the current state of the Program Manager layout. For example, the [Settings] section describes the on-screen location of the Program Manager window. The [Group] section identifies the group window files. Like WIN.INI and SYSTEM.INI, Windows' major configuration files, PROGMAN.INI can also be edited by the user if required. It usually isn't.

program

A collection of instructions that tell the computer what to do. A program is called *software*; hence, program, software and instructions are synonymous. A program is written in a programming language and is converted into the computer's machine language by software called assemblers, compilers and interpreters. A program is made up of:

      1. machine instructions
      2. buffers
      3. constants and counters

Instructions are the directions that the computer will follow (the program's *logic*). Buffers are reserved space, or input/output areas, that accept and hold the data while it's being processed. They can receive any kind of information required by the program.

Constants are fixed values used to compare the data against, such as minimums and maximums and dates. Menu titles and error messages are another example of constants.

Counters, also called *variables*, are reserved space for summing money amounts, quantities, virtually any calculations, including those necessary to keep track of internal operations, such as how many times a function should be repeated.

The program calls for data in an input-process-output sequence. After data has been input into one of the program's buffers from a peripheral device (keyboard, disk, etc.), it is processed. The results are then output to a peripheral device (screen, printer, etc.). If data has been updated, it is output back onto the disk.

The application program, which does the actual data processing, does not instruct the computer to do everything. When it is ready for input or needs to output data, it sends a request to the operating system, which performs those services and then turns control back to the application program.

Following is a conceptual illustration of a program residing in memory. In the physical reality of memory, everything below would be in binary coded form (0s and 1s).

Although represented as small blocks below, machine instructions can be variable in length and they are in some kind of logical sequence. Some of the instructions would be GOTO instructions that point back to the beginning of a routine or to other parts of the program for example.

For an understanding of what the computer does to process data, look up *computer* and read about The 3 C's (calculate, compare and copy).

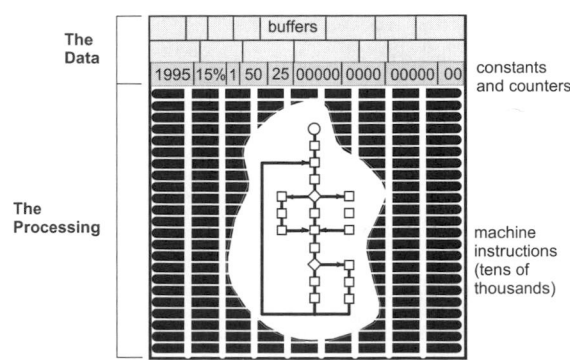

Anatomy of a Program
A program is made up of machines instructions, buffers, constants and counters. The program's logic is embedded within the instructional sequence

program counter
A register or variable used to keep track of the address of the current or next instruction. See *address register* and *instruction register*.

program development
See *system development cycle*.

program generator
See *application generator*.

Program Information File
See *PIF*.

program logic
A sequence of instructions in a program. There are many logical solutions to a problem. If you give a specification to ten programmers, each one may create program logic that is slightly different than all the rest, but the results can be the same. The solution that runs the fastest is usually the most desired, however.

Program logic is written using three classes of instructions: sequential processing, selection and iteration.

  1. Sequential processing is the series of

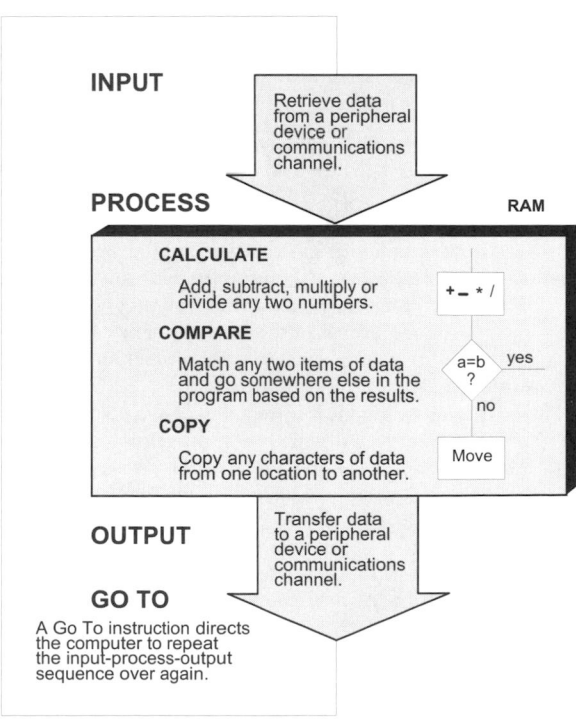

Program Logic
This is the overall logic of a business application, which is also defined as the main loop in a program. The logic contained within the process block can however be extremely complicated.

steps that do the actual data processing. Input, output, calculate and move (copy) instructions are used in sequential processing.

2. Selection is the decision making within the program and is performed by comparing two sets of data and branching to a different part of the program based on the results. In assembly languages, the compare and branch instructions are used. In high-level languages, IF THEN ELSE and CASE statements are used.

3. Iteration is the repetition of a series of steps and is accomplished with DO LOOPS and FOR LOOPS in high-level languages and GOTOs in assembly languages. See *loop*.

programmable

Capable of following instructions. What sets the computer apart from all other electronic devices is its programmability.

programmable calculator

A limited-function computer capable of working with only numbers and not alphanumeric data.

programmable IC

See *PLD*.

program maintenance

Updating programs to reflect changes in the organization's business or to adapt to new operating environments. Although maintaining old programs written by ex-employees is often much more difficult than writing new ones, the task is usually given to junior programmers, because the most talented professionals don't want the job.

Program Manager

The control center for Windows 3.x operation. It provides the means to launch applications and manage the desktop. Program Manager may be replaced with another shell, such as Norton's Desktop for Windows, HP's Dashboard or Quarterdeck's SideBar, all of which provide similar functionality with a different user interface.

programmatic interface

Same as *API*.

programmer

A person who designs the logic for and writes the lines of codes of a computer program. Programming is the heart and soul of developing computer applications, and programmers are the most misunderstood people in the business. They are constantly being criticized for taking longer to write a program than they initially estimated.

It is very difficult for people that have not spent any time programming to understand why programmers are often the world's worst estimators. Programming is very creative, and after a program is put into production, programmers derive a sense of completion that is very satisfying. Thus, the more programs programmers write, the more confidence they have. As a result, they take on what seems like an eternal optimism that the job can be done easily. As their confidence builds with experience, it often seems their estimates are even more absurd. It takes numerous hard knocks to wise up and then double, triple or even quadruple one's initial estimate in order to put reality into it.

It is also very difficult for non-programmers to understand how easy it is to program oneself into a real mess. Programmers love to code and are often in too much of a hurry to dive in instead of sitting back and analyzing the problem carefully on paper. There are a thousand logic solutions for every problem, and it is so easy to pick one that seems to solve the hurdle for the moment, only to find out a month later that the logic is inflexible and making

You didn't write it.

Whoever wrote it is gone.

There's no documentation.

The code is really ugly.

Nobody knows how it works.

Now what?

The Real World of Program Maintenance

Undocumented programs are a huge problem, and this commentary from PROCASE Corporation gets right to the point. The company produced software that created a flowchart from programming source code to make it more understandable.

changes is difficult. Even experienced programmers fall into the trap, which compounds over and over as more patches are made until the program becomes unwieldy and nobody can bring it back into stability. Programs are then reworked and reworked, because they were not designed right from the start. This is why projects take longer and why your favorite program sometimes becomes quirkier in its next version.

It would seem that programming is a profession for bright, young whiz kids, and, in fact, there are tons of them creating and maintaining some of the most widely-used software in the world. Whiz kids, or any left-brained, intelligent person, for that matter, can program with just a little bit of practice. But, it takes years to become an expert at anything. Masters in all professions have earned their stripes by making their mistakes over the course of 10, 20 or even 30 years. When you consider the average age of programmers in most software houses, it is understandable why programs don't always work well. Too many novices make decisions that even more novices have to live with. In addition, programming is such tedious work that those that would eventually become the experts burn out and take other jobs. There is a constant influx of inexperienced souls to this field. See *Freedman's law, application programmer, systems programmer* and *salary survey*. See also *to the recruiter*.

programmer analyst

A person who analyzes and designs information systems and designs and writes the application programs for the system. In theory, a programmer analyst is both systems analyst and applications programmer. In practice, the title is sometimes simply a reward to a programmer for tenure. Which skill is really dominant is of concern when recruiting people with such titles. See *salary survey*.

programming

Creating a computer program. The steps for developing a program are outlined in the illustration on the right.

The logic is generally the most difficult part of programming. However, depending on the programming language, writing the statements may also be laborious. One thing is certain. Documenting the program is considered the most annoying activity by most programmers. See *estimating a programming job*.

programming interface

See *API*.

programming language

A language used to write instructions for the computer. It lets the programmer express data processing in a symbolic manner without regard to machine-specific details.

CREATING A COMPUTER PROGRAM

1. Develop the program logic to solve the particular problem. (See *Boolean logic*).

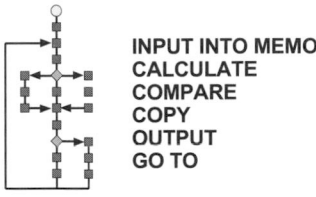

INPUT INTO MEMORY
CALCULATE
COMPARE
COPY
OUTPUT
GO TO

2. Using a text editor, the programmer writes the program in a specific language (coding the program).

3. The assembler or compiler translates the source language into machine language.

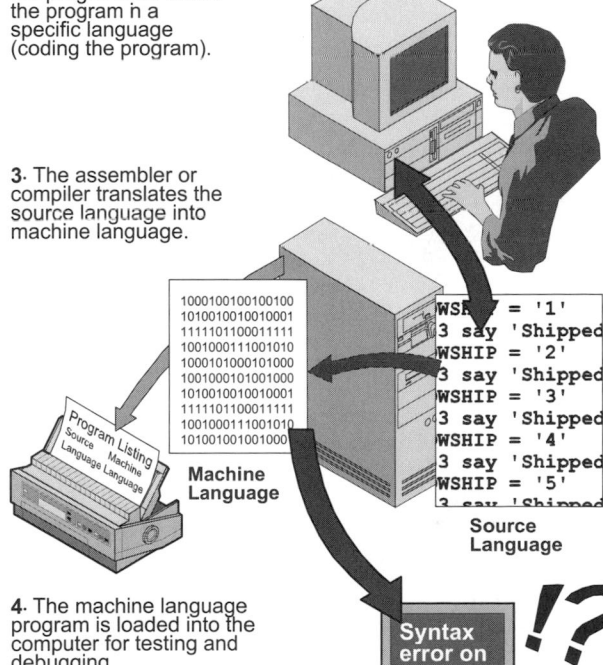

Program Listing
Source Machine
Language Language

Machine
Language

Source
Language

4. The machine language program is loaded into the computer for testing and debugging.

Syntax error on line 132.

5. The program and user documentation is prepared after the testing is completed.

programming language

The statements that are written by the programmer are called *source language*, and they are translated into the computer's *machine language* by programs called *assemblers, compilers* and *interpreters*. For example, when a programmer writes MULTIPLY HOURS TIMES RATE, MULTIPLY must be turned into a code that means multiply, and HOURS and RATE must be turned into memory locations where those items of data are actually located.

Like human languages, each programming language has its own grammar and syntax. There are many dialects of the same language, and each dialect requires its own translating system. Standards have been set by ANSI for many programming languages, and ANSI-standard languages are dialect free. However, it can take years for new features to be included in ANSI standards, and new dialects inevitably spring up as a result.

Programming languages fall into two categories: low-level assembly languages and high-level languages. Assembly languages are available for each CPU family, and each assembly instruction is translated into one machine instruction by the assembler program. With high-level languages, a programming statement may be translated into one or several machine instructions by the compiler.

Following is a synopsis of the major high-level languages. Look up each one for more details. For a list of high-level programming languages designed for client/server development, see *client/server development system*.

Ada
Comprehensive, Pascal-based language used by the Department of Defense.

ALGOL
International language for expressing algorithms.

APL
Used for statistics and mathematical matrices. Requires special keyboard symbols.

BASIC
Developed as a timesharing language in the 1960s. It has been widely used in microcomputer programming in the past, and various dialects of BASIC have been incorporated into many different applications.

C
Developed in the 1980s at AT&T. Widely used to develop commercial applications. UNIX is written in C.

C++
Object-oriented version of C that is popular because it combines object-oriented capability with traditional C programming syntax.

COBOL
Developed in the 1960s. Widely used for mini and mainframe programming. Also available for personal computers.

dBASE
Widely used in business applications. Offshoots of dBASE ("Xbase" languages) are Clipper, Quicksilver, FoxBase and FoxPro.

FORTH
Developed in the 1960s, FORTH is used in process control and game applications.

FORTRAN
Developed in 1954 by IBM, it was the first major scientific programming language. Some commercial applications have been developed in FORTRAN, and it continues to be widely used.

Java
The programming language for the Web. Sun's Java is used to create client/server applications on intranets and the Web.

Computer Desktop Encyclopedia

LISP
Developed in 1960. Used for AI applications. Its syntax is very different than other languages.

Logo
Developed in the 1960s, it is noted for its ease of use and "turtle graphics" drawing functions.

M
Originally MUMPS (Massachusetts Utility MultiProgramming System), it includes its own database. It is widely used in medical applications.

Modula-2
Enhanced version of Pascal introduced in 1979.

Pascal
Originally an academic language developed in the 1970s. Borland commercialized it with its Turbo Pascal.

Prolog
Developed in France in 1973. Used throughout Europe and Japan for AI applications.

REXX
Runs on IBM mainframes and OS/2. Used as a general purpose macro language.

Visual Basic
Version of BASIC for Windows programming from Microsoft that is very popular.

Web Languages
Languages such as JavaScript, Jscript, Perl and CGI are used to automate Web pages as well as link them to other applications running in servers.

programming proficiency & testing
See *aptitude tests*.

program state
An operating mode of the computer that executes instructions in the application program. Contrast with *supervisor state*.

program statement
A phrase in a high-level programming language. One program statement may result in several machine instructions when the program is compiled.

program step
An elementary instruction, such as a machine language instruction or an assembly language instruction. Contrast with *program statement*.

program-to-program communications
Communications between two programs. Often confused with peer-to-peer communications, it is a set of protocols a program uses to interact with another program. Peer-to-peer establishment is the network's responsibility. You can have program-to-program communications in a master-slave environment without peer-to-peer capability.

Progress
An application development system for client/server environments from Progress Software, Corporation, Bedford, MA, (www.progress.com). It supports a variety of clients, including DOS, Windows, OS/2, AIX, HP-UX and Sun. It includes its own relational DBMS, but interfaces to Oracle, Sybase and others. The majority of Progress systems are created by third-party developers. The company was founded in 1984.

progressive scan
Same as *non-interlaced*.

projection panel
See *LCD panel*.

project life cycle
See *full project life cycle* and *system life cycle*.

project manager
Software used to monitor the time and materials on a project. All tasks to complete the project are entered into the database, and the program computes the critical path, the series of tasks with the least amount of slack time. Any change in the critical path slows down the entire project.

Prokey
A keyboard macro processor for DOS and Windows from CE Software, Inc., West Des Moines, IA, (www.cesoft.com), that allows users to eliminate repetitive typing by setting up an occurrence of text or a series of commands as a macro.

Prolog
(**PRO**gramming in **LOG**ic) A programming language used for developing AI applications (natural language translation, expert systems, abstract problem solving, etc.). Developed in France in 1973, it is used throughout Europe and Japan and is gaining popularity in the U.S.

Similar to LISP, it deals with symbolic representations of objects. The following example, written in University of Edinburgh Prolog, converts Fahrenheit to Celsius:

```
convert:- write('Enter Fahrenheit'),
 read(Fahr),
 write('Celsius is '),
 Cent is (5 * (Fahr - 32)) / 9,
 write(Cent),nl.
```

PROM
(Programmable Read Only Memory) A permanent memory chip that is programmed, or filled, by the customer rather than by the chip manufacturer. It differs from a ROM, which is programmed at the time of manufacture. PROMs have been mostly superseded by EPROMs, which can be reprogrammed. See *PROM programmer*.

PROM blower
Same as *PROM programmer*.

PROM programmer
A device that writes instructions and data into PROM chips. The bits in a new PROM are all 1s (continuous lines). The PROM programmer only creates 0s, by "blowing" the middle out of the 1s. Some earlier units were capable of programming both PROMs and EPROMs.

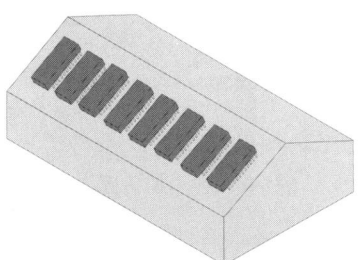

Prom Programmer

prompt
A software message that requests action by the user; for example, "Enter employee name." Command-driven systems issue a cryptic symbol when ready to accept a command; for example, the dot (.) in dBASE, the $ or % in UNIX, and the venerable C:\> in DOS. See *DOS prompt*.

propagation
The transmission (spreading) from one place to another.

propagation delay
The time it takes to transmit a signal from one place to another.

properties
Attributes that are associated with something. Windows uses the term extensively to refer to the configuration of hardware and the characteristics and features of software and data files. In Windows 3.1,

Computer Desktop Encyclopedia

the Properties option in the File menu shows the path of an icon in a Program Group in Program Manager. In Windows 95/98, right clicking on an icon almost always brings up a Properties option that provides details about the file or device.

property list

In a list processing language, an object that is assigned a descriptive attribute (property) and a value. For example, in Logo, **PUTPROP "KAREN "LANGUAGE "PARADOX** assigns the value PARADOX to the property LANGUAGE for the person named KAREN. To find out what language Karen speaks, the Logo statement **PRINT GETPROP "KAREN "LANGUAGE** will generate PARADOX as the answer.

proportional font

A font that uses proportional spacing. See *proportional spacing*.

proportional spacing

Character spacing based on the width of each character. For example, an I takes up less space than an M. In monospacing (fixed), the I and M each take up the same space. See *kerning*.

proprietary protocol

A non-standard communications format and language developed by a single organization. It requires that both sending and receiving devices use the same protocol.

proprietary software

Software owned by an organization or individual. Contrast with *public domain software*.

Protected Mode

In PCs, starting with the 286, an operational state that allows the computer to address all of its memory. It also prevents an errant program from entering into the memory boundary of another. In a 386 and higher machine, it provides access to 32-bit instructions and sophisticated memory management modes.

For example, Windows 95/98 and OS/2 are 32-bit operating systems and their operations are performed in Protected Mode in contrast to the 16-bit Real Mode of DOS and Windows 3.1. See *32-bit processing, Real Mode, Virtual 8086 Mode* and *memory protection*.

Protected Mode driver

A PC driver that is written to the original 32-bit 386 architecture, which allows access to 32-bit instructions and four gigabytes of memory. Protected Mode drivers run in extended memory (above one megabyte).

Windows 95/98 provides Protected Mode, 32-bit drivers for all the popular peripheral devices. If it does not include a driver for a particular device, it loads the 16-bit driver that was used under DOS/Windows 3.x.

protection

See *security, access control, virus* and *file protect ring*.

protection error

See *GPF*.

protocol

Rules governing transmitting and receiving of data. See *communications protocol* and *OSI*.

protocol analyzer

See *network analyzer*.

protocol port

In TCP/IP networks, a number assigned to different types of data in order to distribute incoming traffic to the appropriate program running in the computer. It is not a physical plug or socket, but a logical assignment. See *well-known port*.

protocol stack

The hierarchy of protocols used in a communications network. Network architectures designed in layers, such as TCP/IP, OSI and SNA, are referred to as stacks. See *OSI*.

protocol suite

Same as *protocol stack*.

prototyping

(1) Creating a demo of a new system. Prototyping is essential for clarifying information requirements. The design of a system (functional specs) must be finalized before the system can be built. While analytically-oriented people may have a clear picture of requirements, others may not.

Using fourth-generation languages, systems analysts and users can develop the new system together. Databases can be created and manipulated while the user monitors the progress.

Once users see tangible output on screen or on paper, they can figure out what's missing or what the next question might be if this were a production system. If prototyping is carefully done, the end result can be a working system.

Even if the final system is reprogrammed in other languages for standardization or machine efficiency, prototyping has served to provide specifications for a working system rather than a theoretical one.

(2) See *function prototyping*.

provisioned

Set up for a particular type of telecommunications service. See *provisioning*.

provisioning

Setting up a telecommunications service for a particular customer. Common carriers provision circuits by programming their computers to switch customer lines into the appropriate networks.

proxy server

Also called a *proxy* or *application level gateway*, it is an application that breaks the connection between sender and receiver. All input is forwarded out a different port, closing a straight path between two networks and preventing a hacker from obtaining internal addresses and details of a private network.

Proxy servers are available for common Internet services; for example, an HTTP proxy is used for Web access, and an SMTP proxy is used for e-mail. Proxies generally employ network address translation (NAT), which presents one organization-wide IP address to the Internet. It funnels all user requests to the Internet and fans responses back out to the appropriate users. Proxies may also cache Web pages, so that the next request can be obtained locally. Proxies are only one tool that can be used to build a firewall. See *firewall* and *SOCKS server*. See *LAN* for illustration.

PR/SM

(Processor Resource/Systems Manager) An IBM mainframe feature that allows the CPU to run as multiple logical processors, each capable of running a different operating system and set of applications. Standard on ES/9000 models, it is an upgrade to 3090 processors.

Prt Sc

See *print screen*.

ps

(1) (PicoSecond) See *space/time*.

(2) (PS) (Personal Services) IBM office automation software for PCs, minis and mainframes, which includes word processing, electronic mail and library services.

(3) (PostScript) See *PostScript*.

PS/1

An early IBM home computer series introduced in 1990. The original models featured an integrated monitor and easy-to-open case. The first PS/1 was a 286 with an ISA bus. See *PC*.

PS/2

An IBM personal computer series introduced in 1987, superseding the original PC line. It introduced the

PS/2 Model 50

The 286-based Model 50 was one of IBM's early PS/2 models. The PS/2 introduced the Micro Channel bus, VGA graphics and the 3.5" floppy disk. *(Photo courtesy of IBM Corporation.)*

Computer Desktop Encyclopedia

3.5" floppy disk, VGA graphics and Micro Channel bus. The 3.5" disks and VGA are common in all PCs, but the Micro Channel has since given way to the PCI bus.

S/2 bus

Same as *Micro Channel*.

PS/2 connector

A 6-pin mini DIN plug and socket used to connect a keyboard and mouse to a computer. The PS/2 port was originally used on IBM's PS/2 models and later adapted to all laptops and then desktop PCs. The socket is on the computer. The plug is on the mouse and keyboard cable. See *bus mouse*.

PS/2 keyboard

A keyboard that uses a PS/2 connector to plug into the computer. If the PC does not have a PS/2 socket, a PS/2 keyboard can be plugged into the standard keyboard socket using a PS/2 to PC keyboard adapter.

PS/2 mouse

A mouse that uses a PS/2 plug to connect to the computer. If the PC does not have a PS/2 socket, a PS/2 mouse can be plugged into the PC's serial port using a PS/2 to serial port adapter.

PS/2 port

A hardware interface used to connect a mouse or keyboard. See *PS/2 connector*.

PSCRIPT.DRV

The file name of the Microsoft Windows PostScript driver.

pseudo code

See *intermediate language*.

pseudo compiler

A compiler that generates a pseudo language, or intermediate language, which must be further compiled or interpreted for execution.

pseudo-duplexing

A communications technique that simulates full-duplex transmission in a half-duplex line by turning the line around very quickly.

pseudo language

Same as *intermediate language*.

PSF

(Print Services Facility) Software from IBM that performs the printer rasterization for IBM's AFP and other page description languages. PSF products are available for IBM mainframes, AS/400 and RS/6000 series and output the IPDS format for IBM printers. Various versions also input and output PostScript and PCL (LaserJet) with PSF/AIX for the RS/6000 and SP2 mainframes being the most flexible and providing the most conversion capability.

PSK

See *DPSK*.

PSN

(Packet-Switched Network) A communications network that uses packet switching technology.

PSS

See *EPSS*.

PC Keyboard

PS/2 (mouse, keyboard)

1/2"

5/16"

PS/2 Connector
The PS/2 connector uses a mini version of the common keyboard connector.

PSTN

(Public Switched Telephone Network) The worldwide voice telephone network. Once only an analog system, the heart of most telephone networks today is all digital. In the U.S., most of the remaining analog lines are the ones from your house or office to the telephone company's central office (CO). See *POTS*.

PSW

(Program Status Word) A hardware register that maintains the status of the program being executed.

p-System

See *UCSD p-System*.

PTOCA

(Presentation Text Object Content Architecture) See *MO:DCA*.

PTT

(Postal, Telegraph & Telephone) The governmental agency responsible for combined postal, telegraph and telephone services in many European countries.

PU

(Physical Unit) In SNA, software responsible for managing the resources of a node, such as data links. A PU supports a connection to the host (SSCP) for gathering network management statistics.

PU 2.1

(Physical Unit 2.1) In SNA, the original term for Node Type 2.1, which is software that provides peer-to-peer communications between intelligent devices (PCs, workstations, minicomputers). Only LU 6.2 sessions are supported between Type 2.1 nodes (PU 2.1).

public domain software

Software in which ownership has been relinquished to the public at large. See *freeware* and *shareware*.

public file

A file made available to all other users connected to the system or network. Contrast with *private file*.

public key

The published part of a two-part, public key cryptography system. The private part is known only to the owner. See *RSA* and *cryptography*.

public key cryptography

A cryptographic method that uses a two-part key (code) that is made up of public and private components. To encrypt messages, the published public keys of the recipients are used. To decrypt the messages, the recipients use their unpublished private keys known only to them. See *RSA* and *cryptography*.

public key infrastructure

See *PKI*.

public/private key cryptography

See *public key cryptography*.

publish & subscribe

To provide a source of information that users can selectively retrieve. The service can be free or paid, and the information is typically provided via e-mail or the Web. See *push technology*.

Publish and Subscribe

A Macintosh System 7 capability that provides hot links between files. All or part of a file can be published into an "edition file," which is imported into a subscriber file. When any of the published files are updated, the subscriber file is also updated.

puck

The mouse-like object used to draw on a digitizer tablet. See *mouse*.

pull-down menu

Also called a *drop-down menu* and *pop-down menu*, the common type of menu used with a graphical user interface (GUI). A menu title is displayed that, when selected by clicking it, causes the menu to drop down from that position and be displayed. Items are selected by highlighting the line in the menu and either clicking it or letting go of the mouse button.

pulling glass

Installing optical fiber by pulling it through pipes and conduits.

pull model

See *pull technology*.

pull technology

Specifically requesting information from a particular source. Downloading Web pages with a Web browser is an example of pull technology. Contrast with *push technology*.

pulse code modulation

See *PCM*.

pulse level device

A disk drive or other device that inputs and outputs raw voltages. Data coding/decoding is in the controller the device. Contrast with *bit level device*.

PUMA

(Programmable Universal Micro Accelerator) A Chips and Technolgies' chipset that accelerates graphics operations for the screen and printer.

punch block

Also called a *quick-connect block*, it is a device that interconnects telephone lines from remote points. The wires are pushed, or punched, down into metal teeth that strip the insulation and make a tight connection.

punched card

An early storage medium made of thin cardboard stock that holds data as patterns of punched holes. Each of the 80 or 96 columns holds one character. The holes are punched by a keypunch machine or card punch peripheral and are fed into the computer by a card reader.

Although still used as turnaround documents, punched cards are practically obsolete. However, from 1890 until the 1970s, they were synonymous with data processing. Concepts were simple: the database was the file cabinet; a record was a card. Processing was performed on separate machines called sorters, collators, reproducers, calculators and accounting machines.

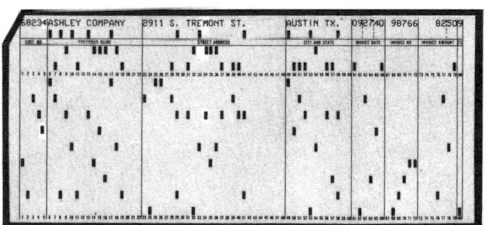

The Punched Card

Stemming from Hollerith's punched card tabulating system in 1890, punched cards "were" data processing for more than 70 years. IBM and Sperry Rand were the two major providers of punched card equipment. This 80-column IBM card shows a typical customer master record. *(Photo courtesy of IBM Corporation.)*

punch in

To press the keys of a keyboard in order to enter data.

purchasing a personal computer

See *how to select a personal computer*.

Pure Java

Refers to initiatives from Sun that specify 100% compliance with its Java specification. The goal is to maintain a consistent, single interface for Java so that all Java Virtual Machines can run all Java programs. See *Holy Grail*.

PURL

(Persistent URL) A URL that points to another URL. PURLs are used when document pages are expected to be moved to different locations from time to time. The PURL is maintained as the official

URL for that resource, and when that PURL is requested, a PURL server redirects the browser to the actual current URL. See also *Perl*.

push client
Software that resides in a user's computer which receives transmissions from Webcast servers from the Internet or intranet. It may be a Web browser with built-in push technology, such as Netscape's Netcaster, or a stand-alone program such as PointCast.

push/pop
Instructions that store and retrieve an item on a stack. Push enters an item on the stack, and pop retrieves an item, moving the rest of the items in the stack up one level. See *stack*.

push/pull tractor
A printer tractor that can be switched from pushing paper onto the platen to pulling it from the platen. Single-sheet continuous forms can be pushed, but most multipart forms and labels must be pulled to prevent jamming.

push technology
A data distribution technology in which selected data is automatically delivered into the user's computer at prescribed intervals or based on some event that occurs. Contrast with *pull technology*, in which the user specifically asks for something by performing a search or requesting an existing report, video or other data type.

Browsing the Web is an example of the pull model, while PointCast and Castanet are push technologies. PointCast was the first Internet service to become extremely popular by pushing selected news and stock quotes into a user's machine at prescribed intervals. See *Castanet, BackWeb* and *Active Channel*.

pushware
Software that uses the push model for delivery of data. See *push technology*.

put
In programming, a request to store the current record in an output file. Contrast with *get*.

PVC
(Permanent Virtual Circuit) A point-to-point connection that is established ahead of time. A group of PVCs defined at the time of subscription to a particular service is known as a virtual private network (VPN). Contrast with *SVC*.

PVCS
A system of version control and configuration management from Intersolv, Inc., Rockville, MD, that runs on DOS, Windows, OS/2 and various UNIX platforms. In 1994, it was the most widely used SCM system on PC LANs.

PVGA
(Paradise VGA) A VGA adapter or VGA chips from the Paradise Division of Western Digital.

PWB
(Printed Wiring Board) An alternate term for printed circuit board. See *printed circuit board*.

Px64
An ITU standard for transmitting audio and video in 64 Kbits/sec ISDN channels (P represents number of channels used). Although video conferencing can be done in only one or two channels, more channels are required for smooth motion.

Px64 uses two screen formats. The CIF (Common Intermediate Format) generates a 352x288 resolution, while QCIF (Quarter CIF) is 176x144. CIF transmits at 36.45 Mbits/sec; QCIF is 9.115 Mbits/sec. See *H.261*.

PXP
(Packet eXchange Protocol) See *PEP*.

Q&A

An integrated file manager and word processor for DOS and Windows from Symantec Corporation, Cupertino, CA, that includes mail merge capability as well as a programming language for customizing data entry forms and reports. Its Intelligent Assistant feature provides a query language that can learn new words from the user.

QAM

(1) (Quadrature Amplitude Modulation) A modulation technique that generates four bits out of one baud. For example, a 600 baud line (600 shifts in the signal per second) can effectively transmit 2,400 bps using this method. Both phase and amplitude are shaped with each baud, resulting in four possible patterns.

(2) (Quality Assessment Measurement) A system used to measure and analyze voice transmission.

QBasic

A BASIC interpreter from Microsoft that comes with DOS starting with DOS 5. It supersedes Microsoft's GW-BASIC and includes REMLINE.BAS, a program that helps convert GW-BASIC programs to QBasic.

QBE

(Query By Example) A method for describing a query originally developed by IBM for mainframes. A replica of an empty record is displayed and the search conditions are typed in under their respective columns (fields). This visual approach has been adopted by nearly every modern query program. Although there are differences from one to another with regard to expressing complicated queries, everything is selected from a menu by the user. The program turns the visual query into the command language, such as SQL, necessary to interrogate the database.

City	State	Balance due
	PA	>=5000

Query By Example

This query selects all Pennsylvania records that have a balance due of $5000 or more.

Q-bus

A bus architecture used in Digital's PDP-11 and MicroVAX series.

QCIF

See *CIF*.

QDOS

(Quick and Dirty Operating System) A CPM-like operating system developed by Seattle Computer Products. Microsoft purchased it for $50,000 and turned it into PC-DOS and MS-DOS. The rest is history.

QEMM

(Quarterdeck EMM) A popular DOS and Windows memory manager from Quarterdeck. QEMM was very popular in the DOS-only days and continues to be used under Windows to manage memory more efficiently.

QFP

(Quad FlatPack) A square, surface mount chip package that has leads on all four sides and comes in several varieties. The QFP itself, PQFP (Plastic QFP), SQFP (Shrink or Small profile QFP) and TQFP (Thin QFP) are plastic and use gull-wing leads. CQFP (Ceramic QFP) chips are ceramic with leads that extend outward like a flatpack chip. See *flatpack* and *chip package*.

QIC

(Quarter Inch Cartridge) A magnetic tape technology used for backup. The "quarter inch" is the width of the

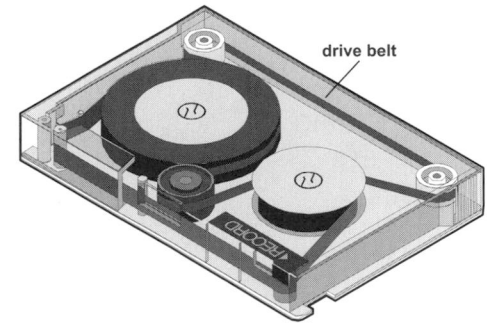

QIC Cartridge

QIC cartridges have supply and takeup hubs which are moved by a drive belt (red) that wraps around them. The belt is pinched between the capstan and drive motor when the cartridge is inserted into the drive.

original tape. QIC comes in two form factors: 3.5" Minicartridges and 5.25" Data Cartridges. Minicartridges have been enhanced with wider and longer tapes (QIC-Wide, QIC-EX and Travan), but Travan has become the most popular. Most drives read and write cartridges one generation back. Minicartridges use a DC-2000 designation, and Data Cartridges use DC-6000. See *Travan, QIC-Wide* and *QIC-EX*. For a summary of all storage technologies, see *storage*. See illustration on next page.

QIC-EX

(Quarter Inch Cartridge-EXtra) A QIC cartridge from Verbatim that uses longer tape and extends the cartridge depth to accomodate it. QIC-EX cartridges are available in .25" tape formats for earlier DC-2000 drives as well as in .315" tape for Travan drives. See *QIC, QIC-Wide* and *Travan*.

QIC-Wide

(Quarter Inch Cartridge-Wide) An enhanced version of QIC tape from Sony that provides more storage capacity. It increases recording density and uses wider .315" tape in a standard QIC Minicartridge with a redesigned housing. QIC-Wide drives support both QIC-Wide and QIC (DC2000) formats. Travan drives also support QIC-Wide tapes. See *QIC, QIC-EX* and *Travan*.

QMF

(Query Management Facility) An IBM fourth-generation language for end-user interaction with DB2.

QMS

(1) (QMS, Inc., Mobile, AL, www.qms.com) A manufacturer of laser printers founded in 1977 by Jim Busby. Initially involved with controllers for printing bar codes and labels, it got into the laser printer business in the mid 1980s. QMS, concurrent with Apple, pioneered the PostScript printer. It also introduced the first auto switching printer and the first Kanji color laser printer.

(2) (Quality Management System) A system that ensures that a manufacturing process or service is performed at a quality level. See *TQM* and *ISO 9000*.

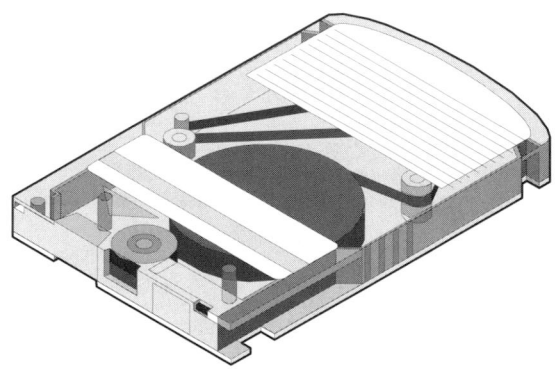

QIC-EXtra Cartridge
Verbatim's QIC-EX cartridge, which is physically extended to hold more tape, can be read and written by many QIC and Travan drives.

QoS

(Quality Of Service) The ability to define a level of performance in a data communications system. For example, ATM networks specify modes of service that ensure optimum performance for traffic such as realtime voice and video. QoS has become a major issue on the Internet as well as in enterprise networks, because voice and video are increasingly travelling over IP-based data networks. See *QoS*.

QppD, QthD

See *TPC*.

QTAM

(Queued Telecommunications Access Method) An early communications program for the System/360 from IBM. It was primarily used to transmit batches of data.

QTW

(QuickTime for Windows) See *QuickTime*.

quadbit

A group of four bits used in QAM modulation.

Quadra

A brand name for certain earlier Macintosh computers. See *Macintosh*.

quadrature amplitude modulation
See *QAM*.

quadrillion
One thousand times one trillion (10 to the 15th power). See *femtosecond*.

quad speed CD-ROM
See *4x CD-ROM*.

quality of service
See *QoS*.

QUAM
See *QAM*.

quantization
(1) The division of a range of values into a single number, code or classification. For example, class A is 0 to 999, class B is 1000 to 9999 and class C is 10000 and above.

(2) In analog to digital conversion, the assignment of a number to the amplitude of a wave. The larger the range of numbers, the finer the increments can be measured, and the more the digital sample represents the analog signal. See *sampling rate* and *quantization error*.

quantization error
The difference between an analog wave and its digital representation. See *quantization*.

quantize
To perform quantization. See *quantization*.

quantum computing
A future technology for designing computers based on quantum mechanics, the science of atomic structure and function. It uses the "qubit," or quantum bit, which can hold several values. Although theoretical, it is believed that if such a device were built, it could factor large numbers 10,000 times faster than today's computers.

quantum cryptography
A future technology for encrypting data that draws on inherent properties of photons. It enables a secret key to be transmitted over a fiber-optic channel without detection.

QuarkImmedia
An extension to QuarkXPress from Quark, Inc., Denver, CO, (www.quark.com), that is used to author multimedia publications on disk, CD-ROM and the Web. Initially slated for the Mac, a Windows version is expected later.

QuarkXPress
A desktop publishing program for the Macintosh and Windows from Quark, Inc., Denver, CO, (www.quark.com). Originally developed for and very popular on the Mac, it is noted for its precise typographic control and advanced text and graphics manipulation.

QuarkXTension
A third-party enhancement to the QuarkXPress desktop publishing program. There are hundreds of QuarkXTensions on the market.

Quarterdeck
(Quarterdeck Corporation, Marina del Rey, CA, www.quarterdeck.com) A software company, founded in 1983, that offers a variety of utilities, diagnostics, connectivity and Internet products for the PC and Macintosh. In the 1980s, with its popular QEMM and DESQview programs, Quarterdeck was the first software company to offer a serious, alternate operating environment for the DOS PC.

quartz crystal
A slice of quartz ground to a prescribed thickness that vibrates at a steady frequency when stimulated by electricity. The tiny crystal, about 1/20th by 1/5th of an inch, creates the computer's heartbeat.

Quattro Pro

See *Corel Quattro Pro*.

qubit

(QUantum BIT) A data bit in quantum computing. Such an entity can hold more than two values. See *quantum computing*.

query

To interrogate a database (count, sum and list selected records). Contrast with *report*, which is usually a more elaborate printout with headings and page numbers. The report may also be a selective list of items; hence, the two terms may refer to programs that produce the same results.

Defining a query for a relational database can be extremely simple or very complex. If the query is based on one matching condition, such as "retrieve all customers who owe us more than $10,000," it is usually pretty easy to define in a query language or program. However, "retrieve all customers who owe us more than $10,000 from purchasing toasters" is not easy. It requires several steps to determine how many toaster orders make up the balance. In fact, this is actually very complicated to program if it is absolutely necessary that the $10,000 be for toaster orders and nothing else.

In addition, relational databases are designed to eliminate redundancy. The idea is to store a data item in one table and not have it duplicated in others. For example, an order record will contain the product number ordered, but often not its description. The description is stored in a product table. Thus, any printout of products ordered and their descriptions requires that the order table be linked to the product table for that query or report. Linking customer, order and product tables is a common example of relating tables to satisfy a query.

Most queries require at least the following conditions to be stated. First, which table or tables is the data coming from. If from two or more tables, what is the link between (typically account number or name). Next, define the selection criteria, which is the matching condition or filter. Lastly, define which fields in the tables are to be displayed or printed in the result.

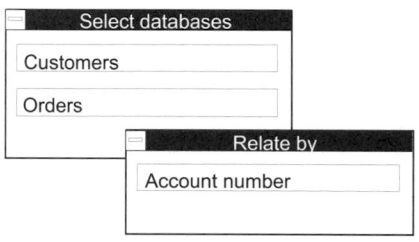

"How many customers in Pennsylvania bought widgits and owe more than $1000?"

Select which databases the data are located in and determine how they are linked.

Select databases
Customers
Orders

Relate by
Account number

Define the matching condition through which the data will be filtered. State which fields are to be in the result.

Filter		
State	=	PA
Balance	>	$1000.00
Product	=	Widgit

Fields
Company
Balance
Product
Quantity

The Query Statement

This diagram depicts the typical conditions that have to be stated when querying a relational database.

query language

A generalized language that allows a user to select records from a database. It uses a command language, menu-driven method or a query by example (QBE) format for expressing the matching condition.

Query languages are usually included in DBMSs, and stand-alone packages are available for interrogating files in non-DBMS applications. See *query program*.

query program

Software that counts, sums and retrieves selected records from a database. It may be part of a large application and be limited to one or two kinds of retrieval, such as pulling up a customer account on screen, or it may refer to a query language that allows any condition to be searched and selected.

Quest disk

A high-capacity, removable hard drive from SyQuest that provides sufficient capacity for DVD mastering as well as general storage. Upon introduction in 1998, it became the fastest, highest-capacity, removable disk on the market. It holds 4.7GB on dual 5.25" platters and connects via the SCSI interface. The Quest uses magnetoresistive (MR) heads and is avialable for Windows, Mac and UNIX (Sun and SGI) machines. See *latest disk drives*. For a summary of all storage technologies, see *storage*. See also *Qwest*.

queue

Pronounced "Q." A temporary holding place for data. See *message queue* and *print queue*.

Quick B

CompuServe's communications protocol for downloading files.

Quest Cartridge
The Quest was introduced in 1998 as the fastest, highest-capacity removable disk on the market.

QuickBASIC

A popular BASIC compiler from Microsoft that adds advanced features to the BASIC language.

QuickBooks

A small business accounting system for Windows from Intuit, Inc., Menlo Park, CA, (www.intuit.com). It works like the popular Quicken program, but is designed to track a whole business.

QuickC

A C compiler and development system from Microsoft that is compatible with Microsoft C and used by the beginner or occasional programmer. QuickC for Windows is a version that provides a Windows-based environment for developing Windows applications. See *Visual C++*.

QuickDraw

The graphics display system built into the Macintosh. It accepts commands from the application and draws the corresponding objects on the screen. It provides a consistent interface that software developers can work with.

QuickDraw GX adds capabilities to QuickDraw, including special graphics effects, more sophisticated font kerning and ligature handling and enhanced printer management. Applications must be programmed for GX in order to take advantage of most of its capabilities.

Quicken

A popular financial management program for PCs and Macs from Intuit, Inc., Menlo Park, CA, (www.intuit.com). It is used to write checks, organize investments and produce a variety of reports for personal finance and small business.

QuickTime

Multimedia extensions to the Macintosh starting with System 7 that add sound and video capabilities. A QuickTime file can contain up to 32 tracks of audio, video, MIDI or other time-based control information. Most major Macintosh DBMSs (database management systems) support QuickTime. Apple also provides a QuickTime for Windows version for Windows-based PCs.

Quicktime VR is the virtual reality version of QuickTime. It allows subjects to be viewed on screen in 3-D space. Scenes are compiled from renderings or from multiple still shots taken of all sides.

QuickWin

A library of C and FORTRAN routines from Microsoft that allows quick porting of DOS applications to the Windows environment. Character-based apps run in resizable windows.

Quinta

(Quinta Division of Seagate Technology, Inc., www.seagate.com/quinta.html) A division within Seagate that is developing a next-generation hard disk. Its Optically Assisted Winchester (OAW) technology employs magnetic and optical methods to increase storage capacity. See *latest disk drives*.

qwerty keyboard

The standard English language typewriter keyboard.

Q, W, E, R, T and Y are the letters on the top left, alphabetic row. Designed in 1868 by Christopher Sholes, who invented the typewriter, the keyboard was organized to slow down a person's typing in order to prevent the keys from jamming. See *Dvorak keyboard*.

Qwest

(Qwest Communications International Inc., Denver, CO, www.qwest.com) A telecommunications company that offers services to telecom carriers, businesses and homes using an extensive fiber optic network throughout the U.S. and Mexico. It started out in 1988 as the SP Construction subsidiary of Southern Pacific Railroad, laying fiber optic cables for other carriers along railroad right-of-ways. In 1991, it became SP Telecom, a subsidiary of Anschutz Corporation (Philip Anschutz owned Southern Pacific).

In the mid 1990s, SP Telecom acquired Qwest Transmission, Inc., a digital microwave carrier and subsequently changed its name. It also began leasing fiber to carriers and has been upgrading its network ever since. In early 1998, it introduced retail long distance service in selected cities at 7.5 cents per minute. Qwest claims its network bandwidth will be greater than AT&T, MCI/WorldCom and Sprint combined by the end of 1999. See *Nacchio's law*.

R

R3000, R4000, etc.
See *MIPS Computer*.

R/2, R/3
An integrated suite of client/server applications from SAP America, Inc., Wayne, PA, (www.sap.com). It is the client/server versions of SAP's R/2 mainframe applications. R/3 includes information systems for manufacturing, distribution, order processing, accounting and human resources. It includes the ABAP/4 Development Workbench. See *BAPI*.

RACF
(Resource Access Control Facility) IBM mainframe security software introduced in 1976 that verifies user ID and password and controls access to authorized files and resources.

rack
A frame or cabinet into which components are mounted.

rack mounted
Built into a cabinet that has a standard panel width of 19" or 23". Electronics such as test instruments, telecommunications components and tape drives are often rack mounted. Such units can be bolted into the rack or placed on shelves. The height of a rack-mounted device is specified in rack units (RUs). One RU is 1.75".

RAD
(Rapid Application Development) Developing systems incrementally and delivering working pieces every three to four months, rather than waiting until the entire project is programmed before implementing it. Over the years, many information projects have failed, because, by the time the implemention took place, the business had changed.

RAD employs a variety of automated design and development tools, including CASE, 4GLs, visual programming and GUI builders, that get prototypes up and running quickly.

RAD was coined years ago by industry guru, James Martin, and focuses on personnel management and user involvement as much as on technology. Joint application development (JAD) is another RAD concept.

radio
The transmission of electromagnetic energy (radiation) over the air or through a hollow tube called a waveguide. Although radio is often thought of as only AM or FM, all airborne transmission is radio, including satellite and line-of-sight microwave.

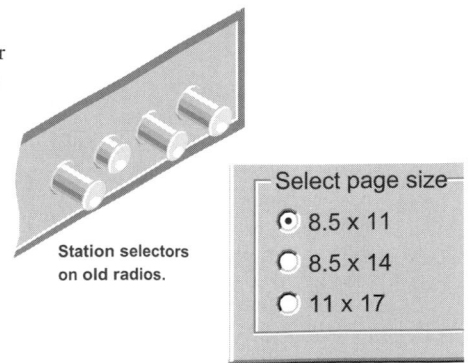

Station selectors on old radios.

radio buttons
A series of on-screen buttons that allow only one selection. If a button is currently selected, it will de-select when another button is selected.

radio frequency
See *RF*.

radio frequency interference
See *RFI*.

Radio Shack
See *Tandy*.

Radio Buttons
This type of selection is used when there is only one choice out of several. Choosing one deselects the others.

radiosity
A rendering method that simulates light reflecting off one surface and onto another. It renders light and shadows more accurately than ray tracing. See *reflection mapping* and *ray tracing*.

RADIUS
(Remote Access Dial-In User Service) An access control protocol that uses a challenge/response method for authentication. It was developed by Livingston Enterprises. See *challenge/response*.

---

radix

The base value in a numbering system. In the decimal numbering system, the radix is 10.

radix point

The location in a number that separates the integral part from the fractional part. For example, in the decimal system, it is the decimal point.

RADSL

See *DSL*.

RAD tool

Any program or utility that speeds up the development and programming of an application. Visual programming tools are widely used to quickly develop graphical front ends.

ragged right

In typography, non-uniform text at the right margin, such as the text you're reading.

RAID

(**R**edundant **A**rray of **I**ndependent **D**isks) A disk subsystem that provides increased performance and/or fault tolerance. Performance is improved by disk striping, which interleaves bytes or groups of bytes across multiple drives, so more than one disk is reading and writing simultaneously. Fault tolerance is achieved by mirroring or parity. Mirroring is 100% duplication of the data on two drives (RAID 1), and parity calculates the data in two drives and stores the result on a third drive (a bit from drive 1 is XOR'd with a bit from drive 2, and the result bit is stored on drive 3). See *OR*.

A RAID system comprises a RAID controller and two or more regular disk drives. The RAID functionality is built into the controller. RAID can also be implemented in ordinary PCs via software only, but with less efficiency and performance.

RAID systems come in all sizes from floor-standing cabinets to a complete system in one full-size drive bay. Self-contained systems often include large amounts of cache and redundant power supplies. In fault-tolerant configurations such as RAID 3 and 5, a failed drive can be hot swapped with a new one, and the RAID controller automatically rebuilds the lost data.

RAID used to mean arrays of "inexpensive" disks, which was the title of a paper written in 1988 at the University of California at Berkeley. RAIDs were contrasted with SLEDs (Single Large Expensive Disks), which were still popular on large computers. Today, all hard disks are inexpensive by comparison, and the RAID Advisory Board (www.raid-advisory.com) changed the name to "independent" disks. For more details, review the white paper from the RAID Advisory Board at www.raid-advisory.com/rabguide.html. See *SAN* and *sector sparing*.

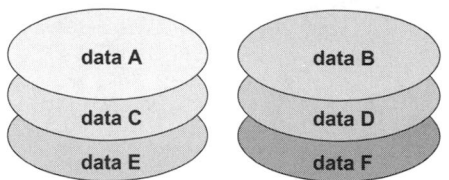

Raid 0 - Striping (for performance)

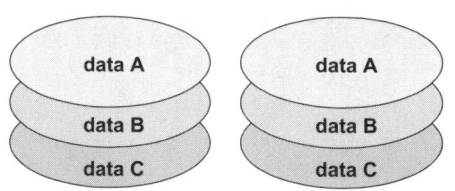

Raid 1 - Mirroring (100% redundant)

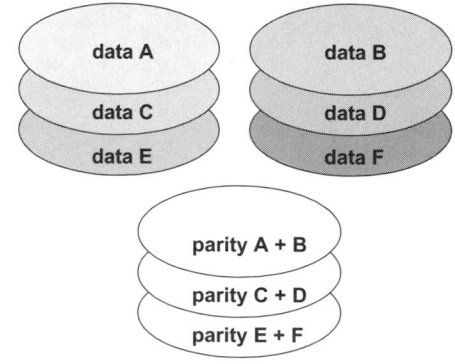

Raid 3 - Striping plus fault tolerance

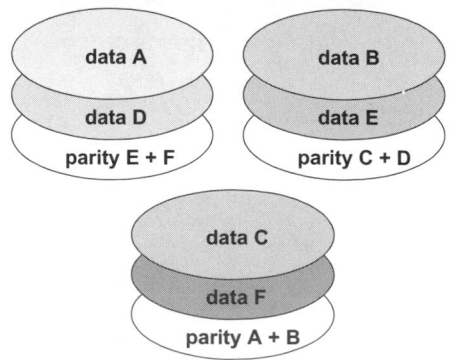

Raid 5 - Striping plus fault tolerance

Computer Desktop Encyclopedia

RAID LEVEL 0
Level 0 is disk striping only, which interleaves data across multiple disks for better performance. It does not provide safeguards against failure.

RAID LEVEL 1
Uses disk mirroring, which provides 100% duplication of data. Offers highest reliability, but doubles storage cost.

RAID LEVEL 2
Bits (rather than bytes or groups of bytes) are interleaved across multiple disks. The Connection Machine used this technique, but this is a rare method.

RAID LEVEL 3
Data is striped across three or more drives. Used to achieve the higest data transfer, because all drives operate in parallel. Parity bits are stored on separate, dedicated drives.

RAID LEVEL 4
Similar to Level 3, but manages disks independently rather than in unison. Not often used.

RAID LEVEL 5
Most widely-used. Data is striped across three or more drives for performance, and parity bits are used for fault tolerance. The parity bits from two drives are stored on a third drive.

RAID LEVEL 6
Highest reliability, but not widely used. Similar to RAID 5, but does two different parity computations or the same computation on overlapping subsets of the data.

RAID LEVEL 10
Actually RAID 1,0. A combination of RAID 1 and 0 (mirroring and striping).

RAM
(Random Access Memory) A group of memory chips, typically of the dynamic RAM (DRAM) type, which functions as the computer's primary workspace. See *memory* and *computer* for an explanation of how memory is used in processing data.

The "random" in RAM means that the contents of each byte can be directly accessed without regard to the bytes before or after it. This is also true of other types of memory chips, including ROMs and PROMs. However, unlike ROMs and PROMs, RAM chips require power to maintain their content, which is why you must save your data onto disk before you turn the computer off. See *computer, memory, dynamic RAM, static RAM* and *SIMM*.

RAMAC
(Random Access Method of Accounting and Control) The first hard disk computer which was introduced by IBM in 1956. All 50 of its 24" platters held a total of five million characters! It was half computer, half tabulator. It had a

The RAMAC, 1956
Part computer, part tabulator, IBM's RAMAC was the first machine with a hard disk. What extraordinary technology of the times. Each 24" platter held a whopping 100KB. *(Photos courtesy of IBM Corporation.)*

drum memory for program storage, but its I/O was wired by plugboard.

After 38 years, IBM resurrected the RAMAC name with the introduction of a high-capacity disk storage system in 1994. The differences between the 1956 and 1994 RAMACs are rather dramatic. Areal density rose from 2,000 to 260 million bits per square inch, increasing total storage capacity from 5MB to 90GB. Access times changed from 600 ms to 9.5 ms.

Rambus DRAM

See *RDRAM*.

RAM cache

See *cache*.

RAM card

(1) A printed circuit board containing memory chips that is plugged into a socket in the computer.

(2) A credit-card-sized module that contains memory chips and battery. See *memory card*.

RAM chip

(Random Access Memory chip) A memory chip. See *dynamic RAM, static RAM, RAM* and *memory*.

RAM cram

Insufficient memory to run applications, especially in older DOS PCs with their 1MB memory limit.

RAMDAC

(Random Access Memory Digital to Analog Converter) The VGA controller chip that maintains the color palette and converts data from memory into analog signals for the monitor.

RAM disk

A disk drive simulated in memory. To use it, files are copied from magnetic disk into the RAM disk. Processing is faster, because there's no mechanical disk action, only memory transfers. Updated data files must be copied back to disk before the power is turned off, otherwise the updates are lost. Same as *E-disk* and *virtual disk*.

RAM doubler

A software technique that compresses the contents of memory, thereby doubling (more or less) its available capacity.

RAMIS

See *CA-RAMIS*.

RAM refresh

Recharging dynamic RAM chips many times per second in order to keep the bit patterns valid.

RAM resident

Refers to programs that remain in memory in order to interact with other programs or to be instantly popped up when required by the user. See *TSR*.

random access

Same as *direct access*.

random noise

Same as *Gaussian noise*.

random number generator

A program routine that produces a random number. Random numbers are created easily in a computer, since there are many random events that take place; for example, the duration between keystrokes. Only a few milliseconds' difference is enough to seed a random number generation routine with a different number each time. Once seeded, an algorithm computes different numbers throughout the session.

range

(1) In data entry validation, a group of values from a minimum to a maximum.

(2) In spreadsheets, a series of cells that are worked on as a group. It may refer to a row, column or rectangular block defined by one corner and its diagonally opposite corner.

ransom note typography

Using too many fonts in a document. The term comes from the text in a ransom note that is pasted together from words cut out of different magazines and newspapers.

The ease with which fonts can be selected in a word processor has led many inexperienced people to use too many fonts in a document or newsletter. Typographers and graphics artists know that only two or three fonts are necessary for the most professional appearance.

rAnSOm NOte tYρOgraphy

It's great to have all these NEAT fonts.

But sometimes people get carried away!

More than three fonts in an entire page generally become tiresome.

There is elegance in simplicity!

But that is not demonstrated here.

RARP

(Reverse ARP) A TCP/IP protocol used by a diskless workstation to obtain its IP address. Upon startup, the client station sends out a RARP request in an Ethernet frame to the RARP server, which returns the layer 3 address for a layer 2 address (performing the opposite function of an ARP). See *BOOTP*.

RAS

(1) (Remote Access Service) A Windows NT Server feature that allows remote users access to the network from their Windows laptops or desktops via modem. See *RRAS* and *remote access server*.

(2) (Reliability Availability Serviceability) Originally an IBM term, it refers to a computer system's overall reliability, its ability to respond to a failure and its ability to undergo maintenance without shutting it down entirely.

(3) (Row Address Strobe) A clock signal in a memory chip used to pinpoint the row of a particular bit in a row-column matrix. See *CAS*.

raster

A pattern of horizontal lines (scan lines) that are displayed on a TV or computer CRT. This is the origin of the term "raster graphics," which refers to bitmapped images, or images comprised of a matrix of pixels. Technically, a raster refers to rows, not columns and rows, and hardware engineers prefer the term "bitmapped" graphics when referring to the images. See *raster scan* and *analog video*.

raster display

A display terminal that uses the raster scan method for creating the image on screen. See *raster scan*. Contrast with *vector display*.

raster graphics

See *bitmapped graphics*.

rasterize

To prepare a page for display or printing. Rasterization is performed by a raster image processor (RIP), which turns text and images into the matrix of pixels (bitmap) that will be displayed on screen or printed on the page. Various conversions may take place. For example, the mathematical coordinates of vector and outline fonts as well as vector drawings must be converted into bitmaps. Existing bitmaps may have to be scaled into different-sized bitmaps.

Unless output is printed on a vector graphics plotter, which literally draws the illustration with pens, all text and graphics must be rasterized into a bitmap for display or printing. See *RIP, font scaler* and *host-based printer*.

raster scan

Displaying or recording a video image line by line. Computer monitors and TVs use this method whereby electrons are beamed (scanned) onto the phosphor coating on the screen a line at a time from left to right starting at the top-left corner. At the end of the line, the beam is turned off and moved back to the left and down one line, which is known as the horizontal retrace (flyback). When the bottom-right corner is reached, a vertical retrace (flyback) returns the gun to the top-left corner. In a TV signal, this is known as the vertical blanking interval.

Rational Rose

An object-oriented analysis and design tool that runs on Windows and UNIX platforms from Rational Software Corporation, Santa Clara, CA, (www.rational.com). It uses the Booch modeling method and is being extended to Rumbaugh's Object Modeling Technique (OMT). Rational is also unifying both approaches.

The base product is used for modeling applications, but versions of Rose are available that generate C++, Smalltalk, Ada, SQLWindows and ObjectPro code.

raw capacity

See *native capacity*.

raw data

Data that has not been processed in any manner. It often refers to uncompressed text that is not stored in any proprietary format. See *ASCII file*.

ray tracing

A rendering method that simulates light reflections, refractions and shadows. It follows a light path from a specific source and computes each pixel in the image to simulate the effect of the light. It is a very process-intensive operation. See *reflection mapping* and *radiosity*.

R:BASE

A relational DBMS for DOS, Windows and OS/2 from Microrim, Inc., Bellevue, WA, (www.microrim.com). It provides a complete programming language as well as an application generator for developing programs. It was the first DBMS to compete with dBASE II in the early 1980s. R:WEB is a runtime version of R:BASE for the Web.

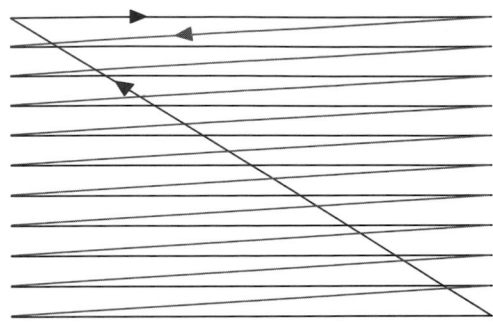

Raster Scan Tracing

Raster displays are imaged a line at a time (black lines), starting at the top-left of the screen and going to the bottom-right. The red lines are the horizontal retraces, and the blue line is the vertical retrace.

Ray Tracing

The shadows in this picture were created by software algorithms that simulate a beam of light from a designated source. Many of the first graphics simulations were done at the University of Utah, and this is one of those first images. *(Photo courtesy of Computer Sciences Department, University of Utah.)*

RBOC

(Regional Bell Operating Company) The regional Bell telephone companies that were spun off of AT&T by court order. Although some have since merged with others, the initial seven companies were Nynex, Bell Atlantic, BellSouth, Southwestern Bell, US West, Pacific Telesis and Ameritech. See *Divestiture*.

RC2, RC4, RC5

A family of secret key cryptographic methods developed by RSA Data Security, Inc., Redwood City, CA (www.rsa.com). Algorithms previously developed by RSA were RC2 and RC4, and all use a variable-length key. RC5 is more secure than RC4 but is slower. RSA Data Security is more widely known for its RSA public key method. See *RSA*.

RCA connector

A plug and socket for a two-wire (signal and ground) coaxial cable that is widely used to connect audio and video components. Rows of RCA sockets are found on the backs of stereo amplifiers and receivers. The prong is 1/8" thick by 5/16" long.

Rdb

See *Oracle Rdb*.

RDBMS

(Relational DataBase Management System) See *relational database*.

RDO

(Remote Data Objects) A programming interface for data access from Microsoft. It is used in Visual Basic to access remote ODBC databases. See *DAO, ADO, OLE DB* and *ODBC*.

RDP

(Remote Desktop Protocol) The presentation services protocol that governs input/output between a Windows terminal client and Windows Terminal Server. It is based on the T.share protocol. See *Windows Terminal Server*.

RDRAM

(Rambus DRAM) A dynamic RAM chip technology from Rambus, Inc., Mountain View, CA, (www.rambus.com), that transfers data at 600 MBytes/sec (up to 10 times faster than conventional DRAMs). It requires modified motherboards, but eliminates the need for memory caches. Rambus licenses its memory designs to other semiconductor companies, which manufacture the chips. Intel and Rambus are expected to come up with a faster version of Rambus to be named nDRAM (Next generation DRAM).

RDS

(Remote Data Services) A set of programming interfaces from Microsoft that enables users to update data on the Internet or intranets from their ActiveX-enabled browser. Formerly ADC (Advanced Data Connector), it was integrated into ADO (Active Data Objects) and renamed RDS. See *ADO*.

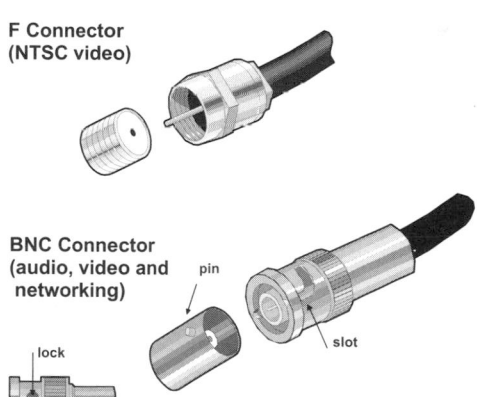

Audio-Video Connectors

Mini-phone (audio)
stereo   mono

RCA Phono connector (audio and video)
Left audio (white)   Right audio (red)   Composite video (yellow)

Phone plug (microphones)
stereo   mono

F Connector (NTSC video)

BNC Connector (audio, video and networking)
pin   slot   lock

read

To input into the computer from a peripheral device (disk, tape, etc.). Like reading a book or playing an audio tape, reading does not destroy what is read.

A read is both an input and an output (I/O), since data is being output from the peripheral device and input into the computer. Memory is also said to be read when it is accessed to transfer data out to a peripheral device or to somewhere else in memory. Every peripheral or internal transfer of data is a read from somewhere and a write to somewhere else.

read channel

A circuit in a disk drive that encodes the data bits into flux changes for recording and decodes the magnetic flux changes into bits for reading.

read cycle

The operation of reading data from a memory or storage device.

reader

A machine that captures data for the computer, such as an optical character reader, magnetic card reader and punched card reader. A microfiche or microfilm reader is a self-contained machine that reads film and displays its contents.

read error

A failure to read the data on a storage or memory device. Although it is not a routine phenomenon, magnetic and optical recording surfaces can become contaminated with dust or dirt or be physically damaged, and cells in memory chips can malfunction.

When a read error occurs, the program will allow you to bypass it and move on to the next set of data, or it will end, depending on the operating system. However, if the damaged part of a disk contains control information, the rest of the file may be unreadable. In such cases, a recovery program must be used to retrieve the remaining data if there is no backup.

readme file

A text file copied onto software distribution disks that contains last-minute updates or errata that have not been printed in the documentation manual.

read notification

A confirmation transmitted back to the sender that an e-mail message has been read.

read only

(1) Refers to storage media that permanently hold their content; for example, ROM and CD-ROM.

(2) A file which can be read, but not updated or erased. See *file attribute*.

read-only attribute

A file attribute that, when turned on, indicates that a file can only be read, but not updated or erased.

readout

(1) A small display device that typically shows only a few digits or a couple of lines of data.

(2) Any display screen or panel.

read-while-write

The ability of a tape drive to write data and read it back for verification immediately so that both operations take place in the same pass.

read/write

(1) Refers to a device that can both input and output or transmit and receive.

(2) Refers to a file that can be updated and erased.

read/write channel

Same as *I/O channel*.

read/write head

A device that reads (senses) and writes (records) data on a magnetic disk or tape. For

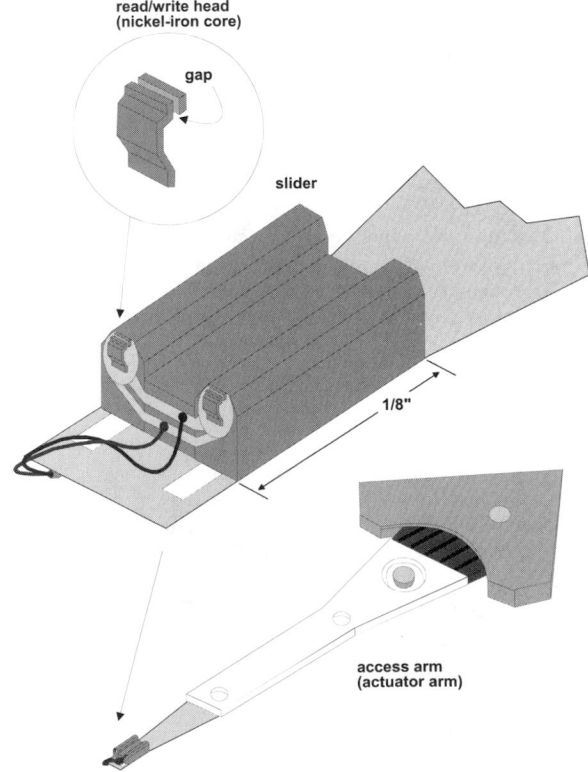

Thin Film Read/Write Head
The read/write heads on today's magnetic disks are so tiny you need a microscope to see them. The heads are attached to a pair of aerodynamically designed rails, known as a "slider," that keep the head at the proper distance from the disk platter.

writing, the surface of the disk or tape is moved past the read/write head. By discharging electrical impulses at the appropriate times, bits are recorded as tiny, magnetized spots of positive or negative polarity.

For reading, the surface is moved past the read/write head, and the bits that are present induce an electrical current across the gap.

read/write memory
Same as *RAM*.

RealAudio
The most popular streaming audio technology for the Internet and intranets from RealNetworks, Inc., Seattle, WA, (www.real.com). A browser equipped with a RealPlayer or RealAudio plug-in enables news, sports and other programs transmitted from RealAudio servers (RealServers) to be heard on the user's computer. Encoders and plug-ins can be downloaded from RealNetworks' Web site. Server software is available for a variety of platforms. RealNetworks was formerly Progressive Networks. See *RealVideo*.

Realizer
See *CA-Realizer*.

RealMagic
An MPEG-1 playback board for PCs from Sigma Designs, Inc., Fremont, CA, (www.sigmadesigns.com). Originally called ReelMagic, it also defined a programming interface that was the basis for OM1, now a de facto standard for interactive games.

RealMedia
A streaming media technology for the Internet from RealNetworks, Inc., Seattle, WA, (www.real.com). Using the Realtime Streaming Protocol (RTSP), it is designed to handle any type of media, including audio, video, MIDI, text, animation and presentations. The RealMedia Architecture (RMA) allows multiple streams to be synchronized simultaneously; for example, sending images intermixed with audio.

Real Mode
An operational state in Intel CPU chips (starting with the 286) in which the computer functions like the first Intel CPU chip (8086/8088), which is limited to accessing one megabyte of memory. DOS applications run in Real Mode, unless they have been enhanced with a DOS extender that allows them to use more memory. See *Protected Mode* and *Virtual 8086 Mode*.

Real Mode driver
A PC driver that is written to the original 16-bit 8086/8088 architecture, which is limited to one megabyte of memory. Real Mode drivers must run within the first megabyte. See *Real Mode*.

RealPlayer
A browser plug-in from Real Networks, Inc., (www.real.com) that plays RealAudio and displays RealVideo transmissions. See *RealAudio* and *RealVideo*.

real storage
Real physical memory in a virtual memory system.

realtime
An immediate response. It refers to process control and embedded systems; for example, space flight computers must respond instantly to changing conditions. It also refers to fast transaction processing systems as well as any electronic operation fast enough to keep up with its real-world counterpart (animating complex images, transmitting live video, etc.).

realtime chat
See *chat*.

realtime clock
An electronic circuit that maintains the time of day. It may also provide timing signals for timesharing operations.

realtime compression

The ability to compress and decompress data without any noticeable loss in speed compared to non-compressed data. PC products such as Stacker and SuperStor let you create a separate compressed drive on your hard disk. All data written to that drive is compressed and decompressed when read back. Realtime compression is included in DOS starting with DOS 6. See *DriveSpace*. See *JPEG*.

realtime conferencing

A "live" teleconferencing session that uses communications equipment fast enough to keep up with the speech and movements of all participants. See *teleconferencing*.

realtime image

A graphics image that can be animated on screen at the same speed as the real-world object.

realtime information system

A computer system that responds to transactions by immediately updating the appropriate master files and/or generating a response in a time frame fast enough to keep an operation moving at its required speed. See *transaction processing*.

realtime operating system

A master control program that can provide immediate response to input signals and transactions.

realtime system

A computer system that responds to input signals fast enough to keep an operation moving at its required speed.

realtime video

The ability to transmit video live without missing any frames. It requires very high transmission capacity. See *ATM*.

RealVideo

A streaming video technology for the Internet and intranets from RealNetworks, Inc., Seattle, WA, (www.real.com). A browser equipped with a RealPlayer or RealVideo plug-in enables video broadcasts from RealVideo servers (RealServers) to be viewed on screen. The material can be statically stored in the server and viewed in full, or it can be an on-going broadcast like that of TV. Plug-ins can be downloaded from RealNetworks' Web site. Server server software is available for a variety of platforms. See *RealAudio*.

reasonable test

A type of test that determines if a value falls within a range considered normal or logical. It can be made on electronic signals to detect extraneous noise as well as on data to determine possible input errors.

reboot

To reload the operating system and restart the computer. See *boot*.

receiver

A device that accepts signals. Contrast with *transmitter*.

recompile

To compile a program again. A program is recompiled after a change has been made to it in order to test and run the revised version. Programs are recompiled many times during the course of development and maintenance. See *compile*.

record

(1) A group of related fields that store data about a subject (master record) or activity (transaction record). A collection of records make up a file.

Master records contain permanent data, such as account number, and variable data, such as balance due. Transaction records contain only permanent data, such as quantity and product code. See *master file* and *transaction file* for examples of record contents.

(2) In certain disk organization methods, a record is a block of data read and written at one time without any relationship to records in a file.

record format

Same as *record layout*.

Computer Desktop Encyclopedia

record layout
The format of a data record, which includes the name, type and size of each field in the record.

record locking
See *file and record locking*.

record mark
A symbol used to identify the end of a record.

records management
The creation, retention and scheduled destruction of an organization's paper and film documents. Computer-generated reports and documents fall into the records management domain, but traditional data processing files do not.

recovery
See *backup & recovery, checkpoint/restart* and *tape backup*.

recruiter information
See *salary survey, to the recruiter, computercruiter, nerd rustler* and *programmer*.

rectifier
An electrical circuit that converts AC into DC current with the use of diodes that act as one-way valves. Contrast with *inverter*.

recursion
In programming, the ability of a subroutine or program module to call itself. It is helpful for writing routines that solve problems by repeatedly processing the output of the same process.

recycle bin
In Windows 95/98, an icon of a waste can used for deleting files. The icon of a file or folder is dragged to the trash can and released. See *trash can*.

redaction
The editing done to sensitive documents before release to the public.

Red Book
(1) The documentation of the U.S. National Security Agency that defines criteria for secure networks. The volumes are "Trusted Network Interpretation of the Trusted Computer System Evaluation Criteria" (NCSC-TG-005) and "Trusted Network Interpetation Environments Guideline: Guidance for Applying the Trusted Network Interpretation" (NCSC-TG-011). It is the network counterpart of the Orange Book for computers. See *NCSC*.

(2) The documentation for the technical specification of audio CDs (CD-DA), which includes such details as sampling and transfer rates. "Red Book audio" refers to digital sound that conforms to the common standard used in music compact discs. See *CD*.

redirection
Diverting data from its normal destination to another; for example, to a disk file instead of the printer, or to a server's disk instead of the local disk.

redirector
In a LAN, software that routes workstation (client) requests for data to the server. In a Windows network, the redirector program is added to the PC to intercept requests for files and printers and direct them to the appropriate remote device if applicable. Starting with Windows 95 and Windows NT 4.0, the redirector recognizes UNC names as well as drive letters that have been mapped to remote servers. The counterpart in NetWare is known as the Requester. See *UNC* and *drive mapping*.

redlining
Identifying text that has been changed in a word processing document by displaying it in a special color, for example. It allows the original author of the text or other users to see ongoing revisions. The term comes from manual editing where a red pen is used to mark up the pages.

redundancy check

In communications, a method for detecting transmission errors by appending a calculated number onto the end of each segment of data. See *CRC*.

Redwood

A magnetic tape technology from StorageTek that uses half-inch, single-hub cartridges similar to IBM's 3480/3490 formats, but employs helical scan recording rather than linear (parallel tracks along the length of the tape). The Redwood SD-3 drive supports 10, 25 and 50GB cartridges (native). StorageTek's Powderhorn library can hold a mix of SD-3 and 3480/3490 cartridges. For a summary of all storage technologies, see *storage*.

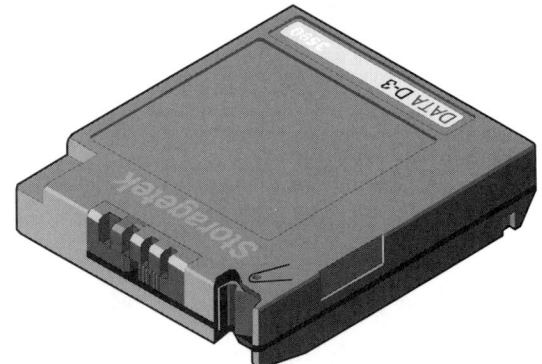

Redwood Cartridge

Redwood cartridges are the same overall size as IBM's 3480/3490 formats, but the door mechanism and internal recording formats are different. Redwood uses helical scan, while IBM uses linear recording.

reengineering

Using information technology to improve performance and cut costs. Its main premise, as popularized by the book "Reengineering the Corporation" by Michael Hammer and James Champy, is to examine the goals of an organization and to redesign work and business processes from the ground up rather than simply automate existing tasks and functions.

According to the authors, reengineering is driven by open markets and competition. No longer, can we enjoy the protection of our own country's borders as we could in the past. Today, we are in a global economy, and worldwide customers are more sophisticated and demanding.

In addition, modern industrialization was based on theories of fragmentation and specialization, which have led to the "left eye" specialist with millions of workers doing dreary, monotonous jobs as well as the creations of departments, functions and business units governed by multiple layers of management. Management has been the necessary glue to control the fragmented workplace.

In order to be successful in the future, the organization will have fewer layers of management and fewer, but more highly-skilled workers that do more complex tasks. Information technology, used for the past 50 years to automate manual tasks, will be used to enable new work models. The successful organization will not be "technology driven," rather it will be "technology enabled."

Although reengineering may, in fact, reduce a department of 200 employees down to 50, it is not just about eliminating jobs. It's goals are customer oriented; for example, it's about processing a contract in 24 hours instead of two weeks or performing a service in one day instead of 10. It's about reducing the time it takes to get a drug to market from eight years to four years or reducing the number of suppliers from 200,000 to 700. Reengineering is about radical improvement, not incremental changes.

reentrant code

A programming routine that can be used by multiple programs simultaneously. It is used in operating systems and other system software as well as in multithreading, where concurrent events are taking place. It is written so that none of its code is modifiable (no values are changed) and it does not keep track of anything. The calling programs keep track of their own progress (variables, flags, etc.), thus one copy of the reentrant routine can be shared by an any number of users or processes.

Conceptually, it is as if several people were each baking a cake from a single copy of a recipe on the wall. Everyone looks at the master recipe, but keeps track of their own progress by jotting down the step they are at on their own scratchpad so they can pick up where they left off. The master recipe is never disturbed.

referential integrity

A database management safeguard that ensures every foreign key matches a primary key. For example, customer numbers in a customer file are the primary keys, and customer numbers in the order file are the foreign keys. If a customer record is deleted, the order records must also be deleted otherwise they are left without a primary reference. If the DBMS doesn't test for this, it must be programmed into the applications.

reflection mapping

A rendering method that simulates light reflecting on an object. It is a much faster method than ray tracing because it maps light over the image rather than actually computing the path the light takes. See *ray tracing* and *radiosity*.

reflective spot

A metallic foil placed on each end of a magnetic tape. It reflects light to a photosensor to signal the end of tape.

reflective VGA

An LCD screen that needs bright ambient light for viewing. Backlit and sidelit screens are much easier to see.

reformat

(1) To change the record layout of a file or database.

(2) To initialize a disk over again.

refraction

The bending of electromagnetic waves as they pass at an angle between materials with different refractive indices. Refraction is an important characteristic in optical systems, which deal with light travelling through optical fibers and lenses. See *refractive index*.

refractive index

A measurement of how light bends in an optical medium such as an optical fiber or lens. The measurement is the ratio of the speed of light in a vacuum compared to the speed of light through the medium. See *refraction*.

refresh

To continuously charge a device that cannot hold its content. CRTs must be refreshed, because the phosphors hold their glow for only a few milliseconds. Dynamic RAM chips require refreshing to maintain their charged bit patterns. See *vertical scan frequency*.

refresh rate

The number of times per second that a device is re-energized, such as a CRT or dynamic RAM chip. See *vertical scan frequency*.

regenerator

(1) In communications, the same as a *repeater*.

(2) In electronics, a circuit that repeatedly supplies current to a memory or display device that continuously loses its charges or content.

ReGIS

(REmote Graphics InStruction) A graphics language from Digital used on graphics terminals and first introduced on the PDP-11.

register

A small, high-speed computer circuit that holds values of internal operations, such as the address of the instruction being executed and the data being processed. When a program is debugged, register contents may be analyzed to determine the computer's status at the time of failure.

In microcomputer assembly language programming, programmers reference registers routinely. Assembly languages in larger computers are often at a higher level.

register level compatibility

A hardware component that is 100% compatible with another device. It implies that the same type, size and names of registers are used.

Registry

The database of configuration settings in Windows 95/98. See *Win 9x Registry*.

regression analysis

In statistics, a mathematical method of modeling the relationships among three or more variables. It is used to predict the value of one variable given the values of the others. For example, a model might estimate sales based on age and gender. A regression analysis yields an equation that expresses the relationship. See *correlation*.

regression testing

In software development, testing a program that has been modified in order to ensure that additional bugs have not been introduced. When a program is enhanced, testing is often done only on the new features. However, adding source code to a program often introduces errors in other routines, and many of the old and stable functions must be retested along with the new ones.

reinstall

To go through the installation process once again, because files have become corrupted. See *reload*.

reintermediation

To provide value as a middleman in order to avoid disintermediation. See *disintermediation*.

related files

Two or more data files that can be matched on some common condition, such as account number or name.

relational algebra

(1) The branch of mathematics that deals with relations; for example, AND, OR, NOT, IS and CONTAINS.

(2) In relational database, a collection of rules for dealing with tables; for example, JOIN, UNION and INTERSECT.

relational calculus

The rules for combining and manipulating relations; for example De Morgan's law, "the complement of a union is equal to the union of the complements."

relational database

A database organization method that links files together as required. In non-relational systems (hierarchical, network), records in one file contain embedded pointers to the locations of records in another, such as customers to orders and vendors to purchases. These are fixed links set up ahead of time to speed up daily processing.

In a relational database, relationships between files are created by comparing data, such as account numbers and names. A relational system has the flexibility to take any two or more files and generate a new file from the records that meet the matching criteria (see *join*).

Routine queries often involve more than one data file. For example, a customer file and an order file can be linked in order to ask a question that relates to information in both files, such as the names of the customers that purchased a particular product.

In practice, a pure relational query can be very slow. In order to speed up the process, indexes are built and maintained on the key fields used for matching. Sometimes, indexes are created "on the fly" when the data is requested.

The term was coined in 1970 by Edgar Codd, whose objective was to easily accommodate a user's ad hoc request for selected data.

Relational terms	Common terms
table or relation	file
tuple	record
attribute	field

relational DBMS

See *relational database* and *DBMS*.

relational operator

A symbol that specifies a comparison between two values.

Computer Desktop Encyclopedia

Relational Operator		Symbol
EQ	Equal to	=
NE	Not equal to	<> or # or !=
GT	Greater than	>
GE	Greater than or equal to	>=
LT	Less than	<
LE	Less than or equal to	<=

relational query

A question asked about data contained in two or more tables in a relational database. The relational query must specify the tables required and what the condition is that links them; for example, matching account numbers. Relational queries are tricky to specify because even the simplest of questions may require data from two or more tables. Both the knowledge of the query language and the database structure is necessary. Even with graphical interfaces that let you drag a line from one field to another, you still need to know how the tables were designed to be related.

relative address

A memory address that represents some distance from a starting point (base address), such as the first byte of a program or table. The absolute address is derived by adding it to the base address.

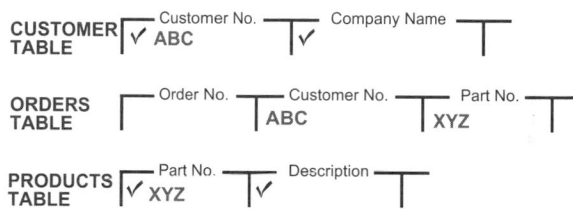

✔ The checkmark is a special symbol inserted to include this field in the result.

An Early Relational Query

In the mid 1980s, Paradox was the first DBMS on a PC that made linking tables easier. Although not as sophisticated as today's methods, the ability to associate relationships by typing sample words was a breakthrough. The Customer No. and Part No. fields are related by "ABC" and "XYZ." Any words would suffice as long as they are the same.

relative movement

A change in position that is based on the current position. For example, it doesn't matter where the mouse is on the desk in relation to the pointer on the screen. When you move it, the pointer starts moving, starting from where it was last positioned.

relative path

An implied path. When a command is expressed that references files, the current working directory is the implied, or relative, path if the full path is not explicitly stated. Contrast with *full path*.

relative URL

A URL that specifies only the document name. The full path is implied by the current document. Contrast with *absolute URL*.

relative vector

In computer graphics, a vector with end points designated in coordinates relative to a base address. Contrast with *absolute vector*.

relay

An electrical switch that allows a low power to control a higher one. A small current energizes the relay, which closes a gate, allowing a large current to flow through.

reload

To load a program from disk into memory once again in order to run it. Reload is entirely different than reinstall. Reinstall means that you have to run the install program from a floppy disk or CD-ROM and perform the installation procedure all over again.

Reloading is common when the program crashes. Reinstalling is much less common, but necessary if program files have become unreadable due to damaged sectors on the disk or because files were accidentally erased. This can also happen due to program error, in which the program erroneously writes incorrect data to some of its own configuration and status files.

relocatable code

Machine language that can be run from any memory location. All modern computers run relocatable code. See *base/displacement*.

Rem

(REMarks) A programming language statement used to document a line. Rem statements are not executed by the compiler. Rem is also used in DOS batch files for comments as well as for disabling instructions. For example, inserting the word **rem** at the beginning of a line in AUTOEXEC.BAT or CONFIG.SYS disables the command.

remedial maintenance

A repair service that is required due to a malfunction of the product. Contrast with *preventive maintenance*.

remote access

See *remote control software*.

remote access concentrator

A remote access server that supports one or more T1/E1 lines, allowing multiple analog and ISDN calls to come in over one port from the telephone company. Remote access concentrators can handle much higher call densities than remote access servers. They include the dial-up protocols, access control and provide the equivalent of a modem pool. See *remote access server*.

remote access router

A networking device used to connect remote sites via private lines or public carriers. The device is required at both ends and provides the protocol conversion between the local area network (LAN) and the wide area network (WAN).

remote access server

A computer in a network that provides access to remote users via analog modem or ISDN connections. It includes the dial-up protocols and access control (authentication) and may be a regular file server with remote access software or a proprietary system such as Shiva's LANRover. The modems may be internal or external to the device. See *remote access concentrator*.

remote access software

See *remote control software*.

remote batch

See *RJE*.

remote boot

Booting up a client machine from the server. This capability is necessary for diskless workstations and network computers, but is also helpful for restarting failed desktop machines. See *boot ROM*.

remote communications

(1) Communicating via long distances.

(2) See *remote control software*.

remote console

A terminal or workstation in a remote location that is used to monitor and control a local computer.

remote control software

Software, installed in both machines, that allows a user at a local computer to have control of a remote computer via modem. Both users run the remote computer and see

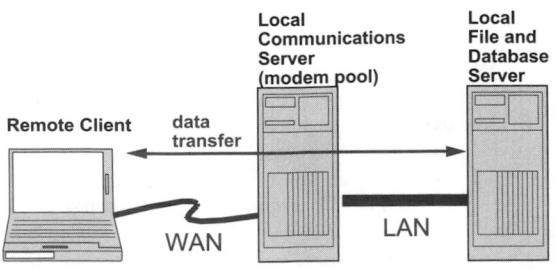

Remote Control
(remote user controls local client PC)

Remote Node
(remote user logged directly onto server)

Computer Desktop Encyclopedia

the same screen. Remote control operation is used to take control of an unattended desktop personal computer from a remote location as well as to provide instruction and technical support to remote users.

Remote control is different than a remote node operation. In remote control, only keystrokes are transmitted from and screen updates are transmitted to the remote machine as all processing takes place in the local computer. All file transfers are done locally or over a high-speed LAN. In a remote node setup, the user is logged onto the network using the phone line as an extension to the network. Thus, all traffic has to flow over a low-speed telephone line.

When working with large files, remote control is faster than remote node, and it gives users the flexibility to do whatever they want on the local machine. However, remote control sessions move screen changes constantly to the remote machine and graphics applications are slow. Remote control usually requires more network ports than remote node for the same number of users. In addition, in remote control, you don't do any local processing in the remote machine so online sessions are often longer than with remote node. See *application sharing*.

Remote Control and Application Sharing
Remote control operation and application sharing are similar if not almost identical in some cases. Application sharing lets two or more users work in the same application which is running in one user's machine. If the application sharing program allows another user to take control of the operating system rather than just a single, specific application, then there is really no difference.

remote echo
The transmission of received data back to the sending station for visual verification. A local echo displays the typed keystrokes from the local machine, but a remote echo displays the data after it has been sent, received and retransmitted back.

remote node
A remote user or workstation. Access to the company LAN is made via POTS or ISDN modem to a connection at the remote access server. See *remote access server* and *remote control software*.

remote-office router
A router specialized to route data to its counterpart in a remote site. Configuring the router is done at the central site, thus network administration is simplified. 3Com pioneered the concept with its Boundary Routing.

remote resource
A peripheral device, such as a disk, modem or printer, that is available for shared use in the network. Contrast with *local resource*.

remote wake-up
The ability for the power in a client station to be turned on by the network. Remote wake-up enables software upgrading and other management tasks to be performed on users' machines after the work day is over. It also enables remote users to gain access to machines that have been turned off.

removable disk
A disk module that is inserted into the drive for reading and writing and removed when not required. Floppy disks, Zip disks, Jaz disks and CD-ROMs are common examples. For a summary of all storage technologies, see *storage*.

render
To draw a real-world object as it actually appears.

rendering
In computer graphics, creating a 3-D image that incorporates the simulation of lighting effects, such as shadows and reflection.

Removable Zip Disk
The Zip has been the most popular removable disk since the introduction of the floppies.

Renderman interface

A graphics format that uses photorealistic image synthesis from Pixar, Inc., Richmond, CA, (www.pixar.com). Developer's Renderman (PCs and UNIX) and Mac Renderman (Macintosh) are Pixar programs that apply photorealistic looks and surfaces to 3-D objects.

Renovator

See *ESL Renovator*.

repeater

(1) A communications device that amplifies or regenerates the data signal in order to extend the transmission distance. Available for both analog and digital signals, it is used extensively in long distance transmission. It is also used to tie two LANs of the same type together. Repeaters work at layer 1 of the OSI model. See *bridge* and *router*.

(2) The term may also refer to a multiport repeater, which is a hub in a 10BaseT network.

Replica

Document exchange software from Farallon Communications, Inc., Alameda, CA, (www.farallon.com), that converts a Windows or Macintosh document into a proprietary file format for viewing on other machines. The Replica viewer can be distributed to the target machines or embedded within the Replica document file itself, turning it into a single-document viewer.

replication

In database management, the ability to keep distributed databases synchronized by routinely copying the entire database or subsets of the database to other servers in the network.

There are various replication methods. Primary site replication maintains the master copy of the data in one site and sends read-only copies to the other sites. In a workflow environment, the master copy can move from one site to another. This is called shared replication or transferred ownership, replication. In symmetric replication, also known as update-anywhere or peer-to-peer replication, each site can receive updates, and all other sites are updated. Failover replication, or hot backup, maintains an up-to-date copy of the data at a different site for backup. See *distributed database* and *mirroring*.

report

A printed or microfilmed collection of facts and figures with page numbers and page headings. See *report writer* and *query*.

report file

A file that describes how a report is printed.

report format

The layout of a report showing page and column headers, page numbers and totals.

report generator

Same as *report writer*.

report writer

Software that prints a report based on a description of its layout. As a stand-alone program or part of a DBMS or file manager, it can sort selected records into a new sequence for printing. It may also print standard mailing labels.

A report is described by entering text for the page header and stating the position of the print columns (data fields) and which ones are totalled or subtotalled. Once created, the description is stored in a report file for future use.

Developed in the early 1970s, report writers (report generators) were the precursor to query languages and were the first programs to generate computer output without having to be programmed.

repository

A database of information about applications software that includes author, data elements, inputs, processes, outputs and interrelationships. A repository is used in a CASE or application development system in order to identify objects and business rules for reuse. It may also be designed to integrate third-party CASE products.

reproducer

An early tabulating machine that duplicated punched cards.

reprographics

Duplicating printed materials using various kinds of printing presses and high-speed copiers.

Requester

See *redirector*.

ResEdit

(Resource Editor) A Macintosh system utility used to edit the resource fork.

reserved word

A verb or noun in a programming or command language that is part of the native language.

reset button

A computer button or key that reboots the computer. All current activities are stopped cold, and any data in memory is lost. On a printer, the reset button clears the printer's memory and readies it to accept new data.

resident module

The part of a program that must remain in memory at all times. Instructions and data that stay in memory can be accessed instantly.

resident program

A program that remains in memory at all times. See *TSR*.

resistor

An electronic component that resists the flow of current in an electronic circuit.

resolution

(1) The degree of sharpness of a displayed or printed character or image. On screen, resolution is expressed as a matrix of dots. For example, the VGA resolution of 640x480 means 640 dots (pixels) across each of the 480 lines. Sometimes the number of colors are added to the spec; for example, 640x480x16 or 640x480x256. The same resolution looks sharper on a small screen than a larger one.

For printers and scanners, resolution is expressed as the number of dots per linear inch. 300 dpi means 300x300, or 90,000 dots per square inch. Laser printers and plotters have resolutions from 300 to 1000 dpi and more, whereas most display screens provide less than 100 dpi. That means jagged lines on screen may smooth out when they print. Scanners have both an optical (physical) resolution and an interpolated resolution, which is computed (see *scanner*).

(2) The number of bits used to record the value of a sample in a digitized signal. See *sampling rate*.

resolve

To change, transform or solve a problem. The

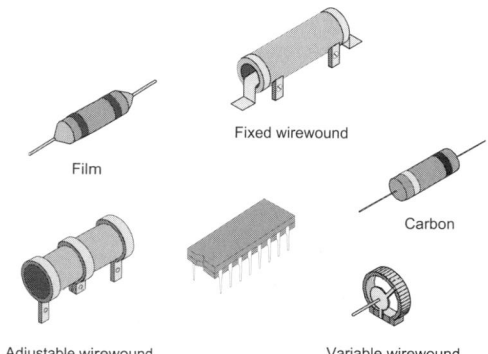

Resistors

There are a wide variety of resistors in use. They can also be built into the circuits of the chip.

Film

Fixed wirewound

Carbon

Adjustable wirewound

Variable wirewound

The aspect ratio of most computer monitors is 4:3.

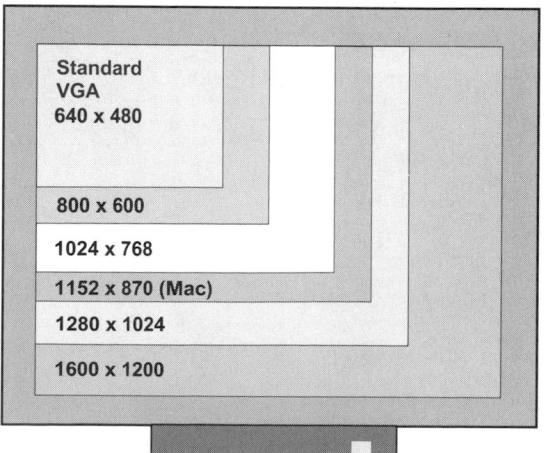

Standard
VGA
640 x 480

800 x 600

1024 x 768

1152 x 870 (Mac)

1280 x 1024

1600 x 1200

Screen Resolutions

These are common screen resolutions. Higher resolutions are available for demanding applications such as document imaging. The higher the resolution, the more information (pixels) can be displayed on screen at one time.

phrase "external references are resolved" refers to determining the addresses that link modules together; that is, solving the unknown links. See *address resolution*.

resource compiler

In a graphical interface (GUI), software that converts and links a resource (menu, dialog box, icon, font, etc.) into the executable program.

resource fork

The resource part of a Macintosh file. For example, in a text document, it contains format codes with offsets into the text in the data fork. In a program, it contains executable code, menus, windows, dialog boxes, buttons, fonts and icons.

resource requirements

The components of a system that are required by software or hardware. It refers to resources that have finite limits such as memory and disk. In a PC, it may also refer to the resources required to install a new peripheral device, namely IRQs, DMA channels, I/O addresses and memory addresses.

response time

The time it takes for the computer to comply with a user's request, such as looking up a customer record.

responsibility

In object technology, a processing step that an object can perform.

restart

To resume computer opertion after a planned or unplanned termination. See *boot, warm boot* and *checkpoint/restart*.

restricted function

A computer or operating system function that cannot be used by an application program.

retrieve

To call up data that has been stored in a computer system. When a user queries a database, the data is retrieved into the computer first and then transmitted to the screen.

return key

Also called the *enter key*, the keyboard key used to signal the end of a line of data or the end of a command. In word processing, return is pressed at the end of a paragraph, and a return code is inserted into the text at that point. See *CR*.

Return (Enter) Key Placement
The correct placement of the return key next to the quote key is very important to the touch typist.

reusability

The ability to use all or the greater part of the same programming code or system design in another application.

reverse engineer

To isolate the components of a completed system. When a chip is reverse engineered, all the individual circuits that make up the chip are identified. Source code can be reverse engineered into design models or specifications. Machine language can be reversed into assembly langauge (see *disassembler*).

reverse polish notation

A mathematical expression in which the numbers precede the operation. For example, 2 + 2 would be expressed as 2 2 +, and 10 - 3 * 4 would be 10 3 4 * -. See *FORTH*.

reverse video

A display mode used to highlight characters on screen. For example, if the normal display mode is black on white, reverse video would be white on black.

revision level

See *version number*.

rewritable

Refers to storage media that can be written, erased and rewritten many times. Magnetic disks and tapes and magneto-optic disks are examples. See *write once*.

REXX

(REstructured EXtended eXecutor) An IBM mainframe structured programming language that runs under VM/CMS and MVS/TSO. It can be used as a general-purpose macro language that sends commands to application programs and to the operating systems. REXX is also included in OS/2. The following REXX example converts Fahrenheit to Celsius:

```
Say "Enter Fahrenheit "
Pull FAHR
Say "Celsius is " (FAHR - 32) * (5 / 9)
```

RF

(Radio Frequency) The range of electromagnetic frequencies above the audio range and below visible light. All broadcast transmission, from AM radio to satellites, falls into this range, which is between 30KHz and 300GHz. See *RF modulation*.

RFC

(Request For Comments) A published document that describes the specifications for a recommended technology. RFCs are used by the Internet Engineering Task Force (IETF) and other standards bodies. RFCs were first used during the creation of the protocols for the ARPAnet back in the 1970s. See *ARPAnet*.

RFI

(Radio Frequency Interference) High-frequency electromagnetic waves that eminate from electronic devices such as chips.

RF/ID

(Radio Frequency/IDentification) An identification system that uses tags that transmit a wireless message. The tag gets its power from a hand-held gun/reading unit.

RF modulation

The transmission of a signal through a carrier frequency. In order to connect to a TV's antenna input, some home computers and all VCRs provide RF modulation of a TV channel, usually Channel 3 or 4. See *FCC class*.

RFP

(Request For Proposal) A document that invites a vendor to submit a bid for hardware, software and/ or services. It may provide a general or very detailed specification of the system.

RFS

(Remote File System) A distributed file system for UNIX computers introduced by AT&T in 1986 with UNIX System V Release 3.0. It is similar to Sun's NFS, but only for UNIX systems.

RF shielding

A material that prohibits electromagnetic radiation from penetrating it. Personal computers and electronic devices used in the home must meet U.S. government standards for electromagnetic interference.

RFT

See *DCA*.

RGB

(Red Green Blue) The color model used for generating video on a display screen. It displays colors as varying intensities of red, green and blue dots. When all three are turned on high, white is produced. As intensities are equally lowered, shades of gray are derived. The base color of the screen appears when all dots are off. See *CMYK* for illustration.

RGB color

The maximum number of colors that can be used for a color image in the computer, which is typically 24-bit color. Contrast with *color palette*. See *24-bit color*.

RGB monitor

(1) A video display screen that requires separate red, green and blue signals from the computer. It generates a better image than composite signals (TV) which merge the three colors together. It comes in both analog and digital varieties.

(2) Sometimes refers to a CGA monitor that accepts digital RGB signals.

Rhapsody

A next-generation operating system for the Macintosh, based on the OpenStep software Apple acquired from NeXT Software. In May 1998, the next-generation Mac OS (Mac OS X) was introduced, and Rhapsody was put on the back burner as a self-contained OS. Object-oriented and other parts of Rhapsody will be used in Mac OS X.

ribbon cable

A thin, flat, multiconductor cable that is widely used in electronic systems; for example, to interconnect peripheral devices to the computer internally.

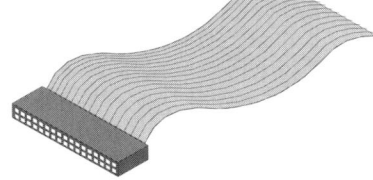

Ribbon Cable
Ribbon cables are widely used to connect peripherals and other electronic components internally. They are rarely used outside of the case or cabinet.

rich e-mail

E-mail messages annotated with graphics, audio and video.

rich text

(1) Text that includes formatting commands for page layout such as fonts, bold, underline, italic, etc. It may also refer to a multimedia document that can include graphics, audio and video.

(2) Text in Microsoft's RTF format. See *RTF*.

RIFF

(1) (Resource Interchange File Format) A file format from Microsoft that can be used to create composite files from existing AVI, WAV, MIDI and other multimedia formats.

(2) An earlier bitmapped graphics format developed for Letraset's ImageStudio and Ready, Set, Go programs for the Macintosh.

right click

To press the right button on the mouse.

right justify

Same as *flush right*.

rightsizing

Selecting a computer system, whether micro, mini or mainframe, that best meets the needs of the application.

rigid disk

Same as *hard disk*.

ring

One stage or level in a set of prioritized stages or levels, typically involved with security and password protection. For example, system-level functions communicate with the OS kernel at the most privileged ring 0, and application programs access the OS at the higher level ring 3.

ring network

A communications network that connects terminals and computers in a continuous loop. See *topology*.

RIP

(1) (Raster Image Processor) The hardware and/or software that rasterizes an image for display or

printing. RIPs are designed to rasterize a specific type of data, such as PostScript or vector graphics images, as well as different kinds of raster data. As desktop computers become more powerful, software RIPs become more appealing than hardware RIPs. Software can be upgraded more easily than hardware, and the operation can be speeded up by installing the software RIP in a faster CPU. See *rasterize*.

(2) (Routing Information Protocol) A simple routing protocol that is part of the TCP/IP protocol suite. It determines a route based on the smallest hop count between source and destination. RIP is a distance vector protocol that routinely broadcasts routing information to its neighboring routers and is known to waste bandwidth. AppleTalk, DECnet, TCP/IP, NetWare and VINES all use incompatible versions of RIP. See *routing protocol*.

(3) (Remote Imaging Protocol) A graphics format from TeleGrafix Communications, Inc., Winchester, VA, (www.telegrafx.com), designed for transmitting graphics over low-speed lines. Using a communications program that supports RIP enables graphical interfaces to be used on a BBS with respectable performance via modem.

RISC

(Reduced Instruction Set Computer) A computer architecture that reduces chip complexity by using simpler instructions. RISC compilers have to generate software routines to perform complex instructions that were previously done in hardware by CISC computers. In RISC, the microcode layer and associated overhead is eliminated.

RISC keeps instruction size constant, bans the indirect addressing mode and retains only those instructions that can be overlapped and made to execute in one machine cycle or less. The RISC chip is faster than its CISC counterpart and is designed and built more economically.

RISC System/6000

See *RS/6000*.

riser card

An expansion card that is used to physically extend a slot for a chip or card in a fully-loaded computer to make room to plug it in. It may also refer to a card that contains several slots used in low-profile, space-saving cabinets. The cards are plugged into the riser card and reside parallel with the motherboard.

RJ-11

(Registered Jack-11) A telephone connector that holds up to four wires. The RJ-11 the common connector used to plug the handset into the telephone and the telphone into the wall. A six-wire variation of RJ-11 is also used.

RJ-21

(Registered Jack-21) An Ethernet cable that uses a 50-pin Telco connector on one end and branches out to 12 RJ-45 connectors on the other.

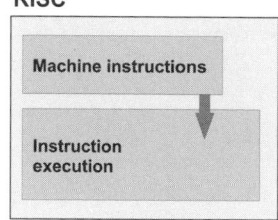
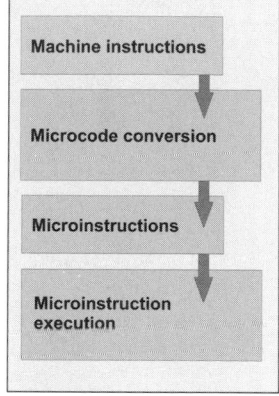

RISC Versus CISC

The RISC machine executes instructions faster because it doesn't have to go through a microcode conversion layer. The RISC compiler does more work than the CISC compiler. It has to generate routines using simpler instructions that would ormally be performed by a single, complex instruction in the CISC computer.

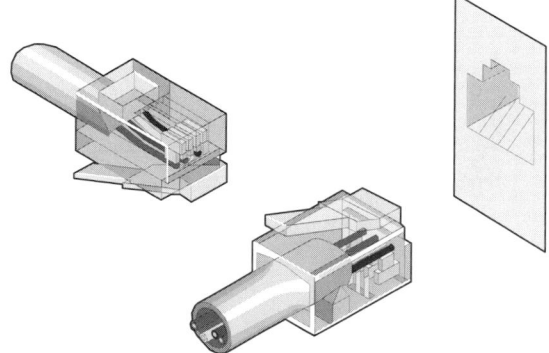

RJ-11 Connectors

Four-wire RJ-11 connectors are used for telephone handsets and wall outlets. There is also a six-wire variation.

RJ-45

(Registered Jack-45) A telephone connector that holds up to eight wires. RJ-45 plugs and sockets are used in 10BaseT Ethernet and Token Ring Type 3 devices.

RJE

(Remote Job Entry) Transmitting batches of transactions from a remote terminal or computer. The receiving computer processes the data and may transmit the results back to the RJE site for printing. RJE hardware at remote sites can employ teleprinters with disk or tape storage or complete computer systems.

RJ-45 Connectors
Eight-wire RJ-45 connectors are used with 10BaseT Ethernet and Type 3 Token Ring networks.

RLE

(Run Length Encoding) A simple data compression method that converts a run of identical characters into a code. A rough example might be []36* where [] is a code and 36* means 36 *'s follow. Microsoft includes an RLE codec in Video for Windows; however, other compression methods are far superior for full-motion video.

RLL

(Run Length Limited) An encoding method commonly used on magnetic disks, including RLL, IDE, SCSI, ESDI, SMD and IPI interfaces. The actual number of bits recorded on the disk is greater than the data bits. Earlier drives inserted extra bits into the data stream so there was more space between signals when reading the data back. As electronics improve, fewer extra bits are inserted, and the ratio of data bits to recorded bits becomes greater.

The "run length" is the number of consecutive 0s before a 1 bit is recorded. For example, RLL 1,7 means there must be at least one 0 between every 1, and the 7 means a maximum of eight time periods between flux transitions. See *hard disk*.

rlogin

(Remote **LOGIN**) A UNIX command that allows users to remotely log onto a server in the network as if they were at a terminal directly connected to that computer. Rlogin is similar to the Telnet command, except that rlogin also passes information to the server about the type of client machine, or terminal, used. See *rsh*.

RMA

(RealMedia Architecture) See *RealMedia*.

RMI

(Remote Method Invocation) A standard from Sun for distributed objects written in Java. RMI is a remote procedure call (RPC), which allows Java objects (software components) stored in the network to be run remotely. Unlike CORBA and DCOM objects, which can be developed in different languages, RMI is designed for objects written only in Java. See *Joe*.

RMON

(Remote **MON**itoring) Extensions to the Simple Network Management Protocol (SNMP) that provide comprehensive network monitoring capabilities. In standard SNMP, the device has to be queried to obtain information. RMON is proactive and can set alarms on a variety of traffic conditions, including specific types of errors. RMON2 can also monitor the kinds of application traffic that flow through the network. The full RMON capabilities are very comprehensive and generally only portions of it are placed into routers and other network devices. See *SNMP*.

RMON probe

A network device that analyzes RMON information. The probe can monitor traffic and set an alarm when a certain condition occurs. It can be used to periodically audit traffic as well as gather statistics that are sent to the management console. RMON probes are often placed permanently into networks.

Computer Desktop Encyclopedia

RMS

(1) (Record Management Services) A file management system used in VAXs.

(2) (Root Mean Square) A method used to measure electrical output in volts and watts.

rn

(ReadNews) A newsreader for Usenet newsgroups. An enhanced version of rn that includes threads is trn. See *Usenet*.

RNI

(Raw Native Interface) A programming interface in Microsoft's Java Virtual Machine used for calling native Windows elements such as GUI routines. RNI is Microsoft's Windows-oriented counterpart of Sun's JNI (Java Native Interface).

robot

A stand-alone hybrid computer system that performs physical and computational activities. It is a multiple-motion device with one or more arms and joints that is capable of performing many different tasks like a human. It can be designed similar to human form, although most industrial robots don't resemble people at all.

It is used extensively in manufacturing for welding, riveting, scraping and painting. Office and consumer applications are also being developed. Robots, designed with AI, can respond to unstructured situations. For example, specialized robots can identify objects in a pile, select the objects in the appropriate sequence and assemble them into a unit.

Robots use analog sensors for recognizing real-world objects and digital computers for their direction. Analog to digital converters convert temperature, motion, pressure, sound and images into binary code for the robot's computer. The computer directs the physical actions of the arms and joints by pulsing their motors.

Huey, Dewey and Louie
Named after Donald Duck's famous nephews, robots at this Wayne, Michigan plant apply sealant to prevent possible water leakage into the car. Huey (top) seals the drip rails while Dewey (right) seals the interior weld seams. Louie is outside of the view of this picture. *(Photo courtesy of Ford Motor Company.)*

robotics

The art and science of the creation and use of robots.

robust

Refers to software without bugs that handles abnormal conditions well. It is often said that there is no software package totally bug free. Any program can exhibit odd behavior under certain conditions, but a robust program will not lock up the computer, cause damage to data or send the user through an endless chain of dialog boxes without purpose. Whether or not a program can be totally bug free will be debated forever. See *industrial strength*.

ROFL

Digispeak for "rolling on the floor laughing."

ROLAP

See *OLAP*.

rollback

A database management system feature that reverses the current transaction out of the database, returning the database to its former state. This is done when some failure interrupts a half-completed transaction.

roll in/roll out

A swapping technique for freeing up memory temporarily in order to perform another task. The current program or program segment is stored (rolled out) on disk, and another program is brought into (rolled in) that memory space. See *pitch-yaw-roll*.

ROM

(Read Only Memory) A memory chip that permanently stores instructions and data. Its contents are created at the time of manufacture and cannot be altered. ROM chips are used to store control routines in personal computers (ROM BIOS), peripheral controllers and other electronic equipment. They are also often the sole contents inside a cartridge that plugs into printers, video games and other systems.

When computers are used in hand-held instruments, appliances, automobiles and any other such devices, the instructions for their routines are generally stored in ROM chips or some other non-volatile chip such as a PROM or EPROM. Instructions may also be stored in a ROM section within a general-purpose computer on a chip. See *PROM, EPROM* and *EEPROM*. Contrast with *RAM*.

ROMable

Machine language capable of being programmed into a ROM chip. Being "read only" the chip cannot be updated and ROMable programs must use RAM or disk for holding changing data.

roman type

The normal typography style in which the vertical lines of the chracters are upright. Contrast with italics, which uses slanted lines.

ROM BIOS

(ROM Basic Input Output System) A PC's BIOS stored in a ROM chip. The first BIOSs were put in ROMs, but later BIOSs have come on flash memory chips, which can be updated in place. See *BIOS*.

ROM BIOS swapping

A technique that alternates areas in the UMA (640K-1M) between ROM BIOSs and the applications as needed.

ROM card

A credit-card-sized module that contains permanent software or data. See *memory card*.

ROM emulator

A circuit that helps debug a ROM chip by simulating the ROM with RAM. The RAM circuit plugs into the ROM socket. Since RAM can be written over, whereas ROM cannot, programming changes can be made easily.

root

A person with unlimited access privileges who can perform any and all operations on the computer. Also called *superuser*. See *root directory*.

root directory

In hierarchical file systems, the starting point in the hierarchy. When the computer is first started, the root directory is the current directory. Access to directories in the hierarchy requires naming the directories that are in its path.

root server

A domain name server that is maintained by Network Solutions, Inc., Herndon, VA. It contains all the primary domain names that are registered, and it is updated daily. The data is replicated on several servers throughout the U.S. and abroad. See *DNS*.

ROP

(1) (Raster Operation) An instruction that manipulates the bits of a bitmapped image .
(2) (RISC Operation) An instruction in a RISC processor.

rot13

A simple cryptography system that substitutes each letter with the 13th letter down the alphabet, rotating back to the beginning. The algorithm that encodes also decodes, because there are 26 letters in the alphabet. It is used to keep messages from the casual observer.

rotational delay

The amount of time it takes for the disk to rotate until the required location on the disk reaches the read/write head.

RO terminal

(Receive Only terminal) A printing device only (no keyboard).

rotoscope

To paint, draw or overlay images onto frames in a movie.

round robin

Continuously repeating sequence, such as the polling of a series of terminals, one after the other, over and over again.

routable protocol

A communications protocol that contains a network address as well as a device address, allowing data to be routed from one network to another. Examples of routable protocols are SNA, OSI, TCP/IP, XNS, IPX, AppleTalk and DECnet. Contrast with *non-routable protocol*. See *routing protocol*.

router

A device that forwards data packets from one local area network (LAN) or wide area network (WAN) to another. Based on routing tables and routing protocols, routers read the network address in each transmitted frame and make a decision on how to send it based on the most expedient route (traffic load, line costs, speed, bad lines, etc.). Routers work at layer 3 in the protocol stack, whereas bridges and switches work at the layer 2.

Routers are used to segment LANs in order to balance traffic within workgroups and to filter traffic for security purposes and policy management. Routers are also used at the edge of the network to connect remote offices. Multiprotocol routers support several protocols such as IP, IPX, AppleTalk and DECnet.

Routers can only route a message that is transmitted by a routable protocol such as IP or IPX. Messages in non-routable protocols, such as NetBIOS and LAT, cannot be routed, but they can be transferred from LAN to LAN via a bridge. Because routers have to inspect the network address in the protocol, they do more processing and add more overhead than a bridge or switch, which both work at the data link (MAC) layer.

Most routers are specialized computers that are optimized for communications; however, router functions can also be implemented by adding routing software to a file

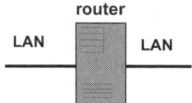

Between LANs
Routers filter traffic from one LAN segment (subnet) to another in order to balance traffic and enforce policy management.

Remote Access
Routers are widely used for remote access changing the LAN frames into the data structures required of the wide area transport.

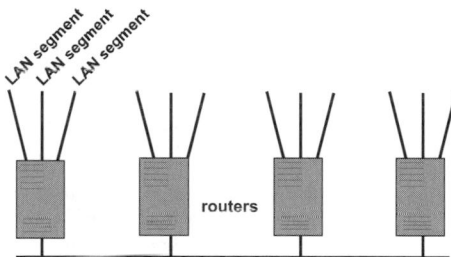

Distributed Router Backbone
Many early networks used a series of routers networked together as a LAN backbone. Typically a router was located on each floor of the building. As more users are added to each segment, traffic can become congested in the shared backbone.

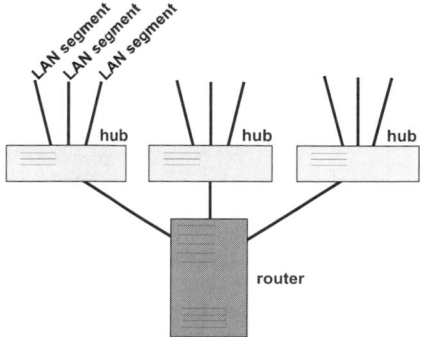

Collapsed Backbone
The collapsed backbone router uses a high-speed backplane to move packets quickly from one port to another. By centralizing the routing in one place, maintenance and troubleshooting is reduced.

server. NetWare, for example, includes routing software. The NetWare operating system can route from one subnetwork to another if each one is connected to its own network adapter (NIC) in the server. The major router vendors are Cisco Systems and Bay Networks.

Routers often serve as an internet backbone, interconnecting all networks in the enterprise. This architecture strings several routers together via a high-speed LAN topology such as Fast Ethernet, FDDI or Gigabit Ethernet. Another approach is the collapsed backbone, which uses a single router with a high-speed backplane to connect the subnets, making network management simpler and improving performance.

In older Novell terminology, a router is a network-layer bridge. Routers also used to be called gateways. For more understanding of how the network layer 3 works within the protocol stack, see *TCP/IP abc's*. See *layer 3 switch, route server* and *routing protocol*.

router protocol

See *routing protocol*.

router table

See *routing table*.

route server

A server that contains a description of a large number of network routes. A route server typically provides a more global view of a geographic area than a router, which is only aware of the destinations that it can reach. See *router* and *routing protocol*.

routine

A set of instructions that perform a task. Same as *subroutine, module, procedure* and *function*.

routing

See *intermediate node routing* and *router*.

routing protocol

A formula used by routers to determine the appropriate path onto which data should be forwarded. The routing protocol also specifies how routers report changes and share information with the other routers in the network that they can reach. A routing protocol allows the network to dynamically adjust to changing conditions, otherwise all routing decisions have to be predetermined and remain static. See *routing table, RIP, OSPF, IGRP, EGP* and *BGP*.

routing switch

See *layer 3 switch*.

routing table

A database in a router that contains the current network topology. See *routing protocol*.

row

A horizontal set of data or components. In a graph, it is called the x-axis. Contrast with *column*.

RPC

(Remote Procedure Call) A programming interface that allows one program to use the services of another program in a remote machine. The calling programming sends a message and data to the remote program, which is executed, and results are passed back to the calling program.

This type of interface is designed to allow

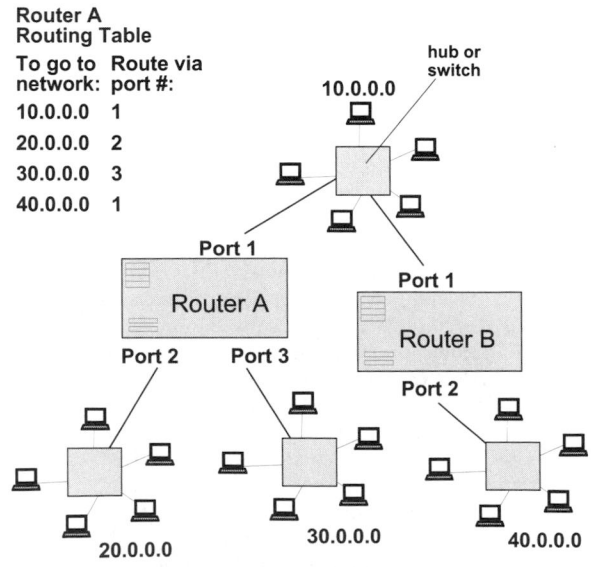

Router A Routing Table	
To go to network:	Route via port #:
10.0.0.0	1
20.0.0.0	2
30.0.0.0	3
40.0.0.0	1

A Routing Table
This is a simpel example of a routing table, showing how packets are directed out the appropriate port.

Computer Desktop Encyclopedia

programs to communicate with each another while freeing the programmer from the nitty gritty networking details. Sun developed the RPC concept as part of its Open Network Computing (ONC) architecture, and a similar type of RPC is used in The Open Group's DCE architecture. Microsoft's DCOM was modelled after the RPC in DCE. CORBA also provides this capability.

RPG

(Report Program Generator) One of the first program generators designed for business reports, introduced in 1964 by IBM. In 1970, RPG II added enhancements that made it a mainstay programming language for business applications on IBM's System/3x midrange computers. RPG III, which added more programming structures, is widely used on the AS/400. RPG statements are written in columnar format.

The following RPG III System/38-AS/400 example changes Fahrenheit to Celsius. The A lines are Data Description Specs (DDS) code. They define a display file and are compiled separately. The F line links RPG code (C lines) to the A lines:

```
A   R FHEITR
A                         6 18'Enter Fahrenheit: '
A     FRHEIT    3Y  0B    6 42DSPATR(PC)
A                           EDTCDE(J)
A                         9 18'Celsius is '
A     CGRADE    3Y  0B    9 42DSPATR(PC)
A                           EDTCDE(J)
FFHEITD   CF   E         WORKSTN
C                   EXFMTFHEITR
C                   Z-ADDO        CGRADE
C     FRHEIT    SUB    32         CGRADE
C     CGRADE    MULT   5          CGRADE
C     CGRADE    DIV    9          CGRADE    H
C                   EXFMTFHEITR
```

rpm

(Revolutions Per Minute) The measurement of the rotational speed of a disk drive. Floppy disks rotate at 300 rpm, while hard disks rotate from 2,400 to 3,600 rpm and more.

RPN

See *reverse polish notation*.

RPQ

(Request for Price Quotation) A document that requests a price for hardware, software or services to solve a specific problem. It is created by the customer and delivered to the vendor.

RRAS

(Routing and Remote Access Service) Software routing and remote access capability in Windows NT. RRAS combines RAS (Remote Access Service) and Multi-Protocol Routing with additional capabilities including packet filtering, demand dial routing and OSPF support.

RS-170

An NTSC standard for composite video signals.

RS-232

(Recommended Standard-232) A TIA/EIA standard for serial transmission between computers and peripheral devices (modem, mouse, etc.). It uses a 25-pin DB-25 or 9-pin DB-9 connector. Its normal cable limitation of 50 feet can be extended to several hundred feet with high-quality cable.

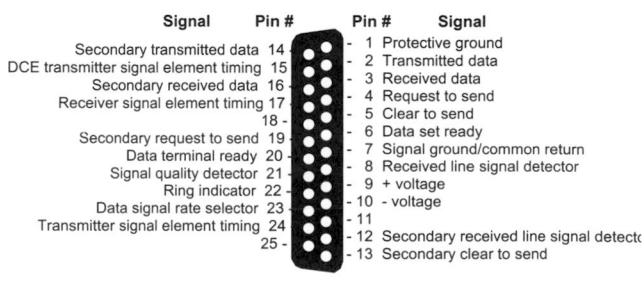

RS-232 defines the purpose and signal timing for each of the 25 lines; however, many applications use less than a dozen. RS-232 transmits positive voltage for a 0 bit, negative voltage for a 1.

In 1984, this interface was officially renamed TIA/EIA-232-E standard (E is the current revision, 1991), although most people still call it RS-232.

RS-422 & 423

A TIA/EIA standards for serial interfaces that extend distances and speeds beyond RS-232. RS-422 is a balanced system requiring more wire pairs than RS-423 and is intended for use in multipoint lines. They use either a 37-pin connector defined by RS-449 or a 25-pin connector defined by RS-530.

RS-449 and RS-530 specify the pin definitions for RS-422 and RS-423. RS-422/423 specify electrical and timing characteristics.

RS-449

Defines a 37-pin connector for RS-422 and RS-423 circuits.

RS-485

A TIA/EIA standard for multipoint communications lines. It can be implemented with as little as a wire block with four screws or with DB-9 or DB-37 connectors. By using lower-impedance drivers and receivers, RS-485 allows more nodes per line than RS-422.

RS-530

Defines a 25-pin connector for RS-422 and RS-423 circuits. It allows for higher speed transmission up to 2Mbits/sec over the same DB-25 connector used in RS-232, but is not compatible with it.

RS/6000

(RISC System/6000) A family of RISC-based workstations and servers from IBM that use the AIX (UNIX) operating system. They are widely used in scientific, industrial and commercial applications. Introduced in 1990, the first RS/6000s used IBM's POWER chip. Starting in 1993, the line began to migrate to the PowerPC chip, a single-chip version of the POWER architecture. Also initially supporting the Micro Channel bus, it later switched to PCI.

RSA

(Rivest-Shamir-Adleman) A highly-secure cryptography method by RSA Data Security, Inc., Redwood City, CA, (www.rsa.com). It uses a two-part key. The private key is kept by the owner; the public key is published.

Data is encrypted by using the recipient's public key, which can only be decrypted by the recipient's private key. RSA is very computation intensive, thus it is often used to create a digital envelope, which holds an RSA-encrypted DES key and DES-encrypted data. This method encrypts the secret DES key so that it can be transmitted over the network, but encrypts and decrypts the actual message using the much faster DES algorithm.

An Early RS/6000
This POWERSERVER 590 is one of many models introduced in IBM's RS/6000 series, which are widely used in scientific, industrial and commercial applications. *(Photo courtesy of IBM Corporation.)*

RSA is also used for authentication by creating a digital signature. In this case, the sender's private key is used for encryption, and the sender's public key is used for decryption. See *digital signature*.

The RSA algorithm is also implemented in hardware. As RSA chips get faster, RSA encoding and decoding add less overhead to the operation. See *cryptography* and *digital certificate*. See illustration on next page.

RSAC

(Recreational Software Advisory Council, Washington, DC, www.rsac.org) A non-profit organization that rates game software and online content. It supports the PICS rating system. See *PICS*.

RSCS

(Remote Spooling Communications Subsystem) Software that provides batch communications for IBM's VM operating system. It accepts data from remote batch terminals, executes them on a priority basis and transmits the results back to the terminals. The RSCS counterpart in MVS is called JES. Contrast with *CMS*, which provides interactive communications for VM.

rsh

(Remote SHell) A UNIX command that enables a user to remotely log into a server on the network and pass commands to it. It is similar to the rlogin command, but provides passing of command line arguments to the command interpreter on the server at the same time. Rsh can be used within programs as well as from the keyboard.

RSI

(Repetitive Strain Injury) Ailments of the hands, neck, back and eyes due to computer use. The remedy for RSI is frequent breaks which should include stretching or yoga postures. See *carpal tunnel syndrome*.

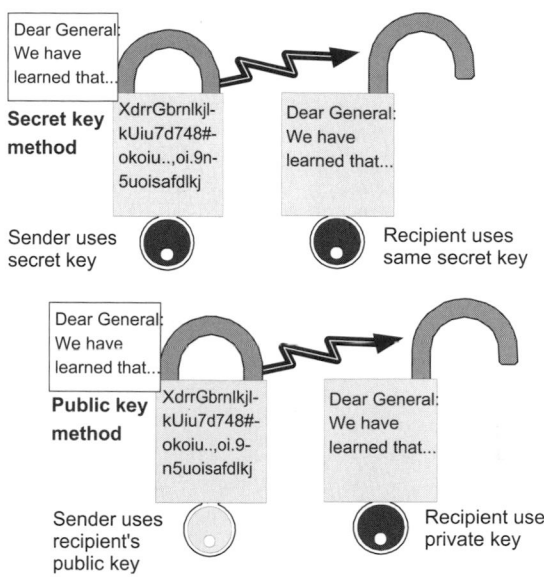

Secret Key vs Public Key

The secret method uses the same key to encrypt and decrypt. The problem is transmitting the key to someone so they can use it. The public key method uses two keys. One kept secret and never transmitted, and the other made public. Sometimes the public key method is used to send the secret key of the private method, and then the message is sent using the private key method.

RSVP

(ReSerVation Protocol) A communications protocol that signals a router to reserve bandwidth for realtime transmission. RSVP is designed to clear a path for audio and video traffic eliminating annoying skips and hesitations. It has been sanctioned by the IETF, because audio and video traffic is expected to increase dramatically on the Internet.

RSX-11

(Resource Sharing eXtension-PDP 11) A multiuser, multitasking operating system from Digital that runs on its PDP-11 series.

RT

A RISC-based workstation from IBM introduced in 1986 that was superseded by the RS/6000 family.

RT-11

A single user, multitasking operating system from Digital that runs on its PDP-11 series.

RTC

See *realtime clock*.

RTF

(Rich Text Format) A Microsoft standard for encoding formatted text and graphics. It was adapted from IBM's DCA format and supports ANSI, IBM PC and Macintosh character sets.

RTFM

(Read The Flaming Manual) The last resort when having a hardware or software problem! The definition of this acronym is rated G. You can figure out what it really means.

This is, of course, a sad but true state of affairs. Most people do not enjoy reading documentation manuals, because they are difficult, if not downright impossible, to understand. The online help is about the same. The reason is that technical documentation is often a last minute rush job with programmers trying to communicate to writers. At times, programmers write the documentation, which is guaranteed to perpetuate the RTFM syndrome.

Some day perhaps, the great minds in the software publishing industry will realize that if they put more time and energy into the design of the menus, buttons and explanations in the first place, they wouldn't be drowning in tech support. User interface design and technical documentation are as difficult as the programming, but this is rarely understood or appreciated.

Until that day arrives, you have several choices for problem resolution if the manual and on-screen help don't help much and all your techy friends are nowhere to be found. You can call tech support and wait on hold, which is usually on your nickel, or you can fax or e-mail your problem and wait a day or more for a reply. Or, you can look it up in one or more good books on the subject. See *user interface* and *how to find a good computer book*.

At Least Get a Laugh

This problem is so pervasive that InfoWorld magazine decided to come up with its "Dumpy" (Documentation User's MalPractice) award for the worst documentation. Although hardly coveted, there are always an inordinate number of candidates.

RTOS

(RealTime Operating System) An operating system designed for use in a realtime computer system. See *realtime system, embedded system, process control* and *OS/9*.

RTP

(1) (Realtime Transport Protocol) An IP protocol that supports realtime transmission of voice and video. An RTP packet rides on top of UDP and includes timestamping and synchronization information in its header for proper reassembly at the receiving end. Realtime Control Protocol (RTCP) is a companion protocol that is used to maintain QoS. RTP nodes analyzes network conditions and periodically send each other RTCP packets that report on network congestion. See *RSVP, RTSP* and *UDP*.

(2) (Rapid Transport Protocol) The protocol used in IBM's High Performance Routing (HPR) system.

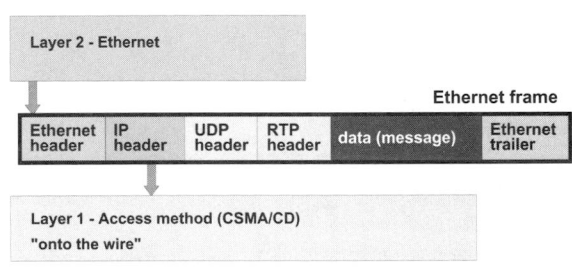

RTP Packet
In a UDP/IP stack, the RTP header is created first and then the packet is moved down the stack to UDP and IP. This shows the RTP packet within an Ethernet frame ready for transmission over the network.

RTS

(Request To Send) An RS-232 signal sent from the transmitting station to the receiving station requesting permission to transmit. Contrast with *CTS*.

RTSP

(RealTime Streaming Protocol) A specification for transmitting audio, video and 3-D animation over the Internet. It was developed by Netscape and Progressive Networks. Contrast with *ASF*.

RTTI

(RunTime Type Information) A facility that allows an object to be queried at runtime to determine its type. One of the fundamental principles of object technology is polymorphism, which is the ability of an object to dynamically change at runtime.

RU

(Rack Unit) A vertical measurement equal to 1.75" for rack-mounted equipment. See *rack mounted*.

rubber banding

In computer graphics, the moving of a line or object where one end stays fixed in position.

rubout key

A keyboard key on a terminal that deletes the last character that was entered.

rule-based expert system

An expert system based on a set of rules that a human expert would follow in diagnosing a problem. Contrast with *model-based expert system.*

ruler line

A graphic representation of a ruler on screen that is used for laying out text and graphics.

rules

(1) A set of conditions or standards which have been agreed upon.

(2) In printing, horizontal and vertical lines between columns or at the top and bottom of a page in order to enhance the appearance of the page.

RUMBA

A family of PC-to-host connectivity programs from Wall Data Inc., Kirkland, WA, (www.walldata.com). On desktop computers connected to minis and mainframes, RUMBA provides a window that emulates a terminal session with these hosts. RUMBA supports Windows and OS/2 clients connected to IBM mainframes, AS/400s, VAXes and other hosts via coax adapters, twinax cards or the network.

Rumbaugh

See *OMT.*

run

(1) To execute a program.

(2) A single program or set of programs scheduled for execution.

run around

In desktop publishing, the flowing of text around a graphic image.

run native

To "run native" is to execute software written for the native mode of the computer. Contrast with running a program under some type of emulation or simulation.

Running native has traditionally been the fastest way to execute instructions on a computer. However, if as expected in the future, machines are so fast they can run emulated programs without any noticeable delay to the user, this will no longer be the important issue it is today.

run on top of

To run as the control program to some other program, which is subordinate to it. Contrast with *run under.*

runt

The frame that remains after a collision on a CSMA/CD medium such as Ethernet. See *runt filtering.*

runt filtering

Discarding runt packets that clog up the network. See *runt.*

runtime

Refers to the actual execution of a program.

runtime version

Software that enables another program to execute on its own or with enhanced capabilities. For example, Visual Basic programs are interpreted, which means Visual Basic applications cannot be executed natively in the computer. They need the runtime module that interprets the Visual Basic code into the machine language of the computer. That actual module in a Windows PC is named VBRUN300.DLL, VBRUN400.DLL, etc.

A full-featured database management system (DBMS) includes a programming language for developing applications. The language is generally interpreted, and the DBMS software must be loaded into the computer in order to run the programs. A runtime version of the DBMS allows the developer to create the application in that language and to package it for customers that have not purchased the DBMS. The runtime version "runs" the application, but does not allow the user access to all the bells and whistles that the owner of the full DBMS has.

In the book "Dvorak Predicts," published by Osborne McGraw-Hill, the well-known computer columnist, John Dvorak, proposes an interesting runtime version. He says that Apple should create a "runtime Mac." As an example, he uses an automobile tune-up kit, suggesting that its probes to the spark plugs, exhaust pipe, etc., be controlled by a computer using the Mac interface for that application only. He claims that the advantages are lower hardware costs if a full-blown Mac isn't required and that the Mac's interface would become widely known if runtime Macs were used for many specialized jobs.

run under

To run within the control of a higher-level program. Contrast with *run on top of*.

RXD

(Receiving Data) See *modem*.

S

S-100 bus

An IEEE 696, 100-pin bus standard used extensively in first-generation personal computers (8080, Z80, 6800, etc.). It is still used in various systems.

S3

(S3 Incorporated, Santa Clara, www.s3.com) A company that specializes in graphics accelerator chips. Founded in 1989 by Dado Banatao and Ronald Yara, it launched the first GUI accelerator on a single chip in 1991 and has continued to be a leader in this field. Its ViRGE technology, introduced in 1995, offered the first 3-D accelerators on a single chip. Earlier chips were the 86C911 and 86C928, whose numbers were derived from the Porsche automobile.

S/360, S/370, S/390

See *System/360, System/370* and *System/390.*

S/3x

See *System/3x.*

SAA

(System Application Architecture) A set of interfaces designed to cross all IBM platforms from PC to mainframe. Introduced by IBM in 1987, SAA includes the Common User Access (CUA), the Common Programming Interface for Communications (CPI-C) and Common Communications Support (CCS). See *CUA, CPI-C* and *CCS.*

Safe Mode

See *Win 9x Safe Mode.*

sag

(1) A momentary drop in voltage from the power source. Contrast with *spike.*

(2) (SAG) (SQL Access Group) See *CLI.*

salary survey

Following is the 1998 Source Edp salary survey of computer professionals, reprinted with permission from Source Services Corporation, Irving, TX. The following salaries are based on an analysis of the current salaries of more than 75,000 computer professionals nationwide. The 20% column below means 20% of the respondents earn that amount or less. The Med (median) represents the figure at which half earn more and half earn less, and 80% means 20% earn that figure or more. See *Source Edp.*

PROGRAMMING	20%-Med-80% (000 US$)		
MAINFRAME			
Jr. programmer	35	38	41
Programmer analyst	44	47	52
Sr. prog/analyst	53	57	65
MIDRANGE			
Jr. programmer	33	36	40
Programmer analyst	42	46	50
Sr. prog/analyst	53	56	62
CLIENT/SERVER/GUI			
Jr. programmer	36	40	44
Programmer analyst	46	51	56
Sr. prog/analyst	56	61	69
SYSTEMS ENGINEER			
Jr. engineer	36	41	46
Engineerer	46	51	58
Sr. engineer	56	64	72
BUSINESS SYSTEMS			
Business analyst	51	55	61
Consultant	59	65	74
EDI analyst	47	53	58
Systems analyst	56	62	66

SPECIALISTS	20%-Med-80% (000 US$)		
Database analyst	55	60	67
Database admin.	62	68	76
LAN admin.	44	48	52
Network engineer	50	58	63
PC software	36	40	44
PC technician	40	43	47
System admin./mgr.	49	54	61
WAN voice analyst	46	51	55
Data comm analyst	54	59	65
WAN administrator	50	54	63
Systems programmer	56	60	65
EDP auditor	43	47	52
Sr. EDP auditor	51	57	65
Technical writer	35	40	45
Systems architect	52	62	72
SALES			
Account rep.	69	75	85
Pre/postsales support	50	59	71
Management	85	94	110

MANAGEMENT
MIS DIRECTOR/CIO
  Small/medium shop   70   77   86
  Large shop   96 111 136
Mgr. business apps   72   82   90
Applications dev.   73   80   89
Technical services   68   76   85
VP/Mgr Systems eng.   75   84   95
VP/Mgr Customer svc. 65   72   86
Project manager   64   71   80
Project leader   57   62   70

DATACENTER
Datacenter manager 59 65 74
Operations support 32 35 42
Operator   33 35 40
Sr. operator   43 46 51
Help desk analyst   38 44 50

INTERNET
Project manager   60 70 80
Engineer   47 55 65
Web programmer   48 53 57
Web graphic designer 44 48 56
Webmaster   40 43 46

Where They Earn It

Seven job categories have been extracted from the survey (note the numbers in the legend below).

  (1) Client/server junior programmer
  (2) Client/server senior prog/analyst
  (3) Business analyst
  (4) LAN administrator
  (5) Technical writer
  (6) Sales rep
  (7) CIO/MIS director (large shop)

NEW ENGLAND	1	2	3	4	5	6	7
Boston	44	68	52	49	45	75	108
Hartford	35	68	48	48	40	65	90
New Hampshire	41	61	65	47	41	74	96
Upper Fairfield, CT	42	70	68	50	45	72	104

MIDDLE ATLANTIC	1	2	3	4	5	6	7
Baltimore	37	62	52	43	35	69	106
Long Island	42	63	52	58	43	65	94
NJ-Central, North	35	58	60	50	41	70	111
New York City	45	75	64	60	46	98	165
Phila, NJ-South	40	60	60	50	40	63	116
Upstate New York	45	60	50	47	38	69	82
Washington, DC	46	69	62	51	42	77	148
Westchester, Lower Fairfld, CT	45	75	58	55	44	90	136

EAST NORTH CENTRAL	1	2	3	4	5	6	7
Cincinnati	36	59	49	48	43	80	101
Cleveland/Akron	37	53	50	41	30	70	96
Columbus	41	62	52	46	33	82	109
Dayton	38	55	51	45	34	79	96
Detroit	35	55	60	48	31	85	132
Grand Rapids	38	64	60	40	36	86	111
Indianpls/Ft. Wayne	34	48	54	46	35	66	85
Louisville	36	54	58	38	38	62	120
Pittsburgh	36	56	53	44	39	75	91

WEST NORTH CENTRAL	1	2	3	4	5	6	7
Chicago	50	60	68	56	45	85	138
Green Bay/Fox Valley	34	56	52	41	32	65	95
Kansas City	32	50	52	42	36	76	108
Milwaukee	37	60	55	43	35	71	110
Minneapolis/St. Paul	40	57	55	45	36	67	119
Omaha/Des Moines	32	47	51	40	35	74	86
St. Louis	38	59	51	48	41	83	111
Wichita/Topeka	32	48	51	41	34	71	93

SOUTH ATLANTIC	1	2	3	4	5	6	7
Atlanta	40	67	55	44	44	109	131
Charlotte	39	63	55	48	35	75	117
Miami	39	68	54	49	36	81	120
Raleigh/Durham	40	64	56	43	36	76	120
Tampa/Orlando	37	56	48	49	31	72	91

SOUTH CENTRAL	1	2	3	4	5	6	7
Dallas/Ft. Worth	42	72	56	50	46	111	163
Houston	39	64	56	49	42	87	135
San Antonio/Austin	41	62	54	49	37	83	122
Tulsa/Oklahoma City	33	49	51	42	35	72	105

MOUNTAIN	1	2	3	4	5	6	7
Denver	38	56	54	46	36	59	96
Phoenix	38	56	53	48	32	60	101
Salt Lake City	36	70	58	53	43	60	116

PACIFIC	1	2	3	4	5	6	7
Los Angeles	41	71	62	52	48	88	152
Orange County	44	72	64	53	48	85	136
Portland	43	72	62	52	45	72	110
San Diego	45	72	66	56	49	80	126
San Fran/San Jose	44	77	64	52	52	116	140
Seattle	45	69	61	50	46	76	110

CANADA	1	2	3	4	5	6	7
Toronto	42	61	55	47	52	99	107

Salsa

A Windows application development system from Wall Data Inc., Kirkland, WA, (www.walldata.com), that uses predefined templates for common business functions. The templates make designing the database more intuitive for non-technical users.

SAM

(1) (Security Accounts Manager) The part of Windows NT that manages the database of usernames, passwords and permissions. A SAM resides in each server as well as in each domain controller. See *PDC* and *trust relationship*.

(2) (Symantec AntiVirus for Macintosh) A popular Macintosh antivirus program from Symantec Corporation, Cupertino, CA.

(3) See *sequential access method*.

Samba

A freeware implementation of the SMB protocol for UNIX machines. It allows a Windows client to share files and printers on a UNIX server. See *SMB*.

sampling

(1) In statistics, the analysis of a group by determining the characteristics of a significant percentage of its members chosen at random.

(2) In digitizing operations, the conversion of real-world signals or movements at regular intervals into digital code. See *sampling rate* and *oversampling*.

sampling frequency, sampling rate

In digitizing operations, the frequency with which

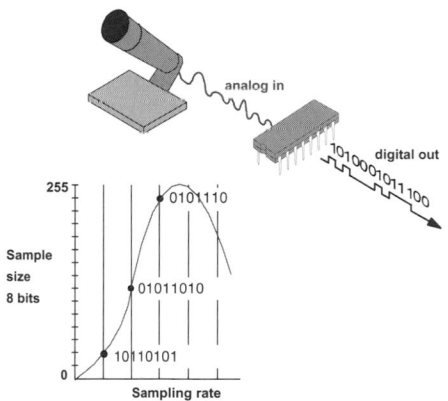

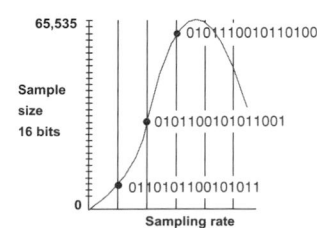

Sampling Sound

The faster the sampling rate and the larger the sample size, the more accurately sound can be digitized. An 8-bit sample breaks the sound wave into 255 increments compared with 65,535 for a 16-bit sample.

samples are taken and converted into digital form. The sampling frequency must be at least twice that of the analog frequency being captured. For example, the sampling rate for hi-fi playback is 44.1KHz, slightly more than double the 20KHz frequency a person can hear. The sampling rate for digitizing voice for a toll-quality conversation is 8,000 times per second, or 8KHz, twice the 4KHz required for the full spectrum of the human voice. The higher the sampling rate, the closer real-world objects are represented in digital form.

Another attribute of sampling is quantizing, which creates a number for the sample. The larger the size of the sample, which is also known as resolution or precision, or just sample size, the more granular the scale and the more accurate the digital sampling. See *oversampling* and *quantization*.

SAN

(1) (Storage Area Network) A back-end network connecting storage devices via peripheral channels such as SCSI, SSA, ESCON and Fibre Channel. There are two ways of implementing SANs: centralized and decentralized. A centralized SAN ties multiple hosts into a single storage system, which is a RAID device with large amounts of cache and redundant power supplies. The cabling distances allow for local as well as campus-wide and metropolitan-wide hookups over peripheral channels rather than an overburdened network. SCSI distances have also been extended. Using fiber, Gigalabs' SCSI switches can communicate over 20 km. This centralized storage topology is commonly employed to tie a server cluster together for failover.

Having data in one place is easier to manage. In addition, some storage systems can copy data for testing, routine backup and transfer between databases without burdening the hosts they serve. The glass house is coming back, not to centralize processing necessarily, but to keep data manageable and safe.

Fibre Channel is a driving force in the SAN arena, because it supports existing peripheral interfaces as well as network interfaces. Fibre Channel (FC) can be configured point-to-point, in an arbitrated loop (FC-AL) or via a switch. With Fibre Channel, the hosts can not only talk to the storage system via SCSI, but they can commuicate with each other via IP over the same topology.

If a centralized storage system is not feasible, a SAN can connect multiple hosts with multiple storage systems. Considering the proliferation of file servers in an enterprise, SANs with distributed storage are expected to be widely employed.

Another related storage device is the network attached storage system (NAS). The NAS is connected

Record Settings ? X

Channels:
○ Mono
● Stereo

Sampling Rate:
○ 11025 Hz
● 22050 Hz
○ 44100 Hz

Sampling Size:
● 8 bits
○ 16 bits

OK
Cancel
Help

Select Stereo or Mono, sample freqency and sample size for the default recording settings.

Sampling Dialog

The recording dialog from Creative Wave Studio, which comes with various Sound Blaster cards, shows the sampling options for digitizing sound into Windows WAV files. *(Screen shot courtesy of Creative Labs, Inc.)*

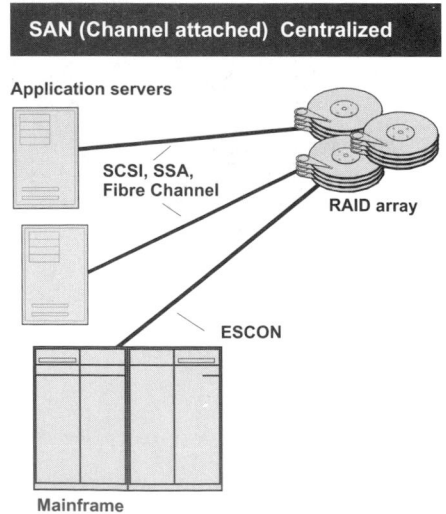

SAN (Channel attached) Centralized

Application servers

SCSI, SSA,
Fibre Channel

RAID array

ESCON

Mainframe

Computer Desktop Encyclopedia

to the front-end communications network (Ethernet, TCP/IP, etc.) just like a file server. Rather than containing a full-blown OS, it typically uses a slim microkernel specialized for handling only I/O requests such as NFS (UNIX), SMB/CIFS (DOS/Windows) and NCP (NetWare).   Adding or removing a NAS system is like adding or removing any network node. In contrast, the channel-attached storage system must be brought down in order to reconfigure it. However, the NAS is subject to the erratic behavior and overhead of the network.

The SAN-NAS terminology is confusing (network attached versus storage area network, etc.). NASs are often contrasted with SANs, but they are also included under the "storage network" umbrella. The major difference is that the SAN is channel attached, and the NAS is network attached. See *SNIA*.

(2) (System Area Network) A high-speed networking architecture used to connect processors and I/O subsystems together. Tandem coined the term with its ServerNet product. See *ServerNet*.

sandbox

See *Java sandbox*.

sans-serif

A typeface style without serifs, which are the short horizontal lines added at the tops and bottoms of the vertical member of the letter. Helvetica is a common sans-serif font.

Santa Cruz Operation

See *SCO*.

SAP

(1) (Service Advertising Protocol) A NetWare protocol used to identify the services and addresses of servers attached to the network. The responses are used to update a table in the router known as the Server Information Table.

(2) (Secondary Audio Program) An NTSC audio channel used for auxiliary transmission, such as foreign language broadcasting or teletext.

(3) (SAP America, Inc., Wayne, PA, www.sap.com) The U.S. branch of the German software company, SAP AG. SAP's R/3 integrated suite of applications and its ABAP/4 Development Workbench became popular starting around 1993 and have gained significant market share in the ERP arena. See *R/3*.

SAS System

(1) Originally called the "Statistical Analysis System," SAS is an integrated set of data management tools from SAS Institute Inc., Cary, NC, (www.sas.com), that runs on PCs to mainframes. It includes a complete programming language as well as modules for spreadsheets, CBT, presentation graphics, project management, operations research, scheduling, linear programming, statistical quality control, econometric and time series analysis and mathematical, engineering and statistical applications.

(2) See *FDDI*.

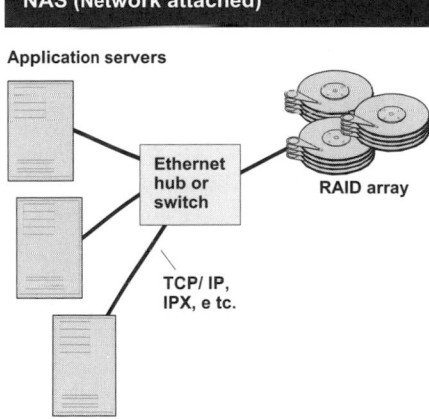

SANs and NASs
SANs are channel attached, and NASs are network attached. They all fall under the "storage network" umbrella.

SATAN

(Security Analysis Tool for Auditing Networks) A utility that analyzes security vulnerabilities on the Internet. In April 1995, it was placed onto the Net as freeware by computer security specialist Dan Farmer.

satellite channel

A carrier frequency used for satellite transmission. See *communications satellite*.

satellite computer

A computer located remotely from the host computer or under the control of the host. It can function as a slave to the master computer or perform offline tasks.

satellite link

A signal that travels from the earth to a communications satellite and back down again. Contrast with *terrestrial link*. See *communications satellite*.

saturation

(1) On magnetic media, a condition in which the magnetizable particles are completely aligned and a more powerful writing signal will not improve the reading back.

(2) In a bipolar transistor, a condition in which the current on the gate (the trigger) is equal to or greater than what is necessary to close the switch.

(3) In a diode, a condition in which the diode is fully conducting.

(4) In a color, the amount of white contained in it. For example, a fully saturated red would be a pure red. The less saturated, the more pastel the appearance. See *chrominance, luminance* and *hue*.

save

To copy the document, record or image being worked on onto a storage medium. Saving updates the file by writing the data that currently resides in memory (RAM) onto disk or tape. Most applications prompt the user to save data upon exiting.

All processing is done in memory (RAM). When the processing is completed, the data must be placed onto a permanent storage medium such as disk or tape.

Save as

A command in the File menu of most applications that lets you make a copy of the current document or image you are working on. It differs from the regular Save command. Save stores your data back into the folder (directory) it originally came from. "Save as" lets you give it a different name and/or put it in a different folder on your hard disk or floppy disk.

If the Save as function provides you with a list of optional file formats, it is used to export a file. Exporting is saving a copy of the current document into a foreign file format. See *foreign file*.

SBC

(1) (SBC Communications Inc., San Antonio, TX, www.sbc.com) A telecommunications company made up of Southwestern Bell, Pacific Bell, Nevada Bell and Cellular One.

(2) See *single board computer*.

Sbus

Originally a proprietary bus from Sun, the Sbus has been released into the public domain. The IEEE standardized a 64-bit version in 1993.

SCA

(Single Connector Attachment) An 80-pin plug and socket used to connect peripherals. With a SCSI drive, it rolls three cables (power, data channel and ID configuration) into one connector for fast installation and removal. An SCA to SCSI adapter allows SCA-configured SCSI drives to fit in traditional SCSI enclosures.

SCADA

(System Control and Data Acquisition, Supervisory Control and Data Acquisition, Security, Control and Data Acquisition). A common process control application that collects data from sensors on the shop floor or in remote locations and sends them to a central computer for management and control.

SCAI

(Switch-to-Computer Applications Interface) A standard for integrating computers to a PBX. See *switch-to-computer*.

scalable

Capable of being changed in size and configuration. It typically refers to a computer, product or system's ability to expand. See *scale*.

scalable font

A font that is created in the required point size when needed for display or printing. The dot patterns (bitmaps) are generated from a set of outline fonts, or base fonts, which contain a mathematical representation of the typeface. The two major scalable fonts are Adobe's Type 1 PostScript and Apple/Microsoft's TrueType.

Although a bitmapped font that is designed from scratch for a particular font size will always look the best, scalable fonts eliminate storing hundreds of different sizes of fonts on disk. In most cases however, only the trained eye can tell the difference. Contrast with *bitmapped font*.

scalar

A single item or value. Contrast with *vector* and *array*, which are made up of multiple values.

scalar processor

A computer that performs arithmetic computations on one number at a time. Contrast with *vector processor*.

scalar variable

In programming, a variable that contains only one value.

scale

(1) To resize a device, object or system, making it larger or smaller. The term is widely used to refer to the expansion capability of hardware or software. For example, "it scales well" means that the device or program can handle increasing numbers of transactions without breaking down or requiring major changes in procedure.

(2) To change the representation of a quantity in order to bring it into prescribed limits of another range. For example, values such as 1249, 876, 523, -101 and -234 might need to be scaled into a range from -5 to +5.

(3) To designate the position of the decimal point in a fixed or floating point number.

scaling

(1) See *scale*.

(2) In the storage industry, obtaining incremental improvements in new products via traditional methods. Evolutionary rather than revolutionary.

SCAM

(SCSI Configured AutoMatically) A subset of Plug and Play that allows SCSI IDs to be changed by software rather than by flipping switches or changing jumpers. Both the SCSI host adapter and peripheral must support SCAM. See *SCSI*.

scan

(1) In optical technologies, to view a printed form a line at a time in order to convert images into bitmapped representations, or to convert characters into ASCII text or some other data code.

(2) In video, to move across a picture frame a line at a time, either to detect the image in an analog or digital camera, or to refresh a CRT display.

(3) To sequentially search a file.

scan converter

A device that changes the video output from a computer to standard TV signals, allowing a regular TV to be used as a computer screen. A VCR can then also be used to record screen output. A scan converter may provide multiple TV formats, such as NTSC and PAL, as well as be able to output digital video such as a D1 signal.

ScanDisk

A utility in Windows 95/98 and DOS (as of Version 6.2) that detects and repairs errors on disk. In Windows 95/98, the ScanDisk Standard option searches for files that have been corrupted. The Thorough option checks the condition of each sector on the disk. For good disk maintenance, periodically run ScanDisk and then Defrag.

scan head

An optical sensing device in an scanner or fax machine that is moved across the image to be scanned.

ScanJet

A family of popular desktop scanners from HP. Monochrome and color models are available.

scan line

One of many horizontal lines in a graphics frame.

scanner

A device that reads a printed page and converts it into a graphics image for the computer. The scanner does not recognize the content of the printed material it is scanning. Everything on the page (text and graphics objects) is converted into one bitmapped graphics image (bitmap), which is a pattern of dots.

Optical character recognition (OCR) systems perform the same scanning operation, but use software to convert the dots into coded ASCII or EBCDIC characters (see *OCR*). Digital cameras are similar to desktop scanners, except that they focus into infinity, whereas desktop scanners accept paper, one page at a time or in a continuous feed like a copy machine (see *digital camera*).

Scanners are optical devices that use CCDs to record the images. They are rated in dots per inch (dpi) by their optical resolution and interpolated resolution, the former being the actual, physical resolution of the device, the latter being a higher resolution that is computed by software. Most all scanners feature 24-bit color, which is generally the maximum number of colors supported in most digital systems. For example, a 24-bit color, 1,200 dpi scanner means each of the 1,200 pixels uses 24 bits to hold color information. However, the 1,200 dpi is often an "enhanced," or interpolated resolution, not the optical resolution. See *optical resolution, interpolated resolution, flatbed scanner, sheet-fed scanner, hand-held scanner, drum scanner, slide scanner, photo scanner* and *digital camera*. See also *virus scanner*.

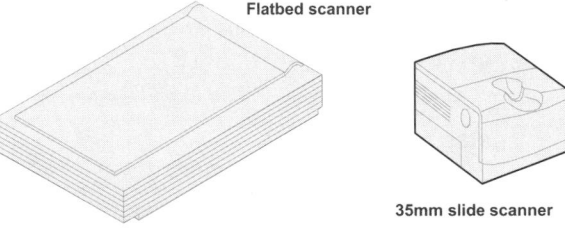

Flatbed scanner

35mm slide scanner

Desktop Scanners

The flatbed scanner on the left is the most common type of desktop scanner. With the addition of a transparancy adapter, which provides a light source from the top, it can scan 35mm slides and large transparencies. The slide scanner on the right is specialized for 35mm slides. The slide is inserted into the slot, and the scanner mechanism moves it past the reading sensors.

scan rate

The number of times per second a scanning device samples its field of vision. See *horizontal scan frequency*.

scan technology

A method for testing chips on the printed circuit board by building the chip with additional input and output pins that are only used for test purposes. Full scan methods test all the registers on the chip. Partial scan tests some of them, and boundary scan tests only the input/output cells. JTAG is the IEEE standard for boundary scan.

scatter plot, scatter diagram

A graph plotted with dots or some other symbol at each data point. Also called a *dot chart*.

scatter read

The capability that allows data to be input into two or more noncontiguous locations of memory with one read operation. See *gather write*.

Computer Desktop Encyclopedia

SCbus
See *SCSA*.

SC connector
A fiber-optic cable connector that uses a push-pull latching mechanism. It is used in FDDI, Fibre Channel and B/ISDN applications. See *fiber-optic connectors*.

scene description language
A method for describing graphics objects to be rendered. Unlike a paint program or image editor, which uses graphical tools for creating images, scene description languages are more like programming source code.

scheduler
The part of the operating system that initiates and terminates jobs (programs) in the computer. Also called a *dispatcher*, it maintains a list of jobs to be run and allocates computer resources as required.

scheduling algorithm
A method used to schedule jobs for execution. Priority, length of time in the job queue and available resources are examples of criteria used.

schema
Pronounced "skeema." The definition of an entire database. Schemas are often designed with visual modeling tools, which automatically create the SQL code necessary to define the table structures. See *subschema*. See *data model* for illustration.

Schottky
A category of bipolar transistor known for its fast switching speeds in the three-nanosecond range. Schottky II devices have switching speeds in the range of a single nanosecond.

SCI
(Scalable Coherent Interface) An IEEE standard for a high-speed bus that uses wire or fiber optic cable. It can transfer data up to 1GBytes/sec.

scientific application
An application that simulates real-world activities using mathematics. Real-world objects are turned into mathematical models and their actions are simulated by executing the formulas.

For example, some of an airplane's flight characteristics can be simulated in the computer. Rivers, lakes and mountains can be simulated. Virtually any objects with known characteristics can be modeled and simulated.

Simulations use enormous calculations and often require supercomputer speed. As personal computers become more powerful, more laboratory experiments will be converted into computer models that can be interactively examined by students without the risk and cost of the actual experiments.

scientific computer
A computer specialized for high-speed mathematic processing. See *array processor, floating point processor* and *supercomputer*.

scientific language
A programming language designed for mathematical formulas and matrices, such as ALGOL, FORTRAN and APL. Although all programming languages allow for this kind of processing, statements in a scientific language make it easier to express these actions.

scientific notation
The display of numbers in floating point form. The number (mantissa) is always equal to or greater than one and less than 10, and the base is 10. For example, 2.345E6 is equivalent to 2,345,000. The number following E (exponent) represents the power to which the base should be raised (number of zeros following the decimal point).

scientific visualization
Using the computer to display real-world objects that cannot normally be seen, such as the shapes of

molecules, air and fluid dynamics and weather patterns. Scientific visualization requires enormous computing resources, and the supercomputer centers and national laboratories throughout the world are always at the forefront of such activity. See *visualization*.

scissoring

In computer graphics, the deleting of any parts of an image which fall outside of a window that has been sized and laid over the original image. Also called *clipping*.

SCL

(1) (Switch-to-Computer Link) Refers to applications that integrate the computer through the PBX. See *switch-to-computer*.

(2) A file extension used for ColoRIX bitmapped graphics file format (640x400 256 colors).

SCM

(1) (Software Configuration Management, Source Code Management) See *configuration management*.

(2) (Service Control Manager) The part of Windows NT that launches background tasks. Developers can write executable programs that run under the control of the SCM.

(3) (Single Chip Module) A chip package that contains one chip. Contrast with *MCM*.

SCO

(The Santa Cruz Operation, Inc., Santa Cruz, CA, www.sco.com) The leading vendor of the UNIX operating system on the Intel x86 platform, which accounts for about one third of all UNIX servers worldwide. SCO has sold licenses for more than two million nodes of UNIX client and server products. Founded in 1979 as a custom programming house, its first operating system was SCO XENIX in 1984. It ran on the Apple Lisa, PC XT and the DEC Pro 350. Subsequently, all SCO products were developed for Intel machines.

In 1995, SCO purchased UnixWare and all the AT&T source code for UNIX System V from Novell. It merged UnixWare and its OpenServer product into a single operating system, which was released in 1998 as SCO UnixWare 7.

SCO Open Desktop, SCO OpenServer

A family of client and server operating systems for the Intel platform from SCO. It is based on UNIX System V Release 3.2 and includes the Motif and X Window user interfaces and standard UNIX networking (TCP/IP, NFS and NIS). SCO OpenServer Desktop is the client version. SCO OpenServer Enterprise is the server version, which has optional SMP support for up to 30 processors. SCO OpenServer Host System is used on computers with dumb terminals.

SCO OpenServer Enterprise was formerly SCO Open Desktop Enterprise. SCO OpenServer Desktop was formerly SCO Open Desktop. SCO OpenServer Host System was originally SCO XENIX.

scope

(1) A CRT screen, such as used on an oscilloscope or common display terminal.

(2) In programming, the visibility of variables within a program; for example, whether one function can use a variable created in another function.

(3) In dBASE, a range of records, such as the "next 50" or "current record to end of file".

SCO UNIX

An enhanced version of UNIX System V Release 3.2 for Intel processors from SCO. In 1989, SCO UNIX was introduced as a major upgrade to SCO XENIX with more security, networking and standards conformance. SCO UNIX servers support dumb terminals, Windows, X terminal and SCO OpenServer clients. The SCO OpenServer line evolved from SCO UNIX.

SCO UnixWare

A family of client and server operating systems for the Intel platform from SCO. It is based on UNIX System V Release 4.2MP and includes SMP support for two processors with optional support for up to 32. As of UnixWare 2.1, it includes NetWare 4.1 file, print and directory services. UnixWare Personal Edition is the client version which comes with the Mosaic Web browser.

UnixWare was originally developed by Univel, a joint venture of Novell and AT&T's UNIX System Labs (USL). In 1993, Novell purchased USL and UnixWare and sold it to SCO two years later. In 1998, SCO released UnixWare 7, which is an enhanced version of UnixWare that combines the UNIX System V

Release 5 kernel with the SCO OpenServer graphical front end. Formerly code named Gemini, UnixWare 7 is intended to provide a migration path to 64-bit computers.

SCP

(Service Control Point) Realtime call processing software from Bellcore that handles 800 number, calling card, collect and third-party billing telephone calls. It runs on Digital processors under VMS, and its counterpart ISCP (Integrated SCP) runs on RS/6000 machines under AIX.

scramble

Same as *encrypt*. The term came from the early days of cryptography which camouflaged analog transmissions with secret frequency patterns. Today, the 0s and 1s are rearranged.

scrambler

A device or software program that encrypts data for security purposes.

scrambling

Encoding data to make it indecipherable. See *cryptography*.

Scrapbook

A Macintosh disk file that holds frequently-used text and graphics objects, such as a company letterhead. Contrast with *Clipboard*, which holds data only for the current session.

scratch disk

A hard disk used to temporarily store data.

scratchpad

A register or reserved section of memory or disk used for temporary storage.

scratch tape

A magnetic tape that can be erased and reused.

screen

The display area of a video terminal or monitor. It is either a CRT or one of the flat panel technologies.

screen angle

The angle at which a halftone screen is placed over an image. Generally, 45 degrees produces the best results. In a digital system, the screen angle is simulated by the placement of the dots within the halftone cells. See *halftone*.

screen capture

Transfering the current on-screen image to a text or graphics file. In Windows, programs such as HiJaak make capturing the screen a snap. You can save the capture as a GIF, BMP or other bitmapped format.

screen dump

Printing the entire on-screen image. On DOS PCs, pressing Shift-PrintScreen prints the current text screen. For DOS graphics, third-party programs work best. On the Macintosh, press Command-shift-3 to create a MacPaint file of the current screen. See *Win 9x Print screen*.

screen font

A font used for on-screen display. For true WYSIWYG systems, screen fonts must be matched as close as possible to the printer fonts. Contrast with *printer font*.

screen frequency

The resolution of a halftone. It is the density of dots (how far they're spaced apart from each other) measured in lines per inch. In a digital system, the screen frequency is simulated by the placement of the dots within the halftone cells. See *halftone*.

screen grabber

A program that saves the current screen image and other screen status information in order for the screen to be restored at a later time.

screen overlay

(1) A clear, fine-mesh screen that reduces the glare on a video screen.

(2) A clear touch panel that allows the user to command the computer by touching displayed buttons on screen.

(3) A temporary data window displayed on screen. The part of the screen that was overlaid is saved and restored when the screen overlay is removed.

screen saver

A utility that prevents a CRT from being etched by an unchanging image. After a specified duration of time without keyboard or mouse input, it blanks the screen or displays moving objects. Pressing a key or moving the mouse restores the screen.

It would actually take many hours to burn in an image on today's color monitors. However, the entertainment provided by these utilities (swimming fish, flying toasters, etc.) has made them very popular.

screen scraper

Also called *frontware*, it is software that adds a graphical user interface to character-based mainframe and minicomputer applications. The screen scraper application runs in the personal computer which is used as a terminal to the mainframe or mini via 3270 or 5250 emulation.

Popular screen scrapers are Star:Flashpoint, Mozart and ESL. Attachmate's QuickApp adds screen scraper capability to development systems such as PowerBuilder, Visual Basic and SQLWindows.

scriplet

See *scriptlet*.

script

(1) A typeface that looks like handwriting or calligraphy.

(2) A program written in a special-purpose programming language such as used in a communications program or word processor. Same as *macro*. See *script language*.

(3) A small program that is used to glue other programs together. It may be written in a full-blown programming language, but it is called a script in this instance.

ScriptActive

A browser plug-in from NCompassLabs, Inc., Vancouver, BC, (www.ncompasslabs.com), that makes Netscape Navigator running under Windows 95 ActiveX compliant. ActiveX is Microsoft's method for running programs on the Internet. See *ActiveX*.

script language

A high-level programming, or command, language that is interpreted (translated on the fly) rather than compiled ahead of time. A script, or scripting, language is not a general-purpose programming language. Although it can be very extensive, it is usually limited to specific functions used to augment the running of an application or system program. Spreadsheet macros and communications scripts are examples. Microsoft's Visual Basic for Applications (VBA) is a script language version of Visual Basic and is used to automate Microsoft applications.

scriptlet

A reusable HTML and script element introduced by Microsoft in Internet Explorer 4.0. It enables an HTML or script fragment to be downloaded once, maintained in a cache and referenced over and over by different HTML pages and scripts.

ScriptX

A multimedia technology from Apple that includes data formats, a scripting language and runtime environment. It is designed for creating applications that can be played on a variety of computers and consumer electronic devices. ScriptX was originally developed by Kaleida, Inc., a joint venture between Apple and IBM, which closed its doors in 1995.

scroll

To continuously move forward, backward or sideways through the text and images on screen or within a window. Scrolling implies continuous and smooth movement, a line, character or pixel at a time, as if the data were on a paper scroll being rolled behind the screen. See *auto scroll*.

scrollable field

A short line on screen that can be scrolled to allow editing or display of larger amounts of data in a small display space. When you type into Look Up in this software, you can type beyond the end of the input box. That's a scrollable field.

scrollable window

A window that contains more data than is visible at one time. Its contents can be scrolled (moved up, down, sideways within the window) in order to view the entire document, image or list of items.

scroll arrow

On-screen arrow that is clicked in order to scroll the screen in the corresponding direction. The screen moves one line, or increment, with each mouse click.

scroll back buffer

Reserved memory that holds a block of transmitted data, allowing the user to browse back through it.

scroll bar

A horizontal or vertical bar that contains a box that looks like an elevator in a shaft. The bar is clicked to scroll the screen in the corresponding direction, or the box (elevator, thumb) is clicked and then dragged to the desired direction.

Scroll Lock

On PC keyboards, a key used to toggle between a scrolling and non-scrolling mode. When on, the arrow keys scroll the screen regardless of the current cursor location. This key is rarely used for its intended purpose, if at all.

SCSA

(Signal Computing System Architecture) An open architecture for transmitting voice and video signals from Dialogic Corporation, Parsippany, NJ, (www.dialogic.com). Its backbone is the SCbus, a 131 Mbps data path that provides up to 2,048 time slots, the equivalent of 1,024 two-way voice conversations at 64 Kbps.v

SCSI

(Small Computer System Interface) Pronounced "scuzzy." SCSI is a hardware interface that allows for the connection of up to seven or 15 peripheral devices to a single expansion board that plugs into the computer called a *SCSI host adapter* or *SCSI controller*. Single boards are also available with two controllers and support up to 30 peripherals. SCSI is widely used from personal computers to mainframes.

Windows 95/98 and the Macintosh provide internal support for SCSI, but Windows 3.1 and DOS do not. Installing SCSI in a Win 3.1 or DOS machine requires adding the appropriate SCSI driver.

ASPI and CAM

Because internal support for SCSI was not provided by DOS and Windows 3.x, there was no benchmark for a standard implementation. As a result, hooking up two SCSI devices often meant plugging in two host adapters, negating SCSI's advantage of connecting multiple peripherals.

ASPI and CAM were created to resolve these differences and provide common

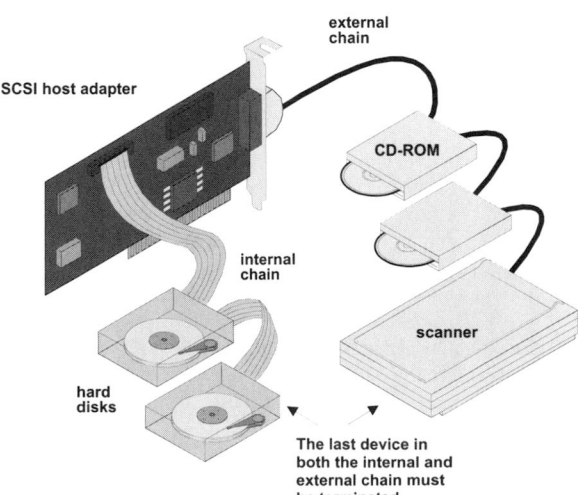

A SCSI Chain

The advantage of SCSI is that several peripherals can be daisy chained to one host adapter, using only one slot in the bus.

interfaces between the drivers and the host adapters. Almost all SCSI products are ASPI and CAM compliant. Windows 95/98 does support popular SCSI host adapters directly. It also supports the ASPI and CAM standards so that older applications and drivers will run even if Windows 95/98 does not support that peripheral with a native driver.

SCSI Is Like a LAN

SCSI is a bus structure itself and functions like a mini-LAN connecting eight or 16 devices. The host adapter counts as one device, thus up to seven or 15 peripherals can be attached depending on the SCSI type. SCSI allows any two devices to communicate at one time (host to peripheral, peripheral to peripheral). See *plugs & sockets* for illustrations of SCSI connectors. Following are SCSI specifications.

Type	Bus Width (bits)	—Cable— Max Length Pins (ft)		Transfer Rate MB/ Sec	Maximum Devices
SCSI-1	8	25	19.7	5	8
SCSI-2	8	50	19.7	5	8
Fast SCSI-2	8	50	9.8	10	8
Wide SCSI-2 or Fast Wide SCSI-2	16	68	9.8	10-20	16
8-bit Ultra SCSI-3	8	50	**	20	8
16-bit Ultra SCSI-3	16	68	**	20-40	16
8-bit Ultra2 SCSI-3	8	50	39.4	40	8
16-bit Ultra2 SCSI-3	16	68	39.4	40-80	16

** 9.8 ft-up to 4 devices
   4.9 ft-5 or more

Version Compatibility

The different SCSI types provide backward and forward compatibility. If a new SCSI host adapter is used with an older SCSI drive, the drive will run at its maximum speed. If an older SCSI host adapter is used with a newer drive, the drive will run at the host adapter's maximum speed.

SCSI and IDE Drives

You can install SCSI hard disk drives in a PC that already contains one or two IDE disk drives. The IDE drive will still be the boot drive, and the SCSI drives will provide additional storage. Follow the instructions in your SCSI host adapter manual carefully to make the correct settings. Some SCSI host adapters provide floppy disk control, which can be disabled since the IDE controller is already handling it.

IDs and Termination

SCSI devices are daisy chained together. External devices have two ports, one for the incoming cable and another for the outgoing cable to the next device. An internal device has a single port that attaches to a ribbon cable with multiple connectors. Each device must be set to a unique ID number, which is normally done by flipping rotary switches on external devices or by setting jumpers on internal ones. The SCSI ID determines the device priority, which starts at 7 and goes to 0 and then from 15 to 8. The host adapter defaults to the highest priority, which is 7.

A subset of Plug and Play, called *SCAM* (SCSI Configured AutoMatically), allows IDs to be set by software rather than manually. Both the host adapter and peripheral must support this.

The device at the end of a SCSI chain must be terminated by either setting a switch or plugging a resistor module into the open port. Usually, host adapters default to terminated. If devices are connected both internally and externally, the host adapter termination must be removed and termination must be applied to the ends of both chains.

Parallel to SCSI

There are adapters that allow SCSI peripherals to be connected via the parallel port. Although the parallel port's transfer rate is considerably less than the SCSI host adapter, it does provide a means to hook up SCSI devices to laptops without PC Card slots and desktop machines without available bus slots.

LUNs

Each SCSI device can be further broken up into eight logical units, identified by logical unit numbers (LUNs) 0 to 7. Although most SCSI disks contain only one disk inside and are addressed as LUN 0, CD-ROM and optical disk jukeboxes contain multiple units. Each disk in these devices can be addressed independently via LUN numbers; for example, a four-disk jukebox could be assigned LUN 0 to 3.

Single Ended, Differential And Low Voltage Differential

There are three types of SCSI signalling. Single-ended SCSI allows devices to be attached to a total cable length of 19.7 feet or 9.8 feet for Fast and Ultra SCSI. Most SCSI devices are single ended.

Differential SCSI is used when devices are spread across a room, because the total cable length is increased to about 80 feet. Differential devices cost more than single-ended ones.

Ultra2 SCSI introduced Low Voltage Differential (LVD) signalling and supports cable lengths up to 39.4 feet. Single-ended SCSI uses a data line and ground. Both Differential SCSI and LVD SCSI use data low and data high lines to increase transmission distance. However, LVD requires less power and is less costly, because the transceivers are built into the controller chips.

SCSI chain

A group of SCSI peripherals connected via a SCSI port. SCSI devices are daisy chained together. The cable goes from the host adapter into device #1, then from #1 to #2 and so on. See *SCSI*.

SCSI switch

A device that cross connects computers to SCSI devices and overcomes many SCSI limitations. The regular SCSI interface is a shared bus, but a SCSI switch, pioneered by GigaLabs, Inc., Sunnyvale, CA, (www.gigalabs.com), provides the full bandwidth between any two devices, greatly increasing overall throughput.

SCSI switches also double the cable distance between devices and minimize access contention, because the devices are not subject to a priority by their ID numbers. In addition, the 7-device or 15-device limit gives way to any number of devices, because the switches can be cascaded. GigaLabs provides remote access between its switches via ATM or with fiber up to 20 km.

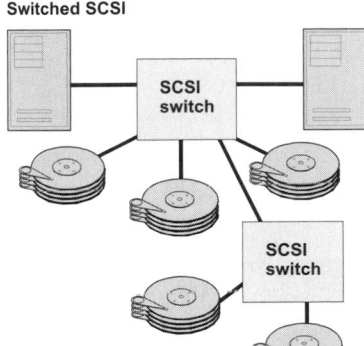

Shared versus Switched
Switched SCSI eliminates many limitations, including bandwidth, cable distance and number of devices. The switch has a backplane capable of handling the full SCSI bandwidth at each of its ports.

scuzzy

See *SCSI*.

SDF

(Standard Data Format) A simple file format that uses fixed length fields. It is commonly used to transfer data between different programs.

```
SDF              Pat Smith    5 E. 12 St.      Rye         NY
                 Bob Jones    200 W. Main St.  Palo Alto   CA

Comma delimited  "Pat Smith","5 E. 12 St.","Rye","NY"
                 "Bob Jones","200 W. Main St.","Palo Alto","CA"
```

SDH

(Synchronous Digital Hierarchy) The European counterpart to SONET. See *SONET*.

SDI

(1) (Switched Digital International) An AT&T dial-up service providing 56 and 64 Kbits/sec digital transmission to international locations.

(2) (Single Document Interface) A Windows function that allows an application to display and lets

the user work with only one document at a time. SDI applications require that the user load the application again for the second and each subsequent document to be worked on concurrently. Contrast with *MDI*.

(3) (Standard Drive Interface) A hard disk interface for VAXs.

(4) (Serial Data Interface) See *serial interface*.

(5) (Strategic Defense Initiative) A high-tech defense system for the U.S. proposed during the Reagan administration.

S-DIMM

(SDRAM-DIMM) SDRAM chips housed on a DIMM module. See *SDRAM* and *DIMM*.

SDK

(Software Developer's Kit) See *developer's toolkit* and *Windows SDK*.

SDLC

(Synchronous Data Link Control) The primary data link protocol used in IBM's SNA networks. It is a bit-oriented synchronous protocol that is a subset of the HDLC protocol. See *SNA, DLC* and *Microsoft DLC*.

SDP

(Streaming Data Procedure) A Micro Channel mode that increases data transfer from 20MB per second to 40MB per second.

SDRAM

(Synchronous DRAM) A type of dynamic RAM memory that is faster than EDO RAM. SDRAM interleaves two or more internal memory arrays so that while one array is being accessed, the next one is being prepared for access. Random access times are the same as EDO RAM, but SDRAM's burst mode obtains the second and subsequent, contiguous characters at a rate of 10ns, some five to six times faster than the first character.

SDRAM-II is a faster SDRAM technology expected in the 1998 timeframe. Also known as DDR DRAM or DDR SDRAM (Double Data Rate DRAM or SDRAM), it allows data reads and writes at twice the speed of the bus.

SDSL

See *DSL*.

SDTV

(StanDard TV) The digital equivalent of the NTSC television format, which has been the broadcast standard since TV's inception. The new Digital TV standard, approved at the end of 1996, provides for many channels of SDTV. See *DTV*.

SDX

(1) See *AIT*.

(2) (Storage Data Acceleration) A technique from Western Digital that improves performance of IDE-based CD-ROM drives. Instead of cabling the drive to the 40-pin IDE interface on the motherboard, it is connected to the Western Digital IDE hard drive with a 10-pin cable. SDX-compliant CD-ROM drives are required.

SE

See *systems engineer* and *service engineer*.

Seagate

(Seagate Technology, Inc., Scotts Valley, CA, www.seagate.com) The largest independent manufacturer of disk drives. Founded in 1979 by Alan Shugart, Tom Mitchell and Doug Mahon, it was the first to offer a 5MByte drive using 5.25" platters making it ideal for the burgeoning desktop computer industry. Seagate became the first company to ship 10 million drives.

In 1989, it aquired Imprimis Technology, a CDC subsidiary making workstation and mainframe drives, nearly doubling Seagate's revenue to $2.5 billion. In 1996, it acquired Conner Peripherals bringing combined revenues to more than eight billion dollars. Starting in the mid 1990s, Seagate acquired several software companies and formed Seagate Software subsidiaries in Europe and the U.S. Seagate Software provides products for asset, network, storage and information management. See *hard disk* for photos of old and new Seagate drives.

seamless integration
An addition of a new application, routine or device that works smoothly with the existing system. It implies that the new feature can be activated and used without problems. Contrast with *transparent*, which implies that there is no discernible change after installation.

search
To look for specific data in a file or an occurrence of text in a file.

search and replace
To look for an occurrence of data or text and replace it with another set of data or text.

search engine
Software that searches for data based on some criteria. Although search engines have been around for decades, they have been brought to the forefront since the World Wide Web exploded onto the scene. See *Web search sites*.

search key
In a search routine, the data entered and used to match other data in the database.

search path
The route to a particular file. See *path*.

seashell
See *C shell*.

Sebring ring
A network of PCI buses that provides up to 512 slots for PCI boards. It links up to 128 PCI buses via a 16-bit dual counter-rotating ring that operates at 266MHz, which achieves a 4.25 GBytes/sec aggregate throughput.

SEC
(Single Edge Connect) Starting with the Pentium II, an Intel hardware module that contains the CPU and an external L2 cache. It plugs into a socket (Slot 1, Slot 2, etc.) on the motherboard which is more similar to a bus slot than an individual chip socket. See *Slot 1*.

SECAM
(Systeme En Couleur Avec Memoire) A color TV standard that was developed in France. It broadcasts 25 interlaced frames per second (50 half frames per second) at 625 lines of resolution. SECAM is used in France and Russia and many countries in Africa, Eastern Europe and the Middle East. See *NTSC* and *PAL*.

secondary cache
See *L2 cache*.

secondary channel
In communications, a subchannel that is derived from the main channel. It is used for diagnostic or supervisory purposes, but does not carry data messages.

secondary index
An index that is maintained for a data file, but not used to control the current processing order of the file. For example, a secondary index could be maintained for customer name, while the primary index is set up for customer account number. See *primary index*.

secondary storage
External storage, such as disk and tape.

second-generation computer
A computer made of discrete electronic components. In the early 1960s, the IBM 1401 and Honeywell 400 were examples.

second-level cache
Same as *L2 cache*. See *cache*.

second source
An alternative supplier of an identical or compatible product. A second source manufacturer is one that holds a license to produce a copy of the original product from another manufacturer.

secret key cryptography
Using the same secret key to encrypt and decrypt messages. The problem with this method is transmitting the secret key to a legitimate person that needs it. See *cryptography*.

sector
The smallest unit of storage read or written on a disk. See *magnetic disk*.

sector interleave
Sector numbering on a hard disk. A one to one interleave (1:1) is sequential: 0,1,2,3, etc. A 2:1 interleave staggers sectors every other one: 0,4,1,5,2,6,3,7.

In 1:1, after data in sector 1 is read, the disk controller must be fast enough to read sector 2, otherwise the beginning of sector 2 will pass the read/write head and must rotate around to come under the head again. If it isn't fast enough, a 2:1 or 3:1 interleave gives it time to read all sectors in a single rotation, eliminating wasted rotations. The best interleave is based on the speed of the particular disk drive. Interleaves are created with the low-level format.

sector map
See *sector interleave*.

sector sparing
Maintaining a spare sector per track to be used if another sector becomes defective. After detecting a bad write, the disk driver or controller writes the data into the spare sector and marks the bad sector as unusable. Existing data can also be moved to the spare sector if the sector is marginal, but the data can be read after several attempts. Sector sparing provides a degree of fault tolerance within the individual disk itself, but RAID provides fault tolerance for the entire disk. See *RAID* and *hot fix*.

secure transaction
A transaction that has been encrypted for online transmission. See *secure Web server*.

secure Web server
A server on the World Wide Web that supports one or more of the major security protocols such as SSL, SHTTP and PCT. See *security protocol*.

SecurID card
An authentication token from Security Dynamics, Inc., Bedford, MA, (www.securid.com), that uses a smart card that authorized users keep in their possession. The card's microprocessor and the host computer are synchronized by a unique number and the time of day. When users log onto a SecurID-enabled host, they type in the number displayed on their cards at that moment as an additional passcode. If the number matches the number that the host computes, the user is presumed to be the valid holder of the card.

security
The protection of data against unauthorized access. Programs and data can be secured by issuing identification numbers and passwords to authorized users of a

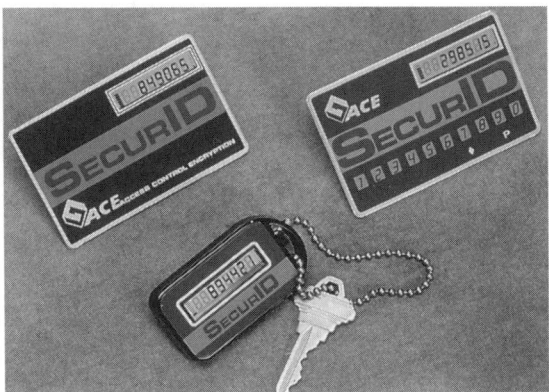

SecurID Card
A variety of SecurID authentication tokens are displayed in this picture. *(Photo courtesy of Security Dynamics, Inc.)*

computer. However, systems programmers, or other technically competent individuals, will ultimately have access to these codes.

Passwords can be checked by the operating system to prevent users from logging onto the system in the first place, or they can be checked in software, such as DBMSs, where each user can be assigned an individual view (subschema) of the database. Any application program running in the computer can also be designed to check for passwords.

Data transmitted over communications networks can be secured by encryption to prevent eavesdropping.

Although precautions can be taken to detect an unauthorized user, it is extremely difficult to determine if a valid user is performing unauthorized tasks. Effective security measures are a balance of technology and personnel management. See *NCSC, ICSA, access control, share-level security, user-level security* and *security audit*.

security audit

An examination of networks and computer systems by an independent consultant to determine an organization's vulnerability to criminal invasion (hackers, viruses, arson, etc.) and natural disasters (fire, tornados, earthquakes, etc.).

security card

A card used for identification purposes which is typically the size of a credit card. See *magnetic stripe, smart card* and *SecurID card*.

security ID

See *security card, SID* and *SecurID card*.

security kernel

The part of the operating system that grants access to users of the computer system.

security levels

See *NCSC*.

security protocol

A communications protocol that encrypts and decrypts a message for online transmission. Security protocols generally also provide authentication. The security protocols that have emerged on the Web are Netscape's SSL, NCSA's SHTTP, Microsoft's PCT and the IETF's IPSec. Web broswers and servers are expected to support all the popular security protocols. See *HTTPS, SHTTP, SSL, PCT* and *IPSec*.

sed

(Stream EDitor) A UNIX editing command that makes changes a line at a time and is used to edit large files that exceed buffer limitations of other editors.

Face Recognition
Face recognition is one of the best ways to authenticate a person. This TrueFace system from Miros uses neural network technology to distinguish a face with different appearances, such as with and without glasses and changing hair styles. *(Photo courtesy of Miros, Inc.)*

seed

(1) The starting value used by a random number generation routine to create random numbers.

(2) (SEED) (Self-Electro-optic-Effect Device) An optical transistor developed by David Miller at Bell Labs in 1986.

seek

(1) To move the access arm to the requested track on a disk.

(2) An assembly language instruction that activates a seek operation on disk.

(3) A high-level programming language command used to select a record by key field.

seek time

The average of the time it takes to move the read/write from its current location to a particular track on a disk. In 1998, Seagate introduced its line of Cheetah hard disks with 5ms seek time. See *access time*.

Seer*HPS

An integrated set of tools for application development from Seer Technologies, Inc., Cary, NC, (www.seer.com). It is object based and repository driven and includes systems analysis tools, application code generation, configuration management and distributed networking facilities. It supports Windows, OS/2, AIX and Sun clients, various servers and databases and connectivity to CICS, IMS and DB2 on the mainframe. The Seer product family includes Seer*SmarkPaks, which are templates that provide the foundation for building vertical market applications.

segment

(1) Any partition, reserved area, partial component or piece of a larger structure. See *overlay*.

(2) One of the bars that make up a single character in an LED or LCD display.

(3) For DOS segment addressing, see *paragraph*.

segmented address space

Memory addressing in which each byte is referenced by a segment, or base, number and an offset that is added to it.

A PC running in 16-bit mode (Real Mode) uses a segmented address space. Memory is broken up into 64KB segments, and a segment register always points to the base of the segment that is currently being addressed. The PC's 32-bit mode is considered a flat address space, but it too uses segments. However, since one 32-bit segment addresses 4GB, one segment covers all of memory.

segmented network

A network that is broken up into groups in order to contain broadcast traffic and improve performance. Contrast with *flat network*. See *LAN segment*.

segment register

A register that points to the base of the current segment being addressed. See *segmented address space*.

SEI

(Software Engineering Institute, Pittsburg, PA, www.sei.cmu.edu) An organization associated with Carnegie Mellon University devoted to the advancement of software engineering. Its Capability Maturity Model (CMM) is used to assess an organization's ability to manage its software development. The results are stated as adhering to one of five levels: Initial, Repeatable, Defined, Managed and Optimizing. The more an organization depends on formal rules to keep projects on schedule and relies less on individual performers, the higher the ranking.

Sel

(SELect) A toggle switch on a printer that takes the printer alternately between online and offline.

selection sort

(1) A sort that starts by searching for the lowest or highest item (alphanumerically) in the list and moving it to the #1 position. The search is repeated starting with the second item, then the third, and so on, until all of items are in the required order. Selection sorts perform numerous comparisons, but fewer data movements than other methods.

(2) A search for specific data starting at the beginning of a file or list. It copies each matching item to a new file so that the selected items are in the same sequence as the original data.

selective calling

In communications, the ability of the transmitting station to indicate which station in the network is to receive the message.

selector channel

A high-speed computer channel that connects a peripheral device (disk, tape, etc.) to the computer's memory.

selector pen

Same as *light pen*.

Selectric typewriter

Introduced in 1961 by IBM, the first typewriter to use a golf-ball-like print head that moved across the paper, rather than moving the paper carriage across the print mechanism. It rapidly became one of the world's most popular typewriters. IBM has always excelled in electromechanical devices. In 1991, IBM's typewriter division was spun off into Lexmark International.

self-booting

Refers to automatically loading the operating system upon startup.

self-checking digit

See *check digit*.

self-clocking

Recording of digital data on a magnetic medium such that the clock pulses are intrinsically part of the recorded signal. A separate timer clock is not required. Phase encoding is a commonly-used self-clocking recording technique.

self-documenting code

Programming statements that can be easily understood by the author or another programmer. COBOL provides more self-documenting code than does C, for example.

self-extracting file

One or more compressed files that have been converted into an executable program which decompresses its contents when run.

self-service application

A software application that allows a user to obtain information or complete a business transaction on the computer that has traditionally required the help of a human representative. Voice response systems and Web sites are widely used for self-service applications. See *kiosk*.

semantic error

In programming, writing a valid programming structure with invalid logic. The compiler will generate instructions that the computer will execute, because it understands the syntax of the programming statements, but the output will not be correct.

semantic gap

The difference between a data or language structure and the real world. For example, in order processing, a company can be both customer and supplier. Since there is no way to model this in a hierarchical database, the semantic gap is said to be large. A network database could handle this condition, resulting in a smaller semantic gap.

semantics

The study of the meaning of words. Contrast with *syntax*, which governs the structure of a language.

semaphore

(1) A hardware or software flag used to indicate the status of some activity.

(2) A shared space for interprocess communications (IPC) controlled by "wake up" and "sleep" commands. The source process fills a queue and goes to sleep until the destination process uses the data and tells the source process to wake up.

semicolon

In programming, the semicolon (;) is often used to separate various elements of an expression. For example, in the C statement **for (x=0; xERROR[Basic syntax error] in:<1ERROR[Basic syntax error] in:0; x++)** the semicolons separate the starting value, number of iterations and increment).

semiconductor

A solid state substance that can be electrically altered. Certain elements in nature, such as silicon, perform like semiconductors when chemically combined with other elements. A semiconductor is halfway between a conductor and an insulator. When charged with electricity or light, semiconductors change their state from nonconductive to conductive or vice versa.

The most significant semiconductor is the transistor, which is simply an on/off switch.

semiconductor device

An elementary component, such as a transistor, or a larger unit of electronic equipment comprised of chips.

sendmail

An SMTP-based mail transport program for UNIX developed at the University of California at Berkeley. The UNIX mail clients commonly used with sendmail are elm, pine, mush and mailx. Sendmail is the MTA (message transfer agent) which stores and forwards the mail. See *messaging system* and *BSD UNIX*.

sensor

A device that measures or detects a real world condition, such as motion, heat or light and converts the condition into an analog or digital representation. An optical sensor detects the intensity or brightness of light, or the intensity of red, green and blue for color systems.

sequel

See *SQL*.

sequence check

Testing a list of items or file of records for correct ascending or descending sequence based on the item or key fields in the records.

sequencer

See *MIDI sequencer*.

Sequent

(Sequent Computer Systems, Inc., Beaverton, OR, www.sequent.com) A computer company founded in 1983 by 17 ex-employees of Intel that specializes in multiprocessing systems for the client/server environment. Sequent pioneered adapting SMP to UNIX and is a leader in the high-end UNIX market.

Sequent's SMP machines are all Intel based and are scalable up to 30 Pentium processors. Its Symmetry series runs the UNIX-based DYNIX/ptx operating system, and the WinServer series runs Windows NT. Its NUMA-Q 2000 line, introduced in 1996, can scale up to 252 processors.

sequential

One after the other in some consecutive order such as by name or number.

sequential access method

Organizing data in a prescribed ascending or descending sequence. Searching sequential data requires reading and comparing each record, starting from the top or bottom of file.

sequential scan

Same as *non-interlaced*.

serial

One after the other.

serial async card

Same as *multiport serial card*.

serial bus

A type of bus that transmits data serially. Ethernet is an example of a serial bus on a network. Serial buses are also expected to become popular for attaching multiple peripherals to computers.

Although both use serial transmission, a serial bus differs from a serial port. The serial port connects the computer to one peripheral device. A serial bus allows for the connection of multiple devices.

serial computer

A single-processor computer that executes one instruction after the other. Contrast with *parallel computer*.

Serial Infrared

See *SIR*.

serial interface

A data channel that transfers digital data in a serial fashion: one bit after the other. Telephone lines use serial transmission for digital data, thus modems are connected to the computer via a serial port. So are mice and scanners. Serial interfaces have multiple lines, but only one is used for data.

For the difference between the serial and parallel ports, see *serial port*. Contrast with *parallel interface*. See *RS-232*

serialize

To convert a parallel signal made up of one or more bytes into a serial signal that transmits one bit after the other.

Serial Line IP

See *SLIP*.

serial matrix printer

See *dot matrix printer*.

serial mouse

A mouse that plugs into the serial port on a PC. Serial mice are the most common type. Contrast with *bus mouse*.

serial number

A unique number assigned by the vendor to each unit of hardware or software. See *signature*.

serial port

A socket on a computer used to connect a modem, mouse, scanner or other serial interface device to the computer. The Macintosh uses the serial port to attach a printer, whereas the PC uses the parallel port. Transferring files between two personal computers can be accomplished by cabling the serial ports of both machines together and using a file transfer program.

The serial port uses DB-9 and DB-25 connectors. On the back of PCs, either one serial port is provided (9-pin connector) or two (one 9- and one 25-pin connector or two 9-pin connectors). Serial port #1 (COM1) is typically used for the mouse, and serial port #2 (COM2) for the modem.

In a PC, serial port circuits are contained on the motherboard (typically two serial ports, one parallel port and one game port). On earlier PCs, they were either on a stand-alone expansion card or on the IDE host adapter card. Contrast with *parallel port*. See *serial interface* and *RS-232*.

serial printer

(1) A printer that uses a serial port for connection to the computer.

(2) A printer that prints one character at a time, such as a dot matrix printer.

Serial SCSI

Running SCSI on Fibre Channel, SSA or FireWire. SCSI is a parallel bus, and the parallel signals must be converted to serial transmission to ride over different transport systems. See *Fibre Channel, SSA, FireWire* and *SCSI*.

serial transmission

Transmitting data one bit at a time. Contrast with *parallel transmission*.

Series/1

An IBM minicomputer series introduced in 1976. It was used primarily as a communications processor and for data collection in process control.

series mode surge suppression

A type of surge suppression that absorbs the surge energy either completely or it absorbs most of it, releasing the residue slowly to neutral. Contrast with *MOV surge suppression*.

serif

Short horizontal lines added to the tops and bottoms of traditional typefaces, such as the Garamond typeface used in this paragraph. Contrast with *sans-serif*.

serpentine recording

A tape recording format of parallel tracks in which the data "snakes" back and forth from the end of one track to the beginning of the next.

server

A computer in a network shared by multiple users. The term may refer to both the hardware and software or just the software that performs the service. For example, Web server may refer to the Web server software in a computer that also runs other applications, or, it may refer to a computer system dedicated to the Web server application. There would be several dedicated Web servers in a large Web site. The following network servers are defined in this book.

```
application server
audio server
database server
fax server
file server
intranet server
mail server
merchant server
modem server
print server
proxy server
remote access server
telephony server
terminal server
video server
Web server
```

server application

(1) An application designed to run in a server. See *client/server*.

(2) Any program that is run in the server, whether designed as a client/server application or not.

(3) See *OLE*.

server based rules

Procedures that are executed on the server. It often refers to messaging systems that can be programmed to do such things as alerting the user when a certain type of mail arrives or automatically replying to specific kinds of mail.

ServerBench

A benchmark from Ziff-Davis that tests the performance of an application server in a client/server environment. It tests Windows clients and a variety of server platforms, including Windows NT, OS/2, NetWare and SCO. See *ZDBOp*.

server farm

A group of network servers that are housed in one location. They might all run the same

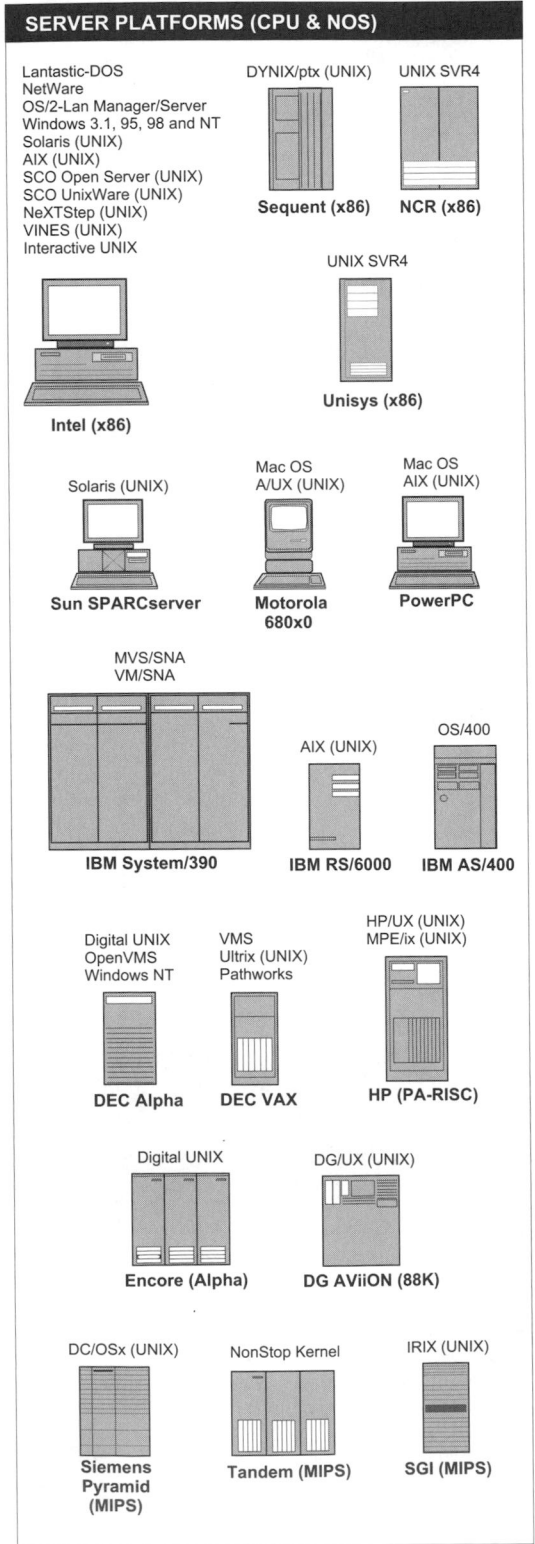

SERVER PLATFORMS (CPU & NOS)

Lantastic-DOS
NetWare
OS/2-Lan Manager/Server
Windows 3.1, 95, 98 and NT
Solaris (UNIX)
AIX (UNIX)
SCO Open Server (UNIX)
SCO UnixWare (UNIX)
NeXTStep (UNIX)
VINES (UNIX)
Interactive UNIX

DYNIX/ptx (UNIX)   UNIX SVR4

Sequent (x86)   **NCR (x86)**

UNIX SVR4

Unisys (x86)

Intel (x86)

Solaris (UNIX)   Mac OS A/UX (UNIX)   Mac OS AIX (UNIX)

Sun SPARCserver   **Motorola 680x0**   **PowerPC**

MVS/SNA
VM/SNA

AIX (UNIX)   OS/400

IBM System/390   **IBM RS/6000**   **IBM AS/400**

Digital UNIX   VMS   HP/UX (UNIX)
OpenVMS   Ultrix (UNIX)   MPE/ix (UNIX)
Windows NT   Pathworks

DEC Alpha   **DEC VAX**   **HP (PA-RISC)**

Digital UNIX   DG/UX (UNIX)

Encore (Alpha)   **DG AViiON (88K)**

DC/OSx (UNIX)   NonStop Kernel   IRIX (UNIX)

Siemens Pyramid (MIPS)   **Tandem (MIPS)**   **SGI (MIPS)**

operating system and applications and use load balancing to distribute the workload between them. See *clustering*.

ServerNet

A clustering technology from Tandem which provides a high-speed interconnect architecture between subsystems. ServerNet I uses switching technology to transfer data at 50 Mbytes/sec in both directions between CPUs, between I/O devices and between CPU and I/O, but not CPU to memory. ServerNet II products transfer at 125 Mbytes/sec. Originally used with Tandem's proprietary fault-tolerant computers, ServerNet is available for NT clusters. See *clustering* and *SAN*.

server program

Software that runs in a server in the network. Contrast with *client program*, which is software that resides in the user's PC or workstation.

server-side

Refers to any operation that is performed at the server. Contrast with *client-side*.

server-side include

An HTML command used to place up-to-date data or boilerplate into a Web page before sending it to the user. For example, it can be used to retrieve the current date and size of downloadable files that are constantly changing. It can be used to insert a boilerplate message where only the boilerplate needs to be changed to bring all the pages up-to-date. HTML pages that contain server-side includes often use the .shtml file extension.

The Include command inserts the contents of another document at the tag location. Echo inserts the contents of an environment variable. Fsize and Flastmod insert size and date of a file, and Config controls the format of the output. The Exec command executes a CGI script. See *SHTML*.

server-side script

A small program run on the server that automates or controls certain functions or links one program to another. On the Web, a CGI script is an example of a server-side script.

service

Functionality derived from a particular software program. For example, network services may refer to programs that transmit data or provide conversion of data in a network. Database services provides for the storage and retrieval of data in a database.

service bureau

An organization that provides data processing and timesharing services. It may offer a variety of software packages, batch processing services (data entry, COLD, COM, etc.) as well as custom programming.

Customers pay for storage of data on the system and processing time used. Connection is made to a service bureau through dial-up terminals, private lines, or other networks, such as Telenet or Tymnet.

Service bureaus also exist that support desktop publishing and presentations and provide imagesetting, color proofing, slide creation and other related services on an hourly or per item basis.

service engineer

A technician that maintains and repairs computers.

service pack

A software patch that is applied to an installed application. It is typically downloaded from the vendor's Web site. When executed, it modifies the application in place.

servlet

A small application that runs on an Internet or intranet server, typically programmed in Java or Perl.

servo

An electromechanical device that uses feedback to provide precise starts and stops for such functions as the motors on a tape drive or the moving of an access arm on a disk.

session

(1) In communications, the active connection between a user and a computer or between two computers.

(2) Using an application program (period between starting up and quitting).

(3) One or more tracks of audio or data that were recorded at one time on a compact disc. See *multisession*.

session layer

The services in the OSI protocol stack (layer 5 of 7) that initiates and manages the communications session. See *OSI*.

SET

(Secure Electronic Transaction) A standard protocol from MasterCard and Visa for securing online credit card payments via the Internet. It is a three-way transaction: the user, merchant and bank must use the SET protocols.

Credit card data and a digital certificate (for authentication) is stored in a plug-in to the user's Web browser. The order is received by a SET-enabled merchant server that passes encrypted payment information to the bank. Approval is electronically sent to the merchant.

set theory

The branch of mathematics or logic that is concerned with sets of objects and rules for their manipulation. UNION, INTERSECT and COMPLEMENT are its three primary operations and they are used in relational databases as follows.

Given a file of Americans and a file of Barbers, UNION would create a file of all Americans and Barbers. INTERSECT would create a file of American Barbers, and COMPLEMENT would create a file of Barbers who are not Americans, or of Americans who are not Barbers. See *fuzzy logic*.

settlement rate

The amount charged by the local access carrier for terminating a call from another country.

set-top box

The cable TV box that "sits on top" of the TV set. A variety of new set-top boxes are emerging for Internet TV and other interactive services.

setup program

(1) Same as *install program*.

(2) See *CMOS setup*.

setup string

A group of commands that initialize a device, such as a printer. See *escape character*.

seven dwarfs

IBM's early competitors in the mainframe business: Burroughs, CDC, GE, Honeywell, NCR, RCA and Univac.

seven-segment display

A common display found on digital watches and readouts that looks like a series of 8s. Each digit is formed by selective illumination of up to seven separately addressable bars.

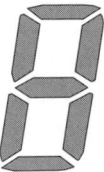

sex changer

See *gender changer*.

SGI

(Silicon Graphics, Inc., Mountain View, CA, www.sgi.com) A manufacturer of graphics workstations and servers founded in 1982 by Jim Clark. SGI shipped its first graphics terminal in 1983 and first workstation in 1984. Computer models include the Indy desktop line, Indigo workstations, CHALLENGE servers and Onyx supercomputers, all running under the IRIX UNIX-based operating system. The hardware is powered by MIPS 64-bit CPUs (MIPS Technologies, Inc., was acquired by SGI in 1992).

SGI has always led the way in computer graphics. Its custom chips and subsystems perform the tedious processing necessary to display objects on screen. Offloading this to the graphics engine frees the CPU to do more application processing, allowing 3-D objects to be animated in realtime. SGI also developed video capabilities in its early years, providing the experience necessary to deliver high-end video servers today.

No matter how much better the graphics get on PCs and Macs, they are always better on SGI workstations. Running a flight simulator on an Indigo workstation is far more realistic than any personal computer or video game. SGI computers are used in a variety of commercial and industrial applications. Airplane manufacturers use them to simulate airflow on new aircraft. Auto companies visualize new car designs and simulate crashes. Medical researchers visualize cell structures. Hollywood creates special effects, such as in "Jurassic Park," "The Abyss" and "The Mask."

In 1996, SGI acquired Cray Research, Inc., and turned it into a wholly-owned subsidiary of the company. SGI and Cray plan to make their product lines binary compatible.

SGML

(Standard Generalized Markup Language) An ISO standard for defining the format in a text document. An SGML document uses a separate Document Type Definition (DTD) file that defines the format codes, or tags, embedded within it. Since SGML describes its own formatting, it is known as a meta-language. SGML is a very comprehensive language that includes hypertext links. The HTML format used on the Web is an SGML document that uses a fixed set of tags. See *HTML* and *XML*.

SGRAM

(Synchronous Graphics RAM) A type of dynamic RAM chip that is similar to the SDRAM technology, but includes enhanced graphics features for use with display adapters. Its Block Write and Mask Write functions allow the frame buffer to be cleared faster and selected pixels to be modified faster.

sh

(SHell) A UNIX command that invokes a different shell. It can be used like a batch file to execute a series of commands saved as a shell.

SHA-1

(Secure Hash Algorithm-1) A popular one-way hash algorithm used to create digital signatures. SHA was developed by the NIST, and SHA-1 is a revision to the standard released in 1994. SHA-1 is similar to the MD4 and MD5 algorithms developed by Rivest, but it is slightly slower and more secure. See *one-way hash function*.

shadow batch

A data collection system that simulates a transaction processing environment. Instead of updating master files (customers, inventory, etc.) when orders or shipments are initiated, the transactions are stored in the computer. When a user makes a query, the master record from the previous update cycle is retrieved; but before it's displayed, it's updated in memory with any transactions that may affect it. The up-to-date master record is then displayed for the user. At the end of the day or period, the transactions are then actually batch processed against the master file.

Dr. James Clark
Clark founded Silicon Graphics in 1982. He has a penchant for starting innovative companies. In 1994, he founded Netscape Communications. *(Photo courtesy of Silicon Graphics, Inc.)*

Virtual Reality
Moving through a 3-D environment in realtime that "really" looks real takes enormous computing power. SGI machines can create this visual reality such as in this picture. *(Photo courtesy of Silicon Graphics, Inc.)*

shadow mask

A thin screen full of holes that adheres to the back of a color CRT's viewing glass. The electron beam is aimed through the holes in the mask onto the phosphor dots. There are generally more holes per inch than the maximum resolution obtainable from that monitor.

shadow RAM

A RAM copy of a PC's ROM BIOS. In order to improve performance, the BIOS, which is stored in a ROM chip, is copied to and executed from RAM. RAM chips are accessed faster than ROMs.

shared DASD

A disk system accessed by two or more computers within a single datacenter. Disks shared in personal computer networks are called file servers or database servers.

shared Ethernet

Refers to the traditional Ethernet topology in which all stations share the total bandwidth of the network. Whether connected via a common cable (10Base5, 10Base2) or a hub (10BaseT), transmission is on a first-come, first-served basis. Contrast with *switched Ethernet*, in which each sender and receiver pair has the full bandwidth of the line.

shared logic

Using a single computer to provide processing for two or more terminals. Contrast with *shared resource*.

shared media LAN

A local area network (LAN) that uses a common path (line, cable, etc.) between all nodes. The total bandwidth of the line is shared among all transmitting stations at any given time. Ethernet, Token Ring and FDDI are the most common shared media LANs. For example, 10BaseT Ethernet provides a total bandwidth of 10 Mbps; 100BaseT and FDDI provide 100 Mbps.

When shared media LANs run out of capacity, they are often replaced with switches to increase bandwidth. The central hub, which functions as a repeater, is replaced with a switch that has the capacity to cross over each sender to the receiver at full wire speed.

shared memory

Memory that can be used by more than one processor. See *SMP* and *MPP*.

shared resource

Sharing a peripheral device (disk, printer, etc.) among several users. For example, a file server and laser printer in a LAN are shared resources. Contrast with *shared logic*.

Shadow mask

Slot mask
NECT CromaClear

Aperture grille
(slot mask)
Sony Trinitron

HUBS AND SWITCHES

Hub versus Switch

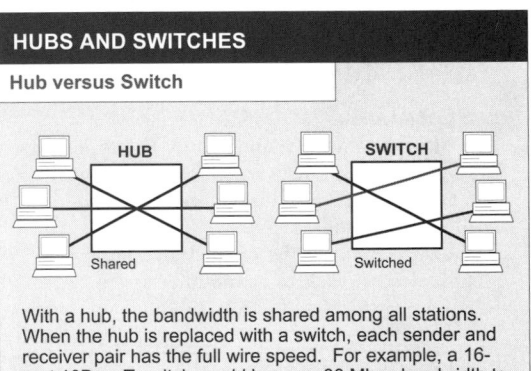

With a hub, the bandwidth is shared among all stations. When the hub is replaced with a switch, each sender and receiver pair has the full wire speed. For example, a 16-port 10BaseT switch would have an 80 Mbps bandwidth to support eight pairs.

Hub and Switch Used Together

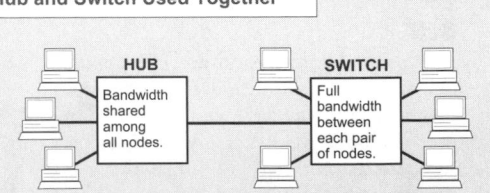

Hubs are used in combination with switches, because not all users may need the speed of an individual switching port.

10/100 Switch (10BaseT and 100BaseT)

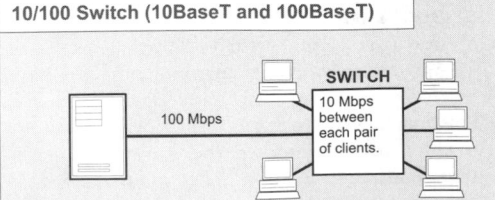

A 10/100 Ethernet switch provides a Fast Ethernet 100 Mbps link to the server and 10 Mbps links between user stations.

shared slot

Typically refers to two different expansion slots that are physically in line with each other in order to save space. Only one of the slots can be used. For example, there may be a PCI/ISA or PCI/EISA shared slot on a motherboard.

share-level security

Access control to a file, printer or other network resource based on knowing the password of that resource. Share-level security provides less protection than user-level security, which identifies each person in the organization. Contrast with *user-level security*.

shareware

Software distributed on a trial basis through the Internet, online services, BBSs, mail-order vendors and user groups. Shareware is software on the honor system. If you use it regularly, you're required to register and pay for it, for which you will receive technical support and perhaps additional documentation or the next upgrade. Paid licenses are required for commercial distribution.

There are tens of thousands of shareware programs, some fantastic, some awful. Shareware vendors compile catalogs with hundreds and thousands of products and sell them by mail or at shows for a small fee. That fee is often misunderstood. It is not the registration fee, rather it is the fee for distributing the shareware to you. See *freeware, public domain software, ASP* and *ZDNet*.

Sharing Violation

An attempt to open a file that is being used by another program. In a normal single-user environment, if an application has already called in a file (document, spreadsheet, etc.), and another program tries to read it, a sharing violation occurs. The solution is to close the file in the application that has "locked" it in order to release it for use by another application.

In a network environment, files can be made sharable for multiple users. If the data is only read and not changed, multiple applications (users) can read the file at the same time. If the file can be updated by multiple users, the operating system or DBMS must manage access to the data via file and record locking or other tracking mechanisms.

Shark disk

A mobile disk drive from Avatar Peripherals, Inc., Milpitas, CA, (www.goavatar.com), that holds 250MB removable cartridges that cost about $39. It comes in parallel port and PC Card versions. The parallel port has a pass-through connector so other parallel devices can remain attached. See *latest disk drives*. For a summary of all storage technologies, see *storage*.

sheet-fed scanner

A scanner that allows only paper to be scanned rather than books or other thick objects. It moves the paper across a stationary scan head. Contrast with *flatbed scanner, hand-held scanner* and *drum scanner*.

sheet feeder

A mechanical device that feeds stacks of cut forms (letterheads, legal paper, etc.) into a printer.

shelfware

Products that remain unsold on a dealer's shelf or unused by the customer.

Shark Cartridge
Shark disks are aimed at providing compact, lightweight removable storage for the portable market.

shell

The outer layer of a program that provides the user interface, or way of commanding the computer. In UNIX, the Bourne shell was the original command processor, with C shell and Korn shell developed later. In DOS, the shell command typically specifies COMMAND.COM, the command processor that interprets commands such as Dir and Type. DOS also came with an optional user interface, known as the DOS Shell, which was a different kind of shell. See *DOS Shell*.

shell account

See *UNIX shell account*.

shell out

To temporarily exit an application, go back to the operating system, perform a function and then return to the application.

shell script

A file of executable UNIX commands created by a text editor and made executable with the Chmod command. It is the UNIX counterpart to a DOS batch file.

shielded twisted pair

See *twisted pair*.

shift register

A high-speed circuit that holds some number of bits for the purpose of shifting them left or right. It is used internally within the processor for multiplication and division, serial/parallel conversion and various timing considerations.

Shiva

(Shiva Corporation, Burlington, MA, www.shiva.com) The leading remote access server manufacturer founded in 1985. Shiva's first products were its NetModem network modems for the Macintosh and later for PCs. Its LANRover is a proprietary remote access server, providing remote users access to LANs via modem. Shiva has also developed the remote access software in Windows 95.

Shlaer-Mellor

An object-oriented analysis and design method developed by Sally Shlaer and Stephen Mellor. The method is applied by partitioning the system into domains. Each domain is analyzed, and the analysis is verified by simulation. A translation method is specified, and the domain models are translated into the object-oriented architecture of the target system.

shocked site

A Web site that contains animations created in Macromedia Director. Users need the Shockwave plug-in for their browser in order to view the files.

Shockwave

A browser plug-in that lets output from Macromedia's Director, Authorware and Freehand software be viewed on the Web. Shockwave is a popular plug-in for viewing animated sequences.

short

In programming, an integer variable. In C, a long is two bytes and can be signed (-32K to +32K) or unsigned (64K). Contrast with *long*.

Short card

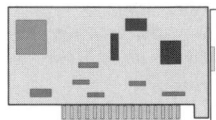

short card

In a PC, a plug-in printed circuit board that is half the length of a full-size board. Contrast with *long card*.

Long card

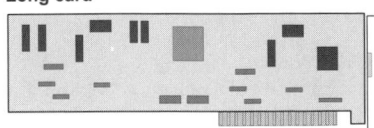

shortcuts

See *Win 9x Shortcuts*.

short-haul modem

In communications, a device that transmits signals up to about a mile. Similar to a line driver that can transmit up to several miles.

shovelware

A large amount of "extras" included on a CD-ROM that add little benefit to the user. Shovelware implies that a lot of freeware, shareware and/or public domain software was added to make it look like a great value. With seven times as much capacity, DVD-ROMs are expected to include even more shovelware than CD-ROMs.

shrink-wrapped software
Refers to store-bought software, implying a standard platform that is widely supported.

SHTML
(Server-parsed HTML) A file extension used to identify HTML pages that contain server-side includes. Server-parsed means that the server scans the page for commands that require additional insertion before the page is sent to the user. See *server-side include* and *parse*.

SHTTP
(Secure HTTP) A protocol that provides secure transactions over the World Wide Web. It is endorsed by NCSA and a variety of organizations. See *security protocol*.

shunt
To divert, switch or bypass.

shut down
To quit all applications and turn off the computer.

SI
See *systems integrator*.

SID
(1) (Society for Information Display, Santa Ana, CA, www.sid.org) A membership organization founded in 1962 devoted to the information display industry. With chapters around the world, SID hosts conferences in the U.S. and abroad and publishes a monthly magazine.

(2) (Security ID) In Windows NT, a unique number assigned to each user and to each workgroup. See *access token*.

sideband
In communications, the upper or lower half of a wave. Since both sidebands are normally mirror images of each other, one of the halves can be used for a second channel to increase the data-carrying capacity of the line or for diagnostic or control purposes.

Sidekick
A personal information manager (PIM) for Windows from Starfish Software, Scotts Valley, CA, (www.starfishsoftware.com). Introduced by Borland in 1984, it was the first popular popup (TSR) program for DOS PCs. It included a calculator, notepad, appointment calendar, phone dialer and ASCII table. Later versions added more notepad commands, calendar alarms, scientific and programming calculators, limited file management and an outliner.

sidetone
In a telephone handset, a small amount of outgoing voice sent back into the caller's speaker to make the caller feel more comfortable.

SIDF
(System Independent Data Format) A tape format designed as a standard for tape backup systems. If widely used, tapes created by one backup software vendor on one platform would be readable by another vendor's software on another platform.

Using a Field Identifier (FID) that identifies the operating system the data was created on, the SIDF format can be extended to support future file systems. Originating from Novell's Storage Management Services (SMS) and governed by the SIDF Association based in Arlington Heights, IL, SIDF is expected to become an international standard.

Siemens Nixdorf
(Siemens Nixdorf Informationssysteme AG, Paderborn, Germany, www.sni-usa.com) The largest European computer firm, which resulted from the 1990 merger of Nixdorf AG and Siemens AG. AG stands for AktienGesellshaft (German for corporation). See *Siemens Pyramid*.

Siemens Pyramid

(Siemens Pyramid Information Systems, San Jose, CA, www.pyramid.com) A computer company that specializes in UNIX-based enterprise servers for commercial markets. Founded as Pyramid Technology in 1981 by former HP employees, it was acquired by Siemens Nixdorf in 1995. Over the years, Pyramid introduced several lines of MIPS-based products, including the Nile, Reliant and RM600 families, many of which include a high-speed mesh interconnect that provides a single point of control for both SMP and MPP systems.

Sieve of Eratosthenes

A benchmark program used to test the mathematical speed of a computer. The program calculates prime numbers based on Eratosthenes's algorithm.

SIG

(Special Interest Group) A group of people that meets and shares information about a particular topic of interest. It is usally a part of a larger group or association.

SIGCAT

(Special Interest Group on CD Applications and Technology, Reston, VA, www.sigcat.org) The world's largest CD-ROM users group, founded by Jerry McFaul in 1986. With more than 10,000 members worldwide, it provides catalogs, publications, regular meetings and conferences.

SIGGRAPH

(Special Interest Group on Computer Graphics, www.siggraph.org) The arm of the ACM that specializes in computer graphics. Providing publications, workshops and conferences, it serves technicians and researchers as well as the artist and business community.

sign

A symbol that identifies a positive or negative number. In digital code, it is either a separate character or part of the byte. In ASCII, the sign is kept in a separate character typically transmitted in front of the number it represents

(+ and - is 2B and 2D in hex).

In EBCDIC, the minus sign can be stored as a separate byte (hex 60), or, more commonly, as half a byte (+ and - is C and D in hex), which is stored in the high-order bits of the least significant byte. For packed decimal, it is in the low-order bits of the least significant byte.

signal

Any electrical or light pulse or frequency. The term is often used when a combination of signals are described, such as power, data and control. See *control signal*.

signal converter

A device that changes the electrical or light characteristics of a signal.

signaling in/out of band

In communications, signaling "in band" refers to sending control signals within the same frequency range as the data signal. For example, a Switched 56 service transmits over a 64 Kbps channel, but uses one out of every eight bits for signaling.

Signaling "out of band" refers to sending control signals outside of the data signal. For example, Basic Rate ISDN (BRI) uses two 64 Kbps channels for data and a separate 16 Kbps channel for signaling.

signal path

A wire, or line, that carries an electrical or light pulse or frequency.

signal processing

See *DSP*.

signal to noise ratio

The ratio of the amplitude (power, volume) of a data signal to the amount of noise (interference) in the line. Usually measured in decibels, it measures the clarity or quality of a transmission channel, audio signal or electronic device.

signature

A unique number built into hardware or software for identification. See *digital signature*.

signature file

A pre-written text file appended to the end of an e-mail message that is used as a closing or end to the message. It typically contains the sender's name and address, but may contain any kind of text or boilerplate that is repetitively sent.

signed document

See *digital signature*.

significant digits

Those digits in a number that add value to the number. For example, in the number 00006508, 6508 are the significant digits.

sign off

Same as *log off*.

sign on

Same as *log on*. See also *Synon/2E*.

silica

Same as *silicon dioxide*.

silica gel

A highly absorbent form of silicon dioxide often wrapped in small bags and packed with equipment to absorb moisture during shipping and storage.

silicon

(Si) The base material used in chips. Next to oxygen, it is the most abundant element in nature and is found in a natural state in rocks and sand. Its atomic structure and abundance make it an ideal semiconductor material. In chip making, it is mined from white quartz rocks and put through a chemical process at high temperatures to purify it. To alter its electrical properties, it is mixed (doped) with other chemicals in a molten state.

Silicon Alley

An area in New York that has become known for its growing number of small, cyberage companies devoted to multimedia and the Internet. It is located in Manhattan's "Soho" district, which does not stand for Small Office Home Office, rather it is SOuth of HOuston Street. See *Silicon Valley*.

silicon compiler

Software that translates the electronic design of a chip into the layout of the logic gates, including the actual masking from one transistor to another. The source of the compilation is either a high-level description or the netlist. See *HDL, netlist* and *logic synthesis*.

silicon dioxide

(SiO^2) A hard, glassy mineral found in such materials as rock, quartz, sand and opal. In MOS chip fabrication, it is used to create the insulation layer between the metal gates of the top layer and the silicon elements below.

silicon disk

A disk drive that is permanently simulated in memory. Typically used in laptops for weight reduction, it requires constant power from a battery to maintain its contents.

silicon foundry

See *foundry*.

Silicon Graphics

See *SGI*.

silicon nitride

(Si_3N_4) A silicon compound capable of holding a static electric charge and used as a gate element on some MOS transistors.

Silicon Valley

An area south of San Francisco, California that is noted for its huge number of computer companies. Thousands of hardware, software and related firms have their headquarters in Silicon Valley, making it the largest confluence of high tech in the U.S.

SIM

(Society for Information Management, Chicago, IL, www.simnet.org) Founded in 1968 as the Society for MIS, it is a membership organization comprised of corporate and division heads of IT organizations. SIM provides a forum for exchange of technical information and offers educational and research programs, competitions and awards.

SimCity 2000

A popular educational game for kids and adults for DOS and Macintosh from Maxis, Inc., Walnut Creek, CA, (www.maxis.com). The purpose is to create a city that prospers due to its well-designed infrastructure. After installing a power plant, electric lines, highways and setting up residential and commercial zones, the people automatically come and build up the city. You can influence the politics, taxation, even determine how much natural disaster befalls the citizens. It's quite amazing!

SIMD

(Single Instruction stream Multiple Data stream) A computer architecture that performs one operation on multiple sets of data, for example, an array processor. One computer or processor is used for the control logic and the remaining processors are used as slaves, each executing the same instruction. Contrast with *MIMD*.

SIMM

(Single In-line Memory Module) A narrow printed circuit board that holds memory chips. It plugs into a SIMM socket on the motherboard or

30-pin SIMM (3.5 x .75")

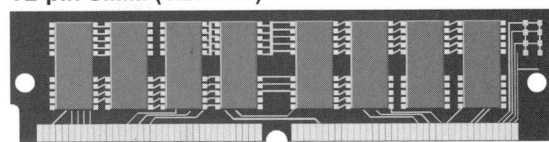

72-pin SIMM (4.25 x 1")

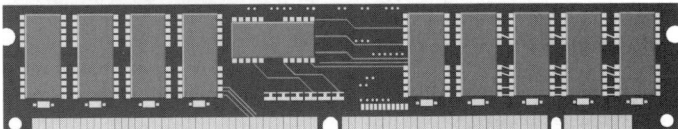

168-pin DIMM (5.375 x 1")

144-pin SODIMM (2.625 x 1")   **72-pin SODIMM (2.375 x 1")**

SIMMs and DIMMs

SIMMs and DIMMs are widely used in desktop computers and servers. The SODIMMs (Small Outline DIMMs) are used in laptops, while 30-pin SIMMs are typically found in older desktop computers.

memory board. The first SIMM format that became popular on personal computers was 3.5" long and used a 30-pin connector. A larger 4.25" format uses 72-pins and contains from one to 64 megabytes of RAM.

SIMMs (Single In-line) evolved into DIMMs (Dual In-line) packages. The difference is in the way the pins are wired. SIMM pins are the same circuit path on both sides of the edge connector. DIMM pins are different on each side, providing double the circuit paths. DIMM modules can be added one at a time on a Pentium motherboard, whereas SIMMs are generally used in pairs and in groups of four on older computers.

PCs use either nine-bit memory (eight bits and a parity bit) or eight-bit memory without parity. Macintoshes use eight-bit memory without parity.

Upgrading Memory - RTFM!

To upgrade to more memory, read your PC's documentation manual. Although it's obvious that you have to put SIMMs in SIMM slots and DIMMs in DIMM slots, the memory chips must also be the same type (EDO, SDRAM, etc.) and the same or faster speed than your existing memory. In addition, your manual should show you all possible combinations of different-sized modules that can be used in the available memory slots.

simplex
One way transmission. Contrast with *half-duplex* and *full-duplex*.

SIMSCRIPT
A programming language used for discrete simulations.

SIMULA
A simulation language originating in the late 1960s that was used to model the behavior of complex systems. SIMULA was the original object-oriented language.

simulation
(1) The mathematical representation of the interaction of real-world objects. See *scientific application*.

(2) The execution of a machine language program designed to run in a foreign computer.

sine
In a right triangle, the ratio of the side opposite an acute angle (less than 90 degrees) and the hypotenuse. The cosine is the ratio between the adjacent side and the hypotenuse. These angular functions are used to compute circular movements.

sine wave
A uniform wave that is generated by a single frequency.

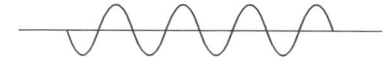

A Sine Wave

single board computer
A printed circuit board that contains a complete computer, including processor, memory, I/O and clock.

single density disk
The first-generation floppy disk.

single-ended configuration
Electrical signal paths that use a common ground, which are more susceptible to noise than *differential configuration*.

single-hub cartridge
A tape cartridge that uses only one spindle and reel. The tape is pulled out of the cartridge and attached to a takeup reel inside the drive. Contrast with *cassette*.

single inheritance
In object-oriented programming, a class that has no more than one parent. Contrast with *multiple inheritance*.

singlemode fiber
An optical fiber with a core diameter of less than 10 microns, used for high-speed transmission and

long distances. It provides greater bandwidth than multimode fiber, but its smaller core makes it more difficult to couple the light source. Contrast with *multimode fiber*.

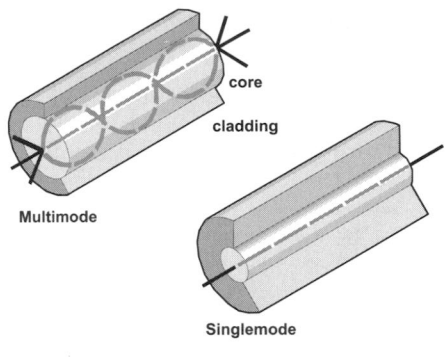

core

cladding

Multimode

single precision

The use of one computer word to hold a numeric value for calculation. Contrast with *double precision*.

single-system image

An operational view of multiple networks, distributed databases or multiple computer systems as if they were one system.

Singlemode

single threading

Processing one transaction to completion before starting the next.

Single UNIX Specification

A common UNIX programming interface governed by X/Open. Formerly known as Spec 1170, it is the latest attempt to unify the UNIX operating system into one set of common programming calls. Products branded by the X/Open organization with the UNIX 95 and UNIX 98 logos conform to Versions 1 and 2 of the specification respectively.

Version 2 of the specfication adds support for realtime processing, threads, Y2K compliance and architecture neutrality. About half of the original APIs were derived from X/Open's XPG4 operating system. Also included are the X/Open Transport Interface (XTI), X and Motif interfaces, UNIX sockets and curses.

sink

A device or place that accepts something. See *heat sink* and *data sink*.

SIP

(1) (Single In-line Package) A type of chip module that is similar to a SIMM, but uses pins rather than edge connectors. SIPs are sometimes called SIPPs (Single In-Line Pin Package).

(2) (SMDS Interface Protocol) The protocol used to support SMDS service. It is composed of the Level 3 Protocol Data Unit (L3_PDU), which contains source and destination addresses and an information field up to 9188 bytes long. See *SMDS*.

(3) (Software Integration Platform) A specification that provides a common format and interface for storing and retrieving geographic data for the petroleum industry.

(4) (Session Initation Protocol) A protocol that provides telephony services similar to H.323, but is less complex.

SIR

(Serial InfraRed) The physical protocol of the IrDA wireless transmission standard. See *IrDA*.

SISD

(Single Instruction stream Single Data stream) The architecture of a serial computer. Contrast with *SIMD* and *MIMD*.

site license

A license to use software within a facility. It provides authorization to make copies and distribute them within a specific jurisdiction.

site map

A hierarchical diagram of the pages on a Web site.

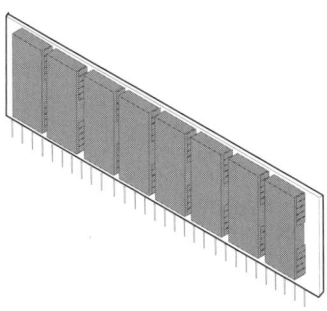

A SIP Module
SIPs use pins to plug the module into the socket whereas SIMMs use edge connectors like most expansion boards.

six degrees of freedom
See *6DOF*.

SIXEL
A graphics language from Digital that supersedes ReGIS. ReGIS to SIXEL conversion programs are available.

skew
(1) The misalignment of a document or punched card in the feed tray or hopper that prohibits it from being scanned or read properly.

(2) In facsimile, the difference in rectangularity between the received and transmitted page.

(3) In communications, a change of timing or phases in a transmission signal.

(4) See *cylinder skew* and *head skew*.

skin effect
Electrons flowing at the outer edges of a wire rather than through the middle. This occurs at very high frequencies.

SKU
(StockKeeping Unit) The number of one specific product available for sale. If a hardware device or software package comes in different versions, there is an SKU for each one.

SkyTel
(SkyTel Corporation, Washington, DC, www.skytel.com) The first nationwide paging service, founded in 1987. It was also the first to integrate voice messaging (dial up and receive the message) as well as alphanumeric text into the pager.

sky wave
A radio signal transmitted into the sky and reflected back down to earth from the ionosphere.

SLA
(Service Level Agreement) A contract between the provider and the user that specifies the level of service that is expected during its term. SLAs are used by vendors and customers as well as internally by IT shops and their end users. They can specify bandwidth availability, response times for routine and ad hoc queries, response time for problem resolution (network down, machine failure, etc.) as well as attitudes and consideration of the technical staff.

SLAs can be very general or extremely detailed, including the steps taken in the event of a failure. For example, if the problem persists after 30 minutes, a supervisor is notified; after one hour, the account rep is contacted, etc.

slamming
The unauthorized switching of your long distance telephone provider. Unethical marketing organizations contact the local telephone company and claim that certain customers have authorized them to handle their long distance. The company may have obtained your name from a list or spoke to you over the phone with a clever hustle whereby you said yes once to another question. Cramming pertains to additional services that you never ordered, such as an 800 number.

slave
A computer or peripheral device controlled by another computer. For example, a terminal or printer in a remote location that only receives data is a slave. When two personal computers are hooked up via their serial or parallel ports for file exchange, the file transfer program may make one computer the master and the other the slave.

slave tube
A display monitor connected to another monitor in order to provide an additional viewing station.

SLDRAM
(Synchronous Link DRAM) An enhanced version of the SDRAM memory technology that uses a multiplexed bus to transfer data to and from the chips rather than fixed pin settings. SLDRAM is expected to support extremely fast transfer rates up into the 3 Gbps range.

The "SL" originally stood for SyncLink, but was dropped since SyncLink is a trade name of MicroGate Corporation products. For information, visit www.sldram.com.

SLED

(Single Large Expensive Disk) The traditional hard disk drive used in minicomputers and mainframes. Such drives were widely used starting in the mid 1960s through the late 1980s. Today, all hard disks are small and inexpensive by comparison. See *RAID*.

sleep

(1) In programming, an inactive state due to an endless loop or programmed delay. A sleep statement in a programming language creates a delay for some specified amount of time.

(2) The inactive status of a terminal, device or program that is awakened by sending a code to it.

slew rate

(1) How fast paper moves through a printer (ips).

(2) The speed of changing voltage.

slice and dice

Refers to rearranging data so that it can be viewed from different perspectives. The term is typically used with OLAP databases that present information to the user in the form of multidimensional cubes similar to a 3-D spreadsheet. See *OLAP*.

slide adapter

See *transparent media adapter*.

slider

A block of material that holds the read/write head of a magnetic disk. See *flying head*.

slide scanner

A scanner that is specialized for scanning 35mm slides. The slide is inserted into the slot and the scanner moves the slide past the read sensors. See *transparent media adapter* and *scanner*.

slideware

Software that is presented in a vendor's "slide" presentation, but that is not anywhere near completion. See *vaporware*.

sliding window

(1) A communications protocol that transmits multiple packets before acknowledgement. Both ends keep track of packets sent and acknowledged (left of window), those which have been sent and not acknowledged (in window) and those not yet sent (right of window).

(2) A view of memory that can be instantly shifted to another location.

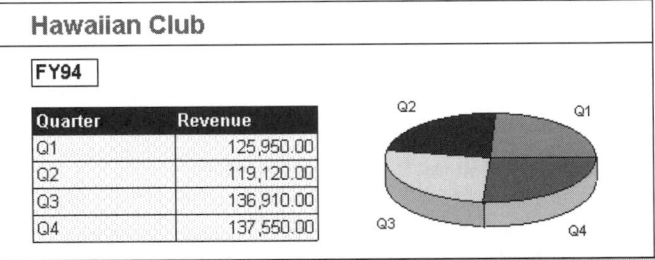

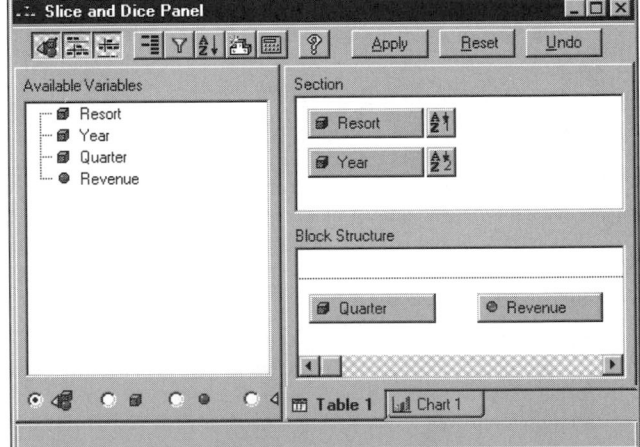

Slice and Dice Dialog

The BusinessObjects query, reporting and OLAP software provides a Slice and Dice Panel that can be called on at any time to rearrange the data. After dragging and dropping the icons into the appropriate windows, BusinessObjects displays the new perspective on screen. The "Section" window shows the breakdown of the overall report, and the "Block Structure" shows the required fields. *(Screen shot courtesy of Business Objects.)*

slime
A dweeb's term for a sales person. See *dweeb*.

SLIP
(Serial Line IP) A data link protocol for dial-up access to TCP/IP networks. It is commonly used to gain access to the Internet as well as to provide dial-up access between two LANs. SLIP transmits IP packets over any serial link (dial up or private lines). See *CSLIP* and *PPP*.

slipstream
To fix a bug or add enhancements to software without identifying such inclusions by creating a new version number.

slot
(1) A receptacle for additional printed circuit boards.

(2) A receptacle for inserting and removing a disk or tape cartridge.

(3) In communications, a narrow band of frequencies. See *time slot*.

(4) May refer to reserved space for temporary or permanent storage of instructions, data or codes.

Slot 1
A receptacle on the motherboard that holds an Intel Single Edge Contact (SEC) cartridge. The cartridge contains up to two CPUs and an L2 cache. It plugs into the slot with a 242-pin edge connector. The Pentium II uses the SEC and Slot 1. See *Slot 2*.

Slot 2
An enhanced Slot 1, which uses a modified SEC (Single Edge Contact) cartridge that holds up to four processors. The L2 cache runs at full processor speed. See *Slot 1*.

slot mask
A type of shadow mask used in CRTs. It refers to two different methods. The first is the aperture grille used in Sony's Trinitron monitors, which uses vertical phosphor stripes and vertical slots in the mask compared to the traditional shadow mask that uses phosphor dots and round holes in the mask.

The second is a combination of traditional shadow mask and aperture grille technologies used in NECT's CromaClear monitors. Sometimes known as a slotted shadow mask, this mask uses elliptical holes and vertical phosphor stripes. See *shadow mask* for illustration.

slot pitch
The distance between like-colored phosphor stripes in a CRT that uses a slot mask. This is slightly closer than the dot pitch in traditional shadow mask CRTs, which measures the diagonal distance between dots. See *slot mask*.

slow scan TV
The transmission of still video frames over telephone lines. Not realtime transmission, it takes several seconds to transmit one frame. Also called *electronic still photography*.

slug
A metal bar containing the carved image of a letter or digit that is used in a printing mechanism.

SMA
(1) (Software Maintenance Association) A membership organization from 1985 to 1996. With chapters worldwide, it was dedicated to advancements in software maintenance.

(2) (Systems Management Architecture) An IBM network management repository.

(3) (Spectrum Manufacturers Association) A DBMS standard for application compatibility.

SMA connector
A fiber-optic cable connector that uses a plug which is screwed into a threaded socket. It was the first connector for optical fibers to be standardized. Two SMA connectors are used for each pair of cables. See *fiber-optic connectors*.

Smalltalk
An operating system and object-oriented programming language that was developed at Xerox PARC.

As an integrated environment, it eliminates the distinction between programming language and operating system. It also allows its user interface and behavior to be customized.

Smalltalk was the first object-oriented programming language to become popular. It was originally used to create prototypes of simpler programming languages and the graphical interfaces that are so popular today. Smalltalk was first run on Xerox's Alto computer, which was designed for it. See *Alto*.

S.M.A.R.T.

(Self Monitoring Analysis and Reporting Technology) A drive technology that reports its own degradation enabling the operating system to warn the user of potential failure. It was included in EIDE drives with the ATA-3 specification.

smart cable

A cable with a built-in microprocessor used to connect two devices. It analyzes incoming signals and converts them from one protocol to another.

smart card

A credit card with a built-in microprocessor and memory used for identification or financial transactions. When inserted into a reader, it transfers data to and from a central computer. It is more secure than a magnetic stripe card and can be programmed to self-destruct if the wrong password is entered too many times. As a financial transaction card, it can be loaded with digital money and used like a travelers check, except that variable amounts of money can be spent until the balance is zero. See *digital money*.

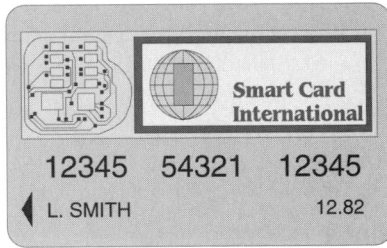

The Smart Card
Widely used in Europe, the smart card is rapidly gaining acceptance in North America.

Smartcom

A family of communications programs for PCs and Macs from Hayes Microcomputer Products, Inc., Atlanta, GA, (www.hayes.com). Versions emulate a several terminals and support a variety of protocols, including the Hayes V-series. Smartcom EZ is for the novice.

Smartdrive

A disk cache program that comes with DOS and Windows. In DOS 4.0 and Windows 3.0, the name of the driver file is SMARTDRV.SYS. Starting with DOS 5 and Windows 3.1, the name of the driver is SMARTDRV.EXE.

SmartFilter

A Web filtering tool for business from Secure Computing Corporation, San Jose, CA, (www.securecomputing.com). SmartFilter adds management control to Internet servers, firewalls and proxy servers. The software uses a URL database that catalogs sites by content (games, investing, sports, sex, cults, etc.), which is updated weekly.

smart hub

See *intelligent hub*.

smart install program

An install program that configures itself automatically based on the hardware environment.

smart network

See *intelligent network*.

smart phone

A telephone with information access features. It is typically a cellular telephone that provides normal voice service as well as any combination of e-mail, fax, pager and limited Web access. See *Internet appliance*.

SmartSuite

A suite of applications for Windows and OS/2 from Lotus that includes the 1-2-3 spreadsheet, Ami

Pro word processor, Freelance Graphics, Approach database, Organizer PIM and Adobe Type Manager. Also included is a common toolbar for launching the applications and selecting predefined macros that provide tighter integration between the applications.

smart terminal

A video terminal with built-in display characteristics (blinking, reverse video, underlines, etc.). It may also contain a communications protocol. The term is often used synonymously with intelligent terminal. See *intelligent terminal* and *dumb terminal*.

SMB

(Server Message Block) The networking protocol used in DOS, Windows and OS/2 networks that allows files and printers to be shared across the network. SMB originated with the NetBIOS protocol used in early DOS networks. SMB services are also available on UNIX servers, which enables Windows workstations to gain access to its files and printers.

The counterpart of SMB in the UNIX world is NFS (Network File System), which is known as a *distributed file system*. NetWare uses the NCP (NetWare Core Protocol) to perform these functions. SMB, NFS and NCP are all high-level protocols that provide open and close file and read and write functions as well as access control. They ride above the transport protocols (NetBEUI, TCP/IP, IPX/SPX), which manage the transfer. See *CIFS, Samba, NFS* and *NCP*.

SMBus

(System Management Bus) A bus used for communicating system requirements. It is used among other things to send charging requirements to the host CPU from the battery.

SMD

(1) (Storage Module Device) A high-performance hard disk interface used with minis and mainframes that transfers data in the 1-4 MBytes/sec range (SMD-E provides highest rate). See *hard disk*.

(2) (Surface Mount Device) A surface mounted chip.

SMDS

(Switched Multimegabit Data Service) A high-speed, switched data communications service offered by the local telephone companies for interconnecting LANs in different locations. It was introduced in 1992 and became generally available nationwide by 1995.

Connection to an SMDS service can be made from a variety of devices, including bridges, routers, CSU/DSUs as well as via frame relay and ATM networks. SMDS can employ various networking technologies. Early implementations use the IEEE 802.6 DQDB MAN technology at rates up to 45 Mbps.

Data is framed for transmission using the SMDS Interface Protocol (SIP), which packages data as Level 3 Protocol Data Units (L3_PDU). The L3_PDU contains source and destination addresses and a data field that holds up to 9188 bytes.

SME

(1) (Small and Medium Enterprises) Refers to organizations that are larger than SOHOs and smaller than the Fortune 1000. The size is subjective ranging from approximately 25 to 500 employees. See *SOHO*.

(2) (Sun Microelectronics) The unit within Sun that develops its chips.

SMF

(1) (Standard Messaging Format) An electronic mail format for Novell's MHS messaging system. The application puts the data into this format in order to send an e-mail message. NGM (NetWare Global Messaging) is based on SMF-71, which supports long addresses and synchronized directories.

(2) (Standard MIDI file) See *MIDI file*.

(3) See *singlemode fiber*.

SMI

(1) (Simple Mail Interface) A subset of functions within the VIM messaging protocol used by applications to send e-mail and attachments.

(2) (Structure of Management Information) A definition for creating MIBs in the SNMP protocol.

(3) (System Management Interrupt) A hardware interrupt in Intel SL Enhanced 486 and Pentium CPUs used for power management. This interrupt is also used for virus checking.

SMIL

(Synchronized Multimedia Integration Language) Pronounced "smile." A format for synchronizing multimedia content on the Web. It uses syntax similar to HTML and enables audio, video and graphics elements to be executed sequentially or in parallel. SMIL supports multimedia streaming protocols such as RTSP.

smiley

See *emoticon.*

S/MIME

See *MIME.*

SMM

(System Management Mode) An energy conservation mode built into Intel SL Enhanced 486 and Pentium CPUs. During inactive periods, SMM initiates a sleep mode that turns off peripherals or the entire system. It retains the computer's status in a protected area of memory called the SMRAM (System Management RAM).

Smoke Test
Not the most sophisticated way to tell if something is w o r k i n g properly, but it's a sure guarantee that it isn't.

smoke test

A test of new or repaired equipment by turning it on. If there's smoke, it doesn't work!

smoothed data

Statistical data that has been averaged or otherwise manipulated so that the curves on its graph are smooth and free of irregularities.

smoothing circuit

An electronic filtering circuit in a DC power supply that removes the ripples from AC power.

SMP

(Symmetric MultiProcessing) A multiprocessing architecture in which multiple CPUs, residing in one cabinet, share the same memory. SMP systems provide scalability. As business increases, additional CPUs can be added to absorb the increased transaction volume.

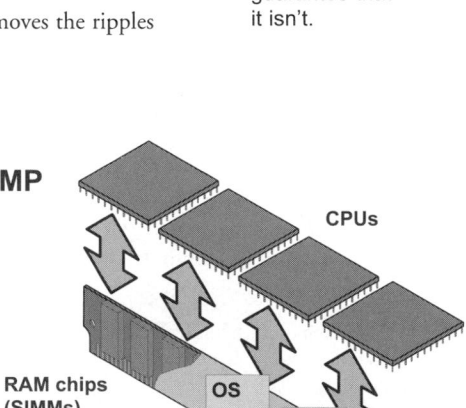

SMP systems range from two to as many as 32 or more processors. However, if one CPU fails, the entire SMP system, or node, is down. Clusters of two or more SMP systems can be used to provide high availability, or fault resilience, in case of failure. If one SMP system fails, the others continue to operate.

A single CPU generally boots the system and loads the SMP operating system, which brings the other CPUs online. There is only one instance of the operating system and one instance of the application in memory. The operating system uses the CPUs as a pool of processing resources, all executing simultaneously, either processing data or in an idle loop waiting to do something.

SMP speeds up whatever processes can be overlapped. For example, in a desktop computer, it would speed up the running of multiple applications simultaneously. If an application is multithreaded, which allows for concurrent operations within the application itself, then SMP will improve the performance of that single application.

Sequent, Pyramid and Encore pioneered SMP on UNIX platforms. SMP servers are also available from IBM, HP, NCR, Unisys and others. Many versions of UNIX as well as proprietary operating systems, such as Windows NT, OS/2 and NetWare, have been designed for or are being revamped for SMP. SMP usage is expected to grow rapidly, and applications are increasingly being designed to take advantage of the SMP architecture. Contrast with *MPP*. See also *NUMA*.

SMPTE

(Society for Motion Picture and TV Engineers, White Plains, NY, www.smpte.org) A professional society for motion picture and TV engineers with more than 9,000 members worldwide. It prepares standards and documentation for TV production. SMPTE time code records hours, minutes, seconds and frames on audio or videotape for synchronization purposes.

SMR

(Specialized Mobile Radio) Communications services used by taxicabs, trucks and other mobile businesses. Throughout the U.S., approximately 3,000 independent operators are licensed by the FCC to provide this service.

SMRAM

See *SMM*.

SMS

(1) (Storage Management System) Software used to routinely back up and archive files. See *HSM*.

(2) (Storage Management Services) Software from Novell that allows data to be stored and retrieved on NetWare servers independent of the file system the data is maintained in (DOS, OS/2, Mac, etc.). It is used to back up data from heterogeneous clients on the network. Various third-party backup products are SMS compliant. See *SIDF*.

(3) (Systems Management Server) Systems management software from Microsoft that runs on Windows NT Server. It requires a Microsoft SQL Server database and is used to distribute software, monitor and analyze network usage and perform various network administration tasks.

(4) (System-Managed Storage) Enhanced data management software for MVS mainframes from IBM. Introduced in 1988, it provides functions such as automatically allocating data, which prevents most out-of-space errors when disk volumes become full. See *DFSMS*.

SMT

(1) (Surface Mount Technology) See *surface mount*.

(2) (Station ManagemenT) An FDDI network management protocol that provides direct management. Only one node requires the software.

SMTP

(Simple Mail Transfer Protocol) The standard e-mail protocol on the Internet. It is a TCP/IP protocol that defines the message format and the message transfer agent (MTA), which stores and forwards the mail. SMTP was originally designed for only ASCII text, but MIME and other encoding methods enable program and multimedia files to be attached to e-mail messages.

SMTP servers route SMTP messages throughout the Internet to a mail server, such as POP3 or IMAP4, which provides a message store for incoming mail. See *POP3, IMAP* and *messaging system*. See also *SNMP*.

smurf attack

An assault on a network that floods it with excessive messages in order to impede normal traffic. It is

SMP and MPP Processing
In SMP, CPUs are assigned to the next available task or thread that can run concurrently. In MPP operation, the problem is broken up into separate pieces, which are processed simultaneously.

accomplished by sending ping requests (ICMP echo requests) to a broadcast address on the target network or an intermediate network. The return address is spoofed to the victim's address. Since a broadcast address is picked up by all nodes on the subnet, it functions like an amplifier, generating hundreds of responses from one request and eventually causing a traffic overload. See *denial of service attack* and *ICMP*.

SNA

(**S**ystems **N**etwork **A**rchitecture) IBM's mainframe network standards introduced in 1974. Originally a centralized architecture with a host computer controlling many terminals, enhancements, such as APPN and APPC (LU 6.2), have adapted SNA to today's peer-to-peer communications and distributed computing environment. Following are some of SNA's basic concepts.

Nodes and Data Links

In SNA, nodes are end points or junctions, and data links are the pathways between them. Nodes are defined as Type 5 (hosts), Type 4 (communications controllers) and Type 2 (peripheral; terminals, PCs and midrange computers).

Type 2.0 nodes can communicate only with the host, and Type 2.1 nodes can communicate with other 2.1 nodes (peer-to-peer) without going to the host.

Data links include high-speed local channels, the SDLC data link protocol and Token Ring.

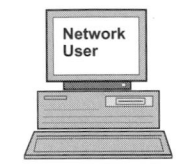

	OSI MODEL		SNA
7	**Application Layer** Type of communication: E-mail, file transfer, client/server.		Transaction Services
6	**Presentation Layer** Encryption, data conversion: ASCII to EBCDIC, BCD to binary, etc.		Presentation Services
5	**Session Layer** Starts, stops session. Maintains order.		Data Flow Control
4	**Transport Layer** Ensures delivery of entire file or message.		Transmission Control
3	**Network Layer** Routes data to different LANs and WANs based on network address.		Path Control
2	**Data Link (MAC) Layer** Transmits packets from node to node based on station address.		Data Link Control
1	**Physical Layer** Electrical signals and cabling.		Physical Control

SSCPs, PUs and LUs

The heart of a mainframe-based SNA network is the SSCP (System Services Control Point) software that resides in the host. It manages all resources in its domain.

Within all nodes of an SNA network, except for Type 2.1, there is PU (Physical Unit) software that manages node resources, such as data links, and controls the transmission of network management information. In Node Type 2.1, Control Point software performs these functions.

In order to communicate user data, a session path is created between two end points, or LUs (Logical Units). When a session takes place, an LU-LU session is established between an LU in the host (CICS, TSO, user appliction, etc.) and an LU in the terminal controller or PC.

An LU 6.2 session provides peer-to-peer communication and lets either side initiate the session.

VTAM and NCP

VTAM (Virtual Telecommunications Access Method) resides in the host and contains the SSCP, the PU for the host, and establishes the LU sessions within the host.

NCP (Network Control Program) resides in the communications controller (front end processor) and manages the routing and data link protocols, such as SDLC and Token Ring.

SNA Layers

SNA is implemented in functional layers starting with the application that triggers the communications down to the bottom layers which transmit packets from station to station. This layering is called a protocol stack. The SNA stack is compared with the OSI model below. Although SNA had major influence on the OSI model, there are differences in implementation.

Computer Desktop Encyclopedia

SNADS

(**SNA D**istribution Services) An IBM messaging protocol used by IBM office automation products such as DISOSS and AS/400 Office. Various messaging gateways and messaging switches support SNADS.

snail mail

Mail sent via the postal system.

snapshot

The saved current state of memory including the contents of all memory bytes, hardware registers and status indicators. It is periodically taken in order to restore the system in the event of failure.

snapshot dump

A memory dump of selected portions of memory.

snapshot printer

See *photo printer*.

snapshot program

A trace program that provides selected dumps of memory when specific instructions are executed or when certain conditions are met.

snap to

A feature in a drawing program that moves a text or graphic element to the closest grid line.

SND file

(**SouND** file) One of several digital audio file formats that were created by Apple, NeXT and others. It typically refers to an uncompressed sound file used on the Macintosh. SND files use the .SND extension. In the Mac, digitized sounds can be stored as SND and AIFF files, or as resources in the resource fork.

sneakernet

Carrying floppy disks from one machine to another to exchange information when you don't have a network.

SNI

(1) (**S**ubscriber **N**etwork **I**nterface) The point of interface between the customer's equipment (CPE) and a communications service from a common carrier.

(2) (**SNA N**etwork **I**nterconnection) Using a mainframe as a gateway between two independent SNA networks.

(3) See *Siemens Nixdorf*.

Sneakernet
The way to transfer data in a workgroup when the network is down. It's a very reliable method.

SNIA

(**S**torage **N**etworking **I**ndustry **A**ssociation, Santa Barbara, CA, www.snia.org) An organization devoted to the advancement of mission-critical storage systems. Founded in 1997, its goal is to determine the standards that must be developed to allow hosts and storage systems to interact via common protocols. SNIA was spearheaded by Strategic Research Corporation's Michael Peterson.

sniffer

Software and/or hardware that analyzes traffic and detects bottlenecks and problems in a network.

snippet

A small amount of something. In the computer field, it often refers to a small piece of program code.

SNMP

(**S**imple **N**etwork **M**anagement **P**rotocol) A widely-used network monitoring and control protocol. Data is passed from SNMP agents, which are hardware and/or software processes reporting activity in each network device (hub, router, bridge, etc.) to the workstation console used to oversee the network. The agents return information contained in a MIB (Management Information Base), which is a data structure that defines what is obtainable from the device and what can be controlled (turned off, on, etc.). Originating in the UNIX community, SNMP has become widely used on all major platforms.

SNMP 2 provides enhancements including security and an RMON (Remote Monitoring) MIB, which provides continuous feedback without having to be queried by the SNMP console. See *RMON*. See also *SMTP*.

SNOBOL

(StriNg Oriented symBOlic Language) One of the first list processing languages (Bell Labs; early 1960s). It was used for text processing and compiler development.

snow

The flickering snow-like spots on a video screen caused by display electronics that are too slow to respond to changing data.

snowflake structure

In a data warehouse, the structure that is created when highly repeated fields are placed into separate tables. The resulting diagram has short and long branches extending from the original dimension that resemble the irregularities of a snowflake. Snowflake structures are generally not recommended as they slow down browsing the data.

SNR

See *signal to noise ratio*.

SOAP

(Simple Object Access Protocol) A protocol from Microsoft for accessing objects on the Web. It employs XML syntax to send text commands across the Internet using HTTP. SOAP is supported in COM, DCOM, Internet Explorer and Microsoft's Java implementation.

socket

(1) A receptacle which receives a plug.

(2) See *UNIX socket*.

Socket 7

The receptacle on the motherboard that holds a Pentium CPU chip. It is also used to hold Pentium chip clones such as the 5x86, 6x86, K5 and K6. See *Slot 1*.

Socket 8

The receptacle on the motherboard that holds a Pentium Pro CPU chip. See *Slot 1*.

socketed

Temporarily attached. For example, a socketed chip plugs into a receptacle and can be pulled out and replaced with relative ease in contrast to a soldered chip.

socket flash

Flash memory that is housed in a standard chip package and plugs into a socket on the circuit board. A flash BIOS is an example. Contrast with *flash card*.

socket mount

A circuit board packaging technique in which a chip or component plugs into a socket. Socket mount devices can be removed and replaced by the user, although the flexible pins on some types of chips make them difficult to insert. Contrast with *surface mount* and *thru-hole*.

socket services

Low-level software that manages a PC Card controller. See *PC Card*.

SOCKS server

(SOCKetS server) A proxy server that functions as a general-purpose TCP/IP proxy and handles any kind of traffic (HTTP, SMTP, FTP, Telnet, etc.). Major Web browsers support SOCKS, and OS/2 4.0 builds it into its TCP/IP stack, enabling all applications to use it. See *proxy server* and *TCP/IP stack*.

Computer Desktop Encyclopedia

SODIMM

(Small Outline-DIMM) A DIMM module with a thinner profile due to the use of TSOP chip packages. SODIMMs are commonly used in laptop computers. See *DIMM* and *TSOP*.

soft

Flexible and changeable. Software can be reprogrammed for different results. The computer's soft nature is its greatest virtue; however, the reason it takes so long to get new systems developed has little to do with the concept. It is based on how systems are developed (file systems vs database management), the programming languages used (assembly vs high-level), combined with the skill level of the technical staff, compounded by the organization's bureaucracy.

soft boot

Same as *warm boot*.

soft copy

Refers to data displayed on a video screen. Contrast with *hard copy*.

soft error

A recoverable error, such as a garbled message that can be retransmitted. Contrast with *hard error*.

soft font

A set of characters for a particular typeface that is stored on the computer's hard disk, or in some cases the printer's hard disk, and downloaded to the printer before printing. Contrast with *internal font* and *font cartridge*.

soft hyphen

A hyphen that prints if it winds up at the end of the line, but does not print otherwise. Contrast with *hard hyphen*. See *discretionary hyphen*.

soft key

A keyboard key that is simulated by an icon on screen.

soft macro

The design of a logic function that specifies how the required logic elements are interconnected, but not the physical wiring pattern on the chip. Contrast with *hard macro*.

soft modem

Software that performs modem functions using the computer's main CPU rather than in modem hardware. Instead of using a dedicated data pump, programmable DSP chips are used. For example, the PowerPC and Intel's MMX Pentiums have instructions that allow it to perform modem functions.

Many modems themselves are already built as soft modems rather than using chips hardwired to a particular modulation technique. Such modems may be upgradable to new modulation methods with new software that can be downloaded or purchased from the vendor.

soft patch

A quick fix to machine language currently in memory that only lasts for the current session.

SoftPC

A family of PC emulation programs from Insignia Solutions, Inc., Santa Clara, CA, (www.insignia.com), that allow DOS and Windows programs to run on the Mac and UNIX workstations.

soft return

A code inserted by the software into a text document to mark the end of the line. When the document is printed, the soft return is converted into the end-of-line code required by the printer. Soft returns are determined by the right margin and change when the margins are changed.

In graphics-based environments, such as in the Macintosh, soft returns are not used as the text must be free to change within movable windows.

With PCs, soft return codes differ; for example, WordPerfect uses a return (ASCII 13) and WordStar uses a line feed (ASCII 10).

Contrast with *hard return*.

soft sectored

A common method of identifying sectors on a disk by initially recording sector information on every track with a format program. Contrast with *hard sectored*.

Soft-Switch

E-mail switching software from Soft-Switch, Wayne, PA, that provides an e-mail backbone for organizations with diverse e-mail systems. It switches between more than 50 messaging protocols using X.400 as the common denominator. Soft-Switch Central runs on IBM mainframes. Soft-Switch LMS runs on AIX computers. A complete system using a UNIX-based Data General computer is also available. Soft-Switch is a division of Lotus, which acquired it in 1995.

software

Instructions for the computer. A series of instructions that performs a particular task is called a *program*. The two major categories of software are *system software* and *application software*. System software is made up of control programs such as the operating system and database management system (DBMS). Application software is any program that processes data for the user (inventory, payroll, spreadsheet, word processor, etc.).

A common misconception is that software is data. It is not. Software tells the hardware how to process the data.

Software is "run."

Data is "processed."

software administration

The on-going management of software applications in an enterprise, which includes the distribution of new software and upgrading of existing software. Improving software administration is one of the main reasons for the creation of the network computer (NC) and NetPC.

software architecture

The design of application or system software that incorporates protocols and interfaces for interacting with other programs and for future flexibility and expandability. A self-contained, stand-alone program would have program logic, but not a software architecture.

software bug

A problem that causes a program to abend (crash) or produce invalid output. Problems that cause a program to abend are invalid data, such as trying to divide by zero, or invalid instructions, which are caused by bad logic that misdirects the computer to the wrong place in the program.

A program with erroneous logic may produce bad output without crashing, which is the reason extensive testing is required for new programs. For example, if the program is supposed to add an amount, but instead, it subtracts it, bad output results. As long as the program performs valid machine instructions on data it knows how to deal with, the computer will run.

software bus

A programming interface that allows software modules to transfer data to each other. Although "bus" is traditionally a hardware term for an interconneting pathway, it is occasionally used in this manner when the focus is on internally transferring large amounts of data from one process to another. See *bus*.

Software Carousel

An early DOS task switching program developed by SoftLogic Solutions, Inc., Manchester, NH. It was one of the first programs that allowed users to switch between several open DOS applications.

software codec

A compression/decompression routine that is implemented in software only without requiring specialized DSP hardware. See *codec*.

software engineer

A person that designs and programs system-level software, such as operating systems and database management systems (DBMSs). Software engineers and systems programmers are sometimes synonymous; however, systems programmers mostly perform administration functions, not traditional programming to create new software.

The title may also be used for programmers in the software industry that create commercial software packages, whether they be system level or application level.

software engineering

The design, development and documentation of software. See *CASE, systems analysis & design, programming, object-oriented programming, software metrics* and *Systemantics*.

Software Engineering Institute

See *SEI*.

software failure

The inability of a program to continue processing due to erroneous logic. Same as *crash, bomb* and *abend*.

software house

An organization that develops custom software for a customer. Contrast with *software publisher*, which develops and markets software packages.

software IC

An object-oriented programming class packaged for sale. The term was coined by The Stepstone Corporation.

software interface

Same as *API*.

software interrupt

An interrupt caused by an instruction in the program. See *interrupt*.

software metering

Limiting the number of users running an application from a centralized source (server) based on the current license agreement.

software metrics

Software measurements. Using numerical ratings to measure the complexity and reliability of source code, the length and quality of the development process and the performance of the application when completed.

software package

An application program developed for sale to the general public. Packaged software is generally designed to appeal to a large audience of users, and although the programs may be tailored to a user's taste by setting various preferences, it is not as individualized as custom-designed and custom-programmed software. Contrast with *custom software*.

software piracy

The illegal copying of software for distribution within the organization or to friends, clubs and other groups or for commercial duplication and resale.

software program

A computer program (computer application). All computer programs are software. Usage of the two words together is redundant, but common.

software programmer

Same as *systems programmer*.

software protection

See *copy protection*.

software publisher

An organization that develops and markets software. It does market research, production and distribution of software. It may develop its own software, contract for outside development or obtain software that has already been written.

software rankings

See *software vendors*.

software reuse

The ability to use software routines over again in new applications. This is the major purpose of object technology.

software RIP

See *RIP*.

software stack

A stack that is implemented in memory. See *stack*.

software tool

A program used to develop other software. Any program or utility that helps a programmer design, code, compile or debug sofware can be called a tool.

software vendors

Following are the top 50 software companies from "The Software 500" in the July 1998 issue of Software Magazine. Consulting, custom services and programming revenues are excluded. See also *hardware vendors*.

```
FROM SOFTWARE MAGAZINE'S "THE SOFTWARE 500"
Ranked by Software Package Revenues Worldwide

Reprinted with the permission of Software Magazine, July 1998,
Wiesner Publishing, LLC, One Research Drive, Westborough, MA 01581.

* = privately held
```

#	NAME, HQ city, (year founded), Web address	Revenues (000 US$)	Employees
1	IBM, Armonk, NY (1924, www.ibm.com	12844	269465
2	MICROSOFT CORP., Redmond, WA (1975), www.microsoft.com	12836	25000
3	COMPUTER ASSOCIATES, Islandia, NY (1976), www.cai.com	4457	11209
4	ORACLE CORP., Redwood Shores, CA (1977), www.oracle.com	4447	33775
5	HITACHI LTD., New York (1947), www.hitachi.com	4023	25000
6	SAP AG (SAP AMERICA), Wayne, PA (1972), www.sap.com	2290	13000
7	FUJITSU LTD., San Jose, CA (1991), www.fsc.fujitsu.com	2000	165000
8	DIGITAL EQUIPMENT, Maynard, MA (1957), www.dec.com	1174	54900
9	SUN MICROSYSTEMS, Mountain View, CA (1981), www.sun.com	1118	21500
10	SIEMENS NIXDORF, Burlington, MA (1990), www.sni-usa.com	1071	35900
11	PARAMETRIC TECHNOLOGY, Waltham, MA (1985), www.ptc.com	1014	4721
12	INTEL CORP., Santa Clara, CA (1968), www.intel.com	1003	63700
13	NOVELL, INC., Provo, UT (1983), www.novell.com	930	4700
14	ADOBE SYSTEMS INC., Mtn. View, CA (1982), www.adobe.com	912	2702
15	SYBASE, INC., Emeryville, CA (1984), www.sybase.com	904	5658
16	HEWLETT-PACKARD, Palo Alto, CA (1939), www.hp.com	886	121900
17	CADENCE DESIGN SYSTEMS, San Jose, CA, www.cadence.com	755	3750
18	SAS INSTITUTE, INC.*, Cary, NC (1976), www.sas.com	727	5208
19	PEOPLESOFT, INC., Pleasanton, CA (1987), www.peoplesoft.com	706	4452
20	BMC SOFTWARE, INC., Houston, TX (1980), www.bmc.com	678	2300
21	UNISYS, Blue Bell, PA (1986), www.unisys.com	664	32600
22	INFORMIX SOFTWARE INC., Menlo Pk, CA ('80), www.informix.com	662	3489
23	ANDERSEN CONSULTING*, Chicago, IL, www.ac.com	660	53426
24	SYNOPSYS INC., Mountain View, CA (1986), www.synopsys.com	651	2812
25	COMPUWARE CORP., Farmingtn Hills, MI ('73), www.compuware.com	647	8078
26	SUNGUARD DATA SYSTEMS INC., Wayne, PA, www.sungard.com	566	4500
27	SYMANTEC CORP., Cupertino, CA (1982), www.symantec.com	552	2205
28	ICL INT'L. COMPUTERS, LTD.*, Reston, VA (1968), www.icl.com	514	2110

29	**THE BAAN CO.N.V.,** Menlo Park, MI (1978), www.baan.com	513	3000
30	**NETWORK ASSOCIATES, INC.,** Santa Clara, CA (1989), www.nai.com	511	1600
31	**AUTODESK INC.,** San Rafael, CA (1982), www.autodesk.com	497	2470
32	**PLATINUM TCHNLGY, INC.,** Okbrk Ter, IL ('87), www.platinum.com	482	4244
33	**BULL INFO. SYSTEMS INC.,** Billerica, MA ('87), www.us.bull.com	443	775
34	**NCR CORP.,** Dayton, OH (1885), www.ncr.com	428	138300
35	**THE LEARNING CO. INC.,** Cmbrdge, MA ('93), www.learningco.com	392	1525
36	**INTERGRAPH CORP.,** Huntsville, AL (1969), www.intergraph.com	391	3800
37	**NETSCAPE COMM. CORP.,** Mtn View, CA ('94), www.netscape.com	384	2310
38	**J.D. EDWARDS & CO.*,** Denver, CO (1977), www.jdedwards.com	377	3577
39	**STERLING SOFTWARE, INC.,** Dallas, TX (1981), www.sterling.com	368	3100
40	**GEAC COMPUTER CORP. LTD,** Markham, Ontario, www.geac.com	335	3000
41	**RATIONAL SOFTWARE CORP.,** SntaClra, CA ('82), www.rational.com	311	1700
42	**SYSTEM SOFTWARE ASSOC. INC.,** Chicago, IL (1981), www.ssax.com	299	2400
43	**CANDLE CORP.*,** Santa Monica, CA (1977), www.candle.com	297	1542
44	**FILEMAKER INC.*,** Santa Clara, CA (1987), www.filemaker.com	275	700
45	**COREL CORPORATION,** Ottawa, Ontario (1985), www.corel.com	261	1456
46	**IDX SYSTEMS CORP.,** Burlington, VT (1969), www.idx.com	251	1900
47	**SEAGATE SFTWRE,** Sctts Vly, CA ('79), www.seagatesoftware.com	246	1534
48	**ENVIRONMENTAL SYSTEMS RSRCH*,** Rdlnds, CA ('69), www.esri.com	241	1300
49	**INFORMATION BUILDERS INC.*,** New York, NY (1975), www.ibi.com	239	1750
50	**STERLING COMRCE INC,** Dbln, OH ('75), www.sterlingcommerce.com	228	1700

SoftWindows

Windows emulation software for the PowerPC and various UNIX platforms from Insignia Solutions, Santa Clara, CA, (www.insignia.com). It allows Windows applications to run on non-Windows platforms. Early versions of SoftWindows provided support for only Standard Mode applications. SoftWindows 2.0 added support for 386 Enhanced Mode. See *PowerMac*.

SOG

(Small Outline Gullwing) Same as *SOIC*.

SOHO

(Small Office/Home Office) Refers to the small business or business-at-home user. This market segment demands as much or more than the large corporation. The small business entrepreneur generally wants the latest, greatest and fastest equipment, and this market has always benefited from high technology, allowing it to compete on a level playing ground with the bigger companies.

SOIC

(Small Outline IC) A small-dimension, plastic, rectangular, surface mount chip package that uses gull-wing pins extending outward. See *gull-wing lead, SOJ* and *chip package*.

SOJ

(Small Outline package J-lead) A small-dimension, plastic, rectangular surface mount chip package with j-shaped pins on its two long sides. See *J-lead, SOP* and *chip package*.

Solaris

A multitasking, multiprocessing operating system and distributed computing environment for Sun's SPARC computers from SunSoft. It provides an enterprise-wide UNIX environment that can manage up to 40,000 nodes from one central station. Solaris is known for its robustness and scalability, which is expected in UNIX-based SMP systems. An x86 version of Solaris is available that can also run applications written for Sun's Interactive UNIX. Solaris was available for the PowerPC, but support was dropped as of Version 2.6.

Solaris includes the SunOS UNIX SVR4-based operating system, ONC networking products (NFS, NIS, etc.) and OpenWindows (Sun's version of X Windows). Also provided are Motif and OPEN LOOK graphical interfaces.

solder

A metal alloy used to bond other metals together. Tin and lead are used in "soft" solders, which melt rather easily. The more tin, the harder the solder, and the higher the temperature required. Copper and zinc are used in "hard" soldering, or brazing, which requires considerably more heat to melt. See *braze*.

solder mask

An insulating pattern applied to a printed circuit board that exposes only the areas to be soldered.

solenoid

A magnetic switch that closes a circuit, often used as a relay.

solid ink printer

A laser-class printer that uses solid wax inks that are melted into a liquid before being used. Instead of jetting the ink onto the paper directly as ink jet printers do, solid ink printers jet the ink onto a drum. A better registration of color is obtained by transferring the ink to the drum first and then to the printer, because the drum can be more tightly controlled than moving paper.

solid logic

Same as *solid state*.

solid modeling

A mathematical technique for representing solid objects. Unlike wireframe and surface modeling, solid modeling systems ensure that all surfaces meet properly and that the object is geometrically correct. Solid models allow for interference checking, which tests to see if two or more objects occupy the same space.

Solid modeling is the most complicated of the CAD technologies, because it simulates an object internally and externally. Solid models can be sectioned (cut open) to reveal their internal features, and they can be stress tested as if they were physical entities in the real world. See *tessellation*.

solid state

An electronic component or circuit made of solid materials, such as transistors, chips and bubble memory. There is no mechanical action in a solid state device, although an unbelievable amount of electromagnetic action takes place within.

For data storage, solid state devices are much faster and more reliable than mechanical disks and tapes, but are more expensive. Although solid state costs continually drop, disks, tapes and optical disks also continue to improve their cost/performance ratio.

The first solid state device was the "cat's whisker" of the 1930s. A whisker-like wire was moved around on a solid crystal in order to detect a radio signal. For a summary of all storage technologies, see *storage*.

solid state disk

A disk drive made of memory chips used for high-speed data access or in hostile environments. Solid state disks are used in battery-powered, hand-held devices as well as in desktop units with hundreds of megabytes of storage that contain their own UPS systems.

Different types of storage chips are used for solid state disks, both volatile and non-volatile. However a solid state disk looks

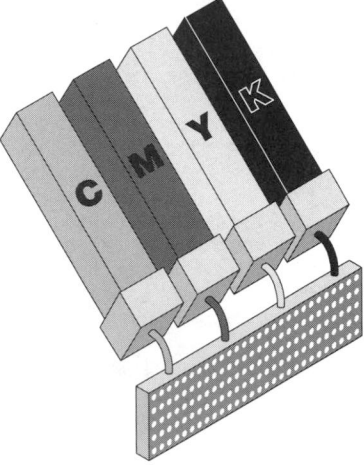

Solid Ink Printhead
Solid wax ink is melted into a liquid before it enters the printhead plumbing. The inks are typically jetted from the nozzles using the piezoelectric drop on demand method. The printhead in this

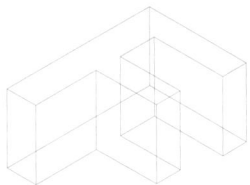

Wireframe

Phantom lines

Shaded (solid) view

Wireframe and Solid Views
The shaded view could be either a solid model or a surface model. You can't tell until you try to slice it in two. *(Redrawn from illustration courtesy of Robo Systems Corporation.)*

Computer Desktop Encyclopedia

like a standard disk drive to the operating system, not a proprietary one that requires additional drivers. See *flash disk*.

solid state memory

Any transistorized, semiconductor or thin film memory that contains no mechanical parts. See *solid state disk*.

solid state relay

A relay that contains no mechanical parts. All switching mechanisms are semiconductor or thin film components.

solver

Mathematical mechanisms that allow spreadsheets to perform goal seeking.

SOM

(1) (System Object Model) An object architecture from IBM that provides a full implementation of the CORBA standard. SOM is language independent and is supported by a variety of large compiler and application development vendors.

It is expected that IBM will promote SOM heavily because its future operating systems are built around objects. DSOM, for distributed SOM, allows objects to be used across the network.

(2) (Self Organizing Map) A two-dimensional map that shows relationships in a neural network.

SONET

(Synchronous Optical NETwork) A fiber optic transmission system for high-speed digital traffic. Employed by telephone companies and common carriers, SONET speeds range from 51 megabits to multiple gigabits per second. SONET is an intelligent system that provides advanced network management and a standard optical interface. It uses a self-healing ring architecture that is able to reroute traffic if a line goes down. SONET backbones are widely used to aggregate lower-speed T1 and T3 lines.

SONET is specified in the Broadband ISDN (BISDN) standard. The European counterpart is SDH. Following are the levels of service. OC (Optical Carrier) refers to the optical signal, and STS (Synchronous Transport Signal) refers to the electrical signal, which is the same speed.

LAN	WAN	WAN
Data, voice, video	Data, voice, video	Data, voice, video
IP (layer 3)	IP (layer 3)	IP (layer 3)
Ethernet (layer 2)	ATM (layer 2)	SONET (layer 1)
Copper	SONET (layer 1)	Fiber
	Fiber	

Transporting IP

In a WAN or over the Internet, IP traffic is widely carried over SONET lines, either using ATM as a management layer or over SONET directly.

```
SONET CIRCUITS

Service            Speed (Mbps)
OC-1     STS-1         51.84  (28 DS1s or 1 DS3)
OC-3     STS-3        155.52  (3 STS-1s)
OC-3c    STS-3c       155.52  (concatenated)
OC-12    STS-12       622.08  (12 STS-1, 4 STS-3)
OC-12c   STS-12c      622.08  (12 STS-1, 4 STS-3c)
OC-48    STS-48      2488.32  (48 STS-1, 16 STS-3)
OC-192   STS-192     9953.28  (192 STS-1, 64 STS-3)
OC-768   STS-768    38813,12  (768 STS-1, 256 STS-3)
```

SOP

(Small Outline Package) A small-dimension, plastic, rectangular surface mount chip with gull-wing pins on its two long sides. See *gull-wing lead, TSOP, SOJ* and *chip package*.

sort

To reorder data into a new sequence. The operating system can typically sort file names and text lists.

Word processors typically allow lines of text to be reordered, and database programs sort records by one or more fields, often generating a new file.

sort algorithm

A formula used to reorder data into a new sequence. Like all complicated problems, there are many solutions that can achieve the same results. One sort algorithm can resequence data faster than another. In the early 1960s, when tape was "the" storage medium, the sale of a computer system may have hinged on the sort algorithm, since without direct access capability, every transaction had to be sorted into the sequence of the master file.

sorter

(1) A sort program.

(2) A person who manually puts data into a specific sequence.

(3) An early tabulating machine that routed punched cards into separate stackers based on the content of a card column. The complete operation required passing the cards through the machine once for each column sorted.

sort field, sort key

A field or fields in a record that dictate the sequence of the file. For example, the sort keys STATE and NAME arrange the file alphabetically by name within state. STATE is the major sort key, and NAME is the minor key.

SOS

(1) (Systems On Silicon) A complete system on a single chip. Increasingly, memory, logic and signal processing components are being combined in one integrated circuit.

(2) (Server Operating System) An operating system that resides on the server.

An Early Sorting Machine
This is a sorter from the Computing-Tabulating-Recording Company in 1917. Punched cards were placed into the hopper and sorted into the respective stackers based on the content of one card column. A 10-digit account number required sorting the cards 10 times. This would have been a great year to buy stock in the company. In 1924, it became IBM. *(Photo courtesy of IBM Corporation.)*

(3) (Silicon On Sapphire) An MOS chip-fabrication method that places a thin layer of silicon over a sapphire substrate (base).

(4) (Sophisticated Operating System) The operating system used on the Apple III.

SOT-23

(Small Outline Transistor) A surface mount package for electronic components (transistor, resistor, etc.). It was the first type of surface mount packaging.

sound bandwidth

A range of sound frequencies. The human ear can perceive approximately from 20 to 20,000Hz, but human voice is confined to within 3,000Hz.

Sound Blaster

A family of sound cards from Creative Labs. The Sound Blaster protocol has become the de facto audio standard for PCs. Monaural versions of Sound Blaster cards were introduced in 1989, and the stereo version, Sound Blaster Pro, in 1992. The Sound Blaster AWE32 and AWE64 are 16-bit sound cards that provide wave table MIDI with 32 and 64 voices respectively.

sound board, sound card

Also called an *audio adapter*, it is a personal computer expansion board that records and plays back sound, providing outputs directly to speakers or an external amplifier. The de facto standard for sound card compatibility in PCs is Creative Labs' Sound Blaster. The Multimedia PC Marketing Council (MPC) sets guidelines for the minimum requirements for sound cards. See *MPC*.

Digital Audio and MIDI

Sound cards play digital audio files and usually support MIDI. Digital audio files contain the actual soundwaves that have been converted into digital form. Without compression, they take up considerable storage space. The native digital audio format for Windows is the wave file (.WAV extension). The Mac uses AIFF, and Sun's AU format is used on the Internet. See *WAV file, AIFF file, AU file* and *sampling rate*.

MIDI files (.MID extension) differ from digital audio, because they contain a coded representation of the musical notes of the instrument; for example, middle C on the piano. MIDI files take up considerably less space than digital audio files, but require a MIDI synthesizer on the sound card. MPC requires MIDI on the board.

There are two kinds of MIDI sound reproduction methods used in sound cards. FM synthesis simulates musical notes. Wave table synthesis (or waveform synthesis) actually holds digitized samples of the notes and produces richer sound.

Another MIDI feature is the number of voices, or notes, that can be played back simultaneously. MPC requires an 8-voice synthesizer, but high-quality sound cards can have up to 64 MIDI voices. See *MIDI* for illustration.

source

(1) One side of a field effect transistor. See *drain*.

(2) (The Source) An online information service in McLean, VA, launched in 1979 and purchased by CompuServe in 1989.

source code

Programming statements and instructions that are written by a programmer. Source code is what a programmer writes, but it is not directly executable by the computer. It must be converted into machine language by compilers, assemblers or interpreters.

In some cases, source code can be machine generated by conversion programs that convert the source code of one programming language or dialect into the source code of another language or dialect. See *lines of code*.

source code compatible

Able to run a program on a different platform by recompiling its source code into that machine code.

source code management

See *configuration management*.

source computer

The computer in which a program is being assembled or compiled. Contrast with *object computer*.

Source Consulting

One of the country's leading full-service consulting firms, specializing in the placement of information technology professionals in short-and long-term assignments. It is a division of Source Services Corporation, Dallas, TX, and has more than 50 offices in the U.S. and one in Canada. See *Source Edp*.

source data

The original data that is handwritten or printed on a source document or typed into the computer system from a keyboard or terminal.

source data acquisition

Same as *source data capture*.

source data capture

Capturing data electronically when a transaction occurs; for example, at the time of sale.

source directory

The directory from which data is obtained.

source disk
The disk from which data is obtained. Contrast with *target disk*.

source document
The paper form onto which data is written. Order forms and employment applications are examples.

source drive
The disk or tape drive from which data is obtained. Contrast with *target drive*.

Source Edp
(Division of Source Services Corporation, Dallas, TX, www.sourceservices.com) A leading full-service staffing firm specializing in the permanent placement of individuals at all levels of information technology. Founded in 1962 by two computer professionals during the industry's first explosive period, Source Edp today has more than 50 offices in the U.S. and one in Canada. See *salary survey*.

source language
The language used in a source program. Contrast with *target language* and *machine language*. See *source code*.

source program
A program in its original form, as written by the programmer. See *source code*.

source route bridging
A communications protocol in which the sending station is aware of all the bridges in the network and predetermines the complete route to the destination station before transmitting. Token Ring uses this method. Contrast with *transparent bridge*. See *SRT*.

source statement
An instructional phrase in a programming language (source language).

SP2
A massively parallel computer system from IBM that supports from two to 512 RS/6000 processors. It runs AIX and uses IBM's POWERparallel architecture, which includes a communications system between processors called the High-Performance Switch. In 1994, the University of New Mexico's Maui High Performance Computing Center installed an SP2 with 400 CPUs, which provides 100 gigaflops of computational power.

SPA
(Software Publishers Association, Washington, DC, www.spa.org) A trade organization of the personal computer software industry that supports legislation for copyright enforcement. It conducts raids on organizations suspected of illegal copying and files lawsuits against violators.

To blow the whistle on a company that has a policy of making illegal copies, call 800/388-PIR8.

space
In digital electronics, a 0 bit. Contrast with *mark*.

space/time
Storage and transmission are measured in the following units. See *binary values*.

SPACE - Bits/bytes			Power of 10	TIME - Fraction of second			Power of 10
Kilo	(K)	Thousand	3	Millisecond	(ms)	Thousandth	-3
Mega	(M)	Million	6	Microsecond	(µs)	Millionth	-6
Giga	(G)	Billion	9	Nanosecond	(ns)	Billionth	-9
Tera	(T)	Trillion	12	Picosecond	(ps)	Trillionth	-12
Peta	(P)	Quadrillion	15	Femtosecond	(fs)	Quadrillionth	-15
Exa	(E)	Quintillion	18	Attosecond	(as)	Quintillionth	-18
Zetta	(Z)	Sextillion	21	Zeposecond	(zs)	Sextillionth	-21
Yotta	(Y)	Septillion	24	Yoctosecond	(ys)	Septillionth	-24

Storage/channel capacity measured in:		Transmission speed measured in:	
CPU word size	bits	Network line/channel	bits/sec
Bus size	bits	Disk transfer rate	bytes/sec
Disk, tape	bytes	Disk access time	ms
Overall memory capacity	bytes	Memory access time	ns
SIMM and DIMM modules	bytes	Machine cycle	μs, ns
Individual memory chip	bits	Instruction execution	μs, ns
		Transistor switching	ns, ps, fs

spaghetti code

Program code written without a coherent structure. The logic moves from routine to routine without returning to a base point, making it hard to follow. It implies excessive use of the GOTO instruction, which directs the computer to branch to another part of the program without a guarantee of returning.

In structured programming, functions are used, which are subroutines that guarantee a return to the instruction following the one that called it.

spam

To send copies of the same message to large numbers of newsgroups or users on the Internet. People spam the Internet to advertise products as well as to broadcast some political or social commentary. See *mail bomb, letter bomb* and *spamdexing*.

spamdexing

Techniques employed by some Web marketers and site designers in order to fool a search engine's spider and indexing programs. The objective is to ensure that their Web sites always appear at or near the top of the list of search engine results.

There are a variety of methods, but one of the most common is "word stuffing," which embeds a particular word in the site dozens or even hundreds of times. The words may be presented in such a way that people who visit the site cannot see them (as white text on a white background, for example), but search engines can. Or they may be quite obvious: line after line of "make money fast" on a page promoting a marketing opportunity.

Another technique is to combine word stuffing with "bait-and-switch," which loads the page with a popular search word such as sex, free, shareware or Windows, even though the word has nothing to do with the site content.

Major search engines such as AltaVista, Excite, and Lycos use special software to try to outsmart the spamdexers. Lycos, for example, automatically gives a lower ranking in its search results to any page that contains a lot of repeated words. But as soon as one method is successfully dealt with, others emerge that call for new and different approaches by the major engines.

Legitimate techniques that site designers can use to make their site more visible to search engines, such as inserting appropriate keywords in the site's ERROR[Basic syntax error] in:<MEERROR[Basic syntax error] in: TA> tags, are often provided along with the search engine's "Search Tips" or "Help" information. Another good source is Search Engine Watch (www.searchenginewatch.com), which covers the major search engines. See *spam*.

Spaghetti Code

There are tons of spaghetti code lurking in the millions of applications that have been written over the years. Spaghetti code is often the result of being in a rush to fix something or change something.

spanning tree algorithm

An algorithm used in transparent bridges that dynamically determines the best path from source to destination. It avoids bridge loops (two or more paths linking one segment to another), which can cause the bridges to misinterpret results.

SPARC

(**S**calable **P**erformance **AR**Chitecture) A family of 32-bit RISC CPUs developed by Sun. The first chip was introduced in 1989 in Sun's SPARCstation 1. Prior to that, Sun used Motorola 680x0 CPUs in its products. The 64-bit UltraSPARC line was introduced in 1995.

SparQ disk

A 1GB removable hard drive from SyQuest. Introduced in 1997, these 3.5" disks are geared to the home market with cartridges in the $30 range when purchased in 3-packs. Parallel port and EIDE versions are available. SparQ cartridges are not compatible with SyQuest's SyJet drives, although the cartridges use a similar case. See *EZFlyer disk, SyJet disk, Quest disk, SyQuest disk* and *latest disk drives*. For a summary of all storage technologies, see *storage*.

SparQ Cartridge
The SparQ is an affordable, removable 1GB disk that is aimed at the consumer market.

spatial data

Data that is represented as 2-D or 3-D images. A geographic information system (GIS) is one of the primary applications of spatial data (land maps).

spatial light modulator

A matrix of shutters that represents a page of binary data. It is used modulate a laser beam for holographic storage. See *holographic storage*.

spawn

To launch another program from the current program. The child program is spawned from the parent program.

SPD

(**S**erial **P**resence **D**etect) An EEPROM chip on a DIMM module that stores information about the memory chips it contains, including size, speed, voltage, row and column addresses and manufacturer.

spec

(1) See *specs* and *specification*.

(2) (SPEC) (Standard Performance Evaluation Corporation, Manassas, VA, www.specbench.org) An organization founded in 1988 to establish standard benchmarks for computers. Its first benchmark was the SPECmark, in which one SPECmark was equivalent in performance to a VAX 11/780. Subsequent SPECint and SPECfp benchmarks measured integer and floating point performance respectively. In 1996, SPEC introduced SPEC CPU95 which includes SPECint95 and SPECfp95, replacing SPECint92 and SPECfp92. A few comparisons of CPU SPEC ratings follow.

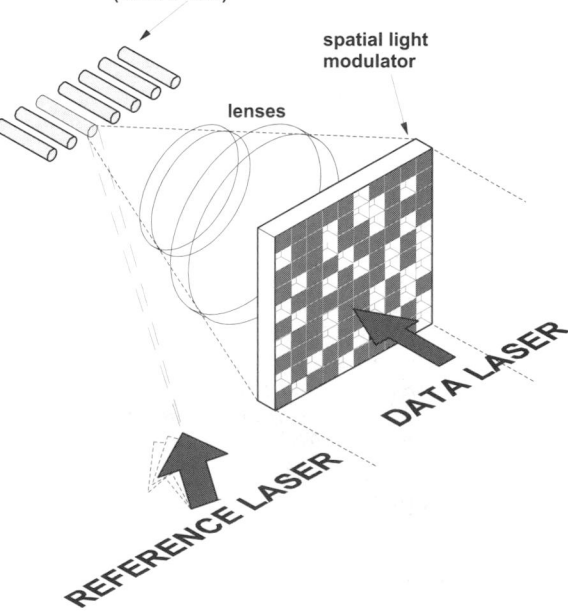

optical cylinders
(1mm x 1cm)

spatial light
modulator

lenses

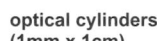

DATA LASER

REFERENCE LASER

The Spatial Light Modulator
The checkerboard-like device modulates the laser beam to create the holographic page when combined with the reference laser.

CPU Chip	SPECint95	SPECfp95
266MHz Pentium II	10.8	6.8
250MHz PPC 604e	11.1	7.8
300MHz UltraSPARC-2	10.4	14.5

SPEC SFS 1 (System File Server) tests NFS server performance. It is also known as the LADDIS test, which was developed by a team of NFS developers. SPECweb96 is a benchmark for Web servers, which is expected to be quickly replaced by SPECweb97. See *benchmark*.

Spec 1170
See *Single UNIX Specification*.

special character
Non-alphabetic or non-numeric character, such as @, #, $, %, &, * and +.

special-purpose computer
A computer designed from scratch for a specific function. Contrast with *general-purpose computer*.

special-purpose language
A programming language designed to solve a specific problem or class of problems. For example, LISP and Prolog are designed for and used extensively in AI applications. Even more specific are languages such as COGO, for civil engineering problems, and APT for directing machine tools. Contrast with *general-purpose language*.

specification
A definition (layout, blueprint, design) of hardware or software. See *specs* and *functional specification*.

specs
(SPECificationS) The details of the components built into a device. See *specification*.

spec sheet
A detail listing of the components of a system.

spectral color
In computer graphics, the color of a single wavelength of light, starting with violet at the low end and proceeding through indigo, blue, green, yellow and orange and ending with red.

spectral response
The variable output of a light-sensitive device that is based on the color of the light it perceives.

spectrum
A range of electromagnetic frequencies. See *electromagnetic spectrum* and *radio*.

speech codec
Also called a *voice codec* or *vocoder*, it is a hardware circuit that converts the spoken word into digital code and vice versa. A speech codec is an audio codec specialized for human voice. By analyzing common vocal tract sounds rather than soundwaves alone, the codec is able to achieve a higher compression ratio, yielding a smaller amount of digital data for transmission. However, if music is encoded with a speech codec, it will not sound good when decoded at the other end.

Although the term generally refers to a chip, it may also refer to just the speech compression method, which can be performed in software. See *audio codec*.

speech compression
Encoding digital speech to take up less storage space and transmission bandwidth. The PCM, ADPCM, CELP and LD-CELP methods are commonly used for speech compression. See *speech codec* and *data compression*.

speech recognition
Same as *voice recognition*.

speech synthesis
Generating machine voice by arranging phonemes (k, ch, sh, etc.) into words. It is used to turn text

input into spoken words for the blind. Speech synthesis performs realtime conversion without a pre-defined vocabulary, but does not create human-sounding speech. Although individual spoken words can be digitized into the computer, digitized voice takes a lot of storage, and resulting phrases still lack inflection.

speed buffering

A technique that compensates for speed differences between input and output. Data is accepted into the buffer at high speed and transferred out at low speed, or vice versa.

Speed Doubler

(1) Software that speeds up the performance of the Mac from Connectix Corporation, San Mateo, CA, (www.connectix.com).

(2) The name given to the technology that doubled the clock speed on Intel's 486 DX2 chips.

Speedo

A scalable font technology from Bitstream Inc., Cambridge, MA, (www.bitstream.com). Speedo fonts use the .SPD extension. See *FaceLift*.

speed of electricity/light

Electricity and light travel at approximately 186,000 miles per second, which is seven times around the equator per second. This inherent speed of Mother Nature is why computers are so fast. Within the tiny chip, electricity has to flow only a couple of millimeters, and, within an entire computer, only a few feet.

As fast as that is, it's never fast enough. There is resistance in the lines, and even though transistors switch in billionths of a second, CAD, image processing and scientific applications are always exhausting the fastest computers.

Speedware

A development system from Speedware Corporation, Toronto, Ontario, (www.speedware.com), that creates programs for the HP 3000, RS/6000 and AS/400. Applications can also be ported to run on DOS and Windows machines with runtime versions of Speedware for those platforms.

spell checker

A separate program or word processing function that tests for correctly-spelled words. It can test the spelling of a marked block, an entire document or group of documents. Advanced systems check for spelling as the user types and can correct common typos and misspellings on the fly.

Spell checkers simply compare words to a dictionary of words, and the wrong use of a correctly-spelled word cannot be detected. See *grammar checker*.

Sperry

See *Unisys*.

SPGA

See *PGA*.

spherization

In computer graphics, turning an image into a sphere.

SPI

(Service Provider Interface) The programming interface for developing Windows drivers under WOSA. In order to provide common access to services, the application (query, word processor, e-mail program, etc.) is written to a particular WOSA-supported interface, such as ODBC or MAPI, and the developer of the service software (database manager, document manager, print spooler, etc.) writes to the SPI for that class of service.

MY SPELL CHECKER

I have a spelling checker,
It came with my PC,
It plainly marks
four my revue
Mistakes I cannot sea.

I've run this poem,
threw it,
I'm sure your
please too no.
It's letter perfect
in its weigh;
My checker
tolled me sew.

SPICE

(Simulation Program with Integrated Circuit Emphasis) A program widely used to simulate the performance of analog electronic systems and mixed mode analog and digital systems. SPICE solves sets of non-linear differential equations in the frequency domain, steady state and time domain and can simulate the behavior of transistor and gate designs. Developed at the University of California at Berkeley, there are enhanced versions of SPICE provided by several software companies.

SPID

(Service Profile IDentifier) A number assigned to an ISDN line by the telephone company that indicates which services the ISDN device can access. The SPID is used by the central office switch, and depending on the type of switch, either one or two SPIDs or none at all are required per line. The SPID is usually the 10-digit ISDN telephone number with a couple of extra digits tacked on. For example, the SPID for the ISDN number (215) 489-2077 might become 21548920770101.

spider

See *crawler*.

spike

Also called a *transient*, it is a burst of extra voltage in a power line that lasts only a fraction of a second. Contrast with *sag*. See *power surge*.

spindle

A rotating shaft in a disk drive. In a fixed disk, the platters are attached to the spindle. In a removable disk, the spindle remains in the drive. Laptops use spindle designations to indicate the number of built-in drives. For example, a two-spindle machine contains a hard drive and a second bay for a floppy or CD-ROM drive. A three-spindle machine means that all three drives (hard disk, floppy and CD-ROM) are built in.

SPL

(1) (Systems Programming Language) The assembly language for the HP 3000 series. See *assembly language* for an SPL program example.

(2) (Structured Programming Language) See *structured programming*.

splash screen

An introductory screen displayed by an application after it is loaded and just before it starts. It generally shows the software company's name and logo. Fancy splash screens may provide some kind of animated graphic to entertain you for a few seconds.

SPLD

(Simple PLD) A programmable logic device that provides an array of logic blocks that can be programmed. See *CPLD, PLD* and *ASIC*.

spline

In computer graphics, a smooth curve that runs through a series of given points. The term is often used to refer to any curve, because long before computers, a spline was a flat, pliable strip of wood or metal that was bent into a desired shape for drawing curves on paper. See *Bezier* and *B-spline*.

split screen

The display of two or more sets of data on screen at the same time. It implies that one set of data can be manipulated independently of the other. This was a popular term with DOS applications and other character-based text screens. Today, a window implies the same thing.

Splitterless ADSL

See *DSL*.

spoofing

(1) In communications, creating fake responses or signals in order to keep a session active and prevent timeouts. For example, a mainframe or mini continuously polls its terminals. If the lines to remote terminals are temporarily suspended because there is no traffic, a local device spoofs the host with "I'm still here" reponses.

(2) Faking the sending address of a transmission in order to gain illegal entry into a secure system.

spooler

See *print spooler* and *spooling*.

spooling

(Simultaneous Peripheral Operations OnLine) The overlapping of low-speed operations with normal processing. It originated with mainframes in order to optimize slow operations such as reading cards and printing. Card input was read onto disk and printer output was stored on disk. In that way, the actual business data processing was done at high speed, since all I/O was on disk.

Today, spooling is used to buffer data for the printer as well as remote batch terminals. See *print spooler*.

spot color

A color that is printed from one printing plate which contains one matched color of ink. Spot colors are used when only one or two solid colors are needed on a page or when a color has to match perfectly and be consistent such as with a company logo or when colors are the trademark of the organization or message. If spot color is used along with process color, then a four-color print job becomes a five or six-color job. Contrast with *process color*.

SPP

(1) (Scalable Parallel Processor) A multiprocessing computer that can be upgraded by adding more CPUs.

(2) (Standard Parallel Port) The parallel port that has been used on PCs since their inception. Contrast with the higher-speed EPP and ECP ports. See *IEEE 1284*.

spreadsheet

Software that simulates a paper spreadsheet, or worksheet, in which columns of numbers are summed for budgets and plans. It appears on screen as a matrix of rows and columns, the intersections of which are identified as cells. Spreadsheets can have thousands of cells and can be scrolled horizontally and vertically in order to view them.

The cells are filled with:

1. labels
2. numeric values
3. formulas

The labels, can be any descriptive text, for example, RENT, PHONE or GROSS SALES.

The values are the actual numeric data used in the budget or plan, and the formulas command the spreadsheet to do the calculations; for example, SUM CELLS A5 TO A10.

Formulas are easy to create, since spreadsheets allow the user to point to each cell and type in the arithmetic operation that affects it. Roughly speaking, a formula is created by saying "this cell PLUS that cell TIMES that cell."

The formulas are the spreadsheet's magic. After numbers are added or changed, the formulas will recalculate the data either automatically or with the press of a key. Since the contents of any cell can be calculated with or copied to any other cell, a total of one column can be used as a detail item in another column. For example, the total from a column of expense items can be carried over to a summary column showing all expenses. If data in the detail column changes, its column total changes, which is then copied to the summary column, and the summary total changes.

Done manually, each change would require recalculating, erasing and changing the totals of each column. The automatic ripple effect allows users to create a plan, plug in different assumptions and immediately see the impact on the bottom line. This "what if?" capability makes the spreadsheet indispensable for budgets, plans and other equation-based tasks.

The spreadsheet originated with VisiCalc in 1978 for the Apple II, and was followed by SuperCalc, Multiplan, Lotus 1-2-3 and a host of others.

CLASSES OF SPREADSHEETS

2-D

Every spreadsheet can create a two-dimensional matrix of rows and columns. In order to summarize data, totals from various parts of the spreadsheet can be summed to another part of the spreadsheet.

3-D

Each cell in the spreadsheet has an X, Y and Z reference. For example, a spreadsheet of expense items by month uses two dimensions, but expense items by month by department requires three.

While this method is superior for consolidating and summarizing data, it lacks some of the flexibility required by sophisticated applications. In addition, all data typically resides in one file as with a standard 2-D spreadsheet.

Multidimensional

Multidimensional spreadsheets support more than three axes and allow the data and the relationships to be viewed from different perspectives. Data is not stored by cell references (A1, B2, etc.), but by name. Formulas are not placed into cells as in a traditional spreadsheet, but are defined separately as in a modeling language; for example, "gross profit=gross sales-cost of goods."

With name references, data can be used in multiple spreadsheets with greater accuracy, and new spreadsheets can be created more easily. However, since data isn't tied to cell references, this method lacks the flexibility and ease of use that caused the traditional 2-D spreadsheet to revolutionize the computer industry.

Analytical Databases

The need for multidimensional views of large amounts of data has given rise to a variety of methods over the years. All sorts of modeling programs have been created, but none have been as easy to use as the spreadsheet. Some combine spreadsheets with traditional database management. For example, TM1 was one of the first programs to provide multiple dimensions and isolate the data from the spreadsheet. This method provides database consistency (the data is not replicated in every spreadsheet) with the ease of use of the spreadsheet for creating the viewing models.

Organizations that analyze large amounts of sales history and other data are increasingly using OLAP (OnLine Analytical Processing) databases. OLAP databases use proprietary algorithms for summarizing data so that multidimensional views can be quickly queried. See *OLAP*.

spreadsheet compiler

Software that translates spreadsheets into stand-alone programs that can be run without the spreadsheet package that created them.

spread spectrum

A radio transmission that continuously changes carrier frequency according to a unique pattern in both sending and receiving devices. It is used for security as well as to allow multiple wireless transmissions in the same space.

sprite

An independent graphic object controlled by its own bit plane (area of memory). Commonly used in video games, sprites move freely across the screen, passing by, through and colliding with each other with much less programming.

sprocket feed

Same as *pin feed*.

SPS

(Standby Power System) A UPS system that switches to battery backup upon detection of power failure.

SPSS

A statistical package from SPSS, Inc., Chicago, (www.spss.com), that runs on PCs, most mainframes and minis and is used extensively in marketing research. It provides over 50 statistical processes, including regression analysis, correlation and analysis of variance. Originally named Statistical Package for the Social Sciences, it was written by Norman Nie, a professor at Stanford. In 1976, he formed SPSS, Inc.

spt

(Sectors Per Track) The number of sectors in one track.

SPX

(Sequenced Packet EXchange) The NetWare communications protocol used to control the transport of messages across a network. SPX ensures that an entire message arrives intact and uses NetWare's IPX protocol as its delivery mechanism. Application programs use SPX to provide client/server and peer-to-peer interaction between network nodes. SPX provides services at layer 4 of the OSI model.

SQFP

See *QFP*.

SQL

(Structured Query Language) Pronounced "SQL" or "see qwill," a language used to interrogate and process data in a relational database. Originally developed by IBM for its mainframes, all database systems designed for client/sever environments support SQL. SQL commands can be used to interactively work with a database or can be embedded within a programming language to interface to a database. Programming extensions to SQL have turned it into a full-blown database programming language.

Some of the major database management systems (DBMSs) that support SQL are DB2, SQL/DS, Oracle, Sybase, SQLbase, INFORMIX and CA-OpenIngres (Ingres).

The following SQL query selects customers with credit limits of at least $5,000 and puts them into sequence from highest credit limit to lowest. The blue words are SQL verbs.

```
SELECT NAME, CITY, STATE, ZIPCODE
FROM CUSTOMER
WHERE CREDITLIMIT > 4999
ORDER BY CREDITLIMIT DESC
```

SQL - A Standard?

The American National Standards Institute (ANSI) has standardized the SQL language, but it does not cover all the bases. Each database management system (DBMS) has its own enhancements, quirks and tricks that, for all intents and purposes, makes SQL non standard. Moving an application from one SQL database to another generally requires hand tailoring to convert some of the SQL statements. So what's new? See *CLI, ODBC* and *IDAPI*. See the illustration in *natural language* for an example of more SQL code.

SQLBase Server

A relational DBMS for DOS, OS/2, NetWare, NT and Sun servers from Centura. It is one of the leading database programs on servers running OS/2 and NetWare. SQLBase has been Centura's flagship product since the company was founded in 1984. See *SQLWindows*.

SQL/DS

(SQL/Data System) A full-featured relational DBMS from IBM for VSE and VM environments that has integrated query and report writing facilities.

SQL engine

A program that accepts SQL commands and accesses the database to obtain the requested data. Users' requests in a query language or database language must be translated into an SQL request before the SQL engine can process it.

SQL Forms

An earlier version of Oracle Forms, an application development tool for client/server systems. See Developer/2000.

SQLJ

(SQL Java) A programming interface that allows SQL statements to be expressed at a high level in a Java program. SQLJ statements are converted into JDBC commands. See *JDBC*.

SQL precompiler

Software that turns SQL commands written within a source program into the appropriate function calls for the database management system (DBMS) being used. After the SQL precompiler stage, the resulting program is translated into machine language by the COBOL compiler or the compiler of whatever language the program is written in. See *embedded SQL*.

SQL Server

A relational DBMS from Sybase that runs on OS/2, Windows NT, NetWare, VAX and UNIX servers. It is designed for client/server use and is accessed by applications using SQL or via Sybase's own QBE and decision support utilities.

SQL Server was also available through Microsoft as Microsoft SQL Server for OS/2 and Microsoft SQL Server for Windows NT. In 1992, Microsoft started to modify the program and eventually rewrote its own version that it sells independently.

SQLWindows

A high-level application development system for Windows from Centura Software Corporation, Menlo Park, CA, (www.centurasoft.com). It is used to write Windows applications that access SQL databases in a client/server environment. SQLWindows Solo is a demonstration version that provides all of the functionality of SQLWindows, but works only on a single machine. See *SQLBase Server* and *Centura*.

SQR

Query and reporting software from SQRIBE Technologies, Menlo Park, CA, (www.sqribe.com). SQR Workbench runs under Windows 95 and NT and provides a graphical front end for designing and viewing complex reports. SQR Server provides native drivers for all the major databases and runs under Windows and most versions of UNIX. It also provides extensions to SQL for more complicated database processing. Output is available as HTML documents.

square wave

A graphic image of a digital pulse as visualized on an oscilloscope. It appears square because it rises quickly to a particular amplitude, stays constant for the duration of the pulse and drops fast at the end of it.

SQUID

(Superconducting Quantum Interference Device) An electronic detection system that uses Josephson junctions circuits. It is capable of detecting extremely weak signals.

SRAM

See *static RAM*.

SRB

See *source route bridging*.

SRI

(SRI International, Menlo Park, CA, www.sri.com) One of the oldest and largest research, technology development and consulting firms in the U.S. Founded in 1946 in conjunction with Stanford University, SRI (then Stanford Research Institute) was created to "promote the application of science in the development of commerce, trade and industry."

Over the years, SRI scientists and researchers have been involved in such fields as health care, information sciences and technology, national defense, chemical engineering, advanced materials and TV and electronics. See *telepresence surgery*.

SRPI

(Server Requester Programming Interface) An IBM programming interface that allows a PC to interact with a mainframe. See *ECF*.

SRT

(1) (Source Routing Transparent) An IEEE-standard that provides bridging between Ethernet and Token Ring networks. Ethernet LANs use transparent bridging, and Token Ring LANs use source route bridging (SRB). The SRT method sends Ethernet packets via transparent bridging and Token Ring packets via SRB.

(2) (Speech Recognition Technology) See *voice recognition*.

SS7

(Signaling System 7) The protocols used in the U.S. telephone system for setting up calls and providing modern transaction services such as caller ID, automatic recall and call forwarding.

SSA

(Serial Storage Architecture) A peripheral interface from IBM that transfers data up to 80 Mbytes/sec. SSA 160 increases the rate to 160 MBps. SSA's ring configuration allows remaining devices to function if one fails. SCSI software can be mapped over SSA allowing existing SCSI devices to be used. While distances of SCSI cables are measured in feet, SSA cable can be up to 25 meters over copper and 2.4 kilometers over fiber.

SSCP

(System Services Control Point) A controlling program in an SNA domain. It resides in the host and is a component within VTAM.

SSD

See *solid state disk*.

SSI

(1) See *server-side include* and *single-system image*.

(2) (Small-Scale Integration) Less than 100 transistors on a chip. See *MSI, LSI, VLSI* and *ULSI*.

SSL

(Secure Sockets Layer) The leading security protocol on the Internet. When an SSL session is started, the browser sends its public key to the server so that the server can securely send a secret key to the browser. The browser and server exchange data via secret key encryption during that session. Developed by Netscape, SSL is expected to be merged with other protocols and authentication methods by the IETF into a new protocol known as Transaction Layer Security (TLS). See *security protocol* and *public key cryptography*.

SSP

(1) (System Support Program) A multiuser, multitasking operating system from IBM that is the primary control program for the System/34 and System/36.

(2) (Switch to Switch Protocol) The protocol used in DLSw which locates resources and routes messages.

ST

An early personal computer series from Atari that used a Motorola 680x0 CPU and included the GEM interface, ROM-based TOS operating system, MIDI interface and three-voice sound chip. The 520ST used 512K of RAM and subsequent 1040ST and STE models used 1MB. Its display was 640x200x16.

ST506

The first hard disk drive for personal computers, introduced in 1979 by Seagate. It was used in drives of 40MB and less and transferred data at 625 KBytes/sec, using the MFM encoding method. ST506 RLL doubled capacity and speed of ST506 MFM drives and transferred data at 937 KBytes/sec. The ST506 RLL controller could be used with later MFM drives that were reformatted for RLL. See *hard disk*.

stack

(1) A set of hardware registers or a reserved amount of memory used for arithmetic calculations or to keep track of internal operations. Stacks keep track of the sequence of routines called in a program. For example, one routine calls another, which calls another and so on. As each routine is completed, the computer returns control to the calling routine all the way back to the first one that started the sequence. Stacks used in this way are LIFO based: the last item, or address, placed (pushed) onto the stack is the first item removed (popped) from the stack.

Stacks are also used to hold interrupts until they can be serviced. Used in this manner, they are FIFO stacks, in which the first item onto the stack is the first one out of the stack.

An "internal stack failure" is a fatal error which means that the operating system has lost track of its next operation. Restarting the computer usually corrects this, otherwise the operating system may have to be re-installed. See *stack dump* and *stack fault*.

(2) See *protocol stack* and *HyperCard*.

stackable hub

A type of Ethernet hub that can be expanded by daisy chaining additional hubs together via dedicated ports for that purpose. They are designed to stack vertically and be treated as a single domain by the network management software.

stack dump
The contents of a stack. A stack dump is often displayed when an error occurs. See *stack*.

stacker
(1) An output bin in a document feeding or punched card machine. Contrast with *hopper*.

(2) (Stacker) A realtime compression program from Stac Electronics, Carlsbad, CA, (www.stac.com), that doubles the disk capacity of a DOS, Windows, Mac or OS/2 computer.

stack fault
An error condition that occurs when the stack is either empty or full. See *stack overflow*.

stack overflow
An error condition that occurs when there is no room in the stack for a new item. Contrast with *stack underflow*.

In DOS, a Stack overflow error message means that there is not enough room on the stack to handle hardware interrupts. Increase the number of stacks in the STACKS= command in the CONFIG.SYS file.

You can also get this message when other things go haywire; for example, a bad expansion board or one that isn't seated properly in the slot can cause erratic signals eventually leading to this message.

stack pointer
An address that identifies the location of the most recent item placed on the stack.

stack underflow
An error condition that occurs when an item is called for from the stack, but the stack is empty. Contrast with *stack overflow*.

stackware
A HyperCard application that is made up of a HyperCard stack (data) and HyperTalk programming.

staging server
A server used to temporarily show certain users new and revised Internet and/or intranet pages before they are put into production.

STAIRS
(STorage And Information Retrieval System) An IBM text document management system for mainframes. It allows users to search for documents based on keywords or word combinations.

stand-alone PC
A PC that is not permanently connected to a local area network (LAN) or wide area network (WAN). Throughout the 1990s, not only have millions of stand-alone PCs been networked in offices, but it is no longer uncommon to find PCs networked in the home so that family members can share printers, scanners and other resources. A single PC connected to the Internet via modem is still considered a stand-alone PC.

standard
A specification for hardware or software that is either widely used and accepted (de facto) or is sanctioned by a standards organization (de jure). See *standards*.

standard cell
A completed design for a logic function on a chip. The function can be as simple as a clock circuit or as complex as a microprocessor, and the functions are combined to make custom-designed chips. Standard cells are more costly than gate arrays, but they are more efficient. Since they are made using blank wafers rather than partially-fabricated ones, they use less silicon real estate. See *gate array* and *ASIC*.

standard deviation
In statistics, the average amount a number varies from the average number in a series of numbers.

Standard Mode
A Windows 3.x operation mode. See *Windows 3.x modes*.

standards

Standards is the most important issue in the computer field. As an unregulated industry, we have wound up with thousands of data formats and languages, but very few standards that are universally used. This subject is as heated as politics and religion to vendors and industry planners.

No matter how much the industry talks about compatibility, new formats and languages appear routinely. The standards makers are always trying to cast a standard in concrete, while the innovators are trying to create a new one. Even when standards are created, they are violated as soon as a new feature is added by the vendor.

If a format or language is used extensively and others copy it, it becomes a de facto standard and may become as widely used as official standards from ANSI and IEEE. When de facto standards are sanctioned by these organizations, they become stable, at least, for a while.

In order to truly understand this industry, it is essential to understand the categories for which standards are created.

STANDARDS CATEGORIES

Machine Languages	Programming Languages
Character Codes	File Management Systems
Hardware Interfaces	Database Mgt. Systems
Storage Media	Text Systems
Operating Systems	Graphics Systems
Communications & Networking	Internet

Standards Categories
These are the major categories of electronic systems that require standards. With so many languages and formats that have become commonplace, developing information systems in today's environment often seems like the Tower of Babel.

Machine Languages

Machine language is the fundamental standard for hardware compatibility. It is the language the CPU understands. All programs that are presented to the computer for execution must be in the machine language of that particular CPU family.

Vendors may produce systems with different machine languages. IBM's mainframe family differs from its AS/400 midrange series, which is also different than its RS/6000 series. Digital's newer Alpha line of computers does not understand the machine language of the many earlier VAX computers that have been installed. For all the major hardware platforms, see *hardware platforms*.

After a program is written, it must be translated (assembled, compiled or interpreted) into the machine language the computer understands. In order to run in a different machine, the program must be reassembled or recompiled into a different machine language.

Since the late 1960s, companies seeking a chunk of the IBM market have designed computers that run the same machine language as the IBM mainframes. RCA's Spectra 70 was the first IBM-compatible mainframe, and companies, such as Amdahl, Itel, National Advanced Systems, Hitachi and Fujitsu have introduced IBM-compatible mainframes at one time or another.

IBM PC machine language compatibility is achieved by using a processor from Intel's x86 family of microprocessors or one of the Intel clone chips.

Machine language compatibility can also be achieved by emulation. An emulator is software (or hardware or both) that executes the machine language of another computer directly. With DOS and Windows emulation in a UNIX workstation or a PowerMac, users can run non-native programs in their computer.

Emulation goes back to the 1950s and 1960s when IBM built a 1401 emulator in its System/360 to ease migration from the very popular 1401s to the new 360s. The terms simulator and emulator are used interchangeably.

Character Codes

The character code built into the computer determines how each letter, digit or special character ($, %, #, etc.) is represented in binary code. Fortunately, there are only two methods in wide use: EBCDIC and ASCII. IBM minis and mainframes use EBCDIC. ASCII is used for most everything else, including all PCs and Macs.

ASCII is a 7-bit code placed into an 8-bit storage unit. The seven bits provide the basic set of 128 ASCII characters. The 8th bit adds storage for another 128 symbols, and these symbols vary from font to font and system to system. For example, the DOS character set contains line drawing and foreign language characters. The ANSI character set places the foreign language characters in different locations. In the Mac, the upper 128 characters can be custom drawn.

When systems are moved from one computer to another, converting between ASCII and EBCDIC is just a small part of the data conversion process. It is done in conjunction with converting file formats from the old to the new systems.

The following is a sample of ASCII and EBCDIC code. See *ASCII chart* and *hex chart*.

Character	ASCII	EBCDIC
space	01000000	00100000
period	01001011	00101110
< sign	01001100	00111100
+ sign	01001110	00101011
$ sign	01011011	00100100
A	11000001	01000001
B	11000010	01000010

Hardware Interfaces

The hardware interface specifies the plugs, sockets, cables and electrical signals that pass through each line between the CPU and a peripheral device or communications network.

Common hardware interfaces for personal computers are the Centronics parallel interface used for printers and the RS-232 interface, typically used for modems, graphics tablets, mice and printers. In addition, the IDE and SCSI interfaces are commonly used for disks and tapes, and the GPIB IEEE 488 standard is used for process control instruments.

The bus in a computer's motherboard, into which additional printed circuit boards are inserted, is a hardware interface. For example, the Micro Channel in IBM's PS/2 series accepts a physically different board than the original PC bus. The PCI bus and the VL-bus also have different pin configurations and are not interchangeable.

LANs, such as Ethernet and Token Ring, dictate the hardware interface as part of their specifications. An Ethernet cable cannot connect to a Token Ring board, and vice versa.

Storage Media

There are many varieties of disk cartridges, floppy disks, reel-to-reel tapes, tape cartridges and tape cassettes. Each one has its own shape and size and can be used only in drives designed to accommodate them.

With removable media, the physical standard is half the compatibility issue. The other half is the recording pattern, which is invisible to the human eye. Magnetic tapes and disks fresh out of the box are blank. The recording tracks are placed onto the surface by the read/write head of the storage drive. Thus, the same floppy disk that stores 720K bytes in one disk drive, can hold 800K if formatted for another. If the computer reads an incompatible tape or reads and writes and incompatible disk, it will signal a read/write error.

For minicomputers and mainframes, half-inch magnetic tape reels and cartridges are the common interchangeable medium. For personal computers, the 3.5" floppy is the woefully-inadequate standard.

Operating Systems

An operating system is a master control program that manages the running of the computer system. In all environments, except for specialized scientific and process control applications, the operating system interacts with the application programs. The application programs must "talk" to the operating system.

If application programs are moved to a different computing environment, they have to be converted to interface with a different operating system. If a new operating system is installed that is not compatible with the old one, the application programs have to be converted to the new operating system.

Communications & Networking

Transmitting between two personal computers is relatively simple. All that's required is a modem and communications program in each computer that uses the same file transfer protocol. Most comm programs support several protocols and are widely used to upload and download files and gain access to a BBS or online service. Connecting to a major online service, such as America Online or CompuServe, is even more straightforward when you use the service's front-end software.

Communications within the enterprise is far more complex. Over the years, organizations have developed islands of computer systems, each with their own networking protocols and access methods. The enterprise is faced with tying mainframes, minis and PCs together for file sharing, electronic mail and routine data processing.

It is a duanting task connecting client machines running DOS, Windows, Mac and Motif with servers that run DOS, Windows, Mac, VMS, MVS and UNIX via protocols such as TCP/IP, IPX and NetBIOS over topologies such as Ethernet, Fast Ethernet, Switched Ethernet, Token Ring, FDDI and ATM using devices such as bridges, routers, hubs, switches and gateways, and there you have it. Oh, add interfacing between multiple mail and messaging systems and managing the entire process from one management console.

To understand the layers of protocols required to transmit a message from one machine to another, review the layers of the OSI model. OSI is a seven-layer reference model for worldwide communications defined by the International Standards Organization (ISO). Originally thought to be the future standard for communications, it was never widely supported. However, it does serve as a teaching model to line up other protocols against. See *enterprise networking, client/server* and *OSI model.*

Programming Langauges

Every software program is written in a programming language, and there is at least one programming language for every major CPU series. There is typically an assembly language and a number of high-level languages for each family. Assembly languages are machine specific, and the machine language they generate runs on only one CPU family. Unless the machine languages are very similar, it is difficult to translate an assembly language program from one CPU series into another.

The high-level programming language was created to eliminate this machine dependency. Programming languages, such as COBOL, FORTRAN and BASIC are designed to run on many different computers. However, due to dialects of each language, compatibility is always an issue. Each compiler vendor keeps adding new features to its language thereby making it incompatible with previous or other versions.

By the time a new feature becomes a standard, a dozen new features have been already implemented. For example, dBASE became a de facto standard business programming language. Since 1981, dBASE spawned competitive products, such as Clipper, QuickSilver, Force III, dbXL and Foxbase, all of which are incomplete versions of dBASE. None of them provides every command in dBASE, and they all provide features not found in dBASE.

There's no rule of thumb for translating one dialect of a programming language into another. The job may be difficult or easy. At times, software is written to translate one dialect into another, as well as one programming language into another. If the translation program cannot translate the program entirely, then manual tailoring is necessary. In these cases, it is often easier to rewrite the program from scratch.

Compatibility can be achieved when a programming language conforms to the ANSI (American National Standards Institute) standard for that language. If the same version of an ANSI COBOL compiler is available for two different CPUs, a program written in ANSI COBOL will run on both machines.

Beyond traditional programming languages such as COBOL and C, known as third-generation languages, or 3GLs, there are more than a hundred software environments used to develop client/server applications on LANs (see *client/server development system*). Each of them attempts to provide less programming-like and more English-like syntax, which is considered a *fourth-generation language*, or 4GL.

They also provide visual development tools to build the graphical user interface by "drawing" the screen and dragging and dropping symbols on it. They may provide the ability to point and click and drag and drop symbols to link objects together rather than by writing programming code. These software-building tools are proliferating and producing even more standards to be dealt with. The programming pools are becoming increasingly fragmented. It's no longer just COBOL, BASIC, dBASE, C and C++. Now it's PowerBuilder, SQLWindows, ObjectView, DYNASTY, OMNIS and JAM and many more. See *programming language.*

File Management Systems

In its simplest form, a data file uses fields of the same length for each item of data, for example, a plain EBCDIC or ASCII file would look like:

```
Chris Smith    34 Main St.    Bangor     ME18567
Pat Jones      10 W. 45 St.   New York   NY10002
```

A common format stemming from the BASIC programming language is an ASCII comma delimited file; for example, the data above would look like the following:

```
"Chris Smith","34 Main St.","Bangor","ME","18567"
"Pat Jones","10 W. 45 St.","New York","NY","10002"
```

Both file formats above are simple, contain only data (except for quotes and commas) and can be easily manipulated by a word processor. However, data files may also contain special codes that identify the way the data is structured within the file. For example, variable length records require a code in each field indicating the size of the field.

Whether fixed or variable length fields, the data in non-DBMS systems is linked directly to the processing. The program must know the layout of the fields in each record that it processes, and it cannot accept records in a different format. In order to process a different file format, the program must be changed.

Incompatible file formats often exist within the same organization because they were developed separately. For example, one record may reserve 40 characters for name, while another holds only 30. As long as a file management system is used rather than a database management system (DBMS), the program that processes the first file structure would have to be changed to process the second.

DBMSs

Database management systems (DBMSs) have their own proprietary formats for storing data. For example, a header record with a unique format that contains identification data is typically placed at the beginning of each file. Codes may also be embedded in each record.

Most DBMSs have an import and export capability that converts popular database formats into their proprietary format. If not, the program usually can import and export a plain EBCDIC or ASCII file, which is stripped of all proprietary codes and can be used as a common denominator between both systems. If conversion facilities cannot be found, a custom program can be written to convert one database format into another if documentation describing the old format is available.

The application program interface (API), or language used by the application program to "talk" to the database, is typically a proprietary language in every DBMS. However, SQL has become the de facto standard database language for client/server environments. In theory, that means any application program requesting data in the SQL language would work with any DBMS that supports SQL. Like everything else however, there are dialects of SQL, and only fundamental expressions can be guaranteed compatible. Whatever special features exist within the DBMS, proprietary syntax is needed to activate them, thus automatically making one DBMS incompatible with another.

Text Systems

Although the basic structure of an English-language text file is standard throughout the world: word, sentence, paragraph, page; every word processing, desktop publishing and typesetting program uses its own codes to set up the layout within a document. For example, the code that turns on boldface in WordPerfect Version 5.0 is [**BOLD**]; in WordStar, it's ^PB.

The codes that define a header, footer, footnote, page number, margin, tab setting, indent and font change are unique to the word processing program in which the document was created or the desktop publishing program into which the text file is converted. Even the codes to end a line and paragraph are not the same.

Document conversion is accomplished with special conversion programs or black boxes. Although every word processing program has a search and replace capability, it may not be effective for converting embedded layout codes from one format to another. In some programs, the search & replace simply does not handle layout codes. In addition, while some systems use one code to turn a function on and another code to turn it off, other systems use the same code for on and off, requiring manual verification and tailoring when using the search & replace function.

Graphics Systems

There are many formats for storing a picture in a computer; but, unlike text and data files, which are primarily made up of alphanumeric characters, graphics formats are more complex.

To begin with, there are the two major categories of graphics: vector graphics (objects made up of lines) and bitmapped graphics (TV-like dots). Images stored in vector format can be moved to another vector system typically without loss of resolution. There are 2-D vector formats as well as 3-D vector formats.

In transferring raster images among different devices, resolution is a major concern. Such transfers can occur without loss of resolution as long as the new format has the same or higher resolution as the older one.

Standard graphics formats allow graphics data to be moved from machine to machine, while standard graphics languages let graphics programs be moved from machine to machine. For example, GKS and PHIGS are major graphics languages that have been adopted by high-performance workstation and CAD vendors. Apple's consistent use of its QuickDraw language helped the Macintosh become popular in graphics-oriented applications.

High-resolution graphics has typically been expensive to implement due to its large storage and fast processing requirements. However, as personal computers become more powerful, graphics are becoming widely used in business applications. The ability to see a person's face or a product's appearance on screen is now as commonplace as text and data.

The Internet
One of the Internet's most significant contributions is that it drives worldwide standards. TCP/IP, HTML, POP, IMAP, LDAP and so on are global standards that have become the glue that is binding the world together electronically. However, these standards are already being updated to newer versions, which is inevitable. At least now, we have a global focal point for compatibility, which is a major improvement.

The Future
After 40 some years of computing, we've managed to create thousands of languages, formats and interfaces in this business. While some of them become bona fide standards endorsed by recognized standards organizations, some of the most widely used are de facto standards. The PC is the perfect example.

While the Internet will help immensely, it will by no means solve all standards issues. There are simply too many. As we forge ahead with new technologies, there is some point where we can no longer cling to the old designs for compatibility. At that time, the new has to break from the past, as the previous infrastructure only holds us back. It's no different than constructing a new building on top of a weak foundation. It seems to be the way of things.

standards bodies
The following organizations set standards for computers, communications and related products throughout the world.

```
U.S.
ANSI   American National Standards Institute
EIA    Electronic Industries Association
IEEE   Institute of Electrical and Electronic Engineers
NIST   National Institute of Standards & Technology


International
ITU    International Telecommunications Union
ISO    International Standards Organization
IEC    International Electrotechnical Commission
```

Star
The Xerox workstation that formally introduced the graphical user interface and desktop metaphor in 1981. It was the inspiration for Xerox's subsequent computers and for Apple's Lisa and Macintosh and all the other graphical user interfaces that followed. See *Alto*. See *GUI* for illustration.

star configuration
See *star network*.

star design
See *star network* and *star schema*.

Star:Flashpoint

A screen scraper from Sterling Software, Atlanta, GA, (www.key.sterling.com), that is used to turn a character-based terminal screen into a Windows front end.

Starlan

A local area network from AT&T that uses twisted pair wire, the CSMA/CD access method, transmits at 1 Mbps and uses a star or bus topology. In 1988, Starlan was renamed Starlan 1, and Starlan 10 was introduced, a 10 Mbps Ethernet version that uses twisted pair or optical fibers.

star network

A communications network in which all terminals are connected to a central computer, controller or hub. PBXs and telephone systems are prime examples as well as Token Ring and 10BaseT Ethernet. See *topology*.

star schema (star query)

A data warehouse design that enhances the performance of multidimensional queries on traditional relational databases. One fact table is surrounded by a series of related tables. Data is joined from one of the points to the center, providing a so called "star query." See *OLAP*.

start bit

In asynchronous communications, the bit transmitted before each character.

Start menu

See *Win 9x Start menu*.

star topology

See *star network*.

start/stop transmission

Same as *asynchronous transmission*.

STARTUP.CMD

(STARTUP.CoMmanD) An OS/2 file that is executed immediately upon startup. It contains instructions that can initialize operating system settings and call in a specific application program. The DOS counterpart is AUTOEXEC.BAT.

StartUp folder

The folder in Windows 95/98 that contains applications (or pointers to applications) that are to be launched when Windows is started. The StartUp folder can be found in the Programs folder under the Start menu at:

```
c:\WINDOWS\Start Menu\Programs\StartUp
```

startup routine

A routine that is executed when the computer is booted or when an application is loaded. It is used to customize the environment for its associated software.

state

The current or last-known status, or condition, of a process, transaction or setting. In object-oriented programming, the state of an object is the combination of the original values in the object plus any modifications made to them. "Maintaining state" means keeping track of data for the next time.

This is an issue on the Web, because Webmasters want to analyze the routes users take when visiting their sites. HTTP does not maintain state between one page request and the next. Server protocols such as NSAPI and ISAPI, as well as cookie files, are used to maintain state about the user. See *NSAPI, ISAPI* and *cookie file*.

stateful inspection

A firewall technology that monitors the state of the transaction so that it can verify that the destination of an inbound packet matches the source of a previous outbound request. See *firewall*.

stateless

Not keeping track of data for the next time. See *state*.

state machine

Also called a *finite state machine*, it is a computing device designed with the operational states required to solve a specific problem. The circuits are minimized, specialized and optimized for the application. For example, chips in audio, video and imaging controllers are often designed as state machines, because they can provide faster performance at lower cost than a general-purpose CPU.

statement

In a high-level programming language, a descriptive phrase that generates one or more machine language instructions in the computer. In a low-level assembly language, programmers write instructions rather than statements, since each source language instruction is translated into one machine language instruction.

state-of-the-art

The most advanced technique or method used.

static

Refers to something that is fixed and unchanging. Contrast with *dynamic*.

static binding

Same as *early binding*.

static column memory

A type of page mode memory that requires less electronic pulsing in order to access the memory bits.

static electricity

A stationary electrical charge that is the result of intentional charging or of friction in low-humidity environments.

static HTML

An HTML page that never changes. See *dynamic HTML*.

static IP address

A permanent IP address that is assigned to a client or server station in a TCP/IP network. Servers are usually assigned static IP addresses, but client stations are typically assigned dynamic IP addresses from a DHCP server. See *dynamic IP address, IP address* and *DHCP*.

static RAM

A memory chip that requires power to hold its content. Static RAM chips have access times in the 10-30ns range. Dynamic RAMs are usually above 30ns, and Bipolar and ECL memories are under 10ns.

 A static RAM bit is made up of a pretzel-like flip-flop circuit that lets current flow through one side or the other based on which one of two transistors is activated. Static RAMs do not require refresh circuitry as do dynamic RAMs, but they take up more space and use more power.

static routing

Forwarding data in a network via a fixed path. Static routing cannot adjust to changing line conditions as can dynamic routing. See *routing protocol*.

static SQL

See *embedded SQL*.

static typing

Same as *early binding*.

station

A computer, workstation or terminal in a network. Same as *node*.

stationery

The term for boilerplate in the Eudora mail client, starting with Version 3.0. Stationery files are stored on disk and brought into new messages or added to replies. See *boilerplate*.

statistical multiplexor

In communications, a device that merges several low-speed channels into a single high-speed channel and vice versa. A standard multiplexor is set up for a fixed number of incoming channels regardless of whether every one is transmitting or not. A statistical multiplexor analyzes the traffic and dynamically changes its pattern of interleaving to use all the available capacity of the outgoing channel.

stat mux

(STATistical MUltipleXor) See *statistical multiplexor*.

status line

An information line displayed on screen that shows current activity.

STB

See *set-top box*.

ST connector

A fiber-optic cable connector that uses a bayonet plug and socket. It was the first de facto standard connector for most commercial wiring. Two ST connectors are used for each pair of cables. See *fiber-optic connectors*.

STD bus

A bus architecture used in medical and industrial equipment due to its small size and rugged design. Originally an 8-bit bus, extensions have increased it to 16 and 32 bits.

stealth URL

A Web site that uses a domain name that is a misspelled version of a popular Web site in order to attract visitors. For example, microsft.com or oracl.com.

stealth virus

A virus that is able to keep itself from being detected. See *polymorphic virus*.

Steelhead

See *RRAS*.

step frame

To capture video images one frame at a time. If a computer is not fast enough to capture analog video in realtime, the video can be forwarded and processed one frame at a time.

stepper motor

A motor that rotates in small, fixed increments and is used to control the movement of the access arm on a disk drive. Contrast with *voice coil*.

stereophonic

Sound reproduction that uses two or more channels. Contrast with *monophonic*.

Sterling Software

(Sterling Software, Dallas, TX, www.sterling.com) A software company founded in 1981 that provides a variety of products for applications and systems management as well as software and services to the U.S. Government. Sterling has grown through numerous acquisitions over the years. Its COOL product line provides a family of application development tools for all major hardware platforms. COOL was derived from products from Knowledgeware and Texas Instruments Software, which it acquired in 1994 and 1997 respectively. Other lines include VISION, SOLVE, SAMS and VM.

stick font

Same as *vector font*.

stick model

A picture made of lines, or vectors. For example, in biomedical applications, the limbs of a person or animal are converted into lines so that the motion can be visually observed and graphically plotted and analyzed.

stiction

(STatic frICTION) A type of hard disk failure in which the read/write heads stick to the platters. The lubricant used on certain drives heats up and liquifies. When the disk is turned off, it cools down and can become like a glue.

STN

(SuperTwisted Nematic) A passive matrix LCD technology that provides better contrast than twisted nematic (TN) by twisting the molecules from 180 to 270 degrees. See *DSTN*.

stochastic

By guesswork; by chance; using or containing random values.

stop bit

In asynchronous communications, a bit transmitted after each character.

stop-motion animation

The original technique used to create an animated sequence. Each frame is created and photographed (or digitized) independently. Contrast with *computer animation*. See *claymation*.

storage

The semi-permanent or permanent holding place for digital data. Storage means disks and tapes, not memory. Memory, which is made of RAM chips, is a temporary workspace for executing instructions and processing data. All storage devices in this book are summarized here.

QIC Tape

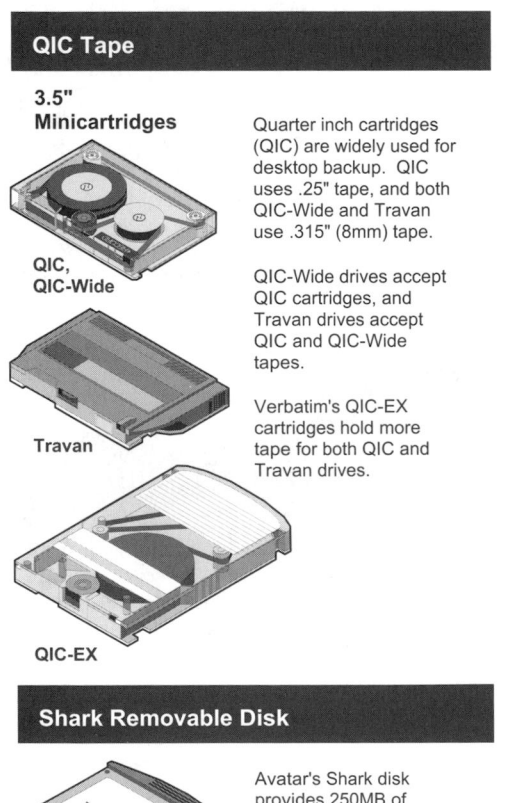

3.5"
Minicartridges

QIC,
QIC-Wide

Travan

QIC-EX

Quarter inch cartridges (QIC) are widely used for desktop backup. QIC uses .25" tape, and both QIC-Wide and Travan use .315" (8mm) tape.

QIC-Wide drives accept QIC cartridges, and Travan drives accept QIC and QIC-Wide tapes.

Verbatim's QIC-EX cartridges hold more tape for both QIC and Travan drives.

Shark Removable Disk

Avatar's Shark disk provides 250MB of removable storage for portable applications. Introduced in 1997, this small hard drive attaches via the parallel port or a PC card.

DAT 4mm Tape

DAT tapes use the DDS recording standard and provide 2 to 12GB of storage. The cartridges look like small audio cassettes, and users love the compact format.

Exabyte 8mm Tape

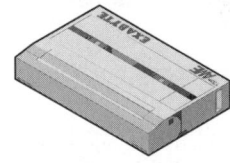

Exabyte's 8mm tapes, provide capacities from 2.5 to 20GB. The Mammoth drive is the high-end unit. The cartridges are smaller than a deck of playing cards.

AIT 8mm Tape

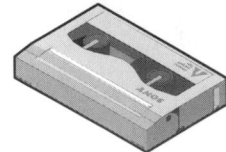

Sony's 8mm drives use Advanced Intelligent Tape (AIT) technology, which includes a built-in head cleaner and EEPROM chip that holds tape status and indexing information. The cartridge holds 25GB.

DLT Tape

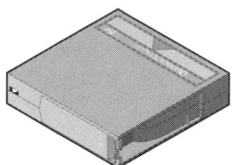

Providing capacities from 10 to 35GB, DLT tapes are widely used in the mid to high-end server market. After insertion, the tape is pulled from the cartridge onto the tapeup reel inside the drive.

3480, 3490, Magstar (3590) Tape

IBM's half-inch tape cartridges provide high performance for archiving and backup on mainframes and midrange systems. Capacities have ranged from 200MB to 10GB. After insertion, the tape is pulled onto the takeup reel inside the drive.

Magstar MP Tape

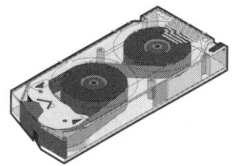

IBM's Magstar MP uses an 8mm, cassete-style cartridge that holds 5GB. Intended for midrange server use, it is especially designed for use in robotic libraries.

Redwood Tape

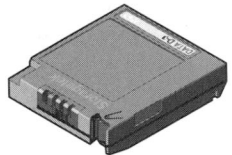

StorageTek's Redwood tapes hold up to 50GB. They use half-inch tape and single-hub cartridges like the 3480/3490s, but are helical scan rather than linear.

Open Reel Tape

The venerable half-inch open reel has been used for half a century. The drives and tapes are still being made for legacy applications.

Pereos Tape

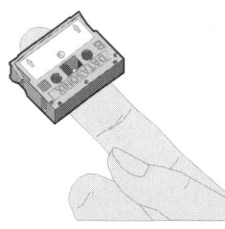

Holding more than a gigabyte (compressed), the Pereos tape is designed for mobile backup. Powered by AA batteries, connection is made via the parallel port.

Floppy Disk

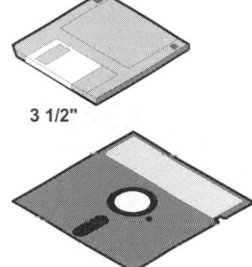

3 1/2"

5 1/2"

The most common removable storage medium is the floppy disk. In the mid 1990s, the 5.25" format gave given way to the 3.5" disk, but its 1.44MB capacity is woefully undersized for today's multimedia files and applications.

Zip Removable Disk

Iomega's Zip disk holds 100MB and was the first, low-cost removable disk to become popular across a broad market segment since the advent of the floppy.

LS-120 Removable Disk

The LS-120 disks are a floppy replacement technology. The drives support 120MB LS-120 media as well as standard 3.5" floppies.

HiFD Removable Disk

Sony's HiFD disk is a floppy replacement technology. The drive supports 200MB HiFD media as well as standard 3.5" floppies.

Fixed Hard Disk

The fixed hard disk, also known as Winchester technology, continues to be the mainstay storage for all types of computers from micro to mainframe.

For personal computers, hard disk capacities have soared with prices under 10 cents per megabyte in 1998. Hard disks will remain the primary storage medium for a number of years, but will be eventually eclipsed by optical disks and other optical storage

Jaz Removable Disk

Iomega's removable Jaz disks come in 1GB and 2GB versions. The 1GB cartridges were introduced in 1995 at a breakthrough $99.

SyJet Removable Disk

The SyJet line supersedes SyQuest's original 5.25" and 3.5" hard disks, which became de facto standards. The first SyJet drive is 1.5GB.

SparQ Removable Disk

SyQuest's SparQ is an affordable 1GB removable hard disk that is aimed at the consumer market.

ORB Removable Disk

Castlewood's ORB disk is expected in 1998, pushing the envelope further with 2.2GB at a very afforable price.

Quest Removable Disk

SyQuest's Quest cartridges hold 4.7GB. They were introduced in 1998 as the fastest, removable, rewritable storage device on the market.

EZFlyer Removable Disk

SyQuest's 3.5" EZFlyer disks hold 230MB, and the drives support the previous EZ135 cartridges.

SyQuest Removable Disk

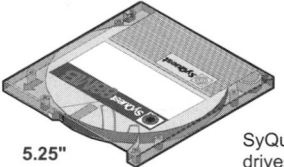

5.25"

3.5"

SyQuest's 3.5" and 5.25" drives became the first de facto standard removable hard disks for personal computers. They have been superseded by the SyJet, SparQ and Quest lines.

Shark Removable Disk

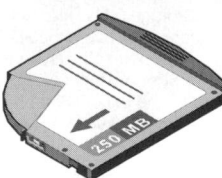

Avatar's Shark disk provides 250MB of removable storage for portable applications. Introduced in 1997, this small hard drive attaches via the parallel port or a PC card.

Click! Removable Disk

Iomega's Click! disk is aimed at PDAs and handheld devices such as digital cameras. A Click! cartridge holds 40MB.

Bernoulli Removable Disk

Iomega's Bernoulli was the first removable storage for personal computers. It was also extremely reliable.

Magneto-optic (MO) Disk

5.25"

3.5"

MO disks provide robust online and archival storage (30-year life).

Double-sided 5.25" disks come in 650MB, 1.3, 2.6 and 5.2GB capacities and must be flipped for each side.

Single-sided 3.5" media come in 128, 230 and 640MB formats.

PD Optical Disk

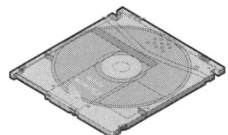

Panasonic's PD is a phase change optical disk that holds 650MB. PD drives support both phase change cartridges and CD-ROMs.

WORM Optical Disk

Ablative

**5.25"
Magneto-optic**

Large-format (12-14") ablative WORM is a declining market, but Philips LMS is supporting future 12" formats.

MO media can also be written in WORM mode that is handled by firmware in the drive.

CD-ROM, CD-R, CD-RW

CD-ROM

The CD-ROM is the de facto standard for software distribution and for publishing large databases. CD-ROMs have a silver cast.

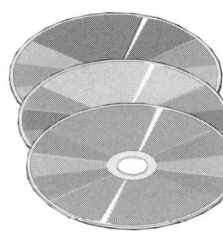

CD-R

Blank CD-R discs can be recorded once and read on any CD-ROM reader. CD-Rs have a gold, blue or green cast.

CD-RWs can be rewritten, but must be read on newer MultiRead CD and DVD drives. CD-RWs have a blue cast.

CD-RW

DVD-ROM, DVD-R, DVD-RAM

DVD-ROM

DVDs look like CDs, but hold from 4 to 28 times as much data. There is a DVD counterpart for every CD type.

DVD-ROMs are silver, read only discs. DVD-Rs are write once and have a pink cast. Rewritable DVD-RAMs can be double sided, so a cartridge is used to protect the surfaces and provide a label area.

DVD-R

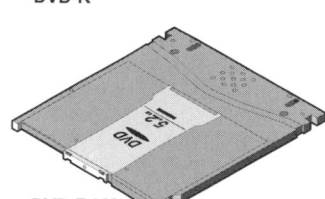

DVD-RAM

OROM Optical ROM Disk

Ioptics' OROM uses 128MB data cards that are read only. Stationary organic LEDs shine through 5000 data "patches" on the card. Each patch is a 2-D image that holds 32KB.

Holographic Storage

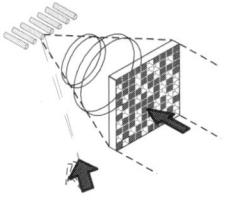

Holographic storage enables huge amounts of data to be stored in an optical material. Rather than reflecting off spinning disks, lasers create interference patterns (holograms) in non-moving optical material.

Some day, all storage devices will be entirely silent.

Solid State Disk

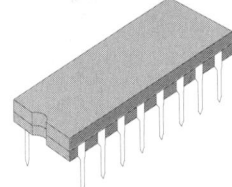

Solid state disks provide the fastest storage access and are made up of banks of RAM that are designed to simulate a hard disk. Units with gigabytes of storage are available. Also included are batteries and a hard disk. In the event of power failure, the RAM contents is copied to the hard disk automatically.

storage area network
See *SAN*.

storage array
A group of disks that work as a unit. It typically refers to a RAID system. See *RAID* and *storage system*.

storage device
A peripheral unit that holds data such as magnetic tape, magnetic disk and optical disk. See *storage* for complete summary.

storage hierarchy
The range of memory and storage devices within the computer system. The following list runs from lowest to highest speed. Items marked with ** are obsolete. See *storage* for complete summary.

```
Punched cards **
Punched paper tape **
Magnetic tape
Floppy disks
CD-ROM
Bubble memory
Optical disks
Magnetic disks (movable heads)
Magnetic disks (fixed heads) **
Low-speed bulk memory
Main memory
Cache memory
Microcode
Registers
```

storage management

The administration of any or all of backup, archival, disaster recovery and hierarchical storage management (HSM) procedures within an organization. See *HSM, ESM, SAN* and *data management.*

storage media

Disks and tapes.

storage network

See *SAN.*

storage subsystem

The part of a computer system that provides the storage. It includes the controller and disk drives. See *storage system.*

storage system

A computer system that provides storage for one or more hosts. See *SAN* and *RAID.*

StorageTek

(Storage Technology Corporation, Louisville, CO, www.storagetek.com) A manufacturer of disk and tape subsystems founded in 1969. Its first products were open reel tape drives for IBM mainframes. Today, it offers a line of 3480/3490 drives and libraries as well as DLT drives and its own Redwood helical scan drives. Its Powderhorn tape library, which supports a mix of Redwood and 3480/3490 tapes holds up to 300TB, the largest nearline storage capacity in the world. StorageTek also also makes a line of RAID disk arrays for IBM. See *Redwood.*

store and forward

The temporary storage of a message for transmission to its destination at a later time. Store and forward techniques allow for routing over networks that are not accessible at all times. For example, messages crossing time zones can be forwarded during daytime at the receiving side, or messages can be forwarded at night in order to obtain off-peak rates. See *messaging protocol.*

store-and-forward switch

A switching device that stores a complete incoming data packet before it is sent out. Such switches are used when incoming and outgoing speeds differ. Contrast with *cut-through switch.*

stored procedure

In a database management system (DBMS), it is an SQL program that is stored in the database which is executed by calling it directly from the client or from a database trigger. When the SQL procedure is stored in the database, it does not have to be replicated in each client. This saves programming effort especially when different client user interfaces and development systems are used. Triggers and stored procedures are built into DBMSs used in client/server environments.

stored program concept

The fundamental computer architecture in which the computer acts upon (executes) internally-stored instructions. See *von Neumann architecture.*

stovepipe application

A stand-alone program. It implies an application that does not integrate with or share data or resources with other applications.

STP

(1) (Shielded Twisted Pair) Telephone wire that is wrapped in a metal sheath to eliminate external interference. See *twisted pair.*

(2) (Spanning Tree Protocol) See *spanning tree algorithm.*

Strand88

A parallel processing programming language developed by AI Ltd., England.

Stratus

(Stratus Computer, Inc., Marlboro, MA, www.stratus.com) A manufacturer of fault-tolerant computers founded in 1980. It supports both the VOS and FTX UNIX operating systems on its XA/R line of i860-based systems. Its earlier XA/2000 line was Motorola 680x0 based. Future systems will use HP's PA-RISC architecture.

stream

(1) A contiguous group of data.

(2) The I/O management in the C programming language. A stream is a channel through which data flows to/from a disk, keyboard, printer, etc.

(3) The data part of a Structured Storage file. See *Structured Storage*.

streaming audio

Audio transmission over a data network. The term implies a one-way transmission to the listener, in which both the client and server cooperate for uninterrupted sound. The client side buffers a few seconds of audio data before it starts sending it to the speakers, which compensates for momentary delays in packet delivery. Audio conferencing, on the other hand, requires realtime two-way transmission for effective results. See *streaming video*.

streaming data

Data that is structured and processed in a continous flow, such as digital audio and video. See *streaming audio* and *streaming video*.

streaming tape

A high-speed magnetic tape drive that is frequently used to make a backup copy of an entire hard disk.

streaming video

Video transmission over a data network. The term implies a one-way transmission to the viewer, in which both the client and server software cooperate for uninterrupted motion. The client side buffers a few seconds of video data before it starts sending it to the screen, which compensates for momentary delays in packet delivery. Videoconferencing, on the other hand, requires realtime two-way transmission for effective results. See *streaming audio*.

Streamline

A Macintosh tracing program from Adobe. It converts scanned or MacPaint images into PostScript files, which can be modified in Adobe Illustrator.

stream-oriented file

A type of file, such as a text document or digital voice file, that is more openly structured than a database file. Text and voice files contain continuous streams of characters, whereas database files contain many small repeating structures (records).

STREAMS

A feature of UNIX System V that provides a standard way of dynamically building and passing messages up and down a protocol stack. STREAMS passes messages from the application "downstream" through the STREAMS modules to the network driver at the end of the stack. Messages are passed "upstream" from the driver to the application. A STREAMS module would be a transport layer protocol such as TCP and SPX or a network layer protocol such as IP and IPX.

STREAMS modules can be dynamically changed (pushed and popped) at runtime, allowing the stack to be used for multiple protocols. Two important STREAMS components are the TLI and LSL interfaces, which provide common languages to the transport and data link layers. See *TLI, LSL, ODI* and *OSI*.

Streettalk

The directory service used in the VINES network operating system from Banyan Systems Inc., Westboro, MA, (www.banyan.com). Streettalk has always been highly regarded and versions are also available for Windows NT. Streettalk Desktop is a 32-bit Windows client program that lets users create folders and keep track of shared documents.

STRETCH

The code name for IBM's first "supercomputer," the 7030, which was started in 1955 and completed in 1961. The first of eight units was delivered to the Los Alamos Scientific Laboratory and was in use for 10 years. STRETCH was IBM's first attempt at building transistorized computers and was designed to "stretch" the speed of its current vacuum tube models by a factor of 100.

The machine was very sophisticated for its time, providing simultaneous execution of business instructions with floating point arithmetic. It was estimated that IBM lost 40 million dollars in developing STRETCH, but that the knowledge gained led to huge profits with its subsequent computers.

stretch blt

An enhanced type of bitblt used for resizing video images. The function expands or contracts the number of bits while moving them from main memory to the display memory. See *bitblt*.

stretching

See *hardware scaling*.

The STRETCH
The STRETCH was the first of IBM's transistorized computers. Its style of cabinetry and console were used in many subsequent computers by the company. *(Photo courtesy of IBM Corporation.)*

string

In programming, a contiguous set of alphanumeric characters that does not contain numbers used for calculations. Names, addresses and error messages are examples of strings. Contrast with *numeric data*.

string handling

The abilty to manipulate alphanumeric data (names, addresses, text, etc.). Typical functions include the ability to handle arrays of strings, to left and right align and center strings and to search for an occurrence of text within a string.

Stringy Floppy

A tape drive developed by Exatron, Sunnyvale, CA, for the Radio Shack TRS-80 personal computer that used a continuous loop cartridge of 1/16" tape. It was faster than the audio cassettes used for data storage on the first TRS-80s, and the company sold several thousand of these "tape wafers." However, soon after, the floppy disk became the norm.

Why not have some fun with such a unique name. Ask your systems people if they've seen the new "Stringy Floppy" on the market, and watch the puzzled expression. Keep a straight face now!

striping

Interleaving or multiplexing data to increase speed. See *disk striping*.

stroke

(1) In printing, the weight, or thickness, of a character. For example, in the LaserJet, one of the specifications of the font description is the stroke weight from -3 to +3.

(2) In computer graphics, a pen or brush stroke. The stroke function lets you set the width of the line being drawn.

stroke font

Same as *vector font*.

stroke weight

The thickness of lines in a font character. The HP LaserJet defines stroke weights from Ultra Thin (-7) to Ultra Black (+7), with Medium, or Text, as normal (0).

stroke writer

Same as *vector display*.

StrongARM

A high-performance RISC-based microprocessor that was jointly developed by Digital and Advanced RISC Machines (ARM). The StrongARM chips are used in Apple's MessagePads (Newtons). In 1997, Intel acquired Digital's chip manufacturing facilities and will continue to produce Digital's flagship Alpha chips. It is expected that Intel will continue to license the ARM architecture and make StrongARM chips.

strong encryption

An encryption method that uses a very large number as its cryptographic key. The larger the key, the longer it takes to unlawfully break the code. Today, 128 bits is considered strong encryption. As computers become faster, the length of the key must be incresed.

strong typing

A programming language characteristic that provides strict adherence to the rules of typing. Data of one type (integer, string, etc.) cannot be passed to a variable expecting data of a different type. Contrast with *weak typing*.

structured analysis

Techniques developed in the late 1970s by Yourdon, DeMarco, Gane and Sarson for applying a systematic approach to systems analysis. It included the use of data flow diagrams and data modeling and fostered the use of implementation-independent graphical notation for documentation.

structured design

A systematic approach to program design developed in the mid 1970s by Constantine, Yourdon, et al, that included the use of graphical notation for effective documentation and communication, design guidelines and recipes to help programmers get started.

structured programming

Techniques that impose a logical structure on the writing of a program. Large routines are broken down into smaller, modular routines. The use of the GOTO statement is discouraged (see *spaghetti code*).

Certain programming statements are indented in order to make loops and other program logic easier to follow. Structured walkthroughs, which invite criticism from peer programmers, are also used.

Structured languages, such as Pascal, Ada and dBASE, force the programmer to write a structured program. However, unstructured languages such as FORTRAN, COBOL and BASIC require discipline on the part of the programmer.

Structured Storage

A file structure from Microsoft for storing compound elements, such as compound documents and the persistent data of COM objects. Contained within one file, its structure looks like a miniature disk drive with the Root storage at the top of the hierarchy and Storages (directories) and streams (data files) below.

stub

A small software routine placed into a program that provides a common function. Stubs are used for a variety of purposes. For example, a stub might be installed in a client machine, and a counterpart installed in a server, where both are required to resolve some protocol, remote procedure call (RPC) or other interoperability requirement.

stub file

A data file or program that stands in for the original file. See *HSM*.

StuffIt

A Macintosh shareware program from Aladdin Systems, Inc., Watsonville, CA, (www.aladdinsys.com), that compresses files onto multiple floppies. A commercial version adds a scripting language, file viewing and supports multiple compression techniques. It was originally developed by Raymond Lau at age 16. StuffIt files use a .SIT extension.

stupid network

See *dumb network*.

style sheet

A master page layout used in document creation systems such as word processing, desktop publishing and the Web. The style sheet is a file that is used to store margins, tabs, fonts, headers, footers and other layout settings for a particular category of document. When a style sheet is selected, its format settings are applied to all the documents created under it, saving the page designer or programmer from redefining the same settings over and over again for each page. See *CSS*.

stylus

A pen-shaped instrument used to "draw" images or point to menus. See *light pen* and *digitizer tablet*.

subarea node

In an SNA network, a system that contains network controlling functions. It refers to a host computer or a communications controller and its associated terminals.

subclass

In programming, to add custom processing to an existing function or subroutine by hooking into the routine at a predefined point and adding additional lines of code.

subdirectory

A disk directory that is subordinate to (below) another directory. In order to gain access to a subdirectory, the path must include all directories above it. See *subfolder*.

subfolder

A folder that is placed within another folder. See *subdirectory*.

submarining

The temporary visual loss of the screen pointer on a passive matrix display screen. See *mouse trails* and *active matrix*.

submenu

An additional list of options within a menu selection. There can many levels of submenus.

subnet, subnetwork

A division of a network into an interconnected, but independent, segment, or domain, in order to improve performance and security. Before the Internet, the vast majority of traffic within an organization moved within subnets. Today, traffic is increasingly routed across subnets.

subnet mask, subnetwork mask

The method used for splitting IP networks into a series of subgroups, or subnets. The mask is a binary pattern that is matched up with the IP address to turn part of the host ID address field into a field for subnets. For example, in a Class C address, the rightmost 8 bits of the address are used for host ID (see *IP address*). The 0 in the default Class C mask 255.255.255.0 has no affect on the host ID. However, the 192 in the mask 255.255.255.192 reserves the two high-order bits for up to four subnets, leaving six bits for host ID addressing as follows:

```
255.255.255.0
11111111.11111111.11111111.00000000

255.255.255.192
11111111.11111111.11111111.11000000
```

subnetting

Dividing a network into smaller subgroups. See *subnet* and *subnet mask*.

subnotebook

A laptop computer that weighs less than four pounds. Subnotebooks often use an external floppy drive to reduce weight, which is inconvenient if you need to exchange data via diskettes in remote locations. For features of a portable computer, see *laptop computer*.

subroutine

A group of instructions that perform a specific task. A large subroutine is usually called a module or procedure; a small one, a function or macro, but all terms are used interchangeably.

subschema

Pronounced "sub-skeema." In database management, an individual user's partial view of the database. The schema is the entire database.

subscribe

To sign up for a service. Signing up for something is often simpler than getting out of it, or unsubscribing. See *unsubscribe*.

subscript

(1) In word processing and mathematical notation, a digit or symbol that appears below the line; for example, I_2O. Contrast with *superscript*.

(2) In programming, a method for referencing data in a table. For example, in the table PRICETABLE, the statement to reference a specific price in the table might be **PRICETABLE (ITEM)**, ITEM being the subscript variable. In a two-dimensional table that includes price and discount, the statement **PRICETABLE (ITEM,DISCOUNT)** could reference a discounted price. The relative locations of the current ITEM and DISCOUNT are kept in two index registers.

subset

A group of commands or functions that do not include all the capabilities of the original specification. Software or hardware components designed for the subset will also work with the original. However, any component designed for the full original specification will not operate with the subset product. Contrast with *superset*.

substrate

The base layer of a structure such as a chip, multichip module (MCM), printed circuit board or disk platter. Silicon is the most widely used substrate for chips. Fiberglass (FR4) is mostly used for printed circuit boards, and ceramic is used for MCMs. Disk substrates are typically aluminum, glass or plastic.

substring

A subset of an alphanumeric field or variable. The substring function in a programming language is used to extract the subset; for example, the programming expression **substr(prodcode,4,3)** extracts characters 4, 5 and 6 out of a product code field or variable.

subsystem

A unit or device that is part of a larger system. For example, a disk subsystem is a part of the computer system. The bus is a part of the computer. A subsystem usually refers to hardware, but it may be used to describe software, although module, subroutine and component are more typically used for software elements.

subtract

In relational database, an operation that generates a third file from all the records in one file that are not in a second file.

subwoofer

A speaker that reproduces the lower end of the audio spectrum. A subwoofer system may include a crossover circuit which switches frequencies approximately 100Hz and under to the subwoofer, while passing the rest of the signal to the main speakers.

suite of applications

See *application suite*.

SuiteSpot

A suite of programs used for building an Internet or intranet Web site from Netscape. It is based on Netscape's Enterprise Server Web server and runs on Windows NT and various UNIX machines. SuiteSpot includes Proxy Server, Catalog Server (index and search), Calendar Server (scheduling), Mail Server (e-mail), News Server (discussions and newsgroups), Media Server (slide presentations with audio), Directory Server (LDAP directory) and Certificate Server (certificate authority).

Mail Server and News Server are called Messaging Server and Collabra Server as of Version 3.0. See *Communicator*.

Sun

(Sun Microsystems, Inc., Mountain View, CA, www.sun.com) A major manufacturer of UNIX-based workstations and servers. In 1981, Bavarian-born Andreas Bechtolsheim was licensing rights to a computer he designed. Named Sun for Stanford University Network and using off-the-shelf parts, it was an affordable workstation for engineers and scientists. In that year, he met Vinod Khosla, a native of India, who convinced him to form a company and expand. Khosla, Bechtolsheim and Scott McNeally, all Stanford MBAs, founded Sun in 1982.

Its first computers, the Sun-1 and subsequent Sun-2 were instant successes in the university market. Sun began to compete against its rival Apollo Computer, an east-coast workstation company, eventually surpassing it in sales (Apollo was later purchased by HP).

Sun has been a major force in open systems. Its computers have always run under UNIX, which was licensed from AT&T and then later purchased outright. Sun and AT&T had formed such a tight alliance for a while that a host of UNIX vendors formed the Open Software Foundation (OSF) in 1988 to keep Sun from dominating UNIX.

In 1984, Bill Joy, head of R&D, designed NFS, which was broadly licensed and became the industry standard for file sharing. Sun later packaged its UNIX components into a complete environment named Solaris, which it later ported to other platforms, including the Intel x86.

Sun used the Motorola 680x0 CPUs in its products until it designed its own RISC-based SPARC chips, which it launched with the SPARCstation 1 in 1989. SPARC technology is also licensed to third parties. The latest version of this architecture is the UltraSPARC, which began shipping in 1995.

Sun is made up of several independent companies spun off as subsidiaries in 1991. For example, Sun Microsystems Computer Company (SMCC) makes hardware, SunSoft, Inc. develops software and Sun Microelectronics makes the SPARC chips.

In 1994, Sun introduced the Java programming language and ushered in a new era for application development on the Internet. Sun is one of the major proponents behind network computers, which are leaner client workstations that download all their software from the server. In 1996, it introduced its first network computer for Java applications, appropriately named the JavaStation. Java CPU chips that execute the Java language directly are also in the works. See *Java* and *network computer*.

The Founders
From left to right: Vinod Khosla, Bill Joy, Andreas Bechtolsheim and Scott McNealy. Although Joy was not a founder, he was hired shortly thereafter and became one of Sun's major contributors. *(Photo courtesy of Sun Microsystems, Inc.)*

The First SPARCstation
In 1989, Sun introduced the SPARCstation 1, the first Sun computer that used the SPARC chip. *(Photo courtesy of Sun Microsystems, Inc.)*

SunOS

Sun's UNIX operating system. SunOS was renamed Solaris. See *Solaris*.

SunSoft

See *Sun*.

Super Audio CD

See *DVD-Audio*.

Superbase

A relational database management (DBMS) and client/server application development system for Windows from Superbase Developers, Inc., Huntington, NY, (www.superbase.com). It includes a database that supports a variety of multimedia types, an object-based Super Basic Language similar to Visual Basic and a suite of visual programming tools. It supports the major SQL databases as well as ODBC-compliant databases.

Superbase has been widely used worldwide. It was originally created in 1984 by Precision Software for the Commodore Amiga and Atari ST. In 1989, it was the first DBMS to run on a Windows computer.

SuperCalc

One of the first spreadsheets which followed in the footsteps of VisiCalc in the early 1980s. It was Computer Associates' first personal computer product.

superclass

In object technology, a high-level class that passes attributes and methods (data and processing) down the hierarchy to subclasses, the classes below it. Abstract superclasses are used as master structures and no objects are created for it. Concrete superclasses are used to create objects.

supercomputer

The fastest computer available. It is typically used for simulations in petroleum exploration and production, structural analysis, computational fluid dynamics, physics and chemistry, electronic design, nuclear energy research and meteorology. It is also used for realtime animated graphics.

superconductor

A material that has little resistance to the flow of electricity. Traditional superconductors operate at -459 Fahrenheit (absolute zero).

Thus far, the major use for superconductors, made of alloys of niobium, is for high-powered magnets in medical imaging machines that use magnetic fields instead of x-rays.

Using experimental materials, such as copper oxides, barium, lanthanum and yttrium, IBM's Zurich research lab in 1986 and the University of Houston in 1987 raised the temperature of superconductivity to -59 degrees Fahrenheit. If superconductors can work at reasonable temperatures, they will have a dramatic impact on the future of computing. See *Josephson junction*.

SuperDisk

A floppy disk drive from Imation Corporation, Oakdale, MN, (www.imation.com), that uses the LS-120 technology. SuperDisks hold 120MB, and SuperDisk drives also read and write standard 1.44MB floppies. See *LS-120* and *latest disk drives*.

SuperDrive

The floppy disk drive used in the Macintosh. It stores 1.44MB of data in its high-density format. It also reads and writes earlier Mac 400 and 800KB disks, as well as Apple II ProDOS, DOS and OS/2 formats. See *SuperDisk*.

super floppy

(1) The "next" high-capacity floppy disk. The Zip and LS-120 disks are likely candidates. In the early 1990s, the Floptical was the super floppy drive for a while, but it did not catch on.

(2) An earlier 3.5" floppy disk introduced by IBM that held 2.88MB. The drives were compatible with standard floppies, but it was not widely used.

superframe

A T1 transmission format made up of 12 T1 frames (superframe) and 24 frames (extended superframe). See *D4*.

SuperKey

An earlier PC keyboard macro processor from Borland that lets users create keyboard macros, rearrange the keyboard and encrypt data and programs.

supermini

A large-scale minicomputer. Note: Supermini is not the same as mini-supercomputer.

SuperNOS

An advanced network operating system. Novell popularized this term for a future product intended to combine NetWare and UnixWare. However, in late 1995, Novell sold UnixWare to The Santa Cruz Operation (SCO), thus abandoning the SuperNOS project.

superscalar

A CPU architecture that allows more than one instruction to be executed in one clock cycle.

superscript

Any letter, digit or symbol that appears above the line; for example, 10^3. Contrast with *subscript*.

superserver

A high-speed network server with very large RAM and disk capacity. Superservers typically support multiprocessing.

superset

A group of commands or functions that exceed the capabilities of the original specification. Software or hardware components designed for the original specification will also operate with the superset product. However, components designed for the superset will not work with the original. Contrast with *subset*.

supertwist

An LCD technology that twists liquid molecules greater than 90 degrees in order to improve contrast and viewing angle. See *LCD*.

superuser

A person with unlimited access privileges who can perform any and all operations on the computer. See *root*.

Super VGA

See *VGA* and *PC display modes*.

supervisor

Same as *operating system*.

supervisor call

The instruction in an application program that switches the computer to supervisor state.

supervisor control program

The part of the operation system that always resides in memory. Same as *kernel*.

supervisor mode

See *supervisor state* and *privileged mode*.

supervisor state

Typically associated with mainframes, it is a hardware mode in which the operating system executes instructions unavailable to an application program; for example, I/O instructions. Contrast with *program state*.

support

(1) The assistance provided by a hardware or software vendor in installing and maintaining its product.

(2) Software or hardware designed to include or work with some other software or hardware product. For example, if computer "supports multiprocessing," it can host more than one CPU internally. If a development system "supports Windows," it is used to create applications for Windows. If a system "supports the major databases," it provides interfaces to those databases.

SUPRA

A relational DBMS from Cincom Systems, Inc., Cincinnati, OH, (www.cincom.com), that runs on IBM mainframes and VAXs. It includes a query language and a program that automates the database design process.

surface

In CAD, the external geometry of an object. Surfaces are generally required for NC (numerical control) modeling rather than wireframe or solids.

surface modeling

A mathematical technique for representing solid-appearing objects. Surface modeling is a more complex method for representing objects than wireframe modeling, but not as sophisticated as solid modeling. Surface modeling is widely used in CAD (computer-aided design) for illustrations and architectural renderings. It is also used in 3-D animation for games and other presentations.

Although surface and solid models appear the same on screen, they are quite different. Surface models cannot be sliced open as can solid models. In addition, in surface modeling, the object can be geometrically incorrect; whereas, in solid modeling, it must be correct. See *tessellation*.

surface mount

A circuit board packaging technique in which the leads (pins) on the chips and components are soldered on top of the board, not through it. Boards can be smaller and built faster. SMT stands for surface mount technology, and an SMD is a surface mount device. Contrast with *socket mount* and *thru-hole*.

surface normal

In 3-D graphics, an imaginary line that is perpendicular to the surface of a polygon. It may be computed at the vertex of a triangle, in which case it is the average of all the vertices of adjoining triangles. Or, it may be computed for each pixel in the triangle as in Phong shading. Surface normals are used to derive the reflectivity of a light source shining onto an object. See *tessellation, triangle, Phong shading* and *Gouraud shading*.

surfing

Scanning online material, such as databases, news clips and forums. The term originated from "channel surfing," the rapid changing of TV channels to find something of interest.

surf the Net

To browse the Internet. The most common Internet browsing today is done on the World Wide Web. See *surfing* and *how to access the Internet*.

surge

See *power surge*.

surge protector

A device that employs some method of surge suppression to protect electronic equipment from excessive voltage (spikes and power surges) in the power line. The most common method uses a metal oxide varistor (MOV) component to shunt the surge to the neutral and ground lines. Another method is series mode, which actually absorbs the energy. Surge protectors may use both methods. See *surge suppression, voltage regulator* and *UPS*.

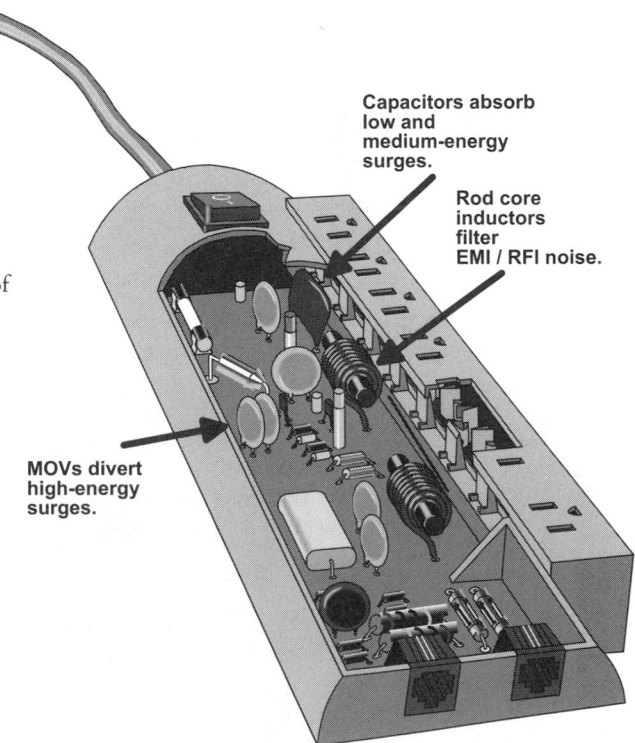

Capacitors absorb low and medium-energy surges.

Rod core inductors filter EMI / RFI noise.

MOVs divert high-energy surges.

Inside a Surge Protector

The SurgeArrest Net7T from American Power shows the internal components used to filter line noise and divert the surges. Note that the capacitors absorb some of the energy, while the MOVs divert the high energy. *(Image courtesy of American Power Conversion Corporation.)*

surge suppression

The diversion of power surges from the incoming hot line to the neutral and/or ground lines. The most common method uses metal oxide varistors (MOVs). See *surge protector*.

surge suppressor

Same as *surge protector*.

SUS

See *Single UNIX Specification*.

suspend and resume

To stop an operation and restart where you left off. In portable computers, the hard disk is turned off, and the CPU is made to idle at its slowest speed. All open applications are retained in memory.

SV

(Scientific Visualization) See *visualization*.

SVC

(Switched Virtual Circuit) A network connection that is established at the time the transmission is required. SVCs are normally implemented in connection-oriented systems such as the analog telephone network and ATM networks. Contrast with *PVC*.

SVD

(Simultaneous Voice and Data) The concurrent transmission of voice and data by modem over a single analog telephone line. The first SVD technologies on the market are MultiTech's MSP, Radish's VoiceView, AT&T's VoiceSpan and the all-digital DSVD, endorsed by Intel, Hayes and others.

SVGA

(Super VGA) Enhancements to the VGA standard that increased resolution to 800x600 and beyond (see *VGA*). The term may be used to refer to 800x600 resolution in general; for example:

```
VGA     640x480
SVGA    800x600
XGA     1024x768
```

S-VHS

(Super-VHS) A video recording and playback system that uses a higher-quality VHS cassette and the S-video technology. VCRs that support S-VHS can also record and play back normal VHS tapes.

SVID

(System V Interface Definition) An AT&T specification for the UNIX System V operating system. SVID Release 3 specifies the interface for UNIX System V Release 4.

S-video

(Super-video) A video technology, also called *Y/C video*, that records and maintains luminance (Y) and color information (C) separately. S-VHS and Hi-8 cameras and VCRs use this method, which provide a better color image than standard VHS and 8mm formats. S-video hookups use a special 5-pin connector rather than the common RCA phono plug.

SVR4

See *System V Release 4.0*.

SVR5

See *SCO UnixWare 7*.

s/w

See *software*.

SwapCrypt

An encryption system from SCM Microsystems Inc., Los Gatos, CA, (www.scmmicro.com), that uses a random number to generate an encryption key. The key is stored on a smart card inserted into a PC

Card slot. The smart card is then required to encrypt and decrypt. The key is also stored on the installation floppy for backup. If laptop data is SwapCrypt'ed, and the machine is stolen, the data cannot be viewed without the smart card. The 128-bit key is theoretically unbreakable, because it is used in conjunction with 160K bits of random data, all of which are stored on the smart card.

swap file
A disk file used to temporarily save a program or part of a program running in memory. See *Windows swap file*.

swapping
Replacing one segment of a program in memory with another and restoring it back to the original when required. In virtual memory systems, it is called paging.

sweet spot
Refers to almost anything that embodies an optimum combination of characteristics and qualities. As a result, it is most efficient, useful or popular, or even the most lucrative product in the line to sell. See also *SuiteSpot*.

switch
(1) A mechanical or electronic device that directs the flow of electrical or optical signals from one side to the other. Switches with more than two ports, such as a LAN switch or PBX, are able to route traffic. See *LAN switch, PBX, data switch* and *transistor*.

With regard to a simple on/off switch, remember...

```
Open is "off."  Closed is "on."
```

(2) In programming, a bit or byte used to keep track of something. Sometimes refers to a branch in a program.

(3) A modifier of a command. See *DOS switch*.

Switched 56
A dial-up digital service provided by local and long distance telephone companies. There is a monthly fee and per-minute charge like the analog voice network. For connection, a DSU/CSU is used instead of a modem. Switched 56 uses a 64 Kbps channel, but one bit per byte is used for in band signaling, leaving 56 Kbps for data.

switched broadband network
A communications network that provides connectivity across a large area at high speed.

switched digital service
See *Switched 56*.

switched Ethernet
An Ethernet network that runs through a high-speed switch. Changing to switched Ethernet means replacing the Ethernet hub with a switch. Instead of sharing 10 Mbps for Ethernet or 100 Mbps for Fast Ethernet among all users on the network segment, the full bandwidth is made available to each sender and receiver pair.

If the switch and network adapters (NICs) provide full-duplex operation, the total bandwidth is 20 Mbps or 200 Mbps between nodes. A major advantage in migrating to switched Ethernet is that the existing NICs are still used. See illustration on next page.

Mechanical switch (manually close)

Source → Output

Semiconductor switch (electronically close)

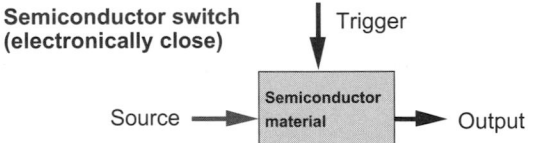

Trigger

Source → Semiconductor material → Output

Mechanical and Semiconductor Switches
The semiconductor switch (transistor) performs the same function as an on/off light switch on the wall. Instead of being manually closed, the switch is electronically closed by pulsing the semiconductor material, which makes it conduct.

switched line

In communications, a link that is established in a switched network, such as the international dial-up telephone system, a Switched 56 digital line or ISDN.

switched multimegabit data service

See *SMDS*.

switched network

(1) The international dial-up telephone system.

(2) A network in which a temporary connection is established from one point to another for either the duration of the session (circuit switching) or for the transmission of one or more packets of data (packet switching).

switched SCSI

See *SCSI switch*.

switch fabric

(1) The internal interconnect architecture used by a switching device, which redirects the data coming in on one of its ports out to another of its ports.

(2) The combination of interconnected switches used throughout a campus or large geographic area, which collectively provide a routing infrastructure.

switching hub

A device that acts as a central switch or PBX, connecting one line to another. In a local area network (LAN), a switching hub gives any two stations on the network the full bandwidth of the line. Contrast with *shared media LAN*, in which all stations share the bandwidth of a common transmission path. See *hub*.

switch router

See *layer 3 switch*.

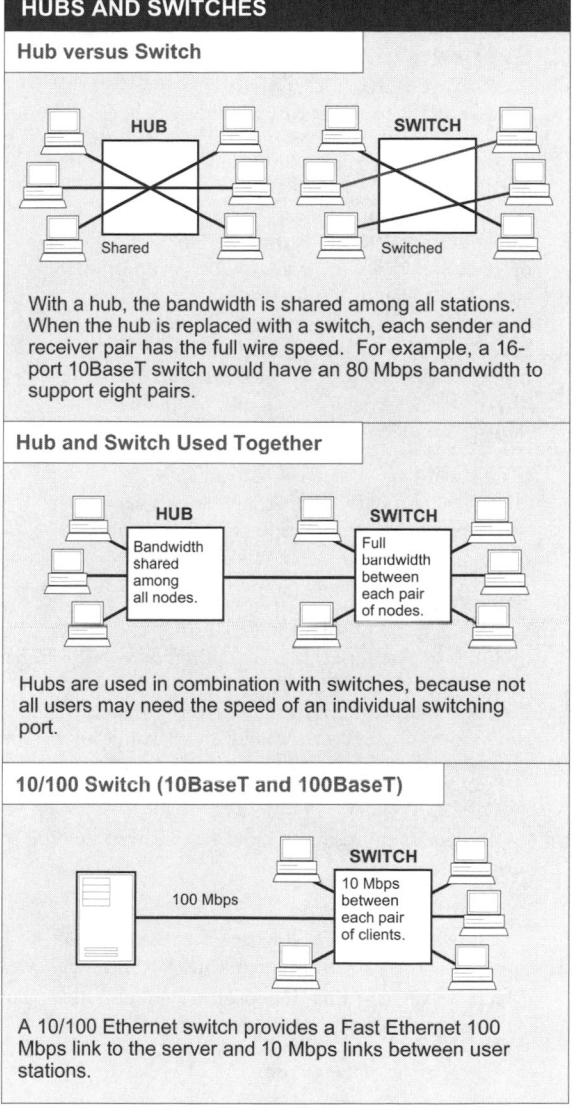

HUBS AND SWITCHES

Hub versus Switch

With a hub, the bandwidth is shared among all stations. When the hub is replaced with a switch, each sender and receiver pair has the full wire speed. For example, a 16-port 10BaseT switch would have an 80 Mbps bandwidth to support eight pairs.

Hub and Switch Used Together

Hubs are used in combination with switches, because not all users may need the speed of an individual switching port.

10/100 Switch (10BaseT and 100BaseT)

A 10/100 Ethernet switch provides a Fast Ethernet 100 Mbps link to the server and 10 Mbps links between user stations.

switch-to-computer

To integrate voice telephone and database access. For example, in customer service applications, using telephone services, such as automatic number identification (ANI) and automatic call distribution (ACD), an incoming call can retrieve and route the customer's file to the next available human agent.

Sybase

(Sybase Inc., Emeryville, CA, www.sybase.com) A software company founded in 1984 that specializes in client/server development products. It was originally known for its SQL Server relational DBMS, but expanded its line in 1995 when it acquired Powersoft, makers of the PowerBuilder application development software. Sybase offers a variety of application development tools, compilers, middleware, database and data warehousing products.

Sybase System

A family of SQL development tools from Sybase that includes SQL Server, SQL Toolset (design, development and control) and Client/Services Interfaces (distributed database architecture). See *SQL Server*.

Sybperl

(**SYB**ase **PERL**) A set of extensions to Perl that provide access to the Sybase database. Sybperl adds the Sybase database APIs to Perl.

SyJet disk

A 1.5GB removable hard drive from SyQuest. Introduced in 1966, it is the successor to SyQuest's original 3.5" disks and comes in parallel port, SCSI and EIDE versions. SyJet media are not compatible with earlier SyQuest drives or the SparQ drives, which are geared for home use. See *SparQ disk, Quest disk, SyQuest disk* and *latest disk drives*. For a summary of all disk technologies, see *storage device*.

SYLK file

(**SY**mbolic **L**in**K** file) A spreadsheet file format originating with Multiplan that is used by a number of spreadsheet programs.

SyJet Cartridge
SyJet disks supersede SyQuest's original 5.25" and 3.5" line, but are not compatible with it.

Symantec

(Symantec Corporation, Cupertino, CA, www.symantec.com) A software company founded in 1982 by Dr. Gary Hendrix. It was acquired by Gordon Eubanks in 1984 and released its Q&A file manager the following year. In 1990, it merged with Peter Norton Computing, Inc., developer of the well-known Norton Utilities and Norton Desktop programs. Since then, it has acquired more than a dozen other software companies, including Central Point Software, maker of PC Tools, and Zortech, developer of of C++ compilers.

symbol

In data compression, a unit of data (byte, floating point number, spoken word, etc.) that is treated independently.

symbolic language

(1) A programming language that uses symbols, or mnemonics, for expressing operations and operands. All modern programming languages are symbolic languages.

(2) A language that manipulates symbols rather than numbers. See *list processing*.

symbol set

Same as *character set*.

symmetric compression

A data compression technique that takes about the same amount of time to compress as it does to decompress. Contrast with *asymmetric compression*.

symmetric DSL

See *ADSL*.

symmetric encryption

Same as *secret key cryptography*.

symmetric multiprocessing

See *SMP*.

Symphony

One of the first integrated software packages for the PC. Developed by Lotus, it included word processing, database, speadsheet, business graphics, communications and a macro language.

sync character

In synchronous communications systems, a special character transmitted to synchronize timing.

sync generator

A device that supplies synchronization signals to a series of cameras to keep them all in phase.

synchronous

Refers to events that are synchronized, or coordinated, in time. For example, the interval between transmitting A and B is the same as between B and C, and completing the current operation before the next one is started are considered synchronous operations. Contrast with *asynchronous*.

synchronous protocol

A communications protocol that controls a synchronous transmission, such as bisync, SDLC and HDLC. Contrast with *asynchronous protocol*.

synchronous transmission

The transmission of data in which both stations are synchronized. Codes are sent from the transmitting station to the receiving station to establish the synchronization, and data is then transmitted in continuous streams.

Modems that transmit at 1200 bps and higher often convert the asynchronous signals from a computer's serial port into synchronous transmission over the transmission line. Contrast with *asynchronous transmission*.

SYN flood attack

An assault on a network that prevents a TCP/IP server from servicing other users. It is accomplished by not sending the final acknowledgment to the server's SYN-ACK response (SYNchronize-ACKnowledge) in the handshaking sequence, which causes the server to keep signalling until it eventually times out. The source address from the client is, of course, counterfeit. SYN flood attacks can either overload the server or cause it to crash. See *denial of service attack*.

Synon/2E

An integrated development environment for AS/400s from Synon, Inc., Larkspur, CA, (www.synon.com). Synon/2E was introduced in the same year as the AS/400 (1988) and is the leading tools product in this market. It provides an upper and lower CASE environment that generates COBOL and RPG code. Synon was founded in England in 1983 by Simon Williams. The name came from and is pronounced "sign on."

Synon's Obsydian is an object-oriented PC-based environment that is used to develop C++ code for Windows clients and RPG code for AS/400 servers.

syntax

The rules governing the structure of a language statement. It specifies how words and symbols are put together to form a phrase.

syntax error

An error that occurs when a program cannot understand the command that has been entered. See *parse*.

synthesis

A combination, derivation or compilation. See *logic synthesis*.

synthesize

To create a whole or complete unit from parts or components. See *synthesis*.

synthesizer

A device that generates sound by creating waveforms electronically (FM synthesis) or from stored samples of musical instruments (wave table synthesis). See *MIDI* and *speech synthesis*.

SyQuest

(SyQuest Technology, Inc., Fremont, CA, www.syquest.com) A manufacturer of removable disk drives, founded in 1982 by Syed Iftikar (Sy's Quest). It originally made 3.9" drives for the military and introduced its first 5.25" drive in 1986, essentially pioneering the removable, hard disk industry for personal computers. Its disks became de facto standards for high-capacity interchange in the graphics arts and printing industries with more than a million units sold by 1994. Since 1995, SyQuest introduced several next-generation products that supersede the original formats. See *SyQuest disk, EZFlyer disk, SyJet disk, SparQ disk* and *Quest disk*.

SyQuest disk

A removable hard drive from SyQuest. Using the SCSI interface, SyQuest's 5.25" drives support 44, 88 and 200MB cartridges. SyQuest's 3.5" drives support 105 and 270MB cartridges. SyQuest disks became de facto standards for transportable interchange of personal computer data. Since 1995, SyQuest introduced several new 3.5" drives that supersede and are not compatible with the original formats. See *EZFlyer disk, SyJet disk, SparQ disk* and *Quest disk*. For a summary of all storage technologies, see *storage*.

SYSCON

(**SYS**tem **CON**figuration) A comprehensive NetWare utility that is used to configure trustee, login and accounting information on NetWare servers.

sysgen

(**SYS**tem **GEN**eration) The installation of a new or revised operating system. It includes selecting the appropriate utility programs and identifying the peripheral devices and storage capacities of the system the operating system will be controlling.

SYSmark

See *BAPCo*.

sysop

(**SYS**tem **OP**erator) Pronounced "siss-op." A person who runs an online communications system or bulletin board. The sysop may also act as mediator for system conferences.

Sysplex

See *Parallel Sysplex*.

SysReq key

(**SYS**tem **REQ**uest key) A keyboard key on a terminal keyboard that is used to get the attention of the central computer. The key exists on PC keyboards, but is rarely used by applications.

system

(1) A group of related components that interact to perform a task.

(2) A *computer system* is made up of the CPU, operating system and peripheral devices.

(3) An *information system* is made up of the database, all the data entry, update, query and report programs and manual and machine procedures.

(4) "The system" often refers to the operating system.

System/3

A batch-oriented minicomputer from IBM. Introduced in 1969, it introduced a new punched card about half the size of previous ones. With the addition of the Communications Control Program (CCP), it could handle interactive terminals.

5.25"

3.5"

SyQuest Cartridges
SyQuest hard disks were the first de facto standard removable hard disks for personal computers. They have been superseded by the SyJet, SparQ and Quest lines.

System/3x

Refers to IBM System/34, System/36 and System/38 midrange computers.

System 7

(1) A major upgrade of the Macintosh operating system introduced in 1991. It included virtual memory, increased memory addressing, hot links (Publish & Subscribe), multitasking (MultiFinder was no longer optional), TrueType fonts and a variety of user interface enhancements.

System 7 Pro added PowerTalk communications, the AppleScript language and QuickTime for sound, movies and animation. System 7.5 advanced the online help with AppleGuide and more sophisticated graphics with QuickDraw GX.

(2) (System/7) A sensor-based minicomputer from IBM introduced in 1970 and used for process control. It was superseded by the Series/1.

System 8

The latest version of the Macintosh operating system introduced in 1997. Designed to take more advantage of the PowerPC chip, it includes an enhanced 3-D look and provides assistance for connecting to the Internet.

System/32

A batch-oriented minicomputer from IBM. Introduced in 1975, it provided a single terminal for operator use. It was superseded by the System/34, which could run System/32 applications in a special mode.

System/34

A multiuser, multitasking minicomputer from IBM, introduced in 1977. The typical system had from a handful to a dozen terminals and could run System/32 programs in a special mode. Most large System/34 users migrated to the System/38, while small users migrated to the System/36.

System/36
This is a small model of the System/36 family. Many applications written for the System/36 have been ported to the AS/400. *(Photo courtesy of IBM Corporation.)*

System/36

A multiuser, multitasking minicomputer from IBM that was introduced in 1983. It superseded the System/34 and is mostly compatible with it. System/34 programs run in the System/36 after recompilation. The typical system supports from a handful to a couple of dozen terminals.

Although superseded by the AS/400, System/36 applications have to be recompiled to run on it. As a result, a large number of System/36s still remain in use. With the announcement of the AS/400 Advanced System/36, which runs System/36 applications natively, it is expected that System/36s will finally begin to fade into history.

System/38

A minicomputer from IBM that includes an operating system with an integrated relational database management system. Introduced in 1978, it was an advanced departure from previous System/3x computers. The typical system handles from a dozen to several dozen terminals. It has been superseded by the AS/400.

System/38
The System/38 was an advanced system for its time, incorporating a relational database management system as part of its core software. Most System/38 applications are now running on AS/400s. *(Photo courtesy of IBM Corporation.)*

System/88

A family of fault-tolerant midrange computers from IBM used for online transaction processing. It uses the System/88 virtual memory and System/88 FTX (Fault Tolerant UNIX) operating systems.

System/360

IBM's first family of computer systems introduced in 1964. It was the first time in history that a complete line of computers was announced at one time. Although considerable enhancements have been made, much of the 360 architecture is still carried over in current-day IBM mainframes. Since its inception, trillions of dollars worth of information systems have been developed for this platform.

The 360, which took four years to develop and cost $5 billion ($24 billion today) was an enormous and risky undertaking. Thomas Watson, Jr. literally "bet his company" on the project. The 360 has been ranked as one of the major business accomplishments in American history alongside of Ford's Model T and Boeing's 707. See *IBM mainframes*.

System/360

On April 7, 1964, the press release for this picture read: "This high-powered System/360 configuration, shown as it will appear in an installation, includes a 2250 display unit, left center. The visual display enables operators to see information that is stored on disk drives, foreground, in core storage, left, or on the drums and tapes in the background." *(Photo courtesy of IBM Corporation.)*

System/370

The mainframe product line introduced in 1970 by IBM (superseding System/360), which added virtual memory and other enhancements. Subsequent series include the 303x, 43xx, 308x, 309x and 9370, all 370-architecture machines. The 370 architecture was brought down to the PC level in 1983 with the PC XT/370, and then again in 1989 with the VM/SP Technical Workstation. See *IBM mainframes*.

System/390

The mainframe product line introduced in 1990 by IBM (superseding System/370) that features ESA/390 architecture and operating systems, ES/9000 hardware (18 models introduced), ESCON fiber optic channels, Sysplex multiprocessing and SystemView.

In 1994, IBM introduced its next generation of System/390 systems known today as Parallel Enterprise Servers or S/390s. These are SMP machines that contain single-chip CMOS CPUs and use less power and dissipate less heat than the bipolar-based ES/9000 models. In 1995, IBM introduced new models that provide up to 10-way SMP within the same machine. Up to 32 10-way systems can be hooked together providing a multiprocessing system with up to 320 CPUs.

As processing requirements increase, customers are migrating from the ES/9000s to clusters of the CMOS-based machines. See *Parallel/Sysplex*.

System 2000

A hierarchical, network and relational DBMS that runs on IBM, CDC and Unisys computers from the SAS Institute, Cary, NC, (www.sas.com). It has been integrated into the SAS System.

system administrator

A person who manages a multiuser computer system. Responsibilities are similar to that of a network administrator. A system administrator would perform systems programmer activities with regard to the operating system and other network control programs. See *salary survey*.

Systemantics

An insightful book on human nature and the systems we build by John Gall (1977). The following is copied with permission from Random House.

A Concise Summary of the Field of General Systematics

Systems are seductive. They promise to do a hard job faster, better, and more easily than you could do it by yourself. But if you set up a system, you are likely to find your time and effort now being consumed in the care and feeding of the system itself. New problems are created by its very presence. Once set up, it won't go away, it grows and encroaches. It begins to do strange and wonderful things. Breaks down in ways you never thought possible. It kicks back, gets in the way, and opposes its own proper function. Your own perspective becomes distorted by being in the system. You become anxious and push on it to make it work. Eventually you come to believe that the misbegotten product it so grudgingly delivers is what you really wanted all the time. At that point encroachment has become complete... **you have become absorbed... you are now a systems person!**

system board

The BIOS on a PC motherboard. Contrast with BIOSs on the peripheral cards. See *BIOS*.

system bus

The primary pathway between the CPU, memory and high-speed peripherals. Same as *local bus*.

system design

See *systems analysis & design* and *information system*.

system development cycle

The sequence of events in the development of an information system (application), which requires mutual effort on the part of user and technical staff.

```
1. SYSTEMS ANALYSIS & DESIGN
   feasibility study
   general design
   prototyping
   detail design
   functional specifications

2. USER SIGN OFF

3. PROGRAMMING
   design
   coding
   testing

4. IMPLEMENTATION
   training
   conversion
   installation

5. USER ACCEPTANCE
```

system development methodology

The formal documentation for the phases of the system development cycle. It defines the precise objectives for each phase and the results required from a phase before the next one can begin. It may include specialized forms for preparing the documentation describing each phase.

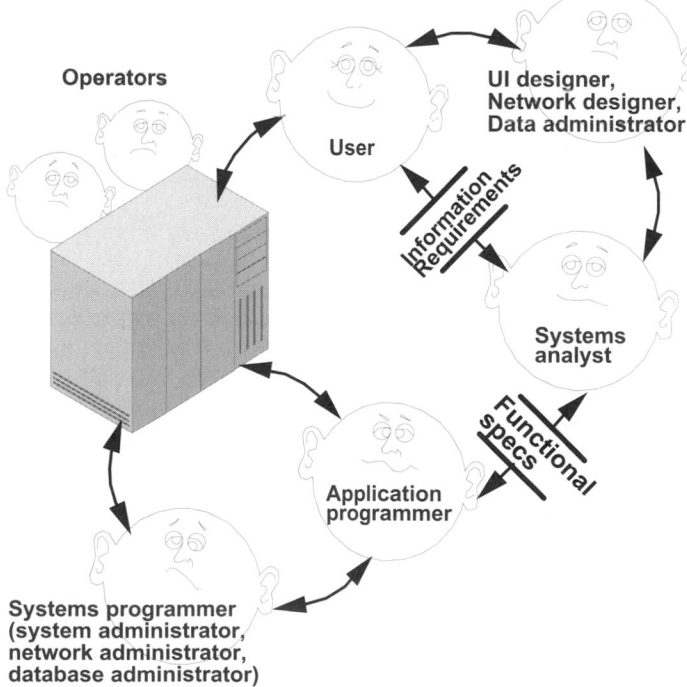

The System Development Cycle
From information requirements to final implementation, the system development cycle is an on-going process. As the business changes, information requirements change, and the cycle continues.

system disk
A disk that contains part or all of the operating system. See *bootable disk*.

system failure
A hardware or operating system malfunction.

system file
An executable file (in machine language) that is part of the operating system or other control program. The term may also refer to a configuration file used by such programs.

system folder
The operating system folder in the Macintosh that contains the System, Finder and MultiFinder, printer drivers, fonts, desk accessories, INITs and cdevs.

system font
The primary font used by the operating system or other control program to display messages and menus unless otherwise directed.

System Halted
A DOS error message that means the computer could not continue due to a hardware or software problem. It can occur if a memory parity error is detected or if a peripheral board goes awry. A program bug can also cause this as well as a virus. Testing memory, testing for viruses and removing peripheral boards one at a time are ways to isolate the problem.

system image
A display of the current contents of memory, which includes the operating system and running programs. For effective management, a cluster of computer systems may be organized as a single system image, in which all systems appear as one. See *virtual server*.

SYSTEM.INI
(SYStem INItialization) A Windows configuration file that describes the current state of the computer system environment. It contains hundreds of entries and is read by Windows on startup. It identifies such things as the drivers in the system, how DOS applications are handled and provides immense detail about internal Windows settings.

The information in SYSTEM.INI is updated by Windows when you change various defaults; however, in order to tweak system performance, the file can be edited with a text editor or a word processor that imports ASCII files.

Most of the time, users do not deal with SYSTEM.INI; however, on occasion, a line in the 386 Enhanced section ([386Enh]) may have to be modified. Sometimes an **EMMExclude=** statement is added or changed to exclude a section of upper memory used by a new peripheral from the general pool of memory that Windows uses. WIN.INI is another major configuration file read by Windows at startup.

Although SYSTEM.INI was created in Windows 3.x, it is still used in Windows 95/98 and NT, although primarily for compatibility with Windows 3.x applications. See *WIN.INI*.

system level
An operation that is performed by the operating system or some other control program.

system life cycle
The useful life of an information system. Its length depends on the nature and volatility of the business, as well as the software development tools used to generate the databases and applications. Eventually, an information system that is patched over and over no longer is structurally sound enough to be expanded.

Tools like DBMSs allow for changes more readily, but increased transaction volumes can negate the effectiveness of the original software later on.

system memory
The memory used by the operating system.

system policy
System-wide rules and regulations that override user settings (user profiles). System policies can be assigned to individual users or to workgroups. See *user profile* and *desktop lockdown*.

system program

A component of system software.

system programmer

See *systems programmer*.

system prompt

An on-screen symbol that indicates the operating system is ready for a command. See *DOS prompt*.

system resources

(1) In a computer system, system resources are the components that provide its inherent capabilities and contribute to its overall performance. System memory, cache memory, hard disk space, IRQs and DMA channels are examples.

(2) In an operating system, system resources are internal tables and pointers set up to keep track of running applications. They may be limited by hardware resources, but are often as not arbitrary limitations within the software itself. See *Windows memory limitations*.

systems

A general term for the department, people or work involved in systems analysis & design activities.

systems administrator

See *system administrator*.

systems analysis & design

The examination of a problem and the creation of its solution. Systems analysis is effective when all sides of the problem are reviewed. Systems design is most effective when more than one solution can be proposed. The plans for the care and feeding of a new system are as important as the problems they solve. See *system development cycle, information system* and *Systemantics*.

systems analyst

The person responsible for the development of an information system. They design and modify systems by turning user requirements into a set of functional specifications, which are the blueprint of the system. They design the database or help design it if data administrators are available. They develop the manual and machine procedures and the detailed processing specs for each data entry, update, query and report program in the system.

Systems analysts are the architects, as well as the project leaders, of an information system. It is their job to develop solutions to user's problems, determine the technical and operational feasibility of their solutions, as well as estimate the costs to develop and implement them.

They develop prototypes of the system along with the users, so that the final specifications are examples of screens and reports that have been carefully reviewed. Experienced analysts leave no doubt in users' minds as to what is being developed, and they insist that all responsible users review and sign off on every detail.

Systems analysts require a balanced mix of business and technical knowledge, interviewing and analytical skills, as well as a good understanding of human behavior. See *salary survey* and *Systemantics*.

systems disk

A disk pack or disk drive reserved only for system software, which includes the operating system, assemblers, compilers and other utility and control programs.

systems engineer

Often a vendor title for persons involved in consulting and pre-sales activities related to computers. See *systems analyst, systems programmer, programmer analyst, application programmer* and *salary survey*.

systems house

An organization that develops custom software and/or turnkey systems for customers. Contrast with *software house*, which develops software packages for sale to the general public. Both terms are used synonymously.

systems integration

Making diverse components work together. See *NASI*.

systems integrator

An individual or organization that builds systems from a variety of diverse components. With increasing complexity of technology, more customers want complete solutions to information problems, requiring hardware, software and networking expertise in a multivendor environment. See *OEM, VAR* and *NASI*.

systems management

(1) The management of systems development, which includes systems analysis & design, application development and implementation. See *system development cycle*.

(2) Software that manages computer systems in an enterprise, which may include any and all of the following functions: software distribution, version control, backup & recovery, printer spooling, job scheduling, virus protection and performance and capacity planning. Depending on organizational philosophy, systems management may include network management or be a part of it. See *network management* and *configuration management*.

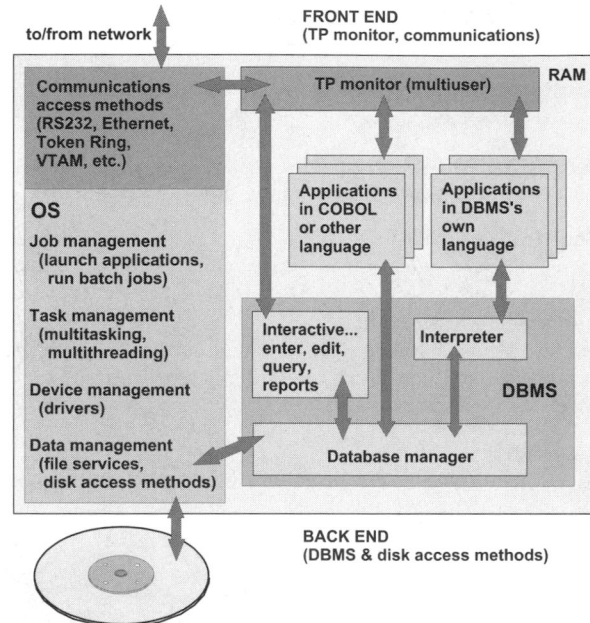

System Software and Application Interaction
This diagram shows the interaction between the system software and application software running in memory.

system software

Programs used to control the computer and develop and run application programs. It includes operating systems, TP monitors, network operating systems and database managers. Contrast with *application program*.

The following diagram shows the flow between system software and application software residing in memory in a multiuser computer. The operating system (OS), TP monitor, database manager and interpreter are considered system software. The applications and interactive DBMS query and edit would be considered application software.

systems person

An umbrella term for an individual that performs systems analysis and consulting in the computer field. See *systems representative, systems analyst, systems engineer* and *software engineer*.

systems program

See *system program* and *system software*.

systems programmer

(1) In the IS department of a large organization, a technical expert on some or all of the computer's system software (operating systems, networks, DBMSs, etc.). They are responsible for the efficient performance of the computer systems.

They usually don't write programs, but perform a lot of technical tasks that integrate vendors' software. They also act as technical advisors to systems analysts, application programmers and operations personnel. For example, they would know whether additional tasks could be added to the computer and would recommend conversion to a new operating or database system in order to optimize performance.

In mainframe environments, there is one systems programmer for about 10 or more application programmers, and systems programmers generally have considerably higher salaries than application programmers. In smaller environments, users rely on vendors or consultants for systems programming assistance. In fact, end users are actually performing systems programmer functions when they install new software or hardware on their own personal computers. See *system administrator* and *salary survey*.

(2) In a computer hardware or software organization, a person who designs and writes system software. In this case, a systems programmer is a programmer in the traditional sense and is often called a *software engineer*. See *salary survey*.

systems representative

An individual that performs presales and post-sales activities for a hardware or software vendor. Depending on the product they represent, systems reps can perform just about any task short of making the actual sale, including systems analysis, programming and general consulting.

system test

Running a complete system for testing purposes. See *unit test*.

system time/date

The on-going time of day in the computer, which is maintained by a battery when the computer is turned off. It is used to time stamp all newly-created files and activate time-dependent processes.

System Tray

An area on the right side of the taskbar on the Windows 95/98 interface used to display the status of various functions, such as speaker volume and modem transmission.

system unit

The primary computer equipment. Housed in a desktop or floor-standing cabinet, it contains such components as the motherboard, CPU, RAM and ROM chips, hard and floppy disks and several input/output ports.

SystemView

An IBM architecture for computer systems management introduced with System/390 that provides an enterprise-wide approach for controlling multiple systems and networks. It will be implemented in stages through the 1990s. NetView is a major component.

System V Interface Definition

See *SVID*.

System V Release 4.0

A unified version of UNIX released in 1989. See *UNIX*.

systolic array

An array of processing elements (typically multiplier-accumulator chips) in a pipeline structure that is used for applications such as image and signal processing and fluid dynamics. The "systolic," coined by H. T. Kung of Carnegie-Mellon, refers to the rhythmic transfer of data through the pipeline like blood flowing through the vascular system.

SYSTEM SOFTWARE

OPERATING SYSTEM
Manages the computer system. Provides file, task and job management. All application programs "talk to" the operating system.

DOS, Windows, OS/2, UNIX, VMS, MVS, VM and Windows NT are examples.

DRIVER
Software that supports a peripheral device, such as a display adapter or CD-ROM. The driver contains the detailed machine language necessary to activate all functions in the device. The operating system commands the driver, which in turn commands the hardware device.

BIOS (Basic Input/Output System)
In a PC, a set of software routines built into a chip that boots the machine and serves as an interface between the drivers and the peripheral devices.

TP MONITOR
Mainframe/midrange program that distributes input from multiple terminals to the appropriate application. This function is also provided in LAN operating systems.

CICS is widely used in IBM mainframes, and Tuxedo and Encina is widely used in UNIX systems.

NETWORK OPERATING SYSTEM
Manage traffic and security between clients and servers in a network. Examples are NetWare, Windows, UNIX, LAN Manager, LAN Server, VINES and LANtastic.

COMMUNICATIONS PROTOCOL
Set of rules, formats and functions for sending data across the network. There are many protocol layers starting at the top application layer to the bottom physical layer

Popular transport protocols are NetBEUI, IPX/SPX and TCP/IP. Popular data link protocols, or access methods, used to transmit data from point to point are Ethernet, Token Ring, SDLC and RS-232.

MESSAGING PROTOCOL
Set of rules, formats and functions for sending, storing and forwarding e-mail in a network. The major messaging protocols are SMTP (Internet), SNADS, MHS, X.400, cc:Mail and Microsoft Mail.

DATABASE MANAGEMENT SYSTEM (DBMS)
Manages the storage, retrieval, security and integrity of the database. A DBMS may provide interactive data entry, updating, query and reporting or rely entirely on the application program for such functions. The DBMS may reside in a mainframe or in a file server in a client/server architecture. Most DBMSs support the SQL language, and many include a complete programming language for application development.

Examples of popular mainframe and client/server DBMSs are DB2, Oracle, Sybase, SQL Server and Informix. Access, dBASE and Paradox are used in PCs.

PROGRAMMING LANGUAGE
Translate source language into machine language using assemblers, compilers, interpreters and application generators. All system software and application software must be programmed in a programming language and turned into machine language for execution.

Examples of programming languages are assembly language, BASIC, FORTRAN, C, C++, Pascal, dBASE, Paradox, Visual Basic and COBOL.

T

T

See *tera*.

T1

(1) A 1.544 Mbps point-to-point dedicated line provided by the telephone companies. The monthly cost is typically based on distance. T1 lines are widely used for private networks and high-speed links to and from Internet service providers.

A T1 line provides 24 64-Kbps voice or data channels. The standard T1 frame is 193 bits long, which holds 24 8-bit voice samples and one synchronization bit with 8,000 frames transmitted per second. See *DS, T-carrier, D4* and *ESF*.

(2) See *Type 1 font*.

T-carrier	Total speed	64 Kbps Channels
T1	1.544 Mbps	24
T2	6.312 Mbps	96
T3	44.736 Mbps	672

T1/E1

Refers to the U.S. T1 line or European E1 equivalent.

T1 font

See *Type 1 font*.

T.2

An ITU standard for Group 1 fax machines. It was introduced in 1968.

T2

A 6.312 Mbps point-to-point dedicated line provided by the telephone companies. A T2 line provides 96 64-Kbps voice or data channels. See *T-carrier* and *DS*.

T3

A 44.736 Mbps point-to-point dedicated line provided by the telephone companies. A T3 line provides 672 64-Kbps voice or data channels. T3 channels are widely used on the Internet. See *T-carrier* and *DS*.

T.4

An ITU standard for Group 3 fax machines that specifies the page dimensions, resolutions and compression scheme. T.4 and T.30, which were introduced in 1980, make up the complete standard for Group 3 fax.

T4

See *100BaseT* and *DS*.

T.6

An ITU standard for Group 4 fax machines. Although introduced in 1984, Group 4 has yet to be implemented on any major scale as it requires high-speed ISDN and DSL technologies for operation.

T.30

An ITU standard for Group 3 fax machines that specifies the handshaking, protocols and error correction. T.4 and T.30, which were introduced in 1980, make up the complete standard for Group 3 fax.

T.120

An ITU standard for realtime data conferencing (sharing data among multiple users). It defines interfaces for whiteboards, application viewing and application sharing. The ITU standard for videoconferencing is H.320.

T.120 is an umbrella term for a series of specifications that define all aspects of data conferencing. The complete standard is made up of the following components.

T.121 - **Generic Application Template** - Common structure for T.120 applications.
T.122 - **Multipoint Communication Service** - Service definition for T.123 networks, which is implemented in T.125.
T.123 - **Audiovisual Protocol Stacks** - Protocol stacks for terminals and MCUs.
T.124 - **Generic Conference Control** - Conference management (establish, terminate, etc.).
T.125 - **Multipoint Communication Service** - Protocol implementation of T.122.
T.126 - **Still Image & Annotation Protocol** - Whiteboards, graphic display and image exchange.
T.127 - **Multipoint Binary Transfer** - Protocol for exchanging binary files.
T.128 - **Audio Visual Control** - Interactive controls (routing, identification, remote control, source selection, etc.)
T.130 - **Realtime Architecture** - Interaction between T.120 and H.320.
T.131 - **Network Specific Mappings** - Transport of realtime data used with T.120 over LANs.
T.132 - **Realtime Link Management** - Creation and routing of realtime data streams.
T.133 - **Audio Visual Control Services** - Controls for realtime data streams.
T.RES - **Reservation Services** - Interaction between devices and reservation systems.
T.Share - **Application Sharing Protocol** - Remote control protocol.
T.TUD - **User Reservation** - Transporting user-defined data.

TA

(Terminal Adapter) See *ISDN terminal adapter*.

tab

(1) To move the cursor on a display screen or the print head on a printer to a specified column (tab stop). There are both horizontal and vertical tab characters in the ASCII character set. See *tab stop*.

(2) A small flap used for quick access that projects out from the end of a page of paper or file folder. Its electronic equivalent on screen can be clicked to gain access to a function.

tabbing

See *tab*.

tab character

A control character in a document that represents movement to the next tab stop. In the ASCII character set, a horizontal tab is ASCII 9, and a vertical tab is ASCII 11. See *ASCII chart*.

tab delimited

A text format that uses tab characters as separators between fields. Unlike comma delimited files, alphanumeric data is not surrounded by quotes.

tab key

A keyboard key that moves the cursor to the next tab stop.

table

(1) In programming, a collection of adjacent fields. Also called an *array*, a table contains data that is either constant within the program or is called in when the program is run. See *decision table*.

(2) In a relational database, the same as a file; a collection of records.

table lookup

Searching for data in a table, commonly used in data entry validation and any operation that must match an item of data with a known set of values.

tablet

See *digitizer tablet*.

tablet cursor

The mouse-like object used to draw on a digitizer tablet. See *mouse*.

table view

A screen display of several items or records in rows and columns. Contrast with *form view*.

tab stop

A location on a horizontal line that has been defined to begin a column of text. Tab stops are necessary for multiple columns when proportional fonts are used. Pressing the space bar several times to move to the next column provides proper alignment only with monospaced characters. With proportional fonts, although the space bar moves a fixed amount, the varying widths of text in one column cause misalignment to the column on the right.

With typewriters, tab stops are mechanical gizmos that halt the movement of the carriage. In word processing, they are column numbers that are maintained by the software.

tabular form

Same as *table view* with respect to printed output.

tabulate

(1) To arrange data into a columnar format.

(2) To sum and print totals.

tabulating equipment

Punched card machines, including keypunches, sorters, collators, interpreters, reproducers, calculators and tabulators.

tabulator

A punched card accounting machine that prints and calculates totals.

TACACS

(Terminal Access Controller Access Control System) An access control protocol used to authenticate a user logging onto the network. TACACS is a simple username/password system. Extended TACACS (XTACACS) adds more intelligence in the server, and TACACS+ adds encryption and a challenge/response option. See *challenge/response*.

tag

(1) A set of bits or characters that identifies various conditions about data in a file and is often found in the header records of such files.

(2) A name (label, mnemonic) assigned to a data structure, such as a field, file or paragraph.

(3) The key field in a record.

(4) A format code used in a document language. See *HTML tag*, *character tag* and *paragraph tag*.

(5) A brass pin on a terminal block that is connected to a wire by soldering or wire wrapping.

tag RAM

A specialized bank of static RAM used to hold addresses. When a stored address matches an input address, a signal is output to perform a function. It is used with hardware devices such as CPU caches to keep track of which memory addresses are stored in the cache.

tag sort

A sorting procedure in which the key fields are sorted first to create the correct order, and then the actual data records are placed into that order.

tag switching

A layer 3 switching technology from Cisco that is used in large enterprise networks (WANs). It uses tags (labels) containing forwarding information. Tag switching uses routers (Tag Edge Routers) that sit on the periphery of the network and make forwarding decisions for all the routers in the backbone. They append this information to each packet in fixed positions of the header that can be quickly examined by interior backbone routers (Tag Edge Switches), saving the time involved in decoding the packet and its associated table lookups.

Tailgate

A conversion layer that lets IDE devices connect to the IEEE 1394 Firewire interface.

Taligent

(Taligent, Inc., Cupertino, CA, subsidiary of IBM, www.taligent.com) A software company formed by Apple and IBM to develop the next-generation operating system. TalOS was to be based on Apple's object-oriented operating system (Pink), but was later disbanded. Taligent delivered its CommonPoint application frameworks and development tools for AIX and OS/2, but they were not widely used. It since turned its focus to class libraries and Web tools and became an IBM subsidiary in 1996.

talk-off

An unintentional command activation when a human voice generates the same tone as a control signal.

Tandem

(Tandem Computers Inc., Cupertino, CA, www.tandem.com) A manufacturer of fault-tolerant computers founded in 1974 by James Treybig. It was the first company to address the transaction processing (OLTP) market for online reservations and financial transfers by providing computers designed from the ground up for fault-tolerant operation. Tandem computers are used in all the major banks, stock exchanges and credit card companies in the world.

Tandem's flagship fault-tolerant product is its MIPS-based Himalaya series which runs the NonStop Kernel operating system, compatible with Tandem's Guardian OS. Tandem also offers a line of UNIX and Windows NT servers. In 1997, Tandem was acquired by Compaq Computer.

James Treybig
Treybig founded Tandem and was at its helm for more than 20 years. *(Photo courtesy of Tandem Computers Incorporated.)*

tandem processors

Two processors hooked together in a multiprocessor environment.

Tandy

(Tandy Corporation, Ft. Worth, TX, www.tandy.com) A manufacturer of PCs and electronics that started as a family leather business in 1919. In 1963, it acquired the nine Radio Shack stores in Boston. Today, it has over 7,000 company-owned stores and franchises.

In 1977, it introduced one of the first personal computers, the TRS-80 Model I. Tandy's Model 100 and 200 lightweight portables were also inspiration to the laptop generation. Its first computers were proprietary, and its initial PCs were non-standard. However, starting with the Model 1000 in 1984, Tandy offered a full line of IBM-compatible PCs.

In 1993, Tandy sold its PC manufacturing facilities to AST and began to eliminate the Tandy brand name on its machines. Radio Shack stores currently offer a variety of machines from AST, IBM and others.

tanstaafl

Digispeak for "there ain't no such thing as a free lunch."

tap

In communications, a connection onto the main transmission medium of a local area network. See *transceiver*.

tape

See *magnetic tape* and *paper tape*.

tape automation

See *tape library*.

tape backup

Using magnetic tape for storing duplicate copies of hard disk files. See *magnetic tape*. For a complete summary of tape, disk and optical storage technologies, see *storage*.

Major Firsts from Tandy
In 1977, Tandy's Radio Shack division introduced the TRS-80. It became widely used in small business and was a major contributor to the personal computer explosion. *(Photo courtesy of Tandy Corporation.)*

tape drive

A physical unit that holds, reads and writes the magnetic tape. See *magnetic tape*.

tape dump

A printout of tape contents without any report formatting.

tape library

A high-capacity data storage system for storing, retrieving, reading and writing multiple magnetic tape cartridges. Also called a *tape automation* system, it contains storage racks for holding the cartridges and a robotic mechanism for moving the cartridge to the drive.

Tape libraries are available for 3480, 3490, Magstar, Magstar MP, DLT, 4mm DAT, 8mm and Travan tape cartridges. Smaller units can have several drives for simultaneous reading and writing and may hold from a handful to several hundred cartridges. Large units support dozens of drives and hold several thousand cartridges.

Accessing data in a tape library can take from 15 seconds to a minute in order to find, retrieve and load a cartridge, making it available for reading and writing.

A Massive Tape Library
StorageTek's RedWood SD-3 tape libary is one of the largest in the world and can hold up to 6,000 helical scan cartridges. Each cartridge holds 50GB, which if fully populated would store 300 terabytes of data. *(Photo courtesy of Storage Technology Corporation.)*

tape mark

A control code used to indicate the end of a tape file.

tape transport

The mechanical part of a tape drive.

TAPI

(Telephony **API**) A programming interface from Microsoft and Intel that is part of Microsoft's WOSA architecture. It allows Windows client applications to access voice services on a server. TAPI is designed to provide interoperability between PCs and telephone equipment, including phone systems and PBXs. See *WOSA*.

tar

(Tape ARchive) A UNIX utility for archiving files, often used in conjunction with "compress."

Targa

A bitmapped graphics file format developed by Truevision, Inc., Indianapolis, IN, (www.truevision.com). It uses the .TGA file extension and handles 16-, 24- and 32-bit color. It is also the trade name of a line of video graphics boards used in high-resolution imaging.

target computer

The computer into which a program is loaded and run. Contrast with *source computer*. See *cross assembler* and *cross compiler*.

target directory

The directory into which data is being sent. Contrast with *source directory*.

target disk

The disk onto which data is recorded. Contrast with *source disk*.

target drive

The drive containing the disk or tape onto which data is recorded. Contrast with *source drive*.

target language

The language resulting from a translation process such as assembling or compiling. Contrast with *source language*.

target machine

Same as *target computer*.

tariff

A schedule of rates for common carrier services.

task

An independent running program. See *multitasking*.

taskbar

An on-screen toolbar that displays the active applications (tasks). Clicking on a taskbar button restores the application to its previous appearance. Windows 95 popularized this feature. See *Win 9x Taskbar*.

task management

(1) The part of the operating system that controls the running of one or more programs (tasks) within the computer at the same time.

(2) Managing personal and office tasks using a to-do list, or task list. This function is typically in a PIM or groupware product.

task swapping

Switching between two applications by copying the current running program to disk or other high-speed storage device (auxiliary memory, EMS, etc.) and loading another program into that program space.

task switching

Switching between active applications. It generally refers to a user purposefully jumping from one application to another, for example, by pressing Alt-Tab in Windows. Task switching can also be performed by a multitasking operating system that continually switches the CPU from one program to another in the background.

Tb, Tbit, TB, Tbyte

See *terabit* and *terabyte*.

Tbits/sec, Tbps, Tb/s; Tbytes/sec, TBps, TB/s

(TeraBits Per Second; TeraBytes Per Second) One trillion bits per second; One trillion bytes per second. See *space/time*.

TCAL

See *thermal recalibration*.

TCAM

(TeleCommunications Access Method) IBM communications software widely used to transfer data between mainframes and 3270 terminals. See *access method*.

T-carrier

A digital transmission service from a common carrier. Introduced by AT&T in 1983 for voice, its use for data has grown steadily. T1 and T3 lines are widely used to create point-to-point private data networks. The cost of the lines is based on the length of the circuit, and it is the customer's responsibility to utilize the lines efficiently. Multiple lower-speed channels can be multiplexed onto a T-carrier line and demultiplexed (split back out) at the other end. Some multiplexors can analyze the traffic load and vary channel speeds for optimum transmission. See *DS, DSU/CSU* and *inverse multiplexor*.

Tcl/Tk

(Tool Command Language/ToolKit) Pronounced "tickle" or "ticklet," it is an interpreted script language that is used to develop a variety of applications, including GUIs, prototypes and CGI scripts. Created for the UNIX platform by John Ousterhout along with students at the University of California at Berkeley, it now runs on PCs and Macs and is primarily supported by SunSoft. Safe-Tcl is an enhanced Tcl interpreter that provides a secure, virus free environment.

Tcl also provides an interface into compiled applications (C, C++, etc.). The application is compiled with Tcl functions, which provide a bi-directional path between Tcl scripts and the executable programs. Tcl provides a way to "glue" program modules together.

TCM

(1) (Trellis-Coded Modulation/Viterbi Decoding) A technique that adds forward error correction to a modulation scheme by adding an additional bit to each baud. TCM is used with QAM modulation, for example.

(2) (Thermal Conduction Module) An IBM circuit packaging technique that seals chips, boards and components into a module that serves as a heat sink. TCMs are mostly water cooled, although some are air cooled.

TCO

(1) (Total Cost of Ownership) The cost of using a computer. It includes the cost of the hardware, software and upgrades as well as the cost of the inhouse staff and/or consultants that provide training and technical support.

(2) Refers to the Swedish Confederation of Professional Employees, which has set stringent standards for devices that emit radiation. TCO 92 added power-saving requirements to the TCO specifications, and TCO 95 added guidelines for recyclable materials and packaging. See *MPR II*.

TCP/IP

(Transmission Control Protocol/Internet Protocol) A communications protocol developed under contract from the U.S. Department of Defense to internetwork dissimilar systems. This de facto UNIX standard, which is the protocol of the Internet, is becoming the global standard for communications.

TCP provides transport functions, which ensures that the total amount of bytes sent is received correctly at the other end. UDP is an alternate transport that does not guarantee delivery. It is widely used for realtime voice and video transmissions where erroneous packets are not retransmitted.

IP provides the routing mechanism. TCP/IP is a routable protocol, which means that all messages contain not only the address of the destination station, but the address of a destination network. This allows TCP/IP messages to be sent to multiple networks within an organization or around the world, hence its use in the worldwide Internet (see *Internet address*). Every client and server in a TCP/IP network requires an IP address, which is either permanently assigned or dynamically assigned at startup. For an explanation of how

the various layers in TCP/IP work, see *TCP/IP abc's*. See also *IP address, NFS, NIS, DNS, DHCP, dumb network* and *IP on Everything*.

TCP/IP abc's

The Internet has pushed its native TCP/IP protocol to the forefront of communications. In so doing, it is enabling the world to migrate to one global data communications system. TCP/IP is a robust and proven technology that was first tested in the early 1980s on ARPAnet, the U.S. military's Advanced Research Projects Agency network, the world's first packet-switched network. TCP/IP was designed as an open protocol that would enable all types of computers to transmit data to each other via a common communications language.

TCP/IP is a layered protocol similar to the ones used in all the other major networking architectures, including IBM's SNA, Windows' NetBIOS, Apple's AppleTalk, Novell's NetWare and Digital's DECnet. Layering means that after an application initiates the communications, the message (data) to be transmitted is passed through a number of stages, or layers, until it actually moves out onto the wire. The data is packaged with a different header at each layer. At the receiving end, the corresponding programs at each protocol layer unpackage the data, moving it "back up the stack" to the receiving application.

TCP/IP is composed of two parts: TCP (Transmission Control Protocol) and IP (Internet Protocol). TCP is a connection-oriented protocol that passes its data to IP, which is a connectionless one. TCP sets up a connection at both ends and guarantees reliable delivery of the full message sent. TCP tests for errors and requests retransmission if necessary, because IP does not.

An alternative protocol to TCP within the TCP/IP suite is UDP (User Datagram Protocol), which does not guarantee delivery. Like IP, it is also connectionless, but very useful for realtime voice and video, where it doesn't matter if a few packets get lost, because it's too late to worry about it if they do.

Although TCP/IP has five layers, it is contrasted to the OSI (Open System Interconnection) seven-layer model, because OSI serves as a universal reference. Once thought to become the worldwide communications standard, OSI gave way to TCP/IP. However, it has become the teaching model for all communications networks, so all efforts of the OSI committee were not in vain.

Application Layer 7

The top layer of the protocol stack is the application layer. It refers to the programs that initiate the communications in the first place. TCP/IP includes several application layer protocols for mail, file transfer, remote access, authentication and name resolution. These protocols are embodied in programs that operate at the top layer just as any custom-made or packaged client/server application would.

FTP, SMTP, Telnet, DNS and WINS

Some of the most widely-known application protocols in the TCP/IP suite are FTP (File Transfer Protocol), SMTP (Simple Mail Transfer Protocol), Telnet, DNS (Domain Name System) and WINS (Windows Internet Name System). FTP programs are widely used to copy files across the network. All TCP/IP-based mail programs use SMTP to send e-mail. Telnet is a terminal emulator that provides access to a remote host. DNS and WINS allow hosts to be given understandable names, and the DNS and WINS servers turn those names into the IP address required by TCP/IP networks.

Except for TCP/IP's own application protocols such as the ones briefly mentioned above, the language and format used in a user's client/server program are not known to TCP/IP. They are known only to the receiving programs that must parse the incoming request to find out what the client is asking for. The data from the programs at the top layer are "handed down" to the lower layers in the stack

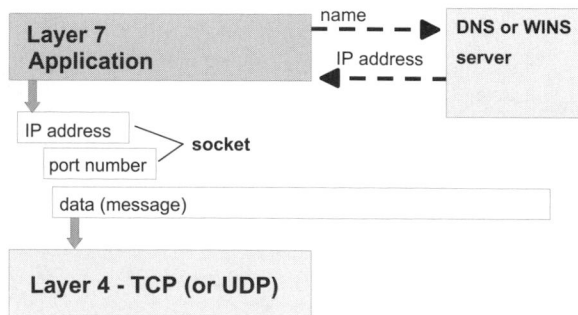

From Application to Transport Layer

The application delivers its data to the communications system by passing a stream of data bytes to the transport layer along with the socket of the destination machine. The dotted lines in this diagram are conceptual. DNS and WINS requests go down the stack (in a UDP packet) like everything else in order to go out onto the network.

for actual transport processing. Then the data is "handed up" the stack to the appropriate application in the receiving machine (server).

IP Addresses

All nodes in a TCP/IP network (clients, servers, routers, etc.) are assigned an "IP address," which is written as four numbers between dots, such as 193.4.64.01. The first part of the address is the network address, and the second part is the host (station) address, also known as the netid and hostid. The network address allows TCP/IP packets to be routed to a different network. The number of bytes used for the netid versus the hostid vary according to a class system, and the first three bits of the first byte determine this ratio (see *IP address* for details).

Ports and Sockets

A program identifies the program it wishes to communicate with by its socket, which is a combination of (1) the server's IP address and (2) the program's port. If it does not know the IP address, but knows the server by name, it uses a Domain Name System server (DNS server) to turn the name into the IP address. In Windows networks, a Windows Internet Name System server (WINS server) is used to map NetBIOS names, which are assigned to Windows machines, to IP addresses.

The port is a logical number assigned to every application. For FTP, SMTP, HTTP and other common applications, there are agreed-upon numbers known as "well-known ports." For example, HTTP applications (World Wide Web) are on port 80, so a Web server is located by its IP address and port 80. An organization's internal client/server applications are given arbitrary ports for its own purposes.

Layers 6 & 5

Although OSI defines layers 6 and 5, TCP/IP does not. The services are indeed performed, if required, but they are not part of the formal TCP/IP stack. For example, Layer 6 (Presentation Layer) is where data conversion (ASCII to EBCDIC, floating point to binary, etc.) and encryption/decryption is performed. Layer 5 is the Session Layer, which is performed in layer 4 in TCP/IP. Thus we jump from layer 7 down to layer 4.

Transport Layer 4 - TCP & UDP

TCP establishes a connection at both ends, creating a "virtual connection" between the two machines before any data can be transmitted. Once established, both sides negotiate the maximum size of a TCP packet. Although TCP supports packets up to 64KB, in most cases, the size will be based on the underlying network, such as Ethernet, which can hold a maximum of 1518 bytes. Token Ring and FDDI support larger frames. TCP attaches a header onto the packet that contains the source and destination ports as well as the sequence number of the packet, and it hands it over to IP along with the destination IP address. (A TCP packet is technically a Protocol Data Unit or segment, but is more often called a packet in common parlance.)

TCP uses a sliding window system, which is an adjustable buffer that allows a number of packets to be received before an

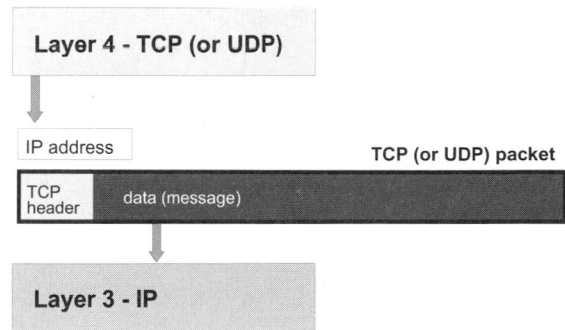

From Transport to Network Layer
TCP and UDP hand over their packets to IP along with the IP address of the destination node. The packet size is typically the size of the underlying data link layer such as Ethernet or Token Ring.

acknowledgement is sent back. The size of the window can be changed as conditions change, and TCP handles this "flow control" in realtime. It also handles the retransmission of packets that have been received with errors.

UDP is an alternative to TCP that does not establish a connection, makes no guarantees and provides no flow control or error detection. Either it doesn't matter as would be the case for realtime audio or video, or the application programs using UDP must themselves include the error detection and recovery that TCP provides.

Network Layer 3 - IP

The IP protocol accepts the packets from TCP or UDP and prepares them for the data link protocol layer below by turning the IP addresses into physical station addresses (MAC addresses) and fragmenting the packets (if necessary) into the required frame size. IP uses the ARP (Address Resolution Protocol) to obtain the MAC address, unless (1) the address has already been ARP'd and is in the cache or (2) there is a predefined configuration file that contains the addresses. An ARP request is broadcast onto the network, and the machine with that IP address responds with its MAC address. If the target machine is in a different network or subnetwork than the source machine, IP supplies the target address of the default gateway, which is the router that can direct the packet to the appropriate network.

IP outputs packets called datagrams, and each datagram is prefixed with an IP header that contains source and destination IP addresses. If IP has to fragment the packet further, it creates multiple datagrams with sequence numbers so that they can be reassembled by IP on the other end. IP hands over each datagram to the data link layer below along with the MAC address (Ethernet address) of the target station or router.

IP supports a very useful feature called mulitcast, which allows one message to be delivered to multiple recipients. That means one IP data stream can travel a long, circuitous route before it is fanned out to all the target stations by the last router.

IP Is the Routing Mechanism

In a large enterprise or on the Internet, the IP protocol is used to route the packets from network to network. Routers contain routing tables that move the datagrams to the next "hop," which is either the destination network or another router. Datagrams can traverse several routers within an enterprise and dozens of routers over the Internet.

Routers that span different types of networks may have to fragment the datagrams even further if they direct them onto routes that use a smaller frame size than the incoming frame; for example, from FDDI to Ethernet.

Routers inspect only the network portion (netid) of the address and direct the incoming datagrams to the appropriate outgoing port for the next hop. Routers move datagrams from one hop to the next as they are mostly aware of only the devices that are directly connected to them. Eventually, if the routing tables are correctly updated, the datagrams reach their destination. Routers use routing protocols to obtain current routing information about the networks and hosts that are directly connected to them.

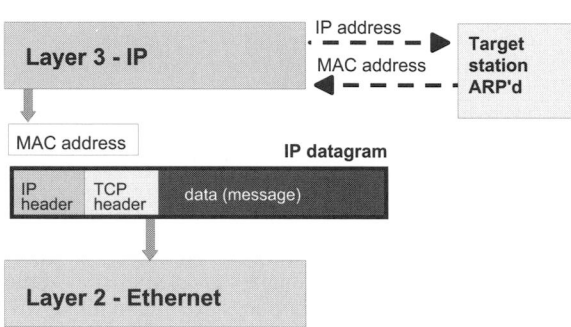

From Network to Data Link Layer

IP datagrams are handed over to Ethernet, Token Ring, ATM or some other data link protocol responsible for moving the data across the wire. The dotted lines in the diagram are conceptual. ARP requests go down the stack like everything else in order to go out onto the network.

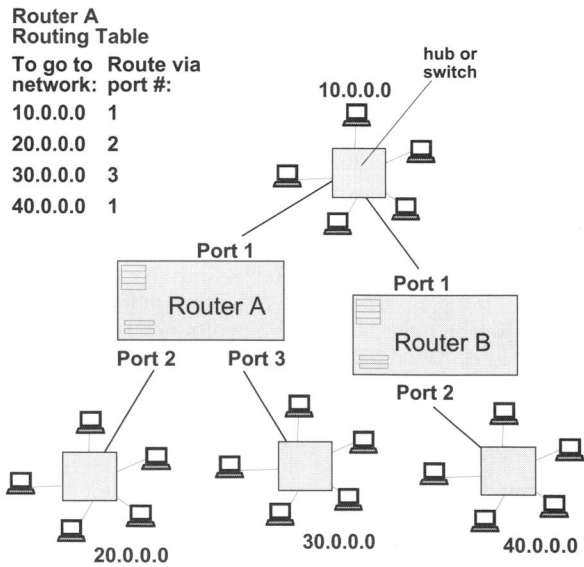

Routing Table Example

If a router receives packets for a remote network, it sends them out the port that will reach the next router. Router ports are entirely different than socket ports. Router ports are physical pathways to and from the router connected via cable. Socket ports are logical assignments made to running programs.

Data Link Layer 2 - Ethernet

IP can connect directly to Ethernet, Token Ring, FDDI, ATM, SONET, X.25, frame relay and other networks. Since Ethernet is the most widely-used data link protocol, or network access method, we use it in our example. Ethernet wraps the IP datagrams into its own frame format, which includes a header with source and destination MAC addresses (station addresses) and a trailer that contains checksum data.

Ethernet uses the CSMA/CD (carrier sense multiple access/collision detection) access method to broadcast the frames onto the wire. If two stations transmit at the same time, their frames collide, and they each back off and wait a random amount of time before trying again (in milliseconds). The data link layer is responsible for reliable node to node transmission. If an Ethernet frame is received with errors, Ethernet handles retransmission until it is received error free.

If IP datagrams start out in a LAN, go to a wide area network (WAN) and then back to an Ethernet again at the other side, the Ethernet frames were converted into WAN frames by a router and back again to Ethernet frames by the router at the other side.

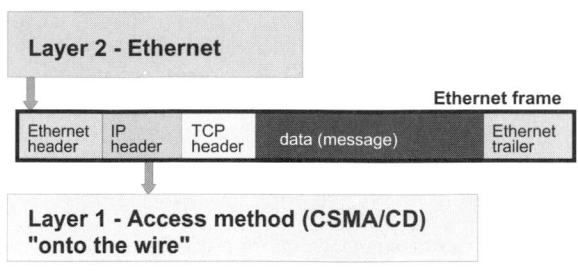

Onto the Wire

The data link layer is responsible for reliable node to node transmission within a subnetwork. When Ethernet frames traverse several routers, the same frames are retransmitted over again by the next router.

Packets, Datagrams or Frames?

The message starts out in one host, goes down the protocol stack, over the wire, and back up the stack on the receiving host. The counterpart protocols unpackage the frames, datagrams and packets and deliver the data to the application for processing.

Although the terms are technically TCP segments, IP datagrams and Ethernet frames, they all ride over packet-switched networks and are frequently called packets at all stages.

LAN	WAN	WAN
Data, voice, video	Data, voice, video	Data, voice, video
IP (layer 3)	IP (layer 3)	IP (layer 3)
Ethernet (layer 2)	ATM (layer 2)	SONET (layer 1)
Copper	SONET (layer 1)	Fiber
	Fiber	

Transporting IP

Transporting IP packets over a LAN is typically done via Ethernet. Over the WAN, IP generally rides over ATM on top of SONET or over SONET directly.

IP Is "The" Standard

IP is becoming the standard protocol for all forms of electronic communications, including data voice and video. New carriers such as Qwest and Level 3 are building their entire infrastructure on IP, and AT&T has announced its future will be IP based. The amount of data communications is increasing far more than voice traffic, and it is expected that all data, voice and video will eventually ride over IP-based networks in the future. See *IP on Everything*.

TCP/IP References

Perhaps the simplest reference ever written on the subject is "An Introduction to TCP/IP" by John Davidson, published by Springer-Verlag (ISBN 0-387-96651-X). Althogh written in 1988 and only 100 pages, it is the easiest read on the subject you will ever find.

The Bibles for TCP/IP have been "Internetworking with TCP/IP," Volumes I, II and III, by Douglas E. Comer. Written in 1991, Volume I covers the essentials from soup to nuts. Published by Prentice-Hall (ISBN 0-13-468505-9).

TCP/IP stack

An implementation of the TCP/IP communications protocol. Network architectures designed in layers, such as TCP/IP, OSI and SNA, are called *stacks*.

TCS

(Transportation Control System) A comprehensive information system for railroad transportation developed by the Missouri Pacific Railroad Company in the late 1960s and early 1970s. It was later implemented by Union Pacific when the companies merged.

TCSEC

See *NCSC*.

TCU

(Transmission Control Unit) A communications control unit controlled by the computer that does not execute internally stored programs. Contrast with *front end processor*, which executes its own instructions.

TDES

(Triple DES) See *DES*.

TDM

(Time Division Multiplexing) A technology that transmits multiple signals simultaneously over a single transmission path. Each lower-speed signal is time sliced into one high-speed transmission. For example, three incoming 1,000 bps signals (A, B and C) can be interleaved into one 3,000 bps signal (AABBCCAABBCCAABBCC). The receiving end divides the single stream back into its original signals.

TDM is the technology used in T-carrier service (DS0, DS1, etc.), which are the leased lines common in wide area networks (WANs). Contrast with *FDM*. See *channel bank*.

TDMA

(Time Division Multiple Access) A satellite and cellular phone technology that interleaves multiple digital signals onto a single high-speed channel. For cellular, TDMA triples the capacity of the original analog method (FDMA). It divides each channel into three subchannels providing service to three users instead of one. See *FDMA, CDMA* and *CDPD*.

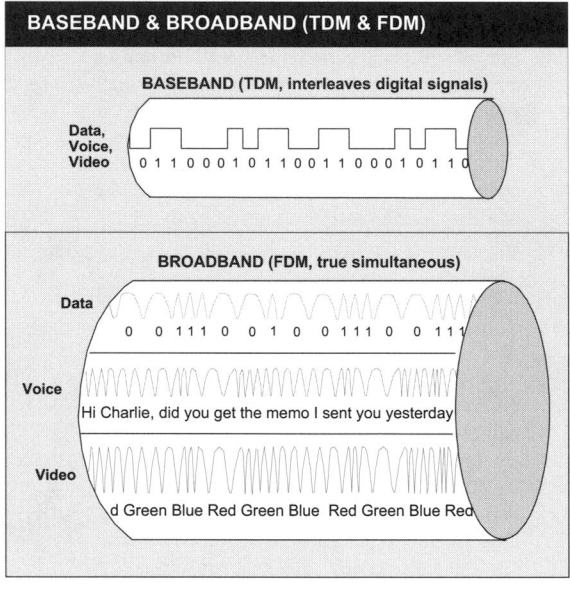

BASEBAND & BROADBAND (TDM & FDM)

BASEBAND (TDM, interleaves digital signals)

Data, Voice, Video
0 1 1 0 0 0 1 0 1 1 0 0 1 1 0 0 0 1 0 1 1 0

BROADBAND (FDM, true simultaneous)

Data
0 0 111 0 0 1 0 0 111 0 0 111

Voice
Hi Charlie, did you get the memo I sent you yesterday

Video
d Green Blue Red Green Blue Red Green Blue Red

Team Enterprise Developer

A client/server application development system from Symantec that supports Windows clients and a variety of databases, including Access, SQL Server, Oracle and Sybase. It is a fully integrated system that is repository-driven. It also includes entity relationship diagrams and version control.

tear down

In communications, to free up a circuit that has been established for a particular session. When the session is completed, the circuit is "torn down" and the components and services involved are available for use by someone else.

tear-off menu

An on-screen menu or palette that can be moved off of its primary position and relocated to any part of the screen.

TechNet

See *Microsoft TechNet*.

technical writer

The person responsible for writing the hardware and software documentation you read in manuals and

Computer Desktop Encyclopedia

in the online help. Considering they are paid the least of all computer professionals, it's no wonder that RTFM is the thing users dread the most. See *RTFM* and *salary survey*.

A Note From the Author

When the great minds in the computer industry wake up and figure out how critical it is to write good, clear documentation, they might pay more attention to it, because it would keep them from drowning in technical support. Describing technical material is as difficult a job as some of the most complex programming.

However, poor programming is invisible. As long as the program works, you have no idea how many resources are being wasted behind the scenes, or if, in fact, the program causes conflicts with your other applications. People are so used to the computer locking up, they take it in stride. But, poor writing is not invisible. It is up front, staring you in the face. You either understand it or you do not.

If the writing in this book is reasonably understandable, it is because I have been writing technical documentation for more than 20 years. I also have nearly 40 years of computer experience to draw on. In addition, I have revised most of the definitions at least a half dozen times, and, in some cases, more times than I can count. And, although it all does get easier after a while, writing this material is still the greatest challenge of my life.

technology

Applying a systematic technique, method or approach to solve a problem. Much of today's technology implies the use of computers. See *high technology*.

technophile

A person that enjoys learning about and using electronics and computers. See *computerphile, hacker* and *dweeb*. Contrast with *technophobic*.

technophobic

Afraid of technology. See *lamer*. Contrast with *technophile*.

tech support

Technical assistance from the hardware manufacturer or software publisher. Unless you have a simple, straightforward question that has nothing to do with a problem you are encountering with your computer, be sure you are at your computer when you call the tech support line.

This is a precise business. Whenever you get an error message, be sure to write down what it says. "I don't quite remember" may be of little value in solving your problem. In addition, in the large companies, some of these people take hundreds of calls all day long and may have little patience with you if you cannot describe the circumstances of your problem in detail.

Intermittent problems are extremely difficult to resolve. If you cannot recreate the problem on screen, there may be very little a tech support person can do to help you.

tech writer

See *technical writer*.

telco

(TELephone COmpany) A company that provides telephone services. It generally refers to the local telephone companies rather than the long-distance suppliers.

tele

("long distance") Operations performed remotely or by telephone.

telecom

Same as *telecommunications*.

Telecom Act of 1996

See *Telecommunications Act of 1996*.

telecommunications

Communicating information, including data, text, pictures, voice and video over long distance. See *communications*.

Telecommunications Act of 1996

Telecommunications legislation passed by the U.S. Congress in 1996. Although it covers many aspects of the field, the most controversial has been the deregulation of local phone service, allowing competition in this arena for the first time. Long-distance carriers (IXCs) and cable TV companies can get into the local phone business, while local telcos (the LECs) can get into long distance. Some of the major provisions follow.

Section 251 - Allows states to regulate prices in the local access market.

Section 254 - Extends universal service to everyone no matter how rural, even if others have to subsidize the expense.

Section 271 - Provides a 14-point checklist of requirements for RBOCs to offer intrastate long-distance service.

It Hasn't Been a Picnic

The RBOCs thought the Act would be a road map for getting into long distance in exchange for ending their local monopolies. What they got were 700 pages of dubious rules that made "deregulating" as complicated as any regulated industry could be. The RBOCs have claimed that the Act discriminates against them and that other large telephone companies have received more favorable treatment. Complaints and lawsuits ensued. Stay tuned.

telecommunity

A society in which information can be transmitted or received freely between all members without technical incompatibilities.

telecommuter

A person that does telecommuting. See *telecommuting, virtual company* and *hoteling*.

telecommuting

Working at home and communicating with the office by electronic means. See *virtual company* and *hoteling*.

teleconferencing

("long distance" conferencing) An interactive communications session between three or more users that are geographically separated. See *audioconferencing, videoconferencing* and *data conferencing*.

telecopying

("long distance" copying) The formal term for fax.

Teledesic

(Teledesic Corporation, Kirkland, WA, www.teledesic.com) A communications company that was spun off from McCaw Cellular in 1994 for the purpose of creating a high-speed, wireless, switched global network. It is designed to handle all kinds of voice, video and data traffic.

Its 288 low-earth orbit (LEO) satellites will blanket the earth, transmit in the 18GHz and 28GHz range and provide the equivalent of 20,000 T1 lines to the world at large. Data is switched from one satellite to another, simulating an Internet in the sky. Using pizza-sized dishes, third-world countries will have the same accessibility as the giant nations.

Teledesic's major investors are Craig McCaw, Bill Gates and AT&T Wireless Services. Expected to be operational in 2003 at a cost of $9 billion, this is the single largest and most ambitious communications project ever undertaken.

telefax

The european term for a fax machine.

telegraph

A low-speed communications device that transmits up to approximately 150 bps. Telegraph grade lines, stemming from the days of Morse code, cannot transmit a voice conversation. See illustration on next page.

telemanagement

Management of an organization's telephone systems, which includes maintaining and ordering new equipment and monitoring the expenses for all telephone calls.

telemarketing

Selling over the telephone.

telematics

The convergence of telecommunications and information processing.

telemedicine

("long distance" medicine) Using videoconferencing for medical diagnosis. With a videoconferencing link to a large medical center, rural health care facilities can perform diagnosis and treatment available only in larger metropolitan areas. A specialist can monitor the patient remotely taking cues from the general practitioner or nurse that is actually examining the patient. A patient's blood can be placed under a microscope in the remote facility and transmitted for examination.

The Days of the Morse Code
Data was transmitted at an equivalent of four to six bits per second in the late 1800s, which was as fast as a human hand could tap out Morse code. The unit on the right is the telegraph key. A metal bar on the receiver (left) simply banged against another bar when the current passed through, creating a clicking sound.

telemetry

Transmitting data captured by instrumentation and measuring devices to a remote station where it is recorded and analyzed. For example, data from a weather satellite is telemetered to earth.

Telenet

One of the first value-added, packet switching networks that enabled terminals and computers to exchange data. Established in 1975, it was later acquired by Sprint and ultimately integrated into the SprintNet network. See also *Telnet*.

telephone

("long distance" + "sound") See *POTS*.

telephone channel

See *voice grade*.

telephone wiring

See *twisted pair*.

telephony

The science of converting sound into electrical signals, transmitting it within cables or via radio and reconverting it back into sound.

telephony server

A computer in a network that provides telephone integration. The term may refer to the entire system or to just the plug-in boards and software. An Internet telephony server links phone lines to the Internet.

Telephony Server NLM

A NetWare NLM that provides an interface between a NetWare server and a PBX. The physical connection is made by cabling the PBX to a card in the server. The NLM provides an open programming interface that allows PBX manufacturers to write drivers for their products.

telepresence surgery

A medical technology developed by SRI International that allows a surgeon to operate long distance. By combining advances in imaging, video, robotics and sensory devices, the system gives doctors the full sensory experience of hands-on surgery. Wearing a pair of specially-polarized glasses and sitting before a console showing a high-resolution 3-D image of the patient, the surgeon is actually doing the operation.

teleprinter

A typewriter-like terminal with a keyboard and built-in printer. In can be a desktop or portable unit. Teleprinters were quite common years ago as input terminals for computers, but have given way to the video screen. Teleprinter-like devices are still used in retail applications where receipts are necessary. As ink jet printers get lighter, they are expected to be built into more notebook computers for sales and similar applications.

The Teleprinter
Teleprinters were widely used starting with the very first computers. They lived well into the 1970s as a computer input device. Any keyboard and printing unit can be called a teleprinter.

teleprocessing

("long distance" processing) An early IBM term for data communications.

teleprocessing monitor

See *TP monitor*.

Telescript

A programming language and software for communications from General Magic. It embeds intelligence in e-mail and other applications allowing them to cooperate with one another and allows messages to move intelligently through diverse public and private networks. Telescript can be added to existing and future operating systems. See *Magic Cap*.

teleservices

(**TELE**phone **SERVICES**) An umbrella term for products and services that integrate telephones and computers. See *IVR*.

teletext

A broadcasting service that transmits text to a TV set that has a teletext decoder. It uses the vertical blanking interval of the TV signal (black line between frames when vertical hold is not adjusted) to transmit about a hundred frames. See *videotex*.

Teletype

The trade name of Teletype Corporation, which refers to a variety of teleprinters used for communications. The Teletype was one of the first communications terminals in the U.S.

teletype interface

See *teletype mode*.

teletype mode

Line-at-a-time output like a typewriter. Contrast with *full-screen mode*.

teletypewriter

A low-speed teleprinter, often abbreviated "TTY."

The Teletype Machine
For years, the clicking and clanging of Teletype machines were familiar sounds in the "wire rooms" of many companies. *(Photo courtesy of Honeywell, Inc.)*.

televaulting

Continuous transmitting of data to vaults for backup purposes. The term was coined by TeleVault Technology Inc.

Telex

An international, dial-up data communications service administered in the U.S. by AT&T, MCI and other providers. In the 1960s, it was the first worldwide, realtime data communications service to use terminals for transmitting and receiving messages. Prior to Telex, telegrams and cablegrams were the primary method for delivering a text message. Although diminishing each year, Telex is still used for commerce in more than 200 countries.

Telex is a low-speed service that transmits Baudot code at 50 bps. It was originally administered worldwide by various carriers and the local PTTs. Western Union handled the U.S., and in 1971, purchased and integrated the Bell System's TXW service. AT&T acquired Western Union's Telex service in 1991.

TeLink

An Xmodem protocol with batch file transfer designed for the Fido BBS. It sends file name, date and size in the first block.

Telnet

A terminal emulation protocol commonly used on the Internet. It allows a user to log onto and run a program from a remote terminal or computer. Telnet was originally developed for ARPAnet and is part of the TCP/IP communications protocol.

Although most computers on the Internet require users to have an established account and password, there are many that allow public access to certain programs, typically, search utilities, such as Archie or WAIS. See also *Telenet*.

Telon

See *CA-Telon*.

TELRIC

(Total Element Long Run Incremental Cost) A calculation method that ILECs can charge CLECs for interconnection and colocation. See *ILEC* and *CLEC*.

temp directory

See *temporary directory*.

TEMPEST

Security against external radiation from data processing equipment. Equipment and cables that meet TEMPEST requirements have extra shielding in order to prevent data signals from escaping and being picked up by unauthorized listeners.

template

(1) A plastic or stiff paper form placed over the function keys on a keyboard to identify their use.

(2) The programmatic and descriptive part of a programmable application; for example, a spreadsheet that contains descriptions and formulas. When the template is filled with data, it becomes a working application.

(3) Same as *style sheet*.

temporary directory

A directory (folder) that is created for some non-permanent usage such as installing an application or compressing or decompressing files. When a file is downloaded from the Internet, it is usually a self-extracting archive, which has to be executed once in order to decompress the files into their original form. Decompressing files in an empty, temporary directory keeps them in one place so they can be deleted later.

temporary font

A soft font that remains in the printer's memory until the printer is reset manually or by software. Contrast with *permanent font*.

ter

Third version. See *bis*.

tera

Trillion (10^{12}). Abbreviated "T." It often refers to the precise value 1,099,511,627,776 since computer specifications are usually binary numbers. See *binary values* and *space/time*.

terabit

One trillion bits. Also Tb, Tbit and T-bit. See *tera* and *space/time*.

terabyte

One trillion bytes. Also TB, Tbyte and T-byte. See *tera* and *space/time*.

teraflops

(tera FLoating point OPerations per Second) One trillion floating point operations per second.

Terastor

(Terastor, Inc., San Jose, CA, www.terastor.com) A company that is developing a next-generation hard disk. Its Near Field Recording (NFR) technology employs magnetic and optical methods to increase storage capacity. See *latest disk drives*.

terminal

(1) An I/O device for a computer that usually has a keyboard for input and a video screen or printer for output. See *ASCII terminal*.

(2) An input device, such as a scanner, video camera or punched card reader.

(3) An output device in a network, such as a monitor, printer or card punch.

(4) A connector used to attach a wire.

terminal adapter

See *ISDN terminal adapter*.

terminal emulation

Using a computer to simulate the type of terminal required to gain access to another computer. See *virtual terminal*.

terminal mode

An operating mode that causes the computer to act like a terminal; ready to transmit typed-in keystrokes and ready to receive transmitted data.

terminal server

(1) A computer or controller used to connect multiple terminals to a network or host computer.

(2) See *Windows-based Terminal Server*.

terminal session

(1) Interacting with a mainframe, minicomputer or UNIX server from a terminal. When a terminal session is activated in a client machine with a GUI (Windows, Mac, etc.), a window for typing in commands is provided. See *3270 emulator, twinax card* and *Telnet*.

(2) The time in which a user is working at a terminal.

terminal strip

An insulated bar that contains a set of screws to which wires are attached.

terminal window

A dialog box that lets you send commands to your modem. In Windows 95/98 Dial-Up Networking (DUN), you have the option of bringing up a terminal window before or after you dial your number.

terminate and stay resident

See *TSR*.

terminator

(1) A character that ends a string of alphanumeric characters.

(2) A hardware component that is connected to the last peripheral device in a series or the last node in a network.

terrestrial link

A communications line that travels on, near or below ground. Contrast with *satellite link*.

tessellation

In surface modeling and solid modeling, the method used to represent 3-D objects as a collection of triangles or other polygons. All surfaces, both curved and straight, are turned into triangles either at the time they are first created or in realtime when they are rendered. The more triangles used to represent a surface, the more realistic the rendering, but the more computation is required.

Triangles may also be discarded at the time they are rendered depending on their distance from the camera. Some applications create multiple models with different amounts of triangles and use the best one depending on distance. The vertices (end points) of the triangles are assigned x-y-z and RGB values, which are used to compute light reflections for shading and rendering.

Tessellation is not used in 2-D graphics. Although 2-D graphics may be used to draw 3-D objects, any simulation of depth and shading must be created by the artist using standard drawing tools, color fills and gradients. See *surface normal* and *triangle*.

test automation software

Software used to test new revisions of software by automatically entering a predefined set of commands and inputs.

test data

A set of data created for testing new or revised programs. It should be developed by the user as well as the programmer and must contain a sample of every category of valid data as well as many invalid conditions.

testing

Running new or revised programs to determine if they process all data properly. See *test data*.

For testing as it pertains to professional certification, see *CCP, NetWare certification* and *Microsoft Certified Professional*. For proficiency and aptitude tests, see *aptitude tests*.

tests

See *certification* and *aptitude tests*.

TeX

A typesetting language used in a variety of typesetting environments. It uses embedded codes within the text of the document to initiate changes in layout including the ability to describe elaborate scientific formulas.

Texas Instruments

See *TI*.

texel

(TEXture ELement) The smallest addressable unit of a texture map. See *texture map*.

text

Words, sentences and paragraphs. Contrast with *data*, which are defined units, such as name and amount due. Text may also refer to alphanumeric data, such as name and address, to distinguish it from numeric data, such as quantity and dollar amounts. A page of text takes about 2,000 to 4,000 bytes. See *text field*.

text based

Also called *character based*, the display of text and graphics as a fixed set of predefined characters. For example, 25 rows of 80 columns. Contrast with *graphics based*.

text box

An on-screen rectangular frame into which you type text. Text boxes are used to add text in a drawing or paint program. The flexibility of the text box is determined by the software. Sometimes you can keep on typing and the box expands to meet your input. Other times, you have to go into a different mode to widen the frame, then go back to typing in more text.

text editing

The ability to change text by adding, deleting and rearranging letters, words, sentences and paragraphs.

text editor

Software used to create and edit files that contain only text; for example, batch files, address lists and source language programs. Text editors produce raw ASCII or EBCDIC text files, and unlike word processors, do not usually provide word wrap or formatting (underline, boldface, fonts, etc.).

Editors designed for writing source code may provide automatic indention and multiple windows into the same file. They may also display the reserved words of a particular programming language in boldface or in a different font, but they do not embed format codes in the file.

text entry

Entering alphanumeric text characters into the computer. It implies typing the characters on a keyboard. See *data entry*.

text field

A data structure that holds alphanumeric data, such as name and address. If a text field holds large, or unlimited, amounts of text, it may be called a memo field. Contrast with *numeric field*.

text file

A file that contains only text characters. See *ASCII file*. Contrast with *graphics file* and *binary file*.

text management

The creation, storage and retrieval of text. It implies flexible retrieval capabilities that can search for text based on a variety of criteria. Although a word processor manages text, it usually has limited retrieval capabilities.

text mode

(1) A screen display mode that displays only text and not graphics.

(2) A program mode that allows text to be entered and edited.

text-to-speech

Converting text into voice output using speech synthesis techniques. Although initially used by the blind to listen to written material, it is now used extensively to convey financial data and other information via telephone for everyone.

texture map

A two-dimensional image of a surface that is used to cover 3-D objects. See *texture mapping*.

texture mapping

In computer graphics, the creation of regular surfaces such as a brick wall and irregular surfaces such as wood grain. A 2-D image of the texture is created, called a *texture map*, which is "wrapped around" a 3-D object using various texture mapping algorithms. The pixels in a texture map are called *texels*. See *point sampling, bilinear interpolation, trilinear interpolation* and *MIP mapping*.

texture memory

Memory on the display adapter used to hold the texture maps. See *texture mapping*.

TFT

(Thin Film Transistor) The term typically refers to active matrix screens on laptop computers. Active matrix LCD provides a sharper screen display and broader viewing angle than does passive matrix. See *LCD* and *thin film*.

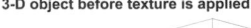
3-D object before texture is applied

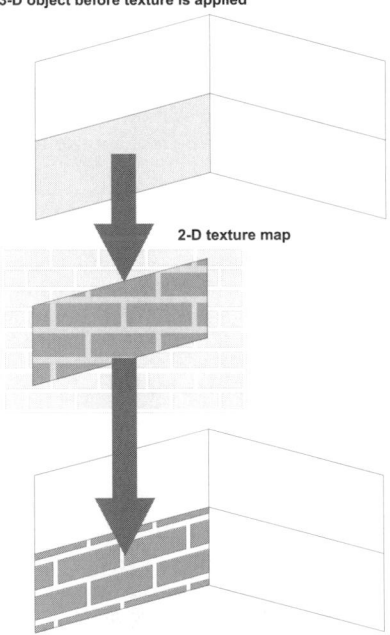
2-D texture map

3-D object after texture is applied

Texture Mapping
Using an algorithm, each pixel in the 3-D object is mapped to a corresponding texel in the texture map. *(Redrawn from illustration courtesy of Intergraph Computer Systems.)*

TFT LCD

(Thin Film Transistor LCD) See *LCD*.

TFTP

(Trivial File Transfer Protocol) A version of the TCP/IP FTP protocol that has no directory or password capability.

TGA

See *Targa*.

The Computer Glossary

The longest-running computer dictionary on the market. First published in 1981, the 8th Edition was introduced in the spring of 1988. The Computer Glossary was the foundation of Computer Desktop Encyclopedia.

The Open Group

See *Open Group*.

thermal calibration

See *thermal recalibration*.

thermal dye transfer

See *dye sublimation printer*.

thermal printer

See *direct thermal printer* and *thermal wax transfer printer*.

thermal recalibration

The periodic sensing of the temperature in hard disk drives in order to make minor adjustments to the alignment of the read/write heads. In an AV drive, this process is performed only in idle periods so that there is no interruption in reading and writing long streams of data.

thermal transfer

See *thermal wax transfer printer* and *direct thermal printer*.

thermal wax transfer printer

A printer that adheres a wax-based ink onto paper. It uses a ribbon containing an equivalent panel of ink for each page to be printed. Monochrome printers have an equivalent black panel for each page to be printed. Color printers have either three (CMY) or four (CMYK) consecutive panels for each page, thus the same amount of ribbon is used to print a full-page image as it is to print a tenth of the page. Coated paper is used, and consumables (ribbon and paper) cost more than other printer technologies, except for dye sublimation printing.

The paper and ribbon are passed together over the printhead, which contains from hundreds to thousands of heating elements. Dots of ink are melted and transferred to the paper. The wax-based ink will adhere to almost any kind of stock, from ordinary paper to complex synthetics and film.

Thermal wax uses the same type of transport mechanism as dye sublimation, but does not produce the same photorealistic

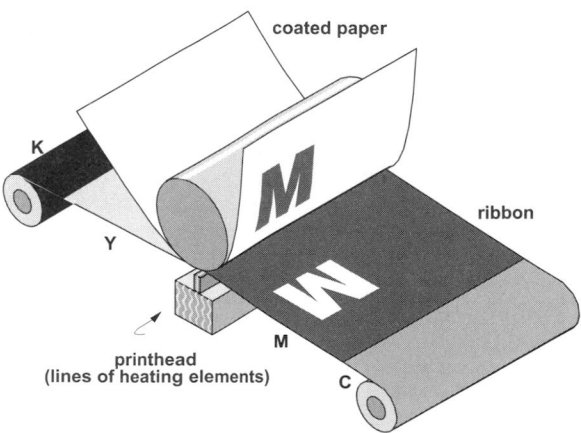

Thermal Wax Transfer Mechanism
The paper and ribbon are passed by the printhead. The ribbon is heated, and dots of ink are transferred to the paper. Monochrome ribbons contain a black panel equivalent in size to each page being printed. Color ribbons contain three (CMY) or four (CMYK) panels for each page to be printed.

output. Like other monochrome and color printers, thermal wax puts down a solid dot of ink and produces shades of gray and colors by placing dots side by side (dithering). Wax transfer does print faster than dye sub and consumables (ribbon and paper) are less expensive. Some printers allow swapping of both ribbons so that thermal wax can be used for draft quality and dye sublimation for final output. See *dye sublimation printer* and *printer*.

thick Ethernet

See *10Base5* and *Ethernet*.

thick film

A layer of magnetic, semiconductor or metallic material that is thicker than the microscopic layers of the transistors on a chip. For example, metallic thick films are silk screened onto the ceramic base of hybrid microcircuits. Contrast with *thin film*.

ThickNet, ThickWire

See *10Base5* and *Ethernet*.

thimble printer

A letter quality printer similar to a daisy wheel printer. Instead of a wheel, characters are formed facing out and around the rim of a thimble-shaped cup. For example, the NEC Spinwriters are thimble printers.

thin client

(1) A "thin processing" client in a client/server environment that performs very little data processing. The client processes only keyboard input and screen output, and all application processing is done in the server. Examples are X Window terminals and Windows terminals. See *X Window* and *Windows terminal*. Contrast with *fat client*, which is a typical desktop PC performing all or most of the application processing.

(2) A "thin storage" client in a network computer environment. The client downloads the program from the server and performs processing just like a PC, but does not store anything locally. All programs and data are on the server. This is a new and different definition for thin client created by the NC community.

thin Ethernet

See *10Base2* and *Ethernet*.

thin film

A microscopically thin layer of semiconductor or magnetic material that is deposited onto a metal, ceramic or semiconductor base. For example, the layers that make up a chip and the surface coating on high-density magnetic disks are called thin films.

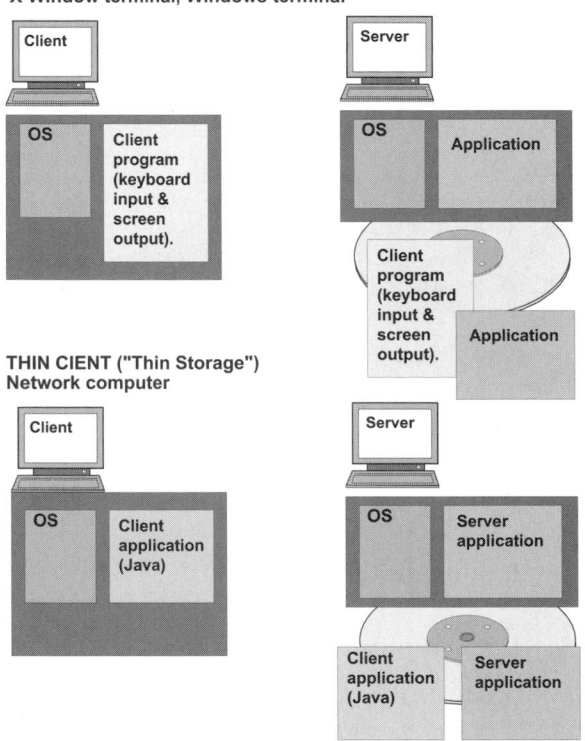

THIN CLIENT ("Thin Processing")
X Window terminal, Windows terminal

THIN CIENT ("Thin Storage")
Network computer

Thin Clients
The original thin client (top) performs no application processing. The network computer definition (below) refers to not providing storage, but it does the same types of client processing as in a PC.

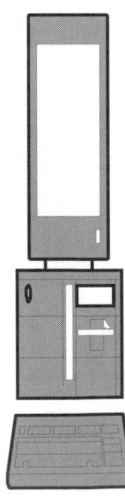

**The Only True
Thin Client!**

thin film head
A read/write head for high-density disks that is made from thin layers of a conducting film deposited onto a nickel-iron core.

ThinkPad
A family of popular notebook computers from IBM. The ThinkPads include IBM's TrackPoint pointing stick, located between the G, H and B keys on the keyboard. The TrackPoint introduced and popularized the pointing stick as a pointing device. The ThinkPads generally offer the largest LCD screens as soon as they become available.

ThinNet
See *10Base2* and *Ethernet*.

thin pipe
A low-speed communications channel. Contrast with *fat pipe*.

thin server
A network-based computer specialized for some server function such as a Web server. Designed for ease of installation, it is typically not expandable and may not even have a keyboard or monitor. Management and control is typically via a Web browser and input/output via the network.

ThinWire
See *10Base2* and *Ethernet*.

third-generation computer
A computer that uses integrated circuits, disk storage and online terminals. The third generation started roughly in 1964 with the IBM System/360.

third-generation language
Also known as a *3GL*, it refers to a high-level programming language such as FORTRAN, COBOL, BASIC, Pascal and C. It is a step above assembly language and a step below fourth-generation language (4GL). For an example of the difference between a 3GL and a 4GL, see *fourth-generation language*.

third normal form
See *normalization*.

third party
An organization that provides an auxiliary product not supplied by the primary manufacturer. Countless third-party add-on and plug-in products keep the computer industry advancing at a rapid pace. It is the third-party vendor that is often the most inventive and innovative.

thrashing
Excessive paging in a virtual memory computer. If programs are not written to run in a virtual memory environment, the operating system may spend excessive amounts of time swapping program pages in and out of the disk.

The goal of virtual memory is to increase internal memory capacity, not to waste time reloading program segments over and over. However, a well-designed virtual memory system tracks page usage and prevents the most-often-used modules from being swapped to disk.

thread
(1) One transaction or message in a multithreaded system. See *multithreading*.

(2) A topic or theme in an Internet newsgroup or groupware program that generates on-going e-mail from interested parties. See *threaded discussion*.

The ThinkPad
IBM's ThinkPad has been popular since its inception. It has introduced innovative features, such as the TrackBall pointing stick, TrackWrite keyboard and ever-increasing screen size.

threaded connector
A plug and socket that uses a threaded mechanism to lock them together. One part is screwed into the other. F and SMA connectors are examples of threaded connectors.

threaded discussion
A running log of remarks and opinions about a subject. Users e-mail their comments, and the computer maintains them in order of originating message and replies to that message. Threaded discussions are used in chat rooms on the Internet and on online services as well as in groupware products.

threading
See *multithreading*.

three degrees of freedom
See *6DOF*.

three-spindle drive
See *spindle*.

three-state logic element
An electronic component that provides three possible outputs: off, low voltage and high voltage.

three-tier client/server
A three-way interaction in a client/server environment, in which the user interface is stored in the client, the bulk of the business application logic is stored in one or more servers, and the data is stored in a database server. See *two-tier client/server*.

threshold
The point at which a signal (voltage, current, etc.) is perceived as valid.

throughput
The speed with which a computer processes data. It is a combination of internal processing speed, peripheral speeds (I/O) and the efficiency of the operating system and other system software all working together.

thru-hole
A circuit board packaging technique in which the leads (pins) on the chips and components are inserted into holes in the board. The leads are bent 90 degrees under the board, snipped off and soldered from below. Contrast with *surface mount*.

thumb
(1) Also called an *elevator*, it is the square box that slides within a scroll bar. The thumb is dragged up and down to position the text or image on screen.

(2) (Thumb) An extension to the architecture of an ARM chip that provides enhanced code density. It stores a subset of 32-bit instructions as compressed 16-bit instructions and decompresses them back to 32 bits upon execution.

thumbnail
A miniature representation of a page or image. A thumbnail program may be stand-alone or part of a desktop publishing or graphics program. Thumbnails take considerable time to generate, but provide a convenient way to browse through multiple images before retrieving the one you need. Programs often let you click on the thumbnail to retrieve it.

thunk
In a PC, to execute the instructions required to switch between segmented addressing of memory and flat addressing. A thunk typically occurs when a 16-bit application is running in a 32-bit address space, and its 16-bit segmented address must be converted into a full 32-bit flat address.

THz
(TeraHertZ) One trillion cycles per second.

TI

(Texas Instruments, Inc., Dallas, TX, www.ti.com) A leading semiconductor manufacturer founded in 1930 as Geophysical Service, an independent contractor specializing in petroleum exploration using sound waves (reflection seismograph method). In 1938, it spun off Geophysical Services, Inc. a Delaware subsidiary to do explorations for others. The parent company was later renamed Coronado Corporation, which ultimately dissolved in 1945.

In 1941, GSI was purchased by three employees and one of the original founders. The next day, the Japanese bombed Pearl Harbor, and the company found itself making equipment that would find enemy submarines, not just oil.

In 1951, GSI's name was changed to Texas Instruments, and soon after began making transistors via a licensing arrangement with Western Electric. In 1954, TI pioneered the first commercial production of transistors made from silicon, and in that same year, introduced the first pocket-sized transistor radio.

In 1958, TI's Jack Kilby demonstrated the first integrated circuit (IC), which incorporated several transistors on a single chip. Three years later, TI demonstrated a working computer using ICs that was six cubic inches in size and weighed only 10 ounces. TI produced a complete computer on a chip in 1971.

In the early 1980s, TI made a large number of low-priced 99/4a home computers. It later introduced desktop PCs, but then discontinued them. Today, TI offers a full line of notebook PCs.

With 1994 revenues of more than ten billion, TI's strength is integrated circuits. However, it also creates computer systems for AI applications, composite metals, electrical control products and consumer electronics, including its well-known line of calculators and educational math and reading machines. As the first to commercialize the silicon transistor, pocket radio, integrated circuit, hand-held calculator, single-chip computer and the LISP chip, TI has a long history of contributions to the electronics and computer industry.

First in Transistors

In 1954, TI pioneered the commercialization of the silicon transistor. In 1958, TI built the first integrated circuit (above) on a bar of germanium. It contained two transistors. These pictures were the beginning of today's commonplace multi-million transistor chips. *(Photo courtesy of Texas Instruments, Inc.)*

TIA

(1) (Telecommunications Industry Association, Arlington, VA, www.tiaonline.org) A membership organization founded in 1988 that sets telecommunications standards worldwide. It was originally an EIA working group that was spun off and merged with the U.S. Telecommunications Suppliers Association (USTSA), sponsors of the annual SUPERCOMM conferences.

(2) Digispeak for "thanks in advance."

TIA/EIA-232

See *RS-232*.

TIA/EIA-568

Standards for wiring buildings for telecommunications.

TIA/EIA-569

Standards for telecommunications wiring and equipment spaces.

TIA/EIA-606

Standards for the administration of telecommunications wiring, equipment and grounding.

TIA/EIA-607

Standards for telecommunications grounding and bonding.

tickle

See *Tcl/Tk*.

tickler

A manual or automatic system for reminding users of scheduled events or tasks. It is used in PIMs, contact management systems and scheduling and calendar systems.

TIFF

(Tagged Image File Format) A widely-used bitmapped graphics file format developed by Aldus and Microsoft that handles monochrome, gray scale, 8-and 24-bit color. TIFF allows for customization, and several versions have been created, which does not guarantee compatibility between all programs.

TIFF files are compressed using several compression methods. LZW provides ratios of about 1.5:1 to 2:1. Ratios of 10:1 to 20:1 are possible for documents with lots of white space using ITU Group III & IV compression methods (fax). See *JPEG*.

tight code

Refers to a program that is written very efficiently. A very experienced and intelligent programmer can produce a program with much tighter code than a novice. The difference can be like night and day.

tightly coupled

Refers to two or more computers linked together and dependent on each other. One computer may control the other, or both computers may monitor each other. For example, a database machine is tightly coupled to the main processor. Two computers tied together for multiprocessing are tightly coupled. Contrast with *loosely coupled*, such as personal computers in a LAN.

tilde

A symbol used in Windows 95/98 to maintain a short version of a long file or directory name for compatibility with Windows 3.1 and DOS. For example, the short version of a file named "Letter to Joe" would be LETTER~1. Then "Letter to Pat" becomes LETTER~2.

The symbol is a Spanish accent that turns an "n" into a "nyeh" sound. The tilde key is located differently on almost every keyboard. Before the tilde, only the backslash (\) key had that distinction. Now we can search high and low for both keys when we need them.

The tilde is also a mathematical symbol that is used to mean the difference between two values or an equivalency between two values.

tile

To display objects side by side. The Tile command in a graphical interface squares up all open windows and displays them in a row and column order.

Tillamook

The code name for a Pentium MMX CPU from Intel designed for notebooks. It was the first Intel chip to use .25 micron technology (down from .35). It requires only 1.8 volts rather than the 2.45 volts needed in Intel's previous Pentium chips designed for portable use. Introduced in late 1997, the first Tillamook models ran at 200 and 233MHz.

timbre

A quality of sound that distinguishes one voice or musical instrument from another. For example, MIDI synthesizers are multi-timbral, meaning that they can play multiple instruments simultaneously.

time base generator

An electronic clock that creates its own timing signals for synchronization and measurement purposes.

timeout

In communications, the intentional ending of an incomplete task. If an acknowledgment, carrier, logon, etc., has not occurred in a specified amount of time, the timeout ends the waiting loop so that the request can be retransmitted or the process terminated. Timeouts are common in communications applications in order to free up a line or port that is tied up with a request that has not been answered in a reasonable amount of time. For each type of situation, there is a default length of time before the timeout is initiated, which typically can be adjusted by the user or network administrator.

timer interrupt

An interrupt generated by an internal clock. See *interrupt*.

timesharing

A multiuser computer environment that lets users initiate their own sessions and access selected databases as required, such as when using online services. A system that serves many users, but for only one application, is technically not timesharing.

time slice

A short interval of time allotted to each user or program in a multitasking or timesharing system. Time slices are typically in milliseconds.

time slot

Continuously repeating interval of time or a time period in which two devices are able to interconnect.

timing clock

See *clock*.

timing signals

Electrical pulses generated in the processor or in external devices in order to synchronize computer operations. The main timing signal comes from the computer's clock, which provides a frequency that can be divided into many slower cycles. Other timing signals may come from a timesharing or realtime clock.

In disk drives, timing signals for reading and writing are generated by holes or marks on one of the platters, or by the way the digital data is actually recorded.

tin

(Threaded Internet Newsreader) A newsreader for Usenet newsgroups that maintains message threads. It is based on the tass newsreader, which was derived from Plato Notes. See *Usenet*.

Tiny BASIC

A subset of BASIC that has been used in first generation personal computers with limited memory.

TIRIS

(Texas Instruments Registration and Identification System) An RF/ID system from TI that uses a 3.6x29mm cylindrical tag. Reading can be done from as far as 40 inches away.

TI-RPC

(Transport-Independent-Remote Procedure Call) A set of functions from Sun for executing procedures on remote computers. It is operating system and network independent and allows the development of distributed applications in multivendor environments.

Tivoli Enterprise Management

A comprehensive suite of applications from IBM subsidiary Tivoli Systems, Inc., Austin, TX, (www.tivoli.com), that provides enterprise-wide network and systems management across all platforms from IBM mainframes to desktop PCs.

TLA

(Three Letter Acronym) The epitome of acronyms! While two-, four- and five-letter acronyms exist, there are more three-letter acronyms. Obviously, three words to describe a concept or product is the most popular.

TLD

(Top Level Domain) The highest level domain category in the Internet naming system. For example, .com, .org and .net are TLDs. See *Internet domain names*.

TLI

(Transport Level Interface) A common interface for transport services (layer 4 of the OSI model). It provides a common language to a transport protocol and allows client/server applications to be used in different networking environments.

Instead of directly calling NetWare's SPX for example, the application calls the TLI library. Thus, any transport protocol that is TLI compliant (SPX, TCP, etc.) can provide transport services to that application. TLI is part of UNIX System V. It is also supported by NetWare 3.x. See *STREAMS*.

TLS

(1) (Transparent LAN service) A communications service from the telephone companies that connects LANs in different locations. The service is typically provided via private lines or FDDI within the carrier's own local access and transport area (LATA).

(2) (Transaction Layer Security) A security protocol from the IETF that is a merger of SSL and other protocols. Expected in 1998, it is also expected to become the security standard on the Internet. TLS uses Triple DES encryption. See *SSL* and *DES*.

TM1

(Tables Manager 1) A multidimensional analysis program for DOS and Windows from Applix, Inc., Westboro, MA, (www.applix.com), that allows data to be viewed in up to eight dimensions. The data is kept in a database, and the formulas are kept in a spreadsheet, which is used as a viewer into the database. TM1 makes it easy to display different slices of the data, and it is designed to import and cross tab large amounts of data. TM1 was originally developed by Sinper Corporation.

TME

See *Tivoli Enterprise Management*.

TMN

(Telecommunications Management Network) A set of international standards for network management from the ITU.

TN

(Twisted Nematic) The first LCD technology. It twists liquid crystal molecules 90 degrees between polarizers. TN displays require bright ambient light and are still used for low-cost applications. See *STN* and *LCD*.

TN3270

A Telnet program that includes the 3270 protocol for logging onto IBM mainframes.

TNT

(1) (Transparent Network Transport) Services from the telephone companies and common carriers that provide Ethernet and Token Ring transmission over MANs and WANs.

(2) A DOS extender from Phar Lap Software, Cambridge, MA, (www.pharlap.com), that allows DOS applications to use various Win32 features, including memory allocation, DLLs and threads.

TOF

(Top Of Form) The beginning of a physical paper form. To position paper in many printers, the printer is turned offline, the forms are aligned properly and the TOF button is pressed.

toggle

To alternate back and forth between two states.

token

See *token passing* and *authentication token*.

token bus network

A LAN access method that uses the token passing technology. Stations are logically connected in a ring but are physically connected by a common bus. All tokens are broadcast to every station in the network, but only the station with the destination address responds. After transmitting a maximum amount of data, the token is passed to the next logical station in the ring. The MAP factory automation protocol uses this method. See *token passing*.

token passing

A communications network access method that uses a continuously repeating frame (the token) that is transmitted onto the network by the controlling computer. When a terminal or computer wants to send a message, it waits for an empty token. When it finds one, it fills it with the address of the destination station and some or all of its message.

Every computer and terminal on the network constantly monitors the passing tokens to determine if it is a recipient of a message, in which case it "grabs" the message and resets the token status to empty. Token passing uses bus and ring topologies. See *token bus network* and *token ring network*.

Token Ring

A local area network (LAN) developed by IBM (IEEE 802.5). It uses a token ring access method and connects up to 255 nodes in a star topology at 4 or 16 Mbps. All stations connect to a central wiring hub called the *MAU* (Multistation Access Unit) using a twisted wire cable. The central hub makes it easier to troubleshoot failures than a bus topology. This is a different type of hub than the one used in 10BaseT twisted pair Ethernet networks.

Token Ring is more deterministic than Ethernet. It ensures that all users get regular turns at transmitting their data. With Ethernet, all users compete to get onto the network.

There are two types of Token Ring networks. Type 1 Token Ring networks allow up to 255 stations per network and use shielded twisted pair wires with IBM style Type 1 connectors. Type 3 Token Rings allow up to 72 devices per network and use unshielded twisted pair (Category 3, 4 or 5) with RJ-45 connectors.

Token Ring is a data link protocol (MAC layer protocol) and functions at layers 1 and 2 of the OSI model. See *data link protocol* and *OSI*.

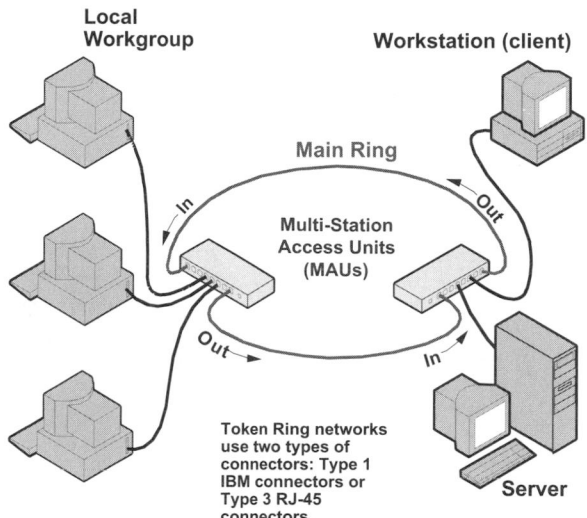

Token Ring networks use two types of connectors: Type 1 IBM connectors or Type 3 RJ-45 connectors.

Token Ring Topology

Token Ring uses a logical ring topology, which provides more equal opportunity for each station to gain access to the network than the broadcast method used by Ethernet. All nodes connect to the MAU.

Token Ring adapter

A network adapter used in a Token Ring network. See *network adapter*.

Token Ring connector

Called a *Type 1 connector* and developed by IBM, it is a combination plug and socket. Flip any connector 180 degrees with the other and they plug together.

Type 1 IBM Connector

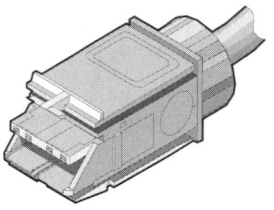

Type 1 connectors are used in Token Ring networks. The same connector is both plug and socket just by flipping one 180 degrees with the other.

token ring network

A LAN access method that uses the token passing technology in a physical ring. Each station in the network passes the token on to the station next to it. Token Ring and FDDI LANs use the token ring access method. See *Token Ring, FDDI* and *token passing*.

TokenTalk

Software for the Macintosh from Apple that accompanies its TokenTalk NB board and adapts the Mac to Token Ring Networks.

toll quality audio

Audio transmission at the quality level of an ordinary long distance telephone call.

toner

An electrically charged ink used in copy machines and laser printers. It adheres to an invisible image that has been charged with the opposite polarity onto a plate or drum or onto the paper itself.

tool

(1) A program used for software development or system maintenance. Virtually any program or utility that helps programmers or users develop applications or maintain their computers can be called a tool.

Examples of programming tools are compilers, interpreters, assemblers, 4GLs, editors, debuggers and application generators. See *toolkit*.

(2) A program that helps the user analyze or search for data. For example, query and report programs are often called query tools and report tools.

(3) An on-screen function in a graphics program; for example, a line draw, circle draw or brush tool.

toolbar

A row or column of on-screen buttons used to activate functions in the application. Some toolbars are customizable, letting you add and delete buttons as required. See *tool palette*.

ToolBook

An application development system for Windows from Asymetrix Learning Systems, Bellevue, WA, (www.asymetrix.com), that uses a "page and book" metaphor analogous to Apple's HyperCard "card and stack." Its OpenScript language is also similar to HyperTalk.

A Toolbar with Tools!
Most toolbar buttons show only pictures, while some have a text explanation too. This toolbar from VTEL's videoconferencing software has real tools on it!

toolbox

See *toolkit* and *toolbar*.

toolkit

An integrated set of software routines or utilities (tools) that are used to develop programs and/or create and maintain databases. See *tool, developer's toolkit, library, class library, Encyclopedia Toolkit* and *CASE*.

tool palette

A collection of buttons grouped together on screen that provide a quick way to select the functions available in the program. A tool palette is typically found in graphics software such as a drawing program or image editor, but a tool palette can be used to provide functions for any kind of program. Tool palettes can generally be customized to display the functions used most often, leaving the rest to be selected by menus. See *toolbar*.

tools vendor

A publisher of development software used by programmers, which includes compilers, debuggers, visual programming utilities and CASE products. A tools vendor may provide a variety of utilities and routines that assist programmers and systems analysts. See *tool*.

TOP

(Technical Office Protocol) A communications protocol for office systems developed by Boeing Computer Services, Seattle, WA, (www.boeing.com). It uses the Ethernet access method and is often used in conjunction with *MAP*, the factory automation protocol developed by GM. TOP is used in the front office, and MAP is used on the factory floor. TOP uses the CSMA/CD access method, while MAP uses token bus.

topdown design

A design technique that starts with the highest level of an idea and works its way down to the lowest level of detail.

topdown programming

A programming design and documentation technique that imposes a hierarchical structure on the design of the program. See *structured programming*.

top level domain

See *Internet domain names*.

top of file

The beginning of a file. In a word processing file, it is the first character in the document. In a data file, it is either the first record in the file or the first record in the index. For example, in a dBASE file that is indexed on name, **goto top** might go to physical record #608 if record #608 is AARDVARK.

topology

(1) In a communications network, the pattern of interconnection between nodes; for example, a bus, ring or star configuration.

(2) In a parallel processing architecture, the interconnection between processors; for example, a bus, grid, hypercube or Butterfly Switch configuration.

TOPS

(1) A multiuser, multitasking, timesharing, virtual memory operating system from Digital that runs on its PDP-6, DECsystem 10 and DECsystem 20 series.

(2) (Transparent OPerating System) A peer-to-peer LAN from Sitka Corporation, Alameda, CA, that uses the LocalTalk access method and connects Apple computers, PCs and Sun workstations. Its Flashcard plugs LocalTalk capability into PCs.

top-tier vendor

A vendor of a product that is highly recognized for its brand name. Examples of top-tier PC vendors are Compaq, HP and IBM.

TopTOOLS

Software from HP that enables system administrators to manage their PCs remotely. It collects configuration data from the PCs in the network and assists in upgrading them with new software and BIOSes.

torn down

See *tear down*.

TOTAL

An early network DBMS from Cincom Systems, Inc., Cincinnati, OH, (www.cincom.com), that ran on a variety of minis and mainframes.

total bypass

Bypassing local and long distance telephone lines by using satellite communications.

to the recruiter

One of the most important things for a recruiter to understand about the psychology of technical people is the split between systems analysis & design and programming.

The skills required of a systems analyst, or the programmer analyst or business analyst who functions as a systems analyst, are different than a programmer or technical professional.

Analysts with experience in a specific type of vertical application, such as insurance and manufacturing, are more valuable to another company with the same application. Since there are fundamentals that apply to all information systems, analysts ocassionally do cross industry lines. For example, good listening and interviewing skills are as important as technical knowledge in designing information systems. An analyst with an abundance of these skills can work with new applications successfully. However, analysts with moderate listening and interviewing skills are generally more successful in the same niche industry, because they are more familiar, hopefully, with the nuances of the business.

Programmers are also sought with application experience, for example, a COBOL programmer in

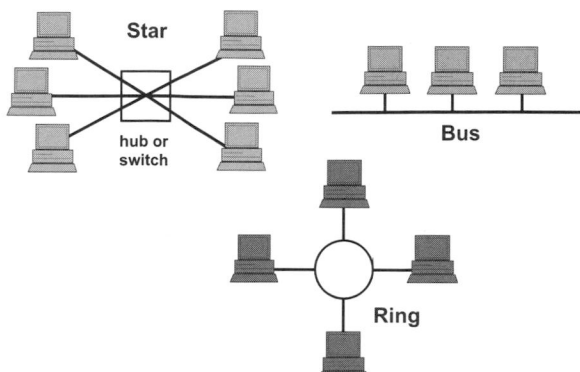

Network Topologies

These are the three major topologies used in networks. Ethernet uses bus, hub and switch topologies. Token Ring uses ring and switch.

banking. However, programmers can cross application boundaries much more easily than systems analysts. Programmers often have little allegiance to their company's industry in the first place, being more concerned with the software environment they work with. It can also take years to learn the nuances of a language, and many programmers do not like to learn a new one.

As far as getting work done on time, it is more important that the programmer have experience with the type of functions required in the program than the nature of the business. If the functional specifications have been well designed, then coding the program is based on the kinds of algorithms required and the complexity of the interface.

Coding routine data processing operations is typically much easier than reworking the user interface, especially if some new kind of user interaction is required that is not part of the GUI library and must be "hand coded." All of it depends on the tools being used and the experience level of the programmer. These variables should not be underestimated, because what can take one programmer a month to do can take another two hours. A programmer's experience, skill level and innate analytic ability can make that much of a difference.

The point is that programmers, as well as technical staff at the programming level, such as systems programmers, systems administrators, network administrators and database administrators, can easily cross industry lines as long as they continue to be involved in their niche hardware and software, such as the hardware platform, programming language, operating system and network protocols. See *programmer, computercruiter* and *nerd rustler.*

touchpad

A stationary pointing device that provides a small, flat surface that you slide your finger over using the same movements as you would a mouse. You can tap on the pad's surface as an alternate to pressing one of the touchpad keys. See *pointing device.*

touch screen

A touch-sensitive display screen that uses a clear panel over on the screen surface. The panel is a matrix of cells that transmit pressure information to the software.

tower

(1) A floor-standing cabinet taller than it is wide. Desktop computers can be made into towers by turning them on their side and inserting them into a floor-mounted base.

(2) (Tower) Series of UNIX-based single and multiprocessor computer systems from NCR that use the Motorola 68000 family of CPUs.

TP

See *twisted pair, TPO, teleprocessing* and *TP monitor.*

TP0-TP4

(Transport Protocol Class 0 to Class 4) The grades of OSI transport layers from least to most complete and specific. TP4 is a full connection-oriented transport protocol.

TPA

(Transient Program Area) See *transient area.*

TPC

(Transaction Processing Performance Council, San Jose, CA, www.tpc.org) An organization devoted to benchmarking transaction processing systems. In order to derive the number of transactions that can be processed in a given timeframe, TPC benchmarks measure the total performance of the system, which includes the computer, operating system, database management system and any other related components involved in the transaction processing operation.

Earlier TPC-A and TPC-B benchmarks produced tpsA and tpsB ratings, which were measured in

Touch Screen
This Richardson Texas firm makes touch screen overlays for PCs and Macs that are used in a wide variety of applications. (Photo courtesy of Keytec, Inc.)

transactions per second. The subsequent TPC-C benchmark yields transactions per minutes expressed in tpmC ratings. The TPC-D benchmark is designed for decision support and tests 17 complex queries. TPC-D results are relative numbers based on the size of the database being queried and yield a single-user Qppd Power metric and a multiple-user QthD Throughput metric.

TPF
(Transaction Processing Facility) An operating system for IBM mainframes specialized for large transaction processing systems such as airline reservations. TPF supports thousands of terminals with a typical response time of two to three seconds. It was formerly called Airline Control Program/Transaction Processing (ACP/TP).

tpi
(Tracks Per Inch) The measurement of the density of tracks recorded on a disk or drum.

TPM
(Transactions Per Minute) The number of transactions processed within one minute. See *TPS*.

tpmC
The rating from the TPC-C benchmark, which measures overall transaction processing performance. See *TPC*.

TP monitor
(TeleProcessing monitor or Transaction Processing monitor) A control program that manages the transfer of data between multiple local and remote terminals and the application programs that serve them. It may also include programs that format the terminal screens and validate the data entered.

In a distributed client/server environment, a TP monitor provides integrity by ensuring that transactions do not get lost or damaged. It may be placed in a separate machine and used to balance the load between clients and various application servers and database servers. It is also used to create a high availability system by switching a failed transaction to another machine.

Examples of popular TP monitors are CICS, a veteran TP monitor used on IBM mainframes and the UNIX-based Tuxedo and Encina products.

TPO
(Twisted Pair Only) Refers to the use of twisted pair wire when other options are available. For example, a TPO suffix at the end of 3com Ethernet adapter model numbers indicates the card has only an RJ45 connector. TP means RJ45 and AUI connectors, TPC is RJ45 and BNC, and COMBO cards provide all three.

TP-PMD
(Twisted Pair-Physical Medium Dependent) An ANSI standard for an FDDI network that uses UTP instead of optical fiber. See *CDDI*.

TPS
(1) (Transactions Per Second) The number of transactions processed within one second. See *TPM*.

(2) (Transaction Processing System) Originally used as an acronym for such a system, it now refers to the measurement of the system (#1 above).

tpsA, tpsB
The rating from the TPC-A and TPC-B benchmarks, which measure overall transaction processing performance. See *TPC*.

TQFP
See *QFP*.

TQM
(Total Quality Management) An organizational undertaking to improve the quality of manufacturing and service. It focuses on obtaining continuous feedback for making improvements and refining existing processes over the long term. See *ISO 9000*.

TR
See *Token Ring*.

trace

See *autotrace*.

Traceroute

An Internet utility that traces the route from the client machine to the remote host being contacted. It reports the IP addresses of all the routers in between. The Windows utility (TRACERT.EXE) is executed from the command line, but programs such as NeoTrace (www.neoworx.com) visually displays the route.

track

A storage channel on disk or tape. On disks, tracks are concentric circles (hard and floppy disks) or spirals (CDs and videodiscs). On tapes, they are parallel lines. Their format is determined by the specific drive they are used in. On magnetic devices, bits are recorded as reversals of polarity in the magnetic surface. On CDs, bits are recorded as physical pits under a clear, protective layer. See *magnetic disk*.

track-at-once

See *disc fixation*.

trackball

A stationary pointing device that contains a movable ball rotated with the fingers or palm. From one to three keys are located in various positions depending on the unit. Years ago, Kensington Microware popularized the trackball with its Turbo Mouse for the Macintosh. See *mouse, pointing stick* and *touchpad*.

tracking

In desktop publishing, the consistent letterspacing of text. Tracking is used to expand or contract the amount of text on a page by expanding or reducing the amount of space between letters. It differs from kerning in that it is applied to an entire font or to a range of text, whereas kerning refers to certain letter pairs.

TrackPoint

The pointing stick used in IBM laptops. IBM introduced and popularized this type of pointing device on its ThinkPad laptops.

trackstick

Same as *pointing stick*.

tractor feed

A mechanism that provides fast movement of paper forms through a printer. It contains pins on tractors that engage the paper through perforated holes in its left and right borders. A "pull" tractor pulls the forms through the printer mechanism, while a "push" tractor pushes the forms. Contrast with *sheet feeder*.

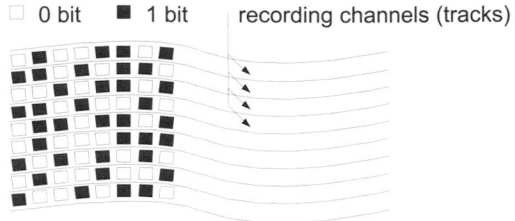

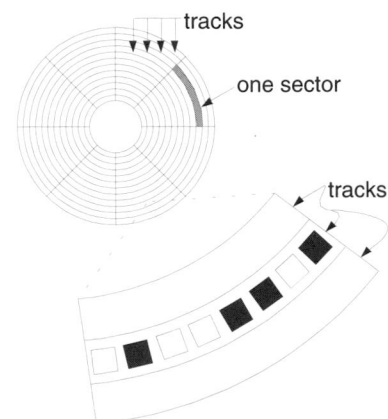

Tracks and Sectors
On disk, tracks are concentric circles. On tape, they are generally parallel with the length, although helical scan tracks run diagonal.

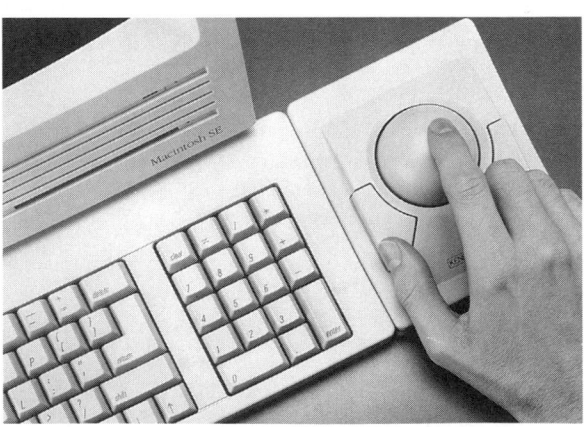

The Turbo Mouse
The Turbo Mouse popularized the trackball for the Macintosh. Later models were developed for the PC. *(Photo courtesy of Kensington Microware, Ltd.)*

Tradacoms

A European EDI standard developed by the Article Numbering Association. See *X12* and *EDIFACT*.

trademarks

The purpose of this book is to provide a meaningful definition of computer science terms and related products, but it is not meant to be a source of trademark registration information. When we know of an origin of a term, we state it. There are thousands of terms in this database that do not include a lineage, because we did not know of it at the time of writing.

We presume that every name of a product is a trademark of its respective organization. If a company creates a name for its product and continues to use it, it is a de facto trademark whether or not it is registered. Among other legal reasons, registration serves to formally document how long a name has been in use.

If a particular technology in this book is attributed to an organization, we do not know if it is a de facto or de jure trademark of that organization. To find out trademark information about a particular item mentioned, please contact the legal counsel of the organization that is mentioned as its creator.

traffic

Data crossing a network. Traffic is a very general term and can refer to transactions and messages of any kind.

trailer

In communications, a code or set of codes that make up the last part of a transmitted message. See *trailer label*.

trailer label

The last record in a tape file. May contain number of records, hash totals and other ID.

training

(1) Teaching the details of a subject. With regard to software, training provides instruction for each command and function in an application. Contrast with *education*.

(2) In communications, the process by which two modems determine the correct protocols and transmission speeds to use.

(3) In voice recognition systems, the recording of the user's voice in order to provide samples and patterns for recognizing that voice.

train printer

An early line printer that used a mechanism similar to a chain printer, except that the characters were not chained together. They were independent type slugs that were pushed around a track by engaging with a drive gear at one end. Train and chain printers gave way to band printers in the early 1980s. See *chain printer* and *printer*.

transaction

An activity or request. Orders, purchases, changes, additions and deletions are typical business transactions stored in the computer. Transactions update one or more master files and serve as both an audit trail and history for future analyses. Ad hoc queries are a type of transaction as well, but are usually just acted upon and not saved. Transaction volume is a major factor in figuring computer system size and speed.

Keeping Transactions in Sync

A major problem in a transaction processing system is ensuring that all master files are updated before the transaction is considered completely processed. For example, if two files must be updated, but a system failure occurs after the first one, but before the second one, the software must be able to roll back the first update and start over later. In a distributed environment, this is called *two phase commit*. See *transaction file*.

transaction environment

A system that processes transactions by updating various files and returning confirmations. It implies a regular, high-volume stream of records entering the system. See *transaction processing, transaction file* and *transaction*.

transaction file

A collection of transaction records. The data in transaction files is used to update the master files, which contain the subjects of the organization. Transaction files also serve as audit trails and history for the organization. Where before they were transferred to offline storage after some period of time, they are increasingly being kept online for routine analyses. See *data warehouse, transaction processing* and *information system*.

Following are the kinds of fields that make up a typical transaction record in a business information system. There can be many more fields depending on the organization. The "key" fields below are the ones that are generally indexed for fast matching against the master record. The account number is usually the primary key, but name may also be used as a primary key. See *master file* for examples of typical master records.

```
     EMPLOYEE PAYROLL RECORD
key  Employee account number
     Today's date
     Hours worked

     ORDER RECORD
key  Customer account number
     Today's date
     Quantity
     Product number

     PAYMENT RECORD
key  Customer number
     Today's date
     Invoice number
     Amount paid
     Check number

     PURCHASE ORDER
key  Purchase order number
     Today's date
     Department
     Authorizing agent
     Vendor account number
     Quantity
     Product number
     Due date
     Total cost

     WAREHOUSE RECEIPT
key  Purchase order number
key  Invoice number
     Today's date
     Quantity
     Product number
```

transaction monitor

See *TP monitor*.

transaction processing

Processing transactions as they are received by the computer. Also called *online* or *realtime* systems, transaction processing means that master files are updated as soon as transactions are entered at terminals or received over communications lines. It also implies that confirmations are returned to the sender.

If you save receipts in a shoebox and add

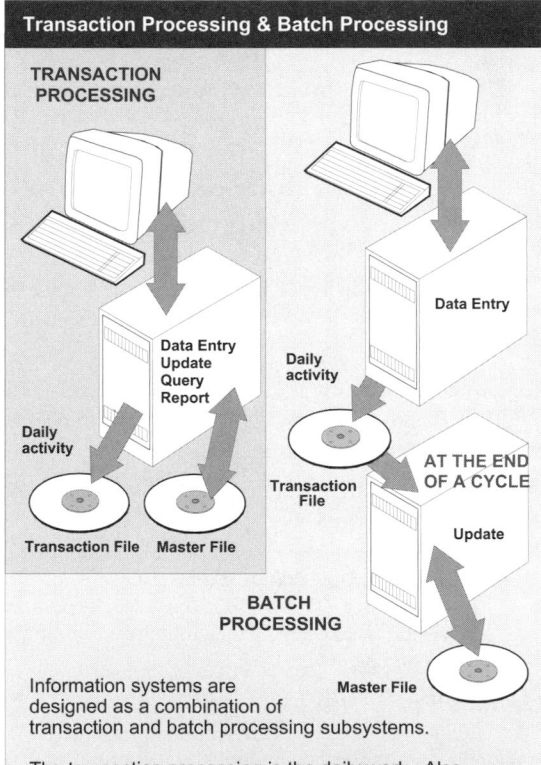

Transaction Processing & Batch Processing

TRANSACTION PROCESSING

Data Entry
Update
Query
Report

Daily activity

Transaction File   Master File

BATCH PROCESSING

Data Entry

Daily activity

Transaction File

AT THE END OF A CYCLE

Update

Master File

Information systems are designed as a combination of transaction and batch processing subsystems.

The transaction processing is the daily work. Also called online transaction processing (OLTP), it means that the database is updated as soon as a transaction is received: a sales order depletes inventory, a stock sale updates the last close, a pledge adds to the fund raising balance. Transaction processing keeps business records up-to-date the moment transactions are keyed into or transmitted to the system.

Batch processing is updating or searching an entire table from beginning to end. A month-end report is a batch job as is printing payroll checks. There are many jobs that can be more economically processed at the end of a cycle. For example, the electronic transactions for telephone calls are stored in the computer until month end, when they are matched against the customer table for updating with all the other telephone transactions at the same time.

Computer Desktop Encyclopedia

them up at the end of the year for taxes, that's batch processing. However, if you buy something and immediately add the amount to a running total, that's transaction processing.

Organizations increasingly rely on computers to keep everything up-to-date all the time. A manager might need to know how many items are left on the shelf, what the latest price of a stock is or what the value of a financial portfolio is at any given moment.

Transaction processing is often called online transaction processing, or *OLTP*. The OLTP market is a demanding one. If a business depends on computers for its day-to-day operations, the computers must stay up and running during business hours. See *two-phase commit, mission critical, industrial strength* and *fault tolerant*.

transceiver

A transmitter and receiver of analog or digital signals. It comes in many forms; for example, a transponder or network adapter.

transcode

To convert from one format to another. It implies conversion between distinct kinds of data, such as from speech into text or from analog video into digital, rather than from one digital format into another.

transcribe

To copy data from one medium to another; for example, from one source document to another, or from a source document to the computer. It often implies a change of format or codes.

transducer

A device that converts one energy into another; for example, a read/write head converts magnetic energy into electrical energy and vice versa. In process control applications, it is used to convert pressure into an electrical reading.

transfer

To send data over a computer channel or bus. "Transfer" generally applies to transmission within the computer system, and "transmit" refers to transmission outside the computer over a line or network.

Transfers are actually copies, since the data is in both locations at the end of the transfer. Input, output and move instructions activate data transfers in the computer.

transfer protocol

See *file transfer protocol*.

transfer rate

Also called *data rate*, it is the transmission speed of a communications or computer channel. Transfer rates are measured in bits or bytes per second.

transfer time

The time it takes to transmit or move data from one place to another. It is the time interval between starting the transfer and the completion of the transfer.

transformer

A device that changes AC voltage. Also called a *power adapter*. It is made of steel laminations wrapped with two coils of wire. The coil ratio derives the voltage change. For example, if the input coil has 1,000 windings, and the output has 100, 120 volts is changed to 12. In order to create direct current (DC), the output is passed through a rectifier.

transient

A malfunction that occurs at random intervals; for example, a rapid fluctuation of voltage in a power line or a memory cell that intermittently fails.

transient area

An area in memory used to hold application programs for processing. The bulk of a computer's main memory is used as a transient area.

transient data

Data that is created within an application session. At the end of the session, it is discarded or reset back to its default and not stored in a database. Contrast with *persistent data*.

transient state

The exact point at which a device changes modes, for example, from transmit to receive or 0 to 1.

transistor

A device used to amplify a signal or open and close a circuit. In a computer, it functions as an electronic switch, or bridge. The transistor contains a semiconductor material that can change its electrical state when pulsed.

In its normal state, the semiconductor material is not conductive. When voltage is applied to it, it becomes conductive and current flows through it. The gate, or base, is the triggering line, and the source and drain or emitter and collector are the two end points.

Transistors, resistors, capacitors and diodes, make up logic gates. Logic gates make up circuits, and circuits make up electronic systems. For the history and evolution of the transistor, see *chip*.

The following illustrations show the stages in the creation of one transistor. Millions of transistors are built on each of several dozen CPU chips on a single wafer. Thus, more than a hundred million transistors are typically fabricated simultaneously.

The invention of the transistor and its increasing miniaturization is the backbone of computer technology.

A run-of-the-mill chip fabrication plant only costs two billion dollars. Wanna be the first on your block to build one?

The Transistor Concept

The transistor is an electronic switch. The switching element is made of semiconductor material which conducts electricity when it is pulsed.

If there is no pulse on the trigger line, the semiconductor element is in a non-conductive state. When it is pulsed, it becomes conductive and current flows from the input to the output.

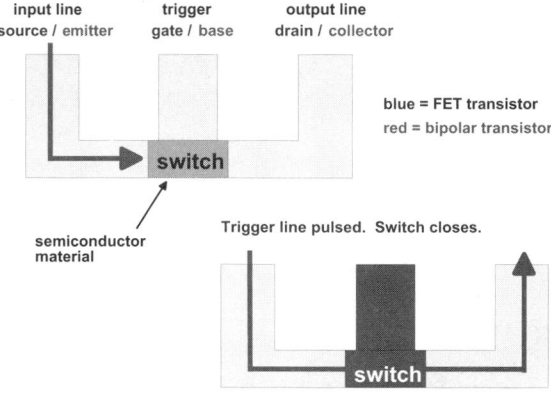

Trigger line not pulsed. Switch is open.

input line	trigger	output line
source / emitter	gate / base	drain / collector

blue = FET transistor
red = bipolar transistor

semiconductor material

Trigger line pulsed. Switch closes.

Conceptual View of a Transistor

Semiconductor material normally acts as an insulator. When it is pulsed with electricity, it becomes electrically conductive for that moment. It simply acts as an electrical bridge.

1 The wafer is covered with an insulation layer and coated with film. Where exposed to light through a photomask, the film and insulation become hard.

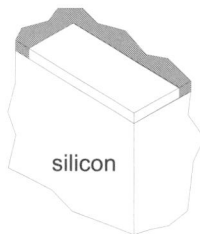

silicon

2 The wafer is subjected to acid, which etches out the unhardened film and insulation exposing the silicon below.

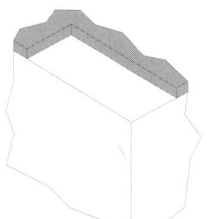

3 Under pressure, chemicals are implanted into the silicon creating a sublayer element that is electrically altered from the rest of the silicon.

This sublayer is only about 1/1000th of an inch deep.

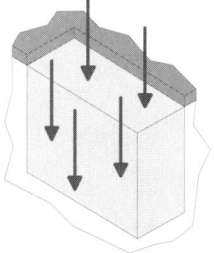

4 The wafer is recovered with insulation and film.

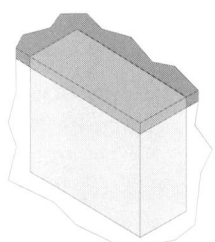

5 The next design is transfered by photomask onto the wafer.

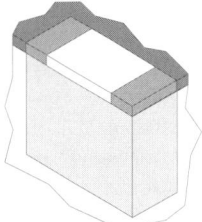

9 The final stage is to tunnel through the insulation again and adhere the aluminum pathways that carry the current to and from the transistor.|The trigger is the signal that activates the transistor, causing the switch to close so current can travel travel from the input line to the output line.

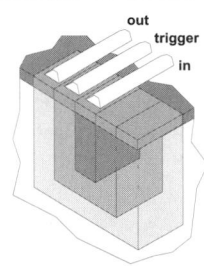

6 A new hole is opened up, and chemicals are implanted to create an element within the sublayer.

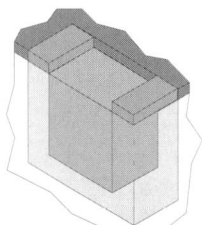

10 When electricity is present on the input line, it cannot bridge over to the output side, because the semiconductor material is not conductive.

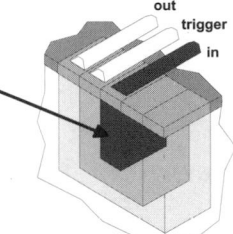

7 The "patient is sewed up" once more, and another design is transferred onto the wafer.

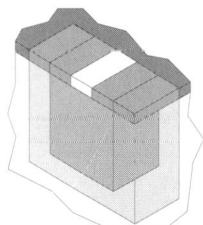

11 When the trigger line is pulsed, the bridge (semiconductor element) becomes conductive.

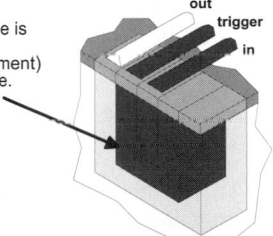

8 The third element is created by the same etching and implantation process.

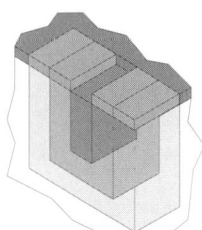

12 When the semiconductor element is conductive, electricity travels from the input to the output.

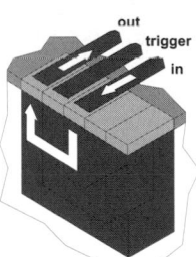

translate

(1) To change one language into another; for example, assemblers, compilers and interpreters translate source language into machine language.

(2) In computer graphics, to move an image on screen without rotating it.

(3) In telecommunictions, to change the frequencies of a band of signals.

translating bridge

A type of bridge that interconnects two different types of LAN protocols, such as Ethernet and Token Ring. Translating bridges are generally complicated devices. However, source routing transparent (SRT) bridging integrates both bridging methods of Ethernet and Token Ring to solve the problem. See *SRT*.

TransLISP PLUS

A version of LISP for PCs developed by Solution Systems, Inc., Wellesley, MA. It provided the ability to link a Microsoft C routine to the LISP library as a function.

transmission

Transferring data over a communications channel.

transmission channel

A path between two nodes in a network. It may refer to the physical cable, the signal transmitted within the cable or to a subchannel within a carrier frequency. In radio and TV, it refers to the assigned carrier frequency.

transmission speed

The rate at which data is moved across a communications channel. Following are the transmission speeds of common LAN and WAN technologies.

transmit

To send data over a communications line. See *transfer*.

transmitter

A device that generates signals. Contrast with *receiver*.

transmogrify

To change into something completely different.

transparent

(1) Refers to a change in hardware or software that, after installation, causes no noticeable change in operation.

(2) In computer graphics, a color that is treated as background which takes on the color of the underlying window or page.

transparent bridge

A common type of network bridge, in which the host stations are unaware of their existence in the network. A transparent bridge learns which node is connected to which port through the experience of examining which node responds to each new station address that is transmitted. Ethernet uses this type of bridge, also called an *adaptive bridge*. Contrast with *source route bridging*. See *spanning tree algorithm*.

transparent LAN service

A communications service from a local telephone company or common carrier that links remote LANs together. It is called transparent because the Ethernet, Token Ring or FDDI network is connected directly to the service at both ends regardless of the technology employed by the carrier in between. The network administrator is not responsible for dealing with a different protocol.

transparent media adapter

A device that allows a flatbed scanner to scan 35mm slides and other film transparencies. It provides a mechanism that shines light through the transparencies.

transponder

A receiver/transmitter on a communications satellite. It receives a microwave signal from earth (uplink), amplifies it and retransmits it back to earth at a different frequency (downlink). A satellite has several transponders.

transport layer

The services in the OSI protocol stack (layer 4 of 7) that provide end-to-end management of the communications session. See *transport protocol* and *OSI*.

LAN Technologies	Bandwidth
Ethernet	10 Mbps (shared)
Switched Ethernet	10 Mbps (node to node)
Fast Ethernet	100 Mbps
Gigabit Ethernet	1000 Mbps
Token Ring	4, 16 Mbps
Fast Token Ring	100, 128 Mbps
FDDI/CDDI	100 Mbps
ATM	25, 45, 155, 622. 2488 Mbps +

To compute actual network throughput, divide bps (bits per sec) by 10 for bytes per second. Then halve the amount to account for overhead. Thus, in a 10 Mbps Ethernet network, there is only 500 thousand bytes per second of usable bandwidth. That means a 10 meg file will take 20 seconds to send. The 10 million bits per second doesn't sound so fast anymore, does it?

WAN Technologies	Bandwidth
UNSWITCHED PRIVATE LINES (point to point)	
T1	24 x 64 Kbps = 1.5 Mbps
T3	672 x 64 Kbps = 44.7 Mbps
Fractional T1	N x 64 Kbps
SWITCHED SERVICES	
Dial-up via modem	9.6, 14.4, 28.8, 33.6, 56 Kbps
ISDN	BRI 64-128 Kbps PRI 1.544 Mbps
Switched 56/64	56 Kbps, 64 Kbps
Packet switched (X.25)	56 Kbps
Frame relay	56 Kbps to 45 Mbps
SMDS	45, 155 Mbps
ATM	25, 45, 155, 622, 2488 Mbps +

Computer Desktop Encyclopedia

transport protocol

A communications protocol responsible for establishing a connection and ensuring that all data has arrived safely. It is defined in layer 4 of the OSI model. Often, the term transport protocol implies transport services, which includes the lower level data link protocol that moves packets from one node to another. See *OSI* and *transport services*.

transport services

The collective functions of layers 1 through 4 of the OSI model.

transputer

(TRANSistor comPUTER) A computer that contains a CPU, memory and communications capability on a single chip. Chips are strung together in hypercube or grid-like patterns to create large parallel processing machines, used in scientific, realtime control and AI applications.

trap

To test for a particular condition in a running program; for example, to "trap an interrupt" means to wait for a particular interrupt to occur and then execute a corresponding routine. An error trap tests for an error condition and provides a recovery routine. A debugging trap waits for the execution of a particular instruction in order to stop the program and analyze the status of the system at that moment.

trapdoor

A secret way of gaining access to a program or online service. Trapdoors are built into the software by the original programmer as a way of gaining special access to particular functions. For example, a trapdoor built into a BBS program would allow access to any BBS computer running that software. A trapdoor can be built into a hash function that enables the output to be converted back into the input. See *one-way hash function*.

trash can

An icon of a garbage can used for deleting files. The icon of a file is dragged to the trash can and released. In the Mac, the trash can is also used to eject a floppy by dragging the icon of the floppy disk onto it. In Windows 95, the equivalent of the trash can is the recycle bin, but it is used only for deleting files and folders, not ejecting floppies.

trashware

Software that is so poorly designed that it winds up in the garbage can.

Travan

A backup tape technology from Imation Enterprises Corporation, Oakdale, MN, (www.imation.com). Travan has evolved from the QIC backup tapes, but uses wider tape, different tape guides and improved magnetic media to yield higher capacities. With Network Series (NS) drives, which provide hardware compression and read-while-write features, Travan tapes are migrating from desktop backup to workgroup server backup. Travan drives may be compatible with QIC, QIC-Wide and QIC-EX cartridges, but it varies from model to model. See *QIC, QIC-Wide* and *QIC-EX*. For a summary of all storage technologies, see *storage*.

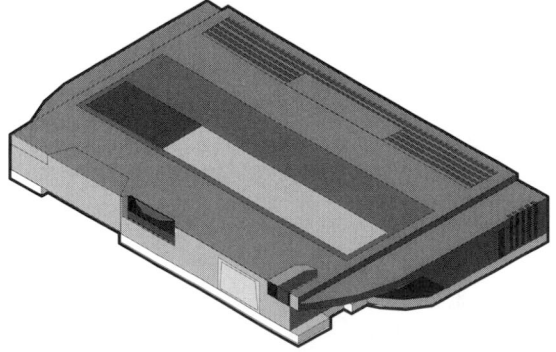

Travan Cartridge
Travan is a member of the QIC family of backup tapes. Travan drives may also be capable of reading earlier QIC, QIC Wide as well as QIC-EX cartridges.

```
TRAVAN NATIVE CAPACITIES
TR-1                    400MB
TR-2 (not popular)      800MB
TR-3                    1.6GB
HP 5GB (TR-4)           2.5GB
Travan 8GB (TR-4)        4GB
Travan NS 8              4GB
Travan 20GB (TR-5)      10GB
Travan NS 20            10GB
```

tray

See *tray card* and *System Tray*.

tray card

The printed insert that goes under the tray in a CD jewel case and wraps around both edges. If the printed cover of the jewel case is only a single piece of paper rather than a booklet, it is often known as the front tray card. See *jewel case*.

tree

A hierarchical structure. See *directory tree*.

treeware

Products derived from trees, namely the documentation manuals.

Trenton Computer Festival (TCF)

The first personal computer show in the U.S. It was started in 1976 by Professor Sol Libes and Dr. Allen Katz, and its two principle organizers were Trenton State College and the Amateur Computer Group of New Jersey (ACGNJ). Expecting only a few hundred people, TCF drew several thousand attendees from all over the country, inspiring the creation of the West Coast Computer Faire shortly thereafter. TCF is held in the spring and also hosts a large outdoor flea market, offering new and used electronic systems and parts.

triangle

A three-sided polygon. In 3-D graphics, the surfaces of 3-D objects are broken down into triangles. Small numbers of triangles are used for flat surfaces, while large numbers are used to mold curved surfaces similar to the way a geodesic dome is constructed. The three points of every triangle (vertices) are computed on an x-y-z scale and must be recomputed each time the object is moved. See *triangle setup* and *geometry calculations*.

triangle setup

In 3-D graphics rendering, computing the rate of change of RGB color values between the points of each triangle (vertices) so that the triangles can be filled with color properly in the rasterization stage. Triangle setup comes after the geometry calculations and before rasterization. In the 3-D world, each object is represented as a collection of triangles. See *graphics accelerator* for illustration.

trichromatic

In computer graphics, the use of red, green and blue to create all the colors in the spectrum.

trigger

A mechanism that initiates an action when an event occurs such as reaching a certain time or date or upon receiving some type of input. A trigger generally causes a program routine to be executed.

In a database management system (DBMS), it is an SQL procedure that is executed when a record is added or deleted. It is used to maintain referential integrity in the database. A trigger may also execute a stored procedure. Triggers and stored procedures are built into DBMSs used in client/server environments. See *intelligent database*.

trilinear interpolation

A texture mapping technique that produces the most realistic images and requires the most computations. This technique is used in conjunction with MIP mapping, which provides texture maps in different depths.

An algorithm is used to map a screen pixel location to a corresponding point on the two nearest texture maps (MIP maps). A weighted average of the attributes (color, alpha, etc.) of the four surrounding texels on each MIP map is computed (bilinear interpolation). Then the weighted average of the two results is applied to the screen pixel. This process is repeated for each pixel forming the object being textured.

The term trilinear refers to the performing of interpolations in three dimensions (horizontal, vertical and depth). See *texture map, MIP mapping, bilinear interpolation* and *point sampling*.

trillion

One thousand times one billion (10 to the 12th power). See *space/time*.

Trilogy

A company founded in 1979 by Gene Amdahl to commercialize wafer scale integration and build supercomputers. It raised a quarter of a billion dollars, the largest startup funding in history, but could not create its 2.5" superchip. In 1984, it abandoned supercomputer development and later the superchip project. In 1985, Trilogy acquired Elxsi Corporation, a manufacturer of VAX-compatible systems, and eventually merged itself into Elxsi.

Trimetra

A family of servers from ICL that are the first products of its Millennium Programme, which is designed to take the company into the 21st century. Trimetra supports the OpenVME, UnixWare and Windows NT environments and comes in high-end SY servers, midrange LY servers and entry-level DY models. Its SY line is expected to provide more than 500 MIPS performance in future models. See *ICL*.

triple precision

The use of three computer words to hold a number used for calculation, providing an enormous amount of arithmetic precision.

triple twist

A supertwist variation that twists crystals to 260 degrees for improved clarity. See *LCD*.

TRITON

The name of earlier versions of Baan software, before the release of BAAN IV. See *BAAN IV*.

Triton chipset

The name Intel previously used for its chipsets. See *Intel chipsets*.

trivestiture

The splitting up of AT&T into three independent companies: AT&T, NCR and Lucent. Unlike the 1984 divestiture, which was court ordered, trivestiture was an internal decision in 1996. See *divestiture*.

trn

(Threaded ReadNews) A popular newsreader for Usenet newsgroups. It is an enhanced version of rn (ReadNews) that includes threads. See *Usenet*.

troff

(Typesetting RunOFF) A UNIX utility that formats documents for typesetters and laser printers. Using a text editor, troff codes are embedded into the text and the troff command converts the document into the required output. See *nroff*.

Trojan horse

A program that appears legitimate, but performs some illicit activity when it is run. It may be used to locate password information or make the system more vulnerable to future entry or simply destroy programs or data on the hard disk. A Trojan horse is similar to a virus, except that it does its damage all at once rather than replicate itself. See *virus*.

trolling

(1) Surfing, or browsing, the Web.

(2) Posting derogatory messages about sensitive subjects on newsgroups and chat rooms to bait users into responding.

(2) Hanging around in a chat room without saying anything, like a "peeping tom."

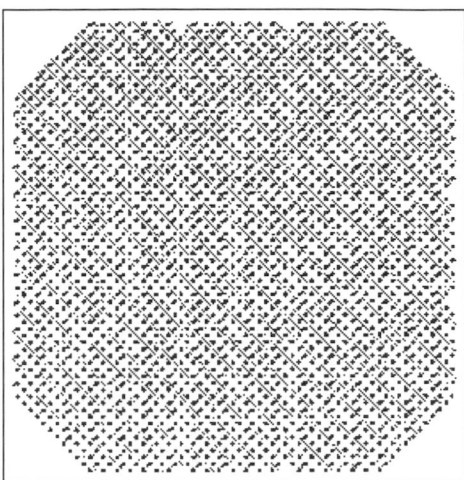

The Trilogy Superchip
The 2.5" square superchip was never completed, because it was too far ahead of its time. Even today, we have not learned how to make chips that are much larger than an inch square. In time perhaps, we'll figure it out, and Amdahl's vision will become a reality. *(Photo courtesy of Elxsi Corporation.)*

troubleshoot

To find out why something does not work and to fix the problem. Troubleshooting a computer often requires determining whether the problem is due to malfunctioning hardware or buggy or out-of-date software. See *debug*.

TRS-80

(Tandy Radio Shack) An early line of personal computers from Tandy. In 1977, the TRS-80, along with the Apple II and the Commodore PET, ushered in the personal computer revolution. The operating system for the TRS-80 was TRS-DOS. See *Tandy* and *personal computer*. See also *TSR*.

True BASIC

An ANSI-standard structured-programming version of BASIC for the PC, Mac and Amiga from True BASIC, Inc., West Lebanon, NH. Developed in 1984 by BASIC's creators, John Kemeny and Thomas Kurtz, it includes many enhancements over original BASIC. It comes in both interpreter and compiler form.

true color

(1) The ability to generate 16,777,216 colors (24-bit color). See *high color*.

(2) The ability to generate photo-realistic color images (requires 24-bit color minimum).

TrueImage

An enhanced PostScript interpreter from Microsoft that prints PostScript Type 1 and TrueType fonts.

TrueType

A scalable font technology that renders fonts for both the printer and the screen. Originally developed by Apple, it was enhanced jointly by Apple and Microsoft. TrueType fonts are used in Windows, starting with Windows 3.1, as well as in the Mac System 7 operating system.

Unlike PostScript, in which the algorithms are maintained in the rasterizing engine, each TrueType font contains its own algorithms for converting the outline into bitmaps. The lower-level language embedded within the TrueType font allows unlimited flexibility in the design. See *TTF file* and *TrueImage*.

True Web Integration

The features in Internet Explorer 4.0 and Windows 98 that add Web integration to the desktop. It includes Active Desktop and Active Channel plus the ability to integrate these functions into the Start menu and Taskbar. It also combines the Explorer file manager and Internet Explorer browser into a common interface, where both can be used to access local and network resources as well as Web pages. See *Active Desktop* and *Active Channel*.

truncate

To cut off leading or trailing digits or characters from an item of data without regard to the accuracy of the remaining characters. Truncation occurs when data is converted into a new record with smaller field lengths than the original.

trunk

A communications channel between two points. It often refers to large-bandwidth telephone channels between major switching centers, capable of transmitting many simultaneous voice and data signals.

trusted computer system

A computer system that cannot be illegally accessed. See *NCSC*.

trusted domain relationship

A trust association between two domains. See *trust relationship*.

trustee

A user or group of users that has been given access rights to files on a network server.

trust relationship

In Windows NT, an association between servers in one domain or an association between one domain and another. It allows a user to log on once and have access to all associated resources without having to be authenticated again. In NT 5.0, the process of defining trust relationships is automated.

truth table

A chart of a logical operation's inputs and outputs. See *Boolean logic*.

TSAPI

(Telephony Services **API**) A telephony programming interface from Novell and AT&T. Based on the international CSTA standard, TSAPI is designed to interface a telephone PBX with a NetWare server to provide interoperability between PCs and telephone equipment.

TSAT

See *VSAT*.

Tseng Labs

(Tseng Labs, Inc., Newtown, PA, www.tseng.com) A manufacturer of chipsets and display adapters for PCs. Founded in 1983, it has continued to provide products that have enhanced the IBM PC display standards. Its ET series (ET3000, ET4000, etc.) of chips have been used in millions of display adapters.

T.share

The remote control part of the T.120 realtime data conferencing protocol. T.share is used in Microsoft's NetMeeting and RDP (Remote Desktop Protocol) is based on it. See *Windows Terminal Server, RDP* and *T.120*.

TSO

(Time Sharing Option) Software that provides interactive communications for IBM's MVS operating system. It allows a user or programmer to launch an application from a terminal and interactively work with it. The TSO counterpart in VM is called CMS. Contrast with *JES*, which provides batch communications for MVS.

TSOP

(Thin Small Outline Package) A very-thin, plastic, rectangular surface mount chip package with gull-wing pins on its two short sides. TSOPs are about a third as thick as SOJ chips. See *gull-wing lead, SOP, SOJ* and *chip package*.

TSR

(Terminate and Stay Resident) Refers to a program that remains in memory when the user exits it in order that it be immediately available at the press of a hotkey. TSRs became popular under DOS to quickly pop up a calendar, calculator or other utility, because task switching was not built into early versions of DOS. But standards for writing TSRs were not codified early on, and TSRs often conflicted with each other and regular applications. Since the advent of Windows 3.0, multiple DOS applications have been conveniently task switched under Windows, which essentially makes a TSR out of every application program.

TSS

See *ITU*.

TTF file

(TrueType Font file) A TrueType font file in Windows that contains the mathematical outlines of each character in the font. In the Mac, the icon of a TrueType file looks like a document, dog-eared on the upper left, with three A's on it. TTF files are stored in the \WINDOWS\SYSTEM or \WINDOWS\FONTS folders. For example, the following files make up the Arial typeface. See *FOT file*.

```
\windows\fonts\arial.ttf      normal
\windows\fonts\ariali.ttf     italics
\windows\fonts\arialbd.ttf    bold
\windows\fonts\arialbi.ttf    bold italics
```

TTFN

Digispeak for goodbye ("ta ta for now").

TT font

See *TrueType*.

TTL
(Transistor Transistor Logic) A digital circuit composed of bipolar transistors wired in a certain manner. TTL logic has been widely used since the early days of digital circuitry. TTL designations may appear on input or output ports of various devices, which indicates a digital circuit in contrast to an analog circuit.

TTS
(Transaction Tracking System) Software that monitors a transaction until completion. In the event of a hardware or software failure, it ensures that the database is brought back to its former state before the attempt to update. See *two-phase commit*. See also *text-to-speech*.

T.TUD
See *T.120*.

TTY
(TeleTYpewriter) See *teletypewriter*.

TTY protocol
A low-speed asynchronous communications protocol with limited or no error checking.

tube
See *CRT* and *vacuum tube*.

tuner
An electronic part of a radio or TV that locks on to a selected carrier frequency (station, channel) and filters out the audio and video signals for amplification and display.

tunneling
Transmitting data structured in one protocol format within the format of another protocol. Tunneling allows other types of transmission streams to be carried within the prevailing protocol. See *IP tunneling*.

TUO
(Technology Upgrade Option) A clause in a computer lease that allows the lessee to upgrade the equipment before the lease term is over. It often states that the same or higher rate of interest applies.

tuple
In relational database management, a record, or row. See *relational database*.

Turbo C
A C compiler from Borland used to create a wide variety of commercial products. It is known for its well-designed debugger. Borland's object-oriented versions of C are Turbo C++ and Borland C++.

TURBOchannel
A 32-bit data bus from Digital introduced in 1990. It has a peak transfer rate of 100 MBytes/sec.

Turbo Pascal
A pascal compiler for DOS from Borland used in a wide variety of applications from accounting to complex commercial products. Turbo Pascal for Windows provides an object-oriented programming environment for Windows development. Borland is responsible for moving the Pascal language from the academic halls to the commercial world.

Turing test
The "acid test" of true artificial intelligence, as defined by the English scientist Alan Turing. In the 1940s, he said "a machine has artificial intelligence when there is no discernible difference between the conversation generated by the machine and that of an intelligent person."

turnaround document
A paper document or punched card prepared for re-entry into the computer system. Paper documents are printed with OCR fonts for scanning Invoices and inventory stock cards are examples.

Computer Desktop Encyclopedia

turnaround time

(1) In batch processing, the time it takes to receive finished reports after submission of documents or files for processing. In an online environment, turnaround time is the same as *response time*.

(2) In half-duplex transmission, the time it takes to change from transmit to receive and vice versa.

turnkey system

A complete system of hardware and software delivered to the customer ready-to-run.

turnpike effect

In communications, a lock up due to increased traffic conditions and bottlenecks in the system.

Turtle Beach

See *Voyetra*.

Turtle Graphics

A method for creating graphic images in the Logo programming language. The "turtle" is an imaginary pen that is given drawing commands, such as go forward and turn right. On screen, the turtle is shaped like a triangle. See *Logo*.

TÜV

(Technischer Überwachungs-Verein) Literally "Technical Watch-Over Association." A German certifying body involved with product safety for the European Community. The "TÜV Rheinland" mark is placed on tested and approved electrical and electronic devices like our UL (Underwriters Laboratory) seal.

Tuxedo

See *BEA TUXEDO*.

TV board

An expansion board in a personal computer that contains a TV tuner. It derives its source from an antenna or cable TV just like any TV set. The accompanying software is used to change the channel and create a video window that is displayed with other windows on screen. In a PC, the board is generally connected to the VGA adapter via the feature connector. The TV board may also cable directly to the computer's monitor or indirectly through the display adapter. See *feature connector*.

TWAIN

(Technology Without An Interesting Name) A programming interface that lets a graphics application, such as an image editing program or desktop publishing program, activate a scanner, frame grabber or other image-capturing device.

tweak

To make minor adjustments in order to improve performance.

tweening

An animation technique that, based on starting and ending shapes, creates the necessary "in-between" frames. See *morphing*.

twinax card

An expansion board in a personal computer that emulates a 5250 terminal, the common terminal on an IBM midrange system (AS/400, System/3x).

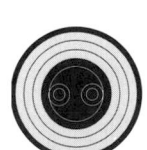

Twinaxial Connector
Twinax connectors are used on IBM System 3x and AS/400 computer systems.

twinax, twinaxial

A type of cable similar to coax, but with two inner conductors instead of one. It is used in IBM midrange (AS/400, System/3x) communications environments.

TWIP

(TWentIeth of a Point) Equal to 1/1440th of an inch.

twisted pair

A thin-diameter wire (22 to 26 guage) commonly used for telephone wiring. The wires are twisted around each other to minimize interference from other twisted pairs in the cable. Twisted pairs have less bandwidth than coaxial cable or optical fiber.

The two major types are unshielded twisted pair (UTP) and shielded twisted pair (STP). UTP is popular because it is very pliable and doesn't take up as much room in ductwork as does shielded twisted pair and other cables.

Shielded twisted pair is wrapped in a metal sheath for added protection against external interference. See *cable categories*.

Shielded and Unshielded Twisted Pairs
The metal shield on the STP cable adds protection against external interference.

two-out-of-five code

A numeric code that stores one decimal digit in five binary digits in which two of the bits are always 0 or 1 and the other three are always in the opposite state.

two-phase commit

A technique for ensuring that a transaction successfully updates all appropriate files in a distributed database environment. All DBMSs involved in the transaction first confirm that the transaction has been received and is recoverable (stored on disk). Then each DBMS is told to commit the transaction (do the actual updating).

Although traditionally two-phase-commit meant updating databases in two or more servers, the term is also applied to updating two different kinds of databases within the same server. See *transaction, transaction file* and *transaction processing*.

two-tier client/server

A two-way interaction in a client/server environment, in which the user interface is stored in the client and the data is stored in the server. The application logic can be in either the client or the server. See *fat client, fat server* and *three-tier client/server*.

The Twisted Pair

two-wire lines

A transmission channel made up of only two wires, such as used in the common dial-up telephone network.

TWX

(TeletypeWriter eXchange Service) A U.S. and Canadian dial-up communications service that became part of Telex. In 1971, the Bell System sold TWX to Western Union. TWX transmits 5-bit Murray code or 7-bit ASCII code at up to 150 bps. See *Telex*.

TX chipset

See *Intel chipsets*.

TXD

(Transmitting Data) See *modem*.

TXT file

See *ASCII file*.

Tymnet

A value-added, packet switching network that enables many varieties of terminals and computers to exchange data. It is now part of Concert Communications Services, owned by MCI and British Telecom (BT). See *Concert*.

type

(1) In data or text entry, to press the keys on the keyboard.

(2) In programming, a category of variable that is determined by the kind of data stored in it. For example, integer, floating point, string, logical, date and binary are common data types.

(3) (Type) In DOS and OS/2, a command that displays the contents of a text file.

Type 1 connector

See *Token Ring connector*.

Type 1 font

The primary type of PostScript font. Each font is composed of a .PFB and .PFM file, which are stored in the \PSFONTS and \PSFONTS\PFM folders. Sometimes, \PSFONTS is in the \WINDOWS folder (\WINDOWS\PSFONTS). In Windows 95/98, Adobe Type Manager lets you view the file names under the Properties of each font. For example, the following files make up the Garamond typeface. See *PostScript*.

```
\psfonts\gdrg____.pfb          normal
\psfonts\gdi_____.pfb          italics
\psfonts\gdsb____.pfb          bold
\psfonts\gdsbi___.pfb          bold italics

\psfonts\pfm\gdrg____.pfm      normal
\psfonts\pfm\gdi_____.pfm      italics
\psfonts\pfm\gdsb____.pfm      bold
\psfonts\pfm\gdsbi___.pfm      bold italics
```

Type 3 font

A type of PostScipt font that is used to create complex designs. See *PostScript*.

typeahead buffer

See *keyboard buffer*.

Type A plug, Type B plug

See *USB*.

type ball

A golf ball-sized element used in typewriters and low-speed teleprinters that contains all the print characters on its outside surface. It was introduced with IBM's Selectric typewriter.

typeface

The design of a set of printed characters, such as Courier, Helvetica and Times Roman.

typeface family

A group of typefaces that include the normal, bold, italic and bold-italic variations of the same design.

type family

See *typeface family*.

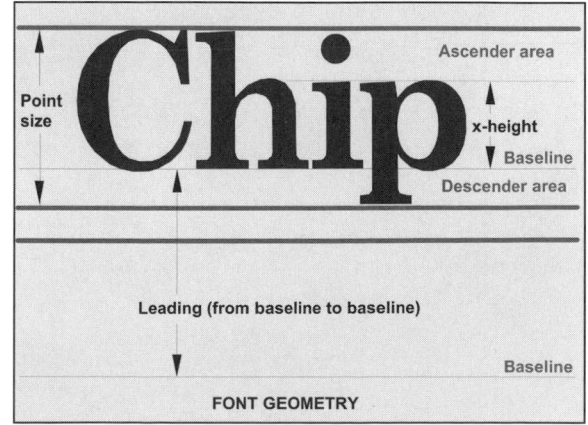

FONT GEOMETRY

type font

A set of print characters of a particular design (typeface), size (point size) and weight (light, medium, heavy). See *font*.

typematic

A keyboard feature that continues to repeat a key as long as it is held down. The speed of the repeating key as well as the time interval before the repeat begins can be set by the DOS Mode command and control panels in Windows and the Mac.

typeover mode

In word processing and data entry, a state in which each character typed on the keyboard replaces the character at the current cursor location. Contrast with *insert mode*.

type scaler

See *font scaler*.

typesetter

See *imagesetter*.

typing

(1) To input data to a typewriter or computer by pressing the keys on the keyboard.

(2) In programming, classifying variables by the kind of data they hold (string, integer, floating point, etc.). Stongly typed languages enforce strict adherance to typing and do not allow data types to be mixed in the same variable. Weakly typed languages provide minimal validation, which can result in processing errors.

U

U

See *RU*.

UA

See *messaging system*.

UAE

(Uninterruptible Application Error) The name of an abend, or crash, in a Windows 3.0 application. When the UAE occurs, an error message is displayed, and the program is generally unable to continue. Starting with Windows 3.1, an abend is known as a GPF (General Protection Fault). See *Application Error* and *abend*.

UART

(Universal Asynchronous Receiver Transmitter) The electronic circuit that makes up the serial port. It converts parallel bytes from the CPU into serial bits for transmission, and vice versa. It generates and strips the start and stop bits appended to each character. Older 8250 and 16450 UARTs are not fast enough for today's modems. A 16550 is required for transmission up to 115,200 bps (115 Kbps).

ISDN users running both 64 Kbps channels are losing performance with a 16-550 UART, because the maximum 115 Kbps is reduced further to 92 Kbps when the start/stop bits are removed. Upgrading to a 16-650 or 16-750 boost real data speed from 92 to 128 Kbps. The 16-650 is the more sophisticated UART, providing hardware flow control that reduces the burden on the CPU. (Dashes added for readability.) See *UART overrun*.

UART	Buffer size	Max speed
8250	None	9,600
16450	1 byte	9,600
16550	16 bytes	115,200
16650	32 bytes	430,800
16750	64 bytes	921,600

UART overrun

A condition in which a UART cannot process the byte that just came in fast enough before the next one arrives.

UBR

(Unspecified Bit Rate) An asynchronous transfer mode (ATM) level of service that does not guarantee available bandwidth. It is very efficient, but not used for critical data.

UCAID

(University Corporation for Advanced Internet Development, Washington, DC, www.ucaid.org) A non-profit consortium founded in 1997 dedicated to developing advanced networking technology. It started as the Internet2 project with 34 universities in late 1996 and grew so large in one year (more than 100 universities and 20 companies) that it became necessary to formalize its administration and coordination. See *Internet2* and *Abilene*.

UCE

(Unsolicited Commercial E-mail) See *spam*.

UCR

(Under Color Removal) A method for reducing amount of printing ink used. It substitutes black for gray color (equal amounts of cyan, magenta and yellow). Thus black ink is used instead of the three CMY inks. See *GCR* and *dot gain*.

UCSD p-System

(University of California at San Diego p-System) An early software development system designed for portability. Source programs (BASIC, Pascal, etc.) were compiled into intermediate "p-code" programs, which were executed by an interpreter in the target machine.

UDA

(Universal Data Access) An umbrella term from Microsoft for its combined set of standards for file and database access. UDA includes ODBC, ADO, OLE DB and RDS.

UDB

See *DB2 UDB*.

UDF

(1) (Universal Disk Format) A file system for optical media developed by the Optical Storage Technology Association (OSTA). It was designed for read-write interoperability between all the major operating systems as well as compatibility between rewritable and write-once media. DVDs are based on the UDF format, which allows them to be used on DVD players and a wide variety of computer systems. See *CD UDF*.

(2) (User Defined Function) A routine that has been defined or programmed by the user of the system and has been included in a standard library of functions. In these cases, "user" typically means programmer, not end user.

UDMA

(Ultra DMA) See *Ultra ATA*.

UDP

(User Datagram Protocol) A protocol within the TCP/IP protocol suite that is used in place of TCP when a reliable delivery is not required. For example, UDP is used for realtime audio and video traffic where lost packets are simply ignored, because there is no time to retransmit. If UDP is used and a reliable delivery is required, packet sequence checking and error notification must be written into the applications. See *RTP*.

UDP/IP

Refers to the use of UDP packets over IP. UDP does not guarantee reliable delivery, whereas TCP does. See *UDP*.

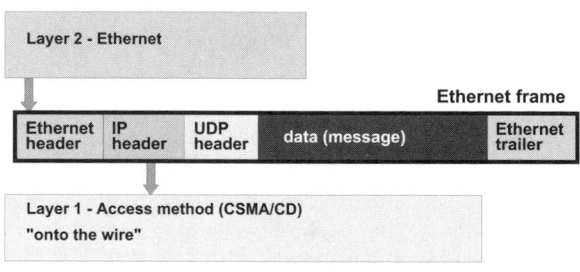

UDP Packet

A UDP packet is framed just like a TCP packet. This shows a UDP packet in an Ethernet frame ready for transmission over the network.

ugly code

Programming source code that is either poorly written or so complex that it is extremely difficult to figure out. See *program maintenance*.

UHF

(Ultra High Frequency) The range of electromagnetic frequencies from 300MHz to 3GHz.

UI

See *UNIX International* and *user interface*.

UIDL

(1) (Unique ID Listing) A POP3 mail server function that assigns a unique number to each incoming mail message. This allows mail to be left on the server after it has been downloaded to the user. Both the mail client and the POP server must support this feature.

(2) (User Interface Definition Language) A language used to describe the elements in a user interface.

UIMX

(User Interface Management System for X Window) Software from Visual Edge Software, Ltd., St. Laurent, Quebec, (www.vedge.com), that allows a user to design and modify Open Look and Motif interfaces.

u-Law

See *mu-Law* and *AU file*.

ULSI

(Ultra Large Scale Integration) More than one million transistors on a chip. See *SSI, MSI, LSI* and *VLSI*.

ULS server

(User Location Service server) A conferencing directory server on a TCP/IP network (intranet, Internet, etc.) that is used to identify participating users. When an audio or videoconferencing program is launched, it sends its user profile and current IP address to the ULS server, so that others can query the server and find out who is currently logged on. Microsoft renamed its directory servers ILS servers (Internet Locator Server), and Netscape Conference uses DLS servers (Dynamic Lookup Service). See *IP telephony*.

Ultra2 SCSI

A SCSI interface that transfers 40 Mbytes/sec for 8-bit versions and 80 Mbytes/sec for 16-bit versions. The maximum cable length is 39.4 feet. See *Ultra SCSI* and *SCSI*.

Ultra ATA, Ultra DMA, Ultra IDE

An enhanced version of the IDE interface that transfers data up to 33 Mbytes/sec. See *IDE* for all the ATA types and speeds.

ultrafiche

Pronounced "ultra feesh." A microfiche that holds up to 1,000 document pages per 4x6" sheet of film. Normal microfiche stores around 270 pages.

UltraJava

A high-end version of Sun's Java chip designed for desktop computers. It is expected to have built-in MPEG compression and use some of Sun's graphics processing found in its UltraSPARC chips.

Ultra SCSI

A SCSI interface that transfers 20 Mbytes/sec for 8-bit versions and 40 Mbytes/sec for 16-bit versions. The maximum cable length is 9.8 feet for up to four deivces or 4.9 feet for five or more. See *Ultra2 SCSI* and *SCSI*.

UltraSPARC

An enhanced series of SPARC chips introduced by Sun in 1995. The UltraSPARC chips are 64-bit CPUs that run all 32-bit SPARC applications.

ultraviolet

An invisible band of radiation at the high-frequency end of the light spectrum. It takes about 10 minutes of ultraviolet light to erase an EPROM chip.

ULTRIX

Digital's version of UNIX for its PDP-11 and VAX series.

UMA

(Upper Memory Area) Memory in a PC between 640K and 1024K. See *UMB*.

UMB

(Upper Memory Block) Unused blocks in the UMA (640K-1M). A UMB provider, such as EMM386.EXE, is software that can load and manage drivers and TSRs in these unoccupied areas. See *PC memory map* for an illustration of the UMB area.

umbrella term

A term used to cover a broad category of functions rather than one specific item. An umbrella term is often a marketing strategy to keep a name visible over a long period.

UML

(Unified Modeling Language) An object-oriented design language from the Object Management Group (OMG). Many design methodologies for describing object-oriented systems were developed in the late 1980s. UML "unifies" the popular methods into a single standard, including Grady Booch's work at Rational Software, Rumbaugh's Object Modeling Technique and Ivar Jacobson's work on use cases.

unary

Meaning one; a single entity or operation, or an expression that requires only one operand.

unbundle

To sell components in a system separately. Contrast with *bundle*.

UNC

(Universal Naming Convention) A standard for identifying servers, printers and other resources in a network, which originated in the UNIX community. A UNC path uses double slashes or backslashes to precede the name of the computer. The path (disk and directories) within the computer are separated with a single slash or backslash, as in the following examples (note that the drive letter is no longer used in the DOS/Windows example):

```
//servername/path      UNIX

\\servername\path      DOS/Windows
```

unconditional branch

In programming, a GOTO, BRANCH or JUMP instruction that passes control to a different part of the program. Constrast with *conditional branch*.

undelete

To restore the last delete operation that has taken place. There may be more than one level of undelete, allowing several or all previous deletions to be restored.

underflow

(1) An error condition that occurs when the result of a computation is smaller than the smallest quantity the computer can store.

(2) An error condition that occurs when an item is called from an empty stack.

underrun

When writing a CD-R disc, the inability for the computer to keep up with the recording process. CD-R discs, prior to using the CD UDF file format, have to be written in one continuous stream that cannot be interrupted. See *CD UDF* and *thermal recalibration*.

underscan

Within the normal rectangular viewing area on a display screen. Contrast with *overscan*.

underscore

The underscore character (_) is often used to make file, field and variable names more readable, when blank spaces are not allowed. For example, NOVEL_1A.DOC, FIRST_NAME and Start_Routine_A.

undo

To restore the last editing operation that has taken place. For example, if a segment of text has been deleted or changed, performing an undo will restore the original text. Programs may have several levels of undo, including being able to reconstruct the original data for all edits performed in the current session.

UNI

(User-to-Network Interface) An interface between the end user and the network. See *NNI*.

Unibus

A bus architecture from Digital that was introduced in 1970 with its PDP-11 series. Unibus peripherals can be connected to a VAX through Unibus attachments on the VAXs.

unicast

To transmit from one station to another, such as from client to server or server to server. Contrast with *multicast*.

Unicenter

See *CA-Unicenter*.

Unicode

A superset of the ASCII character set that uses two bytes for each character rather than one. Able to handle 65,536 character combinations rather than just 256, it can house the alphabets of most of the world's languages. ISO defines a four-byte character set for world alphabets, but also uses Unicode as a subset.

unidirectional

The transfer or transmission of data in a channel in one direction only.

UNIFACE

An application development system for client/server environments from Compuware Corporation, Farmington Hills, MI, (www.compuware.com). It is a repository-driven system that imports a variety of CASE tools. It supports Windows, Mac and OS/2 clients and VMS and UNIX servers. UNIFACE is known for its scalability and deployment on large enterprise-wide applications. Uniface Corporation is part of Uniface International, which was acquired by Compuware of Farmington Hills, MI.

UniForum

(UniForum, Santa Clara, CA, www.uniforum.org) A membership association of computer professionals dedicated to advancing open systems. Membership includes the "UniForum Monthly" magazine and other technical and standards publications, discounts on products and services and eligibility to serve on committees and the Board of Directors.

UNIFY 2000

A relational DBMS for UNIX platforms from Unify Corporation, Sacramento, CA, (www,unify,com). Introduced in 1982, it was the first commercially available RDBMS for UNIX.

Unify VISION

An application development system for client/server environments from Unify Corporation, Sacramento, CA, (www.unify.com). Introduced in 1993, it provides visual programming tools and supports a variety of UNIX platforms and databases. It provides automated application partitioning for developing three-tier client/server architectures. Other Unify Corporation products are the ACCELL/SQL 4GL and UNIFY 2000 relational DBMS.

Unimodem

A driver from Microsoft that provides common telephony services for Windows applications that access data and fax modems. Unimodem is a Telephony Service Provider (TSP) that accepts calls written to the TAPI interface and commands the modem directly.

uninstall

To remove hardware or software from a computer system. In order to remove a software application from a PC, an uninstall program, also called an *uninstaller*, deletes all the files that were initially copied to the hard disk and restores the AUTOEXEC.BAT, CONFIG.SYS, WIN.INI and SYSTEM.INI files if they were modified.

Many applications come with their own uninstall utility. Otherwise, a generic uninstall program can be used to uninstall any application. It must be used when the application is first installed, because it works by monitoring and recording all changes made to the computer system.

uninstaller

Software that helps uninstall applications from a computer. See *uninstall*.

union

In relational database, the joining of two files. See *set theory*.

uniprocessor

A single processor. As more and more computers employ multiprocessing architectures, such as SMP and MPP, the term is used to refer to a system that still has only one CPU. Although most desktop computers are uniprocessor systems, it is expected that dual processor systems will become commonplace on the desktop in the coming years.

UniSQL

An object-oriented DBMS from UniSQL, Austin, TX, (www.unisql.com). UniSQL/X is a relational and object-oriented DBMS for UNIX servers that provides SQL and object access to the database. UniSQL/M adds object-oriented capability to SQL Server, Oracle, Ingres and other relational DBMSs.

Unisys

(Unisys Corporation, Blue Bell, PA, www.unisys.com) A computer manufacturer formed in 1986 as a merger of Burroughs and Sperry corporations, which was the largest merger of computer manufacturers in history.

Sperry started in 1933 in navigational guidance and control equipment. In 1955, it merged with Remington Rand, creator of the UNIVAC I, and became Sperry Rand. Sperry became known for its large-scale mainframes and for providing communications and realtime systems to the military and NASA. In 1971, it absorbed RCA's Spectra 70 computer line and supported it until it phased out.

Burroughs started as a maker of calculating machines and cash registers in 1886. It was first involved with computers by supplying memory for the ENIAC in 1952. A decade later, it introduced the B5000 computer, which was hailed for its advanced operating system. Burroughs computers became well established in the banking and finance industries.

Today, Unisys' A Series and 2200 line, ranging from desktops to high-end mainframes, are current versions of product lines originating from both companies. A full range of UNIX systems, PCs and CTOS-based machines are also available. In addition, Unisys provides integrated solutions for vertical markets as well as business consulting services.

The UNIVAC I
In 1951, Remington Rand had the jump on the computer industry when it introduced the UNIVAC I. For a while, the words "Univac" and "computer" were synonymous. There were more than 40 UNIVAC I's installed. *(Photo courtesy of Unisys Corporation.)*

Burroughs Adding Machine
This adding machine was built circa 1895 and was an example of the exciting new machinery at the turn of the 20th Century. *(Photo courtesy of Smithsonian Institution.)*

unit record equipment
See *tabulating equipment*.

unit test
Running one component of a system for testing purposes. See *system test*.

UNIVAC I
(UNIVersal Automatic Computer) The first commercially-successful computer, introduced in 1951 by Remington Rand. Over 40 systems were sold. Its memory was made of mercury-filled acoustic delay lines that held 1,000 12-digit numbers. It used magnetic tapes that stored 1MB of data at a density of 128 cpi. In 1952, it predicted Eisenhower's victory over Stevenson, and UNIVAC became synonymous with computer (for a while). UNIVAC I's were in use up until the early 1960s. See illustration on next page.

UniVBE

(UNIveral VESA BIOS Extension) A SciTech Software VESA driver from TR Consulting, San Jose, CA, that supports VGA adapters from more than 20 different vendors. It allows DOS applications that are written to the VESA BIOS Extension standard to work with most of the display adapters on the market.

Univel

A joint venture of Novell and USL, which created UnixWare. In 1993, Novell acquired USL and merged it into Novell's Unix Systems Group.

universal client

A computer that can access a wide variety of applications on the network. The Web browser is hailed as a universal client because of its platform-independent ability to reach the Internet and corporate intranets. An e-mail client (mail program) that can access multiple messaging systems could be called a universal client.

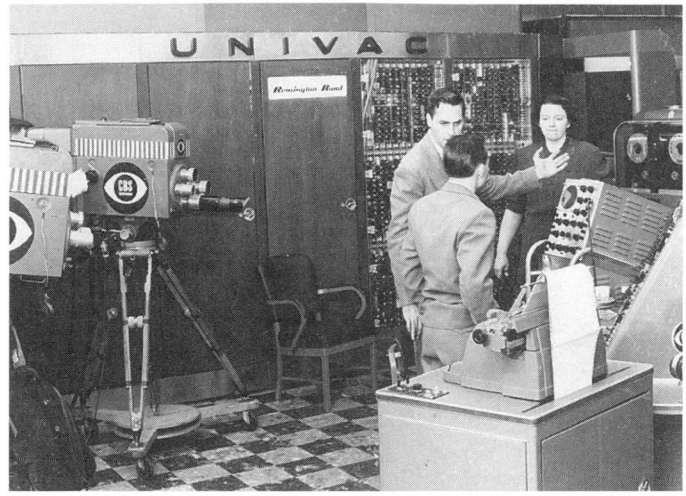

UNIVAC I
The circuitry that filled up the walk-in CPU of the UNIVAC I, now fits on your finger. The UNIVAC I made history in 1952 when it predicted Eisenhower's victory. This picture is news coverage of that event. *(Photo courtesy of Unisys Corporation.)*

universal server

(1) A database management system (DBMS) that stores all types of information including traditional data fields (relational database) as well as graphics and multimedia (object-oriented database). A universal server is an *object-relational DBMS* or *ORDBMS*.

(2) (Universal Server) A universal server from Informix. It supports DataBlades, which are plug-ins designed to manage a particular type of complex data. For example, an image DataBlade might allow a user to search for matching images.

UniVerse

A relational DBMS from VMARK that runs on the major UNIX servers and Windows NT. By 1997, more than a million seats had been sold. UniVerse includes its own BASIC programming environment and provides access to the database via SQL. VMARK provides a variety of tools and enhancements for programming UniVerse applications.

UNIX

A multiuser, multitasking operating system that is widely used as the master control program in workstations and servers. There are many versions of UNIX on the market, and, except for the PC world, where Windows dominates, almost every hardware vendor offers it either as its primary or secondary operating system. Sun and SCO have been major sponsors of UNIX over the years.

UNIX is written in C, and both UNIX and C were developed by AT&T and freely distributed to government and academic institutions, causing it to be ported to a wider variety of machine families than any other operating system. As a result, UNIX became synonymous with "open systems."

UNIX is made up of the kernel, file system and shell (command line interface). The major shells are the Bourne shell (original), C shell and Korn shell. The UNIX vocabulary is exhaustive with more than 600 commands that manipulate data and text in every way conceivable. Many commands are cryptic (see below), but just as Windows hid the DOS prompt, the Motif GUI presents a friendlier image to UNIX users.

Command	UNIX	DOS
List directory	ls	dir
Copy a file	cp	copy
Delete a file	rm	del
Rename a file	mv	rename
Display contents	cat	type
Print a file	lpr	print
Check disk space	df	chkdsk

The History of UNIX

UNIX was developed in 1969 by Ken Thompson at AT&T, who scaled down the sophisticated MULTICS operating system for the PDP-7. The named was coined for a single-user version (UNo) of "multIX." More work was done by Dennis Ritchie, and, by 1974, UNIX had matured into an efficient operating system primarily on PDPs. UNIX became very popular in scientific and academic environments.

Considerable enhancements were made to UNIX at the University of California at Berkeley, and versions of UNIX with the Berkeley extensions became widely used. By the late 1970s, commercial versions of UNIX, such as IS/1 and XENIX, became available.

In the early 1980s, AT&T began to consolidate the many UNIX versions into standards which evolved into System III and eventually System V. Before Divestiture (1984), AT&T licensed UNIX to universities and other organizations, but was prohibited from outright marketing of the product. After divestiture, it began to market UNIX aggressively.

A Lot of Bouncing Around

In 1989, AT&T formed the UNIX Software Operation (USO) division. USO introduced System V Release 4.0 (SVR4), which incorporated XENIX, SunOS, Berkeley 4.3BSD and System V into one UNIX standard. The System V Interface Definition (SVID) was introduced, which defined UNIX compatibility. In 1990, USO became an AT&T subsidiary renamed UNIX System Laboratories, Inc. (USL). In 1993, the UNIX source code was acquired by Novell, and, in 1995, Novell sold it to The Santa Cruz Operation (SCO).

More attempts at unifying UNIX into one standard have been made than for any other operating system. Over the years various industry consortia have tried to make UNIX a shrink-wrapped standard like DOS, Windows and the Mac. However, since UNIX runs on so many different hardware platforms, the only way the same shrink-wrapped UNIX program could ever run on all of them is by the use of an intermediate language similar to Java. The Open Group's ANDF was an attempt at this.

What UNIX application developers really hope for is a single UNIX programming interface (API) so that they only have to recompile the source code for each platform, rather than maintain different versions of the source code. The latest attempt to do this is the Single UNIX Specification governed by X/Open, which brands compliant software with the UNIX logo. X/Open also governs the Common Desktop Environment (CDE), which is a standard user interface for UNIX based on Motif.

UNIX Is Popular

Even with its many versions, UNIX is widely used in mission critical applications for client/server and transaction processing systems. UNIX components are world class standards. The TCP/IP transport protocol and SMTP e-mail protocol are de facto standards on the Internet. NFS allows files to be accessible across the network, NIS provides a "Yellow Pages" directory, Kerberos provides network security, and X Window lets users run applications on remote servers and view the results on their machines. See *X/Open, Open Group, POSIX, CDE* and *BSD UNIX*.

UNIX Is Everywhere

The UNIX versions that are widely used are Sun's Solaris, Digital's UNIX, HP's HP-UX, IBM's AIX and SCO's UnixWare. A large number of IBM mainframes also run UNIX applications, because the UNIX interfaces were added to MVS and OS/390, which have obtained UNIX branding (see *X/Open*). See *client* and *server* and note how many different varieties of UNIX are available.

UNIX 93

An X/Open brand used on a product that is compliant with a number of UNIX-based specifications including XPG3, XPG4, SVID and AT&T source code. In early 1996, X/Open closed this branding. See *X/Open* and *UNIX 95*.

UNIX 95

An X/Open brand used on a product that is compliant with Version 1 of the Single UNIX Specification. See *Single UNIX Specification* and *X/Open*.

UNIX 98

An X/Open brand used on a product that is compliant with Version 2 of the Single UNIX Specification. See *Single UNIX Specification* and *X/Open*.

UNIX International

A non-profit industry association founded to provide direction for UNIX System V. It was disbanded in 1993 after Novell purchased UNIX from AT&T.

UNIX server

A medium to large-scale computer system in a network that runs under UNIX. UNIX servers are widely used as application servers and database servers and are available from a variety of vendors, including Sun, HP, IBM, Digital and others. Sun has been the major proponent of UNIX-based computer systems in the commercial world running on its SPARC processors, and The Santa Cruz Operation (SCO) has been the leading vendor of UNIX on the Intel platform for some time. See *UNIX, server* and *SPARC*.

UNIX shell account

A customer account with an Internet service provider (ISP) that requires the user to enter UNIX commands to send and receive mail and files. Prior to today's graphical interfaces, Internet access was always a command line operation performed by researchers and computer buffs.

UNIX socket

The method of directing data to the appropriate application in a TCP/IP network. The combination of the IP address of the station and a port number make up a socket. See *port number* and *well-known port*.

UNIX to UNIX copy

See *UUCP*.

UnixWare

See *SCO UnixWare*.

unload

To remove a program from memory or take a tape or disk out of its drive.

UNMA

(Unified Network Management Archicture) A network strategy from AT&T for managing multi-vendor networks.

unmark

(1) In word processing, to deselect a block of text, which usually removes its highlight.

(2) To deselect an item that has been tagged for a particular purpose.

unpack

See *pack*.

unqualified address

An incomplete address. For example, a mail program may provide a default name for all recipient addressess that are given without a domain name.

unscramble

Same as *decrypt*. See *scramble*.

unshielded twisted pair

See *twisted pair*.

---

unsubscribe

To cancel a service. It is often possible to unsubscribe to an e-mail service by typing the word "unsubscribe" into a reply message. Contrast with *subscribe*.

unzip

To decompress a file with PKUNZIP. See *PKZIP, PKUNZIP*.

up

Refers to a device that is working.

UPA

(Ultra Port Architecture) A high-speed interconnect between the CPU and memory from Sun. It uses a packet-switched crossbar architecture that can transfer more than a 100 MBytes/sec.

UPC

(Universal Product Code) The standard bar code printed on retail merchandise. It contains the vendor's identification number and the product number, which is read by passing the bar code over a scanner.

update

To change data in a file or database. The terms update and edit are often used synonymously.

uplink

A communications channel from an earth station to a satellite. Contrast with *downlink*.

upload

See *download*.

upper CASE

See *front-end CASE*.

UPS

(Uninterruptible Power Supply) Backup power used when the electrical power fails or drops to an unacceptable voltage level. Small UPS systems provide battery power for a few minutes; enough to power down the computer in an orderly manner. Sophisticated systems are tied to electrical generators that can provide power for days.

A UPS system can be connected to a file server so that, in the event of a problem, all network users can be alerted to save files and shut down immediately.

An online UPS provides a constant source of electrical power from the battery, while the batteries are being recharged from AC power. An offline UPS, also known as a standby power system (SPS), switches to battery within a few milliseconds after detecting a power failure.

The line interactive UPS is a hybrid of the online and standby units. Like the standby unit, it does not constantly draw from the battery, but it switches over to the battery faster when required. In addition, it does not switch to battery when it encounters low voltages. It uses extra power from the the AC source to make up the difference instead.

A surge protector filters out surges and spikes, and a voltage regulator maintains uniform voltage during a brownout, but a UPS keeps a computer running when there is no electrical power. UPS systems typically provide surge suppression and may also provide voltage regulation.

UPS - Now More Than Ever

In order to improve performance, computers are increasingly using write back caches, which means that updated data intended for the disk is temporarily stored in RAM. If a power failure occurs, there is more of a chance that new data will be lost, thus UPS systems are becoming important for all computers.

upstream

See *downstream*.

uptime

The time during which a system is working without failure. Contrast with *downtime*. See *availability*.

---

upward compatible

Also called *forward compatible*. Refers to hardware or software that is compatible with succeeding versions. Contrast with *downward compatible*.

URL

(Uniform Resource Locator) The address that defines the route to a file on the Web or any other Internet facility. URLs are typed into the browser to access Web pages, and URLs are embedded within the pages themselves to provide the hypertext links to other pages.

The URL contains the protocol prefix, port number, domain name, subdirectory names and file name. Port addresses are generally defaults and are rarely specified. To access a home page on a Web site, only the protocol and domain name are required. For example,

```
http://www.computerlanguage.com
```

retrieves the home page at The Computer Language Company's Web site. The http:// is the Web protocol, and www.computerlanguage.com is the domain name.

If the page is stored in another directory, or if a page other than the home page is required, slashes are used to separate the names. For example, http://www.computerlanguage.com/order.html points to the order page.

If a required page is stored in a subdirectory, its name is separated by a slash. Like path names in DOS and Windows, subdirectories can be several levels deep. For example, the components of the following hypothetical URL are described below:

```
http://www.abc.com/clothes/shirts/formal.html
```

```
http://        protocol
www.abc.com/   domain name
clothes/       subdirectory name
shirts/        subdirectory name
formal.html    document name (Web page)
```

Following is a list of the Internet protocols defined by URLs. Most browsers default to HTTP if a prefix is not typed in.

```
Prefix         To gain access to...
http://        World Wide Web server
ftp://         FTP server (file transfer)
news://        Usenet newsgroups
mailto://      e-mail
wais://        Wide Area Information Server
gopher://      Gopher server
file://        file on local system
telnet://      applications on network server
rlogin://      applications on network server
tn3270://      applications on mainframe
```

usability lab

A testing facility for software that deals with its ease of learning and ease of use.

USB

(Universal Serial Bus) A hardware interface for low-speed peripherals such as the keyboard, mouse, joystick, scanner, printer and telephony devices. It also supports MPEG-1 and MPEG-2 digital video. USB has a maximum bandwidth of 1.5 Mbytes/sec, and up to 127 devices can be attached. Peripherals can be plugged in and unplugged without turning the system off. USB ports began to appear on PCs in 1997, and Windows 98 fully supports it.

The devices are plugged directly into a four-pin USB socket on the PC or into a multi-port hub that plugs into the PC or into a device that also functions as a hub for other devices. USB ports on the PC and hubs use a rectangular Type A socket. All cables that are permanently attached to the device have a Type A plug. Devices that use a separate cable have a square Type B socket, and the cable that connects them has both a Type A and a Type B plug. See illustration on next page.

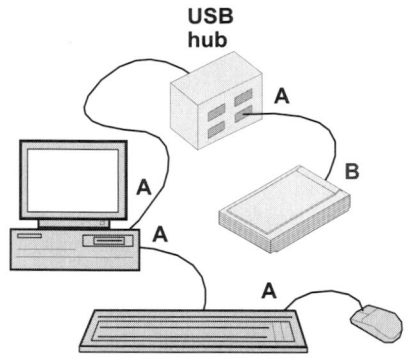

USB Connections
The thin, rectangular A connectors are on the PC and hub. Type B connectors are used on peripherals that have cables which are not permanently attached.

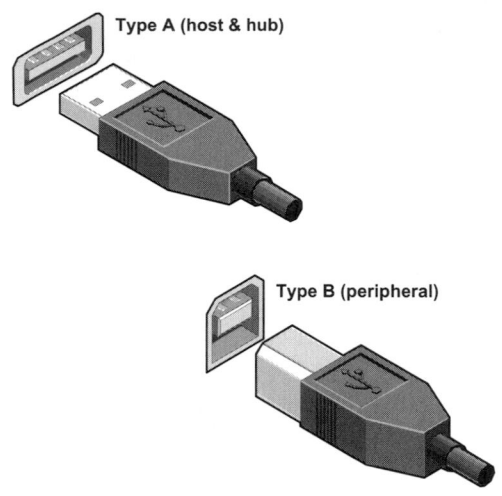

USB Plugs and Sockets

USB hub
A device that increases the number of USB ports on a PC. It cables into the PC's USB port and typically provides four Type A sockets for expansion.

use-case analysis
An object-oriented method for designing information systems by breaking down requirements into user functions. Each use case is a transaction or sequence of events performed by the user. Use cases are studied to determine what objects are required to accomplish them and how they interact with other objects.

Usenet
(USEr NETwork) A public access network on the Internet that provides user news and group e-mail. It is a giant, dispersed bulletin board that is maintained by volunteers who provide news and mail feeds to other nodes. All the news that travels over the Internet is called *NetNews*, and a running collection of messages about a particular subject is called a *newsgroup*. Usenet began in 1979 as a bulletin board between two universities in North Carolina. Today, there are more than 50,000 newsgroups. News can be read with a Web browser or via newsreaders such as nn, rn, trn and tin. See *newsgroup* and *NNTP*.

user
Any individual who interacts with the computer at an application level. Programmers, operators and other technical personnel are not considered users when working in a professional capacity on the computer.

user account
An established relationship between a user and a computer, network or information service. User accounts require a username and password, and new user accounts are given a default set of permissions. See *user profile* and *guest account*.

user agent
The mail client in a messaging system. See *messaging system*.

user area
A reserved part of a disk or memory for user data.

user default profile
A default set of permissions assigned to new uesrs. See *user account* and *user profile*.

user defined

Any format, layout, structure or language that is developed by the user.

user friendly

A system that is easy to learn and easy to use. This term has been so abused that many vendors are reluctant to use it.

user group

An organization of users of a particular hardware or software product. Members share experiences and ideas to improve their understanding and use of a particular product. User groups are often responsible for influencing vendors to change or enhance their products.

The oldest user group in the U.S. still extant is ACGNJ (Amateur Computer Group of New Jersey). Founded in 1974 by Professor Sol Libes, it was one of the first computer clubs organized around microprocessors. ACGNJ also created the Trenton Computer Festival (TCF) in 1976, which it sponsors every year. TCF was the first personal computer show and flea market in the U.S. See *Trenton Computer Festival*.

For contacts and information about the user groups in the U.S. and Canada, visit the User Group Connection at www.ugconnection.org.

userid

(USER IDentification) See *username*.

user interface

The combination of menus, screen design, keyboard commands, command language and online help, which creates the way a user interacts with a computer. If input devices other than a keyboard and mouse are required, this is also included. In the future, natural language recognition and voice recognition will become standard components of the user interface.

The user interface is the most important, yet least-understood area in the software industry as programmers are often the ones responsible for designing everything the user interacts with. This is generally a formula for disaster, because most programmers do not have a clue how to do it. Every application has only a handful of basic functions that users need all the time, yet they are buried in arcane menus and submenus that must be memorized. Worse yet, once bad examples are set by Microsoft or some other major vendor, everybody follows it. Since the most popular applications are often the hardest to learn, users have come to expect that software is just plain difficult, when in fact, it could be made downright simple if educated user interface designers were involved.

Because of the steep learning curves users have gone through, many are afraid to change applications. While the industry touts "productivity gains" for almost every software product, the lost hours frustrating over how to do something, combined with the general reluctance to try something else that could truly be an improvement, all results in lost productivity that cannot be measured. If we are ever to make computers usable for the masses, this issue must be addressed. See *RTFM* and *Freedman's law*.

user-level security

Access control to a file, printer or other network resource based on username. It provides greater protection than share-level security, because users are identified individually or within a group. User-level permissions are stored in a central server and managed by the network administrator. See *share-level security*.

How to Do It Right
Alan Cooper's "About Face" is a must-read primer for user interface designers. It is not only well written, but it is an eye-opening look into an extremely important subject. Numerous examples explain how to do it right, by showing you how easy it is to do it wrong. (IDG Books Worldwide, Inc., 1995, ISBN 1-56884-322-4)

username

The name a person uses to identify himself or herself when logging onto a computer system or online service. Both a username (user ID) and a password are required. In an Internet e-mail address, the username is the left part before the @ sign. For example, KARENB is the username in **karenb@mycompany.com**.

user profile

The preferences and current desktop configuration of a user's machine. User profiles enable several users to work on the same computer with their own desktop setup. When stored in a server, user profiles enable users to obtain their desktop configuration when working at a different machine. See *system policy*.

USL

(UNIX System Laboratories, Inc.) An AT&T subsidiary formed in 1990, responsible for developing and marketing UNIX. In 1993, USL was acquired by Novell and merged into Novell's Unix Systems Group (USG).

USO

(UNIX Software Operation) AT&T's UNIX division before it turned into USL. See *UNIX*.

USR

See *U.S. Robotics*.

U.S. Robotics

(U.S. Robotics, Inc., Skokie, IL, www.usr.com) A modem manufacturer highly regarded for its quality modems. The company manufactures its own chipsets (data pumps) and often leads the industry with innovations. Its HST protocol was a high-speed and reliable modem protocol before V.32bis became a standard. USR's Sportster models have been the best-selling modems in the world. In June of 1997, U.S. Robotics became part of 3Com in the largest merger in data networking history. See *3Com*.

USRT

(Universal Synchronous Receiver Transmitter) An electronic circuit that transmits and receives data on the serial port. It converts bytes into serial bits for transmission, and vice versa, and generates the necessary signals for synchronous transmission.

utilities

See *utility program*.

utility program

A program that supports using the computer. Utility programs, or "utilities," provide file management capabilities, such as sorting, copying, comparing, listing and searching, as well as diagnostic and measurement routines that check the health and performance of the system.

UTP

See *twisted pair*.

UTP Ethernet

(1) (Unshielded Twisted Pair Ethernet) See *Ethernet*.
(2) May refer to pre-IEEE standard twisted pair Ethernet networks.

UTS

(Universal Timesharing System) Amdahl's version of UNIX System V. Release 4.0 is POSIX compliant.

UUcoding

A common method for transmitting non-text files via Internet e-mail, which was originally designed for ASCII text. The UUencode utility encodes the files by converting 8-bit characters into 7-bit ASCII text, and the UUdecode utility decodes it back to its original format at the receiving end. Originating in the UNIX community, UUcoding was one of the first methods for sending binary files as attached files over Internet e-mail. Today, MIME is widely used. See *BinHex, MIME* and *Wincode*

UUCP

(UNIX to UNIX CoPy) A UNIX utility that copies a file from one computer to another. It was widely used for mail transfer. Unlike TCP/IP, which is a routable communications protocol, UUCP provides a point-to-point transmission where a user at one UNIX computer dials up and establishes a session with another UNIX computer. See *bang path*.

UUdecode, UUencode

See *UUcoding*.

UUNET

(UUNET Technologies, Inc., Fairfax, VA, www.uunet.net) Founded in 1987, UUNET was the first commercial Internet service provider. Originally offering e-mail and news, it is now a full Internet service organization providing dial-up and leased line accounts as well as archive space for files and Web pages. UUNET stands for UNIX to UNIX Network. In 1996, UUNET was acquired by MFS Communications, which itself was acquired by WorldCom, Inc., in that same year.

V

V.17

An ITU fax standard (1991) that uses TCM modulation at 12000 and 14400 bps for Group 3. It adds TCM to the V.29 standard at 7200 and 9600 bps to allow transmission over noisier lines. It also defines special functions (echo protection, turn-off sequences, etc.) for half-duplex operation. Modulation use is a half-duplex version of V.32bis.

V.21

An ITU standard (1964) for asynchronous 0-300 bps full-duplex modems for use on dial-up lines. It uses FSK modulation.

V.22

An ITU standard (1980) for asynchronous and synchronous 600 and 1200 bps full-duplex modems for use on dial-up lines. It uses DPSK modulation.

V.22bis

An ITU standard (1984) for asynchronous and synchronous 2400 bps full-duplex modems for use on dial-up lines and two-wire leased lines, with fallback to V.22 1200 bps operation. It uses QAM modulation.

V.23

An ITU standard (1964) for asynchronous and synchronous 0-600 and 0-1200 bps half-duplex modems for use on dial-up lines. It has an optional split-speed transmission method with a reverse channel of 0-75 bps (1200/75, 75/1200). It uses FSK modulation.

V.24

An ITU standard (1964) that defines the functions of all circuits for the RS-232 interface. It does not describe the connectors or pin assignments; those are defined in ISO 2110. In the U.S., EIA-232 incorporates the control signal definition of V.24, the electrical characteristics of V.28 and the connector and pin assignments defined in ISO 2110.

V.25

An ITU standard (1968) for automatic calling and/or answering equipment on dial-up lines. It uses parallel circuits and is similar in function to RS-366 and Bell 801 autodialers used in the U.S. The answer tone defined in V.25 is the first thing heard when calling a modem. It serves a dual function of identifying the answering equipment as being a modem and also disabling the echo suppression and echo cancellation equipment in the network so that a full-duplex modem will operate properly.

V.25bis

An ITU standard (1968) for automatic calling and/or answering equipment on dial-up lines. It has three modes: asynchronous (rarely used), character-oriented synchronous (bisync) and bit-oriented synchronous (HDLC/SDLC). Both synchronous versions are used in IBM AS/400 and other small-to-medium sized computers that do automatic dialing for remote job entry.

Due to the popularity of the Hayes AT Command Set, V.25bis is not used as widely in North America. It does not perform modem configuration functions and is limited to dialing and answering calls.

V.26

An ITU standard (1968) for synchronous 2400 bps full-duplex modems for use on four-wire leased lines. It uses DPSK modulation and includes an optional 75 bps back channel.

V.26bis

An ITU standard (1972) for synchronous 1200 and 2400 bps full-duplex modems for use on dial-up lines. It uses DPSK modulation and includes an optional 75 bps back channel.

V.26ter

An ITU standard (1984) for asynchronous and synchronous 2400 bps full-duplex modems using DPSK modulation over dial-up and two-wire leased lines. It includes a 1200 bps fallback speed and uses echo cancellation, permitting a full-duplex modem to send and receive on the same frequency.

V.27

An ITU standard (1972) for synchronous 4800 bps full-duplex modems for use on four-wire leased lines. It uses DPSK modulation.

V.27bis
An ITU standard (1976) for synchronous 2400 and 4800 bps full-duplex modems using DPSK modulation for use on four-wire leased lines. The primary difference between V.27 and V.27bis is the addition of an automatic adaptive equalizer.

V.27ter
An ITU standard (1976) for synchronous 2400 and 4800 bps half-duplex modems using DPSK modulation on dial-up lines. It includes an optional 75 bps back channel. V.27ter is used in Group 3 fax transmission without the back channel.

V.28
An ITU standard (1972) that defines the functions of all circuits for the RS-232 interface. In the U.S., EIA-232 incorporates the electrical signal definitions of V.28, the control signals of V.25 and the connector and pin assignments defined in ISO 2110.

V.29
An ITU standard (1976) for synchronous 4800, 7200 and 9600 bps full-duplex modems using QAM modulation on four-wire leased lines. It has been adapted for Group 3 fax transmission over dial-up lines at 9600 and 7200 bps.

V.32
An ITU standard (1984) for asynchronous and synchronous 4800 and 9600 bps full-duplex modems using TCM modulation over dial-up or two-wire leased lines. TCM encoding may be optionally added. V.32 uses echo cancellation to achieve full-duplex transmission.

V.32bis
An ITU standard (1991) for asynchronous and synchronous 4800, 7200, 9600, 12000 and 14400 bps full-duplex modems using TCM and echo cancellation. Supports rate renegotiation, which allows modems to change speeds as required.

V.32terbo
An AT&T standard for 19200 bps modems adopted by some modem manufacturers. See *V.34*.

V.33
An ITU standard (1988) for synchronous 12000 and 14400 bps full-duplex modems for use on four-wire leased lines using QAM modulation. It includes an optional time-division multiplexor for sharing the transmission line among multiple terminals.

V.34
An ITU standard (1994) for 28800 bps and (1996) 31200 and 33600 bps modems using QAM modulation. Before V.34, AT&T's V.32terbo and Rockwell International's V.FC modems came on the market to provide greater speed than the V.32bis 14400 bps standard. After V.34 was standardized at 28.8 Kbps, subsequent enhancements that raised speeds to 33.6 Kbps were folded back into V.34, and there was no change in number or designation.

V.35
An ITU standard (1968) for group band modems that combine the bandwidth of several telephone circuits to achieve high data rates. V.35 has become known as a high-speed RS-232 interface rather than a type of modem. The large, rectangular V.35 connector was never specified in V.35, but has become a de facto standard for a high-speed interface.

V.42
An ITU standard (1989) for modem error checking that uses LAP-M as the primary protocol

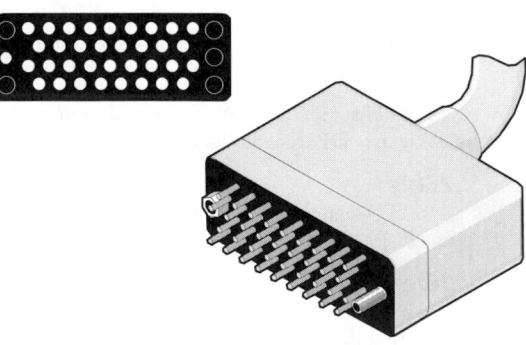

V.35 Connector
V.35 connectors are used for high-speed transmissions that combine various telephone circuits.

Computer Desktop Encyclopedia

and provides MNP Classes 2 through 4 as an alternative protocol for compatibility.

V.42bis
An ITU standard (1989) for modem data compression. It uses the LZW technique to achieve up to a 4:1 ratio. V.42bis implies the V.42 error checking protocol.

V.54
An ITU standard (1976) for various loopback tests that can be incorporated into modems for testing the telephone circuit and isolating transmission problems. Operating modes include local and remote digital loopback and local and remote analog loopback.

V.56
An ITU standard (1972) for a method of testing modems to compare their performance. Newer procedures are currently under study.

V.90
An ITU standard (1998) for a modem that communicates at 56 Kbps downstream and 33.6 Kbps upstream. It is intended for use only with ISPs and online services that are digitally attached to the telephone system. Most service providers are typically connected with high-speed digital T1 or T3 circuits.

In practice, the downstream link isn't generally faster than 45 Kbps in these PCM modems, so called because they use pulse code modulation downstream and standard V.34 upstream. Initially, two incompatible technologies competed in this arena: x2 from U.S. Robotics and K56Flex from Rockwell and Lucent. Such modems can be upgraded to V.90 if they contain software-upgradable memory chips. See *V.34* and *channel bonding*.

V.110
An ITU standard (1984) that specifies how data terminal equipment (DTE) with asynchronous or synchronous serial interfaces can be supported on an ISDN network. It uses rate adaption, which involves a bit-by-bit alignment between the DTE and the ISDN B channel.

V.120
An ITU standard (1988) that specifies how DTEs with asynchronous or synchronous serial interfaces can be supported on an ISDN network using a protocol (similar to LAP-D) to encapsulate the data to be transmitted. It includes the capability of using statistical multiplexing to share a B channel connection between multiple DTEs.

VAC
(Volts Alternating Current) See *volt* and *AC*.

vacuum tube
An electronic device that controls the flow of electrons in a vacuum. It is used as a switch, amplifier or display screen. Used as on/off switches, they allowed the first computers to perform digital computations. Although vacuum tubes have made a comeback in high-end stereo components, most vacuum tubes today are the picture tubes (CRTs) in monitors and TVs.

VAD
(Value Added Dealer) Same as *VAR*.

VADSL
(Very high bit rate Asymmetric DSL) An earlier name for VDSL. See *DSL*.

VAFC
See *VESA Advanced Feature Connector*.

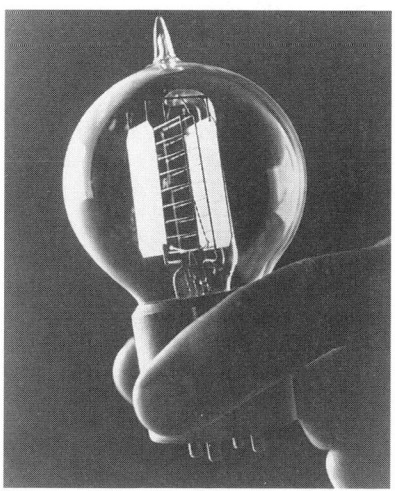

Early Vacuum Tube
Early vacuum tubes were used to amplify signals for radio and other audio devices. This one was made in 1915. Tubes were not used as switches in calculating machines until 1939. *(Photo courtesy of AT&T.)*

validity checking

Routines in a data entry program that tests the input for correct and reasonable conditions, such as numbers falling within a range and correct spelling, if possible. See *check digit*.

value

(1) The content of a field or variable. It can refer to alphabetic as well as numeric data. For example, in the expression, **state** = **"PA"**, PA is a value.

(2) In spreadsheets, the numeric data within the cell.

value-added network

A communications network that provides services beyond normal transmission, such as automatic error detection and correction, protocol conversion and message storing and forwarding. Telenet and Tymnet are examples of value-added networks.

Value Added Process

See *VAP*.

value added reseller

See *VAR*.

vampire tap

A cable connection that is made with a unit that clamps onto and "bites" into the cable, hence the vampire name. Vampire taps are often used to attach thick Ethernet transceivers to the coaxial cable. Without a vampire tap, the cable has to be cut and connectors have to be attached to both ends.

VAN

See *value-added network*.

vandal

A program that performs a clandestine or malicious function such as extracting a user's password or other data or erasing the hard disk. A vandal differs from a virus, which attaches itself to an existing executable program. The vandal is the full executing entity itself which can be downloaded from the Internet in the form of an ActiveX control, Java applet, browser plug-in or e-mail attachment. See *virus*.

VAP

(Value Added Process) Software that enhances or provides additional server functions in a NetWare 286 server. Support for different kinds of workstations, database engines, fax and print servers are examples. The NetWare 386 counterpart is the NLM.

vaporware

Software that is not completed and shipping to customers, but the announced delivery date has passed. At times, major software vendors are criticized for intentionally producing vaporware in order to keep customers from switching to competitive products that offer more features. However, today's commercial software is more difficult than ever to program, and programmers are notorious for being terrible estimators of project time. As a result, shipping dates often slip over and over again.

There is often just as large a gap between management and technical staff in software companies than there is user organizations, private or public. Dates slip because the project is not managed properly, which can be due to management's lack of understanding of the scope of the project as well as a lack of knowledge of the technical competence of the systems and programming staff.

A programming verity: as bad as programmers are at estimating the length of a project, they are equally as optimistic about their ability to meet the requirements and deadlines.

VAR

(Value Added Reseller) An organization that adds value to a system and resells it. For example, it could purchase a CPU and peripherals from different vendors, graphics software from another and package it all together as a specialized CAD system. Although VARs typically repackage products, they might also include programs they have developed themselves. The terms VAR and ISV are often used interchangeably. See *OEM, ISV* and *systems integrator*.

variable

In programming, a structure that holds data and is uniquely named by the programmer. It holds the data assigned to it until a new value is assigned or the program is finished.

Variables are used to hold control values. For example, the C statement **for (x=0; xERROR[Basic syntax error] in:<5ERROR[Basic syntax error] in:; x++)** performs the instructions following it five times. X is a variable set to zero (x=0), incremented (x++) and tested to reach five (xERROR[Basic syntax error] in:<5ERROR[Basic syntax error] in:). Variables also hold data temporarily that is being processed.

Variables are usually assigned with an equal sign; for example, **counter = 1**, places a 1 in COUNTER. Numeric data is unquoted: **counter = 1**, character data requires quotes: **product="abc4344"**. In some languages, the type of data must be declared before it is assigned; for example, in C, the statement, **int counter;** creates a variable that will only hold whole numbers.

A local variable is one that is referenced only within the subprogram, function or procedure it was defined in. A global variable can be used by the entire program.

variable length field

A record structure that holds fields of varying lengths. For example, PAT SMITH would take nine bytes and GEORGINA WILSON BARTHOLOMEW would take 27 plus a couple of bytes that would define the length of the field. If fixed length fields were used, at least 27 bytes would have to be reserved for both names.

There's more programming with variable length fields, because every record has to be separated into fixed length fields after it is brought into memory. Conversely, each record has to be coded into the variable length format before it is written to disk.

The same storage savings can be achieved by compressing data stored on disk and decompressing it when retrieved. All blank spaces in fixed length fields would be filtered out. For acceptable performance, this method must be well integrated into the operating system. See *realtime compression*.

variable length record

A data record that contains one or more variable length fields.

varname

(VARiable NAME) An abbreviation for specifying the name of a variable.

VAX

(Virtual Address eXtension) A family of 32-bit computers from Digital introduced in 1977 with the VAX-11/780 model. VAXes range from desktop personal computers to mainframes all running the same VMS operating system. Large models can be clustered in a multiprocessing environment to serve thousands of users. Software compatibility between models caused the VAX family to achieve outstanding success during the 1980s. VAXes also provide PDP emulation.

VAXcluster

A group of VAXs coupled together in a multiprocessing environment.

VAXELN

A realtime operating environment for VAXs from Digital. It runs under VMS and provides application development in Pascal and other languages. Resulting programs are downloaded into the target systems.

VAXmate

A partially IBM-compatible PC from Digital introduced in 1986, which has been superseded by the DECstation 200 and 300 series in 1989.

The Vax 11/780
The VAX series was an outstanding success and made Digital a major competitor of computers in all sizes from workstation to mainframe in the 1980s. This is a picture of the first VAX model. *(Photo courtesy of Digital Equipment Corporation.)*

VAXstation

A single-user VAX computer that runs under VMS introduced in 1988.

VB

See *Visual Basic*.

VBA

(Visual Basic for Applications) A subset of Visual Basic that provides a common language for customizing Microsoft applications. VBA supports COM, which allows a VBA script to invoke internal functions within Excel, Word and other COM-based programs or to make use of stand-alone, external COM objects. VBA evolved into a common language to consolidate earlier macro and scripting languages. Since 1996, VBA has been licensed to third parties for use in non-Microsoft applications within the Windows environment. Microsoft encourages Windows developers to put VBA support in their software. See *COM, COM automation* and *application programmability*.

VBE

See *VESA BIOS Extension*.

VBE/AI

See *VESA BIOS Extension/Audio Interface*.

VBI

See *vertical blanking interval*.

vBNS

(Very high-speed Backbone Network Service) A high-speed network backbone developed by the National Science Foundation (NSF) and MCI that interconnects several supercomputer centers at 622 Mbps (OC-12). vBNS was expanded to provide backbone services for Internet2. See *Internet2*.

Vbox

(Video **box**) A hardware interface from Sony that attaches up to seven VCRs, videodiscs and camcorders to the serial port. Devices must have the Control-L (LANC) connector.

VBR

(Variable Bit Rate) An asynchronous transfer mode (ATM) level of service that guarantees bandwidth for traffic that is well understood. Realtime variable bit rate (rt-VBR) supports interactive multimedia that requires minimal delays. Non-realtime variable bit rate (nrt-VBR) is used for bursty transaction traffic. See *ATM*.

VBRUN300.DLL

(Visual Basic RUNtime 300.DLL) The Visual Basic runtime module. A Visual Basic application is made up of a series of calls to Visual Basic routines, which are contained in the DLL, and VBRUNxxx.DLL must be available to run them. The number represents the version of Visual Basic (VBRUN300, VBRUN400, etc.).

VB Script

(Visual Basic Script) A programming language for World Wide Web applications from Microsoft. It is an extension to Microsoft's Visual Basic language. See *Jscript*.

VBX

(Visual Basic EXtension) A component software technology from Microsoft that enables a Visual Basic (Windows) program to add funtionality by calling ready-made components (controls). Also called *Visual Basic Controls*, they appear to the end user as just another part of the program. VBXs were Microsofts's first component architecture, and 16-bit VBXs were superseded by 32-bit OCXs. See *OCX* and *ActiveX control*.

Vcache

The disk cache software in Windows 95/98. It is a 32-bit program that dynamically allocates available free memory and replaces the Smartdrive cache in DOS/Windows 3.1.

vCalendar

A standard format for group calendaring and scheduling from Versit.

vCard

A standard format for an electronic business card from Versit. It includes fields for photos, sound and company logos.

V-chip

A chip that blocks objectionable TV programs. The U.S. and Canada have mandated its implementation in new TVs, and other countries are considering it. When fully implemented, TV programs will be transmitted with a rating based on violence and sexual content. The device is actually a programmable closed-caption controller chip that can decode signals sent within the TV's vertical blanking interval. A V-chip set-top box can be used for existing TVs.

VCPI

(Virtual Control Program Interface) A programming interface that allowed DOS-extended programs and Real Mode programs to run together in 386s. It was primarily developed by Quarterdeck to allow its DESQview multitasker to run DOS-extended programs. DPMI succeeded VCPI and provided the same capability for Windows.

VCR

(Video Cassette Recorder) A videotape recording and playback machine that is available in several formats. One inch tape is used for mastering video recordings. Sony Umatic 3/4" tape was widely used in commercial training. VHS 1/2" tape, first used only in the home, has mostly replaced the 3/4" tape. Sony's 1/2" Beta tape, the first home VCR format, is defunct.

Although VCRs are analog recording machines, adapters allow them to store digital data for computer backup.

VDE

(1) (Video Display Editor) A WordStar and WordPerfect-compatible shareware word processor written by Eric Meyer.

(2) (Verband Deutscher Elektrotechniker) The German counterpart of the U.S. Underwriters Lab.

Vdeck

(video deck) A frame-accurate, Super 8mm tape drive from Sony for serial-port connection to a personal computer. It contains an internal Vbox, is controlled by the ViSCA language and has no external play buttons.

VDI

(1) (Video Device Interface) An Intel standard for speeding up full-motion video performance. See *DCI*.

(2) (Virtual Device Interface) An ANSI standard format for creating device drivers. VDI has been incorporated into CGI.

VDM

(Virtual DOS Machine) A DOS session created by OS/2 and Windows NT in order to emulate a DOS environment and run DOS and 16-bit Windows applications. Each application runs in a separate VDM, each one simulating an individual DOS-based PC. VDMs are multitasked along with native applications. Also see *CGM*.

V dot

Refers to the ITU standards for communications that are named starting with a V and followed by a period; for example, V.32bis and V.34.

VDS

(Virtual DMA Services) A programming interface that lets bus mastering devices cooperatively manage DMA channels.

VDSL

See *DSL*.

VDT, VDU

(Video Display Terminal or Unit) A terminal with a keyboard and display screen.

VDT radiation

The electromagnetic radiation emitted from a computer display screen. Exhaustive testing so far seems inconclusive, but vendors recommend keeping the face at least 18 to 20 inches from the screen.

vector

(1) In computer graphics, a line designated by its end points (x-y or x-y-z coordinates). When a circle is drawn, it is made up of many small vectors. See *vector graphics* and *graphics*.

(2) In matrix algebra, a one-row or one-column matrix.

vector display

A display terminal that draws vectors (lines) on the screen. Vector displays, also known as *stroke writers*, were used in the early days of CAD, but gave way entirely to raster displays. See *raster display*.

vector font

A scalable font made of vectors (point-to-point line segments). It is easily scaled as are all vector-based images, but lacks the hints and mathematically-defined curves of outline fonts, such as Adobe Type 1 and TrueType.

vector graphics

In computer graphics, a technique for representing a picture as points, lines and other geometric entities. See *graphics*. Contrast with *bitmapped graphics*.

vector processor

A computer with built-in instructions that perform multiple calculations on vectors (one-dimensional arrays) simultaneously. It is used to solve the same or similar problems as an array processor; however, a vector processor passes a vector to a functional unit, whereas an array processor passes each element of a vector to a different arithmetic unit. See *pipeline processing* and *array processor*.

vector to raster

See *rasterize*.

Vectra

A family of PCs from HP. Vectras are noted for their ruggedness and reliability.

Venn diagram

A graphic technique for visualizing set theory concepts using overlapping circles and shading to indicate intersection, union and complement.

Ventura Publisher

See Corel VENTURA.

verbose

Wordy; long winded. The term is often used as a switch to display the status of some operation. For example, a /v might mean "verbose mode."

verify

In data entry operations, to compare the keystrokes of a second operator with the files created by the first operator.

Verilog

A hardware description language (HDL) used to design electronic systems at the component, board and system level. Developed by Phil Morby, it was initially developed as a simulation language that could also be used to describe the stimulus (test factors). By the late 1980s, Verilog was the de facto standard for proprietary HDLs. After Cadence put it into the public domain, it became an IEEE standard. A Verilog simulator is a separate entity, but the term by itself typically refers to the language (HDL). See *VHDL* and *HDL*.

VERITAS file system

See *VxFS*.

vermil, vermel

See *VRML*.

Veronica

A program that searches the Internet for specific resources by description, not just file name. Using Boolean searches (this AND this, this OR this, etc.), users can search Gopher servers to retrieve a selected group of menus that pertain to their area of interest. See *Gopher*.

VersaCAD

A family of CAD systems for DOS and Macintosh from Computervision, Bedford, MA, (www.cv.com), that features 2-D geometric and construction drafting and 3-D modeling with 16 viewports. The Mac version includes CAD-oriented HyperCard stacks.

version control

The management of source code, bitmaps, documents and related files in a large software project. Version-control software provides a database that is used to keep track of the revisions made to a program by all the programmers and developers involved in it. See *configuration management*.

version number

The identification of a release of software. The difference between Version 2.2 and 2.3 can be night and day, since new releases not only add features, but often correct bugs. What's been driving you crazy may have been fixed!

Numbers, such as 3.1a or 3.11, often indicate a follow-up release only to fix a bug in the previous version, whereas 3.1 and 3.2 usually mean routine enhancements. Version "1.0" drives terror into the hearts of experienced users. The program has just been released, and bugs are still to be uncovered.

Versit

A joint venture of Apple, AT&T, IBM and Siemens that promotes full interoperability for existing and emerging telphony, data communications and computer offerings from different vendors. Versit supports (1) Apple's GeoPort as the primary connector between the computer and the telephone, (2) an enhanced combination of CTI technologies that includes CSTA, (3) digital containers based on Apple's Bento technology, initially defining a "virtual business card" for personal data interchange, and (4) conferencing and messaging standards.

vertex

A corner point of a triangle or other geometric image. Vertices is the plural form of this term.

vertical bandwidth

See *vertical scan frequency*.

vertical bar

The vertical bar character (|), located over the backslash (\) key, is used as an OR operator. For example, the C statement if (x == "a" || x == "b") means "if X is equal to A or B." It is also used as a pipe symbol, which directs the output of one process to another.

vertical blanking interval

The part of a TV signal that is sent between each video frame. In North American TV (NTSC), it takes up the last 45 lines of each 525-line frame. Its purpose is to allow the TV time to reposition its electron beam from the bottom of the current frame (screen) to the top of the next one. This non-viewable part of the signal is used to transmit closed-caption content. See *Intercast* and *V-chip*.

vertical market software

Software packages that are designed for a particular industry such as banking, insurance or manufacturing. Contrast with *horizontal market software*.

vertical recording

A magnetic recording method that records the bits vertically instead of horizontally, taking up less space and providing greater storage capacity. The vertical recording method uses a specialized material for the construction of the disk.

vertical refresh

See *vertical scan frequency* and *interlaced*.

vertical resolution
Number of lines (rows in a matrix). Contrast with *horizontal resolution*.

vertical retrace
See *raster scan*.

vertical scaling
Adding more CPUs within the same computer system. Contrast with *horizontal scaling*.

vertical scan frequency
Also called *refresh rate*, it is the number of times an entire display screen is refreshed, or redrawn, per second. Measured in Hertz, display systems typically range from 56Hz to well over 100Hz. A minimum of 70Hz is recommended to help prevent eye strain. Contrast with *horizontal scan frequency*. See *interlaced*.

vertical scan rate
Same as *vertical scan frequency*.

vertical software
See *vertical market software*.

vertices
The plural of vertex. See *vertex*.

VESA
(Video Electronics Standards Association, San Jose, CA, www.vesa.org) A membership organization founded in 1989 that sets interface standards for the PC, workstation and computing environments. Note the following VESA standards following this entry.

VESA Advanced Feature Connector
A VESA standard point-to-point channel used to transfer video signals between two video controllers, typically between the display adapter and a video capture or TV board. The Advanced Feature Connector (VAFC) increases the original feature connector from 8 to 32 bits and from 40 to 150 Mbytes/sec. The cable is increased from 26 pins to 80. See *VGA feature connector* and *VESA Media Channel*.

VESA BIOS
A BIOS chip on a VGA display adapter that conforms to the VESA BIOS Extension standard.

VESA BIOS Extension
A VESA standard programming interface for Super VGA adapters. IBM set the original VGA standard, but many vendors created proprietary cards with higher resolutions and more colors, all under the Super VGA umbrella.

In Windows, applications call Windows to display everything. Windows then calls the display driver to draw the screen, thus, card vendors solve their incompatibilities by including their own display drivers for Windows.

In DOS, applications draw the screens directly. Since vendors of DOS games and graphics applications increasingly want to use higher resolutions and more colors, the VESA BIOS Extension (VBE) provides a standard interface to write to, including a way to query an adapter for its capabilities and to set resolution and color depth. In order to provide this capability, a software driver, commonly called a *VESA driver*, is provided by the card vendor or the game vendor. See *UniVBE*.

As of VBE Version 2.0, this standard must be implemented in the VGA card's BIOS, not as a software driver. In addition, resolutions are also selectable by pixels (640x480, 800x600, etc.), not just mode number. The VBE can be taken further. Since the card can be interrogated, it is possible to create a universal display driver that asks for and then uses the commands of the card it is driving.

VESA BIOS Extension/Audio Interface
A VESA standard for sound cards. Like the VBE for display adapters (see above), the purpose of the VESA BIOS Extension/Audio Interface (VBE/AI) is to provide a standard sound card interface across all platforms and environments. It also allows sound cards to be programmed using 32-bit instructions.

VESA DDC

(VESA Display Data Channel) A VESA standard communications channel between the display adapter and monitor. DDC requires an additional wire in the cable. The first level implementation (DDC1) provides a unidirectional channel that lets the monitor inform the host of its capabilities. A second bi-directional level (DDC2) allows the host to adjust the monitor. For example, the monitor's switch settings could be put into a software control panel. See *VESA DPMS*.

VESA Display Data Channel

See *VESA DDC*.

VESA display modes

See *VESA BIOS Extension* and *VESA DDC*.

VESA Display Power Management Signaling

See *VESA DPMS*.

VESA DPMS

(VESA Display Power Management Signaling) A VESA standard for signaling the monitor to switch to energy conservation modes. It provides two low energy modes: standby and suspend. See *VESA DDC*.

VESA driver

See *VESA BIOS Extensions*.

VESA/EISA

Refers to an EISA-bus motherboard or system that contains from one to three VL-bus slots.

VESA local bus

See *VL-bus*.

VESA Media Channel

A VESA standard bus for transferring video signals between the display adapter and multimedia boards (TV board, audio/video capture, videoconferencing, etc.). The Media Channel (also VM Channel or VMC) was designed as a high-speed multimedia bus to accommodate realtime audio and video traffic. Up to 16 devices can be connected.

Unlike the VESA Advanced Feature Connector, which is a point-to-point channel, the VMC is a sophisticated packet-oriented, timeshared bus, which can guarantee bandwidth for realtime transmission, even more suited for audio and video than PCI. The VMC can handle up to 16 simultaneous streams of data (audio, video, etc.) and can arbitrate between 8, 16 and 32-bit connections.

vesicular film

A film used to make copies of microforms. It contains its own developer and creates a pink negative or positive copy when exposed to a negative master through ultraviolet light.

V.Everything

A modem from U.S. Robotics that supports a wide variety of modem speeds including all the V.34 standards as well as x2. V.Everything modems can be upgraded to future specifications and standards by downloading new software into their flash memory chips.

VFAT

(Virtual File Allocation Table) The file system used in Windows for Workgroups and Windows 95/98. It provides 32-bit Protected Mode access for file manipulation. VFAT is faster than, but also compatible with, the DOS 16-bit File Allocation Table (FAT). In Windows for Workgroups, VFAT was called *32-bit file access*. In Windows 95/98, it supports long file names up to 255 characters.

V.FC (V.Fast Class)

A modem technology for 28800 bps from Rockwell International endorsed by many modem vendors before V.34 was finalized. V.FC is very similar to V.34, but V.FC modems require an upgraded chip for full compatibility.

VFP

See *Visual FoxPro*.

VFW

See *Video for Windows*.

VGA

(Video Graphics Array) The minimum standard for PC video display, which originated with IBM's PS/2 models in 1987. It supports earlier CGA and EGA modes and requires an analog monitor. VGA was initially 640x480 pixels with 16 colors, but non-IBM vendors quickly boosted resolution and colors to so-called "Super VGA," which was later standardized by VESA. All VGA display adapters today start at 256 colors. See *SVGA, XGA* and *PC display modes*.

VGA adapter, VGA card

A display adapter that provides VGA resolution. Most VGA adapters are capable of 640x480, 800x600 and 1024x768 resolutions with at least 256 colors. Many go up to 1280x1024 with color depth to 16M colors (true color). Most VGA adapters build in graphics acceleration in order to provide respectable scrolling and display speed under Windows. An older VGA card without a graphics accelerator is not recommended for Windows. See *VGA, graphics accelerator* and *video accelerator*.

VGA feature connector

A point-to-point channel used to transfer video signals between two video controllers, typically between the display adapter and a video capture or TV board. Using an 8-bit data path, it provides 40 Mbytes/sec bandwidth. The port is a 26-pin male connector or a 26-pin (13 per side) edge connector at the top of the VGA board. See *VESA Advanced Feature Connector*.

VGA HC

(VGA HiColor) A VGA board that provides 32K or 64K colors using Tseng Labs' ET4000 chip or equivalent.

VGA pass through

A feature of a high-resolution display adapter that is built without standard VGA capability. The standard VGA card in the computer is cabled to the pass through circuit on the high-res adapter. When the high-resolution capability of the adapter is not used, signals from the VGA card pass through the adapter directly to the monitor. The driver that accompanies the high-res adapter turns the pass through circuit on and off.

Pass-through circuits are also built into MPEG boards, allowing both VGA and MPEG signals to go directly to the monitor.

VHD

(Very High Density) A term applied to storage devices from time to time to indicate a higher capacity.

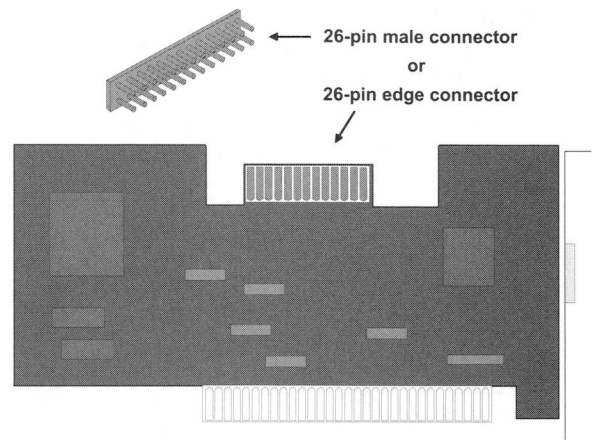

26-pin male connector
or
26-pin edge connector

Feature Connector
The VGA feature connector is either a 26-pin male connector on the chip side of the VGA adapter or a 26-pin (13 pins on each side) edge connector on the top edge. All VGA boards do not have the feature connector.

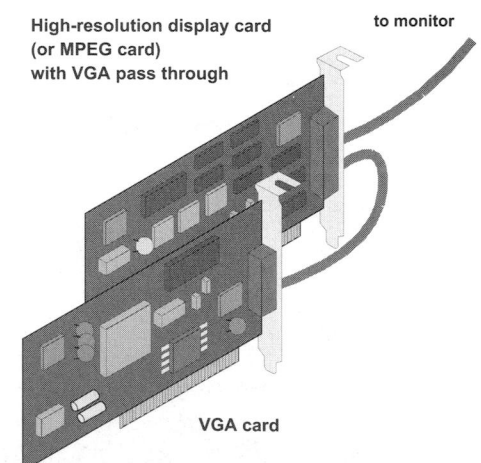

High-resolution display card (or MPEG card) with VGA pass through

to monitor

VGA card

VGA Pass Through
The signals go from the VGA card to the high-resolution adapter and then to the monitor.

VHDL

(VHSIC Hardware Description Language) A hardware description language (HDL) used to design electronic systems at the component, board and system level. VHDL allows models to be developed at a very high level of abstraction. Initially conceived as a documentation language only, most of the language can today be used for simulation and logic synthesis. VHDL is an IEEE standard, but was initially developed for the U.S. military's VHSIC program. See *Verilog* and *HDL*.

VHDSL

(Very High bit rate DSL) See *ADSL*.

VHF

(Very High Frequency) The range of electromagnetic frequencies from 30MHz to 300MHz.

VHS

A VCR format introduced by JVC in 1976 to compete with Sony's Beta format. VHS has become the standard for home and industry, and Beta is now obsolete. SVHS (Super VHS) is a subsequent format that improves resolution.

VHSIC

(Very High Speed Integrated Circuit) Pronounced "vizik." Ultra-high-speed chips employing LSI and VLSI technologies.

vi

(Visual Interface) A UNIX full-screen text editor that can be run from a terminal or the system console. It is a fast, programmer-oriented utility.

via

(1) By means of, by way of. From Latin for "way" or "path."

(2) In a printed circuit board, a conducting pathway between two or more substrates.

video

An audio/visual playback and recording technology used in TV. It also refers to computer screens and terminals. However, there is only one TV/video standard in the U.S., but there are dozens of computer display standards.

Video 1

A video compression/decompression algorithm (codec) from Microsoft that is included in Video for Windows.

video accelerator

A hardware component on a display adapter that speeds up full-motion video. The primary video accelerator functions are color space conversion, which converts YUV to RGB, hardware scaling, which is

The First Video Camera

This is one of the first video cameras, which dates back to the late 1920s. Although some stations were broadcasting TV in the 1930s, RCA began regular transmission in 1939. Below is Felix the Cat, one of the first recording stars. *(Photos courtesy of RCA Corporation.)*

used to enlarge the image to full screen and double buffering which moves the frames into the frame buffer faster. See *graphics accelerator*.

video adapter

See *video capture board, video graphics board* and *display adapter*.

video bandwidth

The maximum display resolution of a video screen, measured in MHz, and calculated by horizontal x vertical resolution x refreshes/sec. For example, 800x600x60 = 28.8MHz. Traditional TV studio recording is limited to 5MHz, and TV broadcasting is limited to 3.58Mhz.

video board

See *display adapter* and *video capture board*.

video camera

A camera that takes continuous pictures and generates a signal for display or recording. It captures images by breaking down the image into a series of lines. The U.S. and Canadian standard (NTSC) is 525 scan lines. Each line is scanned one at a time, and the continuously varying intensities of red, green and blue light across the line are filtered out and converted into a variable signal. Most video cameras are analog, but digital video cameras are also available. See *digital camera*.

video capture board

An expansion board that digitizes full-motion video from a VCR, camera or other video source. The board may also provide digital to analog conversion for recording onto a VCR.

video card

Same as *display adapter*.

Video CD

A compact disc format used to hold full-motion video. Developed by Matsushita, Philips, Sony and JVC, a Video CD holds 74 minutes of VHS-quality video and CD-quality sound. Video CD movies are compressed using the MPEG-1 method and require an MPEG decoder for playback on the computer. They can also be played on certain CD-I and 3DO players. Specifications for this format are defined in the "White Book." See *DVD*.

video codec

A hardware circuit that converts analog video (NTSC, PAL, SECAM) into digital code and vice versa incorporating one of several compression techniques, such as MPEG, Indeo, Cinepak or Video1. The term may refer to only the compression and decompression processing, which can be done in software or in hardware and is separate from the A/D and D/A conversion.

video compression

Encoding digital video to take up less storage space and transmission bandwidth. See *video codec* and *data compression*.

videoconferencing

A video communications session among several people that are geographically separated. This form of conferencing started with room systems where groups of people meet in a room with a wide-angle camera and large monitors and conference with other groups at remote locations. Federal, state and local

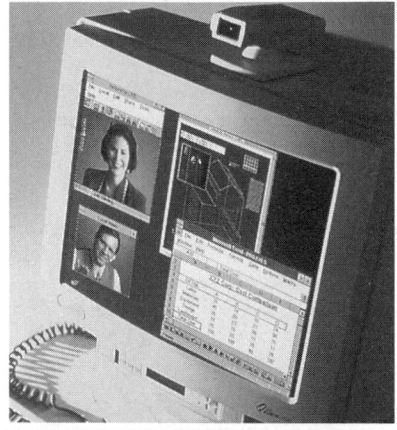

Desktop Videoconferencing
The small video windows in the PC above take a lot less network bandwidth than the full-screen image below. *(Photos courtesy of PictureTel Corporation and VTEL Corporation respectively.)*

governments are making major investments in group videoconferencing for distance learning and telemedicine.

Although the earliest videoconferencing was done with traditional analog TV and satellites, inhouse room systems became popular in the early 1980s after Compression Labs (now part of VTEL) pioneered digitized video systems that were highly compressed and could be transmitted over leased lines and switched digital facilities available from the telephone companies.

WAN, LAN and POTS

The standard for wide area videoconferencing is H.320, which defines the communications handshaking and the H.261 compression algorithm for reducing the digital video into a smaller bandwidth. H.320 runs over ISDN, Switched 56 and T1 lines, with ISDN rapidly becoming the de facto videoconferencing standard. Multiple ISDN lines can be coupled together providing bandwidth in multiples of 64 Kbytes/sec channels.

Desktop videoconferencing over LANs as well as over the plain old telephone system (POTS) is also widely available. Although many proprietary systems have been used, the H.323 and H.324 standards are expected to make interoperable systems mainstream over the next couple of years.

Desktop videoconferencing systems come with a camera and one or two boards for video capture, video compression and ISDN hookup. Many systems are dedicated to videoconferencing, while others use third-party boards that can be used for other ISDN transmission and video purposes. Instead of ISDN adapters, LAN-based systems use network adapters, and POTS-based systems use modems.

Data Conferencing

A concomitant part of videoconferencing is data conferencing, which allows data and documents to be shared by multiple participants. The ITU's T.120 standard provides specifications for whiteboards, application sharing and application viewing (see *data conferencing*). It is expected that all data collaboration software in the future will be T.120 compliant.

The difference between conferencing systems is the number of features in their data conferencing software and the smoothness and quality of the video image, which runs at rates from a handful of frames per second over POTS to 24 and 30 frames per second on high-end systems, both LAN and WAN. Standard TV uses 30 frames per second.

Room Videoconferencing Systems
Videoconferencing got its start with analog-based room systems. Today, digital systems use ISDN, T1 and other high-speed transmission links to provide the necessary bandwidth. *(Photo courtesy of VTEL Corporation respectively.)*

Classroom Videoconferencing
Distance learning is one of the major uses of videoconferencing systems. It enables a teacher to reach an audience that would be otherwise impossible. *(Photo courtesy of VTEL Corporation respectively.)*

Point-to-point and Multipoint

A point-to-point conference between two stations is relatively simple. A multipoint conference between three or more stations is more complex and requires a multipoint control unit, or MCU. The MCU joins the lines and switches the video automatically to the person speaking, or the switching can be directed manually by a user that acts as moderator. Multipoint conferences are also achieved by connecting to a conferencing network service from a common carrier.

Multipoint conferencing over LANs is expected to employ various technologies, including LAN-based MCU servers. ViewPoint Systems of Dallas, TX, pioneered multipoint LAN conferencing entirely in software using the IP multicast feature. Companies such as Datapoint provide full-motion video via an independent video network while running the data conferencing over the LAN.

This industry is expected to explode after the turn of the century and be fueled by personal use as well. Family members will justify the cost of a personal computer or videophone when they can regularly see loved ones in remote locations. Consumer product manufacturers are developing POTS-based systems that hook into the TV. Businesses can increase productivity through telecommuting as well as savings on business trips.

video controller
(1) A device that controls some kind of video function.
(2) Same as *display adapter*.

Video Device Interface
See *VDI*.

video digitizer
Same as *frame grabber*.

videodisc
An optical disc used for full-motion video. See *DVD, LaserDisc* and *Video CD*.

video display board, video display card
See *display adapter* and *video graphics board*.

video display terminal/unit
Same as *video terminal*.

video editing
See *nonlinear video editing*.

video editor
A dedicated computer that controls two or more videotape machines. It keeps track of frame numbers in its own database and switches the recording machine from playback to record. The video editor reads SMPTE time codes provided on professional tape formats.

video effects
See *digital video effects*.

Video for Windows
Full-motion video software for Windows from Microsoft. It is built into Windows 95/98, but has to be installed into Windows 3.1. Video for Windows supports the AVI movie file format and provides the Media Player applet for playing them. The Windows 3.1 installation also includes the VidCap and VidEdit video capture and editor utilities.

In Windows 3.1, the Video 1, RLE and Indeo compression methods are included. Windows 95 added Cinepak compression and provides MCI drivers for Sony ViSCA VCRs and LaserDisc players, which can be precisely controlled by the computer.

The quality of Video for Windows playback depends on CPU speed and the resolution of the video window. At 30 frames per second, the eye perceives a smooth animated sequence. The lower the rate, the more jerky the animation.

videographer
A person involved in the production of video material.

video graphics board
A display adapter that generates text and graphics and accepts video from a camera or VCR. Truevision's Targa board and Vision Technologies Vision board are examples. The terms video graphics board and video display board sound alike, but video display board is another term for display adapter,

which normally does not handle NTSC video.

In time, all display adapters will most likely support analog video, and since almost any combination of the words display, graphics and video, combined with the words board, controller and adapter, are used to refer to a display adapter, it is doubtful whether the term "video graphics board" will survive as originally coined.

video on demand

The ability to start delivering a movie or other video program to an individual Web browser or TV set whenever the user requests it. See *streaming video*.

video overlay

The placement of a full-motion video window on the display screen. There are various techniques used to display video on a computer's screen, depending on whether the video source has been digitized or is still in analog NTSC format.

Since computer monitors are generally analog, NTSC video can be merged with signals coming from the display adapter. Increasingly, faster computer buses (PCI, VL-bus, etc.) and faster video busses (Advanced Feature Connector, VM Channel, etc.), allow for analog video to be digitized and stored with other binary data for output. Then the display adapter turns it into analog scan lines for the monitor.

videophone

(1) A telephone with built-in video capability, including a camera and screen.

(2) (VideoPhone) A line of videophones from AT&T. It uses AT&T's Global VideoPhone Standard technology, which is also licensed to other manufacturers. See *PicturePhone*.

video port

A socket on a computer used to connect a monitor. On a PC, the standard video port is a 15-pin VGA connector. See *VGA*.

video RAM

Also called *VRAM*, it is a type of memory used in a display adapter. It is designed with dual ports so that it can simultaneously refresh the screen while text and images are drawn in memory. It is faster than the common dynamic RAM (DRAM) used as main memory in the computer.

video server

A computer that delivers streaming video for video on demand applications. Video servers may be computers that are specialized for this purpose. The term may just refer to the software that performs this service. See *streaming video*.

videotape

A magnetic tape used for recording full-animation video images. The most widely used videotape format is the 1/2" wide VHS cassette. VHS has all but obsoleted earlier videotape formats for home and commercial use.

video teleconferencing

See *videoconferencing*.

video terminal

A data entry device that uses a keyboard for input and a display screen for output. Although the display screen resembles a TV, it usually does not accept TV/video signals.

videotex

The first attempts at interactive information delivery for shopping, banking, news, etc. Many trials were made, but it never caught on. It used a TV set-top box and keyboard. Data was delivered by phone line and stored in the box as predefined frames with limited graphics that were retrieved by a menu.

Video Toaster

A popular video production system for the Amiga computer from NewTek, Inc., San Antonio, TX, (www.newtek.com). The Toaster includes hardware and software that provides video functions such as digital effects, character generation and 3-D animation. It controls professional analog tape decks and is considered the most affordable broadcast-quality video system on the market.

video window

The display of full-motion video (TV) in an independent window on a computer screen.

view

(1) To display and look at data on screen.

(2) In relational database management, a special display of data, created as needed. A view temporarily ties two or more files together so that the combined files can be displayed, printed or queried; for example, customers and orders or vendors and purchases. Fields to be included are specified by the user. The original files are not permanently linked or altered; however, if the system allows editing, the data in the original files will be changed.

viewer

A program that displays the contents of an electronic (digital) file. Viewers may be stand-alone programs or components within a larger program. They are widely used to display images downloaded from BBSs, online services and the Internet. Viewers for sound and video files are also available.

A viewer typically displays or plays one type of file, whereas a file viewer is a program that supports many different formats. See *file viewer*.

Viewperf

A benchmark created by IBM that is used to test graphics performance. It is endorsed by the OPC Group for OpenGL benchmarking. See *OPC*.

viewport

(1) In the Macintosh, the entire scrollable region of data that is viewed through a window.

(2) Same as *window*.

viewset

A specific mix of tests using the Viewperf benchmark. See *OPC*.

VIM

(Vendor Independent Messaging Interface) A programming interface developed by Lotus, Novell, IBM, Apple, Borland, MCI, WordPerfect and Oracle. In order to enable an application to send and receive mail over a VIM-compliant messaging system such as cc:Mail, programmers write to the VIM interface.

VINES

(VIrtual NEtworking System) A UNIX System V-based network operating system from Banyan Systems Inc., Westboro, MA, (www.banyan.com), that runs on DOS and OS/2-based servers. It provides internetworking of PCs, minis, mainframes and other computer resources providing information sharing across organizations of unlimited size.

Incorporating mainframe-like security with a global directory service called Streettalk, VINES allows access to all network users and resources. Options include printer sharing, e-mail, remote PC dial-in, bridges and gateways.

ViRGE

(VIdeo Rendering Graphics Engine) A family of 2-D and 3-D graphics accelerator chips from S3, first introduced in 1995. See *S3*.

virtual

An adjective that expresses a condition without boundaries or constraints. It is often used to define a feature or state that is simulated in some fashion. However, it has become such a fashionable computer word that it may be a prefix to "virtually" any electronic concept or product without regard to the original meaning of the term.

Virtual 8086 Mode

An operational mode in Intel 386s and up that allows it to perform as multiple 8086 CPUs. Under direction of a control program, each virtual machine runs as a stand-alone 8086 running its own operating system and applications, thus DOS, UNIX and other operating systems can be running simultaneously. All virtual machines are multitasked together.

This mode divides up the computer into multiple address spaces and maintains virtual registers for each virtual machine. This is not the same as the 386's virtual memory mode, which extends main memory to disk.

virtual circuit

(1) A temporary communications path created between devices in a switched communications system. For example, a message from New York to Los Angeles may actually be routed through Atlanta and St. Louis. Within a smaller geography, such as a building or campus, the virtual circuit traverses some number of switches, hubs and other network devices.

(2) A shared circuit that appears private to the users that are communicating with each other. See *PVC* and *SVC*.

virtual company, virtual corporation

An organization that uses computer and telecommunications technologies to extend its capabilities by working routinely with employees or contractors located throughout the country or the world. Using faxes, modems, data and videoconferencing, it implies a high degree of telecommuting as well as remote workgroups and facilities.

The extreme virtual company is one that hires only temporary help and whose office facilities are little more than a post office box and answering machine. See *hoteling*.

virtual connection

A temporary connection made between two nodes.

virtual desktop

An infinitely-large desktop, which is provided either by a virtual screen capability or a shell program that enhances the user interface. See *virtual screen*.

virtual device

See *virtual peripheral* and *VxD*.

virtual device driver

See *VxD* and *VDI*.

virtual disk

See *volume set* and *RAM disk*.

virtual display

A display technology that creates a full screen image in a small space. It enables a hand-held device, such as a pager or hand-held fax machine, to simulate a desktop monitor. See *Private Eye, virtual monitor* and *virtual screen*.

virtual function

In object technology, a function that has a default operation for a base class, but which can be overridden and perform a different operation by a derived class. A derived class inherits the attributes (data) and methods (processing) of a higher-level class.

virtual host

On the World Wide Web, a server that contains multiple Web sites, each with its own domain name. As of the first version of the Web protocol (HTTP 1.0), each Web site on a virtual host must be assigned a unique IP address. HTTP Version 1.1 eliminates this requirement. See *virtual server*.

virtual image

In graphics, the complete graphic image stored in memory, not just the part of it that is displayed at the current time.

FaxView Virtual Display
Reflection Technology's portable fax machine weighs eight ounces, works with most cell phones and stores 25 pages. Its virtual display simulates a 12" monitor and its "virtual keyboard" (lever and buttons on the unit) lets you select menu options. *(Photo courtesy of Reflection Technology, Inc.)*

virtualize

(1) To activate a program in virtual memory.

(2) To create a virtual screen.

virtual LAN

Also called a *VLAN*, it is a logical subgroup within a local area network that is created via software rather than manually moving cables in the wiring closet. It combines user stations and network devices into a single unit regardless of the physical LAN segment they are attached to and allows traffic to flow more efficiently within populations of mutual interest.

VLANs are implemented in port switching hubs and LAN switches and generally offer proprietary solutions. VLANs reduce the time it takes to implement moves, adds and changes.

VLANs function at layer 2. Since their purpose is to isolate traffic within the VLAN, in order to bridge from one VLAN to another, a router is required. The router works at the higher layer 3 network protocol, which requires that network layer segments are identified and coordinated with the VLANs. This is a complicated job, and VLANs tend to break down as networks expand and more routers are encountered. The industry is working towards "virtual routing" solutions, which allows the network manager to view the entire network as a single routed entity. See *802.1q*.

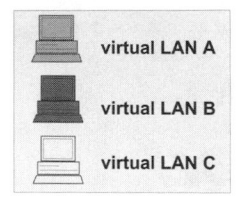

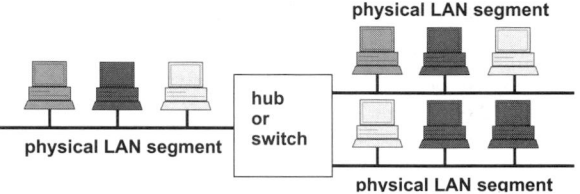

The VLAN
Virtual LANs solve the problem of containing traffic within workgroups that are geographically dispersed. They allow moves, adds and changes to be performed via software at a console rather than manually changing cables in the wiring closet.

virtual library

The worldwide collection of online books, journals and articles available on the Internet.

virtual machine

(1) A computer that runs an operating system that can host other operating systems or multiple copies of itself. Each operating system runs its own set of applications timeshared equally or in some priority with all the other operating systems. Computers can be built with hardware circuits that support a virtual machine environment; for example, the Virtual 8086 Mode in the PC starting with the 386. See *VM* and *Virtual 8086 Mode*.

(2) A computer that has built-in virtual memory capability.

(2) See *Java Virtual Machine*.

virtual memory

Simulating more memory than actually exists, allowing the computer to run larger programs or more programs concurrently. It breaks up the program into small segments, called *pages*, and brings as many pages into memory that fit into a reserved area for that program. When additional pages are required, it makes room for them by swapping them to disk. It keeps track of pages that have been modified, so that they can be retrieved when needed again.

If a program's logic points back and forth to opposite ends of the program, excessive disk accesses, or *thrashing*, can slow down execution.

Virtual memory can be implemented in software only, but efficient operation requires virtual memory hardware. Virtual memory claims are sometimes made for specific applications that bring additional parts of the program in as needed; however, true virtual memory is a hardware and operating system implementation that works with all applications. See *Windows swap file*.

virtual monitor

In the Macintosh, the ability to dynamically configure to any monitor type and to use multiple monitors of different types including displaying the same object across two or more screens.

virtual network

An interconnected group of networks (an internet) that appear as one large network to the user. Optionally, or perhaps ideally, a virtual network can be centrally managed and controlled.

Banyan Systems, creator of VINES, which stands for VIrtual NEtworking System, defines virtual networking as "the ability for users to transparently communicate locally and remotely across similar and dissimilar networks through a simple and consistent user interface." See *virtual LAN*.

virtual operating system

An operating system that can host other operating systems. See *virtual machine*.

virtual peripheral

A peripheral device simulated by the operating system.

virtual printer

A simulated printer. If a program is ready to print, but all printers are busy, the operating system will transfer the printer output to disk and keep it there until a printer becomes available.

virtual processing

A parallel processing technique that simulates a processor for applications that require a processor for each data element. It creates processors for data elements above and beyond the number of processors available.

virtual processor

A simulated processor in a virtual processing system.

virtual reality

An artificial reality that projects the user into a 3-D space generated by the computer. True virtual reality systems require the use of a unique kind of glove, called a *data glove*, and stereoscopic goggles, which are both wired to the computer. The glove lets users point to and manipulate computer-generated objects that are displayed on tiny monitors inside the goggles.

Virtual reality, or VR, can be used to create any illusion of reality or imagined reality and is used both for entertainment and training. Virtual reality has been around for some time now. For example, flight simulators, used to train airplane pilots and astronauts, have provided a very realistic simulation of the environment, albeit extremely expensive.

A variation of virtual reality, known as unencumbered virtual reality or computer automatic virtual environment (CAVE), is becoming popular for entertainment. For example, using a glove, but not goggles, you can play a simulated ballgame such as volley ball or basketball. A video camera captures your movements while you watch yourself on a large screen. You hit a simulated ball that is passed to you by your on-screen opponent and play the game as if it were real.

The term is also used for computer games and interactive environments on the Web that allow you to move from one room or area to another. They of course lack the 360 degree reality that comes from wearing the glove and goggles. See *HMD, CAVE, 6DOF, cyberspace* and *VRML*.

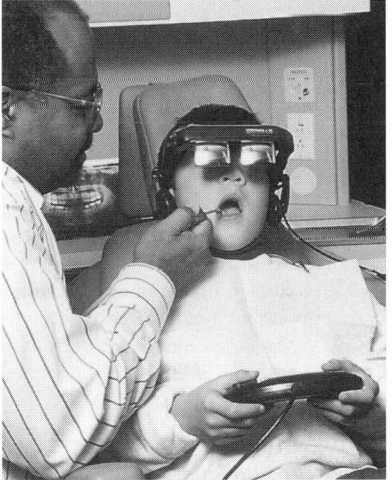

Virtual Reality at the Dentist
In this application, the child is looking through the goggles and manipulating the scenes that he sees with a game controller. *(Photo courtesy of Virtual I-O.)*

virtual root

A root directory that points to another root directory. It allows one root directory to be consistently named although the physical location may change. See *PURL*. See also *virtual circuit*.

virtual route

Same as *virtual circuit*.

virtual routing

An integrated, comprehensive solution to forwarding traffic at high speed in a network. All LAN, WAN and routing protocols are fully supported by all devices in the network so that the entire network can be viewed as a single router at one management console.

It implies the creation of virtual subnets, which are groups of users that are physically located in different areas but are logically treated as a single domain. Virtual subnets combine the logical subdivision provided by layer 2 VLANs with the filtering and firewall benefits of layer 3 routing.

The goal is to provide virtual routing (virtual subnets) in a multivendor environment. Many solutions are expected to tout this capability as ATM is integrated into legacy networks. See *MPOA, I-PNNI* and *IP Switch*.

virtual screen

A viewing area that is larger than the physical borders of the screen. It allows the user to scroll very large documents or multiple documents side by side by moving the mouse pointer beyond the edge of the screen. For example, you might look through an 800x600 screen resolution into a 1600x1200 virtual screen.

virtual server

(1) Same as *virtual host*.

(2) Multiple servers that appear as one server, or one system image, to the operating system or for network administration. See *system image*.

virtual storage

(1) See *virtual memory* and *VTS*.

(2) A storage resource that has infinite capacity and automatically performs all necessary storage management functions such as backup, archiving, disaster recovery and HSM. A totally-integrated system such as this does not now exist, but it is expected in the future.

virtual subnet

See *virtual routing*.

virtual tape

Simulating an infinite number of tape drives to the host system. See *VTS*.

virtual terminal

Terminal emulation that allows access to a foreign system. Often refers to a personal computer gaining access to a mini or mainframe.

virtual toolkit

Development software that creates programs for several computer environments. Its output may require additional conversions or translations to produce executable programs.

virus

Software used to infect a computer. After the virus code is written, it is buried within an existing program. Once that program is executed, the virus code is activated and attaches copies of itself to other programs in the system. Infected programs copy the virus to other programs.

The effect of the virus may be a simple prank that pops up a message on screen out of the blue, or it may destroy programs and data right away or on a certain date. It can lie dormant and do its damage once a year. For example, the Michaelangelo virus contaminates the machine on Michaelangelo's birthday.

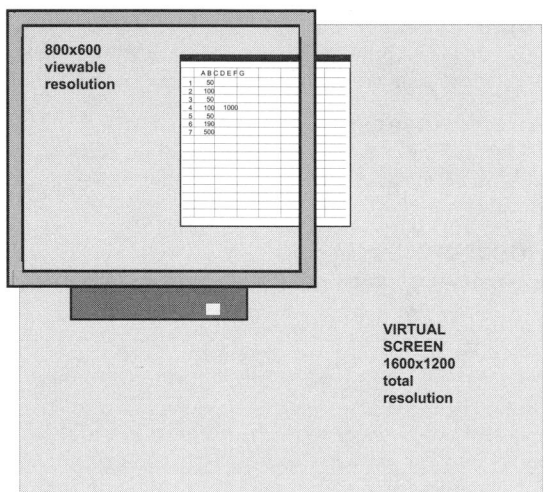

Virtual Screen

In this example, the user can see 800x600 pixels at a time and can pan the entire 1600x1200 pixels by moving the mouse beyond the edge of the viewable screen.

A common type of virus is a boot virus, which is stored in the boot sectors of a floppy disk. If the floppy is left in the drive when the machine is turned off and then on again, the machine is infected, because it reads the boot sectors of the floppy expecting to find the operating system there. Once the machine is infected, the boot virus may replicate itself onto all the floppies that are read or written in that machine from then on until it is eradicated.

In 1996, the National Computer Security Assocation claimed that only about 5% of the more than 6,000 known viruses are harmful. The majority are benign and are more like pranks created for the sheer art of programming. For example, on a certain day of the month, hearing a clicking noise from your speaker every time you press a key is a type of benign virus designed to drive you a little nutty until you figure out what it is.

A virus cannot be attached to data. It must be attached to a runnable program that is downloaded into or installed in the computer. The virus-attached program must be executed in order to activate the virus. Macro viruses, although hidden within documents (data), are similar. It is in the execution of the macro that the damage is done. See *polymorphic virus, stealth virus, worm, boot virus, macro virus* and *vandal.*

Be Careful Out There!
Before you run a shareware, public domain or freeware program, check it with a virus detection program first. In fact, to be 100% safe, every time you insert any new floppy disk into your computer no matter where it came from, check it first. If you're on the Internet, obtain a virus and vandal detector that looks for rogue files that you might have downloaded.

virus scanner
An antivirus program that searches for binary patterns, or signatures, of known viruses that have attached themselves to executable programs. The patterns have to be continually updated, and most antivirus programs work in this manner. Another type of antivirus program takes a blueprint of all existing executables and looks for changes.

virus signature
The binary pattern of the machine code of a particular virus. Antivirus programs compare their database of virus signatures with the files on the hard disk and removable media (including the boot sectors of the disks) as well as within RAM.

VIS
(1) (Voice Information Service) A variety of voice processing service applications.

(2) (Visible Image Size) The actual viewing area on a monitor. In the late 1990s, the industry had an honesty attack and began to provide actual viewing size along with the overall designation (14", 15", 17" etc.) which was exaggerated.

visa
See *VESA.*

ViSCA
(VIdeo System Control Architecture) A Sony protocol for synchronized control of multiple video peripherals. A ViSCA-compatible VCR can be controlled very precisely by the computer. ViSCA is the software interface. Control-L is the hardware plug and socket.

VisiCalc
The first electronic spreadsheet. It was introduced in 1978 for the Apple II. Conceived by Dan Bricklin, a Harvard student, and programmed by a friend, Bob Frankston, it became a major success. It launched an industry and was almost entirely responsible for the Apple II being used in business. Thousands of $3,000 Apples were bought to run the $150 VisiCalc.

VisiCalc was a command-driven program that was followed by SuperCalc, MultiPlan, Lotus 1-2-3 and a host of others, each improving the user interface. Spreadsheets have also been implemented on minis and mainframes, and it all started with VisiCalc.

Visio
A drawing and diagramming program for Windows from Visio Corporation (formerly Shapeware), Seattle, WA, that includes a variety of pre-drawn shapes and picture elements that can be dragged and dropped onto the illustration. Users can define their own elements and place them onto the Visio palette.

Visio Home is a version of Visio designed for personal use and includes elements for landscaping, family trees, decorating, etc.

VisualAge

A family of object-oriented application development software from IBM that includes VisualAge for Basic, VisualAge for C++, VisualAge for COBOL, VisualAge for Java, VisualAge for PacBase and VisualAge for Smalltalk. For example, VisualAge for C++ is a multiplatform environment for writing C++ applications for OS/2, Windows, AS/400, MVS/ESA, AIX and Solaris. It is widely used to write an application on one platform that will be used on another.

Today, the skills of a VisualAge programmer are not implicit, as the term refers to several languages. In the past it implied one or two. The VisualAge name was first used in the late 1980s for Smalltalk, then in 1994 for C++ and later for all the others.

Visual Basic

A version of the BASIC programming language from Microsoft specialized for developing Windows applications. It is similar to Microsoft's QuickBASIC, but not 100% compatible with it. User interfaces are developed by dragging objects from the Visual Basic Toolbox onto the application form.

Visual Basic has become very popular for Windows development and is widely used to write client front ends for client/server applications. Visual Basic for Applications (VBA), a subset of Visual Basic, is a common macro language Microsoft includes with many of its applications.

The Visual Basic program compiles the source code written by the programmer into an intermediate language called *byte code*. In order to run a Visual Basic program, the Visual Basic interpreter, or runtime module, must reside in the target computer. This .DLL file, with a prefix of VBRUN, converts the byte code into the machine language of the computer. The DLL is widely available and typically accompanies a Visual Basic application. See *VB Script*. See *compiler* for illustration.

Visual Basic Control

See *VBX*.

Visual C++

A C and C++ development system for DOS and Windows applications from Microsoft. It includes Visual Workbench, an integrated Windows-based development environment and Version 2.0 of the Microsoft Foundation Class Library (MFC), which provide a basic framework of object-oriented code to build an application upon.

Introduced in 1993, the Standard Edition of Visual C++ replaces QuickC for Windows and the Professional Edition includes the Windows SDK and replaces Microsoft C/C++ 7.0.

Visual Cafe

A family of Java development products from Symantec. Versions for Windows and the Macintosh are available that include a host of Java components and features for rapidly building applications. Visual Cafe added visual programming tools and superseded Cafe, which was Symantec's first-generation Java product that was based on its C++ environment.

As of Version 2.0, Visual Cafe was renamed Visual Cafe for Java and includes Symantec's Visual Page HTML authoring package. The Professional edition includes enhanced debugging and development features. The Database edition includes the dbANYWHERE server, which provides native connectivity to many popular databases.

visual computing

The use of computers for 3-D modelling and animation. See *visualization*.

Visual dBASE

Version 5.5 of dBASE for Windows was renamed Visual dBASE. See *dBASE*.

Visual FoxPro

An Xbase development system for Windows from Microsoft. Originally known as FoxPro for Windows, FoxPro for DOS, etc., Visual FoxPro added object orientation and client/server support. Although FoxPro usage is on the decline, the language is highly regarded by the developers that use it. Many business applications, both large and small, have been written in it.

Starting with Version 5.0, Visual FoxPro added support for ActiveX and is a 32-bit Windows only product. Version 3.0 was the last Macintosh version and 2.6 was the last DOS version.

Visual FoxPro stems from FoxBASE, which was originally developed for DOS by Fox Software and widely praised for its speed and compatibility with dBASE.

Visual InterDev

A Windows-based development system from Microsoft for building dynamic Web applications using Microsoft standards. It is used to write Active Server Pages that can interact with databases and ActiveX-based components in the server.

visualization

Using the computer to convert data into picture form. The most basic visualization is that of turning transaction data and summary information into charts and graphs. Visualization is used in computer-aided design (CAD) to render screen images into 3-D models that can viewed from all angles and which can also be animated. See *scientific visualization* and *information visualization.*

Visual J++

A Windows-based Java development system from Microsoft. It is used to create Java applications that can run on any platform or to create Windows-specific applications that call ActiveX components or Windows directly. Visual J++ also includes a Java compiler.

Visual Objects

See *CA-Visual Objects.*

Visual Page

An HTML authoring package for Windows and the Macintosh from Symantec. It is included with the Visual Cafe for Java development kits. See *Visual Cafe.*

visual programming

Developing programs with tools that allow menus, buttons and other graphics elements to be selected from a palette and drawn and built on screen. It may include developing source code by creating and/or interacting with flow charts that graphically display the logic paths and associated code.

Visual Studio

A suite of development tools from Microsoft that include its major programming languages and Web development package (Visual Basic, Visual C++, Visual FoxPro, Visual J++ and Visual InterDev). The Enterprise Edition includes version control, a database, TP monitor and reference material (Visual SourceSafe, Microsoft SQL Server and Microsoft Transaction Server, Developer Network Library).

visual tool

Any program module or program routine used in a visual programming environment for developing a program or used in a graphics environment for creating drawings or images.

Visual Workbench

See *Visual C++.*

VKD

(Virtual Keyboard Device) In Windows, a built-in virtual device driver that manages the keyboard and allows keystrokes to be sent to the appropriate, active application.

VLAN

See *virtual LAN.*

VLB, VL-bus

(VESA Local-BUS) A peripheral bus from VESA that was primarily used in 486s. It provides a high-speed data path between the CPU and peripherals (video, disk, network, etc.). VL-bus is a 32-bit bus that supports bus mastering and runs at speeds up to 40MHz. It generally provides up to three slots on the motherboard, each slot using one 32-bit Micro Channel connector placed adjacent to the standard ISA, EISA or Micro Channel connector.

VLDB

(Very Large DataBase) An extremely large database. What consitutes a VLDB is debatable, but databases of 100GB or more are generally considered the starting point. A VLDB is also measured by the number of transactions per second and the type of complex queries that it can support.

VLF
(Very Low Frequency) See *low radiation*.

VLIW
(Very Long Instruction Word) A CPU architecture that reads a group of instructions and executes them at the same time. For example, the group (word) might contain four instructions, and the compiler ensures that those four instructions are not dependent on each other so they can be executed simultaneously. Otherwise, it places no-ops (blank instructions) in the word where necessary.

VLSI
(1) (Very Large Scale Integration) Between 100,000 and one million transistors on a chip. See *SSI, MSI, LSI* and *ULSI*.

(2) (VLSI Technology, Inc., Tempe, AZ) A designer and manufacturer of custom chips.

VM
(1) (Virtual Machine) An IBM mainframe operating system, originally developed by its customers and eventually adopted as an IBM system product (VM/SP). It can run multiple operating systems within the computer at the same time, each one running its own programs. CMS (Conversational Monitor System) provides VM's interactive capability. See *Java Virtual Machine* and *Virtual 8086 Mode*.

(2) (Virtual Machine) One instance of a virtual machine in a virtual machine environment. See *virtual machine*.

VM/386
(Virtual Machine/386) An earlier multiuser operating system for 386s developed by IGC Corporation, San Jose, CA. It allowed one PC to serve as a central computer to multiple workstations, each capable of running several DOS and Windows programs simultaneously.

v-mail
(Video mail) The ability to send video clips along with e-mail messages. This is not the same as videoconferencing, which requires realtime capabilities between sender and receiver, but it does require high-speed computers and networks.

VMARK
(VMARK Software, Inc., Westboro, MA, www.vmark.com) A database and tools vendor founded in 1984. Its first and major product was the UniVerse relational DBMS, which was originally host based and then adapted to client/server. UniVerse has been built into many products developed by other software vendors. In 1995, VMARK acquired the Easel Corporation, which brought with it several client/server development packages for Windows and OS/2. Easel's ObjectStudio Smalltalk environment was later sold to Cincom.

VMC, VM Channel
See *VESA Media Channel*.

VME
(Virtual Machine Environment) An operating system from ICL that runs on its Series 39 mainframes. Introduced in 1975, VME is a comprehensive product that provides a variety of utilities for datacenter operations. In late 1992, VME achieved XPG/4 branding for its conformance to open systems standards. In 1994, OpenVME was introduced for the Series 39. See *OpenVME*.

VMEbus
(VersaModule Eurocard bus) A 32-bit bus developed by Motorola, Signetics, Mostek and Thompson CSF. It is widely used in industrial, commercial and military applications with over 300 manufacturers of VMEbus products worldwide. VME64 is an expanded version that provides 64-bit data transfer and addressing.

VMM
(1) (Virtual Machine Manager) The underlying operating system component of Windows. It

manages the computer's memory and virtual machines. The services in the VMM are not directly called by Windows applictions, but are accessible by virtual device drivers (VxDs).

(2) (Virtual Memory Manager) The software that manages virtual memory in a computer.

VMS

(1) (Virtual Memory System) A multiuser, multitasking, virtual memory operating system for the VAX series from Digital. VMS applications run on any VAX from the MicroVAX to the largest unit. See *OpenVMS*.

(2) (Voice Messaging System) See *voice mail*.

VM/SP

See *VM*.

VMTP

(Virtual Message Transaction Protocol) A datagram communications protocol that provides efficient and reliable transmission across networks.

vocoder

(VOice CODER) Same as *speech codec*.

VOD

See *video on demand*.

voice

See *MIDI voices*.

voice channel

A transmission channel or subchannel that has the bandwidth necessary to carry human voice. See *voice grade*.

voice codec

Same as *speech codec*.

voice coil

A type of motor used to move the access arm of a disk drive in very small increments. Like the voice coil of a speaker, the amount of current determines the amount of movement. Contrast with *stepper motor*, which works in fixed increments.

voice compression

Same as *speech compression*.

voice grade

Refers to the bandwidth required to transmit human voice, which is about four thousand Hertz (4KHz).

voice mail

A computerized telephone answering system that digitizes incoming voice messages and stores them on disk. It usually provides auto attendant capability, which uses prerecorded messages to route the caller to the appropriate person, department or mail box.

voice menu

A series of options and the corresponding number to press that are announced to the listener in an IVR or voice processing system.

voice messaging

Using voice mail as an alternative to electronic mail, in which voice messages are intentionally recorded, not because the recipient was not available.

voice navigation

Using voice recognition to select options from a menu.

voice over IP
See *IP telephony* and *IP on Everything*.

voice processing
The computerized handling of voice, which includes voice store and forward, voice response, voice recognition and text to speech technologies.

voice recognition
The conversion of spoken words into computer text. Speech is first digitized and then matched against a dictionary of coded waveforms. The matches are converted into text as if the words were typed on the keyboard.

Speaker-dependent systems require that users enunciate samples into the system in order to tune it to their individual voices. Speaker-independent systems do not require tuning and can recognize limited vocabularies such as numeric digits and a handful of words. For example, such systems have replaced human operators for telephone services such as collect calls and credit card calls.

There are three types of voice recognition applications. Command systems recognized a few hundred words and eliminate using the mouse or keyboard for repetitive commands. This is least taxing on the computer. Discrete voice recognition systems are used for dictation, but require a pause between each word. Continuous voice recognition understands natural speech without pauses and is the most process intensive. Speaker-independent continuous systems that can handle large vocabularies are expected to become mainstream after the turn of the century.

voice response
The generation of voice output by computer. It provides pre-recorded information either with or without selection by the caller. Interactive voice response allows interactive manipulation of a database. See *IVR*.

VoiceSpan
A modem technology for simultaneous voice and data transmission over the same line from AT&T. When the telephone handset is picked up, the modem changes to 4800 bps and modulates the voice over the data. A higher-rate burst mode is expected. See *SVD*.

voice store and forward
The technology behind voice mail and messaging systems. Human voice is digitized, stored in the computer, routed to the recipient's mailbox and retrieved by the user when required.

VoiceView
A modem technology for simultaneous voice and data transmission over the same line from Radish Communications Systems, Inc., Boulder, CO. VoiceView works in different modes. One mode can transmit up to regular V.34 speeds for data only with up to an eight-second delay to change to voice. Another mode, suited for sending small amounts of data, uses 9600 bps for simultaneous voice and data. See *SVD*.

VoIP
(Voice Over IP) See *IP telephony*.

volatile memory
A memory that does not hold its contents without power. A computer's main memory, made up of dynamic RAM or static RAM chips, loses its content immediately upon loss of power.

volt
A unit of measurement of force, or pressure, in an electrical circuit. The common voltage of an AC power line is 120 volts of alternating current (alternating directions). Common voltages within a computer are from 5 to 12 volts of direct current (one direction only).

voltage regulator
A device used to maintain a level amount of voltage in the electrical line. Contrast with *surge suppressor*, which filters out excessive amounts of current, and contrast with *UPS*, which provides backup power in the event of a power failure.

Computer Desktop Encyclopedia

volt-amps

The measurement of electrical usage that is computed by multiplying volts times amps. See *watt*.

volume

(1) A physical storage unit, such as a hard disk, floppy disk, disk cartridge, CD-ROM disc or reel of tape.

(2) A logical storage unit, which is a part of one physical drive or one that spans several physical drives.

volume label

(1) A name assigned to a floppy disk or hard disk by the user when the volume is formatted.

(2) An identifying stick-on label attached to the outside of a tape reel or disk cartridge. The label is handwritten or printed for human viewing.

(3) See *header label*.

volume serial number

A number assigned to a floppy disk or hard disk, which uniquely identifies the volume. It is automatically created by the format program and cannot be modified by the user.

volume set

A logical storage unit that spans several physical drives. The operating system sees the volume set as a contiguous group of storage blocks, but the physical data resides on multiple drives, broken up by various methods. See *RAID* and *disk striping*.

von Neumann architecture

The sequential nature of computers: an instruction is analyzed, data is processed, the next instruction is analyzed, and so on. Hungarian-born John von Neumann (1903-1957), an internationally renowned mathematician, promoted the stored program concept in the 1940s.

Voodoo Graphics

A family of 3-D graphics accelerator chipsets from 3Dfx. Voodoo Graphics chips are used in a variety of 3-D display adapters from major manufacturers. 3Dfx's Voodoo Rush technology adds 3-D capabilities to 2-D adapters. See *3Dfx*.

VOS

An operating system used in Stratus computers. FTX is Stratus' UNIX operating system.

voxel

(VOlume piXEL) A three-dimensional pixel. A voxel represents a quantity of 3-D data just as a pixel represents a point or cluster of points in 2-D data. It is used in scientific and medical applications that process 3-D images.

Voyetra

(Voyetra Turtle Beach, Inc., Yonkers, NY, www.tbeach.com) A manufacturer of sound cards and music software that is a result of a late-1996 merger of Voyetra Technologies and Turtle Beach Systems. Voyetra was founded in 1975 as Octave Electronics, a synthesizer and repair facility in southern New York state. It introduced the Voyetra synthesizer and later moved into software for MIDI sequencer and music-related applications. Voyetra utilities are bundled with numerous sound cards.

Turtle Beach was founded in 1985 in York, PA, and became known for its award-winning Multisound line of high-end sound cards. Its consumer brands are also popular and are named after beaches from around the world such as Malibu, Montego and Daytona.

VPC

(Virtual Processor Complex) An IBM mainframe multiprocessing that uses several computers under tight central control.

V.PCM

An interim name for the V.90 standard. See *V.90*.

VPN

(Virtual Private Network) A private network that is configured within a public network. For years, common carriers have built VPNs that appear as private national or international networks to the customer, but physically share backbone trunks with other customers. VPNs have been built over X.25, Switched 56, frame relay and ATM technologies. Today, there is tremendous interest in building VPNs over the Internet. In order to maintain privacy in a public environment, VPNs use access control and encryption. See *PPTP, L2F, L2TP, IPsec, PVC* and *security.*

VP Planner
An early Lotus-compatible relational spreadsheet from Paperback Software. In 1991, it was taken off the market due to a settlement of Lotus' copyright lawsuit.

VP ratio
(Virtual Processor ratio) The number of virtual processors that a physical processor is simulating.

VPS
(Vectors Per Second) The measurement of the speed of a vector or array processor.

VR
See *virtual reality.*

VRAM
See *video RAM.*

VRC
(Vertical Redundancy Check) An error checking method that generates and tests a parity bit for each byte of data that is moved or transmitted.

VRML
(Virtual Reality Modeling Language) A 3-D graphics language used on the Web. After downloading a VRML page, its contents can be viewed, rotated and manipulated. Simulated rooms can be "walked into." The VRML viewer is launched from within the Web browser.

The first VRML viewer was WebSpace from SGI, whose Open Inventor graphics library was the basis for developing VRML. WebFX, WorldView and Fountain are other Windows viewers, and Whurlwind and Voyager are Mac viewers.

VS
(1) (Virtual Storage) Same as *virtual memory.*

(2) (Virtual Storage) A family of minicomputers from Wang introduced in 1977, which use virtual memory techniques.

VSAM
(Virtual Storage Access Method) An IBM access method for storing data, widely used in IBM mainframes. It uses the B+tree method for organizing data.

VSAT
(Very Small Aperture satellite Terminal) A small earth station for satellite transmission that handles up to 56 Kbits/sec of digital transmission. VSATs that handle the T1 data rate (up to 1.544 Mbits/sec) are called *TSATs.*

VSB
(1) (VME Subsystem Bus) An auxiliary "backdoor" protocol on the VME bus that allows high-speed transfer between devices. It was faster than the main bus before the 64-bit implementation arrived.

(2) (Vestigial SideBand) A digital modulation method developed by Zenith for cable modems.

VSE
See *DOS/VSE.*

VSX
(Verification Suite for X/Open) A testing procedure from X/Open that verifies compliance with their endorsed standards. VSX3 has over 5,500 tests for compliance with XPG3.

VT100, 200, 300, etc.

A series of asynchronous display terminals from Digital for its PDP and VAX computers. Available in text and graphics models in both monochrome and color.

VTAM

(Virtual Telecommunications Access Method) Also ACF/VTAM (Advanced Communications Function/VTAM), it is software that controls communications in an IBM SNA environment. VTAM usually resides in the mainframe under MVS or VM, but may be offloaded into a front end processor that is tightly coupled to the mainframe. It supports a wide variety of network protocols, including SDLC and Token Ring. VTAM can be thought of as the network operating system of SNA.

VTOC

(Volume Table Of Contents) A list of files on a disk. The VTOC is the mainframe counterpart to the FAT table on a PC.

VTR

(VideoTape Recorder) A video recording and playback machine that uses reels of magnetic tape. Contrast with *VCR*, which uses tape cassettes.

VTS

(Virtual Tape Server, Virtual Tape System) A peripheral unit that combines a disk cache and tape library to improve performance and eliminate cartridge waste. Data intended for tape storage is written to the disk cache and later written to tape in the background. If a tape is read frequently, a certain amount of its data is held in the cache, which greatly improves access times over the slow loading process of a robotic library.

Tape files are typically stored on one cartridge no matter how small they are. A VTS provides volume stacking, which stores multiple files on a single volume. The VTS indexes the files and manages them, dramatically improving cartridge efficiency.

IBM's Virtual Tape Server for MVS uses its own Magstar tape library. Sun-based Scimitar systems from Sutmyn Storage Corporation, Santa Clara, CA, (www.sutmyn.com), support the tape library attached to the host.

VUP

(VAX Unit of Performance) A unit of measurement equal to the performance of the VAX 11//80, the first VAX machine.

VX chipset

See *Intel chipsets*.

VxD

(Virtual Device Driver) A special type of Windows driver that allows Windows to perform functions that cannot be done by applications communicating with Windows in the normal manner. VxDs run at the most privileged CPU mode (ring 0) and allow low-level interaction with the hardware and internal Windows functions, such as memory management.

Like DOS TSRs, poorly-written VxDs can conflict and lock up the system. WIN386.EXE (Win 3.1) and VMM32.VXD (Win 95/98) are the VxD files that provide the primary functions (kernel) in Windows.

VxFS

(VERITAS File System) A journaled file system for various UNIX systems from VERITAS Software Corporation, Mountain View, CA, (www.veritas.com), that provides high performance on large volumes of data and fast recovery from system failure. See *journaled file system*.

W

W3C

(World Wide Web Consortium, www.w3.org) An international industry consortium founded in 1994 to develop common standards for the World Wide Web. It is hosted in the U.S. by the Laboratory for Computer Science at MIT.

WAA

(Wide Area Adapter) Any of a variety of ports or adapters that connect to a wide area network (WAN), including RS-232, RS-422 and V.35.

Wabi

(Windows **ABI**) Software from SunSoft that emulates Windows applications under UNIX by converting the calls made by Windows applications into X Window calls. Since it executes native code, it runs Windows applications at the same or higher performance level than a Windows machine. Wabi is an option for Sun's Solaris environment as well as for OEM products.

wafer

(1) The base material in chip making, which goes through a series of photomasking, etching and implantation steps. It is a slice approximately 1/30" thick from a salami-like silicon crystal up to 8" in diameter. Twelve-inch wafers are expected to become popular by the turn of the century. See *chip*.

(2) A small, thin continuous-loop magnetic tape cartridge that has been used from time to time for data storage and specialized applications.

wafer scale integration

The evolution in semiconductor technology that builds a gigantic circuit on an entire wafer. Just as the integrated circuit eliminated cutting apart thousands of transistors from the wafer only to wire them back again on circuit boards, wafer scale integration eliminates cutting apart the chips. All the circuits for an entire computer are designed onto one super-sized chip.

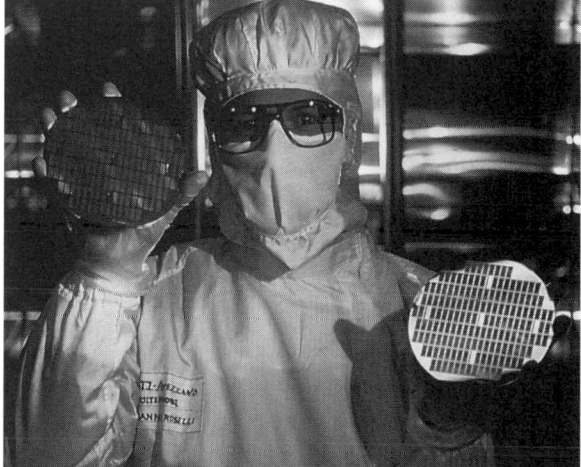

Finished Wafers
The man in the picture is holding up two wafers that have just come off the assembly line in a Texas Instruments plant in Italy. *(Photo courtesy of Texas Instruments, Inc.).*

Thus far, wafer scale integration has not come to fruition (see *Trilogy*); however, the multichip module (MCM), in which several chips are connected closely together in a single package, is expected to be widely used instead.

WAIS

(Wide Area Information Server) A database on the Internet that contains indexes to documents that reside on the Internet. Using the Z39.50 query language, text files can be searched based on keywords.

Information resources on the Internet are called "sources." A directory of WAIS servers and sources is avalable from Thinking Machines Corporation, Cambridge, MA, at address **quake.think.com**. See *Archie* and *Gopher*.

wait state

The time spent waiting for an operation to take place. It may refer to a variable length of time a program has to wait before it can be processed, or to a fixed duration of time, such as a machine cycle.

When memory is too slow to respond to the CPU's request for it, wait states are introduced until the memory can catch up.

wallet

See *digital wallet*.

wallpaper

A pattern or picture used to represent the desktop surface (screen background) in a graphical user interface. GUIs comes with several wallpaper choices, and third-party wallpaper files are available. You can also scan in your favorite picture and make it wallpaper.

If you wonder why you cover a desktop with wallpaper, don't. Very little makes sense in this industry, why should this?

WAN

(Wide Area Network) A communications network that covers a wide geographic area, such as state or country. A LAN (local area network) is contained within a building or complex, and a MAN (metropolitan area network) generally covers a city or suburb. Following is a bandwidth comparison between major LAN and WAN technologies.

WAN analyzer

See *network analyzer*.

wand

A hand-held optical reader used to read typewritten fonts, printed fonts, OCR fonts and bar codes. The wand is waved over each line of characters or codes in a single pass.

Wang

(Wang Laboratories, Inc., Lowell, MA, www.wang.com) A computer services and network integration company. Wang was one of the major early contributors to the computing industry from its founder's invention that made core memory possible, to leadership in desktop calculators and word processors. Founded in 1951 by Dr. An Wang and specializing in electronics, the company became world famous for its desktop calculators by the 1960s.

In the 1970s, Wang introduced its WPS word processor and VS minicomputers. It became North America's largest supplier of small business computers and the world's leader in word processors. Throughout the 1980s, it developed integrated voice and data networks and imaging systems.

In 1992, Wang declared Chapter 11 and recovered 18 months later. Soon after, it acquired Groupe Bull's federal systems integration business, its European imaging installations and its maintenance operations in North America and Australia. Wang has since sold off its software business to specialize in services.

Dr. Wang came from China in 1945 to study applied physics at Harvard. Six years later, he started Wang Labs. In 1988, two years before he died, he was inducted into the National Inventors Hall of Fame for his 1948 invention of a pulse transfer device that let magnetic cores be used for computer memory. The Hall of Fame has recognized an elite group including Edison, Pasteur and Bell.

Dr. An Wang
Dr. Wang was a major force in the early days of computing. His contribution to the invention of core memory significantly advanced the computer industry in the 1950s. His business and word processing systems were used worldwide by the 1970s. *(Photo courtesy of Wang Laboratories, Inc.)*

The Wang Calculator
In 1965, Wang's calculator was a major step forward, because it could generate a natural logarithm with only one keystroke. *(Photo courtesy of Wang Laboratories, Inc.)*

Computer Desktop Encyclopedia

WAP

(1) (Wireless Application Protocol) A wireless standard from Motorola, Ericsson and Nokia for providing most cellular phones with access to e-mail and text-based Web pages. WAP uses the Wireless Markup Language (WML), which is the WAP version of HDML. See *HDML*.

(2) (Wired Access Point) A radio station that transmits and receives wireless data.

wares

We love "wares" in this industry as noted below.

betaware	expireware	infoware	software
bloatware	feeware	liveware	stackware
boardware	firmware	middleware	trashware
brochureware	freeware	nagware	treeware
bridgeware	frontware	payware	vaporware
courseware	groupware	pushware	warmware
crippleware	guiltware	shareware	wetware
crossware	hardware	shelfware	
demoware	hookemware	shovelware	
dribbleware	hyperware	slideware	

warez

Same as *wares*. Slang for software.

warm boot

Restarting the computer by performing a reset operation (pressing reset, Ctrl-Alt-Del, etc.). See *boot, cold boot* and *clean boot*.

warm start

Same as *warm boot*.

warm swap

To pull out a component from a system and plug in a new one without turning the power off. Although often used synonymously with *hot swap*, a unit that is warm swapped must not be functioning. For example, a hard disk cannot be reading or writing while it is pulled out. See *hot swap*.

warmware

Same as *liveware*.

Warnier-Orr diagram

A graphic charting technique used in software engineering for system analysis and design.

WARP

(1) See *OS/2 Warp*.

(2) A parallel processor developed at Carnegie-Mellon University that was the predecessor of iWARP.

Warp Server

The server version of OS/2 from IBM. Warp Server combines OS/2 and Lan Server into one package that was introduced in 1996. Warp Server is generally highly praised and well suited as a Lotus Notes server.

Watcom compilers

A family of C, C++ and FORTRAN compilers for PCs from Sybase Waterloo, a division of Sybase. Originally Watcom International Corporation, Waterloo, Ontario, Watcom compilers have been noted for generating fast, compact code. WATCOM C/386 was the first 32-bit compiler for extended DOS, Windows, OS/2 2.0 and AutoCAD ADS and ADI applications. Watcom was acquired by Powersoft, which was later acquired by Sybase.

Watcom SQL

A relational DBMS for DOS, Windows, NetWare and OS/2 developed by Watcom International Corporation, Waterloo, Ontario. Watcom SQL evolved into Sybase SQL Anywhere when it was acquired by Powersoft and then Sybase.

watermark

See *digital watermark.*

watt

The measurement of electrical power. One watt is one ampere of current flowing at one volt. Watts are typically rated as AMPS x VOLTS; however, AMPS x VOLTS, or VOLT-AMP (V-A) ratings and watts are only equivalent when powering devices that absorb all the energy such as electric heating coils or incandescent light bulbs. With computer power supplies, the actual watt rating is only 60 to 70% of the VOLT-AMP rating.

wave

The shape of radiated energy. All radio signals, light rays, x-rays, and cosmic rays radiate an energy that looks likes rippling waves. To visualize waves, take a piece of paper and start drawing an up and down line very fast while pulling the paper perpendicular to the line.

wave audio

See *digital audio.*

wave file

See *WAV file.*

waveform

The pattern of a sound wave or other electronic signal in analog form.

waveform audio

See *digital audio.*

waveform synthesis

Same as *wave table synthesis.*

waveguide

A rectangular, circular or elliptical tube through which radio waves are transmitted.

wavelength

The distance between crests of a wave, computed by speed divided by frequency (speed / Hz). Wavelength in meters of electromagnetic waves equals 300,000,000 / Hz. Wavelength in meters for sound travelling through the air equals 335 / Hz.

wavelet compression

A lossy compression method used for color images and video. Instead of compressing small blocks of 8x8 pixels (64 bits) as in JPEG and MPEG, the wavelet algorithms compress the entire image with ratios of up to 300:1 for color and 50:1 for gray scale.

Wavelet compression also supports nonuniform compression, where specified parts of the image can be compressed more than others. There are several proprietary methods based on wavelet mathematics, which are available in products from Compression Engines, LLC, (www.cengines.com), InfinOp, Inc., (www.infinop.com) and Summus, Ltd., (www.summus.com). See *lossy compression.*

wavetable

A group of sampled sound waves used in MIDI. See *wavetable synthesis* and *MIDI.*

wave table synthesis

See *wavetable synthesis.*

wavetable synthesis

The technique used by MIDI for creating musical sounds by storing digitized samples of the actual instruments. It provides more realistic sound than the FM synthesis method, which generates the sound waves entirely via electronic circuits. The more notes sampled in the wavetable method, the better the resulting sound recreation. See *MIDI* and *FM synthesis.*

WAV file

The native digital audio format used in Windows. WAV files use the .WAV extension and allow different sound qualities to be recorded. Either 8-bit or 16-bit samples can be taken at rates of 11025 Hz,

22050 Hz and 44100 Hz. The highest quality (16-bit samples at 44100 Hz) uses 88KB of storage per second.

Windows uses WAV files for general system sounds. New WAV files can be placed into the \WINDOWS directory (Win 3.1) or the \WINDOWS\MEDIA folder (Win 95/98) and assigned to various system functions in the Sounds control panel. See *sampling rate*.

wax thermal transfer

See *thermal wax transfer printer*.

WBEM

(Web-Based Enterprise Management) An umbrella term for using Internet technologies to manage systems and networks throughout the enterprise. Both browsers and applications can be used to access the information that is made available in formats such as HTML and XML. Built into Windows 98 and NT 5.0, WBEM uses the Common Information Model (CIM) as the database for information about computer systems and network devices. Originally an initiative of Microsoft, Intel and others, WBEM was passed over to the DMTF in 1998. See *CIM* and *JMAPI*.

WDD

(Windows Distributed Desktop) Software from Tektronix, Wilsonville, OR, that allows UNIX workstations and X terminals access to Windows applications running under an enhanced version of Windows NT Server. An extension to WDD allows remote Windows users access to the server as well.

WDM

(1) (Wavelength Division Multiplexing) A technology that transmits multiple light signals simultaneosly over a single optical fiber. Each signal travels within its unique color band, which is modulated by the data (text, voice, video, etc.). WDM enables the existing fiber infrastructure of the telephone companies and other carriers to be dramatically increased. WDM systems, or DWDM (dense WDM) as it is increasingly being called, have been announced with up to 96 channels, although 16 channels is currently the norm. Trillions of bits per second (Tbps) are expected using this technology. Contrast with *TDM*. See also *FDM*.

(2) (Win32 Driver Model) A device driver architecture from Microsoft that consolidates drivers for Windows 95/98 and Windows NT. It allows a hardware vendor to write one Windows driver for its peripheral device that works with both Win 95/98 and NT.

weak typing

A programming language characteristic that allows different types of data to be moved freely among data structures, as is found in Smalltalk and other earlier object-oriented languages. Contrast with *strong typing*.

Web

See *World Wide Web*.

Web address

The URL of a page on the Web; for example, www.computerlanguage.com. See *URL*.

Web administrator

The Web equivalent of a system administrator. Web administrators are system architects responsible for the overall design and implementation of an Internet Web site or intranet. See *Webmaster*.

Web appliance

See *Internet appliance*.

Web authoring software

A Web site development system that allows Web pages to be visually created like a desktop publishing program. The required HTML, JavaScript or Java code necessary within the pages is automatically generated by the software. It typically displays an entire Web site as a graphical hierarchy of pages and allows existing Web sites to be imported for on-going maintenance. If may include built-in HTML editing capabilities. See *Web development software* and *HTML editor*.

Web based

Any software that runs on or interacts with a Web site, which may be on the Internet or on an inhouse intranet.

WebBench

A benchmark from Ziff-Davis that tests the performance of Web server software. It is a Windows-based program that can test any server platform and can thus be used to guage a Web package running on different hardware or different Web packages running on the same hardware. See *ZDBOp*.

Web box

See *Internet appliance*.

Web browser

The program that serves as your front end to the World Wide Web on the Internet. In order to view a site, you type its address (URL) into the browser's Location field; for example, **www.computerlanguage.com**, and the home page of that site is downloaded to you. The home page is an index to other pages on that site that you can jump to by clicking a "click here" message or an icon. Links on that site may take you to other related sites.

Browsers have a bookmark feature that lets you store references to your favorite sites. Instead of typing in the URL again to visit the site the next time, you select one of the bookmarks.

Although Mosaic was the browser that put the Web on the map, the two major browsers today are Netscape Navigator and Microsoft Internet Explorer. Navigator and Internet Explorer each vie for top recognition by introducing new features and functions that fragment Web sites into competing camps. When a site says "best viewed by Netscape Navigator" or "best viewed by Internet Explorer," it means that the pages were programmed for that particular browser. Using the other browser will ignore some of the page's fancy features until a subsequent release supports them. See *World Wide Web* and *HTML*.

Web cache

See *browser cache*.

Webcast

(1) To send live audio or video programming to several Internet users simultaneously.

(2) To send selected Web-based information (text, graphics, audio, video, etc.) to Internet users based on individual requirements. See *push technology*.

WebCompass

A Web search tool from Quarterdeck. It runs under Windows and polls Web search sites and summarizes the results.

WebCrawler

(www.webcrawler.com) A search site on the Web that searches other search sites. It returns a list of titles first giving you the option of going directly to a specific article or reviewing the summaries of all the hits. See *Web search sites*.

Web designer

A person that creates a Web site. Web designers may use Web authoring software or an HTML editor to create the actual pages, or they may design the overall look and let a Webmaster do the actual coding. See *Webmaster, Web authoring software* and *HTML editor*.

Web development software

Software used to develop Web sites. Although often synonymous with *Web authoring software*, it implies a more programming-oriented set of tools for linking pages to databases and other software components. It generally includes an HTML editor. See *Web authoring software* and *HTML editor*.

Web directories

See *Web white pages, Web yellow pages* and *Web search sites*.

Web enabled

Able to connect to or be used on the Web.

Web-enabled call center

A call center that receives calls from a link on a Web page. Such Web sites include a "talk" button on a page that allows visitors to obtain additional information from a human via IP telephony directly at their computers, providing of course that they have a microphone and speakers attached. If not already installed, the appropriate voice encoding and decoding (codec) plug-in must be downloaded first. See *call center*.

Web farm

A group of Web servers that are controlled locally, but centrally managed. Each Web site is administered by its own Webmaster; however, centralized monitoring provides load balancing and fault tolerance. See *server farm*.

Web filtering

Blocking the viewing of undesirable Internet content. Businesses can block content based on traffic type. For example, Web access might be allowed, but file transfers may not. Content can also be blocked by site, using lists of URLs cataloged by content that are updated frequently. Parents can restrict their children's access with special browsers and filtering programs. See *parental control software*.

Webhead

An enthusiastic and frequent user of the World Wide Web.

Web hosting

Placing a customer's Web page or Web site on a commercial Web server. Many ISPs host a personal Web page at no additional cost above the monthly service fee, while multi-page, commercial Web sites are hosted at a very wide range of prices. The customer's registered domain name is typically used. See *ISP* and *InterNIC*.

Webmaster

A person responsible for the implementation of a Web site. Webmasters must be proficient in HTML as well as one or more scripting and interface languages such as JavaScript and Perl. They may also have experience with more than one type of Web server. See *Web administrator*.

WebNFS

A Web version of the NFS distributed file system from SunSoft. WebNFS-enabled servers and browsers allow access to Web pages as much as 10 times faster than the standard HTTP protocol. Unlike HTTP, which drops the connection after each tiny file is downloaded only to reconnect for the next one, WebNFS downloads multiple files with a single connection. It also provides fault tolerance for large downloads that lose their connection midstream.

Web page

A page in a World Wide Web document. See *World Wide Web* and *Webmaster*.

Web palette

See *Netscape color palette*.

Web PC

See *network computer*.

Web phone

See *Internet telephony*.

Web portal

A Web "supersite" that provides a variety of services including Web searching, news, white and yellow pages directories, free e-mail, discussion groups, online shopping and links to other sites. Web portals are the Web equivalent of the original online services such as CompuServe and AOL.

Webring

(www.webring.org) A navigation system that links related Web sites together. Each ring links sites that pertain to a particular topic.

Web search engines

See *Web search sites, Web white pages* and *Web yellow pages.*

Web search sites

There are various Web sites that maintain databases about the contents of other Web sites. Most sites are free and are paid for by advertising banners, while others charge for the service. Yahoo! was the first search site to gain worldwide attention, and it is still unique, because it is cataloged by humans that create a hierarchical directory by subject. Yahoo! is often called a "directory" rather than a search engine.

Most other sites are highly automated, sending spider programs out on the Web around the clock to collect the text of Web pages. Spiders follow all the links on a page and put all the text into one gigantic database, which is what you search when you use the site. Sometimes, both approaches are offered. For example, Excite lets you search the entire Web or a topic. Similarly, Yahoo! lets you automatically search one of the leading Web search engines. Some sites, such as MetaCrawler, just search other sites.

The Web Site of Search Sites

Be sure to visit www.searchenginewatch.com. The site maintains a list of all major search engines and goes into detail about how they work and explains their significant features.

General-Purpose Sites

Following are popular sites for searching any topic. If you don't find what you want at one site, try another. The spiders don't necessary find the same information at the same time.

```
www.altavista.digital.com
www.dogpile.com
www.excite.com
www.hotbot.com
www.infoseek.com
www.lycos.com
www.metacrawler.com
www.opentext.com
www.search.com
www.webcrawler.com
www.yahoo.com
```

Special-Purpose Sites

Following are popular sites for searching specific topics. For example, Four11 searches a database of the nation's white pages for phone numbers and addresses. Deja News searches a database of postings to Usenet newsgroups. See also *Web white pages* and *Web yellow pages.*

```
Authors & Books,      www.amazon.com
Automobile Buyers Guides,   www.edmunds.com
Book Reviews,    www.nytimes.com/books
Business News,   www.wsj.com
Computer Supersite,   www.cmp.com
Computer Supersite,   www.cnet.com
Computer Supersite,   www.zdnet.com
Consumer Info,   www.consumerworld.org
Education & Career Info,   www.petersons.com
Government (U.S.),   http://thomas.loc.gov
Health & Medicine,   www.healthatoz.com
Jobs & Careers,   www.occ.com
Legal Resources,   www.findlaw.com
Literature (Great Works),   www.promo.net/pg
Mailing Lists (Internet),   www.liszt.com
Maps & Driving Directions,   www.mapquest.com
Microsoft Support,   www.microsoft.com/support
Movies, Actors & Actresses,   www.imdb.com
Music & Videos,   www.cdnow.com
Newsgroups (Usenet),   www.dejanews.com
Package Tracking & Drop Offs,   www.fedex.com
Package Tracking & Drop Offs,   www.ups.com
```

```
Parenting Library,   www.parentsoup.com
Recipes & Cooking,   www.epicurious.com
Research,   www.clearinghouse.net
Research,   www.elibrary.com
Restaurant Menus,   www.menusonline.com
Shareware,   www.shareware.com
Shareware,   www.softseek.com
Subculture,   www.disinfo.com
Tax Forms,   www.1040.com
White Pages (people),   www.four11.com
Yellow Pages (business),   www.zip2.com
Zipcodes,   www.usps.gov
```

Web server

A computer that provides World Wide Web services on the Internet. It includes the hardware, operating system, Web server software, TCP/IP protocols and the Web site content (Web pages). If the Web server is for internal use, it is known as an intranet server.

The term may refer to just the software that performs this service, which accepts requests from Web browsers to download HTML pages and images. It also executes related server-side scripts that automate functions such as searching a database. See *Web site* and *intranet server*.

Search More and Better

Become a great Web searcher with "Search Engines for the World Wide Web" by Alfred and Emily Glossbrenner. This book is easy reading. (Peachpit Press, 1998,

WebShare

An application development system from Radnet, Inc., Cambridge, MA, (www.radnet.com), that is designed to produce groupware applications for the Internet/intranet. The WebShare Server runs under NT in conjunction with the Web server, and client access to the applications is via any Web browser. WebShare uses the BasicScript programming language with extensions for WebShare objects. Access to databases is via ODBC. WebShare 2.0 provides replication to mobile users via its WebShare Mobile file transfer capability.

Web site

A server that contains Web pages and other files which is online to the Internet 24 hours a day. See *World Wide Web, intranet* and *HTTP*.

Webtop

(1) Using a Web browser as the desktop interface in a client machine.

(2) A specification from Sun, IBM and Oracle for a common interface for Java-based network computers.

WebTV

(WebTV Networks Inc., Palo Alto, CA, www.webtv.net) The first Internet TV service that obtained widespread distribution of its set-top boxes in the retail channel. In 1997, it was acquired by Microsoft. WebTV uses an analog modem and telephone line to deliver the Web to the TV set. See *Internet TV*. See *cable modem* for illustation.

Web white pages

Web sites that provide searchable databases of invidivual e-mail addresses and other "people-finding" tools. They typically include residential telephone numbers and street addresses. However, unlike phone company white pages, there is no single source for this information, and you may have to try several sources. There's no guarantee that a person's e-mail address is available in any of these directories. Following are some of the popular white pages sites. See *Web yellow pages* and *Web search sites*.

```
www.bigfoot.com
www.four11.com
www.infospace.com
www.switchboard.com
www.whowhere.com
```

Web yellow pages

Web sites that provide searchable databases of business listings. Some also include additional information such as maps, driving directions, and Web addresses. Following are some of the popular yellow pages sites. See *Web white pages* and *Web search sites*.

```
www.tollfree.att.net
www.bigbook.com
www.bigyellow.com
http://yp.gte.net
www.zip2.com
```

Webzine

A magazine published on the World Wide Web.

Weitek coprocessor

A high-performance math coprocessor from Weitek Corporation. Since 1981, Weitek made coprocessors for CAD and graphics workstations. In 1996, Weitek declared Chapter 11. Later that year, Rockwell Semiconductor Systems agreed to purchase Weitek's assets and hire its employees to start a new multimedia chip design center in San Jose.

well-behaved, well mannered

Refers to programs that do not deviate from a standard. A program that is not well-behaved (ill-behaved) typically bypasses the operating system or some other control program and accesses the hardware directly to improve performance.

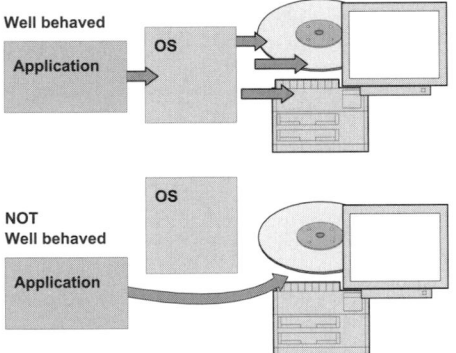

well-known port

A protocol port number that is widely used for a certain type of data on the network. For example, World Wide Web traffic (HTTP packets) is typically assigned port 80. See *protocol port*.

Western Digital

(Western Digital Corporation, Irvine, CA, www.wdc.com) Founded originally as a specialty semiconductor company under the name General Digital in 1970, its name was changed to Western Digital in 1971. In 1976, it introduced the first floppy disk controller, and later, hard disk controllers. In the late 1980s, it introduced a line of display adapters for the PC and also entered the disk drive business. Western Digital's line of award-winning Caviar drives, introduced in 1990, have been widely used in PCs.

Western Electric

See *Lucent*.

wetware

A biological system. It typically refers to the human brain and nervous system.

WfM

(Wired For Management) A specification from Intel for a PC that can be centrally managed in a network. It must be DMI compliant, be accessible by a management server prior to booting, contain instrumentation for component discovery and identification and include remote wake-up capabilities. See *NetPC* and *DMI*.

WFW

See *Windows for Workgroups*.

what if?

Using a spreadsheet as a planning tool. When new data is entered, results are calculated based upon the formulas. Assumptions can be plugged in that ripple through to the bottom line. For example, "what if hourly pay is increased $2?" "What if interest rates are lowered a half a point?"

Computer Desktop Encyclopedia

Whetstones

A benchmark program that tests floating point operations. Results are expressed in Whetstones per second. Whetstone I tests 32-bit, and Whetstone II tests 64-bit operations. See *Dhrystones* and *benchmark*.

WHIRLWIND

The first electronic digital computer with realtime capability and the first to use magnetic core memory. Developed at the Massachusetts Institute of Technology throughout the 1940s, it

WHIRLWIND I
In the early 1950s, the WHIRLWIND was the first computer to use magnetic core memory and provide realtime capabilities. *(Photo courtesy of The MIT Museum.)*

became operational in the early 1950s. The machine was continually enhanced, eventually using 12,000 vacuum tubes and 20,000 diodes and occupying two floors of an MIT campus building. It used 2K words of core memory and magnetic drum and tape for storage.

WHIRLWIND's circuit design, use of CRTs and realtime communications contributed towards the making of future computers. Project members later worked on IBM's 700 series. One in particular, Kenneth Olsen, founded Digital Equipment Corporation.

whiteboard

The electronic equivalent of chalk and blackboard, but between remote users. Whiteboard systems allow network participants to simultaneously view one or more users drawing on an on-screen blackboard or running an application. This is not the same as application sharing where two or more users can interactively work in the application. Only one user is actually running the application from his or her computer. In some systems, the application may not be viewable interactively. A copy of the application window is pasted into the whiteboard, which then becomes a static image for interactive annotation. See *data conferencing* for illustration.

white noise

Same as *Gaussian noise*.

white pages

See *Web white pages* and *DIB*.

white paper

An authoritative report on a topic. There are countless white papers on technology subjects written by vendors, research firms and consultants. Many are now available on the Web.

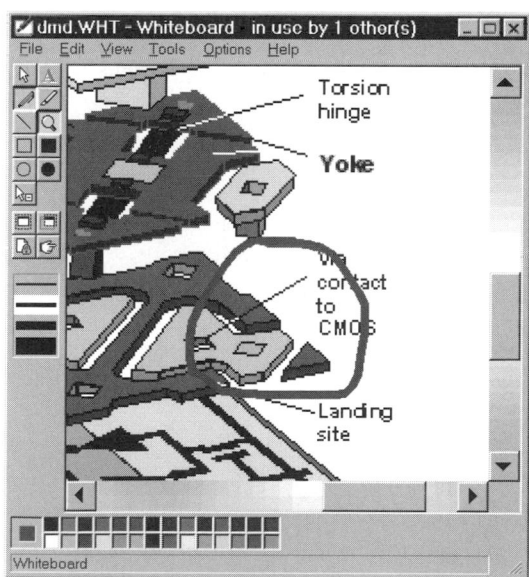

Whiteboards
Whiteboarding offers the most basic data conferencing capability. In this example, a drawing of the DMD pixel under the DLP entry in this book was pasted into a NetMeeting whiteboard. Using the red pen, a particular area of interest was circled.

white point

The measurement of "white" on a color monitor. It can be expressed in degrees Kelvin or as one of the standard illuminants or in x-y coordinates from the CIE Chromaticity Diagram. For example, the most neutral white point is 6500 degrees Kelvin or D65 or x=0.3127/y=0.3290.

whois

An Internet utility used to query a host and find out if a certain user is registered on that system. Originally developed by the military, others followed with their own whois databases, which provide a white pages directory for the organization. See *finger*.

WHQL

(Windows Hardware Quality Labs) A Microsoft facility that provides testing services for hardware and drivers for compliance with its operating systems. WHQL administers various logos that compliant vendors may reprint on their packages; for example, "Designed for Microsoft BackOffice." It was formerly the Microsoft Compatibility Labs (MCL).

wideband

In communications, transmission rates from 64 Kbps to 2 Mbps. Contrast with *narrowband* and *broadband*.

wide-format printer

A printer that prints on very large paper. Such printers typically use ink jet technology to print on a variety of output, including highly-coated glossy paper for signs and posters.

Wide SCSI

A SCSI interface that transfers 16 bits in parallel rather than 8 bits. See *SCSI*.

widget

Pronounced "wih-jit." A popular word for a generic "thing." It is often used to describe examples of made-up products along with other fictitious names; for example, "10 widgets, 5 frabbits and 2 dingits."

widget set

The structures (menu, button, scroll bar, etc.) provided in a graphical interface.

Wide-Format Printer
The DisplayMaker XL60 from ColorSpan prints on matte and glossy paper up to five feet in width. *(Photo courtesy of ColorSpan Corporation.)*

widow & orphan

A "widow" is the last line of a paragraph that appears alone at the top of the next page, and an "orphan" is the first line of a paragraph that appears alone at the bottom of a page. Widow and orphan settings are usually set for a minimum of two lines.

width table

A list of horizontal measurements for each character in a font, used by word processing and desktop publishing programs.

wild cards

Symbols used to represent any value when selecting specific files. In DOS, Windows and UNIX, the asterisk (*) represents any collection of characters, and the question mark (?) represents one single character. Note the following examples:

```
*.exe      All .EXE files
a*.exe     All .EXE files beginning with A
boot.*     All files named BOOT
*.d*       All files with with D— extensions
```

```
?abc        Files such as 1ABC, 2ABC, etc.
??abc       Files such as 10ABC, XXABC, etc.

WINDOWS 95/98 EXCEPTION
*t          Files that end in A (HOT, FAT, etc.)
```

WilTel

(WILliams TELecommunications Group) An international long distance carrier and network services provider, formed in 1987 by a merger of Williams Telecommunications Company and LDX Net, Inc. WilTel grew by acquiring several companies and was the first to offer fractional T3 service and high-capacity, switched digital lines for videoconferencing. In 1994, it was acquired by WorldCom. See *WorldCom*.

wimp interface

(Windows, Icons, Menus and a Pointing device) Same as *GUI*.

Win16 application

An application written for Windows 3.x, which runs within the computer's 16-bit mode of operation. A Win32 application is written for Windows 95, Windows NT or the Win32s extensions to Windows 3.1. See *Win32* and *32-bit processing*.

Win32

The programming interface (API) for 32-bit mode supported in Windows NT and Windows 95/98. When applications are written to Win32, they are activating the PCs native and most efficient internal functions.

Many Win32 functions are also available in Windows 3.1, and Windows 3.1 applications can be written to the Win32 subset (Win32s) to gain improved performance. The Win32s capability did not come with Windows 3.1. If a Windows 3.1 application uses Win32s, it generally installs the Win32s software along with the application.

Win32 application

An application written for Windows 95/98, Windows NT or the Win32s extensions to Windows 3.1. See *Win32* and *32-bit processing*.

Win32s

See *Win32*.

Win95B

Same as *OSR2*.

Win 95 Version number

To find out which version of Windows 95 you have, right click on My Computer, select PROPERTIES and look under the General tab. The first version of Windows 95 was 4.00.950. The second release in late 1996, known as OEM Service Release 2 (OSR2) or Win95B, is identified as 4.00.950 B.

Win 9x/3.1 Differences

Windows 95 and 98 are a mixture of DOS, Windows 3.1 and the Macintosh plus functions and features that are unique. Following are the major differences between Windows 3.1 and Windows 95/98.

In a Nutshell

Windows 95/98 provides faster operation in general, and especially running 32-bit applications. It provides many enhancements over Windows 3.1.

Program Manager has turned into a Macintosh-like desktop with folders and long file names. The Start menu replaces the Program Groups. File Manager has changed to Explorer.

When you turn the machine off, the desktop remains intact from session to session.

DOS is built into and boots with Windows 95/98. AUTOEXEC.BAT, CONFIG.SYS, WIN.INI, SYSTEM.INI and other INI files are maintained for compatibility.

All hardware and environment settings reside in the Registry, and information about files and applications is obtainable and consistent.

Multitasking is now preemptive so two or more programs can execute simultaneously. All active programs are displayed on a Taskbar.

Networking is built in for popular LANs and dial-up communications as well as direct cable connection to portables.

Installing new hardware is easier, but by no means foolproof. Windows 95/98 supports Plug and Play, which many affectionately call "Plug and Pray."

Troubleshooting is somewhat easier because of built-in modes for rebooting in a "clean" state with only the necessary drivers.

The Details

A REAL DESKTOP WITH FOLDERS

Windows 95/98 is like the Macintosh environment, which simulates a real desktop. Items can be placed onto the desktop and left there. When you turn the machine on the next day, the desktop reappears the way you left it.

Windows 95/98 combines the DOS directory structure with Macintosh folders. Directories are now called folders, but you still view them in a hierarchical manner as you did directories and subdirectories in File Manager. You can create a new folder and name it with a long name and place the folder within another folder. Windows 95/98 maintains long file names along with its counterpart DOS 8.3 name by truncating the long name into eight characters so that it can be manipulated with a DOS command (DOS is not dead!).

File extensions are still used in Windows 95/98 to identify and associate program and data files, so extension names such as .EXE, .COM, .DOC and .TXT are still relevant. That means a program name such as "WONDERFUL WORD PROCESSOR.EXE" is valid. File extensions can be hidden from view by selecting OPTIONS/VIEW/HIDE MS-DOS FILE TYPES... from the View menus in Explorer and folders.

MY COMPUTER, NETWORK NEIGHBORHOOD & RECYCLE BIN

The desktop contains three permanent icons that cannot be deleted. My Computer displays all the computer's resources, which includes disk drives and system folders containing the control panels, print spoolers and dial-up networking.

Network Neighborhood displays local area network resources and provides access to setting up the protocols and drivers.

The Recycle Bin is the 1990's counterpart to the Macintosh trash can, which was introduced in 1984. When items are dragged into the Recycle Bin, they remain there, providing an automatic undelete until you purposefully empty the bin.

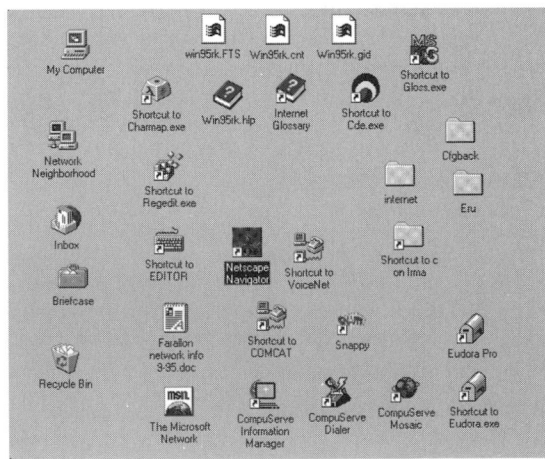

A Crowded Desktop

This is an example of a Windows 95 desktop, which is getting a bit crowded. The Shortcuts are the equivalent to the icons in Program Manager. This desktop is more like the Macintosh than Win 3.1. When you turn on your computer, your desktop is just as messy as you left it. Another major difference from 3.1 is that Windows 95/98 folders (directories) can be placed on the desktop and opened directly by clicking on them without the need of File Manager.

DOS IS ALIVE AND WELL

A new version of DOS, often referred to as DOS 7.0, is built into Windows 95/98 and is actually booted when you turn the computer on. The DOS commands are located in the \WINDOWS\COMMAND folder. Many infrequently-used commands have been dropped, and Windows 95 has added some enhancements. For example, you can launch a Windows application from the command line, and you can reference long file names. You must use quotes if the name has spaces. However, you can use dots as separators; for example:

```
ren   vacitly.txt   "Vacation to Italy Sept. 95.txt"

ren   vacitly.txt   Vacation.Italy.Sept.95.txt
```

If you upgrade an existing system, AUTOEXEC.BAT and CONFIG.SYS are carried forth and used. However, Windows 95/98 directly supports more devices (CD-ROMs, SCSI, etc.) than Windows 3.1, and it provides 32-bit Protected Mode drivers for them, which run in extended memory. Upon installation, if it finds a 16-bit driver that it has a replacement for, it rem's out the old driver in CONFIG.SYS and uses its own.

PROGRAM MANAGER AND THE START MENU

The Windows 3.1 Program Manager has been replaced by the Start menu, which is displayed by pressing Start on the Taskbar. The Start menu contains a Programs submenu, which replaces the group windows in Program Manager. The menu items contain pointers to the respective files, just like the Program Manager group icons were pointers to applications in Windows 3.1.

When applications are installed, they add a menu item in the Programs submenu. Clicking it displays another submenu of application components that can be executed. That submenu used to be a Program Group in Windows 3.1.

The Start menu can be modified by dragging and dropping icons directly onto it or by opening the Start menu window (right click on Start) and treating it as another folder.

When a program is minimized in Windows 95/98, it becomes a button on the Taskbar. Clicking the button restores the application to its previous on-screen appearance. See *Win 9x Taskbar*.

SHORTCUTS

The Start menu is not the only way to access a program. Just as you did with File Manager, you can double click on an executable program in the Explorer to launch it. You can also place a shortcut (pointer) to the program on the desktop by simply dragging it from a folder or an Explorer window and dropping it onto the desktop. Double clicking the shortcut launches the application.

The shortcut accepts a description of the program as did icons in Program Groups in Program Manager.

FILE MANAGER AND EXPLORER

File Manager has been replaced by the Explorer, which is somewhat similar, but displays a variety of icons in its graphical trees instead of the single folder icon in File Manager. One major difference is that Explorer maintains the tree and contents windows independently. You can expand the tree on the left side without disturbing the contents on the right. This allows you to copy individual files to subfolders more easily.

If you want to view the contents of more than one folder at the same time, you have to launch multiple instances of Explorer. With File Manager, you select new window within the same instance of File Manager.

The Explorer can be launched by right clicking the Start menu. If My Computer, Network Neighborhood, the Recycle Bin or a folder is right clicked, selecting EXPLORE launches Explorer with the contents of that item already in view.

To ease the transition to Windows 95/98, Program Manager and File Manager can still be used. The files PROGMAN.EXE and WINFILE.EXE continue to reside in the \WINDOWS directory. Their icons can be dragged to the desktop, creating shortcuts to the them.

CONTROL PANELS

Like Windows 3.1, a series of control panels for environment and hardware settings are provided. Their icons are located within My Computer, which is always present on the desktop. The control panels provide front ends into the Windows 95/98 Registry, which is the database where the actual settings are stored. In Windows 3.1, the Registry stored OLE and file associations. In Windows 95/98, it is the main configuration storehouse.

The contents of most of the control panels are displayed as Properties pages that look like overlapping sheets of paper with tabs at the top for selection. Click on a tab, and a different sheet is displayed. Properties sheets are generally available from the File menu, and right clicking the mouse from various places provides many shortcuts to them.

Windows 95/98 configuration information is generally more consistent and provides more detail than in Windows 3.1.

COMPATIBILITY AND MULTITASKING

WIN.INI, SYSTEM.INI and other .INI files are still maintained in Windows 95/98 for compatibility with Windows 3.1. However, much of the information in these files has been transferred to the Registry.

Windows 95/98 includes preemptive multitasking of 32-bit applications. That ensures, for example, that a communications program running in the background can gain control of the CPU to meet the demands of an incoming transmission. Windows 3.1 is non-preemptive and cannot keep an application from usurping CPU resources.

Both DOS and Windows 95/98 applications can be multitasked preemptively, but not Windows 3.1 applications.

NETWORKING

Windows 95/98 includes extensive networking and supports NetBEUI, IPX/SPX and TCP/IP, the three major transport protocols. A Window 95/98 computer can be configured as a client in a network and exchange information between Windows 95/98, Windows for Workgroups, Windows NT, LAN Manager and NetWare servers.

Network Neighborhood is a permanent icon on the desktop which provides a window into available network resources. Double clicking it displays shared resources as does Connect Network Drive in Windows for Workgroups' File Manager.

Windows 95/98 supports portable computing by providing both modem and cable connections to a Windows 95 host. Dial Up Networking (DUN) lets you log onto the host and access local and remote resources via modem. Direct Cable Connection (DCC) provides the same capability via

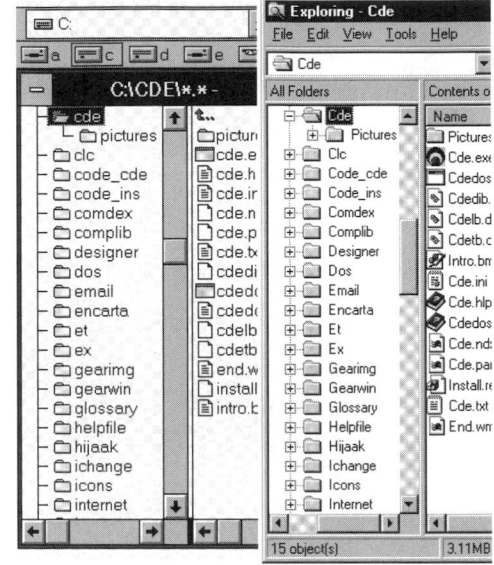

Windows Explorer
Explorer (right) adds some graphic enhancements over File Manager (left). The + and - on the Explorer folder icons say

My Computer and Control Panels
Clicking MY COMPUTER and then CONTROL PANEL displays all the Windows 95/98 control panels. Unlike Windows 3.1, Windows is aware of its display system and contains a display control panel.

the serial or parallel port and also lets you transfer files between two machines.

The Windows 95/98 Briefcase is a special folder that is used to synchronize files between two computers, typically a desktop and laptop. For example, files dragged into a Briefcase and transferred to a laptop and then updated on the road, can automatically update the original files when you get back to the office.

INSTALLATION & PLUG AND PLAY

Windows 95/98 has an installation dialog that helps users install and uninstall new hardware and software. The "Add New Hardware" and "Add/Remove Programs" functions are control panels in My Computer. Windows 95/98-compliant applications must include an uninstall program, which is displayed in the "Add/Remove Programs" dialog.

Windows 95/98 provides 32-bit Protected Mode drivers for a large majority of popular devices on the market, including most display adapters. If a device is not supported, either an older 16-bit driver or a vendor-supplied 32-bit driver can be used.

Windows 95/98 supports Plug and Play, which means that if you install a Plug and Play board you should have a smooth installation without the headaches of setting IRQs, DMAs, I/O and memory addresses as is required in DOS and Windows 3.1. However, even non-Plug and Play devices are easier to install, because Windows 95/98 will alert you to potential conflicts. See *plug and tell*.

TROUBLESHOOTING

Pressing F8 at startup lists a menu of options to help you troubleshoot a problem with the computer. You can boot clean with minimal drivers and standard VGA in order to get back into Windows and figure out the problem. There are several startup options, including booting directly to DOS (who said DOS wasn't around anymore?).

Win 9x abc's

The information under the Win 9x entries is intended for the first-time user of Windows 95 or Windows 98. If you are a Windows 3.1 user, read *Win 9x/3.1 Differences*.

What's a Window?

A window is a rectangular area on screen surrounded by a window frame with a title at the top. When you launch a Windows application, it is displayed in its own window. Each subsequent application is displayed in another.

You can make windows smaller or larger. On large screens, you can keep them side by side.

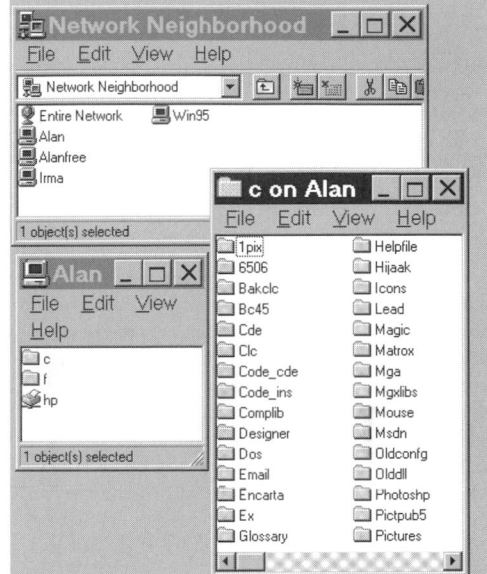

Network Neigborhood
Windows 95/98 is very network savvy. The graphic representation of the Network

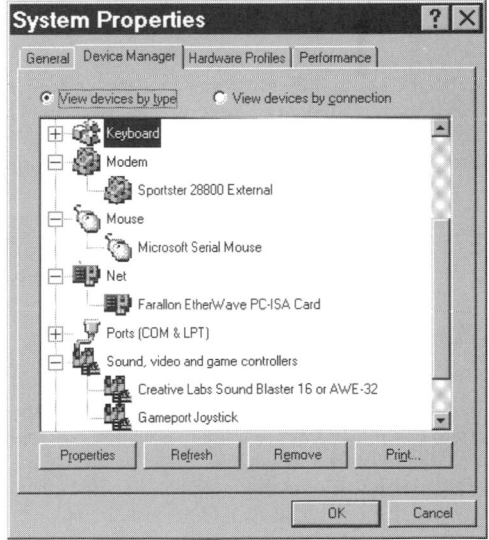

Device Manager
Windows 95/98 is considerably more aware of its peripheral resources than Windows 3.1. In fact, if you a pull a hard drive out of one Windows 95/98 machine and place it into another, Windows may not work unless the system is identical. The version of Windows on that hard disk is tightly configured to that specific PC.

Usually, you'll keep each window full screen so you can see as much of your current document as possible.

Windows 95/98 runs native Windows 95/98 applications (32-bit applications), Windows 3.1 applications (16-bit applications) and DOS applications. Each program runs in a Window and both Windows 3.1 and Windows 95/98 applications appear very similar. One major difference is that Windows 3.1 programs do not support the long file names available in Windows 95. This alone can be a good enough reason to purchase the 32-bit versions of your favorite programs. Plus, new features are generally only added to Windows 95/98 programs, not Windows 3.1.

Desktop, Files and Folders

The desktop in Windows 95 and Windows 98 electronically simulates an office desktop. The screen background is the desktop. When Windows 95/98 is first installed, the desktop contains only a few icons such as My Computer, Network Neighborhood and the Recycle Bin. Additional icons of programs, documents and folders are placed on the desktop by the user. In this respect, Windows 95/98 is like the Macintosh. Data files are represented as icons, which are housed in folders and are moved and copied from one folder to another by dragging and dropping them. Windows 95/98 preserves the desktop from session to session. All icons and open folders reappear in your next Windows session.

As you open each application, it becomes a new screen layer on top of the other layers, and its icon and name are placed on a taskbar at the bottom of the screen. In order to reveal the desktop below, right click on any part of the taskbar that is not covered with an icon and select MINIMIZE ALL WINDOWS.

Windows 95/98 also provides a convenient Start menu that can be customized for your favorite programs, documents and folders. It is your master menu that is always available. You don't really have to put anything on the desktop.

Although Windows 95/98 may be your first venture into Windows, experienced users and tons of documentation refer to directories and subdirectories rather than folders and subfolders, but the terms are synonymous.

Start Menu

The Start menu, which is an ever-present button on the left side of the taskbar, is your master menu and launching pad for applications. Windows 95/98 installation programs make an entry in the Programs submenu which is selected from the Start menu. You can click Start to do everything: access all your programs, documents and control settings, even to turn the computer off.

If you use an application often, drag its icon onto the Start menu button, and it will appear as a selection in alphabetical order the next time you click Start. See *Win 9x Start menu*.

Switching Programs and the Taskbar

The taskbar, which is normally visible at the bottom of the screen, keeps track of your open applications. Whenever a program is launched, its icon and name are placed on the taskbar. To switch to another program, just click its icon/name on the taskbar. Another option for switching programs is to press Alt-Tab. The names and icons of all the programs are made available to you.

The taskbar can be moved to other sides of the screen. It can also be hidden and made to reappear by moving the cursor past the edge of the screen (see *Win 9x Taskbar*).

My Computer and Network Neighborhood

All the resources available to the computer are displayed from two icons that cannot be removed from the desktop: My Computer and Network Neighborhood. They too can be placed in the Start menu.

My Computer displays all local resources, including hard and floppy disks, CD-ROMs, printers and modem connections. For example, double clicking on the hard disk icon opens the hard disk into a window, displaying all its folders, subfolders, documents and files. My Computer also contains the control panels needed to configure the system.

Network Neighborhood displays icons of all the servers in the network. Double clicking on a server displays the folders and printers that have been made sharable for other users.

Desktop Shortcuts

When a folder is opened, any program or data file contained in it can be dragged to the desktop or to the Start button and turned into a Shortcut, which is a pointer to that file. But, unlike Windows 3.1, which only had pointer icons in Program Manager, and they pointed only to applications, Windows 95/98 lets you make a pointer to anything, and the pointer (Shortcut) can be placed on the desktop, in the Start menu or in any other folder. Shortcuts in many different places can all point to the same object.

The Recycle Bin

The Recycle Bin is the 1990s version of the Macintosh Trash Can. Objects are dropped into the Bin for removal, but they are not erased from the disk until the Bin is purposefully emptied. Deleted files can be restored by simply dragging them back from the Bin onto the desktop or into a folder.

Explorer

Windows Explorer (not to be confused with Internet Explorer) provides a file management window whenever you need to view the contents of a folder. You can also look into a folder by selecting down the hierarchy in My Computer, but you can only have once instance of My Computer open, whereas any number of Explorer windows can be opened simultaneously. You can also delete and rename files from Explorer and My Computer. Windows 95/98 generally gives you several ways of doing things. See *Win 9x Explorer*.

The Registry and Properties

The Registry is a Windows 95/98 database that holds all the configuration settings about your current system. Many settings previously stored in the WIN.INI and SYSTEM.INI configuration files in Windows 3.1 are contained in the Windows 95/98 Registry.

Access to the Registry is normally done via the Control Panels and the Properties option. Windows 95/98 divulges a lot of information about its files and functions, and this information is almost always available by either right clicking an object's icon or by selecting Files/Properties from the menu in the active window. You can surgically alter the data in the Registry, but this is not normally required or is it desired. See *Win 9x Properties*.

Summary

Most people use an operating system to launch applications and manage files. These tasks can be learned rather quickly in Windows 95/98, and you may never need to do much else. But, Windows 95/98 is a mixture of DOS, Windows 3.1 and the Macintosh all rolled into one, which makes it rather sophisticated and also very complicated. Mastering the nuances takes some practice.

Win 9x Change window appearance

In Windows, you can move, resize and overlap windows on screen.

Move Window Around Screen
Point to window title bar (top of window) and drag.

Change One Side of a Window
Point to a side. When pointer changes to a double arrow, drag to new location.

Change Two Sides of a Window
Point to a corner. When pointer changes to an angled double arrow, drag to new location.

Turn Window into a Taskbar Button (Minimize)
Click the leftmost button at the top right side of the window (underscore character).

Turn Taskbar Icon back into a Window
Click the taskbar button icon.

Make Window Cover Entire Screen (Maximize)
Click the middle button at the top right side of the window (rectangle).

Restore Window to Previous Size
Click the middle button at the top right side of the window (double rectangles).

Win 9x Clipboard

See *Win 9x Copy between windows*.

Win 9x Copy between windows

To copy text or an image within a document in Windows 95 or 98 and insert it into another, highlight the text or image and select COPY from the Edit menu. Your selected item will be copied into the clipboard. Then switch to the window that contains the destination document. Position the cursor where you want the text or image to appear and select PASTE from the Edit menu. To move the object instead of copying it, select CUT instead of COPY from the Edit menu.

To copy or move data from a DOS window, see *Win 9x Run DOS programs*

Win 9x Create new folder

To create a new folder in Windows 95 or 98, launch Explorer. To get a new, first-level folder on drive C: that is not contained within any other folder, highlight the C: icon at the top of the left window pane by clicking it once. Then do the following:

```
1. Highlight drive or folder icon in left pane.
2. Select NEW from the File menu.
3. Select FOLDER.
4. Look for "New Folder" and type in new name.
5. Press Enter to finish.
```

Subfolders

To create a subfolder, highlight the folder you want to put it in by clicking that folder's icon once in step #1 above.

You can also create subfolders from within any folder window, by selecting NEW from the open window's File menu.

Win 9x Device Manager

The Device Manger Property sheet in Windows 95 and 98 shows the status of all the peripheral devices connected to your computer. To display it, from the Start menu, select Settings/Control Panel/System and then click the DEVICE MANAGER tab.

Win 9x Dial-up Networking

Windows 95/98 Dial-up Networking makes it relatively easy to establish a new connection to a remote dial-up service.

If Dial-up Networking is already installed in My Computer, double click the icon and then double click Make New Connection. Follow the prompts.

If Dial-up Networking is not installed, do the following to install it. You will need your Windows 95/98 CD-ROM.

```
1. Select Settings/Control Panel from Start menu.
2. Select Add/Remove Programs.
3. Click Windows Setup tab.
4. Double click Communications.
5. Enable Dial-up Networking.
6. Click OK and follow prompts.
```

Win 9x Display settings

Settings such as desktop and window colors, screen saver and resolution are in the Display control panel. Right click on any uncovered area on the desktop and select PROPERTIES.

Configuration information about the display adapter is in Device Manager in the System control panel. Double click My Computer, Control Panel and System. Click on the DEVICE MANAGER tab.

Win 9x Explorer

Explorer lets you create and delete folders and copy, move and delete files. In its left window, Explorer displays a hierarchical tree of folders. In its right window, the contents of the currently selected folder are displayed.

Explorer maintains the tree and contents windows independently. For example, you can display the contents of a folder on the right and then expand the tree on the left to display subfolders that you might want to copy or move files into.

Explorer has only one contents window on the right side. However, you can open up as many folders as you wish each into their own window. You can also launch multiple instances of Explorer. Following are the basic operations in Explorer.

Launch Explorer
    Right click Start menu and select EXPLORE.

Display Contents of a Folder
    Click once on the folder in the tree on the left. Its contents will be
    displayed in the right window.
        To open a folder into its own window (not the right side of Explorer),
    click the folder in the tree and select OPEN.

Display Names of Subfolders "Expand the Tree"
    If there is a + to the left of the folder, there are subfolders. To display
    the subfolder hierarchy, click the +. The + changes to a -. To compress
    the tree back again, click the -.

Display Contents of a Subfolder
    Click once on the subfolder icon in the left side of the Explorer window, or
    double click on the subfolder icon in the right side of the window.

Create Folder
    Click the drive or folder icon in which the new folder will be placed, and
    select NEW from the File menu. Then select FOLDER.

Delete Folder
    Click the folder icon and select DELETE from the File menu.

Rename File or Folder
    Click the icon. Select RENAME from the File menu. Or, click the icon name
    twice (but not so fast that it is picked up as a double click). Type in a
    new name and press Enter.

Switch Drives
    Click the drive icon.

Copy or Move File or Folder
    Right click, drag source icon and drop on destination icon. Select COPY or
    MOVE from menu. Note that there is a default selection in the menu. If you
    remember what the defaults are, you can left click and drag and the
    operation will be performed automatically.

TYPE OF FILE	LEFT DRAG ACTION TAKEN
Data file	Move
Program file	Shortcut created

Select Multiple Files
    Hold Ctrl down and click icons. If the file names are contiguous, you can
    lasso them by clicking to the right of the file name on top
    or bottom and dragging to the diagonal corner.

Win 9x Format a disk
    To format a disk, launch Explorer or My Computer. In the left window pane, highlight the icon of the diskette or disk you want to format, and right click the mouse. Select FORMAT and click START.

Win 9x Hardware configuration
    See *Win 9x Device Manager*.

Win 9x IRQs
    To find out which IRQs are assigned in a Windows 95/98 machine, select Device Manager in the System control panel and double click on Computer at the top of the list. The IRQs and current assignments will be displayed. To display the System control panel, select: Start menu, Settings, Control Panel, System.

Win 9x Keyboard commands

Following are the ways to command Windows without a mouse:

MENUS

```
All menus are selectable by pressing Alt and the UNDERLINED letter of the
menu title.  For example, Alt-F for File menu.
```

```
MENU OPTIONS
All menu options are selectable by pressing the UNDERLINED letter of thier
name.  Most of the time, it is the first letter.  However, if two menu
options start with the same letter, one of them will use a letter in
the middle of the name as a keyboard command.
```

```
CANCEL MENU  Esc
```

```
HELP MENU  F1
```

START/STOP

```
DISPLAY START MENU  Ctrl-Esc
LAUNCH APPLICATION FROM ICON  Enter
CLOSE WINDOW  Alt-F4  or  Alt-spacebar, C.
```

GO TO/CHANGE WINDOWS

```
GO TO ALL WINDOWS  Alt-Tab-Tab...
GO BETWEEN LAST TWO  Alt-Tab
GO TO NEXT TABBED SHEET  Ctrl-Tab
MOVE WINDOW  Alt-spacebar, M.  Cursor to new location and press Enter.
RESIZE WINDOW  Alt-spacebar, S.  Cursor to new size and press Enter.
```

MINIMIZE/MAXIMIZE

```
DISPLAY CONTROL MENU  Alt-spacebar
MAXIMIZE  Alt-spacebar  X
MINIMIZE  Alt-spacebar  N
```

CLIPBOARD

```
COPY SELECTED ITEM INTO CLIPBOARD  Ctrl-C
CUT SELECTED ITEM INTO CLIPBOARD  Ctrl-X
PASTE FROM CLIPBOARD  Ctrl-V
HIGHLIGHT TEXT  Hold Shift down while moving the cursor keys.
```

MISCELLANEOUS

```
UNDO LAST OPERATION  Ctrl-Z
TOGGLE DOS FULL SCREEN & WINDOW  Alt-enter
```

Win 9x Long file names

Windows 95 and 98 support file and folder names up to 255 characters in length. It also maintains the name in the 8.3 short form for compatibility with DOS and Windows 3.1 programs that cannot access long file names. The valid characters are the same as in DOS:

```
A-Z,  a-z,  0-9  ! @ # $ % & ( ) ' ` - { } ~
```

as well as:

+ , ; = [ ] . space

File extensions are still used and are attached to the file name with a period as they are in DOS/Windows 3.1. However, you can place dots within the file name. The name **letters to friends.pat.sue.sam.doc** is valid in Windows 95/98. The DOC would be treated as an extension name. The short name that Windows 95/98 creates can be confusing, because it takes the first six letters of the long name and adds the Spanish tilde and a digit. For example, **MY LETTER TO FRIENDS** becomes **MYLETT~1**. Therefore, if you plan on using

Computer Desktop Encyclopedia

```
DOS and Windows 3.1 applications for a while, you will have to be careful how
you name files and folders with Windows 95/98 applications.  If you are not
careful about keeping the first letters different (as you always did in the
past), the resulting 8.3 names Windows 95/98 creates may all look similar or be
too cryptic, so be careful out there among the old and new Windows!
```

The New DOS Handles Long Names

If you use the DOS prompt in Windows 95/98, it will handle the new names. Use quotes if you have spaces, for example:

```
copy oldbudgets newbudgets

copy oldbudgets "new budgets"

copy "old budgets" "new budgets"
```

Win 9x Minimize windows

To remove some of the clutter of your open windows, you can "minimize" a window, turning it into a button on the Taskbar at the bottom of the screen.

To minimize your open window, click on the _ button at the top right corner of the window. The minimized application remains active but out of your way. To turn it back into a window, "maximize" it by clicking the appropriate Taskbar button or pressing Alt-Tab-Tab-etc.

MINIMIZE THEM ALL

You can minimize all your open windows at once by right clicking on an empty area of the Taskbar and selecting MINIMIZE ALL WINDOWS.

DON'T FORGET YOUR MINIMIZED APPLICATIONS

If you forget you have a minimized application, and you double click on the program icon back in the Start menu, on the desktop or in Explorer, you will launch another copy of the application.

Win 9x My Computer

The My Computer icon on a Windows 95/98 desktop serves as a window into all of the resources on the computer. It includes the disk drives and system folders, which contain the control panels, print spoolers and dial-up networking. My Computer displays local resources. Its counterpart for remote resources on the network is the Network Neighborhood, which is also on the desktop.

Win 9x Network Neighborhood

The Network Neighborhood icon on a Windows 95/98 desktop serves as a window into all of the network resources available to the user. Network Neighborhood displays remote resources. Its counterpart for local resources is My Computer, which is also on the desktop.

Win 9x Open With

A dialog box that asks you "Open with what application?" It is displayed when you double click a document to open it, but the document has not been previously associated with an application. Files are associated by file extension (.DOC, .GIF, etc.), and many common associations are predefined in Windows 95/98. To review file associations and create new ones, select VIEW from My Computer or Explorer. Then select OPTIONS (95) or FOLDER OPTIONS (98) and then FILE TYPES.

Win 9x Print screen

To print your current Windows screen, you have to copy it to the clipboard, then paste the clipboard into a graphics or desktop publishing program and print it from there.

To copy the current window into the clipboard, press Alt-PrintScreen. To copy the entire screen with all the windows showing into the clipboard, press PrintScreen.

Then, launch any application that you can paste an image into, such as a paint, drawing or desktop publishing program, and paste the clipboard image into a new document by selecting PASTE from the Edit menu. Print the screen capture from this application.

Win 9x Properties

A Windows 95 or 98 Property sheet displays the current settings of a particular resource in the computer. It is also used to modify the settings and serves as a front end to the Registry, which is the database where these settings are stored (see *Win 9x Registry*).

Property sheets are displayed by selecting the different Control Panels in My Computer as well as from the Properties option in the File menu. Right clicking on various objects also displays them. Following are ways to access some useful Property sheets.

Desktop and Window Colors and Screen Saver
Right click on any uncovered part of the desktop.

Hardware Configuration (CPU and Peripherals)
Double click My Computer, Control Panel and System. Select DEVICE MANAGER.

TaskBar (Hide or Restore, Show Clock)
Right click on any uncovered part of the Taskbar (in between the buttons).

Most All Properties Sheets
Double click My Computer and a Control Panel.

Win 9x Registry

The Registry is a Windows 95/98 database that holds configuration data about the hardware and environment of the PC it has been installed in. It is made up of the SYSTEM.DAT and USER.DAT files. Many settings that were previously stored in WIN.INI and SYSTEM.INI in Windows 3.1 are in the Registry.

The Registry can be edited directly, but that is usually only done for very technical enhancements or as a last resort. Routine access is done via the Control Panels in My Computer and the Properties menu option, which is on the File menu. In addition, right clicking on almost every icon brings you the option of selecting Properties. See *Win 9x Properties*.

Registry Details

To get into the Registry itself, run the Registry Editor program (REGEDIT.EXE) in the \WINDOWS directory. The Registry contains six folders, each named with an HKEY prefix (stands for "Handle to a Key").

HKEY_CLASSES_ROOT
Contains file associations and OLE information. It shows exactly the same thing as the subsequent folder HKEY_LOCAL_MACHINE\Software\Classes.

HKEY_CURRENT_USER
The portion of HKEY_USERS that pertains to the current user. It contains the colors, fonts and attributes for the desktop environment as well as any network connections. If the current user is the only user of the system, HKEY_CURRENT_USER and HKEY_USERS are the same.

HKEY_USERS
Contains the above information for all users of the system. It is the USER.DAT file.

HKEY_LOCAL_MACHINE
Holds a large number of settings for the hardware, system software and applications. Install programs also create folders within this folder and place information in them, taking the place of the INI files commonly used in Windows 3.1.

HKEY_CURRENT_CONFIGURATION
Contains settings for the current display resolution and printers.

HKEY_DYN_DATA
Holds performance statistics which can be viewed with the Windows 95/98 System Monitor (SYSMON.EXE).

Win 9x Run DOS programs

In Windows, you can run and keep DOS programs active along with Windows programs. Pressing Alt-Tab will switch you between all active applications, whether Windows or DOS.

DOS programs are normally run in a window, but they can be run full screen as they normally would in DOS. To switch between a window and full screen, press Alt-Enter.

The advantage of running a DOS program in a window is that you can display a DOS window side by side or overlapped with a Windows windows. Also, you can copy text from a DOS window into the clipboard and paste text from the clipboard into the DOS window. You could even copy text from one DOS program to another.

If you have trouble running a DOS application in Windows, you may have to change its properties. To do that, right click on the DOS program icon and select PROPERTIES.

HOW TO RUN DOS APPLICATIONS IN WINDOWS 95/98

Start DOS Application by Name
Select RUN from the Start menu and type in the path to the program.

Start DOS Application from an Icon
Double click on the program icon in a folder, on the desktop or from Explorer.

Place a DOS Application in the Start Menu
1. Right click Start menu and select OPEN.
2. Drag the DOS program icon into the Start menu window. A Shortcut to the program will be created.
3. Close the window, and a new menu item will be displayed the next time you click the Start menu.

End DOS Application
End your DOS application as you normally would. If the window is still open, click the X button at the top right side of the window.

Run DOS Program in a Window
Press Alt-Enter to toggle between full screen and window modes.

Copy Text from a DOS Window
Click the Mark button (dashed rectangle) on the toolbar. Highlight the text and click the Copy button (double pages).

Copy Text to a DOS Window
Click the Paste button (clipboard) on the toolbar.

Quick Way to Get the DOS Prompt
Right click the Start menu and select MS-DOS PROMPT. See *Win 9x Tips* to put the DOS prompt on the Start menu.

Win 9x Run Windows programs

HOW TO RUN WINDOWS APPLICATIONS IN WINDOWS 95/98

From the Start Menu
Click PROGRAMS from the Start menu. Click the Program Group, then click the program name you want to launch.

From Explorer
Right click Start menu and select EXPLORE. Click on the desired folder icon, then the application icon.

From a Folder on the Desktop
Double click the folder on the desktop. Double click the application or document icon. In order for the document icon to launch the appropriate

software, it must already be associated by extension name to the program.
All popular documents have been associated.

From a Shortcut on the Desktop
Shortcuts have a small northeast-pointing arrow at the bottom left side of
the icon. Double click the icon to launch the program.

By Name
Select RUN from the Start menu. Type in the path to the program name.
To learn more about paths, see *path*.

End Windows Application
Click the rightmost button at the top right side of the window (X) or double
click the application icon at the top left side.

Win 9x Safe Mode
Safe Mode is a Windows 95/98 startup mode used for troubleshooting. It allows the system to boot when it otherwise may not, due often to conflicts from newly-installed hardware. Only the mouse, keyboard and standard VGA drivers are loaded, and all configuration files are bypassed, including the Registry, CONFIG.SYS, AUTOEXEC.BAT and SYSTEM.INI. In this mode, configuration data can be manually edited, but technical knowledge is required.

Windows may automatically boot up in this mode if it detects that the previous session was not shut down properly. To purposely start up in Safe Mode, do the following.

In Windows 95, press F8 when Windows displays the "Starting Windows 95..." message and select Safe Mode from the menu.

In Windows 98, hold the Ctrl key down as soon as you turn the machine on and hold it down until you get the menu, from which you can select the Safe Mode.

Win 9x Shortcuts
Windows 95/98 allows you to create pointers, or Shortcuts, to your program and data files. The Shortcut icons can be placed on the desktop or stored in other folders. Double clicking a Shortcut is the same as double clicking the original file. However, deleting a Shortcut does not remove the original. Shortcut icons have a small arrow in their lower left corner pointing northeast. To find out how to add Shortcuts to the Start menu, see *Win 9x Start menu*.

Create a Shortcut to a Program File
Drag the icon from a folder or Explorer window and drop it on the desktop
or into another folder.

Create a Shortcut to a Data File
Right click and drag the icon from a folder or Explorer window and drop in
on the desktop or into another folder. Select CREATE SHORTCUT.

Create a Shortcut to a Folder
Right click and drag the icon of a folder from within another folder window
or from the Explorer window and drop in on the desktop or into another
folder. Select CREATE SHORTCUT.

Win 9x Start & stop
Windows 95 and 98 are automatically loaded when you start the computer.

To end your Windows 95/98 session, save all the data in your active windows and select SHUT DOWN from the START menu. Wait until the message "It is now safe to turn off your computer" before you turn it off. Newer computers with the latest power management features will automatically be turned off by Windows. When you turn the computer back on, your screen will appear the way you left it.

Win 9x Start menu
The Start menu is a launching pad for applications. For Windows 3.1 users, it takes the place of Program Manager. It is customary for a Windows 95/98 install program to install the program icons in a group within the Programs submenu of the Start menu.

The Start menu can be customized by adding and deleting icons. You can add items to the top of the main Start menu or to the submenus. There are two ways to do the editing. You can right click the Start menu button and select OPEN, or using Explorer, the Start menu is a subfolder in the Windows folder.

Add a Shortcut to the Main Start Menu
Drag an icon from the desktop or from an Explorer window and drop it over the Start menu button. The original file will still remain where it is, and a pointer to it will appear in the Start menu above the line (above Programs).
    In Windows 98, you have the option of dragging an icon from the Programs submenu or any submenu subordinate to it back onto the upper portion of the Start menu (above the line).
    You can also drag an icon (above the line) onto the desktop or to the Recycle bin.
    In Windows 98, you can also rearrange the order of the icons you placed above the line by dragging them to a new location (above the line).

Add a Shortcut to a Start Submenu
Right click the Start menu and select OPEN. Double click on the submenu to open its window and then drag and drop an icon into it.

Delete a Shortcut from the Start Menu
Right click the Start menu and select OPEN. Drag the icons you don't want into the Recycle Bin. If the item is in a submenu, open it and do the same.

Clear items from the Documents Menu
One of the Start menu options is Documents, which contains the last 15 documents worked on by a Windows 95 (not 3.1) application.
    To clear the Documents list, right click the Taskbar, select PROPERTIES, then the tab marked START MENU PROGRAMS and finally CLEAR.

Win 9x Swap file
See *Windows swap file.*

Win 9x Switch windows
In Windows, it's easy to switch between active windows.

Toggle Between ALL Windows
Press Alt-Tab-Tab... Hold Alt down while pressing Tab. Release Alt when the title of the window you want is displayed.

Toggle Between LAST TWO Windows
Press Alt-Tab once.

You Can Click on Any Visible Part of the Window
You can switch to another window by clicking on any part of it. If any side or corner is visible, simply click on it to make it the current topmost window.

Your Window Did Not Go Away Forever!
When you switch windows, the other windows may be temporarily out of view. Just hold Alt down and press Tab several times. Look at the window titles as they appear one after the other. When you get to the one you want, let go of the Alt key.

Win 9x Taskbar
The Windows 95/98 Taskbar is a row of buttons across the bottom of the screen. When an application is minimized (the _ button), it turns into a button on the Taskbar. When the button is clicked, it is restored to its previous position on screen.
    The Taskbar can be moved to the top, right or left side of the screen by clicking any free space on the bar and dragging it there.
    The Taskbar can also be hidden and made to appear when the cursor is moved to the edge of the screen. To hide the Taskbar, right click on any free space on the bar and select AUTO HIDE from the TASKBAR OPTIONS Properties sheet.

Win 9x Tips

Following are a number of ways to help you use Windows 95 or Windows 98.

Move TaskBar to Top, Left or Right of Screen

Click on any uncovered area on the Taskbar and move to any extreme side of the screen.

Make TaskBar Disappear

Right click on any uncovered area button on the Taskbar. Select PROPERTIES and AUTO HIDE.

Fast Way to Get Explorer

Right click the Start menu and select EXPLORE.

Show Extensions with File Names

If file extensions are not visible in Explorer or your folders, select OPTIONS or FOLDER OPTIONS from the View menu in Explorer or your folder.
Under the View tab,
in Windows 95, deselect: "Hide MS-DOS file extensions for..."
in Windows 98, deselect: "Hide file extensions for..."

To show even the hidden system files, select "Show all files."

Find a File that Contains Specific Text

Right click Start menu and select FIND. Define the location of the search with LOOK IN.

Windows 95
Under Advanced tab, type in the text. If you want to confine the search to specific files, choose an option in OF TYPE.

Windows 98
Type in the text into CONTAINING TEXT:. If you want to confine the search to specific files, under the Advanced tab, choose an option in OF TYPE.

Rename My Computer

If you prefer another name for My Computer, right click the icon and select RENAME. Type in the name you want and press Enter.

Recognize a Peripheral Not Turned On at Startup

If a peripheral was turned off when you boot up, the application may not recognize it until Windows rescans the hardware. To perform the rescan, do this:

1. Left click Start menu.
2. Select Settings/Control panel/System
3. Click the DEVICE MANAGER tab.
4. Click REFRESH.

Make the DOS Prompt More Accessible

You can make the DOS prompt a menu option when you right click the Start menu or a folder. If you right click a folder and select the DOS prompt, you are automatically set to the same folder (directory) at the command line. To set this up, do this:

1. In Explorer, select OPTIONS/FILE TYPES from the View menu.
2. Double click the FOLDER icon and select NEW.
3. Type **DOS prompt** in the "Action" line.
4. Type **c:\windows\command.com /k cd** in the "Application used to perform action" line.
5. Select OK/CLOSE/CLOSE.

```
Create a Shortcut to the Device Manager
   You can easily create a Shortcut to the System Control Panel by dragging it
   to the desktop.  However, if you want to immediately display the second
   Properties sheet (Device Manager), you have to do the following:

   1. Right click the desktop and select NEW/SHORTCUT.
   2. Type in the following and select NEXT.
      c:\windows\control.exe sysdm.cpl,system,1
   3. Type Device Manager and select FINISH.
```

Win 9x Typing special characters

In Windows, you can insert special characters into your document that are in the font, but have no corresponding keyboard keys. To see what characters are available in the current font, select the Character Map applet from the Accessories group in the Start menu.

All the characters are displayed on screen. Go to an individual character by clicking on it or using the Arrow keys. Note the keystroke numbers at the bottom right side of the window. For example, if Alt+0171 appears, you would enter that character by holding down the Alt key and pressing 0, 1, 7 and 1 on the numeric keypad on the right side of your keyboard. To change fonts, select a different font from the Font menu at the top left.

You can copy a series of characters from the Character Map to the clipboard and paste them into your document. Press SELECT button to add a character to the Characters to Copy input box. Press COPY to copy the characters to the clipboard. Go into your document, move the cursor to the appropriate location, and select PASTE from the Edit menu.

WinBatch

A Windows batch file program from Wilson WindowWare, Inc., Seattle, WA, (www.windowware.com). Batch files are used to automate repetitive tasks. A WinBatch file is a series of commands that are executed under Windows similar to a DOS batch file. WinBatch files use the .WBT extension.

WinBench

A family of benchmarks from Ziff-Davis that test the display, disk and CD-ROM performance of a PC running Windows 95 or NT. WinBench tests for graphics, disk, 3-D and CD-ROM are rated in WinMarks for their respective benchmarks. The graphics and disk tests are divided into Business (typical business processing) and High-End (graphics intensive). The Winbench test for processor performance (CPU, cache and memory) in a 32-bit environment is rated in CPUmarks.

Benchmarks may change their rating scale with new releases of the software, therefore, the same version of the test must be run to compare results. While WinBench is used to test raw system performance, ZD's Winstone benchmarks test actual application performance. See *Winstone* and *ZDBOp*.

Winchester disk

An early removable disk from IBM that put the heads and platters in a sealed unit for greater speed. Its dual 30MB modules, or 30-30 design, caught the "Winchester rifle" nickname. The term later referred to any fixed hard disk where the heads and platters were not separable.

WinChip

A Pentium MMX-class chip from Centaur Technology, Inc., Austin, TX, (www.winchip.com). The WinChip is optimized for Windows business applications and uses the Socket 7 motherboard socket. The first C6 models were introduced in 1997 at 180MHz and 200MHz. C6+ chips contain enhanced instructions for 3-D graphics. See *MMX*.

The Winchester Disk
IBM's Winchester disk was a removable cartridge, but the heads and platters were built in a sealed unit and were not separable. *(Photo courtesy of IBM Corporation.)*

WinCIM

(WINdows CompuServe Information Manager) CompuServe's client software for Windows, which gives subscribers access to CompuServe's forums and services. Prior to WinCIM, users logged on with a generic communications program and interacted via the command line.

Wincode

A Windows utility written by George Silva that supports the UUcoding and MIME formats for converting binary files into 7-bit ASCII for transmission so they can be attached to e-mail over the Internet. See *UUcoding, BinHex* and *MIME*.

WIN.COM

The DOS program that launches Windows. It displays the Windows startup screen and then loads the Windows kernel and related files. In Windows 3.1, it is called from the DOS prompt manually by typing **win** or from the AUTOEXEC.BAT file. In Windows 95, it is automatically called from DOS, which is loaded when the computer boots.

WinDisk

A driver from Future Domain Corporation that converts Windows 3.1 FastDisk accesses into the SCSI CAM standard supported on its SCSI host adapters.

window

(1) A scrollable viewing area on screen. Windows are generally rectangular, although round and polygonal windows are used in specialized applications. A window may refer to a part of the application, such as the scrollable index window or the text window in the electronic versions of this database, or it may refer to the entire application in a window. See *GUI* and *Win 9x abc's*.

(2) A reserved area of memory.

(3) A time period.

windowing software

See *window system*.

window manager

Software incorporated into all popular GUIs, which displays a window with accompanying menus, buttons and scroll bars. It allows the windows to be relocated, overlapped, resized, minimized and maximized. See *desktop manager*.

Windows

The most widely-used operating system for personal computers. Windows provides a graphical user interface and desktop environment similar to the Macintosh, in which applications are displayed in re-sizable, movable windows on screen.

Starting with Windows for Workgroups, Windows contains built-in networking, which allows users to share files and applications with each other if their PCs are cabled together and equipped with network adapters.

In a network, quite often, Windows clients are connected to UNIX and NetWare servers. Increasingly, Windows NT Server is gaining market share, providing a Windows-only solution for both the client and server.

For fundamentals on how to work with Windows 95/98, see *Win 9x abc's* and various "Win 9x" topics. See also *Windows evolution*.

Advantages of Windows

The single advantage to Windows is the huge wealth of application programs that have been written for it. It is the de facto standard for desktop and laptop computers worldwide with more than 250 million users currently.

Microsoft is in complete control of Windows and does its best to introduce advancements to keep up with the times. Windows supports OLE compound documents, which allows a document to contain multiple elements. When the original elements are changed, the document is automatically changed too.

Microsoft has developed standards for all types of interaction between Windows clients and servers. Its Windows Open System Architecture (WOSA) covers databases, messaging, telephony, software licensing and more, providing a system-wide architecture for application development on the Windows platform.

Computer Desktop Encyclopedia

Windows is supported by Microsoft, the largest independent software company in the world, as well as the Windows industry at large, which includes tens of thousands of software developers.

Disadvantages of Windows

Windows, and especially Windows 95/98, is a complicated operating environment that has its roots in DOS, which was developed for the first PCs. In addition, each version of Windows has to support applications written for previous versions of Windows as well as DOS applications. Certain combinations of hardware and software running together can cause problems, and troubleshooting can be daunting. It's a miracle it works as good as it does.

The Windows installation procedure is inherently flawed, allowing an application when being installed to overwrite shared components that are used by other applications. That means a working application no longer runs properly after another program has been installed. As a result, it has become customary to take a machine that has intermittent, unsolvable crashes and start from scratch by reformatting the hard disk and reinstalling Windows and applications.

Installing new peripherals in a Windows 3.1 machine has been frustrating, to say the least. Windows 95 Plug and Play capability has helped, but has not solved the problem entirely. Windows has its roots in a hardware platform that grew as disorderly as the wild west.

Are There Other Choices?

The primary other choice is the Macintosh. The Mac is easier to use and adding a peripheral is almost as simple as plug it in and go. Mac users kick and scream when they have to use a Windows PC. Just ask them. The major disadvantage is that there are fewer applications available for the Mac, and its market share has been declining.

The confusion and complication in the Windows platform, combined with the explosion of the Internet, opened an opportunity for Microsoft's and Intel's competitors to create the network computer, or NC. The NC provides a non-Windows alternative to users in the corporate world, but this is an entirely new computing environment that is struggling to gain acceptance. Stay tuned! See *network computer*.

Windows 1.0

The original version of Microsoft Windows introduced in late 1985, which provided a graphical interface and windowing environment under DOS. It displayed tiled windows (side by side) and was not popular. See *Windows evolution*.

Windows 2.0

An upgrade to Windows 1.0, introduced in 1988. It supported overlapping and tiled windows and was later renamed Windows/286. Control of Windows was very DOS oriented with programs being launched from an "MS-DOS Executive" window that displayed directory lists not all that different than the DOS Dir command. All display elements (windows, scroll bars, etc.) were two dimensional.

Windows 2.0 ran DOS applications full screen or in a window and supported expanded memory for internal use. Although popular in several circles and adopted by some large organizations, it was not widely used. See *Windows evolution*.

Windows 3.0

A complete overhaul of Microsoft Windows introduced in 1990. It was widely supported because of its improved interface and ability to manage large amounts of memory. Windows 3.0 runs 16-bit Windows and DOS applications on 286s and above. Windows 3.0 substituted the MS-DOS Executive with Program Manager and File Manager. Display elements (windows, scroll bars, etc.) were changed to a three-dimensional appearance. See *Windows evolution*.

Windows 3.1

The first major upgrade to Windows 3.0, introduced in 1992. It added support for multimedia, TrueType fonts, compound documents (OLE) and drag & drop and also provided a more stable environment than Windows 3.0. Windows 3.1 continues to be widely used, but it cannot run Windows 95 applications (32-bit applications). Increasingly, software companies are no longer enhancing their Windows 3.1 applications, having turned their attention to Windows 95 and NT. In order to use the new features, users must upgrade to Windows 95 and obtain the Windows 95 version of their products.

Most Windows 3.1 applications run well under Windows 95 and NT, and many are expected to be widely used for a long time. Although Windows 95 and NT support long file names, Windows 3.1

applications running in these newer environments are still subject to the 8.3 naming convention (file names cannot contain more than eight characters). See *Windows evolution.*

Windows 3.11

An upgrade to and the final release of Windows 3.1.

Windows/386

An early version of Windows for the 386. Using the Virtual 8086 Mode, it was the forerunner of the 386 Enhanced Mode in Windows 3.0. See *Windows evolution.*

Windows 3.x modes

Windows 3.x operates in the following modes of operation:

```
                                 386
                Real   Standard  Enhanced
                Mode   Mode      Mode

Windows 3.0      X       X         X
Windows 3.1              X         X
WFW 3.1                            X
```

386 ENHANCED MODE
```
This is the common mode for Windows 3.1 and the only mode for Windows for
Workgroups (WFW).  It requires at least a 386 and uses the 386's virtual machine
and virtual memory capabilities.  DOS applications can be multitasked in the
background and run in resizable windows.
```

STANDARD MODE (Win 3.0, 3.1)
```
This mode would work on a 286 and it would run faster on a 386 than 386 Enhanced
Mode.  Standard mode was used when applications failed under 386 Enhanced Mode.
```

REAL MODE (Win 3.0)
```
This mode worked on a 286 with as little as 1MB of RAM.  It was used to run
Windows 1.x and 2.x applications and certain DOS applications.
```

Windows 4GL

The predecessor to CA-OpenRoad, it is a client/server development tool for Windows and X terminals. It was originally developed by Ingres Corporation, which was acquired by the Ask Group, and later CA. See *CA-OpenRoad.*

Windows 95

A major upgrade of Windows 3.1 designed to replace Windows 3.11, Windows for Workgroups 3.11 and MS-DOS. Released in August 1995, it is a 32-bit operating system that requires a 386 minimum and will not run in a 286. It is a self-contained operating system that includes a built-in and enhanced version of DOS.

Windows 95 runs Windows 95, Windows 3.x and DOS applications. The user interface provides a desktop and foldering capabilities similar to the Macintosh. The Windows 3.x Program Manager and File Manager are included, but are not the default interface.

Windows 95 includes Plug and Play capabilities and built-in networking for Windows, NetWare, VINES and UNIX networks. The Windows Resources memory limitation has been greatly expanded.

Additional features are the ability to use file names longer than eight characters and to make icons and buttons larger. The latter is a welcome addition for users that run large monitors at high resolutions, causing application windows and their controls to appear much smaller on screen. See *Win 9x abc's.*

Windows 95B

See *OSR2.*

Windows 95J

The Japanese version of Windows 95, which was released by Microsoft and NEC at the end of 1995.

Windows 97

What Windows 98 was to be named, when it was expected in 1997. See *Windows 98.*

Windows 98

A major upgrade to Windows 95. Introduced in June 1998, it includes numerous bug fixes, performance enhancements and support for more hardware, including the Univeral Serial Bus (USB). It supports two monitors, which helps developers working in one resolution and testing in another. Windows 98 tightly integrates Microsoft's Internet Explorer Web browser into the desktop. See *Active Channel* and *Active Desktop*.

Windows 9x

Refers to Windows 95 and/or Windows 98.

Windows accelerator

A display adapter that provides 2-D functions in hardware. See *graphics accelerator*.

Windows-based terminal

A specialized terminal or slimmed-down PC used as a client to Windows Terminal Server. See *Windows terminal*.

Windows-based Terminal Server

See *Windows Terminal Server*.

Windows CE

A version of Windows from Microsoft for handheld PCs (HPCs) and consumer electronics devices. It runs "Pocket" versions of popular applications such as Microsoft Word and Excel.

windows environment

(1) (lower case "w") Any software that provides multiple windows on screen such as Windows, OS/2, Mac, Motif and X Window. Also any application that provides multiple windows for documents or pictures.

(2) (upper case "W") Refers to computers running under a Microsoft Windows operating system.

Windows error messages

See *Application Error*.

Windows evolution

Version 1.0 of Windows was introduced in 1985, but it barely made a dent in the market. Subsequent versions (Windows 2.0, Windows/386) began to make some inroads, and a few companies adopted Windows as their main operating environment. However, it wasn't until Version 3.0 that Windows began to have a major impact on the personal computer world.

WINDOWS 3.x

Windows 3.0 was introduced in 1990 with an improved user interface and the ability to manage more than one megabyte of memory, which was a serious limitation in DOS. Its built-in DOS extender could manage 16MB of RAM, a huge amount for that time, and its Program Manager user interface was widely accepted. It still required DOS to be booted first, but Windows added multitasking, cut and paste capability between applications and centralized printer and font management, all of which were sorely lacking in DOS. Within a couple of years, Windows would become the major desktop operating system worldwide.

Windows 3.1, introduced in 1992, provided a more stable and faster environment. It added multimedia support, TrueType fonts, drag & drop commands and OLE compound documents. Windows for Workgroups was later introduced with built-in networking, allowing PCs to share data and programs when fitted with network adapters.

WINDOWS 95

Windows 95 was introduced in August 1995 with a new user interface that added more Macintosh features. It included preemptive multitasking, which allows multiple programs to be timeshared together more effectively than in Win 3.1, and Plug and Play, which makes adding new peripherals much easier than in Windows 3.1.

Although it was expected users would upgrade to Win 95 more rapidly, Windows 3.1 is still widely used. Unlike Win 3.1, which must be loaded after booting DOS, Windows 95 is self-contained 32-bit operating system that boots with its own version of DOS. Windows 95 can run Windows 3.x and DOS applications as well as applications written specifically for Windows 95. Increasingly, new versions of software are only written for the 32-bit environment.

WINDOWS 98

Windows 98 was introduced in June 1998. It is a major upgrade to Windows 95, incorporating numerous bug fixes and tightly integrating the Web browser into the desktop. It also provides native support for the Universal Serial Bus (USB), which is expected to become very popular.

WINDOWS NT

Windows NT 3.5 was introduced two years before Windows 95. It was the first self-contained Windows operating system, and it was designed primarily for server use. It offers greater crash protection than both Windows 3.1 and Windows 95/98. NT's first user interface was Program Manager. NT 4.0, uses the Windows 95 interface.

Windows NT Server is gaining significant market share as a server operating system. Windows NT Workstation is increasingly being used in desktop machines, but it does not include Plug and Play. Windows NT Workstation 5.0, expected this year, will include Plug and Play and be more suited for desktop and laptop use.

Windows for Workgroups

Also known as *WFW*, it is a version of Windows 3.1 that includes peer-to-peer networking. Users can share files and printers and send messages to other WFW, Windows 95 and Windows NT users on the network. Microsoft's Workgroup Add-On for MS-DOS adds this same networking capability to DOS and Windows 3.1 computers.

WFW's network drivers use a small amount of conventional memory (4-15KB), which helps installation on fully-loaded PCs. WFW also includes 32-bit file access, which bypasses DOS and replaces SmartDrive with another disk cache for increased performance. This is not the same as Windows' 32-bit disk access (FastDisk), which drives the disk controller directly.

Windows help system

Windows provides a help system that most software developers use to provide immediate help to the users of their Windows applications. The help is displayed by pressing F1 or selecting the Help menu in the application. The help windows can remain on screen so that you can try things out while you read the instructions.

Help screens can be developed in a word processor that supports the RTF document format or in specialized help development systems that make it easier to combine text and graphics elements. A help compiler, which comes with various developer's toolkits, converts the RTF files into the final form required by the Windows help system.

Help File Types

Following are the various help files that are created on the fly the first time help is used. They are regenerated if the files are deleted.

```
GID (Global Index)   Master index (hidden file).
CNT (Contents)   Content topics.
FTS (Full Text Search)   Index for text searching.
FTG (Full Text Group)   Links to other help files.
ANN (Annotations)   User annotations.
BMK (Bookmarks)   User bookmarks.
```

Windows history

See *Windows evolution*.

Windows memory limitation

No matter how much memory you have in your Windows 3.1 PC, you never seem to have enough. The more you get used to Windows, the more you want to keep all the applications open that you use during the day. Unfortunately, each one takes up a certain amount of memory.

If you get an "Out of Memory" message often, there are several things you can do as a routine.

1. Keep windows minimized rather than full screen.
2. Keep the clipboard empty.
3. Turn off the desktop wallpaper in Control Panel. Wallpaper uses memory.
4. Check your permanent swap file. The larger the swap file, the more applications can be "rolled out" to disk temporarily.
5. If all else fails, closing one or more applications should give you enough room to open up another application.

System Resources

No matter how much actual RAM or virtual memory (swap file) you have, Windows 3.1 uses six 64K regions of memory (heaps) to keep track of its active applications. When an application is active in a window, each of the application's components (windows, dialog boxes, icons, buttons, etc.) uses up several bytes of this "System Resources" memory.

Windows will tell you there is "Not enough memory..." when either of the regions get close to full. There's nothing you can do but unload one or more applications.

In addition, when these memory regions start to fill more than half way, strange things can occur. Select About from your Program Manager's Help menu and look at System Resources. When this number gets below 30%, watch out, anything can happen.

There are a number of third-party products for Windows 3.1 that improve the resource limitation, including Quarterdeck's QEMM and Helix's Hurricane.

In Windows 95, the situation has improved. Windows 95 uses much larger memory buffers to hold the resources it needs.

Windows Metafile

A Windows file format that holds vector graphics, bitmaps and text. It uses the .WMF file extension for 16-bit Windows and the .EMF extension for 32-bit Windows (see *EMF*). The Windows Metafile is Windows' preferred vector format, since it contains actual Windows commands (GDI calls) to draw the images. It is also used by programs to hold data between sessions, and, Windows sometimes uses it for temporary storage.

A Placeable Metafile is a common variation of the WMF format. It includes a 22-byte header that contains x-y coordinates and resolution. This data is used to compute new coordinates to allow the metafile to be drawn into a display window of any size.

Windows network

Also called a *Microsoft network* or a *Microsoft Windows network*, it is a local area network made up of Windows for Workgroups, Windows 95 and Windows NT computers, which all have built-in networking capabilities.

Windows NT

(Windows New Technology) An advanced 32-bit operating system from Microsoft for Intel x86 and Alpha CPUs. Support for the PowerPC and MIPS platforms was dropped. Introduced in 1993, NT does not use DOS, it is a self-contained operating system that runs 16-bit and 32-bit Windows applications as well as DOS applications.

Features include peer-to-peer networking, preemptive multitasking, multithreading, multiprocessing, fault tolerance and support for the Unicode character set. NT provides extensive security features and continually tests the validity of application requests even after the application has been opened.

Windows NT supports 2GB of virtual memory for applications and 2GB for its own use. Windows NT and Windows NT Workstation are the first and second releases of the client version. Windows NT Advanced Server (NTAS) and Windows NT Server (NTS) are first and second releases of the server version, which supports symmetric multiprocessing (SMP) and provides transaction processing for hundreds of online users. NT includes a dual boot feature.

NT Server is being widely implemented. NT's SMP capability takes advantage of Pentium Pro and Pentium II systems that contain two, four and more CPUs. As these multiprocessor systems become mainstream, NT competes squarely against RISC-based multiprocessor servers running UNIX. NT Workstation is also gaining market share in high-end desktop systems.

The last version of Windows NT with the Program Manager interface was Version 3.51. Introduced in the summer of 1996, Windows NT 4.0 contains the Windows 95 user interface. There are differences in some of the dialog boxes as NT contains features not available in Windows 95, and vice versa. NT 4.0 also includes Microsoft's DCOM interface that allows applications to be distributed across the network.

NT 4.0 does not support Plug and Play, as does Windows 95.

NT Server 4.0 comes with Microsoft's Internet Information Server (IIS), which provides Web server capability.

NT Version 5.0, expected in 1999, adds Plug and Play support, Direct3D support, Active Directory, Zero Administration for Windows (ZAW) and other enhancements.

Version	Date/Intro
3.1	July 1993
3.5	Sept 1994
3.51	Aug 1995
4.0	Aug 1996
5.0	Expected 1999

windows program

(1) Software that adds a windows capability to an existing operating system. See *X Window*.

(2) An application program written to run under Windows. See *Windows*.

Windows requirements

Windows places far more demands of a PC than does DOS. A fast display adapter is also as important as a fast CPU. Today, all VGA cards have built-in graphics acceleration for Windows; however, some are much faster than others. To get more utility and enjoyment from Windows, obtain the largest monitor you can afford. Following are the recommended requirements.

	Word processing, database, spreadsheets	CAD, imaging, multimedia, desktop publishing
CPU	Pentium/266	Pentium II/450
Bus	ISA/PCI	ISA/PCI
RAM	64MB	128MB
Hard disk	4GB	6-9GB
Display system:		
screen size	17"	21"
resolution	800x600	1024x768, 1280x1024, 1600x1200
refresh	72Hz +	72Hz +
CD-ROM	12x	24x
Sound	16 bit	16 bit

Windows Resource Kit

Windows technical documentation from Microsoft written for support personnel. It is a comprehensive document with more than 1000 pages of technical details that includes flow charts and a chapter on troubleshooting.

Windows Resources

See *Windows memory limitation*.

Windows SDK

A set of development utilities for writing Windows applications in Microsoft C. It provides tools for creating custom cursors, fonts and icons, bitmaps, menus and online help.

Windows shell

An add-on user interface for Windows. Numerous shells were created for Windows 3.x to streamline or replace Program Manager by providing such features as foldering, customized toolbars and quick access to the DOS command line. For example, Norton Desktop for Windows was popular. Fewer products were made available for Windows 95.

Windows SNA APIs

Programming interfaces that allow Windows applications to communicate with SNA protocols and functions, such as HLLAPI and APPC.

Windows swap file

A disk file used by Windows for its virtual memory. A virtual memory system temporarily stores segments of the application on disk when there is not enough memory to hold all the programs called for.

WINDOWS 3.1

By default, in 386 Enhanced Mode, Windows 3.1 creates a temporary swap file (WIN386.SWP), which it dynamically enlarges and reduces and then abandons at the end of each session. Creating a permanent swap file (hidden files SPART.PAR and 386SPART.PAR) improves speed because it guarantees an amount of contiguous virtual memory space.

To free up disk space, you can delete or reduce the size of the permanent swap file (select Control Panel/386 Enhanced/Virtual Memory/Change).

WINDOWS 95/98

Windows 95/98 creates only a temporary swap file (WIN386.SWP) that is dynamically sized and abandoned. It can also reside on a compressed drive as long as it is under the control of the DRVSPACE.VXD Protected Mode driver. Windows 95/98 can use the permanent swap file created in Windows 3.1, but cannot reduce its size to less than the original file size.

To adjust the Windows 95/98 swap file, double click on the System Control Panel and select the Performance tab, then Virtual Memory.

WINDOWS NT 4.0

NT 4.0 creates a temporary swap file, or paging file (PAGEFILE.SYS), that is generally equal to the size of memory plus 12MB. It also allows for one additional swap file to be created on each logical partition on the hard disk. To adjust the size of the file, double click on the System Control Panel and select the Performance tab, then Virtual Memory, then Change.

Windows Telephony

See *TAPI*.

Windows terminal

An input/output terminal for a Windows NT server running multiuser software such as WinFrame or Windows Terminal Server. The terminals function like mini and mainframe terminals, where all the processing is done in a central host and only the input and output is performed at the terminal. A Windows terminal can be a full-blown PC, a slimmed-down PC or a specialized terminal for this purpose, the latter being called a "Windows-based terminal." See *ICA, Winterm, WinFrame* and *Windows Terminal Server*. See *network computer* and *thin client* for illustrations.

Windows Terminal Server

Formerly code named Hydra, it is Microsoft's version of the Winframe multiuser architecture. Co-developed with Citrix, it turns an NT server into a centralized, timeshared computer. It uses the T.share presentation services protocol to govern input/output to Windows clients. With additional software from Citrix in the server, clients employing the ICA protocol may also connect to the server. See *WinFrame, T.share* and *ICA*.

Windows versions

Following are all the versions of Windows that have been introduced since 1985. A choice of operating modes is available in Windows 3.x versions only. See *Windows 3.x modes*.

	16 or 32 bit	— Modes — Real	Std.	386	Built-in Networking
Windows 1.0	16				
Windows 286	16				
Windows/386	16				
Windows 3.0	16	X	X	X	
Windows 3.1	16		X	X	
WFW 3.1	16			X	X
Windows 95/98	32				X
Windows NT	32				X

window system

Software that adds a windows capability to an existing system. See *X Window*.

Wind/U

A software porting tool for converting Windows applications written in C or C++ to UNIX and IBM System/390 mainframes from Bristol Technology, Inc., Ridgefield, CT, (www.bristol.com). Originally developed for UNIX only (Wind to Unix), S/390 capability was added later.

WINFILE.EXE

The program name for File Manager in Windows 3.x and Windows 95.

WinFrame

Software from Citrix Systems that turns a Windows NT server into a timeshared central computer. Windows applications are run in the server and only screen changes are sent to the attached PCs, NCs or Winterm terminals. Terminal input and output are governed by Citrix's Intelligent Console Architecture (ICA) protocol, which is also licensed to third parties. WinFrame is comprised of Citrix's MultiWin multiuser technology, Windows NT and ICA. MultiWin is used in Microsoft's own multiuser NT system (see *Windows Terminal Server*). See *MetaFrame*.

WinG

(**WIN**dows **G**ames) A programming interface (API) that lets Windows application developers access the video frame buffer directly. It allows game programs to be written to run as fast in Windows as they do under DOS.

WINGZ

A spreadsheet for the Mac, Windows and various UNIX platforms from Investment Intelligence Systems Group, London, (www.wingz.com). Text, graphs and charts, scanned images, freehand illustration and spreadsheet data can be combined. When data is updated, related graphics and numerical references within the text are changed. WINGZ was originally developed by Informix Software in 1988.

WIN.INI

(**WIN**dows **INI**tialization) A Windows configuration file that describes the current state of the Windows environment. It contains hundreds of entries and is read by Windows on startup. It tells Windows such things as which programs to load or run automatically, if any, what the various screen, keyboard and mouse settings are, what the desktop looks like (icon spacing, wallpaper, colors, etc.) and what fonts are used.

Information in WIN.INI is grouped by section headers, which are names enclosed in brackets. For example, the [Colors] section contains the colors selected by the user for window borders, titles, backgrounds and so forth.

The information in WIN.INI is updated by Windows when you change various defaults; however, the file can also be edited with a text editor or a word processor that imports ASCII files. Sections in WIN.INI are added by many application install programs under their own section header and are used to inform the application about the current defaults.

Although WIN.INI was created in Windows 3.x, it is still used in Windows 95 and NT for font substitutions, but primarily for compatiblity with Windows 3.x applications.

SYSTEM.INI is another major Windows configuration file that is read at startup. See *SYSTEM.INI*.

WINMAIL.DAT

A file sent by Outlook and Microsoft Office programs that contains e-mail formatting information.

WinMark

A unit of measurement of the WinBench benchmarks from Ziff-Davis. See *WinBench* and *ZDBOp*.

Win-OS/2

(**WIN**dows-**OS/2**) The Windows functionality in OS/2 Version 2.x. OS/2 Version 2.x contains the original Windows source code.

WINS

(**W**indows **I**nternet **N**aming **S**ervice) Name resolution software from Microsoft that runs under Windows NT Server and converts NetBIOS names to IP addresses. Windows machines are assigned

NetBIOS names, which must be converted to IP addresses if the underlying transport protocol is TCP/IP.

Windows machines identify themselves to the WINS server, so that other Windows machines can query the server to find the IP address. Since, the WINS server is contacted by IP address, which can be routed across subnets, WINS allows Windows machines on one LAN segment to locate Windows machines on other LAN segments.

When a computer is moved to another subnet and a new IP address is assigned by DHCP, the WINS database is updated. WINS is used in a Windows network, and both DNS and WINS are used in a mixed environment. Microsoft's DNS server integrates the two systems. When a UNIX station wants to resolve the name for a PC, it queries the Microsoft DNS server, which in turn queries the WINS server if it does not already have it. See *DNS*.

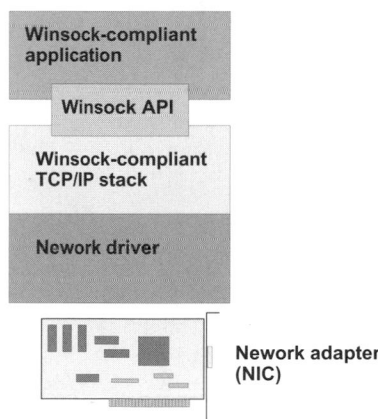

WINS Name Resolution
In an IP network, the application queries a WINS or DNS server to turn the name of the machine it wishes to communicate with into its IP address. See *TCP/IP abc's*.

Winsock API

(**WIN**dows **SOCK**ets API) A common programming interface between a Windows application and the TCP/IP protocol. Most TCP/IP stacks designed to run under Windows and most Windows software that communicates via TCP/IP are Winsock compliant. The Winsock routines are implemented as a dynamic link library (DLL). The WINSOCK.DLL file is included with Windows 95.

Networking and Internet programs often include a WINSOCK.DLL, which may overwrite the one that is present, causing problems with other networking applications that use it. The WINSOCK.DLL is included either to ensure that you have one or because it contains modifications to provide additional functionality at runtime needed by the application.

WINSOCK HIERARCHY

Winsock client

A Windows program that communicates to a TCP/IP-based communications network, such as UNIX or the Internet.

Winstone

A benchmark from Ziff-Davis that tests the performance of a PC running actual Windows applications. ZD Winstone 98 is divided into Business Winstone and High-End Windstone tests. The former uses typical business applications, while the latter uses graphics-intensive applications. ZD's WinBench benchmark is used to test raw system power. See *ZDBOp*.

Wintel

(**WIN**dows In**TEL**) Refers to the world's largest personal computer environment, which is Windows running on an Intel CPU.

Winterm

A family of Windows-based terminals from Wyse Technology, San Jose, CA, (www.wyse.com), designed to work with specialized versions of Windows NT. Citrix's WinFrame software turns a Windows NT machine into a timeshared central computer that runs the applications within the server and sends only screen output to the Winterm clients. A Pentium server with 96MB of RAM can support up to 15 typical Winterm users, and a quad-CPU system with 256MB of RAM can handle up to 60.

The Winterm 2000 family uses an x86 processor, while the Winterm 4000 uses Digital's 200MHz StrongARM processor. The 4000 is a combination Windows terminal and Java-based network computer. The Winterm 2930 is a wireless, pen-based unit for users that are not tied to a desktop.

WinWord

A nickname for the Windows version of the Microsoft Word word processor. The default directory (folder) for the application is \WINWORD. See *Microsoft Word*.

WinXS

A shareware program from Software Online Limited, Sandbach, Cheshire, England, (www.softwareonline.org), that adds UNIX command line capability to Windows. Commands, including grep, cat and uuencode, are provided, giving the user a wealth of useful text and file manipulation capabilities that were never in Windows or even in DOS.

WinZip

A Windows-based utility for zipping and unzipping files from Nico Mac Computing, Bristol, CT, (www.winzip.com). Evaluation copies are available from the Web site.

wired

Connected. Slang for "with it," and "in tune."

wireframe modeling

In CAD, a technique for representing 3-D objects, in which all surfaces are visibly outlined in lines, including the opposite sides and all internal components that are normally hidden from view. Compared to surface and solid modeling, wireframe modeling is the least complex method for representing 3-D images.

wirehead

A person that loves to build, fix and generally tinker with electronics, much like a motorhead enjoys working with cars and engines.

wireless

Radio transmission via the airwaves. Various communications techniques are used to provide wireless transmission including infrared line of sight, cellular, microwave, satellite. packet radio and spread spectrum. See *PCS, FDMA, TDMA, CDMA* and *CDPD*.

wireless bridge

A device that connects two LAN segments together via infrared or microwave transmission.

wireless cable

See *MMDS*.

Wyse Winterm 4300
Wyse Technology's Winterm stations provide Web connectivity and run Windows applications using software that turns an NT server into a timeshared central computer. Only screen changes are sent to the Winterm clients. *(Photo courtesy of Wyse Technology.)*

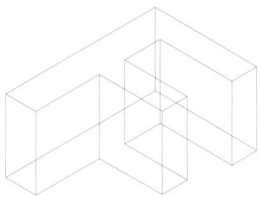

Wireframe

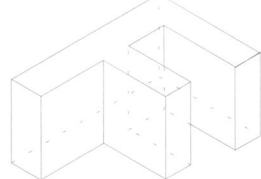

Phantom lines

Shaded (solid) view

wire rate, wire speed

The bandwidth of a particular transmission or networking system. For the example, the wire speed of 10BaseT Ethernet is 10 Mbps. When data is said to run at wire speed or at "wire rate," it implies there is little or no software overhead associated with the transmission and that the data travels at the maximum speed of the hardware.

wire wrap

An early method of wiring circuit boards to each other. The boards were plugged into a backplane that contained metal prongs, which were wired together using a special tool. The tool stripped the end of the wire and coiled it around the prong. Thousands of computers were made with wire wrapped methods.

wiring closet

The central distribution or servicing point for cables in a network.

wizard

Instructional help that guides the user through a series of steps to accomplish a task.

wizzy wig

See *WYSIWYG*.

WMF

See *Windows Metafile*.

WO

See *write once*.

WOLAP

See *OLAP*.

Wolfpack

The code name for Microsoft Cluster Server.

word

(1) The computer's internal storage unit. Refers to the amount of data it can hold in its registers and process at one time. A word is often 16 bits, in which case 32 bits is called a double word. Given the same clock rate, a 32-bit computer processes four bytes in the same time it takes a 16-bit machine to process two.

(2) The primary text element, identified by a word separator (blank space, comma, etc.) before and after a group of contiguous characters.

(3) See *Microsoft Word*.

word addressable

A computer that can address memory only on word boundaries. Contrast with *byte addressable*.

WordBASIC

A subset of Microsoft QuickBASIC with added word processing functions used to customize Microsoft Word word processors.

Word for Windows

The name used for the Windows version of the Microsoft Word word processor when Windows was becoming popular. See *Microsoft Word*.

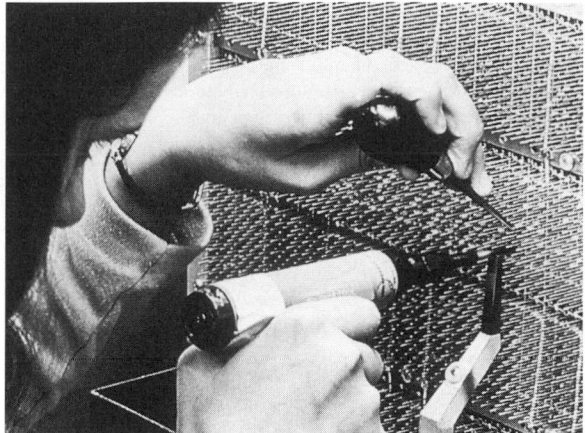

Wire Wrapping
The technician in this picture is wiring circuits together using the wire wrap tool. *(Photo courtesy of Digital Equipment Corporation.)*

Word macro

A script that is executed within a Word document which adds some automatic function for the user. Macros can be created with the Word macro recorder, which stores repetitive keystrokes, or a small program can be written in Visual Basic for Applications (VBA). The macro is executed when the document is opened. See *Word macro virus* and *VBA*.

Word macro virus

A virus written into a macro that is stored in a Word document or template. There are more than 30 different kinds of this virus. When the document is opened, the macro is executed and the virus does its damage. It also attaches itself to the Normal template in Word so that subsequent documents are saved with the virus. Questionable documents can always be opened with macros turned off. See *Word macro* and *letter bomb*.

WordPerfect

See *Corel WordPerfect* and *WordPerfect Corporation*.

WordPerfect Corporation

Founded in 1979 as Satellite Software International by Alan Ashton, Bruce Bastian and Don Owens. In 1980, W. E. Pete Peterson, Bastian's brother-in-law, joined the Utah-based company as office manager and later became executive vice president.

Its first product was a word processor for the Data General minicomputer. In 1982, WordPerfect was introduced for the IBM PC. At the time, WordStar was number one, and there were other word processors available for the PC. Yet, over time, WordPerfect outsold them all and the company was later renamed WordPerfect Corporation. In 1994, the company was acquired by Novell and then by Corel in 1996.

For an interesting inside story by Pete Peterson on how the company got started and grew into a software giant without external financing, read his book, "AlmostPerfect," published by Prima Publishing, Rocklin, CA 95677, 916/786-0426, ISBN 1-55958-477-7.

WordPerfect Office

See *GroupWise*.

WordPerfect Suite

See *Corel WordPerfect Suite*.

Word Pro

A full-featured Windows word processing program from Lotus. It provides groupware features that allow documents to be created and edited collaboratively and also includes version control for tracking document updates. Word Pro is the successor to Ami Pro, which was developed by Samna Corporation and was one of the first full-featured word processors for Windows.

word processing

The creation of text documents. Except for labels and envelopes, it has replaced the electric typewriter in most offices, because of the ease in which documents can be edited, searched and reprinted.

Advanced word processors function as elementary desktop publishing systems. Although there are still machines dedicated only to word processing, most word processing is performed on general-purpose computers using word processing software. Following are the functions of a full-featured word processing program.

Text Editing

Text can be changed by deleting it, typing over it or by inserting additional text within it.

Word Wrap and Centering

Words that extend beyond the right margin are wrapped around to the next line. Text can be centered between left and right margins.

Search and Replace, Move and Copy

Any occurrence of text can be replaced with another block of text. You can mark a block of text and move it elsewhere in the document or copy it throughout the document.

Layout Settings

Margins, tabs, line spacing, indents, font changes, underlining, boldface and italics can be set and reset anywhere within the document.

Headers, Footers and Page Numbering

Headers and footers are common text printed on the top and bottom of every page. Headers, footers and page numbering can be set and reset anywhere within the doucment. Page numbering in optional Roman numerals or alphabetic letters is common.

Style Sheets

After designing a document, its format can be used again. Layout codes (margins, tabs, fonts, etc.) can be stored in a style sheet file and applied to a new document.

Mail Merge

Creates customized letters from a form letter and a list of names and addresses. The list can be created as a document or can be imported from popular database formats.

Math and Sorting

Columns of numbers can be summed and simple arithmetic expressions can be computed. Lines of text can be reordered into ascending (A-Z) or descending (Z-A) sequence.

Preview, Print and Group Print

A document can be previewed before it is printed to show any layout change that may not normally show on screen (page breaks, headers, footers, etc.). Documents can be printed individually or as a group with page numbers consecutively numbered from the first to the last document.

Footnotes and Endnotes

Footnote entries can be made at any place in the document, and the footnotes printed at the end of a page or document.

Spelling Checker and Thesaurus

Spelling for an individual word, marked block of text or an entire document can be checked. When words are in doubt, possible corrections are suggested. Advanced systems can correct the misspellings automatically the next time. A thesaurus displays synonyms for the word at the current cursor location.

File Management

Documents can be copied, renamed and deleted, and directories, or folders, can be created and deleted from within the program. Advanced systems set up a purge list of names or glimpses of document contents in order to allow a user to easily rid the disk of unwanted files.

Advanced Functions

Windows

Allows two or more documents to be worked on at the same time. Text can be moved or copied from one document to the other.

Columns

Columns can be created in all word processors by tabbing to a tab stop. However, true column capability wraps words to the next line within each column. Columns are required for writing resumes with employer information on the left and work history on the right. Script writing also requires column capability. Magazine-style columns flow words from the bottom of one column to the top of the next.

Tables of Contents and Indexes

Tables of contents and indexes can be generated from entries typed throughout the document.

Desktop Publishing

Graphics can be merged into the text and either displayed on screen with the text or in a preview mode before printing. A graphic object can be resized (scaled), rotated and anchored so that it remains with a particular segment of text. Rules and borders can also be created within the text.

Graphics-based Vs Text-based

Graphics-based programs (Windows, Macintosh, etc.) show a close facsimile on screen of the typefaces that will be printed. Text-based programs always show the same type size on screen.

Text-based screens are fine for typing letters and documents with a simple format. They are also very responsive and good for creative writing. Graphics-based systems are necessary for preparing newsletters and brochures that contain a variety of font styles and sizes.

Format Standards

Every major word processing program generates its own proprietary codes for layout settings. For example, in WordStar, ^PB turns on and off boldface. In WordPerfect, [**BOLD**] turns boldface on, and [**bold**] turns it off.

Conversion programs are used to translate documents from one format to another. If a conversion program doesn't exist for the two required formats, multiple search & replace commands can be performed on the original document. However, if the same code turns a mode on as well as off, as in the WordStar example above, the codes have to be changed manually one at a time.

The User Interface

Word processing programs run from the ridiculous to the sublime. Some of the most awkward programs have sold well. As a novice, it's difficult to tell a good one from a bad one. It takes time to explore the nuances. Also, what's acceptable for the slow typist can be horrendous for the fast typist.

Repetitive functions such as centering and changing display attributes (boldface, italics, etc.) should be a snap. Changing margins, tabs, indents and fonts should also be easy.

The most important components in word processing hardware are the keyboard and screen. The feel of a keyboard is personal, but proper key placement is critical. Display screens should have the highest resolution possible, and color screens are better than monochrome as long as the program allows the user to change colors.

word processing machine

A computer that is specialized for only word processing functions.

word processor

(1) Software that provides word processing functions on a computer.

(2) A computer specialized for word processing. Until the late 1970s, word processors were always dedicated machines. Today, personal computers have replaced almost all dedicated word processors.

word separator

A character that separates a word, such as a blank space, comma, period, dash, question mark and exclamation point.

WordStar

A full-featured word processing program for DOS and Windows from The Learning Company. Introduced in 1978 for CP/M machines by MicroPro International Corporation, later renamed WordStar International, it was the first program to give full word processing capabilities to personal computer users at far less cost than the dedicated word processors of the time. WordStar keyboard commands became de facto standards for text manipulation (see *WordStar diamond*).

WordStar diamond

The pattern of W-A-Z, E-S-D-X, and R-F-C keys used with the Ctrl key in WordStar. It allowed all scrolling functions to be done with the left hand in its normal keyboard position. Although it became a de facto standard, this clever system faded into history after IBM moved the Ctrl key on its Enhanced keyboard and the mouse became popular.

word stuffing

See *spamdexing*.

word wheel

A lookup method in which each character that is typed in moves the on-screen index to the closest match. By watching the index move character by character, you can easily tell if you have made a typo. In addition, you can get to the beginning of a word group quickly and then scroll to the word or phrase you are looking for. The DOS and Windows versions of this database use a word wheel.

word wrap

A word processing feature that moves words to the next line automatically as you type based on the current right margin setting. Some word processing programs allow word wrap to be turned off for writing source code.

workflow

The automatic routing of documents to the users responsible for working on them. Workflow is concerned with providing the information required to support each step of the business cycle. The documents may be physically moved over the network or maintained in a single database with the appropriate users given access to the data at the required times. Triggers can be implemented in the system to alert managers when operations are overdue.

The manual flow of documents in an organization is prone to errors. Documents can get lost or be constantly shuffled to the bottom of the in basket. Automating workflow sets timers that ensure that documents move along at a prescribed pace and that the appropriate person processes them in the correct order.

Integrating workflow into existing software applications may require extensive reprogramming, because although independent workflow software can launch a whole application, a workflow system must be able to invoke individual routines within the application. As a result, vendors of application software have teamed up with workflow vendors to provide the appropriate interfaces and/or they have developed their own workflow capability. Workflow standards developed by the Workflow Management Coalition (WFMC) are expected to provide interoperability between workflow software and the applications as well as between different workflow systems.

Workflow software is not the same as workgroup software, otherwise known as *groupware*. Workflow deals with the step-by-step processes, whereas workgroup systems are concerned with information sharing and threaded discussions among users.

For an informative book on the subject of workflow written by the guru in this field, read "The Workflow Imperative" by Thomas M. Koulopoulos, published by Van Nostrand Reinhold, ISBN 0-442-01975-0. See *groupware* for illustration.

workgroup

Two or more individuals who share files and databases. LANs designed around workgroups provide electronic sharing of required data. See *groupware* and *workflow*.

Workgroups

See *Windows for Workgroups*.

workgroup system

Same as *groupware*.

working directory

See *current directory*.

Workplace

An earlier umbrella term from IBM for a set of strategies and system software technologies for developing future products. It included the use of a microkernel-based operating system, object technologies (SOM/DSOM) and voice and pen recognition. Only the term was dropped, not the technology development.

Workplace Shell

The user interface in OS/2 introduced with Version 2.0. The Workplace Shell is extensible and application developers can use Workplace Shell library functions when developing programs.

worksheet

Same as *spreadsheet*.

worksheet compiler

Same as *spreadsheet compiler*.

workstation

(1) A high-performance, single-user microcomputer or minicomputer that is used for graphics, CAD, CAE, simulation and scientific applications. It is typically a RISC-based computer that runs under some variation of UNIX. The major vendors of workstations are Sun, HP, IBM, Digital and SGI. High-end Pentium PCs increasingly compete with workstations in performance.

(2) A personal computer in a network. In this context, a workstation is the same as a client. Contrast with *server* and *host*.

(3) In the telecom industry, a combined telephone and computer.

(4) Any terminal or personal computer.

Workstation

For years, workstations like this one from Sun have been used for applications such as CAD, medical imaging and scientific visualization. They are traditionally UNIX-based and are always pushing the envelope in performance. *(Photo courtesy of Sun Microsystems Computer Company.)*

WorldCom

(WorldCom, Inc., Jackson, MS, www.wcom.com) A major, international telecommunications carrier founded in 1983 as Long Distance Discount Service (LDDS), a reseller of AT&T WATS lines to small businesses. It grew by acquiring many small, and eventually, large long distance and networking organizations, including IDB WorldCom, a leading international carrier, WilTel, a major telecom carrier, and MFS Communications, an international phone company and recent parent of UUNET, a prominent Internet provider. In 1997, the network operations of America Online and CompuServe became part of WorldCom. It also merged with Brooks Fiber and announced its intentions to merge with MCI and become MCI WorldCom.

WorldGate

(WorldGate Communications, Inc., Bensalem, PA, www.wgate.com) An organization founded in 1995 devoted to providing Internet access over your existing TV cable. The technology, which uses an advanced cable set-top box and wireless keyboard, transmits Web data via the vertical blanking interval between TV frames. WorldGate's Channel HyperLinking enables users to link directly to a Web site that is associated with a TV show or commercial. WorldGate sells its service to cable TV companies.

WorldNet

See *AT&T WorldNet*.

World Wide Wait

What many have called the Web while waiting patiently for the next page or file to download. The World Wide Wait is caused by any combination of a slow modem, inundated Web site or overload or router failure in a national, regional or local provider.

World Wide Web

An Internet facility that links documents locally and remotely. The Web document is called a *Web page*, and links in the page let users jump from page to page (hypertext) whether the pages are stored on the same server or on servers around the world. The pages are accessed and read via a Web browser such as Netscape Navigator or Internet Explorer.

The Web became the center of Internet activity, because Web pages, containing both text and graphics, were easily accessible via a Web browser. The Web provides point and click interface to the largest collection of online information in the world, and the amount of information is increasing at a staggering rate. The Web is also turning into a multimedia delivery system as new browser features and browser plug-in extensions, coming at a dizzying pace, allow for audio, video, telephony, 3-D animations and videoconferencing over the Net. Newer browsers also support the Java language, which allow applications of all variety to be downloaded from the Net and run locally.

The fundamental Web format is a text document embedded with HTML tags that provide the formatting of the page as well as the hypertext links (URLs) to other pages. HTML codes are common alphanumeric characters that can be typed with any text editor or word processor. Numerous Web publishing programs provide a graphical interface for Web page creation and automatically generate the codes. Many word processors and publishing programs also export their existing documents to the HTML format, thus Web pages can be created by users without learning any coding system. The ease of page creation has helped fuel the Web's growth.

Web pages are maintained at Web sites, which are computers that support the Web's HTTP protocol. When you access a Web site, you generally first link to its home page, which is an HTML document that serves as an index, or springboard, to the site's contents. Large organizations create and manage their own Web sites. Smaller ones have their sites hosted on

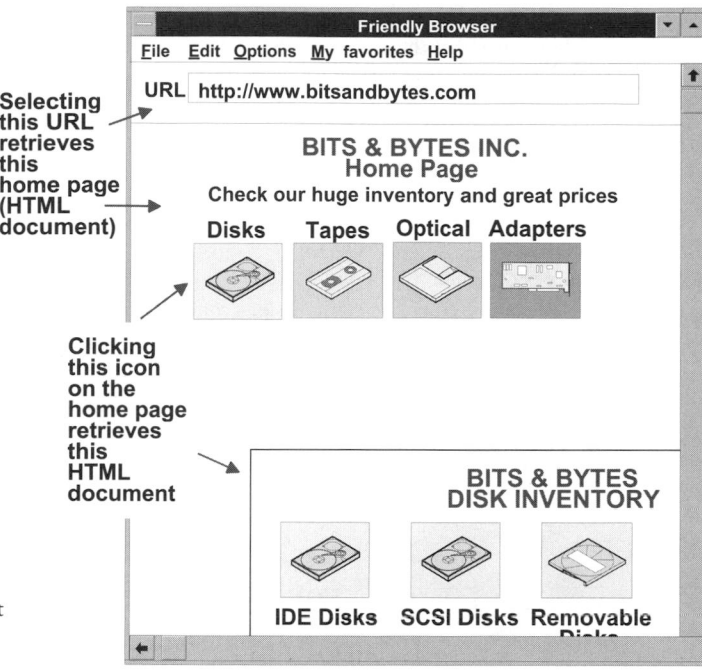

World Wide Web Linking
Accessing a Web document requires typing in the URL (Uniform Resource Locator) address of the home page in your Web browser. The home page contains hypertext links to other documents that can be stored on the same server or on a server anywhere in the world.

servers run by their Internet service providers (ISPs). Countless individuals have developed personal Web home pages as many ISPs include this service with their monthly access charge. Individuals can post their resumes, hobbies and whatever else they want as a way of introducing themselves to the world at large.

The Web spawned the *intranet*, an inhouse, private Web site for internal users. It is protected by a firewall that lets intranet users out to the Internet, but prevents Internet users from coming in.

Where It Came From - Where It's Going

The World Wide Web was developed at the European Center for Nuclear Research (CERN) in Geneva from a proposal by Tim Berners-Lee in 1989. It was created to share research information on nuclear physics. In 1991, the first command line browser was introduced. By the start of 1993, there were 50 Web servers, and the Voila X Window browser provided the first graphical capability for the Web. In that same year, CERN introduced its Macintosh browser, and the National Center for Supercomputing Applications (NCSA) in Chicago introduced the X Window version of Mosaic. Mosaic was developed by Marc Andreessen who later became world famous as a principal at Netscape.

By 1994, there were approximately 500 Web sites, and, by the start of 1995, nearly 10,000. In 1995, more articles were written about the Web than any other subject in the computer field. Today, there are more than a million Web sites with new ones coming online at a staggering rate.

Many believe the Web signifies the beginning of the real information age and envision it as the business model of the 21st century. Others consider it the "World Wide Wait" right now as surfing the Net via modem using an ISP scrambling to keep up with demand is often an exercise in extreme patience.

It seems that everyone has some vested interest in the Web. The telephone and cable companies want to give you high-speed access to it, while the existing ISPs want to gain market share. IS managers are concerned with intranet vulnerability when connected to the Internet. The publishing industry is perplexed over how to manage its copyrighted material on a medium that can send it all over the world in a few seconds. Software vendors are scrambling to make their products Web compatible. Hardware vendors are debating whether the network computer (NC) will replace the personal computer (PC).

Nothing in the computer/communications field has ever come onto the scene with such intensity. Is it really the marketplace of the 21st Century? Stay tuned. It will be interesting.

World Wide Web Consortium

See *W3C*.

WorldWorx

A multimedia network service from AT&T that provides point-to-point and multipoint connections between remote videoconferencing stations.

worm

(1) A destructive program that replicates itself throughout disk and memory, using up the computers resources and eventually putting the system down. See *virus* and *logic bomb*.

(2) A program that moves through a network and deposits information at each node for diagnostic purposes or causes idle computers to share some of the processing workload.

(3) (WORM) (**W**rite **O**nce **R**ead **M**any) An optical disk that can be recorded only once. Updating requires destroying the existing data (all 0s made 1s), and writing new data to an unused part of the disk.

There are two kinds of WORM technologies. Ablative large-format (12-14") WORM is the traditional type, which makes a permanent change in the optical material. Continuous composite write (CCW) WORM is a mode in multifunction 5.25" optical (MO) drives that emulates a WORM drive. The data is not permanently changed, but the drive contains firmware that ensures that recorded areas are not rewritten.

The large-format market is dwindling. Kodak is expected to stop making 14" drives after 1999, leaving only Philips LMS with its 12" line. Philips is switching from the ablative format to phase change in 1999. For a summary of all optical technologies, see *storage device*.

Ablative

5.25" MO

WORM Cartridges
Large-format 12-14" WORM drives have used the ablative technology. Magneto-optic drives have firmware that turns MO media into write-once disks.

WOSA

(**W**indows **O**pen **S**ystem **A**rchitecture) An umbrella term for a variety of programming interfaces from Microsoft designed to provide application interoperability across the Windows environment. It provides a common denominator for front-end Windows applications to access back-end services from different vendors. For example, any WOSA-compliant query program from one vendor can gain access to any WOSA-compliant DBMS from any another vendor. See *SPI*.

WOSA Interface	Provides access to
ODBC	Databases (DBMSs)
MAPI	Messaging systems
TAPI	Telephone network services
LSAPI	Software licensing
Windows SNA	IBM SNA networks
Windows Sockets	Internet, TCP/IP networks
Microsoft RPC	Run remote procedures
Financial Services	Banking services
WOSA/XRT	News, stock market, etc.

WP

See *word processing* and *WordPerfect*.

WPcom

See *write precompensation*.

WPG

(WordPerfect Graphics) A graphics format developed for use in WordPerfect documents. WPG files can contain vector graphics or raster images.

WRAM

(Window **RAM**) A type of RAM developed by Samsung Electronics that is optimized for display adapters. Although faster than VRAM, it uses the same type of dual-ported structure that simultaneously refreshes the screen while text and images are being drawn in the memory. See *video RAM*.

wrist rest

A platform used to raise the wrist to keyboard level for typing.

wrist support

A product that prevents and provides a therapy for carpal tunnel syndrome by keeping the hands in a neutral wrist position.

write

To store data in memory or record data onto a storage medium, such as disk and tape. Read and write is analogous to play and record on an audio tape recorder.

write access

Authorization to record or update data stored in the computer.

write back cache

A disk or memory cache that supports the caching of writing. Data normally written to memory or to disk by the CPU is first written into the cache. During idle machine cycles, the data is written from the cache into real memory or onto disk. Write back caches improve performance, because a write to the high-speed cache is faster than to normal RAM or disk.

A write back cache for disks adds a degree of risk, because the data stays in memory longer. Although it is generally no more than a few seconds until the data is written to disk, if the computer crashes or is shut down before then, the data is lost. A write back cache for memory is no more or less risky than normal memory, because all memory loses its data when the power is turned off. See *write through cache*.

write cycle

The operation of writing data into a memory or storage device.

write error

The inability to store into memory or record onto disk or tape. Malfunctioning memory cells or damaged portions of the disk or tape's surface will cause those areas to be unusable.

write once

Refers to storage media that can be written to but not erased. WORM and CD-R disks are examples. See *rewritable*.

write once CD

See *CD-R*.

write once-run anywhere

Refers to writing software that can run on multiple hardware platforms. Interpreted languages such as Java allow a program to be written once and run in any computer that supports the same version of the Java interpreter. See *network computer*.

write only code

Jokingly refers to source code that is difficult to understand.

write precompensation

Using a stronger magnetic field to write data in sectors that are closer to the center of the disk. In CAV recording, in which the disk spins at a constant speed, the sectors closest to the spindle are packed tighter than the outer sectors.

One of the hard disk parameters stored in a PC's CMOS memory is the WPcom number, which is the track where precompensation begins. See *CMOS setup*.

write protect

A mode that restricts erasing or editing a disk file. See *file protection*.

Write protect error

A DOS error message that means the floppy disk has been protected and data cannot be recorded on it. Either unprotect it or use another disk. See *file protection*.

write protect notch

A small, square cutout on the side of a 5.25" floppy disk used to prevent it from being written and erased. To enable the protection, the notch is covered with self-sticking tape. See *file protection*.

write through cache

A disk or memory cache that supports the caching of writing. Data written by the CPU to memory or to disk is also written into the cache. Write performance is not improved with this method. However, if a subsequent read operation needs that same data, read performance is improved, because the data is already in the high-speed cache. See *write back cache*.

WSI

See *wafer scale integration*.

WTS

See *Windows Terminal Server*.

WUGNET

(Windows Users Group Network, Media, PA, www.wugnet.com) Founded in 1988, it is the oldest and largest independent organization that supports the Windows environment. It provides technical information, software resources and tools, CompuServe forums and newsletters.

WWW

See *World Wide Web*.

WXmodem

(Window **Xmodem**) A faster version of the Xmodem protocol that allows the sending system to transmit data without waiting for the receiving system to acknowledge the transfer.

WYSIWYG

(What You See Is What You Get) Pronounced "wizzy-wig." It refers to displaying text and graphics on screen the same as they will print. To have WYSIWYG text, there must be an equivalent screen font for each printer font used.

The screen and printed results may look the same, but, in fact, it is impossible to get an exact representation because screen and printer resolutions do not match. The typical monitor may display 75 dpi, whereas a low-end desktop printer prints 300 dpi. That means the screen produces approximately 5,000 dots per square inch compared to the printer's 90,000.

WYSIWYG MOL

(WYSIWYG **M**ore **O**r **L**ess) Quite often what you get, when what you want is WYSIWYG!

X

x

(1) In programming, symbol used to identify a hexadecimal number. For example, 0x0A and \x0A specify the hex number 0A.

(2) See *X Window*.

x2

A 56 Kbps modem from U.S. Robotics. X2 was superseded by V.90.

X.3

An ITU standard (1977) for a PAD (packet assembler/disassembler), which divides a data message into packets for transmission over a packet-switched network and reassembles them at the receiving side.

X12

An ANSI protocol for electronic data interchange (EDI). X12 is the primary North American standard for defining EDI transactions. See *Tradacoms* and *EDIFACT*.

X.21

An ITU standard protocol for a circuit switching network.

X.25

An ITU standard (1976) for packet switching networks. Public X.25 communications networks have been available worldwide for many years, which provide a switched data service at 56 Kbps or less. Such networks are widely used for point of sale (POS) terminals, credit card verifications and automatic teller machine (ATM) transactions. New packet-switched networks employ frame relay and SMDS technologies rather than X.25. See *packet switching, frame relay* and *SMDS*.

X.28

An ITU standard (1977) for exchange of information between a DTE and a PAD; commonly known as PAD commands.

X.29

An ITU standard (1977) for exchange of information between a local PAD and a remote PAD; procedures for interworking between PADs.

X.32

An ITU standard (1984) for connecting to an X.25 network by dial up. It defines how the network identifies the terminal for billing and security purposes and how default parameters are negotiated for the connection.

X.75

An ITU standard for connecting X.25 networks.

x86

Also 80x86. Refers to the Intel 8086 CPU family used in PCs, which includes the 8086, 8088, 80186, 80286, 386, 486, Pentium, Pentium MMX, Pentium Pro and Pentium II. This is the largest installed base of computers worldwide.

x86 based

Refers to a computer that uses an Intel CPU (486, Pentium, etc.) or a clone chip.

x86 PROCESSORS

	CPU	Clock Speed (MHz)	Bus Size	Max RAM	Floppy Disk	Typical Hard disk	Operating Systems
16-bit CPUs	8088	5	8	1M	5.25" 360K	10-20MB	DOS DR DOS
	8086	5-10	16	1M			
	286	6-12	16	16M	5.25" 1.2MB	20-80MB	DOS DR DOS Windows 3.0 OS/2 1.x
32-bit CPUs	386DX	16-40	32	4G	5.25" 1.2MB	60- 200MB	DOS DR DOS OS/2 1.x OS/2 2.x Windows 3.x Windows NT Windows 95
	386SX	16-33	32	4G			
	386SL	20-25	32	4G	3.5" 1.44MB		
	486DX	25-100	32	4G		200- 500MB	UNIX (SCO) Solaris Linux Misc. DOS multiuser
	486SX	20-40	32	4G			
	Pentium	60- 200	64	4G		500MB- 16GB	
	Pentium MMX	150- 233	64	4G			
	Pentium Pro	150- 200	64	64G			
	Pentium II	233- 400	64	4G			
	Celeron	266- 300	64	4G			
	Pentium II Xeon	400- 450	64	64G			

x86 clone, X86 compatible

A CPU chip that is compatible with various models of the Intel x86 family. Companies such as AMD and Cyrix make x86 clones.

X.400

An OSI and ITU standard messaging protocol. It is an application layer protocol (layer 7 in the OSI model). X.400 has been defined to run over various network transports including Ethernet, X.25, TCP/IP and dial-up lines. See *messaging protocol, XAPIA* and *CMC*. The format of an X.400 address is:

```
c=  /admd=  /prmd=  /o=  /s=  /g=

    c    country
 admd    administrative management domain (public e-mail service)
 prmd    private management domain (inhouse e-mail)
    o    organization
    s    surname
    g    given name
```

X.400 API Association

See *XAPIA*.

X.445

An ITU standard for sending X.400 traffic over standard telephone lines. It is also known as the Asynchronous Protocol Specification (APS).

X.500

An OSI protocol for managing online directories of users and resources. X.500 can be used to support X.400 and other messaging systems, but it is not restricted to e-mail usage. It provides a hierarchical structure that fits the world's classification system: countries, states, cities, streets, houses, families, etc. The goal is to have a directory that can be used globally.

An X.500 directory is called a Directory Information Base (DIB) or white pages. The program that maintains the DIBs is called a Directory Server Agent (DSA). A Directory Client Agent (DCA) is used to search DSA sites for names and addresses.

The X.500 specification was published in 1988, and the 1993 edition is interoperable with it. The 1993 edition includes replication and access control. Using the Directory Information Shadowing Protocol (DISP), replication allows a portion of the Directory Information Tree (DIT) to be copied between nodes.

Access control provides a method to allow or deny access to a particular attribute of a directory entry based on the identity of the requesting user.

X500

See *X.500*.

X.509

A widely-used specification for digital certificates that has been a recommendation of the ITU since 1988. See *digital certificate*.

XA

See *CD-ROM XA* and *370/XA*.

XAPIA

(X 4.00 **API A**ssociation) A consortium dedicated to standardizing X.400 and other specifications, such as the CMC messaging API.

x-axis

See *x-y matrix*.

Xbase

Refers to dBASE-like languages such as Clipper and FoxPro. Originally almost identical to dBASE, new commands and features over the years have made Xbase languages only partially dBASE compatible.

X-based

See *X Window* and *Xbase*.

X Bitmap

A black and white bitmapped graphics format used in the UNIX environment. It uses the .XBM extension and is often used as a hypertext icon on a Web page. Many Web browsers treat the white parts of the image as transparent, or background, which takes on the color of the underlying window.

XBM

The file extension used by an X Bitmap image. See *X Bitmap*.

XCMD

(eXternal CoMmanD) A user-developed HyperCard command written in a language such as C or Pascal. See *XFCN*.

XDB Enterprise Server

A relational database management system (DBMS) for DOS, Windows, Windows NT and OS/2 from XDB Systems, Inc., Columbia, MD, (www.xdb.com). XDB is fully compatible with IBM's DB2 database.

XDF

(EXtended Density Format) A floppy disk format that extends the capacity of a 1.44MB floppy to about 1.86MB.

XDR

(EXternal Data Representation) A data format developed by Sun that is part of its networking standards. It deals with integer size, byte ordering, data representation, etc. and is used as an interchange format. Different systems convert to XDR for sending and from XDR upon receipt.

xDSL

Refers to DSL technologies in general, including ADSL, HDSL, SDSL and VDSL. See *DSL*.

xe file

See *EXE file*.

Xeon

A Pentium II CPU chip designed for server and high-end workstation use. Introduced in the summer of 1998 at 400MHz, it includes additional error checking and system management features as well as L2 cache from 512MB to 2MB. It introduces the System Management Bus (SMBus) interface, which includes a Processor Information ROM (PIROM) that contains data about the processor and an empty EEPROM that can be used by manufacturers or resellers to track their own information such as usage and service information. Using Intel's Extended Server Memory Architecture, the Pentium II Xeon chip can address 64GB of memory.

xerography

See *electrophotographic*.

Xerox

(Xerox Corportion, Stamford, CT, www.xerox.com) A major manufacturer of analog and digital copy machines, computer printers and document management systems. Corporate headquarters are in Stamford, CT, while manufacturing and marketing is in Rochester, NY.

In 1906, the Haloid Company was founded in Rochester to manufacture and sell photographic paper. In 1947, it acquired the license to Chester Carlson's basic xerographic patents from Batelle Development Corporation and sold the first xerographic copier in 1950. In 1958, the company changed its name to Haloid Xerox, and three years later, to Xerox Corporation.

The Xerox 914 copier, introduced in 1959, was an outstanding success, and the xerography technology catapulted the company into a major corporation. Over the years, Xerox acquired a wide variety of companies in computers, financial services, publishing and education, many of which it sold or spun off later on.

Its creation in 1970 of PARC (Palo Alto Research Center) resulted in major contributions to the computer industry, including the development of the first workstation with a graphical user interface, the mouse and Ethernet. As copy machines and printers merge into the world of networked document management, Xerox is at the forefront of this market, while continuing to research and develop new technologies.

The name Xerox means "dry writing" in Greek. The word xero means "dry," and graphy means "write." Carlson's invention used a dry, granular ink which replaced the messy liquid ink of the times.

XFCN

(eXternal FunCtioN) A user-developed HyperCard function that is written in a language, such as C or Pascal. XFCNs usually return a value. See *XCMD*.

xfr

Often used as an abbreviation for "transfer" in may electronic and communications terms and phrases.

XGA

(EXtended Graphics Array) An IBM video display standard introduced in 1990 that extended VGA to 132-column text and interlaced 1024x768x256 resolution. XGA-2 added non-interlaced 1024x768x64K. The term may be used to refer to 1024x768 resolution in general; for example:

```
XGA    1024x768
SVGA   800x600
VGA    640x480
```

The First Xerox Machine
The first xerographic copier was sold in 1950. Although manually operated, it provided the experience and revenue to develop the 914. *(Photo courtesy of Xerox Corporation.)*

x-height

In typography, the height of the letter x in lower case. Point size includes the x-height, the height of the ascender and the height of the descender. See *typeface* for illustration.

XICS

(X Window interface to the Internet Chess Server) A graphical interface to the Internet Chess Server (ICS), which allows people to play chess over the Internet. X Window displays the chess board and allows mouse moves rather than typing and receiving text. See *ICS*.

XIE

(X Image Extension) Extensions to the X Window system that enhance its graphics capability. It allows the desktop terminal or PC (the server) to retrieve various types of compressed images from the client and be able to manipulate them.

Remember, in X, the client and server are the opposite of what they are in client/server. See *X Window*.

XIP

(Execute In Place) The ability to execute a program directly from a memory card.

XL

See *Excel*.

Xlib

(X LIBrary) Functions in the X Window System. See *X toolkit*.

X library

See *Xlib*.

XLISP

A microcomputer version of the LISP programming language that has been in the public domain for a number of years.

Xmark

See *XPC*.

XMI

A high-speed bus from Digital used in large VAX machines.

XML

(EXtensible Markup Language) A document format for the Web that is more flexible than HTML. While HTML uses only predefined tags to describe elements within the page, XML allows tags to be defined by the developer of the page. Thus, tags for virtually any data items such as product, sales rep and amount due, can be used for specific applications, allowing Web pages to function like database records.

XML is a subset of the SGML document language, and HTML is a document type of SGML. See *HTML* and *SGML*.

Xmodem

The first widely-used file transfer protocol for personal computers, developed by Ward Christensen for CP/M machines. Xmodem programs typically support the earlier checksum method and the subsequent CRC method of error detection. Xmodem transmits 128-byte blocks. Xmodem-1K improves speed with 1KB blocks. Xmodem-1K-G transmits without acknowledgment for error-free channels or when modems are self correcting, but transmission is cancelled upon any error.

XMP

(X/Open Management Protocol) A high-level network management protocol governed by X/Open. Network management software written to the XMP interface is shielded from the details of the underlying SNMP or CMIP protocols.

XMS

(1) (eXtended Memory Specification) A programming interface that allows DOS programs to use extended memory in 286s and up. It provides a set of functions for reserving, releasing and transferring data to and from extended memory without conflict, including the high memory area (HMA). See *HIMEM.SYS* and *DOS extender*.

XMS, VCPI and DPMI all deal with extended memory. However, XMS allows data and programs to be stored in and retrieved from extended memory, whereas the VCPI and DPMI interfaces allow programs to "run" in extended memory.

(2) See *cross memory services*.

XMT

In communications, an abbreviation for transmit.

XNOR

(eXclusive NOR) See *NOR*.

XNS

(Xerox Network Services) An early networking protocol suite developed at Xerox's Palo Alto Research Center (PARC). XNS has been the basis for many popular network architectures including Novell's NetWare, Banyan's VINES and 3Com's 3+.

XNS Layer	XNS Protocols	OSI Layers	NetWare Protocols
4 Application		7	
3 Control		5 & 6	
2 Transport	SPP, PEP	4	SPX
1 Internet	IDP	3	IPX
0 Transmission	Ethernet	1 & 2	

xon-xoff

In communications, a simple asynchronous protocol that keeps the receiving device in synchronization with the sender. When the buffer in the receiving device is full, it sends a "transmit off" signal to the sending device, telling it to stop transmitting. When the receiving device is ready to accept more, it sends the sending device a "transmit on" signal to start again.

X/Open

(X/Open, San Francisco, CA, division of The Open Group, www.opengroup.org) A consortium of international computer vendors founded in 1984 to resolve standards issues. Incorporated in 1987 and based in London, North American offices are in San Francisco. In 1996, it merged with OSF into The Open Group. Its purpose is to integrate evolving standards in order to achieve an open environment. XPG are X/Open specifications, and VSK are X/Open testing and verification procedures.

In late 1993, Spec 1170 was announced to provide a common programming interface for UNIX in order to unify all the various versions of the operating system. Containing more than 1,100 APIs, Spec 1170 later evolved into the Single UNIX Specification, which is branded by X/Open.

X/Open is also responsible for governing the Common Desktop Environment (CDE), a standard user interface for UNIX above and beyond X and Motif, which are part of the Single UNIX Specification. The first CDE products were introduced in early 1995. See *Open Group*.

X/Open Portability Guide

Known as the *XPG*, it is a set of standards that specify compliance with X/Open's Common Application Environment (CAE). XPG3 (1989) and XPG4 (1992) define operating systems, languages and protocols, etc. About half of the Single UNIX Specification (formerly Spec 1170) was taken from XPG4. The term "base" with XPG (XPG3 base, XPG4 base, etc.) refers to a minimum number of required APIs.

XOR

See *OR*.

XPC

(X Performance Characterization) A graphics benchmark that tests X Window performance. In 1993, the XPC project group created Xmark93, which rates a broad set of X functions in Xmarks. See *GPC*.

XPG

See *X/Open Portability Guide*.

X Pixelmap

An 8-bit bitmapped graphics format used in the UNIX environment. It uses the .XPM extension and is similar to the X Bitmap format, but provides 256 colors. X Pixelmaps are often used for X Window icons and hypertext icons on Web pages.

Xplor

(Xplor International, Torrance, CA 90505, www.xplor.org) A membership organization founded in 1981 dedicated to enhancing the use of electronic document systems. With more than 2,000 organizations as members, benefits include newsletters, surveys, catalogs and conferences. In addition, Xplor offers certification as an Electronic Document and Printing Professional (EDPP) to members and non-members with experience in electronic publishing.

XPM

The file extension used by an X Pixelmap image. See *X Pixelmap*.

X protocol

The message format of the X Window System.

X server

The receiving computer in an X Window system. The X server displays the application that is running on a remote machine, which is the X client. See *X Window*.

X standard

See *X Window* and *X.400*.

XT

(1) (EXtended Technology) The first IBM PC with a hard disk, introduced in 1983. It still used the same 8088 CPU as the original PC and included 128KB of RAM and a 10MB hard drive. See *PC*.

(2) (Xt) See *X toolkit*.

XTACACS

See *TACACS*.

XT bus

See *PC bus*.

XT class

Refers to first-generation PCs, which includes the first floppy-disk PC, the actual "XT" PC with a hard disk and all compatibles that use the 8088 or 8086 or compatible CPU and an 8-bit bus.

X terminal

A terminal with built-in X server capability.

XTI

(X/Open Transport Interface) A common programming interface between the application and the transport layer of the communications protocol. It is governed by The Open Group.

XT interface

See *XT bus*.

X toolkit

Development software for building X Window applications. Typically includes a widget set, X Toolkit Intrinsics (Xt) libraries for managing the widget set and the X Library (Xlib).

XTP

(Xpress Transfer Protocol) A research transport protocol designed by Greg Chesson of Silicon Graphics. It is a type of lightweight protocol designed for high-speed networks and provides services at layers 3 and 4 of the OSI model.

XTP is flexible and can select rate and flow control. In order to handle different traffic; for example, transactions versus realtime video, XTP's "universal receiver" has the transmitting station tell the receiver when to acknowledge. ANSI's version is called HSTP (High Speed Transport Protocol).

XTree

Introduced in 1985 by the Xtree Company, it was the first program to help DOS users manage hard disks by providing a hierarchical display of directories. Versions for Windows came later, and XtreeGold added file viewers.

Xtrieve

A menu-driven query language and report writer from Novell that accesses Btrieve files.

XVT

(EXtensible Virtual Toolkit) A C++ developers toolkit for creating user interfaces across multiple environments from XVT Software, Inc., Boulder, CO, (www.xvt.com). Programmers design the user interface by calling XVT functions, which are then translated to Windows, OS/2, Motif or the Mac.

X Window

(X Window System) Also called *X Windows* and *X*, it is a windowing system developed at MIT, which runs under UNIX and all major operating systems. It lets users

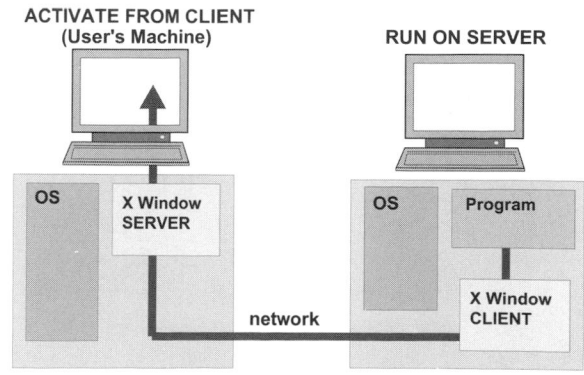

X Window Servers Run on Clients

It is correct to say that the X Window server runs on your client, and the X Window client runs on your server. Hey, all's fair in love and computers!

run applications on other computers in the network and view the output on their own screen.

X Window generates a rudimentary window that can be enhanced with GUIs, such as Open Look and Motif, but does not require applications to conform to a GUI standard. The window manager component of the GUI allows multiple resizable, relocatable X windows to be viewed on screen at the same time.

X client software resides in the computer that performs the processing and X server software resides in the computer that displays it. Both components can also be in the same machine. This seems opposite to today's client/server terminology, but the concept is that the server is "serving up" the image. See *thin client* and *XIE*.

x-y matrix

A group of rows and columns. The x-axis is the horizontal row, and the y-axis is the vertical column. An x-y matrix is the reference framework for two-dimensional structures, such as mathematical tables, display screens, digitizer tablets, dot matrix printers and 2-D graphics images.

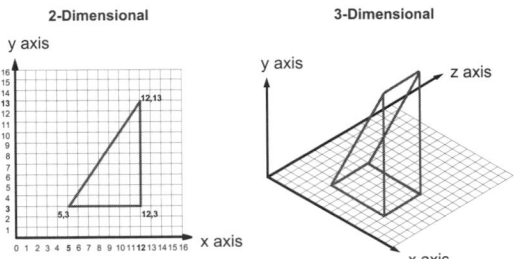

xy matrix

See *x-y matrix*.

x-y monitor

In graphics, the display screen of a vector display terminal. The entire vector display comprises the monitor and vector graphics controller.

x-y plotter

Same as *plotter*.

XyWrite for Windows

The Windows version of the XyWrite word processor from The Technology Group, Baltimore, MD. It is a full-featured Windows word processor that accepts XyWrite and ASCII files and automatically converts IBM's DCA documents into XyWrite format. XyWrite for Windows maintains the flexibility that made its DOS predecessors popular among writers and editors. It also retains the XyWrite method for displaying format codes on screen. See *XyWrite III Plus*.

XyWrite III Plus

Pronounced "zy-write." A word processing program that has been used extensively in the newspaper and magazine business as well as by professional writers. Developed by XyQuest, Inc., Billerica, MA, it was the most customizable DOS word processor ever developed and the first DOS program to provide complete typographic control over the page layout.

XyWrite generates a pure ASCII file with commands embedded in high-order DOS characters that display as unobtrusive triangles. Their contents can be easily revealed at any time.

x-y-z matrix

A three-dimensional structure. The x and y axes represent the first two dimensions; the z axis, the third dimension. In a graphic image, the x and y denote width and height; the z denotes depth.

Y2K

See *Year 2000 problem*.

Y2K compliant

Capable of correctly processing any data that deals with a date beyond the year 1999. See *Year 2000 problem*.

YAAP

(Yet Another Authentication Protocol) A proposed access control protocol from Microsoft designed to replace RADIUS and TACACS+.

yacc

(Yet Another Compiler Compiler) A UNIX compiler that is used to create C compilers. Part of its code is included in the generated compiler. See *bison*.

Yahoo!

(www.yahoo.com) The first search site on the Web to gain worldwide attention. Yahoo! indexes much of its material manually rather than from automated spiders that roam the Web indexing everything in sight. See *Web search sites*.

Yahooligans!

(www.yahooligans.com) A special version of the Yahoo! site aimed at kids from 7 to 12. It works just like the regular Yahoo! directory. Every site that is retrieved has been reviewed by Yahoo! staffers, judged suitable for kids and placed into the appropriate category or categories.

Yankee Group

(the Yankee Group, Boston, MA, www.yankeegroup.com) A major market research, analysis and consulting firm founded in 1970 by Howard Anderson. It provides general consulting and Planning Services in the computer and communications field. Planning Services are a package of services on a particular topic that includes reports, personal consulting, conference attendance and electronic delivery of material.

yaw

See *pitch-yaw-roll*.

y-axis

See *x-y matrix*.

Y/C video

See *S-video*.

Year 2000 problem

Also known as the *Y2K problem*, it is the inability of older hardware and software to recognize the century change in a date. The reason they cannot is because the year is stored with only two digits; for example, 12-11-42 instead of 12-11-1942. Thus, when the year changes from 1999 to 2000, the date becomes 01-01-00, but the system thinks it is January 1, 1900, not January 1, 2000.

Many financial transactions match dates in an electronic record with today's date or with a future date. If the computer system does not handle the dates correctly, bills will not get paid, notices will not get triggered, actions will not be taken, virtually all software that deals with dates will cause problems after the turn of the century in a system that cannot recognize the millenium change.

The solution to this "millenium bug" is mammoth. It requires upgrading hardware to support four-digit years, converting files and databases to four-digit years and converting all the software that references dates. Enterprises have large numbers of legacy data files and huge numbers of programs that deal with them. Each reference to a date must be changed in every program, and finding them can be extremely difficult. There are many legacy systems that are still running every day, but the programmers that wrote the software are long gone, and the programs may lack documentation or even the original source code. Even if the changes can be made, the time it takes to test them all is inordinately taxing on the IS staff that is trying to run the daily work as well as implement new applications to accomodate our fast-changing world.

The problem originated with punched cards that go back to the early 1900s. In order to cram an entire order or customer record into typically less than 100 character columns, which was the physical size of the card, the year field was shortened to two digits. After all, why waste two columns for the "19" when it was going to be "19" for such a long time. When punched card systems were converted to magnetic tape and disk during the 1960s, the 21st century still seemed too far away to worry about. Likewise, many computer systems were built to keep track of the time of day using two-digit years.

Saving two columns (characters, bytes) in a punched card may have been appropriate 50 years ago, but the lack of attention to this matter over the years is now estimated to cost as much as $600 billion to correct, and many believe everything will not be totally fixed by 2000. There just is not enough time and resources to do the job.

It's Happening Already!

We don't have to wait until January 1, 2000 to experience the Y2K problem. For example, how about a company that wants to delete all customers that have not ordered anything for the past five years. The program logic would be to add 5 years to the date of the customer's last order and then compare the result to this year.

Making the Point
This advertising graphic for the TICTOC Year 2000 compliance software from Isogon Corporation, (www.isogon.com) makes a strong point. TICTOC is used to test Y2K compliance for MVS applications by setting fictitious dates on a job-by-job basis. *(Image courtesy of Isogon Corporation.)*

Suppose the customer last ordered in 1995 and this year were 1996. Add 5 to 1995, and you have 2000, except that in a system that is not Y2K compliant, you get 1900 instead. Since 1996 is greater than 1900, the customer would be deleted. See *data aging* and *Year 2038 problem*.

Year 2038 problem

Another date problem, which results from computing dates into the year 2038 and beyond in 32-bit operating systems. UNIX and other C applications represent time as the number of seconds from January 1, 1970. The 32-bit variable (time_t) that stores this number overflows in the year 2038 and becomes January 1, 1970 again. However, even today, any date caculations forecasted beyond that time will be erroneous. Switching to 64-bit computing solves the problem. See *Year 2000 problem*.

Yellow Book

The standard for the physical format of a CD-ROM disk. The ISO 9660 standard defines the logical format for the disk. See *CD*.

Yellow Pages

See *NIS, naming service* and *Web yellow pages*.

yield

In semiconductor manufacturing, the percentage of chips that work out of one wafer.

YIQ

The color model used for color TV. The Y stands for luminosity or lightness, which was the original black and white TV signal. The I and Q were added to make color TV backward compatible with the black and white standard. Known as chromacity, the I and Q signals are the color differences that are derived from the difference between red, blue and the luminosity (I=red-Y, Q=blue-Y).

Ymodem

A file transfer protocol that adds batch file processing to Xmodem. Multiple files can be sent at the same time. It is faster than Xmodem and sends the file name before sending the data. Ymodem-G transmits without acknowledgment for error-free channels or when modems are self correcting, but transmission is cancelled upon any error.

yocto

Septillionth (10 to the -24th power). See *space/time*.

yotta

Septillion (10^{24}). See *space/time*.

YUV

The native signal format of video. When video is digitized and compressed (MPEG, Indeo, etc.), it is kept in YUV format, because it takes less storage than the RGB equivalent. In order to display YUV data on a monitor, it must be converted into RGB, which is known as *color space conversion*.

Z

A mathematical language used for developing the functional specification of a software program. Developed in the late 1970s at Oxford University, IBM's CICS software is specified in Z.

Z39.50

An ANSI standard query language that is a simplified version of SQL. It is used on the Internet to search for documents. See *WAIS*.

Z80

A family of 8-bit microprocessors from Zilog. The original Z80 chip was the successor to the Intel 8080 and was widely used in first-generation personal computers that used the CP/M operating system. Subsequent Z180, Z280 and Z380 chips have been widely used in embedded systems, and hundreds of millions of them have been shipped.

Z8000

A 16-bit microprocessor from Zilog that was the successor to the Z80. The Z8000 is no longer made.

ZAI

(Zero Administration Initiative) A slogan for lower cost network administration using NetPCs. See *NetPC*.

ZAK

(Zero Administration Kit) A series of wizards that assist network administrators in using system policies and user profiles in Windows 95 and NT. See *ZAW, system policy* and *user profile*.

zap

A command that typically deletes the data within a file but leaves the file structure intact so that new data can be entered.

ZAW

(Zero Administration for Windows) Features in Windows NT 5.0 that provide central administration of Windows PCs and NetPCs in a network. For example, it provides for more automatic distribution of new software and upgrades. Support for ZAW is also expected in Windows 98. See *ZAK*.

z-axis

The third dimension in a graphics image. The width is the x-axis and the height is the y-axis.

ZBR

See *zone bit recording*.

z buffer

A memory buffer in a graphics accelerator that is used to speed up the rendering of 3-D images. It holds the depth of each pixel (z axis), and as an image is drawn, each pixel is matched against the z buffer location. If the next pixel in line to be drawn is below the one that is already there, it is ignored. See *graphics accelerator* for illustration.

Z-CAV, Z-CLV

See *CAV* and *CLV*.

ZDBOp

(Ziff-Davis Benchmark Operation, www.zdbop.com) A division of the Ziff-Davis Publishing Company that develops and supports the benchmark programs that all the Ziff-Davis magazines use to test computer products. The Winstone, WinBench, MacBench, NetBench, ServerBench, BatteryMark, BrowserComp and WebBench benchmarks are widely distributed and free at its Web site. See *benchmark*.

ZDNet

(ZDNet, Cambridge, MA, www.zdnet.com) Formerly ZiffNet, ZDNet is a shareware and technical information service for PC users from Ziff-Davis Publishing Company. It contains a wide of variety of shareware and public domain software that can be downloaded. ZD Net can be accessed via the Web as well as from CompuServe and America Online.

zebra strip
A packaging device that allows quick alignment of electronic devices on a printed circuit board. It is a small rubber strip with carbon bands running around it. It allows contact to be made from the pads on the board to the pads on the device by whichever bands happen to line up at both points.

zeen
See *zine*.

zeon
See *Xeon*.

zepto
Sextillionth (10^{-21}). See *space/time*.

zero administration
An umbrella term for improved network administration functions in Windows products. See *ZAW* and *ZAK*.

zero-slot LAN
Refers to transmitting between computers over a serial or parallel port, thus freeing up an expansion slot normally used by LAN cards (NICs).

zero suppression
Eliminating leading zeros for readability. For example, 00000001542 becomes 1542.

zero wait state
Refers to a high-speed memory that transfers its data immediately upon being accessed without waiting one or more machine cycles to respond.

zetta
Sextillion (10 to the 21st power). See *space/time*.

ZiffNet
See *ZDNet*.

ZIF socket
(Zero Insertion Force socket) A type of socket designed for easy insertion of chips that have a high density of pins. The chip is dropped into the socket's holes and a lever is pulled down to lock it in.

Zilog
(Zilog, Inc., Campbell, CA, www.zilog.com) A semiconductor manufacturer that was founded in 1974. It was a subsidiary of Exxon from 1980 to 1989 and went public in 1991. Zilog's Z80 chip was the CPU in CP/M machines, which helped to create the personal computer industry. Today, Zilog makes a variety of microprocessors and microcontrollers, and the Z80 family is still a major part of it.

zinc air
A rechargeable battery technology that provides more charge per pound than nickel cadmium or nickel hydride and does not suffer from the memory effect. It uses a carbon membrane that absorbs oxygen, a zinc plate and potassium hydroxide as the electrolyte. AER Energy Systems, Smyrna, GA, is the pioneer in this battery technology.

zine
Pronounced "zeen." See *Webzine* and *e-zine*.

zip
(1) To compress a file with PKZIP. See *PKZIP*.

(2) (ZIP) (Zig-Zag Inline Package) A chip package similar to a DIP, but both rows of pins come out of one side in an alternating pattern. See *DIP* and *chip package*.

(3) (ZIP) A proprietary messaging protocol from IBM. PROFS uses ZIP for its e-mail transport.

Zip disk

A 3.5" removable disk drive from Iomega. It uses design concepts from Iomega's Bernoulli technology as well as hard disks to provide 100MB removable cartridges that cost about $15. The drive is bundled with software that can catalog the disks and lock the files for security. See *latest disk drives*. For a summary of all storage technologies, see *storage*.

Zip file

See *zipped file* and *Zip disk*.

zipped

Compressed into the PKZIP format. See *zipped file*.

zipped file

A file compressed by PKZIP, PKZip for Windows, WinZip or other compression utility that compresses data into the PKZIP format. See *PKZIP*.

Zip Cartridge
Since the introduction of the Zip in 1995, it has become the most popular removable storage medium since the floppy.

Zmodem

A file transfer protocol that has become very popular because it handles noisy and changing line conditions very well, including satellite transmission. It sends file name, date and size first, uses variable length blocks and CRC error correction.

If a transmission is interrupted using Zmodem or Ymodem, Zmodem will transmit only the remainder of the file on the next try. This feature is extremely valuable when sending large files over noisy lines.

zone bit recording

Breaking a disk into recording zones using Z-CAV or Z-CLV methods. See *CAV* and *CLV*.

zoned CAV, zoned CLV

See *CAV* and *CLV*.

zoned constant angular velocity

See *CAV*.

zoned constant linear velocity

See *CLV*.

Zoo

A freeware compression program, including source code, used in UNIX, DOS and other environments.

zoom

To change from a distant view to a more close-up view (zoom in) and vice versa (zoom out). An application may provide fixed or variable levels of zoom. A display adapter may also have built-in zoom capability.

Zoomed Video Port

See *ZV Port*.

Zortech compilers

A series of C and C++ compilers from Zortech Inc., which was acquired by Symantec in 1991. Zortech compilers became Symantec compilers.

ZV Port

(Zoomed Video Port) An extension to the PC Card (PCMCIA) standard that provides a high transfer rate for video applications on portable computers. Video data goes directly to the display controller, bypassing the CPU and system bus, allowing full-screen, full-motion playback of digital video. The ZV Port is built into the notebook computer and activated by plugging in an MPEG PC Card that is ZV Port-compliant.

The ZV Port equivalent on a desktop computer is the pass through capability built into the MPEG board. The MPEG board is cabled directly to the monitor and provides a pass through for the VGA signals from the display adapter. See *VGA pass through*.

ZyIMAGE

Document management software for Windows from ZyLAB International, Inc., Rockville, MD, (www.zylab.com), that provides storage and retrieval for text documents, dBASE files and TIFF images. It provides full indexing on text, spreadsheet and data files and allows keywords to be appended to TIFF files. ZyIMAGE includes the ZyINDEX system.

ZyINDEX

Text management software for DOS and Windows from ZyLAB International, Inc., Rockville, MD, (www.zylab.com). It indexes the full text of word processing documents, spreadsheets and dBASE files. ZyINDEX works with Calera Recognition Systems WordScan OCR program to provide integrated scanning, optical character recognition and indexing. See *ZyIMAGE*.

zywrite

See *XyWrite for Windows* and *XyWrite III Plus*.

0-9

0K

(Zero Kilobytes) Typically references motherboards that do not include memory as priced.

0x

In programming, the symbol for a hexadecimal number. See *x*.

1-bit DAC

(1-bit Digtal to Analog Converter) A serial method of converting digital samples back into analog form for amplification. Each bit of the sample is converted into its analog weight rather than all bits of the sample converted in parallel. See *ladder DAC*.

1-Meg Modem

A data access device from Northern Telecom, Toronto, (www.nortel.com), that provides up to 960 Kbps downstream and up to 120 Kbps upstream over a standard telephone line. It uses 10BaseT Ethernet to connect to the computer, while an RJ-11 passthrough allows a phone, fax or analog modem to use the line simultaneously. The telephone company's switch must be upgraded, which can be done on a subscriber by subscriber basis.

1x DVD-ROM

A first-generation DVD-ROM drive that provides a transfer rate of 1350KB per second. It uses the CLV method and reads CD-ROMs at 8x speed, but generally cannot read CD-R and CD-RW disks. See *2x DVD-ROM* and *CLV*.

1-2-3

See *Lotus 1-2-3*.

1.2M, 1.44M

Refers to the 1.2MB 5.25" and the 1.44MB 3.5" floppy disks. See *floppy disk*.

10/100 card

An Ethernet network adapter (NIC) that supports both 10BaseT (10 Mbps) and 100BaseT (100 Mbps) access methods. Most cards autonegotiate at startup, enabling them to run at the higher speed if supported by the device they are connected to (hub or switch).

10/100 hub, 10/100 switch

An Ethernet hub or switch that automatically senses the speed (10 Mbps or 100 Mbps) of the network adapter connected to it. See *10/100 card*.

10Base2, 10Base5, 10BaseF, 10BaseT

See *Ethernet*.

10-way

Typically refers to a 10-CPU symmetric multiprocessing (SMP) system. See *SMP*.

10x CD-ROM

A CD-ROM drive that spins 10 times as fast as the first CD-ROM. It provides 1.5MB per second data transfer.

12-way

Typically refers to a 12-CPU symmetric multiprocessing (SMP) system. See *SMP*.

12x CD-ROM

A CD-ROM drive that spins 12 times as fast as the first CD-ROM. It provides 1.8MB per second data transfer.

14.4

Refers to the speed of modems that transmit at 14,400 bits per second.

16x CD-ROM

A CD-ROM drive that spins 16 times as fast as the first CD-ROM. It provides 2.4MB per second data transfer.

16:9

The aspect ratio of HDTV (High Definition TV), which is like the wide screen in movie theaters. It is wider than the 4:3 aspect ratio of computer monitors and standard TV. The 16:9 size is also called the *letterbox format.*

16-bit

See *bit specifications.*

16-bit characters

See *Unicode.*

16-bit color

Using two bytes per pixel in a color image. Up to 65,536 colors can be represented in the color palette. Most graphics formats provide 8-bit color or 24-bit color; however, display adapters generally have an intermediate 16-bit color range and can display 65,536 colors. See *bit depth* and *bit specifications.*

16-bit computer

A computer that uses a 16-bit word length. It processes two bytes (16 bits) at a time. See *32-bit processing.*

16-bit driver

A driver written for a 16-bit environment. It often refers to drivers written for DOS or Windows 3.x machines in contrast to 32-bit drivers written for Windows 95/98 or Windows NT. For example, when users upgrade a PC from Windows 3.1 to Windows 95/98, they have to replace the 16-bit Windows 3.1 display adapter driver with the 32-bit Windows 95/98 version.

16-bit sample

See *sampling rate.*

16-bit sound

A sound card that processes 16-bit sound samples. The more data in the sample, the more accurately sound can be digitized. See *sampling rate.*

16-bit version

A program that runs in a 16-bit environment. It typically refers to a program that was written for a DOS or Windows 3.1 PC in contrast with a 32-bit version that was written for Windows 95/98 or Windows NT.

16CIF

See *CIF.*

16 million colors

See *24-bit color.*

18-track

See *Magstar.*

100BaseT (100BaseFX)

Also called *Fast Ethernet,* it is a high-speed version of Ethernet (IEEE 802.3u standard). 100BaseT transmits at 100 Mbps rather than 10 Mbps. Like regular Ethernet, Fast Ethernet is a shared media LAN. All nodes share the 100 Mbps bandwidth. 100BaseT uses the same CSMA/CD access method as regular Ethernet with some modification. Three cabling variations are provided. 100BaseTX uses two pairs of Category 5 UTP, 100BaseT4 uses four pairs of Category 3, and 100BaseFX uses multimode optical fibers and is primarily intended for backbone use. See *100VG-AnyLAN.*

100BaseVG, 100VG-AnyLAN

A 100 Mbps version of Ethernet developed by HP that was able to transport both Ethernet and Token Ring frames. It was a shared media LAN like Ethernet, but employed the Demand Priority access method rather than CSMA/CD, allowing realtime voice and video to be given high priority. For a while, 100VG-AnyLAN was also called "Fast Ethernet," but the IEEE 802.3u Fast Ethernet became the standard.

128-bit
See *bit specifications*.

128-bit graphics accelerator
A display adapter that has a pathway 128 bits wide between its on-board graphics processor and memory (video RAM).

1000BaseLX, 1000BaseSX, 1000BaseTX
See *Gigabit Ethernet*.

1024x768, 1280x1024
Standard super VGA resolutions of 1,024 columns by 768 rows (lines) and 1280 columns by 1024 rows respectively. In the specification 1024x768x64K, the 64K is the number of colors. See *resolution*.

1284
See *IEEE 1284*.

1394
See *FireWire*.

1401
A second-generation IBM computer introduced in 1959 and used until the late 1960s. It had 16K of core memory, six tape drives and used punched cards for input. It was an outstanding success due to its reliability. Some 18,000 units were installed. For migration, 1401 emulators were built into IBM's 360 series.

IBM 1401
The 1401 was very successful. Its architecture and machine language were simple and straightforward. *(Photo courtesy of IBM Corporation.)*

16450, 16550
See *UART*.

2-D
(2 Dimensional) Refers to objects that are constructed on two planes (x and y, height and width, row and column, etc.). Two-dimensional structures are also used to simulate 3-D images on screen.

2-D accelerator
See *graphics accelerator*.

2-D graphics
The creation, display and manipulation of objects in the computer in two dimensions. Drawing programs and 2-D CAD programs allow objects to be drawn on an x-y scale as if they were drawn on paper. Although 3-D images can be drawn in 2-D programs, their views are static. They can be scaled larger or smaller, but they cannot be rotated to different angles as with 3-D objects in 3-D graphics programs. They also lack the automatic lighting effects of 3-D programs. Any desired shadows must be created by the artist using color fills or gradients. See *graphics* and *3-D graphics*.

2-tier architecture
See *two tier client/server*.

2-way
In both directions.

2x CD-ROM
A CD-ROM drive that spins twice as fast (300KB/sec) as the first-generation CD-ROM drive.

2x DVD-ROM
A DVD-ROM drive that spins twice as fast as first-generation DVD-ROMs. It provides 2700KB per second data transfer. The drives read CD-ROMs at a varying rate (CAV) between 8x and 20x, and they can read CD-Rs and possibly CD-RWs. See *1x DVD-ROM* and *CAV*.

24-bit color

Using three bytes per pixel in a color image. Also called *true color* and *RGB color*, up to 16,777,216 colors can be represented in the color palette. See *bit depth* and *bit specifications*.

24x7

Non-stop operation 24 hours a day, 7 days a week. Same as *7x24*.

24x CD-ROM

A CD-ROM drive that spins 24 times as fast as the first CD-ROM. It provides 3.6MB per second data transfer.

28.8

Refers to the transmission speed of a modem that can transmit up to 28,800 bits per second. See *V.34*.

256-bit

See *bit specifications*.

286

The second generation of the Intel x86 family of CPU chips. The term may refer to the chip or to a PC that uses it. Introduced in 1982, it is the successor to the 8088/8086 chips used in the first PCs. The 286 broke the infamous one-megabyte memory barrier, but although faster than the previous generation, it was never capable of supporting Windows and other graphics-based applications. See *AT class* and *x86*.

286 CPU Technical Specs

A 16-bit multitasking microprocessor in a 68-pin PGA, PLCC or LCC package. Has 15 16-bit registers including eight general-purpose. Operational modes: "Real Mode" performs as a fast 8086 CPU and addresses 1MB memory. "Protected Mode" addresses 16MB physical and 1GB virtual memory and provides access to memory protection capabilities. Contains 134,000 transistors.

2780 & 3780

Standard communications protocols for transmitting batch data. The numbers originated with early IBM remote job entry (RJE) terminals that included a card reader and a printer.

2B1Q

(2 Binary 1 Quaternary) An encoding method used in ISDN in which each pair of binary digits represents four discrete amplitude and polarity values.

3+Open

An OS/2-based network operating system from 3Com that supported DOS, OS/2 and Mac clients. It was discontinued in 1993.

3+Share

A DOS-based network operating system from 3Com that supported DOS and Mac clients. It was discontinued in 1993.

3Com

(3Com Corporation, Santa Clara, CA, www.3com.com) Founded in 1979 by Bob Metcalfe, 3Com is a leading communications hardware vendor, offering a wide variety of network adapters, hubs and related products. In 1997, 3Com and U.S. Robotics agreed to merge. Retaining the 3Com name, it creates a $5 billion dollar company with more than 12,000 employees and is the largest merger in the history of the data networking industry.

3Com used to develop and support a line of network operating systems, which it discontinued in 1993. 3+Share was a DOS-based network operating system for PC and Mac clients. 3+Open was OS/2 based and supported DOS, OS/2 and Mac clients.

3-D

(3 Dimensional) Refers to objects that are constructed on three planes (x, y and z). A 2-D drawing program can be used to illustrate a 3-D object; however, in order to automatically rotate the object as a self-contained entity, a 3-D drawing program must be used.

3-D accelerator

See *graphics accelerator*.

3-D animation

Animating objects that appear in a three-dimensional space. They can be rotated and moved like real objects. 3-D animation is at the heart of games and virtual reality, but it may also be used in presentation graphics to add flair to the visuals. See *geometry calculations, VRML* and *surface modeling*.

3-D audio

Audio reproduction that simulates sounds coming from all directions. Using signal processing techniques as well as multiple speakers, 3-D audio is used in virtual reality and home theater systems.

3-D chat

A chat room environment that incorporates 3-D images. See *chat room, VRML* and *avatar*.

3-D digitizer

A graphics input system that records x, y and z coordinates of a real object. Contact is made with various points on the object's surface by a light sensor, sound sensor, robotic instrument or pen.

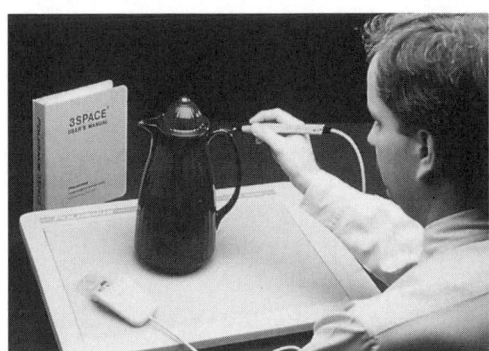

Digitizing Three Dimensions
The 3DRAW PRO 3-D digitizer system from Polhemus uses a pen to touch the object's surface. This 3SPACE technology records the x, y and z coordinates of the tip position in 3-dimensional space and outputs directly into popular CAD and graphics programs. *(Photo courtesy of Polhemus, Inc.)*

3D Fax

A Windows program from InfoImaging Technologies, Inc., Pleasanton, CA, (www.infoimaging.com), that allows binary files to be transmitted via fax. The sending software encodes the file into a printed image that is sent to the recipient's fax machine. The image is scanned into the computer and 3D Fax decodes it back to its original file format.

3Dfx

(3Dfx Interactive, San Jose, CA, www.3dfx.com) A company that specializes in 3-D accelerator chips and arcade game subsystems geared to the entertainment market. Founded in 1994, 3Dfx is known for its Voodoo Graphics processors which are used in a variety of products. See *Voodoo Graphics*.

3-D graphics

The creation, display and manipulation of objects in the computer in three dimensions. 3-D CAD and 3-D graphics programs allow objects to be created on an x-y-z scale (width, height, depth). As 3-D entities, they can be rotated and viewed from all angles as well as be scaled larger or smaller. They also allow lighting to be applied automatically in the rendering stage. See *graphics, Gouraud shading, Phong shading* and *2-D graphics*.

3-D modeling

The ability to create three-dimensional images. See *surface modeling* and *solid modeling*.

3DO

A multimedia and video game technology from 3DO Company, Redwood City, CA, (www.3do.com), that is licensed to manufacturers and developers. The first 3DO player was

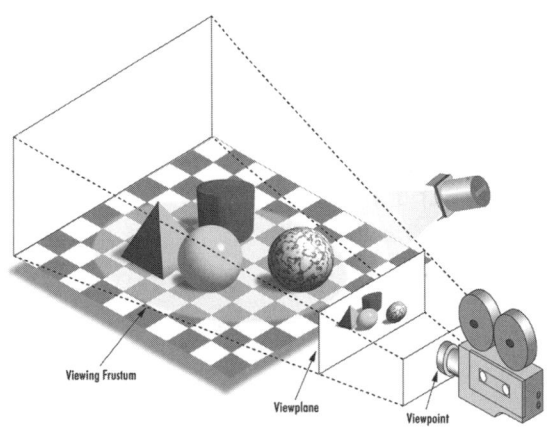

The 3-D Stage
In 3-D graphics, objects are created on a 3-dimensional stage where the current view is derived from the camera angle and light sources, similar to the real world. *(Image courtesy of Intergraph Computer Systems.)*

Panasonic's Realistic Entertainment Active Learning (REAL) Multiplayer, which plays audio CDs and can be fitted for Video CDs.

3DO developers are able to create games from a large library of royalty-free sound effects, music, stills, clip art and film. The technology provides very high speeds for animation and can also provide a 3-D capability that is viewed through glasses.

3DO was founded by Trip Hawkins, one of Apple's earliest employees and founder of Electronic Arts software company. In 1990, Hawkins left Electronic Arts to start 3DO.

3DOF
See *6DOF*.

3-D sound
See *3-D audio*.

3D Studio
A 3-D modeling and animation program from Autodesk, Inc., Sausalito, CA, (www.autodesk.com). 3D Studio is the DOS version, and 3D Studio Max is the Windows version. It was the first program to bring professional animation and 3-D rendering from high-end workstations to the PC. Its 2D Shaper module lets you create 2-D shapes that become the cross sections of the 3-D models. 3D Lofter creates the underlying framework of the 3-D model, and 3D Editor is used to prepare the scene for rendering. In Release 4, the Keyframer animation module includes inverse kinematics, which links components so that they move together. See *Character Studio*.

3GL
See *third-generation language*.

3-tier architecture
See *three tier client/server*.

3.3v
(**3.3** Volts) Refers to the amount of voltage required by the chips on newer personal computer motherboards. See *5v*.

3.5"
(1) Refers to the common 3 1/2 inch microfloppy disk used in personal computers.
(2) Refers to disk drives and other devices with a 3 1/2 inch wide form factor.

32-bit
See *bit specifications*.

32-bit color
Using 24 bits per pixel to represent a color image in a computer, plus an additional eight bits for an alpha channel. See *24-bit color, alpha channel, bit depth* and *bit specifications*.

32-bit computer
A computer that uses a 32-bit word length. It processes four bytes (32 bits) at a time. See *32-bit processing*.

32-bit driver
A driver written for a 32-bit environment. It often refers to drivers written for Windows 95/98 or Windows NT in contrast to 16-bit drivers written for DOS and Windows 3.x. For example, when users upgrade a PC from Windows 3.1 to Windows 95/98, they have to replace the Windows 3.1 display adapter driver with the Windows 95/98 version. In this case, they are replacing the 16-bit driver with a 32-bit driver.

32-bit file access
See *Windows for Workgroups*.

32-bit processing
Refers to programs running in a 32-bit computer. A 32-bit computer processes four bytes at a time compared with two bytes in a 16-bit computer or one byte in an 8-bit computer. Starting with the 386

chip, Intel CPUs have been built with a split personality for compatibility with earlier models. They have both 16- and 32-bit modes of operation, the 32-bit mode being the native mode with more advanced capabilities.

In 16-bit mode, or Real Mode, a program executes 16-bit instructions. In Protected Mode, a program has access to both 16- and 32-bit instructions, the maximum amount of RAM, virtual memory and virtual machine capabilities as well as memory protection, which keeps one program from crashing another.

DOS applications run in Real Mode, while Windows 3.1 switches back and forth between Real Mode and Protected Mode. OS/2, UNIX, Windows 95/98, Windows NT and other 32-bit operating systems run in Protected Mode when running 32-bit applications.

The 32-bit mode does not result in two times as much real work getting done as in 16-bit mode, because it relates to internal processing and not every instruction or unit of data takes advantage of the four bytes. In addition, program design as well as disk and bus speed play important roles in a computer's performance. While the speed may improve a little or a lot, depending on the program being run, 32-bit processing for the PC means as much a break from the past architecture as it does faster speed.

32-bit version

A program that runs in a 32-bit environment. It typically refers to a program that was written for a Windows 95/98 or Windows NT machine in contrast with a 16-bit version that was written for DOS or Windows 3.1.

32-bit Windows

Refers to Windows NT and Windows 95/98, which use the 32-bit native mode of the Intel CPU. The 32-bit mode became available starting with the 386. The term explicitly excludes Windows 3.1 and previous versions of Windows. See *Win32*.

32x CD-ROM

A CD-ROM drive that spins a maximum of 32 times as fast as the first CD-ROM. It provides a maximum of 4.8MB per second data transfer.

33.3

Refers to the transmission speed of a modem that can transmit up to 33,300 bits per second. See *V.34*.

36-track

See *Magstar*.

360

See *System/360*.

360K

May refer to the 360K 5.25" minifloppy disk used with PCs.

370

See *System/370*.

370 architecture

Refers to a computer that will run IBM mainframe applications. See *System/370* and *IBM mainframes*.

370/XA

(370 EXtended Architecture) A major enhancement (1981) to System/370 architecture which improved multiprocessing, introduced a new I/O system and increased addressing from 24 to 31 bits (16MB to 2GB).

386

The third generation of the Intel x86 family of CPU chips. The term may refer to the chip or to a PC that uses it. Introduced in 1986, it is the successor to the 286, and although adequate for DOS applications, it is very slow for Windows and other graphics-based programs. The 386 was the first chip in the x86 line to provide 32-bit processing and provides both 16-bit and 32-bit modes. It added enhanced memory management, allowing both extended and expanded (EMS) memory to be allocated on demand. The 386 architecture has been followed in all of Intel's subsequent CPUs (486, Pentium, etc.). See *PC* and *x86*.

386 CPU Technical Specs

A 32-bit multitasking microprocessor in a 132-pin PGA package. Supports 8, 16 and 32-bit data types. Has 32 32-bit registers including eight general-purpose. Operational modes: "Real Mode" performs as a fast 8086 CPU and addresses 1MB memory. "Protected Mode" addresses 4GB physical and 64TB virtual memory and provides access to memory management, paging and memory protection capabilities (see *32-bit processing*). "Virtual 8086 Mode" is a Protected Mode subset that runs tasks as if each were in an individual 8086 CPU. See *Virtual 8086 mode*.

The 386 contains 275,000 transistors and uses 1.5 micron technology (transistor elements are as small as 1.5 microns).

386DX

See *386*.

386 Enhanced Mode

An operational mode in Windows 3.x. See *Windows 3.x modes*.

386EX

A version of the 386 designed for embedded systems. It is similar to the 386SL, but includes a clock, timers, DMA control and serial and parallel ports. A version for extreme temperatures is also available. The 386SL's integrated cache controller and tag RAM are not included.

386MAX

A DOS memory manager for 386s and up from Qualitas, Inc., Bethesda, MD, (www.qualitas.com), that is noted for its advanced capabilities. BlueMAX is a version for PS/2 models.

386SL

A version of the 386SX designed for laptops. It has built in power management, and its variable clock rate allows it to idle for long suspend and resume periods. Except for memory and video controller, the 386SL and the 82360SL chip make up almost the entire computer. See *x86*.

386SLC

An IBM version of the 386SX that includes an internal 8KB memory cache. It includes power management capabilities and runs as fast as a 386DX.

386SX

A version of the 386 from Intel that runs at slower speeds than the 386DX, addresses only 16MB of memory (not 4GB) and supports only a 16-bit data bus (not 32). It uses less power and dispells less heat than the 386DX. See *386SL* and *x86*.

387

Math coprocessor for the 386.

390

See *System/390*.

303x

A series of medium to large-scale IBM mainframes introduced in 1977, which includes the 3031, 3032 and 3033. See *IBM mainframes*.

308x

A series of large-scale IBM mainframes introduced in 1980, which includes the 3081, 3083 and 3084. See *IBM mainframes*.

3090

A series of large-scale IBM mainframes introduced in 1986. Before the ES/9000 models (System/390), 3090s were the largest mainframes in the System/370 line. Models 120, 150 and 180 are single CPUs. Models 200 through 600 are multiprocessor systems (first digit indicates the number of CPUs). The E, S and J models represent increased speed respectively. See *IBM mainframes*.

3270

A family of IBM mainframe terminals and related protocols (includes 3278 mono and 3279 color terminal). See *3270 emulator*.

3270 Data Stream
The format for transmitting data from an application to a 3270-type terminal.

3270 emulator
A plug-in board that converts a personal computer or workstation into an IBM mainframe terminal. The first 3270 emulator was the Irma board from Attachmate Corporation.

3480, 3490, 3590
See *Magstar*.

3770
The standard communications protocol for batch transmission in an IBM SNA environment. It also refers to early remote batch terminals that used punched cards and floppy disks as input.

3780
See *2780 & 3780*.

37xx
IBM communications controllers that includes the 3704, 3705, 3720, 3725 and 3745 models. The 3704 and 3705 are early units, and the 3745 models are newer and more versatile. The 3745 includes a cluster controller that can connect 512 terminals, eight token ring networks and 16 T1 lines.

4CIF
See *CIF*.

4DOS
A popular DOS command processor from JP Software Inc., East Arlington, MA, (www.jpsoft.com), that replaces DOS' COMMAND.COM file. It includes enhanced commands that allow multiple files to be referenced with a single command. For example, you can copy several files with different names with one copy statement, which would require a copy statement for each file in DOS.

4GL
See *fourth-generation language*.

4mm tape
See *DAT*.

4-way
Typically refers to a 4-CPU symmetric multiprocessing (SMP) system. See *SMP*.

4x CD-ROM
A CD-ROM drive that spins four times as fast as the first CD-ROM. It provides 600KB per second data transfer.

404 error
The error message that is commonly displayed when a Web browser cannot locate a Web page or CGI script. The link to a Web page (URL) is static like a telephone number in a telephone book. A Web site can use software to search each link that it references for validity, but there is no program that can automatically find the new address for the missing link. The Webmaster can also replace the 404 message with something more understandable. See *link rot*.

411
See *Web white pages*.

430FX, 430HX, 430MX, 430TX, 430VX
See *Intel chipsets*.

440BX, 440FX, 440LX
See *Intel chipsets*.

450BX, 450GX
See *Intel chipsets*.

486

The fourth generation of the Intel x86 family of CPU chips. The term may refer to the chip or to a PC that uses it. Introduced in 1989, it is the successor to the 386, and depending on clock speed, can be up to five times as fast. It provides very acceptable performance for DOS applications, but is bare minimum for Windows and other graphics-intensive programs. The 486 has a built-in math coprocessor.

Later versions of the chip offered double and triple the internal speed while maintaining the same external speeds (see *DX2* and *DX4*). See *OverDrive CPU, PC* and *x86*.

486 CPU Technical Specs

A 32-bit multitasking microprocessor that uses the same registers and operational modes as the 386 (see *32-bit processing*). It obtains its speed from an internal 8KB memory cache that it quickly fills in burst mode. The chip is housed in a 168- or 169-pin PGA package.

The 486DX chip contains 1.2 million transistors; the 486SX contains 1.1 million. Both use 1.0 micron technology (transistor elements are as small as one micron).

486DX

A designation for the 486 CPU to distinguish it from the DX2 and DX4 models. See *486*.

486DX2

See *DX2*.

486SL

A version of the 486 from Intel designed for laptops. It runs on 3.3 volts (instead of 5) and includes power management features like the 386SL.

486SLC

(1) A 486SX-compatible CPU from Cyrix that is pin compatible with the 386SX, has a 1K cache and uses a 16-bit bus. It provides an upgrade path for 386SXs.

(2) The IBM version of the 486SX.

486SX

A slower version of the 486DX without the math coprocessor. 486SXs can be upgraded to 486DX2s with Intel's OverDrive chip, which includes the coprocessor. The DX2 chip is plugged into the empty coprocessor socket, disabling the original CPU. See *486*.

487

The math coprocessor for the 486.

4004

The first microprocessor. Designed by Marcian E. "Ted" Hoff at Intel in 1971, it was a 4-bit, general-purpose CPU initially developed for the Japanese Busicom calculator.

43xx

A series of medium-scale IBM mainframes initially introduced in 1979, which include the 4300, 4321, 4331, 4341, 4361 and 4381.

5.1 channel

A digital audio recording and playback system for home theater. It includes five channels (left, right, center, rear/surround left and right) plus a subwoofer channel. The major 5.1 channel standards are Dolby AC-3 and Philips Musicam.

5.25"

Refers to disk drives and other devices with a 5 1/4 inch wide form factor.

The 4004

With only 2,300 transistors, this general-purpose CPU launched Intel into the microprocessor business. Few could have envisioned the company would become the powerhouse that it is today. *(Photo courtesy of Intel Corporation.)*

5v

(5 Volts) Refers to the amount of DC electricity required by the chips on most personal computer motherboards. The power supply converts 120v alternating current (AC) into 5v direct current (DC). It also generates 12v for the disk drives. See *3.3v*.

5x86

A Pentium-class CPU chip from Cyrix that runs in 486 motherboards. It is similar in power to a 75MHz to 90MHz Pentium chip.

56 Kbps modem

See *V.90*.

586

A Pentium-class chip made by a company other than Intel. The 486 was the last numeric designation used by Intel. What was to be the 586 became the Pentium, thus, Pentium-class chips from non-Intel manufacturers are often designated as 586s and Pentium Pro-class chips as 686s.

5100

The first IBM desktop computer (1974). It came with up to 64K of RAM, a built-in tape drive and used APL or BASIC. Eight inch floppy disks became available in 1976.

5250

A family of terminals and related protocols for IBM midrange computers (System 3x, AS/400).

5250 emulator

Same as *twinax card*.

6DOF

(6 Degrees Of Freedom) The amount of motion supported in a robotics or virtual reality system. Six degrees provides x, y and z (horizontal, vertical and depth) and pitch, yaw and roll. Three degrees of freedom (3DOF) provides x, y and z only. See *pitch-yaw-roll*.

6-way

Typically refers to a 6-CPU symmetric multiprocessing (SMP) system. See *SMP*.

6x86

A Pentium-class CPU chip from Cyrix that is available in a variety of clock speeds. The 100MHz 6x86 is similar in power to a 133MHz Pentium chip. IBM produces the 6x86 for Cyrix and also sells and uses the chip.

6x86MX

A Pentium II-class CPU chip from Cyrix. Initial models run at 200MHz and 233MHz. The 6x86MX was code named M2.

6x CD-ROM

A CD-ROM drive that spins six times as fast as the first CD-ROM. It provides 900KB per second data transfer.

64-bit

See *bit specifications*.

64-bit graphics accelerator

A display adapter that has a pathway 64 bits wide between its on-board graphics processor and memory (video RAM).

601

The first model of the PowerPC chip. See *PowerPC*.

603

A low-power PowerPC chip designed for notebooks and portable applications. See *PowerPC*.

604

The second model of the PowerPC chip. Depending on clock speed, it runs applications from 50 to 100% faster than the 601. The 604e is a version of the 604 that has enhanced architecture for improving DOS and Windows emulation. See *PowerPC*.

615

An IBM version of the PowerPC that was expected to be able to execute PowerPC and x86 instructions natively.

620

A high-end model of the PowerPC chip, expected in 1997, but never came to fruition. See *PowerPC*.

640K

(640 **Kilobytes**) Typically refers to the first 640 kilobytes of memory in a PC, known as *conventional memory*. See *PC memory* and *PC memory map*.

640x480

Standard VGA resolution of 640 columns by 480 rows (lines). In the specification 640x480x16, the 16 is the number of colors. See *resolution*.

650

IBM's first major computer success. Introduced in 1954, it read data from punched cards and magnetic tapes. It used a fixed-head magnetic drum that rotated at 12,500 rpm for its internal memory of from 1,000 to 2,000 10-digit

IBM 650

The 650 was IBM's first successful computer system. Punched cards were used for input, but permanent records were stored on magnetic tape. *(Photo courtesy of IBM Corporation.)*

words. Magnetic disks, which IBM pioneered on its 305 RAMAC, were made available to the 650 in 1956.

By the end of the 1950s, there were more than 1,500 units installed, making it the most widely-used computer in the world. The 650 added high-speed computational ability to punched card data processing shops, which were the norm in those days.

686

A Pentium Pro-class chip made by a company other than Intel. The 486 was the last numeric designation used by Intel. What was to be the 586 became the Pentium, thus, Pentium-class chips from non-Intel manufacturers are often designated as 586s and Pentium Pro-class chips as 686s.

6502

An 8-bit microprocessor from Rockwell International Corporation used in the Apple II and earlier Atari and Commodore computers.

6800

An 8-bit microprocessor from Motorola. The 6801 is a computer-on-a-chip version.

68000

A family of 32-bit microprocessors from Motorola that are the CPUs in Macintoshes and a variety of workstations. It is also known as the 68K or 680x0 series.

```
Model   Bus size  Max RAM
68000   16        16MB
68020   32        4GB
68030   32        4GB     (built-in cache)
68040   32        4GB     (2x fast as 68030)
68060   32        4GB     (last 680x0 model)
```

Computer Desktop Encyclopedia

680x0

Refers to the Motorola 68000 family of CPU chips or to applications that are written for that chip. See *68000*.

7-bit ASCII

The original ASCII character code, which provides for 128 different characters. Internet mail as well as certain PBXs support 7-bit ASCII, not the 8-bit byte. In order to transmit proprietary file formats and binary executables over these systems, the 8-bit data must be encoded into a 7-bit format using such encoding methods as MIME, UUcoding and BinI Iex.

7-track

Refers to older magnetic tape formats that recorded 6-bit characters plus a parity bit on seven parallel tracks along the length of the tape. See *half-inch tape*.

IBM's First Computer

At General Electric's Aircraft Jet Engine Plant in Evendale, Ohio, this 1954 photo shows GE manager Herbert Grosch explaining the 701 to former president Ronald Reagan. Reagan was a TV personality for GE at the time. *(Photo courtesy of IBM Corporation.)*

7x24

Non-stop operation 7 days a week; 24 hours a day. Same as *24x7*.

701

IBM's first computer which was introduced in 1952. It was designed for scientific work and research, which later led to the development of the high-level FORTRAN language. Nineteen machines were built, a record volume for such a machine in that era. Its internal memory contained 2,048 36-bit words of Williams electrostatic storage tube memory and 8,192 words of magnetic drum memory. It used magnetic tapes for storage and was one of the first machines to use plastic-based tapes instead of metal tapes.

702

IBM's first commercial computer designed for business data processing. It was introduced in 1955.

720K

May refer to the 720K microfloppy disk used in PCs.

750

See *i750*.

786

Refers to non-Intel CPUs that are successors to the Pentium Pro class. The 486 was the last numeric designation used by Intel. What was to be the 586 became the Pentium. Thus, CPUs competing with the Pentium Pro are designated as 686s, and so on.

8-bit

See *bit specifications*.

8-bit color

Using one byte per pixel in a color image. Up to 256 colors can be represented in the color palette. Various graphics formats are limited to 256 colors; for example, GIF images, which are widely used on the Web, are 8-bit color. See *bit depth* and *bit specifications*.

8-bit sample

See *sampling rate*.

8-bit sound

A sound card that processes 8-bit sound samples. The more data in the sample, the more accurately sound can be digitized. See *sampling rate*.

8mm tape

A high-capacity magnetic tape technology developed by Exabyte that uses the helical scan method. Drives are sold direct and through OEMs. Using the international 8mm format established in 1984, Exabyte introduced an 8mm drive for digital storage in 1987. The cartridges held 2.5GB, a breakthrough capacity for the time. In 1996, Exabyte introduced the Mammoth drive, a capstan-less version of its 8mm line, which supports AME-based 20GB cartridges and earlier MP-based cartridges. The lack of capstan reduces wear and tear on the tape, because the capstan has to press against the medium to move it.

   Tape libraries hold from 500GB to more than 1TB. Drives are expected in 1999 that hold 60GB with an increase in transfer rate from 3 to 12MB/sec.

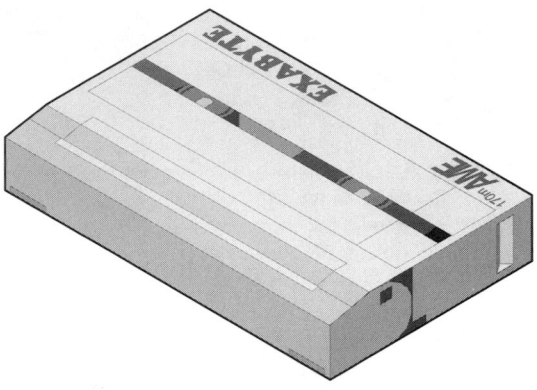

Mammoth Cartridge
The 20GB storage capacity may be large, but the cartridges are smaller than a deck of playing cards.

8-way

Typically refers to an 8-CPU symmetric multiprocessing (SMP) system. See *SMP*.

8x CD-ROM

A CD-ROM drive that spins eight times as fast as the first CD-ROM. It provides 1.2MB per second data transfer.

8.3

Often refers to the method used to name files in DOS and Windows 3.x. The file name is up to eight characters long and the file extension is up to three characters long. See *DOS file names*.

88K

See *88000*.

88Open

A consortium founded in 1988 that provides information and certification for the Motorola 88000-based platform. Companies such as Data General, Encore and Harris offer products using the 88K chips.

800x600

Standard super VGA resolution of 800 columns by 600 rows (lines). In the specification 800x600x256, the 256 is the number of colors. See *resolution*.

802.1

An IEEE standard for network management. See *IEEE 802*.

802.11

An IEEE standard for wireless communications. Approved in the summer of 1997, 802.11 provides 1 and 2 Mbps transmission using either a frequency hopping modulation technique or direct sequence CDMA. Higher speeds are expected in the future.

802.12

See *100VG-AnyLAN*.

802.1p

An IEEE standard for providing quality of service (QoS) in 802-based networks. 802.1p uses three bits (defined in 802.1q) to allow switches to reorder packets based on priority level. It also defines the

Generic Attributes Registration Protocol (GARP) and the GARP VLAN Registration Protocol (GVRP). GARP lets client stations request membership in a multicast domain, and GVRP lets them register into a VLAN. See *IEEE 802* and *QoS*.

802.1q

An IEEE standard for providing VLAN identification and quality of service (QoS) levels. Four bytes are added to an Ethernet frame, increasing the maximum frame size from 1518 to 1522 bytes. Three bits are used to allow eight priority levels (QoS) and 12 bits are used to identify up to 4096 VLANs. See *virtual LAN*.

802.2

An IEEE standard that specifies the data link layer for various media access methods. See *IEEE 802*.

802.3

An IEEE standard for a CSMA/CD local area network access method, which is widely implemented in Ethernet. The 802.3u standard covers Fast Ethernet, and 802.3ab and 3z cover Gigabit Ethernet. See *IEEE 802*.

802.3ab

See *802.3z*.

802.3u

See *802.3*.

802.3z

An IEEE standard for Gigabit Ethernet over optical fiber. It provides for full-duplex transmission from a switch to a client station or another switch and half-duplex over a shared channel using the CSMA/CD access method. The 802.3ab copper cabling counterpart is expected to be standardized in 1999.

802.4

An IEEE standard for a token bus local area network access method, which is used in the MAP factory automation protocol. See *IEEE 802*.

802.5

An IEEE standard for a token ring local area network access method, which is widely implemented in Token Ring. See *IEEE 802*.

802.6

An IEEE standard for a DQDB metropolitan area network access method. See *IEEE 802*.

860

See *i860*.

8080

An Intel 8-bit CPU chip introduced in 1974. It was the successor to the first commercial 8-bit microprocessor (8008) and precursor to the x86 family. It contained 4,500 transistors and other electronic components.

8086

Introduced in 1978, the CPU chip that defines the base architecture of Intel's x86 family (XT, AT, 386, 486, Pentium). 8086s are used in some XT-class machines. See *PC* and *x86*.

8086 CPU Technical Specs

A 16-bit microprocessor in a 40-pin CERDIP package. Has 14 16-bit registers including eight general-purpose. Addresses 1MB memory using base addresses contained in segment registers. Contains 29,000 transistors.

8087

The math coprocessor for the 8086/8088.

8088

The Intel CPU chip used in first-generation PCs (XT class). It is a slower version of the 8086, chosen for migration from CP/M programs, the predominate business applications of the early 1980s. See *PC* and *x86*.

8088 CPU Technical Specs

Same as the 8086 CPU except that is uses an 8-bit data bus instead of a 16-bit data bus. Designed to ease conversion from 8-bit, Z80-based CP/M programs. Contains 25,000 transistors.

8100

An IBM minicomputer introduced in 1978 that was designed for departmental computing and used the DPPX/SP operating system.

8250A

See *UART*.

8259A

Known as a Programmable Interrupt Controller, it is the interrupt controller chip used in a PC. It is superseded by the 82489DX chip. See *IRQ* and *PIC*.

8514

The IBM monitor used with its 8514/A display adapter.

8514/A

An early high-resolution PC display adapter with 2-D graphics acceleration from IBM. Designed for Micro Channel machines and as a second monitor for dual screen display, it provided an interlaced 1024x768x256 resolution. Third parties provided non-interlaced versions for the ISA bus.

80286, 80287

See *286*.

80386, 80386DX, 80387

See *386*.

80386SL

See *386SL*.

80386SX

See *386SX*.

80486

See *486*.

80486SX

See *486SX*.

80487

See *487*.

80860

See *860*.

80x86

See *x86*.

82385

An Intel controller chip that manages the memory cache in 386 and 486 CPUs.

82489DX

Known as the Advanced Programmable Interrupt Controller, it is the successor to the 8259A interrupt controller. The 82489DX is enhanced for multiprocessing. See *IRQ* and *PIC*.

Computer Desktop Encyclopedia

88000

A family of 32-bit RISC microprocessors from Motorola. The 88100 is the first processor in the 88000 family. Introduced in 1988, it incorporates four built-in execution units that allow up to five operations to be performed in parallel. Although the 88000 processors are very sophisticated chips, they never took off in the marketplace. See *88Open*.

9-track

Refers to magnetic tape that records 8-bit bytes plus parity on nine parallel tracks along the length of the tape. This is the common format for half-inch open reels. See *half-inch tape*.

9221

A series of CMOS-based mainframes from IBM introduced in 1992. These were rack-mounted, entry-level mainframes that were part of the ES/9000 line. The 9221s were not widely used. See *Parallel Enterprise Server*.

9370

A series of IBM entry-level mainframes introduced in 1986 that use the 370 architecture. In 1990, the Enterprise System models (ES/9370) were introduced, which used the Micro Channel bus and a 386 for I/O processing. A Model 14 biprocessor system added a second 386 for DOS and OS/2 applications with a high-speed link between the 386 and 370 processors.

9660

See *ISO 9660*.

9672

The model number designation for IBM's CMOS-based mainframes. See *Parallel Enterprise Server*.